AN INDEX OF THE SOURCE RECORDS OF MARYLAND

AN INDEX OF THE

SOURCE RECORDS OF MARYLAND

Genealogical, Biographical, Historical

BY

ELEANOR PHILLIPS PASSANO
(MRS. EDWARD BOTELER PASSANO)
Honorary State Historian, Maryland Society of the National Society, Daughters of the American Revolution

With a new introduction by
P. W. FILBY

GENEALOGICAL · PUBLISHING Co., Inc

Originally published: Baltimore, 1940
Reprinted, with permission, by
Genealogical Publishing Co., Inc.
Baltimore, 1967, 1974, 1984, 1994

Library of Congress Catalogue Card Number 67-17943
International Standard Book Number 0-8063-0271-2
Made in the United States of America

The Publishers

Gratefully Dedicate

This Reprint

to the Diligence and

Competence of

the Late

Eleanor Phillips Passano

This book is dedicated

with affection and esteem

to the memory of my friend

Mrs. John Grey Hopkins Lilburn
(ANNE ELIZABETH THOMAS)

Regent of the Maryland Society

of the National Society

of the

Daughters of the American Revolution

INTRODUCTION

This work by the late Mrs. Passano, long out-of-print and to some extent out-of-date, is primarily a reference book for libraries and genealogical researchers. In principle any older work which falls under the classification of bibliography or index should be updated before being reprinted and an effort made to bring out a revised edition of the original work. But this monumental work defies correction or addition, simply because the task of checking all entries and adding those of the past twenty-six years would take too long and meanwhile genealogists, historians and others would not have available any copy of the work in any form for years.

Under these circumstances a reprint of the only source book of Maryland containing records and references in such detail is welcome. Many users have found errors and omissions; records were sometimes taken from books or papers which have since been lost, or from lists which were in themselves faulty; many new sources have been printed or have been discovered since 1940; and the locations of some of the material have been changed. Nevertheless, *Passano* is still the only record of its kind. It is undoubtedly the first work which should be used when Maryland genealogical research is undertaken, and it is invaluable for out-of-State researchers with Maryland family connections.

There are several main sources of reference and a number of sections to the book. By far the most useful at present are the 362 pages (of a total of 478) listing all the then known references to Maryland records of genealogical, biographical, and historical interest on families or individuals who have lived in Maryland, and noting where this material was then available for consultation. At the Maryland Historical Society the staff have realized that their difficulty in finding referenced manuscript family material is the result of Mrs. Passano's copying from a card catalog which was faulty and has since been reworked. Many family records listed do not now exist in the Library. The same is substantially true of the D.A.R. Library, and in both libraries there is often doubt because Mrs. Passano quoted titles quite different from those now used by these two institutions. Some of the titles listed as manuscripts have since been collected into bound volumes. Still, this part of the work will stand up best, and since it occupies three quarters of the book it alone warrants a reprint.

But the same is not true of the State, county and church records. Mrs. Passano did not distinguish between the Land Office and the Hall of Records, and anything in either office was cited as Hall of Records. This did not matter when they were colocated, but the Land Office's new location has caused some confusion. As a result of the ballot of November 8, 1966, however, the records of the Hall of Records and the Land Office are to be consolidated, and questions on records in the Land Office and in the Hall of Records should be sent to the Hall of Records.

The county records which Mrs. Passano listed are substantially correct but incomplete, since vast changes in location of repositories have taken place since 1940. (She relied upon the Historical Records Survey compiled under the Works Progress Administration, which had in process the publication of a detailed description of all State and county records - never completed.) All the land and probate records, either the originals or photostats or microfilms, are now to be found in the courthouses and in the Hall of Records. The judgement records are held by the Hall of Records, at least to the mandatory surrender period of April 28, 1788, the date when Maryland adopted the Federal Constitution. In fact, for county records there is now no need to consult *Passano*. In 1963 the Hall of Records issued *The County Courthouses and Records of Maryland. Part 2: The Records,* by Radoff, Skordas and Jacobsen (Hall of Records Commission, Publ. no. 13, Annapolis. $5). There is no other work to replace the *Passano* index of family records, but the Hall of Records publication is an essential reference work to accompany *Passano.*

The church records (parish registers of baptisms, marriages, deaths, vestry minutes, etc.) present a special problem, since the holdings of churches are often transferred. For example, all of the now extant records of the Episcopal Diocese of Easton are at the Hall of Records, mainly in the original, but sometimes on microfilm. This is true also of the Washington Diocese. For the Maryland Diocese, that is, the diocese with its See in Baltimore, some records are at the Hall of Records, some with the parishes, and some at the Maryland Historical Society. The Maryland Diocesan Library manuscripts include a vast amount of material on the early history of all the parishes of all three dioceses.

Apart from the above, the following movements of records have occurred. The Peabody Institute Library is now the Peabody Branch of the Enoch Pratt Free Library, but I am assured that the genealogy and local history (all of it printed material) will remain at the Peabody. The Library of the Maryland Diocese in Baltimore has left the Peabody; most of the printed works have been sent to the General Theological Seminary, New York (but this does not in any way affect the references in *Passano*), and the Diocesan manuscripts will be in the Thomas and Hugg Memorial Building of the Maryland Historical Society early in 1967. The Milton S. Eisenhower Library of The Johns Hopkins University, the Enoch Pratt Free Library, the Library of Congress and the D.A.R. Library in Washington, D.C., report no changes of location.

Mrs. Passano often referred to "personal list" or to "(name) personal list". In many cases it has never been determined which collections she referred to, but since some may have since been deposited in libraries, it would be worth checking with the Maryland Historical Society to ascertain whether their present whereabouts is known. Mrs. Passano also referred to "Mrs. - - chart". These are almost always the charts in the Colonial Dames volumes, housed at the Maryland Historical Society. It is also useful to know that the papers of the Historical Society of Harford County, though not listed in *Passano,* and the vast collection of Scharf Papers (formerly at The Johns Hopkins Library) are now in the Maryland Historical Society (Ms. 2000 and Ms. 1999 respectively).

Most of the printed works of reference listed in the rest of the books have stood the test of time and are still the chief sources. Many have been reprinted, and a number of new ones have appeared, but in the main the lists are still useful. Since 1940 many of the standard works have been acquired by the libraries mentioned by Mrs. Passano, and it is usually possible to find them at the library where the manuscript is held.

For much of the above information I am indebted to Dr. Morris Radoff, Archivist of the State of Maryland, Mrs. Millard F. Walsh, Librarian, N.S.D.A.R. Library, Mr. John D. Kilbourne, Curator, Pennsylvania Historical Society, Mr. F. Garner Ranney, Curator, Maryland Diocesan Library, and Miss Hester Rich and Mr. Thomas Eader of the Maryland Historical Society.

The addresses of the institutions listed in the present work are given below. Each institution wishes to state that no research can be done by its staff.

MHS — Library of the Maryland Historical Society,
201 West Monument St.,
Baltimore, Md. 21201.

DAR — D. A. R. Library, 1776 D St., N. W.,
Washington, D. C. 20006.

Lib. Cong. — Library of Congress, Washington, D. C. 20540.

JHU — The Milton S. Eisenhower Library,
The Johns Hopkins University,
Homewood, Charles & 34th Sts.,
Baltimore, Md. 21218.

Md. Dioc. Lib. — Library of the Maryland Diocese in
Baltimore, at the Maryland Historical Society,
201 West Monument St.,
Baltimore, Md. 21201.

Enoch Pratt Lib. — Enoch Pratt Free Library
Cathedral & Mulberry Sts.
Baltimore, Md. 21201.

Hall of Records — Hall of Records, State of Maryland,
Annapolis, Md. 21401.

P. W. FILBY
January 1967

PREFACE

It was my pleasure and privilege to serve as State Historian under Mrs. John Grey Lilburn, then Regent of the Maryland Society of the Daughters of the American Revolution. During this association I not only was deeply impressed by her executive ability and leadership, but was drawn close to her in comradeship. I soon learned to respect her and love her for her great charm and culture.

Mrs. Lilburn was a direct descendant of Leonard Calvert, the first Governor of Maryland. She was born in Saint Mary's County where the early years of her life were spent. She is now resting in Trinity Churchyard, in Old Saint Mary's City.

Upon her untimely death, knowing her great interest and zeal in the preservation of the early records of her State, I was moved to compile a book as a memorial to her—to be my work as State Historian.

The original scope was modest in its conception; the book was to be an index of the church records of Maryland. It soon became evident, however, that this could not be made complete, because many records had been destroyed by fire or lost through carelessness. Nevertheless, the work brings together many records previously unknown, which I hope will prove valuable.

Since church records and county records overlap, it was necessary to broaden the scope of the work and include court house records. Here again many early records had been destroyed or lost.

After a preliminary survey of this field, I learned that the Historical Records Survey compiled under the Works Progress Administration will include a rather detailed description of all State and County records. Records of some counties have been completed and published in mimeographed form, and presumably the project will eventually cover all counties. Not wishing to duplicate this material, I have given only a brief outline of this group of records.

At the suggestion of the late Charles L. Fickus, then librarian of the Maryland Historical Society, I decided to include a list of

Maryland family names. A majority are of colonial families; others are of more recent families, migrating from neighboring states. These have been gathered from private records, both printed and manuscript, family histories, biographies, and pedigrees. The list contains some 20,000 names, cross-indexed, and I hope will facilitate and broaden the usefulness of the book.

A large number of these records will be found in the Library of Congress, the D. A. R. Library in Washington, the Enoch Pratt, Maryland Diocesan, Maryland Historical Society and Peabody Libraries in Baltimore; also in some of our county libraries where there is a local interest in the preservation of records.

Although the work is not complete, it is my hope that those interested in tracing family lines in Maryland will find it valuable. No doubt errors as well as omissions will be discovered but I present "my child," representing six years work, and ask that it be accepted for its virtues, if any it has, rather than be condemned and criticized for its sins, which will be sins of omission.

ELEANOR PHILLIPS PASSANO.

Towson, Baltimore County, Maryland.

ACKNOWLEDGMENT

I wish to express my indebtedness to the many who have assisted in the compilation of this work, providing access to information, facilitating my efforts, and aiding in many ways.

The Maryland Historical Society gave full access to their marvelous collection of records. To Miss Florence J. Kennedy, assistant librarian of the Society, I am especially grateful. I am grateful, too, for the splendid coöperation of the late Dr. James A. Robertson, former archivist of the Hall of Records, Annapolis.

I appreciate the courteous assistance of Mr. Louis H. Diehlman, of the Peabody Library, and Mr. James W. Foster, in charge of the Maryland Room of the Enoch Pratt Library; also the unusual privileges accorded by Mrs. Mary T. Walsh, librarian of the N. S., D. A. R. Library, and the courtesy of those at the Library of Congress in granting access to the Maryland manuscripts.

The D. A. R. chapters were extremely helpful in locating the church records in the various counties, and this kindness I acknowledge to Mrs. Frederick J. Cotton, Anne Arundel Chapter; Mrs. James McAllister, Dorset Chapter; Mrs. T. Scott Offutt, Francis Scott Key Chapter; Mrs. William Slemmer, Frederick Chapter; Mrs. John M. Lynch and Mrs. Thomas S. George, General Mordecai Gist Chapter; Miss Minnie B. Cairnes, Governor William Paca Chapter; Miss Mollie Howard Ash, Head of Elk Chapter; Mrs. W. Irvin Walker, Major Samuel Turlbutt Wright Chapter; Dr. Esther Dole, Old Kent Chapter, and Miss Katherine Todd and Mrs. William Tilghman, Samuel Chase Chapter.

To others who have helped to compile the church records I am most grateful: to Dr. Peter Guilday, for the bibliography of Catholic records, to Miss Harriet P. Marine, for the bibliography of records in Park Avenue Friends Meeting House, Baltimore, to Mrs. A. Viola Horisberg, for the bibliography of records in Homewood Friends Meeting House, Baltimore, and to Dr. Alexander E. Pearce, for the bibliography of manuscript histories of the Presbyterian churches in Maryland at the Department of History, Witherspoon Building, Philadelphia.

Many of the clergy of Maryland have aided. The late Dr. Willys Rede, former librarian of the Maryland Diocese gave me full access to its wonderful collection of manuscripts and records. I shall always remember his kindness and courtesy.

Last but not least I wish to thank my sister, Mary W. Isaac, and Miss Lucile A. Bull, editor of the Waverly Press, for their untiring efforts in working over the manuscript.

There are doubtless others that should be named. The omissions, if any, are not intentional, for I am grateful to all for their assistance and kindness.

CONTENTS

Index of Names 1

Bibliography 363

State Records—General 363

General, 363; Account Books, 365; Boundaries, 365; Calendars, Reports, 365; Canal Companies, 366; Constitutions, 366; Courts, 366; Deeds, 367; Historic Papers, Letters, Journals, Diaries, 367; Land Records, 368; Laws, 368; Marriages, 369; Maps, 369; Rainbow Series, 370; Rent Rolls, 370; Wills, 371

State Records—County 371

Counties arranged alphabetically

Bibliography 380

Biography 381

History, Biography, and Travel 382

Genealogy 395

Maryland, 395; American, 397; Great Britain, 398

Magazines, Newspapers 399

Fiction 400

Church Records 401

General Church History of Maryland, 401; Baptist, 404; Christian, 405; Church of God, 405; Churches of the Brethren, 405; Dunkard, Dunker, or Tunker, 405; Lutheran, 405; Methodist, 408; Moravian, 412; Presbyterian, 413; Protestant Episcopal, 415; Quaker, 426; Reformed, 431; Roman Catholic, 433; Swedenborgen, 435; Unitarian, 435; United Brethren in Christ, 435

Tombstone Inscriptions 436

Arranged alphabetically by counties

Census, Lists, Commissions, etc. 441

General, 441; Census of Maryland, 441; Commissions, Lists, Directories, etc., in Maryland, 442; Early Settlers of America, Passengers, Ships, 443; Early Settlers of Maryland, Passengers, Ships, 444; Maryland Lists, 447; National Lists, 449; Population Census, 450

War Records 450

General and Miscellaneous, 450; Colonial and French and Indian Wars, 451; Revolutionary War—Maryland, 451; Revolutionary War—General, 457; War of 1812, 461; Civil War, 462; World War, 463

Star Spangled Banner 463

Patriotic Clubs and Societies 463

Early Eastern Colleges 465

Bibliography of Other States, containing references to Maryland Families 467

California, 467; Connecticut, 467; Delaware, 467; District of Columbia, 467; Kentucky, 469; New England, 470; New Jersey, 470; New York, 470; North Carolina, 470; Ohio, 471; Pennsylvania, 473; Rhode Island, 474; South Carolina, 474; Virginia, 474; West Virginia, 478

INDEX OF NAMES

* Genealogy. † Biography. ‡ History. Symbols and abbreviations at ends of items indicate libraries in which records can be located. MHS=Library of the Maryland Historical Society; DAR=D. A. R. Library in Washington; Lib. Cong.=Library of Congress; JHU=Library of the Johns Hopkins University; Md. Dioc. Lib.=Library of the Maryland Diocese in Baltimore.

A

Abadie-Beall. Americans of gentle birth and their ancestors. Pittman. V. 2, pp. 2–3. MHS; DAR.

Abb. Mt. Olivet Cemetery, Frederick. Md. Geneal. Rec. Com., 1934–35, p. 111. Mss. DAR.

Abel. Old Md. families. Bromwell. MHS; DAR.

St. Paul's Parish, Balto. V. 2, 4, 5. Mss. MHS.

†Abel, John J. Biog. file, Enoch Pratt Lib.

†Abell. Abell family. Steiner. Repr. from Men of mark in Md., Balto., 1910, v. 2 and 4. DAR; Enoch Pratt Lib.

Ancestors of Arunah Shepherdson Abell. Ms. MHS.

Balto., its hist., its people. Hall. V. 2. MHS; DAR.

†Biog. file, Enoch Pratt Lib.

†Encyc. of Amer. biog. Amer. Hist. Soc., N. Y., v. 1, p. 366. MHS.

Geneal. and mem. encyc. of Md. Spencer. V. 1, pp. 13–22, 39–42, 66–67; v. 2, pp. 428–30. MHS; DAR.

†Hist. of Balto. City and Co. Scharf. P. 622. MHS.

†Men of mark in Md. Johnson. V. 2; v. 4. DAR; Enoch Pratt Lib.

O'Daniel-Hamilton ancestry in Md. and Ky. O'Daniel. Pp. 73–83. MHS.

Patriotic Md. Md. Soc. of S. A. R., 1930. MHS; DAR.

Peter Mills and Mary Shirtcliffe Mills, St. Mary's Co. Mills. 1936, bd. ms. MHS; DAR.

Talbott of "Poplar Knowle." Shirk. MHS; DAR.

Tercentenary hist. of Md. Andrews. V. 3, p. 683. MHS; DAR.

Abell, A. S. Monumental city. Howard. MHS; DAR.

***Abell, Arunah S.** Ancestors, 1806–88. Horace A. Abell. Rochester, N. Y., 1936. Mimeog. MHS.

†Balto., hist. and biog. Richardson and Bennett. 1871, pp. 153–67. MHS; DAR.

Abell, Sam'l, Jr. Will dated 1774. Misc'l Will Book, v. 5. DAR.

***Abell, W. W.** Coat of arms. Burke's landed gentry. 1939. MHS.

Abell, Walter D. Wise. Abridged Compendium of American Genealogy. Virkus. V. 6, p. 608. DAR.

Abell Family. Hist. of Balto. Lewis Pub. Co., 1912, v. 2, pp. 3, 10, 14, 16, 17, 18. DAR.

Abell Line. Origins of Clements-Spalding families of Md. and Ky. Clements. Pp. 73–87. MHS.

Abell-Smith-Winsatt, Md. and Ky. Family notes. Ms. File case, DAR.

Abbess. St. Paul's Parish, Balto. V. 1. Mss. MHS.

***Abbett, Abbott.** Wicomico Co. families. Tilghman. Ms, p. 13. DAR.

Abbey. St. Paul's Parish, Balto. V. 2. Mss. MHS.

Abbot. Old Kent. Hanson. P. 228. MHS; DAR.

Abbot Family. Tercentenary hist. of Md. Andrews. V. 2, p. 457. MHS; DAR.

***Abbott.** Abbott-Denison-Willie families. Spencer Miller. Repr. from N. Y. Geneal. and Biog. Rec., Jan., 1936. MHS.

*Abbott-Denison-Willie families, early ancestors, of Bishops, Stratford Co., Herts, Eng. Pamph. MHS.

Balto., hist. and biog. Richardson and Bennett. 1871, p. 149. MHS; DAR.

*Bible rec. Md. O. R. Soc., v. 2, pp. 85–93.

†Hist. of Frederick Co. Williams. V. 2, p. 869. MHS; DAR.

†Med. Annals Md. Cordell. 1903, p. 297. MHS.

†Men of mark in Md. Johnson. V. 3, p. 254. DAR; Enoch Pratt Lib.

St. Paul's Parish, Balto. V. 2, 3. Mss. MHS.

St. Stephens Parish, Cecilton, Md. MHS; DAR.

See Bordley-Abbott-Laird-Winder.

See Abbett.

Abbott, Talbot Co. Bible rec., 1689–1864. Md. O. R. Soc. Bul., no. 2, pp. 85–93.

Abbott, Abbett. Wicomico Co. families. Bible rec. Ms. DAR.

Abercrombie. Balto., its hist., its people. Hall. V. 3. MHS; DAR.

Gulf State His. Mag., v. 1, p. 350. MHS.

†Med. Annals Md. Cordell. 1903, p. 297. MHS.

St. Paul's Parish, Balto. V. 1, 2. Mss. MHS.

Abercrombie, Phila. Bible rec. Pub. Geneal. Soc. Pa., v. 8, p. 284.

***Abercrombie, Ronald T.** Burke's landed gentry. 1939. MHS.

Abercrombie Family. Bible rec. Ga. Geneal. Rec. Com., 1936–37, p. 17. Typed, bd. DAR.

Bible rec. Geneal. Soc. Pa. Pub., v. 8, pp. 284–89. DAR.

Abert. Abridged Compendium of American Genealogy. Virkus. V. 1, p. 371. DAR.
Abington, St. Mary's and Calvert Cos. M. H. Mag., 1930, v. 25, no. 3, p. 251–55.
Abraham, Abrahams. St. Paul's Parish, Balto. V. 1, 2. Mss. MHS.
†**Abrahams.** Hist. of Balto. City and Co. Scharf. P. 386. MHS.
Monumental City. Howard. MHS; DAR.
Abrams. White Geneal. Tree. MHS.
Acheson. St. Paul's Parish, Balto. Vol. 1. Mss. MHS.
Acheson Family. Amer. biog. directories. H. B. F. Macfarland. 1908, p. 2. DAR.
†**Achey, Charles F.** (1831). Hist. of Free Masonery in Md. Schultz. 1884.
Achilles. Naturalizations in Md., 1666–1765; Laws. Bacon. MHS.
Ackworth. Old Somerset. Torrence. MHS; DAR.
Rec. of Stepney Parish. MHS; DAR.
Somerset Co. Court Book. Tilghman. 1937. Ms. DAR.
See Acworth.
Acton. Founders of Anne Arundel and Howard Cos. Warfield. P. 145. MHS; DAR.
St. Paul's Parish, Balto. V. 1. Mss. MHS.
***Acworth, Akworth, Ackworth.** Wicomico Co. families. Tilghman. Ms, pp. 2, 96, 101. DAR.
Adair. *See* Ardery. Abridged Compendium of American Genealogy. Virkus. V. 4, pp. 31–32. MHS.
Adam. Peale Geneal. Coll. Ms. MHS.
Adams. Adams family in London, Va., and Somerset Co., Md. Ms. MHS.
*Adams family of London, Va., and Md. Lida Bosler Hunter. 1927. Ms. MHS.
Adams family of Somerset and Worcester Cos.. and probably of Va.; also of Concklin, N. Y. Mrs. Minor Ljungstedt. Ms. File case, DAR.
Bible rec. D. A. R. Mag., Oct., 1932, v. 66, no. 10, pp. 672–74.
*Biog. geneal. of Adams (Va.) families, with some collateral branches. T. W. Adams. 1928, 57 pp. DAR.
Col. families of U. S. A. Mackenzie. V. 1, pp. 3–5; v. 2, pp. 8–9; v. 6, pp. 8–12; v. 7. MHS; DAR.
See Dexter, James, U.S.N. Abridged Compendium of American Genealogy. Virkus. V. 6, p. 23. DAR.
See Griffin, Mrs. F. L. Abridged Compendium of American Genealogy. Virkus. V. 1, p. 923. DAR.
Hist. of Balto. Lewis Hist. Pub. Co., 1912, v. 2, p. 454. DAR.
†Hist. of Frederick Co. Williams. V. 1, pp. 111, 113, 114. MHS; DAR.
†Hist. scholarship in U. S., 1876–1901, as revealed in correspondence of Herbert B. Adams. W. Stull Holt. Balto., J. H. U. Studies, series 26, no. 4, 314 pp. MHS; Enoch Pratt Lib.
See Layton. Abridged Compendium of American Genealogy. Virkus. V. 6, p. 357. DAR.
Leverton family, Kent Co., Bible Rec. Md. Geneal. Rec. Com., 1932–33, v. 5. Mss. DAR.
*Lineage Bk. Daughters of Amer. Colonists. V. 4, pp. 33–34. MHS; DAR.
Md. Geneal. Bul., v. 6, pp. 27, 37; v. 7, p. 1.
†Med. Annals Md. Cordell. 1903, pp. 297–98. MHS.
Miss. M. W. Davis chart. MHS.
Mrs. C. C. Hall chart. MHS.
Old Somerset. Torrence. MHS; DAR.
Peale Geneal. Coll. Ms. MHS.
Rehobeth P. E. churchyard, Somerset Co. Md. Geneal. Rec. Com., 1937, Mrs. Lines. Mss. DAR.
Revolutionary pensions rec. of Nathan, Peter and William Adams. Unbd. ms. DAR.
Revolutionary war pension abst. Natl. Geneal. Soc. Quart., v. 17, no. 4, p. 57.
Somerset Co. Court Book. Tilghman. 1937. Ms. DAR.
Talbott of "Poplar Knowle." Shirk. MHS; DAR.
Tercentenary hist. of Md. Andrews. V. 2, p. 567; v. 3, p. 692. MHS; DAR.
Turner Geneal. Coll. Ms. MHS.
*Wicomico Co. families. Tilghman. Ms, pp. 9, 27, 46, 107. DAR.
Wm. Turpin, Dorchester Co., Bible rec. D. A. R. Mag., v. 66, no. 10, p. 672.
***Adams,** Charles Co. Notes. Amer. Hist. Reg., 1895, v. 1, p. 567. MHS.
†Biog. cyc. of rep. men of Md. and D. C. P. 93. MHS; DAR.
Adams, Del. De Ford chart. MHS.
Adams, Fork Dist., Dorchester Co. Bible rec. of Dorchester and Somerset Cos. and Del. P. 3. DAR.
Adams, Md. and Va. Adamses in North Neck of Va. (Upper Co.) and some nearby counties of Md. Amer. Geneal. and New Haven Geneal. Mag., v. 13, pp. 82, 233. DAR.
Va. Mag. Hist. and Biog., 1902, v. 8, pp. 312, 420; v. 9, pp. 200, 313, 432.
Adams, Snow Hill. Bible rec. of Dorchester and Somerset Cos. and Del. Pp. 4–5. DAR.
Bible rec. Ms. MHS.
Adams, Edward, Fork Dist., Dorchester Co. Bible rec. D. A. R. Mag., v. 66, no. 10, p. 673.
Adams, Colonel Edward, Dorchester Co. Bible rec. Ms. MHS.
***Adams, Henry.** Geneal. J. Gardner Bartlett, for Edward Dean Adams. Priv. pr., 1927. MHS.
†**Adams, Herbert B.** Biog. dict. of U. S. J. H. Lamb Co., v. 1, p. 21.
Memorial. Daniel Coit Gilman. 1902. MHS; Enoch Pratt Lib.
†**Adams, Herbert Baxter** (1850) (educator). Appleton's cyc. of Amer. biog., v. 1, p. 14.
†**Adams, Oscar Fay.** Dict. of Amer. authors. 1905.
Adams, Peter. Revolutionary services, Caroline Co. Ms. DAR.
Adams, Peter, Caroline Co. Family notes. Ms. File case, DAR.
Adams, Prof. T. S. Encyc. of Amer. biog. Amer. Hist. Soc., new series, v. 1, p. 368. MHS; DAR.
***Adams, Thomas.** Hist. of Thomas and Hastings families of Amherst, Mass. Herbert Baxter Adams. Amherst, Mass., priv. pr., 1880. MHS.
Adams Family. Hist. sketches of Campbell, Pilcher and kindred families. M. C. Pilcher. 1911, p. 309. DAR.
Adams Family, Caroline Co. Geneal. and Revolutionary rec. Ms. MHS.

*__Adams Family,__ London, Va., and Somerset Co. Adams family of London, Va., and Somerset Co. Lida Bosler-Hunter. 1927. Ms. MHS.
__Adams Family,__ Md. and Va. Va. Mag. Hist. and Biog., v. 8, pp. 312, 420; v. 9, pp. 200, 313, 432. MHS; DAR.
__Adams-Hughlett.__ Bible rec. of Dorchester and Somerset Cos. and Del. Pp. 6–7. DAR.
__Adams-Mallalieu.__ Bible rec. of Dorchester and Somerset Cos. and Del. Pp. 9, 10. DAR.
__Adams-Waltham.__ Revolutionary war pension rec. of Nathan, Peter and William Adams and Michael Waltham of Md. Mss. DAR.
*__Adams, Addams.__ Branch of Philip Adams family of Md. K. Adams. 1929. MHS.
St. Paul's Parish, Balto. V. 1, 2, 3, 4. Mss. MHS.
__Adamson.__ Beall and Bell families. Beall. MHS.
The Beckwiths. Beckwith. P. 40.
__Addair.__ St. Paul's Parish, Balto. V. 1. Mss. MHS.
__Addams.__ *See* Adams.
See Long-Addams-Crew.
__Addams-Robertson-Wright.__ Notes. D. A. R. Mag., v. 60, no. 9, p. 573.
__Adderley.__ St. Paul's Parish, Balto. V. 1. Mss. MHS.
__Addison.__ Americans of gentle birth and their ancestors. Pitman. P. 5. MHS; DAR.
Ances. rec. and portraits. Col. Dames of Amer., 1910, v. 1, p. 357; v. 2, pp. 671, 687. MHS; DAR.
Mrs. R. Barton, Jr., charts. MHS.
Chart, photos., complete in 1 sheet. Cary Geneal. Coll. Ms. MHS.
Col. families of U. S. A. Mackenzie. V. 1; v. 6. MHS; DAR.
Garrison Church. Allen. P. 77. MHS; DAR.
Geneal. of Va. family of Lomax. Lib. Cong.
†Hist. of Frederick Co. Williams. V. 2, p. 1285. MHS; DAR.
Lehr chart. MHS.
Lineage Bks., Natl. Soc. of Daughters of Amer. Col., v. 3, p. 25. MHS; DAR.
*Lineage Bk. Daughters of Founders and Patriots, v. 16, p. 50. MHS.
Md. families. Culver. Ms. Personal list.
†Med. Annals Md. Cordell. 1903, p. 298. MHS.
†One hundred years ago, or life and times of Walter Dulany Addison, 1769–1848. Chart. E. H. Murray. Phila., 1895. MHS.
Parr chart. MHS.
Peale Geneal. Coll. Ms. MHS.
Pedigree of Edmund Pendleton Hunter Harrison. Soc. Col. Wars Md. Culver. 1940. MHS; DAR.
Pedigree of Franklin Buchanan Owen. Soc. Col. Wars Md. Culver. 1940. MHS; DAR.
Pedigree of Pleasants Pennington. Soc. Col. Wars Md. Culver. 1940. MHS; DAR.
Pedigree of Tilghman Goldsborough Pitts. Soc. Col. Wars Md. Culver. 1940. MHS; DAR.
Pedigree of Raphael Semmes. Soc. Col. Wars Md. Culver. 1940. MHS; DAR.
Pedigree of Henry Lee Smith, Sr. Soc. Col. Wars Md. Culver. 1940. MHS; DAR.
Pedigree of Rev. Sam'l Tagart Steele. Soc. Col. Wars Md. Culver. 1940. MHS; DAR.
St. Paul's Parish, Balto. V. 2, 4. Mss. MHS.
*Side lights on Md. hist. Richardson. V. 2, p. 1. MHS; DAR.
Miss Kate Steele chart. MHS.
*The Sun, Balto., Nov. 27, 1904.
Tercentenary hist. of Md. Andrews. V. 2, p. 515; v. 4, p. 289. MHS; DAR.
The Times, Balto., Sunday, Dec. 13, 1885; Sunday, Jan. 10, 24, 1886. Newsp. clipp. MHS.
See Sprigg-Addison-Cresap-Lamar-Gordon.
__Addison,__ Prince George Co. McH. Howard pedigree chart, plate 2. Soc. Col. Wars, Md. Johnston. 1905, pp. 42, 138. MHS.
*__Addison, James Allison.__ Encyc. of Amer. biog. Amer. Hist. Soc., 1928, v. 33, p. 31.
__Addison, Col. John__ (16— to 1707). Some early col. Marylanders. M. H. Mag., 1919, v. 14, pp. 388–89.
__Addison, Mrs. Murray.__ Abridged Compendium of American Genealogy. Virkus. V. 1, p. 47. DAR.
__Addison, Taylor.__ Md. Soc., War of 1812, no. 56. Ms. MHS.
__Addison Family.__ Amer. biog. directories. H. B. F. Macfarland. 1908, p. 4. DAR.
Ames Geneal. Coll. Ms. MHS.
†Pictures of city of Wash. 1898, p. 162. DAR.
*The Times, Balto., Dec. 13, 1885; Jan. 10, 1886.
__Adkins.__ Buckingham Pres. churchyard, Worcester Co., Hudson. Bd. ms. MHS; DAR.
†Men of mark in Md. Johnson. V. 3, p. 215. DAR; Enoch Pratt Lib.
Mt. Olive M. P. churchyard, Worcester Co. Md. Geneal. Rec. Com., 1937, Mrs. Lines. Mss. DAR.
Rec. of Stepney Parish. MHS; DAR.
*Wicomico Co. families. Tilghman. Ms, pp. 50, 116. DAR.
See Nuttler-Taylor-Parsons-Adkins.
__Adkins Family.__ Tercentenary hist. of Md. Andrews. V. 2, p. 506. MHS; DAR.
__Adler.__ Balto., its hist., its people. Hall. V. 3. MHS; DAR.
__Adlington.__ St. Paul's Parish, Balto. V. 2. Mss. MHS.
†__Adlum.__ Sketch of nurseries. Rec. Columbia Hist. Soc., v. 10, p. 38.
__Adlum, John.__ Newsp. clipp. File case, DAR.
†__Adreon.__ Med. Annals Md. Cordell. 1903, p. 298. MHS.
__Adrian.__ My family memoirs. Hughes. 1931, pp. 50, 59. MHS; DAR.
†__Adt.__ Men of mark in Md. Johnson. V. 3. DAR; Enoch Pratt Lib.
*__Aemon.__ Wicomico Co. families. Tilghman. Ms, p. 109. DAR.
__Affley.__ Cary Geneal. Coll. Ms. MHS.
__Aggis.__ St. Paul's Parish, Balto. V. 1. Mss. MHS.
__Aghen.__ St. Paul's Parish, Balto. V. 1. Mss. MHS.
__Aglionby-Yates,__ Va. The Sun, Balto., Aug. 19, 1906.
__Agnew.__ Amer. Armory and Blue Book. Matthews. 1911–12, p. 412.
*Book of Agnews. M. V. Agnew. 1926. DAR.
†Hist. of life of David Hayes Agnew, M.D., LL.D. J. Adams Howe, Phila.
*Lineage Bk. Daughters of Amer. Colonists. V. 1, p. 202. MHS; DAR.
St. Paul's Parish, Balto. V. 1. Mss. MHS.

Agnew, James. His forbears and descendants. D. A. R. Mag., v. 62, no. 6, p. 346.
Agnus. Balto., its hist., its people. Hall. V. 2. MHS; DAR.
†**Ahalt.** Hist. of Frederick Co. Williams. V. 2, pp. 988, 1045, 1086, 1164, 1265, 1339, 1474, 1485, 1573. MHS; DAR.
†**Ahl.** Med. Annals Md. Cordell. 1903, p. 298. MHS.
Ahrens, Mrs. George Adolf (Bertha Ellen Hall). Chart. Col. Dames, Chap. I. MHS.
Aiken. Focke Geneal. Coll. Ms. MHS.
†Med. Annals Md. Cordell. 1903, p. 298. MHS.
Aiken Family. Jerome hist. and geneal., and ancestry of Sarah Noble. Pp. 63-64. Mss. MHS.
†**Ainslie, Peter.** Appleton's cyc. of Amer. biog., 1922, v. 9.
†Men of mark in Md. Johnson. V. 1, p. 31. DAR; Enoch Pratt Lib.
†Working with God, story of twenty-five years pastorate in Balto. 1915. Enoch Pratt Lib.
Aires, Airs. Rec. of Stepney Parish. MHS; DAR.
Airey. Cary Geneal. Coll. Ms. MHS.
Robert Gilmor chart, MHS.
*Hist. Dorchester Co. Jones. 1925, p. 276. MHS; DAR.
Trinity Church cemetery, Dorchester Co. Md. O. R. Soc. Bul., no. 3, pp. 42-52.
Airey, Thomas. Revolutionary rec. Ms. DAR.
Airey, Thomas, Dorchester Co. Revolutionary rec. Ms. File case, DAR.
Airey Family. Ames Geneal. Coll. Ms. MHS.
Airs. *See* Aires.
Aisquith. St. Paul's Parish, Balto. V. 2. Mss. MHS.
†**Aitken.** Med. Annals Md. Cordell. 1903, p. 299. MHS.
Akels. St. Paul's Parish, Balto. V. 1. Mss. MHS.
Akworth. *See* Acworth.
Albaugh. First settlement of Germans in Md. Schultz. 1896. MHS.
Frederick Co. tombstone inscriptions. Gruder. Natl. Geneal. Soc. Quart., 1919, v. 8, nos. 1, 2.
†Hist. of Balto. City and Co. Scharf. P. 689. MHS.
†Hist. of Frederick Co. Williams. V. 2, pp. 1261, 1283, 1519. MHS; DAR.
Albaugh Family. Tercentenary hist. of Md. Andrews. V. 4, p. 360. MHS; DAR.
†**Albaugh Family,** Md. and Pa. Hist. of Bedford, Somerset and Fulton Cos., Pa. 1884, p. 284. DAR.
Albee-Strong-Miller. Abridged Compendium of American Genealogy. Virkus. V. 4, p. 675. MHS.
†**Albert.** Balto., hist. and biog. Richardson and Bennett. 1871, p. 169. MHS; DAR.
Botfield and allied families. Ms. DAR.
Hagerstown tombstone inscriptions. Gruder. Natl. Geneal. Soc. Quart., 1919, v. 8, nos. 1, 2.
Harvey chart. MHS.
Med. Annals Md. Cordell. 1903, p. 299. MHS.
Mrs. T. R. Brown chart. MHS.
Zion Reformed Church, Hagerstown. Md. Geneal. Rec. Com., 1934-35. Mss. DAR.
Albert, Andrew (born in Germany Apr. 20, 1753; died in Pa., 1841). Greenway Mss. Geneal. Coll. Binder's title, Taylor, no. 2. MHS.
Albert Family. Md. Geneal. Rec. Com., 1937, pp. 102-03. DAR.
Albough, Jacob. Md. Soc., War of 1812, v. 1, no. 57. Ms. MHS.
Albright, Philip. Geneal rec. of George Small, etc. Small. MHS.
Alcock. Cary Geneal. Coll. Ms. MHS.
Gary chart. MHS.
†Med. Annal. Md. Cordell. 1903, p. 299. MHS.
St. Paul's Parish, Balto. V. 2, 3. Mss. MHS.
Alden. Coll. of Amer. epitaphs and inscriptions. Alden. 1814, v. 1. MHS.
Alden, John, of Plymouth colony. Pedigree of Julian White Ridgely. Soc. Col. Wars Md. Culver. 1940. MHS; DAR.
Alder. St. Paul's Parish, Balto. V. 1, 3. Mss. MHS.
See Alter.
Alderson. St. Paul's Parish, Balto. V. 1, 2. Mss. MHS.
Aldin. St. Paul's Parish, Balto. V. 1. Mss. MHS.
Aldrich. Pedigree of Rev. Sam'l Tagart Steele. Soc. Col. Wars Md. Culver. 1940. MHS; DAR.
†**Aldridge.** Hist. of Allegany Co. Thomas and Williams. V. 2. MHS; DAR.
Lehr chart. MHS.
St. Paul's Parish, Balto. V. 1. Mss. MHS.
Alexander. Alexander family, Md., N. C., Ohio, Pa. F. A. Butterworth. Ms. File case, DAR.
†Bench and Bar of Md. Sams and Riley. 1901, v. 2, p. 600. Lib. Cong.; MHS; Peabody Lib.
Carlyle family and Carlyle house. Spencer. P. 24. MHS.
*Chart, with genealogies. F. T. A. Junkin. Balto., 1888. MHS.
Col. families of U. S. A. Mackenzie. V. 3, p. 7; v. 6, p. 18. MHS; DAR.
Descendants of John Alexander, Scotland, and his wife Margaret Glasson, Chester Co., Pa., 1736. J. E. Alexander. 1878, 220 pp. DAR.
*Geneal.; chart of Alexander and other families. Comp. by Francis T. A. Junkin. Priv. pr. 1908, 2nd and revised ed. MHS.
Ghiselin chart. Cary Geneal. Coll. Ms. MHS.
†Hist. of Cecil Co. Johnston. MHS; DAR.
†John Henry Alexander, LL.D. (Born in Annapolis, 1812; died in Balto., 1867.) J. G. Proud. 1868.
Lineage Bks., Natl. Soc. of Daughters of Amer. Col., v. 3, pp. 277-78. MHS; DAR.
Md. families. Culver. Ms. Personal list.
†Med. annals Md. Cordell. 1903, pp. 299, 422. MHS.
Pedigree of Mark Alexander Herbert Smith. Soc. Col. Wars Md. Culver. 1940. MHS; DAR.
*Rec. of family of house of Alexander, 1640-1909. Descendants of William Alexander, Cecil and Somerset Cos. F. A. Butterworth. Priv. pr., Chicago, 1909.
St. Paul's Parish, Balto. V. 1, 2, 3. Mss. MHS.
Selden chart. MHS.
Somerset Co. Court Book. Tilghman. 1937. Ms. DAR.

*The Sun, Balto., Nov. 5, 19, 1905; Jan. 6, 1906.
Mrs. Wm. L. Watson chart. MHS.
Alexander, Va. Chart. Ancestors and descendants of John and Sussannah (Pearson) Alexander. Col. T. E. Cassidy and Mrs. E. A. H. Cassidy. Blue print. Washington, 1929–30. File case, DAR.
Va. geneal. Hayden. MHS; DAR.
Posey chart. MHS.
Alexander, Va., Princeton and New York. Chart. W. Alexander. 1714. File case, DAR.
Alexander, Mrs. Charles Butler (Margaret Sterrett Moss). Chart. (Mostly W. Va. families.) Col. Dames, Chap. I. MHS.
†**Alexander, David Henry,** Wash. Amer. Clan Gregor Year Book, 1934, p. 64. MHS; DAR.
Alexander, E. D., Annapolis. Abridged Compendium of American Genealogy. Virkus. V. 1, p. 128. DAR.
†**Alexander, John H.** Memoir. William Pinkney. Balto., John Murphy, 1867.
†**Alexander, John Henry,** (1812–67). First geologist of state of Md. M. H. Mag., 1929, v. 24, no. 2, p. 145–51.
†**Alexander, Robt.** Hist. of Md. Scharf. V. 2, p. 297. MHS.
Md. loyalist. M. H. Mag., 1906, v. 1, pp. 316–23.
†**Alexander, Thomas Harwood.** Sketch. M. H. Mag., 1930, v. 25, pp. 167–69.
***Alexander Family.** Rec. W. M. Clemens. N. Y., ltd. ed., 1914. MHS; DAR.
Alford, A. G. Md. Soc., War of 1812, v. 2, no. 177. Ms. MHS.
Alger. Chart of Com. John Rodgers. DAR.
†**Alger, Philip Rounseville** (U. S. A., 1859–1912). In memoriam. Pamph. File case, DAR; Enoch Pratt Lib.
†**Algire.** Med. Annals Md. Cordell. 1903, p. 300. MHS.
Alman. St. Stephens Parish, Cecilton, Md. MHS; DAR.
Allan, Va. Ahrens chart. MHS.
Allandale. Harford Co. Hist. Soc. Mss. Coll. JHU.
Allanson. Thomas Allanson, Lord of Christian Temple Manor and Ford-Smoot. Mrs. Mary T. Layton. Mss. DAR.
Allen. Bond chart. MHS.
Diffenderfer family, arrived in Phila., 1727. Ms. File case, DAR.
Hist. graves of Md. and D. C. Ridgely. MHS.
McCormick chart. MHS.
†Med. Annals Md. Cordell. 1903, p. 300. MHS.
†Men of mark in Md. Johnson. V. 3. DAR; Enoch Pratt Lib.
Peale Geneal. Coll. Ms. MHS.
St. Paul's Parish, Balto. V. 1, 2, 3, 4. Mss. MHS.
Sater geneal. Bd. ms. MHS.
Zimmerman-Waters and allied families. Allen. MHS; DAR.
Allen, Calvert Co. Mrs. G. R. Veazey chart. MHS.
†**Allen, Mrs. Brasseya** (born in Ireland; married Rev. J. Allen, church in Harford Co., 1795). Poets and Prose writers of Md. Perine.
Allen, Dorothy Edmondstone Zimmerman. Amer. Clan Gregor Year Book, 1917, p. 68. MHS; DAR.
Allen, Capt. John. St. Steven's graveyard, Cecil Co. Md. Geneal. Rec. Com., 1934–35, pp. 213–14. Mss. DAR.
†**Allen, Paul** (born in R. I., 1755; died in Balto., 1826). Poets and prose writers of Md. Perine.
Allen-Coale. Abridged Compendium of American Genealogy. Virkus. V. 4, pp. 23–24. DAR.
Allender. Patriotic Md. Md. Soc. of S. A. R., 1930. MHS; DAR.
†Med. Annals Md. Cordell. 1903, p. 300. MHS.
St. Paul's Parish, Balto. V. 1, 2. Mss. MHS.
See Ellender.
Alley. St. Paul's Parish, Balto. V. 1. Mss. MHS.
Allgire, from Md. Tercentenary hist. of Md. Andrews. V. 3, p. 163. MHS; DAR.
Allin. St. Stephen's Parish, Cecilton, Md. MHS; DAR.
Allingsworth. Somerset Co. Court Book. Tilghman. 1937. Ms. DAR.
***Alliphan.** Wicomico Co. families. Tilghman. Ms, p. 112. DAR.
Allison. Bantz geneal. notes. Ms. MHS.
Mrs. R. Barton, Jr., charts. MHS.
Clark chart.
Coll. of Amer. epitaphs and inscriptions. Alden. 1814, v. 5. MHS.
*Frederick Co. families. Markell. Ms. Personal list.
Pedigree of Howard Elmer Ashbury. Soc. Col. Wars Md. Culver. 1940. MHS; DAR.
St. Paul's Parish, Balto. V. 1, 2. Mss. MHS.
Southerland-Latham and allied families. Voorhees. P. 108. Bd. ms. MHS.
Allison Family. Ms. MHS.
Allnutt. Americus Dawson Farm, Montgomery Co. Md. Geneal. Rec. Com., 1926, p. 76. Mss. DAR.
M. E. Church burial ground, Laytonsville, Montgomery Co. Md. Geneal. Rec. Com., 1934–35, pp. 69–82. Mss. DAR.
Monocacy Cemetery, Beallsville, Montgomery Co. Md. Geneal. Rec. Com., 1926–27. Mss. DAR.
Mothers' Delight stones, moved from Americus Dawson farm, near Dawsonville, to Monocacy Cemetery. Md. Geneal. Rec. Com., v. 2, p. 76. Mss. DAR.
Talbott of "Poplar Knowle." Shirk. MHS; DAR.
Allnutt, Calvert Co. Sweetser chart. MHS.
Allstons. *See* Alstons.
***Allyn-Foote-Webb-Cooch-Wilkins.** Geneal.; ancestry and descendants of Nancy Allyn (Foote) Webb, Rev. Edward Webb and Joseph Wilkins Cooch. Mary Evarts (Webb) Cooch. Pr. for priv. distribution, Wilmington, Del., Star Publishing Co., 1919. MHS; DAR.
Alpin. MacAchaia, King of Scotland. Line of descent from Adam and Eve, 4000 B.C. Amer. Clan Gregor Year Book, 1926–27, p. 28. MHS; DAR.
Alpin, MacAlpin, Gregor, MacGregor, Magruder. "My race is royal." Amer. Clan Gregor Year Book, 1919, p. 54. MHS; DAR.
Alpine-Gregor-McGregor-Magruder, 787–1928, 25 generations. Md. Geneal. Rec. Com., 1933–34, pp. 287–92. Mss. DAR.

Alricks. Miss Margaret M. Steele chart. MHS.
See Heslop-Alricks. Lineage Bks., Natl. Soc. of Daughters of Amer. Col., v. 3, p. 250. MHS; DAR.
Alricks, Peter, Del. and Pa. Pedigree of Lewis Warrington Cottman. Soc. Col. Wars Md. Culver. 1940. MHS; DAR.
Alricks-Haughton. Lineage Bks., Natl. Soc. of Daughters of Amer. Col., v. 3, p. 9. MHS; DAR.
Alsop. Cary Geneal. Coll. Ms. MHS.
***Alstons, Allstons.** Alstons and Allstons of North and South Carolina. J. A. Groves. Atlanta, Ga., Franklin Printing and Publishing Co., 1902, 1st ed. MHS.
Alter, Alder. Hagerstown tombstone inscriptions. Gruder. Natl. Geneal. Soc. Quart., 1919, v. 8, nos. 1, 2.
†Alvey. Bench and Bar of Md. Sams and Riley. 1901, v. 2, p. 473. Lib. Cong.; MHS; Peabody Lib.
Centenary of Catholicity in Ky. Webb. 1884. MHS.
†Hist. of Allegany Co. Thomas and Williams. V. 1. MHS; DAR.
†Men of mark in Md. Johnson. V. 1. DAR; Enoch Pratt Lib.
Alward. Naturalizations in Md., 1666–1765; Laws. Bacon. MHS.
Alwell. St. Paul's Parish, Balto. V. 1. Mss. MHS.
Amas. St. Paul's Parish, Balto. V. 1. Mss. MHS.
Ambler. Marshall family, Westmoreland Co., Va. Pp. 42–45.
Va. families. Du Bellett.
Ambler, J. M. Abridged Compendium of American Genealogy. Virkus. V. 1, p. 99. DAR.
Ambrose. Marriages, 1704–1823. Parrish family. Boyd. MHS; DAR.
Naturalizations in Md., 1666–1765; Laws. Bacon. MHS.
Trinity P. E. churchyard, Long Green. Typed ms. MHS; DAR.
Ames. Ames Geneal. Coll. (N. C., Md. and Va. families). Md. families listed. Mss. MHS.
†Med. Annals Med. Cordell. 1903, p. 301. MHS.
Ames, James Sweetman, Pedigree chart. Ms. MHS.
Ames, Mrs. Joseph S. (Mary Boykm Williams) (married first Thomas Bullitt Harrison). Chart. (Mostly S. C. families.) Col. Dames, Chap. I, MHS.
Amler. St. Paul's Parish, Balto. V. 1. Mss. MHS.
†Ammidon. Men of mark in Md. Johnson. V. 2. DAR; Enoch Pratt Lib.
Whitridge chart. MHS.
Amonscoars. St. Paul's Parish, Balto. V. 1. Mss. MHS.
***Amos.** Amos-Paca-Smith. Lineage Bk. Daughters of Amer. Colonists. V. 2, pp. 93–94. MHS; DAR.
See Anderson. Col. families of U.S.A. Mackenzie. V. 4, p. 3. MHS.
Bonsal charts. MHS.
See Glenn. Col. families of U. S. A. Mackenzie. V. 3, p. 187. MHS; DAR.
Hist. of Harford Co. Preston. 1901, p. 357. MHS; DAR.
Harford Co. Hist. Soc. Mss. Coll. JHU.
Machen chart. MHS.
Md. families. Culver. Ms. Personal list.
Md. Geneal. Bull., v. 3, p. 29.
†Med. Annals Md. Cordell. 1903, p. 301. MHS.
Pedigree of Pleasants Pennington. Soc. Col. Wars Md. Culver. 1940. MHS; DAR.
Pedigree of Anthony Morris Tyson. Soc. Col. Wars Md. Culver. 1940. MHS; DAR.
Mrs. Pennington chart. MHS.
Perin chart. MHS.
Tercentenary hist. of Md. Andrews. V. 2, p. 685; v. 4, p. 735. MHS; DAR.
M. Van V. Tyson pedigree chart, plate 1. Soc. Col. Wars, Md. Johnston, 1905, p. 117. MHS.
Amos, Wm., Harford Co. W. S. Myers pedigree chart. Soc. Col. Wars, Md. Johnston. 1905, pp. 76, 138. MHS.
Amos, William, Sr., Balto. Co. Copy of will, 1757–59. Ms. MHS.
Amoss. Geneal. of descendants of George and Sarah Smedley. Cope. Pp. 806–07. MHS; DAR.
*Smithsons of Harford Co. Md. Geneal. Rec. Com., 1932–33, pp. 151, 153, 154. Mss. DAR.
***Ancell.** Descendants of Edward Ancell, Va. B. L. Ancell. Pamph., 1933. DAR.
†Anders. Hist. of Frederick Co. Williams. V. 2, pp. 923, 924, 1140, 1327. MHS; DAR.
Hist. of West. Md. Scharf. V. 1, p. 617; v. 2, p. 900. MHS; DAR.
Anderson. Abr. Compend. Amer. Geneal. Virkus. V. 1, p. 421. DAR.
Balto., its hist., its people. Hall. V. 3. MHS; DAR.
*Boone-Anderson-Scothoron. Homer Eiler. Topeka, Kans., 1929. MHS.
Buckingham Pres. churchyard. Worcester Co., Hudson. Bd. ms. MHS; DAR.
†Carrollton Manor, Md. Grove. 1921, p. 76. DAR.
Col. families of U. S. A. Mackenzie. V. 4, p. 3. MHS.
Eiler-Anderson-Boon-Sothoron-Witten. Eiler. 1929, pamph. MHS.
*Frederick Co. families. Markell. Ms. Personal list.
Geneal. of family of Gideon Gilpin. MHS.
Hist. of Allegany Co. Thomas and Williams. V. 2, pp. 713–14, 1216–18. MHS; DAR.
*Hist. Dorchester Co. Jones. 1902, p. 277, 1925, p. 277. MHS; DAR.
†Hist. of Frederick Co. Williams. V. 2, p. 1028. MHS; DAR.
Hist. of Harford Co. Preston. 1901, p. 182. MHS; DAR.
MacSherry chart. MHS.
†Med. Annals Md. Cordell. 1903, pp. 301–03. MHS.
Moravian Church of York, Pa., register of 1780. Pub. Geneal. Soc. Pa., v. 4, p. 345.
Mt. Carmel burial ground, Unity, Montgomery Co. Md. Geneal. Rec. Com., 1934–35, p. 85. Mss. DAR.
*Mullikin, family Bible rec. Mss., in Binder. DAR.
See Mullikin-Anderson-Woodward-Hall. DAR.
Naturalizations in Md., 1666–1765; Laws. Bacon. MHS.

See Nelson, Mrs. W. B. Abr. Compend. Amer. Geneal. Virkus. V. 1, p. 419. DAR.
*Old Kent. Hanson. Pp. 364–68. MHS. DAR.
Old Somerset. Torrence. MHS; DAR.
Peale Geneal. Coll. Ms. MHS.
Portrait and biog. rec. of Sixth Cong. Dist. of Md. 1898, pp. 686, 691. MHS; DAR.
Rec. of Stepney Parish. MHS; DAR.
St. Paul's Parish, Balto. V. 1, 2, 3. Mss. MHS.
Tercentenary hist. of Md. Andrews. V. 2, pp. 73, 658, 705; v. 4, p. 744. MHS; DAR.
*The Sun, Balto., April 1, 8, 19, 1906.
Uhler Bible rec. Md. Geneal. Rec. Com., v. 2. DAR.
*Wicomico Co. families. Tilghman. Ms., pp. 20, 40, 100, 104, 115. DAR.
See Zoller. Lineage Bks., Natl. Soc. of Daughters of Amer. Col., v. 2, p. 187. MHS; DAR.
See Eiler-Boone-Anderson-Scothoron.
See Uhler-Anderson-Burgess-Galloway.

Anderson, Baltimore Co. Talbott of "Poplar Knowle". Shirk. MHS; DAR.

Anderson, Absolom, Anne Arundel Co. (1772–1832.) Ms. DAR.

†**Anderson, Capt. Richard.** Hist. of Md. Scharf. V. 2, p. 406. MHS.

Anderson, Wm., Sr. And his wife, Elizabeth Willet. Ms. MHS.

***Anderson Family.** Gravestones, Velvoir, Md. D. C. Geneal. Rec. Com., 1930–32, v. 2, p. 62. Typed, bd. DAR.
*Old Kent Chapter. Bible rec. East. Shore of Md., 1926–29, pp. 36–37. Mss. Bk. DAR.

Anderson-Owen-Beall. Geneal. Anderson. Index to. Mss. DAR.
*Geneal. in part. G. J. Anderson. Richmond, Va., 1909, 159 pp. DAR.

Anderton. Anderton and Andrews; arrivals in Md., 1634–84. Md. Geneal. Bull., v. 2, no. 2, p. 14.

†**Andre.** Med. Annals Md. Cordell. 1903, p. 303. MHS.

Andrew. Bond chart. MHS.
St. Paul's Parish, Balto. V. 1. Mss. MHS.
Somerset Co. Court Book. Tilghman. 1937. Ms. DAR.

Andrew-Platt Family. Chart, printed. File case, DAR.

Andrews. Anderton and Andrews; arrivals in Md., 1634–84. Md. Geneal. Bull., v. 2, no. 2, p. 14.
Geneal. and alliances, New Eng., Md. and Pa. C. B. Wyker (Mrs. John D.) Cincinnati, Ohio, Methodist Book Concern, 1917. MHS.
Chart, photos. of ms. File case, DAR.
Col. families of Amer. Lawrence. V. 3, p. 301. MHS.
Eldridge chart. MHS.
*Geneal. and alliances. Clara Berry Wyker. Decatur, Ala., 1917. DAR.
Geneal. of Andrews family and alliances, descendants of John, who settled in Md. in 1654. Robert S. Andrews. East Orange, N. J., 1893. Pa. Hist. Soc. Lib.
Geneal. of Henrietta Chauncy Wilson. Upshur. Bk. of photos. MHS.
†Hist. of Balto. City and Co. Scharf. P. 669. MHS.
Photos. Newsp. clipp. Scrap Book. MHS.
St. Paul's Parish, Balto. V. 1, 2, 3, 5. Mss. MHS.
Somerset Co. Court Book. Tilghman. 1937. Ms. DAR.

Andrews, Calvert Co. See Shaw. Abr. Compend. Amer. Geneal. Virkus. V. 1, p. 608. DAR.

†**Andrews, Matthew Page.** Balto. in Amer. literature. Holly.
†Tercentenary hist. of Md. V. 4, pp. 688–93.

†**Andrews, Richard Snowden** (1830–1903) (Lieut. Col. commanding First Md. Artillery C.S.A.). Memoir. Tunstall Smith. 1910, 151 pp. MHS; DAR.

Andrews, Sally Magruder (Ferneyhough), Va. Amer. Clan Gregor, Year Book, 1914, p. 82. MHS; DAR.

***Andrews Family.** Anderson families (in his Groome families connections). 1907, p. 82. DAR.
Garrison Church, St. Thomas Parish. Allen. Pp. 43–44. DAR.
Photos. MHS.
Tercentenary hist. of Md. Andrews. V. 4, p. 636, MHS; DAR.
Thomas Book. Thomas. P. 194. Lib. Cong.; MHS.

Andrews-Bonner-Carroll-Corkran-Medford Families. Geneal., data. Andrews Scrap Book. MHS.

Angell. Ances. rec. and portraits. Col. Dames of Amer., 1910, p. 772, MHS; DAR.

Angle. Abr. Compend. Amer. Geneal. Virkus. V. 1, p. 423. DAR.

†**Angleberger.** Hist. of Frederick Co. Williams. V. 2, pp. 1468, 1609. MHS; DAR.

Angleing. St. Paul's Parish, Balto. V. 1. Mss. MHS.

Anglen. St. Paul's Parish, Balto. V. 1. Mss. MHS.

Ankeney. Spessard family. Spessard. MHS; DAR.

Ankeny Line. Gaither, Va. and Md. Col. and Revolutionary families of Phila. Jordan. 1933, v. 1, pp. 144–67.

Anleton. Naturalizations in Md., 1666–1765; Laws. Bacon. MHS.

Anhan. Hist. of Allegany Co. Thomas and Williams. V. 1, pp. 552–54; v. 2, pp. 812–14. MHS; DAR.
†Hist. of Frederick Co. Williams. V. 2, pp. 864, 1502, 1503. MHS; DAR.
Hist. of Wash. Co. Williams. 1906, p. 446. MHS., DAR.
†Hist. of West. Md. Scharf. V. 1, p. 593. MHS; Dar.
†Med. Annals Md. Cordell. 1903, pp. 303–04. MHS.

Annis. St. Paul's Parish, Balto. V. 1. Mss. MHS.

Anson-Sanborn. Chart. DAR.

Antes. Dukehart and collateral lines. Ms. MHS.
Life and times of Henry Antes (1701–75), German hero of col. Pa. Rev. E. McMinn. 1886, 305 pp. MHS; DAR.
Ms. MHS.

Anthony. Pattison wills. Md. Geneal. Rec. Com., 1929, pp. 7–42; 1930–31. Mss. DAR.
St. Paul's Parish, Balto. V. 2. Mss. MHS.

Anthony, John (born in Spain 1756; died at home near Galena, Kent Co.; married Sophia Briscoe). Md. Geneal. Rec. Com., 1937–38, pp. 68–69. Mss. DAR.
***Anthony Family.** Bible rec. in Md. Bible Rec., Stuart, p. 35. Typed, bd. DAR.
Anthony-Cooper. Bible. Upper Penins. East. Shore. Pp. 37–43. MHS; DAR.
Apple. Henkel Family Assoc., July, 1930, No. 2, p. 26. MHS; DAR.
†Hist. Frederick Co. Williams. MHS; DAR.
†**Apple, Rev. J. H.,** Frederick Co. Biog. dict. of U. S. J. H. Lamb Co., v. 1, p. 108.
Apple, J. R., Pa. Abr. Compend. Amer. Geneal. Virkus. V. 1, p. 426. DAR.
Apple, Appleman. St. Paul's Parish, Balto. V. 1. Mss. MHS.
Appleby. Culver pedigree chart. MHS.
St. Paul's Parish, Balto. V. 1. Mss. MHS.
Appleby, Montgomery Co. Pedigree of Francis Barnum Culver. Soc. Col. Wars Md. Culver. 1940. MHS; DAR.
†**Applegarth.** Biog. cyc. of rep. men of Md. and D.C. P. 93. MHS; DAR.
Appleman. *See* Apple.
Appleton. St. Paul's Parish, Balto. V. 2, 3. Mss. MHS.
Appleton, Sam'l., Mass. Pedigree of Rufus King Goodenow, Jr. Soc. Col. Wars Md. Culver. 1940. MHS; DAR.
Appold. Balto., its hist., its people. Hall. V. 2. MHS., DAR.
Col. families of U. S. A. Mackenzie. V. 1, p. 382. MHS.
Appold-Campbell. Abr. Compend. Amer. Geneal. Virkus. V. 1, p. 57. DAR.
Appold-Dryden Family. Bible rec. Ms. MHS.
Arback, St. Paul's Parish, Balto. V. 1. Mss. MHS.
†**Archer.** Bench and bar of Md. Sams and Riley. 1901, v. 1, p. 291. Lib. Cong.; MHS; Peabody Lib.
†Biog. cyc. of rep. men of Md. and D.C. Pp. 40–44. MHS; DAR.
Col. families of U. S. A. Mackenzie. V. 1, pp. 9–11; v. 2, pp. 19–30. MHS; DAR.
*Frederick Co. families. Markell. Ms. Personal list.
Harford Co. Hist. Soc. Mss. Coll. JHU.
Hist. of Harford Co. Preston. MHS; DAR.
†Hist. of Md. Scharf. V. 2, p. 597. MHS.
Ms., 12 pp. Inst. Amer. Geneal., 440 Dearborn St., Chicago.
Md. families. Culver. Ms. Personal list.
†M. H. Mag., v. 12, p. 201.
†Med. Annals Md. Cordell. 1903, pp. 304–06, 746–52. MHS.
Patriotic Md. Md. Soc. of S. A. R., 1930. MHS; DAR.
Pedigree of George Webb Constable. Soc. Col. Wars Md. Culver. 1940, MHS; DAR.
Plummer family. A. P. H. Ms. MHS.
St. Paul's Parish, Balto. V. 3. Mss. MHS.
St. Stephens Parish, Cecilton, Md. MHS; DAR.
Stump family of Cecil and Harford Cos. Pamph. MHS.
***Archer, C. Graham.** Burke's landed gentry. 1939. MHS.
***Archer, John.** Harford Co. Geneal., 1741–1876. Md. Geneal. Rec. Com., 1929, pp. 72–78. DAR.
Arden. Wills. Ms. MHS.
Arenson. Naturalizations in Md., 1666–1765; Laws. Bacon. MHS.
Armat. See Hunter. Col. families of U. S. A. Mackenzie. V. 1, p. 274. MHS; DAR.
Armer. St. Paul's Parish, Balto. V. 1, 2. Mss. MHS.
Armistead. Amer. Armory and Blue Book. Matthews. 1911–12, p. 361.
Amer. of gentle birth, and their ancestors. Pittman. V. 1. MHS; DAR.
*Armistead family of Va. Pr. for Wm. S. Appleton. Boston, David Clapp & Son, 1899.
Balch chart. MHS.
Cary Geneal. Coll. Ms. MHS.
Col. families of U. S. A. Mackenzie. V. 1, p. 12. MHS; DAR.
Family of Armistead of Va. Pr. for W. S. Appleton. Boston, David Clapp & Son, 1899, pamph. Lib. Cong.; MHS.
Lehr chart. MHS.
Moale-Croxall-North chart. Cary Geneal. Coll. Ms. MHS.
St. Paul's Parish, Balto. V. 2, 3. Mss. MHS.
Selden chart. MHS.
Va. geneal. Hayden. MHS; DAR.
*The Sun, Balto., Sept. 16, 23, 30, Oct. 7, 1906.
†**Armistead, Lt.-Col. George.** Hist. of Md. Scharf. V. 3, p. 104. MHS.
Armistead, Geo. Md. Soc., War of 1812, v. 3, no. 209. Ms. MHS.
Armistead Family, Va. Rec. Ancestry of Benjamin Harrison. Keith. MHS; DAR.
Armistead Line, Va. W. A. Moale pedigree charts, plate 1. Soc. Col. Wars, Md. Johnston. 1905, pp. 72, 138. MHS.
Armistead-Harrison Line, Va. W. H. Gill pedigree chart. Soc. Col. Wars, Md. Johnston. 1905, p. 26. MHS.
†**Armitage.** Med. Annals Md. Cordell. 1903, p. 306. MHS.
St. Paul's Parish, Balto. V. 1, 2. Mss. MHS.
Armor. Wm. Conway of Md. and Pa. Ms. File case, DAR.
Armour. Foeke Geneal. Coll. Ms. MHS.
Jenkins-Courtney chart. MHS.
St. Paul's Parish, Balto. V. 1. Mss. MHS.
†**Armstrong.** Bench and Bar of Md. Sams and Riley. 1901, v. 2, p. 609. Lib. Cong.; MHS; Peabody Lib.
Fox-Ellicott-Evans families. Evans. MHS; DAR.
*Garrett Co. pioneer families. Hoye. MHS; DAR.
†Med. Annals Md. Cordell. 1903, p. 306. MHS.
Mountain Democrat, Garrett Co. Newsp. clipp. MHS; DAR.
Peale Geneal. Coll. Ms. MHS.
St. Paul's Parish, Balto. V. 1, 2, 3. Mss. MHS.
St. Stephens Parish, Cecilton, Md. MHS; DAR.
Zion Reformed Church, Hagerstown. Md. Geneal. Rec. Com., 1934–35. Mss. DAR.
†**Armstrong, Alexander.** Encyc. of Amer. biog. Amer. Hist. Soc., new series, v. 1, p. 218. MHS; DAR.
Armstrong, Horatio Gates. Pedigree chart. Soc. Col. Wars, Md. Johnston. 1905, pp. 1, 138. MHS.
Arnald. Early Quaker rec., Anne Arundel and

Calvert Cos., 1665–1889. Pub. Geneal. Soc. Pa., v. 3, no. 3, pp. 197–200.

Arnall. St. Paul's Parish, Balto. V. 1. Mss. MHS.

Arnelled. Early Quaker rec., Anne Arundel and Calvert Cos., 1665–1889. Pub. Geneal. Soc. Pa., v. 3, no. 3, pp. 197–200.

†**Arnest.** Med. Annals Md. Cordell. 1903, p. 306. MHS.

Arnett, Dorchester Co. Marriages. Md. Geneal. Bull., v. 3, no. 4, p. 29.

Arnold. Col. families of Amer., Lawrence. V. 9, p. 138. MHS.
De Ford chart. MHS.
†Hist. Frederick Co. Williams. MHS; DAR.
Mrs. G. C. Jenkins chart. MHS.
†Med. Annals Md. Cordell. 1903, p. 306. MHS.
Sacred Heart R. C. churchyard, Bushwood, St. Mary's Co. Md. Geneal. Rec. Com., 1929. Mss. DAR.
St. Paul's Parish, Balto. V. 1, 3, 4, 5. Mss. MHS.

Arnold, Mrs. Carrington Gindrat (Cassandra Laurence Lee). Chart. Col. Dames, Chap. I. MHS.

***Arnold-Luckey.** Rec. Our family ties. MHS.

Aron. St. Stephens Parish, Cecilton, Md. MHS; DAR.

Arrowsmith. Col. families of Amer. Laurence. V. 10, p. 33. See also Arrowsmith, of N. Y., v. 16, pp. 286–312. MHS.
St. Paul's Parish, Balto. V. 1. Mss. MHS.

***Arrowsmith,** N. Y. and Balto. Burke's landed gentry. 1939, p. 2989. MHS.

Arthington. St. Paul's Parish, Balto. V. 1. Mss. MHS.

Arthur. Smithson-Rumsey rec. bk. Ms. MHS.

Arthurs. Lineage Bk., Order of Washington, p. 26. MHS; DAR.

Arthurs, E. Ferguson. Md. Soc., War of 1812, v. 2, no. 140. Ms. MHS.
Pedigree chart. Soc. Col. Wars, Md. Johnston. 1905, p. 2. MHS.

Artis. Fresh Pond Neck cemetery, home of Bennetts. Md. O. R. Soc. Bull., no. 3, pp. 57–58.

Artz. Hagerstown tombstone inscriptions. Gruder. Natl. Geneal. Soc. Quart., 1919, v. 8, nos. 1, 2.

Arundal. St. Paul's Parish, Balto. V. 1. Mss. MHS.

***Arundel.** Early geneal. hist. of house of John Pym Yeatman, Esq. London, Mitchell and Hughes, 1882. MHS.

Arundell. Md. gleanings in Eng. Wills. M. H. Mag., 1907. v. 2, no. 3.

***Asbury.** Church. Wicomico Co. families. Tilghman Ms., p. 128. DAR.

†**Asbury, Bishop,** Francis. Hist. of Md. Scharf. V. 2, p. 557. MHS.
†H. M. Du Bose. (Francis Asbury, 1745–1816, was made first Meth. bishop in Amer. at Christmas Conference, 1784, in Lovely Lane Meeting House, Balto.) 1916. DAR.
Life and work. Asbury Lowry. Amer. Soc. Church Hist. Papers, N. Y., 1894, v. 6.

Asford. *See* Ashford.

Ash Family. Md. Geneal. Rec. Com. 1938–39, pp. 84–86. Mss. DAR.

Ashburner. St. Paul's Parish, Balto. V. 1, 2. Mss. MHS.

Ashbury, Howard Elmer. Pedigree. Soc. Col. Wars. Md. Culver. 1940. MHS; DAR.

Ashby. Balto., its hist, its people. Hall. V. 2. MHS; DAR.
*Garrett Co. pioneer families. Haye. MHS; DAR.
*Geneal. and mem. encyc. of Md. Spencer. V. 2, p. 437. MHS; DAR.
Md. Soc., War of 1812, v. 4, no. 326. Ms. MHS.
†Med. Annals Md. Cordell. 1903, p. 307. MHS.
†Men of mark in Md. Johnson. V. 2. DAR; Enoch Pratt Lib.
Mountain Democrat, Garrett Co. Newsp. clipp. MHS; DAR.

***Ashby,** Va. The Sun, Balto., Dec. 3, 10, 1905.

Ashby, Bernard. Pedigree. Soc. Col. Wars Md. Culver. 1940. MHS; DAR.

Ashby, Bladen (Revolutionary hero). Md. Geneal. Rec. Com., 1937–38, p. 39. Mss. DAR.

Ashcom. Md. Families. Culver. Ms. Personal list.

Ashcom Family. Sketch, 1643–1931. (Copy.) Md. Geneal. Rec. Com., 1932–33, pp. 27–35. Mss. DAR.

Ashford, Asford. St. Stephens Parish, Cecilton, Md. MHS; DAR.

Ashhurst. Hazelhurst charts. MHS.

Ashley. St. Paul's Parish, Balto. V. 1, 2. Ms. MHS.

Ashley-Elburn. Rec. contrib. by Miss Isabel Fowler, Chestertown, Md. Md. Geneal. Rec. Com., 1938–39, pp. 104–06. Mss. DAR.

***Ashman.** Ashman-Cromwell-Hines. Lineage Bk. Daughters of Amer. Colonists. V. 4, p. 198. MHS; DAR.
Chart. Geneal. and chart of Chenoweth and Cromwell families of Md. and Va. Chenoweth. MHS.
Griffith geneal. Griffith. MHS; DAR.
Lineage Bks., Natl. Soc. of Daughters of Amer. Col., v. 4, p. 198. MHS; DAR.
Md. families. Culver. Ms. Personal list.
Chenoweth-Cromwell geneal. and charts. MHS.
W. W. Coleman pedigree chart. Soc. Col. Wars, Md. Johnston. 1905, p. 17. MHS.
Rogers Coll. Ms. MHS.
St. Paul's Parish, Balto. V. 1. Mss. MHS.
St. Thomas' Parish, Balto. Co. Bd. ms. MHS. Also: Md. Geneal. Rec. Com., 1937, pp. 109–82. Mss. DAR.

***Ashman Family.** Anne Arundel Co. gentry. Newman. Pp. 567–75. MHS; DAR.

***Ashman-Cromwell-Jacob-Taylor-Towson-Trehearn-Wilmott.** The Sun, Balto., Aug. 11, 18, 1907.

Ashmore. St. Paul's Parish, Balto. V. 1. Mss. MHS.

Ashton. Mrs. H. De Courcy Wright Thom chart. MHS.
Peale Geneal. Coll. Ms. MHS.
*The Sun, Balto., Dec. 8, 15, 1907; Jan. 19, July 21, Oct. 11, 1908.
St. Paul's Parish, Balto. V. 2, 3. Mss. MHS.
See Jewett-Ashton.

Askew. St. Paul's Parish, Balto. V. 1, 2. Mss. MHS.

Askew, Askue, Askey, Asque (1765). Natl. Geneal. Soc. Quart., v. 10, no. 2, p. 87.

Askey. *See* Askew.
Askin. St. Paul's Parish, Balto. V. 1. Mss. MHS.
Askue. *See* Askew.
Asplen. Trinity Church cemetery, Dorchester Co. Md. O. R. Soc. Bull., no. 3, pp. 42–52.
Aspril. Bible rec. Upper Penins. East. Shore, p. 164–66. MHS; DAR.
See Vandergrift-Aspril.
Asque. *See* Askew.
Asquith. St Paul's Parish, Balto. V. 1. Mss. MHS.
Asterman. St. Paul's Parish, Balto. V. 1. Mss. MHS.
Aston, Walter, Va. Pedigree of Charles Morton Stewart. Soc. Col. Mars Md. Culver. 1940. MHS; DAR.
Astor. Cary Geneal. Coll. Ms. MHS.
Atchinson. *See* Athison.
***Athey.** Index to. "Geneal. of Athey family in Amer., 1642–1932," by C. E. Athey. A. T. Coons. Ms. DAR.
See Bransford. Abr. Compend. Amer. Geneal. Virkus. V. 1, p. 486. DAR.
*"Geneal. of Athey family in Amer., 1642–1932." C. E. Athey. DAR.
***Athey-Marsh.** Lineage Bks. Daughters of Amer. Colonists. V. 2, p. 66; v. 3, p. 133; v. 4, p. 275. MHS; DAR.
Athison, Atchinson. St. Paul's Parish, Balto. V. 1, 3. Mss. MHS.
Atkey. St. Stephens Parish, Cecilton, Md. MHS; DAR.
Atkin. Ances. rec. and portraits. Col. Dames of Amer., 1910, p. 20. MHS; DAR.
Atkins. Md. gleanings in Eng. Wills. M. H. Mag., 1907, v. 2, no. 3.
Memoir and geneal. of Md. and Pa. family of Mayer. Mayer. Pp. 145–47. MHS; DAR.
St. Stephens Parish, Cecilton, Md. MHS; DAR.
Atkinson. Chart, photos., complete in 1 sheet. Cary Geneal. Coll. Ms. MHS.
†Med. Annals Md. Cordell. 1903, pp. 307–08. MHS.
Rec. of Stepney Parish. MHS; DAR.
St. Paul's Parish, Balto. V. 1, 2, 3, 4, 5. Mss. MHS.
***Atkinson,** Va. The Sun, Balto., May 14, 1905.
Atkinson, Mrs. A. Duval (Patty Taylor). Chart. (Mostly Va. families.) Col. Dames, Chap. I. MHS.
†Atkinson, Wilmer. Autobiog. M. H. Mag., 1922, v. 17, p. 228. (Rev.) MHS.
***Atkinson Family,** Buck Co., Pa. Atkinson family of Buck Co., Pa. Oliver Hough. Repr. from Pa. Mag. of Hist. and Biog., v. 30, 31. J. B. Lippincott Co., 1908. MHS.
(Md. connections.) Pa. Mag., v. 30, p. 220, 332, 479; v. 31, p. 157, 175, 429.
Atkinson Family, Somerset Co. Bible rec. Ms. MHS.
Atlee, Pa. Geneal. Newsp. clipp. File case, DAR.
*Burke's landed gentry. 1939. MHS.
***Atlee Family.** Descendants of Judge Wm. Augustus Atlee and Col. Sam'l John Atlee, Lancaster Co., Pa. Phila., 1884, 130 pp. DAR.
***Atwarter, Waters.** Pennington Papers. Ms. MHS.
***Atwater.** Register; descendants in the male line of David Atwater (died 1692), New Haven, Conn., to fifth generation. E. E. Atwater. New Haven, Conn., 1851. MHS.
Waters, Atwater. Ms. MHS.
Atwaters. *See* Harris-Atwaters.
Atwell. Patriotic Md. Md. Soc. of S. A. R., 1930. MHS; DAR.
Atwood Family. Old Catholic Md. Treacy. P. 117. DAR.
***Audley.** Pedigrees; comp. for George Audley, Liverpool, by Aleyn Lyell Reade. London and Bradford, 1932, 2 pts. MHS.
Auld. Elliott-Auld families. Ms. MHS.
S. G. Hopkins chart. MHS.
Pedigree of T. Edward Hambleton. Soc. Col. Wars Md. Culver. 1940. MHS; DAR.
Sater geneal. Bd. ms. MHS.
Auld, Talbot Co. F. S. Hambleton pedigree chart. Soc. Col. Wars, Md. Johnston. 1905, p 33. MHS.
Auld, Mrs. James. McHenry chart. MHS.
Auld Family. Chart. Thomas F. Sears. Photos. from orig. Ms. MHS.
Ault. McSpadden-Love-Meigs-Clendinen-Von Bibber-Pope chart. MHS.
St. Paul's Parish, Balto. V. 4, 5. Mss. MHS.
Austen-Gardiner Line. Balto., its hist., its people. Hall. V. 2, p. 299. MHS., DAR.
Austin. Meade relations. Prichard. DAR.
†Med. Annals Md. Cordell. 1903, p. 308. MHS.
*Wicomico Co. families. Tilghman. Ms., pp. 123–24. DAR
Austin Family, Caroline Co. Marriages, 1805–11. Geneal. Mag. Amer. Ancestry, N. Y., 1916, v. 5, no. 7.
Avelin. St. Paul's Parish, Balto. V. 1. Mss. MHS.
Averill. Col. families of U. S. A. Mackenzie. V. 1, pp. 15–17. MHS; DAR.
Averly. St. Paul's Parish, Balto. V. 1, Mss. MHS.
Avery. Dorsey and allied families. Ms. MHS.
Old Somerset. Torrence. MHS; DAR.
Sacred Heart R. C. churchyard, Bushwood, St. Mary's Co. Md. Geneal. Rec. Com., 1929. Mss. · DAR.
St. Paul's Parish, Balto. V. 1. Mss. MHS.
Somerset Co. Court Book. Tilghman, 1937. Ms. DAR.
***Avery, Capt. John.** Captain John Avery, President Judge at Whorekill in Delaware Bay, and his descendants. E. J. Sellers. Phila., 1893. MHS.
***Avery-Fairchild-Park Families.** Avery-Fairchild-Park families. Sam'l Putman Avery. Harford, Conn., 1919, 1st ed. MHS.
†Avirett, Col. J. W. Encyc. of Amer. biog., Amer. Hist. Soc., N. Y., 1928, v. 33, p. 188.
†Men of mark in Md. Johnson. V. 1. DAR; Enoch Pratt Lib.
Avis. St. Paul's Parish, Balto. V. 1. Mss. MHS.
†Awalt. Encyc. of Amer. biog. Amer. Hist. Soc., new series, v. 1, p. 57. MHS; DAR.
Awbrey-Vaughan. Lloyd family hist. of Wales, Pa., and Md. DAR.
***Axtell.** Pennington Papers. Ms. MHS.
***Aydelott.** Family association bulletins. George C. Aydelott. Mimeog. MHS.
***Aydelotte.** Wicomico Co. families. Tilghman. Ms., p. 13. DAR.

Ayers. St. Paul's P. E. churchyard, Berlin, Worcester Co. Hudson. Bd. ms. MHS; DAR. Also: Md. Geneal. Rec. Com., 1937, Mrs. Lines. Mss. DAR.
St. Paul's Parish, Balto. V. 1. Mss. MHS.
Aylett. Chart, photos., 2 sheets. Cary Geneal. Coll. Ms. MHS.
Corbin chart. Cary Geneal. Coll. Ms. MHS.
Mrs. H. De Courcy Wright Thom chart. MHS.
Ayloffe. Cary Geneal. Coll. Ms. MHS.
Ayre-Ayres-Eyres. Col. and Revolutionary families of Pa. Amer. Hist. Soc., N. Y., 1934, p. 3.
Ayres. Buckingham Pres. churchyard, Worcester Co., Hudson. Bd. ms. MHS; DAR.
Chew family. Culver. M. H. Mag., 1935, v. 30 no. 2, pp. 157–75.
Dawson family of Md. Ms. File case, DAR.
De Ford chart. MHS.
Ayres, Balto. Co. Beirne chart. MHS.
Ayres Line. Col. and Revolutionary lineages in Amer. 1939, v. 2, p. 127. MHS.
Ayres Line, Gaither, Va. and Md. Col. and Revolutionary families of Phila. Jordan. 1933, v. 1, pp. 144–67.
Ayton. Laytonsville M. E. churchyard, Montgomery Co. Md. Geneal. Rec. Com., 1934–35, p. 69. Mss. DAR.
Ayton, Henry. Copy of will. Ms. File case, DAR.

B

Babcock. St. Paul's Parish, Balto. V. 1. Mss. MHS.
†**Babcock, Rev. M.D.** (1858–1901). Account of his life. C. E. Robinson.
Babington. St. Paul's Parish Balto. V. 1. Mss. MHS.
Babinton. St. Stephens Parish, Cecilton, Md. MHS; DAR.
Babylon. Babylon family, around Westminster, Carroll Co. W. B. and M. C. Duttera. Bd., Ms. MHS.
*Family hist. Duttera Brothers. Salisbury, N. C., 1936, typed. MHS.
Bache. Mrs. Emory Whitridge chart. MHS.
Bache, The, in Warley. H. P. Kendall. 1927. MHS.
Bachtel Family. Tombstone inscriptions, Chewsville Dist., Wash. Co., 1780–1883. Md. Geneal. Rec. Com., 1935–36, p. 8. Mss. DAR.
Bachtell. Beards' Luth. graveyard, Washington Co. Md. Geneal. Rec. Com., 1935–36. Mss. DAR.
Spessard family. Spessard. MHS; DAR.
†**Bacon.** Rev. Thomas Bacon, 1745–68, incumbent of St. Peter's, Talbot Co., and All Saints, Frederick Co. Rev. Ethan Allen. Amer. Quart. Church Review, 1865, v. 17, pp. 430–51.
Bacons, Va., and their Eng. ancestry. Excerpt. DAR.
Sara R. Baldwin chart. MHS.
Bible rec., Kent Co. Md. Geneal. Rec. Com., 1937, Parran, p. 205. Mss. DAR.
†Hist. of West. Md. Scharf. V. 1, pp. 462–64. MHS; DAR.
St. Paul's Parish, Balto. V. 2. Mss. MHS.
Bacon, Nathan, Mass. line. Ms. MHS.
Bacon, Nathaniel, Mass. Chart. In folder marked Ames charts. MHS.
†**Bacon, Rev. Thomas.** Hist. of printing in col. Md. Wroth. P. 95.
†(1700–68). Hist. of Talbot Co. Tilghman. V. 1, pp. 272–300. MHS; DAR.
Bacon Family, Kent Co. Births, marriages and deaths, 1818–74. Md. Geneal. Rec. Com., 1937. DAR.
Bacon-Chew. Lineage Bks., Natl. Soc. of Daughters of Amer. Col., v. 2, p. 215. MHS; DAR.
†**Baden.** Med. Annals Md. Cordell. 1903, p. 309. MHS.
St. Paul's Parish, Balto. V. 2, 3. Mss. MHS.
Baechtel, Baeghtle, Beaghthe, Bechtel. Hagerstown tombstone inscriptions. Gruder. Natl. Geneal. Soc. Quart., 1919, v. 8, nos. 1, 2.
Baer. Frederick Co. tombstone inscriptions. Gruder. Natl. Geneal. Soc. Quart., 1919, v. 8, nos. 1, 2.
Baer, Bear. Patriotic Md. Md. Soc. of S. A. R., 1930. MHS; DAR.
Bagby. Bagby family tree. Rev. Alfred Bagby. Richmond, Va., 1897.
King and Queen Cos., Va.; hist. and geneal. Bagby. 1908.
Bagfort. St. Paul's Parish, Balto. V. 1. Mss. MHS.
Bahler. St. Paul's Parish, Balto. V. 1, 2. Mss. MHS.
Bahn. Peale Geneal. Coll. Ms. MHS.
Baile. Bible rec., Carroll Co. Md. Geneal. Rec. Com., 1932–33, p. 56. Mss. DAR.
Englar family. Barnes. MHS; DAR.
Roop geneal. Pamph. MHS.
Bailey. Ances. rec. and portraits. Col. Dames of Amer., 1910, v. 2, p. 820. MHS; DAR.
*Ancestry of Joseph Trowbridge and Catherine Goddard Weaver. J. T. Bailey. Priv. pr., Phila., 1892. MHS.
Bible rec., 1796–84. Md. Geneal. Rec. Com., 1939–40, pp. 161–62. Mss. DAR.
Jackson family gathering. 1878.
M. E. churchyard Snow Hill, Worcester Co., Hudson. Bd. ms. MHS; DAR.
Pedigree of Duncan Keener Brent. Soc. Col. Wars Md. Culver. 1940. MHS; DAR.
Rec. of Stepney Parish. MHS; DAR.
See Baily.
See Barnes-Bailey.
***Bailey, Bayley.** Wicomico Co. families. Tilghman. Ms, pp. 97, 116, 124. DAR.
Bailliere. Abr. Compend. Amer. Geneal. Virkus. V. 6, p. 48. DAR.
Bailliere, Mrs. Thomas Gaither (Marion Cromwell Riggs). Chart. Col. Dames, Chap. I. MHS.
Baily, Bailey. St. Paul's Parish, Balto. V. 1, 2, 3. Mss. MHS.
†**Bain.** Med. Annals Md. Cordell. 1903, p. 310. MHS.
†**Bainbridge.** Commodore Bainbridge. J. Barnes.
Bainbridge family tree. (Md. ref.) Photos. of ms. File case, DAR.
Bainbridge Line. Col. and Revolutionary lineages of Amer., 1939, v. 3, pp. 392–93. MHS.
***Baine,** Wicomico Co. families. Tilghman. Ms. p. 107. DAR.
Baird, Pa. Col. families of U. S. A. Mackenzie. V. 6. MHS; DAR.
Baird Family. Ms. File case, DAR.
Baker. Ances. rec. and portraits. Col. Dames of Amer., 1910, v. 2, p. 560. MHS; DAR.

Baker. Baker family, Md., Pa. and Ohio, 1756–1840. John Wood Baker. Ms. File case, DAR.
Henry Baker and some of his descendants. Miles White, Jr., Balto. Repr. from Pub. South. Hist. Soc., Sept., Nov., 1901, v. 5, no. 6. Pamph. MHS.
Bowie-Claggett chart. MHS.
Buckingham Pres. churchyard, Worcester Co., Hudson. Bd. ms. MHS; DAR.
Evergreen cemetery, Worcester Co., Hudson. Bd. ms. MHS; DAR.
Geneal. of Henrietta Chauncy Wilson. Upshur. Bk. of photos. MHS.
See Guernsey-Baker. Lineage Bks., Natl. Soc. of Daughters of Amer. Col., v. 1, no. 1. MHS; DAR.
†Hist. of Frederick Co. Williams. MHS; DAR.
†Med. Annals Md. Cordell. 1903, pp. 310–11. MHS.
†Men of mark in Md. Johnson. V. 3. DAR; Enoch Pratt Lib.
M. E. churchyard, Snow Hill. Worcester Co., Hudson. Bd. ms. MHS; DAR.
Monumental City. Howard. MHS; DAR.
Mt. Carmel Burial Ground, Montgomery Co. Md. Geneal. Rec. Com., 1934, p. 85. Mss. DAR.
Patriotic Md. Md. Soc. of S. A. R., 1930. MHS; DAR.
Peale Geneal. Coll. Ms. MHS.
Rec., Kent Co. Md. Geneal. Rec. Com., 1934–35, p. 177. Mss. DAR.
Rumsey-Smithson Bible rec. Md. Geneal. Rec. Com., 1932–33, v. 5, pp. 63–142. DAR.
Rumsey-Smithson family rec. bk. Md. Geneal. Rec. Com., 1932, pp. 63–158. DAR
St. Paul's Parish, Balto. V. 1, 2, 3, 4, 5. Mss. MHS.
St. Stephens Parish, Cecilton, Md. MHS; DAR.
St. Thomas' Parish, Balto. Co. Bd. ms. MHS. Also: Md. Geneal. Rec. Com., 1937, pp. 109–82. Mss. DAR.
Smithson-Rumsey rec. bk. Ms. MHS.
Steiner geneal. Steiner. 1896. MHS.
*The Sun, Balto., May 28 (Judith); Aug. 27, 1905.
Tombstone inscriptions, Bond Chapel, near Pomona, Kent Co. Md. O. R Soc. Bull., No. 2, p. 78. MHS.
Miss Sara E. White chart. MHS.
*Wicomico Co. families. Tilghman. Ms, p. 114. DAR.
William and Mary Quart., 1st series, v. 6, p. 94.
Young Bible rec. Ms. MHS.
See Brooke-Baker.
See Herbert-Baker.
See Hopkins-Kinsey-Baker.
See Jean-Baker-George.
See Taylor-Roberts-Standiford-Patterson-Reardon-Baker-Reisinger-Scharf.
Baker, Frederick Co. Lineage Bks., Natl. Soc. of Daughters of Amer. Col., v. 1, p. 1. MHS; DAR.
†**Baker, Bernard.** Men of mark in Md. Johnson. V. 1. DAR; Enoch Pratt Lib.
†**Baker, Charles, J.** Balto., hist. and biog. Richardson and Bennett. 1871, pp. 177–80. MHS; DAR.
†Hist. of Balto. City and Co. Scharf. Pp. 459–61. MHS.
Baker, Henry. And some of his descendants. Miles White, Jr. Pub. Southern Hist. Assoc., Nov., 1901, v. 5, pp. 388–400, 477–96. Reprint. MHS.
†**Baker, Capt. John.** Geneal. and mem. encyc. of Md. Spencer. V. 2 p. 723. MHS; DAR.
Baker Line. Mrs. T. B. Harrison chart. MHS.
Baker-Hargarader-Dehoff. Baker-Hargarader-De Hoff families, Frederick Co. J. M. Kellogg. Ms., 136 pp. File case, DAR.
Baker-Reed-Young-Wroth, Kent Co. Bible, marriage and tombstone rec., 1796–1802. Md. Geneal. Rec. Com., 1934–35, p. 175. DAR.
Bakie. Trinity P. E. churchyard, Long Green. Typed ms. MHS; DAR.
Balabrega, Ballebraga. St. Paul's Parish, Balto. V. 1. Mss. MHS.
Balch. Abr. Compend. Amer. Geneal. Virkus. V. 1, p. 35. DAR.
Amer. Armory and Blue Bk. Matthews. 1908, p. 146. DAR.
Beall and Bell families. Beall. MHS.
Brooke family of Whitchurch, etc. Balch. Pp. 43–55. MHS; DAR.
*Genealogica; coat of arms. Thomas Willing Balch. Allen, Lane and Scott, Phila., 1907, 1st. ed. MHS.
Genealogica. Thomas Willing Balch. Phila., 1907. Review by Dr. Christopher Johnston. M. H. Mag., 1907, v. 2, p. 275.
Harford Co. Hist. Soc. Mss. Coll. JHU.
Letters and papers; geneal. notes. Pamph. MHS.
See Nevin. Abr. Compend. Amer. Geneal. Virkus. V. 1, p. 638. DAR.
Pa. Mag., v. 29, p. 252.
See Sears, M. E. B. Abr. Compend. Amer. Geneal. Virkus. V. 1, p. 950. DAR.
Balch, Francis Du Pont. Pedigree chart. Soc. Col. Wars, Md. Johnston. 1905, p. 3. MHS.
†**Balch, Rev. Stephen Bloomer** (pioneer preacher of Georgetown, D. C.). Rec. Columbia Hist. Soc., v. 15, p. 73.
Hist. of Bethel Presbyterian Church. Cross. P. 26. DAR.
Balch, T. Willing. Amer. Armory and Blue Bk. Matthews. 1908, p. 31. DAR.
Balch, Mrs. Thomas Willing (Dulany Whiting). Chart. Col. Dames, Chap. I. MHS.
Phila. newsp. clipping. File case, DAR.
Baldry. St. Paul's Parish, Balto. V. 1. Mss. MHS.
Baldwin. Ances. rec. and portraits. Col. Dames of Amer. 1910, v. 1, pp. 80, 84, 92. MHS; DAR.
*Ancestry. Millie E. Baldwin. San Francisco, Frank Bastmond Co., 1904. MHS.
Anne Arundel Co. tombstone inscriptions. Ms. DAR.
Bailliere chart. MHS.
Baldwin family of Md. E. B. Baldwin. Ms. Inst. Amer. Geneal., 440 Dearborn St., Chicago, 1925.
Col. families of U. S. A. Mackenzie. V. 3, p. 456; v. 7, p. 249. MHS; DAR.
Eldridge chart. MHS.
*Founders of Anne Arundel and Howard Cos. Warfield. Pp. 158–60. MHS.
Griffith chart. Cary Geneal. Coll. Ms. MHS.
Mrs. C. C. Hall chart. MHS.
Hamill chart. MHS.

Lineage Bks., Natl. Soc. of Daughters of Amer. Col., vol. 2, p. 117 MHS; DAR
Md. families. Culver. Ms. Personal list.
Maulsby family in Amer. Barnard. DAR; Peabody Lib.
†Med. Annals Md. Cordell. 1903, p. 311. MHS.
†Men of mark in Md. Johnson. V. 1, pp. 48, 53. DAR; Enoch Pratt Lib.
Milligan chart. MHS.
Patriotic Md. Md. Soc. of S. A. R., 1930. MHS; DAR.
Mrs. C. L. Riggs chart. MHS.
*George Donald Riley. Riley. DAR.
Posey chart. MHS.
Prentice chart. MHS.
Tompkins chart. MHS.
Townley geneal. chart. MHS.
Welsh Hyatt and kindred. Welsh. Sec. 8, p. 196. MHS; DAR.
Mrs. G. H. Williams, Jr., chart. MHS.
Baldwin, Charles Gambrill. Pedigree. Soc. Col. Wars Md. Culver. 1904. MHS; DAR.
Md. Soc., War of 1812, v. 4 no. 348. Ms. MHS.
Baldwin, Francis Joseph. Pedigree. Soc. Col. Wars Md. Culver. 1940. MHS; DAR.
Baldwin, Mrs. Frank Gambrill (Katherine Williams Harrison). Chart. Col. Dames, Chap. I. MHS.
Baldwin, Mrs. Henry Du Pont (Margaret Eyre Taylor). Chart. (Many Va. families.) Col. Dames, Chap. I. MHS.
Baldwin, J. S. Her life and ancestry. Pamph. MHS.
Baldwin, Miss Sara Rodman. Chart. Col. Dames, Chap. I. MHS.
***Baldwin, Summerfield.** His autobiography; his ancestry; with editorial and newspaper comments. Balto., Norman T. A. Munder Co., 1925. MHS; DAR.
Pedigree. Soc. Col. Wars Md. Culver. 1940. MHS; DAR.
Baldwin Family. Geneal. Ms. MHS.
Baldwin Line. Copied from Riley family. Md. Geneal. Rec. Com., 1934–35, p. 424. Mss. DAR.
Baldwin-Brewer-Disney-Maccubin, and others, Anne Arundel Co. Copies of deeds, depositions, wills and court proceedings, relating to lands owned by these families, 1690–1758. Ms. MHS.
Baldwin-Woodward. Chart, photos., 2 sheets. Cary Geneal. Coll. Ms. MHS.
***Baldwyn.** Early comers to the Province. Georgians in Anne Arundel Co. Atlanta Jour., Sept. 22, 1906. Newsp. clipp. File case, MHS.
Bale. Cary Geneal. Coll. Ms. MHS.
Md. families. Culver. Ms. Personal list.
Rogers Coll. Ms. MHS.
See Beall.
Ball. Col. families of U. S. A. Mackenzie. V. 2; v. 7, (Va. and Md.). MHS; DAR.
Early Virginians in Md. Va. Mag. Hist. and Biog., v. 21, pp. 324–26.
Forgotten member of Ball family (Md. in 1659). Md. Geneal. Rec. Com., 1935–36, pp. 297–303. Ms. DAR.
Forgotten member of Ball family, Va. and Md. Va. Hist. and Geneal. Mag., v. 7, p. 440; v. 8, pp. 80, 297–303.
Griffith geneal. Griffith. MHS; DAR.
Rev. Joseph Hull (1595) and some of his descendants. Hull. 1904, p. 21. MHS.
Md. families. Culver. Ms. Personal list.
Monnet family geneal. Monette. MHS.
Pedigree of Francis Barnum Culver. Soc. Col. Wars Md. 1904. MHS; DAR.
Pedigree of Gustavus Warfield Evans. Soc. Col. Wars Md. Culver. 1940. MHS; DAR.
Pedigree of John Ridgely Fisher. Soc. Col. Wars Md. Culver. 1940. MHS; DAR.
Pedigree of Henry Irvine Keyser, II. Soc. Col. Wars Md. Culver. 1940. MHS; DAR.
Pedigree of Towsend Scott, IV. Soc. Col. Wars Md. Culver. 1940. MHS; DAR.
St. Paul's Parish, Balto. V. 1, 2. Mss. MHS.
Selden chart. MHS.
Smallwood-Ball family notes. Ms. MHS.
*The Sun, Balto., Jan. 8, 1905 (Va.); July 15, 22, 1906; Nov. 1, 1908.
Sydney-Smith and Clagett Price families. Price. MHS; DAR
Mr. H. De Courcy Wright Thom chart. MHS.
Va. geneal. Hayden. MHS; DAR.
See Collison-Hodson-Ball.
See Dorsey-Ball.
See Hodson-Collison-Ball-Jones-Lankford.
See Purnell.
Ball, Talbot Co. Culver pedigree chart. MHS.
H. Mullikin pedigree chart, plate 2. Soc. Col. Wars, Md. Johnston. 1905, pp. 75, 139. MHS; DAR.
Ball, Va. Ances. rec. and portraits. Col. Dames of Amer., 1910, v. 1, p. 134; v. 2, p. 814. MHS; DAR.
Ball, Mary and Abraham Milton, Kent Co. Marriage certificate. Md. Geneal. Rec. Com., 1924–25, v. 1, p. 2. DAR.
***Ball, Col. Wm.,** Va. Coat of arms. Burke's landed gentry. 1939. MHS.
*Col. Wm. Ball of Va., great-grandfather of Washington. E. L. W. Heck. 1928. DAR.
Descendants. Henry I. Kirk. 1933, 4 vols. Ms. MHS.
W. H. Gill pedigree chart. Soc. Col. Wars, Md. Johnston. 1905, p. 26. MHS.
Millenbeck, Lancaster Co., Va. (V. 3 contains Pa. pioneer family.) Henry I. Kirk. 3 vols. Ms. MHS.
Pedigree of John Baker Thompson Hull. Soc. Col. Wars Md. Culver. 1940. MHS; DAR.
***Ball Family.** Rec.: Great Britain, Ireland, and Amer. Wm. Ball Wright. York, Eng., 1908.
Ball Family, Talbot Co. Patriotic Marylander, v. 2, no. 2, p. 57. MHS; DAR.
Ball-Mahan-Pullen-Wright families, Va. Ms. File case, DAR.
†Ballard. Med. Annals Md. Cordell. 1903, p. 311. MHS.
Old Somerset. Torrence. MHS; DAR.
St. Paul's Parish, Balto. V. 1, 2. Mss. MHS.
*The Sun, Balto., Jan. 5, 1908.
Ballard Family. Bible rec. Turner Geneal. Coll. Ms. MHS.
Ballebraga. *See* Balabrega.
†Balridge. Papers relating to early hist. of Md. Streeter. 1876. MHS.
Baltimore, The Lords. Exhibition of portraits at War Memorial. Pamph. DAR.
Baltzell. Dorsey and allied families. Ms. MHS.
†Hist. of Frederick Co. Williams. MHS; DAR.

†Baltzell. Med. Annals Md. Cordell. 1903, p. 311. MHS.
Samuel Carpenter of Phila. Carpenter. P. 139. MHS.
Bancroft. Bailliere chart. MHS.
Col. families of U. S. A. Mackenzie. V. 4. MHS. DAR.
***Bancroft, J. Towsend.** Burke's landed gentry. 1939. MHS.
Bandel, Littleton Chandler. Md. Soc., War of 1812, v. 2, no. 154. Ms. MHS.
Baney Family, Frederick Co. Ms. File case, DAR.
Banister. Blair-Banister-Braxton families. Horner. MHS.
Bank. *See* Bounds-Bank.
†Bankard. Biog. cyc. of rep. men of Md. and D. C. P. 180. MHS; DAR.
Hist of Balto. City and Co. Scharf. P. 774. MHS.
Bankhead. Mrs. Newhall chart. MHS.
Bankhead Family. William and Mary Quart., 2nd series, vol. 9, p. 303.
Banks. Cary Geneal. Coll. Ms. MHS.
†Day-Star of Amer. Freedom. Davis. P. 223. MHS.
†Hist. of Balto. City and Co. Scharf. P. 856. MHS.
Mt. Calvary Church burial ground, Cooksvill Pike, Montgomery Co. Md. Geneal. Rec. Com., 1934. Mss. DAR.
Mt. Calvary Church burial ground, Howard Co. Md. Geneal. Rec. Com., 1934-35, pp. 95-99. Mss. DAR.
St. Paul's Parish, Balto. V. 1, 2, 3. Mss. MHS.
St. Thomas' Parish, Balto. Co. Bd. ms. MHS. Also: Md. Geneal. Rec. Com., 1937, pp. 109-82. Mss. DAR.
Smithson-Rumsey rec. bk. Ms. MHS.
*The Sun, Balto., June 4, 11, 1905.
Wicomico Co. families. Bible rec. Ms. DAR.
*Wicomico Co. families. Tilghman. Ms., pp. 1, 6, 60, 77. DAR.
Bankson. St. Paul's Parish, Balto. V. 1, 2. Mss. MHS.
Bankston. St. Paul's Parish, Balto. V. 1. Mss. MHS.
Bannaker. St Paul's Parish, Balto. V. 1. Mss. MHS.
Banncker. St Paul's Parish, Balto. V. 1. Mss. MHS.
†Banneker, Benjamin. Memoir. J. S. Norris. Md. Hist. Soc. Pub 1845, v. 1, no. 5. MHS.
†Sketch of life. Mrs. M E.. Tyson. Md. Hist. Soc. Pub., v. 3, no. 8.
Banning. Amer. Armory and Blue Book. Matthews. 1911-12, pp. 45, 253.
Col. families of U. S. A. Mackenzie. V. 3. MHS; DAR.
*Geneal. and biog. Amer. Hist. Soc., priv. pr., N. Y., 1925. MHS.
(1733-98). Hist. of Talbot Co. Tilghman. V. 1, p. 325. MHS; DAR.
St. Paul's Parish, Balto. V. 1. Mss. MHS.
Some notable families of southern states. Armstrong. V. 1, pp. 25-31. DAR.
Banning, E., III, Talbot Co. Abr. Compend. Amer. Geneal. Virkus. V. 1, p. 91. DAR.
†Banning, Col. Jeremiah (1733-98). Hist. of Talbot Co. Tilghman. V. 1, pp. 325-52. MHS; DAR.
Will. Ms. MHS.
Banning Family, Md. and Va. Ms. File case, DAR.
Bannon. Founders of Anne Arundel and Howard Cos. Warfield. P. 324. MHS; DAR.
Banor. *See* Benner.
Bansley. St. Paul's Parish, Balto. V. 1. Mss. MHS.
Bantz. Col. families of Amer. Lawrence. V. 2, p. 50. MHS.
D. A. R. Mag., v. 70, no. 3, p. 205.
*Frederick Co. families. Markell. Ms. Personal list.
Geneal. notes. Ms. MHS.
†Med. Annals Md. Cordell. 1903, p. 312. MHS.
See Kerr-Bantz.
Barbarin. St. Paul's Parish, Balto. V. 1, 2. Mss. MHS.
Barber. Christ P. E. Church cemetery, Cambridge. Steele. 1936. MHS; DAR.
*Geneal. of Barber family; descendants of Robert Barber, Lancaster Co., Pa., 1699. Edwin Atlee Barber. Phila., Wm. F. Fell Co., 1890.
†Med. Annals Md. Cordell. 1903, p. 312. MHS.
†Men of mark in Md. Johnson. V. 3. DAR; Enoch Pratt Lib.
Old Kent. Hanson. P. 123. MHS; DAR.
Pedigree of John Seymour Taliaferro Waters. Soc. Col. Wars Md. Culver. 1940. MHS; DAR.
St. Paul's Parish, Balto. V. 1, 2, 3, 5. Mss. MHS.
Barber, "Luckland," St. Mary's Co. Bible rec., 1803-45, incl. Briscoe, Hanson, Plummer, Yates. Natl. Geneal. Soc. Quart., v. 22, no. 4, pp. 89-92.
Tombstone inscriptions. Natl. Geneal. Soc. Quart., v. 22, no. 4, p. 93.
Barber, Luke, "Wickham Hall." Will, 1654. Ms. File case, DAR
Barber-Billingsley. Bible rec. Natl. Geneal. Soc. Quart., Dec., 1934.
***Barbour.** Va. The Sun, Balto., Jan. 14, 21, 1906.
Barckstrasser. Hagerstown tombstone inscriptions. Gruder. Natl. Geneal. Soc. Quart., 1919, v. 8, nos. 1, 2.
Barclay. N. Y. Geneal. and Biog. Rec., v. 8, p. 140.
Old Kent. Hanson. P. 295. MHS; DAR.
St. Paul's Parish, Balto. V. 1, 2, 3. Mss. MHS.
Barcroft. Abr. Compend. Amer. Geneal. Virkus. V. 4, p. 620. MHS.
Barcus-Porter. Note. D. A. R. Mag., v. 67, no. 4, p. 241.
Bard. Abr. Compend. Amer. Geneal. Virkus. V. 4, p. 333. MHS.
Bardwell. St. Paul's Parish, Balto. V. 1. Mss. MHS.
Bare. Cummings chart. Lib. Cong.; MHS; DAR.
Bargner. Peale Geneal. Coll. Ms. MHS.
†Barkdall. Hist. of Allegany Co. Thomas and Williams. V. 2. MHS; DAR.
Barkdoll. Spessard family. Spessard. MHS; DAR.
Barker. Ances. rec. and portraits. Col. Dames of Amer. 1910. P. 65. MHS; DAR.

Greenway Mss. Geneal. Coll. Binder's title, Hawkins-Bordley. MHS.
†Med. Annals Md. Cordell. 1903, p. 312. MHS.
St. Paul's Parish, Balto. V. 1, 2, 3, 4. Mss. MHS.
St. Stephens Parish, Cecilton, Md. MHS; DAR.
Barkett. St. Paul's Parish, Balto. V. 1. Mss. MHS.
Barkley. Edmund Beauchamp of East. Shore of Md. D. A. R. Mag., v. 66, no. 4, pp. 234-38. April 1932.
Rec. of Stepney Parish. MHS; DAR.
Barkman. Hagerstown tombstone inscriptions. Gruder. Natl. Geneal. Soc. Quart., 1919, v. 8, nos. 1, 2.
Barlow. St. Paul's Parish, Balto. V. 1. Mss. MHS.
***Barlow Family.** Bible rec., incl. Bennet and Kelly. Photos. DAR.
*Geneal., comprising the ancestry and descendants of Jonathan and Plain Rogers, Del. Co., N. Y. G. Barlow. Incl. geneal. of Lydia Cosgrove and George Phillips of Balto., pp. 283-92. 1891. MHS.
Barnabe, Barnabee, Barnaby. Old Somerset. Torrence. MHS; DAR.
Barnaby, Cecil Co. Perin chart. MHS.
Segrave chart. MHS.
Barnaby. St. Paul's Parish, Balto. V. 1. Mss. MHS.
See Barnabe.
Barnance. St. Paul's Parish, Balto. V. 1. Mss. MHS.
†**Barnard.** Hist. of Allegany Co. Thomas and Williams. V. 2. MHS; DAR.
St. Paul's Parish, Balto. V. 1. Mss. MHS.
Barnell Family, Ky. and Pa. With Md. ref. Ms. File case, DAR.
Barnes. Ances. rec. and portraits. Col. Dames of Amer., 1910, v. 2, p. 809. MHS; DAR.
Barnes Family Assoc. T. C. Barnes, secretary. Grafton Press. MHS.
Cary Geneal. Coll. Ms. MHS.
Dorsey and allied families. Ms. MHS.
*Frederick Co. families. Markell. Ms. Personal list.
Geneal. Dixie Mag., Aug., 1899, v. 2, no. 2, p. 286. MHS.
†Hist. of Frederick Co. Williams. MHS; DAR.
Hooe-Barnes of Va. and Md., from Va. Geneal. Hayden. MHS.
Mrs. B. S. Johnston chart. MHS.
Md. families. Culver. Ms. Personal list.
Mason chart. MHS.
Med. Annals Md. Cordell. 1903, p. 312. MHS.
See O'Carroll. Focke Geneal. Coll. Ms. MHS.
Patriotic Md. Md. Soc. of S. A. R., 1930. MHS; DAR.
Portrait and biog. rec. of East. Shore of Md. 1898. Pp. 366, 922, see DeKafft, p. 408. MHS; DAR.
Portrait and biog. rec. of Harford and Cecil Cos. 1897. Pp. 125, 165. MHS; DAR.
St. Paul's Parish, Balto. V. 1, 2, 3. Mss. MHS.
St. John's R. C. Church cemetery, Montgomery Co. Md. Geneal. Rec. Com., 1926, p. 27. Mss. DAR.
Tombstone rec. of Dorchester Co. Jones. DAR.
Whitehead chart. MHS.
See Hooe-Barnes.
Barnes, Va. Chart, showing Lovelace-Gorsuch-Todd Line. Va. Mag. Hist. and Biog., v. 17, p. 292.
*The Sun, Balto., Dec. 31, 1905.
Barnes, Henry F., Princess Anne. Bible rec. Ms. MHS.
Barnes, N. P. Bible rec. Ms. MHS.
Barnes-Bailey. Barnes-Bailey geneal. Walter D. Barnes. Balto., 1939. MHS.
Barnes Family. Chart. Walter Barnes, Balto. Blue print. MHS.
Barnes Family, Montgomery Co. Ms. File case, DAR.
Barnes-Robertson. Revolutionary war pension rec. of James Barnes and Charles Robertson of Md. D. A. R. Mag., v. 62, no. 10, pp. 626-29.
Barnes-Tasker Families. Dixie Mag., Sept., 1899, v. 2, no. 3. MHS.
Barnet. Trinity Church cemetery, Dorchester Co. Md. O. R. Soc. Bull., no. 3, pp. 42-52.
Barnet, Barnett. St. Paul's Parish, Balto. V. 1, 2, 3, 4. Mss. MHS.
Barnett. Ances. rec. and portraits. Col. Dames of Amer., p. 128. MHS; DAR.
Barney. Chart, photos., complete in 1 sheet. Cary Geneal. Coll. Ms. MHS.
Few facts in connection with life of Com. Joshua Barney. W. F. Adams. 1910, 9 pp. DAR.
Field book of Revolution. Lossing. V. 2, p. 644.
Harford Co. Hist. Soc. Mss Coll. JHU.
†Memoir of Com. Joshua Barney. Mary C. Barney. Boston, 1832. MHS; DAR.
St. Paul's Parish, Balto. V. 1, 2, 3, 4. Mss. MHS.
St. Thomas' Parish, Balto. Co. Bd. ms. MHS. Also: Md. Geneal. Rec. Com., 1937, pp. 109-82. Mss. DAR.
Sailor of fortune. Life and adventures of Comdre. Barney, U.S.N. Hulbert Footner. N. Y., Harper, 1940, 323 pp. MHS.
†**Barney, Commodore Joshua.** Hero of battle of Bladensburg. M. I. Weller. Rec. Columbia Hist. Soc., v. 14, pp. 67-165.
*Geneal. material. W. F. Adams. 1912. DAR.
U. S. N., 1776-1812. Everett Hosmer Barney, George Murray Barney. Comp. by Wm. F. Adams. Springfield, Mass., priv. pr. 1912. MHS; DAR.
†Balto., hist. and biog., Richardson and Bennett. 1871, pp. 181-84. MHS; DAR.
†Hero of two wars. D. A. R. Mag., v. 53, p. 596.
Revolutionary war heroes. Cole. Bklet. Enoch Pratt Lib.
Will, 1818. Misc'l Will Bk., v. 2. DAR.
***Barnhill.** Burke's landed gentry. 1939. MHS.
Barnhouse. St. Paul's Parish, Balto. V. 1. Mss. MHS.
***Barnitz.** Md. Geneal. Bull., v. 10, no. 1, pp. 4-6. MHS; DAR.
Barnsley. St. Paul's Parish, Balto. V. 1. Mss. MHS.
***Barnum.** Geneal. rec. of Barnum family; male descendants of Thomas Barnum, 1625-95; coat of arms. E. L. and F. Barnum. 1912. MHS.
Peale Geneal. Coll. Ms. MHS.

Barnwell. Ances. rec. and portraits. Col. Dames of Amer. 1910. Pp. 378-81, 503. MHS. DAR.
***Barr.** The Sun, Balto., Dec. 11, 1904.
Barr, David (1705-87). Will. Ms. DAR.
Barrack. Hist. of Frederick Co. Williams. V. 2, pp. 1091, 1163, 1616. MHS; DAR.
Barrat, Barratt. St. Stephens Parish, Cecilton, Md. MHS; DAR.
Barratt. Col. families of U. S. A. Mackenzie. V. 3. MHS; DAR.
Polk family. Polk. P. 481-82. MHS; DAR.
Barratt, Cecil Co. Turner. Geneal. Coll. Ms. MHS.
Barratt, Barret, Barrett. St. Paul's Parish, Balto. V. 1, 2, 3. Ms. MHS.
Barraud, Va. Mrs. Henry Du Pont Baldwin chart. MHS.
***Barraud Family.** Old Kent. Hanson. Pp. 168-69, 171-73. MHS; DAR.
Barre. Old Somerset. Torrence. MHS; DAR.
Barret. Barret family, Va. G. W. Chappelear. Harrisonburg, Va., 1934. DAR.
See Barratt.
†**Barrett.** Med. Annals Md. Cordell. 1903, p. 313. MHS.
See Barratt.
Barrett, John L. Md. Soc., War of 1812, v. 1, no. 45. Ms. MHS.
Barrett, John Minot. Md. Soc., War of 1812, v. 3, no. 298. Ms. MHS.
Barrette. Naturalizations in Md., 1666-1765; Laws. Bacon. MHS.
***Barrick.** Frederick Co. families. Markell. Ms. Personal list.
Hist. of Frederick Co Williams. V. 2, pp. 1195, 1604. MHS; DAR.
Tercentenary hist. of Md. Andrews. V. 3, p. 733. MHS; DAR.
Barrington. Smithson-Rumsey rec. bk. Ms. MHS.
***Barrington Family.** Bible rec. Copiah Chapter, DAR., Miss., 1934, p. 5. Typed, bd. DAR.
Barroll. Abr. Compend. Amer. Geneal. Virkus. V. 1, p. 901. DAR.
Amer. Armory and Blue Book. Matthews. 1911-12, p. 102.
Ances. rec. and portraits Col. Dames of Amer. 1910, v. 2, pp. 474, 475-76. MHS; DAR.
Barroll in Great Britain and Amer., 1554-1910. Coat of arms; pedigree charts. H. H. Barroll. Balto., J. H. Saumenig & Co., 1910. MHS.
Beall chart. Cary Geneal. Coll. Ms. MHS.
Pedigree and hist. of Washington family. Welles. P. 219. MHS.
Pedigree of Henry Irvine Keyser, II. Soc. Col. Wars Md. Culver. 1940 MHS; DAR.
Port. and biog. rec. of Cecil and Harford Cos. 1897. Pp. 257-58. MHS; DAR.
St. Paul's Parish, Balto. V. 2, 3, 4. Ms. MHS.
St. Stephens Parish, Cecilton, Md. MHS; DAR.
Shrewsbury churchyard, Kent Co. Md. O. R. Soc., v. 2, pp. 46-54. MHS.
†Tercentenary hist. of Md. Andrews. V. 4, p. 74. MHS; DAR.
Mrs. H. De Courcy Wright Thom chart. MHS.
Barroll, Hope Horsey, Jr. Pedigree. Soc. Col. Wars Md. Culver. 1940. MHS; DAR.
Barroll, Mrs. Lee (Josephine Tunstall Smith). 3 charts, containing the Fairfax line, Prince George Co., and Smith, Va. Col. Dames, Chap. I. MHS.
Barroll, Levin Wethered. Pedigree. Soc. Col. Wars Md. Culver. 1940. MHS; DAR.
Barroll Family. Bible rec. Ms. MHS.
(13 generations.) Horwitz chart. MHS.
Tercentenary hist. of Md. Andrews. V. 3, p. 722; v. 4, p. 74. MHS; DAR.
***Barron.** Barron family. G. L. C. Ward. Typed, bd. DAR.
Beall and Bell families. Beall. MHS.
*Bible rec. D. C. Geneal. Rec. Com., 1932-34, v. 11, pp. 3-7. Typed, bd. DAR.
†Med. Annals Md. Cordell. 1903, p. 313. MHS.
Pedigree of Edward Boteler Passano. Soc. Col. Wars Md. Culver. 1940. MHS; DAR.
Barron, Capt. Oliver. Revolutionary muster rolls, 1901, v. 2, p. 4. DAR.
***Barron Family.** Rec., Prince George Co. Mss. DAR.
Barry. Amer. Armory and Blue Book. Matthews. 1911-12, p. 250.
†William R. Barry, president of Md. School for Deaf. B. E. C. Wyand. Frederick, Md., 1904.
†Med. Annals Md. Cordell. 1903, p. 313. MHS.
St. Paul's Parish, Balto. V. 1, 2, 3. Ms. MHS.
Sharpless family geneal. Cope. P. 1092. MHS; DAR.
Barry, Joanna, Wash., D. C. Will proved, Nov. 9, 1811. D. A. R. Mag., v. 61, no. 10, p. 785.
Barry, Com. John (1745-1803). Amer. Catholic Hist. Soc. of Phila. Rec., 1896, v. 7.
†Amer. Catholic hist. researches, new series, v. 6, p. 312. DAR.
†Biog. sketches of eminent Amer. patriots. Taggart. MHS.
†(1745-1802). Sketches of his life and achievements. 2 pamph. DAR.
Bartges. Scholl, Sholl, Shull family. Scholl. P. 787. MHS; DAR.
Bartgis. Hist. of Frederick Co. Williams. V. 1, p. 249; v. 2, p. 858.
Mt. Olivet Cemetery, Frederick. Md Geneal. Rec. Com., 1934-35, p. 111. Mss.. DAR.,
†**Bartholow.** Hist. of West. Md. Scharf. V. 2, p. 893. MHS; DAR.
†Med. Annals Md. Cordell. 1903, p. 313. MHS.
Bartholow Family. Hist. of West. Md. Scharf. P. 893.
Barthslow. Mt. Calvary Church burial ground, Howard Co. Md. Geneal. Rec. Com. 1934-35, pp. 95-99. Mss. DAR.
Bartleet. Cox (Cock) family. Leef and Webb. Ms. MHS.
Bartlett. Balto., its hist., its people. Hall. V. 2, 3. MHS; DAR.
Burton ancestry. Ms. MHS.
Centreville cemetery. Md. O. R. Soc. Bull., no. 1, pp. 41-47.
Hist. of Balto. Lewis Hist. Pub. Co., 1912, v. 2, pp. 172-74; v. 3, p. 599. DAR.
Matthews-Price chart. MHS.
†Men of mark in Md. Johnson. V. 3. DAR; Enoch Pratt Lib.
Pedigree of Maurice Edward Skinner. Soc. Col. Wars Md. Culver. 1940. MHS; DAR.

St. Paul's Parish, Balto. V. 1, 2, 3. Mss. MHS.
Tercentenary hist. of Md. Andrews. V. 2, p. 636; v. 3, p. 418; v. 4, p. 635. MHS; DAR.
Third Haven Friends Meeting House, Easton. Vital rec. MHS. Also: Natl. Geneal. Soc. Quart., v. 11, no. 1, pp. 9–14.
*Throckmorton pedigree chart. Gardiner. Ms. DAR.
Turner family. Forman. Pp. 11, 84. MHS.
†**Bartlett,** Mass. Md. Hist. of Balto. City and Co. Scharf. Pp. 406, 426. MHS.
Bartlett, J. Kemp, Talbot Co. Abr. Compend. Amer. Geneal. Virkus. V. 1, p. 214. DAR.
†**Bartol, James C.,** Harford Co. Balto. hist. and biog. Richardson and Bennett. 1871, pp. 185–88. MHS; DAR.
Barton. ·Amer. of gentle birth and their ancestors. Pittman. V. 1, p. 7. MHS; DAR.
Ances. rec. and portraits. Col. Dames of Amer. 1910, p. 36. MHS; DAR.
Barton and allied families. Ms. File case, DAR.
†Bench and bar of Md. Sams and Riley. 1901, v. 2, p. 639. Lib. Cong.; MHS; Peabody Lib.
Epitaphs. Hist. of West. Md. Scharf. V. 2, p. 1472. MHS; DAR.
*Frederick Co. families. Markell. Ms. Personal list.
Hist. of Frederick Co. Williams. V. 2, p. 1505. MHS; DAR.
Md. families. Culver. Ms. Personal list.
Md. tombstone rec. Md. Geneal. Rec. Com., 1937, Parran, pp. 25, 29. Mss. DAR.
Port. and biog. rec. of Cecil and Harford Co. 1897, pp. 539–40. MHS; DAR.
Rucker family. Whitley.
St. Paul's Parish, Balto. V. 1, 2. Mss. MHS.
Smithsons of Harford Co. Md. Geneal. Rec. Com., 1932–33, pp. 148–62. Mss. DAR.
Southerland-Latham and allied families. Voorhees. P. 101. Bd. Ms. MHS.
Tercentenary hist. of Md. Andrews. V. 2, p. 263; v. 3, pp. 183, 299; v. 4, p. 141. MHS; DAR.
***Barton,** Va. The Sun, Balto., Oct. 8, 1905.
Barton, Miss Agnes Priscilla. Barton chart. Col. Dames, Chap. I. MHS.
Barton, Carlyle. Pedigree. Soc. Col. Wars Md. Culver. 1940. MHS; DAR.
Abr. Compend. Amer. Geneal. Virkus. V. 1, p. 214. DAR.
Barton, Miss Elizabeth Hawkins. Chart. Col.
Barton, Randolph. Pedigree chart. Soc. Col. Wars, Md. Johnston. 1905, p. 4. MHS.
Barton, Randolph, Jr. Pedigree. Soc. Col. Wars Md. Culver. 1940. MHS; DAR.
Barton, Mrs. Randolph, Jr. (Eleanor Addison Morison). Chart. Col. Dames, Chap. I. MHS.
Mrs. A. R. Rogers chart. MHS.
Mrs. M. J. Henry chart. MHS.
Sidney Morison chart. MHS.
Barton, Wm. Pedigree of Morris Gregg. Soc. Col. Wars Md. Culver. 1940. MHS; DAR.
Barton Family. Miscellaneous data. Ms. MHS.
*Prominent Va. families. L. Pecquet du Bellet. 1907, v. 1, p. 170; v. 2, pp. 671, 745–50. DAR.
Barton Family, Charles Co. Ms. MHS.
Barton-Morison. Appendix chart. Mrs. Randolph Barton, Jr., and Miss Sidney Buchanan Morrison. Chart. Col. Dames, Chap. I. MHS.
***Bartow.** Bartow family in Eng. Evelyn Bartow. 1886, 1890, 2 pamph. MHS.
*Geneal., containing every one of the name Bartow, descended from Dr. Thomas Bartow. E. B. Bartow. Balto., Innes & Co., 1878. Lib. Cong.; MHS.
*Supplement to Bartow geneal. Evelyn Bartow. Balto., 1879. Lib. Cong.; MHS.
Bartow, Thomas. Geneal. rec. of George Small, etc. Small. MHS.
Bartran. St. Paul's Parish, Balto. V. 1. Mss. MHS.
Baruch. Sara R. Baldwin chart. MHS.
Barwell. St. Paul's Parish, Balto. V. 1, 3. Mss. MHS.
Basel. Rahn and allied families. Ms. MHS.
Basel Family. Ms. MHS.
Baseman. St. Paul's Parish, Balto. V. 1. Mss. MHS.
***Baseman Family.** Outline. Md. Geneal. Bull., v. 10, no. 3, p. 26. MHS; DAR.
Bashaw. St. Paul's Parish, Balto. V. 1. Mss. MHS.
***Baskerville.** Additional geneal., supplemental ed. Patrick Hamilton Baskerville. Richmond, Va., 1917.
Geneal. Patrick Hamilton Baskerville. Richmond, Va., Wm. Ellis Jones Son, Inc., 1912.
Basset, Bassett. Cary Geneal. Coll. Ms. MHS.
***Basset, Bassett,** Va. The Sun, Balto., July, 14, 21, 28; Aug. 4, 1907.
†**Bassett.** Hist. of Cecil Co. Johnston. MHS. DAR.
Bassett, Va. Rec. Ancestry of Benjamin Harrison. Keith. MHS; DAR.
Bassett-DuPuy-Woodson (all Va.). Americans of gentle birth and their ancestors. Pitman. P. 10. MHS.
Bassler. Catonsville pioneers of Luth. faith. Natl. Geneal. Soc. Quart., v. 9, no. 2, p. 29.
†**Batchelor.** Med. Annals Md. Cordell. 1903, p. 314. MHS.
St. Paul's Parish, Balto. V. 2, 3. Mss. MHS.
Batdorf (Potterf), Casper. (Md. ref.) Natl. Geneal. Soc. Quart., v. 23, p. 87.
Bateman. Graves. Greensboro churchyard. Md. Geneal. Rec. Com., 1935–36, p. 168. Mss. DAR.
Greensboro old churchyard. Md. Geneal. Rec. Com., 1935–36, p. 168. Mss. DAR.
See Linthicum family. Focke Geneal. Coll. Ms. MHS.
Bateman Line. Hamilton family of Charles Co. Kelly. MHS.
Bates. Cary Geneal. Coll. Ms. MHS.
St. Paul's Parish, Balto. V. 1, 2, 3. Mss. MHS.
Bateson. St. Paul's Parish, Balto. V. 1, 2. Mss. MHS.
***Batiste.** Bible rec. Ms. MHS.
Batson. St. Paul's Parish, Balto. V. 1. Mss. MHS.
Battee. Ances. rec. and portraits. Col. Dames of Amer., 1910, v. 2, p. 605. MHS; DAR.
Hazelhurst chart. MHS.

Battee, Brewer, Boteler (1669), **Gibson, Grundy, Harris, Lingan, Maccubin, Peale, Ridgely, Robinson.** Family rec. Comp. by Mrs. Clapham Murray. Bk. of photos. MHS.
Batten Family. Md. Geneal. Rec. Com., 1938–39, p. 88. Mss. DAR.
Batterton. Amer. Guthrie and allied families. Guthrie. Bk. 4. DAR.
Bauers. *See* Bowers.
Baugh, Anneslie Bond. Geneal. through Beall, Bond, Magruder families, 1660–1936. Md. Geneal. Rec. Com., 1937–38, pp. 204–06. Mss. DAR.
Baugher. Hist. of Frederick Co. Williams. V. 2, p. 1527. MHS; DAR.
Lanahan chart. MHS.
Mrs. Sherlock Swann chart. MHS.
Baughman. Balto., its hist., its people. Hall. V. 3. MHS; DAR.
Hist. of Frederick Co. Williams. V. 1, p. 251; v. 2, pp. 696, 1384.
Baughman, C. C. Md. Soc., War of 1812, v. 2, no. 184. Ms. MHS.
Baughman, Edwin Austin. Pedigree. Soc. Col. Wars Md. Culver. 1940. MHS; DAR.
Md. Soc., War of 1812, v. 2, no. 185. Ms. MHS.
Baughman, Greer H. Md. Soc., War of 1812, v. 2, no. 183. Ms. MHS.
Baughman, Louis Victor. Pedigree chart. Soc. Col. Wars, Md. Johnston. 1905, p. 5. MHS.
†Men of mark in Md. Johnson. V. 3. DAR; Enoch Pratt Lib.
Baughman Family. Carrollton Manor, Frederick Co. Grove. 1921, p. 17. DAR.
Hist. of Carrollton Manor, Frederick Co. Jarboe. P. 62. DAR.
Hist. of Balto. Lewis Pub. Co., 1912, v. 3, p. 589. DAR.
Tercentenary hist. of Md. Andrews. V. 3, p. 681. MHS; DAR.
Baumgardner. Hist. of Frederick Co. Williams. V. 2, pp. 733, 1291. MHS; DAR.
†**Baumgardner Family.** Hist. of Lancaster Co., Pa. Ellis and Evans. 1883, v. 1, p. 528. DAR.
Baumgartner. *See* Bous-Baumgartner-Cavander.
Bauman. *See* Bowman.
Bavinton. St. Stephens Parish, Cecilton, Md. MHS; DAR.
†**Baxley.** Med. Annals Md. Cordell. 1903, p. 315. MHS.
St. Paul's Parish, Balto. V. 1, 2. Mss. MHS.
Baxter. Ances. rec. and portraits. Col. Dames of Amer. P. 125. MHS; DAR.
St. Paul's Parish, Balto. V. 1, 2, 3. Mss. MHS.
St. Thomas' Parish, Balto. Co. Bd. ms. MHS. Also: Md. Geneal. Rec. Com., 1937, pp. 109–82. Mss. DAR.
***Baxter Family.** File case, DAR.
Bay Family. Tercentenary hist. of Md. Andrews. V. 2, p. 560. MHS; DAR.
Bayard. Amer. Guthrie and allied families. Guthrie. Bk. 4. DAR.
Ances. rec. and portraits, Col. Dames of Amer. 1910. V. 1, p. 61. MHS; DAR.
Col. John Bayard, 1738–1807, and Bayard family in America. Gen. J. G. Wilson. Repr. from N. Y. Geneal. Rec., April, 1885. Pamph. MHS.
Cary Geneal. Coll. Ms. MHS.
†Col. John Bayard. Appleton's Cyc.
Descendants of Joran Kyn. Pa. Mag., v. 6, p. 208; v. 7, p. 299.
Robert Gilmor chart. MHS.
†Hist. of Cecil Co. Johnston. MHS; DAR.
Hist. of Del. Scharf. 1888. V. 1, pp. 279, 533, 569, 577, 586, 589; v. 2, p. 959, DAR.
Judge Bayard's London diary, 1795–96. J. G. Wilson. N. Y. Geneal. and Biog. Rec., 1892, v. 23.
Memorial of Col. John Bayard. By J. G. Wilson, read before the N. J. Hist. Soc., Jan. 16, 1878. N. J. Hist. Soc. Pro.
Naturalizations in Md., 1666–1765; Laws. Bacon. MHS.
Pedigree. Geneal. of McKean family of Pa. Buchanan. P. 142. MHS.
*Pennington Papers. Ms. MHS.
St. Paul's Parish, Balto. V. 1, 3. Mss. MHS.
St. Stephens Parish, Cecilton, Md. MHS; DAR.
See Schindell. Lineage Bk., Order of Washington. MHS; DAR.
*The Sun, Balto., Sept. 9, 1885. (Article on Bohemia Manor.)
Bayard, Cecil Co. Notes. D. A. R. Mag., Jan., 1938, v. 72, no. 1, p. 63.
Bayard, Del. Abr. Compend. Amer. Geneal. Virkus. V. 1, p. 221. DAR.
***Bayard, Col. John** (1738–1807). And Bayard family in Amer. N. Y. Geneal. and Biog. Rec., April, 1885, v. 16, no. 2, pp. 49–72.
Bayard, Richard H. The Sun, Balto., July 8, 1889.
Bayard Family. Ancient families of Bohemia Manor. 1888. Pp. 46–71. MHS; DAR.
Newsp. clipp. File case, DAR.
*N. J. Cyc. N. J., 1923, v. 1, p. 78. DAR.
N. J. Hist. Soc. Proc., 3rd series, 1897, v. 2, p. 101. DAR.
*N. Y. Geneal. and Biog. Rec., v. 8, pp. 15–16. MHS; DAR.
Bayard family of America and Judge Bayard's London diary of 1795–96. Huguenot Soc. of Amer. Proc. N. Y., 1883–84, v. 1.
*Rec. of Peter Bayard (born 1732; died 1817). Ms. DAR.
Bayard, Col. Nicholas Line, New York. C. W. L. Johnson pedigree chart, plate 1. Soc. Cols. Wars, Md. Johnston. 1905, pp. 49, 139. MHS.
Bayer. Mt. Olivet Cemetery, Frederick. Md. Geneal. Rec. Com., 1934–35, p. 111. Mss. DAR.
Bayer-Boyer. Peale Geneal. Coll. Ms. MHS.
Bayler. Hist. of Allegany Co., Thomas and Williams. V. 2, pp. 720–21. MHS; DAR.
Bayles. *See* Bayless.
Bayless, Baylis. Col. families of U. S. A. Mackenzie. V. 2. MHS; DAR.
Hist. of Harford Co. Preston. Pp. 181, 182. MHS; DAR.
Patriotic Md. Md. Soc. of S. A. R., 1930. MHS; DAR.
Bayless Family. Descendants of Nathaniel Bayless of Md.; with some Keen family data. DAR.
Photos. and ms. File case, DAR.
Hist. of Balto. Lewis Pub. Co., 1912, v. 2, p. 329. MHS; DAR.

Bayless Family, Harford Co. See Cochran-Beard-Carr-Ross-Wassan families. Ms. File case, DAR.
Bayless, Bayles. Balto., its hist., its people. Hall. V. 2. MHS; DAR.
Bayley. Coale chart. MHS.
Pedigree of John Philemon Paca. Soc. Col. Wars Md. Culver. 1940. MHS; DAR.
St. Paul's Parish, Balto. V. 1, 2, 3. Mss. MHS.
See Bailey.
Bayley (Mrs. Mary Nixon-Goldsborough) (born 1788). N. Y. Geneal. and Biog. Rec., v. 8, p. 94.
Baylies Line. Hooper family. Col. and Revolutionary families of Pa. Jordan. 1932, v. 4, p. 223.
Baylis. *See* Bayless.
Baylor. Ances. rec. and portraits. Col. Dames of Amer. 1910, p. 140. MHS; DAR.
Balch chart. MHS.
Baylor Family. Tercentenary hist. of Md. Andrews. V. 2, p. 961. MHS; DAR.
Bayly. Christ P. E. Church cenetery, Cambridge. Steele. 1936. MHS; DAR.
Done Bible rec. Ms. MHS.
Haynie Bible rec. Ms. MHS.
*Hist. Dorchester Co. Jones. 1925, p. 277. MHS; DAR.
Mt. Olivet Cemetery, Frederick. Md. Geneal. Rec. Com., 1934–35, p. 111. Mss. DAR.
Bayly Family. Amer. biog. directories. H. B. F. Macfarland. 1908, p. 28. DAR.
Baynard. Whiteley chart. MHS.
See Whiteley. Col. families of U. S. A. Mackenzie. V. 1, p. 581. DAR.
Baynard Family. Rec. of Tred Avon Friends Meeting House, Talbot Co. Bd. mss. MHS.
Baynard Family, Talbott Co., **and Thomas Family,** Talbot Co. Bible rec. from 1779. D. C. Geneal. Rec. Com., v. 31, pp. 107–09. Typed, bd. DAR.
Bayne. Col. and Revolutionary families of Pa. Amer. Hist. Soc., N. Y., 1934, p. 11.
Dawson family of Md. Ms. File case, DAR.
*St. Mary's Co. Burke's landed gentry. 1939. MHS.
See Castle. Abr. Compend. Amer. Geneal. Virkus. V. 1, p. 91. DAR.
Bayne, William. Copy of will. File case, DAR.
***Bayne Family.** Md. Geneal. Rec. Com., 1932, p. 22. DAR.
Tercentenary hist. of Md. Andrews. V. 4, p. 468. MHS; DAR.
Bayne-Boswell. Abr. Compend. Amer. Geneal. Virkus. V. 4, pp. 213–14. MHS.
Baynes. Baynes of Md., 1652–1729. Md. Geneal. Rec. Com., 1932, v. 5, p. 22. DAR.
Bays. St. Paul's Parish, Balto. V. 1. Mss. MHS.
Baysand. St. Paul's Parish, Balto. V. 1. Mss. MHS.
***Baytop Family.** Times-Dispatch, Richmond, Va., May 10, 1910. DAR.
Baytop-Catlett. Hist. of two Va. families, transplanted from Co. Kent, Eng.: Thomas Baytop and John Catlett. Dr. and Mrs. W. C. Stubbs. New Orleans, 1918. DAR.
Bazeman. St. Paul's Parish, Balto. V. 1. Mss. MHS.
Beach. St. Paul's Parish, Balto. V. 1, 2. Mss. MHS.
***Beach Family.** Mag. comp. by A. H. Beach and Cora M. Beach. Jan. 1, 1926–Oct., 1927. MHS.
Beacham. *See* Beachim.
***Beachamp.** Wicomico Co. families. Tilghman. Ms., p. 100. DAR.
Beachey. Hist. of Allegany Co. Thomas and Williams. V. 2, pp. 724–25. MHS; DAR.
Hist. of West. Md. Scharf. V. 2, p. 1530. MHS; DAR.
Beachey-Humrickhouse-Jacques, Hixon-Gregory. Abr. Compend. Amer. Geneal. Virkus. V. 4, p. 646. MHS.
Beachgood. St. Paul's Parish, Balto. V. 1. Mss. MHS.
Beachim, Beacham. St. Paul's Parish, Balto. V. 1, 2, 3. Mss. MHS.
Beachley. Hist. of Frederick Co. Williams. V. 2, pp. 857, 1102, 1315, 1476. MHS; DAR.
***Beachy Family.** Garrett Co. families. Hoye. P. 11. In Binder, DAR.
Beadle. Md. families. Culver. Ms. Personal list.
Beadle, Beedle, Bedle. St. Stephens Parish, Cecilton, Md. MHS; DAR.
Beaghthe. *See* Baechtel.
Beal. Hist. of Allegany Co. Thomas and Willams. V. 1, pp. 94, 102, 138, 142, 379; v. 2, pp. 725–26, 726–28, 892, 987, 1230–32 MHS; DAR.
*Kith and kin. Dixon. P. 18. DAR.
Trinity P. E. churchyard, St. Mary's City. Md. O. R. Soc. Bull., no. 3, p. 59.
See Beall.
Beale. Anne Arundel Co. gentry. Newman. Pp. 1–2. MHS; DAR.
Founders of Anne Arundel and Howard Cos. Warfield. Pp. 65, 101–04. MHS; DAR.
*Frederick Co. families. Markell. Ms. Personal list.
Mrs. Alexander Gordon chart. MHS.
Jackson chart. MHS.
Rogers Coll. Ms. MHS.
Smithsons of Harford Co. Md. Geneal. Rec. Com., 1932–33, pp. 160, 162. Mss. DAR.
See Beall.
***Beale, Charles Frederick Tiffany.** Pub. Soc. Col. Wars of D. C., 1901. MHS.
***Beale, Samuel.** Wilson Mss. Coll., no. 42. MHS.
***Beale, Beall.** Anne Arundel Co. gentry. Newman. MHS; DAR.
*Founders of Anne Arundel and Howard Cos. Warfield. Pp. 101–04. MHS; DAR.
***Beale, Beall, Bell.** Balto. Herald, Mar. 15, 1903; Jan. 31, 1904. MHS.
Col. families of U. S. A. Mackenzie. V. 1, p. 349; v. 2, pp. 82–105 (W. Va. and Md.); v. 7, p. 254. MHS; DAR.
St. Barnabas P. E. churchyard. Typed ms. MHS; DAR.
*St. Mary's R. C. Church cemetery, Montgomery Co. Hist. of West. Md. Scharf. V. 1, pp. 731–50. MHS; DAR.
Semmes Geneal. Coll. Ms. MHS.
John Swadner and his descendants. Evans. 1919. Typed, bd. MHS.
See Abadie-Beall. Amer. of gentle birth, and their ancestors. Pittman. V. 2, pp. 2–3. MHS; DAR.
Beall. See Abadie. Abr. Compend. Amer. Geneal. Virkus. V. 1, pp. 227, 407. DAR.

Beall. Abr. Compend. Amer. Geneal. Virkus. V. 4, p. 705; MHS; v. 6, pp. 127, 250. DAR.
Amer. Armory and Blue Book. Matthews. 1911–12, p. 192.
Amer. Clan Gregor Year Book 1929, p. 55 (Jack Beall, Tex.); 1934, p. 71. MHS; DAR.
*Ancestral beginnings in Amer. of McGregor, Magruder, Beall, Price, Phillips, Bland, McKisick, Young and related families. Caroline B. Price. Austin, Texas 1928. DAR.
Ances. rec. and portraits. Col. Dames of Amer., 1910, v. 2, pp. 465–69, 802. MHS; DAR.
Ancestry and descendants of Gustavus Beall and Thomas Heugh Beall. J. H. Shinn. Wash., D. C., Geneal. and Hist. Pub. Co., 1911, pamph. MHS.
Anderson-Owen-Beall Geneal. in part. Anderson. Richmond, Va., 1909, pp. 78–142. DAR.
*Beall and Edwards families and their descendants 360–1892. A. S. Edwards. 1910. DAR.
Beall family. Land grant papers, pp. 7–27. Mss. DAR.
George Beall, 1695–1780; George Beall, 1729–1807; Col. war service. Col. Ninian Beall, 1625–1717. Moses. DAR.
Mordecai Beall (1742–77); also Collins and South family rec. of Ky. File case, DAR.
†Col. Ninian Beall (1625–1717). C. C. Magruder, Jr. 41 pp. MHS; DAR.
Col. Ninian Beall, 1625–1717; Col. George Beall, 1695–1780; Col. George Beall, 1729–1807; owners of Rock of Dumbarton estate, 2175 acres, on which Georgetown was located. Zebina Moses. Pamph. Wash. D. C., 1908, File case, DAR.
*Samuel Beall (born in 1749) and Celina (born 1762). Bible rec. D. C. Geneal. Rec. Com., 1928–30. Typed, bd. DAR.
†"Bellevue", home of Natl. Soc. of Col. Dames. Mrs. J. R. Lamar. M. H. Mag., June, 1929, v. 24, no. 2, pp. 99–112.
Col. Joseph Belt. Hist. papers of Soc. Col. Wars. Magruder. 1909. MHS; DAR.
Bible rec. Ga. Geneal. Rec. Com., 1933 pp., 45–46. File case, DAR.
Bible rec. of Samuel (born in 1749) and Celina (born in 1762). D. C. Geneal. Rec. Com., 1928–30. Typed, bd. DAR.
Bible rec., 1760–1826. Natl. Geneal. Soc. Quart., v. 24, p. 87.
Bowie-Claggett chart. MHS.
Brooke family of Whitchurch, etc. Balch. MHS; DAR.
Cemetery Creek, Anne Arundel Co., tombstone inscriptions. Founders of Anne Arundel and Howard Cos. Warfield. P. 333. MHS; DAR.
Cemetery near Carroll Chapel, Forest Glen. Md. Geneal. Rec. Com., v. 2, p. 27. Mss. DAR.
Chart, Photos., complete in 1 sheet. Cary Geneal. Coll. Ms. MHS.
Robt. Smith Chew and his ancestors in Md. and Va. 1938, pp. 74–81. Typed. in binder, DAR.
Col. families of Amer. Lawrence. V. 15, p. 171; v. 16, p. 79. MHS.
Col. war service, George Beall (1695–1780) and George Beall (1729–1807). In Ninian Beall (1625–1717), Zebina Moses. File case, DAR.
Col. wars service of Col. Ninian Beall. Mss MHS; DAR.
See Daniel. Linage Bks., Natl. Soc. of Daughters of Amer. Col., v. 3, p. 92. MHS; DAR.
Descendants of Sam'l Beall Sr., and his wife Jane Edmondston. Mss. File case, DAR.
D. C. Geneal. Rec. Com., 1932–34, v. 10, p. 124.
†Early days of Wash. Mackall. Pp. 53, 64. DAR.
*Frederick Co. families. Markell. Ms. Personal list.
Gartrell-Beall family of Md. Mss. DAR.
*Geneal. of Alexander Beall (1649–1744). Mo. Geneal. Rec. Com., 1936. Mss. DAR.
*Geneal. of Alexander Beall (1649–1744). Kansas, Mo., 1936. Typed. DAR.
Harford Co. Hist. Soc. Mss. Coll. JHU.
†Hist. of Allegany Co. Thomas and Williams V. 1; v. 2. MHS; DAR.
Hist. of Carrollton Manor, Frederick Co. Grove. 1928, p. 381. DAR.
Hist. of Frederick Co. Williams. V. 1, pp. 8, 84. MHS; DAR.
†Hist. of Natl. capital. Bryan. 1914, p. 101. DAR.
†Hist. of West. Md. Scharf. V. 1, pp. 472, 596, 731; v. 2, p. 933. MHS; DAR.
Ky. Bible and tombstone rec. File case, DAR.
*Lineage Bks., Natl. Soc. of Daughters of Amer. Col., v. 1, p. 41; v. 2, p. 157; v. 3, pp. 4, 221, 246; v. 4, p. 215; v. 5, pp. 74, 127–30. MHS; DAR.
See Longcope; Price. Abr. Compend. Amer. Geneal. Virkus. V. 1, p. 695. DAR.
Md. families. Culver. Ms. Personal list.
*Md. Geneal. Rec. Com., 1932–33, pp. 176–178. DAR.
See Nevin. Abr. Compend. Amer. Geneal. Virkus. V. 1, p. 638. DAR.
Old Kent. Hanson. P. 245. MHS; DAR.
Orme Geneal. chart. MHS.
Richard Owens and Rachel Beall. Ms. DAR.
Patriotic Md. Md. Soc. of S. A. R., 1930. MHS; DAR.
Pedigree and hist. of Washington family. Welles. P. 197. MHS.
Pedigree of Coleman Randall Freeman. Soc. Col. Wars Md. Culver. 1940. MHS; DAR.
Pedigree of Henry Irvine Keyser, II. Soc. Col. Wars Md. Culver. 1940. MHS; DAR.
Pedigree of Charles O'Donnell Mackall. Soc. Col. Wars Md. Culver. 1940. MHS; DAR.
Pedigree of James Donnell Tilghman. Soc. Col. Wars Md. Culver. 1940. MHS; DAR.
Pa. Mag., v. 21, p. 507; v. 22, p. 508.
Portrait and biog. rec. of Sixth Cong. Dist. of Md. 1898. P. 673. MHS; DAR.
Price ancestral data (maternal). Bd. ms. MHS.
*Repr. from Daily News, Cumberland, Md., May 20, 1896. MHS.
St. John's R. C. Church cemetery, Montgomery Co. Md. Geneal. Rec. Com., 1926, p. 27. Mss. DAR.
Segrave chart. MHS.
*Side lights on Md. hist. Richardson. V. 2, p. 5. MHS; DAR.
Tercentenary hist. of Md. Andrews. V. 4, p. 427. MHS; DAR.
Mrs. H. DeCourcy Wright Thom chart. MHS.
*The Sun, Balto., Jan. 31, 1904.

Zimmerman-Waters and allied families. Allen. Pp. 92–103, 104. MHS; DAR.
Zion Reformed Church, Hagerstown. Md. Geneal. Rec. Com., 1934–35. Mss. DAR.
See Anderson-Owen-Beall.
See Beale.
See Sewall-Brooke-Darnall-Beall.

***Beall,** Md. and Va. Family rec. of Zephaniah Beall (born 1753; died 1809; married Elizabeth Magruder). Ms. DAR.

***Beall, Alexander.** Lineage Bk., Daughters of Founders and Patriots, v. 10, p. 35; v. 14, p. 106; v. 21, p. 108. MHS.

***Beall, Fielder M. M.** Col. families of U. S., descended from immigrants who arrived before 1700. Wash., D. C., 296 pp. DAR.

***Beall, Col. Joshua.** Md. Geneal. Rec. Com., 1932, pp. 243–45. DAR.
Land grant. Md. Geneal. Rec. Com., v. 5, pp. 243–45. DAR.

Beall, Mary, Georgetown, D. C. Abs. of will proved Nov. 11, 1806. D. A. R. Mag., June, 1927, v. 61, no. 6, p. 469.

Beall, Col. Ninian (born in Largo, Fifeshire, Scotland, 1625; died in Prince George Co., 1717). C. C. Magruder. Soc. Col. Wars, Hist. Papers, no. 6. MHS; DAR.
F. Du Pont Balch pedigree chart. Soc. Col. Wars, Md. Johnston. 1905, pp. 3, 139. MHS.
(1624–1717). Children (generally accepted number is 12): John, Thomas, Ninian, Jr., Charles, George, Sarah, Hester, Jane, Marjery, Rachel, James. Ms. list inserted in back of pamph. Col. Ninian Beall, C. C. Magruder. DAR.
(1624–1717). Children: Ninian, Jr., Jane, Charles, Hester, Margery, Mary and George. Rec. in old diary in possession of Mrs. Mary Beall, Gaithersburg, Md., mother of Louis C. Beall, Kensington, Md., and have been copied under title "Beall families of Frederick and Montgomery Cos." Md. Geneal. Rec. Com., 1932–33, p. 176. DAR.
Chart. File case, DAR.
†J. H. Univ. studies, Hist. and Political Sciences, 1890, no. 3. MHS; Enoch Pratt Lib.
McCall-Tidwell families. McCall. P. 466. MHS; DAR.
Memoir, 1625–1717. C. C. Magruder. Repr. from New Eng. Hist. and Geneal. Reg., by Soc. Col. Wars, in D. C., Jan. 2, 1911. Pamph. MHS; DAR.
Some descendants of Eng. and Scotland. File case, DAR.

Beall, Rezin (1723–1809). Descendant of Brig. Gen. Rezin Beall. File case, DAR.

***Beall, Richard,** Prince George Co. Will. D. C. Geneal. Rec. Com., 1932–34, v. 12, pp. 196–98. Typed, bd. DAR.

Beall, Samuel. Bible rec., 1749–1851. Natl. Geneal. Soc. Quart., v. 18, no. 1, p. 20.

Beall, Thomas. Oklahoma Geneal. Rec. Com., 1934, pp. 16–21. Typed, bd. File case, DAR.

Beall, Zephaniah (born 1753; died 1807; married Elizabeth Magruder). File case, DAR.

***Beall, Zepheniah,** Montgomery Co. Lineage Bk. Daughters of Founders and Patriots. V. 23, p. 127. MHS; DAR.

***Beall Family.** Amer. Hist. Soc.: Amer. families; geneal. and heraldic. Pp. 317–19. In vault, DAR.
*Alexander Beall (1649–1744). Kansas City, Mo., 1932(?). Typed. DAR.
*Bible rec. Ga. Geneal. Rec. Com., 1933, pt. 4, pp. 45–46. Typed, bd. DAR.
*D. C. Geneal. Rec. Com., 1932–34, v. 10, p. 124. Typed, bd. DAR.
*Robert Smith Chew and his ancestors in Md. and Va. Pollock. 1938, pp. 74–81. Typed; in Binder. DAR.
*Some descendants of Ninian Beall of Scotland and Md. Mss. DAR.
Tercentenary hist. of Md. Andrews. V. 4, p. 427. MHS; DAR.
*Wilson Mss. Coll., no. 25. MHS.
With wills of Josiah and Samuel Beall. Ms. File case, DAR.

Beall Family, Frederick and Montgomery Cos. (1624–1907). Md. Geneal. Rec. Com., 1932–33; pp. 176–78. Mss. DAR.

Beall Line. Col. and Revolutionary lineages of Amer. 1939, v. 3, pp. 289–98. MHS.

Beall Line, Beck, Pa. Col. and Revolutionary families of Phila. Jordan. 1933, v. 1, pp. 329–39.

Beall-Gantt-Brooke. Welsh-Hyatt and kindred. Supplement. Welsh. P. 13. MHS; DAR.

Beall-Kennedy Families, Md. and Ky. Ms. File case, DAR.

Beall, Beale, Bell. Cary Geneal. Coll. Ms. MHS.
*Beall and Bell families. Additional index to 1937. F. M. Beall. Ms. DAR.

***Beall, Bell.** Beall and Bell families. Col. families of U. S. prior to 1700. Bale, Beal, Beale, Beall, Bell. F. M. Beall. 296 pp. Wash., D. C., Charles H. Potter Co., 1929. MHS; DAR.

Bealmear. Wills of Francis Bealmear, Anne Arundel Co., 1780, and Francis Bealmear, Balto. Co., 1834. Absolom Anderson of Md. Pp. 2, 22. Mss. File case, DAR.

Bealmear, Elizabeth Brewer, Anne Arundel Co. Will 1803. In: Absolom Anderson. Ms., p. 5. DAR.

Bean. Bean family of Va., now W. Va. J. Bean Wilson. Athens, Ohio, pamph. MHS.
Cemetery near Carroll Chapel, Forest Glen. Md. Geneal. Rec. Com. v. 2, p. 28. Mss. DAR.
Fresh Pond Neck cemetery, home of Bennetts. Md. O. R. Soc. Bull., no. 3, pp. 57–58.
†Hist. of Washington Co. Williams. 1906, v. 2, p. 1138. MHS; DAR.
St. John's R. C. Church cemetery, Montgomery Co. Md. Geneal. Rec. Com., 1926, p. 27. Mss. DAR.

Bean, George, Prince George Co. Will, 1797, and other court rec. File case. Mss. DAR.

***Bean Family,** Hardy Co., Va.; now W. Va. Bean family. Josephine Bean Wilson. Aug., 1917, no. 1. MHS.

***Beans.** Amer. Clan Gregor Year Book, 1916, p. 35. MHS; DAR.
†Med. Annals Md. Cordell. 1903, p. 316. MHS.
Pedigree of Charles O'Donnell Mackall. Soc. Col. Wars Md. Culver. 1940. MHS; DAR.
Rec. Columbia Hist. Soc., v. 16, pp. 150–89.

‡Beans, Dr. William. Incidental cause of authorship of Star Spangled Banner. C. C. Magruder. Repr. from Rec. Columbia Hist. Soc., v. 22, pp. 207–25. Wash. D. C., 1919. DAR.

†**Bear.** Med. Annals Md. Cordell. 1903, p. 309. MHS.
See Baer.
†**Bear, John W.** Life and travels of John W. Bear, Buckeye blacksmith (born in Frederick, 1800). Balto., 1873.
Beard. Ances. rec. and portraits. Col. Dames of Amer., 1910, v. 1, p. 247. MHS; DAR.
Baust or Emanuel Reformed churchyard, Carroll Co. Md. Geneal. Rec. Com., 1935-36. Mss. DAR.
Beards' Luth. graveyard, Washington Co. Md. Geneal. Rec. Com., 1935-36. Mss. DAR.
Elliott chart. MHS.
Founders of Anne Arundel and Howard Cos. Warfield. Pp. 49, 88, 106-07. MHS; DAR.
Hist. of Frederick Co. Williams. V. 2, pp. 859, 1251. MHS; DAR.
Hist. of Washington Co. Williams. 1906, v. 1, p. 543. MHS; DAR.
Hist. of West. Md. Scharf. V. 2, p. 1304. MHS; DAR.
Md. tombstone rec. Md. Geneal. Rec. Com., 1937, Parran, pp. 14, 21, 25. Mss. DAR.
†Men of mark in Md. Johnson. V. 4, p. 392. DAR; Enoch Pratt Lib.
Pedigree of Charles McKnew Park. Soc. Col. Wars Md. Culver. 1940. MHS; DAR.
Ringgold-Elliott chart. MHS.
See Cochran-Beard-Carr-Ross-Wassan.
Beard, Rich. Pedigree of Benedict Henry Hanson, Jr. Soc. Col. Wars Md. Culver. 1940. MHS; DAR.
Beard, Stephen. And his descendants. S. W. Townsend. Ms. MHS.
Beard Family. Index. Ms. MHS.
Tercentenary hist. of Md. Andrews. V. 2, p. 984; v. 4, p. 501. MHS; DAR.
Beasaman. St. Paul's Parish, Balto. V. 1. Mss. MHS.
Beaseman. St. Thomas' Parish, Balto. Co. Bd. ms. MHS. Also: Md. Geneal. Rec. Com., 1937, pp. 109-82. Mss. DAR.
Beasley. Peale Geneal. Coll. Ms. MHS.
St. Paul's Parish, Balto. V. 2. Mss. MHS.
Beasley Family, Va. Lineage. Ms. File case, DAR.
Beasman Family. Bible. Md. Geneal. Bull., V. 1, no. 3, p. 17.
Beason. *See* Beeson.
Beastin, Beaston, Beeston, Beston. St. Stephens Parish, Cecilton, Md. MHS; DAR.
Beaston. *See* Beastin.
†**Beaston, Thomas** (1806-75). Hist. of Talbot Co. Tilghman. V. 1, pp. 607-13. MHS; DAR.
Beatle, Beetle. St. Stephens Parish, Cecilton, Md. MHS; DAR.
Beatty. Amer. Guthrie and allied families. Guthrie. Bk. 4. DAR.
*Coat of arms. Burke's landed gentry. 1939. MHS.
Dorsey and allied families. Ms. MHS.
Faith Pres. Church (Glendy Graveyard). Mss. MHS.
*Frederick Co. families. Markell. Ms. Personal list.
Hist. of Frederick Co. Williams. V. 2, p. 795. MHS; DAR.
†Hist. of West. Md. Scharf. V. 1, pp. 457, 470; v. 2, pp. 1017, 1034-35. MHS; DAR.
†Med. Annals Md. Cordell. 1903, pp. 316-17. MHS.
Port. and biog. rec. of Cecil and Harford Cos., 1897, p. 576. MHS; DAR.
St. Paul's Parish, Balto. V. 1, 2. Mss. MHS.
Spessard family. Spessard. MHS; DAR.
Tercentenary hist. of Md. Andrews. V. 4, p. 102. MHS; DAR.
Beatty, J. E. Md. Soc., War of 1812, v. 2, no. 197. Ms. MHS.
Beatty, John. Frederick Co. D. A. R. Mag., v. 57, no. 12, p. 742.
Beatty, Captain Wm., of Md. Line (1776-81). Personal or family papers, journal and letters. Mss. MHS.
***Beatty Family.** Beatty family. Effie L. Henry. (Ayton, Cissel, Green, Luck and Orme data.) Wash., D. C., typed, bd., 66 pp. DAR.
For boys and girls of Cambridge, Ohio. 1937 (?), pp. 10-12. In Binder. DAR.
Old Northwest. Geneal. Soc. Quart., Columbus, Ohio., April, 1905, v. 8, no. 2. MHS.
Pa. geneal. Egle. Pp. 68-81. MHS.
(Showing Jenkins, McCormick, Ryan, Sheets, Wilson and allied families.) Col. and Revolutionary lineages of Amer. 1939, v. 3, pp. 48-74. MHS.
***Beatty Family,** Md. and Ky. Family rec. and will of James Beatty (born in Md., 1742; died in Ky., 1820). Ms. DAR.
Beatty-Carmack, Frederick Co. Will probated, May 13, 1746. D. A. R. Mag., v. 57, no. 12, p. 743.
Beauchamp. Abr. Compend. Amer. Geneal. Virkus. V. 4, p. 598, MHS; v. 6, p. 719, DAR.
Beauchamp of Md. D. A. R. Mag., v. 66, p. 234.
Branch of Philip Adams family of Md. Adams. MHS.
M. E. churchyard, Snow Hill, Worcester Co., Hudson. Bd. ms. MHS; DAR.
Old Somerset. Torrence. MHS; DAR.
Somerset Co. Court Book. Tilghman. 1937. Ms. DAR.
Turner Geneal. Coll. Ms. MHS.
***Beauchamp, Edmund.** Seven generations. D. A. R. Mag., April, 1932, v. 66, no. 4, pp. 234-38.
Beauchamp Family. Chart. Descendants of Edmund Beauchamp. Printed. File case. DAR.
*Descendants of Edmund Beauchamp of East., Shore of Md. Ms. DAR.
*Wilson Mss. Coll., no. 62. MHS.
Beauchamp-Hackett-Layton-Turpin-Wilson-Willis. Families of East. Shore of Md. Md. geneal. rec. D. A. R. Mag., Sept., 1933, v. 67, no. 9, pp. 583-88.
Beauchamp-Smoot-Turpin-White-Willis-Wilson Families. Md. geneal. rec., Caroline, Charles, Dorchester, Somerset, Talbot and Worcester Cos. Incl. deeds, depositions, marriages and wills (127), 1663-1814. D. A. R. Mag., v. 67, no. 9, pp. 583-88.
Beaven. *See* Clark-Beaven.
Beaven Line. Origins of Clements-Spalding families of Md. and Ky. Clements. Pp. 66-72. MHS.
Beaven, Bevan. Data. Will of Charles Bevan, Prince George Co., 1690; will of Charles

Beavan, Jr., Prince George Co., 1761; 2 photos. and indenture between Richard Beaven and Richard Benedict Gardiner of Charles Co. 1810. Ms. MHS.
Patriotic Md. Md. Soc. of S. A. R., 1930. MHS; DAR.
Turner Geneal. Coll. Ms. MHS.
Beavens. Fisher family. Morse. MHS.
Patriotic Md. Md. Soc. of S. A. R., 1930. MHS; DAR.
Bechtel. *See* Baechtel.
Beck. Dulaney churchyard, near Massey, Kent Co. Md. Geneal. Rec. Com., 1933–34, pp. 210–12. Mss. DAR.
Evans family chart. Hull. Mss. MHS.
Hagerstown tombstone inscriptions. Gruder. Natl. Geneal. Soc. Quart., 1919, v. 8, nos. 1, 2.
†Hist. of Washington Co. Williams. 1906, v. 2, p. 1241. MHS; DAR.
St. Paul's churchyard, Kent Co. Md. O. R. Soc. Bull., no. 2, pp. 54–65. MHS.
Beck, Pa. Col. and Revolutionary families of Phila. Jordan. 1933, v. 1, pp. 329–39.
Becker. Peale Geneal. Coll. Ms. MHS.
***Becket.** Frederick Co. families. Markell. Ms. Personal list.
***Beckham Family.** Beckham family in Va., and branches thereof in Ky., Tenn., Pa., and W. Va. J. M. Beckham. Richmond, 1910.
Beckley. Mt. Paran Pres. churchyard, Harrisonville, Balto. Co. Typed ms. MHS; DAR.
Beckwith. Lineage Bks., Natl. Soc. of Daughters of Amer. Col., v. 2, p. 207. MHS; DAR.
*The Beckwiths, descendants of George Beckwith who came to Md. in 1648. P. Beckwith. Albany, N. Y., Joel Munsell's & Son, 1891.
See Cooke.
Beckwith, Va. See Linthicum family. Focke Geneal. Coll. Ms. MHS.
***Beckwith, Marvin,** Southington. Marvin Beckwith. Priv. pr., Elkorn, Wis., 1899. MHS.
Beddeson. St. Paul's Parish, Balto. V. 1. Mss. MHS.
Bedford. Allyn - Foote - Webb - Cooch - Wilkins geneal. Cooch. Bd. ms. MHS.
Ancestry and descendants of Nancy Allyn (Foote) Webb, etc. Cooch. MHS; DAR.
Mrs. R. F. Brent chart. MHS.
Coll. of Amer. epitaphs and inscriptions. Alden. 1814, v. 5. MHS.
Horwitz chart. MHS.
Ms. MHS.
Pedigree of Hope Horsey Barroll. Soc. Col. Wars Md. Culver. 1940. MHS; DAR.
St. Paul's Parish, Balto. V. 2. Mss. MHS.
Bedinger. *See* Bittinger and Bedinger.
Bedinger, Pa. and W. Va. Lee of Va., 1642–1892. E. J. Lee. Lib. Cong.; MHS.
Bedle. *See* Beadle.
***Bedsworth.** Wicomico Co. families. Tilghman. Ms., p. 121. DAR.
Bee. Turner Geneal. Coll. Ms. MHS.
Beedle. Greenway chart. MHS.
Howard-Montague-Warfield geneal. chart. Culver and Marye. MHS.
See Beadle.
Beedle-Foster-Kennedy-Walker. Harford Co. Hist. Soc. Mss. Coll. JHU.
Beeks. Branch of Philip Adams family of Md. Adams. MHS.
Beeman. St. Paul's Parish, Balto. V. 1, 2. Mss. MHS.
Beems. St. Paul's Parish, Balto. V. 1. Mss. MHS.
Beers, Walter Whitney. Md. Soc., War of 1812, v. 4, no. 345. Ms. MHS.
***Beers Family.** Beers Family Assoc.; Walter Whitney Beers, sec., 1219 Fidelity Bldg., Balto.
Beeson. Col. families of Amer. Lawrence. V. 2, p. 38. MHS.
*Frederick Co. families. Markell. Ms. Personal list.
(Md. in 1666). Geneal. J. L. Beeson. Milledgeville, Ga. Pamph. MHS.
Naturalizations in Md., 1666–1765; Laws. Bacon. MHS.
Beeson (Beason) Family, Pa. Col. and Revolutionary lineages of Amer. 1939, v. 3, pp. 142–48. MHS.
Beeston. St. Paul's Parish, Balto. V. 1. Mss. MHS.
See Beastin.
Beetle. *See* Beatle.
***Begole Line,** Hagerstown, Md., (1784 or 86). Encyc. of Amer. biog. Amer. Hist. Soc., N. Y., 1928, v. 33, p. 216.
Beirne, Mrs. Francis Foulke (Rosamond Harding Randall). Chart. Col. Dames, Chap. I. MHS.
Bela. St. Paul's Parish, Balto. V. 1. Mss. MHS.
Belamy. St. Paul's Parish, Balto. V. 1. Mss. MHS.
Bell. Bell family in Amer. Wm. M. Clemens. N. Y., 1913, pamph. (Bell of Md., p. 32.) MHS.
Bible rec., 1801–1924. Md. Geneal. Rec. Com., 1937, p. 20. Mss. DAR.
*Founders of the Bell family. R. M. Bell. 1929. DAR.
Hagerstown tombstone inscriptions. Gruder. Natl. Geneal. Soc. Quart., 1919, v. 8, nos. 1, 2.
Lanahan chart. MHS.
Last will and testament of James Bell, Revolutionary soldier of Md.; with Bible rec. Pamph. DAR.
Ms. MHS.
Md. families. Culver. Ms. Personal list.
Merryman family. Culver. M. H. Mag., 1915, v. 10, pp. 176, 286.
Patriotic Md. Md. Soc. of S. A. R., 1930. MHS; DAR.
Pattison wills. Md. Geneal. Rec. Com., 1929, pp. 7–42; 1930–31. Mss. DAR.
Pedigree of John Edward Hurst. Soc. Col. Wars Md. Culver. 1940. MHS; DAR.
St. Paul's churchyard, Kent Co. Md. O. R. Soc. Bull., no. 2, pp. 54–65. MHS.
St. Paul's Parish, Balto. V. 1, 2, 3, 4. Mss. MHS.
St. Stephens Parish, Cecilton, Md. MHS; DAR.
Mrs. Sherlock Swann chart. MHS.
Wicomico Co. families. Bible rec. Ms. DAR.
*Wicomico Co. families. Tilghman. Ms, pp. 2, 3, 35, 98, 99, 100, 107, 115. DAR.
See Beale.
See Beall.
***Bell Family.** Bell family in Amer. Wm. M. Clemens. N. Y., 1913. MHS.

***Bell Family.** Bell family of Md. 1894, 45 pp.
*Bell family of Md. 4 supplements, 1895, 1897, 19 pp.
Bell-Cashell. Graves; tombstones on hilltop near site of Hawling's River P. E. Chapel, 1761, Montgomery Co., Md. Geneal. Rec. Com., 1934, p. 60. DAR.
Bellfrage. St. Paul's Parish, Balto. V. 1. Mss. MHS.
Bellicane. Naturalizations in Md., 1666–1765; Laws. Bacon. MHS.
Bellnap (Mrs. Wm. Graham). Bowdoin, Jr., chart. MHS.
Belmar. See Linthicum family. Focke Geneal. Coll. Ms. MHS.
Belt. Ancestry of Mrs. Fulton Ray Gordon, nee Ellen Marjorie Gray. D. C. Geneal. Rec. Com., 1932–34, p. 121. Typed, bd. DAR.
Beall and Bell families. Beall. MHS.
†Col. Joseph Belt (1680–1761). C. C. Magruder. 1909. MHS; DAR.
Bowie-Claggett chart. MHS.
Britton Scrap Book. V. 1. Ms. MHS.
Cary Geneal. Coll. Ms. MHS.
Chart, photos., 1 sheet. Cary Geneal. Coll. Ms. MHS.
See Daniel. Lineage Bks., Natl. Soc. of Daughters of Amer. Col., v. 3, p. 92. MHS; DAR.
Family geneal. Christopher Johnston. M. H. Mag., 1918, v. 8, pp. 195–202.
*Frederick Co. families. Markell. Ms. Personal list.
James Hook and Virginia Eller. Hook. MHS; DAR.
Lineage. Christopher Johnston. M. H. Mag., 1913, v. 8, no. 2, pp. 195–208.
Md. families. Culver. Ms. Personal list.
Mayflower ancestors of Bertha Brownell Belt. Photos. DAR.
†Med. Annals Md. Cordell. 1903, pp. 317–18. MHS.
Mullikins of Md. Baker. MHS; DAR.
Parrish family. Boyd. MHS; DAR.
Patriotic Md. Md. Soc. of S. A. R., 1930. MHS; DAR.
Pedigree of Maurice Falconer Rodgers. Soc. Col. Wars Md. Culver. 1940. MHS; DAR.
Pedigree of Levin Gale Shreve. Soc. Col. Wars Md. Culver. 1940. MHS; DAR.
Pedigree of James Donnell Tilghman. Soc. Col. Wars Md. Culver. 1940. MHS; DAR.
St. Barnabas P. E. churchyard. Typed ms. MHS; DAR.
St. Paul's Parish, Balto. V. 1, 2, 3, 4. Mss. MHS.
Segrave chart. MHS.
*Side lights on Md. hist. Richardson. V. 2, p. 11. MHS; DAR.
*The Sun, Balto., Oct. 16, 30, Nov. 13, 1904; March 26, 1909 (Col. Joseph Belt, Chevy Chase).
Talbott of "Poplar Knowle." Shirk. MHS; DAR.
See Lucas-Belt-Lawrence-West.
See Moore-Belt.
†Belt, Col. Joseph. Col. Joseph Belt. C. C. Magruder.
Hist. papers of Soc. Col. Wars of D. C., no. 5, p. 36, 1909. C. C. Magruder. Repr., Advertiser and Republican Print, Annapolis, 1909, pamph. MHS; DAR.
Belt Line. Beck, Pa. Col. and Revolutionary families of Phila. Jordan. 1933, v. 1, pp. 329–39.
Belt-Bier. Col. families of U. S. A. Mackenzie. V. 2, p. 640. MHS; DAR.
Belt-Price-Pitts. Marriages, 1778–1856. Parrish family. Boyd. MHS; DAR.
Benchoff. Spessard family. Spessard. MHS; DAR.
Bend, Wm. Bradford. St. Paul's Parish, Balto. V. 1, 2. Mss. MHS.
Coll. of Amer. epitaphs and inscriptions. Alden. 1814, v. 1, pp. 105–06. MHS.
Bender. Hagerstown tombstone inscriptions. Gruder. Natl. Geneal. Soc. Quart., 1919, v. 8, nos. 1, 2.
White Geneal. Tree. MHS.
Bender-Fisk-Morfit Families. Ms. File case, DAR.
Bendergrass. St. Paul's Parish, Balto. V. 1. Mss. MHS.
Benezet, Daniel. Geneal. rec. of George Small, etc. Small. MHS.
Benfield. St. Paul's Parish, Balto. V. 1. Mss. MHS.
Benjamin. Col. families of U. S. A. Mackenzie. V. 1, pp. 18–22. MHS; DAR.
Peale Geneal. Coll. Ms. MHS.
St. Paul's Parish, Balto. V. 1. Mss. MHS.
***Benner** or **Banor.** Frederick Co. families. Markell. Ms. Personal list.
Bennet. Barlow family Bible rec. Photos. DAR.
†Men of mark in Md. Johnson. V. 1. DAR; Enoch Pratt Lib.
Bennet, Gov. Richard. Geneal. M. H. Mag., v. 9, no. 4, p. 307.
†(Gov. of Va., 1652–55.) M. H. Mag., 1914, v. 9, pp. 307–15.
Bennet, Richard, Jr. Notes. Will of 1667. M. H. Mag., 1906, v. 1, pp. 73–75.
Bennet, Bennett. Somerset Co. Court Book. Tilghman. 1937. Ms. DAR.
St. Paul's Parish, Balto. V. 1, 2, 3, 4. Mss. MHS.
Bennett. Abs. of Va. land patents. Va. Mag. Hist. and Biog., v. 3, p. 55.
*Bennett and allied families; addenda to Bullard and allied families. Edgar J. Bullard. Detroit, Mich., 1931.
*Balto.: its hist. and its people. Hall. V. 3, p. 678. MHS; DAR.
*Bantz geneal. notes. Ms. File case A, MHS.
Bible rec. Upper Penins. East Shore., p. 210.
Browne-Cochrane-Brooke-Neale-Bennett chart. File case, MHS.
Centreville Record, Feb. 4, 1893. Newsp. clipp. MHS.
*C. H. B. Turner Geneal. Coll. Ms. MHS.
Christ P. E. Church cemetery, Cambridge. Steele. 1936. MHS; DAR.
Col. families of East. Shore and their descendants. Emory. 1900, p. 227. MHS.
Cummings chart. Lib. Cong.; MHS; DAR.
Data. William and Mary Quart., first series, v. 2, pp. 29, 157. (incomplete).
Few abs. from will book at Annapolis. William and Mary Quart., 1st series, v. 13, p. 27.
Founders of Anne Arundel and Howard Cos. Warfield. MHS; DAR.
Fresh Pond Neck cemetery, "St. Michael's

Manor," home of Bennett's, St. Mary's Co., 1806. Md. O. R. Soc. Bull., no. 3, pp. 57–58. MHS.
Hamilton family, of Charles Co. Kelly. P. 49. MHS.
Hist. graves of Md. and D. C. Ridgely. MHS.
Lineage Bks., Natl. Soc. of Daughters of Amer. Col., v. 1, p. 314. MHS; DAR.
Md. families. Culver. Ms. Personal list.
Neale family of Md. The Times, Balto., Sunday, Dec. 27, 1885. Scrap Book, no. 7. MHS.
*Pennington Papers. Ms. MHS.
Rec. of Stepney Parish. MHS; DAR.
Spring Hill Cemetery, Talbot Co. Md. O. R. Soc. Bull., no. 1, pp. 35–41. MHS.
Revolutionary war service of Patrick Bennett. Md. Geneal. Rec. Com., 1932–33. Mss. DAR.
*Side lights on Md. hist. Richardson. V. 2, p. 13. MHS; DAR.
Southerland-Latham and allied families. Voorhees. Bd. Ms. MHS.
Trinity P. E. churchyard, St. Mary's City. Md. O. R. Soc. Bull., no. 3, p. 59.
*The Sun, Balto., Oct. 9, 1904.
Turner Geneal. Coll. Ms. MHS.
Virginians and Marylanders at Harvard College in 17th century. William and Mary Quart., 2nd series, v. 13, no. 1, p. 1.
*Va. Mag. Hist. and Biog., v. 3, pp. 56, 187, 311.
*Wicomico Co. families. Tilghman. Ms, pp. 98, 99, 100, 104, 117, 118, 120. DAR.
See Bennet.
See Browne-Cochrane-Brooke-Neale-Bennett.
See Mayo-Poythress-Bland-Bennett.

Bennett, John. Abr. Compend. Amer. Geneal. Virkus. V. 1, p. 457. MHS; DAR.

***Bennett, Richard.** Richard Bennett (gov. of Va., 1652–55. J. T. Tichenor. Mss. File case A, MHS.
B. B. Browne pedigree chart. Soc. Col. Wars, Md. Johnston. 1905, pp. 8, 139. MHS.
Will. William and Mary Quart., 1905, v. 13, pp. 27–28. MHS.

***Bennett Family.** Bennett family in Md. The Times, Dec. 20, 1885.
Md. and Va. Notes. Ms. File case, DAR.

Benny. Trinity P. E. churchyard, St. Mary's City. Md. O. R. Soc. Bull., no. 3, p. 59.

Bens. Frederick Co. tombstone inscriptions. Gruder. Natl. Geneal. Soc. Quart., 1919, v. 8, nos. 1, 2.

Benson. Ances. rec. and portraits. Col. Dames of Amer., 1910, v. 2, p. 691. MHS; DAR.
Beirne chart. MHS.
*Bensons in Md., 1790. Natl. Geneal. Soc. Quart., 1914, v. 3, no. 2, p. 10.
Mrs. Wm. Graham Bowdoin chart. MHS.
Britton Scrap Book. V. 1. Ms. MHS.
Chew family. Culver. M. H. Mag., 1935, v. 30, no. 2, pp. 157–75.
Laytonsville M. E. churchyard, Montgomery Co. Md. Geneal. Rec. Com., 1934–35, p. 69. Mss. DAR.
Mrs. J. F. Lee chart. MHS.
Md. families. Culver. Ms. Personal list.
M. E. Church burial ground, Laytonsville, Montgomery Co. Md. Geneal. Rec. Com., 1934–35, pp. 69–82. Mss. DAR.
†Med. Annals Md. Cordell. 1903, pp. 318–19. MHS.
Patriotic Md. Md. Soc. of S. A. R., 1930. MHS; DAR.
Pedigree of Charles Clarke Duke. Soc. Col. Wars Md. Culver. 1904. MHS; DAR.
Price family and other Gunpowder friends, Balto. Co. Newsp. clipp. File case A, MHS.
St. Paul's Parish, Balto. V. 4. Mss. MHS.
St. Stephens Parish, Cecilton, Md. MHS; DAR.
Somerset Co. Court Book. Tilghman. 1937. Ms. DAR.
(1814–96). Tombstone inscriptions of Berlin. C. H. B. Turner Geneal. Coll. Ms. MHS.
Turner Geneal. Coll. Ms. MHS.
*Wicomico Co. families. Tilghman. Ms, pp. 4, 27. DAR.

Benson, Cecil Co. Miss Sidney Price chart. MHS.

Benson, Somerset Co. Bible rec. Ms. MHS.

Benson, Capt. James. H. Mullikin pedigree chart, plate 2. Soc. Col. Wars, Md. Johnston. 1905, pp. 75, 139. MHS.

Benson, M. A. Wyse (Mrs. Wm. S.), Balto. Co. Abr. Compend. Amer. Geneal. Virkus. V. 6, p. 71. DAR.

Benson, O. Suter, M.D. Md. Soc., War of 1812, v. 3, no. 300. Ms. MHS.

†Benson, Perry (1757–1827). Hist. of Talbot Co. Tilghman. V. 1, pp. 303–24. MHS; DAR.

Bentalou, Col. Paul (1735–1826). Revolutionary war heroes. Cole. Bklet. Enoch Pratt Lib.
Westminster churchyard. Patriotic Marylander, v. 2, no. 4, pp. 54–60. MHS; DAR.

Bentham. St. Stephens Parish, Cecilton, Md. MHS; DAR.

Bentley. Geneal. notes of Thomas family. Thomas. P. 37. MHS; DAR.
Monumental city. Howard. MHS; DAR.
Pocahontas and her descendants. Robertson. MHS; DAR.

Bentley Family. Thomas Book. Thomas. P. 200. Lib. Cong.; MHS.

Bently. St. Paul's Parish, Balto. V. 1, 2. Mss. MHS.

Bentz. Frederick Co. tombstone inscriptions. Gruder. Natl. Geneal. Soc. Quart., 1919, v. 8, nos. 1, 2.

Bereton. *See* Berreton.

Bergen. St. Paul's Parish, Balto. V. 1, 2. Mss. MHS.

***Berkeley, Berkley.** Va. The Sun, Balto., May 6, 13, 20, 1906.

Berkely, Loudon and Middlesex Co., Va. Cary Geneal. Coll. Ms. MHS.

Berkley. Balto., its hist., its people. Hall. V. 3. MHS; DAR.
See Berkeley.

Berkley, Loudon Co., Va. Chart, photos. (unfinished). A. Cary Geneal. Coll. Ms. MHS.

Berkley Family, Va. and Md. William and Mary Quart., 2nd series, v. 3, pp. 180–99.

Berkum. Somerset Co. Court Book. Tilghman. 1937. Ms. DAR.

***Bernabeu.** Bartow geneal. Bartow. Pp. 57, 144–46, 212. Lib. Cong.; MHS.

Bernard. Bond family geneal. Ms. MHS.
Tiernan families. Tiernan. 1901. MHS; DAR.

Bernard, A. D. Md. Soc., War of 1812, v. 1, no. 132. Ms. MHS.
Bernard, Gov. John, Line, Va. C. B. Tiernan pedigree chart. Soc. Col. Wars, Md. Johnston. 1905, pp. 113, 139. MHS.
Bernard, R. Constable. Md. Soc., War of 1812, v. 3, no. 290. Ms. MHS.
Pedigree. Soc. Col. Wars Md. Culver. 1940. MHS; DAR.
Bernard-Reade-Throckmorton, Va. Eng. ancestry. Va. Mag. Hist. and Biog., v. 6, pp. 407-11, charts; v. 7, p. 103, corrections; v. 8, pp. 83-89, 309-12.
Bernnett. Trinity P. E. churchyard, Long Green. Typed ms. MHS; DAR.
Berreton, Bereton. Hist. of Waltham family. Md. Geneal. Rec. Com., 1935-36, p. 71. Mss. DAR.
Berridge, Berrige. St. Paul's Parish, Balto. V. 1. Mss. MHS.
Berrige. *See* Berridge.
Berry. Abr. Compend. Amer. Geneal. Virkus. V. 4, p. 623. MHS.
Amer. Clan Gregor Year Book, 1917, pp. 28-30; 1928, p. 22; 1931, pp. 29-30. MHS; DAR.
Balto., its hist., its people. Hall. V. 3. MHS; DAR.
Bowies and their kindred. Bowie. MHS; DAR.
Col. families of U. S. A. Mackenzie. V. 1, pp. 23-25; v. 2. MHS.
*Frederick Co. families. Markell. Ms. Personal list.
Griffith geneal. Griffith. MHS; DAR.
*Lineage Bk., Daughters of Founders and Patriots, v. 3, p. 99; v. 6, p. 82; v. 21, p. 102. Mass. rec. MHS; DAR.
Md. families. Culver. Ms. Personal list.
Monnet family geneal. Monette. MHS.
Naturalizations in Md., 1666-1765; Laws. Bacon. MHS.
Notes. Ms. MHS.
Pedigree of Tilghman Vickers Morgan. Soc. Col. Wars Md. Culver. 1940. MHS; DAR.
Pedigree of Maurice Edward Skinner. Soc. Col. Wars Md. Culver. 1940. MHS;DAR.
Pedigree of Wm. Emory Waring, Jr. Soc. Col. Wars Md. Culver. 1940. MHS; DAR.
Preston at Patuxent. MHS.
See Purnell. Abr. Compend. Amer. Geneal. Virkus. V. 1, p. 921. DAR.
Rumsey-Smithson family rec. bk. Md. Geneal. Rec. Com., 1932, pp. 63-158. DAR.
St. Barnabas P. E. churchyard. Typed ms. MHS; DAR.
St. Paul's Parish, Balto. V. 1, 2, 3. Mss. MHS.
Berry, Talbot Co. H. Mullikin pedigree charts, plate 1. Soc. Col. Wars, Md. Johnston. 1905, p. 74. MHS.
Berry, Jasper Maudiut, Jr. Pedigree. Soc. Col. Wars Md. Culver. 1940. MHS; DAR.
†**Berry, J. Summerfield.** Balto., hist. and biog. Richardson and Bennett. 1871, pp. 189-93. MHS; DAR.
Berry, Thomas Lansdale. Pedigree. Soc. Col. Wars Md. Culver. 1940. MHS; DAR.
Md. Soc., War of 1812, v. 3, no. 255. Ms. MHS.
***Berry, Wm.,** Battle Creek, Calvert Co. Some col. mansions and those who lived in them. Glenn. 2nd series, 1900, v. 2, pp. 389-94. MHS. Also: Preston at Patuxent. Pamph. repr. from above. MHS.
Berry Family, Charles Co. M. H. Mag., 1928, v. 23, no. 1, pp. 13-20.
Berry Line. Origins of Clements Spalding families of Md. and Ky. Clements. Pp. 42-51. MHS.
***Berry-Bruff-Dixon-Troth.** Preston-on-the-Patuxent. MHS.
Berryman. Cary Geneal. Coll. Ms. MHS.
Marriages in Va. and Ky. D. A. R. Mag., v. 66, no. 8, pp. 538-39; no. 9, p. 604.
Berryman Family, Va. With Gerrard notes. Ms. File case, DAR.
Berte. Naturalizations in Md., 1666-1765; Laws. Bacon. MHS.
Berton. St. Paul's Parish, Balto. V. 1, 2. Mss. MHS.
Besse. St. Paul's Parish, Balto. V. 1. Mss. MHS.
Besson. Blackwell chart. MHS.
Britton Scrap Book. V. 1. Ms. MHS.
Cary Geneal. Coll. Ms. MHS.
Col. families of Amer. Lawrence. V. 2, p. 38. MHS.
Howard-Montague-Warfield geneal. chart. Culver and Marye. MHS.
Besson Family. Md. Geneal. Rec. Com., 1933-34, pp. 37-39. Mss. DAR.
Beston. *See* Beastin.
Beswick. Polk family. Polk. Pp. 470-74. MHS; DAR.
Still Pond Church and cemetery. Md. O. R. Soc. Bull., no. 2, pp. 65-75.
†**Bethell.** Encyc. of Amer. biog. Amer. Hist. Soc., new series, v. 1, p. 62. MHS; DAR.
Betterton Line. Turner family. Forman. Pp. 50-55; chart, p. 53. MHS.
Betts. Old Somerset. Torrence. MHS; DAR.
St. Paul's Parish, Balto. V. 1, 2, 3. Mss. MHS.
Somerset Co. Court Book. Tilghman. 1937. Ms. DAR.
***Bevan.** Lineage Bk. Daughters of Amer. Colonists. V. 1, p. 372. MHS; DAR.
*Lineage Bk., Daughters of Founders and Patriots, v. 13, p. 98; v. 16, pp. 24, 59. MHS; DAR.
†Men of mark in Md. Johnson. V. 2. DAR; Enoch Pratt Lib.
See Beaven.
Bevan, H. Cromwell. Amer. armory and blue bk. Matthews. 1908, p. 89. DAR.
Bevends. Somerset Co. Court Book. Tilghman 1937. Ms. DAR.
Beverly. Selden chart. MHS.
***Beverly,** Va. The Sun, Balto., Aug. 21, 1904.
Biamer. St. Paul's Parish, Balto. V. 1. Mss. MHS.
Biays. Md. families. Culver. Ms. Personal list.
Patriotic Md. Md. Soc. of S. A. R., 1930. MHS; DAR.
St. Paul's Parish, Balto. V. 4. Mss. MHS.
Biays, Miss Cassandra. Lee chart. MHS.
Biays, J. Phillips. Md. Soc., War of 1812, v. 3, no. 294. Ms. MHS.
Biays, Tolly A. Md. Soc., War of 1812, v. 3, no. 249. Ms. MHS.
Bibb. Cook Bible rec. Ms. MHS.
Bickerton. Winston of Va. Torrence. P. 88. MHS; DAR.

Bickham. St. Paul's Parish, Balto. V. 1, 2. Mss. MHS.
Bickley (Biclet) Line. Gaither Va. and Md. Col. and Revolutionary families of Phila. Jordan. 1933, v. 1, pp. 144–67.
Biclet. *See* Bickley.
Bidderson. St. Paul's Parish, Balto. V. 1. Mss. MHS.
Biddison. St. Paul's Parish, Balto. V. 1. MSS. MHS.
Biddle. Amer. Armory and Blue Book. Matthews. 1911–12, p. 28.
Coll. of Amer. epitaphs and inscriptions. Alden. 1814, v. 5. MHS.
St. Paul's Parish, Balto. V. 1, 2. Mss. MHS.
Shrewsbury churchyard, Kent Co. Md. O. R. Soc., v. 2, pp. 46–54. MHS.
Biddle, Cecil Co. Bible rec. Upper Penins. East. Shore, p. 236.
Biddle, Mrs. J. Wilmer (Elizabeth Southall Clarke). Chart. Col. Dames, Chap. I. MHS.
Biddle Family. Pa. and Cecil Co. (1687). Pub. Geneal. Soc. Pa., v. 11, no. 1, p. 1.
Bidwell. St. Paul's Parish, Balto. V. 1. Mss. MHS.
Bier. Diffenderfer family, arrived in Phila., 1727. Ms. File case. DAR.
See Belt-Bier.
Biers. St. Paul's Parish, Balto. V. 1, 2. Mss. MHS.
Bigelow. Balto., its hist., its people. Hall. V. 3. MHS; DAR.
Bigelow-Poultney. Col. families of U. S. A. Mackenzie. V. 5, pp. 54–65, 61 (Poultney, Balto.). MHS; DAR.
Bigg. Md. gleanings in Eng. Wills. Md. H. Mag., 1907, v. 2, no. 3.
Biggs. Bible rec. Natl. General. Soc. Quart., v. 10, no. 3, p. 110
†Hist. of Frederick Co. Williams. MHS; DAR.
†Hist. of West. Md. Scharf. V. 1, pp. 581 583. MHS; DAR.
Lineage Bks., Natl. Soc. of Daughters of Amer. Col., v. 4, p. 17. MHS; DAR.
St. James Parish Rec., Anne Arundel Co. Ms. MHS.
St. Stephens Parish, Cecilton, Md. MHS; DAR.
Tom's Creek M. E. Church cemetery. Md. Geneal. Rec. Com., 1932–33, p. 70. Mss. DAR.
Biggs, John. Frederick Co. Copy of will, 1760. Ms. File case, DAR.
Biggs Family. Frederick Co. Bible and tombstone rec., 1743–1917. Md. General. Rec. Com., 1930–31, v. 4, pp. 9–23, 27–60, DAR.
Biglands. Rec. of Stepney Parish. MHS; DAR.
†Biglow, Wm. Men of mark in Md. Johnson. V. 2. DAR; Enoch Pratt Lib.
Billings. Christ P. E. Church cemetery, Cambridge. Steele. 1936. MHS; DAR.
Miss Kate Steele chart. MHS.
Billingslea. Harford Co. Hist. Soc. Mss. Coll. JHU.
Md. Geneal. Bull., v. 5, p. 8.
†Med. Annals Md. Cordell. 1930, p. 321. MHS.
Pedigree of John Milton Reifsnider. Soc. Col. Wars Md. Culver. 1940. MHS; DAR.
Rumsey-Smithson Bible rec. Md. Geneal. Rec. Com., 1932–33, v. 5, pp. 63–142. DAR.
Rumsey-Smithson family rec. bk. Md. Geneal. Rec. Com., 1932, p. 141. DAR.
Billingsley. Barber-Billingsley Bible rec. Natl. Geneal. Soc. Quart., Dec., 1934.
*Burke's landed gentry. 1939. MHS.
Cummings chart. Lib. Cong.; MHS; DAR.
Md. families. Culver. Ms. Personal list.
Talbott of "Poplar Knowle." Shirk. MHS; DAR.
Billingsley Family. Charles Co. Ms. File case, DAR.
Billop. St. Barnabas P. E. churchyard. Typed ms. MHS; DAR.
Bilson. St. Paul's Parish, Balto. V. 1, 2, 3. Mss. MHS.
Bingham. Beards' Luth. graveyard, Washington Co. Md. Geneal. Rec. Com., 1935–36. Mss. DAR.
Birch. Still Pond Church and cemetery. Md. O. R. Soc. Bull., no. 2, pp. 65–75.
Tombstone inscriptions, Still Pond churchyard, Kent Co. Md. O. R. Soc., v. 2. MHS.
St. Paul's Parish, Balto. V. 1, 3. Mss. MHS.
Birckhead. Amer. Clan Gregor. Year Book, 1936, p. 48. MHS; DAR.
*Birckheads of Md. Allen Kerr Bond. From Md. Gazette, Annapolis, Md., Dec., 1927. MHS.
Col. families of Amer. Laurence. V. 12, p. 262. MHS.
Early Quaker rec., Anne Arundel and Calvert Cos., 1665–1889. Pub. Geneal. Soc. Pa., v. 3, no. 3, pp. 197–200.
Harford Co. Hist. Soc. Mss. Coll. JHU.
Mrs. R. N. Jackson chart. MHS.
†Med. Annals Md. Cordell. 1903, p. 321. MHS.
Monumental City. Howard. MHS; DAR.
†Mt. Royal and its owners. M. H. Mag., 1931, v. 26, no. 4, pp. 311–15.
Patriotic Md. Md. Soc. of S. A. R., 1930. MHS; DAR.
St. Paul's Parish, Balto. V. 1, 2, 3. Mss. MHS.
Talbott of "Poplar Knowle." Shirk. MHS; DAR.
Tombs. St. James Parish rec., Anne Arundel Co. Ms. MHS.
Birckhead, Lennox. Md. Soc., War of 1812, v. 2, No. 143. Ms. MHS.
Bird. Ances. rec. and portraits. Col. Dames of Amer., 1910, v. 1, p. 650. MHS; DAR.
Balto., its hist., its people. Hall. V. 3. MHS; DAR.
Dorsey and allied families. Ms. MHS.
King and Queen Cos., Va.; hist. and geneal. Bagby. 1908.
Patriotic Md. Md. Soc. of S. A. R., 1930. MHS; DAR.
Rec. of Stepney Parish. MHS; DAR.
St. Paul's Parish, Balto. V. 2, 4. Mss. MHS.
St. Stephens Parish, Cecilton, Md. MHS; DAR.
*The Sun, Balto., Nov. 17, 1907.
See Lake-Bird.
Bird, Mrs. Imogen Reid, (Imogen Reid) (married Wilson Edgeworth Bird). Chart. Col. Dames, Chap. I. MHS.
†Birely. Hist. of Frederick Co. Williams. MHS; DAR.

Birkhead. Md. gleanings in Eng. Wills. M. H. Mag., 1909, v. 4, no. 3.
Birkner. Catonsville pioneers of Luth. faith. Natl. Geneal. Soc. Quart., v. 9, no. 2, p. 29.
Birney. Gantz family geneal. Ms. MHS.
Birney-Carroll-Fitzhugh. Cemetery rec., Williamsburg, N. Y. (Many inscriptions of Md. births from 1761.) Ms. MHS.
†**Birnie.** Med. Annals Md. Cordell. 1903, p. 322. MHS.
†Men of mark in Md. Johnson. V. 3. DAR; Enoch Pratt Lib.
Birshall. St. Paul's Parish, Balto. V. 1. Mss. MHS.
Biscoe. Ancestry of Rosalie Morris Johnson. Johnson. 1905. MHS. DAR.
Done Bible rec. Ms. MHS.
Dorsey Papers. MS. MHS.
Hist. graves of Md. and D. C. Ridgley. , MHS.
Pedigree of Richard Dennis Steuart. Soc. Col. Wars Md. Culver. 1940. MHS; DAR.
St. Paul's Parish, Balto. V. 2, 3. Mss. MHS.
*Scruggs geneal. MHS.
See Childs-Biscoe-Goodwin.
†**Biser.** Hist. of Allegany Co. Thomas and Williams. V. 2. MHS. DAR.
†Hist. of Frederick Co. Williams. MHS; DAR.
Bishop. All Hallow's P. E. churchyard, Snow Hill, Worcester Co. Hudson. Bd. ms. MHS; DAR. Also: Md Geneal. Rec. Com., 1935-36, p. 24. Mss. DAR.
John Neill of Lewes, Del., 1739. Pr. for family, Phila., 1875.
Makemie Memorial Pres. churchyard, Snow Hill, Worcester Co. Hudson. Bd. ms. MHS; Dar. Also: Md. Geneal. Rec. Com., Mrs. Lines. Mss. DAR.
M. E. churchyard, Snow Hill, Worcester Co., Hudson. Bd. ms. MHS; DAR.
†Med. Annals. Md. Cordell. 1903, p. 322. MHS.
Pedigree of Lewis Warrington Cottman. Soc. Col. Wars Md. Culver. 1940. MHS; DAR.
St. Paul's Parish, Balto. V. 1, 2, 3. Mss. MHS.
Worcester Co. militia, 1794. Covington. Pp. 157, 161. MHS.
Bishop-Booth, Bishopville, Md. Notes. D.A.R. Mag., v. 70, no. 5, p. 455.
Bissell, Benj. Md. Soc., War of 1812, v. 3, no. 256. Ms. MHS.
Bitters. St. Paul's Parish, Balto. V. 1. Mss. MHS.
***Bittinger.** Garrett Co. pioneer families. Hoye. MHS; DAR.
Mountain Democrat, Garrett Co. Newsp. clipp. MHS; DAR.
Bittinger and Bedinger Families. Geneal. hist. Ms. index, 1938. DAR.
Bittle, David F. (born near Myersville, Frederick Co., 1811; son of Thomas and Mary Beale Bittle). Quart. Rev. of Evangelical Luth. Church, Gettysburg, 1877, pp. 541-70.
Bixler, Wm. H. Harrison. Md. Soc., War of 1812, v. 3, no. 273 Ms. MHS.
Black. Mt. Paran Pres. churchyard, Harrisonville, Balto. Co. typed ms. MHS; DAR.
St. Paul's Parish, Balto. V. 1, 2, 3, 4. Mss. MHS.
Talbott of "Poplar Knowle." Shirk. MHS; DAR.
†**Black, Crawford H.** Men of mark in Md. Johnson. V. 2. DAR.; Enoch Pratt Lib.
Black, H. Crawford. Balto., its hist., its people. Hall. V. 2. MHS; DAR.
Black, Mrs. H. Crawford (Ida Perry). Chart. Col. Dames, Chap. I. MHS.
Black Family. Marriages. Geneal. Mag. Amer. Ancestry, N. Y., 1916, v. 6, no. 11.
*Marriages in U. S. 1628-1865. W. M. Clemens. 1916.
*Old Kent. Hanson. Pp. 175, 183. MHS. DAR.
Black Family, Pa. (Wife, Elizabeth Burget, of Frederick Co.) Ms. File case, DAR.
***Blackburn.** Geneal.; with notes on Washington family. Vinnetta W. Ranke, 1466 Columbia Road, Wash., D. C. DAR.
*The Sun, Balto., Jan. 5, 1908.
Blackburn-Dent-Fowke. Abr. Compend. Amer. Geneal. Virkus. V. 4, p. 547. MHS.
Blackford, Mrs. Wm. Steenberger (Julia Whitridge). Chart. Col. Dames, Chap. I. MHS.
†**Blackiston.** Bench and bar of Md. Sams and Riley. 1901, v. 2, p. 533. Lib. Cong.; MHS; Peabody Lib.
†Biog. cyc. of rep. men of Md. and D. C. P. 100. MHS; DAR.
Blackiston, Blackistone family. Christopher Johnston. M. H. Mag., 1907, no. 1, pp. 54-64, 172-79.
*Geneal. and mem. encyc. of Md. Spencer. V. 2, pp. 470-79. MHS; DAR.
Mrs. T. R. Brown chart. MHS. ·
Old graveyard at Still Pond Upper Penins. East. Shore. Bd. mss. MHS; DAR.
Pedigree of Lee Cummins Cary. Soc. Col. Wars Md. Culver. 1940. MHS; DAR.
Pedigree of Wm. Handy Collins Vickers. Soc. Col. Wars Md. Culver. 1940. MHS; DAR.
Blackiston, Kent Co. Mrs. J. Hall Pleasants, Jr., chart. MHS.
Blackiston, Wilmer (Revolutionary soldier); died 1813, aged 72 yrs.; buried St. Paul's cemetery, Kent Co.) Md. Geneal. Rec., Com., 1933-34, p. 232. Mss. DAR.
Blackiston, Blackistone. Balto., its hist., its people. Hall. V. 2. MHS; DAR.
Col. families of Amer. Laurence. V. 15, pp. 158-63. MHS.
Geneal. and memorial encyc. of Md. Spencer. 1909, v. 2, p. 470. MHS; DAR.
Shrewsbury churchyard. Md. O. R. Soc. Bull., no. 2, pp. 46-54.
*The Sun, Balto., Dec. 4, 1904.
Blackistone. Blackiston, Blackistone family. Christopher Johnston. M. H. Mag., 1907, v. 2, no. 1, p. 54; no. 2, p. 172.
Thomas chart. Cary Geneal. Coll. Ms. MHS.
See Blackiston.
Blackmore Family, Pa. (in Md. 1774). Ms. File case, DAR.
Blackwell, Mrs. Josiah Low (Helen Barton Campbell). Chart. Col. Dames, Chap. I. MHS.
Blackwells, Va. Geneal. and services of Gen. John Blackwell. Md. Geneal. Rec. Com., 1935-36, pp. 288-295. DAR.

Bladen. Ances. rec. and portraits. Col. Dames of Amer., 1910, v. 1, p. 285. MHS; DAR.
†Bench and bar of Md. Sams and Riley. 1901, v. 1, p. 176. Lib. Cong.; MHS; Peabody Lib.
Bladen family. Christopher Johnston. M. H. Mag., 1910, v. 5, p. 297–99; 1913, v. 8, no. 3, p. 302–3.
Bowie-Claggett chart. MHS.
Cary Geneal. Coll. Ms. MHS.
Col. families of U. S. A. Mackenzie. V. 4, p. 278. MHS. DAR.
Fairfax family notes. Ms. MHS.
Md. gleanings in Eng. Wills. M. H. Mag., 1907. V. 2, no. 3.
St. Ann's churchyard, Annapolis. Md. O. R. S. Bull., no. 3, pp. 55–56.
St. Paul's Parish, Balto. V. 1. Mss. MHS.
*Side lights on Md. Hist. Richardson. V. 2, p. 16. MHS. DAR.
*The Sun, Balto., May 29, 1904.
Tasker chart. Cary Geneal. Coll. Ms. MHS.
Bladen, Hon. William. Notes. Pa. Mag., v. 28, p. 121.
Bladen Family. Geneal. notes; charts. Ms. MHS.
Blades. Somerset Co. Court Book. Tilghman. 1937. Ms. DAR.
Blaidenburgh. St. Stephens Parish, Cecilton, Md. MHS; DAR.
Blaine. Bible records, 1725. Turner Geneal. Col. Ms. MHS.
†**Blair.** Bench and bar of Md. Sams and Riley. 1901, v. 2, p. 364. Lib. Cong.; MHS; Peabody Lib.
Chart, photos., complete in 1 sheet. Cary Geneal. Coll. Ms. MHS.
†Francis Preston Blair family in politics. W. E. Smith. Macmillan Co., 1933, 2 vols., 516 pp. MHS.
†Hist. of West. Md. Scharf. V. 1, p. 764. MHS; DAR.
Lee of Va., 1642–1892. E. J. Lee. P. 399. Lib. Cong.; MHS.
Lineage Bks., Natl. Soc. of Daughters of Amer. Col., v. 3, p. 188. MHS; DAR.
Marriage rec. of Frederick Co. Markell. Md. Geneal. Rec. Com., 1938–39. Mss. DAR.
St. Joseph's R. C. churchyard, Worcester Co., Hudson. Md. O. R. Soc. Bull., no. 3, p. 64.
St. Paul's Parish, Balto. V. 2, 3. Mss. MHS.
***Blair,** Va. Blairs of Richmond, Va. 1933. DAR.
Blair, E. D. C. Abr. Compend. Amer. Geneal. Virkus. V. 1, p. 473. DAR.
†**Blair, Montgomery.** Public career and services as postmaster general. Rec. Columbia Hist. Soc., v. 13, pp. 126–57.
***Blair-Banister-Braxton.** (Carter Braxton family, Va.) Blair-Banister-Braxton families, before and after the Revolution. Frederick Horner. J. B. Lippincott Co., 1898. MHS.
Blake. Ancestry of Mrs. Fulton Ray Gordon, née Ellen Marjorie Gray. D. C. Geneal. Rec. Com., 1932–34, p. 122. Typed, bd. DAR.
T. J. Chew Pedigree chart. Soc. Col. Wars, Md. Johnston. 1905, p. 14. MHS.
Col. families of U. S. A. Mackenzie. V. 2. MHS. DAR.
See Gordon. Abr. Compend. Amer. Geneal. Virkus. V. 1, p. 300. DAR.
See Martin. Abr. Compend. Amer. Geneal. Virkus. V. 1, p. 206.
Md. gleanings in Eng. Wills. M. H. Mag., 1908, v. 3, no. 2.
†Med. Annals of Md. Cordell. 1903, p. 323. MHS.
†Men of mark in Md. Johnson. V. 3. DAR; Enoch Pratt Lib.
Patriotic Md. Md. Soc. of S. A. R., 1930. MHS; DAR.
*Pennington Papers. Ms. MHS.
St. Paul's Parish, Balto. V. 2, 3. Mss. MHS.
*The Sun, Balto., May 22, 1904.
Blake, Anne Arundel Co. Milligan Chart. MHS.
Blake, Calvert Co. Mrs. G. R. Veazey chart. MHS.
Blake, Benson, Jr. Pedigree. Soc. Col. Wars Md. Culver. 1940. MHS; DAR.
Blakenstein. Naturalizations, in Md., 1666–1765; Laws. Bacon. MHS.
Blakiston. Pedigree of Bennet Biscoe Norris. Soc. Col. Wars Md. Culver. 1940. MHS. DAR.
Pedigree of John Philemon Paca. Soc. Col. Wars Md. Culver. 1940. MHS; DAR.
Blakiston, Col. Nehemiah. St. Mary's Co. L. A. Knott pedigree chart. Soc. Col. Wars, Md. Johnston. 1905 pp. 57, 139. MHS.
Blanch. Old cemetery, Denton, Caroline Co. Md. Geneal. Rec. Com., 1935–36, p. 168. Mss. DAR.
Blanchard. Beirne chart. MHS.
Cosden family data. Ms. MHS.
St. Paul's Parish, Balto. V. 3. Mss. MHS.
Bland. Ancestral beginnings in Amer. of McGregor, Magruder, Beall, Price, Phillips, Bland, McKisick, Young and related families. Caroline B. Price. 1928. DAR.
Balto., its hist., its people. Hall. V. 2. MHS; DAR.
†Bench and bar of Md. Sams and Riley. 1901, v. 1, p. 268. Lib. Cong.; MHS; Peabody Lib.
Cemetery Creek, Anne Arundel Co., Tombstone inscriptions. Founders of Anne Arundel and Howard Cos. Warfield. P. 333. MHS; DAR.
King and Queen Cos., Va.; hist. and geneal. Bagby. 1908.
Lee of Va.; 1642–1892. E. J. Lee. P. 137. Lib. Cong.; MHS.
Pedigree. Familiae Minorum Gentium, v. 2, Harleian Soc. Pub., London. MHS.
Pocahontas and her descendants. Robertson. MHS; DAR.
Ruffin and other geneal. Pr. chart. Henry.
Sketch and geneal. of Theoderic Bland. Md. Geneal. Bull., v. 1, p. 11.
Miss E. K. Thom chart. MHS.
Times Dispatch, Richmond, Va., Feb. 12, 1905. Newsp. clipp. MHS.
See Mayo-Poythress-Bland-Bennett.
Bland, Va. Ances. rec. and portraits. Col. Dames of Amer. 1910, v. 1, pp. 279–81. MHS; DAR.
Genesis of U. S. Riverside Press, v. 2.
W. H. De C. W. Thom pedigree charts. Soc. Col. Wars, Md. Johnston. 1905, pp. 107, 140. MHS.
*The Sun, Balto., Oct. 30, 1904.
Bland, Mrs. Anna. Va. Mag., v. 10, p. 372. See Codd, p. 375.

***Bland, John Randolph.** Men of mark in Md. Johnson. V. 3. DAR; Enoch Pratt Lib.
Bland, Richard Howard. Burke's landed gentry. 1939, p. 2992. MHS.
***Bland Line.** Geneal. and mem. encyc. of Md. Spencer. V. 2, p. 595. MHS; DAR.
Blandford. Children of Alex P. and M. C. Hill. Ms. MHS.
Blandy. Chart of Com. John Rodgers. DAR.
Blaney. Bowie-Claggett chart. MHS.
Naturalizations in Md., 1666–1765; Laws. Bacon. MHS.
Blay. Graveyard, Blay's range, Kent Co. Ms. DAR.
***Blay Family.** Old Kent. Hanson. P. 313. MHS. DAR.
Bleakley. Bleakley Bible rec. Ms. MHS.
†Bledsoe. Men of mark in Md. Johnson. V. 3. DAR; Enoch Pratt Lib.
***Blenkensop Family.** Arch. of Georgetown Univ., Wash., D. C., v. 130, no. 3.
Blinio. St. Paul's Parish, Balto. V. 1. Mss. MHS.
Bliss. Fox-Ellicott-Evans families. Evans. MHS; DAR.
Blizzard. St. Paul's Parish, Balto. V. 3. Mss. MHS.
Blodget. G. H. Stickney, pedigree chart. Soc. Col. Wars, Md. Johnston. 1905, p. 98. MHS.
†Bloede, Victor G. Men of mark in Md. Johnson. V. 2. DAR; Enoch Pratt Lib.
Bloomer. St. Paul's Parish, Balto. V. 3. Mss. MHS.
†Bloomfield, Maurice R. Biog. dict. of U. S. J. H. Lamb Co., v. 1, p. 332.
Bloyce, Bloyes, Bloys, Bloyse. Old Somerset. Torrence. MHS. DAR.
Bloyes. *See* Bloyce.
Bloys. *See* Bloyce.
Bloyse. *See* Bloyce.
Blue Family, Va. With Reeves and Yates data. Descendants from Thomas Reeves of Md. 29 mss. File case, DAR.
Bluford. St. Paul's Parish, Balto. V. 1, 2. Mss. MHS.
Blundell. St. Paul's Parish, Balto. V. 1, 2. Mss. MHS.
Blunston. Lloyd family hist. of Wales, Pa., and Md. DAR.
Blunt. Bantz geneal. notes. Ms. MHS.
***Blunt Family.** Geneal.; chart. MHS.
***Blyden.** Wicomico Co. families. Tilghman. Ms, pp. 5, 126. DAR.
Blyden-Malone. Wicomico Co. families. Bible rec. Ms. DAR.
Board. St. Paul's Parish, Balto. V. 1. Mss. MHS.
Boarman family. C. F. Thomas. Balto. May 12, 1897, pamph. MHS.
*Boarman-Neale-Gill-Mathews. Lineage Bk. Daughters of Amer. Colonists. V. 2, pp. 54–55. MHS; DAR.
Boarmans of South. Md. Land grants, copies of Wills, during 17th and 18th cent. Ms. MHS.
Children of Alex P. and M. C. Hill. Ms. MHS.
†Hist. of Balto. City. and Co. Scharf. P. 898. MHS.
Boarman. See Keith. Abr. Compend. Amer. Geneal. Virkus. V. 1, p. 665. DAR.
Lineage Bks., Natl. Soc. of Daughters of Amer. Col., v. 2, p. 54. MHS; DAR.
Pedigree of Alfred Jenkins Tormey. Soc. Col. Wars Md. Culver. 1940. MHS; DAR.
Semmes and allied families. Semmes. P. 216. MHS.
Taney and allied families. Silverson. MHS; DAR.
*The Sun, Balto., Sept. 9, 16, 23, 1906.
Miss Eliza Thomas chart. MHS.
Thomas chart. Cary Geneal. Coll. Ms. MHS.
Boarman, Eleanor. Will. Patriotic Marylander, v. 2, no. 2, p. 63. MHS; DAR.
Boarman, Maj. William. J. A. and F. de S. Jenkins pedigree chart. Soc. Col. Wars, Md. Johnston. 1905, pp. 46, 140. MHS.
Some early col. Marylanders. M. H. Mag., 1920, v. 15, p. 319.
***Boarman Family.** Descendants of Wm. Boarman who came to Md., 1645. C. F. Thomas. Balto., John Murphy Co., 1934. MHS; DAR.
*Geneal. Balto., John Murphy Co., 1897. MHS.
Boarman Line. Col. and Revolutionary lineages of Amer. 1939, v. 2, p. 67. MHS.
Boarman, Boreman, Borman. Geneal.; descendants of William Boarman, who came to Amer. 1645. C. F. Thomas. Balto., John Murphy & Co., 1935, pamph. MHS; DAR.
Boarman (Boreman), Thomas. Geneal. MS. File case, DAR.
Boarman, Borman Line. Lilburn family. Col. and Revolutionary families of Phila. Jordan. 1933, v. 1, pp. 382–98.
Bobart, C. C. Md. Soc., War of 1812, v. 1, No. 100. MHS.
Bobbett. St. Paul's Parish, Balto. V. 2. Mss. MHS.
Bobbin. St. Paul's Parish, Balto. V. 1. Mss. MHS.
Boblet. St. Paul's Parish, Balto. V. 1. Mss. MHS.
***Boddie.** Boddie and allied families. J. T. and J. B. Boddie. Priv. pr., 1918. MHS.
Boddy. Bible rec., Kent Co. Md. Geneal. rec. Com., 1933–34, p. 220. Mss. DAR.
Bodien. Mrs. J. Hall Pleasants, Jr., chart. MHS.
Wallis chart. MHS.
Bodieu. Naturalizations in Md., 1666–1765; Laws. Bacon. MHS.
Bodly. St. Paul's Parish, Balto. V. 2. Mss. MHS.
Body. St. Paul's Parish, Balto. V. 1. Mss. MHS.
Somerset Co. Court Book. Tilghman. 1937. Ms. DAR.
Boehm. Peale Geneal. Coll. Ms. MHS.
Turner Geneal. Coll. Ms. MHS.
†Boerstler. Med. Annals Md. Cordell. 1903, p. 324. MHS.
Boggert. St. Paul's Parish, Balto. V. 2. Mss. MHS.
Boggett. St. Paul's Parish, Balto. V. 1. Mss. MHS.
Boggs. Balto., its hist., its people. Hall. V. 3. MHS., DAR.
J. H. Cottman pedigree chart. Soc. Col. Wars, Md. Johnston. 1905, p. 18. MHS.
C. D. Fisher pedigree chart. Soc. Col. Wars, Md. Johnston. 1905, p. 25. MHS.

Mrs. A. G. Ober chart. MHS.
Boggs, Andrew. Pedigree of Lewis Warrington Cottman. Soc. Col. Wars Md. Culver. 1940. MHS; DAR.
***Boggs, Edith Fenton.** Lineage Bk. Daughter of Founders and Patriots. V. 18, pp. 35-36. MHS; DAR.
Boggs, F. H. Md. Soc., War of 1812, v. 1, no. 85. Ms. MHS.
Boggy. St. Paul's Parish Balto. V. 1. Mss. MHS.
***Bohannen Family.** Wilson Mss. Coll., no. 70. MHS.
Bohanning. St. Stephens Parish, Cecilton, Md. MHS; DAR.
Bohanon. Patiortic Md. Md. Soc. of S. A. R., 1930. MHS; DAR.
***Bohun, Boon,** Frederick Co. Lineage Bk. Daughter of Amer. Colonists, v. 3, p. 222. MHS., DAR.
Boice, Boyce, Boist, Buse, Buss. Old Somerset. Torrence. MHS. DAR.
Boies, Cecil Co., Col. families of U. S. A. Mackenzie. V. 6, pp. 375-79. MHS.
Boist. *See* Boice.
Bolden. St. Stephens Parish, Cecilton, Md. MHS; DAR.
Bolling. Abr. Compend. Amer. Geneal. Virkus, v. 1, p. 397. DAR.
Ancest. rec. and portraits. Col. Dames of Amer., 1910, v. 1, p. 325. MHS; DAR.
*Memoir of portion of Bolling family in Eng. and Va. Wynne's Hist. Documents from Old Dominion Press, no. 4. Printed for priv. distribution, Richmond, Va., W. H. Wade Co., 1868. MHS.
Pocahontas and her descendants, Robertson. MHS; DAR.
Rec. of Nicholas Meriwether of Wales, and descendants in Va. and Md. Griffith. P. 57.
Ruffin and other geneal. Pr. chart. Henry.
Times Dispatch, Richmond, Va., Oct. 4, 1903. Newsp. clipp.
See Rolfe.
Bolling, Va. W. M. Cary pedigree charts. Soc. Col. Wars, Md. Johnston. 1905, pp. 11, 140. MHS.
Col. families of U. S. A. Mackenzie. V. 2. MHS; DAR.
Tiernan families. Tiernan. 1901, p. 408. MHS; DAR.
Va. Mag., Hist. and Biog., v. 7, pp. 352-54.
Bolling, Robt., Va. Pedigree of John Triplett Haxall. Soc. Col. Wars Md. Culver. 1940. MHS; DAR.
Bolling Family (1803). Orig. ms. in handwriting of John Randolph of Roanoke. Copy in MHS.
Bolling Line, Va. C. B. Tiernan pedigree chart. Soc. Col. Wars, Md. Johnston. 1905, p. 113. MHS.
***Bolling-Rolfe.** The Sun, Balto., Nov. 12, 19, 1905.
***Bolton.** Geneal. and biog. account of family of Bolton in Eng. and Amer. R. Bolton. Bolton in Md., pp. 69-70, 86, 112, 115. N. Y., John A. Gray, 1862. MHS.
St. Paul's Parish, Balto. V. 1. Mss. MHS.
Tombstone rec. of Glendy burying ground. Md. Geneal. Rec. Com., 1933-34, pp. 171-78. Mss. DAR.
Bolton, Mrs. F. Nelson (Mary Harrison Thompson). Chart. Col. Dames, Chap. I, MHS.
Bolton, John, Chestertown. Hist. of Byberry and Moreland. Martindale. MHS.
†**Bonaparte.** Bench and Bar of Md. Sams and Riley. 1901, v. 2, p. 522. Lib. Cong., MHS; Peabody Lib.
†Bonapartes of Amer. C. E. Macartney and Maj. G. Dorrance. 287 pp. MHS; Enoch Pratt Lib.
†Bonapartes of New World. Elinor M. O'Donoghne. 1932.
Col. families of U. S. A. Mackenzie. V. 1, p. 602; v. 5. MHS; DAR.
Golden bees. D. M. Henderson. (Story of Betsy Patterson (Madame Bonaparte); picture of Balto. in early 1800's.) 1928. (Fiction.)
Greenway Mss. Geneal Coll. Binder's title, Hawkins-Bordley. MHS.
No hearts to break. Susan Ertz. (Tale of colorful story of Betsy Patterson, beautiful Balto. girl, who married Jerome Bonaparte, 1803.) N. Y.; Appleton-Century Co., London; 1937. (Fiction.) DAR.
†**Bonaparte, Madame.** Life and letters. E. M. Didier. N. Y., Scribners, 1879.
Bonaparte, Charles J. Bonapartes of Amer. Macartney and Dorrance. MHS; Enoch Pratt Lib.
†Men of mark in Md. Johnson. V. 1. DAR; Enoch Pratt Lib.
†Hist. reg. Hill. V. 2, pp. 197-203. MHS.
***Bonaparte-Patterson.** Marriage in 1803. W. T. R. Saffell. Illus. 1873.
Bonar Family, Va. Ms. File case, DAR.
Bond. Ancest. rec. and portraits. Col. Dames of Amer., 1910, v. 2, p. 690. MHS; DAR.
Balto., its hist., its people. Hall. V. 3. MHS; DAR.
†Bench and bar of Md. Sams and Riley, 1901, v. 2, pp. 420, 469. Lib. Cong.; MHS; Peabody Lib.
*Bond-Brice-Johnson. Lineage Bk. Daughters of Amer. Colonists. V. 3, pp. 218-19. MHS., DAR.
Brooks chart. MHS.
Chart. Harford Co. Hist. Soc. Mss. Coll. JHU.
Chart, photos. Cary Geneal. Coll. Ms. MHS.
Chart, 1669. Md. Geneal. Rec. Com., 1932-33. Mss. DAR.
Chew family. Culver. M. H. Mag., 1935, v. 30, no. 2, pp. 157-75.
Col. families of U. S. A. Mackenzie. V. 3. MHS; DAR.
Englar family. Barnes. MHS; DAR.
Gantt geneal. Ms. MHS.
Geneal. and memorial encyc. of Md. Spencer. V. 1. MHS; DAR.
Gibbs chart. MHS.
Griffith geneal. Griffith. MHS; DAR.
F. S. Hambleton pedigree chart. Soc. Col. Wars, Md. Johnston. 1905, p. 33. MHS.
Hist. of Harford Co. Preston. MHS; DAR.
Mrs. R. N. Jackson chart. MHS.
Mrs. J. F. Lee chart. MHS.
*Lineage Bk., Daughters of Founders and Patriots, v. 22, p. 49. MHS; DAR.
Lineage Bks., Natl. Soc. of Daughters of Amer. Col., v. 3, p. 219. MHS; DAR.
Macsherry chart. MHS.
Md. families. Culver. Ms. Personal list.
Md. gleanings in Eng. Wills. M. H. Mag., 1908, v. 3, no. 2; 1909, v. 4, no. 2.

Bond. McCormick chart. MHS.
†Med. Annals. Md. Cordell. 1903, pp. 225–26. MHS.
†Men of mark in Md. Johnson. V. 2, v. 4. DAR; Enoch Pratt Lib.
Monnet family geneal. Monette. MHS.
†Mt. Royal and its owners. M. H. Mag., 1931, v. 26, no. 4, pp. 311–15.
Obituary of Sarah, consort of Thomas W. Bond, Abingdon, Harford Co., Oct. 4, 1833. D. C. Geneal. Rec. Com., 1932–34, v. 10, pp. 162–63. Typed, bd. DAR.
Patriotic Md. Md. Soc. of S. A. R., 1930. MHS; DAR.
Pedigree of Duncan Keener Brent. Soc. Col. Wars Md. Culver. 1940. MHS; DAR.
Pedigree of T. Edward Hambleton. Soc. Col. Wars Md. Culver. 1940. MHS; DAR.
Pedigree of Maurice Falconer Rodgers. Soc. Col. Wars Md. Culver. 1940. MHS; DAR.
Pedigree of Maurice Edward Skinner. Soc. Col. Wars Md. Culver. 1940. MHS; DAR.
Pedigree of Rev. Sam'l Tagart Steele. Soc. Col. Wars Md. Culver. 1940. MHS; DAR.
Miss C. Petre chart. MHS.
St. Paul's Parish, Balto. V. 1, 2, 3. Mss. MHS.
St. Thomas' Parish, Balto. Co. Bd. ms. MHS. Also: Md. Geneal. Rec. Com., 1937, pp. 109–82. Mss. DAR.
Sater geneal. Bd. Ms. MHS.
Sharpless family geneal. Cope. Pp. 203, 206, 320–23, 527. MHS; DAR.
Miss Kate Steele chart. MHS.
*Story of Bonds of earth. A. K. Bond. Balto., Pegasus Press, 1930.
Taney and allied families. Silverson. MHS; DAR.
Taylor Bible rec. Ms. MHS.
†The Sun, Balto., April 28, May 5, 1907.
Miss Sara E. White chart. MHS.
See Colgate-Onion-Bond-Waters.
See Dempsey-Nourse-Bond.
See Hall-Bond-Cromwell-Delaport-Harris-Reisinger-Reardon.

Bond, Daniel. Copy of will from Court of Chancery, 1779. Md. Geneal. Rec. Com., 1932–33. Mss. DAR.

Bond, H. W. Abr. Compend. Amer. Geneal. Virkus. V. 1, p. 480; DAR.; v. 4, pp. 160, 384. MHS.

Bond (James) Family (1730). Pa. Mag., v. 36, p. 254.

Bond, Richard. Ms. File case, DAR.

Bond Family. Bible rec. Gorsuch and allied families. Harrison. Mss. MHS.
Chart. Beverley Bond, Jr. Blue print. MHS.
Chart. (Peter born 1706.) MHS.
Geneal., 1660–1905. Ms. MHS.
*Wilson. Mss. Coll., no. 73. MHS.

Bond Family, Md. and N. J. Ms. File case, DAR.

Bond Line. Col. and Revolutionary lineages of Amer. 1939, v. 1, p. 477. MHS.

Bond-Morris. Morris family of Phila. Moon. V. 1, p. 317. MHS.

Bone. St. Paul's Parish, Balto. V. 1, 2. MSS. MHS.

Bonfeald. St. Paul's Parish, Balto. V. 1. Mss. MHS.
Newsp. clipp. Scrap Book. MHS.
See Andrews-Bonner-Carroll-Corkran-Medford.
See Medford-Bonner-Carroll-Corkran-Stevens.

Bonner. St. Paul's Parish, Balto. V. 1, 2. Mss. MHS.

Bonnerville. St. Mary's P. E. churchyard, Pocomoke, Worcester Co., Hudson. Bd. ms. MHS; DAR.

Bonnett. Gaither, Va. and Md. Col. and Revolutionary families of Phila. Jordan. 1933, v. 1, pp. 144–67.

Bonney. Pedigree of Leigh Bonsal. Soc. Col. Wars Md. Culver. 1940. 'MHS; DAR.

Bonns. St. Paul's Parish, Balto. V. 1. Mss. MHS.

Bonsal. Ancest. rec. and portraits. Col. Dames of Amer., 1910, v. 2, p. 778. MHS; DAR.
St. Paul's Parish, Balto. V. 1, 2, 3. Mss. MHS.
Mrs. J. G. Thomas chart. MHS.
Miss Sara E. White chart. MHS.

Bonsal, Miss Evelyn Pleasants. Chart. Col. Dames, Chap. I. MHS.

†Bonsal, Leigh. Men of mark in Md. Johnson. V. 2 DAR; Enoch Pratt Lib.
Pedigree. Soc. Col. Wars Md. Culver. 1940. MHS; DAR.

Bonsal, Mrs. Leigh (Mary Camilla Pleasants). Chart. Col. Dames, Chap. I. MHS.

Bonstead. St. Paul's Parish, Balto. V. 2. Mss. MHS.

Bonvile. *See* Churchill-Crocker-Fox-Coplestone-Bonville-Ellicott.

Boogher. Abr. Compend. Amer. Geneal. Virkus. V. 1, pp. 480–81. DAR.
Amer. of gentle birth, and their ancestors. Pittman. V. 1, p. 31. MHS; DAR.
Col. families of U. S. A. Mackenzie. V. 3. MHS; DAR.
*Gleanings in Va. hist. W. F. Boogher. Washington, D. C., 1903.

Booker. St. Paul's Parish, Balto. V. 1, 2. Mss. MHS.

Boon. Bible rec., Caroline Co. Md. Geneal. Rec. Com., 1937, Parran, pp. 195–98. Mss. DAR.
Eiler-Anderson-Boon-Sothoron-Witten. Eiler. 1929, pamph. MHS.
St. Paul's Parish, Balto. V. 1. Mss. MHS.
Wilkinson-Brann-Boon family of Balto. Photos. DAR.
See Bohun.

Boon Family, Kent Co. Rec. of births, marriages and deaths, 1778–1913. Md. Geneal. Rec. Com., 1937, pp. 195–98. DAR.

***Boone.** Bible rec. In Ky. Bible rec., pp. 24, 31. Mss. DAR.
*Boone-Anderson-Scothoron. Homer Eiler. Topeka, Kans., 1929. MHS.
Boone Family Assoc., Inc. Organized 1925. Bulletin, v. 1, June, 1928. (Robert Boone, Anne Arundel Co., 1931, v. 2, no. 7.) MHS; DAR.
Boone. W. A. Galloway. Ohio Arch. Hist. Soc. Pub., v. 13, p. 263. DAR.
Bromwell geneal. Ms. Lib. Cong.; MHS.
Carlyle family. William and Mary Quart., 1st series, v. 18, pp. 201, 278.
Centenary of Catholicity in Ky. Webb. 1884. MHS.
Col. families of U. S. A. Mackenzie. V. 3, p. 128. MHS; DAR.

*Frederick Co. families. Markell. Ms. Personal list.
Graves, Trinity Reformed Church cemetery, Boonsboro, Wash. Co. Hist. of West. Md. Scharf. V. 2, p. 1263.
Hist. of Frederick Co. Williams. V. 2, pp. 1230, 1239. MHS; DAR.
Hist. West. Md. Scharf. V. 2, p. 1261. MHS; DAR.
Lineage Bks., Natl. Soc. of Daughters of Amer. Col., v. 2, p. 61. MHS; DAR.
New light on Daniel Boone's ancestry. J. C. Morton. Ky. State Hist. Soc. Reg., Louisville, Jan., 1903, v. 1, no. 1.
Old Md. families. Bromwell. MHS; DAR.
Patriotic Md. Md. Soc. of S. A. R., 1930. MHS; DAR.
Pioneer families of Mo. Bryan and Rose.
Semmes and allied families. Semmes. MHS.
See Eiler-Boone-Anderson-Scothoron.
See Howard-Dorsey-Boone.

***Boone**, Pa. Geneal. Pa. Mag. Hist. and Biog., 1897, v. 21. MHS.

Boone, Miss Camilla Herbert. Chart. Col. Dames, Chap. I. MHS.
Posey chart. MHS.

†**Boone, Daniel** (born in Buck's Co., Pa., 1734; to N. C.; died in Mo., 1821; married Rebecca Bryan, 1755). Amer. Monthly Mag., v. 13, p. 129; v. 24, p 99. DAR.
†Daniel Boone (1734–1820) and wilderness road. H. A. Bruce. N. Y., 1911, 349 pp. DAR.
†Daniel Boone, backwoodsman. 1908. DAR.
Daniel Boone. L. P. Kellogg. Ky. Hist. Reg., v. 32, pp. 187–98. DAR.
†Boone Narrative. W. R. Jillson. 61 pp., facsim. Louisville, Ky., 1932. DAR.
†Daniel Boone. Master of Wilderness. J. Bakeless. Morrow, 1939, 480 pp.
†Daniel Boone. Ruben G. Thwaites. Appleton, 1902.
†Boone's wilderness road. A. B. Hulbert. Cleveland, 1903.

Boone, Humphrey. Pedigree of James Etchberger Hancock. Soc. Col. Wars Md. Culver. 1940. MHS; DAR.

†**Boone, Marshall D.** Hist. of Frederick Co. Williams. V. 2, pp. 1239–40.

***Boone, Wm. Kennedy.** Coat of arms. Burke's landed gentry. 1939. MHS.

Boone, Mrs. Wm. Kennedy (Anne Gordon Herbert). Chart. Col. Dames, Chap. I. MHS.

***Boone Family.** Anne Arundel Co. gentry. Newman. Pp. 531–48. MHS; DAR.
*Arch. of Georgetown Univ., Wash., D. C., v. 280, no. 1.
*Boone family. Geneal. hist. of descendants of George and Mary Boone, who came to Amer., 1717. H. A. Spraker. Also biog. sketch of Daniel Boone, pioneer, by one of his descendants. Rutland, Vt., The Tuttle Co., 1922.
*Boone-Railford, 1763–1834. Ms. DAR.
*Bulletins. MHS; DAR.
*Carrollton Manor, Md. Grove. 1921, p. 12. Ms. File case, DAR.
*Geneal. Mag., 1913, pp. 113–28, 143, 169. DAR.
*Hist. of Carrollton Manor, Frederick Co. Jarboe. P. 61. DAR.
†Old Catholic Md. Treacy. P. 149. DAR.
Rec., marriages in Md. Geneal. Mag. Amer. Ancestry, N. Y., 1916, v. 7, nos. 8, 9, 11.
*Rec. W. M. Clemens. 1917.
*Wash. Geneal. Rec. Com., 1931–32, p. 55. Typed, bd. DAR.

Boone Line. Posey chart. MHS.

Boone-Talbott-Pumphrey. Bible rec. Natl. Geneal. Soc. Quart., v. 20, no. 3, p. 78.

Booth. Clay family of Pa. Ms. File case, DAR.
Col. families of U. S. A. Mackenzie. V. 1, pp. 26–29. MHS; DAR.
†Darling of misfortune, Edwin Booth. Richard Lockridge. 1932.
Descendants of Mordecai, of "Mordecai's Mount," Gloucester Co., Va., 1650, and Thomas Booth, of "Wareneck," Gloucester Co., Va., 1685. Dr. and Mrs. Wm. Carter Stubbs. N. O. 1923. MHS.
Life and art of Edwin Booth. W. Winter. N. Y., Macmillan; London; 1894, 2nd ed.
Life and crime of John Wilkes Booth. G. A. Townsend. 1865. Pamph. Enoch Pratt Lib.
†Mad Booths of Md. S. Kimmel. Bobbs, 1939. Ms. MHS.
Old Somerset. Torrence. MHS. DAR.
St. Paul's Parish, Balto. V. 1, 2, 3. Mss. MHS.
†Sketches of Tudor Hall and Booth family. Ella V. Mahoney. Bel Air, Md. 1925. MHS; DAR.
†This one mad act. Unknown story of John Wilkes Booth and his family. Izola Forrester. Boston, Hale, Chushman & Flint, 1937.
†Unlocked book; memoir of John Wilkes Booth. By his sister Asia Booth Clarke; with foreword by Eleanor Farjeon. 205 pp. Putman, N. Y., 1938. Enoch Pratt Lib.
See Bishop-Booth.
See Cooke-Booth.
See Neil-Booth-Reynolds.

†**Booth, Edwin.** Cavalcade of Amer. Edited by D. R. Fox and A. M. Schlesinger. V. 2.
Last tragedian. Otis Skinner. Doubleday, 1939.
(tragedian; born at Booth Farm, Belair, Harford Co., Nov. 13, 1833; died in N. Y., June 7, 1893; buried at Mount Auborn, Boston). Encyc. of Amer. biog., v. 1.

†**Booth, John Wilkes.** Man who killed Lincoln. Philip Van Doren Stern. (In form of novel.)
†What became of him? M. H. Mag., 1913, v. 8, p. 327.

†**Booth, Junius Brutus.** Address before Anne Arundel Co. Hist. Soc. W. Stump Forwood. 41 pp., typed. File case, DAR.

Booth Family, Va. (With Cooke ref.) William and Mary Quart., 2nd series, v. 6, pp. 259–64.

Booth, Boothe. Persons found in search of federal census. Ms. DAR.

Boothe. Wathen Prayer Book rec. Ms. MHS.
*Wicomico Co. families. Tilghman. Ms., pp. 118, 122–24. DAR.
See Booth.

Bootman. Md. tombstone rec. Md. Geneal. Rec. Com., 1937, Parran, p. 14. Mss. DAR.

Boovey. St. Paul's Parish, Balto. V. 1. Mss. MHS.

Boquets. *See* Judd-Sutton-Boquets.

Borden. Dorsey-Duvall-Coale-Buchanan-Borden-Brooke and allied families. Newsp. clipp. and other printed matter. MHS.

Borden Family. Miscellaneous family data. Ms. MHS.
Bordley. Ances. rec. and portraits. Col. Dames of Amer. 1910, v. 2, p. 668. MHS; DAR.
Barroll in Great Britain and Amer. Barroll. Pp. 65–67. MHS.
Mrs. R. Barton, Jr., charts. MHS.
Beall and Bell families. Beall. MHS.
Bible rec., 1793–1920. D. C. Geneal. Rec. Com., v. 32, pp. 46–48. Typed, bd. DAR.
†Biog. cyc. of rep. men of Md. and D. C. P. 49. MHS; DAR.
Col. families of East. Shore and their descendants. Emory. 1900, pp. 191, 228–37. MHS.
Descendants of Col. Thomas White. Morris. MHS.
*Family notes from 1697. Md. O. R. Soc., v. 2, pp. 30–34.
Greenway Mss. Geneal. Coll. Binder's title, Hawkins-Bordley. MHS.
Hist. of Talbot Co. Tilghman. V. 2, p. 545. MHS; DAR.
Md. families. Culver. Ms. Personal list.
†Med. Annals Md. Cordell. 1903, pp. 327–28. MHS.
*Old Kent. Hanson. P. 81. MHS; DAR.
Peale Geneal. Coll. Ms. MHS.
Portrait and biog. rec. of East. Shore of Md. 1898, p. 155. MHS; DAR.
St. Paul's churchyard, Kent Co. Md. O. R. Soc. Bull., no. 2, pp. 54–65. MHS.
St. Paul's Parish, Balto. V. 2, 3. Mss. MHS.
St. Stephens Parish, Cecilton, Md. MHS; DAR.
*Side lights on Md. hist. Richardson. V. 2, p. 261. MHS; DAR.
Thomas Book. Thomas. P. 207. Lib. Cong.; MHS.
"Whorton Manor" graveyard. Md. O. R. Soc. Bull., no. 2, p. 80. MHS.
Bordley, John Beale. Hist. of Md. Scharf. V. 2, p. 46.
Bordley, Stephen. Hist. of Md. Scharf. V. 2, p. 18.
Bordley, Thomas. Geneal. Hist. of Md. Scharf. V. 2, pp. 429–30.
***Bordley Family.** Bordley family of Md. and their descendants. E. Bordley Gibson. Edited by E. Mifflin. Phila., Henry B. Ashmead, 1865. MHS.
Md. O. R. Soc. Bull., no. 2, pp. 30–34. MHS; DAR.
Bordley Line. J. S. Williams pedigree chart. Soc. Col. Wars, Md. Johnston. 1905, p. 125. MHS.
Bordley-Abbott-Laird-Winder. Bordley-Abbott-Laird-Winder families (East. Shore of Md.). F. E. Old, Jr. Ms. MHS.
Bordley-Hawkins. Greenway Mss. Geneal. Coll. MHS.
Bordley-Lloyd-Paca Families. Wye Island. R. Wilson. Lippincott Mag., v. 19. MHS.
Boreing. St. Paul's Parish, Balto. V. 1. Mss. MHS.
***Boreman** (*see* **Boarman**). The Sun, Balto. Sept. 9, 16, 23, 1906.
Borman. *See* Boarman.
Borroway Family (Pa.)-**Leightheiser.** Ms. File case, DAR.
†**Börstler, Christian** (Md. pioneers). Deutsch-Americkanische Geschichtsblatter, Chicago, 1901.
Bose. Dorsey and allied families. Ms. MHS. Howland chart. MHS.
†**Bose, William** (1796–1875). M. H. Mag., 1933, v. 28, pp. 1, 3.
Bosler. Branch of Philip Adams family of Md. Adams. MHS.
Bosley. Balto; its hist., its people. Hall. V. 2. MHS; DAR.
Bond chart. MHS.
Bond family geneal. Ms. MHS.
†Hist. of Balto. City and Co. Scharf. Pp. 884, 913. MHS.
Keene family. Jones. MHS; DAR.
Lineage Bks., Natl. Soc. of Daughters of Amer. Col., v. 2, p. 61. MHS; DAR.
Md. families. Culver. Ms. Personal list.
†Med. Annals Md. Cordell. 1903, p. 328. MHS.
Parrish family. Boyd. MHS; DAR.
St. Paul's Parish, Balto. V. 1, 2, 3. Mss. MHS.
Talbott of "Poplar Knowle." Shirk. MHS; DAR.
Trinity P. E. churchyard, Long Green. Typed Mss. MHS.
†**Bosley, Wm. H.** Men of mark in Md. Johnson. V. 2. DAR; Enoch Pratt Lib.
Bosley Family. Ms. File case, DAR.
Bosley-Bowen-Merryman Families. Copies of wills. Ms. MHS.
Bosley, Bozeley, Balto. Co. Hardwick family, Md. and Va. William and Mary Quart., 2nd series, v. 23, pp. 63–66.
Bosline. St. Paul's Parish, Balto. V. 1. Mss. MHS.
***Bosman.** Bozman. Side lights on Md. hist. Richardson. V. 2, p. 264. MHS; DAR.
Old Somerset. Torrence. MHS; DAR.
Boss. McClellan chart. MHS.
Bossman. Somerset Co. Court Book. Tilghman. 1937. Ms. DAR.
†**Bostetter.** Hist. of Allegany Co. Thomas and Williams. V. 2. MHS. DAR.
Bostetter Family. Graveyard, Conococheague Dist., Wash. Co. Md. Geneal. Rec. Com., 1935–36. Mss. DAR.
Bostetter Family, Washington Co. Tombstone inscriptions. Md. Geneal. Rec. Com., 1935–36. DAR.
***Boston.** Burke's landed gentry. 1939. MHS.
Col. families of U. S. A. Mackenzie. V. 3. MHS; DAR.
Old Somerset. Torrence. MHS; DAR.
St. Paul's Parish, Balto. V. 1, 2. Mss. MHS.
Somerset Co. Court Book. Tilghman. 1937. Ms. DAR.
Southern Bapt. Church cemetery, Worcester Co. Md. Geneal. Rec. Com., 1937, Mrs. Lines. Mss. DAR.
Boswell. Mt. Carmel burial ground, Unity Montgomery Co. Md. Geneal. Rec. Com., 1934–35, p. 85. Mss. DAR.
St. Paul's Parish, Balto. V. 1. Mss. MHS.
Boswell, Charles Co. Abr. Compend. Amer. Geneal. Virkus. V. 4, p. 65. MHS.
Boswell, Va. Balto., its hist., its people. Hall. V. 3. MHS; DAR.
***Bosworth.** Wicomico Co. families. Tilghman. Ms., p. 105. DAR.
Boteler. Ancest. rec. and portraits. Col. Dames of Amer., 1910, v. 2, p. 593–96. MHS; DAR.

Ancestry of Lieut. and Mrs. Wm. B. Stork. Ms. MHS.
Battee, Brewer Boteler, etc., family rec. Murray. Photos. MHS.
Duckett chart. MHS.
Hist. of Frederick Co. Williams. V. 2, p. 1080. MHS; DAR.
†Hist. of lower Shenandoah, Va. Norris. P. 557.
†Hist. of Washington Co. Williams. 1906, v. 2, p. 1036. MHS; DAR.
†Med. Annals Md. Cordell. 1903, p. 328. MHS.
Pedigree of Harry Willson Falconer. Soc. Col. Wars Md. Culver. 1940. MHS; DAR.
Pedigree of Edward Boteler Passano. Soc. Col. Wars Md. Culver. 1940. MHS; DAR.
Pedigree of Maurice Falconer Rodgers. Soc. Col. Wars Md. Culver. 1940. MHS; DAR.
†Portrait and biog. rec. of Sixth Cong. Dist. of Md. 1898, p. 239. MHS; DAR.
†Shenandoah Valley pioneers. Cartnell. DAR.
See Lingan.

Boteler, Alex. Robinson. Shepherdstown Register, May 16, 1815; unpub. autobiog., 1880. Newsp. clipp. MHS.

Botfield. Botfield and allied families, originally of Talbot Co., 1706–1937. Md. Geneal. Rec. Com., 1937, Parran, pp. 78–102. Mss. DAR.

***Bothom.** Wicomico Co. families. Tilghman. Ms., p. 112. DAR.

Botner. St. Paul's Parish, Balto. V. 1, 2. Mss. MHS.

Botts. Portrait and biog. rec. Harford and Cecil Cos., pp. 365–66, 562–63. MHS; DAR.

†**Bouchell, Peter.** Hist. of Cecil Co. Johnston. MHS; DAR.

Bouchell, Boushall, Boushell. St. Stephen's Parish, Cecilton, Md. MHS; DAR.

Bouchelle. Bohemia Manor. Mallory. P. 43. MHS.
Descendants of Joran Kyn. Pa. Mag., v. 7, p. 299.

†**Boucher, Jonathan.** M. H. Mag., 1930, v. 25, pp. 305–09.
†(Rector of St. Anne's Parish, Annapolis, 1770–75). M. H. Mag., v. 7, 8, 9, 10.

Boughton. Brisko-Brisco-Briscoe and some family connections. Ramey. P. 31. Ms. MHS.
†Hist. of Allegany Co. Thomas and Williams. V. 2. MHS; DAR.
St. Paul's Parish, Balto. V. 2. Mss. MHS.

†**Bouie.** Portrait and biog. rec. of Sixth Cong. Dist. of Md. 1898, p. 158. MHS; DAR.

†**Boulden.** Med. Annals Md. Cordell. 1903, p. 329. MHS.
St. Paul's Parish, Balto. V. 2. Mss. MHS.

Boulden, C. Newton. Md. Soc., War of 1812, v. 3, no. 292. Ms. MHS.

***Boulden, Capt. Thomas.** Md. Geneal. Rec. Com., 1937–38, pp. 55–60. Mss. DAR.

Boulden Family. Abr Compend. Amer. Geneal. Virkus. V. 4, pp. 479, 532, 678.
(Dunbar-Ash line). Md. Geneal. Rec. Com., 1938–39, p. 82. Mss. DAR.
Md. Geneal Rec. Com., 1938–39, p. 60–80. Mss. DAR.

Boulden, Bouldin, Boulding. St. Stephens Parish, Cecilton, Md. MHS; DAR.

Boulden, Boulding, Bouldin Families. Births, marriages and deaths in North Sassafras or St. Stephens Parish, Cecil Co., 1693–1714. Md. Geneal. Rec. Com., 1932, v. 5. DAR.

Bouldin. Glendy churchyard, Balto. Md. Geneal. Rec. Com., 1933–34. Mss. DAR.
Col. families of U. S. A. Mackenzie. V. 3, p. 217. MHS; DAR.
Heath family. Brooks. Ms. MHS.
Lineage Bks., Natl. Soc. of Daughters of Amer. Col., v. 1, p. 17. MHS; DAR.
N. Dakota Hist. Quart., Jan., 1930, v. 4, no. 2. MHS.
See Boulden.
See Edwards, Faris, Bouldin.

Bouldin, Augustus. Md. Soc., War of 1812, v. 1, no. 58. Ms. MHS.

Boulding. *See* Boulden.

Boulton Line. Col. and Revolutionary lineages of Amer. 1939. V. 1, p. 526. MHS.

Bounds. McSpadden-Love-Meigs-Clendinen-Von Bibber-Pope chart. MHS.
Rec. of Stepney Parish. MHS; DAR.
Tombstone inscriptions from Friendship Churchyard, Worcester Co. Md. Geneal. Rec. Com., 1937–38, p. 137. Mss. DAR.
*Wicomico Co. families. Tilghman. Ms., pp. 6, 66, 109, 128. DAR.

Bounds Family. Data. Md. Geneal. Rec. Com., 1938–39, p. 193. Mss. DAR.

Bounds-Bank. Wicomico Co. families. Bible rec. Ms. DAR.

Bouquet. Naturalizations, in Md., 1666–1765. Laws. Bacon. MHS.

Bourdillon. Bantz geneal. notes. Ms. MHS.
St. Paul's Parish, Balto. V. 1. Mss. MHS.

†**Bourne.** Med. Annals Md. Cordell. 1903, p. 329. MHS.

Bous-Baumgartner-Cavander. Notes. D. A. R. Mag., v. 68, no. 2, p. 121.

Boushell. *See* Bouchell.

Boutcher, Va. Sydney-Smith and Clagett-Price families. Price. MHS; DAR.

Boute. St. Paul's Parish, Balto. V. 1. Mss. MHS.

Bovey. Hagerstown tombstone inscriptions. Gruder. Natl. Geneal. Soc. Quart., 1919, v. 8, nos. 1, 2.

Boward. Hagerstown tombstone inscriptions. Gruder. Natl. Geneal. Soc. Quart., 1919, v. 8, nos. 1, 2.
Spessard family. Spessard. MHS; DAR.

Bowditch. Fisher family. Morse. MHS.
Fisher family, Sussex Co., Del. and Md. Ms. MHS.

***Bowdle,** Calvert Co. Lineage Bk., Daughters of Founders and Patriots, v. 11, p. 901. MHS.
Pedigree of Granville Bowdle Hopkins. Soc. Col. Wars Md. Culver. 1940. MHS; DAR.

***Bowdle,** Talbot Co. Lineage Bk., Daughters of Founders and Patriots, v. 21, pp. 21–22; v. 22, pp. 133–34. MHS.

Bowdle, Thomas, of Eng., to Calvert Co., 1659. Typed, ms. MHS.

Bowdle Family. Man-Needles-Hambleton families. Needles. P. 47. MHS; DAR.

Bowdoin. Balto., its hist., its people. Hall. V. 2. MHS; DAR.
Mrs. Howard Bruce chart. MHS.
Christ P. E. Church cemetery, Cambridge. Steele. 1936. MHS; DAR.

†**Bowdoin.** Geneal. and mem. encyc. of Md. Spencer. V. 1, p. 68. MHS; DAR.
Turner Geneal. Coll. Ms. MHS.
Bowdoin, Md. and Va. Ances. rec. and portraits. Col. Dames of Amer. 1910, v. 2, pp. 477, 477–81, 486. MHS; DAR.
Bowdoin, Miss Frances Murray. Chart. Col. Dames, Chap. I. MHS.
Mrs. Howard Bruce chart. MHS.
Bowdoin, Mrs. Henry Johns (Julia Morris Murray). Chart. Col. Dames, Chap. I. MHS.
Bowdoin, Mrs. Wm. Graham, Jr. (Elinor McLane). Chart. Col. Dames, Chap. I. MHS.
Bowdoin, Mrs. William Graham (Katharine Gordon Price). Chart. Col. Dames, Chap. I. MHS.
Bowen. All Hallows P. E. churchyard, Snow Hill, Worcester Co. Hudson. Bd. Ms. MHS; DAR. Also: Md. Geneal. Rec. Com., 1935–36, p. 24. Mss. DAR.
Amer. Armory and Blue Book. Matthews. 1911–12, p. 361.
Bible rec., 1778–1839. Md. Geneal. Bull., v. 5, p. 17.
Buckingham Pres. churchyard, Worcester Co. Hudson. Bd. ms. MHS; DAR.
Geneal. of family of Gideon Gilpin. MHS.
Lineage Bks., Natl. Soc. of Daughters of Amer. Col., v. 2, p. 61. MHS; DAR.
†Med. Annals Md. Cordell. 1903, p. 329. MHS.
M. E. churchyard, Snow Hill, Worcester Co., Hudson. Bd. ms. MHS; DAR.
†Old Buckingham by the Sea, East. Shore of Md. Page. DAR.
Patriotic Md. Md. Soc. of S. A. R., 1930. MHS; DAR.
Purnell family tree. MHS.
St. Paul's P. E. churchyard, Berlin, Worcester Co. Hudson. Bd. ms. MHS; DAR. Also: Md. Geneal. Rec. Com., 1937, Mrs. Lines. Mss. DAR.
St. Paul's Parish, Balto. V. 1, 2, 3. Mss. MHS.
Stansbury chart. Cary Geneal. Coll. Ms. MHS.
See Bosley-Bowen-Merryman.
See Davenport-Sabritt-Ross-Bowen.
Bowen, Snow Hill. Bible records. Turner Geneal. Col. Ms. MHS.
***Bowen,** Va. The Sun, Balto., Sept. 25, 1904.
Bowen, Bowin. St. Stephens Parish, Cecilton, Md. MHS; DAR.
Bowerman. St. Paul's Parish, Balto. V. 2, 3. Mss. MHS.
Bowers. Beard's Luth. graveyard, Washington Co. Md. Geneal. Rec. Com., 1935–36. Mss. DAR.
Bible rec., Kent Co. Md. Geneal. Rec. Com., 1933–34, p. 220. Mss. DAR.
†Hist. of Frederick Co. Williams. MHS; DAR.
Mrs. E. W. Poe chart. MHS.
St. Paul's Parish, Balto. V. 2. Mss. MHS.
Spessard family. Spessard. MHS; DAR.
Still Pond Church and cemetery. Md. O. R. Soc. Bull., no. 2, pp. 65–75.
Trinity P. E. churchyard, Long Green. Typed ms. MHS; DAR.
Bowers, Kent Co. Manning chart. MHS.
Bowers Family. Ms. File case, DAR.
Bowers, Bauers, Pa, to Wolford, Md. Ms. File case, DAR.
Bowie. Abr. Compend. Amer. Geneal. Virkus. V. 6, p. 84. DAR.
Amer. Clan Gregor Year Book, 1909–10, p. 59; 1916, pp. 25–28; 1919, p. 99; 1934, p. 67. MHS; DAR.
Ancestry of Rosalie Morris Johnson. Johnson. 1905. MHS; DAR.
Balto., its hist., its people. Hall. V. 2. MHS; DAR.
*Bowies and their kindred. Geneal. and biog. W. W. Bowie. Washington, D. C., Cromwell Bros., 1899, 523 pp. MHS; DAR.
Bowie-Claggett chart. MHS.
Mrs. A. C. Bruce chart. MHS.
*Burke's landed gentry. 1939. MHS.
Mrs. Charles Carter chart. MHS.
Chart, photos. Cary Geneal. Coll. Ms. MHS.
†Chesapeake Bay Country. Earle. P. 215. MHS.
Chew family. Culver. M. H. Mag., 1935, v. 30, no. 2, pp. 157–75.
Children of Alex P. and M. C. Hill. Ms. MHS.
Col. families of U. S. A. Mackenzie. V. 1, p. 331; v. 7, p. 245. MHS; DAR.
See Dorsey-Bowie-Claggett. Lineage Bks., Natl. Soc. of Daughters of Amer. Col., v. 3, p. 162. MHS; DAR.
Duckett chart. MHS.
"Fairview," home of Gov. Oden Bowie, near Bowie, Prince George Co. Private burying ground, 1745–1904. Ms. MHS; DAR.
Founders of Anne Arundel and Howard Cos. Warfield. P. 251 (Gov. Robert), 287 (Gov. Oden). MHS.
Geneal. and memorial encyc. of Md. Spencer. V. 2, p. 386. MHS; DAR.
Geneal. notes of Thomas family. Thomas. P. 39. MHS; DAR.
Ghiselin chart. Cary Geneal. Coll. Ms. MHS.
Mrs. C. C. Hall chart. MHS.
Hist. graves of Md. and D. C. Ridgely. MHS.
Iglehart chart. MHS.
Lineage Bk., Order of Washington, pp. 32–35. MHS; DAR.
Md. families. Culver. Ms. Personal list.
†M. H. Mag., v. 12, p. 202.
See McMahon. Abr. Compend. Amer. Geneal. Virkus. V. 1, p. 199. DAR.
†Med. Annals Md. Cordell. 1903, p. 329. MHS.
Patterson-Lamar. Bible rec. Md. Geneal. Rec. Com., 1932, p. 20. DAR.
Patriotic Md. Md. Soc. of S. A. R., 1930. MHS; DAR.
Pedigree of Leigh Bonsal. Soc. Col. Wars Md. Culver. 1940. MHS; DAR.
Pedigree of Charles O'Donnell Mackall. Soc. Col. Wars Md. Culver. 1940. MHS; DAR.
Stones from Bowie Davis place, Montgomery Co. Md. Geneal. Rec. Com., 1934, p. 61. Mss. DAR.
*The Sun, Balto., Jan. 28, Feb. 4, 1906 (Md.); Jan. 6, 13, Va. 1907.
Mrs. G. Ross Veazey chart. MHS.
Mrs. G. H. Williams, Jr., chart. MHS.
See Duckett-Bowie.
See Purnell.
See Worthington-Bowie.

Bowie, Howard S. Amer. armory and blue bk. Matthews. 1908, p. 108. DAR.
***Bowie, Oden.** Geneal. and mem. encyc. of Md. Spencer. V. 2, pp. 386–98. MHS; DAR.
†Governors of Md. Buchholz. P. 192. MHS.
†**Bowie, Robert.** Governors of Md. Buchholz. P. 57. MHS.
Bowie, Washington, Jr. Pedigree chart. Soc. Col. Wars, Md. Johnston. 1905, p. 6. MHS.
***Bowie Family.** Arch. of Georgetown Univ., Wash., D. C., v. 287.
Bowie-Claggett. Chart; paternal ancestry of Claggett Bowie. Wm. Bowie. Blue print, Ms., 1929. MHS.
Bowin. *See* Bowen.
Bowland. Turner Geneal. Coll. Ms. MHS.
Bowles. Balch chart. MHS.
Bible rec., 1764–1840, Washington Co. D. A. R. Mag., Sept., 1936, v. 70, no. 9, p. 1021.
Daughters of Md.; Mother of Texas. Bell. MHS; DAR.
*Frederick Co. families. Markell. Ms. Personal list.
Gooch, Gouge, Goffe, Gough. William and Mary Quart., 1st series, v. 5, p. 112.
Md. gleanings in Eng. Wills. M. H. Mag., 1907, v. 2, no. 2.
Tasker chart. Cary Geneal. Coll. Ms. MHS.
Tombstone rec. Md. Geneal. Rec. Com., 1937, Parran, pp. 1, 25. Mss. DAR.
Bowles, Wash. Co. Bible rec., 1766–1863. D. A. R. Mag., v. 70, no. 9, p. 1021.
Bowles, James, St. Mary's Co. W. A. Moale pedigree charts. Soc. Col. Wars, Md. Johnston. 1905, pp. 72, 140. MHS.
Will, 1727. M. H. Mag., v. 2, no. 2, p. 181.
Bowles-Plater. Chart, photos., complete in 2 sheets. Cary Geneal. Coll. Ms. MHS.
Bowley. *See* Bowly.
Bowlin. Centenary of Catholicity in Ky. Webb. 1884. MHS.
St. Paul's Parish, Balto. V. 1, 2. Mss. MHS.
Bowling, Wm. I. Revolutionary pension abs. Natl. Geneal. Soc. Quart., v. 24, p. 51.
Bowly. Bolton chart. MHS.
Pedigree of Eustis Thompson. Soc. Col. Wars Md. Culver. 1940. MHS; DAR.
Bowly, Balto. Co. (1715–1849). J. G. and M. G. Wilson pedigree chart. Soc. Col. Wars, Md. Johnston. 1905, p. 129. MHS.
Bowly, Daniel (Revolutionary soldier). St. Paul P. E. graveyard. Patriotic Marylander, v. 2, no. 4, pp. 54–60. MHS; DAR.
Bowly Family. Ames Geneal. Coll. Ms. MHS.
Bowly, Bowley. Cary Geneal. Coll. Ms. MHS.
St. Paul's Parish, Balto. V. 1, 2, 3. Mss. MHS.
Bowman. Geneal. of Henrietta Chauncy Wilson. Upshur. Bk. of photos. MHS.
M. E. Church burial ground, Laytonsville, Montgomery Co. Md. Geneal. Rec. Com., 1934–35, pp. 69–82. Mss. DAR.
Mt. Carmel burial ground, Unity, Montgomery Co. Md. Geneal. Rec. Com., 1934–35, p. 85. Mss. DAR.
Rev. Joseph Hull (1595) and some of his descendants. Hull. 1904. MHS.
Bowman, Edmund, Va. Pedigree of Sam'l King Dennis. Soc. Col. Wars Md. Culver. 1940. MHS; DAR.
Bowman, Maj. Edmund. Pedigree of John Custis Handy. Soc. Col. Wars Md. Culver. 1940. MHS; DAR.
Bowman, Bauman. Hagerstown tombstone inscriptions. Gruder. Natl. Geneal. Soc. Quart., 1919, v. 8, nos. 1, 2.
***Bowyer.** Pedigree of Keturah Watts Clayton Hill 1849–1907. (Family of John Philip Hill). Charts. Sir George Bowyer. London. Mss. MHS.
†Men of mark in Md. Johnson. V. 3. DAR; Enoch Pratt Lib.
St. Paul's Parish, Balto. V. 1, 2. Mss. MHS.
Boyce. Cannon-Riley-Truitt-Houston-Kollock. Stow. Ms. MHS.
Mrs. Charles Carter chart. MHS.
W. W. Coleman pedigree chart. Soc. Col. Wars, Md. Johnston. 1905, p. 17. MHS.
Md. families. Culver. Ms. Personal list.
Mulford chart. MHS.
St. Paul's Parish, Balto. V. 2. Mss. MHS.
Somerset Co. Court Book. Tilghman. 1937. Ms., DAR.
See Boice.
See Loney-Boyce-Day-Garrett-Ross-Stansbury.
Boyce, A. Page. Md. Soc., War of 1812, v. 2, no. 166. Ms. MHS.
Boyce, Hayward Easter. Md. Soc., War of 1812, v. 3, no. 244. Ms. MHS.
Boyce, Mrs. Hayward (Annabel Lee George). Col. Dames, Chap. I. MHS.
Mrs. Marshall L. Price chart.
Boyce Family, Del. and Worcester Co. With geneal. J. C. Stowe. 1935. Ms. MHS.
Boyd. Abr. Compend. Amer. Geneal. Virkus. V. 6, p. 674. DAR.
Amer. Guthrie and allied families, Guthrie. Bk. 4. DAR.
†Bench and bar of Md. Sams and Riley. 1901, v. 2, p. 530. Lib. Cong.; MHS; Peabody Lib.
Boyd Family. Journal; devoted mainly to Southern Boyds and allied families. No. 1, Mar., 1925. Willis M. Boyd, editor. Cartersville, Ga., Tribune Pub. Co. MHS; DAR.
†Col. David French Boyd and his life work. Louisiana State Univ. Bull., June, 1904. MHS.
Buckingham Pres. churchyard, Worcester Co., Hudson. Bd. ms. MHS; DAR.
Chart. Family record of John and Mary Boyd. Photos. File case, DAR.
*Descendants of John and Mary (Fulton) Boyd. Chart. Photos. DAR.
Descendants of Valentine Hollingsworth, Sr. Stewart. MHS.
*Frederick Co. families. Markell. Ms. Personal list.
Hagerstown tombstone inscriptions. Gruder. Natl. Geneal. Soc. Quart., 1919, v. 8, nos. 1, 2.
†Hist. of Allegany Co. Thomas and Williams. V. 2. MHS. DAR.
†Med. Annals Md. Cordell. 1903, p. 19. MHS.
Notes on Thomas Boyd family, 1716. E. K. Voorhees, Atlanta, Ga. Revised, 1930. Typed, bd. MHS; File case, DAR.
Patriotic Md. Md. Soc. of S. A. R., 1930. MHS; DAR.
St. Paul's Parish, Balto. V. 1, 2, 3. Mss. MHS.
*Side lights on Md. hist. Richardson. V. 2, p. 267. MHS; DAR.

***Boyd.** The Sun, Balto., Oct. 27, Nov. 3, 1907.
Boyd, J. Knox Polk. Md. Soc., War of 1812, v. 2, no. 167. Ms. MHS.
Boyd, Dr. John (1746–99). Revolutionary war heroes. Cole. Bklet. Enoch Pratt Lib.
Westminster churchyard. Patriotic Marylander, v. 2, no. 4, pp. 54–60. MHS; DAR.
***Boyd, Thomas.** Patriots of Revolutionary period interred in D. C. Balch. Rec. of Columbia Hist. Soc., v. 19, v. 20.
***Boyd Family.** Boyd family. S. L. Boyd. K. C. Gottschalk, geneal. 1935. DAR.
*Journal. March, 1925, no. 1. MHS.
*Notes on Thomas Boyd family. Edw. Kinsey Voorhees. Atlanta, Ga., 1931. Mimeog. MHS; DAR.
Pa. Military rec. Pamph. DAR.
Boyd-Cole-Malone. Parrish family. Boyd. MHS; DAR.
Boyden. Col. families of U. S. A. Mackenzie. V. 3. MHS; DAR.
Boyds, Md. and Va. Ms. File case, DAR.
***Boydstun Family.** Boydstun family. G. C. Weaver. Cincinnatti, Ohio, Powell & White, 1927. MHS; DAR.
Ms. File case, DAR.
Boye. St. Paul's Parish, Balto. V. 1. Mss. MHS.
Boyed. St. Paul's Parish, Balto. V. 1. Mss. MHS.
Boyer. Geneal. Asa Emory Phillips. Wash., D. C., 1935, pamph. MHS.
*Monsieur Boyer (with books). A. E. Phillips. Photo-Process Pub., 1935. MHS.
St. Stephens Parish, Cecilton, Md. MHS; DAR.
See Bayer.
Boykin. Ances. rec. and portraits. Col. Dames of Amer. V. 1, p. 44. MHS; DAR.
Rec. of Boykins of Va., 1685. Edw. M. Boykin. S. C., 1876, pamph. MHS.
Boykin Family, Va. Ms. File case, DAR.
***Boykin Family,** Va., S. C., Ga., and Ala. Boykin family. Edw. Boykin. Camden, S. C., 1876. MHS.
Boyle. St. Paul's Parish, Balto. V. 1, 2. Mss. MHS.
†**Boyle, Capt. Thomas.** Hist. of Md. Scharf. V. 3, p. 135.
Boynton. Tilghman chart. MHS.
Boys. Naturalizations in Md., 1666–1765; Laws. Bacon. MHS.
Bozeley. *See* Bosley.
Bozman. Barroll in Great Britain and Amer. Barroll. P. 77. MHS.
Dobbin chart. MHS.
Done Bible rec. Ms. MHS.
(1755–1823). Hist. of Talbot Co. Tilghman. V. 1, p. 375. MHS. DAR.
Md. families. Culver. Ms. Personal list.
Pedigree of Harrison Tilghman. Soc. Col. Wars Md. Culver. 1940. MHS; DAR.
Pedigree of Levin Gale Shreve. Soc. Col. Wars Md. Culver. 1940. MHS; DAR.
Sketches of Bozman family. J. W. Bozman. Meridian, Miss., 1885, pamph. MHS.
Somerset Co. Court Book. Tilghman. 1937. Ms. DAR.
Tilghman chart. MHS.
†**Bozman, John Leeds.** Biog. cyc. of rep. men of Md. and D. C. P. 291. MHS; DAR.
†First historian of Md. S. A. Harrison. Balto., M. H. S. Fund. Pub., no. 26, 1888. MHS.
†(Historian; 1755–1823.) Hist. of Talbot Co. Tilghman. V. 1, pp. 375–88. MHS; DAR.
(1753–1823). Sketches of Bozman family. Bozman. 1885, chap. 12, p. 143. MHS.
Bozman Family. Ames Geneal. Coll. Ms. MHS.
Burial place, 1700. Geneal. notes of Chamberlaine family. P. 11. MHS.
*Sketches. J. W. Bozman. Chart. Meridian, Miss., Mercury Pub. Co., 1885. Pamph., 167 pp. MHS.
†**Brace.** Hist. of Allegany Co. Thomas and Williams. V. 2. MHS; DAR.
†Hist. of West. Md. Scharf. V. 2, pp. 1402–06. MHS; DAR.
St. Stephens Parish, Cecilton, Md. MHS; DAR.
***Bracken.** Boyd family. Boyd. DAR.
Brackenbury. St. Stephens Parish, Cecilton, Md. MHS; DAR.
Braddock, Gunpowder Falls. Abr. Compend. Amer. Geneal. Virkus. V. 1, p. 905.
Braderhouse. St. Paul's Parish, Balto. V. 2. Mss. MHS.
†**Bradford.** Bench and bar of Md. Sams and Riley. 1901, v. 2, p. 383. Lib. Cong.; MHS; Peabody Lib.
Bond chart. MHS.
Coll. of Amer. epitaphs and inscriptions. Alden. 1814, v. 1. MHS.
Descendants of Wm. and Sarah Bradford; married 1764. Ms. File case, DAR.
Ellicott-Campbell chart. MHS.
*Frederick Co. families. Markell. Ms. Personal list.
Griffith geneal. Griffith. MHS; DAR.
Harford Co. Hist. Soc. Mss Coll. JHU.
Hist. of Harford Co. Preston. MHS; DAR.
†Hist. of Printing in Col. Md. Wroth. MHS.
†Med. Annals Md. Cordell. 1903, p. 330. MHS.
Patriotic Md., Md. Soc. of S. A. R., 1930. MHS; DAR.
St. Paul's Parish, Balto. V. 1, 3. Mss. MHS.
St. Stephens Parish, Cecilton, Md. MHS; DAR.
*Semmes Geneal. Coll. Ms. MHS.
Whittaker folder. Ms. MHS.
Bradford, S. C. Ms. MHS.
Bradford-Du Pont, Del. Abr. Compend. Amer. Geneal. Virkus. V. 1, pp. 222–24.
Bradford-Miller Families, Md. and Pa. Ms. File case, DAR.
†**Bradford, Gov. Augustus Williamson.** Founders of Anne Arundel and Howard Cos. Warfield. P. 284. MHS; DAR.
Governors of Md. Buchholz. P. 178. MHS.
†Inaugural address, 1862. (Dealing wholly with Civil War.) Annapolis, 1862, 15 pp.
Bradford, Sam'l Webster. Md. Soc., War of 1812, v. 3, no. 205. Ms. MHS.
Bradley. Children of Alex P. and M. C. Hill. Ms. MHS.
Portrait and biog. rec. of East. Shore of Md. 1898, pp. 456, 851. MHS; DAR.
St. Joseph's R. C. churchyard, Worcester Co., Hudson. Md. O. R. Soc. Bull., no. 3, p. 64.
St. Paul's Parish, Balto. V. 1, 2, 4. Mss. MHS.
***Bradley-Mills,** Dorchester Co. Lineage Bks., Daughters of Amer. Col., v. 3, p. 222. MHS; DAR.

Bradshaw. Cotton chart. MHS.
Hagerstown tombstone inscriptions. Gruder. Natl. Geneal. Soc. Quart., 1919, v. 8, nos. 1, 2.
St. Paul's Parish, Balto. V. 1, 2. Mss. MHS.
Bradshaw, Kent Co. Mrs. T. R. Brown chart. MHS.
Bradshawe. Somerset Co. Court Book. Tilghman. 1937. Ms. DAR.
Brady. Md. tombstone rec. Md. Geneal. Rec. Com., 1937, Parran, pp. 1, 25. Mss. DAR.
St. Paul's Parish, Balto. V. 1, 2, 4. Mss. MHS.
Braithwaite. Col. families of U. S. A. Mackenzie. V. 1, p. 348. MHS; DAR.
St. Paul's Parish, Balto. V. 1. Mss. MHS.
Braithwaite Family (1636). 2 charts. Ms. File case, DAR.
Brámall. *See* Bromwell.
Bramble. Christ P. E. Church cemetery, Cambridge. Steele. 1936. MHS; DAR.
†Hist. of Allegany Co. Thomas and Williams. V. 2, p. 749. MHS.
Tombstone rec. of Dorchester Co. Jones. DAR.
Bramble Family. Ms. File case, DAR.
Bramhall. *See* Bromwell.
Bramwell. Col. families of U. S. A. Mackenzie. V. 6, p. 421. MHS; DAR.
Griffith geneal. Griffith. MHS; DAR.
Old Md. families. Bromwell. MHS; DAR.
St. Thomas' Parish, Balto. Co. Bd. ms. MHS. Also: Md. Geneal. Rec. Com., 1937, pp. 109-82. Mss. DAR.
Bramwell, George. Garrison Church. Allen. P. 148-49. MHS; DAR.
***Branch.** Branchiana, being partial account of Branch family in Va. J. Branch Cabell. Richmond, Va., Whittel & Shepperson, 1907. MHS.
Pocahontas and her descendants. Robertson. MHS; DAR.
St. Paul's Parish, Balto. V. 1. Mss. MHS.
***Branch,** Abington. Branch of Abington, founder of Branch family in Va. J. Branch Cabell. Richmond, Va., Wm. Ellis Jones' Sons, Inc., 1911. 1st ed. MHS.
***Branch,** Va. Burke's landed gentry. 1939. MHS.
Lineage Bks., Natl. Soc. of Daughters of Amer. Col., v. 1, p. 187. MHS; DAR.
Branch, C. H. Harden. Md. Soc., War of 1812, v. 2, no. 147. Ms. MHS.
Branch, Henry. Md. Soc., War of 1812, v. 2, no. 146. Ms. MHS.
Branch, Rev. Henry. Bell, Bolling, Cary, Rolfe rec. of Va. Pedigree. Soc. Col. Wars Md. Culver. 1940. MHS; DAR.
Branch Family, Va. Ms. File case, DAR.
†**Brandenberg.** Hist. of Frederick Co. Williams. MHS; DAR.
Mt. Carmel burial ground, Unity, Montgomery Co. Md. Geneal. Rec. Com., 1934-35, p. 85. Mss. DAR.
Brandt. Ances. rec. and portraits. Col. Dames of Amer., 1910, v. 1, pp. 194-201. MHS; DAR.
Balto., its hist., its people. Hall. V. 2. MHS; DAR.
Cary Geneal. Coll. Ms. MHS.
See Gross-Weiss-Brandt families Ms. MHS.
Poundstone chart. MHS.
*Side lights on Md. hist. Richardson. V. 2, p. 276. MHS; DAR.
Turner chart. MHS.
Brandt, Miss Miriam. Chart. Col. Dames, Chap. I. MHS.
Branklin. St. Stephens Parish, Cecilton, Md. MHS; DAR.
Brann. Wilkinson-Brann-Boon family of Balto. Photos. DAR.
Brannan. *See* Brannen.
Brannen, Brannan. St. Paul's Parish, Balto. V. 1, 3. Mss. MHS.
Brannock. Trinity Church burial ground, near Cambridge, Md. Md. Geneal. Rec. Com., 1937-38, pp. 93-104. Mss. DAR.
Trinity Church cemetery, Dorchester Co. Md. O. R. Soc. Bull., no. 3, pp. 42-52.
Bransford Family. Chart, photos. Edw. S. Lewis. Wm. and Mary Quart., v. 8, series 2, p. 34. MHS.
Bransford-Athey. Abr. Compend. Amer. Geneal. Virkus. V. 1, p. 486. DAR.
Branson. St. Paul's Parish, Balto. V. 1, 2, 3. Mss. MHS.
Brant. St. Paul's Parish, Balto. V. 2, 3. Mss. MHS.
***Brantfafer, Adam.** Family Association Bulletins. MHS.
***Braselton (Brazelton).** Lineage Bks., Daughters of Amer. Col., v. 3, p. 144. MHS; DAR.
Brashear. Abr. Compend. Amer. Geneal. Virkus. V. 6, pp. 123, 732. DAR.
*Frederick Co. families. Markell. Ms. Personal list.
Lineage Bks., Natl. Soc. of Daughters of Amer. Col., v. 1, p. 80. MHS; DAR.
†Med. Annals Md. Cordell. 1903, p. 331. MHS.
See Oakley. Abr. Compend. Amer. Geneal. Virkus. V. 1, p. 749. DAR.
Pedigree of Richard Walker Worthington. Soc. Col. Wars Md. Culver. 1940. MHS; DAR.
Brashears. Cary Geneal. Coll. Ms. MHS.
*Geneal. and mem. encyc. of Md. Spencer. V. 2, p. 406. MHS; DAR.
†Men of mark in Md. Johnson. V. 3. DAR; Enoch Pratt Lib.
Pedigree of Mareen Duvall. Soc. Col. Wars Md. Culver. 1940. MHS; DAR.
*Semmes Geneal. Coll. Ms. MHS.
See Brasseur.
***Brashears Family.** Wilson Mss. Coll., no. 37, D. MHS.
Brashier. Griffith geneal. Griffith. MHS; DAR.
***Brasseur** or **Brashears.** Side lights on Md. hist. Richardson. V. 2, p. 283. MHS; DAR.
***Brassieur,** Md. and Va. Brassieur family of Md. and Va. O. E. Monette.
***Brattan, Brattin.** Wicomico Co. families. Tilghman. Ms, pp. 98, 102, 123. DAR.
Bratten Bible records. Turner Geneal. Col. Ms. MHS.
Buckingham Pres. churchyard, Worcester Co., Hudson. Bd. ms. MHS; DAR.
M. E. churchyard, Snow Hill, Worcester Co., Hudson. Bd. ms. MHS; DAR.
Brattin. *See* Bratton.
Bratton. *See* Gillespie-Brittain-Bratton.

Brauner. St. Charles R. C. Church graveyard, Indianhead, Charles Co. Md. Geneal. Rec. Com., 1933–34, p. 137. Mss. DAR.
Brauns Family, Balto. Hist. George C. Keidel. Ms. MHS.
Brausby, J. C. Md. Soc., War of 1812, v. 1, no. 76. Ms. MHS.
Brawner. Col. families of U. S. A. Mackenzie. V. 1, p. 406. MHS; DAR.
Lineage Bks., Natl. Soc. of Daughters of Amer. Col., v. 2, p. 95. MHS; DAR.
*Semmes Geneal Coll. Ms. MHS.
Brawner, Charles Co. Abs. of will, 1767. D. A. R. Mag., Oct., 1927, no. 10, p. 785.
Brawner, Edward, Charles Co. Will probated, Jan. 3, 1767. D. A. R. Mag., v. 61, no. 10, p. 785.
Braxton. Blair-Banister-Braxton families. Horner. MHS.
Braxton, Carter. Sketch of life of Carter Braxton, Va., with members of Carter Braxton Chapter, D. A. R., Balto., descended from him. William Tyler Page, descendant, and author of American Creed, accepted April 1918, in House of Representatives, in behalf of Amer. people, made honorary member. Pamph., 20 pp. MHS.
Braxton-Carter Line, Va. Mrs. Renshaw chart. MHS.
Braxton (Carter)-Stiles. Lineage Bks., Natl. Soc. of Daughters of Amer. Col., v. 3, p. 305. MHS; DAR.
Bray. Burbank family. Sedgley. MHS.
Ms. MHS.
†Narrative of events connected with rise and progress of P. E. church in Md. Hawks. 1839, chap. 4, p. 94.
Somerset Co. Court Book. Tilghman. 1937. Ms. DAR.
†Bray, Rev. Thomas. His life and selected works relating to Md. B. C. Steiner, Balto., M. H. S. Fund. Pub., no. 37, 1901. MHS.
†Thomas Bray and Md. parochial libraries. J. T. Wheeler. M. H. Mag., 1939, v. 34, no. 3, p. 246.
Brazelton, Braselton. Lineage Bks., Natl. Soc. of Daughters of Amer. Col., v. 3, p. 144. MHS; DAR.
Breading. Ewing geneal. with kin in Amer. Kittredge and Ewing. 1919, pp. 11–12. MHS.
†Breathed. Hist. of West. Md. Scharf. V. 2, pp. 1258–59. MHS; DAR.
Md. tombstone rec. Md. Geneal. Rec. Com., 1937, Parran, p. 1. Mss. DAR.
Bredell. Buckingham Pres. churchyard, Worcester Co., Hudson. Bd. ms. MHS; DAR.
Breeset. St. Paul's Parish, Balto. V. 1. Mss. MHS.
Breidenhardt. Jacobs chart. MHS.
Machen chart. MHS.
Breidenhart. Greenway chart. MHS.
Peale Geneal. Coll. Ms. MHS.
Bremond-Brooke-Beall. Abr. Compend. Amer. Geneal. Virkus. V. 1, p. 407. DAR.
Brendel. Hagerstown tombstone inscriptions. Gruder. Natl. Geneal. Soc. Quart., 1919, v. 8, nos. 1, 2.
***Brengle.** Brengle family of Frederick. B. C. Steiner. M. H. Mag., 1912, v. 7, pp. 91–98, 219.
Frederick Co. tombstone inscriptions. Gruder. Natl. Geneal. Soc. Quart., 1919, v. 8, nos. 1, 2.
†Hist. of Frederick Co. Williams. MHS; DAR.
Hist. of Shriver family. Shriver. Pp. 84–89. MHS.
Home guard, Frederick Co., April, 1861. M. H. Mag., v. 7, no. 2, p. 196.
Scholl, Sholl, Shull family. Scholl. P. 784. MHS; DAR.
Talbott of "Poplar Knowle." Shirk. MHS; DAR.
Brent. Ances. rec. and portraits. Col. Dames of Amer., 1910, v. 2, pp. 521–31, 532, 534–38, 565. MHS; DAR.
Cemetery near Carroll Chapel, Forest Glen. Md. Geneal. Rec. Com., v. 2, p. 27. Mss. DAR.
Clark chart. MHS.
Col. families of U. S. A. .Mackenzie. V. 1; v. 4; v. 7, p. 101 (Giles Brent line). MHS; DAR.
*Descendants of Hugh Brent, immigrant to Isle of Wight Co., 1642. C. H. Brent. 1936. DAR.
Dorsey Papers. Ms. MHS.
Family graveyard, Hancock, Wash. Co. Hist. of West. Md. Scharf. V. 2, p. 1255.
Geneal. Assoc. Pub. Crozier. V. 3.
Hist. graves of Md. and D. C. Ridgely. MHS.
†Hist. of West. Md. Scharf. V. 2, p. 1120. MHS; DAR.
R. B. Keyser pedigree chart, plate 2. Soc. Col. Wars, Md. Johnston. 1905, p. 56. MHS.
Lineage Bks., Natl. Soc. of Daughters of Amer. Col., v. 2, p. 66. MHS; DAR.
Manly chart. MHS.
Md. families. Culver. Ms. Personal list.
Md. Geneal. Bull., v. 3, p. 28.
†Md.'s royal family. Giles Brent and Mary Kittamaqund, Indian. E. Rigby. M. H. Mag., 1934, v. 29, pp. 259–68.
Md. tombstone rec. Md. Geneal. Rec. Com., 1937, Parran, p. 8. Mss. DAR.
†Mistress Margaret Brent, spinster. Julia C. Spruill. M. H. Mag., 1934, v. 29, pp. 259–68.
Old Georgetown cemetery, Georgetown, D. C. Natl. Geneal. Soc. Quart., v. 23, no. 3, pp. 85, 104.
Old N. W. Geneal. Soc. Quart., Columbus, Ohio, 1900, v. 3, pp. 64–67. MHS.
*Pennington Papers. Ms. MHS.
Portraits. Va. Mag. Hist. and Biog., v. 20, p. 99.
Prayer Book rec. Ms. MHS.
Rec. from Trinity parish, Charles Co. Va. Mag. Hist. and Biog., v. 21, p. 96.
St. John R. C. Church cemetery, Montgomery Co. Md. Geneal. Rec. Com., 1926, p. 27. Mss. DAR.
Semmes and allied families. Semmes. MHS.
*Semmes Geneal. Coll. Ms. MHS.
*Side lights on Md. hist. Richardson. V. 2, p. 21. MHS; DAR.
Brent, Charles Co. Cary Geneal. Coll. Ms. MHS.
Brent, Lancaster Co., Va. Cary Geneal. Coll. Ms. MHS.
***Brent,** Md. and Va. Brents of Md. and Va. W. B. Chilton.
De Bow's Review, v. 26, pp. 487–502.
Brent, Va. Mrs. T. C. Jenkins chart. MHS.
*The Sun, Balto., March 27, 1904.

Brent, Duncan Keener. Pedigree. Soc. Col. Wars Md. Culver. 1940. MHS; DAR.
Brent, Duncan Keener, Jr. Pedigree. Soc. Col. Wars Md. Culver. 1940. MHS; DAR.
Brent, Giles. E. A. and F. de S. Jenkins pedigree chart. Soc. Col. Wars, Md. Johnston. 1905, pp. 46, 140. MHS.
Brent, Henry (nephew of Arch Bishop Carroll), Charles Co. Birth rec.; Ms. MHS.
Baptism, 1787. Ms. MHS.
***Brent, J. Lancaster.** Burke's landed gentry. 1939. MHS.
†**Brent, John Carroll.** Life and character; address. J. B. Blake. Oldest inhabitants of District, Assoc. Wash., 1876.
Brent, Joseph Lancaster. Pedigree. Soc. Col. Wars Md. Culver. 1940. MHS; DAR.
Pedigree chart. Soc. Col. Wars, Md. Johnston. 1905, p. 7. MHS.
†**Brent, Margaret.** First woman in Amer. to claim right to vote in legislative body. J. L. Thomas. Bath Telegram, Dec. 22, 1883. MHS.
Will. Va. Mag. Hist. and Biog., v. 16, p. 98.
Brent, Mrs. Robert Fenwick (Alice G. Harris). Chart. Col. Dames, Chap. I. MHS.
Brent Family (1487; to Md. 1637; moved to Va. 1645). Va. Mag. Hist. and Biog., v. 12, pp. 439–445; v. 13; v. 14; v. 15, pp. 95, 194, 324, 450; v. 16, pp. 96, 98, 211; v. 17, pp. 81, 194, 308, 420; v. 18; v. 19, pp. 94, 95, 100, 206, 317, 433; v. 20, pp. 96, 99, 321, 433; v. 21, p. 96; v. 22.
*De Bow's Review, May, 1859.
*Graveyard near Hancock, Washington Co., 1787–1875 (11 stones). Hist. of West. Md. Scharf. V. 2, p. 1255. MHS; DAR.
*Old Kent. Hanson. Pp. 17–19. MHS; DAR.
Brent (Va.)-Langhorne. Chart, photos. complete in 2 sheets. Cary Geneal. Coll. Ms. MHS.
***Brents,** Md. and Va. Va. Mag. Hist. and Biog., v. 16, p. 96.
Brereton. Abr. Compend. Amer. Geneal. Virkus. V. 1, pp. 488–89. DAR.
Amer. Armory and Blue Book. Matthews. 1911–12, p. 159.
†Med. Annals Md. Cordell. 1903, p. 331.
Somerset Co. Court Book. Tilghman. 1937. Ms. DAR.
Brereton, Capt. St. Paul's Parish, Balto. V. 1. Mss. MHS.
Bresee. Hist. of Balto. City and Co. Scharf. Pp. 489–90. MHS.
†**Bretton.** Day-Star of Amer. Freedom. Davis. P. 224. MHS; DAR.
†Papers relating to early hist. of Md. Streeter. 1876. MHS.
Brevard. Harford Co. Hist. Soc. Mss. Coll. JHU.
Brevard, Md. and N. C. line. Geneal. of Mays family. Mays. P. 249. MHS.
Brevard Family, Md. and N. C. Ms. File case, DAR.
Brewer. Ances. rec. and portraits. Col. Dames of Amer., 1910, v. 2, p. 602. MHS; DAR.
Balto., its hist., its people. Hall. V. 2. MHS; DAR.
Battee, Brewer, Boteler, etc., family rec. Murray. Photos. MHS.
†Bench and Bar of Md. Sams and Riley, 1901, v. 2, pp. 415, 597. Lib. Cong.; MHS; Peabody Lib.
†Biog. cyc. of rep. men of Md. and D. C. P. 65. MHS; DAR.
Cary Geneal. Coll. Ms. MHS.
Cemetery Creek, Anne Arundel Co., tombstone inscriptions. Founders of Anne Arundel and Howard Cos. Warfield. P. 333. MHS; DAR.
*Founders of Anne Arundel and Howard Cos. Warfield. P. 320. MHS; DAR.
Geneal. of Henrietta Chauny Wilson. Upshur. Bk. of photos. MHS.
Hill, Mass. Col. and Revolutionary families of Phila. Jordan. 1933, v. 1, pp. 293–322.
Hist. graves of Md. and D. C. Ridgely. MHS.
†Hist. of Balto. City and Co. Scharf. P. 639. MHS.
Lineage Bks., Natl. Soc. of Daughters of Amer. Col., v. 1, p. 83. MHS; DAR.
Md. gleanings in Eng. Wills. M. H. Mag., 1910, v. 5.
†Med. Annals Md. Cordell. 1903, p. 332. MHS.
Monumental City. Howard. MHS; DAR.
Mrs. E. N. Morison chart. MHS.
Patriotic Md. Md. Soc. of S. A. R., 1930. MHS; DAR.
Peale Geneal. Coll. Ms. MHS.
See Peale-Brewer-Ridgely. Lineage Bks., Natl. Soc. of Daughters of Amer. Col., v. 2, p. 201. MHS; DAR.
Pedigree of John B. Philip C. Hall. Soc. Col. Wars Md. Culver. 1940. MHS; DAR.
Pedigree of Edward Hammond. Soc. Col. Wars Md. Culver. 1940. MHS; DAR.
(7 generations.) Pedigree of Thomas Carroll Roberts. Soc. Col. Wars Md. Culver. 1940. MHS; DAR.
*George Donald Riley. Riley. DAR.
St. Paul's Parish, Balto. V. 1, 2. Mss. MHS.
*The Sun, Balto., Dec. 25, 1904; Jan. 1, 1905.
Whiteley chart. MHS.
See Baldwin-Brewer-Disney-Maccubin.
See Magruder.
Brewer Family. Ames. Geneal. Coll. Ms. MHS.
Copied from Riley family. Md. Geneal. Rec. Com., 1934–35, pp. 379–82, 394. Mss. DAR.
Brewer Line. Hill family of Hourston and Spaxton, Eng., Mass., Md., and New Eng., 1334–1934. P. 314. MHS.
Brewer Line, Anne Arundel Co. J. P. Hill pedigree chart, plate 2. Soc. Col. Wars, Md. Johnston. 1905, pp. 37, 140. MHS.
Brewington. Hist. Salisbury, Wicomico Co. Truitt. DAR.
†**Brewington, Marion B.** Men of mark in Md. Johnson. V. 1. DAR; Enoch Pratt Lib.
***Brewington, Bruenton, Bruereton.** Wicomico Co. families. Tilghman. Ms, pp. 4, 7, 8, 95, 97–99, 115. DAR.
Brezler. Hagerstown tombstone inscriptions. Gruder. Natl. Geneal. Soc. Quart., 1919, v. 8, nos. 1, 2.
Brian. St. Paul's Parish, Balto. V. 1, 2. Mss. MHS.
Briance. St. Paul's Parish, Balto. V. 2. Mss. MHS.

Briant. St. Paul's Parish, Balto. V. 1. Mss. MHS.

Briarly, Bryarly, Harford Co., Gilpin chart. MHS.

Brice. Abr. Compend. Amer. Geneal. Virkus. V. 1, p. 494. DAR.
Bible rec. Upper Penins. East. Shore., p. 133.
* Brice and allied families. Ms. DAR.
Brice-Govane-Howard tombstone inscriptions. Ms. MHS.
Cemetery Creek, Anne Arundel Co., Tombstone inscriptions. Founders of Anne Arundel and Howard Cos. Warfield. P. 333. MHS; DAR.
Col. mansions of Md. and Del. Hammond. 1914. MHS.
Dorsey chart. MHS.
Col. Nicholas Duvall Family Records. Price. Bd. ms. MHS.
*Founders of Anne Arundel and Howard Cos. Warfield. Pp. 156–58. MHS; DAR.
Harford Co. Hist. Soc. Mss. Coll. JHU.
Howard-Govane-Woodward-Law Bible rec. Ms. MHS.
Lineage Bks., Natl. Soc. of Daughters of Amer. Col., v. 1, p. 41; v. 3, p. 219. MHS; DAR.
Patriotic Md. Md. Soc. of S. A. R., 1930. MHS; DAR.
*Pennington Papers. Ms. MHS.
St. Paul's Parish, Balto. V. 2, 3. Mss. MHS.
Tombstone rec. found on Brice farm, near Sassafras, Kent Co. Md. Geneal. Rec. Com., 1934–35, p. 195. Mss. DAR.
See Cummings-Brice.

***Brice,** Annapolis. The Sun, Balto., Jan. 6, 13, 20, 1907.

Brice, Rev. John, Harford Co. D. A. R. Mag., July, 1935, v. 69, no. 7, p. 433.

Brice Family. Descendants of James Brice, with Smith data. Ms. File case, DAR.
Family Rec. Bk. of photos. MHS.
*Old Kent. Hanson. Pp. 82–84. MHS; DAR.

Brice, Bryce Family. Ms. File case, DAR.

Bridger. Mrs. Henry Du Pont Baldwin chart. MHS.

Bridgerum. Cummings chart. Lib. Cong.; MHS; DAR.

†**Bridges.** Hist. of Washington Co. Williams. 1906, v. 2, p. 1062. MHS; DAR.
Md. tombstone rec. Md. Geneal. Rec. Com., 1937, Parran, p. 14. Mss. DAR.

†**Brien.** Portrait and biog. rec. of Sixth Cong. Dist. of Md. 1898, p. 306. MHS; DAR.
St. Paul's Parish, Balto. V. 3. Mss. MHS.

Briggs. St. Paul's Parish, Balto. V. 2. Mss. MHS.

†**Briggs, Isaac** (1763–1825). Sketch of his life. M. H. Mag., 1912, v. 7, pp. 409–19.

Bright. Bailliere chart. MHS.
Riggs of Anne Arundel, Frederick and Montgomery Cos. prior to 1663. Pamph. MHS.

Brinckloe. Pedigree of Malcolm Van Vechten Tyson. Soc. Col. Wars Md. Culver. 1940. MHS; DAR.

Bringler. Col. families of U. S. A. Mackenzie. V. 7, p. 115. MHS; DAR.
Pedigree of Duncan Keener Brent. Soc. Col. Wars Md. Culver. 1940. MHS; DAR.
Thomas family of Talbot Co. Spencer. P. 95. MHS; DAR.

Brinton. Burton ancestry. Ms. MHS.
Peale Geneal. Coll. Ms. MHS.
*Lineage Bks., Daughters of Amer. Col., v. 4, p. 157. MHS; DAR
See Briscoe.
See Brisko.

Briscoe. Abr. Compend. Amer. Geneal. Virkus. V. 1, p. 480; v. 6, p. 29. DAR.
Amer. Armory and Blue Bk. Matthews. 1908, p. 107. DAR
Bantz geneal. notes. MS. MHS.
Barber, "Luckland," St. Mary's Co. Bible rec. Natl. Geneal. Soc. Quart., v. 22, no. 4, pp. 89–92.
†Bench and bar of Md. 1901, v. 2, p. 652. Lib. Cong.; MHS; Peabody Lib.
Brooke-Baker chart. MHS; DAR.
Cary Geneal. Coll. Ms. MHS.
Col. families of Amer. Lawrence. V. 16, p. 84. MHS.
Col. families of U. S. A. Mackenzie. V. 3, pp. 84–88; v. 4, pp. 191–92. MHS; DAR.
Descendants of Col. Thomas White. Morris. MHS.
First John Briscoe of Md. Natl. Geneal. Soc. Quart., v. 21, no. 3, p. 73.
†Med. Annals Md. Cordell. 1903, p. 332. MHS.
Pedigree of Rev. James Mitchell Magruder. Soc. Col. Wars Md. Culver. 1940. MHS; DAR.
Porcher chart. MHS.
St. Paul's Parish, Balto. V. 1, 2, 3, 4. Mss. MHS.
Scruggs geneal. Dunklin. M. H. Mag., 1914, v. 9, p. 88.
*Semmes Geneal. Coll. Ms. MHS.
*Side lights on Md. hist. Richardson. V. 2, p. 28. MHS; DAR.
Still Pond Church and cemetery. Md. O. R. Soc. Bull., no. 2, pp. 65–75.
*The Sun, Balto., July 5, 1903.
Times Dispatch, Richmond, Va., June 5, 1904. Newsp. clipp.
Tombstone inscriptions. D. C. Geneal. Rec. Com., v. 35, p. 103. Typed, bd. DAR.
See Brisko.
See Smoot-Briscoe.

Briscoe, James. Wills of Wm. Wilkinson and James Briscoe, 1779. Mss. DAR.

Briscoe, Philip. Md. pensioner on Miss. pension rolls. D. A. R. Mag., v. 69, no. 11, p. 685.

Briscoe, Philip and Maria. Bible rec. Ms. MHS.

Briscoe, Col. Philip. Some descendants. M. H. Mag., 1927, v. 22, pp. 40–53.

Briscoe Family. Ms. File case, DAR.
*Old Kent. Hanson. Pp. 121–24; arms, p. 121. MHS; DAR.
Rec., Cecil Co., 1767–1836. Md. Geneal. Rec. Com., 1932–33. Mss. DAR.

Briscoe Family, Cecil Co. (1767–1836). Md. Geneal. Rec. Com., 1932–33, p. 53. Mss. DAR.

Briscoe Line. Lilburn family. Col. and Revolutionary families of Phila. Jordan. 1933, v. 1, pp. 382–98.

Briscoe-Anderson. Abr. Compend. Amer. Geneal. Virkus. V. 4, p. 408. MHS.

Briscoe-Smith. Bible rec., 1743–1848. D. A. R. Mag., May, 1939, v. 73, no. 5, pp. 89–90.

Briscoe, Brisco. Scruggs geneal. Dunklin. Pp. 171–79.

Brish. Frederick Co. tombstone inscriptions. Gruder. Natl. Geneal. Soc. Quart., 1919, v. 8, nos. 1, 2.
Brisko. Brisko-Brisco-Briscoe and some family connections. Mary E. Ramey. Ms. MHS.
Brispoe. Naturalizations in Md., 1666–1765; Laws. Bacon. MHS.
Bristor, J. Whitridge. Md. Soc., War of 1812, v. 3, no. 248. Ms. MHS.
Bristor, Wm. B. Md. Soc., War of 1812, v. 3, no. 291. Ms. MHS.
Bristow. St. Paul's Parish, Cecilton, Md. MHS; DAR.
Brittain. *See* Gillespie-Brittain-Bratton.
Brittingham. St. Martin's P. E. Church, Worcester Co. Md. Geneal. Rec. Com., 1937, Mrs. Lines. Mss. DAR.
St. Paul's P. E. churchyard, Berlin, Worcester Co. Hudson. Bd. ms. MHS; DAR. Also: Md. Geneal. Rec. Com., 1937, Mrs. Lines. Mss. DAR.
Southern Bapt. Church cemetery, Worcester Co. Md. Geneal. Rec. Com., 1937, Mrs. Lines. Mss. DAR.
Turner Geneal. Coll. Ms. MHS.
*Wicomico Co. families. Tilghman. Ms, p. 109. DAR.
See Parker-Brittingham.
Britton. Chart; arms. (Traced back to Charlemagne.) Compiled for Mrs. Winchester Britton III (Edythe Clements Shipley). MHS.
Magna Charta Dame line of Milliscent Howard Britton (through Britton), 1066–1932. Md. Geneal. Rec. Com., 1933–34, p. 35. Mss. DAR.
Md. Royal and Baronial Scrap Book, being the ancestry of Edythe Clements Shipley Britton. Charts; coat of arms. 2 v. Ms. MHS.
Patriotic Md. Md. Soc. of S. A. R., 1930. MHS; DAR.
Britton, Edyth Clements (Shipley). Rec. (condensed) for Soc. of Magna Charta Dames, 1609–1903. Md. Geneal. Rec. Com., 1933–34, pp. 22–34. Mss. DAR.
Britton-Shipley. Abr. Compend. Amer. Geneal. Virkus. V. 6, p. 91. DAR.
Broad. Cary Geneal. Coll. Ms. MHS.
Cole-Price chart. Cary Geneal. Coll. Ms. MHS.
St. Paul's Parish, Balto. V. 1. Mss. MHS.
Broadbent. Price family and other Gunpowder Friends. Death notices; photos. of newsp. clipp. MHS.
Broadnax. Geneal. of family of Dr. Robert H. Broadnax, Dinwiddie Co., Va., 1803–1901. Md. Geneal. Rec. Com., 1934. DAR.
Broadnax, Dr. Robert H., Dinwiddie Co., Va. (Married Mary Ann Tolly Love, Feb. 17, 1827; died April 23, 1850.) Geneal. Md. Geneal. Rec. Com., 1933–34, p. 66. Mss. DAR.
***Broadwater.** Frederick Co. families. Markell. Ms. Personal list.
†Hist. of West. Md. Scharf. V. 2, p. 1530. MHS; DAR.
Broadwater Family. Mountain Democrat, Garrett Co., Sept. 27, 1934. Newsp. clipp. MHS; DAR.
Brock. *See* Humphries-Pope-Brock-Parker.
***Brockenborough,** Va. The Sun, Balto., Oct. 23, Nov. 6, 1904.
Brockenbrough. Cary Geneal. Coll. Ms. MHS.
Brockenbrough, Wm., Va. Ms. File case, DAR.
Brodie. St. Barnabas P. E. churchyard. Typed ms. MHS; DAR.
Brogden. Trinity P. E. churchyard, Long Green. Typed ms. MHS; DAR.
Brogden, Mrs. John Gittings (Katherine MacSherry). Chart. Col. Dames, Chap. I. MHS.
Brogden, Miss Mary Stevenson. Chart. Col. Dames, Chap. I. MHS.
***Brogden Family.** Old Kent. Hanson. P. 88. MHS; DAR.
Brogunier. Zion Reformed Church, Hagerstown. Md. Geneal. Rec. Com., 1934–35. Mss. DAR.
Brombaugh. *See* Brumbach.
Brome. Col. families of U. S. A. Mackenzie. V. 1, p. 35. MHS; DAR.
*The Sun, Balto., June 28, 1903.
Bromel. *See* Bromwell.
Bromhall. *See* Bromwell.
Bromley. Somerset Co. Court Book. Tilghman. 1937. Ms. DAR.
Bromley, J. L. Md. Soc., War of 1812, v. 2, no. 144. Ms. MHS.
Bromwell. Bromwell families of Eng., from notes collected in London. By Henrietta E. Bromwell. Denver, Col., 1913. Ms; index in separate binding. MHS.
Chart of Bromwell family of Mass. (complete, with dates of all births, marriages and deaths) dating from three Mayflower ancestors to date (200 names). Md. Geneal. Rec. Com., 1938–39. Mss. DAR.
Geneal.; incl. descendants of William Bromwell and Beulah Hall. Henrietta E. Bromwell. Denver, Col., 1910. Bd. ms. Lib. Cong.; MHS.
Griffith geneal. Griffith. MHS; DAR.
†Med. Annals Md. Cordell. 1903, p. 333. MHS.
*(Bromwell, Bramall, Brumwell, Bromel, Bramhall, Bromhall, Bramwell.) Old Md. families. H. E. Bromwell. V. 1, pedigree chart, pr. in Denver, Col., 1916; v. 2, notes collected in Eng., typed and bd., 1916. MHS; DAR Peabody Lib.
Revolutionary rec. Bromwell geneal. Bromwell. P. 95. MHS.
Trinity Church burial ground, near Cambridge, Md. Md. Geneal. Rec. Com., 1937–38, pp. 93–104. Mss. DAR.
Trinity Church cemetery, Dorchester Co. Md. O. R. Soc. Bull., no. 3, pp. 42–52.
Turner family. Forman. Pp. 96–97. MHS.
Bronson. Rogers Coll. Ms. MHS.
***Brook.** Balto. Herald, Mar. 29, 1903. Newsp. clipp. MHS.
See Greville-Brook.
Brooke. Abr. Compend. Amer. Geneal. Virkus. V. 6, p. 738. DAR.
Advocate, Mar. 1, 1883. Newsp. clipp. MHS.
Ances. rec. and portraits. Col. Dames of Amer., 1910, v. 1, p. 357; v. 2, pp. 469, 553–55, 686. MHS; DAR.
Application for Membership to Natl. Soc. Col. Dames of Amer. Ms. MHS.
Beall and Bell families. Beall. MHS.
Beall chart. Cary Geneal. Coll. Ms. MHS.

Brooke. Bible rec., 1706–1849. Md. Geneal. Rec. Com., 1926–27, v. 2, pp. 59–62. Mss. DAR.
Boarman geneal. Thomas. 1935. MHS; DAR.
Bowie-Claggett chart. MHS.
Bowies and their kindred. Bowie. MHS; DAR.
J. L. Brent pedigree chart. Soc. Col. Wars, Md. Johnston. 1905, pp. 7, 141. MHS.
Mrs. R. F. Brent chart. MHS.
Brooke family. Christopher Johnston. M. H. Mag., 1906, pp. 66–73, 184–89, 284–98, 376–78.
Robert Brooke (1652) and Thomas Brooke (1720). Sketches. Pa. Soc. of Col. Governors, v. 1. MHS.
Brooke family. E. B. C. Bowen. M. H. Mag., 1934, v. 29, no. 2, pp. 152–69; 1935, v. 30, no. 2, p. 180, corrections.
Brooke family of Md. Christopher Johnston, Jr. Advocate, Montgomery Co., Mar. 1, 1883. Scrap Bk. MHS.
*Brooke family of Whitchurch, Hampshire, Eng. Together with account of Acting Governor Robert Brooke and Col. Ninian Beall of Md. and some of their descendants. T. W. Balch. Phila., Allen, Lane and Scott, 1899, 1st ed. MHS; DAR.
B. B. Browne pedigree chart. Soc. Col. Wars, Md. Johnston. 1905, p. 8. MHS.
Browne-Cochrane-Brooke-Neale-Bennett chart. File case, MHS.
*Burke's landed gentry. Amer. Families. 1939. MHS.
Chart. B. B. Browne. Framed, MHS. Corrections; Md. Hist. Mag., 1924, v. 19, p. 401–2.
Children of Alex P. and M. C. Hill. Ms. MHS.
C. Johnston pedigree chart, plate 2. Soc. Col. Wars, Md. Johnston. 1905, p. 54. MHS.
Col. families of U. S. A. Mackenzie. V. 1; v. 3; v. 4; v. 5; v. 6; v. 7, p. 178. MHS; DAR.
Copy of note book about Brooke and allied families. File case A. MHS.
Daughter of Md.; Mother of Texas. Bell. MHS; DAR.
Descendants of Col. Thomas White. Morris. MHS.
Dorsey-Duvall-Coale-Buchanan-Borden-Brooke and allied families. Newsp. clipp. and other printed matter. MHS.
Dorsey Papers. Ms. MHS.
Duckett chart. MHS.
Freeman family. Col. and Revolutionary families of Phila. Jordan. 1933, v. 1, pp. 323–28.
*Geneal. V. 1 and 2. Ms. MHS.
*Geneal. R. D. Culver. Ind. 1924. MHS.
Geneal. and memorial encyc. of Md. Spencer. 1909, v. 1. MHS; DAR.
Geneal. of family of Gideon Gilpin. MHS.
Hamilton family of Charles Co. Kelly. MHS.
†Hist. of West. Md. Scharf. V. 1, pp. 774–75. MHS; DAR.
R. B. Keyser pedigree chart, plate 2. Soc. Col. Wars, Md. Johnston. 1905, p. 56. MHS.
Mrs. H. DeCourcy Wright Thom Keyser chart. MHS.
King and Queen Cos., Va.; hist. and geneal. Bagby, 1908.
*Lineage Bk., Daughters of Founders and Patriots. V. 18, pp. 84–85. MHS; DAR.
Lineage Bks., Natl. Soc. of Daughters of Amer. Col., v. 1, p. 87; v. 2, p. 66, 257; v. 4, p. 85. MHS; DAR.
Manly chart. MHS.
Marshall of Marshall Hall. Natl. Geneal. Soc. Quart., v. 19, no. 1, p. 1; no. 4, pp. 86–96.
Md. families. Culver. Ms. Personal list.
Memorial to Thomas Potts, Jr. James. MHS.
Memoirs of Roger Brooke Taney. Tyler. MHS.
Neale family of Md. The Times, Balto., Sunday, Dec. 27, 1885. Scrap Book, no. 7. MHS.
Our Brooke geneal. R. Dillon Culver. (Thomas Brooke, Wash. Co., 1734–88, p. 1.) Veedersburg, Ind., 1924, pamph. MHS.
Parr chart. MHS.
Patriotic Md. Md. Soc. of S. A. R., 1930. MHS; DAR.
Pedigree of Edwin Austin Baughman. Soc. Col. Wars Md. Culver. 1940. MHS; DAR.
Pedigree of Duncan Keener Brent. Soc. Col. Wars Md. Culver. 1940. MHS; DAR.
Pedigree of Walter Ireland Dawkins. Soc. Col. Wars Md. Culver. 1940. MHS; DAR.
Pedigree of Coleman Randall Freeman. Soc. Col. Wars Md. Culver. 1940. MHS; DAR.
Pedigree of Henry Irvine Keyser, II. Soc. Col. Wars Md. Culver. 1940. MHS; DAR.
Pedigree of W. Wallace McKaig. Soc. Col. Wars Md. Culver. 1940. MHS; DAR.
Pedigree of Charles O'Donnell Mackall. Soc. Col. Wars Md. Culver. 1940. MHS; DAR.
Pedigree of Franklin Buchanan Owen. Soc. Col. Wars Md. Culver. 1940. MHS; DAR.
Pedigree of Rev. Sam'l. Tagart Steele. Soc. Col. Wars Md. Culver. 1940. MHS; DAR.
Pedigree of Alfred Jenkins Tormey. Soc. Col. Wars Md. Culver. 1940. MHS; DAR.
Pedigree of Malcolm Van Vechten Tyson. Soc. Col. Wars Md. Culver. 1940. MHS; DAR.
Pedigree of Wm. Emory Waring, Jr. Soc. Col. Wars Md. Culver. 1940. MHS; DAR.
Pedigree of Mason Locke Weems Williams. Soc. Col. Wars Md. Culver. 1940. MHS; DAR.
*Pennington Papers. Ms. MHS.
Portfolio; contains rubbings from brasses of Brooke family of Whitchurch, Hampshire, Eng. Ms. MHS.
Posey chart. MHS.
Price ancestral data (maternal). Bd. Ms. MHS.
Raisin chart. MHS.
St. Barnabas P. E. churchyard. Typed ms. MHS; DAR.
St. Joseph's R. C. churchyard, Worcester Co., Hudson. Md. O. R. Soc. Bull., no. 3, p. 64.
St. Paul's Parish, Balto. V. 1. Mss. MHS.
Semmes and allied families. Semmes. MHS.
*Semmes. Geneal. Coll. Ms. MHS.
*Side lights on Md. hist. Richardson. V. 2, p. 32. MHS. DAR.
Some Md. and Va. ancestors. Bell. Natl. Geneal. Soc. Quart., v. 19, no. 4, pp. 86–96.
Miss Kate Steele chart. MHS.
Stevenson chart. MHS.
Student at Harvard, 1650. Ms. MHS.
*The Sun, Balto., Nov. 29, 1903; Sept. 25, Oct. 9 (Va.), 1904.
Taney and allied families. Silverson. MHS; DAR.
Thomas Book. Thomas. Pp. 218–23. Lib. Cong.; MHS.
Miss Eliza Thomas chart. MHS.

Virginians and Marylanders at Harvard College in 17th century. William and Mary Quart., 2nd. series, v. 13, no. 1, p. 1.
Zimmerman-Waters and allied families. Allen. Pp. 112–25. MHS. DAR.
See Beall-Gantt-Brooke.
See Bremond. Abr. Compend. Amer. Geneal. Virkus. V. 1, p. 407. DAR.
See Browne-Cochrane-Brooke-Neale-Bennett.
See Cooke.
See Sewall-Brooke-Darnall-Beall.
See Sewall-Darnall-Brooke-Calvert-Lee.

Brooke, John. Will, 1763. Ms. File case, DAR.

Brooke, Mary. Corrections. J. B. C. Nicklin. M. H. Mag., 1926, v. 26, pp. 285–323; 1935, v. 30, pp. 180–81.

Brooke, Robt., acting Gov. of Md., 1652. Pa. Soc. of Col. Gov., v. 1.
Geneal., 1602–1828. Edw. Stabler, Jr. 2 vols. Ms. Filing Case A. MHS.
*Note. H. H. Hall. M. H. Mag., 1910, v. 5, p. 200.
(To Md. in 1650.) Chart; arms. Dr. B. B. Browne. Printed in London, for Douglas H. Thomas, Balto., 1912. MHS; DAR.

Brooke, Thomas, acting Gov. of Md., 1720. Pa. Soc. of Col. Gov., v. 1.

***Brooke Family.** Wilson Mss. Coll., no. 6. MHS.

Brooke Family, Va. Va. Mag. Hist. and Biog., v. 9, pp. 315, 435, through v. 20.

Brooke Line. Col. and Revolutionary lineages of Amer. 1939, v. 2, pp. 69–74. MHS.
Lilburn family. Col. and Revolutionary families of Phila. Jordan. 1933, v. 1, pp. 382–98.
T. M. Smith pedigree charts, plate 2. Soc. Col. Wars, Md. Johnston. 1905, p. 96. MHS.

Brooke-Baker. Pedigree chart of Robert Brooke and Mary Baker. De La Brooke, St. Mary's Co. Printed in Eng. for Ellen B. Culver Bowen. 52 coats of arms. Mitchell, Hughes, Clarke, London. MHS; DAR.

Brooke-Hill-Perry. Abr. Compend. Amer. Geneal. Virkus. V. 4, pp. 488–89. DAR.

Brooke-Plunkett. Chart. From Robert Gilmor Papers. Photos. of mss. MHS.

Brooke-Taylor. Chart, photos., complete in 1 sheet. Cary Geneal. Coll. Ms. MHS.

***Brooke-Zimmerman.** Lineage Bk. Daughters of Amer. Colonists. V. 4, p. 85. MHS; DAR.

Brookings, Cecil Co. Abr. Compend. Amer. Geneal. Virkus. V. 1, pp. 497–98. DAR.

Brooks. Bible rec. Upper Penins. East. Shore., p. 244–50. MHS; DAR.
Brooks family and Hellings family. Ms. File case, DAR.
Cole-Price chart. Cary Geneal. Coll. Ms. MHS.
Col. families of U. S. A. Mackenzie. V. 5, p. 88. MHS.
Wm. Conway of Md. and Pa. Ms. File case, DAR.
Descendants of Joran Kyn. Pa. Mag., v. 7, p. 299.
Gaylord or Gaillard family. Brooks. MHS.
Harryman chart. Cary Geneal. Coll. Ms. MHS.
McCormick chart. MHS.
McCormick family. Pa. Geneal. Egle. P. 416. MHS.
Monumental City. Howard. MHS; DAR.
Patriotic Md. Md. Soc. of S. A. R., 1930. MHS; DAR.
St. Paul's Parish, Balto. V. 1, 2, 3, 4. Mss. MHS.
Mrs. J. G. Thomas. Chart. MHS.
Wallis chart. MHS.

Brooks, Chauncy. Geneal. and memorial encyc. of Md. Spencer. 1909, v. 2, p. 546. MHS; DAR.

Brooks, Walter B. Geneal. and memorial encyc. of Md. V. 2, p. 374. MHS; DAR.

Brooks, Mrs. Walter Booth (Caroline Cole). Chart. Col. Dames, Chap. I. MHS.

Brooks-Gaylord Line. Balto., its hist., its people. Hall. V. 2. MHS; DAR.

***Brooks-Woolford.** Notes. D. A. R. Mag., Oct., 1914, v. 45, p. 45.

Brookshaw, Brookshawe. Somerset Co. Court Book. Tilghman. 1937. Ms. DAR.

Broome. Gantt geneal. Ms. MHS.
†Med. Annals Md. Cordell. 1903, p. 333. MHS.
St. Paul's Parish, Balto. V. 2. Mss. MHS.

Broord. Naturalizations in Md., 1666–1765; Laws. Bacon. MHS.

Brosius. Md. tombstone rec. Md. Geneal. Rec. Com., 1937, Parran, pp. 1, 25. Mss. DAR.

Brotherton. St. Paul's Parish, Balto. V. 1, 2. Mss. MHS.

Brothres. St. Paul's Parish, Balto. V. 1. Mss. MHS.

Broughton. St. Paul's Parish, Balto. V. 2. Mss. MHS.
Somerset Co. Court Book. Tilghman. 1937. Ms. DAR.

Broughton, Draughton. Rehobeth P. E. churchyard, Somerset Co. Md. Geneal. Rec. Com., 1937, Mrs. Lines. Mss. DAR.

***Broun Family,** Va. Broun Family of Va. Copied by Henry I. Kirk. Jan., 1927. Ms. MHS.

Brow. St. Paul's Parish, Balto. V. 1. Mss. MHS.

Browder-Calvert. Abr. Compend. Amer. Geneal. Virkus. V. 4, p. 693. MHS.

Brower. St. Paul's Parish, Balto. V. 2. Mss. MHS.

Browhan. Christ P. E. Church cemetery, Cambridge. Steele. 1936. MHS; DAR.

Brown. Ancestry of Rosalie Morris Johnson. Johnson. 1905. MHS; DAR.
Mrs. Lee Barroll chart. MHS.
Mrs. R. Barton, Jr., charts. MHS.
Beall and Bell families. Beall. MHS.
†Bench and Bar of Md. Sams and Riley. 1901, v. 2, pp. 484, 647. Lib. Cong.; MHS; Peabody Lib.
Bible rec. Upper Penins. East. Shore. Bd., Mss. MHS; DAR.
Britton Scrap Book V. 1. Ms. MHS.
*Dr. Gustavus Brown, Charles Co. J. T. Howard Repr., pamph., 1937. MHS.
†Doctors Gustavus Brown of lower Md. E. F. Cordell. Balto., 1902.
(33 mss.) See Burchinal-Howard families. Ms. File case, DAR.
Centreville cemetery. Md. O. R. Soc. Bull., no. 1, pp. 41–47.
Col. families of U. S. A. Mackenzie. V. v. 2, p. 148; v. 5. MHS. DAR.

Brown. Cummings chart. Lib. Cong.; MHS; DAR.
†Day-Star of Amer. Freedom. Davis. p. 229. MHS. DAR.
See Elkins. Abr. Compend. Amer. Geneal. Virkus. V. 1, p. 588; v. 6, p. 210. DAR.
See Field. Abr. Compend. Amer. Geneal. Virkus. V. 1, p. 599. DAR.
First families of Md. The Post, Balto., Feb. 2, 3, 4, 6, 7, 8, 1933. Newsp. clipp., bd. MHS.
Frederick Co. tombstone inscriptions. Gruder. Natl. Geneal. Soc. Quart., 1919, v. 8, nos. 1, 2.
Gantt geneal. Ms. MHS.
Griffith geneal. Griffith. MHS; DAR.
Hazelhurst charts. MHS.
†(146 ref). Hist. of Frederick Co. Williams. MHS; DAR.
†Hundred years of merchant banking. J. C. Brown. M.H.S.
Md. families. Culver. Ms. Personal list.
Meade relations. Prichard. DAR.
†Med. Annals Md. Cordell. 1903, pp. 326, 333–35. MHS.
Mt. Carmel burial ground, Unity, Montgomery Co. Md. Geneal Rec. Com., 1934–35, p. 85. Mss. DAR.
Old Somerset. Torrence. MHS; DAR.
Pedigree of Duncan Keener Brent. Soc. Col. Col. Wars Md. Culver. 1940. MHS; DAR.
Perin chart. MHS.
Portrait and biog. rec. of Sixth Cong. Dist. of Md. 1898, pp. 387, 714, 726. MHS; DAR.
Rec. of Stepney Parish. MHS; DAR.
Rogers. Coll. Ms. MHS.
Rumsey-Smithson family rec. bk. Md. Geneal. Rec. Com., 1932, pp. 63-158. DAR.
St. Barnabas P. E. churchyard. Typed ms. MHS; DAR.
St. Paul's churchyard, Kent Co. Md. O. R. Soc. Bull., no. 2, pp. 54–65. MHS.
St. Paul's Parish, Balto. V. 1, 2, 3, 4, 5. Mss. MHS.
St. Thomas' Parish, Balto. Co. Bd. ms. MHS. Also: Md. Geneal. Rec. Com., 1937, pp. 109–82. Mss. DAR.
Smithson-Rumsey rec. bk. Ms. MHS.
*The Sun, Balto., June 7, 1903 (Scotch).
Thomas Book. Thomas. P. 224. Lib. Cong.; MHS.
White Geneal. Tree. MHS.
Whiting-Little-Horner-Brown. Va. families. MHS.
Mrs. J. Whitridge Williams chart 1. MHS.
*Wicomico Co. families. Tilghman Ms. pp. 56, 96. DAR.
See Smith, (Samuel)-McKim-Spear-Brown.
See Tyler-Brown.
See Wilkinson-Brown-Bullitt-Gregoire.

Brown, Buck's Co., Pa. Cary Geneal Coll. Ms. MHS.

Brown, Dorchester Co. Lineage Bks., Natl. Soc. of Daughters of Amer. Col., v. 2, p. 297; v. 3, p. 107. MHS; DAR.

Brown, Talbot Co. H. Mullikin pedigree chart, plate 1. Soc. Col. Wars, Md. Johnston. 1905, p. 74. MHS.

Brown, Va. Peale Geneal. Coll. Ms. MHS.

†**Brown, Abel.** Garrison Church. Allen. MHS; DAR.

***Brown, Abell.** Side lights on Md. Hist. Richardson. V. 2, p. 302. MHS; DAR.

Brown, Alexander. Abr. Compend. Amer. Geneal. Virkus. V. 1, p. 502. DAR.
*Alexander Brown and his descendants, 1764–1916. Mary E. Brown. East Orange, N. J., Abbey Printshop, priv. pr., 1917.
†Balto., hist. and biog. Richardson and Bennett. 1871, pp. 195–98. MHS; DAR.
†Chronicles of Balto. Scharf. 1874, p. 468. MHS; DAR.
†Hist. of Balto. City and Co. Scharf. Pp. 474–75. MHS.
†Men of mark in Md. Johnson. V. 4. DAR; Enoch Pratt Lib.
Monumental City. Howard. MHS; DAR.

†**Brown, Arthur G.** Men of mark in Md. Johnson. V. 1. DAR; Enoch Pratt Lib.

***Brown, B. B.** Folder. MHS.

***Brown, David.** And his descendants of Rich Hill, 1708. Ms. MHS.

†**Brown, Frank.** Governors of Md. Buchholz. P. 248. MHS.
†Hist of West. Md. Scharf. V. 2, pp. 870, 874. MHS; DAR.

†**Brown, G. Stewart.** Geneal. and mem. encyc. of Md. Spencer. V. 2, p. 414. MHS; DAR.

†**Brown, G. W.** Balto., hist. and biog. Richardson and Bennett. 1871, pp. 199–206. MHS; DAR.

Brown, George. Geneal. and memorial encyc. of Md. Spencer. V. 2, p. 371. MHS; DAR.

Brown, Dr. Gustavus. Sydney-Smith and Clagett-Price families. Price. P. 279. MHS; DAR.

Brown, Dr. Gustavus, Port Tobacco. Immediate descendants. D. C. Geneal. Rec. Com., 1936–37, v. 31, pt. 2, pp. 323–24. DAR.

Brown, Dr. Gustavus, Rich Hill, Charles Co. Va. geneal. Hayden. Pp. 147–201. MHS; DAR.

Brown, James Dorsey, Jr. Pedigree. Soc. Col. Wars Md. Culver. 1940. MHS; DAR.

†**Brown, Joshua** (1717–98), Nottingham, Md., and Pa. Index to biog. sketches pub. in "The Friend," v. 26, v. 27. Pub. Geneal. Soc. Pa., v. 3, no. 2, pp. 109–34.

Brown, Samuel. Bible rec., 1747–1847. Md. O. R. Soc. Bull., 1913, no. 3, pp. 34–36.
Patriotic Md. Md. Soc. of S. A. R., 1930. MHS; DAR.

Brown, Mrs. Thomas Richardson (Jean McComb Albert). Chart. Col. Dames, Chap. I. MHS.

***Brown, William.** William Brown of Md. Boston, Houghton Mifflin Co., 1895.
Chart of William Brown (from Scotland to Va.). Descendants. E. M. Weeks, Wash. File case, DAR.

Brown Family. Anne Arundel Co. Notes. Md. Geneal. Bull., v. 1, p. 32.
*Bible rec. MHS.
*Side lights on Md. hist. Richardson. V. 2, p. 286. MHS; DAR.

***Brown Family,** Balto. Family of Nathaniel and Mary Ann (Hopkins) Morison. Leaflet. MHS.

Brown Family, Columbiana, Ohio. Chart (Md., Ohio, Pa., and Va. Maj. W. C. Brown, U. S. A. Retired. Printed Jan. 11, 1936. File case, DAR.

***Brown-Griffith,** Dorchester Co. Lineage Bk. Daughters of Amer. Colonists, V. 3, pp. 5, 107. MHS; DAR.

Brown-Howard Families. Bible rec., 1774–1913. Md. Geneal. Rec. Com., v. 1, pp. 6–9. Mss. DAR.

Brown-Little Families, Carroll and Frederick Cos. Ms. File case, DAR.

Brown-Smith. Bible rec. of Dorchester and Somerset Cos. and Del. Pp. 11–12. DAR.

Brown-Toadvin. Bible rec. Md. Geneal. Rec. Com., 1937–38, p. 137. Mss. DAR.

Brown, Browne. Col. families of Amer. Lawrence. V. 2, pp. 36–37. MHS.
*Founders of Anne Arundel and Howard Cos. Warfield. Pp. 164–70, 296 (Gov. Frank), 490–93. MHS; DAR.
Geneal. of Henrietta Chauncy Wilson. Upshur. Bk. of photos. MHS.

Brown, Browne, Family. Md. Geneal. Rec. Com., 1933–34, pp. 48–49. Mss. DAR.

***Brown, Browne, Thomas.** Richardson. Burke's landed gentry. 1939. MHS.

Brownback. *See* Brumbach.

Browne. Autobiography of Summerfield Baldwin. MHS; DAR.
Col. families of U. S. A. Mackenzie. V. 1; v. 2, pp. 148–46; v. 6; v. 7. MHS; DAR.
Dorsey and allied families. Ms. MHS.
See Hoff. Abr. Compend. Amer. Geneal. Virkus. V. 1, p. 364. DAR.
Md. gleanings in Eng. Wills. M. H. Mag., 1907, v. 2, no. 3.
†Med. Annals Md. Cordell. 1903, p. 336. MHS.
Memoir. Roll of house of Lacy. Balto., 1928.
*Memorial. The Chad, 1638–1888. Isabel Brown Bulbley. Brooklyn, N. Y; pr. for family. MHS.
Naturalizations in Md., 1666–1765; Laws. Bacon. MHS.
*Old Kent. Hanson. P. 370. MHS; DAR.
Patriotic Md. Md. Soc. of S. A. R., 1930. MHS; DAR.
Pedigree and hist. of Washington family. Welles. P. 220. MHS.
Mrs. Morris Whitridge chart. MHS.
See Brown.

Browne, Balto. Dosey chart. MHS.

Browne, Bennet Bernard, M.D. Pedigree chart. Soc. Col. Wars, Md. Johnston. 1905, p. 8. MHS.

***Browne, Robert,** Wrighton. Side Lights on Md. hist. Richardson. V. 2, p. 307. MHS; DAR.

†Browne, William Hand (1828–1912). In memoriam. JHU; Enoch Pratt Lib.
Abr. Compend. Amer. Geneal. Virkus. V. 1, p. 365. DAR.

Browne - Cochrane - Brooke - Neale - Bennett Families. Chart. B. B. Browne. 1894. MHS.

Browner. Bible rec. D. C. Geneal Rec. Com., v. 31, pt. 1, pp. 66–67. Typed, bd. DAR.

Browning. St. Paul's Parish, Balto. V. 1, 2, 3. Mss. MHS.
St. Stephens Parish, Cecilton, Md. MHS; DAR.

Browning, Edward, Sr., Montgomery Co. Geneal.; died prior to 1776. Ms. File case, DAR.

Browning, Joshua. Geneal. Ms. File case, DAR.

Broxon. St. Stephens Parish, Cecilton, Md. MHS; DAR.

Bruce. Cabells and their kin. Brown. MHS.
†Hist of Allegany Co. Thomas and Williams. V. 1; v. 2. MHS; DAR.
†Hist. of West. Md. Scharf. V. 2, pp. 900, 1528. MHS; DAR.
Ind. Mag. Hist., March, 1927, v. 23, no. 1, p. 63. MHS.
†Med. Annals Md. Cordell. 1903, p. 336. MHS.
*Old Kent. Hanson. P. 263. MHS; DAR.
Peale Geneal. Coll. Ms. MHS.
St. Paul's Parish, Balto. V. 2, 3, 4. Mss. MHS.
See Morrison-Bruce.
See Wallace-Bruce.

Bruce, Charles Co. Abr. Compend. Amer. Geneal. Virkus. V. 1, p. 906. DAR.

Bruce, Va. Geneal. Va. Mag. Hist. and Biog., v. 11, pp. 197, 328, 441; v. 12, pp. 93–96, 446–53.
James chart. MHS.
*The Sun, Balto., Sept. 24 (Va.), Oct. 1, 1905.

Bruce, Mrs. Albert Cabell (Helen Eccleston Whitridge). Chart. Col. Dames, Chap. I. MHS.

Bruce, Mrs. Howard (Mary Graham Bowdoin). Chart. Col. Dames, Chap. I. MHS.

Bruce, O. Herman. Md. Soc., War of 1812, v. 3, no. 258. Ms. MHS.

Bruce, Wm. Cabell. Abr. Compend. Amer. Geneal. Virkus. V. 1, p. 506. DAR.
Balto. Va. Mag. Hist. and Biog., v. 12, p. 95.

Bruce-McPherson. Revolutionary war pension abs. Natl. Geneal. Soc. Quart., 1931, v. 19, no. 4, p. 110.

Bruder. Frederick Co. tombstone inscriptions. Gruder. Natl. Geneal. Soc. Quart., 1919, v. 8. nos. 1, 2.

Bruenton, Brewington. Wicomico Co. Families. Bible rec. Ms. DAR.
See Brewington.

Bruereton. *See* Brewington.

Bruff. Auld chart. MHS.
†Hist. of Balto. City and Co. Scharf. P. 413. MHS.
Hist. of Talbot Co. Tilghman. V. 2, p. 540. MHS; DAR.
Md. families. Culver. Ms. Personal list.
Morris family of Phila. Moon. V. 2, p. 647. MHS.
Preston at Patuxent. MHS.
St. Paul's Parish, Balto. V. 2. Mss. MHS.
*Some col. mansions and those who lived in them. Glenn. 2nd series, 1900, v. 2, pp. 390, 391, 394. MHS. Also: Preston at Patuxent. Pamph. repr. from above. MHS.
See Berry-Bruff-Dixon-Troth.

***Brumbach.** Geneal. Brumbaugh, Brumback, Brombaugh, Brownback, and many other connected families. B. G. M. Brumbaugh. N. Y., Fred H. Hitchcock, 1913.

Brumbaugh. Elliott chart. MHS.
Hagerstown tombstone inscriptions. Gruder. Natl. Geneal. Soc. Quart., 1919, v. 8, Nos. 1, 2.
See Brumbach.

Brumbaugh, Pa. Abr. Compend. Amer. Geneal. Virkus. V. 4, pp. 325, 474. MHS.

Brumfield, Jerome E. Md. Soc., War of 1812, v. 3, No. 225. Ms. MHS.

Brumwell. *See* Bromwell.
Brune. Abr. Compend. Amer. Geneal. Virkus. V. 1, p. 507. DAR.
†Balto., hist. and biog. Richardson and Bennett, 1871, pp. 207–10. MHS; DAR.
Beirne Chart. MHS.
†Bench and Bar of Md. Sams and Riley. 1901, v. 2, pp. 508, 524. Lib. Cong.; MHS; Peabody Lib.
Col. families of U. S. A. Mackenzie. V. 1, pp. 50–52. MHS; DAR.
Naturalizations in Md., 1666–1765; Laws. Bacon. MHS.
Monumental City. Howard. MHS; DAR.
Miss E. B. Randall chart. MHS.
St. Paul's Parish, Balto. V. 2, 3, 4. Mss. MHS.
Bruner Family. Ms. File case, DAR.
Brunner. First settlement of Germans in Md. Schultz. 1896. MHS.
*Frederick Co. families. Markell. Ms. Personal list.
Frederick Co. tombstone inscriptions. Gruder. Natl. Geneal. Soc. Quart., 1919, v. 8, nos. 1, 2.
†Hist. of Frederick Co. Williams. MHS; DAR.
Patriotic Md. Md. Soc. of S. A. R., 1930. MHS; DAR.
Brush. Mrs. W. H. Harris, Jr., chart. MHS.
Brush, E. N. Abr. Compend. Amer. Geneal. Virkus. V. 1, p. 158. DAR.
Brush, Graham. Abr. Compend. Amer. Geneal. Virkus. V. 1, p. 508. DAR.
Brush, Murray Peabody. Abr. Compend. Amer. Geneal. Virkus. V. 1, p. 508. DAR.
Pedigree. Soc. Col. Wars Md. Culver. 1940. MHS; DAR.
Brustchar. St. Paul's Parish, Balto. V. 2. Mss. MHS.
Bryan. Anne Arundel Co. tombstone inscriptions. Ms. DAR.
Col. families of U. S. A. Mackenzie. V. 1, pp. 53–55; v. 6, pp. 104–08; v. 7, pp. 119–23. MHS; DAR.
Hist. Dorchester Co. Jones. 1925, pp. 290–96. MHS; DAR.
Martin family, 1680–1934. Porcher. P. 37. DAR.
St. Paul's Parish, Balto. V. 1, 2, 3, 4. Mss. MHS.
†Bryan, Wm. S. Men of mark in Md. Johnson. V. 1, pp. 70, 76. DAR; Enoch Pratt Lib.
Bryan, Wm. Shepard, Jr. Geneal. and mem. encyc. of Md. Spencer. V. 1, p. 293. MHS; DAR.
Bryan Family. Bible rec., Kent Co. Md. Geneal. Rec. Com., 1932–33, v. 5. Mss. DAR.
Chart, photos. MHS.
Bryant. Col. families of U. S. A. Mackenzie. V. 2, pp. 150–56. MHS; DAR.
St. Paul's Parish Balto. V. 1. Mss. MHS.
†Tercentenary hist. of Md. Andrews. V. 2, p. 634. MHS; DAR.
Bryarly. Miss Cassandra Lee chart. MHS.
See Briarly.
Bryce. *See* Brice.
†Brydon. Hist. of Allegany Co. Thomas and Williams. V. 1, p. 1297, v. 2, pp. 896–98, 1270–72. MHS; DAR.
Brysen. St. Paul's Parish, Balto. V. 1. Mss. MHS.
Buchanan. Amer. Armory and Blue Book. Matthews. 1911–12, pp. 230, 386.
†Balto. Richardson and Bennett. 1871, p. 211. MHS; DAR.
Mrs. R. Barton, Jr., charts. MHS.
Miss M. S. Brogden chart. MHS.
*Buchanan and allied families (Pa.). C. E. Buchanan Rex. Norristown, Pa., Eureka Printing Co., 1931. DAR.
*Buchanan line. Mrs. R. T. Lemon. 1938. Ms. DAR.
H. D. G. Carroll Ms. Book. In H. F. Thompson Papers. MHS.
Chart, photos., 1 sheet. Cary Geneal. Coll. Ms. MHS.
Col. families of U. S. A. Mackenzie. V. 3. MHS; DAR.
Dorsey and allied families. Ms. MHS.
Dorsey-Duvall-Coale-Buchanan-Borden-Brooke and allied families. Newsp. clipp. and other printed matter. MHS.
Duckett chart. MHS.
Col. Nicholas Duvall family Records, Price. Bd. ms. MHS.
First families of Md. The Post, Balto., Feb. 2, 3, 4, 6, 7, 8, 1933. Newsp. clipp., bd. MHS.
Geneal. and mem. encyc. of Md. Spencer. V. 2, pp. 268–670. MHS; DAR.
Geneal. of descendants of Dr. Wm. Shippen, the Elder, Phila. Buchanan. P. 11. MHS.
See Harrison. Abr. Compend. Amer. Geneal. Virkus. V. 1, p. 167.
†Hist. of Allegany Co. Thomas and Williams. V. 1, v. 2. MHS; DAR.
Hist. of Talbot Co. Tilghman. V. 1, p. 587. MHS; DAR.
Hist. of Washington Co. Williams. Pp. 132, 452.
Hist. of West. Md. Scharf. V. 2, pp. 1115–16. MHS; DAR.
Howard-Montague-Warfield geneal. chart. Culver and Marye. MHS.
Mrs. T. C. Jenkins chart. MHS.
Md. families. Culver. Ms. Personal list.
†Med. Annals Md. Cordell. 1903, pp. 278, 337. MHS.
Milligan chart. MHS.
Pedigree. Geneal. of McKean family of Pa. Buchanan. P. 128, pedigree; pp. 214–16. children of Admiral Franklin Buchanan. MHS.
Pedigree of Francis Joseph Baldwin. Soc. Col. Wars Md. Culver. 1940. MHS; DAR.
Pedigree of Franklin Buchanan Owen. Soc. Col. Wars Md. Culver. 1940. MHS; DAR.
Pedigree of Wm. Handy Collins Vickers. Soc. Col. Wars Md. Culver. 1940. MHS; DAR.
Public Parks of Balto., no. 3, p. 12, MHS; DAR.
St. Paul's Parish, Balto. V. 1, 2, 3, 5. Mss. MHS.
St. Thomas' Parish, Balto. Co. Bd. ms. MHS. Also: Md. Geneal. Rec. Com., 1937, pp. 109–82. Mss. DAR.
Sherburne chart. MHS.
*The Sun, Balto. Oct. 27, Nov. 3, 1907.
West. Nottingham Cemetery. M. H. Mag., 1923, v. 18, p. 55.
(9 mss.) See Burchinal-Howard families. Ms. File case, DAR.

See Johnson-Buchanan.

Buchanan, Admiral Franklin, (1800–74; Confederates States Navy). Hist of Talbot Co. Tilghman. V. 1, pp. 587–99. MHS; DAR.
†First superintendent of Naval Academy at Annapolis. C. L. Lewis. 1929.
†(1800–74). M. H. Mag., v. 12, p. 203.

Buchanan, Dr. George (1698–1750). W. S. G. Williams pedigree chart. Soc. Col. Wars, Md. Johnston. 1905, pp. 128, 141. MHS.

†Buchanan, James M. Balto., hist. and biog. Richardson and Bennett. 1871, pp. 212–16. MHS; DAR.

Buchanan, John. Revolutionary rec. (died in Md. 1795). D. A. R. Mag.; v. 69, no. 3, p. 158.

†Buchanan, R. C. M. H. Mag., v. 12, p. 203.

Buchanan, Roberdeau, Incl. biog. of Gen. Daniel Roberdeau. 196 pp. Wash., D. C., 1876. DAR.
(1732–1804). Revolutionary war heroes. Cole. Bklet. Enoch Pratt Lib.

Buchanan, Gen. Wm. Westminister churchyard. Patriotic Marylander, v. 2, no. 4, pp. 54–60. MHS; DAR.

Buchanan Family. Ames Geneal. Coll. Ms. DAR.
Bantz Geneal. notes. Ms. MHS.
Buchanan family reminiscences. M. H. Mag., Sept., 1940, v. 35, no. 3, pp. 262–69.
*Chart. Ms. MHS.
Natl. Geneal. Soc. Quart., v. 24, p. 85; v. 25, pp. 14, 67.
Newsp. clipp. MHS.
Pedigree charts. Ms. MHS.
*Rec. Wm. M. Clemens. N. Y. pamph. ltd. ed. MHS.
*Wilson Mss. Coll., no. 9; no. 70. MHS.

Buchanan-Gittings. Abr. Compend. Amer. Geneal. Virkus. V. 4, p. 684. MHS.

***Buchanan-Lloyd.** Old Kent. Hanson. Pp. 34–35, 49, 181. MHS; DAR.

***Buchannan.** Wicomico Co. families. Tilghman. Ms., p. 97. DAR.

Buck, Balto. Co. Bible rec. Upper Penins. East. Shore., p. 219.
Bible rec. Md. Geneal. Rec. Com., 1924–25, v. 1, p. 11. Mss. DAR.
Bible rec. in Md. Bible rec: Sarah E. Stuart and Frances E. Stuart. 1926, p. 207. Typed., bd. DAR.
*Buck family of Buck's Co., Pa. W. J. Buck. Phila., 1893. MHS.
*Buck family of Va. Walter H. Buck. Balto., 1936, 1st ed. MHS.
Christ P. E. Church cemetery, Cambridge. Steele. 1936. MHS; DAR.
†Hist. of Washington Co. Williams. 1906, v. 2, p. 1167. MHS; DAR.
Md. families. Culver. Ms. Personal list.
†Med. Annals Md. Cordell. 1903, p. 338. MHS.
Merryman family. Culver. M. H. Mag., 1915, v. 10, pp. 176, 286.
*Rec. Eight family Bibles. MHS.
St. Paul's Parish, Balto. V. 1, 2, 3. Mss. MHS.
†Tercentenary hist. of Md. Andrews. V. 2, p. 293. MHS; DAR.

Buck, Rev. George. Md. Soc., War of 1812, v. 1, no. 135. Ms. MHS.

***Buck Family.** Bible rec., 1778–1891. Md. Geneal. Rec. Com., v. 1, pp. 12–13. DAR.

Buck Family, Va. Ms. MHS.

Buck-Simmonds-Trew. Bible rec. 3 Bibles. MHS.

Buckey. Frederick Co. tombstone inscriptions. Gruder. Natl. Geneal. Soc. Quart., 1919, v. 8, nos. 1, 2.
Getzendanner family of Frederick Co. 1890, pamph. MHS; DAR.
Hist. of Frederick Co. Williams. V. 2, pp. 854, 1068, 1129, 1596. MHS; DAR.
John Swadner and his descendants. Evans. 1919. Typed, bd. MHS.

***Buckingham.** Chronicles of Little, Lee, and Albert Buckingham families. MHS.
Geneal. of ancestors and descendants of John and Hannah (Fincher) Russell. Russell. 1887, 1889, pamph. MHS.
St. Paul's Parish, Balto., v. 1, 4. Mss. MHS.

Buckingham, Eng. and Balto. Bible rec., 1798–1855. Natl. Geneal. Soc. Quart., v. 22, no. 2 p. 45.
Little-Lee-Albert Buckingham families. Millie A. Little. 1936. MHS.
Russell family. Russell. 1889, 2nd ed. MHS.
†Tercentenary hist. of Md. Andrews. V. 4, p. 108. MHS; DAR.

Buckingham, C. Wesley. Md. Soc., War of 1812, v. 1, no. 28. Ms. MHS.

†Buckingham, Mrs. Grace (Laucks). Encyc. of Amer. biog. Amer. Hist. Soc., N. Y., 1928, v. 33, p. 174 (Pa. and Balto).

Buckingham Family. Notes. Ms. MHS.

***Buckler.** Buckleriana. Notices of family Buckler; coat of arms; charts. C. A. Buckler. Buckler of Baltimore, U. S. A., p. 11. London, 1886, 81 pp. MHS.
Hist. sketch of P. F. Eichelberger. Eichelberger.
†Med. Annals Md. Cordell. 1903, pp. 338–39. MHS.
Riggs of Anne Arundel, Frederick and Montgomery Cos. prior to 1663. Pamph. MHS.
St. Paul's Parish, Balto. V. 1, 3, 4. Mss. MHS.

Buckler, Mrs. H. Warren (Mary Coleman Herbert). Chart. Col. Dames, Chap. I. MHS.
Neill chart. MHS.

Buckler Line. Neill chart. MHS.

***Buckles Family,** Shepherdstown, W. Va. Notes. Ms. DAR.

Buckley. Geneal. notes of Thomas family. Thomas. MHS; DAR.
Lineage Bks., Natl. Soc. of Daughters of Amer. Col., v. 4, p. 17, MHS; DAR.
Patriotic Md. Md. Soc. of S. A. R., 1930. MHS; DAR.
Rec. of Stepney Parish. MHS; DAR.
St. Paul's Parish, Balto. V. 1, 2. Mss. MHS.
Thomas Book. Thomas. Lib. Cong.; MHS.
*Wilson Mss. Coll., no. 80. MHS.

Buckman Family. Garrison Church. Allen. P. 128. MHS; DAR.

Buckner. St. Paul's Parish, Balto. V. 1. Mss. MHS.

Budd. Peale Geneal. Coll. Ms. MHS.

Budd, Thomas, N. J. Pedigree of Townsend Scott, IV. Soc. Col. Wars Md. Culver. 1940. MHS; DAR.

Buely. Dobbin chart. MHS.

Buffington. Gen. Tobias Emerson Stansbury chart. MHS.
†Med. Annals Med. Cordell. 1903, p. 339. MHS.
Bulger. St. Paul's Parish, Balto. V. 1. Mss. MHS.
Bull. Harford Co. Hist. Soc. Mss. Coll. JHU.
Portrait and biog. rec. of Harford and Cecil Cos. 1897. Pp. 151, 173. MHS; DAR.
Rumsey-Smithson Bible rec. Md. Geneal. Rec. Com., 1932–33, v. 5, pp. 63–142. DAR.
Rumsey-Smithson family rec. bk. Md. Geneal. Rec. Com., 1932, pp. 124–29. DAR.
St. Paul's Parish, Balto. V. 1, 2. Mss. MHS.
Smithson-Rumsey rec. bk. Ms. MHS.
***Bull, Edmund** (1811–75). Ms. File case, MHS.
Bull, Robt. Berry. Md. Soc., War of 1812, v. 1, no. 129. Ms. MHS.
***Bullard.** Bullard and allied families. Edgar J. Bullard. Detroit, Mich., 1930. MHS.
Geneal. Pamph. MHS.
*Geneal. supplementary to Bullard and allied families. Pub. by E. J. Bullard. Port Austin, Mich., 1928. MHS.
Bullen. St. Paul's Parish, Balto. V. 1, 2. Mss. MHS.
Spring Hill Cemetery, Talbot Co. Md. O. R. Soc. Bull., no. 1, pp. 35–41. MHS.
Bullevent. St. Paul's Parish, Balto. V. 1. Mss. MHS.
Bullitt. Col. families of U. S. A. Mackenzie. V. 7. MHS; DAR.
See Wilkinson-Brown-Bullitt-Gregoire.
Lineage Bk., Order of Washington, pp. 48–55. MHS; DAR.
Bulloch. Col. families of U. S. A. Mackenzie. V. 2, pp. 157–62. MHS; DAR.
Bullock. Bible rec. of Dorchester and Somerset Cos. and Del. Pp. 13–21. DAR.
Bullock, Balto. French chart. MHS.
Bumap. Monumental City. Howard. MHS; DAR.
Bungey. St. Paul's Parish, Balto. V. 1. Mss. MHS.
†**Bunnecke, G.** Geneal. and mem. encyc. of Md. Spencer. V. 2, p. 730. MHS; DAR.
Bunting. Patriotic Md. Md. Soc. of S. A. R., 1930. MHS; DAR.
Burbage. Buckingham. Pres. churchyard, Worcester Co., Hudson. Bd. ms. MHS; DAR.
***Burbank Family.** And Bray, Welcome, Sedgley and Welsh families. G. B. Sedgley. Farmington, Me., Knowlton & McLeary Co., 1928, 1st ed. MHS.
Ms. MHS.
Burbeck. Lloyd family hist. of Wales, Pa., and Md. DAR.
***Burch.** Lineage Bk. Daughters of Amer. Col., v. 4, pp. 55–56. MHS; DAR.
Sacred Heart R. C. churchyard, Bushwood, St. Mary's Co. Md. Geneal. Rec. Com., 1929. Mss. DAR.
Burchanell. Lambdin chart. MHS.
***Burchardt.** Frederick Co. families. Markell. Ms. Personal list.
†**Burchinal.** Biog. cyc. of rep. men of Md. and D. C. P. 44. MHS; DAR.
Burchinal-Howard. Burchinal-Howard families. Contains 33 Brown mss; and 9 Buchanan mss. Ms. File case, DAR.
Burckhartt. Frederick Co. Abr. Compend. Amer. Geneal. Virkus. V. 6, p. 519. DAR.
Burd. Peale Geneal. Coll. Ms. MHS.
Burdsall. Matthews-Price chart. MHS.
Burford. Cary Geneal. Coll. Ms. MHS.
Mrs. G. C. Jenkins chart. MHS.
Burford, Thomas. Some early Col. Marylanders. M. H. Mag., 1920, v. 15, p. 65.
Burford, Thomas, Charles Co. McH. Howard pedigree chart. Soc. Col. Wars, Md. Johnston. 1905, pp. 42, 141. MHS.
Pedigree of Tilghman Goldsborough Pitts. Soc. Col. Wars Md. Culver. 1940. MHS; DAR.
Pedigree of Pleasants Pennington. Soc. Col. Wars Md. Culver. 1940. MHS; DAR.
Burgain. St. Paul's Parish, Balto. V. 1. Mss. MHS.
*Wicomico Co. families. Tilghman. Ms., p. 107. DAR.
Burgan. St. Paul's Parish, Balto. V. 1. Mss. MHS.
***Burges, Burgess.** Pennington Papers. Geneal. Ms. MHS.
See Burgess.
Burgess. Ances. rec. and portraits. Col. Dames of Amer. 1910, v. 2, p. 615. MHS; DAR.
Blakiston churchyard, Kent Co., Del., near Millington. Md. Geneal. Rec. Com., 1933–34, pp. 204–07, Mss. DAR.
Mrs. R. F. Brent chart. MHS.
Cary Geneal. Coll. Ms. MHS.
Col. families of Amer. Lawrence. V. 5, p. 88; v. 16, p. 86. MHS.
Descent of Lottie Repp Caldwell, from William the Conqueror. D. C. Geneal. Rec. Com., v. 34, pp. 30–33. Typed, bd. DAR.
*Founders of Anne Arundel and Howard Cos. Warfield. Pp. 49–55, 370, 438–39. MHS. DAR.
Griffith geneal. Griffith. MHS. DAR.
Hist. Graves of Md. and D. C. Ridgely. MHS.
*Lineage Bks. Natl. Soc. of Daughters of Amer. Col., v. 2, pp. 117, 339; v. 3, p. 276; v. 4, pp. 132, 310. MHS; DAR.
W. A. and S. W. Merritt pedigree charts, plate 2. Soc. Col. Wars, Md. Johnston. 1905, pp. 68, 141. MHS.
Parr chart. MHS.
Patriotic Md. Md. Soc. of S. A. R., 1930. MHS; DAR.
Pedigree of Harry Willson Falconer. Soc. Col. Wars Md. Culver. 1940. MHS; DAR.
Pedigree of Charles Worthington Hoff. Soc. Col. Wars Md. Culver. 1940. MHS; DAR.
Pedigree of Rt. Rev. Rogers Israel. Soc. Col. Wars Md. Culver. 1940. MHS; DAR.
Pedigree of W. Wallace McKaig. Soc. Col. Wars Md. Culver. 1940. MHS; DAR.
Pedigree of John Philemon Paca. Soc. Col. Wars Md. Culver. 1940. MHS; DAR.
Pedigree of Pleasants Pennington. Soc. Col. Wars Md. Culver. 1940. MHS; DAR.
Pedigree of Maurice Falconer Rodgers. Soc. Col. Wars Md. Culver. 1940. MHS; DAR.
Pedigree of Levin Gale Shreve. Soc. Col. Wars Md. Culver. 1940. MHS; DAR.
Pedigree of St. George Leakin Sioussat. Soc. Col. Wars Md. Culver. 1940. MHS; DAR.
Pedigree of Harrison Tilghman. Soc. Col. Wars Md. Culver. 1940. MHS; DAR.

Pedigree of Mrs. J. Whitridge Williams chart 2. MHS.
Pedigree of Mason Locke Weems Williams. Soc. Col. Wars Md. Culver. 1940. MHS; DAR.
Revolutionary war pension abs., Natl. Geneal. Soc. Quart., v. 17, no. 4, p. 63.
St. Paul's churchyard, Kent Co. Md. O. R. Soc. Bull. no. 2, pp. 54–65. MHS.
St. Paul's Parish, Balto. V. 1, 2. Mss. MHS.
*Side lights on Md. hist. Richardson. V. 2, p. 36. MHS; DAR.
*The Sun, Balto., Nov. 1, 8, 15, 22, Dec. 6, 27, 1903.
Talbott of "Poplar Knowle". Shirk. MHS; DAR.
Uhler Bible rec. Md. Geneal. Rec. Com., v. 2. DAR.
Uhler Bible rec. Ms. MHS.
Warfields of Md. Warfield. MHS.
See Burges.
See Uhler-Anderson-Burgess-Galloway.
Burgess Family, Md. and Va. Ms. File case, DAR.
Burgess Line. Col. and Revolutionary lineages in Amer. 1939, v. 2, p. 125. MHS.
Gaither, Va. and Md. Col. and Revolutionary families of Phila. Jordan. 1933, v. 1, pp. 144–67.
Burgess, Burges. Col. families of U. S. A. Mackenzie. V. 6, pp. 363–68. MHS; DAR.
Burgesser. Zion Reformed Church, Hagerstown. Md. Geneal. Rec. Com., 1934–35. Mss. DAR.
Burghes. St. Paul's Parish, Balto. V. 1. Mss. MHS.
Burgis. St. Stephens Parish, Cecilton, Md. MHS; DAR.
Burgoyne. St. Paul's Parish, Balto. V. 1. Mss. MHS.
Times Dispatch, Richmond, Va., Nov. 22, 1903. Newsp. clipp.
Burk. St. Paul's Parish, Balto. V. 1. Mss. MHS.
St. Stephens Parish, Cecilton, Md. MHS; DAR.
Burke. Col. families of East. Shore and their descendants. Emory. 1900, pp. 174–83. MHS.
Md. families. Culver. Ms. Personal list.
St. Paul's Parish, Balto. V. 2. Mss. MHS.
Trinity P. E. churchyard, St. Mary's City. Md. O. R. Soc. Bull., no. 3, p. 59.
Burkele. Naturalizations in Md., 1666–1765. Laws. Bacon. MHS.
†**Burkett, Burkhardt.** Hist. of West. Md. Scharf. V. 1, p. 606. MHS; DAR.
Burkhardt. *See* Burkett.
Burkhart. Cummings chart. Lib. Cong., MHS; DAR.
Hagerstown tombstone inscriptions. Gruder. Natl. Geneal. Soc. Quart., 1919, v. 8, nos. 1, 2.
Burland. St. Paul's Parish, Balto. V. 1, 2. Mss. MHS.
Burleson. Abr. Compend. Amer. Geneal. Virkus. V. 1, p. 519. DAR.
Burn, Burns. St. Paul's Parish, Balto. V. 1, 2, 3. Mss. MHS.
Burnam. St. Stephens Parish, Cecilton, Md. MHS; DAR.
Burnet, Burnett. St. Paul's Parish, Balto. V. 1, 2, 3. Mss. MHS.
Burnett. St. John's R. C. Church cemetery, Montgomery Co. Md. Geneal. Rec. Com., 1926, p. 27. Mss. DAR.
Burnham. St. Stephens Parish, Cecilton, Md. MHS; DAR.
Burnor. St. Paul's Parish, Balto. V. 1. Mss. MHS.
Burns. Balto., its hist., its people. Hall. V. 2. MHS; DAR.
David and Marcia Burns. S. Helen Fields. Pamph. DAR.
†Hist. of Balto. City and Co. Scharf. Pp. 471–72. MHS.
Holdens Cemetery, Kent Co. Md. Geneal. Rec. Com., 1932, v. 5, p. 211. Mss. DAR.
Monumental City. Howard. MHS; DAR.
See Burn.
Burns, Daniel Tombstone, 1867. Mt. Olivet U. B. Church, Pleasant Walk, Frederick Co.
***Burns, David and Marcia.** David and Marcia Burns. S. H. Field. DAR.
†**Burns, Francis.** Balto., hist. and biog. Richardson and Bennett. 1871, pp. 217–19. MHS; DAR.
Burrage. Mrs. Charles Carter chart. MHS.
Chart, photos., complete in 1 sheet. Cary. Geneal. Coll. Ms. MHS.
Sweeter chart. MHS.
Mrs. G. H. Williams, Jr., chart. MHS.
Burrell. Cummings chart. Lib. Cong., MHS; DAR.
St. Paul's Parish, Balto. V. 2. Mss. MHS.
Burrell Family. Monnet family geneal. Monette. Pp. 370, 392, 409, 1112–15. MHS.
Burris. Dulaney churchyard, near Massey, Kent Co. Md. Geneal. Rec. Com., 1933–34, pp. 210–12. Mss. DAR.
Quisenberry family. Quisenberry. MHS.
See Clark-Burriss.
Burroughs. Dent family of Md. Ms. File case, DAR.
Makemie Memorial Pres. churchyard, Snow Hill, Worcester Co. Hudson. Bd. ms. MHS; DAR. Also: Md. Geneal. Rec. Com., Mrs. Lines. Mss. DAR.
Md. gleanings in Eng. Wills. M. H. Mag., 1907, v. 2, no. 3.
Miss Kate Steele chart. MHS.
Burrows. St. Paul's Parish, Balto. V. 1, 2. Mss. MHS.
Burton. Ancestry of Georgie H. B. Burton, Lexington, Ky. Data collected by herself, and edited by H. M. Fich. 1933. Ms. MHS.
*Ancestry of Georgia. H. B. Burton, of Lexington, Kentucky. (Mostly Va. Families.) Charts and Ms. Bd. 1933. MHS.
*Chronicles of Col. Va., relating to Burtons of Valley of James and Appomattox rivers, with especial reference to ancestry of Jesse Burton of Lynchburg (1750?–95). F. B. Harrison. Priv. pr., 1933. MHS; DAR.
Fisher family, Sussex Co., Del., and Md. Ms. MHS.
Fisher family. Morse. MHS.
Geneal. of Henrietta Chauncy Wilson. Upshur. Bk. of photos. MHS.
Harrison-Waples and allied families. Harrison. MHS.
St. Paul's Parish, Balto. V. 1, 2, 3, 4. Mss. MHS.
Smithson-Rumsey rec. bk. Ms. MHS.

Burton, Henry and Abell, Va. With notes on the Harmon family. Ms. File case, DAR.
Burton, Robert. Pedigree chart, plates 1 and 2. Soc. Col. Wars, Md. Johnston. 1905, pp. 9–10. MHS.
Burton-Diefendorf-Hendree-Machen-Paine. Abr. Compend. Amer. Geneal. Virkus. V. 4, p. 657. MHS.
Burwell. Cary Geneal. Coll. Ms. MHS.
Selden chart. MHS.
See Harrison-Burwell.
***Burwell,** Va. The Sun, Balto., May 12, 19, 26, June, 2, 1907.
Burwell, Lewis, Va. Pedigree of Leigh Bonsal. Soc. Col. Wars Md. Culver. 1940. MHS; DAR.
Burwell Line, Va. W. A. Moale pedigree charts, plate 1. Soc. Col. Wars, Md. Johnston. 1905, pp. 72, 141. MHS.
Buse. Somerset Co. Court Book. Tilghman. 1937. Ms. DAR.
See Boice.
***Busey, Sam'l.** Will, 1770. D. C. Geneal. Rec. Com., 1930–32, v. 5, p. 183. Typed, bd. DAR.
***Busey Family.** Souvenir, with autobiog. sketch. S. C. Busey. (Md. ref., pp. 13–16.) 1896. DAR.
†**Bush** (killed in action, War of 1812). M. H. Mag., v. 12, p. 203.
St. Paul's Parish, Balto. V. 1, 2. Mss. MHS.
*Wicomico Co. families. Tilghman. Ms., p. 125. DAR.
See Cannan-Bush-Calder-Joiner-Meeks.
Bushrod. Ances. rec. and portraits. Col. Dames of Amer. V. 2, p. 450. MHS; DAR.
*Bushrod family. J. Fautleroy. William and Mary Quart., 2nd series, v. 16, p. 319.
Cary Geneal. Coll. Ms. MHS.
Mrs. H. De Courcy Wright Thom chart. MHS.
Busick. Still Pond Church and cemetery. Md. O. R. Soc. Bull., no. 2, pp. 65–75.
Buss. *See* Boice.
†**Bussard.** Hist. of Frederick Co. Williams. MHS; DAR.
Bussey. See Hewes. Abr. Compend. Amer. Geneal. Virkus. V. 1, p. 340. DAR.
Harford Co. Hist. Soc. Mss. Coll. JHU.
Patriotic Md. Md. Soc. of S. A. R., 1930. MHS; DAR.
Bussy, Bussey. St. Paul's Parish, Balto. V. 2. Mss. MHS.
†**Busteed, C. A.** Men of mark in Md. Johnson. V. 4, p. 406. DAR; Enoch Pratt Lib.
Butcher. Md. gleanings in Eng. Wills. M. H. Mag., 1907, v. 2, no. 3.
Buthaey. St. Paul's Parish, Balto. V. 1. Mss. MHS.
Butler. Denison family of Mass. to Harford Co. Ms. DAR.
*Geneal. C. A. Claypool. Typed in Binder. DAR.
Geneal. of Henrietta Chauncy Wilson. Upshur. Bk. of photos. MHS.
Geneal. Rogers Coll. Ms. MHS.
†Hist. of Allegany Co. Thomas and Williams. V. 2, pp. 764–68. MHS; DAR.
Hist. of Harford Co. Preston. P. 192. MHS; DAR.
Hist. of Talbot Co. Tilghman. 1915. V. 1, p. 64. MHS; DAR.
Md. families. Culver. Ms. Personal list.
Md. gleanings in Eng. Wills. M. H. Mag., 1907, v. 2, no. 3.
Portrait and biog. rec. of Harford and Cecil Cos. 1897. Pp. 145, 478–79, 516–17. MHS; DAR.
Rodgers Bible rec. Ms. MHS.
St. Barnabas P. E. churchyard. Typed ms. MHS; DAR.
St. Thomas' Parish, Balto. Co. Bd. ms. MHS. Also: Md. Geneal. Rec. Com., 1937, pp. 109–82. Mss. DAR.
*The Sun, Balto., Nov. 27, 1904.
See Ormonde.
Butler, Mass. Chart, photos., complete in 1 sheet. Cary Geneal. Coll. Ms. MHS.
Butler-Houston-Ellicott, Frederick Co. 2 family Bibles. DAR.
Butler-Wells-White. Notes. D. A. R. Mag., v. 70, no. 2, pp. 129–30.
Butler, Buttler. St. Paul's Parish, Balto. V. 1, 2, 3. Mss. MHS.
Butt. Col. Nicholas Duvall family rec. Price. Bd. ms. MHS.
Butt, Anne Aundel Co. tombstone inscriptions. Ms. DAR.
Butt Family, Md. and Va. Ms. File case, DAR.
Butterfield. Butterfield and allied families. Chart. L. B. Clarke. (Mostly New Eng.) MHS.
Butterworth. Gibbs chart. MHS.
St. Paul's Parish, Balto. V. 1. Mss. MHS.
Buttler. *See* Butler.
Button. St. Paul's Parish, Balto. V. 1, 2. Mss. MHS.
***Buxton.** Frederick Co. families. Markell. Ms. Personal list.
Byas. St. Paul's Parish, Balto. V. 2. Mss. MHS.
Bye. Warner hist. Osler. MHS.
***Bye, Thomas.** Thomas Bye of Buckingham, Pa. A. E. Bye. (Thomas Bye married daughter of Andrew Ellicott.)
Byerly. Frederick Co. tombstone inscriptions. Gruder. Natl. Geneal. Soc. Quart., 1919, v. 8, nos. 1, 2.
Hist. of St. Paul's Evan. Luth. Church, Balto. Co. MHS.
Byers. Hist. and geneal. rec. of descendants of Paul Weitzel. Hayden. 1883, pamph. MHS.
Md. tombstone rec. Md. Geneal. Rec. Com., 1937, Parran, pp. 1, 2. Mss. DAR.
Byrd. Southern Bapt. Church cemetery, Worcester Co. Md. Geneal. Rec. Com., 1937, Mrs. Lines. Mss. DAR.
Cary Geneal. Coll. Ms. MHS.
Selden chart. MHS.
Byrd, from Va. to Somerset Co. Turner Geneal. Coll. Ms. MHS.
Byrd, Va. Abr. Compend. Amer. Geneal. Virkus. V. 1, p. 525. DAR.
*The Sun, Balto., Aug. 7, 1904.
Byrd, J. E. Md. Soc., War of 1812, v. 3, no. 213. Ms. MHS.
Byrd, Col. Wm., Va. W. A. Moale pedigree charts. Soc. Col. Wars, Md. Johnston. 1905, pp. 72, 141. MHS.
†**Byrne.** Med. Annals Md. Cordell. 1903, pp. 340–44. MHS.
Byrnside. *See* Clark-Byrnside.
Byron. St. Paul's Parish, Balto. V. 1. Mss. MHS.
Byus. Christ P. E. Church cemetery, Cambridge. Steele. 1936. MHS; DAR.

Trinity Church cemetery, Dorchester Co. Md. O. R. Soc. Bull., no. 3, pp. 43–52. MHS.
Bywaters. St. Paul's Parish, Balto. V. 1. Mss. MHS.
See Read-Corbin-Luttrell-Bywaters.

C

***Cabell.** Cabells and their Kin. A. Brown. N. Y., Houghton, Mifflin & Co.; Cambridge, Riverside Press; 1895. MHS. (2nd ed., 1938, v. 2, includes 1895 to present time; Richmond, Va.)
*Descendants in Mo. Joseph H. Mudd, Hyattsville, Md. From Mo. Review. MHS.
Pocahontas and her descendants. Robertson. MHS; DAR.
Mrs. Albert Ritchie chart. MHS.
Cabell, Va. Col. families of U. S. A. Mackenzie. V. 7. MHS; DAR.
*The Sun, Balto., June 25, July 2, 1905.
Cable. St. Paul's Parish, Balto. V. 1, 2. Mss. MHS.
Cacy. *See* Casey.
Cadle. St. Paul's Parish, Balto. V. 1, 2. Mss. MHS.
Cadwalader. Descendants of Joran Kyn. Pa. Mag., v. 6, p. 207.
Descendants of Joran Kyn of New Sweden. Keen. MHS; DAR.
Morris family of Phila. Moon. V. 1, p. 201. MHS.
Cadwalader, Gen. John. Hist. of Md. Scharf. V. 2, p. 291. MHS.
(Revolutionary soldier; died Feb. 11, 1786, aged 44 yrs. 1 month 1 day; buried Shrewsbury cemetery, Kent Co.) Md. Geneal. Rec. Com., 1933–34, p. 232. Mss. DAR.
Cadwalader, Cadwallader. Col. families of U. S. A. Mackenzie. V. 3. MHS; DAR.
Cadwalder, Pa. Col. and Rev. families of Pa. Jordan. 1932, v. 4, pp. 92–97.
Cadwalder, Thomas F. Md. Soc., War of 1812, v. 3, no. 267. Ms. MHS.
Cadwalder Family. Newsp. clipp. File case, DAR.
Cadwallader. *See* Cadwalader.
Cadwell. Md. gleanings in Eng. Wills. M. H. Mag., 1907, v. 2, no. 3.
Cady. Monocacy Cemetery, Beallsville, Montgomery Co. Md. Geneal. Rec. Com., 1926–27. V. 2, pp. 70–73. Mss. DAR.
Caffrey. St. Paul's Parish, Balto. V. 1. Mss. MHS.
Caile. Ances. rec. and portraits. Col. Dames of Amer. 1910, v. 1, pp. 58, 320. MHS; DAR.
Mrs. Frank G. Baldwin chart. MHS.
Bolton chart. MHS.
Christ P. E. Church cemetery, Cambridge. Steele. 1936. MHS; DAR.
M. H. Mag., 1916, v. 11, p. 76.
See Harrison-Haskins-Caile-Loockerman.
Cailson. St. Paul's Parish, Balto. V. 1. Mss. MHS.
Cain. Diffenderfer family, arrived in Phila., 1727. Ms. File case, DAR.
*Frederick Co. families. Markell. Ms. Personal list.
St. Paul's Parish, Balto. V. 1. Mss. MHS.
See Kain.
Caine. Old Somerset. Torrence. MHS; DAR.
†Cairnes. Med. Annals Md. Cordell. 1903, p. 341. MHS.
See Rutledge-Stump-Jennings.
Cake Family. Indenture. Ms. File case, DAR.
Calberson. St. Paul's Parish, Balto. V. 1. Mss. MHS.
Calder. Bible rec., Kent Co. Md. Geneal. Rec. Com., 1937, Parran, p. 213. Mss. DAR.
See Cannan-Bush-Calder-Joiner-Meeks.
See Norris-Calder.
Caldron. St. Paul's Parish, Balto. Mss. MHS.
Caldwell. McSpadden-Love-Meigs-Clendinen-Von Bibber-Pope chart. MHS.
(1783). Natl. Geneal. Soc. Quart., July, 1914, v. 3, no. 2, p. 9.
Rumsey-Smithson Bible rec. Md. Geneal. Rec. Com., 1932–33, v. 5, pp. 63–142. DAR.
St. Paul's Parish, Balto. V. 1, 2. Mss. MHS.
See Scrogin. Col. families of U. S. A. Mackenzie. V. 7, p. 477. MHS; DAR.
†Sketch of Elias Boudinot Caldwell of Wash. Rec. Columbia Hist. Soc., 1914, v. 3; v. 24, pp. 204–13.
Smithson-Rumsey rec. bk. Ms. MHS.
*The Sun, Balto., Sept. 3, 10, 1905.
*Wicomico Co. families. Tilghman. Ms., p. 96. DAR.
Caldwell, Scotland. Natl. Geneal. Soc. Quart., v. 3, no. 1, p. 12.
Caldwell, Dr. J. J., N. Y. (Born 1836; married Ann Ridgely Love Jan. 5, 1864.) With data on Miller-Turner families. Md. Geneal. Rec. Com., 1933–34, pp. 269–70. Mss. DAR.
Caldwell, Lottie Repp. Descent from William the Conqueror. D. C. Geneal. Rec. Com., v. 34, pp. 30–33. Typed, bd. DAR.
Caldwell Family, Kent Co., Del. Pub. Geneal. Soc. Pa., v. 6, no. 1, p. 190–200, 321.
Caleb. St. Paul's Parish, Balto. V. 1. Mss. MHS.
Calef. St. Paul's Parish, Balto. V. 1. Mss. MHS.
Calf. St. Paul's Parish, Balto. V. 1. Mss. MHS.
Calhoun. All Hallow's P. E. churchyard, Snow Hill, Worcester Co. Hudson. Bd. ms. MHS; DAR. Also: Md. Geneal. Rec. Com., 1935–36, p. 24. Mss. DAR.
Descendants of Joran Kyn of New Sweden. Keen. MHS; DAR.
Pedigree of Iredell Waddell Iglehart. Soc. Col. Wars Md. Culver. 1940. MHS; DAR.
St. Thomas' Parish, Balto. Co. Bd. ms. MHS. Also: Md. Geneal. Rec. Com., 1937, pp. 109–82. Mss. DAR.
Sherburne chart. MHS.
See Whitridge. Col. families of U. S. A. Mackenzie. V. 5, pp. 540–48. MHS; DAR.
Calhoun, Pa. to S. C. Some notable families of south. States. Armstrong. V. 1. DAR.
Calhoun, James (1743–1816). Revolutionary war heroes. Cole. Bklet. Enoch Pratt Lib.
St. Paul's Parish, Balto. V. 1. Mss. MHS.
Westminster churchyard. Patriotic Marylander, v. 2, no. 4, pp. 54–60. MHS; DAR.
Calhoun Family. Ames Geneal. Coll. Ms. MHS.
Calkins. Data. Md. Geneal. Rec. Com., 1929, p. 115. Mss. DAR.
Denison family of Mass. to Harford Co. Ms. DAR.

Callahan. St. Paul's Parish, Balto. V. 1. Mss. MHS.
*Wicomico Co. families. Tilghman. Ms., p. 118. DAR.
Callahan, John. Abs. of will, 1803. D. A. R. Mag., Jun, 1929, v. 61, no. 6, p. 469.
Annapolis. Will proved, Nov. 22, 1803. D. A. R. Mag., v. 61, no. 6, p. 469.
Callahan-Lednum-Willis-Wright. Rec., 1780–1892. Copy from old Bible, belonging to Martin Maloney of Wright family of Caroline and Dorchester Cos. (Not previously pub.) Nicolite Quakers of East. Shore of Md. Bible rec. of Dorchester and Somerset Cos. and Del. Pp. 66–67. DAR.
Callan. Md. tombstone rec. Md. Geneal. Rec. Com., 1937, Parran, p. 2. Mss. DAR.
Callaway. Somerset Co. Court Book. Tilghman. 1937. Ms. DAR.
Callegan. St. Paul's Parish, Balto. V. 1. Mss. MHS.
Calliflower. Mt. Carmel burial ground, Unity, Montgomery Co. Md. Geneal. Rec. Com., 1934–35, p. 85. Mss. DAR.
†**Callister** (pronounced Collister). Hist. of Talbot Co. Tilghman. V. 1, pp. 83–103. MHS; DAR.
†**Callister, Henry.** Hist. of Talbot Co. Tilghman. V. 1, pp. 83–103. MHS; DAR.
†Md. Merchant and his friends, 1750. L. C. Wroth. M. H. Mag., 1911, v. 6, no. 3, pp. 213–39.
†Merchant of Oxford, Md., 1755, and others, who assisted Frenth exiles of Arcadia. Hist. of Md. Scharf. V. 1, p. 476.
Calloway. Old Somerset. Torrence. MHS; DAR.
Rec. of Stepney Parish. MHS; DAR.
Somerset Co. Court Book. Tilghman. 1937. Ms. DAR.
*Wicomico Co. families. Tilghman. Ms., p. 116. DAR.
Calmes. Black chart. MHS.
Calver. St. Paul's Parish, Balto. V. 1. Mss. MHS.
***Calvert.** Amer. Armory and Blue Bk. Matthews. 1908, p. 250. DAR.
*Abr. Compend. Amer. Geneal. Virkus. V. 1, p. 50. DAR.
Americans of gentle birth and their ancestors. Pittman. P. 224. MHS.
Ancestry of Rosalie Morris Johnson. Johnson. 1905. MHS; DAR.
Ances. rec. and portraits. Col. Dames of Amer. 1910, v. 1, pp. 158–64, 165, 166; v. 2, pp. 562–65. MHS; DAR.
Mrs. Lee Barroll chart. MHS.
†Bench and Bar of Md. Sams and Riley. 1901, v. 1, p. 77. Lib. Cong.; MHS; Peabody Lib.
†Biog. cyc. of rep. men of Md. and D. C. Pp. 60–64, 78. MHS; DAR.
Boarman geneal. Thomas. 1935. MHS; DAR.
See Browder. Abr. Compend. Amer. Geneal. Virkus. V. 4, p. 693. MHS.
Mrs. A. C. Bruce chart. MHS.
*Burke's landed gentry. 1939. MHS.
Calvert and Darnall gleanings from Eng. wills. Mrs. Russell Hastings. M. H. Mag., v. 21, no. 4, p. 303; v. 22, pp. 1, 115, 211, 307.
Benedict Leonard Calvert, Esq., Gov. of Md., 1727–31. Bernard C. Steiner. M. H. Mag., v. 3, no. 3, pp. 191–227, 283–341.
Calvert family. E. L. Didier. Lippincott, v. 6, p. 531.
Calvert family. J. B. C. Nicklin. M. H. Mag., 1921, v. 16, pp. 50–9, 189–204, 313–18, 389–94.
‡Calvert family. Beginnings of Md. in Eng. and Amer. A. B. Bibbins. 1934. MHS; DAR.
†Frederick Calvert. T. F. Henderson. MHS.
‡George Calvert and Cecilius Calvert, barons of Balto. Wm. Hand Brown. Amer. Commonwealth Series, Dodd, N. Y., 1890. MHS; DAR; Enoch Pratt Lib.
‡Life of Sir George Calvert, baron of Balto. Lewis W. Wilhelm. Balto., M. H. S. Fund Pub., no. 20, 1884. MHS.
†George Henry Calvert (born in Prince George Co., 1803; died, 1889. Bibliog. of work of Calvert. H. B. Tompkins.
Calverts. S. D. Page. Pa. Soc. Col. Gov., v. 1. MHS.
Cary Geneal. Coll Ms MHS.
Chart, photos. Cary Geneal. Coll. Ms. MHS.
*Col. families of U. S. A. Mackenzie. V. 2, p. 163; v. 4, p. 398; v. 6, p. 287. MHS; DAR
Col. mansions of Md. and Del. Hammond. 1914. MHS.
Descendants of Francis Calvert, 1751–1823. J. B. Nicklin. M. H. Mag., 1930, v. 25, no. 1, p. 30–49.
Discourse on life of George Calvert, first Lord Baltimore. J. P. Kennedy. M. H. S. Pub., v. 1, no. 3. MHS.
Ellicott Campbell chart. MHS.
Fairfax family notes. Ms. MHS.
*Frederick Co. families. Markell. Ms. Personal list.
Genesis of U. S. Riverside Press, v. 2.
See Guthrie. Abr. Compend. Amer. Geneal. Virkus. V. 1, p. 314. DAR.
Hollingsworth chart. Cary Geneal. Coll. Ms. MHS.
Hurst chart. MHS.
Iglehart chart. MHS.
‡Leaves from Calvert Papers. G. Hill. London, W. Milligan & Co., 1894. MHS.
†Life of Leonard Calvert G. W. Burnap. Lib. of Amer. biog., 2nd series, Boson, Little, 1864, v. 19, pp. 1–229. Enoch Pratt Lib.
*Lineage Bk. Daughters of Amer. Col., v. 2, p. 45. MHS; DAR.
‡Lords Baltimore. John G. Morris. Balto., J. Murphy, 1874 MHS.
Md. families. Culver. Ms. Personal list.
Maternal ancestry of Sir George Calvert. Correction. F. B. Culver. M. H. Mag., 1934, v. 29, no. 4, p. 330.
†Med. Annals Md. Cordell. 1903, p. 342. MHS.
Morning Herald, Balto., April 24, May 18, 1898 Newsp. clipp. MHS.
Motto. Francis C. Culver. M. H. Mag., 1925, v. 20, p. 378–79.
See Nicklin. Abr. Compend. Amer. Geneal. Virkus. V. 1, p. 743; v. 4, pp. 409–10. MHS.
†Papers relating to early hist. of Md. Streeter. 1876. MHS.
Pedigree charts. M. H. Mag., 1907, v. 2, no. 4, p. 369.
Pedigree from Hearne's Diary. (Bodleian mss.) MHS.

Pedigrees of all Lords Baltimore. Genealogist Peerage of United Kingdom, v. 1, pp. 226–27. MHS.
Pedigree of Edwin Austin Baughman. Soc. Col. Wars Md. Culver. 1940. MHS; DAR.
Pedigree of Duncan Keener Brent. Soc. Col. Wars Md. Culver. 1940. MHS; DAR.
(9 generations.) Pedigree of Howard Mohler Campbell. Soc. Col. Wars Md. Culver. 1940. MHS; DAR.
Pedigree of Benj. Patten Nicklin. Soc. Col. Wars Md. Culver. 1940. MHS; DAR.
Pedigree of Richard Dennis Steuart. Soc. Col. Wars Md. Culver. 1940. MHS; DAR.
Pedigree of Alfred Jenkins Tormey. Soc. Col. Wars Md. Culver. 1940. MHS; DAR.
Pedigree. Report of G. D. Butchaell, Deputy Ulster King of Arms, of John, 3rd Lord Baltimore. Ms. MHS.
Mrs. E. W. Poe chart. MHS.
Mrs. A. Randall chart. MHS.
Review of Hon. J. P. Kennedy's discourse on life and character of George Calvert, first Lord Baltimore. B. U. Campbell. Balto., 1846.
Riverdale home of the Calverts. Scrap Book. MHS.
St. Paul's Parish, Balto., v. 1, 2, 3. Mss. MHS.
Semmes and allied families. Semmes. MHS.
*Side lights on Md. hist. Richardson. V. 2, p. 39. MHS; DAR.
Some notes concerning Sir George Calvert, 1579–1632, First Lord Baltimore and his family, from Eng. rec. M. H. Mag., 1932, v. 27, no. 4, p. 334.
Some old Eng. letters. M. H. Mag., 1914, v. 9, no. 2, pp. 107–56.
*The Sun, Balto., May 17, Dec. 13, 1903.
Mrs. G. R. Veazey chart. MHS.
See Pendleton-Orrick-Strother-Calvert.
See Sewall-Darnall-Brooke-Calvert-Lee.
See Swingate.
Calvert, Va. Va. Mag. Hist. and Biog., v. 5, pp. 189, 436; v. 6, p. 73.
Calvert, Benedict Leonard, the Younger. M. H. Mag., 1906, v. 1, p. 274–77.
‡**Calvert, Cecil.** Memoir of baron of Balto., proprietor of Md. Minn. Hist. Soc., St. Paul, Minn., 1879.
Calvert, Cecilius. Maryland's greatest politician. South. Hist. Assoc. Pub., 1898, v. 2.
Calvert, Charles Baltimore. Amer. Armory and Blue Book. Matthews. 1908, p. 128. DAR.
(1663–1733.) And some of his descendants. J. B. C. Nicklin. M. H. Mag., 1929, v. 24, no. 2, p. 126–32.
(Fifth Lord Baltimore.) Forgotten love story. M. H. Mag., 1922, v. 17, pp. 308–18.
Parentage. M. H. Mag., 1906, v. 1, p. 289–91.
Calvert, George. At Oxford. B. Smith. M. H. Mag., 1931, v. 26, pp. 109–30.
Hist. of Md. Bozman. Pp. 232–60. MHS.
†Hist. of Md. Scharf. V. 1, pp. 29, 47, 52; v. 1, p. 380 (Cecilius); v. 1, p. 395 (Charles); v. 1, p. 441 (Frederick); v. 2, pp. 136–39. MHS.
†(First Lord Baltimore; 1846.) U. S. Catholic Mag., v. 5, pp. 193–20, 340–76.
(1700–71.) Some of his descendants, 1731–1931. J. B. C. Nicklin. M. H. Mag., 1931, v. 26, pp. 283–307, 315–41.
Terra Mariae. Neill. Pp. 1–55. MHS.
Will, 1634. M. H. Mag., v. 1, p. 363.
Eng. beginnings in Md. A. B. Bibbons. M. H. Mag., 1933, v. 28, pp. 283–308.
Calvert, Leonard (1606–1647). L. V. Baughman pedigree chart. Soc. Col. Wars, Md. Johnston. 1905, pp. 5, 141. MHS.
The Times, Balto., 1885. Newsp. clipp. Scrap Book. MHS.
Calvert Family. Ames Geneal. Coll. Ms. MHS.
Grants, deeds, documents to land in Eng. Personal letters and heraldic documents. Calvert Papers. Mss., MHS. Also: Fund Pub. no. 28, pp. 61, 126, Balto., 1889, MHS.
(Lords Baltimore.) Ms. File case, DAR.
Memorabelia. M. H. Mag., 1915, v. 10, no. 4, p. 372; 1916, v. 11, p. 282; 1921, v. 16, p. 386.
Morris family of Phila. Moon. V. 2, p. 579; v. 5, pp. 203, 206, 256. MHS.
Notes. Ms. MHS.
Pedigree of George, First Baron. Ms. MHS.
Calvert Line. Lilburn family. Col. and Revolutionary families of Phila. Jordan. 1933, v. 1, p. 382–98.
***Calvert-Darnall.** Gleanings from Eng. wills. M. H. Mag., 1927, v. 23, pp. 1–22, 115–36, 211–45, 307–49.
Calwell. Hist. of Harford Co. Preston. MHS; DAR.
· Somerset Co. Court Book. Tilghman. 1937. Ms. DAR.
Cam. St. Paul's Parish, Balto. V. 2. Mss. MHS.
Cambel. St. Paul's Parish, Balto. V. 1. Mss. MHS.
Cambell. St. Paul's Parish, Balto. V. 1, 2. Mss. MHS.
Spring Hill cemetery, Easton. Md. O. R. Soc. Bull., no. 1, pp. 35–41.
Cambell, Rose Croft, St. Mary's Co. Tombstone inscriptions. Md. O. R. Soc. Bull., no. 3, p. 58.
Cambell Family, Del. Co., N. Y. (Md. ref.) Md. Geneal. Rec. Com., 1934–35, pp. 148–74. Mss. DAR.
Cambell Family, "The Lookout," Chattanooga, Tenn. From Alfred the Great, William the Conqueror and Charlemagne. Emigrants; Revolutionary war service. Md. ref. MHS.
Cambron. Centenary of Catholicity in Ky. Webb. 1884. MHS.
O'Daniel-Hamilton ancestry in Md. and Ky. O'Daniel. Pp. 35–48. MHS.
Cambron (Cameron) Family, from Md. to Ky., 1785. Ms. MHS.
Camby. St. Paul's Parish, Balto. V. 2. Mss. MHS.
See Ramsay. Abr. Compend. Amer. Geneal. Virkus. V. 1, p. 536. DAR.
Camel. St. Paul's Parish, Balto. V. 1. Mss. MHS.
Cameron. Quisenberry family. Quisenberry. MHS.
See Cambron.
Camp. *See* Campe.
Campbell. Amer. Clan Gregor Year Book, 1911–12, p. 55. MHS; DAR.
Ancestry of Rosalie Morris Johnson. Johnson. 1905. MHS; DAR.
See Appold. Abr. Compend. Amer. Geneal. Virkus. V. 1, p. 57. DAR.
Christ P. E. Church cemetery, Cambridge. Steele. 1936. MHS; DAR.
Coale chart. MHS.

Campbell. Crain chart. MHS.
Cummings chart. Lib. Cong., MHS; DAR.
Dorsey and allied families. Ms. MHS; DAR.
Ellicott-Campbell chart. MHS.
Hagerstown tombstone inscriptions. Gruder. Natl. Geneal. Soc. Quart., 1919, v. 8, nos. 1, 2.
Mulford chart. MHS.
Patriotic Md. Md. Soc. of S. A. R., 1930. MHS; DAR.
St. Paul's Parish, Balto. V. 3. Mss. MHS.
St. Stephens Parish, Cecilton, Md. MHS; DAR.
Spring Hill Cemetery, Talbot Co. Md. O. R. Soc. Bull., no. 1, pp. 35–41. MHS.
*Wicomico Co. families. Tilghman. Ms, p. 40. DAR.
*Wilson Mss. Coll., no. 29, A, B, C, D; no. 73. MHS.
Winchester-Owings chart. Cary Geneal. Coll. Ms. MHS.
Whitehead chart. MHS.
Campbell, Howard Mohler. Pedigree. Soc. Col. Wars Md. Culver. 1940. MHS; DAR.
Campbell Family, Del. Co., N. Y., from Scotland, 1774. Md. Geneal. Rec. Com., 1934–35, pp. 148–74. Mss. DAR.
Campbell-Crist. Lineage Bks., Natl. Soc. of Daughters of Amer. Col., v. 2, p. 256. MHS; DAR.
Campe, Camp. St. Paul's Parish, Balto. V. 1, 2. Mss. MHS.
Camperson. Naturalizations in Md., 1666–1765; Laws. Bacon. MHS.
Campion. Cottman family chart. MHS.
Campison. Somerset Co. Court Book. Tilghman. 1937. Ms. DAR.
Campson. Somerset Co. Court Book. Tilghman. 1937. Ms. DAR.
Can, Cann. St. Stephens Parish, Cecilton, Md. MHS; DAR.
***Canby, William,** Brandywine, Del. His descendants—fourth to seventh generations—in Amer. Phila., pr. for priv. circulation, 1883.
Canby, Phila. (1683). Morris family of Phila. Moon. V. 2, p. 660. MHS.
Canby Family. Thomas Book. Thomas. P. 384. Lib. Cong.; MHS.
Cane. St. Paul's Parish, Balto. V. 1, 2. Mss. MHS.
Cann. St. Paul's Parish, Balto. V. 1, 2. Mss. MHS.
See Can.
Cannadah. St. Paul's Parish, Balto. V. 1. Mss. MHS.
Cannan Family. Rec., Kent Co., 1752–1933. Md. Geneal. Rec. Com., 1937, Parran, pp. 210–15. Mss. DAR.
Cannan-Bush-Calder-Joiner-Meeks Families, Kent Co. (1749–1908). Geneal. notes. Md. Geneal. Rec. Com., 1937. Mss. DAR.
Cannodey. St. Paul's Parish, Balto. V. 1. Mss. MHS.
Cannon. Abr. Compend. Amer. Geneal. Virkus. V. 4, p. 85. MHS.
Cannon-Riley-Truitt-Houston-Kollock. J. Carroll Stow, Balto. Typed, bd., 23 pp. MHS.
Pedigree of Nicholas Leeke Dashiell. Soc. Col. Wars Md. Culver. 1940. MHS; DAR.
St. Paul's Parish, Balto. V. 1, 2, 3. Mss. MHS.
Tombstone rec. of Dorchester Co. Jones. DAR.
See Cannon.
Cannon, Dorchester Co. Abr. Compend. Amer. Geneal. Virkus. V. 4, p. 492. MHS.
*And Mecklenburg, N. C. Lineage Bk., Daughters of Founders and Patriots, v. 22, pp. 156–57. MHS; DAR.
Cannon, Sussex Co., Del. Bible rec. of Dorchester and Somerset Cos. and Del. P. 22. DAR.
***Canon, Cannon.** Wicomico Co. families. Tilghman. Ms, pp. 35, 112. DAR.
Cansten, Isaac. Westminster churchyard. Patriotic Marylander, v. 2, no. 4, pp. 54–60. MHS; DAR.
***Cantrall,** Va. The Sun, Balto., Jan. 1, 1905.
Cantrell. Cary Geneal. Coll. Ms. MHS.
Cantwell. Cary Geneal. Coll. Ms. MHS.
Capble, Capel. St. Paul's Parish, Balto. V. 1. Mss. MHS.
Capel. *See* Capble.
Capewell. 1st annual geneal. and heraldic report, July 21, 1906. Also 2nd. Clarence S. Capewell and Larence L. Capewell. Balto., W. H. Richards. MHS; DAR.
Capewell Family. Capewell family. Clarence L. Capewell. Balto., July 21, 1906. 1st geneal. and heraldic report. MHS.
Caphort. St. Paul's Parish, Balto. V. 1. Mss. MHS.
Caphost. St. Paul's Parish, Balto. V. 1. Mss. MHS.
Capp. *See* Kapp.
Carbach-Wright. Ms. File case, DAR.
Carback. Bible rec., 1763–1874. Md. Geneal. Rec. Com., 1924–25, v. 1, p. 16. Mss. DAR.
St. Paul's Parish, Balto. Vol. 1, 2. Mss. MHS.
Carberry. Mayors of Corporation of Washington. Clark. Repr. from Columbia Hist. Soc., 1916, v. 19. Pamph. File case, DAR.
*Patriots of Revolutionary period interred in D. C. Balch. Rec. of Columbia Hist. Soc., v. 19, v. 20.
St. Ingoes churchyard, St. Mary's Co. Md. O. R. Soc. Bull., no. 3, p. 58.
†Carberry, Henry. Hist. of Md. Scharf. V. 3, p. 49. MHS.
Carberry Family, Md. and Wash., D. C. Ms. File case, DAR.
Carcaud. Talbott of "Poplar Knowle." Shirk. MHS; DAR.
†Carder. Hist. of Allegany Co. Thomas and Williams. V. 2. MHS; DAR.
Carere. Va. Mag. Hist. and Biog., v. 19, p. 433.
Carey. Balto., its hist., its people. Hall. V. 3. MHS; DAR.
Buckingham Pres. churchyard, Worcester Co. Hudson. Bd. ms. MHS; DAR.
McCormick chart. MHS.
St. Paul's Parish, Balto. V. 2. Mss. MHS.
St. Paul's P. E. churchyard, Berlin, Worcester Co. Hudson. Bd. ms. MHS; DAR. Also: Md. Geneal. Rec. Com., 1937, Mrs. Lines. Mss. DAR.
Somerset Co. Court Book. Tilghman. 1937. Ms. DAR.
Thomas Book. Thomas. Pp. 239–41. Lib. Cong.; MHS.
Carey, Mrs. Francis King (Anne Galbraith Hall). Chart. Col. Dames, Chap. I. MHS.
Carey-Kimber. Morris family of Phila. Moon. V. 3, p. 1037. MHS.
***Carey, Cary.** Wicomico Co. families. Tilghman. Ms., pp. 80, 91, 99, 114. DAR.

†**Carl.** Hist. of Allegany Co. Thomas and Williams. V. 2. MHS; DAR.
Carleton. Col. families of U. S. A. Mackenzie. V. 3. MHS; DAR.
Carlile. Charts. Wm. Preston of Newcastle upon Tyne, Eng., and Phila., Pa., and allied families. Belsterling. MHS.
†**Carlton.** Hist. of Allegany Co. Thomas and Williams. V. 2. MHS; DAR.
Carlyle. Balch chart. MHS.
Barroll chart. MHS.
*Carlyle family and descendants of John and Saral (Fairfax) Carlyle. Carlyle house and its associations. R. H. Spencer. Richmond, Va., Whittel & Shepperson, 1910, 58 pp. MHS.
Pedigree of Mark, Alexander Herbert Smith. Soc. Col. Wars Md. Culver. 1940. MHS; DAR.
Posey chart. MHS.
Carlyle Family. William and Mary Quart., 1st series, v. 18, pp. 201, 278.
***Carmack.** Frederick Co. families. Markell. Ms. Personal list.
Lineage Bks., Natl. Soc. of Daughters of Amer. Col., v. 3, p. 3. MHS; DAR.
See Beatty-Carmack.
Carmack, William, Frederick Co. Copy of will. Ms. File case, DAR.
Carmack Family. Ms. File case, DAR.
Carmady. St. Paul's Parish, Balto. V. 1. Mss. MHS.
Carman. Rumsey-Smithson Bible rec. Md. Geneal. Rec. Com., 1932–33, v. 5, pp. 63–142. DAR.
Smithson-Rumsey rec. Bk. Ms. MHS.
***Carman, Phebe Pruden.** Thomas C. and Phebe Pruden Carman. A. P. Carman. Urbana-Champaign, Ill., 1935. MHS.
***Carman, Thomas C.** Thomas C. and Phebe Pruden Carman. A. P. Carman. Urbana-Champaign, Ill., 1935. MHS.
***Carmean.** Wicomico Co. families. Tilghman. Ms., pp. 107, 108, 112. DAR.
Carmichael. Mrs. R. F. Brent chart. MHS.
†Diplomatic career of Wm. Carmichael. F. B. Streeter. M. H. Mag., 1913, v. 8, pp. 119–40.
Early hist. of Hollyday family. Hollyday. MHS; DAR.
†Hist. of Md. Scharf. V. 2, p. 348. MHS.
See Hollyday. Col. families of U. S. A. Mackenzie. V. 2, p. 336. MHS. DAR.
‡Mission of Wm. Carmichael to Spain. J. H. U., series 46, no. 1, 1928. MHS.
St. Paul's Parish, Balto. V. 1, 2. Mss. MHS.
Carmichael-Paca-Tilghman-Veazey. Hist. family reminiscences; Revolutionary Md. Balto. American, Oct. 24, 1881. Newsp. clipp. MHS.
Carnan. Carne and allied family notes. Coues. Ms. MHS
Chart, photos. Cary Geneal. Coll. Ms. MHS.
Dorsey and allied families. Ms. MHS.
Dorsey chart. MHS.
*Garrison Church. Allen. Pp. 138–42. MHS; DAR.
Gist chart. Cary Geneal. Coll. Ms. MHS.
Milligan chart. MHS.
Moale-Croxall-North chart. Cary Geneal. Coll. Ms. MHS.
Mrs. E. N. Morison chart. MHS.
Miss C. Petre chart. MHS.
Peale Geneal. Coll. Ms. MHS.
Pedigree of Raphael Semmes. Soc. Col. Wars Md. Culver. 1940. MHS; DAR.
Mrs. A. Randall chart. MHS.
Ridgely chart. Cary Geneal. Coll. Ms. MHS.
Mrs. A. R. Rogers chart. MHS.
St. Paul's Parish, Balto. V. 1, 2. Mss. MHS.
St. Stephens Parish, Cecilton, Md. MHS; DAR.
St. Thomas' Parish, Balto. Co. Bd. ms. MHS. Also: Md. Geneal. Rec. Com., 1937, pp. 109–82. Mss. DAR.
Carnan, Thomas C., and Phebe Pruden Carnan Family. Notes. Ms. MHS.
Carnan Family. Ames Geneal. Coll. Ms. MHS.
Carne. Carne and allied family notes and wills. Ellicott Coues. Ms. MHS.
Carnes. St. Paul's Parish, Balto. V. 1. Mss. MHS.
†**Carothers.** Men of mark in Md. Johnson. V. 1. DAR; Enoch Pratt Lib.
Carpender. Ancestry of Rosalie Morris Johnson. Johnson. 1905. MHS; DAR.
***Carpenter.** Carpenter and allied families. Geneal. and biog. Prepared and pr. for Miss A. L. Carpenter by Amer. Hist. Soc. Inc., N. Y., 1931. MHS.
*Carpenter family of Lancaster. A. Y. Cassanova. Philipsburg. Repr. from Pa.-German, Feb., 1910, v. 11, no. 2. MHS.
*Frederick Co. families. Markell. Ms. Personal list.
Some col. mansions and those who lived in them. Glenn. 2nd series, 1900, v. 2, p. 377. MHS. Also: Preston at Patuxent. Pamph. repr. from above. MHS.
*The Sun, Balto., June 14, 1903.
St. Paul's Parish, Balto. V. 1, 2. Mss. MHS.
***Carpenter, Samuel.** Samuel Carpenter of Phila. and his descendants. E. Carpenter and his son Gen. L. H. Carpenter, U.S.A. Pr. for priv. circulation, Phila., J. B. Lippincott Co., 1912, 1st ed. MHS.
***Carpentier.** Geneal. of family in Holland. E. J. Sellers. Phila., 1909. MHS.
***Carpentier, De Carpentier.** Carpentier, De Carpentier; allied ancestry. E. J. Sellers. Phila., 1928. MHS; DAR.
Carper. Peck family of Va. and Sharpesburg. William and Mary Quart., 2nd series, v. 13, pp. 273–76.
Carr. Clark chart. MHS.
Old Somerset. Torrence. MHS; DAR.
Pennington Papers. Ms. MHS.
Mrs. A. Randall chart. MHS.
St. Paul's Parish, Balto. V. 1, 2. Mss. MHS.
See Cochran-Beard-Carr-Ross-Wassan.
Carr, A. J. Md. Soc., War of 1812, v. 1, no. 20. Ms. MHS.
Carr, J. E., Jr. Md. Soc., War of 1812, v. 1, no. 10. Ms. MHS.
Carr, Wm. E. Md. Soc., War of 1812, v. 1, no. 119. Ms. MHS.
Carr Family. Ames Geneal. Coll. Ms. MHS.
Carr Family, Va. William and Mary Quart., 1st series, v. 8, p. 106.
Va. Mag., Hist. and Biog., v. 2, p. 221; v. 3, p. 208.
Carrell. Jenkins-Courtney chart. MHS.
Willcox and allied families. Willcox. MHS; DAR.
†**Carrere.** Med. Annals Md. Cordell. 1903, p. 343. MHS.

Carrick. St. Paul's Parish, Balto. V. 1, 4. Mss. MHS.

†**Carrico.** Med. Annals Md. Cordell. 1903, p. 343. MHS.

Carrico, Peter, Family. Chart. (France and Md.) DAR.

Carrington. Bond chart. MHS.
- Cabells and their kin. Brown. MHS.
- Griffith geneal. Griffith. MHS; DAR.
- Introduction to geneal. of Judge Paul and Priscilla (Sims) Carrington. J. B. Killebrew. S. Hist. Assoc., 1901, v. 5.
- Pedigree of Duncan Keener Brent. Soc. Col. Wars Md. Culver. 1940. MHS; DAR.
- Portrait and biog. rec. of Sixth Cong. Dist. of Md. 1898, p. 744 (under Nelson, p. 743). MHS; DAR.

Carrington Family, Barbadoes and Va. Rec. Natl. Geneal. Soc. Quart., June, 1939, v. 27, no. 2, pp. 33–34.

†**Carroll.** Bench and bar of Md. Sams and Riley. 1901, v. 1, p. 83. Lib. Cong.; MHS; Peabody Lib.
- †Biog. cyc. of rep. men of Md. and D. C. Pp. 76–78. MHS; DAR.
- †Biog. sketch of Most Rev. John Carroll. John Carroll Brent. Balto., 1843. MHS.
- Bolton chart. MHS.
- Carne and allied family notes. Coues. Ms. MHS.
- H. D. G. Carroll Ms. Book. In H. F. Thompson Papers. MHS.
- *Carroll family data, Md., N. C., etc. Charles C. Carroll, Ia. File case A, MHS.
- Carroll family, Howard Co. Inventory of co. and town rec. PWA. MHS; DAR.
- *Carroll of Carrollton and Duddington. Wilson Miles Cary Ms. Geneal. Coll. Chart. F. 40. MHS.
- *Carroll of "The Caves." Sir J. Bernard Burke, Ulster, Ireland, bk. photos., 1879. MHS.
- Carrolls of Doughoregan Manor and Carrollton. Ancestors and descendants of Charles, 1688. Some col. mansions. Glenn. Pp. 361–63. MHS.
- Mrs. Charles Carter chart. MHS.
- Caton chart. Cary Geneal. Coll. Ms. MHS.
- (1737–1937). Celebration of bicentenary of birth of Charles Carroll of Carrollton; pageant of episodes in his life, at Homewood, Johns Hopkins Univ., Monday, Sept. 30, 1937. Scrap Book. Gift of John H. Scarff, Oct., 1937. MHS.
- Cemetery near Carroll Chapel, Forest Glen. Md. Geneal. Rec. Com., v. 2, p. 29. Mss. DAR.
- *Chapel; tombstone records. Hist. of West. Md. Scharf. V. 1, p. 759. MHS; DAR.
- †Charles Carroll, barrister: The man. W. S. Holt. M. H. Mag., June, 1936, v. 31, pp. 112–26.
- ‡Charles Carroll bicentenary. John H. Scarff. Lord Balto. Press, 1938, 142 pp. MHS; DAR; Enoch Pratt Lib.
- †Charles Carroll of Carrollton. J. C. Carpenter. MHS.
- Charles Carroll of Carrollton. Charts. DAR.
- †Charles Carroll of Carrollton (1737–1832; born in Annapolis; buried in chapel of Doughoregan Manor, Howard Co.) J. Gurn. 1932.
- †Charles Carroll of Carrollton. L. A. Leonard. N. Y., Moffat, 1913. Enoch Pratt Lib.
- †Charles Carroll of Carrollton. Mag. Amer. Hist., Feb., 1878, v. 2, pt. 1, pp. 101–06. MHS.
- Charles Carroll of Carrollton; eulogy. J. Sergeant. Phila., 1833, 45 pp.
- †Charles Carroll of Carrollton, last surviving signer of Declaration of Independence. Horace Edwin Hayden, Wilkesbarre, Pa.
- Col. mansions of Md. and Del. Hammond. 1914. MHS.
- Correspondence of "first citizen," Charles Carroll of Carrollton and "Antilon" Daniel Dulany, Jr., 1773. With hist. of Gov. Eden's administration, 1769–76. Elihu S. Riley. Balto., 1902.
- See De Kergorlay. Abr. Compend. Amer. Geneal. Virkus. V. 1, p. 580. DAR.
- Descendants of Valentine Hollingsworth, Sr. Stewart. MHS; DAR.
- Dorsey and allied families. Ms. MHS.
- Dorsey Papers. Ms. MHS.
- Duddington. Abr. Compend. Amer. Geneal. Virkus. V. 1, p. 83. DAR.
- *Founders of Anne Arundel and Howard Cos. Warfield. Pp. 266 (Gov. Thomas King), 291 (Gov. John Lee), 501–18. MHS; DAR.
- Hill family of Hourston and Spaxton, Eng., Mass., Md., and New Eng., 1334–1934. Pp. 303–04. MHS.
- *Hist. Dorchester Co. Jones. 1925, pp. 296–301. MHS; DAR.
- †(41 ref.) Hist. of Frederick Co. Williams. MHS; DAR.
- Home of Charles Carroll of Carrollton. Mag. Amer. Hist., Nov., 1889, v. 22, pp. 354–57. MHS.
- ‡Home of Charles Carroll of Carrollton. Martha J. Lamb. MHS.
- Rev. Joseph Hull (1595) and some of his descendants. Hull. 1904, p. 16. MHS.
- ‡Journal of Charles Carroll of Carrollton, during visit to Canada, 1776, as commissioner from Congress. With memoir and notes. Brantz Mayer. Balto., John Murphy, 1845, 1876. MHS; DAR.
- Justus Engelhart Kulm. J. Hall Pleasants. 1937, pamph. MHS.
- Life and times of Archbishop Carroll. (Born near Upper Marlboro, Prince George Co., June 8, 1735; son of Daniel and Eleanor (Darnall) Carroll; died 1815; first bishop of R. C. Church in Amer., 1789.) J. G. Shea. N. Y., 1888. MHS.
- †Life and times of John Carroll. Peter Guilday. N. Y., Encyc. Press., 1922. MHS; Enoch Pratt Lib.
- †Life of Anna Ella Carroll (born in Somerset Co., 1815; died, 1894). Blackwell.
- *Life of Charles Carroll of Carrollton, 1737–1832, with his correspondence and public papers. Pedigree charts; coat of arms. Kate M. Rowland. 2 v. N. Y., G. P. Putnam & Sons, 1898. MHS.
- Md. families. Culver. Ms. Personal list.
- Md. Gazette, Annapolis, Oct. 2, 1755 (2 deaths). Newsp. clipp. MHS.

Medford family, Dorchester Co. Ms. MHS.
Milligan chart. MHS.
"Mount Clare." Mrs. T. C. Jenkins chart. MHS.
No Name Mag., v. 3, pp. 14, 41. MHS.
John O'Donnell of Balto. Cook. MHS.
Patriotic Md. Md. Soc. of S. A. R., 1930. MHS; DAR.
Peale Geneal. Coll. Ms. MHS.
Pedigree of Charles Gambrill Baldwin. Soc. Col. Wars Md. Culver. 1940. MHS; DAR.
Pedigree of Edward Hammond. Soc. Col. Wars Md. Culver. 1940. MHS; DAR.
Pedigree. Miss C. Petre chart. MHS.
*Regarding Carroll portraits. Pennington Papers. Ms. MHS.
St. Ann's churchyard, Annapolis. Md. O. R. S. Bull., no. 3, pp. 55–56.
St. John's R. C. Church cemetery, Montgomery Co. Md. Geneal. Rec. Com., 1926, p. 27. Mss. DAR.
St. Paul's Parish, Balto. V. 1, 2, 3, 4. Mss. MHS.
St. Stephens Parish, Cecilton, Md. MHS; DAR.
*Semmes Geneal. Coll. Ms. MHS.
*Side lights on Md. hist. Richardson. V. 2, p. 54. MHS; DAR.
Somerset Co. Court Book. Tilghman. 1937. Ms. DAR.
The Monumental City. Howard. MHS; DAR.
Tombstone rec. Rogers Coll. Ms. MHS.
Trinity Church cemetery, Dorchester Co. Md. O. R. Soc. Bull., no. 3, pp. 42–52.
Va. Mag. Hist. and Biog., v. 19, p. 95–100.
Will, with codicil of Charles Carroll, barrister, 1781–83. Md. Geneal. Rec. Com., 1935–36, pp. 204–09. Mss. DAR.
See Andrews-Bonner-Carroll-Corkran-Medford.
See Birney-Carroll-Fitzhugh.
**See* King-Carroll Line.
See Medford-Bonner-Carroll-Corkran-Stevens.
See O'Carroll.

Carroll, Sweet Air, Balto. Co. Hist. of Balto. City and Co. Scharf. P. 908.

Carroll, "The Caves." J. B. B. Ulster. Bk. of photos. MHS.

Carroll, Charles, of Carrollton. Ames Geneal. Coll. Ms. MHS.
Barrister of Annapolis. Will 1781–83. Md. Geneal. Rec. Com., 1935–36, pp. 33–38. Mss. DAR.
Biog. of signers of Declaration of Independence. Joseph M. Sanderson. 1820–27, v. 7, pp. 237–61.
†Biog. sketches of distinguished Marylanders. Boyle. MHS; DAR.
*Biog. sketches of eminent Amer. patriots. Taggart. 1907, pp. 46–121. MHS.
Chart. DAR.
†Hist. of Balto. City and Co. Scharf. P. 705. MHS.
*†Hist. of Md. Scharf. V. 2, pp. 123–31, 214–16. MHS.
†(1737–1832). M. H. Mag., v. 12, pp. 205–06; v. 13, p. 76.
Modern encyc. McDannald. 1933.
*Notes. M. H. Mag., 1910, v. 5, p. 70.
Patriotic Marylander, v. 3, no. 3, pp. 167–76. (Portrait, p. 169.) MHS; DAR.
Unpublished letters. Ms. MHS.

Carroll, Dr. Charles, Annapolis. M. H. Mag., v. 18, p. 197.

Carroll, D. G. Abr. Compend. Amer. Geneal. Virkus. V. 1, p. 78; v. 6, p. 122. DAR.

†**Carroll, D. H.** Men of mark in Md. Johnson. V. 1. DAR; Enoch Pratt Lib.

†**Carroll, Daniel.** Hist. of Md. Scharf. V. 2, p. 540. MHS.

Carroll, David H. Balto., its hist., its people. V. 3. MHS; DAR.

***Carroll, Douglas Gordon.** Coat of arms. Burke's landed gentry. 1939. MHS.

Carroll, Gough. Bible rec., 1745–1888. M. H. Mag., 1930, v. 25, pp. 302–04.

Carroll, Harry Dorsey Gough. Bible rec., 1793–1866. M. H. Mag., Dec., 1927, v. 22, no. 4.
Family Bible, 1793–1866, births and deaths. M. H. Mag., 1927, v. 22, pp. 377–80.
†Hist. of Balto. City and Co. Scharf. P. 908. MHS.

***Carroll, Howell.** Bible rec. File case A, MHS.

†**Carroll, Archbishop John.** Balto., hist. and biog. Richardson and Bennett. 1871, pp. 225–27. MHS; DAR.
†Biog. sketches of distinguished Marylanders. Boyle. MHS; DAR.
†Hist. of Md. Scharf. V. 2, pp. 220–21. MHS.
Life and times of John Carroll (1735–1815), Archbishop of Balto. Pedigree chart. Peter Guilday. N. Y., Encyclopedia Press. MHS.
†Lives of Catholic heroes and heroines of Amer. J. O. K. Murray.
Modern encyc. McDannald. 1933.

Carroll, John Butterworth Randol. (Carroll, 8 generations.) Pedigree. Soc. Col. Wars Md. Culver. 1940. MHS; DAR.

†**Carroll, John Lee.** Governor of Md. Buchholz. P. 213. MHS.

Carroll, Patrick. Prayer book rec. Md. Geneal. Bull., v. 2, p. 6.
Will. Md. Geneal. Bull., v. 1, p. 26.

Carroll, Polly. Marriage to Richard Caton, Nov. 30, 1787. Catonsville pioneers of Luth. faith. Natl. Geneal. Soc. Quart., v. 9, no. 2, p. 29.

Carroll, S. Sterett. Amer. Armory and Blue Bk. Matthews. 1908, p. 272. DAR.

†**Carroll, Thomas King.** Governor of Md. Buchholz. P. 109. MHS.
Graves. Trinity Church burial ground, near Cambridge, Md. Md. Geneal. Rec. Com., 1937–38, pp. 93–104. Mss. DAR.

***Carroll Family.** Arch. of Georgetown Univ., Wash., D. C., v. 287.
*Arms. Old Kent. Hanson. Pp. 137–55. MHS; DAR.
Lee of Va., 1642–1892. E. J. Lee. P. 385. Lib. Cong.; MHS.
Thomas Book. Thomas. Pp. 242–43. Lib. Cong.; MHS.

***Carroll Family,** Md. and N. C. Notes. Ms. MHS.

Carroll-Chase-Paca-Stone. Data; "The Declaration of Independence." D. A. R. Mag., v. 60, no. 8, pp. 473–76.

***Carroll-Darnall.** Wilson Miles Cary Ms. Geneal. Coll. 3 charts photos. F. 40. MHS.

Carroll - Howard - Brown - Buchanan - Lee - O'Donnell. First families of Md. The Post, Balto., Feb. 2, 3, 4, 6, 7, 8, 1933. Newsp. clipp., bd. MHS.
Carroll Maccubin Families. Ames Geneal. Coll. Ms. MHS.
Carroll McCubbin. Wilson Miles Cary Ms. Geneal. Coll. 2 charts. F. 64. MHS.
Carroll, O'Carroll. Col. family of U. S. A. Mackenzie. V. 1, pp. 66–77; v. 2, p. 170. (Charles Carroll of Carrollton); v. 3; v. 4; v. 6; v. 7. MHS; DAR.
*Geneal. chart. Repr. from Jour. of Royal Hist. and Archaeolog. Assoc. of Ireland, Oct., 1883, v. 6, no. 56, 4th series. MHS.
*The Sun, Balto., May 1, 1904; Feb. 19, 1905.
†**Carshee.** Men of mark in Md. Johnson. V. 3. DAR; Enoch Pratt Lib.
Carsley. Southern Bapt. Church cemetery, Worcester Co. Md. Geneal. Rec. Com., 1937, Mrs. Lines. Mss. DAR.
Carson. Dorsey and allied families. Ms. MHS.
Peale Geneal. Coll. Ms. MHS.
Perin chart. MHS.
Harford Co. Hist. Soc. Mss. Coll. JHU.
St. Paul's Parish, Balto. V. 2, 3, 4. Mss. MHS.
Carson, Carsons. Col. families of U. S. A. Mackenzie. V. 1, p. 73. MHS; DAR.
*Pennington Papers. Ms. MHS.
Carter. Abr. Compend. Amer. Geneal. Virkus. V. 1, pp. 85–86. DAR.
Ancestry of Rosalie Morris Johnson. Johnson. 1905. MHS; DAR.
Balto; its hist., its people. Hall. V. 2. MHS; DAR.
†Bench and bar of Md. Sams and Riley. 1901, v. 2, p. 574. Lib. Cong.; MHS; Peabody Lib.
Mrs. A. C. Bruce chart. MHS.
Carter family tree. New edition. Prepared by Mrs. M. C. Oliver. 1897.
Certificate of service in Amer. Revolution. Ms. File case, DAR.
Chart. Coats of arms, complete in 1 Sheet. Cary Geneal. Coll. Ms. MHS.
Col. families of U. S. A. Mackenzie. V. 1 (Bernard Carter); v. 5; v. 7. MHS; DAR.
*Geneal., 1652–1912. Descendants of Captain Thomas Carter of Bradford, Lancaster Co., Va., with geneal. notes of many allied families. J. L. Miller.
Geneal. of Augusta Maitland (Carter) Libby, of Denver, Col., 1704–1933. Ms. MHS.
Hazelhurst charts. MHS.
†Hist. of Allegany Co. Thomas and Williams. V. 2. MHS; DAR.
Humphrey Cissel farm, Montgomery Co. Md. Geneal. Rec. Com., 1926–27, p. 75. Mss. DAR.
Iglehart chart. MHS.
Journal and letters. P. V. Fithian (tutor at Nomini Hall, Va., 1773–74). Princeton Hist. Assoc., 1900.
Md. gleanings in Eng. Wills. M. H. Mag., 1907, v. 2, no. 4; 1910, v. 5.
Md. tombstone rec. Md. Geneal. Rec. Com., 1937, Parran, pp. 14, 25. Mss. DAR.
"Nomini Hall," Va. (Robt. Carter married Francis Tasker, Apr. 2, 1754, daughter of Benj. and Ann Tasker of Md.) New Eng. Hist. and Geneal. Reg., v. 79, p. 330.
Rec. of Cope family. Cope. Pp. 130–34. MHS.
Mrs. Renshaw chart. MHS.
Rucker family. Whitley.
St. Charles R. C. Church graveyard, Indianhead, Charles Co. Md. Geneal. Rec. Com., 1933–34, p. 137. Mss. DAR.
Somerset Co. Court Book. Tilghman. 1937. Ms. DAR.
John Swadner and his descendants. Evans. 1919. Typed, bd. MHS.
St. Paul's Parish, Balto. V. 1, 2, 3. Mss. MHS.
St. Thomas' Parish, Balto. Co. Bd. ms. MHS. Also: Md. Geneal. Rec. Com., 1937, pp. 109–82. Mss. DAR.
Times Dispatch, Richmond, Va., May 1, 1904. Newsp. clipp.
Trinity P. E. churchyard, Long Green. Typed ms. MHS; DAR.
Va. families. Du Bellett.
See Law-Carter.
Carter, Prince George Co. Mrs. G. R. Veazey Chart. MHS.
Carter, Va. Some notable families of south. States. Armstrong. V. 2, pp. 61–74. DAR.
†**Carter, Bernard.** Biog. cyc. of rep. men of Md. and D. C. P. 135. MHS; DAR.
†Hist. of Balto. City and Co. Scharf. P. 702. MHS.
Carter, Mrs. Charles. (Sarah Carroll Daingerfield). Chart. Col. Dames, Chap. I. MHS.
Raisin chart. MHS.
***Carter, Giles,** Va. Geneal. memoir. Gen. G. A. C. Ports. 1909.
Carter, J. Ridgely. Abr. Compend. Amer. Geneal. Virkus. V. 6, p. 124. DAR.
†**Carter, M. H.** Men of mark in Md. Johnson. V. 3. DAR; Enoch Pratt Lib.
Carter Family. Chart; coat of arms. R. R. Carter, Shirley, Va. 1896. Ms. MHS; DAR.
Descendants of Col. John Carter, Va.; with portraits. Some col. mansions. Glenn. V. 1, pp. 217–94.
Carter Family, Va. Lee of Va., 1642–1892. E. J. Lee. Pp. 356–62. Lib. Cong.; MHS.
Carter Family, Va. and Pa. Ms. File case, DAR.
Carter Line. Mrs. A. Randall chart. MHS.
Carter (Bernard) Line. Law-Carter families. Col. and Revolutionary families of Pa. Jordan. 1932, v. 4, p. 560.
Carton. Chart of Com. John Rodgers. DAR.
Carton, Miss Eugenia Whyte. Chart. Col. Dames, Chap. I. MHS.
Carton, Mrs. Laurence R. (Eliza Cradilla Whyte). Chart. Col. Dames, Chap. I. MHS.
***Cartwright.** Frederick Co. families. Markell. Ms. Personal list.
Naturalizations in Md., 1666–1765; Laws. Bacon. MHS.
Carty. St. Paul's Parish, Balto. V. 1, 2. Mss. MHS.
Carver. Fox-Ellicott-Evans families. Evans. MHS; DAR.
Hist. of Byberry and Moreland. Martindale. MHS.
***Carver Family.** Gilbert family, Carver family, Duffield family. J. C. Martindale. DAR.

***Carvil.** Lineage Bk. Daughters of Amer. Colonists, v. 4, p. 312. MHS; DAR.
Sherburne chart. MHS.
Carvill, St. Mary's Co. Pedigree of Thomas Gardener Hill. Soc. Col. Wars Md. Culver 1940. MHS; DAR.
Carvill, Maj. John, St. Mary's Co. M. W. Hill pedigree chart. Soc. Col. Wars, Md. Johnston. 1905, pp. 39, 141. MHS.
Carvill-Hall Matthews. Harford Co. Hist. Soc. Mss. Coll. JHU.
†Carville. Bench and bar of Md. Sams and Riley. 1901, v. 1, p. 77. Lib. Cong.; MHS; Peabody Lib.
Crumpton graveyard. Md. Geneal. Rec. Com., 1933-34, pp. 193-203. Mss. DAR.
Carvills, Carvel Hall. St. Paul's P. E. churchyard, Kent Co. Md. O. R. Soc. Bull., no. 2, pp. 54-65.
Cary. Aylett chart. Cary Geneal. Coll. Ms. MHS.
Barroll chart. MHS.
Cary Geneal. Coll., Mss. B, 14, 2, Folders 20, 36, 47, 60, 81. MHS.
†Wilson Miles Cary. J. S. Ames. M. H. Mag., 1916, v. 11, pp. 190-92.
Chart, photos., complete in 1 sheet. Cary Geneal. Coll. Ms. MHS.
Clark chart. MHS.
Col. families of U. S. A. Mackenzie. V. 1 (Wilson Miles Cary); v. 7. MHS; DAR.
Curle chart. Cary Geneal. Coll. Ms. MHS.
*Devon Carys. F. Harrison. N. Y., priv. pr., De Vinne Press, 1920, 2 vols. MHS.
Geneal. of Page family, Va. Page. Pp. 105-08, 258-59. MHS; DAR.
Rev. Joseph Hull (1595) and some of his descendants. Hull. 1904, p. 27. MHS.
Pocahontas and her descendants. Robertson. MHS; DAR.
St. Paul's Parish, Balto. V. 1. Mss. MHS.
Selden chart. MHS.
Times Dispatch, Richmond, Va., May 29, 1904. Newsp. clipp.
Va. families. Du Bellett.
See Carey.
See Mc Henry-Cary.
See Scarsbrook-Scarsbrooke-Harwood-Cary.
Cary, Va. Abr. Compend. Amer. Geneal. Virkus. V. 1, p. 541. DAR.
Mrs. Lee Barroll chart. MHS.
*Carys. Essay in geneal. F. Harrison. N. Y., priv. pr., De Vinne Press, 1919. MHS; DAR.
Rec. Ancestry of Benjamin Harrison. Keith. MHS; DAR.
*The Sun, Balto., Nov. 25, Dec. 2, 9, 1906.
Cary, Lee Cummins. Pedigree. Soc. Col. Wars Md. Culver. 1940. MHS; DAR.
Cary, Miles. Pedigree of Henry Lee Smith, Sr. Soc. Col. Wars Md. Culver. 1940. MHS; DAR.
***Cary, Sally.** Sally Cary. W. M. Carey. N. Y., priv. pr., 1916. MHS.
Cary, Wilson, "Ceeleys," Va. And his family; chart. Va. Mag. Hist. and Biog., 1902, v. 9, pp. 104-11.
Will, 1772. Va. Mag. Hist. and Biog., v. 10, p. 189.
Pedigree charts, plates 1 and 2. Soc. Col. Wars, Md. Johnston. 1905, pp. 11-12, 142. MHS.
***Cary Family.** Cary family in Eng. H. G. Cary. Boston, 1906.
Casey. Ances. rec. and portraits. Col. Dames of Amer., 1910, v. 2, p. 658. MHS; DAR.
Casey, Cacy. Bible rec. Upper Penins. East. Shore, pp. 21-29. MHS; DAR.
Casey, Cassey. St. Paul's Parish, Balto. V. 1, 2. Mss. MHS.
***Cash,** Prince George Co. Lineage Bk. Daughters of Amer. Col., v. 2, p. 69. MHS; DAR.
Cashell. Mt. Carmel burial ground, Unity, Montgomery Co. Md. Geneal. Rec. Com., 1934-35, p. 85. Mss. DAR.
See Bell-Cashell.
Cashman. St. Paul's Parish, Balto. V. 1. Mss. MHS.
Casho, Jacob (Jacques Cacheau) (born in France 1750; died in Cecil Co. 1823). Md. Geneal. Rec. Com., 1937-38, pp. 63-65. Mss. DAR.
Port. and biog. rec., Harford and Cecil Co. Md. Geneal. Rec. Com., 1937-38. Mss. DAR.
Caskey. St. Paul's Parish, Balto. V. 1, 3. Mss. MHS.
***Caskie Family,** Va. Caskie Family of Va. J. A. Caskie. 1928. DAR.
***Cason.** The Sun, Balt., Aug. 6, 1905.
Cassard, Jesse L. Md. Soc., War of 1812, v. 1, no. 63. Ms. MHS.
Cassard, John. Md. Soc., War of 1812, v. 2, no. 200. Ms. MHS.
Cassard, Wm. L. Md. Soc., War of 1812, v. 1, no. 59. Ms. MHS.
Cassel. Roop geneal. Pamph. MHS.
Cassel, Leonard. Memoir. C. D. Smith. Balto. Methodist Print., 1896.
Cassey. *See* Casey.
***Casteel.** Newsp. clipp. MHS.
Castell Family. Mountain Democrat, Garrett Co., Sept. 6, 1934. Newsp. clipp. MHS; DAR.
Castle. Biggs family. Ms. DAR.
*Geneal.; chart. Also Swaine and Tyler. MHS.
†Hist. of Frederick Co. Williams. MHS; DAR.
Castleman. Abr. Compend. Amer. Geneal. Virkus. V. 1, p. 91. DAR.
Caswell. St. Paul's Parish, Balto. V. 1, 2. Mss. MHS.
Cate. Mrs. Wm. Graham Bowdoin, Jr., chart. MHS.
Catesby. Capt. Roger Jones, of London and Va. Browning.
Cathall. *See* Cathol.
Cathcart. Balto., its hist., its people. Hall. V. 2. MHS; DAR.
Cathcart, Asbury Roszel. Md. Soc., War of 1812, v. 3, no. 204. Ms. MHS.
†Cathell. Med. Annals Md. Cordell. 1903, p. 344. MHS.
Patriotic Md. Md. Soc. of S. A. R., 1930. MHS; DAR.
***Cathol, Cathall.** Wicomico Co. families. Tilghman. Ms, pp. 80, 94, 96, 97, 113. DAR.
Catlett. Pocahontas and her descendants. Robertson. MHS; DAR.

Catlett. St. Paul's Parish, Balto. V. 3. Mss. MHS.
Zimmerman-Waters and allied families. Allen. Pp. 18–28. DAR; MHS.
See Baytop-Catlett.
Catlett, Va. Geneal. of Mays family. Mays. P. 194. MHS.
Catlin. Chestertown cemetery. Md. O. R. Soc. Bull., no. 1, pp. 18–29.
Old Somerset. Torrence. MHS; DAR.
Wicomico Co. families. Bible rec. Ms. DAR.
*Wicomico Co. families. Tilghman. Ms., p. 9. DAR.
Cato. St. Paul's Parish, Balto. V. 1. Mss. MHS.
†**Caton.** Mrs. Richard Caton (nee Mary Carroll). M. H. Mag., 1922, v. 17, pp. 74–89.
Chart, complete in 1 sheet. Cary Geneal. Coll. Ms. MHS.
Marriage of Richard Caton and Polly Carroll, Nov. 30, 1787. From Md. Jour. and Balto. Advertiser. Catonsville pioneers of Lutheran faith. Natl. Geneal. Soc. Quart., v. 9, no. 2, p. 29.
*Pennington Papers. Ms. MHS.
St. Paul's Parish, Balto. V. 1. Mss. MHS.
†**Caton, Richard.** M. H. Mag., 1921, v. 16, pp. 299–313.
Cator. Balto; its hist., its people. Hall. V. 3. MHS; DAR.
Md. families. Culver. Ms. Personal list.
†**Cator, Benj. F.** Balto., hist. and biog. Richardson and Bennett. 1871, pp. 229–31. MHS; DAR.
Cattell. Descendants of Joran Kyn of New Sweden. Keen. MHS; DAR.
Sherburne chart. MHS.
Cattell, S. C. Cary Geneal. Coll. Ms. MHS.
Cattell, Wm., S. C. Pedigree of Iredell Waddell. Iglehart. Soc. Col. Wars Md. Culver. 1940. MHS; DAR.
Cattle (Mo.)-**Brown-Fowke.** Abr. Compend. Amer. Geneal. Virkus. V. 4, p. 93. MHS.
Cattlin. Somerset Co. Court Book. Tilghman 1937. Ms. DAR.
†**Caughy.** Geneal. and mem. encyc. of Md. Spencer. V. 2, p. 706. MHS; DAR.
Caulk. Md. families. Culver. Ms. Personal list.
St. Paul's Parish, Balto. V. 1. Mss. MHS.
St. Stephens Parish, Cecilton, Md. MHS; DAR.
Causey. Makernie Memorial Pres. churchyard, Snow Hill, Worcester Co. Hudson. Bd. ms. MHS; DAR. Also: Md. Geneal. Rec. Com., Mrs. Lines. Mss. DAR.
M. E. churchyard, Snow Hill, Worcester Co., Hudson. Bd. ms. MHS; DAR.
Patriotic Md. Md. Soc. of S. A. R., 1930. MHS; DAR.
*Wicomico Co. families. Tilghman. Ms, p. 56. DAR.
Causey Line, Anne Arundel Co. from 1668. Vale family, Pa. Col. and Revolutionary families of Phila. Jordan. 1933, v. 1, pp. 168–86.
Causin. Cary Geneal. Coll. Ms. MHS.
†**Caussin.** Med. Annals Md. Cordell. 1903, p. 345. MHS.
Cavalier. St. Paul's Parish, Balto. V. 1. Mss. MHS.
Cavander. *See* Bous-Baumgartner-Cavander.
Cavender. St. Paul's P. E. churchyard, Berlin, Worcester Co. Hudson. Bd. ms. MHS; DAR. Also: Md. Geneal. Rec. Com., 1937, Mrs. Lines. Mss. DAR.
Cawood. *See* Caywood.
See Cole-Cawood.
†**Cawood, Stephen,** Charles Co. Two forgotten heroes, 1675–76. M. H. Mag., 1924, v. 19, pp. 339–40.
***Caywood, Cawood,** Va. The Sun, Balto., Sept. 3, 1905.
Cazier. St. Paul's Parish, Balto. V. 1. Mss. MHS.
See Ford-Foster-Cazier.
Cecil. Cary Geneal. Coll. Ms. MHS.
Cecil, St. Mary's Co. Abr. Compend. Amer. Geneal. Virkus. V. 1, p. 92; v. 6, pp. 232, 735. DAR.
***Cecil Family,** Md. and Va. From Rocky Mountain Herald, Denver, Col., July 18, 1931. MHS.
***Cecil, Cissel.** Founders of Anne Arundel and Howard Cos. Warfield. P. 430. MHS; DAR.
Celeston. St. Paul's Parish, Balto. V. 1. Mss. MHS.
Cellar. St. Paul's Parish, Balto. V. 1. Mss. MHS.
Chace. Chase Chronicle. Bulletin of Chase-Chace family. MHS; DAR.
Chader. St. Paul's Parish, Balto. V. 1, 2. Mss. MHS.
Chaille. Patriotic Md. Md. Soc. of S. A. R., 1930. MHS; DAR.
Sketches of John Slemmons Stevenson and Rev. Samuel Mc Master. Stevenson. P. 24. MHS.
Worcester Co. militia, 1794. Covington. P. 160. MHS.
Chaille-Long. Notes. M. H. Mag., v. 6, no. 3, p. 254.
†**Chaille-Long, Charles.** M. H. Mag., v. 12, pp. 206–08.
Ms. list of Md. authors. Steiner. P. 120. Enoch Pratt Lib.
Chaires. Bible rec. from Bible in possession of G. E. Chaires, Chestertown (orig. Queen Anne Co.), 1770–1846. Md. Geneal. Rec. Com., 1937–38, pp. 70–72. Mss. DAR.
Chaires Family. Notes. D. A. R. Mag., v. 67, no. 8, p. 512.
†**Chaisty.** Med. Annals Md. Cordell. 1903, p. 346. MHS.
Chalfant. Jackson family gathering. 1878.
Chalmer. St. Paul's Parish, Balto. V. 1, 2. Mss. MHS.
†**Chalmers.** Bench and bar of Md. Sams and Riley. 1901, v. 1, p. 191. Lib. Cong.; MHS; Peabody Lib.
***Chalmers,** Va. The Sun, Balto., Feb. 26, 1905.
†**Chalmers, George.** Hist. of Md. Scharf. V. 2, p. 298. MHS.
***Chamberlaine.** Gale and Chamberlaine family rec. Ms. MHS.
Gale family pedigree, Somerset and Cecil Cos. Ms. MHS.
*Geneal. notes of Chamberlaine family of Md. (East. Shore). Comp. from rec. and Ms. found among papers of John Bozman Kerr, Balto., John B. Piet, 1880. MHS
Gittings chart. MHS.
Hist. and geneal. of Earles of Secancus. Earle. Md. descendants of James Earle, John of Md. in Revolution. DAR.

Hist. of Talbot Co. Tilghman. V. 1, pp. 531–75. MHS; DAR.
Lehr chart. MHS.
Md. families. Culver. Ms. Personal list.
†Med. Annals Md. Cordell. 1903, p. 346. MHS.
Pedigree of Harrison Tilghman. Soc. Col. Wars Md. Culver. 1940. MHS; DAR.
Pedigree of Levin Gale Shreve. Soc. Col. Wars Md. Culver. 1940. MHS; DAR.
St. Stephens Parish, Cecilton, Md. MHS; DAR.
Spring Hill Cemetery, Talbot Co. Md. O. R. Soc. Bull., no. 1, pp. 35–41. MHS.
Tilghman chart. MHS.
Chamberlaine, Perryville. Abr. Compend. Amer. Geneal. Virkus. V. 1, p. 95. DAR.
Chamberlaine, Samuel, Talbot Co. (1697–1773). W. A. and S. W. Merritt pedigree charts, plate 2. Soc. Col. Wars Md. Johnston. 1905, pp. 68, 142. MHS.
†**Chamberlain, Sam'l, Jr.,** (1742–1811). Hist. of Talbot Co. Tilghman. V. 1, pp. 552–54. MHS; DAR.
***Chamberlaine Family.** Old Kent. Hanson. Pp. 247, 288. MHS; DAR.
Chamberlaine, Chamberlayne. St. Paul's Parish, Balto. V. 1, 2, 3. Mss. MHS.
Chamberland. Harford Co. Hist. Soc. Mss. Coll. JHU.
St. Paul's Parish, Balto. V. 1, 2. Mss. MHS.
Chamberlayne. *See* Chamberlaine.
†**Chambers.** Bench and bar of Md. Sams and Riley. 1901, v. 2, p. 378. Lib. Cong.; MHS; Peabody Lib.
Bible rec., Md. Geneal. Rec. Com., 1938–39, pp. 94–97. Mss. DAR.
†Biog. cyc. of rep. men of Md. and D. C. P. 97. MHS; DAR.
Chart of Com. John Rodgers. DAR.
Fisher family. Morse. MHS.
Fisher family, Sussex Co., Del., and Md. Ms. MHS.
Md. families. Culver. Ms. Personal list.
Orme geneal. chart. MHS.
Pedigree of Joseph Lee Wickes. Soc. Col. Wars Md. Culver. 1940. MHS; DAR.
Mrs. E. W. Poe chart. MHS.
St. Paul's Parish, Balto. V. 1, 2. Mss. MHS.
Somerset Co. Court Book. Tilghman. 1937. Ms. DAR.
Chambers, Kent Co. Manning chart. MHS.
Chambers, Col. Benj. (Wars of 1776 and 1812. buried in Chester cemetery, Kent Co.) Md. Geneal. Rec. Com., 1933–34, p. 232. Mss. DAR.
Chambers, R. M. Md. Soc., War of 1812, v. 1, no. 18. Ms. MHS.
Chambers Family. Lee of Va., 1642–1892. E. J. Lee. P. 101. Lib. Cong.; MHS.
Chamier. St. Paul's Parish, Balto. V. 1. Mss. MHS.
Chamnis. St. Paul's Parish, Balto. V. 1, Mss. MHS.
Champlain. St. Paul's Parish, Balto. V. 2. Mss. MHS.
Chancellor. Abr. Compend. Amer. Geneal. Virkus. V. 6, p. 131. DAR.
†Hist. of Balto. City and Co. Scharf. P. 751. MHS.
Somerset Co. Court Book. Tilghman. 1937. Ms. DAR.
Chancellor Family, Va. Ms. File case, DAR.
***Chancellor-Fitzgerald-Cooper.** The Sun, Balto., Jan. 8, 1905.
***Chandlee.** Hist. of Cecil Co. Johnston. Pp. 157–158. MHS; DAR.
*Chandlee line. Thomas Chandlee.
Chandlee Line. Turner family. Forman. Pp. 60, 88–89. MHS.
Chandler. Cary Geneal. Coll. Ms. MHS.
Daughter of Md.; Mother of Texas. Bell. MHS; DAR.
*Old Kent. Hanson. P. 175. MHS; DAR.
Our real granddaughters and their ancestry. D. A. R. Mag., Nov., 1933, v. 67, no. 11, p. 686.
*Rec. of descendants of George and Jame Chandler, who emigrated to Pa. from Wiltshire, Eng., 1687. 1937. DAR.
St. Paul's Parish, Balto. V. 2, 3, 4. Mss. MHS.
See Thoroughgood-Chandler.
Chandler, Joseph, Balto. Co. (born 1798). D. A. R. Mag., v. 67, no. 11, p. 686.
Chandless. St. Paul's Parish, Balto. V. 1, 3. Mss. MHS.
†**Chaney.** Men of mark in Md. Johnson. V. 4, p. 110. DAR; Enoch Pratt Lib.
St. Barnabas P. E. churchyard. Typed ms. MHS; DAR.
St. Paul's Parish, Balto. V. 1, 2. Mss. MHS.
†**Chaney, R. G.** Men of mark in Md. Johnson. V. 4, p. 117. DAR; Enoch Pratt Lib.
Chanlor. St. Paul's Parish, Balto. V. 1. Mss. MHS.
Chaplain. Christ P. E. Church cemetery, Cambridge. Steele. 1936. MHS; DAR.
Md. families. Culver. Ms. Personal list.
†Med. Annals Md. Cordell. 1903, p. 347. MHS.
***Chapline.** Chaplines from Md. and Va. Coat of arms. M. J. Dare. Washington, D. C., Franklin Press, 1902.
Col. families of U. S. A. Mackenzie. V. 2, MHS; DAR.
†Hist. of Frederick Co. Williams. MHS; DAR.
Portrait and biog. rec. of Sixth Cong. Dist. of Md. 1898, p. 345. MHS; DAR.
*Side lights on Md. hist. Richardson. V. 2, p. 61. MHS; DAR.
*The Sun, Balto., July 24, 31, 1904.
***Chapline,** Frederick Co. Data. M. H. Mag. Mar. 1933, v. 23, no. 1, p. 74.
Chapman. Miss M. S. Brogden chart. MHS.
Burton ancestry. Ms. MHS.
Chart, photos. cary Geneal Coll. Ms. MHS.
*Geneal., 1610–1931. E. R. Chapman. Pamph. 1931. DAR.
†Med. Annals Md. Cordell. 1903, pp. 347–48. MHS.
Mt. Paran Pres. churchyard, Harrisonville, Balto. Co. Typed ms. MHS; DAR.
*Pennington Papers. Ms. MHS.
St. Paul's Parish, Balto. V. 1, 2, 3. Mss. MHS.
Chapman, Va. Abr. Compend. Amer. Geneal. Virkus. V. 1, p. 546. DAR.
Chappell. Amer. Guthrie and allied families. Guthrie. Bk. 4. DAR.
***Chappin Family,** Pa. (comes into Md.). DAR.
Chard. St. Paul's Parish, Balto. V. 1, 2. Mss. MHS.
Charfinch. St. Paul's Parish, Balto. V. 1. Mss. MHS.

†**Charles.** Hist. of Allegany Co. Thomas and Williams. V. 1. MHS; DAR.
St. Paul's Parish, Balto. V. 1, 2. Mss. MHS.
***Charles Family.** Arch. of Georgetown Univ., Wash., D. C., v. 287.
***Charlescroft.** Wicomico Co. families. Tilghman. Ms., p. 96. DAR.
Charlton. Bantz. Geneal. notes. Ms. MHS.
De Ford chart. MHS.
*Frederick Co. families. Markell. Ms. Personal list.
Patriotic Md. Md. Soc. of S. A. R., 1930. MHS; DAR.
Mrs. E. C. Venable chart. MHS.
Charlton, Frederick Co. McH. Howard pedigree chart, plate 2. Soc. Col. Wars, Md. Johnston. 1905, p. 42. MHS.
***Charlton Family.** Arch. of Georgetown Univ., Wash., D. C., v. 287.
Charshee. Balto., its hist., its people. Hall. V. 2. MHS; DAR.
Chartres, Chartress. St. Paul's Parish, Balto. V. 1, 2. Mss. MHS.
Chase. Ances. rec. and portraits. Col. Dames of Amer. 1910, v. 2, p. 621. MHS; DAR.
Bantz geneal. notes. Ms. MHS.
†Bench and Bar of Md. Sams and Riley. 1901, v. 1, pp. 154, 172. Lib. Cong.; MHS; Peabody Lib.
†Biog. cyc. of rep. men of Md. and D. C. Pp. 183–84. MHS; DAR.
Cemetery Creek, Anne Arundel Co., Tombstone inscriptions. Founders of Anne Arundel and Howard Cos. Warfield, pp. 333, 335. MHS; DAR.
Chart, photos., 2 sheets. Cary Geneal. Coll. Ms. MHS.
Christ P. E. Church cemetery, Cambridge. Steele. 1936. MHS; DAR.
*Chronicle. Bulletin of Chase-Chace family. MHS; DAR.
Col. mansions of Md. and Del. Hammond. 1914. MHS.
Founders of Howard and Anne Arundel Cos. Warfield. Pp. 187–89. MHS; DAR.
*Geneal.; ancestral card index. MHS.
*Geneal. tree. DAR.
Hist. Salisbury, Wicomico Co. Truitt. DAR.
Lawrence-Chase-Townley-estate. Hill. P. 38. MHS.
Lawrence-Townley and Chase-Townley estates in Eng. Usher. Lib. Cong.; MHS.
Machen chart. MHS.
Patriotic Md. Md. Soc. of S. A. R., 1930. MHS; DAR.
Russell-Lux Bible rec. Photos. MHS.
St. Paul's Parish, Balto. V. 1, 2, 3. Mss. MHS.
See Carroll-Chase-Paca-Stone.
Chase, Rev. Richard (was rector of Westminster, and All Hallow's Parishes, Anne Arundel Co.). Townley geneal. chart. MHS.
†**Chase, Judge Samuel** (1741–1811; born in Somerset Co.; son of Thomas Chase, rector of Somerset Parish). Biog. of signers of Declaration of Independence. Sanderson. Phila., 1820–27, v. 9, p. 181.
†Balto., hist. and biog. Richardson and Bennett. 1871, pp. 233–35. MHS; DAR.
Biog. of signers of Declaration of Independence. Joseph M. Sanderson. 1820–27, v. 7, pp. 185–235.
*Chronicles of Balto. Scharf. 1874, p. 305. MHS; DAR.
†Md. in natl. politics. Essary. 1915.
†(1741–1811). M. H. Mag., v. 12, pp. 208–09.
Rept. of trial of Samuel Chase, before High Court of Impeachment. Balto., 1805, 336 pp., with appendix.
(Revolutionary soldier). St. Paul's P. E. graveyard. Patriotic Marylander, v. 2, no. 4, pp. 54–60. MHS; DAR.
*The Sun, Balto., Dec. 31, 1879.
Chase, Thorndike. Glendy churchyard. Patriotic Marylander, v. 2, no. 4, pp. 54–60. MHS; DAR.
***Chase Family.** Arch. of Georgetown Univ., Wash., D. C., v. 287.
***Chase-Townley** and **Lawrence-Townley.** Hist. of estates in Eng. James Usher. N. Y., 1883. MHS.
***Chastain Family.** Arch. of Georgetown Univ., Wash., D. C., v. 287.
***Chastin.** The Sun, Balto., July 7, 1907.
†**Chatard.** Med. Annals Md. Cordell. 1903, p. 348. MHS.
***Chatfield Family.** Arch. of Georgetown Univ., Wash., D. C., v. 287.
Chattel, Chattle. St. Paul's Parish, Balto. V. 1, 2. Mss. MHS.
***Chauncey Family.** Arch. of Georgetown Univ., Wash., D. C., v. 287.
Chauncy. Geneal. of Henrietta Chauncy Wilson. Upshur. Bk. of photos. MHS.
Chavannes. Balto., its hist., its people. Hall. V. 2. MHS; DAR.
Chawfinch. St. Paul's Parish, Balto. V. 1, Mss. MHS.
***Cheadle Family.** Arch. of Georgetown Univ., Wash., D. C., v. 287.
***Cheatham Family.** Arch. of Georgetown Univ., Wash., D. C., v. 287.
Cheeseman. Fischer family. Morse. MHS.
Fisher family, Sussex Co., Del., and Md. Ms. MHS.
Somerset Co. Court Book. Tilghman. 1937. Ms. DAR.
***Cheeseman Family.** Arch. of Georgetown Univ., Wash., D. C., v. 287.
Cheesman. Andrew's Scrap Book. MHS.
***Cheever Family.** Arch. of Georgetown Univ., Wash., D. C., v. 287.
***Chelton.** Bible rec. C. H. B. Turner Geneal. Coll. Ms. MHS.
Chenault. Quisenberry family. Quisenberry. MHS.
Cheney. Autobiography of Summerfield Baldwin. MHS; DAR.
Sara R. Baldwin chart. MHS.
de Ghize chart. MHS.
Md. families. Culver. Ms. Personal list.
Peale Geneal. Coll. Ms. MHS.
Pedigree of Charles Gambrill Baldwin. Soc. Col. Wars Md. Culver. 1940. MHS; DAR.
Pedigree of Mareen Duvall. Soc. Col. Wars Md. Culver. 1940. MHS; DAR.
St. Paul's Parish, Balto. V. 2. Mss. MHS.
St. Thomas' Parish, Balto. Co. **Bd. ms.** MHS. Also: Md. Geneal. Rec. Com., 1937, pp. 109–82. Mss. DAR.
Taney and allied families. Silverson. MHS; DAR.
See Jacob-Cheney.

*Cheney Family. Anne Arundel Co. gentry. Newman. Pp. 348-52. MHS; DAR.
*Arch. of Georgetown Univ., Wash., D. C., v. 287.
Chenoweth. Abr. Compend. Amer. Geneal. Virkus. V. 1, p. 908. DAR.
Amer. Armory and Blue Bk. Matthews. 1908, p. 132. DAR.
Col. families of U. S. A. Mackenzie. V. 1, p. 86; v. 2, p. 178. MHS; DAR.
St. Thomas' Parish, Balto. Co. Bd. ms. MHS. Also: Md. Geneal. Rec. Com., 1937, pp. 109-82. Mss. DAR.
Talbott of "Poplar Knowle." Shirk. MHS; DAR.
Chenoweth, John, to Md. 1700. D. A. R. Mag., v. 58 (also marked 59), no. 2, p. 109.
Chenoweth Family. Hist. Address of Capt. Wm. F. Cobb, 1912. Newsp. clipp. MHS.
*Arch. of Georgetown Univ., Wash., D. C., v. 287.
Chenoweth Family, Va. and Md. Tylers' Quart. Mag., v. 3, pp. 186-93.
*Chenoweth-Cromwell. Geneal. and charts of the Chenoweth and Cromwell families of Md. and Va. Alex Crawford Chenoweth, C.E. Redfield Press, New York, 1894. MHS.
Chenowith. Index to hist. of Chenowith family by C. C. Hiatt. Mrs. Brumbaugh. 1925. Ms. DAR.
St. Paul's Parish, Balto. V. 2. Mss. MHS.
Cherbonnier, A. Victor. Md. Soc., War of 1812, v. 3, no. 220. Ms. MHS.
*Cherry Family. Arch. of Georgetown Univ., Wash., D. C., v. 287.
†Cheseledyne. Bench and bar of Md. Sams and Riley. 1901, v. 1, p. 75. Lib. Cong.; MHS; Peabody Lib.
Cheshire Family. Ms. File case, DAR.
Chesley. Lineage Bks., Natl. Soc. of Daughters of Amer. Col., v. 2, p. 102. MHS; DAR.
*Mrs. Charles Howard Lloyd chart. Col. Dames Amer., Chap. I. MHS.
Med. Annals Md. Cordell. 1903, p. 349. MHS.
*Chesley, St. Mary's Co., Lineage Bk. Daughters of Amer. Colonists, v. 2, p. 102; v. 5, p. 51. MHS; DAR.
Pedigree of Culbreth Hopewell Warner. Soc. Col. Wars Md. Culver. 1940. MHS; DAR.
Chester. St. Paul's Parish, Balto. V. 1, 2. Mss. MHS.
Chester Family. Arch. of Georgetown Univ., Wash., D. C., v. 287.
*Cheston. Burke's landed gentry. 1939. MHS.
Md. gleanings in Eng. Wills. M. H. Mag., 1907, v. 2, no. 4.
†Med. Annals Md. Cordell. 1903, p. 349. MHS.
St. Paul's Parish, Balto. V. 2, 3. Mss. MHS.
Cheston, Kent Co. Col. and Revolutionary families of Pa. Amer. Hist. Soc., N. Y., 1934.
Cheston Family. Thomas Book. Thomas. Pp. 244-46. Lib. Cong.; MHS.
Chettle. St. Paul's Parish, Balto. V. 1. Mss. MHS.
*Chetwood Family. Arch. of Georgetown Univ., Wash., D. C., v. 287.
*Chevalier Family. Arch. of Georgetown Univ., Wash., D. C., v. 287.
Cheves. St. Paul's Parish, Balto. V. 1. Mss. MHS.
Chew. Abr. Compend. Amer. Geneal. Virkus. V. 6, pp. 136, 141, 301, 384. DAR.
Abs. of Va. land patents. Va. Mag., Hist. and Biog., v. 1, p. 87.
See Andrews, Mo. Abr. Compend. Amer. Geneal. Virkus. V. 4, p. 543. MHS.
Ances. rec. and portraits. Col. Dames of Amer., 1910, v. 1, p. 219; v. 2, pp. 499, 777. MHS; DAR.
Ancestry. Geneal. hist. of Endress family. Endress. Pp. 97-107. MHS.
Beirne chart. MHS.
Bowies and their kindred. Bowie. MHS; DAR.
*Burke's landed gentry. 1939. MHS.
H. D. G. Carroll. Ms. Book. In H. F. Thompson Papers. MHS.
Chart of Com. John Rodgers. DAR.
Chart, photos., 3 sheets. Cary Geneal. Coll. Ms. MHS.
†Benjamin Chew (1722-1810), head of Pa. judiciary system under colony and commonwealth. B. A. Kinkle. Phila., Univ. of Pa. Press, 1932.
Chew family. F. C. Culver. M. H. Mag., 1935, v. 30, no. 2, p. 157-75.
*Robert Smith Chew and his ancestors to Md. and Va. E. T. Pollock. 1938. Typed, in Binder. DAR.
Clark chart. MHS.
Col. families of Amer. Lawrence. V. 3, p. 305; v. 5, p. 89; v. 16, p. 92. MHS.
Col. families of U. S. A. Mackenzie. V. 1; v. 2. MHS; DAR.
See Cotton. Abr. Compend. Amer. Geneal. Virkus. V. 1, p. 568. DAR.
Cotton chart. MHS.
De Ford chart. MHS.
Descendants of Col. Thomas White. Morris. MHS.
Dorsey and allied families. Ms. MHS.
Early Quaker rec. Anne Arundel and Calvert Cos., 1665-1889. Pub. Geneal. Soc. Pa., v. 3, no. 3, pp. 197-200.
Eldridge chart. MHS.
See Ewen-Chew-Hutchins, etc. Lineage Bks., Natl. Soc. of Daughters of Amer. Col., v. 4, p. 269. MHS; DAR.
*Founders of Anne Arundel and Howard Cos. Warfield. Pp. 109-12. MHS; DAR.
Gantt geneal. Ms. MHS.
Geneal. notes of Thomas family. Thomas. MHS; DAR.
Harford Co. Hist. Soc. Mss. Coll. JHU.
†Hist. of Md. Scharf. V. 2, p. 399. MHS.
Hopkins and allied families. P. 21. Bd. ms. MHS.
S. G. Hopkins chart. MHS.
McH. Howard pedigree charts, plate 1. Soc. Col. Wars, Md. Johnston. 1905, pp. 41, 142. MHS.
Mrs. J. F. Lee chart. MHS.
*Lineage Bk. Daughters of Amer. Colonists. V. 2, p. 117; v. 3, pp. 145-46, 260-61; v. 4, p. 310; v. 5, p. 3. MHS; DAR.
Macsherry chart. MHS.
Md. families. Culver. Ms. Personal list.
†Med. annals Md. Cordell. 1903, pp. 349-50. MHS.

Chew. John O'Donnell of Balto. Cook. MHS.
*Old Kent. Hanson. P. 39. MHS; DAR.
J. P. Paca pedigree chart. Soc. Col. Wars, Md. Johnston. 1905, p. 80. MHS.
Patriotic Md. Md. Soc. of S. A. R., 1930. MHS; DAR.
Peale Geneal. Coll. Ms. MHS.
Pedigree of Coleman Randall Freeman. Soc. Col. Wars Md. Culver. 1940. MHS; DAR.
Pedigree of Charles Worthington Hoff. Soc. Col. Wars Md. Culver. 1940. MHS; DAR.
Pedigree of Charles Morris Howard. Soc. Col. Wars Md. Culver. 1940. MHS; DAR.
Pedigree of Rt. Rev. Rogers Israel. Soc. Col. Wars Md. Culver. 1940. MHS; DAR.
Pedigree of Henry Irvine Keyser, II. Soc. Col. Wars Md. Culver. 1940. MHS; DAR.
Pedigree of John Philemon Paca. Soc. Col. Wars Md. Culver. 1940. MHS; DAR.
Pedigree of Maurice Falconer Rodgers. Soc. Col. Wars Md. Culver. 1940. MHS; DAR.
Pedigree of Mason Locke Weems Williams. Soc. Col. Wars Md. Culver. 1940. MHS; DAR.
See Pegues. Abr. Compend. Amer. Geneal. Virkus. V. 1, p. 422. DAR.
See Ramsay. Abr. Compend. Amer. Geneal. Virkus. V. 1, p. 536. DAR.
St. Paul's Parish, Balto. V. 2. Mss. MHS.
*Side lights on Md. Hist. Richardson. V. 2, p. 65. MHS; DAR.
*The Sun, Balto., Aug. 2, 1903.
Mrs. H. De Courcy Wright Thom chart. MHS.
Thomas-Chew-Lawrence. Thomas. MHS.
Times Dispatch, Richmond, Va., July 16, 1905. Newsp. clipp.
Van Dyke-Johns-Montgomery-Manlove. chart. Cary Geneal. Coll. Ms. MHS.
Mrs. E. C. Venable chart. MHS.
See Bacon-Chew.
Chew, Md. and Pa. Descendants of John, 1622. Thomas Book, pp. 252–75, of Va. pp. 276–84. Lib. Cong.; MHS; DAR.
***Chew, Samuel.** Hist. reg. Hill. V. 1, pp. 97–99. MHS.
Chew, Samuel Claggett, M.D. Pedigree chart. Soc. Col. Wars, Md. Johnston. 1905, p. 13. MHS.
Chew, Thomas John. Pedigree chart. Soc. Col. Wars, Md. Johnston. 1905, p. 14. MHS.
***Chew Family.** Arch. of Georgetown Univ., Wash., D. C., v. 287.
Morris family of Phila. Moon. V. 3, p. 907. MHS.
Chew Family, Md. to Pa. Ms. File case, DAR.
Chew Family, Md. to Va. Ms. File case, DAR.
Chew Line. Balto., its hist., its people. Hall. V. 3, p. 512. MHS; DAR.
Col. and Revolutionary lineages in Amer. 1939, v. 2, p. 126. MHS.
Gaither, Va. and Md. Col. and Revolutionary families of Phila. Jordan. 1933, v. 1, pp. 144–67.
(1590–1881.) M. L. W. Williams pedigree chart. Soc. Col. Wars, Md. Johnston. 1905, p. 126. MHS.
(1590–1885.) P. H. Tuck pedigree chart. Soc. Col. Wars, Md. Johnston. 1905, p. 115. MHS.
Chew-Fleming-Johns-Neely (Pa.)-**Philpot-Usher.** Abr. Compend. Amer. Geneal. Virkus. V. 4, p. 572. MHS.
Chew-O'Donnell. Ances. rec. and portraits. Col. Dames. Amer. 1910. p. 519. MHS; DAR.
Chew-Thomas-Worthington Family. Notes. L. B. Brown. Ms. MHS.
Chewning. Amer. Clan Gregor Year Book, 1912, p. 120; 1916, p. 81. MHS; DAR.
Chicard. St. Paul's Parish, Balto. V. 1. Mss. MHS.
Chichester. Coale chart. MHS.
Chichester, Va. Crain chart. MHS.
Whitehead chart. MHS.
Chick. St. Stephens Parish, Cecilton, Md. MHS; DAR.
***Chiffelle.** Pennington Papers. Ms. MHS.
Chilcoat, Chilcote. St. Paul's Parish, Balto. V. 1. Mss. MHS.
Chilcoate. Matthews-Price chart. MHS.
Chilcote. *See* Chilcoat.
Child. Mrs. R. N. Jackson chart. MHS.
St. Stephens Parish, Cecilton, Md. MHS; DAR.
See Childs.
Childs. Children of Alex P. and M. C. Hill. Ms. MHS.
†G. W. Hist of Md. Scharf. V. 3, p. 711. MHS.
Monumental City. Howard. MHS; DAR.
St. Stephens Parish, Cecilton, Md. MHS; DAR.
Childs, J. R., Cecil Co. Abr. Compend. Amer. Geneal. Virkus. V. 4, p. 100. MHS.
Childs, Rebecca, consort of Samuel Childs. Inscriptions from tombstone no longer standing; "Holland Point" on Patuxent River, Calvert Co. Md. Geneal. Rec. Com., 1932–33, p. 21. Mss. DAR.
Childs-Biscoe-Goodwin Families, Calvert Co. Rec., 1796–1844. Md. Geneal. Rec. Com., 1932–33, v. 5. Mss. DAR.
Childs, Child. St. Paul's Parish, Balto. V. 1, 3, 4. Mss. MHS.
Chilton. Col. Families of U. S. A. Mackenzie. V. 1, p. 89. MHS; DAR.
Chipley Family, East. Shore of Md. Rec., 1790–1930. Ms. File case, DAR.
Chiselin. Carey Geneal. Coll. Ms. MHS.
***Chisholm.** The Chisholms. J. A. Nydegger. Md. Chisholms, p. 39. 1922. MHS; DAR.
St. Paul's Parish, Balto. V. 2. Mss. MHS.
Chisman. Cary Geneal. Coll. Ms. MHS.
Chisolm. Abr. Compend. Amer. Geneal. Virkus. V. 1, p. 547. DAR.
Col. Families of U. S. A. Mackenzie. V. 6. MHS; DAR.
†Med. Annals Md. Cordell. 1903, p. 350. MHS.
***Chisolm,** S. C. Geneal. (1254–1914). W. G. Chisolm. N. Y. Knickerbocker Press, 1914. MHS.
***Chisolm,** S. C. and Md. Burke's landed gentry. 1939. MHS.
Chisolm, Wm. Garnett. Rec. of Pope, Warner, Washington and Yeardley of Va. Pedigree. Soc. Col. Wars Md. Culver. 1940. MHS; DAR.
Chissam. Somerset Co. Court Book. Tilghman. 1937. Ms. DAR.
Chiswell. Bible rec., 1747–1915. Md. Geneal.

Rec. Com., 1932–33, v. 5. pp. 220–22. Mss. DAR.
*Chittam. Wicomico Co. families. Tilghman. Ms, p. 107. DAR.
Choate. Mt. Paran Pres. churchyard, Harrisonville, Balto. Co. Typed ms. MHS; DAR.
St. Paul's Parish, Balto. V. 1, 2. Mss. MHS.
Chowning Family, Lancaster Co., Va. (About 1730). Reference to Redwood family of Balto. Ms. File case, DAR.
†**Chrisfield.** Bench and bar of Md. Sams and Riley. 1901, v. 2, p. 409. Lib. Cong.; M.H.S; Peabody Lib.
Christhilf, Edw. Md. Soc., War of 1812, v. 1, no. 8. Ms. MHS.
***Christian.** Frederick Co. families. Markell. Ms. Personal list.
Naturalizations in Md., 1666–1765; Laws. Bacon. MHS.
Christian Family, Va. Chart; ancestors and descendants. Blue print. File case, DAR.
Christie. Chart of Com. John Rodgers. DAR.
Harford Co. Hist. Soc. Mss. Coll. JHU.
See Zoller. Lineage Bks., Natl. Soc. of Daughters of Amer. Col., v. 2, p. 187. MHS; DAR.
Christison. Wenlocke Christison and early Friends in Talbot Co. S. A. Harrison. Balto., M. H. S. Fund Pub., no. 12, 1878. MHS.
†Wenlocke Christison's plantation, "The Ending of Controversie." H. C. Forman. M. H. Mag., Sept., 1939, v. 34, no. 3, pp. 223–27.
†(Quaker Annals.) Hist. of Talbot Co. Tilghman. V. 1, pp. 103–2. MHS; DAR.
Christopher. Md. Geneal. Bull., v. 3, p. 30. Notes. Turner Geneal. Col Ms. MHS.
Somerst Co. Court Book. Tilghman. 1937. Ms. DAR.
Rec. of Stepney Parish. MHS; DAR.
St. Paul's Parish, Balto. V. 1, 2. Mss. MHS.
*Wicomico Co. families. Tilghman. Ms., pp. 67, 96, 99, 111, 113. DAR.
Chukshank. Bible rec. Upper Penins. East. Shore, p. 1.
†**Chunn.** Med. Annals Md. Cordell. 1903, p. 351. MHS.
Church. St. Paul's Parish, Balto. V. 2. Mss. MHS.
Churchill. Cary Geneal. Coll. Ms. MHS.
Churchill, Rt. Hon. Winston S. Jerome hist. and geneal., and ancestry of Sarah Noble. P. 50. Mss. MHS.
Churchill-Crocker-Fox-Coplestone-Bonville-Ellicott. Families of Devonshire, Eng., and some of their descendants. W. M. Ellicott. M. H. Mag., 1931, v. 26, no. 4, p. 362–80.
Churchman. St. Paul's Parish, Balto. V. 2, 3. Mss. MHS.
Churchman Family. Hist. of Cecil Co. Johnston. P. 525. MHS; DAR.
Cibble. *See* Kibble.
Cipriani. Sarah Smith Hood Bible rec. Ms. MHS.
Cissel. Cemetery near Carroll Chapel, Forest Glen. Md. Geneal. Rec. Com., v. 2. Mss. DAR.
Centenary of Catholicity in Ky. Webb. 1884. MHS.
Humphrey Cissel farm, near Poolesville, Montgomery Co. Tombstone inscriptions, 1822–85 (Cissel stones removed to Monocacy Cemetery, Beallsville). Md. Geneal. Rec. Com., 1926–27, p. 75. Mss. DAR.
Monocacy Cemetery, Beallsville, Montgomery Co. Md. Geneal. Rec. Com., 1926–27. Pp. 70–73. Mss. DAR.
See Cecil.
Cissel-Hobbs-Hammond-Ridgely. Abr. Compend. Amer. Geneal. Vierkus. V. 4, p. 676. MHS.
Clabaugh. Family hist. of John Hyder and Catherine Delaplaine Beam. 1909, pamph. MHS.
*Frederick Co. families. Markell. Ms. Personal list.
Clagett. Ancestry of Mrs. Fulton Ray Gordon, nee Ellen Marjorie Gray. D. C. Geneal. Rec. Com., 1932–34, pp. 122–24. Typed bd. DAR.
*Burke's landed gentry. Amer. families. 1939, p. 2995. MHS.
Mrs. Charles Carter chart. MHS.
†Chesapeake bay country. Earle. P. 209. MHS.
Mrs. C. C. Hall chart. MHS.
See Maynard family. Focke Geneal. Coll. Ms. MHS.
†Med. annals Md. Cordell. 1903, pp. 351–52. MHS.
Pedigree of Tilghman Vickers Morgan. Soc. Col. Wars Md. Culver. 1940. MHS; DAR.
Pedigree of Thomas Carroll Roberts. Soc. Col. Wars Md. Culver. 1940. MHS; DAR.
Pedigree of Wm. Emory Waring, Jr. Soc. Col. Wars Md. Culver. 1940. MHS; DAR.
Pedigree of Mason Locke Weems Williams. Soc. Col. Wars Md. Culver. 1940. MHS; DAR.
Sydney-Smith and Clagett-Price families. Price. MHS; DAR.
Mrs. G. H. Williams, Jr., chart. MHS.
*Wilson Mss. Coll., no. 42. MHS.
See Claggett.
See Eichar-Clagett.
See Offutt.
Clagett, Nathaniel. Will, 1807. D. A. R. Mag. v. 61, no. 8, p. 608.
Clagett Family. Bible. DAR.
*Descendants of John Clagett, son of Capt. Thomas, 1st. Additional notes. N. G. Florence. Ms. DAR.
*Ms. DAR.
Clagett, Claggett. St. Paul's Parish, Balto. V. 1, 2, 3. Mss. MHS.
***Clagget Family.** Arch. of Georgetown Univ., Wash., D. C., v. 287.
Claggets. Claggets (unpub. branch). Mrs. Turpin Layton. Md. Geneal. Rec. Com., 1938–39, 25 pp. Mss. DAR.
Claggett. Balto., its hist., its people. Hall. V. 2. MHS; DAR.
*Baptist church; burial records. Hist. of West. Md. Scharf. V. 1, p. 172. MHS; DAR.
The Beckwiths. Beckwith. Pp. 30–31.
Cary Geneal. Coll. Ms. MHS.
Chew family. Culver. M. H. Mag., 1935, v. 30, no. 2, pp. 157–75.
S. C. Chew pedigree chart. Soc. Col. Wars, Md. Johnston. 1905, p. 13. MHS.
See Daniel. Lineage Bks., Natl. Soc. of Daughters of Amer. Col., v. 3, p. 92. MHS; DAR.
Dorsey and Allied Families. Ms. MHS.

Claggett. *See* Dorsey-Bowie-Claggett. Lineage Bks., Natl. Soc. of Daughters of Amer. Col., v. 3, p. 162. MHS; DAR.
*Frederick Co. Families. Markell. Ms. Personal list.
†Hist. of West. Md. Scharf. V. 1, pp. 544, 761. MHS; DAR.
Life and times of Thomas J. Claggett (1743 (?)–1816), first bishop of Md., and first bishop consecrated in Amer. (Buried in Claggett burial ground, Croome, Prince George Co., 1898; remains removed and reinterred in Episcopal Cathedral, Wash., D. C.) G. G. Utley. 1913. Peabody Lib.; Lib. Cong.
Lillard, family of col. Va. Lillard. P. 248. MHS.
Maddox family. Col. and Revolutionary families of Phila. Jordan. 1933, v. 1, pp. 401–02.
Md. Families. Culver. Ms. Personal list.
Patriotic Md. Md. Soc. of S. A. R., 1930. MHS; DAR.
Pedigree of Jasper Mauduit Berry, Jr. Soc. Col. Wars Md. Culver. 1940. MHS; DAR.
*Pennington Papers. Ms. MHS.
*Presbyterian church, Darnestown, Montgomery Co.; burial records. Hist. of West. Md. Scharf. V. 1, p. 761. MHS; DAR.
*Side lights on Md. hist. Richardson. V. 2, p. 67. MHS. DAR.
Miss Margaret M. Steele chart. MHS.
Va. geneal. Hayden. MHS; DAR.
See Bowie-Claggett.
See Clagett.

Claggett, Bishop. Hist. of Md. Scharf. V. 2, p. 552. MHS.

Claggett, Nathaniel, Prince George Co. Abs. of will, 1809. D. A. R. Mag., Aug., 1927, v. 61, no. 8, p. 608.

Claggett Family. Bible rec. Ms. DAR.
*Claggett family of Md. M. T. Layton. Ms. DAR.
*Coat of arms. The Sun, Balto., March 13, 1904.

Claggett Line (1680–1843). M. L. W. Williams pedigree chart. Soc. Col. Wars, Md. Johnston. 1905, pp. 126, 142. MHS.

Claggett Line, Beck, Pa. Col. and Revolutionary families of Phila. Jordan. 1933, v. 1, pp. 329–39.

Claggett, Clagett. Bowies and their kindred. Bowie. MHS. DAR.

Claiborne. Claiborne, rebel W. H. Carpenter. Phila., 1845.
William Claiborne of Kent Island. J. H. Claiborne. William and Mary Quart., 2nd series, v. 1, p. 73.
‡Founders of Md. Neill. 1879.
Genealogical table of descendants of Secretary William Claiborne. G. M. Claiborne. J. P. Bell Co., Lynchburg, Va., 1900.
See Harris-Claiborne.

Claiborne, Va. Col. families of Amer. Lawrence. V. 5, p. 296. MHS.
Pedigree of Duncan Keener Brent. Soc. Col. Wars Md. Culver. 1940. MHS; DAR.

†Claiborne, Capt. Wm., Kent Island. Hist of Talbot Co. Tilghman. V. 1, pp. 493–521. MHS; DAR.

Clairborne. St. Paul's Parish, Balto. V. 1, 2. Mss. MHS.

***Clairborne,** Va. The Sun, Balto., June 3, 21, 1903.

Clairborne Family. Arch. of Georgetown Univ., Wash., D. C., v. 287.

Clandenin. Somerset Co. Court Book. Tilghman. 1937. Ms. DAR.

Clandening. Somerset Co. Court Book. Tilghman. 1937. Ms. DAR.

†Clapham. Encyc. of Amer. biog. Amer. Hist. Soc., N. Y., v. 9, p. 142. MHS.
Md. Families. Culver. Ms. Personal list.
St. Paul's Parish Balto. V. 1, 2, 3. Mss. MHS.

Clapham, Josias, Va. C. Johnston pedigree chart. Soc. Col. Wars, Md. Johnston. 1905, pp. 54, 142. MHS.

Claplatel. St. Paul's Parish, Balto. V. 1. Mss. MHS.

***Clapman.** Pennington Papers. Ms. MHS.

Clapp. Ances. Rec. and Portraits. Col. Dames of Amer., 1910, v. 2, p. 763. MHS; DAR.

***Clapp Family.** Arch. of Georgetown Univ., Wash., D. C., v. 287.

Claragahn. St. Paul's Parish, Balto. V. 2. Mss. MHS.

Clark. Amer. Armory and Blue Book. Matthews. 1911–12, p. 402.
Balto., Its Hist., Its People. Hall. V. 2, 3. MHS; DAR.
†Bench and Bar of Md. Sams and Riley. 1901, v. 2, p. 514. Lib. Cong.; MHS; Peabody Lib.
Centenary of Catholicity in Ky. Webb. 1884. MHS.
†Day-Star of Amer. Freedom. Davis. P. 195. MHS; DAR.
See Glenn. Col. Families of U. S. A. Mackenzie. V. 3, p. 183. MHS; DAR.
Griffith geneal. Griffith. MHS; DAR.
Md. Families. Culver. Ms. Personal list.
†Med. Annals Md. Cordell. 1903, pp. 352–53. MHS.
Patriotic Md. Md. Soc. of S. A. R., 1930. MHS; DAR.
Peale Geneal. Coll. Ms. MHS.
*Private burying ground, Montgomery Co., 1752–1817 (4 stones). Hist. of West. Md. Scharf. V. 1, p. 720. MHS; DAR.
Robinson chart. MHS.
St. Stephens Parish, Cecilton, Md. MHS; DAR.
Trinity P. E. Churchyard, Long Green. Typed ms. MHS; DAR.
See Ober-Nash-Clark.

Clark, E. Judson. Abr. Compend. Amer. Geneal. Virkus. V. 1, p. 553. DAR.

†Clark, Edw. L. Geneal. and mem. encyc. of Md. Spencer. V. 2, p. 703. MHS; DAR.

†Clark, Ernest J. Men of mark in Md. Johnson. V. 2, DAR; Enoch Pratt Lib.

***Clark, Gaylord Lee.** Burke's landed gentry. 1939. MHS.

Clark, Mrs. Gaylord Lee (Julia Brent Keyser). Chart. Col. Dames, Chap. I. MHS.

†Clark, J. C. Men of mark in Md. Johnson. V. 4. DAR; Enoch Pratt Lib.

Clark, John, Balto. Co. Will probated Dec. 19, 1754. D. A. R. Mag., v. 65, no. 8, p. 505.

Clark, Wm. Bullock. Amer. armory and blue bk. Matthews. 1908, p. 260. DAR.
Pedigree chart, plates 1 and 2. Soc. Col. Wars, Md. Johnston. 1905, pp. 15–16. MHS.

Clark, Mrs. Wm. Bullock (Ellen Clark Strong). Abr. Compend. Amer. Geneal. Virkus. V. 1, p. 554. DAR.
Chart. (Mostly Mass. families.) Col. Dames, Chap. I. MHS.
Clark Family, S. C. Col. families of Amer. Lawrence. V. 14, p. 129. MHS.
***Clark-Beaven.** Lineage Bk. Daughters of Founders and Patriots, v. 16, p. 81; v. 17, p. 104. MHS.
Clark-Burriss, Bible rec., East. Shore of Md. Contrib. by Mrs. H. W. Helwig of Youngstown, Ohio. Md. Geneal. Rec. Com., 1938–39, pp. 123–25. Mss. DAR.
Clark-Byrnside. Bible rec., Monroe Co., Va. (now W. Va.). D. A. R. Mag., Jan. 1936, v. 70, no. 1, pp. 58–59.
Clark, Clarke. Founders of Anne Arundel Co. Warfield. Pp. 533–35. MHS; DAR.
St. Paul's Parish, Balto. V. 1, 2, 3, 4. Mss. MHS.
Clark, Clarke Line, New Eng. N. W. Williams pedigree chart. Soc. Col. Wars, Md. Johnston. 1905, p. 127. MHS.
Clarke. Col. Nicholas Duvall Family Records. Price. Bd. ms. MHS.
Gallaher, O'Gallaher, family of Ireland. Ms. File case, DAR.
Monumental City. Howard. MHS, DAR.
*Semmes Geneal. Coll. Ms. MHS.
See Clark.
Clarke, Addison Downing. Greenway Mss. Geneal. Coll. Binder's title, Hawkins-Bordley. MHS.
Clarke, William, Anne Arundel Co. (Married Lavinia Warfield, Sept. 30, 1780.) D. A. R. Mag., v. 71, no. 2, p. 162.
Clarkson. Centenary of Catholicity in Ky. Webb. 1884. MHS.
St. Paul's Parish, Balto. V. 2. Mss. MHS.
*Semmes Geneal. Coll. Ms. MHS.
Clarkson, N. Y. (1690). Ms. File case, DAR.
***Clarkson Family.** Arch. of Georgetown Univ., Wash., D. C., v. 287.
†**Clarvoe.** Med. Annals Md. Cordell. 1903, p. 353. MHS.
†**Clary.** Hist of Frederick Co. Williams. MHS; DAR.
***Clary Family.** Arch. Georgetown Univ., Wash., D. C., v. 287.
***Clautice.** Geneal. and mem. encyc. of Md. Spencer. V. 1, p. 301. MHS; DAR.
Claxton. Descendants of Joran Kyn. Pa. Mag., v. 7, p. 464.
†**Claxton, Thomas, Jr.** (killed in action, 1813). M. H. Mag., v. 12, p. 209.
Clay. Clay family of Pa., 1716, with family connections in Kent Co., Md., and Del. Ms. File case, DAR.
St. Paul's Parish, Balto. V. 1, 2. Mss. MHS.
***Clay Family.** Arch. of Georgetown Univ., Wash., D. C., v. 287.
Clayland. St. Paul's Parish, Balto. V. 2. Mss. MHS.
Turner Geneal. Coll. Ms. MHS.
Miss G. Eyre Wright chart. MHS.
Clayland Family. Ms. MHS; DAR.
Claypole. *See* Claypool.
Claypool. Border settlers of northwest Va. Pp. 311, 409.
Howard lineage. Weaver. Pp. 119–22.
Rasin-Claypool. Ms. MHS.
Rasin-Claypool line. Balto.: its hist., its people. C. C. Hall. V, 3, p. 765. MHS.
Claypool, John, Va. Will. Ms. File case, DAR.
Claypool, Claypoole, Claypole. Ringgold-Elliott chart. MHS.
***Claypoole.** Arms. Old Kent. Hanson. P. 310. MHS; DAR.
See Claypool.
See Raisin.
Claypoole, Pa. Geneal. Pa. Mag., 1890, v. 14, pp. 86–87.
***Claypoole Family.** Arch. of Georgetown Univ., Wash., D. C., v. 287.
(1653.) Morris family of Phila. Moon. V. 1, p. 297; v. 2, p. 622. MHS.
Claypoole, Claypole. St. Paul's Parish, Balto. V. 2, 3. Mss. MHS.
Howard lineage. Weaver. MHS.
Clayton. Bible rec., Kent Co. Md. Geneal. Rec. Com., 1937 Parran,. Mss. DAR.
Cary Geneal. Coll. Ms. MHS.
Clayton family. 1933. Corrections. Mss. DAR.
Clayton family, Del. Corrections. Mss. MHS.
Clayton family. H. F. Hepburn. Hist. Soc. of Del., Wilmington, 1904, pamph. MHS.
Corrections to Clayton family. 1933. Ms. DAR.
Dulaney churchyard, near Massey, Kent Co. Md. Geneal. Rec. Com., 1933–34, pp. 210–12. Mss. DAR.
Gittings chart. MHS.
Md. Geneal. Rec. Com., 1938–39, p. 75. Mss. DAR.
Patriotic Md. Md. Soc. of S. A. R., 1930. MHS; DAR.
Pedigree of John B. Philip C. Hall. Soc. Col. Wars Md. Culver. 1940. MHS; DAR.
Revolutionary war pension abs. Natl. Geneal. Soc. Quart., v. 17, no. 4, p. 68.
St. Barnabas P. E. churchyard. Typed ms. MHS; DAR.
St. Paul's Parish, Balto. V. 2, 3, 4. Mss. MHS.
Southerland-Latham and allied families. Voorhees. Bd. Ms. MHS.
White Geneal. Tree. MHS.
See Davies-Clayton.
See Hart-Shehan-Clayton-Meloir.
Clayton, Va. Hill family of Hourston and Spaxton, Eng., Mass., Md., and New Eng., 1334–1934. MHS.
Clayton, Samuel, Queen Anne's Co. (1685–1739). W. H. De C. W. Thom pedigree charts. Soc. Col. Wars, Md. Johnston. 1905, pp. 108, 142. MHS.
***Clayton Family.** Arch. of Georgetown Univ., Wash., D. C., v. 287.
*Clayton family. 1933. DAR.
*Clayton family. H. F. Hepburn, Esq. Read before Hist. Soc. Del., Feb. 15, 1904. Hist. Soc. Del., Wilmington, 1904, pamph. MHS.
Line of descent of Maj. Philip Clayton, of "Catapla". (From copy of letter.) Ms. MHS.
*Old Kent. Hanson. P. 235. MHS; DAR.
Clayton Line, Kent Co., Del. Col. and Revolutionary families of Pa. Amer. Hist. Soc., N. Y., 1934, p. 197. (Clayton, Md., p. 199.)

Clayton Line, Va. J. P. Hill pedigree chart, plate 2. Soc. Col. Wars, Md. Johnston. 1905, p. 37. MHS.
***Clayton-Dashiell.** Lineage Bk., Daughters of Founders and Patriots, v. 23, pp. 53–54. MHS; DAR.
Claytor. *See* Owens-Claytor-Maynard-Rutter-Welsh.
Claytor Family, Anne Arundel Co. (1801). Md. Geneal. Rec. Com., 1932, v. 5, p. 44. DAR.
Clayville. Makemie Memorial Pres. churchyard, Snow Hill, Worcester Co. Hudson. Bd. ms. MHS; DAR. Also: Md. Geneal. Rec. Com., Mrs. Lines. Mss. DAR.
M. E. churchyard, Snow Hill, Worcester Co. Hudson. Bd. ms. MHS; DAR.
Clawson Family, Caroline, Cecil and Queen Anne Cos. Bible rec. Pub. Geneal. Soc. Pa., v. 11, pp. 78–80.
Clemens. Robins family tree. MHS.
Clement. Col. families of U. S. A. Mackenzie. V. 1, pp. 97–100. MHS; DAR.
Clements. Bible rec. Upper Penins. East. Shore, pp. 44–49. MHS; DAR.
Britton chart. MHS.
Britton Scrap Book. V. 1. Ms. MHS.
Chestertown cemetery. Md. O. R. Soc. Bull., no. 1, pp. 18–29.
Md. Geneal. Rec. Com., 1933–34, pp. 28, 30, 31, 50–60. Mss. DAR.
Middendorf chart. MHS.
Naturalizations in Md., 1666–1765; Laws. Bacon. MHS.
Patriotic Md. Md. Soc. of S. A. R., 1930. MHS; DAR.
St. Stephens Parish, Cecilton, Md. MHS; DAR.
*Semmes Geneal. Coll. Ms. MHS.
See Harrison-Clements.
Clements, Charles Co. Jenkins-Courtney chart. MHS.
Clements, Surry Co., Va. and Balto. Tyler's Quart., 1935–36, v. 17, pp. 125–27; 250–57. MHS.
†**Clements, Alday.** Men of mark in Md. Johnson. V. 4, DAR; Enoch Pratt Lib.
Clements, Richard. Bible rec., 1783–1867. Ms. MHS.
Clements Family, Caroline Co. Bible rec. M. H. Mag., 1917, v. 12, p. 387.
***Clements-Spalding.** Origins of Clements-Spalding and allied families of Md. and Ky. J. W. S. Clements, Louisville, Ky. Standard Press, 1928, 1st ed. MHS.
Clemm. Hist. sketch of P. F. Eichelberger. Eichelberger.
Pedigree of Philip Livingston Poe. Soc. Col. Wars Md. Culver. 1940. MHS; DAR.
Mrs. E. W. Poe chart. MHS.
St. Paul's Parish, Balto. V. 2, 3. Mss. MHS.
Steiner geneal. Steiner. 1896. MHS.
See Shultz-Clemm-Poe.
Clemson. Bible rec., 1757–1846. Note. (Came from Lancaster Co., Pa, into Md. prior to Revolutionary war; founder of Clemson family in Md.) Typed, 2 pp. MHS.
*Clemson family. A. Y. Casanova. Westminster, Md. Typed. MHS.
†Hist. of West. Md. Scharf. V. 1, pp. 602–03. MHS; DAR.
Jones family, "Clean Drinking Manor," Montgomery Co. Ms. MHS.
St. Paul's Parish, Balto. V. 2. Mss. MHS.
St. Stephens Parish, Cecilton, Md. MHS; DAR.
Clemson Family, Carroll Co. Tombstone rec. Md. Geneal. Rec. Com., 1933–34, pp. 146–49. Mss. DAR.
Clemsted. St. Paul's Parish, Balto. V. 2. Mss. MHS.
Clendenin. Md. families. Culver. Ms. Personal list.
Peale Geneal. Coll. Ms. MHS.
Clendenin, James, Harford Co. (1737). Ms. File case, DAR.
Clendinen. McSpadden-Love-Meigs-Clendinen-Von Bibber-Pope chart. MHS.
†Med. Annals Md. Cordell. 1903, pp. 354–55. MHS.
Tombstone rec. of Glendy burying ground. Md. Geneal. Rec. Com., 1933–34, pp. 171–78. Mss. DAR.
Clendinen Family. Chart. J. Vincent Meigs. Blue print, 1906. Ms. File case, DAR.
Clerk. St. Paul's Parish, Balto. V. 2. Mss. MHS.
†**Clerke.** Papers relating to early hist. of Md. Streeter. 1876. MHS.
Cleveland. Grover Cleveland pedigree. Ms. MHS.
Cleveland-Iddings. Abr. Compend. Amer. Geneal. Virkus. V. 4, p. 112. MHS.
Clever. St. Paul's Parish, Balto. V. 2. Mss. MHS.
Cliff, Talbot Co. H. Mullikin pedigree charts, plate 1. Soc. Col. Wars, Md. Johnston. 1905, pp. 74, 143. MHS.
†**Cline.** Hist. of Frederick Co. Williams. MHS; DAR.
Portrait and biog. rec. of Sixth Cong. Dist. of Md. 1898, p. 791. MHS; DAR.
Clingman. *See* Wagner-Clingman.
***Clinkssales.** Clinkssales family of Southern Md. Wilson Mss. Coll., no. 120. MHS.
***Clocker.** Wilson Mss. Coll., no. 8, B. MHS.
Clokey, Ohio. Parrish family. Boyd. MHS; DAR.
Close. Biggs family. Ms. DAR.
Mrs. H. De Courcy Wright Thom chart. MHS.
Clotworthy. *See* Reeves-Clotworthy.
Cloud. Data. Natl. Geneal. Soc. Quart., April, 1912, v. 1, no. 1, p. 22.
Harford Co. Hist. Soc. Mss. Coll. JHU.
Cloud, W. W. Abr. Compend. Amer. Geneal. Virkus. V. 1, p. 556. DAR.
Cloud Family. Our family ancestors. Potts. Lib. Cong; DAR.
Cloudley. *See* Cloudsley.
Cloudsley, Cloudley. St. Paul's Parish, Balto. V. 2, 3. Mss. MHS.
†**Clough.** Med. Annals Md. Cordell. 1903, p. 355. MHS.
***Clssna** (?). Frederick Co. families. Markell. Ms. Personal list.
Clunet. St. Paul's Parish, Balto. V. 2. Mss. MHS.
***Coade.** Wilson Mss. Coll., no. 8, B. MHS.
Coal, Coale, Cole. St. Paul's Parish, Balto. V. 1, 2, 3, 4. Mss. MHS.
Coale. See Allen. Abr. Compend. Amer. Geneal. Virkus. V. 4, p. 23. MHS.
Bible rec. Ms. MHS.
Col. families of Amer. Lawrence. V. 16, p. 82. MHS.

Col. families of U. S. A. Mackenzie. V. 2. MHS; DAR.
Col. and Revolutionary families of Pa. Jordan. 1932, v. 4, p. 593.
Descendants of William of Md. Thomas Book. Thomas. Pp. 289–91. Lib. Cong.; MHS.
Dorsey-Duval-Coale-Buchanan-Borden-Brooke and allied families. Newsp. clipp. and other printed matter. MHS.
Early Quaker rec., Anne Arundel and Calvert Cos., 1665–1889. Pub. Geneal. Soc. Pa., v. 3, no. 3, pp. 197–200.
Ellicott-Campbell chart. MHS.
Ellicott-King chart. MHS.
†Hist. of Allegany Co. Thomas and Williams. V. 2. MHS; DAR.
Hist. sketch of P. F. Eichelberger. Eichelberger.
†Med. Annals Md. Cordell. 1903, pp. 18, 355. MHS.
Pedigree. Geneal. of McKean family of Pa. Buchanan. Pp. 149, 152. MHS.
Pedigree of Corbin Braxton Dallam. Soc. Col. Wars Md. Culver. 1940. MHS; DAR.
Pedigree of Maurice Edward Skinner. Soc. Col. Wars Md. Culver. 1940. MHS; DAR.
Portrait and biog. rec. of Harford and Cecil Cos. 1897, pp. 128, 291. MHS; DAR.
Mrs. Renshaw chart. MHS.
Thomas-Chew-Lawrence. Thomas. MHS.
Turner family. Forman. P. 43. MHS.
See Coal.
Coale, Anne Arundel Co. G. M. Sharp pedigree chart, plate 1. Soc. Col. Wars, Md. Johnston. 1905, p. 91. MHS.
Coale, Mrs. Wm. Ellis (Anne Esther Colston). Chart. Col. Dames, Chap. I. MHS.
Coale Family. Data. Ms. MHS.
Coard. Buckingham Pres. churchyard, Worcester Co. Hudson. Bd. ms. MHS; DAR.
Coates. Abr. Compend. Amer. Geneal. Virkus. V. 1, p. 395. DAR.
Cummings chart. Lib. Cong.; MHS; DAR.
*Geneal. of Moses and Susanna Coates, who settled in Pa., 1717. Truman Coates. 1906.
Ingrham family. Md. Geneal. Rec. Com., 1938–39, pp. 142–67. Mss. DAR.
Jones family, "Clean Drinking Manor," Montgomery Co. Ms. MHS.
†Med. Annals Md. Cordell. 1903, p. 356. MHS.
St. Paul's Parish, Balto. V. 1, 2. Mss. MHS.
†Coates, John, Md. (1751–1810; first Grand Master of Masons in Md.). Hist. of Talbot Co. Tilghman. V. 1, pp. 575–78. MHS; DAR.
Coates Family, Pa. Newsp. clipp. File case, DAR.
Coats. *See* Courts.
***Coats,** Pa. Burke's landed gentry. 1939. MHS.
Cobb, C. H. Md. Soc., War of 1812, v. 1, no. 92. Ms. MHS.
Cobb Family. Dulaney family. Dulaney. MHS.
***Cobbs,** Va. The Sun, Balto., Nov. 10, 17, 24, Dec. 1, 8, 1907; Jan. 26, Feb. 2. 1908.
Cobelance, Coblentz. Patriotic Md. Md. Soc. of S. A. R., 1930. MHS; DAR.
†Coblentz. Med. Annals Md. Cordell. 1903, p. 356. MHS.
See Cobelance.
†Coblentz, Emory L. Men of mark in Md. Johnson. V. 4. DAR; Enoch Pratt Lib.
Cochran. Balto., its hist., its people. Hall. V. 3. MHS; DAR.
*Chronicles of Cochrans. I. Cochran Haughton. Columbus, Ohio, T. J. Heer Printing Co., 2 vols. DAR.
Glendy churchyard, Balto. Md. Geneal. Rec. Com., 1933–34. Mss. DAR.
Hamilton family of Charles Co. Kelly. MHS.
St. Paul's Parish, Balto. V. 2, 3. Mss. MHS.
Cochran Family. Descendants of Nathaniel. Ms. File case, DAR.
*Kirkendbright and N. Y. Cochran family. J. H. Callender. Priv. pr., N. Y., 1931. MHS.
Cochran-Beard-Carr-Ross-Wassan Families. Ms., 12 pp. File case, DAR.
Cochrane Browne-Cochrane-Brooke-Neale-Bennett chart. File case, MHS.
Cochrill. St. Paul's Parish, Balto. V. 2. Mss. MHS.
Cock. St. Stephens Parish, Cecilton, Md. MHS; DAR.
See Cox.
Cock, Cocke. St. Paul's Parish, Balto. V. 2, 3. Mss. MHS.
Cocke family of Va.; giving hundreds of family connections. W. R. Cocke, Jr. 1931, pamph. File case, DAR.
Cocke family of Va. Va. Mag. Hist. and Biog., 1895–96. V. 3, pp. 282–92, 405–14; 1896–97. V. 4, pp. 86–96, 212–17, 322–32, 431–50; 1897–98. V. 5, pp. 71–89, 181–94. MHS.
Mrs. G. R. Veazey chart. MHS.
Cocke, Richard, Va. Pedigree of Duncan Keener Brent. Soc. Col. Wars Md. Culver. 1940. MHS; DAR.
Pedigree of Charles Morton Stewart. Soc. Col. Wars Md. Culver. 1940. MHS; DAR.
Cocke, Wm., Va. Pedigree of Henry Holladay Latané. Soc. Col. Wars Md. Culver. 1940. MHS; DAR.
Cocke-Johnson. Abr. Compend. Amer. Geneal. Virkus. V. 4, p. 660. MHS.
Cockey. Arnold chart. MHS.
†Chesapeake Bay Country. Earle. P. 344. MHS.
D. A. R. Mag., v. 70, no. 5, pp. 457–58.
Deeds, indentures, tombstone rec. and wills. Rogers Coll. Ms. MHS.
Descendants of Col. Thomas White. Morris. Pp. 133–34. MHS.
Dorsey chart. MHS.
Elliott chart. MHS.
*Garrison Church. Allen. P. 150. MHS; DAR.
Harford Co. Hist. Soc. Mss. Coll. JHU.
Hist. graves of Md. and D. C. Ridgely. MHS.
†Hist. of Balto. City and Co. Scharf. Pp. 843–44. MHS.
Legge-Washington families. Galloway. Ms. MHS.
Md. families. Culver. Ms. Personal list.
†Med. Annals Md. Cordell. 1903, p. 357. MHS.
Patriotic Md. Md. Soc. of S. A. R., 1930. MHS; DAR.
Pedigree of Richard Walker Worthington. Soc. Col. Wars Md. Culver. 1940. MHS; DAR.
Ringgold-Elliott chart. MHS.

Cockey. St. Paul's Parish, Balto. V. 1, 2, 3, 4. Mss. MHS.
St. Thomas' Parish, Balto. Co. Bd. ms. MHS. Also: Md. Geneal. Rec. Com., 1937, pp. 109–82. Mss. DAR.
Talbott of "Poplar Knowle". Shirk. MHS; DAR.
*The Sun, Balto., June 24, July 1, Oct. 28, 1906.
Western Run Parish book. Allen. Bd. ms. MHS.
See Legge.
See Tucker-Cockey.
Cockey, E. C. Ms. MHS.
Cockey, John. Bible rec. Ms. MHS.
†**Cockey, Joshua F.** Men of mark in Md. Johnson. V. 3. DAR; Enoch Pratt Lib.
Cockey, Thomas, Balto. Co. Family data, 1724–64. Ms. File case, DAR.
Cockey Family. Chart. E. C. Cockey. Ms. MHS.
Copied from Riley family. Md. Geneal. Rec. Com., 1934–35, p. 411. Mss. DAR.
Focke Geneal. Coll. Ms. MHS.
Cockrell. Abr. Compend. Amer. Geneal. Virkus. V. 1, p. 559; v. 4, p. 457. MHS.
†**Cockrill.** Med. Annals Md. Cordell. 1903, p. 357. MHS.
Cocks. Tombstone rec. of Glendy burying ground. Md. Geneal. Rec. Com., 1933–34, pp. 171–78. Mss. DAR.
Mrs. Wm. T. Howard, Jr., chart. MHS.
Whitridge chart. MHS.
Codd. Balto., its hist., its people. Hall. V. 3. MHS; DAR.
†Men of mark in Md. Johnson. V. 4. DAR: Enoch Pratt Lib.
St. Paul's Parish, Balto. V. 2. Mss. MHS.
Codd, Cecil Co. Va. Mag., v. 10, p. 375.
Coddington Family. Mountain Democrat, Garrett Co., Jan. 3, 1935. Newsp. clipp. MHS; DAR.
Cody. Naturalizations in Md., 1666–1765; Laws. Bacon. MHS.
***Coe, Ward Baldwin.** Burke's landed gentry. 1939. MHS.
***Coe-Ward.** Memorial and immigrant ancestors. 1897. DAR.
Coffin. Evergreen cemetery, Worcester Co., Hudson, Bd. ms. MHS; DAR.
Coffman, J. (veteran). Md. Soc., War of 1812, v. 1, no. 73. Ms. MHS.
Coggins. Botfield and allied families. Ms. DAR.
Cogswell. Hazelhurst charts. MHS.
Cohen. Bible. Photos. MHS.
Cemetery, 1217 W. Saratoga St., Balto., 1793–1920. Typed ms. MHS.
*Cohens of Md. A. Baroway. M. H. Mag., 1923, v. 18, pp. 537–76; 1924, v, 19, pp. 54–77.
***Cohen, Mendes.** Geneal. and mem. encyc. of Md. Spencer. V. 2, pp. 675–78. MHS; DAR.
Cohill. Md. tombstone rec. Md. Geneal. Rec. Com., 1937, Parran, p. 29. Mss. DAR.
Cohn. Done Bible rec. Ms. MHS.
***Coit.** Gilman-Coit chart. MHS.
Hazelhurst charts. MHS.
Pamph., with geneal. MHS.
Colbert, E. Abbott. Md. Soc., War of 1812, v. 3, no. 235. Ms. MHS.
Colbert, P. Maulsby. Md. Soc., War of 1812, v. 4, no. 343. Ms. MHS.
Colbourn. Mt. Zion P. E. churchyard, Worcester Co. Md. Geneal. Rec. Com., 1937, Mrs. Lines. Mss. DAR.
Colburn. Descendants of Col. Thomas White. Morris. P. 134. MHS.
Colburne. St. Paul's Parish, Balto. V. 3. Mss. MHS.
Cole. Ances. rec. and portraits. Col. Dames of Amer., 1910, v. 2, p. 546. MHS; DAR.
J. L. Brent pedigree chart. Soc. Col. Wars, Md. Johnston. 1905, p. 7. MHS.
Brooks chart. MHS.
*Chart of descendants of Richard Cole, 1717–1781. R. F. Cole. MHS.
Col. families of Amer. Lawrence. V. 5, p. 92. MHS.
J. T. Dennis pedigree chart, plate 2. Soc. Col. Wars, Md. Johnston. 1905, p. 22. MHS.
Dorsey Papers. Ms. MHS.
Founders of Anne Arundel and Howard Cos. Warfield. P. 133. MHS; DAR.
†Geneal. and mem. encyc. of Md. Spencer. V. 1, p. 152. MHS; DAR.
Harryman chart. Cary Geneal. Coll. Ms. MHS.
Mrs. G. C. Jenkins chart. MHS.
Md. families. Culver. Ms. Personal list.
McCormick chart. MHS.
†Med. Annals Md. Cordell. 1903, pp. 358–59. MHS.
Parrish family. Boyd. MHS; DAR.
Pedigree of Duncan Keener Brent. Soc. Col. Wars Md. Culver. 1940. MHS; DAR.
Price family and other Gunpowder Friends. Death notices; photos. of newsp. clipp. MHS.
Raisin chart. MHS.
St. Stephens Parish, Cecilton, Md. MHS; DAR.
*Semmes Geneal. Coll. Ms. MHS.
See Vander Horst. Abr. Compend. Amer. Geneal. Virkus. V. 1, p. 867. DAR.
J. A. Wilson pedigree chart, plate 1. Soc. Col. Wars, Md. Johnston. 1905, p. 130. MHS.
See Coal.
See Dye-Cole.
Cole, Abraham. Copy of will, 1822. Ms. File case, DAR.
†**Cole, Giles,** Charles Co. Two forgotten heroes, 1675–76. M. H. Mag., 1924, v. 19, pp. 339–40.
Cole, J. C. de G. Md. Soc., War of 1812, v. 1, no. 115. Ms. MHS.
·**Cole, R. C.** Md. Soc., War of 1812, v. 1, no. 97. Ms. MHS.
Cole, R. F., Worcester Co. and Tex. Abr. Compend. Amer. Geneal. Virkus. V. 4, p. 118. MHS.
Cole, Thomas. Glendy churchyard. Patriotic Marylander, v. 2, no. 4, pp. 54–60. MHS; DAR.
Cole Family, Harford Co. Serton or Saxon family, Monmouth, N. J. Md. Geneal. Rec. Com., v. 2, pp. 17–22. DAR.
Cole Family, Va. Chart; some descendants of Richard Cole, 1717–1781, of Louisa Co., Va. R. F. Cole. MHS.
‡**Cole-Cawood.** Two forgotten heroes, Giles Cole and Stephen Cawood, Charles Co. M. H. Mag., 1924, v. 19, p. 339.
Cole-Price. Chart, photos., 2 sheets. Cary Geneal. Coll. Ms. MHS.
Colebourne. Somerset Co. Court Book. Tilghman. 1937. Ms. DAR.

Colegate. Arnold chart. MHS.
See Clement. Col. families of U. S. A. Mackenzie. V. 1, pp. 97–100. MHS; DAR.
Hopkinson family, Phila. Col. and Revolutionary families of Pa. Jordan. 1932, v. 4.
St. Paul's Parish, Balto. V. 1, 2. Mss. MHS.
Colegate Line. Hopkinson, Phila. Col. and Revolutionary families of Phila. Jordan. 1933, v. 1, pp. 22–86.
Colegate-Dale. Harford Co. Hist. Soc. Mss. Coll. JHU.
Colehound. Somerset Co. Court Book. Tilghman. 1937. Ms. DAR.
Coleman. Brandt chart. MHS.
Cary Geneal. Coll. Ms. MHS.
Crumpton graveyard. Md. Geneal. Rec. Com., 1933–34, pp. 193–203. Mss. DAR.
See Dickenson. Abr. Compend. Amer. Geneal. Virkus. V. 1, p. 911. DAR.
Griffith geneal. Griffith. MHS; DAR.
Hist. of Harford Co. Preston. MHS; DAR.
Pedigree of Thomas Murray Maynadier. Soc. Col. Wars Md. Culver. 1940. MHS; DAR.
Pedigree of Mark Alexander Herbert Smith. Soc. Col. Wars Md. Culver. 1940. MHS; DAR.
St. Paul's Parish, Balto. V. 1, 2, 3, 4. Mss. MHS.
Somerset Co. Court Book. Tilghman. 1937. Ms. DAR.
*Wicomico Co. families. Tilghman. Ms., p. 129. DAR.
Coleman, Va. Posey chart. MHS.
†**Coleman, Rev. John.** Garrison Church. Allen. Pp. 57–66. MHS; DAR.
Hist. of Harford Co. Preston. MHS; DAR.
Coleman, Wm. Wheeler. Pedigree chart. Soc. Col. Wars, Md. Johnston. 1905, p. 17. MHS.
***Coles,** Va. The Sun, Balto., Sept. 4, Nov. 6, Dec. 4, 18 (Va.), 1904.
***Coles Family,** Va. Its numerous connections from emigration to Amer. to year 1915. W. B. Coles. N. Y., 1931, 1st ed. MHS; DAR.
Coleston. Somerset Co. Court Book. Tilghman. 1937. Ms. DAR.
Colgate. Abr. Compend. Amer. Geneal. Virkus. V. 1, pp. 359, 563. DAR.
Focke Geneal. Coll. Mss. MHS.
†Med. Annals Md. Cordell. 1903, p. 359. MHS.
Colgate, Colegate-Von Meyer. Abr. Compend. Amer. Geneal. Virkus. V. 4, p. 170. MHS.
Colgate-Onion-Bond-Waters. Harford Co. Hist. Soc. Mss. Coll. JHU.
Colleman. Naturalizations in Md., 1666–1765; Laws. Bacon. MHS.
Colier. Rec. of Stepney Parish. MHS; DAR.
Colke. Naturalizations in Md., 1666–1765; Laws. Bacon. MHS.
Colleberry, Kellenberger. John Swadner and his descendants. Evans. 1919. Typed, bd. MHS.
***Collett.** Copies of two orig. letters written by John Collett, dated London, May 9, 1650, and Amsterdam July 14, 1656. Mss. File case, MHS.
*Descendants of John D. Collett. Appendix, 1928. MHS.
*Descendants of John D. Collett (1578–1659) of Eng. and U. S. Chart. 1929. MHS; DAR.
*(Born in Eng., 1578; died in Balto., 1659.) Geneal. of descendants of John Collett. J. D. Collett, 1929, 131 pp. MHS; DAR.
Md. families. Culver. Ms. Personal list.
M. H. Mag., v. 8, no. 2, p. 203.
Collett Family, Eng. Chart. John Collett. Ms. File case, DAR.
***Collett-Utye.** Notes. M. H. Mag., 1913, v. 8, pp. 203–04.
***Collier.** Burke's landed gentry. 1939. MHS.
Cary Geneal. Coll. Ms. MHS.
*Semmes Geneal. Coll. Ms. MHS.
Somerset Co. Court Book. Tilghman. 1937. Ms. DAR.
Wicomico Co. families. Bible rec. Ms. DAR.
*Wicomico Co. families. Tilghman. Ms., pp. 10–11, 32, 66, 99, 116–22. DAR.
See Humphreys-Collier.
Collins. All Hallow's P. E. churchyard, Snow Hill, Worcester Co. Hudson. Bd. Ms. MHS; DAR. Also: Md. Geneal. Rec. Com., 1935–36, p. 24. Mss. DAR.
Bible rec., 1771–1881. Bible now owned by Dr. C. E. Collins, Crisfield, Md. Md. Geneal. Rec. Com., 1938–39, pp. 208–09. Mss. DAR.
Buckingham Pres. churchyard, Worcester Co. Hudson. Bd. ms. MHS; DAR.
Cannon-Riley-Truitt-Houston-Kollock, Stow. Ms. MHS.
Centreville cemetery. Md. O. R. Soc. Bull., no. 1, pp. 41–47.
Makemie Memorial Pres. churchyard, Snow Hill, Worcester Co. Hudson. Bd. ms. MHS; DAR. Also: Md. Geneal. Rec. Com., Mrs. Lines. Mss. DAR.
†Med. Annals. Md. Cordell. 1903, p. 359. MHS.
Rec. of Stepney Parish. MHS; DAR.
St. Paul's Parish, Balto. V. 1, 2, 3, 4. Mss. MHS.
St. Stephens Parish, Cecilton, Md. MHS; DAR.
Somerset Co. Court Book. Tilghman. 1937. Ms. DAR.
Turner Geneal. Coll. Ms. MHS.
*Wicomico Co. families. Tilghman. Ms., pp. 12, 68, 94, 119–20. DAR.
Wicomico Co. families. Bible rec. Ms. DAR.
See Hall-Collins-Elliott-Tingley.
See White-Collins.
***Collins,** Va. Burke's landed gentry. 1939. MHS.
Collins, Maj. Brice, Md. and N. C. (1758–1823). Ms. File case, DAR.
Collins, G. Gordon. Md. Soc., War of 1812, v. 3, no. 295. Ms. MHS.
†**Collins, Wm.** Men of mark in Md. Johnson. V. 1. DAR; Enoch Pratt Lib.
Collins Family. Data. Coll. by J. C. Stow. Ms. MHS.
Collins-Law-Polk, Del. and Md. Bible rec., 1737–1853. Md. Geneal. Bull., v. 6, pp. 13–15, 25.
Collison. *See* Hodson-Collison-Ball-Jones-Lankford.
Collison-Hodson-Ball. Bible rec. of Dorchester and Somerset Cos. and Del. Pp. 36–39. DAR.
Collmus, C. Carroll. Md. Soc., War of 1812, v. 3, no. 234. Ms. MHS.

Colson. Fox-Ellicott-Evans families. Evans. MHS; DAR.
Colston. Ances. rec. and portraits. Col. Dames of Amer., 1910, v. 2, pp. 728, 819. MHS; DAR.
Balto., its hist., its people. Hall. V. 2. MHS; DAR.
See Beckley. Abr. Compend. Amer. Geneal. Virkus. V. 1, p. 452. DAR.
Robert Brooke chart. MHS; DAR.
Coale chart. MHS.
Col. families of U. S. A. Mackenzie. V. 1. MHS; DAR.
Crain chart. MHS.
Geneal. rec. of family of Thomas. Thomas. MHS.
Patriotic Md. Md. Soc. of S. A. R., 1930. MHS; DAR.
*Old Kent. Hanson. Pp. 131–32. MHS; DAR.
Stevenson chart. MHS.
*The Sun, Balto., April 8, 1906 (Va.); Nov. 10, 17, 1907.
Trinity Church burial ground, near Cambridge, Md. Md. Geneal. Rec. Com., 1937–38, pp. 93–104. Mss. DAR.
Whitehead chart. MHS.
Colston, Va. Chart, photos. Cary Geneal. Coll. Ms. MHS.
Colston, Frederick Morgan. Pedigree. Soc. Col. Wars Md. Culver. 1930. MHS; DAR.
Colston, Wm. Line, Va. D. H. Thomas pedigree chart, plate 1. Soc. Col. Wars, Md. Johnson. 1905, pp. 109, 143. MHS.
Colton. Geneal. of family of Gideon Gilpin. MHS.
†Hist. of Balto. City and County. Scharf. P. 634. MHS.
Coly, Daniel (died 1729). Grave in St. Paul's cemetery, Kent Co. Md. Geneal. Rec. Com., 1933–34, p. 233. Mss. DAR.
Combe. Christ P. E. Church cemetery, Cambridge. Steele. 1936. MHS; DAR.
Combes, Maj. Wm., Talbot Co. H. Mullikin pedigree charts, plate 1. Soc. Col. Wars, Md. Johnson. 1905, pp. 74, 143. MHS.
Combs. Abr. Compend. Amer. Geneal. Virkus. V. 1, p. 274. DAR.
Cummings chart. Lib. Cong.; MHS; DAR.
†Hist. of West. Md. Scharf. V. 2, pp. 1542–43. MHS; DAR.
See Coombs.
Combs, Coombs. Col. families of U. S. A. Mackenzie. V. 3. MHS; DAR.
***Comegys.** Comegys family in Amer. Wm. Wirt Comegys, Greensboro, Md. Mss. MHS.
Comegys family in Amer. Wm. Wirt Comegys. 3 typed and bd. copies. MHS; Pa. Hist. Soc.; N. Y. Hist. Soc.
Kent Co. Bible rec. Md. Geneal. Rec. Com., 1933–34, p. 243. Mss. DAR.
Bible rec. Md. Geneal. Rec. Com., 1937. Parran. Mss. DAR.
Lineage Bks., Natl. Soc. of Daughters of Amer. Col., v. 1, p. 222. MHS; DAR.
Md. families. Culver. Ms. Personal list.
Morris family of Phila. Moon. V. 3, p. 1061. MHS.
Naturalizations in Md., 1666–1765; Laws. Bacon. MHS.
*Revolutionary patriots of Comegys family. Ellen I. S. Wallis. D. A. R. Mag., Jan., 1933, v. 67, no. 1, pp. 15–18; Feb., 1933, no. 2, pp. 86–88.
St. Paul's Parish, Balto. V. 2. Mss. MHS.
Turner family. Forman. P. 70. MHS.
W. A. and S. W. Merritt pedigree charts, plate 1. Soc. Col. Wars, Md. Johnston. 1905, pp. 67, 143. MHS.
Comegys Family. From ms. list of Md. militia, Revolutionary war, Kent Co. Muster Roll, 1775, 27th Batt., 5th Co. MHS; DAR.
*Old Kent. Hanson. Pp. 224–29. MHS; DAR.
Revolutionary patriots, Md., 1661, with geneal. D. A. R. Mag., v. 67, no. 1, p. 15; no. 2, p. 86.
***Comiston.** Wicomico Co. families. Tilghman. Ms., p. 96. DAR.
Comly. Hist. of Byberry and Moreland. Martindale. MHS.
Compton. Balto., its hist., its people, Hall. V. 2. MHS; DAR.
†Biog. cyc. of rep. men of Md. and D. C. P. 39. MHS; DAR.
Comptons. Edited by C. V. Compton, San Antonio, Tex. Md. rec. of Comptons, Oct., 1939, v. 1, no. 4, pp. 19–20. MHS.
*Semmes Geneal. Coll. Ms. MHS.
Spessard family. Spessard. MHS; DAR.
Conable. *See* Cunnabell.
Conavroe. *See* Conroe.
***Conaway.** Wilson Mss. Coll., no. 8, B. MHS.
Conaway, Connaway. St. Paul's Parish, Balto. V. 1, 2. Mss. MHS.
Condon. St. Stephens Parish, Cecilton, Md. MHS; DAR.
Conger. St. Stephens Parish, Cecilton, Md. MHS; DAR.
Conier, Kent Co. Pedigree of Richard Dennis Steuart. Soc. Col. Wars Md. Culver. 1940. MHS; DAR.
Conier. *See* Conner.
Conklin, Wm. Glendy churchyard. Patriotic Marylander, v. 2, no. 4, pp. 54–60. MHS; DAR.
Conklin-Gibson. Tombstone rec. of Glendy burying ground (vault). Md. Geneal. Rec. Com., 1933–34, pp. 171–78. Mss. DAR.
Conkling. Mrs. R. F. Brent chart. MHS.
Conn. Bible rec., 1725–1831, from original owner, Richard Isaac Wilkes Conn. D. C. Geneal. Rec. Com., 1936–37, v. 31, pt. 2, p. 312. DAR.
See Guyton-Kirr-Rush-Holland-Conn.
Conn, James. D. A. R. Mag., v. 71, no. 2, p. 164.
Connable. *See* Cunnabell.
Connard. Somerset Co. Court Book. Tilghman. 1937. Ms. DAR.
Connaway. *See* Conaway.
Connel, Connell. St. Paul's Parish, Balto. V. 1, 2. Mss. MHS.
Connell. Abr. Compend. Amer. Geneal. Virkus. V. 6, p. 467. DAR.
Connelly, Connoley, Connolly, Connoly. St. Paul's Parish, Balto. V. 1, 2, 3. Mss. MHS.
†**Conner.** Day-Star of Amer. Freedom. Davis. P. 220. MHS.

Mt. Carmel Burial Ground, Montgomery Co. Md. Geneal. Rec. Com., 1934, p. 85. Mss. DAR.
St. Paul's Parish, Balto. V. 1, 2, 3. Mss. MHS.
*Wicomico Co. families. Tilghman. Ms., p. 17. DAR.
Conner, Kent Co. Pedigree of George Webb Constable. Soc. Col. Wars Md. Culver. 1940. MHS; DAR.
***Conner, Conier.** Old Kent. Hanson. Pp. 79–80. MHS; DAR.
Somerset Co. Court Book. Tilghman. 1937. Ms. DAR.
Connier. *See* Conner.
Connolly. Old cemetery, Denton, Caroline Co. Md. Geneal. Rec. Com., 1935–36, p. 168. Mss. DAR.
Trinity P. E. churchyard, Long Green. Typed ms. MHS; DAR.
See Connelly.
Connoway, Conoway. St. Paul's Parish, Balto. V. 1, 2. Mss. MHS.
Conoley. St. Stephens Parish, Cecilton, Md. MHS; DAR.
Conoway. *See* Connoway.
Conrad. Western Run Parish book. Allen. Bd. ms. MHS.
Conrad, James Madison Monroe. Md. Soc., War of 1812, v. 1, no. 87. Ms. MHS.
Conrad, Townsend N. Md. Soc., War of 1812, v. 1, no. 116. Ms. MHS.
Conroe, Conavroe. Florence Eyster Weaver chart. MHS.
Constable. Chestertown cemetery. Md. O. R. Soc. Bull., no. 1, pp. 18–29.
Hist. graves of Md. and D. C. Ridgely. MHS.
Pedigree of Richard Constable Bernard. Soc. Col. Wars Md. Culver. 1940. MHS; DAR.
St. Paul's churchyard, Kent Co. Md. O. R. Soc. Bull., no. 2, pp. 54–65. MHS.
St. Paul's Parish. Balto. V. 1, 3. Mss. MHS.
St. Paul's P. E. churchyard, Kent Co. Md. O. R. Soc. Bull., no. 2, pp. 54–65.
Stump family of Cecil and Harford Cos. Pamph. MHS.
Constable, George Webb. Pedigree. Soc. Col. Wars Md. Culver. 1940. MHS; DAR.
***Constable Family.** Old Kent. Hanson. Pp. 85–87. MHS; DAR.
Constantine. Mt. Paran Pres. churchyard, Harrisonville, Balto. Co. Typed ms. MHS; DAR.
St. Paul's Parish, Balto. V. 2, 3. Mss. MHS.
Contee. Ances. rec. and portraits. Col. Dames of Amer., 1910, v. 2, p. 726. MHS; DAR.
Bowie chart. Cary Geneal. Coll. Ms. MHS.
Bowies and their kindred. Bowie. MHS; DAR.
Robert Brooke chart. MHS; DAR.
Col. families of U. S. A. Mackenzie. V. 2, pp. 199–206. MHS; DAR.
Duckett chart. MHS.
Geneal. rec. of family of Thomas. Thomas. MHS.
Lineage Bks., Natl. Soc. of Daughters of Amer. Col., v. 2, p. 66. MHS; DAR.
Md. Geneal. Rec. Com., 1932–33, pp. 208–09. Mss. DAR.
See Meredith. Abr. Compend. Amer. Geneal. Virkus. V. 1, p. 725. DAR.
Portrait and biog. rec. of Sixth Cong. Dist. of Md. 1898. See Viers, p. 721. MHS; DAR.
St. Barnabas P. E. churchyard. Typed ms. MHS; DAR.
St. Paul's Parish, Balto. V. 2. Mss. MHS.
Side lights on Md. hist. Richardson. V. 2, p. 71. MHS; DAR.
Stevenson chart. MHS.
*The Sun, Balto., Nov. 20, 1904.
Contee, Alexander (1691–1740). D. H. Thomas pedigree chart, plate 1. Soc. Col. Wars, Md. Johnson. 1905, pp. 109, 143. MHS.
†**Contee, Benj.** Hist. of Md. Scharf. V. 2, p. 573. MHS.
Contee, Duval and Jarboe. Huguenots in Md. Patriotic Marylander, v. 1, no. 4, p. 36. MHS; DAR.
†**Contee, John.** M. H. Mag., v. 12, p. 210.
Contee, Richard. Md. Soc., War of 1812, v. 1, no. 42. Ms. MHS.
***Contee Family.** Old Kent. Hanson. P. 127. MHS; DAR.
Contrell. Cary Geneal. Coll. Ms. MHS.
Conway, Conwell. Whiteley chart. MHS.
Wm. Conway of Md. and Pa.; born in Wales, 1742; in Cecil Co., 1771. Gives marriage of Wm. Conway and Ruth (Adams) Conway. Ms. File case, DAR.
Maulsby family in Amer. Barnard. DAR; Peabody Lib.
St. Paul's Parish, Balto. V. 1, 2. Mss. MHS.
Va. geneal. Hayden. MHS; DAR.
Conway, Thomas, Va. and Pa. Ms. File case, DAR.
Conway Family, Va. Md. Geneal. Rec. Com., 1935–36, p. 281. DAR.
Conway-Stansbury. Abr. Compend. Amer. Geneal. Virkus. V. 4, p. 120. MHS.
Conwell. *See* Conway.
Conyngham. Mrs. Talbot T. Speer chart. MHS.
***Cooch.** Ancestry and descendants of Nancy Allyn (Foote) Webb, etc. Cooch. MHS; DAR.
Geneal. Ms. MHS.
Cooch, Thomas, Jr., Del. D. A. R. Mag., v. 73, no. 6, p. 56.
†**Coode, John.** Hist. of Md. Scharf. V. 1, p. 309. MHS.
Cook. Balto., its hist., its people. Hall. V. 3. MHS; DAR.
Bible rec. Ms. MHS.
*Burke's landed gentry. 1939. MHS.
Md. gleanings in Eng. Wills. M. H. Mag., 1908, v. 3, no. 2.
Mt. Calvary Church burial ground, Howard Co. Md. Geneal. Rec. Com., 1934–35, pp. 95–99. Mss. DAR.
Talbott of "Poplar Knowle." Shirk. MHS; DAR.
See Cooke.
Cook, Mass., R. I. and Md. Col. families of Amer. Lawrence. V. 10, pp. 1–34. MHS.
Cook, John (son of John Cook). Born at Bush, Sept. 25, 1681; first event on register of St. George's (old Spesutia) Church, Harford Co. Ms. MHS.
Cook-James. Abr. Compend. Amer. Geneal. Virkus. V. 4, pp. 567–68. MHS.

*Cook-James. Cook-James and allied families. Jane James Cook. 1 vol., illuminated levant. Natl. Americana Soc., N. Y., 1931.
†Cook, Cooke. Med. Annals Md. Cordell. 1903, pp. 360–61. MHS.
*Pennington Papers. Ms. MHS.
St. Paul's Parish, Balto. V. 1, 2, 3. Mss. MHS.
St. Stephens Parish, Cecilton, Md. MHS; DAR.
*The Sun, Balto., Aug. 11, 18, 25, Sept. 1 (Va.), 8 (Va.), 1907.
Cook, Koch. Hagerstown tombstone inscriptions. Gruder. Natl. Geneal. Soc. Quart., 1919, v. 8, nos. 1, 2.
Cook (Cooke), Mordecai. Virkus. V. 1, Abr. Compend. Amer. Geneal., p. 579. DAR.
Cooke. Amer. Clan Gregor Year Book, 1919, p. 44; 1926–27, p. 23. MHS; DAR.
Balto., its hist., its people. Hall. V. 3. MHS; DAR.
*Cooke, Dorchester Co. Lineage Bk., Daughters of Founders and Patriots, v. 21, p. 134. MHS
Cooke, Ebenezer, Cecil Co. Md. O. R. Soc. Bull., no. 2, pp. 94–96.
Cooke, Wm. Dewey. Md. Soc., War of 1812, v. 2, no. 187. Ms. MHS.
Cooke-Booth. Descendants of Mordecai Cooke, "Mordecai's Mount," Gloucester Co., Va., 1650, and Thomas Booth, "Ware Neck," Gloucester Co., Va., 1685. Coat of arms. Dr. and Mrs. Wm. Carter Stubbs. New Orleans, 1923. Bd. Ms. MHS.
Col. families of Amer. Lawrence. V. 10, p. 47. MHS.
*Cooke-Brooke-Beckwith Families. Hist. Dorchester Co. Jones. 1925, pp. 279–90. MHS; DAR.
Booth family. William and Mary Quart., 2nd series, v. 6, pp. 259–64.
*Descendants of Mordecai, of "Mordecai's Mount," Gloucester Co., Va., 1650, and Thomas Booth, of "Wareneck," Gloucester Co., Va., 1685. Dr. and Mrs. Wm. Carter Stubbs. New Orleans 1923. MHS.
Dorsey Papers. Ms. MHS.
Miss Katherine Lurman chart. MHS.
Pedigree of Rev. Sam'l Tagart Steele. Soc. Col. Wars Md. Culver. 1940. MHS; DAR.
See Cook.
See Gordon-Knox-Fitzhugh-Cooke.
See Robertson.
Cooke, Cook. Maulsby family in Amer. Barnard. DAR; Peabody Lib.
Selden chart. MHS.
Cooksey. Anne Arundel Co. tombstone inscriptions. Ms. DAR.
St. Paul's Parish, Balto. V. 2. Mss. MHS.
Cooley. Glison-Sellman-Murphy-Cooley Bible rec. Ms. DAR.
John White Bible rec. Ms. MHS.
Coombs. Christ P. E. Church cemetery, Cambridge. Steele. 1936. MHS; DAR.
Coombs, Combs. Centenary of Catholicity in Ky. Webb. 1884. MHS.
*Semmes Geneal. Coll. Ms. MHS.
Hamilton family of Charles Co. Kelly. MHS.
Coomes. Darby geneal. Darby. MHS.
St. Paul's Parish, Balto. V. 2. Mss. MHS.
Cooper. Beards' Luth. graveyard, Washington Co. Md. Geneal. Rec. Com., 1935–36. Mss. DAR.
Bible rec. Upper Penins. East. Shore, p. 37.
*Frederick Co. families. Markell. Ms. Personal list.
Gibbs chart. MHS.
†Med. Annals Md. Cordell. 1903, p. 361. MHS.
Old Somerset. Torrence. MHS; DAR.
Price ancestral data (paternal). Bd. Ms. MHS.
Rec. of Stepney Parish. MHS; DAR.
St. Paul's Parish, Balto. V. 1, 2, 4. Mss. MHS.
St. Stephens Parish, Cecilton, Md. MHS; DAR.
*Wicomico Co. families. Tilghman. Ms, p. 121. DAR.
See Chancellor.
Cooper, Benjamin, Talbot Co. Copy of will, 1789. Ms. File case, DAR.
†Cooper, H. A. Balto., hist. and biog. Richardson and Bennett. 1871, pp. 237–39. MHS; DAR.
Cooper, Jonathan (born in Md., 1758; died in Ill., 1845). Copy of will. Ms. File case, DAR.
Cooper, Peter. Monumental City. Howard. MHS; DAR.
*Cope. Rec. of Cope family from Eng. to Pa. about 1682. G. Cope. Phila., King and Baird, 1861. MHS.
Cope, Pa. Abr. Compend. Amer. Geneal. Virkus. V. 1, p. 270. DAR.
Cope Family, Pa. And Cope chart by Gilbert Cope. Ms. File case, DAR.
Cope-Garrett. Ancestral chart of Gilbert Cope and Anna Garrett, his wife, 1879, West Chester, Pa., with additions and corrections, 1920. Lib. Cong.
Copeland. Mrs. Talbot T. Speer chart. MHS.
Pedigree of Charles Morton Stewart. Soc. Col. Wars Md. Culver. 1940. MHS; DAR.
Copen. *See* Coppen.
Copenhaven, Koppenhaven Family, Pa. With Dannecker data. Md. ref. Ms. File case, DAR.
*Copes. Wicomico Co. families. Tilghman. Ms, p. 96. DAR.
Coplestone. *See* Churchill-Crocker-Fox-Coplestone-Bonvile-Ellicott.
Copley. Copley family or fossil seal. Patriotic Marylander, v. 2, no. 2, pp. 19–37. MHS; DAR.
†Papers relating to early hist. of Md. Streeter. 1876. MHS.
†Copley, Lionel. First royal gov. of Md. M. H. Mag., 1922, v. 17, pp. 163–77.
Coppage. Cummings chart. Lib. Cong.; MHS; DAR.
Coppen, Copen, Copping. St. Stephens Parish, Cecilton, Md. MHS; DAR.
Copper. Bible rec., Kent Co. Md. Geneal. Rec. Com., 1933–34, pp. 240–42. Mss. DAR.
Still Pond Church and cemetery. Md. O. R. Soc. Bull., no. 2, pp. 65–75.
Coppidge. Lambdin chart. MHS.
Copping. *See* Coppen.
Copson. Md. gleanings in Eng. Wills. M. H. Mag., 1907, v. 2, no. 3.
Corban. St. Paul's Parish, Balto. V. 1. Mss. MHS.
Corbett. Md. tombstone rec. Md. Geneal, Rec. Com., 1937. Parran, pp. 15, 16. Mss. DAR.

Corbin. Chart, photos., 1 sheet. Cary Geneal. Coll. Ms. MHS.
Geneal. H. I. Kirk. Ms, in six ms boxes in the vault. MHS.
Geneal. of Va. family of Lomax. Lib. Cong.
King and Queen Cos., Va.; hist. and geneal. Bagby. 1908.
Patriotic Md. Md. Soc. of S. A. R., 1930. MHS; DAR.
St. Paul's Parish, Balto. V. 1, 2. Mss. MHS.
Selden chart. MHS.
Mrs. H. De Courcy Wright Thom chart. MHS.
See Read-Corbin-Luttrell-Bywaters.
***Corbin,** Va. The Sun, Balto., Oct. 2, Nov. 6, 20, 1904.
Corbin, Henry, Va. Pedigree of James Donnell Tilghman. Soc. Col. Wars Md. Culver. 1940. MHS; DAR.
Corbin Family, Md. and Ky. Ms. File case, DAR.
Corbit. Wm. Conway of Md. and Pa. Ms. File case, DAR.
Corcoran. Trinity P. E. churchyard, Long Green. Typed ms. MHS; DAR.
Cord. Somerset Co. Court Book. Tilghman. 1937. Ms. DAR.
Corddry. M. E. churchyard, Snow Hill, Worcester Co., Hudson. Bd. ms. MHS; DAR.
Cordea. Naturalizations in Md., 1666–1765; Laws. Bacon. MHS.
†Cordell. Med. Annals Md. Cordell. 1903, p. 361. MHS.
†Cordell, Eugene F. Men of mark in Md. Johnson. V. 2. DAR; Enoch Pratt Lib.
Corey. Bible rec. Upper Penins. East. Shore., p. 217.
Coriell, Dr. Louis Duncan. Pedigree. Soc. Col. Wars Md. Culver. 1940. MHS; DAR.
Corkran. Medford family, Dorchester Co. Ms. MHS.
†Men of mark in Md. Johnson. V. 4. DAR; Enoch Pratt Lib.
Newsp. clipp. Scrap Book. MHS.
See Andrews-Bonner-Carroll-Corkran-Medford.
See Medford-Bonner-Carroll-Corkran-Stevens.
Cornelius. Bible rec. Upper Penins. East. Shore, pp. 30–36. MHS; DAR.
St. Thomas' Parish, Balto. Co. Bd. ms. MHS. Also: Md. Geneal. Rec. Com., 1937, pp. 109–82. Mss. DAR.
Cornelius, T. Reese. Md. Soc., War of 1812, v. 4, no. 307. Ms. MHS.
Cornell. Rev. Joseph Hull (1595) and some of his descendants. Hull. 1904, p. 23. MHS.
Cornise. Frederick Co. tombstone inscriptions. Gruder. Natl. Geneal. Soc. Quart., 1919, v. 8, nos. 1, 2.
Cornwaleys. Thomas Cornwaleys, commissioner and counsellor. G. B. Stratemier. MHS.
See Cornwallis.
†Cornwaleys, Cornwallis. Papers relating to early hist. of Md. Streeter. 1876. MHS.
‡Cornwallis. Capt. Thomas Cornwallis. H. J. Berkley. MHS.
See Cornwaleys.
‡Cornwallis, Thomas. Founders of Md. Neill. 1879.
‡Cornwallis, Cornwaleys. Thomas Cornwallis. (Cornwaleys) and early Md. colonists. Edw. D. Neill. Repr. from New Eng. Hist. and Geneal. Reg., April, 1889, v. 43. Boston, 1889.
Coroxall. St. Paul's Parish, Balto. V. 1. Mss. MHS.
†Correll. Med. Annals Md. Cordell. 1903, p. 362. MHS.
Corse. Col. families of Amer. Lawrence. V. 2, p. 280; v. 9, p. 66. MHS.
†Med. Annals Md. Cordell. 1903, p. 362. MHS.
Mrs. E. C. Venable chart. MHS.
Corse, Kent Co. Morris family of Phila. Moon. V. 1, p. 180; v. 2, p. 629. MHS.
Mrs. J. Hall Pleasants, Jr., chart. MHS.
Corse, Coursey. Evans family chart. Hull. Mss. MHS.
†Corse, De Corse. Hist. of Balto. City and Co. Scharf. P. 929. MHS.
Cosby. Abr. Compend. Amer. Geneal. Virkus. V. 1, p. 567. DAR.
Cosden. St. Stephens Patish, Cecilton, Md. MHS; DAR.
Cosden Family. Data, 1640. M. H. Jamar. Ms. MHS.
***Cosgrove, Lydia.** Geneal. of Barlow family. Barlow. MHS.
Cosins. Naturalizations in Md., 1666–1765; Laws. Bacon. MHS.
†Coskery. Med. Annals Md. Cordell. 1903, p. 363. MHS.
Cost. Patriotic Md. Md. Soc. of S. A. R., 1930. MHS; DAR.
Costa. Naturalizations in Md., 1666–1765; Laws. Bacon. MHS.
Costin. Miss G. Eyre Wright chart. MHS.
Turner Geneal. Coll. Ms. MHS.
Costin, Costine. Somerset Co. Court Book. Tilghman. 1937. Ms. DAR.
Cotten, Edyth Johns (Mrs. Bruce). Abr. Compend. Amer. Geneal. Virkus. V. 1, p. 568. DAR.
Formerly Mrs. Jesse Tyson. Chart. Col. Dames, Chap. I. MHS.
Cottingham. All Hallow's churchyard, Snow Hill. Md. Geneal. Rec. Com., 1935–36, p. 24. Mss. DAR.
Old Somerset. Torrence. MHS; DAR.
Somerset Co. Court Book. Tilghman. 1937. Ms. DAR.
Cottingham Family, Somerset Co. (1700–1854). Ancestors of Arthur Orision Dillon. Dillon. 1927, pp. 40–43. MHS; DAR.
Cottman. All Hallow's churchyard, Snow Hill. Md. Geneal. Rec. Com., 1935–36, p. 24. Mss. DAR.
Balto., its hist., its people. Hall. V. 2. MHS; DAR.
Cottman family chart. H. Clifford Campion. 1911. MHS.
Md. families. Culver. Ms. Personal list.
McCormick chart. MHS.
Rehobeth P. E. churchyard, Somerset Co. Md. Geneal. Rec. Com., 1937, Mrs. Lines. Mss. DAR.
Somerset Co. Court Book. Tilghman. 1937. Ms. DAR.
Cottman, James Hough. Pedigree chart, Soc. Col. Wars, Md. Johnston. 1905. p. 18. MHS.
Cottman, Lewis Warrington. Pedigree. Soc. Col. Wars Md. Culver. 1940. MHS; DAR.
Cottman, Mrs. Thomas Edmund (Margaret Darlington Bennett). Chart. Col. Dames, Chap. I. MHS.

Cottman-Lux-Detrick. Rec., 1669–1862. Md. Geneal. Rec. Com., 1932–33, pp. 338–48. Mss. DAR.
Coudon. Abr. Compend. Amer. Geneal. Virkus. V. 6, p. 306. DAR.
Stump family of Cecil and Harford Cos. Pamph. MHS.
†**Coudon,** Cecil Co. Biog. cyc. of rep. men of Md. and D. C. P. 327. MHS; DAR.
Coudy. Md. tombstone rec. Md. Geneal. Rec. Com., 1937, Parran, p. 2. Mss. DAR.
Coues. Carne and allied family notes. Coues. Ms. MHS.
Coulbourn. Mt. Olive M. P. churchyard, Worcester Co. Md. Geneal. Rec. Com., 1937, Mrs. Lines. Mss. DAR.
Rehobeth P. E. churchyard, Somerset Co. Md. Geneal. Rec. Com., 1937, Mrs. Lines. Mss. DAR.
Patriotic Md. Md. Soc. of S. A. R., 1930. MHS; DAR.
See Coulbourne.
Coulbourne, Coulbourn. Old Somerset. Torrence. MHS.
Coulson. Harford Co. Hist. Soc. Mss. Coll. JHU.
St. Paul's Parish, Balto. V. 1, 2. Mss. MHS.
Coulter. Dorsey and allied families. Ms. MHS.
*Frederick Co. families. Markell. Ms. Personal list.
See Gambrill. Abr. Compend. Amer. Geneal. Virkus. V. 1, p. 116. DAR.
†Med. Annals Md. Cordell. 1903, p. 363. MHS.
Patriotic Md. Md. Soc. of S. A. R., 1930. MHS; DAR.
St. Paul's Parish, Balto. V. 3. Mss. MHS.
Council. Southern Bapt. Church cemetery, Worcester Co. Md. Geneal. Rec. Com., 1937, Mrs. Lines. Mss. DAR.
†**Councilman.** Med. Annals Md. Cordell. 1903, p. 363. MHS.
Counselman. St. Paul's Parish, Balto. V. 3. Mss. MHS.
Coupard. St. John's R. C. Church cemetery, Montgomery Co. Md. Geneal. Rec. Com., 1926, p. 27. Mss. DAR.
†**Coupland, R. S.** Men of mark in Md. Johnson. V. 2. DAR; Enoch Pratt Lib.
Courci. *See* De Coursey.
Coursey. Dobbin chart. MHS.
Evans family chart. Hull. Mss. MHS.
Mrs. H. F. Johnston chart. MHS.
Pedigree of Duncan Keener Brent. Soc. Col. Wars Md. Culver. 1940. MHS; DAR.
Thomas family of Talbot Co. Spencer. MHS; DAR.
See De Courcy.
Coursey Line. Col. and Revolutionary lineages in Amer. 1939, v. 3, p. 235. MHS.
Coursey, De Courcy. Miss G. Eyre Wright chart. MHS.
Courtenay. Abr. Compend. Amer. Geneal. Virkus. V. 1, p. 568; v. 6, p. 165. DAR.
Burton ancestry. Ms. MHS.
Col. families of U. S. A. Mackenzie. V. 2; v. 7, p. 180. MHS.
Patriotic Md. Md. Soc. of S. A. R., 1930. MHS; DAR.
St. Paul's Parish, Balto. V. 1, 2. Mss. MHS.
Courtney. Amer. Armory and Blue Book. Matthews. 1911–12, p. 393.
Col. families of U. S. A. Mackenzie. V. 1, p. 284. MHS; DAR.
E. A. and F. De Sales Jenkins pedigree chart. Soc. Col. Wars, Md. Johnston. 1905, p. 46. MHS.
*Jenkins-Courtney chart. MHS.
King and Queen Cos., Va.; hist. and geneal. Bagby. 1908.
Marriage rec., 1781–1892, Harford Co. Md. Geneal. Rec. Com., 1934–35, p. 108. DAR.
Middendorf chart. MHS.
Pedigree of Charles O'Donovan. Soc. Col. Wars Md. Culver. 1940. MHS; DAR.
Courts. Courts graves, "Deep Falls." Md. O. R. S. Bull., no. 3. MHS.
Jones family, "Clean Drinking Manor," Montgomery Co. Ms. MHS.
†Med. Annals Md. Cordell. 1903, p. 364. MHS.
*Wilson Mss. Coll., no. 96. MHS.
Courts, Betsey. Will proved Mar. 8, 1808. D. A. R. Mag., v. 61, no. 8, p. 608.
Courts Line. Lilburn family. Col. and Revolutionary families of Phila. Jordan. 1933, v. 1, pp. 382–98.
Courts Line, Gaither, Va. and Md. Col. and Revolutionary families of Phila. Jordan. 1933, v. 1, pp. 144–67.
***Courts, Coats.** Semmes Geneal. Coll. Ms. MHS.
Cousin. Harford Co. Hist. Soc. Mss. Coll. JHU.
Coutanceau. Coutanceau and Waughop families, St. Mary's Co., Md., and Va. Christopher Johnston. William and Mary Quart., 1st series, v. 22, p. 271.
Couter. Zion Reformed Church, Hagerstown. Md. Geneal. Rec. Com., 1934–35. Mss. DAR.
Coventon. St. Paul's Parish, Balto. V. 1, 2. Mss. MHS.
Cover. Biggs family. Ms. DAR.
Covey. Gillingham family. Gillingham. P. 79. MHS; DAR.
Covington. All Hallow's P. E. churchyard, Snow Hill, Worcester Co. Hudson. Bd. ms. MHS; DAR. Also: Md. Geneal. Rec. Com., 1935–36, p. 24. Mss. DAR.
Amer. Clan Gregor Year Book, 1917, pp. 56–62 (Gen. Leonard); 1929, p. 40 (Alexander). MHS; DAR.
Cary Geneal. Coll. Ms. MHS.
Christ P. E. Church cemetery, Cambridge. Steele. 1936. MHS; DAR.
Col. families of U. S. A. Mackenzie. V. 1, p. 332. MHS; DAR.
De Ford chart. MHS.
Early hist. of Hollyday family. Hollyday. MHS; DAR.
†Memoir of Leonard Covington. B. L. C. Wailes. Natchez, 1928, 64 pp. MHS.
Old Somerset. Torrence. MHS; DAR.
Pedigree of Lee Cummings Cary. Soc. Col. Wars Md. Culver. 1940. MHS; DAR.
Pedigree of Rev. James Mitchell Magruder. Soc. Col. Wars Md. Culver. 1940. MHS; DAR.
Pedigree of Levin Gale Shreve. Soc. Col. Wars Md. Culver. 1940. MHS; DAR.
St. Paul's P. E. churchyard, Berlin, Worcester Co. Hudson. Bd. ms. MHS; DAR. Also:

Md. Geneal. Rec. Com., 1937, Mrs. Lines. Mss. DAR.
Side lights on Md. hist. Richardson. V. 2, p. 309. MHS; DAR.
Sketches of John Slemmons Stevenson and Rev. Samuel McMaster. Stevenson. P. 16. MHS.
Somerset Co. Court Book. Tilghman. 1937. Ms. DAR.
Tilghman chart. MHS.
Turner Geneal. Coll. Ms. MHS.
*Wicomico Co. families. Tilghman. Ms, pp. 44–45, 125. DAR.

Covington, Henry, Queen Anne Co. Will dated July 7, 1805. D. A. R. Mag., v. 67, no. 6, p. 384.

Covington, Brig.-Gen. Leonard. Hist. of Md. Scharf. V. 3, p. 101. MHS.

†**Cowan.** John K. Cowan. W. Irving Cross. M. H. Mag., 1925, v. 20, pp. 1–29.
St. Paul's Parish, Balto. V. 1, 2, 3. Mss. MHS.
St. Stephens Parish, Cecilton, Md. MHS; DAR.

Coward. Old Md. families. Bromwell. MHS; DAR.

Cowarden. St. Stephens Parish, Cecilton, Md. MHS; DAR.

Cowart. Tombstone rec. of Dorchester Co. Jones. DAR.

Cowden. Hist. of Allegany Co. Thomas and Williams. V. 2, pp. 798–800. MHS; DAR.

***Cowden Family.** Bible rec. Md. Geneal. Rec. Com., 1932–33, pp. 40–41. DAR.

Cowden-Ridgely-Jamison. Bible rec., 1724–1845, from Bible in possession of Dr. James L. Ridgely, Forest Park, Balto. Md. Geneal. Rec. Com., 1932–33, pp. 40–41. Mss. DAR.

Cowdery Family. Tercentenary hist. of Md. Andrews. V. 4, p. 621. MHS; DAR.

†**Cowen.** Bench and bar of Md. Sams and Riley. 1901, v. 2, p. 654. Lib. Cong.; MHS; Peabody Lib.
Scrap books relating to John K. Cowen. W. Irving Cross. 4 vols. MHS.

†**Cowen, John K.** M. H. Mag., 1925, v. 20, no. 1, p. 1.

†**Cowherd.** Hist. of Allegany Co. Thomas and Williams. V. 2. Pp. 1258–59. MHS; DAR.
Tercentenary hist. of Md. Andrews. V. 2, p. 415. MHS; DAR.
Tyler's Quart. Mag., v. 12, p. 245. MHS; DAR.

Cowin. Somerset Co. Court Book. Tilghman. 1937. Ms. DAR.

Cowman. Col. Nicholas Duvall family records. Price. Bd. ms. MHS.
Price ancestral data (maternal) Ms. MHS.
Mrs. M. L. Price chart. MHS.
Talbott of "Poplar Knowle." Shirk. MHS; DAR.
Thomas-Chew-Lawrence. Thomas. MHS.

Cowman Family. Thomas Book. Thomas. P. 291. Lib. Cong.; MHS.

Cox. Ances. rec. and portraits. Col. Dames of Amer. 1910. Pp. 30–36. MHS; DAR.
Col. families of East. Shore and their descendants. Emory. 1900, pp. 144, 184–87. MHS.
Jennings Hand Bible rec. Photos. MHS.
Lineage and descendants of Sarah Cox, Earleville, Cecil Co., 1675–1937. Ms. MHS; File case, DAR.
*Lineage and descendants of Sarah Cox, 1675–1937: Mrs. Walter Miles, great-granddaughter, 3907 Jocelyn St., Washington, D. C. Typed. MHS.
*Lineage Bk. Daughters of Amer. Colonists. V. 5, p. 145. MHS; DAR.
†Med. Annals Md. Cordell. 1903, p. 364. MHS.
Pedigree of Benedict Henry Hanson, Jr. Soc. Col. Wars Md. Culver. 1940. MHS; DAR.
Rec. of Stepney Parish. MHS; DAR.
St. Paul's Parish, Balto. V. 1, 2, 3. Mss. MHS.
St. Stephens Parish, Cecilton, Md. MHS; DAR.
Tercentenary hist. of Md. Andrews. V. 2, p. 760. MHS; DAR.
Turner Geneal. Coll. Ms. MHS.
*Wicomico Co. families. Tilghman. Ms, p. 113. DAR.
See Hutchins-Cox.

Cox, Isaac. Revolutionary war pension. Natl. Geneal. Soc. Quart., Sept., 1938, v. 26, no. 3, p. 54.

Cox, John. Copy of will, 1785, Cecil Co. Md. Geneal. Rec. Com., 1934–35, p. 255. Mss. DAR.

Cox, Rebbecca. Copy of will, 1793, Cecil Co. Md. Geneal. Rec. Com., 1934–35, p. 256. Mss. DAR.

Cox-Morehead. Data. D. A. R. Mag., v. 60, no. 9, p. 570.

***Cox, Cock.** Cecil Co. Lineage Bk., Daughters of Founders and Patriots, v. 22, pp. 48, 93. MHS; DAR.

Cox (Cock) Family, from Balto. to Cecil Co.; Davy from London; and George family of Talbott Co.; with notes on Bartlett, Hammond, Troth and Turner families. Mrs. Rachel Cox Leef and Celeste Webb. Ms. MHS.

Cox, Cock Family, Cecil Co. Geneal. notes. Ms. File case, DAR.

Coxe. Old Kent. Hanson. P. 297. MHS; DAR.

Coy. Revolutionary war pension abst. Natl. Geneal. Soc. Quart., v. 20, no. 2, p. 57.
Tercentenary hist. of Md. Andrews. V. 3, p. 49. MHS; DAR.

***Cozens Family,** Wash., D. C. Notes. Amer. Clan Gregor Year Book, 1937, p. 109. MHS; DAR.

Crabb. Black chart. MHS.
Griffith geneal. Griffith. MHS; DAR.
Pedigree of Walter Ireland Dawkins. Soc. Col. Wars Md. Culver. 1940. MHS; DAR.
See Sprigg. Col. families of U. S. A. Mackenzie. V. 2, p. 699. MHS; DAR.

Crabb, Ralph. Pedigree of James Mather Sill. Soc. Col. Wars Md. Culver. 1940. MHS; DAR.

Crabb Family. Monnet family geneal. Monette. Pp. 1102–08. MHS.
*Robert Smith Chew and his ancestors to Md. and Va. Pollock. 1938, pp. 115–16. Typed, in Binder. DAR.

Crabbe. Md. families. Culver. Ms. Personal list.
Orme geneal. chart. MHS.

Crabbin. St. Paul's Parish, Balto. V. 2. Mss. MHS.

Cracroft. St. Paul's Parish, Balto. V. 1. Mss. MHS.

Craddock, J. N. Md. Soc., War of 1812, v. 1, no. 78. Ms. MHS.
Craddock, Cradock. St. Paul's Parish, Balto. V. 1, 3. Mss. MHS.
Cradock. Amer. Armory and Blue Book. Matthews. 1911–12, p. 194.
*Coat of arms. Burke's landed gentry. 1939. MHS.
Hist. of West. Md. Scharf. V. 2, p. 1495. MHS; DAR.
Garrison Church. Allen. MHS; DAR.
Hist. graves of Md. and D. C. Ridgely. MHS.
†Hist. of Balto. City and Co. Scharf. Pp. 841, 858–62. MHS.
†Md. Annals Md. Cordell. 1903, p. 364. MHS.
St. Thomas' Parish, Balto. Co. Bd. ms. MHS. Also: Md. Geneal. Rec. Com., 1937, pp. 109–82. Mss. DAR.
See Craddock.
Cragg. St. Paul's Parish, Balto. V. 2. Mss. MHS.
Cragin. *See* McCarteney-McKenny-Cragin.
Craig. Christ P. E. Church cemetery, Cambridge. Steele. 1936. MHS; DAR.
Lukens chart. MHS.
†Med. Annals Md. Cordell. 1903, p. 365. MHS.
Old Md. families. Bromwell. MHS; DAR.
St. Paul's Parish, Balto. V. 1, 2, 3. Mss. MHS.
Talbott of "Poplar Knowle." Shirk. MHS; DAR.
Craig, John. Ms. File case, DAR.
***Craig Family,** Pa. (1708–1895). Craig family of Pa. W. M. Clemens. 1921. DAR.
†**Craik.** Boyhood memories of Dr. James Craik (Va.). Va. Mag. Hist. and Biog., April, 1938, v. 46, no. 2, p. 135.
Fitzhugh family. Va. Mag. Hist. and Biog., v. 8, p. 95.
†Hist. of Allegany Co. Thomas and Williams. V. 1. MHS; DAR.
Craik, Fairfax Co., Va. Coll. of Amer. epitaphs and inscriptions. Alden. 1814, v. 5. MHS.
Crain, Mrs. Bennett (Helen Hampton Young). Chart. Col. Dames, Chap. I. MHS.
Crainer. John Swadner and his descendants. Evans. 1919. Typed, bd. MHS.
Cralle-Drane-Nuthall-Sprigg. Abr. Compend. Amer. Geneal. Virkus. V. 4, p. 694. MHS.
†**Cramer.** (106 ref.) Hist. of Frederick Co. Williams. MHS; DAR.
†Patriotic Md. Md. Soc. of S. A. R., 1930. MHS; DAR.
Steiner geneal. Steiner. 1896. MHS.
Zion Reformed Church, Hagerstown. Md. Geneal. Rec. Com., 1934–35. Mss. DAR.
***Cramer-Kramer.** Frederick Co. families. Markell. Ms. Personal list.
Crammer. Southern Bapt. Church cemetery, Worcester Co. Md. Geneal. Rec. Com., 1937, Mrs. Lines. Mss. DAR.
Cramphim. Lineage Bks., Natl. Soc. of Daughters of Amer. Col., v. 2, p. 299. MHS; DAR.
Crandall. All Hallow's Church Parish rec., Anne Arundel Co. Ms. MHS.
Austin's Geneal. Dict. MHS.
St. Barnabas P. E. churchyard. Typed ms. MHS; DAR.
Vital rec. of Rhode Island. MHS.
White Geneal. tree. MHS.
Crane. Abr. Compend. Amer. Geneal. Virkus. V. 1, p. 571. DAR.
Fresh Pond Neck cemetery, home of Bennetts. Md. O. R. Soc. Bull., no. 3, pp. 57–58.
Freshpond Neck tombstone inscriptions. Md. O. R. Soc. Bull., no. 3, p. 75. MHS.
*Geneal. of Crane family. E. B. Crane. Worcester, Mass., Press of Charles Hamilton, 1900, 2 vols.
†Med. Annals Md. Cordell. 1903, pp. 365–66. MHS.
Patriotic Md. Md. Soc. of S. A. R., 1930. MHS; DAR.
†**Crane, Anne Moncure.** Biog. sketches of distinguished Marylanders. Boyle. MHS; DAR.
Crane, Jonathan, Conn. Pedigree of Arthur Gordon Turner. Soc. Col. Wars Md. Culver. 1940. MHS; DAR.
Crane, Wm. H. Md. Soc., War of 1812, v. 4, no. 302. Ms. MHS.
Crane Family (1843–59). Md. Geneal. Rec. Com., v. 4, pp. 66–67. DAR.
Cranforth. St. Paul's Parish, Balto. V. 1. Mss. MHS.
Cranwell. Zion Reformed Church, Hagerstown. Md. Geneal. Rec. Com., 1934–35. Mss. DAR.
Cranwell, J. Harford. Amer. Armory and Blue Bk. Matthews. 1908, p. 77. DAR.
***Crapster.** Founders of Anne Arundel and Howard Cos. Warfield. Pp. 449–50. MHS; DAR.
Cratiot. Cary Geneal. Coll. Ms. MHS.
Crawford. Beall and Bell families. Beall. MHS.
Bond chart. MHS.
Chart. Geneal. tables of descendants of John Hamilton, Va. MHS.
Crawford family of Amer. Wm. M. Clemens. 1914, pamph. MHS.
Faith Pres. Church (Glendy Graveyard). Mss. MHS.
*Frederick Co. families. Markell. Ms. Personal list.
Gantz family geneal. Ms. MHS.
Gillingham family. Gillingham. P. 78. MHS; DAR.
Glendy churchard. Patriotic Marylander, v. 2, no. 4, pp. 54, 60. MHS; DAR.
Hagerstown tombstone inscriptions. Grunder. Natl. Geneal. Soc. Quart., 1919, v. 8, nos. 1, 2.
Laytonsville M. E. churchyard, Montgomery Co. Md. Geneal. Rec. Com., 1934–35, p. 69. Mss. DAR.
†Med. Annals Md. Cordell. 1903, pp. 182, 366, 758–70. MHS.
M. E. Church burial ground, Laytonsville, Montgomery Co. Md. Geneal. Rec. Com., 1934–35, pp. 69–82. Mss. DAR.
St. Paul's Parish, Balto. V. 1, 2, 3, 4. Mss. MHS.
Trinity Church cemetery, Dorchester Co. Md. O. R. Soc. Bull., no. 3, pp. 42–52.
Trinity Church burial ground, near Cambridge, Md. Md. Geneal. Rec. Com., 1937–38, pp. 93–104. Mss. DAR.

*Wicomico Co. families. Tilghman. Ms., p. 111. DAR.
Crawford Family. Rec. Wm. M. Clemens. N. Y., 1914, ltd. ed. MHS.
Craycroft. Cary Geneal. Coll. Ms. MHS.
*Semmes Geneal. Coll. Ms. MHS.
***Creager.** Frederick Co. families. Markell. Ms. Personal list.
Creager, Henry (born in Md., 1795). D. A. R. Mag., v. 71, no. 12, p. 1111.
Creague. St. Paul's Parish, Balto. V. 1. Mss. MHS.
Creal. Md. Geneal. Bull., v. 4, p. 18. MHS. DAR.
Creal, Philip, Harford Co. Ms. File case, DAR.
Creek, Krick. Hagerstown tombstone inscriptions. Gruder. Natl. Geneal. Soc. Quart., 1919, v. 8, nos. 1, 2.
Creighton. *See* Hunter. Col. families of U. S. A. Mackenzie. V. 1, p. 274. MHS. DAR.
St. Paul's Parish, Balto. V. 2. Mss. MHS.
Tombstone rec. of Dorchester Co. Jones. DAR.
†**Cresap.** Biog sketch of life of Capt. Michael Cresap, Cumberland, Md. Pr. for author (John J. Jacob), by J. W. Buchanan, 1928.
Capt. Cresap's company's roll, 1775. M. H. Mag., 1927, v. 22, p. 399.
†Capt. Michael Cresap and Indian Logan. W. Va. Hist. Mag., v. 3, no. 2, pp. 144–52.
Col. Thomas Cresap. M. Thurston, Shepherdstown, W. Va., in cooperation with Natl. Highway Asso., Wash. D. C., and N. Y. City, 1923. MHS.
Hannah Johnson, Cresap. A. P. Silver. Newsp. clipp. MHS.
Cresap Soc. Bulletins, Oct.–Dec., 1937, vs. 1–15. MHS; DAR.
*Cresap Society, natl. organization of descendants of Col. Thomas Cresap, West. Md., Pathfinder, pioneer and patriot. Bull. no. 1, Oct., 1935–No. 8, May, 1936. MHS.
†Hist. of Allegany Co. Thomas and Williams. V. 1. MHS; DAR.
*Hist of Cresaps. J. O. Cresap and B. Cresap. Foreword by F. Tallmadge. Cresap Soc., McComb, Miss., 491 pp. and index. MHS.
†Hist. of Md. Scharf. V. 2, pp. 181–83. MHS.
†Hist. of West. Md. Scharf. V. 1, pp. 75–77, 102–03; v. 2, pp. 1458–59. MHS; DAR.
†Life of Col. Thomas Cresap. M. L. C. Stevenson. Pub. of Ohio Archaeolog. Hist. Soc., 1901, v. 10, no. 2. MHS.
Ms. MHS.
Patriotic Md. Md. Soc. of S. A. R., 1930. MHS; DAR.
†Story of Thomas Cresap, Md. pioneer. L. C. Wroth. (Col. Thomas Cresap first selected trail over mountains, 1754, known as Braddock's Road, only road to West; Cresap memorial, erected to Thomas Cresap, 1919, at Cumberland, Allegany Co.) Pr. by Cresap Soc., Columbus, Ohio, 1928.
*The Sun, Balto. Dec. 9, 16, 23, 30, 1906.
See Logan and Cresap.
See Sprigg-Addison-Cresap-Lamar-Gordon.
Cresap, Daniel. Born Jan. 29, 1727; earliest birth rec. on register, All Saints P. E. Church, Frederick. MHS.
Cresap, Hannah Johnson. Excerpts from paper by A. P. Silver. Ms. MHS.
***Cresap, Michael.** Cresap Soc. Bull., nos. 2 and 3. MHS.
†**Cresap, Thomas.** Early chapters in development of Potomac route to West. Rec. Columbia Hist. Soc., v. 15, pt. 1, pp. 96–99.
Md. pioneer. From Soc. Coll. M. H. Mag., 1914, v. 9, pp. 1–37.
Cresap, Col. Thomas. Chart. Mrs. C. E. B. Towt. 1924. Printed by Cresap Society, Columbus, Ohio, 1930. MHS.
Cresap-Logan. Cresap-Logan. M. L. Stevenson. West Va. Hist. Mag., 1903, v. 3, no. 2. MHS.
Cressop, Michael. Obit. notice. N. Y. Gazette and Weekly Mercury, Oct. 23, 1775. Photost. Newsp. clipp. File case, DAR.
†**Creswell.** Bench and bar of Md. Sams and Riley. 1901, v. 2, p. 362. Lib. Cong.; MHS; Peabody Lib.
†Men of mark in Md. Johnson. V. 3. DAR; Enoch Pratt Lib.
Portrait and biog. rec. of Harford and Cecil Cos. 1897, pp. 119, 263, MHS. DAR.
St. Paul's Parish, Balto. V. 2. Mss. MHS.
Crew. Old Somerset. Torrence. MHS. DAR. (28 stones.) Still Pond churchyard, Kent Co. Md. O. R. Soc., v. 2, pp. 65–75. MHS.
See Long-Addams-Crew.
Crewe. Branch of Philip Adams family of Md. Adams. MHS.
Crewe Family. See Adams family, London, Va., and Somerset Co. Ms. MHS.
Crichton. St. Paul's Balto. V. 4. Mss. MHS.
***Crise** or **Krise.** Frederick Co. families. Markell. Ms. Personal list.
Crise, Kreiss, Kries, Kreuss Family (1749). Ms. File case, DAR.
Crisfield, Chestertown. Abr. Compend. Amer. Geneal. Virkus. V. 1, p. 572. DAR.
Crismand. Naturalization in Md., 1666–1765; Laws. Bacon. MHS.
***Crist.** Lineage Bk. Daughters of Amer. Colonists. V. 2, p. 256. MHS., DAR.
See Campbell-Crist.
***Crist Family.** Wilson Mss. Coll., no. 79. MHS.
Criswell. St. Paul's Parish, Balto. V. 1. Mss. MHS.
Crittenden. Chart; descendants of Thomas Turpin Crittenden, son of Major Thomas Turpin Crittenden and Judith Harris. Elizabeth W. Putnam. 1937. MHS.
Crittenden, Wm. L. Md. Soc., War of 1812, v. 3, No. 266. Ms. MHS.
***Crittenden-Harris.** Chart. MHS.
***Crittenden-McMechen.** Chart. MHS.
***Crocker.** Burke's landed gentry. 1939. MHS.
St. Paul's Parish, Balto. V. 2. Mss. MHS.
St. Stephens Parish, Cecilton, Md. MHS; DAR.
See Churchill-Crocker-Fox-Coplestone-Bonvile-Ellicott.
Crocket, Crockett. St. Paul's Parish, Balto. V. 1, 2, 3. Mss. MHS.
Crockett. Barroll in Great Britain and Amer. Barroll. Pp. 93–94, 101. MHS.
Pedigree of Henry Irvine Keyser, II. Soc. Col. Wars Md. Culver. 1940. MHS; DAR.
Rec. Stepney Parish. MHS; DAR.
Mrs. H. DeCourey Wright Thom chart. MHS.

Crockett. Wicomico Co. families. Tilghman. Ms, pp. 100, 103, 106, 119, 124. DAR.
See Crocket.

Crommelin, Jean. Geneal. rec. of George Small, etc. Small. MHS.

Cromwell. Amer. Armory and Blue Book. Matthews. 1911-12, p. 261.
Bailiere chart. MHS.
Balto. American, Feb. 11, 1885. Newsp. clipp. MHS.
Blackwell chart. MHS.
Chart, photos., complete in 1 sheet. Cary Geneal. Coll. Ms. MHS.
Col. families of U. S. A. Mackenzie. V. 1, p. 597 DAR; v. 4, p. 479. MHS.
Cromwell and allied families. Typed, priv. distributed.
Cromwell family. F. B. Culver. M. H. Mag., 1918, v. 13, pp. 386-403.
Cromwell family F. B. Culver. Corrections. M. H. Mag., 1919, v. 14, p. 80.
*Frederick Co. families. Markell. Ms. Personal list.
Frederick Co. tombstone inscriptions. Gruder. Natl. Geneal. Soc. Quart., 1919, v. 8, nos. 1, 2.
Geneal. and chart of Chenoweth and Cromwell families of Md. and Va. Chenoweth. MHS.
*Hammond-Cromwell families. Amer. Hist. Reg., 1895, v. 2, pp. 867-73. MHS.
Hist. graves of Md. and D. C. Ridgely. MHS.
†Hist. of Allegany Co. Thomas and Williams. V. 1. MHS.
Jenkins-Courtney chart. MHS.
Lineage Bks., Natl. Soc. of Daughters of Amer. Col., v. 4, p. 198. MHS; DAR.
Md. families. Culver. Ms. Personal list.
Med. Annals Md. Cordell. 1903, pp. 366-67. MHS.
Merryman family. Culver. M. H. Mag., 1915, v. 10, pp. 176, 286.
See Samuel Owings geneal. Focke Geneal. Coll. Ms. MHS.
Pedigree of James Etchberger Hancock. Soc. Col. Wars Md. Culver. 1940. MHS; DAR.
Mrs. C. L. Riggs chart. MHS.
Rogers Coll. Ms. MHS.
St. Paul's Parish, Balto. V. 2. Mss. MHS.
St. Thomas Parish, Balto. Co. Bd. ms. MHS. Also: Md. Geneal. Rec. Com., 1937, pp. 109-82. Mss. DAR.
*Side lights on Md. hist. Richardson. V. 2, p. 73. MHS;DAR.
*The Sun, Balto., Oct. 11, 1903; Aug. 11, 18, 1907.
See Bond-Cromwell-Delaport-Harris-Reisinger-Reardon.
See Chenoweth-Cromwell.

Cromwell, A. Grant. Md. Soc., War of 1812, v. 4, no. 311. Ms. MHS.

Cromwell, B. F. Md. Soc., War of 1812, v. 3, no. 275. Ms. MHS.

†Cromwell, W. K. Men of mark in Md., Johnson, v. 3, DAR; Enoch Pratt Lib.

***Cromwell Family.** Anne Arundel Co. gentry. Newman. Pp. 576-622. MHS; DAR.
(1671). Ms. File case, DAR.

Cromwell Family, Va., and Md. Ms. File case, DAR.

Cromwell-Gist. Chart. Gist family of S. C. and its Md. antecedents. Gee. P. 5. MHS; DAR.

†Cronise. Hist. of Frederick Co. Williams. MHS; DAR.
Patriotic Md. Md. Soc. of S. A. R., 1930. MHS; DAR.

†Cronmiller. Med. Annals Md. Cordell. 1903, p. 367. MHS.

Crook, Cecil Co. Hardwick family, Md. and Va. William and Mary Quart., 2nd series, v. 23, pp. 59-69.
Fox-Ellicott-Evans families. Evans. MHS; DAR.

Crook, Crooks. St. Paul's Parish, Balto. V. 1, 2, 3, 4. Mss. MHS.

***Crooke.** Lineage Bk. Daughters of Amer. Colonists. V. 5, pp. 308, 309, 310. MHS; DAR.

Crooks. Mt. Paran Pres. churchyard, Harrisonville, Balto. Co. Typed ms. MHS; DAR.
See Crook.

Crookshanks. St. Paul's Parish, Balto. V. 1. Mss. MHS.

Cropper. M. E. churchyard, Snow Hill. Worcester Co., Hudson. Bd. ms. MHS; DAR.
†Old Buckingham by the Sea, East. Shore of Md. Page. DAR.
Tombstone inscriptions of Princess Anne and Snow Hill. Turner Geneal. Coll. Ms. MHS.

Cropper, Snow Hill. Turner. Geneal. Coll. Ms. MHS.

Crosby. Amer. Armory and Blue Book. Matthews. 1911-12, pp. 201, 343.
Bible rec. Ms. MHS.

Crosdale. St. Paul's Parish, Balto. V. 2, 3. Mss. MHS.

Cross. Glendy churchyard, Balto. Md. Geneal. Rec. Com., 1933-34. Mss. DAR.
†M. H. Mag., v. 12, p. 211.
Monocacy Cemetery, Beallsville, Montgomery Co. Md. Geneal. Rec. Com., 1926-27, v. 2, pp. 70-73. Mss. DAR.
Pedigree of Andrew Noel Trippe. Soc. Col. Wars Md. Culver. 1940. MHS; DAR.
*William Cross of Botetourt Co., Va., and his descendants, 1733-1932. J. N. Cross. 1932. DAR.
St. Paul's Parish, Balto. V. 1, 2, 3. Mss. MHS.
St. Thomas Parish, Balto. Co. Bd. ms. MHS. Also: Md. Geneal. Rec. Com., 1937, pp. 109-82. Mss. DAR.

Cross, Cecil Co. A. C. and J. McC. Trippe pedigree chart. Soc. Col. Wars, Md. Johnson. 1905, p. 114. MHS.

Cross, Andrew (War of 1812). Glendy churchyard. Patriotic Marylander, v. 2, no. 4, pp. 54-60. MHS; DAR.

Cross, John (Revolutionary Soldier; War of 1812) Glendy churchyard. Patriotic Marylander v. 2, no. 4, pp. 54-60. MHS; DAR.

†Cross, W. Irvin. Men of mark in Md. Johnson. V. 4, DAR; Enoch Pratt Lib.

Cross, Wm. (War of 1812). Glendy churchyard. Patriotic Marylander, v. 2, no. 4, pp. 54-60. MHS; DAR.

Crossan, Pa. Gibbs chart. MHS.

Crossland Family. The Sun, Balto., July 8, 1883.

Crossley. Still Pond cemetery, Kent Co. Md. O. R. Soc., v. 2. MHS.

Croswell. Uhler Bible rec. Ms. MHS.

Crothers, Austin L. Balto., its hist., its people. Hall. V. 2. MHS; DAR.
†Governors of Md. Buchholz. P. 276. MHS.
Crouch. Rec. of Stepney Parish. MHS; DAR.
St. Paul's Parish, Balto. V. 2. Mss. MHS.
St. Stephens Parish, Cecilton, Md. MHS; DAR.
Somerset Co. Court Book. Tilghman. 1937. Ms. DAR.
*Wicomico Co. families. Tilghman. Ms, pp. 62, 96. DAR.
Crouse. Bigges family. Ms. DAR.
Patriotic Md. Md. Soc. of S. A. R., 1930. MHS; DAR.
St. Paul's Parish, Balto. V. 3. Mss. MHS.
Crouse, Frederick Co. Lineage Bk., Order of Washington, p. 27. MHS; DAR.
Crouth. *See* Smith-Crouth.
Crow. Griffith geneal. Griffith. MHS; DAR.
Robins family tree. MHS.
St. Paul's P. E. churchyard, Kent Co. Md. O. R. Soc. Bull., no. 2, pp. 54-65.
St. Paul's Parish, Balto. V. 1, 2. Mss. MHS.
St. Stephens Parish, Cecilton, Md. MHS; DAR.
***Crow Family.** Wilson Mss. Coll., no. 37, D. MHS.
Crowder. St. Paul's Parish, Balto. V. 1, 2. Mss. MHS.
Crowell. Patriotic Md. Md. Soc. of S. A. R., 1930. MHS; DAR.
Crowley. Chew family. Culver. M. H. Mag., 1935, v. 30, no. 2, pp. 157-75.
Croxall. Cary Geneal. Coll. Ms. MHS.
Col. Families of U. S. A. Mackenzie. V. 2. MHS. DAR.
Pedigree of Frances Joseph Baldwin. Soc. Col. Wars Md. Culver. 1940. MHS; DAR.
Pedigree of Wm. Winchester Eareckson. Soc. Col. Wars Md. Culver. 1940. MHS; DAR.
Pedigree of Arthur Lafayette Jones. Soc. Col. Wars Md. Culver. 1940. MHS; DAR.
Pedigree of Wm. Handy Collin Vickers. Soc. Col. Wars Md. Culver. 1940. MHS; DAR.
See Moale-Croxall-North.
Croyle. Lineage Bks., Natl. Soc. of Daughters of Amer. Col., v. 3, p. 82. MHS; DAR.
Crrichton. St. Paul's Parish, Balto. V. 3. Mss. MHS.
Cruikshank Family (1749-1848). Md. Geneal. Rec. Com., v. 4, pp. 66-67.
Crukshank. Bible rec. Upper Penins. East. Shore. Pp. 1-4. MHS; DAR.
***Crum.** Frederick Co. families. Markell. Ms. Personal list.
†(55 ref.) Hist. of Frederick Co. Williams. MHS; DAR.
†Med. Annals Md. Cordell. 1903, p. 368. MHS.
John Swadner and his descendants. Evans. 1919. Typed, bd. MHS.
Crumbaugh, Krumbach, Family. Ms. File case, DAR.
Crummer. St. Paul's Parish, Balto. V. 2. Mss. MHS.
Crumpton, Kent Co. Graveyard. Ms. DAR.
Cruse. Hilles chart. MHS.
J. I. Dennis pedigree chart, plate 2. Soc. Col. Wars, Md. Johnston. 1905, p. 22. MHS.
Crutchley. Autobiography of Summerfield Baldwin. MHS; DAR.
Sara R. Baldwin chart. MHS.
Cary Geneal. Coll. Ms. MHS.
Hamill chart. MHS.
Prentice chart. MHS.
Pedigree of Charles Gambrill Baldwin. Soc. Col. Wars Md. Culver. 1940. MHS; DAR.
Cruzen Line. Balto., its hist., its people. Hall. V. 3. MHS; DAR.
†Cuddy. Med. Annals Md. Cordell. 1903, p. 368. MHS.
***Cudmore.** Autobiography of P. Cudmore. 1896. MHS.
Autobiog. of P. C. Cudmore, with geneal. F. P. Cudmore. 1885, pamph. MHS.
Beirne chart. MHS.
†Cugle. Men of mark in Md. Johnson. V. 4. DAR; Enoch Pratt Lib.
Culberson. St. Paul's Parish, Balto. V. 2. Mss. MHS.
Culbert. St. Paul's Parish, Balto. V. 2. Mss. MHS.
†Culbreath. Memoir of Thomas Culbreath, representative of 15th and 16th Congress. E. T. Tubbs.
†Culbreth. Hist. of Caroline Co. Noble. MHS.
†Men of mark in Md. Johnson. V. 1. DAR; Enoch Pratt Lib.
Pedigree of Culbreth Hopewell Warner. Soc. Col. Wars Md. Culver. 1940. MHS; DAR.
Culbreth-Hardcastle Line, Caroline and Queen Anne Cos. C. H. Warner pedigree chart. Soc. Col. Wars, Md. Johnston. 1905, p. 123. MHS.
Cullamore, Cullimore. St. Paul's Parish, Balto. V. 2, 3. Mss. MHS.
***Cullar.** Boyd family. Boyd. DAR.
Cullen. Amer. Armory and Blue Book. Matthews. 1911-12, p. 392.
†Med. Annals Md. Cordell. 1903, p. 368. MHS.
St. Paul's Parish, Balto. V. 2. Mss. MHS.
Somerset Co. Court Book. Tilghman. 1937. Ms. DAR.
***Cullen, Thomas S.** Burke's landed gentry. 1939. MHS.
***Culler.** Hist. of Frederick Co. Williams. MHS, DAR.
Cullimore. *See* Cullamore.
***Culpeper** (proprietors of N. Neck). Geneal. Fairfax Harrison. Priv. pr. by Old Dominion Press, Va., 1926. MHS.
Culver. Amer. Armory and Blue Book. Matthews. 1911-12, p. 391.
Abr. Compend. Amer. Geneal. Virkus. V. 1. p. 574. DAR.
Col. families of U. S. A. Mackenzie. V. 4. MHS.
*Culver and allied families. Geneal.; chart. Francis Barnum Culver. Baltimore. MHS.
†Med. Annals Md. Cordell. 1903, p. 368. MHS.
*Wicomico Co. families. Tilghman. Ms. p. 107. DAR.
Culver, Francis B. Md. Soc., War of 1812, v. 1, no. 107. Ms. MHS.
Culver, Francis Barnum. Pedigree. Charts. Soc. Col. Wars Md. Culver. 1940. MHS; DAR.
Cumming. Dorsey and allied families. Ms. MHS.

Cummings. Cemetery near Carroll Chapel, Forest Glen. Md. Geneal. Rec. Com., v. 2. Mss. DAR.
Howland chart. MHS.
Morris family of Phila. Moon. V. 1, p. 180; v. 2, p. 766; v. 3, pp. 934–35. MHS.
St. John's R. C. Church cemetery, Montgomery Co. Md. Geneal. Rec. Com., 1926, p. 27. Mss. DAR.
St. Paul's Parish, Balto. V. 2. Mss. MHS.
Table of descent of William Cummings of Frederick Co. (born near Inverness, Scotland 1725) and his wife (died in 1793) of Eastern Shore of Md. Montgomery Cummings. Washington, D. C., 1905. Lib. Cong., M.H.S; DAR.
Cummings, East. Shore. Abr. Compend. Amer. Geneal. Virkus. V. 1, p. 954. DAR.
Cummings, Frederick Co. Abr. Compend. Amer. Geneal. Virkus. V. 1, p. 909. DAR.
Cummings, Harmon, Md. Revolutionary soldiers buried in northwest. S. C. Natl. Geneal. Soc. Quart., v. 21, no. 2, p. 46.
Cummings, John. Revolutionary war pension abs. Natl. Geneal. Soc. Quart., v. 23, p. 51.
***Cummings Family.** Chart. DAR.
Cummings-Brice. Farm, near Sassafras, Kent Co. Burial ground. Md. Geneal. Rec. Com., 1934–35. Mss. DAR.
Cummins. Pedigree of Lee Cummins Cary. Soc. Col. Wars Md. Culver. 1940. MHS; DAR.
Revolutionary war pension abs. Natl. Geneal. Soc. Quart., v. 23, no. 2, p. 51.
St. Paul's Parish, Balto. V. 1, 3. Mss. MHS.
***Cummins Family.** Old Kent. Hanson. P. 188. MHS. DAR.
***Cunnabell, Connable, Conable Family.** V. 1, 1650–1886; v. 2, 1886–1935. R. Connable. Md. ref., pp. 21, 24, 25, 74. N. Y., East Aurora, 1935, 183 pp. MHS.
***Cunningham.** Boyd family. Boyd. DAR.
†Hist. of West. Md. Scharf. V. 2, p. 1233. MHS; DAR.
Machen chart. MHS.
Cunningham Family. Ms. MHS.
Cunningham, Cunnyngham. St. Paul's Parish, Balto. V. 1, 2. Mss. MHS.
Curfman. Hagerstown tombstone inscriptions. Gruder. Natl. Geneal. Soc. Quart., 1919, v. 8, nos. 1, 2.
Curl, Jarrett (veteran). Md. Soc., War of 1812, v. 1, no. 73. Ms. MHS.
Curle. Chart, photos., complete in 1 sheet. Cary. Geneal. Coll. Ms. MHS.
Currethers. West. Nottingham Cemetery. M. H. Mag., 1923, v. 18, p. 55.
†Currey. Med. Annals Md. Cordell. 1903, p. 369. MHS.
St. Stephens Parish, Cecilton, Md. MHS; DAR.
Curry. Bible rec., Harford Co. Md. Geneal. Rec. Com., 1934-35, p. 108. Mss. DAR.
Curson. St. Paul's Parish, Balto. V. 1, 2. Mss. MHS.
Curtain. St. Paul's Parish, Balto. V. 1, 2. Mss. MHS.
Curtis. Clay family of Pa. Ms. File case, DAR.
Edmund Beauchamp of East. Shore of Md. D. A. R. Mag., v. 66, no. 4, pp. 234–38.
Naturalizations in Md., 1666–1765; Laws. Bacon. MHS.
Old Somerset. Torrence. MHS; DAR.
St. Paul's Parish, Balto. V. 1, 2, 3. Mss. MHS.
Curtis, Curtiss. Somerset Co. Court Book. Tilghman. 1937. Ms. DAR.
***Curzon.** Curzon family of N. Y. and Balto., and their Eng. descent. J. H. Pleasants Balto., 1919. MHS.
Deford chart. MHS.
Cushing. Ancest. rec. and portraits. Col. Dames of Amer., 1910, v. 2, p. 760. MHS; DAR.
Col. families of U. S. A. Mackenzie. V. 7, p. 434. MHS; DAR.
Mrs. Wm. T. Howard, Jr., chart. MHS.
McClellan chart. MHS.
Cushing, Daniel, Mass. Pedigree of George D. F. Robinson, Jr. Soc. Col. Wars Md. Culver. 1940. MHS; DAR.
Cushing Family. Col. and Revolutionary families of Pa. Amer. Hist. Soc., N. Y., 1934, pp. 593–604.
Cushing Line, Mass. W. Whitridge pedigree chart. Soc. Col. Wars, Md. Johnston. 1905, p. 124. MHS.
Cushing-Whitridge Line. Balto., its hist., its people. V. 2, p. 278. MHS; DAR.
Cushwa. Hagerstown tombstone inscriptions. Gruder. Natl. Geneal. Soc. Quart., 1919, v. 8, nos. 1, 2.
†Hist. of West. Md. Scharf. V. 2, p. 1245. MHS; DAR.
Portrait and biog. rec. of Sixth Cong. Dist. of Md. 1898, p. 535. MHS; DAR.
†Cushwa, Victor. Men of mark in Md. Johnson. V. 4, DAR; Enoch Pratt Lib.
***Custer.** Garrett Co. pioneer families. Hoye. MHS; DAR.
†Hist. of West. Md. Scharf. V. 2, p. 1531. MHS; DAR.
Custer Family. Mountain Democrat, Garrett Co., Feb. 21, 1935. Newsp. clipp. MHS; DAR.
Custis. Ancestry of Rosalie Morris Johnson. Johnson. 1905. MHS; DAR.
Col. and Revolutionary families of Pa. Amer. Hist. Soc., N. Y., 1934, pp. 22–24.
Geneal. of Henrietta Chauncey Wilson. Upshur. Bk. of photos. MHS.
*Hist. Dorchester Co. Jones. 1925, p. 301. MHS. DAR.
Jacobs chart. MHS.
*Mrs. Charles Howard Lloyd chart. Col. Dames Amer., Chap. 1. MHS.
See Munoz. Abr. Compend. Amer. Geneal. Virkus. V. 1, p. 627. DAR.
Pedigree of James Donnell Tilghman. Soc. Col. Wars Md. Culver. 1940. MHS; DAR.
Turner Geneal. Coll. Ms. MHS.
Mrs. Wm. L. Watson chart. MHS.
Mrs. Morris Whitridge chart. MHS.
See Hill-Custis.
Custis, Va. Ances. rec. and portraits. Col. Dames of Amer., 1910, v. 1, pp. 290, 345.
J. T. Dennis pedigree chart, plate 2. Soc. Col. Wars, Md. Johnston. 1905, pp. 22, 143. MHS.
Harrison-Waples and allied families. Harrison. P. 88. MHS.
(Md. ref.) Natl. Geneal. Soc. Quart., v. 3, no. 3, p. 2.
Prior to 1650. (11 generations.) Pedigree of Wm. Parke Custis Munoz. Soc. Col. Wars Md. Culver. 1940. MHS; DAR.

*The Sun, Balto., Dec. 15, 22, 29, 1907; Jan. 5, 12, 19, 1908.
Custis Family. Lee of Va., 1642–1892. E. J. Lee. Pp. 456–61. Lib. Cong.; MHS.
Custis Line. Col. and Revolutionary lineages in Amer. 1939, v. 2, p. 114. MHS.
Custis-Gillet-Martin-McMaster Families. Turner. Geneal Coll. Ms. MHS.
Custis-Teakle. Chart, photos. Cary Geneal. Coll. Ms. MHS.
Custis-Teackle-Upshur Line, Va. Harvey chart. MHS.
Mrs. Howard Bruce chart. MHS.
Miss Minna Lurman chart. MHS.
Cutfield. St. Paul's Parish, Balto. V. 1. Mss. MHS.
Cuthbert. Cummings chart. Lib. Cong., MHS; DAR.
***Cuthbertson.** Ancient diary of Rev. John Cuthbertson, first Reformed Presbyterian missionary to come to Amer. from Scotland. Register of baptisms and marriages, 1751–1791 (some date to 1720). S. Helen Fields. Headquarters Middle Octoraror, Lancaster Co., Pa., visits into Del., Md., N. J., N. Y. and Va., etc. (5000 families.) Lancaster Press, Pa., 1934. DAR.
Cutler. Md. Geneal. Rec. Com., 1932–33, pp. 208–09. Mss. DAR.
Cutsail. Lehman family in Md. Lehman. 1935, pamph., p. 59. MHS; DAR.
***Cutt Family,** N. H. Old Kent. Hanson. P. 153. MHS; DAR.
Cutting. Geneal. of Henrietta Chauncey Wilson. Upshur. Bk. of photos. MHS.
***Cuyman.** Frederick Co. families. Markell. Ms. Personal list.

D

Dabney. Cary Geneal. Coll. Ms. MHS.
Origin of Dabney family of Va. Va. Mag., Hist. and Biog. V. 45, no. 2, pp. 121–43.
*Sketch of Dabneys of Va. W. H. Dabney. Chicago, S. D. Chiles Co., 1888.
Dabridgecourt. Note on the pedigree pub. in the Topographer and Genealogist, 1, 197–207. M. H. Mag., 1913, v. 8, p. 203.
Dade. Monocacy Cemetery, Beallsville, Montgomery Co. Md. Geneal. Rec. Com., 1926–27. pp. 70–73. Mss. DAR.
Va. geneal. Hayden. MHS; DAR.
Dade Family. Portrait and biog. rec. of Sixth Cong. Dist. of Md. 1898, p. 769. MHS. DAR.
Dade Family, Va. Tyler's Quart. Mag., 1934–35, v. 16, pp. 47, 48, 157–75, 243–45; 1935–36, v. 17, pp. 49–58; 243–45. MHS.
Daffin. Abr. Compend. Amer. Geneal. Virkus. V. 4, p. 136 (showing Dickinson). MHS.
St. Inigoes churchyard, St. Mary's Co. Md. O. R. Soc. Bull., no. 3, p. 58.
Daffour. Naturalizations in Md., 1666–1765; Laws. Bacon. MHS.
†**Dagworthy, Capt.** Hist. of Md. Scharf. V. 1, p. 447. MHS.
Dagworthy, Brig-Gen. John (of Revolution). Memoir. Hist. Soc. of Del. Papers, No. 10. Wilmington, 1895.
†Proc. at unveiling of monument erected to his memory, May 30, 1908 (born at Trenton, N. J., 1721; died in Sussex Co., Del., 1784; in command of Md. troops, French and Indian War, 1756–58). Hist. Soc. of Del., Wilmington, 1908, pamph. Ms. File case, DAR.
Dail. *See* Dale.
Daingerfield. Carter chart. MHS.
Cary Geneal. Coll. Ms. MHS.
Raisin chart. MHS.
Daingerfield Family, Va. Ms. File case, DAR.
***Dale.** Burke's landed gentry. 1939. MHS.
Col. families of U. S. A. Mackenzie. V. 1, p. 97. MHS. DAR.
Md. families. Culver. Ms. Personal list.
Turner Geneal. Coll. Ms. MHS.
Dale, Eloise Featherston Posey (born in Holly Springs, Marshall Co., Miss.). Geneal., 1760–1836. Md. Geneal. Rec. Com., 1937–38, p. 169. Mss. DAR.
Dale Family, Del., Md. and Pa. Ms. File case, DAR.
Dale Line. Hopkinson, Phila. Col. and Revolutionary families of Phila. Jordan. 1933, v. 1, pp. 22–86.
Dale-Read, Worcester Co. Notes. D. A. R. Mag., v. 71, no. 4, p. 356.
Dale, Dail, Joppa, Md. (1720). Hopkinson family, Phila. Col. and Revolutionary families of Pa. Jordan. 1932, v. 4, p. 10.
Daley. St. Paul's Parish, Balto. V. 2. Mss. MHS.
Dall. Miss Katherine Lurman chart. MHS.
St. Paul's Parish, Balto. V. 1, 2, 3. Mss. MHS.
Dallam. Col. and Revolutionary families of Pa. Jordan. 1922, v. 4, p. 302.
Deford chart. MHS.
Gilpin chart. MHS.
Harford Co. Hist. Soc. Mss. Col. JHU.
Hist. of Harford Co. Preston. MHS; DAR.
Howard-Govans-Woodward-Law Bible rec. Ms. MHS.
Miss Cassandra Lee chart. MHS.
Marriage rec., 1781–1892, Harford Co. Md. Geneal. Rec. Com., 1934–35, p. 108. DAR.
Md. families. Culver. Ms. Personal list.
Maulsby family in Amer. Barnard. DAR; Peabody Lib.
†Med. Annals Md. Cordell. 1903, p. 369. MHS.
Patriotic Md. Md. Soc. of S. A. R., 1930. MHS; DAR.
Pedigree of Edmund Pendleton Hunter Harrison. Soc. Col. Wars Md. Culver. 1940. MHS; DAR.
Portrait and biog. rec. of Harford and Cecil Cos. 1897, pp. 129, 380, 474. MHS. DAR.
Tombstones, 1739–1866, on Cranberry Farm, near Aberdeen, Harford Co. Md. Geneal. Rec. Com., 1929, p. 60. Mss. DAR.
Dallam, Corbin Braxton. Pedigree. Rec. of Armistead, Ball Braxton, Carter, Corbin Fauntleroy, and Tayloe of Va. Soc. Col. Wars Md. Culver. 1940. MHS; DAR.
Dallam, H. Gough. Md. Soc., War of 1812, v. 3, no. 201. MHS.
***Dallam Family** (1690–1929). And brief story of Eng. family, 1066–1690. D. E. Dallam. Published for priv. circulation, Phila., George H. Buchanan Co., 1929. Pamph. MHS; DAR.

Dalrymple. St. Paul's Parish, Balto. V. 1, 2, 3. Mss. MHS.
Dalrymple Family. Col. and Revolutionary lineages of Amer. 1939, v. 3, pp. 400–18. MHS.
***Dalters.** Wicomico Co. families. Tilghman. Ms., p. 114. DAR.
Dalton. Ancest. rec. and portraits. Col. Dames of Amer., 1910, v. 2, p. 655. MHS; DAR.
Hughes family of Va. Horton. MHS.
Daly. Balto., its hist., its people. Hall. V. 3. MHS; DAR.
Dame. Balto., its hist., its people. Hall. V. 2. MHS; DAR.
*Burke's landed gentry. 1939. MHS.
†Dame, Wm. H. Men of mark in Md. Johnson. V. 2. DAR; Enoch Pratt Lib.
Dancy. Amer. Armory and Blue Book. Matthews. 1911–12, p. 131.
Dancy, Bryan Grimes. Pedigree. Soc. Col. Wars Md. Culver. 1940. MHS; DAR.
Dancy, F. B. Abr. Compend. Amer. Geneal. Virkus. V. 1, p. 55. DAR.
Dancy, Frank Battle. Pedigree. Soc. Col. Wars Md. Culver. 1940. MHS; DAR.
Dancy, Frank Battle, Jr. Pedigree. Soc. Col. Wars Md. Culver. 1940. MHS; DAR.
Dancy, Wm. Grimes. Pedigree. Soc. Col. Wars Md. Culver. 1940. MHS; DAR.
Dandridge. Dandridge family of Va. (With Washington-Custis notes; ref. to Denison family, Harford Co., and Smith family, Calvert Co.). Wilson Miles Cary. William and Mary Quart., 1st series, v. 5, pp. 30, 81.
Henley chart. Cary Geneal. Coll. Ms. MHS.
Pocahontas and her descendants. Robertson. MHS; DAR.
Daneker, E. T. Md. Soc., War of 1812, v. 1, no. 7. Ms. MHS.
Dangerfield, Va. Col. families of U. S. A. Mackenzie. V. 1, p. 69. MHS; DAR.
Dangerfield Family. Willis family, Va. (Md. ref.) William and Mary Quart., 1st, series, v. 5; v. 6, p. 206; v. 8, p. 96.
Dangerman. Naturalizations in Md., 1666–1765; Laws. Bacon. MHS.
Daniel. Daniel families of south. states. C. B. Heineman. 2 folders, typed, pp. 1–125, 126–233. Wash. D. C., 1934. MHS.
Med. Annals Md. Cordell. 1903, p. 369. MHS.
***Daniel,** Va. Lineage Bk., Daughters of Founders and Patriots, v. 22, p. 43, MHS; DAR.
Geneal. Hayden. MHS; DAR.
Daniel-Claggett-Beall-Belt. Lineage Bks, Natl. Soc. of Daughters of Amer. Col., v. 3, p. 92. MHS; DAR.
Danison. Naturalizations in Md., 1666–1765; Laws. Bacon. MHS.
Dannecker. Copenhaven, Pa., family. Ms. File case, DAR.
Dannwolf. Frederick Co. tombstone inscriptions. Gruder. Natl. Geneal. Soc. Quart., 1919, v. 8, nos. 1, 2.
Danridge. Col. families of U. S. A. Mackenzie. V. 1. MHS; DAR.
Darbey, Darby. St. Paul's Parish, Balto. V. 1, 2, 4. Mss. MHS.
Darby. Americus Dawson farm, Montgomery Co. Md. Geneal. Rec. Com., 1926, p. 76. Mss. DAR.
*Geneal., ancestors and descendants of George Darby, Montgomery Co., 1726–88. R. C. Darby. Collected 1912, 1913, 1914. Atlanta, Ga. MHS.
Graves; Old German Baptist Churchyard, near old Germantown, Montgomery Co. Md. Geneal. Rec. Com., 1934–35, p. 83. DAR.
Hackett Bible rec. Bible rec. of Dorchester and Somerset Cos. and Del. P. 31. DAR.
†Hist. of West. Md. Scharf. V. 2, p. 1130. MHS; DAR.
*Lineage Bk. Daughters of Amer. Colonists. V. 5, p. 405. MHS; DAR.
Lineage Bks., Natl. Soc. of Daughters of Amer. Col., v. 1, p. 235. MHS; DAR.
Mothers Delight stones, moved from Americus Dawson farm near Dawsonville to Monocacy Cemetery. Md. Geneal. Rec. Com., v. 2, p. 76. Mss. DAR.
Old German Baptist Church, near Germantown, Montgomery Co. Tombstone inscriptions. Md. Geneal. Rec. Com., 1934–35, p. 83. Mss. DAR.
Patriotic Md. Md. Soc. of S. A. R., 1930. MHS; DAR.
Rogers Bible rec. Ms. MHS.
Wicomico Co. families. Tilghman. Ms. P. 120. DAR.
See Darbey.
Darby Family, Montgomery Co., Geneal. R. C. Darby, Atlanta, Ga. Ms. MHS.
Darcey. Darcey and Hannah Peach tombstone rec., June 30, 1842. Natl. Geneal. Soc. Quart., July, 1917, v. 6, no. 2.
D'Arcey, D'Arcy. St. Paul's Parish, Balto. V. 2, 3. Mss. MHS.
***Darcy-Dorsey.** Side lights on Md. hist. Richardson. V. 2, p. 86. MHS; DAR.
***D'Arcy.** Chart. See Dorsey family papers. Ms. MHS.
Col. families of U. S. A. Mackenzie. V. 2, p. 616. MHS; DAR.
Mrs. Alexander Gordon chart. MHS.
Hilles chart. MHS.
Lineage Bks., Natl. Soc. of Daughters of Amer. Col., v. 2, p. 298. MHS; DAR.
Md. families. Culver. Ms. Personal list.
W. T. Wilson pedigree chart. Soc. Col. Wars, Md. Johnston. 1905, p. 136. MHS.
See D'Arcey.
See Dorsey.
†Dare. Med. Annals Md. Cordell. 1903, p. 370. MHS.
See Derr.
Darnall. Abr. Compend. Amer. Geneal. Virkus. V. 1, p. 577, DAR; v. 4, p. 335. MHS.
Ancestry of Rosalie Morris Johnson. Johnson. 1905. MHS; DAR.
*Burke's landed gentry. 1939. MHS.
Calvert and Darnall gleanings from Eng. wills. Hastings. M. H. Mag., v. 21, no. 4, p. 303; v. 22, pp. 1, 115, 211, 307.
Carroll-Darnall charts. MHS.
Mrs. Charles Carter chart. MHS.
Cary Geneal. Coll. Ms. MHS.
Children of Alex P. and M. C. Hill. Ms. MHS.
Col. families of U. S. A. Mackenzie. V. 1, p. 66. MHS; DAR.
Col. Henry Darnall and his family. Rec. Columbia Hist. Soc., v. 26, pp. 129–45.
Justus Engelhart Kulm. J. Hall Pleasants. 1937, pamph. MHS.

Md. families. Culver. Ms. Personal list.
Parr chart. MHS.
*Pennington Papers. Ms. MHS.
Semmes and allied families. Semmes. MHS.
*Semmes Geneal. Coll. Ms. MHS.
Side lights on Md. hist. Richardson. V. 2, p. 75. MHS; DAR.
*The Sun, Balto., March 30, April 3, 1904.
See Calvert-Darnall.
Neale family of Md. The Times, Balto., Sunday, Dec. 27, 1885. Scrap Book, no. 7. MHS.
See Sewall-Brooke-Darnall-Beall.
See Sewall-Darnall-Brooke-Calvert-Lee.
Darnall-Talbot. Chart, photost., complete in 1 sheet. Cary Geneal. Coll. Ms. MHS.
Darrington. St. Paul's Parish, Balto. V. 1, 2. Mss. MHS.
Darumple-Tucker-Kent Families. Records. Monnet family geneal. Monette. Pp. 356–69. MHS.
***D'Ary Family.** Bible rec. Ms. MHS.
Dashiel. *See* Dashiell.
Dashield. (Over 150 rec.) Rec. of Stepney Parish. MHS; DAR.
Dashiell, of Wicomico Hundred. Abr. Compend. Amer. Geneal. Virkus. V. 6, p. 443. DAR.
Atkinson family (Somerset Co.). Bible rec. Ms. MHS.
Bible rec. from Bible owned by Isaac Jones Dashiell, Tyakin, Md., 1809–59. Md. Geneal. Rec. Com. 1937–38, p. 138. Mss. DAR.
†Biog. cyc. of rep. men of Md. and D. C. P. 606. MHS; DAR.
Chart, photos., complete in 1 sheet. Cary Geneal. Coll. Ms. MHS.
Col. and Revolutionary families of Pa. Amer. Hist. Soc., N. Y., 1934, p. 653.
Col. families of U. S. A. Mackenzie. V. 4, p. 129. MHS; DAR.
De Ford chart. MHS.
Handy and their kin. Handy.
Hist. of Balto. City and Co. Scharf. P. 744. MHS.
Law-Davies Bible rec. Ms. MHS.
Lineage Bks., Natl. Soc. of Daughters of Amer. Col., v. 1, p. 309; v. 4, p. 327. MHS; DAR.
Makemie Memorial Pres. churchyard, Snow Hill, Worcester Co. Hudson. Bd. ms. MHS; DAR. Also: Md. Geneal. Rec. Com., Mrs. Lines. Mss. DAR.
Md. families. Culver. Ms. Personal list.
†Med. Annals Md. Cordell. 1903, p. 370. MHS.
Old Somerset. Torrence. MHS; DAR.
Patriotic Md. Md. Soc. of S. A. R., 1930. MHS; DAR.
Pedigree of Charles Thabor Le Viness, III. Soc. Col. Wars Md. Culver. 1940. MHS; DAR.
Pedigree of Pleasants Pennington. Soc. Col. Wars Md. Culver. 1940. MHS; DAR.
(8 generations.) Pedigree of John Fowler Phillips. Soc. Col. Wars Md. Culver. 1940. MHS; DAR.
Pedigree of Ralph Robinson. Soc. Col. Wars Md. Culver. 1940. MHS; DAR.
Pedigree of Lloyd Bankson Whitham. Soc. Col. Wars Md. Culver. 1940. MHS; DAR.
Portrait and biog. rec., East. Shore of Md., 1898, pp. 423, 536, 572, 592, 654, 796, 840. MHS; DAR.
Elizabeth Ridgely Bible rec. Ms. MHS.
Somerset Co. Court Book. Tilghman. 1937. Ms. DAR.
*Somerset Co., Lineage Bk. Daughters of Amer. Col., v. 1, pp. 255, 309; v. 4, p. 327. MHS; DAR.
*Somerset Co. Lineage Bk., Daughters of Founders and Patriots, v. 13, p. 26; v. 18, p. 44. MHS.
*Wicomico Co. families. Tilghman. Ms. pp. 10, 88, 99, 117, 118, 123–25, 128, 129. DAR.
*Wilson Mss. Coll., no. 7; no. 143. MHS.
See Clayton-Dashiell.
See Wimbrough-Dashiell-Howard.
Dashiell, N. Leake. Md. Soc., War of 1812, v. 2, no. 162. Ms. MHS.
Dashiell, Nicholas Leeke. Pedigree chart. Soc. Col. Wars, Md. Johnston. 1905, pp. 19, 144. MHS.
Pedigree Soc. Col. Wars Md. Culver. 1940. MHS; DAR. See Pedigree Book, 1905, p. 19.
Dashiell, Mrs. Nicholas L. (nee Marine). Abr. Compend. Amer. Geneal. Virkus. V. 1, p. 202. DAR.
***Dashiell Family.** Rec., 1663–1927. B. J. Dashiell. Balto., The Sun Printing Office, 1928, 1929, 1932, 3 vols. MHS; DAR.
Dashiell, Dashiel. St. Paul's Parish, Balto. V. 1, 2, 3. Mss. MHS.
Daughaday, Baltimore Co. Abr. Compend. Amer. Geneal. Virkus. V. 1, p. 578. DAR.
†Daugherty. Med. Annals Md. Cordell. 1903, p. 371. MHS.
Dauntress, Naturalizations in Md., 1666–1765; Laws. Bacon. MHS.
Davenport. Abr. Compend. Amer. Geneal. Virkus. V. 6, p. 244. DAR.
Florence Eyster Weaver chart. MHS.
St. Paul's Parish, Balto. V. 3. Mss. MHS.
Davenport Family. Chart. MHS.
Davenport-Sabritt-Ross Bowen. Bible rec. Ms. MHS.
Daves. Col. families of U. S. A. Mackenzie. V. 2. MHS; DAR.
Daves, John Collins. Pedigree chart. Soc. Col. Wars, Md. Johnston. 1905, p. 20. MHS.
†Notes and queries. M. H. Mag., Mar., 1940, v. 35, no. 1, p. 89.
Davidge. Autobiography of Summerfield Baldwin. MHS; DAR.
Sara R. Baldwin chart. MHS.
Cary Geneal. Coll. Ms. MHS.
Eldridge chart. MHS.
Hamill chart. MHS.
John Beal Davidge, M.D. (born at Annapolis, 1769; died 1829). Ms. list of Md. authors. Md. Room, Enoch Pratt Lib.
Lineage Bks., Natl. Soc. of Daughters of Amer. Col., v. 2, p. 117. MHS; DAR.
Md. families. Culver. Ms. Personal list.
Med. Annals Md. Cordell. 1903, pp. 302, 371. MHS.
Pedigree of Charles Gambrill Baldwin. Soc. Col. Wars Md. Culver. 1940. MHS; DAR.
Pedigree of Wm. Winchester Eareckson. Soc. Col. Wars Md. Culver. 1940. MHS; DAR.
St. Paul's Parish, Balto. V. 2, 3. Mss. MHS.
Troup-Davidge. Ames Geneal. Coll. Ms. MHS.

Davidson, Anne Arundel Co. tombstone inscriptions. Ms. DAR.
Col. families of East. Shore and their descendants. Emory. 1900, pp. 195-99. MHS.
Buckingham Pres. churchyard, Worcester Co., Hudson. Bd. ms. MHS; DAR.
†Med. Annals Md. Cordell. 1903, pp. 371-72. MHS.
Patriotic Md. Md. Soc. of S. A. R., 1930. MHS; DAR.
Portrait and biog. rec. of East. Shore of Md. 1898, pp. 291, 465. MHS; DAR.
St. Paul's Parish, Balto. V. 1, 2, 3. Mss. MHS.

Davidson, Gen. John, Annapolis. Will proved Mar. 5, 1807. D. A. R. Mag., v. 61, no. 6, p. 470.

Davies. Cabells and their kin. Brown. MHS.
John Swadner and his descendants. Evans. 1919. Typed, bd. MHS.
Law-Davies Bible rec. Ms. MHS.
St. Paul's Parish, Balto. V. 1. Mss. MHS.
*The Sun, Balto., Jan 22, 1905; Oct. 21, 28, Nov. 4, Va., 1906.
Mrs. Wm. L. Watson chart. MHS.

Davies-Clayton, Va. Tyler's Quart. Mag., v. 8, pp. 140, 207.

Davis. All Hallow's churchyard, Snow Hill. Md. Geneal. Rec. Com., 1935-36, p. 24. Mss. DAR.
Abr. Compend. Amer. Geneal. Virkus. V. 6, p. 37. DAR.
Anne Arundel Co. Bailliere chart. MHS.
Balto., its hist., its people. Hall. V. 2, 3. MHS; DAR.
†Bench and bar of Md. Sams and Riley. 1901, v. 1, p. 325. Lib. Cong.; MHS; Peabody Lib.
†Biog. cyc. of rep. men of Md. and D. C. P. 346. MHS; DAR.
Cary Geneal. Coll. Ms. MHS.
Col. families of Amer. Lawrence. V. 6, p. 271. MHS.
Col. families of U. S. A. Mackenzie. V. 1; v. 5. MHS; DAR.
Davis Family Rec. C. H. S. Davis. Monthly journal devoted to hist. and geneal. of Davis family. (Md. Davis, no. 5.) Meriden, Conn., 1867-1868, nos. 1-6. MHS.
See Elkins. Abr. Compend. Amer. Geneal. Virkus. V. 1, p. 588. DAR.
†(1817-1865.) Encyc. of Amer. biog. Amer. Hist. Soc., N. Y., v. 9, p. 228. MHS.
*Founders of Anne Arundel and Howard Cos. Warfield. Pp. 113-16, 323 (Henry Winter). MHS; DAR.
*Frederick Co. families. Markell. Ms. Personal list.
Geneal. of Henrietta Chauncy Wilson. Upshur. Bk. of photos. MHS.
Hist. graves of Md. and D. C. Ridgely. MHS.
†(82 ref.) Hist. of Frederick Co. Williams. MHS; DAR.
†Hist. of West. Md. Scharf. V. 1, p. 606. MHS; DAR.
Life of Henry Winter Davis. B. C. Steiner. M. H. Mag., 1916, v. 11, p. 300.
Md. families. Culver. Ms. Personal list.
Md. tombstone rec. Md. Geneal. Rec. Com., 1937, Parran, p. 2. Mss. DAR.
†Med. Annals Md. Cordell. 1903, pp. 372-74. MHS.
*Miscellaneous Md. families and Davis family. Ms. MHS.
Old Somerset. Torrence. MHS; DAR.
Patriotic Md. Md. Soc. of S. A. R., 1930. MHS; DAR.
Pattison wills. Md. Geneal. Rec. Com., 1929, pp. 7-42; 1930-31. Mss. DAR.
Pedigree of George Ross Veazey. Soc. Col. Wars Md. Culver. 1940. MHS; DAR.
Pedigree of Richard Walker Worthington. Soc. Col. Wars Md. Culver. 1940. MHS; DAR.
Mrs. N. S. Pendleton, Jr., chart. MHS.
Mrs. Pennington chart. MHS.
Revolutionary war pension abst. Natl. Geneal. Soc. Quart., v. 23, no. 2, p. 51.
Riggs of Anne Arundel, Frederick and Montgomery Cos. prior to 1663. Pamph. MHS.
St. Paul's P. E. churchyard, Berlin, Worcester Co. Hudson. Bd. ms. MHS; DAR. Also; Md. Geneal. Rec. Com., 1937, Mrs. Lines. Mss. DAR.
St. Paul's Parish, Balto. V. 1, 2, 3, 4. Mss. MHS.
St. Stephens Parish, Cecilton, Md. MHS; DAR.
St. Thomas' Parish, Balto. Co. Bd. ms. MHS. Also: Md. Geneal. Rec. Com., 1937, pp. 109-82. Mss. DAR.
Side lights on Md. hist. Richardson. V. 2, p. 77. MHS; DAR.
Sommerset Co. Court Book. Tilghman. 1937. Ms. DAR.
Stones from Bowie Davis place, near Brookfield, Montgomery Co. 1768-1890. Md. Geneal. Rec. Com., 1934-35, p. 61. Mss. DAR.
*The Sun, Balto., July 17, 31, 1904.
Talbott of "Poplar Knowle." Shirk. MHS; DAR.
Mrs. H. De Courcy Wright Thom chart. MHS.
Trinity P. E. churchyard, St. Mary's City. Md. O. R. Soc. Bull., no. 3, p. 59.
Mrs. Morris Whitridge chart. MHS.
*Wicomico Co. families. Tilghman. Ms, pp. 3, 52, 67, 107, 111, 113, 114, 128. DAR.
See Cotten. Abr. Compend. Amer. Geneal. Virkus. V. 1, p. 568. DAR.
See Zimmerman-Davis.

Davis, Cecil Co. Blackford chart. MHS.

Davis, Kent Co. Cotton chart. MHS.

Davis, Worcester Co. Col. families of Amer. Lawrence. V. 3, pp. 364-73; v. 6, pp. 271-87. MHS.

Davis, E. Steuart. Abr. Compend. Amer. Geneal. Virkus. V. 1, p. 106. DAR.

Davis, Henry Gassaway. Col. families of Amer. Lawrence. V. 2, pp. 30-52. MHS.
Monumental City. Howard. MHS; DAR.

†**Davis, Henry Winter.** Balto., hist and biog. Richardson and Bennett. 1871, pp. 241-44. MHS; DAR.

Davis, Ignatius, Worcester Co. Bible rec. 3 pts. Md. Geneal. Bull., v. 2, p. 12; v. 8, p. 41. MHS; DAR.

†**Davis, Jesse A.** Men of mark in Md. Johnson. V. 2. DAR; Enoch Pratt Lib.

Davis, J. Staige, Va. and Md. Abr. Compend. Amer. Geneal. Virkus. V. 4, p. 566. MHS.

Davis, Mrs. John Staige. (Katharine Gordon Bowdoin) Chart. Col. Dames, Chap. I. MHS.
Mrs. Wm. Graham Bowdoin chart. MHS.
Mrs. Howard Bruce charts. MHS.

†**Davis, John.** Autobiog., (1770–1864), Hagerstown, Md. M. H. Mag., 1935, v. 30, pp. 11–39.
†M. H. Mag., v. 12, p. 212.
Davis, Miss Kathleen. chart. Col. Dames, Chap. I. MHS.
Davis, Miss Mary Winter. Chart. Col. Dames, Chap. I. MHS.
Davis, Septimus, Harford Co. and Conn. Pedigree. Soc. Col. Wars Md. Culver. 1940. MHS; DAR.
Davis, S. Griffith, Aberdeen. Abr. Compend. Amer. Geneal. Virkus. V. 1, p. 811. DAR.
Davis, Wm. Revolutionary war pension abs. Natl. Geneal. Soc. Quart., v. 23, p. 51.
Davis Family. Allied families of Delaware. Sellers. MHS.
*Arch. of Georgetown Univ., Wash., D. C., v. 287.
Coat of arms. Hester Dorsey Richardson. Repr. from Balto. Sun, July 17, 1904, pamph. MHS.
Coat of arms. Side lights on Md. hist. Richardson. 1904. MHS.
Copied from Riley family. Md. Geneal. Rec. Com., 1934–35, p. 398. Mss. DAR.
*Rec., with geneal. 33 pp. MHS.
***Davis Family,** St. Mary's Co. Davis family. C. H. Davis. MHS.
Davis Line. Gaither, Va., and Md. Col. and Revolutionary families of Phila. Jordan. 1933, v. 1, pp. 144–67.
Davis-Harned. Mountain Democrat, Garrett Co., Dec. 6, 1934. Newsp. clipp. MHS; DAR.
***Davis-Lewis-Parish Line,** Va. The Sun, Balto., Jan. 22, 1905.
Davison, Mrs. R. Barton, Jr., charts. MHS.
*The Sun, Balto., March 4, 11, 1906.
St. Paul's Parish, Balto. V. 1. Mss. MHS.
Davison, Gen. John, Annapolis. Abs. of will. D. A. R. Mag., June, 1927, v. 61, no. 6, p. 470.
Davy. St. Paul's Parish, Balto. V. 1. Mss. MHS.
Davy, London. Cox (Cock) family. Leef and Webb. Ms. MHS.
Dawe, Daw. St. Paul's Parish, Balto. V. 2, 3. Mss. MHS.
Dawkins. Amer. Armory and Blue Book. Matthews. 1911–12, p. 312.
Geneal. and memorial encyc. of Md. Spencer. V. 2, p. 417. MHS; DAR.
Md. Families. Culver. Ms. Personal list.
Taylor Bible rec. Ms. MHS.
*Wilson Mss. Coll., no. 53; no. 80. MHS.
Dawkins, St. Mary's Co. Col. families of U. S. A. Mackenzie. V. 4; v. 5, pp. 165–70. MHS; DAR.
***Dawkins, Judge W. I.** Geneal. and mem. encyc. of Md. Spencer. V. 2, p. 415. MHS; DAR.
Pedigree. Soc. Col. Wars. Md. Culver. 1940. MHS; DAR.
Dawkins, Walter L. Amer. Armory and Blue Book. Matthews. 1908, p. 46. DAR.
Dawley. Pedigree of Leigh Bonsal. Soc. Col. Wars Md. Culver. 1940. MHS; DAR.
Dawson. Auld chart. MHS.
Americus Dawson farm, near Dawsonville, Montgomery Co. (Mother's Delight stones moved to Monocacy Cemetery, Beallsville.) Tombstones, 1797–1866. Md. Geneal. Rec. Com., 1926, p. 76. Mss. DAR.
Coll. of family rec. with biog. sketches of various families and individuals bearing name Dawson. C. C. Dawson. 1874. DAR.
Col. families of U. S. A. Mackenzie. V. 4, pp. 115–20. MHS; DAR.
Darby geneal. Darby. MHS.
Dawson family of Md. Ms. File case, DAR.
Descent. Col. and Revolutionary families of Pa. Amer. Hist. Soc., N. Y., 1934, p. 7.
*Frederick Co. families. Markell. Ms. Personal list.
*Lineage Bk. Daughters of Amer. Colonists. V. 1, p. 269. MHS; DAR.
Mann-Needles-Hambleton families. Needles. MHS; DAR.
Md. families. Culver. Ms. Personal list.
†Med. Annals Md. Cordell. 1903, p. 374. MHS.
Monocacy Cemetery, Beallsville, Montgomery Co. Md. Geneal. Rec. Com., 1926–27, pp. 70–73. Mss. DAR.
Mothers' Delight stones, moved from Americus Dawson farm, near Dawsonville, to Monocacy Cemetery. Md. Geneal. Rec. Com., v. 2, p. 76. Mss. DAR.
St. Paul's Parish, Balto. V. 1, 2, 3. Mss. MHS.
Spring Hill Cemetery, Talbot Co. Md. O. R. Soc. Bull., no. 1, pp. 35–41. MHS.
Torrence and allied families. Torrence. Pp. 483–84. MHS; DAR.
***Dawson,** Talbot Co. Lineage Bk., Daughters of Founders and Patriots. V. 23, pp. 149–50. MHS; DAR.
Dawson, Nicholas, Frederick Co. Copy of will, 1806. Ms. File case, DAR.
***Dawson Family.** Chart. MHS.
Dawson Family, Talbot Co. Chart. Dr. Thomas Sears. Ms. MHS.
Day. Bond chart. MHS.
Day data. Md. Geneal. Bull. April 1938. V. 9, no. 2. MHS; DAR.
St. Paul's Parish, Balto. V. 1, 2, 3. Mss. MHS.
Day, Edward. Died in Balto. Co., 1746. Bible rec. Gorsuch and allied families. Harrison. Mss. MHS.
Md. families. Culver. Ms. Personal list.
†Med. Annals Md. Cordell. 1903, p. 374. MHS.
Mrs. C. L. Riggs chart. MHS.
Sharar-Perine-Day Bible rec. Ms. MHS.
See Loney-Boyce-Day-Garrett-Ross-Stansbury.
Day, Wm., Md. Revolutionary soldiers buried in northwest S. C. Natl. Geneal. Soc. Quart., v. 21, no. 2, p. 46.
Day Line, Mass. and Md. Taylor family, Balto. Co. Col. and Revolutionary families of Phila. Jordan. 1933, v. 1, pp. 260–67.
Deaderick, Va. Some notable families of south. states. Armstrong. V. 1, pp. 59–75. DAR.
Deagan. Lanahan chart. MHS.
Md. Families. Culver. Ms. Personal list.
Deagen. Mrs. Sherlock Swann chart. MHS.
***Deakins.** Wilson Mss. Coll., no. 23. MHS.
***Deakins,** Charles Co., 1665. Lineage Bk., Daughters of Founders and Patriots. V. 18, p. 136. MHS; DAR.
***Deakins,** Georgetown, Md., (1720–1800). Lineage Bk. Daughters of Amer. Colonists. V. 2, p. 241. MHS; DAR.

***Deakins, Wm., Jr.** Patriots of Revolutionary period interred in D. C. Balch. Rec. of Columbia Hist. Soc., v. 19, v. 20.
Deal. *See* Diehl.
Deal, J. T., Jr. Md. Soc., War of 1812, v. 1, no. 3. Ms. MHS.
Deale. Gary chart. MHS.
Hazelhurst chart. MHS.
Pedigree of Henry Irvine Keyser, II. Soc. Col. Wars Md. Culver. 1940. MHS; DAR.
Somerset Co. Court Book. Tilghman. 1937. Ms. DAR.
†Dean. Hist. of Allegany Co. Thomas and Williams. V. 1, pp. 605–6. MHS; DAR.
†Hist. of Frederick Co. Williams. V. 2, pp. 842, 1197. MHS; DAR.
*Marriage rec. of some descendants of Wm. Dean of col. Md. Ms. MHS.
Maulsby family in Amer. Barnard. DAR; Peabody Lib.
St. Paul's Parish, Balto. V. 1, 2. Mss. MHS.
Tombstone rec. of Dorchester Co. Jones. DAR.
*Wicomico Co. families. Tilghman. Ms, p. 96. DAR.
Dean, W. J. Abr. Compend. Amer. Geneal. Virkus. V. 6, p. 184. DAR.
Deane. Ances. rec. and portraits. Col. Dames of Amer., p. 214. MHS; DAR.
Patriotic Md. Md. Soc. of S. A. R., 1930. MHS; DAR.
Mrs. E. W. Poe chart. MHS.
Deane, Kent Co. Manning chart. MHS.
***Deardorf.** Frederick Co. families. Markell. Ms. Personal list.
Deardorff. Mrs. James McHenry chart. MHS.
Deaver. Cary Geneal. Coll. Ms. MHS.
Gibbs chart. MHS.
Patriotic Md. Md. Soc. of S. A. R., 1930. MHS; DAR.
Revolutionary war pension abs. Natl. Geneal. Soc. Quart., v. 23, no. 2, p. 52.
Deaver, Talbot Co. Revolutionary war pension abs. Natl. Geneal. Soc. Quart., v. 23, p. 53.
Deaver, John and Mary. Md. pension. Natl. Geneal. Soc. Quart., v. 23, no. 2, p. 42.
Debrulagh. Somerset Co. Court Book. Tilghman. 1937. Ms. DAR.
Debruter. Naturalizations in Md., 1666–1765; Laws. Bacon. MHS.
Debutts. St. Paul's Parish, Balto. V. 1, 3. Mss. MHS.
DeButts. Balch chart. MHS.
†Med. Annals Md. Cordell. 1903, p. 374. MHS.
De Carpentier. *See* Carpentier.
†Decatur. Chesapeake Bay Country. Earle. P. 439. MHS.
Edmundson family. Focke Geneal. Coll. Mss. MHS.
*Geneal.; descendants of Stephen Decatur of Rhode Island, 1746. W. Decatur Parsons. Decatur family in Md., pp. 14–22. 500 copies. N. Y., 1921. MHS.
†Romantic Decatur. C. L. Lewis. 1937, 296 pp. DAR.
†Decatur, Com. Stephen. Biog. cyc. of rep. men of Md. and D. C. P. 376. MHS; DAR.
†(Born at "Sinepuxent," Berlin, Md., Jan., 5, 1779; killed in duel with Commodore Barron, Mar. 22, 1820). M. H. Mag., v. 12, pp. 214, 383.
†Daredevil champion of our early navy. D. A. R. Mag., v. 65, p. 3.
Obituary copied from Md. Gazette. D. A. R. Mag., Apr., 1914, p. 260.
***Decatur Family.** Decatur family. W. Decatur Parsons. N. Y., 1921, 55 pp. DAR.
De Chappotin. Ances. rec. and portraits. Col. Dames of Amer., 1910, p. 709. MHS; DAR.
Dechert. Hagerstown tombstone inscriptions. Gruder. Natl. Geneal. Soc. Quart., 1919, v. 8, nos. 1, 2.
De Cocye. St. Paul's Parish, Balto. V. 2. Mss. MHS.
De Cormis. Col. families of U. S. A. Mackenzie. V. 1. MHS: DAR.
Decorse, Kent Co. Md. Geneal. Rec. Com., 1932–33, v. 5. DAR.
DeCorse. Bible rec., Kent Co., 1819–1914. Md. Geneal. Rec. Com., 1932–33, p. 315. Mss. DAR.
See Corse.
DeCourcy. Bankhead family. William and Mary Quart., 2nd series, v. 9, p. 303.
†Chesapeake Bay Country. Earle. P. 347. MHS.
Col. families of East. Shore and their descendants. Emory. 1900, p. 111, 224. MHS.
Col. mansions of Md. and Del. Hammond. 1914. MHS.
Day-Star of Amer. Freedom. G. L. L. Davis. 1855, p. 83. MHS; DAR.
De Courcy's of My Lord's Gift. Cheston and Courcy upon Wye, Queen Anne Co. Geneal. Soc. Pa., Mss. Coll.
Geneal. and mem. encyc. of Md. Spencer. V. 2, pp. 596, 597. MHS; DAR.
Gittings chart. MHS.
Side lights on Md. hist. Richardson. V. 2, p. 81. MHS; DAR.
*The Sun, Balto., July 12, 1903.
Thomas family of Talbot Co. Spencer. P. 41. MHS; DAR.
Turner family. Forman. P. 37. MHS.
See Coursey.
See Taylor.
De Courcy, Coursey. Mrs. H. F. Johnston chart. MHS.
De Courcy, Coursey Line, Md. (from 1649). W. H. De C. W. Thom pedigree charts, plate 2. Soc. Col. Wars, Md. Johnston. 1904, pp. 108, 143. MHS.
De Coursey. De Coursey family. Thomas H. H. Patterson. Typed. Geneal. Soc. Pa., Mss. Coll.
See Patterson. Abr. Compend. Amer. Geneal. Virkus. V. 1, p. 601. DAR.
***De Coursey, Samuel Wickes.** Old Kent. Hanson. P. 97. MHS; DAR.
De Coursey, de Courcy, Courci. Cary Geneal. Coll. Ms. MHS.
Deems. St. Paul's Parish, Balto. V. 2. Mss. MHS.
Tercentenary hist. of Md. Andrews. V. 3, p. 456. MHS; DAR.
Deemy. Amer. Clan Gregor Year Book, 1913, p. 60. MHS; DAR.
Deen. St. Paul's Parish, Balto. V. 1. Mss. MHS.
†Deets. Med. Annals Md. Cordell. 1903, p. 375. MHS.
†Portrait and biog. rec. of Sixth Cong. Dist. of Md. 1898. p. 813. MHS; DAR.

†**Deetz.** Hist. of Allegany Co. Thomas and Williams. V. 1. MHS; DAR.
***Defoe Family.** Hist. of Cecil Co. Johnston. Pp. 526–34. MHS; DAR.
Deford. Lanahan chart. MHS.
Mrs. Sherlock Swann chart. MHS.
†**Deford, Benj.** Balto., hist. and biog. Richardson and Bennett. 1871, pp. 245–46. MHS; DAR.
Deford, Mrs. Robert Bell (Dorothea Hoffman). Chart. Col. Dames, Chap. I. MHS.
De Ford. Mrs. E. C. Venable chart. MHS.
De Ford, Mrs. William (Lydia Hollingsworth Howard). Chart. Col. Dames, Chap. I. MHS.
de Forest. Walloon family in Amer. Mrs. R. W. de Forest. Houghton, Mifflin Co., 1914. MHS.
De Gant. *See* Gantt.
de Ghize, Countess Alef (Eleanor May Jencks). Chart. Col. Dames, Chap. I. MHS.
Dehay. St. Paul's Parish, Balto. V. 1. Mss. MHS.
De Hoff. *See* Baker-Hargarader-De Hoff.
Deiffenderfer. *See* Diffenderfer.
Deitrick. Hist. sketch of P. F. Eichelberger. Eichelberger.
De Kergorlay. Abr. Compend. Amer. Geneal. Virkus. V. 1, p. 580. DAR.
de la Bistrate. Ellicott-Campbell chart. MHS.
Delahay, Talbot Co. H. Mullikin pedigree charts. plate 1. Soc. Col. Wars, Md. Johnston. 1905, p. 74. MHS.
Delahaye. Descendants. Old Md. families. Bromwell. MHS; DAR.
Delamaire. Naturalizations in Md., 1666–1765; Laws. Bacon. MHS.
Delany. *See* Lindsay. Abr. Compend. Amer. Geneal. Virkus. V. 1, p. 689. DAR.
Delaplaine. Family hist. of John Hyder and CatherineDelaplaine. Beam. 1909, pamph, MHS.
*Frederick Co. families. Markell. Ms. Personal list.
*Wilson Mss. Coll. no. 25, A and B; no. 101. MHS.
Delaplaine, Phila. Coll. of Amer. epitaphs and inscriptions. Alden, 1814, v. 5, pp. 173, 175. MHS.
Delaplane. Amer. Clan Gregor Year Book, 1930, pp. 12–13. MHS; DAR.
Md. tombstone rec. Md. Geneal. Rec. Com., 1937, Parran, p. 2. Mss. DAR.
Delaport. *See* Bond-Cromwell-Delaport-Harris-Reisinger-Reardon.
***De Lashmutt.** Frederick Co. families. Markell. Ms. Personal list.
***De Laurcal.** Thompson Bible rec. Ms. File case, MHS.
Dell, T. Medairy. Md. Soc., War of 1812, v. 3, no. 227. Ms. MHS.
†**Dellinger.** Hist. of Allegany Co. Thomas and Williams. V. 2, MHS; DAR.
†**De Loughery.** Med. Annals Md. Cordell. 1903, p. 375. MHS.
De Lozier. St. Paul's Parish, Balto. V. 2. Mss. MHS.
Delpart. St. Paul's Parish, Balto. V. 2. Mss. MHS.
De Macklot. Cary Geneal. Coll. Ms. MHS.
De Marin. *See* Marine.
Dement, Md. prior to 1671. Rec. of families of Calif. pioneers. Pub. by Calif. State Com. on Geneal. Research, D. A. R. V. 2, p. 44. MHS; DAR.
Demitt, Demmitt. St. Paul's Parish, Balto. V. 1, 2. Mss. MHS.
Demouderer. Naturalizations in Md., 1666–1765; Laws. Bacon. MHS.
Dempsey. St. Paul's Parish, Balto. V. 2. Mss. MHS.
Dempsey, Margaret, Balto. Will, Dec. 26, 1867. D. C. Geneal. Rec. Com., 1932–34, v. 10, pp. 246–48. Typed, bd. DAR.
Dempsey-Nourse-Bond. Bible rec. D. C. Geneal. Rec. Com., v. 10, pp. 32–35. Typed bd. DAR.
***Demuth Family.** Demuth family and Moravian Church. Pamph. DAR.
***Denison.** Abbott-Denison-Willie families, early ancestors, of Bishops. Stratford Co., Herts, Eng. Pamph. MHS.
*Abbott-Denison-Willie families. Spencer Miller. Repr. from N. Y. Geneal. and Biog. Rec., Jan., 1936. MHS.
Denison family of Mass. to Harford Co. Md. Geneal. Rec. Com., 1929, p. 112–14. DAR.
Butler chart. Cary Geneal. Coll. Ms. MHS.
Dorsey chart. MHS.
Mrs. T. C. Jenkins chart. MHS.
Rodgers Bible rec. Ms. MHS.
Denison Family, Harford Co. Dandridge family of Va. William and Mary Quart., 1st series, v. 5, pp. 30, 81.
Denmead. St. Paul's Parish, Balto. V. 2, 3. Mss. MHS.
Denmead, Garner Wood. Pedigree. Soc. Col. Wars Md. Culver. 1940. MHS; DAR.
Dennis. Amer. Armory and Blue Book. Matthews. 1911–12, p. 110.
Abr. Compend. Amer. Geneal. Virkus. V. 1, pp. 245–46. DAR.
Balto., its hist., its people. Hall. V. 2. MHS; DAR.
Col. families of U. S. A. Mackenzie. V. 4, pp. 125–33. MHS; DAR.
Custis-Teakle chart. Cary Geneal. Coll. Ms. MHS.
Hist. graves of Md. and D. C. Ridgely. MHS.
Md. families. Culver. Ms. Personal list.
Old Somerset. Torrence. MHS; DAR.
Pedigree of John Custis Handy. Soc. Col. Wars Md. Culver. 1940. MHS; DAR.
St. Andrews P. E. churchyard, Princess Anne, Somerset Co. Md. O. R. Soc. Bull., no. 1, pp. 29–32.
St. Paul's Parish, Balto. V. 1, 2, 3. Mss. MHS.
Sketches of John Slemmons Stevenson and Rev. Samuel McMaster. Stevenson. Pp. 18–19. MHS.
Somerset Co. Court Book. Tilghman. 1937. Ms. DAR.
Tombstones at "Beverly," Worcester Co., 1728–1899. Bible rec. of Dorchester and Somerset Cos. and Del. P. 25. DAR.
Turner Geneal. Coll. Ms. MHS.
*Wicomico Co. families. Tilghman. Ms, pp. 78–79. DAR.
Wicomico Co. families. Bible rec. Ms. DAR.
Worcester Co. militia, 1794. Covington. Pp. 157, 161. MHS.

Dennis. *See* Hicks-Dennis-Edmondson-Phillips-Travers-White.
Dennis, James Teackle. Md. Soc., War of 1812, v. 1, no. 104. Ms. MHS.
Pedigree chart, plates 1 and 2. Soc. Col. Wars, Md. Johnston. 1905, pp. 21, 144. MHS.
†Dennis, James Upshur. Biog. cyc. of rep. men of Md. and D. C. P. 342. MHS; DAR.
Dennis, John McPherson. Pedigree. Soc. Col. Wars Md. Culver. 1940. MHS; DAR. See Pedigree Book, 1905, p. 21.
†Sketch. Md. Manual, 1933, p. 301.
Dennis, Sam'l King. Pedigree. Soc. Col. Wars Md. Culver. 1940. MHS; DAR.
***Dennis Line.** Geneal. tables of paternal lines of Dennis family as prepared prior to June 1890. Judge John Upshur Dennis, Balto. 1938, 61 pp. MHS.
Denny. Botfield and allied families. Ms. DAR.
*East. Shore of Md. Wilson Mss. Coll., no. 45; no. 76. MHS.
Md. Geneal. Bull., v. 7, p. 23. MHS; DAR.
†Med. Annals Md. Cordell. 1903, p. 375. MHS.
Pedigree of Harrison Tilghman. Soc. Col. Wars Md. Culver. 1940. MHS; DAR.
Rumsey-Smithson Bible Rec. Md. Geneal. Rec. Com., 1932–33, v. 5, pp. 63–142. DAR.
Rumsey-Smithson family rec. bk. Md. Geneal. Rec. Com., 1932, p. 131. DAR.
Smithson-Rumsey rec. Bk. Ms. MHS.
Denny, Dr. Wm. St. Paul's Parish, Balto. V. 2. Mss. MHS.
Denny-Chapman. Abr. Compend. Amer. Geneal. Virkus. V. 1, p. 544. DAR.
Denny-Roberts. Bible rec. Ms. MHS.
***Denson, Denston.** Wicomico Co. families. Tilghman. Ms, pp. 1, 95, 99. DAR.
Dent. Amer. Armory and Blue Book. Matthews. 1911–12, p. 258.
Abr. Compend. Amer. Geneal. Virkus. V. 6, pp. 149, 647. DAR.
Ancestors of Judge Thomas and Rebecca (Wilkinson) Dent, their descendants and connections. Alexander Hamilton Bell, Esq. To be pub. in Natl. Geneal. Soc. Quart.
Ancest. rec. and portraits. Col. Dames of Amer., 1910, v. 2, p. 469. MHS; DAR.
Ancestry of Rev. Hatch Dent. F. B. Culver. M. H. Mag., 1924, v. 19, p. 193–96.
†Bench and bar of Md. Sams and Riley. 1901, v. 1, p. 302. Lib. Cong.; MHS; Peabody Lib.
Bowie-Claggett chart. MHS.
Brooke family of Whitchurch, etc. Balch. p. 21. MHS; DAR.
Robert Brooke chart. MHS; DAR.
Carne and allied family notes. Coues. Ms. MHS.
Cary Geneal. Coll. Ms. MHS.
Col. families of U. S. A. Mackenzie. V. 3, pp. 152–54; v. 6. MHS; DAR.
Data. D. A. R. Mag., Dec., 1931, v. 65, no. 12, p. 758.
Daughter of Md.; Mother of Texas. Bell. MHS; DAR.
Dent Family of Md. from Eng. to Amer. about 1660. (Julia Bray Dent was wife of Ulysses Simpson Grant, President of U. S.) Ms. File case, DAR.
Gary chart. MHS.
See Grant. Abr. Compend. Amer. Geneal. Virkus. V. 1, p. 301. DAR.
†Hist. of Allegany Co. Thomas and Williams. V. 1. MHS; DAR.
Lineage Bk., Order of Washington, pp. 108, 124. MHS; DAR.
Lineage Bks., Natl. Soc. of Daughters of Amer. Col., v. 2, p. 66; v. 3, p. 326. MHS; DAR.
Marshall of Marshall Hall. Natl. Geneal. Soc. Quart., v. 19, no. 1, p. 1; no. 4, pp. 86–96.
Md. families. Culver. Ms. Personal list.
†Med. Annals. Md. Cordell. 1903, pp. 375–76. MHS.
Old cemetery rec. Md. Geneal. Rec. Com., 1935–36. Mss. DAR.
Patriotic Md. Md. Soc. of S. A. R., 1930. MHS; DAR.
Pedigree of Wm. Bernard Duke. Soc. Col. Wars Md. Culver. 1940. MHS; DAR.
Pedigree of Coleman Randall Freeman. Soc. Col. Wars Md. Culver. 1940. MHS; DAR.
Pedigree of George Harrison. Soc. Col. Wars Md. Culver. 1940. MHS; DAR.
Pedigree of W. Wallace McKaig. Soc. Col. Wars Md. Culver. 1940. MHS; DAR.
Pedigree of Bennet Biscoe Norris. Soc. Col. Wars Md. Culver. 1940. MHS; DAR.
Some Md. and Va. ancestors. Bell. Natl. Geneal. Soc. Quart., v. 19, no. 4, pp. 86–96.
See Marshall-Dent.
D. H. Thomas pedigree chart. Soc. Col. Wars, Md. Johnston. 1905, pp. 109, 144. MHS.
Dent, Peter, Charles Co. D. A. R. Mag., v. 65, no. 12, p. 758.
***Dent, Col. Wm.** Lineage Bk. Daughters of Amer. Colonists. V. 3, p. 326. MHS; DAR.
Dent Family, Md. and Ohio. Ms. File case, MHS.
***Dent-Magruder-Trueman Family.** Notes. Natl. Geneal. Soc. Quart., Dec., 1937, v. 25, no. 4, pp. 104–13.
Denwood. Ancestry of Rosalie Morris Johnson. Johnson. 1905. MHS; DAR.
Ances. rec. and portraits. Col. Dames. of Amer., 1910, v. 1, pp. 149, 344; v. 2, p. 682. MHS; DAR.
Frances Murray Bowdoin chart. MHS.
Carey chart. MHS.
Cary Geneal. Coll. Ms. MHS.
Miss M. W. Davis chart. MHS.
De Ford chart. MHS.
Done Bible rec. Ms. MHS.
Dorsey and allied families. Ms. MHS.
Mrs. C. C. Hall chart. MHS.
*Hist. Dorchester Co. Jones. 1925, p. 303. MHS; DAR.
Geneal. of Henrietta Chauncy Wilson. Upshur Bk. of photos. MHS.
Gillis-Winder chart. Cary Geneal. Coll. Ms. MHS.
Md. families. Culver. Ms. Personal list.
Md. gleamings in Eng. Wills. M. H. Mag., 1907, v. 2, no. 4.
Old Somerset. Torrence. MHS; DAR.
Pedigree of Gustav Wm. Lurman. Soc. Col. Wars Md. Culver. 1940. MHS; DAR.
Side lights on Md. hist. Richardson. V. 2, p. 311. MHS; DAR.
Somerset Co. Court Book. Tilghman. 1937. Ms. DAR.
Mrs. Morris Whitridge chart. MHS.

*Wicomico Co. families. Tilghman. Ms., p. 111. DAR.
Mrs. G. H. Williams, Jr., chart. MHS.
Denwood Family. Holliday Papers. Ms. MHS.
Denwood-Hooper. Ancest. rec. and portraits. Col. Dames of Amer., 1910, v. 2, p. 682. MHS; DAR.
***Derby.** Wicomico Co. families. Tilghman. Ms., p. 96. DAR.
***Dern.** Frederick Co. families. Markell. Ms. Personal list.
Dern, George. Bible rec., 1806–1931. Md. Geneal. Rec. Com., 1932–33, p. 61. Mss. DAR.
Derochbrune, Lewis (shipwright), Balto. Will proved June 5, 1802. D. A. R. Mag., 1926. V. 61, no. 6, p. 470.
de Roth, Mrs. Herbert C. (Lydia H. De Ford). Chart. Col. Dames, Chap. I. MHS.
Mrs. Wm. De Ford chart. MHS.
Mrs. E. C. Venable chart. MHS.
Derr. Baust or Emanuel Reformed churchyard, Carroll Co. Md. Geneal. Rec. Com., 1935–36. Mss. DAR.
†Hist. of Frederick Co. Williams. MHS; DAR.
†Med. Annals Md. Cordell. 1903, p. 376. MHS.
Steiner geneal. Steiner. 1896. MHS.
Derr, Dare. Frederick Co. tombstone inscriptions. Gruder. Natl. Geneal. Soc. Quart., 1919, v. 8, nos. 1, 2.
Derrickson. Turner Geneal. Coll. Ms. MHS. *See* Williams-Derrickson.
Dertzbauch. Frederick Co. tombstone inscriptions. Gruder. Natl. Geneal. Soc. Quart., 1919, v. 8, nos. 1, 2.
Derydor. St. Paul's Parish, Balto. V. 1. Mss. MHS.
Desjardins. Naturalizations in Md., 1666–1765; Laws. Bacon. MHS.
Deterly. Hagerstown tombstone inscriptions. Gruder. Natl. Geneal. Soc. Quart., 1919, v. 8, nos. 1, 2.
Detrick. *See* Cottman-Lux-Detrick.
Dettmar. Catonsville pioneers of Luth. faith. Natl. Geneal. Soc. Quart., v. 9, no. 2, p. 29.
Detweiler. Hagerstown tombstone inscriptions. Gruder. Natl. Geneal. Soc. Quart., 1919, v. 8, nos. 1, 2.
†Devecmon. Bench and bar of Md. Sams and Riley. 1901, v. 2, p. 457. Lib. Cong.; MHS; Peabody Lib.
†Deveemon, W. Coombs. Men of mark in Md. Johnson. V. 3. DAR; Enoch Pratt Lib.
Devereaux. M. E. churchyard, Snow Hill, Worcester Co., Hudson. Bd. ms. MHS; DAR.
Devereux. Abr. Compend. Amer. Geneal. Virkus. V. 1, p. 43. DAR.
†Deveries. Biog. cyc. of rep. men of Md. and D. C. P. 178. MHS; DAR.
Founders of Anne Arundel and Howard Cos. Warfield. P. 488. MHS; DAR.
Monumental City. Howard. MHS; DAR.
Mt. Paran Pres. churchyard, Harrisonville, Balto. Co. Typed ms. MHS; DAR.
John Swadner and his descendants. Evans. 1919. Typed, bd. MHS.
Devilbiss. Englar family. Barnes. MHS; DAR.
†Hist. of Frederick Co. Williams. MHS; DAR.
John Swadner and his descendants. Evans. 1919. Typed, bd. MHS.
Roop geneal. Pamph. MHS.
Devilbiss, Charles. Bible rec. Ms. MHS.
*New Windsor, Md. Bible rec. Ms. MHS.
Devilbiss Family. Rec. Ms. MHS.
Devries. Whitridge chart. MHS.
***Dew.** Hist. and geneal. of Dew family. Descendants of Col. Thomas Dew of Va. E. Dew White. (Also families in Md., N. C., Tenn.) Heraldry. Chart. Greenville, N. C. 349 pp. MHS.
Marriage rec., 1795–1931. Ms. MHS.
Marriages, 1796–1854, Balto. Co. Md. Geneal. Bull., v. 4, p. 4. MHS; DAR.
Gen. Tobias Emerson Stansbury chart. MHS.
*Stansbury-Dew chart. MHS.
St. Paul's Parish, Balto. Vol. 1, 2. Mss. MHS.
Dew Family, Va. Chart, with books, photos. Jan. 15, 1932. MHS.
Dewees. U. B. cemetery, Sabillasville. Young. Natl. Geneal. Soc. Quart., Sept., 1938, v. 26, no. 3, p. 61 (to be contd.).
Dewey. Rumsey-Smithson Bible rec. Md. Geneal. Rec. Com., 1932–33, v. 5, pp. 63–142. DAR.
Dewitt. St. Paul's Parish, Balto. V. 1, 2. Mss. MHS.
De Wolf. Ancest. rec. and portraits. Col. Dames of Amer., 1910, v. 2, p. 701. MHS; DAR.
Mrs. J. Whitridge Williams chart 2. MHS.
Deye. Arnold chart. MHS.
See Clement. Col. families of U. S. A. Mackenzie. V. 1, pp. 97–100. MHS; DAR.
†D'Hinojosa, Alexander (last Dutch gov. of Del.). Hist. of Talbot Co. Tilghman. V. 1, pp. 521–31. MHS; DAR.
Dhymiossa. Naturalizations in Md., 1666–1765; Laws. Bacon. MHS.
***Dial.** Scruggs geneal. MHS.
Dias. Somerset Co. Court Book. Tilghman. 1937. Ms. DAR.
***Dick.** Dick and allied families. Pamph. DAR.
*Eng. ancestry of Mrs. Frank Madison Dick (nee Minette G. Mills) connecting with several Md. and Va. ancestors of Mrs. Dick. L. S. Olson. 1932, pamph. DAR.
St. Paul's Parish, Balto. V. 1, 2. Mss. MHS.
Dick, Christina, Bladensburg, Md. Abs. of will, 1801. D. A. R. Mag., v. 61, no. 6, p. 470.
(Daughter of Robert Dick, Bladensburg, Prince George Co.) Will proved Oct. 6, 1804. D. A. R. Mag., v. 61, no. 6, p. 470.
***Dick, Frank Madison.** Burke's landed gentry. 1939. Pp. 2996–97. MHS.
†Encyc. of Amer. biog., new series, v. 9, p. 238.
Dick, Thomas, Bladensburg, Md. Will proved June 10, 1803. D. A. R. Mag., v. 61, no. 6, p. 470.
Dick-Dixon. Lineage Bks., Natl. Soc. of Daughters of Amer. Col., v. 3, p. 221. MHS; DAR.
***Dickens.** Alstons of North and South Carolina. Groves. P. 303. MHS.
Dickenson. Pedigree of Tilghman Goldsborough Pitts. Soc. Col. Wars Md. Culver. 1940. MHS; DAR.
See Dickinson.

Dickenson, Talbot Co. D. A. R. Mag., April, 1928, v. 62, no. 4, p. 245.
Dickerson. All Hallow's P. E. churchyard, Snow Hill, Worcester Co. Hudson. Ms. MHS; DAR. Also Md. Geneal. Rec. Com., 1935–36, p. 24. Mss. DAR.
Bond chart. MHS.
Mt. Olive M. P. churchyard, Worcester Co. Md. Geneal. Rec. Com., 1937, Mrs. Lines. Mss. DAR.
Old Somerset. Torrence. MHS; DAR.
Sharar-Perine-Day Bible rec. Ms. MHS.
Tercentenary hist. of Md. Andrews. V. 2, p. 768. MHS; DAR.
Turner Geneal. Coll. Ms. MHS.
*Wicomico Co. families. Tilghman. Ms., p. 100. DAR.
Dickes. Somerset Co. Court Book. Tilghman. 1937. Ms. DAR.
Dickes, Dicks. St. Paul's Parish, Balto. V. 1, 2. Mss. MHS.
Dickeson. Somerset Co. Court Book. Tilghman. 1937. Ms. DAR.
Dickey. Balto., its hist., its people. Hall. V. 2. MHS; DAR.
Hist. of Allegany Co. Thomas and Williams. V. 1, pp. 562–64. MHS; DAR.
Hist. of Balto. Lewis Hist. Pub. Co., 1912, v. 2, p. 225. DAR.
Tercentenary hist. of Md. Andrews. V. 4, p. 707. MHS; DAR.
Dickey, C. H. Md. Soc., War of 1812, v. 1, no. 79. Ms. MHS.
†Men of mark in Md. Johnson. V. 3. DAR; Enoch Pratt Lib.
Dickey, P. Sadtler. Md. Soc., War of 1812, v. 1, no. 72. Ms. MHS.
†Dickey, Wm. A. Men of mark in Md. Johnson. V. 2. DAR; Enoch Pratt Lib.
Dickey Family. Bible rec., 1828–1921. D. C. Geneal. Rec. Com., v. 31, pp. 131–32. Typed, bd. DAR.
*D. C. Geneal. Rec. Com., v. 31, pt. 1, pp. 131–32. Typed, bd. DAR.
Dickinson. Abr. Compend. Amer. Geneal. Virkus. V. 4, p. 136. MHS.
Christ P. E. Church cemetery, Cambridge. Steele. 1936. MHS; DAR.
Col. mansions of Md. and Del. Hammond. P. 251. MHS.
*Dickinson family of East. Shore of Md. Drapper. Typed. DAR.
Griffin family. Streets. P. 70. MHS.
†Hist. of Caroline Co. Noble. MHS.
(1732–1808). Hist. of Talbot Co. Tilghman. V. 1, p. 352. MHS; DAR.
†Hist. of Pocomoke City. Murray. 1883, pp. 68, 102, 128. DAR.
Mrs. R. N. Jackson chart. MHS.
†Life and character of John Dickinson (born in Talbot Co., 1732; died in Wilmington, Del., 1808). Pub. Hist. Soc. Del., 1901, pamph. File case, DAR.
Md. families. Culver. Ms. Personal list.
†Med. Annals Md. Cordell. 1903, pp. 376–77. MHS.
Pocomoke Pres. churchyard, Worcester Co. Hudson. Bd. ms. MHS; DAR.
St. Paul's Parish, Balto. V. 1. Mss. MHS.
Thomas family of Talbot Co. Spencer. P. 84. MHS; DAR.
Thomas Hobson and some of his descendents. Tyler's Quart. Mag., v. 8, pp. 127–33.
†Dickinson, Hon. John (1732–1808). Hist. of Talbot Co. Tilghman. V. 1, pp. 352–67. MHS; DAR.
Dickinson Family, Caroline and Talbot Cos. Ms. File case, DAR.
Dickinson, Dickenson. Third Haven Friends Meeting House, Easton. Vital rec. MHS. Also: Natl. Geneal. Soc. Quart., v. 11, no. 1, pp. 9–14.
Dicks. *See* Dickes.
†Dickson. Med. Annals Md. Cordell. 1903, p. 377. MHS.
Mt. Paran Pres. churchyard, Harrisonville, Balto. Co. Typed ms. MHS; DAR.
Didier. Mrs. Alexander Gordon chart. MHS.
Greenway Mss. Geneal. Coll. Binder's titles, Taylor, nos. 1 and 2. MHS.
Hilles chart. MHS.
Md. families. Culver. Ms.. Personal list.
St. Paul's Parish, Balto. V. 2. Mss. MHS.
Turner family. Forman. P. 84. MHS.
Didier, Henry, (1747–1822). Revolutionary war heroes. Cole. Bklet. Enoch Pratt Lib.
Diederick. Hagerstown tombstone inscriptions. Gruder. Natl. Geneal. Soc. Quart., 1919, v. 8, nos. 1, 2.
Diefendorff. Burton ancestry. Ms. MHS.
Dieffenderfer. Hist. of West. Md. Scharf. V. 1, p. 66. MHS; DAR.
***Dieffenderfer Family,** Pa. Bible rec. Ga. Geneal. Rec. Com., 1933, pt. 5, p. 17. Typed, bd. DAR.
***Diehl.** Geneal. E. H. Diehl. 1930. DAR.
Zion Reformed Church, Hagerstown. Md. Geneal. Rec. Com., 1934–35. Mss. DAR.
Diehl, Nicholas, Pa. Revolutionary service. Md. Geneal. Rec. Com., 1936, p. 69. DAR.
***Diehl (Deal) Family.** Geneal. of Conrad Diehl and descendants, 1763–1933. Supplement to Diehl geneal., by Diehl, 1930. 1933. Ms. DAR.
Dietrich. Balto., its hist., its people. Hall. V. 3. MHS; DAR.
***Dietrick.** Coat of arms. Family of Holland. J. Howard Randerson. MHS.
†Diffenderfer. Diffenderfers and Frieses. Soc. for Hist. of Germans in Md. 5th ann. rept., 1891, pp. 91–95.
Griffith geneal., Griffith. MHS; DAR.
Diffenderfer, Deiffenderfer Family. Arrived in Phila., 1727. Ms. File case, DAR.
†Diffenderffer. Med. Annals Md. Cordell 1903, p. 377. MHS.
Tercentenary hist. of Md. Andrews. V. 3, p. 963. MHS; DAR.
Digges. Mrs. Henry Du Pont Baldwin chart. MHS.
Bible (line of Gov. Edw. Digges, Va.), 1793–1881. Ms., 5 pp. MHS.
*Burke's landed gentry. 1939. MHS.
H. D. G. Carroll Ms. Book. In H. F. Thompson Papers. MHS.
Children of Alex P. and M. C. Hill. Ms. MHS.
†Chronicles of col. Md. Thomas. 1913, p. 351. MHS; DAR.
Columbia Hist. Soc. Rec., v. 21, p. 11; v. 23, p. 215.

Digges of Va. L. G. Tyler. William and Mary Quart., v. 1, pp. 80–89, 141–54, 208–13.
See Col. John Fitzgerald. Aide-de-Camp to Gen. Washington. Ms. File case, DAR.
Founders of Anne Arundel and Howard Cos. Warfield. P. 55. MHS; DAR.
Gittings chart. MHS.
Historic Digges family. D. A. R. Mag., v. 57, no. 3, p. 125.
Hist. of Digges family. D. A. R. Mag., Oct., 1933, v. 67, no. 10, pp. 617–21.
Mrs. G. C. Jenkins chart. MHS.
Justus Engelhart Kulm. J. Hall Pleasants. 1937, pamph. MHS.
Lineage Bks., Natl. Soc. of Daughters of Amer. Col., v. 1, p. 81. MHS; DAR.
Md. families. Culver. Ms. Personal list.
Pedigree of representative Va. planter. (Md. ref.) William and Mary Quart., 1st series, v. 1, pp. 80–89, 141–54, 208–13.
Pedigree of Richard Dennis Steuart. Soc. Col. Wars Md. Culver. 1940. MHS; DAR.
Pedigree of Alfred Jenkins Tormey. Soc. Col. Wars Md. Culver. 1940. MHS; DAR.
St. John's R. C. Church cemetery, Montgomery Co. Md. Geneal. Rec. Com., 1926, p. 27. Mss. DAR.
Semmes and allied families. Semmes. MHS.
Side lights on Md. hist. Richardson. V. 2, p. 84. MHS; DAR.
Va. Mag. Hist. and Biog., v. 19, p. 206.
See Hill-Digges.
Digges (Diggs), Sir Dudley. His Eng. ancestry and Digges line in Amer. E. R. Ramsburg. D. A. R. Mag., v. 57, no. 3, p. 125–39.
†Pictures of city of Wash. 1898, p. 177. DAR.
(1729–90). Sketch. Va. Mag. Hist. and Biog., v. 17, p. 381.
Digges, Col. Edward, Va. Pedigree. William and Mary Quart., 1st series, v. 1, pp. 80, 140.
***Digges Family.** Arch. of Georgetown Univ., Wash., D. C., v. 130, no. 1.
*Bible. MHS.
*B. B. Brown folder. MHS.
Lee of Va., 1642–1892. E. J. Lee. P. 311. Lib. Cong.; MHS.
Digges Line, Va. L. A. Knott pedigree chart. Soc. Col. Wars, Md. Johnston. 1905, pp. 57, 144. MHS.
Digges, Diggs. Cary Geneal. Coll. Ms. MHS.
Col. families of U. S. A. Mackenzie. V. 1, p. 68; v. 7. MHS; DAR.
*Semmes Geneal. Coll. Ms. MHS.
*Pennington Papers. Ms. MHS.
*The Sun, Balto., May 8, Oct. 9, 1904.
Diggs. Dundas-Hesselius. P. 120. MHS.
†Hist. of West. Md. Scharf. V. 1, pp. 687, 760. MHS; DAR.
See Digges.
†DiGiorgia. Men of mark in Md. Johnson. V. 4. DAR; Enoch Pratt Lib.
***Dikes-Dykes.** Wicomico Co. families. Tilghman. Ms, pp. 15, 16. DAR.
Dill. Abr. Compend. Amer. Geneal. Virkus. V. 6, p. 656. DAR.
Catonsville pioneers of Luth. faith. Natl. Geneal. Soc. Quart., v. 9, no. 2, p. 29.
†Men of mark in Md. Johnson. V. 4, p. 248. DAR; Enoch Pratt Lib.
Mt. Carmel burial ground, Unity, Montgomery Co. Md. Geneal. Rec. Com., 1934–35, p. 85. Mss. DAR.
Orme geneal. chart. MHS.
Tercentenary hist. of Md. Andrews. V. 4, p. 527. MHS; DAR.
***Dill Family.** Arch. of Georgetown Univ., Wash. D. C., v. 287.
***Dillard Family.** Arch. of Georgetown Univ., Wash., D. C., v. 287.
Dillehunt. St. Paul's Parish, Balto. V. 1, 2, 3. Mss. MHS.
Diller. Dillers of Md. C. H. Diller. Abst. of paper read at first Diller reunion, New Holland, Pa., June, 1910. Pa.-German, Lititz, Pa., 1910, v. 11, pp. 534–35.
†Hist. of Frederick Co. Williams. V. 2, p. 1118. MHS; DAR.
†Med. Annals Md. Cordell. 1903, p. 378. MHS.
Dillon. Ancestors of Arthur Orision Dillon, and his poems. A. O. Dillon. 1927, 111 pp. pamph. MHS; DAR.
Brooke-Baker chart. MHS; DAR.
Our Brooke geneal. Culver. 1924, pamph., p. 1. MHS.
St. Paul's Parish, Balto. V. 2. Mss. MHS.
Tercentenary hist. of Md. Andrews. V. 2, p. 284, MHS; DAR.
***Dillon Family.** Arch. of Georgetown Univ., Wash., D. C., v. 287.
Dimmit, Dimmett. St. Paul's Parish, Balto. V. 1, 2. Mss. MHS.
Dimmitt. Md. families. Culver. Ms. Personal list.
Talbott of "Poplar Knowle." Shirk. MHS; DAR.
Dimmock. St. Paul's Parish, Balto. V. 4. Mss. MHS.
***Dimock Family.** Arch. of Georgetown Univ., Wash., D. C., v. 287.
Dingy. St. Paul's P. E. churchyard, Berlin, Worcester Co. Hudson. Bd. ms. MHS; DAR. Also: Md. Geneal. Rec. Com., 1937, Mrs. Lines. Mss. DAR.
Dinus. John Swadner and his descendants. Evans. 1919. Typed, bd. MHS.
Dirickson. Fisher family. Morse. MHS.
†Men of mark in Md. Johnson. V. 3. DAR; Enoch Pratt Lib.
Pedigree of Lee Cummins Cary. Soc. Col. Wars Md. Culver. 1940. MHS; DAR.
Purnell family tree. MHS.
St. Martin's P. E. Church, Worcester Co. Md. Geneal. Rec. Com., 1937, Mrs. Lines. Mss. DAR.
St. Paul's P. E. churchyard, Berlin, Worcester Co. Hudson. Bd. ms. MHS; DAR. Also: Md. Geneal. Rec. Com., 1937, Mrs. Lines. Mss. DAR.
Disharoon. Mt. Zion P. E. churchyard, Worcester Co. Md. Geneal. Rec. Com., 1937, Mrs. Lines. Mss. DAR.
*Wicomico Co. families. Tilghman. Ms., pp. 19, 45–48, 64–65, 95, 98–99, 115, 125–26. DAR.
See Malone-Disharoon-Stanford.
Disharoone. Somerset Co. Court Book. Tilghman. 1937. Ms. DAR.
***Dismukes Family.** Wilson Mss. Coll., no. 90. MHS.
Disney (1854). Old Md. Bibles. M. H. Mag., 1934, v. 29, no. 4, pp. 322–30; corrections, v. 30, p. 370.
St. Paul's Parish, Balto. V. 2, 4. Mss. MHS.

Disney. *See* Baldwin-Brewer-Disney-Maccubin.
***Disney-Linthicum Families,** Anne Arundel Co. Marriages. Md. Geneal. Bul., v. 10, no. 2, p. 22. MHS; DAR.
***Distler.** Burke's landed gentry. 1939, p. 2997. MHS.
Ditman. Abr. Compend. Amer. Geneal. Virkus. V. 1, p. 249. DAR.
Ditty. Founders of Anne Arundel and Howard Cos. Warfield. P. 324. MHS; DAR.
Dixon. Abr. Compend. Amer. Geneal. Virkus. V. 1, pp. 214, 544. DAR.
Balto., its hist., its people. Hall. V. 2. MHS; DAR.
Edmund Beauchamp of East. Shore of Md. D. A. R. Mag., v. 66, no. 4, pp. 234–38.
Christ P. E. Church cemetery, Cambridge. Steele. 1936. MHS; DAR.
Mrs. W. H. Harris chart. MHS.
†Hist. of Allegany Co. Thomas and Williams. V. 2. MHS; DAR.
Old Somerset. Torrence. MHS; DAR.
Pocahontas and her descendants. Robertson. MHS; DAR.
Preston at Patuxent. MHS.
Purnell family tree. MHS.
St. Paul's Parish, Balto. V. 1, 2, 3, 4. Mss. MHS.
Sketches of John Slemmons Stevenson and Rev. Samuel McMaster. Stevenson. P. 21. MHS.
*Some col. mansions and those who lived in them. Glenn. 2nd series, 1900, v. 2, pp. 390, 392, 394. MHS. Also: Preston at Patuxent. Pamph. repr. from above. MHS.
Somerset Co. Court Book. Tilghman. 1937. Ms. DAR.
Taliaferro family, Va. Tyler's Quart. Mag., v. 11, pp. 241–51.
Third Haven Friends Meeting House, Easton. Vital rec. MHS. Also: Natl. Geneal. Soc. Quart., v. 11, no. 1, pp. 9–14.
Trinity Church cemetery, Dorchester Co. Md. O. R. Soc. Bull., no. 3, pp. 42–52.
See Berry-Bruff-Dixon-Troth.
***Dixon,** Talbot Co. Burke's landed gentry. 1939. MHS.
Dixon-Dick. Lineage Bks., Natl. Soc. of Daughters of Amer. Col., v. 3, p. 221. MHS; DAR.
Doane. *See* Done.
***Doane Family.** Deacon John Doane of Plymouth and Dr. John Doane of Md., and their descendants. A. A. Doane. Boston, 1902, 1st ed. MHS.
Dobbin. Ances. rec. and portraits. Col. Dames of Amer., 1910, v. 1, p. 359. MHS; DAR.
Cary Geneal. Coll. Ms. MHS.
Dorsey and allied families. Ms. MHS.
Dorsey chart. MHS.
Griffith geneal. Griffith. MHS; DAR.
Howland chart. MHS.
Pedigree of Thomas Dobbin Penniman. Soc. Col. Wars Md. Culver. 1940. MHS; DAR.
St. Inigoes churchyard, St. Mary's Co. Md. O. R. Soc. Bull., no. 3, p. 58.
St. Paul's Parish, Balto. V. 2, 3. Mss. MHS.
*The Sun, Balto., Aug. 19, 1906.
Dobbin, Mrs. Robert A., Jr. (Maria Kerr Hemsley). Chart. Col. Dames, Chap. I. MHS.
Dobbin Family. Ms. MHS.
Dobson. Auld chart. MHS.
†Hist. of Cecil Co. Johnston. P. 323. MHS; DAR.
Whiteley chart. MHS.
Dockery. Christ P. E. Church cemetery, Cambridge. Steele. 1936. MHS; DAR.
Docura. Rec. from two family Bibles. Ms. MHS.
Dodd. Mt. Carmel Burial Ground, Montgomery Co. Md. Geneal. Rec. Com., 1934, p. 85. Mss. DAR.
See Harris-Dodd.
Dodderer. *See* Dotterer.
See Duddra.
Doddridge. Col. Nicholas Duvall family rec. Price, Bd. ms. MHS.
***Doddridge, Hon. Philip.** W. Va. Hist. Mag., v. 2, no. 1, p. 54.
Doddridge Family, Md. and Pa. (John Doddridge, born in Md. 1745; married Mary Wells; died 1791.) Ms. File case, DAR.
Dodge. Brandt chart. MHS.
Dodge, R. I. Col. and Revolutionary families of Pa. Jordan. 1932, v. 4, pp. 305–43.
***Dodge Family.** Report of first reunion, Salem, Mass., July 10, 1679 (?). Robert Dodge. N. Y., 1879. MHS.
Dodson. Anne Arundel Co. tombstone inscriptions. Ms. DAR.
Balto., its hist., its people. Hall. V. 3. MHS; DAR.
Doebler, Valentine Sherman. Pedigree. Soc. Col. Wars Md. Culver. 1940. MHS; DAR.
Doffler. Frederick Co. tombstone inscriptions. Gruder. Natl. Geneal. Soc. Quart., 1919, v. 8, nos. 1, 2.
Dohme. Balto., its hist., its people. Hall. V. 3. MHS; DAR.
†Dohme, A. R. L. Men of mark in Md. Johnson. V. 3. DAR; Enoch Pratt Lib.
Doll. Frederick Co. tombstone inscriptions. Gruder. Natl. Geneal. Soc. Quart., 1919, v. 8, nos. 1, 2.
†Men of mark in Md. Johnson. V. 1. DAR; Enoch Pratt Lib.
Patriotic Md. Md. Soc. of S. A. R., 1930. MHS; DAR.
Donahoe. Somerset Co. Court Book. Tilghman. 1937. Ms. DAR.
Donaldson. Abr. Compend. Amer. Geneal. Virkus. V. 1, p. 223. DAR.
†Bench and bar of Md. Sams and Riley. 1901, v. 2, p. 587. Lib. Cong.; MHS; Peabody Lib.
*Burke's landed gentry. 1939, pp. 2997–98. MHS.
Donaldson family. Portraits. J. W. Donaldson. 1931, pamph. MHS.
Donaldson family of Va. Some notable families of south. States. Armstrong. V. 2, pp. 87–128. DAR.
Dorsey and allied families. Ms. MHS.
Dorsey chart. MHS.
Manning chart. MHS.
†Med. Annals Md. Cordell. 1903, pp. 379, 842–47. MHS.
*Pennington Papers. Ms. MHS.
St. Paul's Parish, Balto. V. 1, 2, 3. Mss. MHS.
†Sketch of life of Thomas Donaldson. G. W. Brown. Balto., Cushing & Bailey, 1881. MHS.
†Donaldson, J. L. (1814–85). M. H. Mag., v. 12, p. 214.

***Donaldson Family.** Book of portraits. John Donaldson. MHS.
***Donaldson-Forster.** Donaldson family, Va., and Forster family, Md. Ms. File case, DAR.
Done, Doane. Done Bible rec. Ms. MHS.
Col. families of East. Shore and their descendants. Emory. 1900, p. 200. MHS.
Donellen. Cary Geneal. Coll. Ms. MHS.
Donelson, Col. John. Ancestry. County Court Note Book. Ljungstedt.
***Donelson Family.** Stockley geneal. Leaflet. MHS.
Doniphan. Cary Geneal. Coll. Ms. MHS.
Donnell. Cary Geneal. Coll. Ms. MHS.
Howland chart. MHS.
Jacobs chart. MHS.
*Mrs. Charles Howard Lloyd chart. Col. Dames Amer., Chap. I. MHS.
Pedigree of Gustav Wm. Lurman. Soc. Col. Wars Md. Culver. 1940. MHS; DAR.
Miss Minna Lurman chart. MHS.
Richard Dobbs Spaight of N. C. Wheeler. 1880, pamph. MHS.
St. Paul's Parish, Balto. V. 2, 3. Mss. MHS.
Mrs. Talbot T. Speer chart. MHS.
Mrs. Wm. L. Watson chart. MHS.
Donnell, O'Donnell. Sir George Yeardley. Upshur. P. 36. MHS.
Donnellan. Barroll in Great Britain and Amer. Barroll. P. 93. MHS.
St. Paul's Parish, Balto. V. 2. Mss. MHS.
Mrs. H. De Courcy Wright Thom chart. MHS.
Donnelly. Geneal. and mem. encyc. of Md. Spencer. V. 1, p. 297. MHS; DAR.
St. Paul's Parish, Balto. V. 2. Mss. MHS.
***Donoho.** Wicomico Co. families. Tilghman. Ms., p. 75. DAR.
Donougho. St. John's R. C. Church cemetery, Montgomery Co. Md. Geneal. Rec. Com., 1926, p. 27. Mss. DAR.
Donovan. Christ P. E. Church cemetery, Cambridge. Steele. 1936. MHS; DAR.
St. Paul's Parish, Balto. V. 1, 2. Mss. MHS.
***Doodes.** Pennington Papers. Ms. MHS.
Doran, I. Joseph (1844–1919). With written corrections. Pamph. MHS.
Dorman. Pedigree of Charles Thabor Le Viness, III. Soc. Col. Wars Md. Culver. 1940. MHS; DAR.
Rec. of Stepney Parish. MHS; DAR.
Somerset Co. Court Book. Tilghman. 1937. Ms. DAR.
Wicomico Co. families. Bible rec. Ms. DAR.
*Wicomico Co. families. Tilghman. Ms, pp. 5, 14, 107, 111, 119, 124–25. DAR.
Dormer Line. Gaither, Va. and Md. Col. and Revolutionary families of Phila. Jordan. 1933, v. 1, pp. 144–67.
Dormott. Washington ancestry and rec. Hoppin. V. 2. MHS; DAR.
See Veazey-Dormott-Husband.
Dorners. Hist. sketch of P. F. Eichelberger. Eichelberger.
Dorney, C. Polk. Md. Soc., War of 1812, v. 4, no. 319. Ms. MHS.
Doroney. Geneal. Mag. Amer. Ancestry, New York, 1916, v. 4, no. 1.
Dorrance, C. S. Md. Soc., War of 1812, v. 4, no. 318. Ms. MHS.
Dorrell, Dorrall. St. Stephens Parish, Cecilton. Md. MHS; DAR.
Dorsett. Amer. Clan Gregor Year Book, 1924, pp. 30–31. MHS; DAR.
Dorsett-McColl. Amer. Clan Gregor, Year Book, 1935, p. 78. MHS; DAR.
Dorsey. Abr. Compend. Amer. Geneal. Virkus. V. 6, pp. 248, 519, 683. DAR.
Ancest. rec. and portraits. Col. Dames of Amer., 1910, v. 1, pp. 150, 250; v. 2, p. 568, 615. MHS; DAR.
Bailliere chart. MHS.
Barroll chart. MHS.
Mrs. R. Barton, Jr., charts. MHS.
Beall and Bell families. Beall. MHS.
Bible rec., 1744–1900. Ms. File case, DAR.
Bible rec. Natl. Geneal. Soc. Quart., v. 5, no. 3, p. 46.
Bonsal charts. MHS.
Britton Scrap Book. V. 1. Ms. MHS.
Brooks chart. MHS.
Mrs. Howard Bruce chart. MHS.
H. D. G. Carroll Ms. Book. In H. F. Thompson Papers. MHS.
Cary Geneal. Coll. Ms. MHS.
Carton chart. MHS.
Chart; line of descent from Edward Dorsey, Captain Henry Ridgely. Colonel John Worthington, Colonel Nicolas Greenberry. Matthew Howard, Major General John Hammond. (Coat of Arms.) Compiled by Henry Ridgely Evans. Printed Washington, D. C., 1898. Lib. Cong., MHS.
Col. families of Amer. Lawrence. V. 3, p. 298; v. 5, p. 85; v. 16, p. 92. MHS.
Col. mansions of Md. and Del. Hammond. 1914. MHS.
Cummings chart. Lib. Cong.; MHS; DAR.
D. A. R. Mag. June, 1932, v. 66, no. 6, p. 361.
D'Arcy. Col. families of U. S. A. Mackenzie. V. 2, p. 616. MHS; DAR.
Donaldson family. Donaldson. 1931, pamph. MHS.
*Dorsey and allied families. Ms. MHS; Also: Md. Geneal. Rec. Com., 1935–36, pp. 9–24. DAR.
Dorsey chart. MHS.
Dorsey-Duval-Coale-Buchanan-Borden-Brooke and allied family data. Newsp. clipp. and other printed matter. MHS.
*Dorsey family of Md., and their descendants. Geneal., Jour. of Amer. Ancestry, N. Y., Nov., 1912, 2, no. 18. MHS.
Katherine Costigan Dorsey. Dorsey Papers. Geneal. Coll. Mss. MHS.
*Dorsey of Md. Wilson Mss. Coll., no. 37. MHS.
Ford and other lines. Md. Geneal. Rec. Com., 1932–33, pp. 7–20. Mss. DAR.
Founders of col. families, Ridgely, Dorsey and Greenberry. Evans. MHS; DAR.
*Frederick Co. families. Markell. Ms. Personal list.
Gale family pedigree, Somerset and Cecil Cos. Ms. MHS.
*Gallup family sketch. File case A, MHS.
Griffith chart. Cary Geneal. Coll. Ms. MHS.
Griffith geneal. Griffith. MHS; DAR.
Hammond Dorsey Bible rec. Ms. MHS.
*Hist. Dorchester Co. Jones. 1925, pp. 304–07. MHS; DAR.
†(84 ref.) Hist. of Frederick Co. Williams. MHS; DAR.
Hist. graves of Md. and D. C. Ridgely. MHS.

Dorsey. Howard - Montague -Warfield geneal. chart. Culver and Marye. MHS.
Howland chart. MHS.
†Identity of Edward Dorsey I. M. H. Mag. Mar., 1938, v. 33, pp. 27–55.
Mrs. T. C. Jenkins chart. MHS.
*Lineage Bk., Daughters of Founders and Patriots, v. 12, p. 96. MHS.
*Lineage Bks., Natl. Soc. of Daughters of Amer. Col., v. 1, pp. 40–41; v. 2, p. 298; v. 3, pp. 13, 51, 87, 162; v. 4, p. 298; v. 5, p. 152. MHS; DAR.
Manly chart. MHS.
*Md. Dorseys and their descendants. Geneal. Journal of Amer. Ancestry, N. Y., Nov., 1912, v. 2, no. 8. MHS.
Md. families. Culver. Ms. Personal list.
†Med. Annals Md. Cordell. 1903, pp. 380–81. MHS.
Milligan chart. MHS.
W. A. Moale pedigree charts, plate 2. Soc. Col. Wars, Md. Johnston. 1905, p. 73. MHS.
Mrs. E. N. Morison chart. MHS.
Mt. Calvary Church burial ground, Cooksvill Pike, Montgomery Co. Md. Geneal. Rec. Com., 1934. Mss. DAR.
Mt. Calvary Church burial ground, Howard Co. Md. Geneal. Rec. Com., 1934–35, pp. 95–99. Mss. DAR.
Mt. Carmel burial ground, Montgomery Co. Md. Geneal. Rec. Com., 1934, p. 85. Mss. DAR.
Neill chart. MHS.
Peale Geneal. Coll. Ms. MHS.
Patriotic Md. Md. Soc. of S. A. R., 1930. MHS; DAR.
Pedigree of Francis Joseph Baldwin. Soc. Col. Wars Md. Culver. 1940. MHS; DAR.
Pedigree of Duncan Keener Brent. Soc. Col. Wars Md. Culver. 1940. MHS; DAR.
Pedigree of Gustavus Warfield Evans. Soc. Col. Wars Md. Culver. 1940. MHS; DAR.
Pedigree of Edward Hammond. Soc. Col. Wars Md. Culver. 1940. MHS; DAR.
Pedigree of Charles Worthington Hoff. Soc. Col. Wars Md. Culver. 1940. MHS; DAR.
Pedigree of Charles Thomas Holloway. Soc. Col. Wars Md. Culver. 1940. MHS; DAR.
Pedigree of Benedict Henry Hanson, Jr. Soc. Col. Wars Md. Culver. 1940. MHS; DAR.
Pedigree of Rt. Rev. Rogers Israel. Soc. Col. Wars Md. Culver. 1940. MHS; DAR.
Pedigree of Howard Hall Macy Lee. Soc. Col. Wars Md. Culver. 1940. MHS; DAR.
Pedigree of Thomas Murray Maynadier. Soc. Col. Wars Md. Culver. 1940. MHS; DAR.
Pedigree of Tilghman Vickers Morgan. Soc. Col. Wars Md. Culver. 1940. MHS; DAR.
Pedigree of Thomas Dobbin Penniman. Soc. Col. Wars Md. Culver. 1940. MHS; DAR.
Pedigree of Pleasants Pennington. Soc. Col. Wars Md. Culver. 1940. MHS; DAR.
Pedigree of Tilghman Goldsborough Pitts. Soc. Col. Wars Md. Culver. 1940. MHS; DAR.
Pedigree of Dorsey Richardson. Soc. Col. Wars Md. Culver. 1940. MHS; DAR.
Pedigree of Townsend Scott, IV. Soc. Col. Wars Md. Culver. 1940. MHS; DAR.
Pedigree of Levin Gale Shreve. Soc. Col. Wars Md. Culver. 1940. MHS; DAR.
Pedigree of Mark Alexander Herbert Smith. Soc. Col. Wars Md. Culver. 1940. MHS; DAR.
Pedigree of John Ogle Warfield, Jr. Soc. Col. Wars Md. Culver. 1940. MHS; DAR.
Pedigree of Wm. Emory Waring, Jr. Soc. Col. Wars Md. Culver. 1940. MHS; DAR.
Pedigree of Mason Locke Weems Williams. Soc. Col. Wars Md. Culver. 1940. MHS; DAR.
Pedigree of Richard Walker Worthington. Soc. Col. Wars Md. Culver. 1940. MHS; DAR.
Pedigree of Andrew Jackson Young, Jr. Soc. Col. Wars Md. Culver. 1940. MHS; DAR.
Mrs. Pennington chart. MHS.
Miss C. Petre chart. MHS.
Mrs. E. W. Poe chart. MHS.
John Price, emigrant, Jamestown Col., 1620. Price. MHS.
Raisin chart. MHS.
Mrs. A. Randall chart. MHS.
Rec. of Nicholas Meriwether of Wales, and descendants in Md. and Va. Griffith. P. 134.
Mrs. C. L. Riggs chart. MHS.
St. Paul's Parish, Balto. V. 1, 2, 3, 4. Mss. MHS.
St. Thomas' Parish, Balto. Co. Bd. ms. MHS. Also: Md. Geneal. Rec. Com., 1937, pp. 109–82. Mss. DAR.
Segrave chart. MHS.
See Shouse. Abr. Compend. Amer. Geneal. Virkus. V. 1, p. 827. DAR.
Mrs. Edw. Simpson chart. MHS.
Talbott of "Poplar Knowle." Shirk. MHS; DAR.
Trinity Church burial ground, near Cambridge, Md. Md. Geneal. Rec. Com., 1937–38, pp. 93–104. Mss. DAR.
Trinity Church cemetery, Dorchester Co. Md. O. R. Soc. Bull., no. 3, pp. 42–52.
Warfields of Md. Warfield. MHS.
Welsh-Hyatt and kindred. Welsh. 1928. Sec. 6, p. 178. MHS; DAR.
Welsh-Hyatt and kindred. Supplement. Welsh. Pp. 21, 22, 23, 24. MHS; DAR.
Mrs. G. H. Williams, Jr., chart. MHS.
W. S. G. Williams pedigree chart. Soc. Col. Wars, Md. Johnston. 1905, p. 128. MHS.
Mrs. J. Whitridge Williams chart 2. MHS.
See Ford-Dorsey-Hyland, etc.
See Howard-Dorsey-Boone.
See Ridgely-Dorsey-Evans.
See Simmons-Torrence-Dorsey.
See Worthington-Dorsey.

Dorsey, Hockley. Side lights on Md. hist. Richardson. V. 2, p. 87. MHS; DAR.

†**Dorsey,** Washington Co. Hist. of West. Md. Scharf. V. 2, pp. 1134–38. MHS; DAR.

Dorsey, Caleb, "Hockley," Howard Co. (1686–1742). Md. Geneal. Rec. Com., 1935–36, p. 25. DAR.
Md. Geneal. Rec. Com., 1935–36, pp. 196–200. Mss. DAR.
Notes. D. A. R. Mag., v. 65, no. 9, p. 568; v. 66, no. 6, p. 361.

***Dorsey, Charles.** Charles Dorsey and his descendants. Mrs. Charles B. Thurman. Pamph., 36 pp. MHS.
Revolutionary soldier of Md. and his descendants. Pamph. MHS.

Dorsey, Comfort. D. A. R. Mag., v. 68, no. 4, p. 239.

Dorsey, Edward. Sydney-Smith and Clagett-Price families. Price. P. 273. MHS; DAR.
*__Dorsey, Edw.-Wyatt, Nicholas.__ Notes, from land rec. N. B. Nimmo. M. H. Mag., 1937, v. 32, pp. 47–51.
Dorsey, Maj. Edward. R. B. Keyser pedigree chart, plate 2. Soc. Col. Wars, Md. Johnston. 1905, pp. 56, 144. MHS.
Dorsey, George. Bible rec. Ms. DAR.
Family Bible. DAR.
Dorsey, Harriet, Carroll Co. Copy of will, 1864. Md. Geneal. Rec. Com., 1938–39, pp. 35–42. Mss. DAR.
Dorsey, Col. John. S. C. Chew pedigree chart. Soc. Col. Wars, Md. Johnston. 1905, pp. 13 144. MHS.
*__Dorsey Family.__ Anne Arundel Co. gentry. Newman. Pp. 3–146. MHS; DAR.
*Clippings from The Sun, Balto., 1908.
*Clipp. from The Sun, Balto., 1909. MHS.
*Founders of Anne Arundel and Howard Cos. Warfield. Pp. 55–67, 338–47, 353, 390–409, 437–38, 441–64, 480–85, 489–90, 493–96. MHS; DAR.
Gallup family sketch. Ms. MHS.
Geneal. Mag. Amer. Ancestry, New York, 1916, v. 2, no. 18, p. 345.
(1657). Dorsey family. H. A. Browne. Balto., 1926. Peabody Lib.
Md. Geneal. Rec. Com., 1933–34, pp. 26, 40–45 Mss. DAR.
Mountain Democrat, Garrett Co., Oct. 25, 1934. Newsp. clipp. MHS; DAR.
Dorsey Family, Md. and Tenn. Ms. File case, DAR.
Dorsey Line. Col. and Revolutionary lineages of Amer. 1939, v. 1, pp. 282–87. MHS.
Geneal. and mem. encyc. of Md. Spencer. V. 2, pp. 610–14. MHS; DAR.
Dorsey-Ball. Col. families of U. S. A. Mackenzie. V. 7. MHS; DAR.
Dorsey-Bowie-Claggett. Lineage Bks., Natl. Soc. of Daughters of Amer. Col., v. 3, p. 162. MHS; DAR.
Dorsey-Darcy. Side lights on Md. hist. Richardson. V. 2, p. 86. MHS; DAR.
Dorsey-Linthicum. Bible rec. Ms. MHS.
Dorsey-Pue. Bible rec., 1760–1924. Md. Geneal. Rec. Com., 1935–36, pp. 175–95. Mss. DAR.
Dorsey-Pue, Howard Co. Bible rec., 1760–1924. Md. Geneal. Rec. Com., 1935–36, v. 8, p. 4. DAR.
Dorsey-Riggs Line. Geneal. and memorial encyc. of Md. Spencer. V. 2, p. 610. MHS; DAR.
Dorsey-Wyatt. Md. Geneal. Rec. Com., 1933–34, p. 46. Mss. DAR.
Notes on Edward Dorsey and Nicholas Wyatt. Nannie Ball Nimmo. M. H. Mag., Mar., 1937, v. 32, pp. 47–50.
Dorsey, D'Arcy. Chart; descendants of the Dorsey family in Md. from 1657. H. A. Brown. Printed Balto., 1926. MHS.
Geneal., Mag. Amer. Ancestry, N. Y., 1916, v. 3, nos. 10, 12.
*The Sun, Balto., June 26, July 3, 1904; Jan. 12, 19, 26, Feb. 2, 9, 16, March 1, 8, 1908.
Dotterer. Dukehart and collateral lines. Ms. MHS.
†Hist. of Frederick Co. Williams. MHS; DAR.
Dotterer Family. Bible rec. Natl. Geneal. Soc. Quart., 1925, v. 14, p. 47.
Dotterer, Dodderer. Strassburger family and allied families. Strassburger. Pp. 357–74. MHS.
†**Doub.** Hist. of Allegany Co. Thomas and Williams. V. 2. MHS; DAR.
†Hist. of Washington Co. Williams. 1906, v. 2, pp. 1049, 1114. MHS; DAR.
Spessard family. Spessard. Pp. 15, 52. MHS; DAR.
Doub, Abraham (Mar., 1853). Mt. Zion U. B Church, Myersvill, Frederick Co.
Doughadie. St. Paul's Parish, Balto. V. 2. Mss. MHS.
Dougherty. Makemie Memorial Pres. churchyard, Snow Hill, Worcester Co. Hudson Bd. ms. MHS; DAR. Also: Md. Geneal. Rec. Com., Mrs. Lines. Mss. DAR.
St. Mary's churchyard, Tyaskin, Md. Md. Geneal. Rec. Com., 1938–39, pp. 187–92. Mss. DAR.
St. Paul's Parish, Balto. V. 2. Mss. MHS.
Somerset Co. Court Book. Tilghman. 1937. Ms. DAR.
Turner Geneal. Coll. Ms. MHS.
Dought. Amer. Guthrie and allied families. Guthrie. Bk. 4. DAR.
Doughty. Bible rec. Md. Geneal. Bull., v. 2, p. 6. MHS; DAR.
Douglas. Ances. rec. and portraits. Col. Dames of Amer., 1910, v. 1, p. 198. MHS; DAR.
†Bench and bar of Md. Sams and Riley. 1901, v. 2, p. 614. Lib. Cong.; MHS; Peabody Lib.
Bible rec. D. A. R. Mag., Oct., 1932, v. 66, no. 10, pp. 672–74.
Col. families of Amer. Lawrence. V. 9, p. 120. MHS.
Fox-Ellicott-Evans families. Evans. MHS; DAR.
*Geneal. coat of arms. C. H. J. Douglas. Incl. Benj. Douglas of Charles Co. (born 1743), p. 509. Providence, E. L. Freeman & Co., 1879. MHS.
*Hist. Dorchester Co. Jones. 1902. MHS.
Lineage Bks., Natl. Soc. of Daughters of Amer. Col., v. 4, p. 309. MHS; DAR.
Md. families. Culver. Ms. Personal list.
Pedigree of Coleman Randall Freeman. Soc. Col. Wars Md. Culver. 1940. MHS; DAR.
Portrait and biog. rec. of Sixth Cong. Dist. of Md. 1898, p. 205. MHS; DAR.
St. Stephens Parish, Cecilton, Md. MHS; DAR.
Stevenson chart. MHS.
Wm. Turpin, Dorchester Co., Bible rec. D. A. R. Mag., v. 66, no. 10, p. 672.
See Douglass.
Douglas, Hurlock, Md. Bible rec. of Dorchester and Somerset Cos. and Del. Pp. 26–28. DAR.
Douglas, B. Dunn. War of 1812, v. 2, no. 151. Ms. MHS.
Douglas, R. Dunn. Md. Soc., War of 1812, v. 2, no. 149. Ms. MHS.
Douglas, R. Graham Dunn. War of 1812, v. 2, no. 150. Ms. MHS.
Douglas Line. Freeman family. Col. and Revolutionary families of Phila. Jordan. 1933, v. 1, pp. 323–28.
Douglas (Va.)-**Hale** (Md.). Americans of gentle birth and their ancestors. Pitman. P. 169. MHS.
Douglas-Smoot. D. A. R. Mag., v. 66, no. 10, p. 673.

Douglas, Douglass Chart, 1 sheet. Cary Geneal. Coll. Ms. MHS.
*Semmes Geneal. Coll. Ms. MHS.
Douglass. See Freeman. Abr. Compend. Amer. Geneal. Virkus. V. 1, p. 920. DAR.
†Hist. of Balto. City and Co. Scharf. Pp. 383-84. MHS.
Pocahontas and her descendants. Robertson. MHS; DAR.
St. Paul's Parish, Balto. V. 1, 2, 3, 4. Mss. MHS.
*Wicomico Co. families. Tilghman. Ms, p. 120. DAR.
See Douglas.
Douglass Family. Douglas family of Md. F. L. Huidekoper, Switzerland, May, 1930. Ms. MHS.
Douglass, Douglas. Abr. Compend. Amer. Geneal. Virkus. V. 1, p. 257; v. 6, p. 591. DAR.
Douglay. St. Paul's Parish, Balto. V. 2, Mss. MHS.
Doulin. *See* Dowland.
Douthat. McCormick chart. MHS.
See Douthet.
Douthet, Douthat, Douthit, Douthitt, Prince George Co., 1742. Family geneal. Presented by R. S. Douthat, 1934. Ms. MHS.
Douthitt. *See* Douthet.
Douw, Mrs. John de Peyster (Anne Morss Olyphant). Chart. Col. Dames, Chap. I. MHS.
Dove. Harford Co. Hist. Soc. Mss. Coll. JHU.
Dowd. St. Paul's Parish, Balto. V. 2. Mss. MHS.
Dowdee. Naturalizations in Md., 1666-1765; Laws. Bacon. MHS.
Dowland, Doulin. Rumsey-Smithson family rec. bk. Md. Geneal. Rec. Com., 1932, p. 132. DAR.
Rumsey-Smithson Bible rec. Md. Geneal. Rec. Com., 1932-33, v. 5, pp. 63-142. DAR.
***Dowman.** The Sun, Balto., May 7, 1905.
Downe. Md. gleanings in Eng. Wills. M. H. Mag., 1908, v. 3, no. 2.
Downes. Elbert chart. MHS.
Mt. Carmel burial ground, Montgomery Co. Md. Geneal. Rec. Com., 1934, p. 85. Mss. DAR.
Old Somerset. Torrence. MHS; DAR.
Somerset Co. Court Book. Tilghman. 1937. Ms. DAR.
Downey. Abr. Compend. Amer. Geneal. Virkus. V. 1, p. 259. DAR.
†Hist. of West. Md. Scharf. V. 1, p. 606. MHS; DAR.
St. Paul's Parish, Balto. V. 2, 3. Mss. MHS.
Talbott of "Poplar Knowle." Shirk. MHS; DAR.
Downing. Col. families of U. S. A. Mackenzie. V. 1, p. 599; v. 4, p. 400. MHS; DAR.
Gillett-Miller families. Ms. MHS.
St. Paul's Parish, Balto. V. 2. Mss. MHS.
*Wicomico Co. families. Tilghman. Ms, p. 126. DAR.
Downing Family, Northumberland Co., Va. Md. Geneal. Rec. Com., 1935-36, p. 286. DAR.
Downings, Northumberland Co., Va. Md. Geneal. Rec. Com., 1935-36, p. 286. Mss. DAR.
Downs. Bible rec. Upper Penins. East. Shore. Pp. 150, 152. MHS; DAR.
Md. Geneal. Bul., v. 4, pp. 19, 27. MHS; DAR.
Mt. Carmel burial ground, Unity, Montgomery Co. Md. Geneal. Rec. Com., 1934-35, p. 85. Mss. DAR.
St. Paul's Parish, Balto. V. 2. Mss. MHS.
Downs, S. A. Md. Soc., War of 1812, v. 1, no. 5, Ms. MHS.
†Downs, Downes. Med. Annals Md. Cordell. 1903, p. 382. MHS.
Doyle. Griffith geneal. Griffith. MHS; DAR.
Hagerstown tombstone inscriptions. Gruder. Natl. Geneal. Soc. Quart., 1919, v. 8, nos. 1, 2.
†Hist. of West. Md. Scharf. V. 2, p. 1244. MHS; DAR.
Trinity P. E. churchyard, Long Green. Typed ms. MHS; DAR.
Willcox and allied families. Willcox. MHS; DAR.
Doyne. Cary Geneal. Coll. Ms. MHS.
Col. and Revolutionary families of Pa. Amer. Hist. Soc., N. Y., 1934, p. 8.
Pedigree of Duncan Keener Brent. Soc. Col. Wars Md. Culver. 1940. MHS; DAR.
Semmes and allied families. Semmes. MHS.
*Semmes Geneal. Coll. Ms. MHS.
Taney and allied families. Silverson. MHS; DAR.
***Drain.** Hist. Dorchester Co. Jones. 1925, p. 307. MHS; DAR.
Drainbridge. Selden chart. MHS.
***Drane.** Garrett Co. pioneer families. Haye. MHS; DAR.
*Lineage Bks.; Natl. Soc. of Daughters of Amer. Col., v. 4, p. 25. MHS; DAR.
See Harding.
Drane, Ga. Amer. Clan Gregor Year Book, 1928. pp. 26, 49; 1931, p. 35. MHS; DAR.
Drane Family. Mountain Democrat, Garrett Co., Jan. 17, 1934. Newsp. clipp. MHS; DAR.
***Draper.** Early hist. of Draper family of Sussex Co., Del. E. J. Sellers. Phila., 1929. Ltd. ed. MHS.
Old Somerset. Torrence. MHS; DAR.
Draper, Edwin. Sketch of Pike Co. pioneer. (Solomon Draper, born in Tenn., 1807; his great-great-grandfather born in Md., 1715.) Ms. File case, DAR.
Draper Family. Descendants of Francis Swayne. Swayne. P. 103. MHS.
Draper and allied families of Delaware. Sellers. MHS.
*Notes. Photos. MHS.
Draughton. *See* Broughton.
Drefs - Boarman - Bretton - Carberry - Neal - Newman-Shoemaker. Abr. Compend. Amer. Geneal. Virkus. V. 4, p. 161. MHS.
†Dreyer. Hist. of Allegany Co. Thomas and Williams. V. 2. MHS; DAR.
***Drinker.** Wicomico Co. families. Tilghman. Ms, p. 126. DAR.
Driscole. St. Stephens Parish, Cecilton, Md. MHS; DAR.
Driscoll. St. Paul's Parish, Balto. V. 1, 2. Mss. MHS.
***Driskell.** Wicomico Co. families. Tilghman. Ms, p. 100. DAR.
Driskill. Rec. of Stepney Parish. MHS; DAR.
Somerset Co. Court Book. Tilghman. 1937. Ms. DAR.

Driver, Caroline Co., Samuel Carpenter of Phila. Carpenter. P. 113. MHS.
†**Drum.** Men of mark in Md. Johnson. V. 1. DAR; Enoch Pratt Lib.
Portrait and biog. rec. of Sixth Cong. Dist. of Md. 1898, p. 185. MHS; DAR.
Drury. Burton ancestry. Ms. MHS.
Glendy churchyard, Balto. Md. Geneal. Rec. Com., 1933-34. Mss. DAR.
Ellen Emmerich Mears. Col. and Revolutionary families of Phila. Jordan. 1933, v. 1, pp. 412-15.
Drury, Charles, Anne Arundel Co. Copy of will, 1766. Ms. File case, DAR.
Drury-Simmons, Anne Arundel Co. D. A. R. Mag., Jan. 1936, v. 70, no. 1, p. 54.
Dryden. Dryden and allied families. Notes made by Mr. T. P. Dryden. Ms. MHS.
Makemie Memorial Pres. churchyard, Snow Hill, Worcester Co. Hudson. Bd. ms. MHS; DAR. Also: Md. Geneal. Rec. Com., Mrs. Lines. Mss. DAR.
M. E. churchyard, Snow Hill. Worcester Co., Hudson. Bd. ms. MHS; DAR.
Pocomoke Pres. churchyard, Worcester Co. Hudson. Bd. ms. MHS; DAR.
See Appold-Dryden.
See Owings-Dryden-Harris.
Dryden, Joshua. Bible rec., 1814; incl. Hurst, Keire, Owings, Rogers and Swinton. Ms. MHS.
Dubley. Births, 1727-91. Md. Geneal. Rec. Com., v. 4, pp. 66-67. DAR.
Dubois. Hazelhurst charts. MHS.
St. Paul's Parish, Balto. V. 2. Mss. MHS.
†**Du Bois.** Hist. of West Md. Scharf. V. 2, p. 917. MHS; DAR.
Du Bourg. Pedigree of Duncan Keener Brent. Soc. Col. Wars Md. Culver. 1940. MHS; DAR.
†**Ducatel.** Med. Annals Md. Cordell. 1903, p. 383. MHS.
†**Ducker.** Hist. of Balto. City and Co. Scharf. P. 868. MHS.
Ducket. Bowie-Claggett chart. MHS.
See Duckett.
Duckett. Ances. rec. and portraits. Col. Dames of Amer., 1910, v. 1, p. 89. MHS; DAR.
Autobiography of Summerfield Baldwin. MHS; DAR.
Sara R. Baldwin chart. MHS.
Boydstun family. Weaver. P. 112. MHS; DAR.
Mrs. A. C. Bruce chart. MHS.
Cary Geneal. Coll. Ms. MHS.
Chart, 1675-1935. A. A. Selden. Photos. of ms., 1937. MHS.
Col. Nicholas Duvall family Records. Price. Bd. ms. MHS.
"Fairview," home of Gov. Oden Bowie, near Bowie, Prince George Co. Private burying ground, 1745-1904. Ms. MHS; DAR.
*Frederick Co. families. Markell. Ms. Personal list.
Hamill chart. MHS.
Hist. of Byberry and Moreland. Martindale. MHS.
Iglehart chart. MHS.
Md. families. Culver. Ms. Personal list.
†Med. Annals Md. Cordell. 1903, p. 383. MHS.
Moale-Croxall-North chart. Cary Geneal. Coll. Ms. MHS.
Murdoch chart. Cary Geneal. Coll. Ms. MHS.
Pedigree of Charles Gambrill Baldwin. Soc. Col. Wars Md. Culver. 1940. MHS; DAR.
Pedigree of Mareen Duvall. Soc. Col. Wars Md. Culver. 1940. MHS; DAR.
Pedigree of Charles O'Donnell Mackall. Soc. Col. Wars Md. Culver. 1940. MHS; DAR.
Pedigree of Richard Dennis Steuart. Soc. Col. Wars Md. Culver. 1940. MHS; DAR.
Prentice chart. MHS.
Mrs. M. L. Price chart. MHS.
Selden chart. MHS.
Selden-Duckett Bible rec. Ms. MHS.
Mrs. G. R. Veazey chart. MHS.
Duckett, Jacob. Will, 1764. Ms. File case, DAR.
Duckett Family. Arms and charts. Howard lineage. Weaver. Pp. 86-104. MHS.
†**Duckett-Bowie.** Chesapeake Bay Country. Earle. Pp. 201, 205-06. MHS.
Duckett, Ducket. Col. families of U. S. A. Mackenzie. V. 3, p. 607; v. 7, p. 238. MHS; DAR.
Dudderar. Patriotic Md. Md. Soc. of S. A. R., 1930. MHS; DAR.
Dudderar, Conrad, Pa. (Md. ref.) Ms. File case, DAR.
***Duddra-Dodderer.** Some descendants of George Philip Duddra (or Dodderer). Wm. B. Duttera. Salisbury, N. C., 1934, bklet. and four supplements, 225 pp., typed, Dushore, Pa., 1933. Revised 1934. All in MHS.
*Supplement to descendants of George Philip Duddra (or Dodderer). Wm. B. Duttera. 1937, typed, bd., 223 pp. MHS.
Dudley. Man-Needles-Hambleton families. Needles. MHS; DAR.
Marriages, 1706. Md. Geneal. Rec. Com., v. 4, pp. 66-67. DAR.
Dudweiler. Hagerstown tombstone inscriptions. Gruder. Natl. Geneal. Soc. Quart., 1919, v. 8, nos. 1, 2.
Duer. Bible rec. Pa. Mag. Hist. and Biog., v. 39, p. 218.
White chart. Cary Geneal. Coll. Ms. MHS.
Duer, Henry Lay. Pedigree chart. Soc. Col. Wars, Md. Johnston. 1905, p. 23. MHS.
Duff. St. Paul's Parish, Balto. V. 2, 3. Mss. MHS.
†**Duffey.** Bench and bar of Md. Sams and Riley. 1901, v. 2, p. 603. Lib. Cong.; MHS; Peabody Lib.
***Duffey Family.** Data of John Duffey, Cecil Co. (born, 1752; died, 1843). Ms. DAR.
Duffield. Hist. of Byberry and Moreland. Martindale. MHS.
Ingrham family. Md. Geneal. Rec. Com., 1938-39, pp. 142-67. Mss. DAR.
Makemie Memorial Pres. churchyard, Snow Hill, Worcester Co. Hudson. Bd. ms. MHS; DAR. Also: Md. Geneal. Rec. Com., Mrs. Lines. Mss. DAR.
Memorial to Thomas Potts, Jr. James. MHS.
John Neill of Lewes, Del., 1739. Pr. for family, Phila., 1875.
St. Paul's Parish, Balto. V. 2. Mss. MHS.
***Duffield, John Potts.** Memoir. Spence's letters of early history of the Presbyterian Church in Amer.

Duffield Family. Bible rec. Phila. Chap., Geneal. Rec. Com., vi, pp. 51–73. Typed, bd. DAR.
*Gilbert family, Carver family, Duffield family. J. C. Martindale. DAR.
Duffy. St. Paul's Parish, Balto. V. 2, 3. Mss. MHS.
Dugan. Mrs. R. Barton, Jr., charts. MHS.
Miss M. S. Brogden chart. MHS.
*Buchanan family. Col. families of U. S. Mackenzie. V. 3, pp. 111–13.
*Burke's landed gentry. 1939. MHS.
Geneal. and memorial encyc. of Md. Spencer. V. 2. MHS; DAR.
Lehr chart. MHS.
St. Paul's Parish, Balto. V. 1, 2. Mss. MHS.
Tercentenary hist. of Md. Andrews. V. 4, p. 223. MHS; DAR.
Mrs. G. H. Williams, Jr., chart. MHS.
***Dugan, Cumberland.** Geneal. and mem. encyc. of Md. Spencer. V. 2, pp. 668–70. MHS; DAR.
Dugdale. Faith Pres. Church (Glendy Graveyard). Mss. MHS.
Duhamel. Holdens Cemetery, Kent Co. Md. Geneal. Rec. Com., 1932, v. 5, p. 211. Mss. DAR.
Du Hamel, East. Shore. Abr. Compend. Amer. Geneal. Virkus. V. 1, p. 274. DAR.
Duhattoway. Naturalizations in Md., 1666–1765; Laws. Bacon. MHS.
Duke. Beall and Bell families. Beall. MHS.
Brisko-Brisco-Briscoe and some family connections. Ramey. Ms. MHS.
Cary Geneal. Coll. Ms. MHS.
†Rev. Wm. Duke (born in Balto. Co., 1757; died, 1840). Poets and prose writers of Md. Perine.
Gantt geneal. Ms. MHS.
Hist. graves of Md. and D. C. Ridgely. MHS.
Hist. of Allegany Co. Thomas and Williams. V. 1, p. 574; v. 2, pp. 846–48. MHS; DAR.
Md. families. Culver. Ms. Personal list.
†Med. Annals Md. Cordell. 1903, p. 383. MHS.
Pedigree of Jasper Mandiut Berry, Jr. Soc. Col. Wars Md. Culver. 1904. MHS; DAR.
Pedigree of John Hurst Morgan. Soc. Col. Wars Md. Culver. 1940. MHS; DAR.
Tercentenary hist. of Md. Andrews. V. 4, p. 359. MHS; DAR.
Duke, Calvert Co. G. M. Mackenzie pedigree chart, plate 1. Soc. Col. Wars, Md. Johnston. 1905, p. 61. MHS.
Duke, St. Mary's Co. Col. families of U. S. A. Mackenzie. V. 1, p. 139; v. 6, p. 197. MHS; DAR.
Duke, Charles Clarke. Pedigree. Soc. Col. Wars Md. Culver. 1940. MHS; DAR.
Duke, Wm. Bernard. Pedigree. Soc. Col. Wars Md. Culver. 1940. MHS; DAR.
Duke-Shepard-Van Meter, Pa. D. A. R. Mag., Sept., 1927, v. 61, no. 9, p. 706.
Duke-Shepherd-Van Metre Families. Geneal. from civil, church, family and military rec. and documents. S. G. Smyth. Lancaster, Pa. 1909.
Dukehart. Dukehart and collateral lines, of Antes, Dotterer, Latrobe, Murphy, etc. Morton McT. Dukehart. Typed, bd., 1933. MHS.
Dukes. Somerset Co. Court Book. Tilghman. 1937. Ms. DAR.
Dukes, A. Thompson. Md. Soc., War of 1812, v. 3, no. 239. Ms. MHS.
Dulaney. Balto., its hist., its people. Hall. V. 3. MHS; DAR.
Col. families of Md. Emory. 1900, pp. 11–12, 230. MHS; DAR.
Hist. of Balto. Lewis Pub. Co., 1912, v. 3, p. 810. DAR.
†Hist. of Frederick Co. Williams. V. 1, p. 24. MHS; DAR.
*Something about the Dulaney family and sketch of Southern Cobb family, 1700–1920. Charts. B. L. Dulany. Washington, D. C. MHS.
Tercentenary hist. of Md. Andrews. V. 2, p. 190; v. 4, p. 890. MHS; DAR.
*The Sun, Balto., March 26, 1905.
Dulany. Anne Arundel Co. tombstone inscriptions. Ms. DAR.
Balch chart. MHS.
†Bench and bar of Md. Sams and Riley. 1901, v. 1, pp. 167, 170, 192. Lib. Cong.; MHS; Peabody Lib.
Bolton chart. MHS.
*Burke's landed gentry. 1939. P. 2998. MHS.
Cary Geneal. Coll. Ms. MHS.
Daniel Dulany's "considerations," 1765. M. H. Mag., 1911, v. 6, pp. 374–406; 1912, v. 7, p. 26–59.
†Hon. Daniel Dulany, 1722–97. R. H. Spencer. M. H. Mag., 1911, v. 6, pp. 145–63.
†Daniel Dulany, the Elder. Pa. Mag. of Hist. and Biog. 1900, v. 24, pp. 395–96.
†Hon. Daniel Dulany, the Elder, (1685–1753). R. H. Spencer. M. H. Mag., 1918, v. 13, pp. 20–28.
†Hon. Daniel Dulany, the younger (1722–97). R. H. Spencer. M. H. Mag., 1918, v. 13, pp. 149–60.
Fairfax family notes. Ms. MHS.
*Founders of Anne Arundel and Howard Cos. Warfield. Pp. 184–87. MHS; DAR.
†Hist. of Balto. City and Co. Scharf. P. 904. MHS.
St. Ann's churchyard, Annapolis. Md. O. R. Soc. Bull., no. 3, pp. 55–56.
†Sketches of Balto. Boyles. 1877. MHS.
Tasker chart. Cary Geneal. Coll. Ms. MHS.
†Dulany, Daniel. Amer. at Eton in col. days. Va. Mag., v. 13, pp. 210–11.
†Biog. sketch. J. H. B. Latrobe. Pa. Mag. of Hist. and Biog., Jan., 1879, v. 3, pp. 1–10.
†Biog. sketches of distinguished Marylanders. Boyle. MHS; DAR.
Coll. of Amer. epitaphs and inscriptions. Alden. 1814, v. 5. MHS.
†Daniel Dulany, the Elder, and Daniel Dulany, the Greater. Hist. of Md. Scharf. V. 1, pp. 545–46. MHS.
†Md. gossip in 1775. Pa. Mag. of Hist. and Biog., Jan., 1879, v. 3, pp. 144–49.
*Biog. cyc. of rep. men of Md. and D. C. P. 380. MHS; DAR.
Dulany, J. Highambotham. Md. Soc., War of 1812, no. 93. Ms. MHS.
Dulany, J. Mason. Md. Soc., War of 1812, v. 1, no. 48. Ms. MHS.

Dulany, Wm. J. C. Md. Soc., War of 1812, v. 1, no. 95. Ms. MHS.
Dulany, W. Mason. Md. Soc., War of 1812, v. 1, no. 49. Ms. MHS.
Dulany Family. Ames Geneal. Coll. Ms. MHS.
Goldsborough Geneal. Coll. Ms. MHS.
†**Dulin.** Med. Annals Md. Cordell. 1903, p. 384. MHS.
Dumler. Trinity P. E. churchyard, Long Green. Typed ms. MHS; DAR.
Dunbar. Harford Co. Hist. Soc. Mss. Coll. JHU.
†Med. Annals Md. Cordell. 1903, p. 384. MHS.
†**Dunbar, Wm. H.** Men of mark in Md. Johnson. V. 2. DAR; Enoch Pratt Lib.
Dunboyne. *See* Ormonde.
*__Duncan.__ Burke's landed gentry. 1939. MHS.
Patriotic Md. Md. Soc. of S. A. R., 1930. MHS; DAR.
Pedigree of George Ross Veazey. Soc. Col. Wars Md. Culver. 1940. MHS; DAR.
St. Paul's Parish, Balto. V. 1. Mss. MHS.
Tercentenary hist. of Md. Andrews. V. 4, pp. 261, 597. MHS; DAR.
Duncan, Charles, from Scotland to Md., 1761. Ms. File case, DAR.
Duncan, John, N. C. Mc Call-Tidwell families. Mc Call. MHS; DAR.
Dunckle, Johann Daniel. Geneal. rec. of George Small, etc. Small. MHS.
*__Dundas Family.__ Arch. of Georgetown Univ., Wash., D. C., v. 156, no. 4.
*__Dundas-Hesselius.__ Dedicated to the Clan Dundas, past, present and future. Hist. Pub. Soc., Phila., 1938. MHS.
Dunham. Robins family tree. MHS.
St. Martin's P. E. Church, Worcester Co. Md. Geneal. Rec. Com., 1937, Mrs. Lines. Mss. DAR.
Dunken. St. Paul's Parish, Balto. V. 2. Mss. MHS.
Dunker. Burial rec., 1813–63. MHS.
*__Dunkin.__ Scruggs geneal. MHS.
Dunkin, L. H. Tombstone rec. of Glendy burying ground (vault). Md. Geneal. Rec. Com., 1933–34, pp. 171–78. Mss. DAR.
Dunkinson. St. Inigoes churchyard, St. Mary's Co. Md. O. R. Soc. Bull., no. 3, p. 58.
Dunlap. Trinity P. E. churchyard, Long Green. Typed ms. MHS; DAR.
Dunn. Amer. Guthrie and allied families. Guthrie. Bk. 4. DAR.
Col. families of U. S. A. Mackenzie. V. 2. MHS; DAR.
Md. families. Culver. Ms. Personal list.
Pedigree of Duncan Keener Brent. Soc. Col. Wars Md. Culver. 1940. MHS; DAR.
Pedigree of George Webb Constable, Soc. Col. Wars Md. Culver. 1940. MHS; DAR.
Pedigree of Joseph Lee Wickes. Soc. Col. Wars Md. Culver. 1940. MHS; DAR.
St. Paul's Parish, Balto. V. 1, 2. Mss. MHS.
Dunn, Kent Co. W. A. and S. W. Merritt pedigree charts, plate 1. Soc. Col. Wars, Md. Johnston. 1905, pp. 67, 144. MHS.
*__Dunn Family,__ Kent Co. M. H. Mag., 1912, v. 7, pp. 329–33.
Dunnavin. Cummings chart. Lib. Cong.; MHS; DAR.
†**Dunnington.** Med. Annals Md. Cordell. 1903, p. 385. MHS.
Dunnock. Trinity Church cemetery, Dorchester Co. Md. O. R. Soc. Bull., no. 3, pp. 42–52.
†**Dunott.** Med. Annals Md. Cordell. 1903, pp. 385–86. MHS.
Dunstable. St. Paul's Parish, Balto. V. 1. Mss. MHS.
Dunton, Phila. and Md. Col. families of U. S. A. Mackenzie. V. 6. MHS; DAR.
Dunton, Henry Hurd. Pedigree. Soc. Col. Wars Md. Culver. 1940. MHS; DAR.
Dunton, Wm. Rush, Jr. Pedigree. Soc. Col. Wars Md. Culver. 1940. MHS; DAR.
du Pont. Donaldson family. Donaldson. 1931, pamph. MHS.
Du Pont Family, Del. Col. and Revolutionary lineages of Amer. 1939, v. 1, pp. 1–110. MHS.
Dupuy. Family rec. of John Dupuy (1756–1832), son of John Bartholomew and Esther Dupuy (Va.). Photos. DAR.
*Huguenot Bartholomew Dupuy, and his descendants Dupuys and Lockermans, etc. B. H. Dupuy. Louisville, Ky., Courier Journal Job Printing Co., 1908.
Plummer family. A. P. H. Ms. MHS.
*__Dupuy,__ Va. The Sun, Balto., Dec. 11, 1904.
*Notes. D. A. R. Mag., Aug., 1932, v. 66, no. 8, p. 539.
*__Dupuy Family.__ Charts. C. M. Dupuy. Pr. for priv. circulation, J. B. Lippincott Co., Phila., 1910, 1st ed. MHS.
Dupuy Family, Va. Ms. File case, DAR.
DuPuy. *See* Bassett-DuPuy-Woodson.
*__Du Puy, Bartholomew.__ Col. men and times. Harper. 1916.
Du Puy Family, France, Va. and Ky. Col. men and times. Harp. Pp. 369–417. MHS.
Durand. Few abs. from will book at Annapolis. William and Mary Quart., 1st series, v. 13, p. 27.
Durbin. St. Paul's Parish, Balto. V. 1. Mss. MHS.
Durborough. Beards' Luth. graveyard, Washington Co. Md. Geneal. Rec. Com., 1935–36. Mss. DAR.
Pedigree of Malcolm Van Vechten Tyson. Soc. Col. Wars Md. Culver. 1940. MHS; DAR.
Durborow. M. Van V. Tyson pedigree chart, plate 4. Soc. Col. Wars, Md. Johnston. 1905, p. 120. MHS.
Durham. Rumsey-Smithson. Bible rec. Md. Geneal. Rec. Com., 1932–33, v. 5, pp. 63–142. DAR.
Rumsey-Smithson family rec. bk. Md. Geneal. Rec. Com., 1932, pp. 111–12, 116–24. DAR.
St. Paul's Parish, Balto. V. 1, 3. Mss. MHS.
Smithson-Rumsey rec. bk. Ms. MHS.
Durst. Mt. Olivet Cemetery, Frederick. Md. Geneal. Rec. Com., 1934–35, p. 111. Mss. DAR.
Dushane. Gantt geneal. Ms. MHS.
Dutitree. Naturalizations in Md., 1666–1765; Laws. Bacon. MHS.
Dutro. St. Paul's Parish, Balto. V. 1. Mss. MHS.
†**Dutrow.** Hist. of Frederick Co. Williams. MHS; DAR.
Tombstone inscriptions. Some descendants of Philip Duttera (or Dotterer). 1934. Lutheran Cemetery, Middletown, Frederick Co., p. 135; Mt. Olivet Cemetery, Frederick Co., p. 135. MHS.

Duttera. Babylon family. Duttera. Ms. MHS.
Dutton, T. Matthews. Md. Soc., War of 1812, v. 1, no. 31. Ms. MHS.
Duval. Bowie-Claggett chart. MHS.
Chart, photos., complete in 1 sheet. Cary Geneal. Coll. Ms. MHS.
Dorsey-Duval-Coale-Buchanan-Borden-Brooke and allied families. Newsp. clipp. and other printed matter. MHS.
Eldridge chart. MHS.
*Frederick Co. families. Markell. Ms. Personal list.
†Hist. of Allegany Co. Thomas and Williams. V. 2. MHS; DAR.
Md. families. Culver. Ms. Personal list.
See Contee-Duval-Jarboe.
See Duvall.
Duval, Duvall. Lineage Bks., Natl. Soc. of Daughters of Amer. Col., v. 4, pp. 132, 189. MHS; DAR.
†Med. Annals Md. Cordell. 1903, pp. 386–87. MHS.
***Duval, Duvall Family.** Copied from Amer. Hist. Reg., Aug., 1895. MHS.
***Du Val.** Lineage Bk. Daughters of Amer. Colonists. V. 4, p. 189. MHS; DAR.
Du Val Family, Anne Arundel Co. Ms., MHS; also N. Y. G. B. Soc. Lib.
***Du Val Family,** Va. Du Val family of Va. B. B. Grabowskie. 1931. DAR.
Duvall. Abr. Compend. Amer. Geneal. Virkus. V. 1, p. 282. DAR.
(Magruder descendants of Mareen Duvall, Huguenot immigrant). Amer. Clan Gregor Year Book, 1935, pp. 56–62. MHS; DAR.
Ances. rec. and portraits. Col. Dames of Amer., 1910, v. 1, p. 252. MHS; DAR.
Anne Arundel Co. tombstone inscriptions. MS. DAR.
Balto. Morning Herald, April 5, 1903. Newsp. clipp. Scrap Book. MHS.
†Bench and bar of Md. Sams and Riley. 1901, v. 1, p. 214. Lib. Cong., MHS; Peabody Lib.
*Burke's landed gentry. 1939. MHS.
Chart, photos. of ms., 7 sections. Luther W. Welsh. MHS; DAR.
Col. families of Amer. Lawrence. V. 3, p. 307. MHS.
Day Star of Amer. Freedom. Davis. MHS.
Duckett chart. MHS.
Col. Nicholas Duvall family rec. Ms., bd. MHS.
*Duvall family of Md. Amer. Hist. Reg., 1895, v. 2, pp. 1474–76. MHS.
Duvall's of Md. Huguenot Soc. Amer. Pro., N. Y., 1903, v. 3, pt. 2.
*Founders of Anne Arundel and Howard Cos. Warfield. Pp. 104–06. MHS; DAR.
*Geneal. and mem. encyc. of Md. Spencer. V. 1, pp. 132–41. MHS; DAR.
Geneal. of family of Stockett, 1558–1892. Stockett. Pamph., p. 24. MHS; DAR.
†Hist. of Frederick Co. Williams. MHS; DAR.
Laytonsville M. E. churchyard, Montgomery Co. Md. Geneal. Rec. Com., 1934–35, p. 69. Mss. DAR.
*Lineage Bk. Daughters of Amer. Colonists. V. 4, p. 132. MHS; DAR.
Mrs. D. G. Lovell chart. MHS.
Patriotic Md. Md. Soc. of S. A. R., 1930. MHS; DAR.
Pedigree of Edward Hammond. Soc. Col. Wars Md. Culver. 1940. MHS; DAR.
Pedigree of Benedict Henry Hanson, Jr. Soc. Col. Wars Md. Culver. 1940. MHS; DAR.
Pedigree of Thomas Dobbin Penniman. Soc. Col. Wars Md. Culver. 1940. MHS; DAR.
Pedigree of Maurice Falconer Rodgers. Soc. Col. Wars Md. Culver. 1940. MHS; DAR.
Pedigree of James Mather Sill. Soc. Col. Wars Md. Culver. 1940. MHS; DAR.
Pedigree of John Ogle Warfield, Jr. Soc. Col. Wars Md. Culver. 1940. MHS; DAR.
Mrs. M. L. Price chart. MHS.
St. Paul's Parish, Balto. V. 2, 3, 4. Mss. MHS.
Side lights on Md. hist. Richardson. V. 2, p. 94. MHS; DAR.
Stockett-Duvall Bible rec. Ms. MHS.
*The Sun, Balto., April 3, 1904.
Welsh-Hyatt and kindred. Welsh. Sec. 11, p. 204. MHS; DAR.
See Duval.
See Hall-Duvall.
†Duvall, Gabriel. Hist. of Md. Scharf. V. 2, p. 597. MHS.
Duvall, Dr. Jeremiah. Biog. Ms. MHS.
***Duvall, Col. Nicholas.** Family rec.; with Price connections, 1684–1909. Maj. H. Brooks Price. Bd. ms. MHS.
Duvall, R. Warren. Md. Soc., War of 1812, v. 3, no. 210. Ms. MHS.
†Duvall, Richard. Men of mark in Md. Johnson. V. 2. DAR; Enoch Pratt Lib.
Duvall, Richard Isaac. Geneal. and memorial encyc. of Md. Spencer. V. 1, p. 132. MHS; DAR.
Duvall, Richard Mareen. Pedigree. Soc. Col. Wars Md. Culver. 1940. MHS; DAR.
Duvall Family. Bible rec. Ms. MHS.
Col. and Revolutionary lineages of Amer. 1939, v. 2, pp. 192–200. MHS.
Data, presented by Mrs. Richard Duvall. Typed. MHS.
From Amer. Hist. Register, Aug., 1895. Typed. MHS.
The Huguenot, April, 1932, v. 2, no. 3.
*Wilson Mss. Coll., no. 37, A; no. 128. MHS.
Duvall Family, Md. and Ohio. Ms. File case, DAR.
Duvall Lines. Mullikins of Md. Baker. MHS; DAR.
Duvall-Farmer-Waters Line. Welsh-Hyatt and kindred. Supplement. Welsh. P. 27. MHS; DAR.
***Duvall-Hall-Tyler Families.** Copied by Miss M. Rebecca Duvall, from Mr. R. M. Duvall's copy of original, by Mr. Justice Gabriel Duvall, with interpolations by Miss Duvall. Ms. MHS.
Duvall-Lovejoy-Sprigg Line. Welsh-Hyatt and kindred. Supplement. Welsh. P. 5. MHS; DAR.
Duvall-Stockett Line. Welsh-Hyatt and kindred. Supplement. Welsh. P. 25. MHS; DAR.
Duvall, Duval, Du Val. Col. families of U. S. A. Mackenzie. V. 1, pp. 146–51; v. 7, p. 244. MHS.
***Du Vals.** Duvals of Ky. from Va. (1794–1935). M. G. Buchanan. DAR.

Duyer. Bible rec. Upper Penins. East. Shore., pp. 18–20. MHS; DAR.
Dwerhagen. Hagerstown tombstone inscriptions. Gruder. Natl. Geneal. Soc. Quart., 1919, v. 8, nos. 1, 2.
Dwyer. Laytonsville M. E. churchyard, Montgomery Co. Md. Geneal. Rec. Com., 1934–35, p. 69. Mss. DAR.
Mt. Carmel burial ground, Montgomery Co. Md. Geneal. Rec. Com., 1934, p. 85. Mss. DAR.
Still Pond Church and cemetery. Md. O. R. Soc. Bull., no. 2, pp. 65–75.
Still Pond cemetery, Kent Co. Md. O. R. Soc., v. 2. MHS.
Dye. Rogers Coll. Ms. MHS.
St. Paul's Parish, Balto. V. 2. Mss. MHS.
Dye-Cole. Bible rec. of Ohio. Photos. DAR.
Dyer. Bible rec. Ms. DAR.
Geneal. notes of Chamberlaine family. MHS.
†Med. Annals Md. Cordell. 1903, p. 387. MHS.
Patriotic Md. Md. Soc. of S. A. R., 1930. MHS; DAR.
See Dyre.
St. Paul's Parish, Balto. V. 3. Mss. MHS.
Dyer Family. Jerome hist. and geneal., and ancestry of Sarah Noble. P. 61. Mss. MHS.
Dykes. Wicomico Co. families. Bible rec. Ms. DAR.
See Dikes.
Dymoke. Chart of Sir Lionel Dymoke. Patriotic Marylander, v. 2, no. 1, p. 19. MHS; DAR.
***Dynmock.** Wicomico Co. families. Tilghman. Ms, p. 7. DAR.
Dyre. Dyre family chart. MHS.
Dyre, Dyer. Cary Geneal. Coll. Ms. MHS.
Dyre, Dyer, Family. Chart. Blue print. 1906. MHS; DAR.
Dyson. Dryden and allied families. Ms. MHS.
†Med. Annals Md. Cordell. 1903, p. 387. MHS.

E

Eader. Beard's Luth. graveyard, Washington Co. Md. Geneal. Rec. Com., 1935–36. Mss. DAR.
Lehman family in Md. Lehman. 1935, pamph., p. 56. MHS; DAR.
Mt. Olivet Cemetery, Frederick. Md. Geneal. Rec. Com., 1934–35, p. 111. Mss. DAR.
Steiner geneal. Steiner. 1896. MHS.
Zion Reformed Church, Hagerstown. Md. Geneal. Rec. Com., 1934–35. Mss. DAR.
Eager. Ances. rec. and portraits. Col. Dames of Amer., 1910, v. 2, pp. 499, 776. MHS; DAR.
Col. families of U. S. A. Mackenzie. V. 1, p. 267. MHS; DAR.
De Ford chart. MHS.
Mrs. J. F. Lee chart. MHS.
Pedigree of Charles Morris Howard. Soc. Col. Wars Md. Culver. 1940. MHS; DAR.
St. Paul's Parish, Balto. V. 1. Mss. MHS.
Mrs. E. C. Venable chart. MHS.
Eager, George, Anne Arundel Co. McH. Howard pedigree chart, plate 1. Soc. Col. Wars, Md. Johnston. 1905. Pp. 41, 144. MHS.
Eaglestone. St. Paul's Parish, Balto. V. 1, 3. Mss. MHS.
Eakle. Hagerstown tombstone inscriptions. Gruder. Natl. Geneal. Soc. Quart., 1919, v. 8, nos. 1, 2.
†Ealer. Med. Annals Md. Cordell. 1903, p. 388. MHS.
†Eareckson. Med. Annals Md. Cordell. 1903, p. 388. MHS.
Eareckson, Wm. Winchester. Pedigree. Soc. Col. Wars Md. Culver. 1940. MHS; DAR.
Eareckson Family. Ms. File case, DAR.
***Earl.** Lineage Bk. Daughters of Amer. Colonists. V. 1, pp. 48, 270, 298. MHS; DAR.
Earle. Barroll in Great Britain and Amer. Barroll. P. 73. MHS.
*Biog. cyc. of rep. men of Md. and D. C. P. 133. MHS; DAR.
†Chesapeake Bay Country. Earle. Pp. 334, 337. MHS.
Col. families of East. Shore and their descendants. Emory. 1900. MHS.
Geneal notes of Chamberlaine family. MHS.
*Hist. and geneal. of Earles of Secancus. I. N. Earle. Md. descendants of James Earle, John of Md. in Revolution. Marquette, Mich., 1925, 828 pp. DAR.
Hist. graves of Md. and D. C. Ridgely. MHS.
Md. families. Culver. Ms. Personal list.
†Med. Annals Md. Cordell. 1903, p. 388. MHS.
Mt. Calvary Church burial ground, Cooksville Pike, Montgomery Co. Md. Geneal. Rec. Com., 1934. Mss. DAR.
Mt. Calvary Church burial ground, Howard Co. Md. Geneal. Rec. Com., 1934–35, pp. 95–99. Mss. DAR.
Newsp. clipp. Scrap Book #7, p. 19. MHS.
*Old Kent. Hanson. Pp. 231–37. MHS; DAR.
St. Paul's churchyard, Kent Co. Md. O. R. Soc. Bull., no. 2, pp. 54–65, MHS.
See Highland-Earle-Patton.
Earle Family. Land of legendary lore. Ingraham. MHS.
Portrait and biog. rec. of East. Shore of Md. 1898, pp. 830, 835. MHS; DAR.
Earle Family, Bishop's Stortford Co., Herts, Eng. Ms. MHS.
Early. Rucker family. Whitley.
Eastburn. St. Paul's Parish, Balto. V. 2. Mss. MHS.
Easter. Balto., its hist., its people. Hall. V. 3. MHS; DAR.
Papers. Ms. MHS.
Easter, A. Miller. Md. Soc., War of 1812, v. 1, no. 38. Ms. MHS.
Easter, J. Miller. Md. Soc., War of 1812, v. 3, no. 224. Ms. MHS.
Easter-Webster-Tinges. Abr. Compend. Amer. Geneal. Virkus. V. 4, p. 568, MHS; v. 6, p. 207. DAR.
Easton. Mt. Carmel Burial Ground, Montgomery Co. Md. Geneal. Rec. Com., 1934, p. 85. Mss. DAR.
St. Paul's Parish, Balto. V. 1. Mss. MHS.
Eaton. Ancestry of Lieut. and Mrs. Wm. B. Stork. Ms. MHS.
Md. Geneal. Bull., v. 3, p. 24.
Ebberts. Mt. Olivet Cemetery, Frederick. Md. Geneal. Rec. Com., 1934–35, p. 111. Mss. DAR.
Ebert. Frederick Co. tombstone inscriptions. Gruder. Natl. Geneal. Soc. Quart., 1919, v. 8, nos. 1, 2.
†Eby. Hist. of Washington Co. Williams. 1906, v. 2, p. 1068. MHS; DAR.

Eby. U. B. cemetery, Sabillasville. Young. Natl. Geneal. Soc. Quart., Sept., 1938, v. 26, no. 3, p. 61 (to be contd.)
†Eccleston. Bench and bar of Md. Sams and Riley. 1901, v. 2, p. 414. Lib. Cong.; MHS; Peabody Lib.
†Biog. cyc. of rep. men of Md. and D. C. P. 402. MHS; DAR.
Christ P. E. Church cemetery, Cambridge. Steele. 1936. MHS; DAR.
*Hist. Dorchester Co. Jones. 1925, p. 308. MHS; DAR.
Lineage of Sarah Eliz. Pritchard. 1929, typed, bd. MHS.
Manning chart. MHS.
Mrs. E. W. Poe chart. MHS.
St. Paul's churchyard, Kent Co. Md. O. R. Soc. Bull., no. 2, pp. 54–65, MHS.
Whitridge chart. MHS.
St. Paul's Parish, Balto. V. 3. Mss. MHS.
†Eccleston, J. Houston. Men of mark in Md. Johnson. V. 2. DAR; Enoch Pratt Lib.
Eccleston Family. Lineage of Sarah Elizabeth Pritchard, wife of Rear Admiral Arthur John Pritchard, U.S.N. 1925. Bd. Ms. MHS.
***Eccleston Family,** Dorchester Co. Wilson. Mss. Coll., no. 8, A. MHS.
Eccleston Family, Lancastershire, Eng.; also in Buckinghamshire to Dorchester Co., Md., 1645. Typed, bd. MHS.
***Eckenrode.** (Pa.) Lineage Bk. Daughters of Amer. Colonists. V. 2, pp. 95–96, 183. MHS; DAR.
Eddy. Ruf-Height-Eddy-Sumner-Hatch and allied families. Ms. MHS.
Eddy Family. Ms. MHS.
Edelen. Children of Alex P. and M. C. Hill. Ms. MHS.
O'Daniel-Hamilton ancestry, in Md. and Ky. O'Daniel. Pp. 87–95. MHS.
Patriotic Md. Md. Soc. of S. A. R., 1930. MHS; DAR.
Pedigree of Francis Joseph Baldwin. Soc. Col. Wars Md. Culver. 1940. MHS; DAR.
Semmes and allied families. Semmes. MHS.
***Edelen, Richard.** Semmes Geneal. Coll. Ms. MHS.
Edelin. Centenary of Catholicity in Ky. Webb. 1884. MHS.
†Med. Annals Md. Cordell. 1903, p. 389. MHS.
Eden. Col. families of U. S. A. Mackenzie. V. 2, pp. 247–50. MHS; DAR.
†Hist. of Md. Scharf. V. 2, p. 218. MHS.
†Life and administration of Sir Robert Eden. B. C. Steiner. J. H. U., Series 16, no. 7, 9. Balto., J. H. Press, 1898. MHS; Enoch Pratt Lib.
*Some hist. notes on Eden family. Rev. Robert Allan Eden, Vicar of Old St. Pancras, London. Illus., folded pedigree. Blades East Blades, London, 1907, 58 pp. MHS.
***Eden Family.** Hist. notes. Robt. Allan Eden. Misc. Mss. MHS.
*Miscellaneous material. Rev. Robert Allan Eden. Ms. Some hist. notes on Eden family in B. C. Steiner's copy of above book. MHS.
Notes. Robert Eden. Ms. MHS.
Edgar. Md. gleanings in Eng. Wills. M. H. Mag., v. 2, no. 3.
Naturalizations in Md., 1666–1765; Laws. Bacon. MHS.
Tombstone rec. of Dorchester Co. Jones. DAR.
Edge. Geneal. of family of Gideon Gilpin. MHS.
Edgeworth. Ances. rec. and portraits. Col. Dames of Amer., 1910, v. 2, p. 658. MHS; DAR.
Edley. Wathen Prayer Book rec. Ms. MHS.
Edmond. Lambdin chart. MHS.
Edmonds. Md. families. Culver. Ms. Personal list.
†Men of mark in Md. Johnson. V. 2. DAR; Enoch Pratt Lib.
Edmondson. Barroll in Great Britain and Amer. Barroll. P. 77. MHS.
Mrs. R. N. Jackson chart. MHS.
Md. families. Culver. Ms. Personal list.
*Old Kent. Hanson. P. 33. MHS; DAR.
Pattison Bible. Md. Geneal. Bull., v. 4, p. 13. MHS; DAR.
Revolutionary rec. D. A. R. Mag., v. 68, no. 5, p. 283.
Talbott of "Poplar Knowle." Shirk. MHS; DAR.
Mrs. H. DeCourcy Wright Thom chart. MHS.
Tombstone rec. of Dorchester Co. Jones. DAR.
Florence Eyster Weaver chart. MHS.
*Wicomico Co. families. Tilghman. Ms., p. 74. DAR.
See Edmondstone.
See Hicks-Dennis-Edmondson-Phillips-Travers-White.
Edmondson-Turbutt Families. Ames Geneal. Coll. Ms. MHS.
Edmonston. Beall and Bell families. Beall. MHS.
*Burke's landed gentry. 1939. MHS.
Lineage Bks., Natl. Soc. of Daughters of Amer. Col., v. 1, p. 83. MHS; DAR.
Orme geneal. chart. MHS.
Patriotic Md. Md. Soc. of S. A. R., 1930. MHS; DAR.
Pedigree of Coleman Randall Freeman. Soc. Col. Wars Md. Culver. 1940. MHS; DAR.
Edmonston, Wm. Md. and Va. Ms. File case, DAR.
Edmonston Family. Ms. File case, DAR.
Edmondston, Edmonson. Price ancestral data (maternal). Bd. Ms. MHS.
See Orem-Edmondstone.
Edmondstone, Edmondson. Ances. rec. and portraits. Col. Dames of Amer., 1910, v. 2, p. 468. MHS; DAR.
Pattison Bible rec. Ms. MHS.
*The Sun, Balto., Feb. 23, 28, 1904.
Edmonson. St. Paul's Parish, Balto. V. 2. Mss. MHS.
See Edmondston.
Edmonstone. Zimmerman Waters and allied families. Allen. Pp. 76–91. MHS; DAR.
Edmundson Family, Pa., to Frederick Co., and Balto., 1765. And allied families of Decatur, Ingram, Miller and Parrine. Focke Geneal. Coll. Mss. MHS.
***Edwards.** Beall and Edwards families and their descendants 360–1892. A. S. Edwards. 1910. DAR.
Cary Geneal. Coll. Ms. MHS.
Dent family of Md. Ms. File case, DAR.

†Hist. of Allegany Co. Thomas and Williams. V. 1. MHS; DAR.
Joseph Hull (1595) and Tome of his Descendants. Hull. 1904, p. 18. MHS.
†Med. Annals Md. Cordell. 1903, p. 389. MHS.
Portrait and biog. rec. of Sixth Cong. Dist. of Md. 1898, pp. 694, 710. MHS; DAR.
Quaker cemetery, Millington, Kent Co., 1802–1906. Md. Geneal. Rec. Com., 1932–33, v. 5. Mss. DAR.
St. Paul's Parish, Balto. V. 1, 2, 3, 4. Mss. MHS.
*The Sun, Balto, Oct. 30, Nov. 6 (Va.), 1904.
See St. Clair-Edwards.
***Edwards Family.** Anne Arundel Co. Gentry. Newman. Pp. 147–51. MHS; DAR.
Edwards Family, Md. and Ky. Ms. File case, DAR.
Edwards, Faris (Farris, Faries), Bouldin Families. Bible rec. Md. Geneal. Rec. Com., v. 5, p. 201, DAR. Md. MSS.
Egerton. Descendants of Col. Thomas White. Morris. MHS.
*Egerton family. F. B. Culver. M. H. Mag., Sept., 1940, v. 35, no. 3, pp. 292–302.
Eggan. Wm. Conway Md and Pa. Ms. File case, DAR.
Eggleston. Cary Geneal. Coll. Ms. MHS.
Eggleston, Maj. Azariah. *See* Egleston, Bigod.
Eggleston-DuPuy (Va). **Colgate Purnell-Von Meyer** (Md). Abr. Compend. Amer. Geneal. Virkus. V. 4, p. 170; v. 4, p. 676. MHS.
Egleston. Bigod Egleston and his descendants. Caldwell Woodruff, 1937, of Settrington, Yorkshire, Eng. and Windsor, Conn. With a record line of Major Azariah Egleston. With short account of Heriot of S. C. and Scotland and Woodruff of Ga.; Caldwell Woodruff, Linthicum Heights, Anne Arundel Co., Md. Typed, 90 pp. MHS.
Egleston, Bigod. Bigod Egleston and his descendants, Caldwell Woodruff, Linthicum Heights, Md. Bigot Egleston of Settrington, Yorkshire, Eng., and Windsor, Conn., with rec. of line of Maj. Azariah Eggleston. With short account of Heriot of S. C. and Scotland and Woodruff, Ga. 1937, typed. MHS.
***Ehlen.** Burke's landed gentry. 1939. MHS.
Ehlen, Florence M. (Snowden). Abr. Compend. Amer. Geneal. Virkus. V. 1, p. 81. DAR.
Eichar. Bowies and their kindred. Bowie. Pp. 422–26. MHS; DAR.
Eichar-Clagett. Bible rec., 1810–1922. D. C. Geneal. Rec. Com., v. 31, pt. 1, pp. 91–95. Typed, bd. DAR.
Eichelberger. Abr. Compend. Amer. Geneal. Virkus. V. 4, pp. 274 (Pa.), 332. MHS.
†Bench and bar of Md. Sams and Riley. 1901, v. 2, pp. 618, 630. Lib. Cong.; MHS; Peabody Lib.
Data, 1693–1869. Md. Geneal. Rec. Com., 1932–33, p. 218. Mss. DAR.
Hagerstown tombstone inscriptions. Gruder. Natl. Geneal. Soc. Quart., 1919, v. 8, nos. 1, 2.
†Hist. of Frederick Co. Williams. V. 1, pp. 398, 589; v. 2, pp. 974, 1357. MHS; DAR.
*Hist. sketch of Philip Frederick Eichelberger, who came from Ittlingen, Germany, 1728, and his Descendants, with family register. A. W. Eichelberger. Hanover, Pa., Hanover Harold Print, 1901.
Md. tombstone rec. Md. Geneal. Rec. Com., 1937, Parran, pp. 13, 15, 18. Mss. DAR.
†Med. Annals Md. Cordell. 1903, p. 390. MHS.
Monumental City. Howard. MHS; DAR.
Rec., 1693–1869. Md. Geneal. Rec. Com., 1932–33. DAR.
Portrait and biog. rec. of Sixth Cong. Dist. of Md. 1898, p. 427. MHS; DAR.
Tercentenary hist. of Md. Andrews. V. 4, p. 268. MHS; DAR.
***Eichelberger Family.** Md. Geneal. Rec. Com., 1932–33, p. 218. DAR.
Eilbeck. Mason chart. MHS.
Eilbeck, Charles Co. Pedigree of Francis Joseph Baldwin. Soc. Col. Wars Md. Culver. 1940. MHS; DAR.
Eiler, Iler-Anderson-Boon-Sothoron-Witten. Our ancestors; rec. of these families, Frederick Co. Homer Eiler. Grenola, Kansas, J. S. Dancy, 1929, pamph. MHS.
Eiler (Iler - Boone - Anderson - Scothoron. Written by Homer Eiler. Topeka, Kansas, 1929. MHS.
Elbert. Tercentenary hist. of Md. Andrews. V. 4, p. 773. MHS; DAR.
Elbert (Hugh) Family, Kent Island. Chart. Oswald Tilghman. Printed Easton, 1898; supplemental chart of descendants of Dr. Downes Elbert. MHS.
Elbrow. Md. gleanings in Eng. Wills. M. H. Mag., 1907, v. 2, no. 4.
Elburn. *See* Ashley-Elburn.
***Elder.** Ancestors and descendants of Thomas Elder, 1748–1832. Ms. DAR.
Ances. rec. and portraits. Col. Dames of Amer., 1910, p. 568. MHS; DAR.
Gist chart. Cary Geneal. Coll. Ms. MHS.
Britton Scrap Book. V. 1. Ms. MHS.
Brooks chart. MHS.
Cary Geneal. Coll. Ms. MHS.
Centenary of Catholicity in Ky. Webb. 1884. MHS.
Col. Families of Amer. Lawrence. V. 5, p. 92. MHS.
Dorsey and allied families. Ms. MHS.
*Elder family in Md. Ms. DAR.
Hist. of Emmitsburg. Helman. P. 17. DAR.
†Hist. of Frederick Co. Williams. V. 1, pp. 11, 81, 324; v. 2, pp. 834, 835. MHS; DAR.
†Hist. of West. Md. Scharf. V. 2, pp. 461, 581–83. MHS; DAR.
Jenkins-Courtney chart. MHS.
Mrs. B. S. Johnston chart. MHS.
Lineage Bks., Natl. Soc. of Daughters of Amer. Col., v. 2, pp. 22, 95, 298. MHS; DAR.
Manly chart. MHS.
Md. families. Culver. Ms. Personal list.
*Old Kent. Hanson. P. 42–3. MHS; DAR.
Pedigree of Francis Joseph Baldwin. Soc. Col. Wars Md. Culver. 1940. MHS; DAR.
St. Joseph's churchyard, Emmitsburg. Md. O. R. Soc. Bull., no. 3, pp. 64–66. MHS.
St. Paul's Parish, Balto. V. 3. Mss. MHS.
St. Thomas Parish, Balto. Co. Bd. ms. MHS. Also: Md. Geneal. Rec. Com., 1937, pp. 109–82. Mss. DAR.
Elder, Wm. Will, 1773. D. C. Geneal. Rec. Com., 1930–32, v. 3, pp. 2–4. Typed. DAR.
***Elder Family.** Bible rec. Ga. Geneal. Rec. Com., 1933, pt. 4, p. 26. Typed., bd. DAR. Ms. File case, DAR.

***Elder Family,** Pa. Descendants of Robert Elder (1732–1818; Married Elizabeth Towson, 1769). In: Elder family in Md. Ms. DAR.

†**Elderdice,** Men of mark in Md. Johnson. V. 1, v. 4, p. 158. DAR; Enoch Pratt Lib.
Tercentenary hist. of Md. Andrews. V. 2, p. 667. MHS; DAR.

Elderkin. St. Paul's Parish, Balto. V. 2, 3. Mss. MHS.

Eldred. St. Paul's Parish, Balto. V. 2. Mss. MHS.

Eldridge. M. E. Church South cemetery, near Poolesville, Montgomery Co. Md. Geneal. Rec. Com., 1926. Mss. DAR.

Eldridge, Mrs. Frederick (Louisa Lee Andrews). Chart. Col. Dames, Chapt. I. MHS.

Elexon. Naturalizations in Md., 1666–1765; Laws. Bacon. MHS.

Elgin. Portrait and biog. rec. of Sixth Cong. Dist. of Md., 1898, p. 256. MHS; DAR.

Eliason. St. Stephens Parish, Cecilton, Md. MHS; DAR.

Eliot. Abr. Compend. Amer. Geneal. Virkus. V. 4, p. 171. MHS.

Elkington. Geneal. of Henrietta Chauncey Wilson. Upshur. Bk. of photos. MHS.

Elkins. Amer. biog. directories. H. B. F. Macfarland. 1908, p. 142. DAR.
Memorials of Reading, Howell, Yerkes, Watts, Latham and Elkins families. Leach.

Elkins, Pa. and Va. Col. and Revolutionary families of Pa. Amer. Hist. Soc., N. Y.,1934, p. 145.

Elkins, Hallie Davis (Mrs. Stephen B.). Abr. Compend. Amer. Geneal. Virkus. V. 1, p. 588. DAR.

***Elkins Family.** See card index (35 ref.) in DAR.

Elkins - Brown - Gassaway. Abr. Compend. Amer. Geneal. Virkus. V. 6, p. 210.

†**Ellegood.** Bench and bar Md. Sams and Riley. 1901, v. 2, p. 562. Lib. Cong.; MHS; Peabody Lib.
†Men of mark in Md. Johnson. V. 4. DAR; Enoch Pratt Lib.
Wicomico Co. families. Bible rec. Ms. DAR.
*Wicomico Co. families. Tilghman. Ms. pp. 17–18, 108. DAR.

Ellender. St. Paul's Parish, Balto. V. 2. Mss. MHS.

Ellender, Allender. Patriotic Md. Md. Soc. of S. A. R., 1930. MHS; DAR.
(Revolutionary soldier). Greenmount Cemetery. Patriotic Marylander, v. 2, no. 4, pp. 54–60. MHS; DAR.

Ellery. St. Paul's Parish, Balto. V. 2. Mss. MHS.

***Ellet, Mrs. Eliz.** Memoirs. Arch. of Georgetown Univ., Wash., D. C., v. 139, no. 12.

Ellett. Pocahontas and her descendants. Robertson. MHS; DAR.
Samuel Carpenter of Phila. Carpenter. P. 84. MHS.

†**Ellicott.** Mrs. S. K. Alexander. Columbia Hist. Soc. Rec., v. 1, pp. 158–20. MHS; DAR.
Amer. biog. directories. H. B. F. Macfarland. 1908, p. 143. DAR.
Abr. Compend. Amer. Geneal. Virkus. V. 1, pp. 87–88. DAR.
Mrs. J. G. Brogden chart. MHS.
Butler-Houston-Ellicott family Bibles. DAR.
See Carroll. Col. families of U. S. A. Mackenzie. V. 3, p. 131. MHS; DAR.
Col. families of Amer. Lawrence. V. 9, pp. 121–23. MHS.
Ellicott City tombstone inscriptions, Howard Co., 1733–1920. M. H. Mag., 1924, v. 19, p. 200–2.
Ellicott family, Howard Co. Inventory of co. and town rec. PWA. MHS; DAR.
Ellicott's Mills, Tyson. 1871.
Emory-Price. Bible rec. M. H. Mag., 1931, v. 26, pp. 198–201.
†Founders of Anne Arundel and Howard Cos. Warfield. Pp. 496–501.
Fox-Ellicott-Evans families. Evans. MHS; DAR.
Geneal. and memorial encyc. Md. Spencer. V. 1, p. 235. MHS; DAR.
Geneal. notes of Thomas family. Thomas. MHS; DAR.
See George. Col. fam. of U. S. A. Mackenzie. V. 2, p. 296. MHS; DAR.
†Hist. of Balto. City and Co. Scharf. Pp. 373–76. MHS.
M. H. Mag., 1931, v. 26, p. 369.
Md. families. Culver. Ms. Personal list.
John O'Donnell of Balto. Cook. MHS.
Pedigree of Malcolm Van Vechten Tyson. Soc. Col. Wars Md. Culver. 1940. MHS; DAR.
St. Paul's Parish, Balto. V. 2, 3, 4. Mss. MHS.
†Sketch of Maj. Andrew Ellicott, designer of city of Wash. Mrs. J. E. Reese. Ms. DAR.
†Sketch of life of Maj. Andrew Ellicott. Sally K. Alexander. Rec. Columbia Hist. Soc., 1899, v. 2, pp. 158–202.
Sketch of life of Maj. Andrew Ellicott. South. Hist. Asso., 1899, v. 2.
Tercentenary hist. of Md. Andrews. V. 4, pp. 350, 769. MHS; DAR.
*The Sun, Balto., March 12, 1905.
See Churchill-Crocker-Fox-Coplestone-Bonville-Ellicott.
See Emory-Price.

†**Ellicott,** Washington Co. Hist of West. Md. Scharf. V. 2, pp. 1028–34. MHS; DAR.

†**Ellicott, Andrew.** Astronomer, surveyor and soldier of hundred years ago. Grafton Mag. of Hist. and Geneal., 1908–09, v. 1, pp. 32–42.
Col. families of Amer. Lawrence. V. 9, pp. 121–22. MHS.
†Col. Hist. Soc. Rec., v. 2, p. 1899. MHS.
D. A. R. Mag., July, 1931, v. 65, no. 7, p. 407.
Ellicott-King chart. MHS.
Family data from newspapers anf from orig. family tree, etc. Ms. File case. DAR.
Fox chart. MHS.
†His life and letters. C. Van C. Mathews. Grafton Press, 1908.
Warner hist. Osler. MHS.

Ellicott, Andrew, Pa. and Md. Revolutionary soldiers buried at West Point. D. A. R. Mag. v. 65, no. 7, pp. 405–08.

***Ellicott, Andrew and Joseph.** Plans of Washington and Village of Buffalo. Dr. G. H. Bartlett. 1922. Repr. from Pub. Buffalo Hist. Soc., 1922, v. 26. MHS.

Ellicott (Andrew)-Fox Line. T. M. Smith pedigree charts, plate 2. Soc. Col. Wars, Md. Johnston. 1905, p. 96. MHS.

Ellicott, Mrs. William M. (Anna Goldwaite Campbell). Chart. Col. Dames, Chap. I. MHS.

Ellicott, Mrs. William M. (Elizabeth G. King). Chart. Col. Dames, Chap. I. MHS.
***Ellicott, Wm. Miller.** Burke's landed gentry. 1939. MHS.
Pedigree chart. Soc. Col. Wars, Md. Johnston. 1905, p. 24. MHS.
***Ellicott Family.** Md. Geneal. Rec. Com., 1926–27, v. 2, pp. 1–7. DAR.
Thomas Book. Thomas. Pp. 294–302. Lib. Cong.; MHS.
Ellicott Family, Ellicott City, Howard Co. Few facts about family. Md. Geneal. Rec. Com., 1926–27, v. 2, p. 1–7. DAR.
Ellicott Line. Geneal. and mem. encyc. of Md. Spencer. V. 1, pp. 235–37. MHS; DAR.
***Ellingsworth.** Wicomico Co. families. Tilghman. Ms., pp. 99, 103, 106. DAR.
***Elliot Family,** in Pa. See card index (21 ref.) in DAR.
Elliott. Ances. rec. and portraits. Col. Dames of Amer. 1910, pp. 374, 519. MHS; DAR.
Cannon-Riley-Truitt-Houston-Kollock. Stow. Ms. MHS.
Wm. Conway of Md. and Pa. Ms. File case, DAR.
S. G. Hopkins chart. MHS.
Machserry chart. MHS.
Mrs. James McHenry chart. MHS.
†Med. Annals Md. Cordell. 1903, p. 390. MHS.
Portrait and biog. rec. of Sixth Cong. Dist. of Md. 1898, p. 473. MHS; DAR.
(39 rec.) St. Paul's Parish, Balto. V. 2, 3, 4. Mss. MHS.
Tercentenary hist. of Md. Andrews. V. 4, pp. 734, 770. MHS; DAR.
See Hall-Collins-Elliott-Tingley.
See Ringgold-Elliott.
See Waggaman-Elliott.
Elliott, of S. C. Johnstone chart. MHS.
†Elliott Jesse Duncan. Hist. of Md. Scharf. V. 3, p. 28. MHS.
†(1782–1845). M. H. Mag., v. 12, p. 215.
Elliott, T. Ireland. Md. Soc., War of 1812, v. 1, no. 118. Ms. MHS.
Elliott Family, Kent Island. Chart, showing the Elliott-Hambleton (Hampleton), Ringgold, lines of descent. Adele Elliott Valentine. Photos., 1920. MHS.
***Elliott Family,** Md. and Ky. Sam'l Elliott, born in Md., 1745; died in Ky., 1825; married Mary Oldham, 1768. Ms. DAR.
Elliott-Auld. Chart. From Hist. Talbot Co. Tilghman. MHS.
Elliott-Auld Families. Ms. MHS.
Elliott-McDonnald. Bible rec. Ms. MHS.
Ellis. Ancestry of Lieut. and Mrs. Wm. B. Stork. Ms. MHS.
†Med. Annals Md. Cordell. 1903, pp. 390–91. MHS.
Pedigree of Duncan Keener Brent. Soc. Col. Wars Md. Culver. 1940. MHS; DAR.
St. Paul's Parish, Balto. V. 1, 2, 3. Mss. MHS.
Somerset Co. Court Book. Tilghman. 1937. Ms. DAR.
Ellis, Phila. Abr. Compend. Amer. Geneal. Virkus. V. 1, p. 94. DAR.
***Ellis, Lieut.-Col. Thomas.** Burke's landed gentry. 1939. MHS.
Ellis Family. Morris family of Phila. Moon. V. 2, p. 654; v. 5, p. 228. MHS.
Ellis-Shelton Line. J. S. Tapscott pedigree chart. Soc. Col. Wars, Md. Johnston. 1905, p. 106. MHS.
Ellis, Elliss. Old Somerset. Torrence. MHS; DAR.
*Wicomico Co. families. Tilghman. Ms. pp. 81, 108, 117, 121–24. DAR.
Ellison. St. Paul's Parish, Balto. V. 2, 4. Mss. MHS.
Elliss. *See* Ellis.
Ellsberry, "Bohemia Manor," Md., and Ohio. Washington ancestry and rec. Hoppin. V. 2. MHS; DAR.
Elmer. Pedigree of Howard Elmer Ashbury. Soc. Col. Wars Md. Culver. 1940. MHS; DAR.
Elms. Mt. Carmel Burial Ground, Montgomery Co. Md. Geneal Rec. Com., 1934, p. 85. Mss. DAR.
Elmsworth. Rec. of Stepney Parish. MHS; DAR.
***Elphinstone.** Burke's landed gentry. 1939. MHS.
Elsey. Ms. MHS.
***Elshem.** Wicomico Co. families. Tilghman. Ms., p. 113. DAR.
Elson Family, Va., and Md. Ms. File case, DAR.
Elsworth. St. Paul's Parish, Balto. V. 2. Mss. MHS.
Elten-Eltynge-Eltinge Elting Family. 1632–1918 (10 generations). Md. Geneal. Rec. Com., v. 3, pp. 45–49. DAR.
Elting. Md. Geneal. Rec. Com., v. 3, pp. 45–49. DAR.
***Elting-Shepherd Family,** Md. and Va. W. Va. Hist. Mag., April, 1903, v. 3, no. 2, pp. 119–27.
†Eltinge. Hist. of West. Md. Scharf. V. 2, p. 918. MHS; DAR.
Md. Geneal. Rec. Com., v. 3, pp. 45–49. DAR.
Pedigree of Charles O'Donovan. Soc. Col. Wars Md. Culver. 1940. MHS; DAR.
See Ferree-Eltinge.
Elton. Mrs. T. B. Harrison chart. MHS.
Eltonhead. Ancest. rec. and portraits. Col. Dames of Amer., 1910; v. 2, p. 544–46. MHS; DAR.
*Mrs. Charles Howard Lloyd chart. MHS. Col. Dames Amer., Chap. 1. MHS.
Conway family, Va. Ms. DAR.
Geneal. of Va. family of Lomax. Lib. Cong.
Md. families. Culver. Ms. Personal list.
Pedigree of Corbin Braxton Dallam. Soc. Col. Wars Md. Culver. 1940. MHS; DAR.
Eltynge Md. Geneal. Rec. Com., v. 3, pp. 45–49. DAR.
Elwell Family, Va. Col. families of U. S. Mackenzie. V. 5, pp. 202–06.
Ely. Dorsey and allied families. Ms. MHS.
Frederick Co. tombstone inscriptions. Gruder. Natl. Geneal. Soc. Quart., 1919, v. 8, nos. 1, 2.
*Geneal. and mem. encyc. of Md. Spencer. V. 2, p. 454. MHS; DAR.
St. Paul's Parish, Balto. V. 2. Mss. MHS.
Warner hist. Osler. MHS.
See Rogers-Ely-Prigg.
Ely, Cecil Co. Bible rec. Pub. Geneal. Soc. Pa., v. 10, p. 82.
†Elzey. Med. Annals Md. Cordell. 1903, p. 391. MHS.
Old Somerset. Torrence. MHS; DAR.

†**Elzey.** Rec. of Stepney Parish. MHS; DAR.
Somerset Co. Court Book. Tilghman. 1937. Ms. DAR.
Turner Geneal. Coll. Ms. MHS.
†**Elzey, Gen. Arnold.** Biog. Sketches of Distinguished Marylanders. Boyle. MHS; DAR.
†(1816-71). M. H. Mag., v. 12, p. 215.
Elzey Family, "Almodington," Somerset Co. Ms. MHS.
Elzey-Waters. Geneal. notes. Ms. MHS.
†**Embrey.** Hist. of West. Md. Scharf. V. 2, pp. 1225. MHS; DAR.
Emerson. Balto., its hist., its people. Hall. V. 2. MHS; DAR.
Old cemetery, Denton, Caroline Co. Md. Geneal. Rec. Com., 1935-36, p. 168. Mss. DAR.
Mrs. Wm. L. Watson chart. MHS.
Emerson, Samuel, Caroline Co. Will, 1812. Ms. File case, DAR.
***Emerson-Evitts,** East. Shore of Md. Wilson Mss. Coll., no. 63. MHS.
Emmart. Balto., its hist., its people. Hall. V. 3. MHS; DAR.
Emmerich. Ellen Emmerich Mears. Col. and Revolutionary families of Phila. Jordan. 1933, v. 1, pp. 412-15.
***Emory.** Burke's landed gentry. 1939. MHS.
†Chesapeake Bay Country. Earle. P. 330. MHS.
Col. families of East. Shore and their descendants. Emory. 1900, p. 187. MHS.
Col. families of U. S. A. Mackenzie. V. 1, p. 159. MHS; DAR.
Emory family Bible rec. M. H. Mag., 1917, v. 12, pp. 164-65.
†Hist. of Balto. City and Co. Scharf. P. 914. MHS.
†Life of Rev. John Emory, D.D. Written by his eldest son. 1841. MHS.
Md. families. Culver. Ms. Personal list.
McDonnald-Elliott Bible rec. Ms. MHS.
†Med. Annals Md. Cordell. 1903, p. 391. MHS.
Morris family of Phila. Moon. V. 3, p. 933. MHS.
Patriotic Md. Md. Soc. of S. A. R., 1930. MHS; DAR.
Pedigree of Ralph Robinson. Soc. Col. Wars Md. Culver. 1940. MHS; DAR.
Price and Emory families. M. H. Mag., 1931, v. 26, no. 2, p. 198.
St. Paul's Parish, Balto. V. 2, 3. Mss. MHS.
Spring Hill Cemetery, Talbot Co. Md. O. R. Soc. Bull., no. 1, pp. 35-41. MHS.
Mrs. Emory Whitridge chart. MHS.
See Sudler-Emory.
Emory, Kent and Queen Anne Cos. Howard-Montague-Warfield geneal, chart. Culver and Marye. MHS.
Emory, Queen Anne Co. G. N. Mackenzie, 3rd, pedigree chart. Soc. Col. Wars, Md. Johnston. 1905, p. 64. MHS.
Emory, Thomas Lane, Belair. Bible rec. Pub-Geneal. Soc. Pa., v. 11, p. 80.
†**Emory, Wm. Hemsley** (1811-87). M. H. Mag., v. 12, p. 216.
***Emory Family.** Corrections. Emory-Price family. M. H. Mag., 1931, v. 26, pp. 198-201.
*M. H. Mag., 1928, v. 23, pp. 363-72.
*Some old Bible rec., 1751-1836. F. B. Culver. M. H. Mag., 1917, v. 12, pp. 164-65.
Emory-Price. Bible rec., additions and corrections. M. H. Mag., 1931, v. 26, pp. 198-201.
***Endress, Im Hof.** Geneal. hist. of Endress family. W. F. Endress. Knickerbocker Press, 1926, 1st ed. MHS.
Engel. Roop geneal. Pamph. MHS.
England. Ancestry of Wm. Haines. Cregar. MHS.
Balto., its hist., its people. Hall. V. 2. MHS; DAR.
Griffith geneal. Griffith. MHS; DAR.
England, Charles. Md. Soc., War of 1812, v. 2, no. 176. Ms. MHS.
Englar. Roop geneal. Pamph. MHS.
Englar, Carroll Co. Newsp. clipp., bd. MHS.
***Englar Family.** Descendants of Philip Englar, 1736-1817, traced five generations. Charts V. Englar Barnes. Taneytown, Md., Carroll Record Print, 1929, pamph. MHS; DAR.
Geneal. descendants of Philip Englar, 1736-1817. Taneytown, Md., Carroll Record Print, pamph. DAR.
Miscellaneous papers. Ms. MHS.
Engle. St. Paul's Parish, Balto. V. 1, 2, 4. Mss. MHS.
Engle Family. Natl. Geneal. Soc. Quart., v. 25, p. 98.
*Shenandoah Valley. W. Va. Hist. Mag., v. 5, no. 2, pp. 153-56.
Engler-Wedge. Lineage Bks., natl. Soc. of Daughters of Amer. Col., v. 4, pp. 47, 61. MHS; DAR.
English. Col. families of U. S. A. Mackenzie. V. 4, pp. 142-47 (Del.); v. 7, p. 476. MHS; DAR.
Cummings chart. Lib. Cong.; MHS; DAR.
Orme geneal. chart. MHS.
Rec. of Stepney Parish. MHS; DAR.
St. Stephens Parish, Cecilton, Md. MHS; DAR.
Enloes. Naturalizations in Md., 1666-1765; Laws. Bacon. MHS.
Enloes, Inloes. Md. Geneal. Rec. Com., 1938-39, pp. 182-85. Mss. DAR.
Enlow. *See* Thompson-Enlow.
Enlow, Jeremiah. Bible rec. Md. Geneal. Bull., v. 3, p. 30; v. 4, p. 29; v. 5, p. 13. MHS; DAR.
Enn. Christ P. E. Church cemetery, Cambridge. Steele. 1936. MHS; DAR.
†**Ennals, Col. Thomas** (War of 1812). M. H. Mag., 1910, v. 5, p. 252.
Ennalls. Abr. Compend. Amer. Geneal. Virkus. V. 6, pp. 30, 437. DAR.
Ances. rec. and portraits. Col. Dames of Amer., 1910, v. 1, p. 148; v. 2, p. 681. MHS; DAR.
Mrs. Howard Bruce chart. MHS.
Christ P. E. Church cemetery, Cambridge. Steele. 1936. MHS; DAR.
Col. families of Amer. Lawrence. V. 16, p. 91. MHS.
*Hist. of Dorchester Co. Jones. 1925, pp. 310-14. MHS; DAR.
Md. families. Culver. Ms. Personal list.
Memorial to Thomas Potts, Jr. James. P. 248. MHS.
Pedigree of Franklin Buchanan Owen. Soc. Col. Wars Md. Culver. 1940. MHS; DAR.
Pedigree of Pleasants Pennington. Soc. Col. Wars Md. Culver. 1940. MHS; DAR.
Pedigree of Tilghman Goldsborough Pitts.

Soc. Col. Wars Md. Culver. 1940. MHS; DAR.
Pedigree of Maurice Edward Skinner. Soc. Col. Wars Md. Culver. 1940. MHS; DAR.
Pedigree of Rev. Sam'l Tagart Steele. Soc. Col. Wars Md. Culver. 1940. MHS; DAR.
Mrs. E. W. Poe chart. MHS.
Miss Kate Steele chart. MHS.
*The Sun, Balto., May 6, 1906.
See Waggaman-Ennalls.
Ennalls-Haskins-Dupuy. Chart. Dupuy family. Dupuy. P. 68. MHS.
Ennalls-Waggaman Families, Somerset Co. William and Mary Quart., 1st series, 1894, v. 2, pp. 98, 135.
Ennalls Line. Col. and Revolutionary lineages of Amer. 1939, v. 3, p. 287. MHS.
Ennis. Evergreen cemetery, Worcester Co., Hudson. Bd. ms. MHS; DAR.
Md. gleanings in Eng. Wills. M. H. Mag., 1907, v. 2, no. 3.
St. Paul's P. E. churchyard, Berlin, Worcester Co. Hudson. Bd. ms. MHS; DAR. Also: Md. Geneal. Rec. Com., 1937, Mrs. Lines. Mss. DAR.
St. Paul's Parish, Balto. V. 1, 2. Mss. MHS.
Turner Geneal. Coll. Ms. MHS.
Ensor. Bohemia Manor. Mallory. P. 23. MHS.
Cary Geneal. Coll. Ms. MHS.
Cole-Price chart. Cary Geneal. Coll. Ms. MHS.
Descendants of Joran Kyn. Pa. Mag., v. 7, p. 299.
*Hist. of Cecil Co. Johnston. P. 178. MHS; DAR.
Md. families. Ms. Personal list.
See McArthur, L. A. Abr. Compend. Amer. Geneal. Virkus. V. 1, p. 703. DAR.
Merryman family. Culver. M. H. Mag., 1915, v. 10, pp. 176, 286.
Stansbury chart. Cary Geneal. Coll. Ms. MHS.
St. Paul's Parish, Balto. V. 1, 2. Mss. MHS.
Ensor, John S. Geneal. and mem. encyc. of Md. Spencer. V. 1, p. 202. MHS; DAR.
Ensor Family (1739–1840). Md. Geneal. Rec. Com., 1937. Parran. Pp. 106–07. Mss. DAR.
*Wilson Mrs. Coll., no. 4. MHS.
Ensor Family, Balto. Co. Geneal. notes, 1739–1905. Md. Geneal. Rec. Com., 1937, p. 106. DAR.
Ensor-Oldham, Cecil and Balto. Cos. Bible rec. Upper Penins. East. Shore, p. 251–57. MHS; DAR.
Entler, York, Pa., and Md. A. L. Thomsen, H. I. Thomsen, J. J. Thomsen pedigree chart. Soc. Col. Wars, Md. Johnston. 1905, p. 112. MHS.
Eppes. Ances. rec. and portraits, Col. Dames of Amer., 1910, v. 1, p. 276. MHS; DAR.
***Eppes,** Va. The Sun, Balto., June 3, 10, 1906.
Epps. St. Paul's P. E. churchyard, Berlin, Worcester Co. Hudson. Bd. ms. MHS; DAR. Also: Md. Geneal. Rec. Com., 1937, Mrs. Lines. Mss. DAR.
†Epstein, Jacob. Men of mark in Md. Johnson. V. 3. DAR; Enoch Pratt Lib.
Epsy Family, Ireland, Pa. and Md. (1610–1930). Md. Geneal. Rec. Com., 1933–34, pp. 187–90. Mss. DAR.
Ergood (married Harve de Grace, 1837). Bible rec. natl. Geneal. Soc. Quart., v. 25, p. 86.
†Erich. Med. Annals Md. Cordell. 1903, p. 392. MHS.
Erickson. Naturalizations in Md., 1666–1765; Laws. Bacon. MHS.
St. Paul's Parish, Balto. V. 2. Mss. MHS.
Erskine. Natl. Geneal. Soc. Quart., v. 7, no. 3, pp. 45–48.
Erskine, Cecil Co. Abr. Compend. Amer. Geneal. Virkus. V. 1, p. 593. DAR.
Erwin. Copy of will of Robert Erwin, and copies of Erwin and allied rec. from court house in Cecil Co. Geneal. Soc. Pa. Mss. Coll.
***Eskridge,** Va. The Sun, Balto., Sept. 17, 1905.
Este. Mrs. A. G. Ober chart. MHS.
See Reynolds. Abr. Compend. Amer. Geneal. Virkus. V. 1, p. 794. DAR.
Estep. Col. families of U. S. A. Mackenzie V. 7, p. 241. MHS; DAR.
Md. families. Culver. Ms. Personal list.
***Estep Family.** Wilson. Mss. Coll., no. 10. MHS.
Etherington. St. Stephens Parish, Cecilton, Md. MHS; DAR.
Etting. Newsp. clipp. Scrap Book no. 7. MHS.
†Etting, Solomon (1764–1847). M. H. Mag., 1920, v. 15, pp. 1–20.
Etting Family. Hist. Typed. File case, MHS.
***Etzer.** Frederick Co. families. Markell. Ms. Personal list.
John Swadner and his descendants. Evans. 1919. Typed, bd. MHS.
Eubank. Third Haven Friends Meeting House, Easton. Vital rec. MHS. Also: Natl. Geneal. Soc. Quart., v. 11, no. 1, pp. 9–14.
Evains. Rec. of Stepney Parish. MHS; DAR.
Evans. Amer. families, geneal. and heraldic. Amer. Hist. Soc., pp. 303–07. In vault, DAR.
Ancestry of Rosalie Morris Johnson. Johnson. 1905. MHS; DAR.
Bible rec. Upper Penins. East. Shore. Pp. 5–8, 137. MHS; DAR.
†Biog. cyc. of rep. men of Md. and D. C. P. 171. MHS; DAR.
Botfield and allied families. Ms. DAR.
Chart. of Edith Corse Evans. Amy Hull. Mss. MHS.
Col. and Revolutionary families of Phila. Jordan. V. 1. DAR.
Descendants of Valentine Hollingsworth, Sr. Stewart. MHS; DAR.
Dorsey chart. MHS.
Fox-Ellicott-Evans families. Evans. MHS; DAR.
Greenway chart. MHS.
Hist. of Balto. Lewis Pub. Co., 1912, v. 2, p. 482. DAR.
*Hist. of Nathaniel Evans and his descendants. J. D. Evans. MHS.
†Hist. of Frederick Co. Williams. V. 2, p. 1089. MHS; DAR.
Jackson family gathering. 1878.
Md. to W. Va. Col. and Revolutionary families of Phila. Jordan. 1933, v. 1, pp. 402–04.
†Med. Annals Md. Cordell. 1903, pp. 392–93. MHS.
†Memoir of Hugh Davey Evans, founded on recollections, written by himself. Hall Harrison. (Balto., 1792–1869; in Harford Co., 1870.) MHS.

Evans. Patriotic Md. Md. Soc. of S. A. R., 1930. MHS; DAR.
Portrait and biog. rec. of Harford and Cecil Cos. 1897. Pp. 126–28, 579–80. MHS; DAR.
Somerset Co. Court Book. Tilghman. 1937. Ms. DAR.
(48 references.) St. Paul's Parish, Balto. V. 1, 2, 3, 4. Mss. MHS.
Tercentenary hist. of Md. Andrews. V. 2, p. 823; v. 3, pp. 18, 277; v. 4, pp. 433, 553. MHS; DAR.
Wicomico Co. families. Bible rec. Ms. DAR.
*Wicomico Co. families. Tilghman. Ms, pp. 19, 76, 100, 118, 121. DAR.
See Key-Evans.
See Ridgely-Dorsey-Evans.
Evans, Cecil Co. Carton charts. MHS.
Evans, Queen Anne Co. Bible rec. Upper Penins. East. Shore, pp. 52, 137.
Evans, Dr. Amos Alexander. Extracts from diary, 1812–13. Patriotic Marylander, v. 3, no. 3, p. 177. MHS; DAR.
†(Born near Elkton, Md., 1785; died at Elkton, 1848). M. H. Mag., v. 12, p. 216.
Evans, C. R. Md. Soc., War of 1812, v. 3, no. 269. Ms. MHS.
Evans, Lieut. Griffith (Revolutionary soldier). St. Paul's P. E. graveyard. Patriotic Marylander, v. 2, no. 4, pp. 54–60. MHS; DAR.
Evans, Gustavus Warfield. Pedigree. Soc. Col. Wars Md. Culver. 1940. MHS; DAR.
Evans, Henry Cotheal. Pedigree. Soc. Col. Wars Md. Culver. 1940. MHS; DAR.
†Evans, Mary Garrettson (The Sun, Balto., 1888). Ladies of press. Ross. 1936.
Evans, Stuart, Sarah and Frances E. Bible rec. Md. Geneal. Rec. Com., 1926, pp. 6, 128. Typed bd. DAR.
Evans Family. Bible rec., Kent Co., 1773–1864. Md. Geneal. Rec. Com., 1932–33, pp. 321–22. Mss. DAR.
*Bible rec. Md. Geneal. Rec. Com., 1932–33, pp. 321–22. DAR.
Bible rec. Photos. DAR.
Dupuy family. Dupuy. Pp. 85–91. MHS.
*Hist. of Cecil Co. Johnston. Pp. 485–95. MHS; DAR.
Evans-Mountain Family. Old Kent Chapter, D. A. R. Bible rec. of East. Shore of Md. Md. Geneal. Rec. Com., 1926–29, pp. 31–35. Mss. Book. DAR.
Evans-Reynolds-DuPuy. Chart. Dupuy family. Dupuy. P. 83. MHS.
†Evelin. Papers relating to early hist. of Md. Streeter. 1876. MHS.
***Evelyn.** Evelyns in Amer., 1608–1805. (Evelyns on Kent Island, Md., 1636, pp. 1–45.) G. D. Scull. Oxford Parker Co., 1881, pr. for priv. circu., 392 pp. MHS; DAR.
Evenson. St. Paul's Parish, Balto. V. 1. Mss. MHS.
†Everden, Thomas (died in Md. 1710). Index to biog. sketches pub. in "The Friend," v. 26, v. 27. Pub. Geneal. Soc. Pa., v. 3, no. 2, pp. 109–34.
Everdson, Everson. St. Stephens Parish, Cecilton, Md. MHS; DAR.
Everett. Legacies of R., 1831. Ms. MHS.
*Old Kent. Hanson. P. 261. MHS; DAR.
Everett, John, Balto. Co. Will probated April 26, 1758. D. A. R. Mag., v. 65, no. 8, p. 506.
***Everhart.** Everhart-Miller and allied families. A. E. Miller. 1931. DAR.
*Frederick Co. families. Markell. Ms. Personal list.
*Hist. of Everhart and Shower family, 1744–1883, embracing six generations. O. T. Everhart. Incl. account of Weaver family of Frederick Co. Also sketch of Manchester, Md. Hanover, York Co., Pa., 1883.
Hist. of West. Md. Scharf. V. 1, p. 454. MHS; DAR.
St. Paul's Parish, Balto. V. 1, 2. Mss. MHS.
Tercentenary hist. of Md. Andrews. V. 4, p. 594. MHS; DAR.
†Everheart, Lawrence, Frederick Co. Hist. of Md. Scharf. V. 2, p. 408. MHS.
Everit, John, Balto. Co. Will probated May 12, 1760. D. A. R. Mag., v. 65, no. 8, p. 505.
***Everly.** Frederick Co. families. Markell. Ms. Personal list.
Eversfield. Bowies and their kindred. Bowie. MHS; DAR.
Bowie chart. Cary Geneal. Coll. Ms. MHS.
Mrs. Charles Carter chart. MHS.
Carlyle family and Carlyle house. Spencer. P. 24. MHS.
Mrs. C. C. Hall chart. MHS.
†Med. Annals Md. 1903, pp. 392–93. MHS.
Pedigree of Thomas Carroll Roberts. Soc. Col. Wars. Md. Culver. 1940. MHS; DAR.
Pedigree of Wm. Emory Waring, Jr. Soc. Col. Wars. Md. Culver. 1940. MHS; DAR.
Mrs. G. H. Williams, Jr., chart. MHS.
***Eversfield Line.** Arms. The Sun, Balto., April 9, 1905.
Eversol. M. E. Church, South cemetery, near Poolesville, Montgomery Co. Md. Geneal. Rec. Com., 1926. Mss. DAR.
Everson. *See* Everdson.
Everton. St. Paul's Parish, Balto. V. 1, 2, 4. Mss. MHS.
Evett. *See* Evitt.
Evitt, Evett. St. Stephens Parish, Cecilton, Md. MHS; DAR.
***Evitts.** *See* Emerson-Evitts.
Ewell. Amer. Armory and Blue Book. Matthews. Pt. 3.
Balto., its hist., its people. Hall. V. 3. MHS; DAR.
Hist. of Balto. Lewis Pub. Co., 1912, v. 3, p. 639.
Ewell, Va. Col. families of U. S. A. Mackenzie. V. 5, pp. 202–06. MHS; DAR.
Va. geneal. Hayden. MHS; DAR.
Ewell, Va. and Md. Amer. Clan Gregor Year Book, 1909–10, p. 63; 1914, pp. 39–44; 1915, p. 75; 1916, p. 36; 1917, p. 65; 1919, p. 97; 1921, p. 44. MHS; DAR.
***Ewell Family,** East. Shore of Md. Wilson Mss. Coll., no. 75. MHS.
Ewen. See Robertson, Mrs. H. Abr. Compend. Amer. Geneal. Virkus. V. 1, p. 802. DAR.
Talbott of "Poplar Knowle." Shirk. MHS; DAR.
Ewens. Ancest. rec. and portraits. Col. Dames of Amer., 1910, v. 2, p. 567. MHS; DAR.
Cary Geneal. Coll. Ms. MHS.
See Ewen-Hutchins-Kinsey-Thomas. Lineage Bks., Natl. Soc. of Daughters of Amer. Col., v. 4, p. 269. MHS; DAR.
*Lineage Bk., Daughters of Amer. Colonists,

v. 2, pp. 61, 297–98; v. 4, pp. 268–69; v. 5, pp. 208–09. MHS; DAR.
Md. families. Culver. Ms. Personal list.
Pedigree of Morris Gregg. Soc. Col. Wars Md. Culver. 1940. MHS; DAR.
Pedigree of Benedict Henry Hanson, Jr. Soc. Col. Wars Md. Culver. 1940. MHS; DAR.
Pedigree of Charles Worthington Hoff. Soc. Col. Wars Md. Culver. 1940. MHS; DAR.
Ewin. Geneal. Letter from Richard Ewin. Ms. File case, MHS.
***Ewing.** Balto. Co. Lineage Bk. Daughters of Amer. Colonists. V. 1, p. 278. MHS; DAR.
*Clan Ewing of Scotland. E. W. R. Ewing. Ballston, Va., Cobden Pub. Co., 1923.
*Ewing geneal.; with cognate branches. P. K. Ewing and M. E. W. Ewing. 1919. DAR.
Ewing geneal. with kin in Amer. P. K. Kittredge and M. E. Ewing. Houston, Tex., agent J. H. Witney, 1919. MHS; DAR.
*Frederick Co. families. Markell. Ms. Personal list.
†Hist. of Balto. City and Co. Scharf. P. 839. MHS.
In John Heard family, Va. McCall-Tedwell families. McCall. Pp. 557–59. MHS; DAR.
McSpadden-Love-Meigs-Clendinen-Von Bibber-Pope chart. MHS.
Ewing, Cecil Co. and St. Louis, Mo. Abr. Compend. Amer. Geneal. Virkus. V. 1, pp. 595–96. DAR.
Ewing, Mrs. Henry Gordon (Carolyn Winslow Sanford). Chart. Col. Dames, Chap. I. MHS.
†Eyler. Hist. of Frederick Co. Williams. V. 2, pp. 733, 836, 837, 1455. MHS; DAR.
Eyre. Ances. rec. and portraits. Col. Dames of Amer. 1910. P. 485. MHS; DAR.
J. T. Dennis pedigree chart, plate 2. Soc. Col. Wars, Md. Johnston. 1905, p. 22. MHS.
Miss G. Eyre Wright chart. MHS.
Eyre, Va. Mrs. Henry DuPont Baldwin chart. MHS.
Eyres. *See* Ayre.
***Eyster.** Bible rec. D. C. Geneal. Rec. Com., 1937–38, v. 37, p. 130. Typed, bd. DAR.
Florence Eyster Weaver chart. MHS.
***Eyster, George** (1757–1836). Revolutionary soldier; married Mary M. Slagle. (Chart of Florence Eyster Weaver on line.) Ms. DAR.
***Eyster Family.** Hist. of Emmitsburg. Helman. P. 60.

F

Fackler. Hagerstown tombstone inscriptions. Gruder. Natl. Geneal. Soc. Quart., 1919, v. 8, nos. 1, 2.
Fackney. St. Paul's Parish, Balto. V. 1. Mss. MHS.
Fagan, Fegan. Branch of family tree. (James Fagan, born in Kent Co. about 1720–25; died about 1791–95.) Ms. File case, DAR.
Fahnestock. Abr. Compend. Amer. Geneal. Virkus. V. 6, p. 687. DAR.
Balto., its hist., its people. Hall. V. 3. MHS; DAR.
Col. families of Amer. Lawrence. V. 3, pp. 289–90, 302. MHS.
Fahnestock, Mrs. Gibson. Ancestry. Mrs. Frederick Eldridge chart. MHS.
(Caroline Snowden Andrews). Chart. Col. Dames, Chap. I, MHS.
***Fahnestock Family.** Memorial in U. S. A. K. and W. F. Fahnestock. Descendants of Diedrick Fahnestock, born in Germany, Feb. 2, 1696, died in Amer. Oct. 10, 1775. Family register, 1696–1877, pp. 25–68; Fahnestocks in Balto., pp. 61–2, 68. Harrisburg, Pa., S. W. Fleming, 1879. MHS.
Fahrney. Englas family. Barnes. MHS; DAR.
†Hist. of Washington Co. Williams. 1906, v. 2, p. 1253. MHS; DAR.
Fairbank. Col. families of U. S. A. Mackenzie. V. 4, p. 299. MHS; DAR.
Fairbanks, Talbot Co. Evans family chart. Hull. Mss. MHS.
Fairchild. *See* Avery-Fairchild-Park Families.
Fairfax. Amer. Armory and Blue Book. Matthews. 1911–12, p. 306.
Ancestral rec. and portraits. Col. Dames of Amer., 1910, v. 2, pp. 641–49. MHS; DAR.
Balch chart. MHS.
Barroll chart. MHS.
Boone chart. MHS.
Bowie-Claggett chart. MHS.
Chart. Ancestors and descendants of Col. David Funsten. Randolph. P. 32. MHS.
Fairfax family notes of Eng. Ms. MHS.
General notes of Thomas family. Thomas. MHS; DAR.
Md. families. Culver. Ms. Personal list.
Neill chart. MHS.
Pedigree of Mark Alexander Herbert Smith. Soc. Col. Wars Md. Culver. 1940. MHS; DAR.
See Smith. Abr. Compend. Amer. Geneal. Virkus. V. 6, p. 744. DAR.
*The Sun, Balto., Jan. 15, 1905.
Va. families. Du Bellett.
See Smith.
Fairfax, Charles Co. Side lights on Md. hist. Richardson. V. 2, p. 313. MHS; DAR.
Fairfax, Va. and Md. Col. families of U. S. A. Mackenzie. V. 2, pp. 264–83. MHS; DAR.
***Fairfax, John Walter.** Burke's landed gentry. 1939. MHS.
Fairfax Family. Lee of Va., 1642–1892. E. J. Lee. P. 147. Lib. Cong., MHS.
Thomas Book. Thomas. Pp. 303–12. Lib. Cong.; MHS.
Fairfax Line. Mrs. Lee Barroll chart. MHS.
Fairlamb. Sharpless family geneal. Cope. P. 1165. MHS; DAR.
Falconer, Harry Willson. Pedigree. Soc. Col. Wars Md. Culver. 1940. MHS; DAR.
Falconer, Faulkner. St. Paul's Parish, Balto. V. 2, 3. Mss. MHS.
Fales. St. Paul's Parish, Balto. V. 2. Mss. MHS.
Fallin. Tombstone rec. of Dorchester Co. Jones. DAR.
Fallowfield. Centreville cemetery. Md. O. R. Soc. Bull., no. 1, pp. 41–47.
Falls. Manning chart. MHS.
Mrs. E. W. Poe chart. MHS.
Faries. *See* Edwards, Faris, Bouldin.
Faris. *See* Edwards, Faris, Bouldin.
Faris-Pitt. Bible rec. Ms. MHS.
Farman. *See* Foreman-Farman-Forman.
Farmer. *See* Duvall-Farmer-Waters.
Farmer Family. Miss Inex Osborn. Harford Co. Hist. Soc. Mss. Coll. JHU.
Farnadis. See Smithson. Hist. of Harford Co. Preston. MHS; DAR.

†**Farnandis.** Chesapeake Bay Country. Earle. P. 248. MHS.
Griffith geneal. Griffith. MHS; DAR.
†**Farquhar.** Hist. of West. Md. Scharf. V. 2, p. 790. MHS; DAR.
Plummer family. A. P. H. Ms. MHS.
Sharpless family geneal. Cope. Pp. 202, 518. MHS; DAR.
Farquhar, Sandy Springs. Abr. Compend. Amer. Geneal. Virkus. V. 1, pp. 101–02. DAR.
Farquhar Family. Thomas Book. Thomas. P. 313. Lib. Cong.; MHS.
Farquharson. Christ P. E. Church cemetery, Cambridge. Steele. 1936. MHS; DAR.
Farrington. Rec. of Stepney Parish. MHS; DAR.
Farris. *See* Edwards, Faris, Bouldin.
Farrow. All Hallow's P. E. churchyard, Snow Hill, Worcester Co. Hudson. Bd. ms. MHS; DAR. Also: Md. Geneal. Rec. Com., 1935–36, p. 24. Mss. DAR.
†**Farrow, J. Miles.** Men of mark in Md. Johnson. V. 2. DAR; Enoch Pratt Lib.
Fassitt. Bible rec., from Bible owned by T. J. Fassitt, Berlin, Md., 1850–1910. (First birth 1776.) Md. Geneal. Rec. Com., 1937–38, p. 139. Mss. DAR.
Buckingham Pres. churchyard, Worcester Co. Hudson. Bd. ms. MHS; DAR.
Evergreen cemetery, Worcester Co. Hudson. Bd. ms. MHS; DAR.
†Med. Annals Md. Cordell. 1903, p. 394. MHS.
†Old Buckingham by the Sea, East. Shore of Md. Page. DAR.
Pattison Bible rec. Ms. MHS.
St. Paul's P. E. churchyard, Berlin, Worcester Co. Hudson. Bd. ms. MHS; DAR. Also: Md. Geneal. Rec. Com., 1937, Mrs. Lines. Mss. DAR.
See Gilliss-Fassitt.
Fassitt, Worcester Co. Pub. Geneal. Soc. Pa., v. 8, p. 197 (footnote).
Fassitt-McGregor. Bible rec., 1774–1878. Bible owned by Miss McGregor, Berlin, Md. Md. Geneal. Rec. Com., 1937–38, pp. 140–41. Mss. DAR.
Faulkner. Hist. Graves of Md. and D. C. Ridgely. MHS.
Spring Hill Cemetery, Talbot Co. Md. O. R. Soc. Bull., no. 1, pp. 35–41. MHS.
See Falconer.
Faunt Le Roy. John Swadner and his descendants. Evans. 1919. Typed, bd. MHS.
***Fauntleroys,** Va. The Sun, Balto., Nov. 11, 1906.
Fause. *See* Fouse.
Faw. *See* Lowe Bible rec. Ms. MHS.
Fawcett. McClellan chart. MHS.
†**Feaga.** Hist. of West. Md. Scharf. V. 1, p. 558. MHS; DAR.
†**Fearhake.** Men of mark in Md. Johnson. V. 1. DAR; Enoch Pratt Lib.
***Fearson,** 1720–1792. Lineage Bk. Daughters of Amer. Colonists. V. 1, p. 31. MHS; DAR.
St. Paul's Parish, Balto. V. 1, 2, 3. Mss. MHS.
Young Bible rec. Ms. MHS.
***Fearson,** Port Tobacco. Lineage Bk., Daughters of Founders and Patriots, v. 14, p. 94. MHS.
Fearson, Pezivel, Charles Co. Will, 1727. Ms. File case, DAR.
Fechtig. Hagerstown tombstone inscriptions. Gruder. Natl. Geneal. Soc. Quart., 1919, v. 8, nos. 1, 2.
Fechtig, Wash. Co. Beatty family. Pa. geneal. Egle. P. 78–81. MHS.
Feddeman. Hist. Graves of Md. and D. C. Ridgely. MHS.
*Old Kent. Hanson. P. 233. MHS; DAR.
Spring Hill Cemetery, Talbot Co. Md. O. R. Soc. Bull., no. 1, pp. 35–41. MHS.
Federline. St. John's R. C. Church cemetery, Montgomery Co. Md. Geneal. Rec. Com., 1926, p. 27. Mss. DAR.
Fee. Abr. Compend. Amer. Geneal. Virkus. V. 6, p. 41. DAR.
Fegan. *See* Fagan.
Feige. *See* Fike.
Feigley, Fugely, Figely. Hagerstown tombstone inscriptions. Gruder. Natl. Geneal. Soc. Quart., 1919, v. 8, nos. 1, 2.
Feldner. Balto., its hist., its people. Hall. V. 2. MHS; DAR.
Fell. Bond chart. MHS.
Bond family geneal. Ms. MHS.
F. S. Hambleton pedigree chart. Soc. Col. Wars, Md. Johnston. 1905, p. 33. MHS.
Md. families. Culver. Ms. Personal list.
Mrs. James McHenry chart. MHS.
Pedigree of T. Edward Hambleton. Soc. Col. Wars Md. Culver. 1940. MHS; DAR.
St. Paul's Parish, Balto. V. 1. Mss. MHS.
†**Fell, Thomas.** Biog. dict. of U. S. J. H. Lamb Co., v. 1, p. 332.
†Men of mark in Md. Johnson. V. 1. DAR; Enoch Pratt Lib.
***Fell Family.** Arch. of Georgetown Univ., Wash., D. C., v. 287.
Bible rec. Gorsuch and allied families. Harrison. Mss. MHS.
Fellers, Fellows. St. Paul's Parish, Balto. V. 1, 2. Mss. MHS.
Fellows. Col. families of U. S. A. Mackenzie. V. 5. MHS; DAR.
St. Stephens Parish, Cecilton, Md. MHS; DAR.
Fenby. Tombstone rec. of Glendy burying ground. Md. Geneal. Rec. Com., 1933–34, pp. 171–78. Mss. DAR.
Fendall. Beall and Bell families. Beall. MHS.
Bowies and their kindred. Bowie. MHS; DAR.
Family data of Amer. Fendalls. (John Fendall born in Charles Co., 1672; married Elizabeth Hanson.) Typed, 8 pp. MHS.
Founders of Anne Arundel and Howard Cos. Warfield. P. 47. MHS; DAR.
Lee Mag. of Va., May, 1925, v. 3, no. 1, p. 16. MHS.
*Lineage Bk. Daughters of Amer. Colonists. V. 4, p. 301. MHS; DAR.
Pedigree of Garner Wood Denmead. Soc. Col. Wars Md. Culver. 1940. MHS; DAR.
St. Paul's Parish, Balto. V. 3. Mss. MHS.
*Semmes Geneal. Coll. Ms. MHS.
Mrs. G. R. Veazey chart. MHS.
***Fendall Family.** Arch. of Georgetown Univ., Wash., D. C., v. 287.
Notes. M. H. Mag., v. 1, no. 3, p. 291.
Fenley, Finley. Col. and Revolutionary families of Pa. Amer. Hist. Soc., N. Y., 1934, p. 14.
Fenner. Ances. rec. and portraits. Col. Dames of Amer., 1910, v. 1, p. 189. MHS; DAR.
Fenton. St. Paul's Parish, Balto. V. 1, 2, 3. Mss. MHS.

†**Fenton, M. C.** Men of mark in Md. Johnson. V. 4. DAR; Enoch Pratt Lib.
***Fenton Family.** Arch. of Georgetown Univ., Wash., D. C., v. 287.
***Fenwick.** Allied ancestry. Ancestry of Thomas Fenwick of Sussex Co., Del. E. J. Sellers. Md. ref., pp. 26–27. Phila., 1916. MHS.
Ancest. rec. and portraits. Col. Dames of Amer., 1910, v. 2, p. 539–44. MHS; DAR.
J. L. Brent pedigree chart. Soc. Col. Wars, Md. Johnston. 1905, p. 7. MHS.
Children of Alex Pand. M. C. Hill. Ms. MHS.
Clark chart. MHS.
Conway family, Va. Ms. DAR.
†Day-Star of Amer. Freedom. Davis. P. 207. MHS; DAR.
†Right Rev. Edw. Dominic Fenwick, O.P. V. F. O'Daniel. 2nd ed., 1921. DAR.
Few abs. from will book at Annapolis. William and Mary Quart., 1st series, v. 13, p. 27.
Graves (5 stones), Charles Co., 1794–1824. Md. Geneal. Rec. Com., 1935–36, p. 33. DAR.
Hist. graves of Md. and D. C. Ridgely. MHS.
R. B. Keyser pedigree chart, plate 2. Soc. Col. Wars, Md. Johnston. 1905, p. 56. MHS.
Manly chart. MHS.
Md. families. Culver. Ms. Personal list.
†Med. Annals Md. Cordell. 1903, p. 395. MHS.
Parr chart. MHS.
Patriotic Md. Md. Soc. of S. A. R., 1930. MHS; DAR.
Pedigree of Duncan Keener Brent. Soc. Col. Wars Md. Culver. 1940. MHS; DAR.
Raisin chart. MHS.
St. Inigoes churchyard, St. Mary's Co. Md. O. R. Soc. Bull., no. 3, p. 58.
St. John's R. C. Church cemetery, Montgomery Co. Md. Geneal. Rec. Com., 1926, p. 27. Mss. DAR.
*Semmes Geneal. Coll. Ms. MHS.
Side lights on Md. hist. Richardson. V. 2, p. 98. MHS; DAR.
Tiernan families. Tiernan. 1901, p. 369. MHS; DAR.
Tombstones, Charles Co. Md. Geneal. Rec. Com., 1935–36, p. 33. Mss. DAR.
*The Sun, Balto., Oct. 30, Nov. 20, 1904; Dec. 16, 1906.
Fenwick, St. Mary's Co. Abs. of will, 1806. D. A. R. Mag., Aug., 1927, v. 61, no. 8, p. 607.
Fenwick, James, St. Mary's Co. Will 1806. D. A. R. Mag., v. 61, no. 8, p. 607.
***Fenwick Family.** Arch. of Georgetown Univ., Wash., D. C., v. 130, no. 7.
(Magna Charta claims.) Ms. File case, DAR.
Fenwick Family, Somerset Co. Allied families of Delaware. Sellers. MHS.
***Fenwick Family,** Southern Md. Wilson Mss. Coll., no. 50. MHS.
Ferdinando. Naturalizations in Md., 1666–1765; Laws. Bacon. MHS.
Ferguson. Christ. P. E. Church cemetery, Cambridge. Steele. 1936. MHS; DAR.
Dorsey and allied families. Ms. MHS.
*Ferguson family in Scotland and Amer. (Contents: Hist. of Ferguson family in Scotland, by James Ferguson; Hist. of Md. branch of Ferguson family in Amer., by Martin Luther Ferguson.) Canandaigua, N. Y., Times, 1905.
Hist. graves of Md. and D. C. Ridgely. MHS.
†Med. Annals Md. Cordell. 1903, p. 395. MHS.
Papers. Letters and documents, 1761–81, showing Ferguson family, and Slemons notes. Not indexed. Ms. MHS.
St. Paul's Parish, Balto. V. 1, 2, 3. Mss. MHS.
Ferguson, J. Henry. Pedigree. Soc. Col. Wars Md. Culver. 1940. MHS; DAR.
Ferguson, Levi, and Kezia B. (Jessop). Ferguson marriage license, 1855. Ms. MHS.
***Ferguson Family.** Arch. of Georgetown Univ., Wash., D. C., v. 287.
Graves, Port Tobacco, Charles Co., 1768–1922. Md. Geneal. Rec. Com., 1932–33. DAR.
The Pilot, Union Bridge, Friday, Aug. 4, 1911. Newsp. clipp. Ferguson papers. MHS.
Ferguson-Morris (Pa.)-Hill. Abr. Compend. Amer. Geneal. Virkus. V. 4, pp. 179–80. MHS.
†**Ferree.** Hist. of West. Md. Scharf. V. 2, pp. 916–17. MHS; DAR.
Ferree-Eltinge, Carroll Co. Hist. of West. Md. Scharf. V. 2, pp. 916–17.
***Ferrel Family.** Arch. of Georgetown Univ., Wash., D. C., v. 287.
***Ferris Family.** Arch. of Georgetown Univ., Wash., D. C., v. 233, no. 6.
Fesler. Mrs. E. Worthington chart. MHS.
Fiddis. Chestertown cemetery. Md. O. R. Soc. Bull., no. 1, pp. 18–29.
Fidlar. McClellan chart. MHS.
Field. *See* Fields.
Field-Williamson-Stevenson. Chart, photos., 3 sheets. Cary Geneal. Coll. Ms. MHS.
Fielding-Reid. Col. families of U. S. A. Mackenzie. V. 7. MHS; DAR.
Fields. Md. tombstone rec. Md. Geneal. Rec. Com., 1937, Parran, p. 3. Mss. DAR.
*Wicomico Co. families. Tilghman. Ms, p. 59. DAR.
Fields, Field. St. Paul's Paris, Balto. V. 1, 2, 3, 4. Mss. MHS.
Figely. *See* Feigley.
Fightmaster. St. Paul's Parish, Balto. V. 1. Mss. MHS.
Fike, Feige, Fyke. Mountain Democrat, Garrett Co., Dec. 13, 1934. Newsp. clipp. MHS; DAR.
Fillingham, Fillingham. St. Stephens Parish, Cecilton, Md. MHS; DAR.
Finch. Md. gleanings in Eng. Wills. M. H. Mag., 1909, v. 4, no. 2.
Finch, Francis. Will. Md. Geneal. Bull., v. 1, p. 30. MHS; DAR.
Fincher. Russell family. Russell. 1889, 2nd ed. MHS.
Findlay, John Van Lear. Torrence and allied families. Torrence. P. 282. MHS; DAR.
Findley. John O'Donnell of Balto. Cook. MHS.
Finlay, Findlay. St. Paul's Parish, Balto. V. 1, 2. Mss. MHS.
***Finley.** Boyd family. Boyd. DAR.
Cummings chart. Lib. Cong.; MHS; DAR.
*Finleys of Md., 1638–1878. Md. Geneal. Rec. Com., 1932, v. 5, pp. 1–19. DAR.
See Fenley.
Finley, Charles Beatty. Pedigree. Soc. Col. Wars. Md. Culver. 1940. MHS; DAR.
Finley, Charles Beatty, Jr. Pedigree. Soc. Col. Wars Md. Culver. 1940. MHS; DAR.

Finley, Findlay, Lineage. Torrence and allied families. Torrence. Pp. 187–295; John Van Lear Findlay, p. 282. MHS; DAR.
Finn. St. Paul's Parish, Balto. V. 1. Mss. MHS.
Finney. Descendants of Joran Kyne of New Sweden. Keen. MHS; DAR.
Descendants of Joran Kyn. Pa. Mag., v. 7, p. 464.
Finney, Rev. Wm. Hist. of Bethel Presbyterian Church. Cross. P. 27. DAR.
Finotti. Children of Alex P. and M. C. Hill. Ms. MHS.
Fischer. Gary chart. MHS.
Pedigree of Henry Irvine Keyser, II. Soc. Col. Wars Md. Culver. 1940. MHS; DAR.
See Fisher.
***Fish.** Wicomico Co. families. Tilghman. Ms., p. 101. DAR.
***Fishbourne.** Wharton family, Phila. Pa. Mag. Hist. and Biog., v. 1, p. 324 (contd.).
Fishbourne, Talbot Co. Samuel Carpenter of Phila. Carpenter. P. 160. MHS.
Fisher. Balto., its hist., its people. Hall. V. 2, p. 181 (William A.); v. 3, p. 835 (J. Harmanus); v. 3, p. 837 (Charles D.); v. 3, p. 840 (Edward Mc); v. 3, p. 842 (Richard). MHS; DAR.
†Bench and bar of Md. Sams and Riley. 1901, v. 2, p. 594. Lib. Cong.; MHS; Peabody Lib.
See Bruce, Wm. Cabell. Abr. Compend. Amer. Geneal. Virkus. V. 1, p. 506. DAR.
Dorsey and allied families. Ms. MHS.
Fox-Ellicott-Evans families. Evans. MHS; DAR.
†Geneal. and mem. encyc. of Md. Spencer. V. 1, pp. 34–38; v. 2, pp. 443, 542. MHS; DAR.
†Hist. of Balto. City and Co. Scharf. Pp. 383–85, 702. MHS.
†Hist. of Frederick Co. Williams. MHS; DAR.
Laytonsville M. E. churchyard, Montgomery Co. Md. Geneal. Rec. Com., 1934–35, p. 69. Mss. DAR.
Marshall family, Westmoreland Co., Va. Pp. 42–45.
†Med. Annals Md. Cordell. 1903, p. 396. MHS.
Mt. Paran Pres. churchyard, Harrisonville, Balto. Co. Typed ms. MHS; DAR.
Miss C. Petre chart. MHS.
Fisher, Charles D. Geneal. and memorial encyc. of Md. Spencer. V. 1, p. 34. MHS; DAR.
Pedigree chart. Soc. Col. Wars, Md. Johnston. 1905, p. 25. MHS.
Fisher, Hermanus. Bible rec. Md. Geneal. Rec. Com., 1938–39, p. 107. Mss. DAR.
†**Fisher, J. I.** Balto., hist. and biog. Richardson and Bennett. 1871, p. 250. MHS; DAR.
Fisher, John Ridgely. Pedigree. Soc. Col. Wars Md. Culver. 1940. MHS; DAR.
Fisher, Richard. Geneal. and memorial encyc. of Md. Spencer. V. 2, p. 443. MHS; DAR.
Fisher, Mrs. Wm. A., Jr. (Anne Baylor). Chart. (Va. families.) Col. Dames, Chap. I. MHS.
***Fisher Family.** Old Kent. Hanson. Pp. 62–63. MHS; DAR.
Fisher Family, Montgomery Co., (1790) and Ky. Ms. File case, DAR.
***Fisher Family,** Sussex Co., Del. Descendants of Isaac Montgomery (1817–1875) and Sarah Jane (Vaughn) Fisher (1822–1907). Chart. W. S. Morse. Seaford, Del., 1909. MHS.
Fisher Family, Sussex Co., Del., and Md. Charts. Typed, bd. MHS.
Fisher Line. Mrs. A. G. Ober chart. MHS.
Fisher, Fischer. St. Paul's Parish, Balto. V. 1, 2, 3, 4. Mss. MHS.
Fishpaw. St. Paul's Parish, Balto. V. 1, 2. Mss. MHS.
Fishwick. Christ P. E. Church cemetery, Cambridge. Steele. 1936. MHS; DAR.
St. Paul's Parish, Balto. V. 1, 2. Mss. MHS.
Fisk. *See* Bender-Fisk-Morfit.
Fitch. Cary Geneal. Coll. Ms. MHS.
***Fitchet.** Wicomico Co. families. Tilghman. Ms, p. 2. DAR.
Fitchett. *See* Stick. Abr. Compend. Amer. Geneal. Virkus. V. 4, p. 629. MHS.
Fitchgarrell. St. Stephens Parish, Cecilton, Md. MHS; DAR.
***Fite.** Biog. and geneal. rec. of Fite families in U. S.
Freeborn Garrettson Waters Bible rec. Ms. MHS.
Tombstone rec., Mt. Olive Cemetery Focke Geneal. Coll. Ms. MHS.
Fite, Heinrich. Biog. and geneal. rec. of Fite families in U. S.
Fite-Owings-Stinchcomb. Tombstone inscriptions from Mt. Olive cemetery, Randallstown, Balto. Co. Ms. MHS.
Fite, Sipes and Stinchcomb. Tombstone inscriptions in Mt. Olive cemetery, Balto. Co. Ms. MHS; DAR.
Fitzgerald. Carne and allied family notes. Coues. Ms. MHS.
St. Paul's Parish, Balto. V. 1, 2, 4. Mss. MHS.
See Chancellor.
Fitzgerald, Col. John, (Aide-de-Camp to Gen. Washington; Col. in Militia, Alexandria, Va.) Will of Jane (Digges) Fitzgerald, daughter of George Digges, of Warburton Manor, now Fort Washington, Md. Ms. File case, DAR.
Fitzgerald-Dorsey-Tilden. Abr. Compend. Amer. Geneal. Virkus. V. 4, p. 183. MHS.
Fitzhugh. Abr. Compend. Amer. Geneal. Virkus. V. 1, p. 603. DAR.
Ancestry. Geneal. hist. of Endress family. Endress. Pp. 89–94. MHS.
Dorchester Parish rec. Ms. MHS.
Fitzhugh family of Va. Va. Mag. Hist. and Biog., v. 7, pp. 196, 317, 425; v. 8, pp. 91–95 (ref. Craik, p. 95; Frisby, p. 92), 209, 314–317; v. 9, p. 99.
†Hist. of Balto. City and Co. Scharf. P. 904. MHS.
†Hist. of West. Md. V. 2, pp. 1026–27. MHS; DAR.
†Hist. of Washington Co. Williams. 1906, v. 1, p. 138. MHS; DAR.
Md. families. Culver. Ms. Personal list.
*Old Kent. Hanson. Pp. 135, 283. MHS; DAR.
Rousby chart. Cary Geneal. Coll. Ms. MHS.
St. John's Parish, Hagerstown. Md. Geneal. Rec. Com., 1939–40. Mss. DAR.
St. Paul's Parish, Balto. V. 2. Mss. MHS.
*The Sun, Balto., June 18, Dec. 17, 24, 1905.
Trinity Church burial ground, near Cambridge, Md. Md. Geneal. Rec. Com., 1937–38, pp. 93–104. Mss. DAR.

See Birney-Carroll-Fitzhugh.
See Gordon-Knox-Fitzhugh-Cooke.
Fitzhugh, Va. Balch chart. MHS.
Thomas Book. Thomas. Pp. 315-16. Lib. Cong.; MHS.
*The Sun, Balto., June 18, Dec. 17, 24, 1905.
Fitzhugh, George Lee Mason. Amer. at Eton in col. days. Va. Mag. Hist. and Biog., v. 13, p. 211.
Fitzhugh, William. Digest, letters and charts. Va. Mag. Hist. and Biog., v. 45, pp. 144-46.
***Fitzhugh-Knox.** Allied families of Va. Fitzhugh Knox. Related families of Baylor, Brown, King Carter, Digges, Edmonds, Gordon, Horner, Page, Selden and Tayloe. 1932. DAR.
Fitzhugh Fitzhughs. Col. families of U. S. A. Mackenzie. V. 1, pp. 70, 365. MHS; DAR.
Fitzhughs. *See* Fitzhugh.
Fitz Randolph, Nathaniel, N. J. Pedigree of Anthony Morris Tyson. Soc. Col. Wars Md. Culver. 1940. MHS; DAR.
†**Flake.** Hist. of Allegany Co. Thomas and Williams. V. 2. MHS; DAR.
‡**Fleet, Henry.** Founders of Md. Neill. 1879.
†Hist. of Md. Scharf. V. 1, p. 14. MHS.
†**Fleete.** Papers relating to early hist. of Md. Streeter. 1876. MHS.
See Patten, Jeanie M. (Coyle). Abr. Compend. Amer. Geneal. Virkus. V. 1, p. 760. DAR.
Fleete, Henry. Pedigree of Benedict Henry Hanson, Jr. Soc. Col. Wars Md. Culver. 1940. MHS; DAR.
Fleetwood. St. Paul's Parish, Balto. V. 1, 2. Mss. MHS.
***Fleming.** Fleming family in col. Md. R. Fleming Bopes. N. Y., 1938, 61 pp., typed, in binder. MHS.
†Med. Annals Md. Cordell. 1903, p. 397. MHS.
Fleming, Allison Sweeney. Md. Soc., War of 1812, v. 2, no. 191. Ms. MHS.
Fleming, John, Montgomery Co. Copy of will, 1797. Ms. File case, DAR.
Fleming, John, Sr., Montgomery Co. Will probated Jan. 16, 1797. D. A. R. Mag., v. 61, no. 10, p. 784.
Abs. of will. D. A. R. Mag., Oct., 1927, v. 61, no. 10, p. 784.
Fleming Family (Md., 1714). Ms. File case, DAR.
Fleming-Keith. Chart, photos., complete in 2 sheets. Cary Geneal. Coll. Ms. MHS.
***Flemming.** Wicomico Co. families. Tilghman. Ms., p. 107. DAR.
Fletchall, Thomas. Bible rec. Ms. DAR.
Fletcher. Rec. of Stepney Parish. MHS; DAR.
Turner Geneal. Coll. Ms. MHS.
*Wicomico Co. families. Tilghman. Ms., pp. 2, 97, 107. DAR.
See Walker-Rider-Fletcher.
Fletcher, Hurlock. Bible rec. of Dorchester and Somerset Cos. and Del. P. 29. DAR.
***Fletcher,** Pa. and Md. Burke's landed gentry. 1939. P. 2999. MHS.
†**Flexner.** Med. Annals. Md. Cordell. 1903, p. 398. MHS.
Fling. *See* Ford-Fling.
Flinn. St. Paul's Parish, Balto. V. 1. Mss. MHS.
***Flint.** Wicomico Co. families. Tilghman. Ms., pp. 96-97. DAR.
Flint, John Thomas, Ga. Amer. Clan Gregor Year Book, 1929, p. 74. MHS; DAR.
Flood. St. Paul's Parish, Balto. V. 1. Mss. MHS.
Flora. Beards' Luth. graveyard, Washington Co. Md. Geneal. Rec. Com., 1933-36. Mss. DAR.
Flournoy Family. Geneal. data. Ms. MHS.
Letter presented by Mrs. Ida M. Shirk. Ms. MHS.
Flower, J. Sebastian. Md. Soc., War of 1812, v. 3, no. 211. Ms. MHS.
***Flower Family,** St. Inigoes. Arch. of Georgetown Univ., Wash., D. C., v. 90, no. 9.
Flowers. Smithson-Rumsey rec. bk. Ms. MHS.
***Floyd.** Geneal. of Va. and Ky. Floyd families. N. J. Floyd. Balto., Williams & Wilkins Co., 1912. DAR.
***Floyd Family.** Floyd family. N. J. Floyd. 1912. Index. DAR.
Fluegal. Baust or Emanuel reformed churchyard, Carroll Co. Md. Geneal. Rec. Com., 1935-36. Mss. DAR.
Foard. St. Paul's Parish, Balto. V. 1. Mss. MHS.
Foard, Hezekiah, Cecil Co. Md. Geneal. Rec. Com., 1937-38, pp. 61-62. Mss. DAR.
†**Foard, Norval E.** Men of mark in Md. Johnson. V. 1. DAR; Enoch Pratt Lib.
Foard, Ford. Britton Scrap Book. V. 1. Ms. MHS.
Chart. M. H. Mag., 1922, v. 17, p. 230.
Foard, Ford Family, Cecil Co. Chart. M. E. Wood. Printed. MHS.
***Focke.** Pedigree of Mrs. Rachel Healy Focke, through Little family of Marshfield, Mass. Bd. ms. MHS.
See Reese. Abr. Compend. Amer. Geneal. Virkus. V. 1, p. 792. DAR.
Focke, Ferdinand. Focke geneal. Coll. MHS. Incl. charts, marriages, wills, etc. (Principally on the Owen, Owens, Owings family of Balto. Co.) With geneal. data. Ms. MHS.
Md. Soc., War of 1812, v. 3, no. 281. Ms. MHS.
Focke, Frederick. Bible rec. Focke Geneal. Coll. Ms. MHS.
Focke, H. Smull. Md. Soc., War of 1812, v. 4, no. 327. Ms. MHS.
Focke, Walter Davis. Pedigree. Soc. Col. Wars Md. Culver. 1940. MHS; DAR.
Md. Soc., War of 1812, v. 3, no. 282. Ms. MHS.
†**Fogle.** Hist. of Frederick Co. Williams. MHS; DAR.
Patriotic Md. Md. Soc. of S. A. R., 1930. MHS; DAR.
Fogle Family, Frederick Co. (1831-1931). Md. Geneal. Rec. Com., 1932-33, p. 219. Mss. DAR.
Foley. McCormick chart. MHS.
Folger. Mrs. Frank G. Baldwin chart. MHS.
Md. families. Culver. Ms. Personal list.
Folger, Capt. Frederick. Westminster churchyard. Patriotic Marylander, v. 2, no. 4, pp. 54-60. MHS; DAR.
†**Fonerden.** Med. Annals Md. 1903, p. 398. MHS.
***Fontaine.** Memoirs of Huguenot family. Translated and compiled from original autobiography of Rev. James Fontaine. George F. Putman & Co., 1853. MHS.
See Fountaine.

Fontaine Family (1500–1913). Md. Geneal. Rec. Com., 1935–36, pp. 35–47. Mss. DAR.
Fontaine Family, Eng., Va. and Snow Hill, Md., 1500–1913. Md. Geneal. Rec. Com., 1935–36, pp. 35–47. DAR.
Fontaine, Fountaine. Selden chart. MHS.
Fooke. Patriotic Md. Md. Soc. of S. A. R., 1930. MHS; DAR.
Fooks. Patriotic Md. Md. Soc. of S. A. R., 1930. MHS; DAR.
Trinity Church burial ground, near Cambridge, Md. Md. Geneal. Rec. Com., 1937–38, pp. 93–104. Mss. DAR.
Trinity Church cemetery, Dorchester Co. Md. O. R. Soc. Bull., no. 3, pp. 42–52.
See Fowke.
***Fooks, Fowke.** Wicomico Co. families. Tilghman. Ms, pp. 38, 100, 114, 128. DAR.
Foord. Thomas chart. Cary Geneal. Coll. Ms. MHS.
See Ford.
***Foote.** Ancestry and descendants of Nancy Allyn (Foote) Webb, etc. Cooch. MHS; DAR.
Ms. MHS.
See Allyn-Foote-Webb-Cooch-Wilkins.
†Footer, Thomas. Men of mark in Md. Johnson. V. 3. DAR; Enoch Pratt Lib.
Forbas. Naturalizations in Md., 1666–1765; Laws. Bacon. MHS.
Forbes. Abr. Compend. Amer. Geneal. Virkus. V. 1, p. 799. DAR.
†Med. Annals Md. Cordell. 1903, p. 398. MHS.
Patriotic Md. Md. Soc. of S. A. R., 1930. MHS; DAR.
***Forbes, George.** Burke's landed gentry. 1939. MHS.
Force. Zion Reformed Church, Hagerstown. Md. Geneal. Rec. Com., 1934–35. Mss. DAR.
Ford. Balto., its hist., its people. Hall. V. 2. MHS; DAR.
Bible rec. Md. Geneal. Rec. Com., 1938–39, p. 114. Mss. DAR.
Britton chart. MHS.
Beck, Pa. Col. and Revolutionary families of Phila. Jordan. 1933, v. 1, p. 336.
Blakiston churchyard, Kent Co., Del., near Millington. Md. Geneal. Rec. Com., 1933–34, pp. 204–07. Mss. DAR.
Chew family. Culver. M. H. Mag., 1935, v. 30, no. 2, pp. 157–75.
Done Bible rec. Ms. MHS.
*Hyland family, Cecil Co. Ms. MHS.
Md. families. Culver. Ms. Personal list.
†Med. Annals. Md. Cordell. 1903, p. 398. MHS.
Patriotic Md. Md. Soc. of S. A. R., 1930. MHS; DAR.
Rumsey-Smithson Bible rec. Md. Geneal. Rec. Com., 1932–33, v. 5, pp. 63–142. DAR.
St. Paul's P. E. churchyard, Kent Co. Md. O. R. Soc. Bull., no. 2, pp. 54–65.
St. Paul's Parish, Balto. V. 1, 2, 4. Mss. MHS.
St. Stephens Parish reg., Cecil Co. Ms. MHS.
St. Stephens Parish, Cecilton, Md. MHS; DAR.
St. Thomas' Parish, Balto. Co. Bd. ms. MHS. Also: Md. Geneal. Rec. Com., 1937, pp. 109–82. Mss. DAR.
*Semmes Geneal. Coll. Ms. MHS.
Southerland-Latham and allied families. Voorhees. P. 106. Bd. ms. MHS.
Wathen Prayer Book rec. Ms. MHS.
See Foard.
See Foster-Ford-Sampson.
See Tilghman-Hyland-Ford.
Ford, Cecil Co. Data. Md. Geneal. Rec. Com., 1933–34, pp. 24, 25. Mss. DAR.
*Ford rec. Md. Geneal. Rec. Com., v. 1, pp. 30–45. DAR.
Ford, H. Jones. Md. Soc., War of 1812, v. 2, no. 196. Ms. MHS.
***Ford, Stephen Hyland.** Burke's landed gentry. 1939. MHS.
Ford, Thomas G. Md. Soc., War of 1812, v. 1, no. 43. Ms. MHS.
Ford Family. Chart comp. by Maria Ford Massey (Mrs. Herman Biddle). Md. Geneal. Rec. Com., 1937–38. Mss. DAR.
*Chart. Mrs. Joseph Y. Jeans. MHS; also Geneal. Soc. Pa. Ms. Coll.
Ms. File case, DAR.
*Five geneal. charts in Mss., comp. by Maria Ford Massey (Mrs. Herman Biddle). (1) Kenneth MacAlpine; (2) Bruce, Barons of Skelton and Annandale; (3) Charlemange; (4) Ford family of Md.; (5) Magna Carta Barons. Md. Geneal. Rec. Com., 1937–38. Mss. DAR.
Ford Family, Cecil Co. Ms. MHS.
Ford Family, Charles Co. Ms. MHS.
Ford - Dorsey - Howard - Hyland - Ridgely-Tilden-Warfield-Watkins Families (1667–1910). Md. Geneal. Rec. Com., 1932–33. DAR.
Ford-Fling. Note. D. A. R. Mag., v. 71, no. 11, p. 1025.
Ford-Foster-Cazier. Bible rec., 1770–1845. Ms., MHS; Also in: Md. Geneal. Rec. Com., 1932–33, v. 5, photos., DAR.
Ford-Hopkins. Col. and Revolutionary families of Pa. Amer. Hist. Soc., N. Y., 1934, pp. 877–80.
Ford-Plowden. Marriage of Lewis Ford and Eliz. Plowden, St. Mary's Co. Natl. Geneal. Soc. Quart., Sept., 1938, v. 26, no. 3, p. 63.
***Ford, Wm.-Preston, Sarah** marriage certificate 1670. Notes from public rec. Hodges. M. H. Mag., 1915, v. 10, pp. 284–85.
Ford-Smoot. Thomas Allanson, Lord of Christian Temple Manor. Layton. Mss. DAR.
Ford-Stevenson. Notes. D. A. R. Mag., v. 70, no. 6, p. 574.
Ford, Foard, Cecil Co. Patriotic Marylander, v. 1, no. 3, p. 61. MHS; DAR.
†Foreman. Med. Annals Md. Cordell. 1903, p. 399. MHS.
Pedigree of Maurice Edward Skinner. Soc. Col. Wars Md. Culver. 1940. MHS; DAR.
†Foreman, Gen. Thomas M. Hist. of Cecil Co. Johnston. P. 409. MHS; DAR.
***Foreman-Farman-Forman.** Geneal., descendants of William Foreman, from London, Eng., in 1675; settled near Annapolis. Supplemented by single lines of families of ancestors of writer, paternal great-grandmother, his grandmother, his own mother and the descendants of Edward Frisbie, original Settler of Brandford, Conn. E. E. Farman. N. Y., Tobias A. Wright, 1911. MHS.
***Forington.** Wicomico Co. families. Tilghman. Ms., p. 126. DAR.

Forman. Clay family of Pa. Ms. File case, DAR.
Elbert chart. MHS.
*Geneal. Comp. principally by A. S. Danbridge, for Mrs. E. P. Dismakes of Georgia. Begins with the Formans of Kent Co., Md., 1674. Md. ref., pp. 95, 98. Cleveland, Ohio, Forman-Bassett Hatch Co., 1903. MHS.
Md. families. Culver. Ms. Personal list.
Pedigree of Joseph Lee Wickes. Soc. Col. Wars Md. Culver. 1940. MHS; DAR.
Mrs. E. W. Poe chart. MHS.
*Three Revolutionary soldiers: Jonathan Forman (1755–1809), Thomas Marsh Forman (1758–1845), David Forman (1745–1797). C. Forman. Cleveland, Ohio, Forman-Bassett-Hatch Co., 1902. MHS.
St. Paul's Parish, Balto. V. 2. Mss. MHS.
See Foreman-Farman-Forman.
Forman, Kent Co. Manning chart. MHS.
Forman, Gen. David, Kent Co. Will probated, Natchez, Miss., 1796. D. A. R. Mag., v. 67, no. 10, p. 649.
Formans. Rec., Kent Co. Md. Geneal. Rec. Com., 1938–39, pp. 100–02. Mss. DAR.
***Forney.** Frederick Co. families. Markell. Ms. Personal list.
Hist. of Shriver family. Shriver. Pp. 102–09. MHS.
†Med. Annals Md. Cordell. 1903, p. 399. MHS.
St. Paul's Parish, Balto. V. 2. Mss. MHS.
Swope family. Swope. MHS.
†See Young. Hist. of Balto. City and Co. Scharf. P. 442. MHS.
***Forney Family.** Forney family. L. Forney Bittinger. Siewickly, Pa.
Forrest. See Henry. Col. families of U. S. A. Mackenzie. V. 1, pp. 229–36. MHS; DAR.
*The Sun, Balto., July 24, 1904.
†Forrest, Gen. Uriah. Hist. of Md. Scharf. V. 2, p. 572. MHS.
*Patriots of Revolutionary period interred in D. C. Balch. Rec. of Columbia Hist. Soc., v. 19, v. 20.
Forrester. See Hope. Abr. Compend. Amer. Geneal. Virkus. V. 1, p. 924. DAR.
St. Paul's Parish, Balto. V. 2. Mss. MHS.
Forster. Ancest. rec. and portraits. Col. Dames of Amer., 1910, v. 2, p. 559. MHS; DAR.
See Donaldson-Forster.
Forsyth. St. Paul's Parish, Balto. V. 2. Mss. MHS.
Forsythe. Balto., its hist., its people. Hall. V. 3. MHS; DAR.
Founders of Anne Arundel and Howard Cos. Warfield. P. 486. MHS; DAR.
†Forsythe, Wm. H., Jr. Men of mark in Md. Johnson. V. 2. DAR; Enoch Pratt Lib.
†Fort, Fortt. Med. Annals Md. Cordell. 1903, p. 399. MHS.
Fortt. Md. families. Culver. Ms. Personal list.
St. Thomas' Parish, Balto. Co. Bd. ms. MHS. Also: Md. Geneal. Rec. Com., 1937, pp. 109–82. Mss. DAR.
Forwood. Col. families of U. S. A. Mackenzie. V. 1. MHS; DAR.
†Med. Annals Md. Cordell. 1903, p. 399. MHS.
See Paca-Smithson-Forwood.
Fossett. Geneal. of descendants of George and Sarah Smedley. Cope. Pp. 337, 638, 639. MHS; DAR.
Foster. Balto., its hist., its people. Hall. V. 3. MHS; DAR.
Bible rec., Kent Co., 1817–1868. Md. Geneal. Rec. Com., 1932–33, pp. 325–27. Mss. DAR.
Miss M. S. Brogden chart. MHS.
Foster family. D. I. Foster. Pamph. MHS.
Foster-Ford-Sampson and allied families. Mrs. Anna Foster Ford. Priv. pr., Amer. Hist. Soc., N. Y., 1930.
*Fosters and Foster Barham. Descendants of Roger Foster of Edreston. A. H. Foster-Barham. London, 1897. MHS.
M. E. Church South cemetery, near Poolesville, Montgomery Co. Md. Geneal. Rec. Com., 1926. Mss. DAR.
St. Paul's Parish, Balto. V. 1, 2. Mss. MHS.
St. Stephens Parish, Cecilton, Md. MHS; DAR.
Sater geneal. Bd. Ms. MHS.
See Beedle-Foster-Kennedy-Walker.
See Ford-Foster-Cazier.
See Jones-Foster-Kennedy.
See Kenedy-Foster.
Foster, C. Dulany. Md. Soc., War of 1812, v. 3, no. 222. Ms. MHS.
†Foster, Ruben. Men of mark in Md. Johnson. V. 3. DAR, Enoch Pratt Lib.
Foster, Seth, Great Choptank Island (1659). Hist. of Talbot Co. Tilghman. V. 2, p. 531. MHS; DAR.
***Foster Family.** B. B. Brown folder. MHS.
Cary Geneal. Coll. Ms. MHS.
Foster Family, Md. and Ind. Will of John D. Foster, Talbot Co., 1875; Benjamin and Catherine (Prather) Foster, married Feb. 14, 1798; Benjamin, died 1844, aged 69 years, Fountain Co., Ind.) Ms. File case, DAR.
Fotterell. Dorsey and allied families. Ms. MHS.
Fouey. Md. gleanings in Eng. Wills. M. H. Mag., 1908, v. 3, no. 2.
Foulke. Col. families of U. S. A. Mackenzie. V. 7, p. 304. MHS; DAR.
Orme geneal. chart. MHS.
See Fowke-Foulke.
Fountain. *See* Fountaine.
Fountaine. Edmund Beauchamp of East. Shore of Md. D. A. R. Mag., v. 66, no. 4, pp. 234–38.
Naturalizations in Md., 1666–1765; Laws. Somerset Co. Court Book. Tilghman. 1937. Ms. DAR.
See Fontaine.
Fountaine, Fountain, Fontaine. Old Somerset. Torrence. MHS; DAR.
***Fouse, Fause.** Geneal. of descendants of Theobald Fouse, incl. many other connected families. G. M. Brumbaugh and John G. Fouse. Balto., Williams & Wilkins Co., 1914.
Fout. Mt. Olivet cemetery, Frederick. Md. Geneal. Rec. Com., 1934–35, p. 111. Mss. DAR.
Foutz. See Hoover. Abr. Compend. Amer. Geneal. Virkus. V. 1, p. 370. DAR.
†Fowble. Hist. of Balto. City and Co. Scharf. P. 867. MHS.
Fowcate. Naturalizations in Md., 1666–1765; Laws. Bacon. MHS.
Fowke. Ancest. rec. and portraits. Col. Dames of Amer., 1910, v. 2, p. 641. MHS; DAR.
Cary Geneal. Coll. Ms. MHS.

Fowke. Crain chart. MHS.
Daughter of Md., Mother of Texas. Bell. MHS; DAR.
*Lineage Bk. Daughters of Amer. Colonists. V. 5, pp. 411–13. MHS; DAR.
Marshall of Marshall Hall. Natl. Geneal. Soc. Quart., v. 19, no. 1, p. 1; no. 4, pp. 86–96.
Md. families. Culver. Ms. Personal list.
*Repr. from Ohio Archeological Hist. Quart., Columbus, Ohio, April, 1929. MHS.
Some Md. and Va. ancestors. Bell. Natl. Geneal. Soc. Quart., v. 19, no. 4, pp. 86–96.
Sydney-Smith and Clagett-Price families. Price. MHS; DAR.
*The Sun, Balto. Sept. 17, 1905 (Va.); July 14, 1907 (Md.).
Va. geneal. Hayden. MHS; DAR.
See Fooks.
See Mitchell-Smith-Fowke.
Fowke, Va. and Md. Va. gleanings in Eng. Va. Mag. Hist. and Biog., v. 29, pp. 348–49.
Fowke, Col. Gerard Fowke, Va., and Md. from 1651. M. H. Mag., 1921, v. 16, pp. 1–19.
Fowke Line. Col. and Revolutionary lineages of Amer. 1939, v. 1, pp. 273–74; v. 3, pp. 119–22. MHS.
Fowke, Fooks. Fowke (Fooks) family. H. C. Fookes, Balto. Federalsburg, J. W. Stowell Printing Co., 1928, pamph., 47 pp. MHS; DAR.
Mason chart. MHS.
Fowke-Foulke. Repr. from Hayden's Va. Geneal. Pamph. MS.
Fowler. Bible rec., Kent Co. Md. Geneal. Rec. Com., 1938–39, pp. 126–27. Mss. DAR.
Maddox family. Col. and Revolutionary families of Phila. Jordan. 1933, v. 1, pp. 401–02.
See Mays. Abr. Compend. Amer. Geneal. Virkus. V. 1, p. 722. DAR.
Mrs. E. N. Morison chart. MHS.
St. Paul's Parish, Balto. V. 1, 2, 4. Mss. MHS.
*Wicomico Co. families. Tilghman. Ms., p. 101. DAR.
Fowler, Anne Arundel Co. Mrs. A. R. Rogers chart. MHS.
Fowler, Miss Alice Silvie. Chart. Col. Dames, Chap. I. MHS.
Fowler, Miss Amelia De Pau. Chart. Col. Dames, Chap. I. MHS.
***Fowler Family.** Anne Arundel Co. Gentry. Newman. Pp. 549–56. MHS; DAR.
*Incomplete geneal. H. A. Fowler. (Md. family.) Kansas City, 1913.
Fownes. St. Paul's Parish, Balto. V. 2. Mss. MHS.
Fownes, John, Balto. D. A. R. Mag., June, 1927, v. 61, no. 6, p. 470.
Balto. (Merchant). Will proved Oct. 7, 1802. D. A. R. Mag., v. 61, no. 6, p. 470.
***Fox.** Chart, genealogy of Fox family of Cornwall. (Andrew Ellicott and Mary Fox). J. L. Pratt. Republican Office, 1843. MHS.
Early marriages of Fox family in U. S., 1828–65. Wm. M. Clemens. N. Y., 1916, 1st ed. ltd. Lib. Cong.
†Hist. of Frederick Co. Williams. MHS; DAR.
Peale Geneal. Coll. Ms. MHS.
St. Paul's Parish, Balto. V. 1, 2. Mss. MHS.
T. M. Smith pedigree charts, plate 2. Soc. Col. Wars, Md. Johnston. 1905, p. 96. MHS.
See Churchill-Crocker-Fox-Coplestone-Bonvile-Ellicott.
***Fox Family.** Marriages in U. S., 1628–1865. W. M. Clemens. 1916.
***Fox-Ellicott-Evans Families.** Fox-Ellicott-Evans families of Md.; Hist. accounts; and different families connected with them, 1645–1882. C. W. Evans. Buffalo, Baker-Jones Co., 1882. 281 pp. MHS; DAR.
Fox-Nelson-Prosser-Ring Families, Va. Bible rec. Ms. DAR.
Foxhall, Mrs. H. De Courcy Wright Thom chart. MHS.
Foxley. Mrs. Emory Whitridge chart. MHS.
Foxwell. Tombstone rec. of Dorchester Co. Jones. DAR.
Foy and Allied Families. 6 charts. Ella Foy O'Gorman. Printed 1932. MHS.
Fraizer. Marriages. Dorchester Co. Marriages. Md. Geneal. Rec. Com., v. 4, p. 80. DAR.
Frame-Lowndes. Ances. rec. and portraits. Col. Dames of Amer., 1910, v. 1, p. 285. MHS; DAR.
***Frampton Family.** Frampton family. J. S. Wrightnour.
France. Bible rec., Kent Co. Md. Geneal. Rec. Com., 1933–34, p. 220. Mss. DAR.
Francis. Dobbin chart. MHS.
Naturalizations in Md., 1666–1765; Laws. Bacon. MHS.
St. Paul's churchyard, Kent Co. Md. O. R. Soc. Bull., no. 2, pp. 54–65. MHS.
Pedigree of Levin Gale Shreve. Soc. Col. Wars Md. Culver. 1940. MHS; DAR.
Pedigree of Harrison Tilghman. Soc. Col. Wars Md. Culver. 1940. MHS; DAR.
St. Paul's P. E. churchyard, Kent Co. Md. O. R. Soc. Bull., no. 2, pp. 54–65.
St. Paul's Parish, Balto. V. 1, 2. Mss. MHS.
Thomas family of Talbot Co. Spencer. P. 120. MHS; DAR.
Tilghman chart. MHS.
Francis, Kent Co. Col. families of Amer. Lawrence. V. 12, p. 96. MHS.
Francis, Joseph (born in Md., 1742). D. A. R. Mag., v. 71, no. 12, pp. 1109–10.
***Francis Family.** Old Kent. Hanson. Pp. 296–97. MHS; DAR.
Francis-Watkins-Lloyd. Md. Geneal. Rec. Com., 1933–34, pp. 102–07. Mss. DAR.
Frank. Tercentenary hist. of Md. Andrews. V. 2, p. 820; v. 3, p. 713. MHS; DAR.
Frankland. St. Paul's Parish, Balto. V. 1. Mss. MHS.
Franklin. Ances. rec. and portrait. Col. Dames of Amer. 1910. P. 70. MHS; DAR.
Balto., its hist., its people. Hall. V. 3. MHS; DAR.
Buckingham Pres. churchyard, Worcester Co., Hudson. Bd. ms. MHS; DAR.
Gary chart. MHS.
Hazelhurst chart. MHS.
Hist. of Allegany Co. Thomas and Williams. V. 1, p. 56; v. 2, pp. 1032–33. MHS; DAR.
†Hist. of Frederick Co. Williams. V. 1, p. 42. MHS; DAR.
John Neill of Lewes, Del., 1739. Pr. for family, Phila., 1875.
Makemie Memorial Pres. churchyard, Snow Hill, Worcester Co. Hudson. Bd. ms. MHS;

DAR. Also: Md. Geneal. Rec. Com., Mrs. Lines. Mss. DAR.
Old Buckingham by the Sea, East. Shore of Md. Page. DAR.
Purnell family tree. MHS.
Taliaferro family, Va. Tyler's Quart. Mag., v. 11, pp. 241–51.
Turner Geneal. Coll. Ms. MHS.
Worcester Co. militia, 1794. Covington. P. 156. MHS.
†**Franklin,** Snow Hill, Md. Biog. cyc. of rep. men of Md. and D. C. P. 507. MHS; DAR.
†**Franklin, Walter S.** Men of mark in Md. Johnson. V. 1. DAR; Enoch Pratt Lib.
†**Frantz.** Hist. of Allegany Co. Thomas and Williams. V. 2. MHS; DAR.
Frantz, Md. and Pa. Abr. Compend. Amer. Geneal. Virkus. V. 6, p. 711. DAR.
Frazee. Frazee family of Md. (in N. J. prior to 1700). C. E. Haye. Rep. from Mountain Democrat, Garrett Co., Jan. 10, 1935. MHS; File case, DAR.
Portrait and biog. rec. of Sixth Cong. Dist. of Md. 1898. Pp. 474, 552, 614. MHS; DAR.
Frazier. Burial ground, near Mutual, Calvert Co. Frazier-Magruder stones. Md. Geneal. Rec. Com., 1938–39, p. 21. Mss. DAR.
Hist. of Allegany Co. Thomas and Williams. V. 1, pp. 84–88. MHS; DAR.
†Hist. of Caroline Co. Noble. MHS.
†Hist. of Frederick Co. Williams. V. 2, p. 1160. MHS; DAR.
St. Paul's Parish, Balto. V. 2. Mss. MHS.
*Some account of Capt. John Frazier and his descendants, with notes on West and Checkley families. Priv. pr., 1910. DAR.
***Frazier, Capt. John.** Some account of his descendants. J. G. Leach. Phila., priv. pr., J. B. Lippincott Co., 1910. MHS.
***Frazier Family.** Bible rec. Old Kent Chapter, East. Shore of Md. Md. Geneal. Rec. Com., 1926–27, pp. 12–24. DAR.
Burying ground, near Preston (East. Shore of Md.). Md. Geneal. Rec. Com., 1937, Parran, p. 76. Mss. DAR.
*Wilson Mss. Coll., No. 8, A. MHS.
***Frazier Family,** Md. and Ohio. Bible rec. of George Frazier and Rebecca Smith; married, 1780; with will of George Frazier, Trumbull Co., Ohio, dated 1810. Ms. DAR.
Freaks. Somerset Co. Court Book. Tilghman. 1937. Ms. DAR.
Freaner. Zion Reformed Church, Hagerstown. Md. Geneal. Rec. Com., 1934–35. Mss. DAR.
Frederick. St. Paul's Parish, Balto. V. 2, 4. Mss. MHS.
Frederick, Lord Baltimore. Deed Jan. 16, 1761, to Francis Hall. Prince George Co. D. C. Geneal. Rec. Com., 1937, v. 35, pp. 72–77. Typed, bd. DAR.
Will. Putnam's Monthly Mag., new series, v. 1, pp. 282–83. DAR.
Freeborn. Greenway chart. MHS.
Lambdin chart. MHS.
Freeburger. St. Paul's Parish, Balto. V. 2. Mss. MHS.
Freeburger, A. C. Md. Soc., War of 1812, v. 1, no. 12. Ms. MHS.
Freeland. Man-Needles-Hambleton families. Needles. MHS; DAR.
†Med. Annals Md. Cordell. 1903, p. 401. MHS.
Rolle family rec., Talbot Co. Ms. MHS.
Freeman. Col. and Revolutionary families of Phila. Jordan. 1933, v. 1. pp. 323–28.
Edmund Beauchamp. D. A. R. Mag., April, 1932, v. 66, no. 4, p. 235.
Md. families. Culver. Ms. Personal list.
Naturalizations in Md., 1666–1765; Laws. Bacon. MHS.
†Papers relating to early hist. of Md. Streeter. 1876. MHS.
St. Paul's P. E. churchyard, Kent Co. Md. O. R. Soc. Bull., no. 2, pp. 54–65. MHS.
St. Paul's Parish, Balto. V. 1, 2. Mss. MHS.
Somerset Co. Court Book. Tilghman. 1937. Ms. DAR.
See Matthiason.
Freeman, Charles Co. Abr. Compend. Amer. Geneal. Virkus. V. 1, p. 920. DAR.
Freeman, Coleman Randall. Pedigree. Soc. Col. Wars Md. Culver. 1940. MHS; DAR.
Freeman, Eliza Jane. Sampler, 1834. Md. Geneal. Rec. Com., 1933–34, p. 152. Mss. DAR.
***Freeman, John Douglas.** Burke's landed gentry. 1939. MHS.
Freeman-Brooke-Dent-Douglas-Howard. Abr. Compend. Amer. Geneal. Virkus. V. 4, p. 648, 665. MHS.
***Freeny.** Wicomico Co. families. Tilghman. Ms., p. 101. DAR.
Freer. St. Paul's Parish, Balto. V. 2. Mss. MHS.
French. Balch chart. MHS.
Deed; Susannah French to Elijah Chaney, 1802, Anne Arundel Co. Md. Geneal. Rec. Com., 1933–34, pp. 5–6. Mss. DAR.
Patriotic Md. Md. Soc. of S. A. R., 1930. MHS; DAR.
St. Paul's Parish, Balto. V. 1, 2, 4. Mss. MHS.
French, Lieut. A. R. (1806–90). N. Y. Geneal. and Biog. Rec., v. 22, p. 56 (notes and queries).
French, Chester Lee. Md. Soc., War of 1812, v. 3, no. 202. Ms. MHS.
French, Emm. Will, 1780. Md. Geneal. Rec. Com., 1933–34, pp. 7–8. Mss. DAR.
French, Mrs. H. Findley (Helen Clark). Chart. Col. Dames, Chap. I. MHS.
French, William, Anne Arundel Co. Private; oath of fidelity in war of 1776; land rec., ab. of wills; marriage and birth rec.; 1790–1915. Md. Geneal. Rec. Com., 1933–34, pp. 1–4. Mss. DAR.
French Line. Col. and Revolutionary lineages of Amer. 1939, v. 1, p. 497. MHS.
French (Va.)-**Chapman.** Abr. Compend. Amer. Geneal. Virkus. V. 4, pp. 194–95. MHS.
Fretz. Dulaney churchyard, near Massey, Kent Co. Md. Geneal. Rec. Com., 1933–34, pp. 210–12. Mss. DAR.
Frey. Hist. of Shriver family. Shriver. Pp. 142–43. MHS.
See Fry.
Frick. Ances. rec. and portraits. Col. Dames of Amer., 1910, v. 1, pp. 130, 350. MHS; DAR.
Balto., its hist., its people. Hall. V. 2. MHS; DAR.

†**Frick.** Bench and bar of Md. Sams and Riley. 1901, v. 2, p. 577. Lib. Cong.; MHS; Peabody Lib.
Carey Geneal. Coll. Ms. MHS.
Geneal. and memorial encyc. of Md. Spencer. V. 2, pp. 620–30. MHS; DAR.
†Nicholas Hasselback, printer. McCreary. MHS.
†Hist. of Balto. City and Co. Scharf. Pp. 699–701. MHS.
Jacobs chart. MHS.
†Med. Annals Md. Cordell. 1903, pp. 542, 795–802, 807–17. MHS.
Mrs. J. Pleasants chart. MHS.
Mrs. E. Worthington chart. MHS.
†**Frick, Frank.** Men of mark in Md. Johnson. V. 1. DAR; Enoch Pratt Lib.
***Frick, Judge Frederick Wm.** Geneal. and mem. encyc. of Md. Spencer. V. 2, pp. 620–30. MHS; DAR.
Frick, James Swan. Abr. Compend. Amer. Geneal. Virkus. V. 1, p. 919, DAR.
Frick, Mrs. James Swan (Elise Winchester Dana). Chart. (New Eng. families.) Col. Dames, Chap. I. MHS.
Friedenwald. Balto., its hist., its people. Hall. MHS; DAR.
†Med. Annals Md. Cordell. 1903, p. 402. MHS.
†**Friedenwald, Harry.** Men of mark in Md. Johnson. V. 2. DAR; Enoch Pratt Lib.
Friend. Abr. Compend. Amer. Geneal. Virkus. V. 4, p. 574. MHS.
Friend Family, Youghiogheny Valley. Rec. with geneal. S. R. White. Ms. MHS.
†**Friese.** Diffenderfers and Frieses. Soc. for Hist. of Germans in Md. 5th ann. rept., 1891, pp. 91–95.
Zion Reformed Church, Hagerstown. Md. Geneal. Rec. Com., 1934–35. Mss. DAR.
Frietz. St. Paul's Parish, Balto. V. 2. Mss. MHS.
Frincham. St. Paul's Parish, Balto. V. 2. Mss. MHS.
Frisbie. *See* Frisbee-Frisbie.
Frisby. Barroll in Great Britain and Amer. Barroll. P. 86. MHS.
Blackford chart. MHS.
Fitzhugh family. Va. Mag. Hist. and Biog., v. 8, p. 92.
Frisby family. F. B. Culver. M. H. Mag., 1936, v. 31, pp. 337–53.
Howard-Montague-Warfield geneal. chart. Culver and Marye. MHS.
Parr chart. MHS.
Pedigree of Benedict Henry Hanson, Jr. Soc. Col. Wars Md. Culver. 1940. MHS; DAR.
Pedigree of Pleasants Pennington. Soc. Col. Wars Md. Culver. 1940. MHS; DAR.
Pedigree of Harrison Tilghman. Soc. Col. Wars Md. Culver. 1940. MHS; DAR.
Pedigree of Levin Gale Shreve. Soc. Col. Wars Md. Culver. 1940. MHS; DAR.
Pedigree of Richard Dennis Steuart. Soc. Col. Wars Md. Culver. 1940. MHS; DAR.
*Pennington Papers. Ms. MHS.
Mrs. J. Hall Pleasants, Jr., chart. MHS.
Raisin chart. MHS.
St. Paul's Parish, Balto. V. 2. Mss. MHS.
St. Stephens Parish, Cecilton, Md. MHS; DAR.
Frisby, Cecil Co. W. A. and S. W. Merritt pedigree charts, plate 2. Soc. Col. Wars, Md. Johnston. 1905, pp. 68, 145. MHS.
Frisby, James, Fairlee, Kent Co. Tory maid. Stimpson.
***Frisby Family.** Old Kent. Hanson. Pp. 81, 302. MHS; DAR.
Frisdy. Pedigree of George Webb Constable. Soc. Col. Wars Md. Culver. 1940. MHS; DAR.
Fritchie. Frederick Co. tombstone inscriptions. Gruder. Natl. Geneal. Soc. Quart., 1919, v. 8, nos. 1, 2.
Fritz. Hagerstown tombstone inscriptions. Gruder. Natl. Geneal. Soc. Quart., 1919, v. 8, nos. 1, 2.
Frock. Babylon family. Duttera. P. 35. Ms. MHS.
***Frost.** Geneal. in five families, 1634. N. S. Frost. Pt. 5, Frost line, Frostburg, Md. 1926, pamph. MHS.
†Hist. of Allegany Co. Thomas and Williams. V. 1. MHS; DAR.
St. Paul's Parish, Balto. V. 1, 2. Mss. MHS.
***Frost,** Frostburg. Hist. of West. Md. Scharf. V. 2, pp. 1476–77. MHS; DAR.
Frost, Howard Co. M. H. Mag., 1939, v. 34, no. 3, p. 304.
†**Frost, Wm. A. Crawford.** Men of mark in Md. Johnson. V. 2. DAR; Enoch Pratt Lib.
Frost Family, Reisterstown, Balto. Co. Focke Geneal. Coll. Mss. MHS.
Fry. John Hawkins, Fells Point, Bible rec. Ms. MHS.
Fry, Frey. St. Paul's Parish, Balto. V. 2, 4. Mss. MHS.
†**Fuch, Otto** (born in Prussia, Oct., 1839; died 1906). M. H. Mag., v. 12, p. 217.
†**Fuchs, Carl G.** Men of mark in Md. Johnson. V. 1. DAR; Enoch Pratt Lib.
Fugate Family. Pocock family notes. Typed, p. 15. MHS.
Fugely. *See* Feigley.
Fulford. St. Paul's Parish, Balto. V. 2. Mss. MHS.
Fulford, Maj. John (Revolutionary soldier). St. Paul's P. E. graveyard. Patriotic Marylander, v. 2, no. 4, pp. 54–60. MHS; DAR.
Fulham. *See* Fullam.
Fullam, Wm. Freeland. Pedigree. Soc. Col. Wars Md. Culver. 1940. MHS; DAR.
Fullam, Fulham. Col. families of U. S. A. Mackenzie. V. 6. MHS; DAR.
Fullemvider. Bromwell geneal. Ms. Lib. Cong.; MHS.
Fullenvider, Hagerstown. Bromwell geneal. Bromwell. Pp. 200–15. MHS.
Fuller. Col. families of U. S. A. Mackenzie. V. 7, p. 208. MHS; DAR.
†Hist. of Allegany Co. Thomas and Williams. V. 1. MHS; DAR.
Trinity P. E. churchyard, Long Green. Typed ms. MHS; DAR.
Fuller, Rev. Richard. Monumental City. Howard. MHS; DAR.
Fullerton. Md. gleanings in Eng. Wills. M. H. Mag., 1907, v. 2, no. 3.
*Wicomico Co. families. Tilghman. Ms., p. 96. DAR.

Fulton. Geneal. and memorial encyc. of Md. Spencer. V. 1, p. 1. MHS; DAR.
†Hist. of Frederick Co. Williams. MHS; DAR.
†Med. Annals Md. Cordell. 1903, p. 403. MHS.
St. Paul's Parish, Balto. V. 2, 4. Mss. MHS.
Fulton, Wm. M. Copy of will, 1806. Ms. File case, DAR.
Fulton Line. Col. and Revolutionary families of Pa. Amer. Hist. Soc., N. Y., 1934, p. 815.
†**Funck.** Med. Annals Md. Cordell. 1903, p. 403. MHS;
See Funk.
***Funck, Funk.** Brief hist. of Bishop Henry Funk and other Funk pioneers. Complete Geneal. register. A. J. Fretz. Elkhart, Ind., Mennonite Pub. Co., 874 pp. DAR.
Fundenberg. Abr. Compend. Amer. Geneal. Virkus. V. 6, p. 687. DAR.
†Hist. of Allegany Co. Thomas and Williams. V. 1. MHS; DAR.
Data. Md. Geneal. Rec. Com., 1932-33, p. 217. Mss. DAR.
***Funk.** Frederick Co. families. Markell. Ms. Personal list.
*Hist. of Washington Co. Williams. 1906, v. 2, p. 992. MHS; DAR.
Md. families. Culver. Ms. Personal list.
Taney and allied families. Silverson. MHS; DAR.
Zion Reformed Church, Hagerstown. Md. Geneal. Rec. Com., 1934-35. Mss. DAR.
See Funck.
†**Funk, Jacob J.** Men of mark in Md. Johnson. V. 1. DAR; Enoch Pratt Lib.
Funk Family. Bible rec. from two family bibles, 1819-82. Ms. File case, DAR.
Funk, Funck. Hagerstown tombstone inscriptions. Gruder. Natl. Geneal. Soc. Quart., 1919, v. 8, nos. 1, 2.
***Funsten.** Ancestors and descendants of Colo. David Funsten and his wife Susan Everard Mead. H. S. F. Randolph. N. Y., Knickerbocker Press, 1926. MHS.
Furgerson. *See* Furguson.
Furguson-Duvall-Hall-Tyler Families. Notes. Ms. MHS.
Furguson or **Furgerson.** Col. Nicholas Duvall family rec. Price. Bd. ms. MHS.
Furlong. St. Paul's Parish, Balto. V. 2. Mss. MHS.
Furnis. Somerset Co. Court Book. Tilghman. 1937. Ms. DAR.
Furniss. Turner. Geneal. Coll. Ms. MHS.
Furnival. St. Paul's Parish, Balto. V. 1, 2. Mss. MHS.
Furry. Hagerstown tombstone inscriptions. Gruder. Natl. Geneal. Soc. Quart., 1919, v. 8, nos. 1, 2.
†**Fussel.** Med. Annals Md. Cordell. 1903, p. 403. MHS.
Fussell, Annie E. Life and death, 1829-59. Ms. MHS.
†**Futcher.** Med. Annals Md. Cordell. 1903; p. 403. MHS.
Somerset Co. Court Book. Tilghman. 1937. Ms. DAR.
Fyke. *See* Fike.

G

Gadd. Keene family. Jones. MHS; DAR.
Gadsby. St. Paul's Parish, Balto. V. 2. Mss. MHS.
***Gaffney Family.** Arch. of Georgetown Univ., Wash., D. C., v. 379.
Gail. Balto., its hist., its people. Hall. V. 2. MHS; DAR.
†Men of mark in Md. Johnson. V. 1. DAR; Enoch Pratt Lib.
Gaillard. *See* Gaylord.
Gain. St. Paul's Parish, Balto. V. 1. Mss. MHS.
†**Gaines.** Med. Annals. Md. Cordell. 1903, p. 404. MHS.
Gaither. Ances. rec. and portraits. Col. Dames of Amer., 1910, v. 1, p. 247. MHS; DAR.
Balto., its hist., its people. Hall. V. 2. MHS; DAR.
Britton Scrap Book. V. 1. Ms. MHS.
*Burke's landed gentry. 1939. MHS.
Col. families of Amer. Lawrence. V. 5, p. 87; v. 16, p. 85. MHS.
Col. families of U. S. A. Mackenzie. V. 6. MHS; DAR.
Dorsey chart. MHS.
*Early comers to the Province. Georgians in Anne Arundel Co. Atlanta Jour., Sept. 22, 1906. Newsp. clipp. File case, MHS.
*Founders of Anne Arundel and Howard Cos. Warfield. Pp. 107-09, 419-28, 425-28 (N. C.). MHS; DAR.
Graves. Worthington Place, 1 mile west of Unity, Montgomery Co. Md. Geneal. Rec. Com., 1934-35, p. 90. Mss. DAR.
Hist. Graves of Md. and D. C. Ridgely. MHS.
†Hist. of West. Md. Scharf. V. 1, pp. 599-600. MHS; DAR.
Hood family Bible rec. Pamph. MHS.
Lineage Bks., Natl. Soc. of Daughters of Amer. Col., v. 2, p. 117. MHS; DAR.
Md. families. Culver. Ms. Personal list.
Mt. Calvary Church burial ground, Howard Co. Md. Geneal. Rec. Com., 1934-35, pp. 95-99. Mss. DAR.
Mt. Carmel burial ground, Unity, Montgomery Co. Md. Geneal. Rec. Com., 1934-35, p. 85. Mss. DAR.
*Owings-Gaither Hood-Thomas Bible rec. Ms. File case, MHS.
Pedigree of Harry Willson Falconer. Soc. Col. Wars Md. Culver. 1940. MHS; DAR.
Pedigree of Charles Worthington Hoff. Soc. Col. Wars Md. Culver. 1940. MHS; DAR.
Pedigree of Maurice Falconer Rodgers. Soc. Col. Wars Md. Culver. 1940. MHS; DAR.
Private cemetery. Md. Geneal. Rec. Com., 1934-35. DAR.
Stones from Bowie Davis place, Montgomery Co. Md. Geneal. Red. Com., 1934, p. 61. Mss. DAR.
Warfields of Md. Warfield. MHS.
Welsh-Hyatt and kindred. Welsh. Sec. 9, p. 199. MHS; DAR.
Gaither, Va. and Md. Col. and Revolutionary families of Phila. Jordan. 1933, v. 1, pp. 144-67.
†**Gaither, Henry.** Hist. of Md. Scharf. V. 3, p. 49. MHS.

Gaither (John) Family Line, Va. and Md. (John Gaither born 1600.) Natl. Geneal. Soc. Quart., v. 25, no. 3, p. 96.
***Gaither, T. H.** Geneal. and mem. encyc. of Md. Spencer. V. 2, pp. 572–76. MHS; DAR.
***Gaither Family.** Anne Arundel Co. Gentry. Newman. Pp. 353–91. MHS; DAR.
*Col. and Revolutionary families of Pa. Jordan. 1932, v. 4, pp. 130–52.
Md. Geneal. Rec. Com., 1933–34, pp. 62–65. Mss. DAR.
Galbraith. Carey chart. MHS.
Mrs. W. H. Harris chart. MHS.
Peale Geneal. Coll. Ms. MHS.
Galbraith Family. Torrence and allied families. Torrence. Pp. 487–90. MHS; DAR.
Gale. Done Bible rec. Ms. MHS.
*Gale and Chamberlaine family rec. Ms. MHS.
Geneal. notes of Chamberlaine family. MHS.
Md. families. Francis B. Culver. Ms. Personal list.
Pedigree of Levin Gale Shreve. Soc. Col. Wars Md. Culver. 1940. MHS; DAR.
Rec. of Stepney Parish. MHS; DAR.
St. Paul's churchyard, Kent Co. Md. O. R. Soc. Bull., no. 2, pp. 54–65. MHS.
St. Paul's Parish, Balto. V. 2. Mss. MHS.
*See Col. Arthur Lee Shreve. Burke's Landed Gentry Amer. Families. 1939. MHS.
Side lights on Md. hist. Richardson. V. 2, p. 102. MHS; DAR.
Still Pond cemetery, Kent Co. Md. O. R. Soc., v. 2. MHS.
*Wicomico Co. families. Tilghman. Ms., pp. 34, 101, 118. DAR.
Gale, George (born 1756; died 1815). Tombstone rec., North-Elk Parish, Cecil Co.
***Gale Family.** Old Kent. Hanson. P. 315. MHS; DAR.
Gale Family, Somerset and Cecil Cos. Pedigree, showing Chamberlaine, Dorsey, Hollyday, Shreve and other families, 1756–. Alward Chamberlaine. Typed. MHS.
Gallagher. Geneal. and mem. encyc. of Md. Spencer. V. 1, p. 166. MHS; DAR.
St. Paul's Parish, Balto. V. 2. Mss. MHS.
See Gallaher.
†**Gallagher, John.** M. H. Mag., v. 12, p. 218.
Gallaher, Va.: Col. families of U. S. A. Mackenzie. V. 4, pp. 159–63. MHS.
*The Sun, Balto. Jan. 29, Feb. 12, 1905; Oct. 28, Nov. 4, 1906.
Gallaher, O'Gallaher. Family of Ireland. Ms. File case, DAR.
Gallatin. St. Paul's Parish, Balto. V. 2. Mss. MHS.
Gallaway. St. Stephens Parish, Cecilton, Md. MHS; DAR.
Galloway. Amer. ancestry of Frederick Louis and Reginald Shippen Huidekoper. 1931, pamph., p. 13. MHS; DAR.
Balch letters and papers. Pamph., p. 70. MHS.
*Burke's landed gentry. 1939. MHS.
Cary Geneal. Coll. Ms. MHS.
Chew family. Culver. M. H. Mag., 1935, v. 30, no. 2, pp. 157–75.
Col. mansions of Md. and Del. Hammond. 1914. MHS.
Cotton chart. MHS.
De Ford chart. MHS.
Descendants of Joran Kyn. Pa. Mag., v. 6, p. 332.
Dorsey and allied families. Ms. MHS.
Early Quaker rec., Anne Arundel and Calvert Cos., 1665–1889. Pub. Geneal. Soc. Pa., v. 3, no. 3, pp. 197–200.
McH. Howard pedigree chart, plate 1. Soc. Col. Wars, Md. Johnston. 1905, p. 41. MHS.
See Huidekoper. Abr. Compend. Amer. Geneal. Virkus. V. 4, p. 295. MHS.
Mrs. J. F. Lee chart. MHS.
Md. families. Culver. Ms. Personal list.
Pedigree of Charles Morris Howard. Soc. Col. Wars Md. Culver. 1940. MHS; DAR.
Price ancestral data (maternal). Bd. ms. MHS.
Rumsey-Smithson Bible rec. Md. Geneal. Rec. Com., 1932–33, v. 5, pp. 63–142. DAR.
Rumsey-Smithson family rec. bk. Md. Geneal. Rec. Com., 1932, pp. 63–158. DAR.
St. Paul's Parish, Balto. V. 1, 2, 4. Mss. MHS.
Smithsons of Harford Co. Md. Geneal. Rec. Com., 1932–33, pp. 157. Mss. DAR.
Talbott of "Poplar Knowle." Shirk. MHS; DAR.
Thomas-Chew-Lawrence. Thomas. MHS.
Uhler Bible rec. Ms. MHS.
Uhler Bible rec. Md. Geneal. Rec. Com., v. 2. DAR.
See Uhler-Anderson-Burgess-Galloway.
Galloway Family. Thomas Book. Thomas. Pp. 317–20. Lib. Cong.; MHS.
Galloway Family, Talbot Co. Invoices. Ms. MHS.
Gallup Family. Sketch, with reference to Dorsey family. Ms. MHS.
Galt. Bolton chart. MHS.
Cummings chart. Lib. Cong.; MHS; DAR.
Elliott chart. MHS.
Galt Family. Ames Geneal. Coll. Ms. MHS.
*Notes on origin and their hist. with geneal. notes. H. S. Galt, Peiping, China. In Scotland, Pa., Va., Md., pp. 51–52, 126–34; Canada, Denmark. Pamph. MHS.
Gambel. Balto., its hist., its people. Hall. V. 3. MHS; DAR.
Gamble. Harford Co. Hist. Soc. Mss. Coll. JHU.
†Med. Annals Md. Cordell. 1903, p. 404. MHS.
St. Paul's P. E. churchyard, Kent Co. Md. O. R. Soc. Bull., no. 2, pp. 54–65.
Gamble Family. Ames Geneal. Coll. Ms. MHS.
Gambrill. Anne Arundel Co. tombstone inscriptions. Ms. DAR.
J. S. Baldwin; her life and ancestry. Pamph. MHS.
*Founders of Anne Arundel and Howard Cos. Warfield. Pp. 373–74. MHS; DAR.
Hist. Graves of Md. and D. C. Ridgely. MHS.
Hist. sketch of P. F. Eichelberger. Eichelberger.
Md. families. Culver. Ms. Personal list.
†Med. Annals Md. Cordell. 1903, p. 405. MHS.
Monumental City. Howard. MHS; DAR.
Pedigree of Charles Gambrill Baldwin. Soc. Col. Wars Md. Culver. 1940. MHS; DAR.

Pedigree of Wm. Winchester Eareckson. Soc. Col. Wars Md. Culver. 1940. MHS; DAR.
St. Paul's Parish, Balto. V. 2. Mss. MHS.
†**Gambrill, H. N.** Balto., hist. and biog. Richardson and Bennett. 1871, pp. 255–59. MHS; DAR.
†**Gambrill, J. H., Jr.** Men of mark in Md. Johnson. V. 4. DAR; Enoch Pratt Lib.
Gambrill Family. Md. Geneal. Rec. Com., 1938–39, pp. 168–72. Mss. DAR.
***Game.** Wicomico Co. families. Tilghman. Ms., pp. 97, 111. DAR.
†**Gans.** Geneal. and mem. encyc. of Md. Spencer. V. 2, pp. 637–42. MHS; DAR.
Gantt. See Addison. Abr. Compend. Amer. Geneal. Virkus. V. 1, p. 47. DAR.
Balto. Herald, May 10, 1903. Newsp. clipp. MHS.
Bowie-Claggett chart. MHS.
Cary Geneal. Coll. Ms. MHS.
S. C. Chew pedigree chart. Soc. Col. Wars, Md. Johnston. 1905, p. 13. MHS.
Col. families of U. S. A. Mackenzie. V. 1, pp. 186–89. MHS. DAR.
Geneal. of de Gant, Gaunt, Gauntt, Gantt and descendants. (Also contains list of members of Old South River Club, 1742–1885.) Typed, bd., 270 pp., 14 charts. Ms. MHS.
*Geneal. of de Gant, Gaunt, Gauntt, Gantt Family. Charles S. Gantt. Balto., 1937, typed. MHS.
†Henry Lawrence Gantt, leader in industry. L. P. Alford. (Gantt family in Md., 1660.) Amer. Soc. of Mechan. Eng., N. Y., 1934.
Hist. graves of Md. and D. C. Ridgely. MHS.
†Md. Annals Md. Cordell. 1903, p. 405. MHS.
Monnet family geneal. Monette. MHS.
Patriotic Md. Md. Soc. of S. A. R., 1930. MHS; DAR.
Pedigree of Thomas Carroll Roberts. Soc. Col. Wars Md. Culver. 1940. MHS; DAR.
Pedigree of Wm. Emory Waring, Jr. Soc. Col. Wars Md. Culver. 1940. MHS; DAR.
Pedigree of Mason Locke Weems Williams. Soc. Col. Wars Md. Culver. 1940. MHS; DAR.
*The Sun, Balto., Oct. 1, 8, 15, 29, 1905.
See Beall-Gantt-Brooke.
***Gantt,** Anne Arundel Co. Lineage Bk., Daughters of Founders and Patriots, v. 21, p. 12. MHS.
Tombstone inscriptions. Ms. DAR.
***Gantt,** Prince George and Anne Arundel Cos. Wilson Mss. Coll., no. 42. MHS.
Gantt (Thomas) Family Line (Md. 1660). Natl. Geneal. Soc. Quart., v. 25, no. 3, p. 97.
Gantz. Abr. Compend. Amer. Geneal. Virkus. V. 1, p. 919. DAR.
Gantz Family. Geneal. (incomplete). Ms. MHS.
†**Garber.** Hist. of Frederick Co. Williams. MHS; DAR.
Gardener. Bleakley Bible rec. Ms. MHS.
St. Paul's Parish, Balto. V. 1. Mss. MHS.
Gardiner. Boarman geneal. Thomas. 1935. MHS; DAR.
Centenary of Catholicity in Ky. Webb. 1884. MHS.
Col. families of U. S. A. Mackenzie. V. 4, p. 443. MHS; DAR.
De Ford chart. MHS.
Dorsey Papers. Ms. MHS.
Hist. graves of Md. and D. C. Ridgely. MHS.
†Md. Annals Md. Cordell. 1903, p. 405. MHS.
Parr chart. MHS.
Pedigree of Charles Morris Howard. Soc. Col. Wars Md. Culver. 1940. MHS; DAR.
Pedigree of Edward Key. Soc. Col. Wars Md. Culver. 1940. MHS; DAR.
Raisin chart. MHS.
St. Paul's Parish, Balto. V. 1, 2. Mss. MHS.
Semmes and allied families. Semmes. P. 204. MHS.
*Semmes Geneal. Coll. Ms. MHS.
*The Sun, Balto. March 18, 25, May 6, 1906.
Miss Eliza Thomas chart. MHS.
See Heuisler-Gardiner.
Gardiner, Capt. Luke, St. Mary's Co. T. C. Jenkins pedigree chart. Soc. Col. Wars, Md. Johnston. 1905, pp. 47, 145. MHS.
Some early col. Marylanders. M. H. Mag., 1921, v. 16, p. 19.
Gardiner Family. Ms. MHS.
Gardiner-Austen Line. Balto., its hist., its people. Hall. V. 2, p. 299; v. 3, p. 515. MHS; DAR.
Abr. Compend. Amer. Geneal. Virkus. V. 4, p. 665. MHS.
***Gardiner, Gardner.** Geneal. Washington, D. C. DAR.
†**Gardner.** Md. Annals Md. Cordell. 1903, p. 405. MHS.
Patriotic Md. Md. Soc. of S. A. R., 1930. MHS; DAR.
St. Paul's Parish, Balto. V. 1, 2. Mss. MHS.
(Née Stone.) Whiteley chart. MHS.
See Gardiner.
Gardner, Balto. Co. Mrs. H. H. Wrenn chart. MHS.
†**Gardner, Asa B., Jr.** Men of mark in Md. Johnson. V. 4. DAR; Enoch Pratt Lib.
Gardner, Thomas. Glendy churchyard. Patriotic Marylander, v. 2, no. 4, pp. 54–60. MHS; DAR.
Gardner Family. Lee of Va., 1642–1892. E. J. Lee. P. 477. Lib. Cong.; MHS.
Gare. *See* Ghare.
Garish. St. Paul's Parish, Balto. V. 2. Mss. MHS.
Garland. St. Paul's Parish, Balto. V. 2. Mss. MHS.
***Garlitz.** Garrett Co. pioneer families. Hoye. MHS; DAR.
Garlitz Family. Mountain Democrat, Garrett Co., Feb. 7, 1935. Newsp. clipp. MHS; DAR.
Garlough Family. With Todd of Pa. Geneal., Md. (and Ohio, 1808). Ms. File case, DAR.
Garmons. St. Paul's Parish, Balto. V. 2. Mss. MHS.
Garner. Carroll Co. Newsp. clipp., bd. MHS.
Pedigree of Garner Wood Denmead. Soc. Col. Wars Md. Culver. 1940. MHS; DAR.
†**Garnett.** Men of mark in Md. Johnson. V. 2. DAR; Enoch Pratt Lib.
†Papers relating to early hist. of Md. Streeter. 1876. MHS.
St. Paul's Parish, Balto. V. 2. Mss. MHS.
Garnett, King and Queen Cos., Va.; hist. and geneal. Bagby. 1908.

Garnett, Va. Va. Mag. Hist. and Biog., v. 42, pp. 72, 166, 256, 358.
Garnett, Va. and Md. Col. families of U. S. A. Mackenzie. V. 1. MHS; DAR.
Garnett, Thomas, Kent Co. Land grant. Md. Geneal. Rec. Com., v. 1, pp. 51–53. DAR.
Garnett-Mercer. Biog. sketch of Hon. James Mercer Garnett, Elmwood, Essex Co., Va.; with Mercer-Garnett and Mercer geneal. J. M. Garnett. 1910. DAR.
***Garnett-Mercer Families,** Essex Co., Va. Geneal. J. M. Garnett. Richmond, Whittet, Shepperson Printers, 1916. MHS.
Garrets. Naturalizations in Md., 1666–1765; Laws. Bacon. MHS.
Garretson. Talbott of "Poplar Knowle." Shirk. MHS; DAR.
Garretson-Griffith. Greenway Mss. Geneal. Coll. Binder's title, Hawkins-Bordley. MHS.
Garrett. Anne Arundel Co. tombstone inscriptions. Ms. DAR.
Autobiography of Summerfield Baldwin. MHS; DAR.
Sara R. Baldwin chart. MHS.
Baldwin-Woodward chart. Cary Geneal. Coll. Ms. MHS.
Balto., its hist., its people. Hall. V. 2. MHS; DAR.
Brooks chart. MHS.
Chart, photos., 2 sheets. Cary Geneal. Coll. Ms. MHS.
Founders of Anne Arundel and Howard Cos. Warfield. Pp. 121–23. MHS; DAR.
†Geneal. and mem. encyc. of Md. Spencer. V. 1, pp. 23–25; v. 2, p. 359. MHS; DAR.
Gilpin chart. MHS.
Greenway chart. MHS.
Hamill chart. MHS.
†Hist. of Balto. City and Co. Scharf. Pp. 331, 475. MHS.
Hist. of Caroline Co., Va. Wingfield.
Key and allied families. Lane. DAR.
Lloyd family hist. of Wales, Pa., and Md. DAR.
Md. families. Culver. Ms. Personal list.
Md. Geneal. Bull., v. 7, p. 2. MHS; DAR.
Md. gleanings in Eng. Wills. M. H. Mag., 1907, v. 2, no. 3.
Parrish family. Boyd. MHS; DAR.
Monumental City. Howard. MHS; DAR.
Pedigree of Charles Gambrill Baldwin. Soc. Col. Wars Md. Culver. 1940. MHS; DAR.
Prentice chart. MHS.
St. Ann's churchyard, Annapolis. Md. O. R. S. Bull., no. 3, pp. 55–56.
St. Paul's Parish, Balto. V. 4. Mss. MHS.
Whitridge chart. MHS.
*Wicomico Co. families. Tilghman. Ms, p. 128. DAR.
See Cope-Garrett.
See Loney-Boyce-Day-Garrett-Ross-Stansbury.
Garrett, Kent, London, Ireland, Anne Arundel Co., Md., Louisa Co. and Williamsburg, Va. Cary Geneal. Coll. Ms. MHS.
Garrett, John W. Abr. Compend. Amer. Geneal. Virkus. V. 1, p. 118. DAR.
†Balto., hist. and biog. Richardson and Bennett. 1871, pp. 261–70. MHS; DAR.
Geneal. and mem. encyc. of Md. Spencer. V. 2, p. 359. MHS; DAR.
†Hist. of West. Md. Scharf. V. 2, pp. 1511–16. MHS; DAR.
Descendants of Joran Jyn of New Sweden. Keen. MHS; DAR.
***Garrett Family,** Garrett family, Janeville, Ireland and Louisa Co., Va. Lester Durand Gardner. Chart. Supplement to article in William and Mary Quart., 1932, v. 12, pp. 13–25. Pamph. MHS; DAR.
Garrett Family, Louisa Co., Va. Ms., MHS; ms., File case, DAR.
Pamph. MHS; DAR.
Garrettson. Greenway chart. MHS.
Griffith-Garrettson rec. Pamph. DAR.
Harford Co. Hist. Soc. Mss. Coll. JHU.
†Hist. of Balto. City and Co. Scharf. Pp. 864, 920. MHS.
Miss Cassandra Lee chart. MHS.
Pedigree of Septimus Davis. Soc. Col. Wars Md. Culver. 1940. MHS; DAR.
Rumsey-Smithson Bible rec. Md. Geneal. Rec. Com., 1932–33, v. 5, pp. 63–142. DAR.
Smithson-Rumsey rec. bk. Ms. MHS.
*Wicomico Co. families. Tilghman. Ms, p. 95. DAR.
Garrettson-Whitson. Rumsey-Smithson family rec. bk. Md. Geneal. Rec. Com., 1932, pp. 134, 135. DAR.
Garrit. St. Paul's Parish, Balto. V. 2. Mss. MHS.
***Garrott.** Frederick Co. families. Markell. Ms. Personal list.
†Med. Annals Md. Cordell. 1903, p. 406. MHS.
Garth Family. Sketch. M. H. Mag., 1911, v. 6, p. 420.
Gartrell. Gartrell-Beall families of Md. Mss. DAR.
Garver Line. Gaither, Va. and Md. Col. and Revolutionary families of Phila. 1933, v. 1, pp. 144–67.
Garvey. St. Paul's Parish, Balto. V. 1, 2. Mss. MHS.
Gary. Abr. Compend. Amer. Geneal. Virkus. V. 1, p. 119. DAR.
Balto., its hist., its people. Hall. V. 3. MHS; DAR.
Founders of Howard and Anne Arundel Cos. Warfield. P. 535. MHS; DAR.
†Hist. of Balto. City and Co. Scharf. P. 408. MHS.
Whitridge chart. MHS.
†**Gary, E. S.** Men of mark in Md. Johnson. V. 1. DAR; Enoch Pratt Lib.
†**Gary, J. S.** Balto., hist. and biog. Richardson and Bennett. 1871, pp. 271–74. MHS; DAR.
†**Gary, James A.** Men of mark in Md. Johnson. V. 2. DAR; Enoch Pratt Lib.
Gary, Mrs. James A., Jr. (Anne Franklin Keyser). Chart. Col. Dames, Chap. I. MHS.
Gash. St. Paul's Parish, Balto. V. 1, 2. Mss. MHS.
***Gaskins,** Va. The Sun, Balto., Dec. 18, 1904.
Gassaway. Abr. Compend. Amer. Geneal. Virkus. V. 4, p. 688. MHS.
Anne Arundel Co. tombstone inscriptions. Ms. DAR.
Beall and Bell families. Beall. MHS.
Britton Scrap Book. V. 1. Ms. MHS.

Col. families of Amer. Lawrence. V. 2, p. 37. MHS.
*Early Comers to the Province. Georgians in Anne Arundel Co. Atlanta Jour., Sept. 22, 1906. Newsp. clipp. File case, MHS.
See Elkins. Abr. Compend. Amer. Geneal. Virkus. V. 6, p. 210.
*Founders of Anne Arundel and Howard Cos. Warfield. Pp. 170–74, 380–85. MHS; DAR.
Geneal., 1746–1818. Geneal. Mag. of Amer. Ancestry. N. Y. July, 1916, v. 6, p. 101.
Griffith geneal. Griffith. MHS; DAR.
Howard-Montague-Warfield geneal. chart. Culver and Marye. MHS.
*Lineage Bk. Daughters of Amer. Colonists. V. 2, p. 256. MHS; DAR.
Patriotic Md. Md. Soc. of S. A. R., 1930. MHS; DAR.
St. Anne's churchyard, Annapolis. Md. O. R. S., Bull., no. 3, pp. 55–56.
Gassaway, Louis Dorsey. Pedigree. Soc. Col. Wars Md. Culver. 1940. MHS; DAR.
Gassaway-Larkin. Chart, photos., complete in 2 sheets. Cary Geneal. Coll. Ms. MHS.
*Side lights on Md. hist. Richardson. V. 2, p. 317. MHS; DAR.
Talbott of "Poplar Knowle." Shirk. MHS; DAR.
*The Sun, Balto., July 3, 1904; also mentioned in The Sun, April 15, 1908 (letter).
Warfields of Md. Warfield. MHS.
Gassman. Zion Reformed Church, Hagerstown. Md. Geneal. Rec. Com., 1934–35. Mss. DAR.
†**Gatch.** Hist. of Balto. City and Co. Scharf. P. 931. MHS.
Md. families. Culver. Ms. Personal list.
Lineage Bks., Natl. Soc. of Daughters of Amer. Col., v. 2, p. 150. MHS; DAR.
Gatchell. Gantz family geneal. Ms. MHS.
St. Paul's Parish, Balto. V. 3. Mss. MHS.
Gates. St. John's R. C. Church cemetery, Montgomery Co. Md. Geneal. Rec. Com., 1926, p. 27. Mss. DAR.
†**Gatton.** Med. Annals Md. Cordell. 1903, p. 406. MHS.
Gaulbert. White geneal. tree. MHS.
Gault. Hagerstown tombstone inscriptions. Gruder. Natl. Geneal. Soc. Quart., 1919, v. 8, nos. 1, 2.
Mrs. A. G. Ober chart. MHS.
Peale Geneal. Coll. Ms. MHS.
***Gault Family.** Geneal. Pt. 1. Ms. MHS.
Gaunt. *See* Gantt.
Gaunt, Fielder, Frederick Co. Will proved Nov. 24, 1807. D. A. R. Mag. June 1927, v. 61, no. 6, p. 470.
Gaunt Line. Col. and Revolutionary lineages of Amer. 1939, v. 1, p. 503. MHS.
Gauntt. *See* Gantt.
***Gaut.** Boyd family. Boyd. DAR.
Gautier. St. Paul's Parish, Balto. V. 2. Mss. MHS.
Gay. Rogers Bible rec. Ms. MHS.
Russell-Lux Bible rec. Photos. MHS.
St. Paul's Parish, Balto. V. 1. Mss. MHS.
Gaylord. Mrs. B. S. Johnston chart. MHS.
See Brooks.
***Gaylord, Gaillard.** Gaylord or Gaillard family. Isabel Brooks. Balto., John S. BridgesCo., 1928. MHS.
Gears, Geers. St. Stephens Parish, Cecilton, Md. MHS; DAR.
Gebhard. St. Paul's Parish, Balto. V. 2. Mss. MHS.
***Gedder.** Wicomico Co. families. Tilghman. Ms, p. 97. DAR.
Geddes. Amer. Clan Gregor Year Book, 1930, p. 54. MHS; DAR.
Geddis, Geddes. St. Paul's Parish, Balto. V. 1, 2. Mss. MHS.
***Gee Family.** Charles and Hannah Gee of Va. W. J. Fletcher. 1937. DAR.
Geers. *See* Gears.
Geewicks. *See* Gilwicks.
Gehr. Hagerstown tombstone inscriptions. Gruder. Natl. Geneal. Soc. Quart., 1919, v. 8, nos. 1, 2.
Gehring, J. G., II. Md. Soc., War of 1812, v. 1, no. 102. Ms. MHS.
Geiger. See Price. Col. families of U. S. A. Mackenzie. V. 3, p. 414. MHS; DAR.
Hagerstown tombstone inscriptions. Gruder. Natl. Geneal. Soc. Quart., 1919, v. 8, nos. 1, 2.
Geiman. Roop geneal. Pamph. MHS.
†**Geisinger, David.** M. H. Mag., v. 12, p. 219.
Geissinger, (Ohio)-**Dorsey.** Abr. Compend. Amer. Geneal. Virkus. V. 4, p. 201. MHS.
Geist. Naturalizations in Md., 1666–1765; Laws. Bacon. MHS.
Gelston Family. Descendants of Judge Hugh Gelston of Southampton, L. I. N. Y. Geneal. and Biog. Rec., 1871, v. 2, no. 3, pp. 131–38. MHS.
†**Geltmacher.** Hist. of Washington Co. Williams. 1906, v. 1, p. 745. MHS; DAR.
Gelwicks. Hagerstown tombstone inscriptions. Gruder. Natl. Geneal. Soc. Quart., 1919, v. 8, nos. 1, 2.
Gemmill. I. U. Church cemetery. Md. O. R. Soc. Bull., no. 2, pp. 76–78.
***Gentry Family.** Gentry family in Amer., 1676–1909; New Kent Co., Va. R. Gentry. N. Y., Grafton Press, 1909.
***Geoghegan.** Hist. Dorchester Co. Jones. 1925, p. 315. MHS; DAR.
George. Bible rec., Kent Co. Md. Geneal. Rec. Com., 1937. Parran. Mss. DAR.
Bible rec., 1797–1922. Md. Geneal. Rec. Com., 1932–33, v. 5, p. 216. DAR.
†Biog. cyc. of rep. men of Md. and D. C. P. 309. MHS; DAR.
Boyce chart. MHS.
Col. families of U. S. A. Mackenzie. V. 2, pp. 295–98. MHS; DAR.
Fox-Ellicott-Evans families. Evans. MHS; DAR.
†Hist. of Balto. City and Co. Scharf. Pp. 467–68. MHS.
Jenkins-Courtney chart. MHS.
†Men of mark in Md. Johnson. V. 4. DAR; Enoch Pratt Lib.
See Miller, Mrs. Sarah Fenner. Abr. Compend. Amer. Geneal. Virkus. V. 1, p. 728. DAR.
Pedigree of Maurice Edward Skinner. Soc. Col. Wars Md. Culver. 1940. MHS; DAR.
Mrs. M. L. Price chart. MHS.
See Jean-Baker-George.
George, James. Faith Pres. Church (Glendy Graveyard). (Vault, 1836). Mss. MHS.

George, Mrs. John C. (Amabel Lee). Chart. Col. Dames, Chap. I. MHS.
†**George, P. T.** Balto., hist. and biog. Richardson and Bennett. 1871, pp. 275–77. MHS; DAR.
***George Family.** Bible rec. contrib. by Mrs. T. S. George, Towson, Md. Md. Geneal. Bull., v. 10, no. 4, p. 40; v. 11, p. 17.
Thomas Book. Thomas. Pp. 321–22. Lib. Cong.; MHS.
George Family, Talbot Co. Cox (Cock) family. Leef and Webb. MS. MHS.
Gephart. Frederick Co. tombstone inscriptions. Gruder. Natl. Geneal. Soc. Quart., 1919, v. 8, nos. 1, 2.
†Hist. of Allegany Co. Thomas and Williams. V. 1. MHS; DAR.
Gerard. Ances. rec. and portraits. Col. Dames of Amer., 1910, v. 2, p. 547. MHS; DAR.
Cary Geneal. Coll. Ms. MHS.
Mason chart. MHS.
Lineage Bks., Natl. Soc. of Daughters of Amer. Col., v. 1, p. 372. MHS; DAR.
Pedigree of Duncan Keener Brent. Soc. Col. Wars Md. Culver. 1940. MHS; DAR.
Pedigree of Coleman Randall Freeman. Soc. Col. Wars Md. Culver. 1940. MHS; DAR.
Pedigree of Bennet Biscoe Norris. Soc. Col. Wars Md. Culver. 1940. MHS; DAR.
Side lights on Md. hist. Richardson. V. 2, p. 103. MHS; DAR.
*The Sun, Balto., Aug. 30, 1903.
See Stanard. Abr. Compend. Amer. Geneal. Virkus. V. 1, p. 951. DAR.
Gerard, Thomas. E. A. and F. de S. Jenkins pedigree chart. Soc. Col. Wars, Md. Johnston. 1905, pp. 46, 145. MHS.
German. St. Paul's Parish, Balto. V. 1, 4. Mss. MHS.
Gerock. Coll. of Amer. epitaphs and inscriptions. Alden. 1814, v. 5, MHS.
Gerrard. Ancestry of Rosalie Morris Johnson. Johnson. 1905. MHS; DAR.
Mrs. A. C. Bruce chart. MHS.
Mrs. Howard Bruce chart. MHS.
Ellicott-Campbell chart. MHS.
Md. families. Culver. Ms. Personal list.
Notes. Berryman family of Va. Ms. DAR.
Mrs. A. Randall chart. MHS.
*Wilson. Mss. Coll., no. 8, B. MHS.
Gerritson. Bible rec. Upper Penins. East. Shore. Pp. 68–86. MHS; DAR.
†**Getting.** Hist. of Washington Co. Williams. 1906, v. 2, p. 1126. MHS; DAR.
Getty. Bible rec., Carroll Co., 1611–1926. Md. Geneal. Rec. Com., 1932–33, pp. 57–59. Mss. DAR.
†Hist. of Allegany Co. Thomas and Williams. V. 1. MHS; DAR.
Getz. Frederick Co. tombstone inscriptions. Gruder. Natl. Geneal. Soc. Quart., 1919, v. 8, nos. 1, 2.
Getzendanner. First settlement of Germans in Md. Schultz. 1896, p. 40. MHS.
Frederick Co. tombstone inscriptions. Gruder. Natl. Geneal. Soc. Quart., 1919, v. 8, nos. 1, 2.
Getzendanner family of Frederick Co. Waxahackie, Texas, 1890, pamph. MHS; DAR.
†Hist. of Allegany Co. Thomas and Williams. V. 2. MHS; DAR.
†Hist. of Frederick Co. Williams. MHS; DAR.
Md. tombstone rec. Md. Geneal. Rec. Com., 1937, Parran, p. 15. Mss. DAR.
Mt. Olivet Cemetery, Frederick. Md. Geneal. Rec. Com., 1934–35, p. 111. Mss. DAR.
See Shriner. Lineage Bks., Natl. Soc. of Daughters of Amer. Col., v. 3, p. 121. MHS; DAR.
Steiner geneal. Steiner. 1896. MHS.
***Getzendanner Family,** Frederick Co. Getzendanner family. By W. H. Getzendanner. Texas, Waxachie, 1890. MHS; DAR.
***Getzendanner-Steiner (Stoner).** Lineage Bk. Daughters of Amer. Colonists, v. 3, p. 121. MHS; DAR.
Geyer. First settlement of Germans in Md. Schultz. 1896, p. 41. MHS.
Ghare, Gare. Hagerstown tombstone inscriptions. Gruder. Natl. Geneal. Soc. Quart., 1919, v. 8, nos. 1, 2.
†**Ghiselin, Cesar** (1693–1733). First gold- and silversmith, Phila. Pa. Mag. of Hist. and Biog., v. 57, pp., 244–59.
Ghiselm. Mrs. Charles Carter chart. MHS.
Chart, photos., complete in 1 sheet. Cary Geneal. Coll. Ms. MHS.
Mrs. C. C. Hall chart. MHS.
Maccubin-Lusby chart. Cary Geneal. Coll. Ms. MHS.
Md. families. Culver. Ms. Personal list.
†Med. Annals Md. Cordell. 1903, p. 407. MHS.
Mrs. G. H. Williams, Jr., chart. MHS.
Gibb. Tombstone inscriptions of Princess Anne and Snow Hill. Turner Geneal. Coll. Ms. MHS.
Gibb or **Gibbes.** Turner Geneal. Coll. Ms. MHS.
***Gibb** or **Gibbs.** Pennington Papers. Ms. MHS.
†**Gibbons.** Life of Cardinal Gibbons, Archbishop of Balto. Allen Sinclair Wills. 1922. MHS.
Lloyd family hist. of Wales, Pa., and Md. DAR.
†Med. Annals Md. Cordell. 1903, p. 408. MHS.
St. Paul's Parish, Balto. V. 1, 2. Mss. MHS.
St. Stephens Parish, Cecilton, Md. MHS; DAR.
†**Gibbons, James Cardinal.** Men of mark in Md. Johnson. V. 1. DAR; Enoch Pratt Lib.
Gibbs. Mary E. Jenkins Surratt, maternal line. Md. Geneal. Bull., v. 1, pp. 1–3.
See Gibb.
Gibbs, Mrs. Edward Everett (Ann Crossan Cooper Ranson). Chart. Col. Dames, Chap. I. MHS.
***Gibbs Family.** Memoir; Warwickshire, Eng., and U. S. Phila., 1879. MHS.
Gibson. Amer. Armory and Blue Book. Matthews. Pt. 4.
Ances. rec. and portraits. Col. Dames of Amer., 1910, v. 2, pp. 588–91. MHS; DAR.
Battee, Brewer, Boteler, etc., family rec. Murray. Photos. MHS.
Centreville cemetery. Md. O. R. Soc. Bull., no. 1, pp. 41–47.
Elbert chart. MHS.
*Gibson and allied families. Mrs. Clapham Murray. Photos. of family rec. MHS.
Gorsuch chart. Cary Geneal. Coll. Ms. MHS.
†Hist. of West Md. Scharf. V. 2, p. 1496. MHS; DAR.

Jackson family gathering. 1878.
Md. families. Culver. Ms. Personal list.
†Med. Annals Md. Cordell. 1903, pp. 409, 802-07. MHS.
Pedigree of Dr. Christopher Johnston, Jr. Soc. Col. Wars Md. Culver. 1940. MHS; DAR.
Pedigree of James Donnell Tilghman. Soc. Col. Wars Md. Culver. 1940. MHS; DAR.
Revolutionary war pension abs. Natl. Geneal. Soc. Quart., v. 23, no. 2, p. 54.
St. Paul's Parish, Balto. V. 1, 2, 3, 4. Mss. MHS.
See Conklin-Gibson.
Gibson, George Thornburgh Macauley. Pedigree. Soc. Col. Wars Md. Culver. 1940. MHS; DAR.
†**Gibson, Col. Jacob** (1759-1818). Hist. of Talbot Co. Tilghman. V. 1, pp. 231-56. MHS; DAR.
Gibson, James. Glendy churchyard. Patriotic Marylander, v. 2, no. 4, pp. 54-60. MHS; DAR.
Gibson, John. Revolutionary pensions abs. Natl. Geneal. Soc. Quart., v. 23, p. 54.
†**Gibson, Woolman Hopper.** Men of mark in Md. Johnson. V. 4. DAR; Enoch Pratt Lib.
Gibson-Harrison. Tombstone rec. from St. Michael's Parish, Talbot Co. Md. O. R. Soc. Bull., no. 1, p. 54.
Giffin, Wallis. Pedigree. Soc. Col. Wars Md. Culver. 1940. MHS; DAR.
Gilbert. Hagerstown tombstone inscriptions. Gruder. Natl. Geneal. Soc. Quart., 1919, v. 8, nos. 1, 2.
Hist. of Byberry and Moreland. Martindale. MHS.
†Hist. of Frederick Co. Williams. MHS; DAR.
St. Paul's Parish, Balto. V. 2. Mss. MHS.
Gilbert, James. Deeds, plats and other papers relating to lands in Carroll Co., 1812-48. Ms. File case, MHS.
*Gilbert family, Carver family. Duffield family. J. C. Martindale. DAR.
Gilbert Family, Carroll Co. Ms. MHS.
Gilberthorpe. St. Paul's Parish, Balto. V. 1, 2. Mss. MHS.
Gilchrist. Mt. Paran Pres. churchyard, Harrisonville, Balto. Co. Typed ms. MHS; DAR.
Gildea. St. Joseph's R. C. churchyard. Md. O. R. Soc. Bull., no. 3, p. 64.
Gilder. Abr. Compend. Amer. Geneal. Virkus. V. 1, p. 156. DAR.
Gildersleeve. Colston chart. Cary Geneal. Coll. Ms. MHS.
†**Gildersleeve, Basil L.** Men of mark in Md. Johnson. V. 1. DAR; Enoch Pratt Lib.
Gildz. Frederick Co. tombstone inscriptions. Gruder. Natl. Geneal. Soc. Quart., 1919, v. 8, nos. 1, 2.
Giles. Balto., its hist., its people. Hall. V. 3. MHS; DAR.
Early Quaker rec., Anne Arundel and Calvert Cos., 1665-1889. Pub. Geneal. Soc. Pa., v. 3, no. 3, pp. 197-200.
Mrs. E. W. Poe chart. MHS.
Rec. of Stepney Parish. MHS; DAR.
St. Paul's Parish, Balto. V. 1, 2. Mss. MHS.
Giles, Balto. Co. Manning chart. MHS.
†**Giles, W. F.** Balto., hist. and biog. Richardson and Bennett. 1871, pp. 279-83. MHS; DAR.
Gill. Balto., its hist., its people. Hall. V. 2. MHS; DAR.
Cary Geneal. Coll. Ms. MHS.
Dorsey chart. MHS.
Founders of Anne Arundel and Howard Cos. Warfield. P. 130. MHS; DAR.
Gary chart. MHS.
†Geneal. and mem. encyc. of Md. Spencer. V. 1, p. 75. MHS; DAR.
Hazelhurst chart. MHS.
See Henderson. Abr. Compend. Amer. Geneal. Virkus. V. 4, p. 575. MHS.
†Med. Annals Md. Cordell. 1903, p. 410. MHS.
Patriotic Md. Md. Soc. of S. A. R., 1930. MHS; DAR.
Pedigree of Duncan Keener Brent. Soc. Col. Wars Md. Culver. 1940. MHS; DAR.
Pedigree of Henry Irvine Keyer, II. Soc. Col. Wars Md. Culver. 1940. MHS; DAR.
*Pennington Papers. Ms. MHS.
Price ancestral data (paternal). Bd. Ms. MHS.
Rogers Coll. Ms. MHS.
St. Paul's Parish, Balto. V. 1, 2. Mss. MHS.
St. Thomas' Parish, Balto. Co. Bd. ms. MHS. Also: Md. Geneal. Rec. Com., 1937, pp. 109-82. Mss. DAR.
*The Sun, Balto., Oct. 21, 1906.
Western Run Parish book. Allen. Bd. ms. MHS.
Mrs. J. Whitridge Williams chart 1. MHS.
Gill, Charles Co. Lineage Bks., Natl. Soc. of Daughters of Amer. Col., v. 2, p. 54. MHS; DAR.
†**Gill, Gen. John.** Garrison Church. Allen. P. 151. MHS; DAR.
*Geneal. and memorial encyc. of Md. Spencer. V. 2, p. 631. MHS; DAR.
Gill, Mrs. John (Miss Louisa Wallace Spence). Chart. Col. Dames, Chap. I. MHS.
Gill, N. R. Md. Soc., War of 1812, v. 1, no. 112. Ms. MHS.
Gill, R. Lee. Md. Soc., War of 1812, v. 1, no. 113. Ms. MHS.
†Men of mark in Md. Johnson. V. 2. DAR; Enoch Pratt Lib.
Gill, R. Lee George, Jr. Abr. Compend. Amer. Geneal. Virkus. V. 6, p. 688. DAR.
Gill, Roger Taney. Md. Soc., War of 1812, v. 1, no. 114. Ms. MHS.
†**Gill, Gen. Wm. Dorman.** Geneal. and mem. encyc. of Md. Spencer. V. 2, pp. 697. MHS; DAR.
Gill, William Harrison. Pedigree chart. Soc. Col. Wars, Md. Johnston. 1905, p. 26. MHS.
Md. Soc., War of 1812, v. 1, no. 52. Ms. MHS.
Gilles. Early Quaker rec., Anne Arundel and Calvert Cos., 1665-1889. Pub. Geneal. Soc. Pa., v. 3, no. 3, pp. 197-200.
Thomas-Chew-Lawrence. Thomas. MHS.
Gillespie Family. Thomas Book. Thomas. P. 56. Lib. Cong; MHS.
Gillespie-Brittain-Bratton. Bible rec. Pub. Geneal. Soc. Pa., v. 11, pp. 73-75.
Gillet. Abr. Compend. Amer. Geneal. Virkus. V. 1, p. 165. DAR.
Dorsey chart. MHS.
Turner Geneal. Coll. Ms. MHS.
*Wicomico Co. families. Tilghman. Ms, p. 4. DAR.

Gillet, Charles Berkley. Pedigree. Soc. Col. Wars Md. Culver. 1940. MHS; DAR.
Gillet, Francis Warrington. Pedigree. Soc. Col. Wars Md. Culver. 1940. MHS; DAR.
Gillet, James McClure. Pedigree. Soc. Col. Wars Md. Culver. 1940. MHS; DAR.
Gillet-Miller. Gillett-Miller families, 1755-1859. Ms. MHS.
***Gillett, George Martin.** Burke's landed gentry. 1939. MHS.
†Men of mark in Md. Johnson. V. 2. DAR; Enoch Pratt Lib.
Pedigree. Soc. Col. Wars Md. Culver. 1940. MHS; DAR.
†Gillingham. Med. Annals Md. Cordell. 1903, p. 410. MHS.
St. Paul's Parish, Balto. V. 2. Mss. MHS.
***Gillingham Family.** Descendants of Yeamans Gillingham. H. E. Gillingham. Phila., 901. MHS; DAR.
Gillips. Dorsey and allied families. Ms. MHS.
Gillis. H. D. G. Carroll. Ms. Book. In H. F. Thompson Papers. MHS.
Miss M. W. Davis chart. MHS.
Mrs. C. C. Hall chart. MHS.
Handy and their kin. Handy.
Salisbury, Wicomico Co. Truitt. DAR.
Rec. of Stepney Parish. MHS; DAR.
Somerset Co. Court Book. Tilghman. 1937. Ms. DAR.
Mrs. E. C. Venable chart. MHS.
Wicomico Co. families. Bible rec. Ms. DAR.
*Wicomico Co. families. Tilghman. Ms, pp. 20, 22, 44, 97, 129. DAR.
Mrs. G. H. Williams, Jr., chart. MHS.
See Handy-Gillis.
Gillis-Winder. Chart, photos. (2). Cary Geneal. Coll. Ms. MHS.
Gilliss. Carey chart. MHS.
DeFord chart. MHS.
Ms. MHS.
Md. families. Culver. Ms. Personal list.
†Med. Annals Md. Cordell. 1903, p. 411. MHS.
Old Somerset. Torrence. MHS; DAR.
Pedigree of Charles Morris Howard. Soc. Col. Wars Md. Culver. 1940. MHS; DAR.
Gilliss-Fassitt. Bible rec., 1772-1855. Md. Geneal. Rec. Com., 1938-39, p. 212. Mss. DAR.
***Gillman, Gilman.** Searches into hist. of Gillman or Gilman family. A. W. Gillman. 1895. DAR.
Gillmeyer. Jenkins-Courtney chart. MHS.
Gillmyer. St. Joseph's R. C. churchyard. Md. O. R. Soc. Bull., no. 3, p. 64.
Gilman. Col. families of U. S. A. Mackenzie. V. 1, p. 193. MHS; DAR.
Life of Daniel Coit Gilman. Fabian Franklin. N. Y., 1910.
St. Paul's Parish, Balto. V. 2. Mss. MHS.
See Gillman.
Gilman, Daniel Coit. Ances. rec. and portraits. Col. Dames of Amer., 1910, v. 1, pp. 260-62, 264, 269-73, 275. MHS; DAR.
†Men of mark in Md. Johnson. V. 1. DAR; Enoch Pratt Lib.
New Eng. Pedigree charts, plates 1 and 2. Soc. Col. Wars, Md. Johnston. 1905, pp. 27-28. MHS.
Gilman, Miss Elizabeth. Chart. Col. Dames, Chap. I. MHS.
Gilman-Coit. Pedigree chart. MHS.
Gilmer. William and Mary Quart., 1st series, v. 6, p. 94.
Gilmor. Ances. rec. and portraits. Col. Dames of Amer., 1910, v. 1, pp. 288, 290, 291. MHS; DAR.
Balto., its hist., its people. Hall. V. 3. MHS; DAR.
†Bench and bar of Md. Sams and Riley. 1901, v. 2, p. 656. Lib. Cong.; MHS; Peabody Lib.
Cary Geneal. Coll. Ms. MHS.
Caton chart. Cary Geneal. Coll. Ms. MHS.
*Chart. Ms. MHS.
†Diary of Robert Gilmor; also short biog. M. H. Mag., 1922, v. 17, pp. 231-68, 319-347.
Gilmor Papers. Ms. MHS.
Robert Gilmor chart. MHS.
Glen Ellen, birthplace of Col. Henry Gilmor. The Jeffersonian, Towson, Md., July, 19, 1930. Newsp. clipp. MHS.
Harvey chart. MHS.
No Name Mag., v. 2, p. 174. MHS.
*Pennington Papers. Ms. MHS.
St. Paul's Parish, Balto. V. 2, 3. Mss. MHS.
Sir George Yeardley. Upshur. Pp. 33, 34, 35. MHS.
†Gilmor, Robt. (1748-1822). Balto., hist. and biog. Richardson and Bennett. 1871, p. 285. MHS; DAR.
(1748-1822). Revolutionary war heroes. Cole. Bklet. Enoch Pratt Lib.
(Born in Balto., Mar. 8, 1833.) Greenway Mss. Geneal. Coll. Binder's title, Taylor, no. 2. MHS.
*Chart. Ms. MHS.
Westminster churchyard. Patriotic Marylander, v. 2, no. 4, pp. 54-60. MHS; DAR.
Gilmor Family. Ames Geneal. Coll. Ms. MHS.
Gilpin. Balto., its hist., its people. Hall. V. 2. MHS; DAR.
†Biog. cyc. of rep. men of Md. and D. C. P. 262. MHS; DAR.
*Geneal. and memorial encyc. of Md. Spencer. V. 2, p. 480-85. MHS; DAR.
*Geneal. of family of Gideon Gilpin of Chester Co., Pa., 1696. Charts. J. E. Gilpin. Families Anderson, Bowen, Brooke, Colton, Edge, Goldsmith, Henderson, Hughes, Painter, Palmer, Sampson, Smith, Stabler, Stokes, Sullivan and others. July, 1897. MHS.
Harlan family geneal., Chester Co., Pa. Harlan. Pp. 680-82. MHS.
Husband and allied families. Ms. MHS.
Patriotic Md. Md. Soc. of S. A. R., 1930. MHS; DAR.
Thomas-Chew-Lawrence. Thomas. MHS.
***Gilpin,** Pa. and Md. The Sun, Balto., March 19, April 23 (An Old Manor), 1905.
Gilpin, Mrs. Arthington (Grace Howard Munnkhuysen) (married first Edwin Pugh Baugh). Chart. Col. Dames, Chap. I. MHS.
Gilpin, H. Brooke. Abr. Compend. Amer. Geneal. Virkus. V. 1, p. 285. DAR.
†Gilpin, Henry. Men of mark in Md. Johnson. V. 1. DAR; Enoch Pratt Lib.
***Gilpin Family.** From Richard, in 1206, in line to Joseph Gilpin, emigrant to Amer., and something of Amer. Gilpins and their descendants to 1916. W. T. Robert's Co., Wash., D. C. DAR.

Hist. of Cecil Co. Johnston. P. 511. MHS; DAR.
Thomas Book. Thomas. Pp. 327-38. Lib. Cong.; MHS.
Gilwicks, Geewicks. Hagerstown tombstone inscriptions. Gruder. Natl. Geneal. Soc. Quart., 1919, v. 8, nos. 1, 2.
Ginevan. St. Paul's Parish, Balto. V. 2. Mss. MHS.
Girdletree, about 1 mile from Snow Hill. Births, marriages and deaths, 1846-1894. Turner Geneal. Coll. Ms. MHS.
†**Gisriel, Wm.** Men of mark in Md. Johnson. V. 3, DAR; Enoch Pratt Lib.
Gist. Bible rec., Carroll Co., 1712-1830. Md. Geneal. Rec. Com., 1930-31, p. 24. Ms. DAR.
Bible rec., from Bible in home of Dow Gist, London, Ohio. D. A. R. Mag., May, 1936, v. 70, no. 5, p. 457.
Bible rec., from Bible owned by Mrs. S. H. Gatskell, McIntosh, Fla. D. A. R. Mag., May, 1936, v. 70, no. 5, p. 458.
Bible rec. from home of Robert Gist, near Westminster, Md. D. A. R. Mag., May, 1936, v. 70, no. 5, p. 458.
Bible rec., London, Ohio, 1837-61. D. A. R. Mag., v. 70, no. 5, pp. 457-58.
†Biog. of Gen. Mordecai Gist. MHS.
Brooks chart. MHS.
Mrs. T. R. Brown chart. MHS.
Charts, 1623. Md. Geneal. Rec. Com., 1932-33. Mss. DAR.
Chart of descent of Col. Joshua Gist. Md. Geneal. Rec. Com., 1937-38. Mss., folder. DAR.
Chart of descent of Gen. Mordecai Gist. Md. Geneal. Rec. Com., 1937-38. Mss., folder. DAR.
Chart, photos., 3 sheets. (Gist, Md. and Va., 1 sheet.) Cary Geneal. Coll. Ms. MHS.
Col. families of Amer. Lawrence. V. 5, p. 92. MHS.
Col. families of U. S. A. Mackenzie. V. 1, p. 267; v. 6. MHS; DAR.
Descendants of Joran Kyn of New Sweden. Keen. MHS; DAR.
Descendants of Joran Kyn. Pa. Mag., v. 5, p. 451.
*Garrison Church. Allen. Pp. 129-31. MHS; DAR.
Brig. Gen. Mordecai Gist. B. Gist Lynch. D. A. R. Mag., v. 65, no. 12, p. 720-24.
Harvey chart. MHS.
Hist. of Frederick Co. Williams. V. 1, pp. 217-28. MHS; DAR.
*Hist. of West Md. Scharf. V. 1, p. 75; v. 2, pp. 791, 920. MHS; DAR.
Lambdin chart. MHS.
Md. families. Culver. Ms. Personal list.
McCormick chart. MHS.
Patriotic Md. Md. Soc. of S. A. R., 1930. MHS; DAR.
Rogers Coll. Ms. MHS.
St. Paul's Parish, Balto. V. 1. Mss. MHS.
St. Thomas' Parish, Balto. Co. Bd. ms. MHS. Also: Md. Geneal. Rec. Com., 1937, pp. 109-82. Mss. DAR.
Sherburne chart. MHS.
Side lights on Md. hist. Richardson. V. 2, p. 106. MHS; DAR.
*The Sun, Balto., Sept. 27, 1903.
Tombstone inscriptions, 1816-1907 from graveyard on farm of Robert Gist, near Westminster, Md. Md. Geneal. Rec. Com., 1930-31, p. 25. Mss. DAR.
Valuable papers of Gist family. Hall Rec.
Wilson Mss. Coll., no. 143. MHS.
Gist, Christopher (1706). Pioneer; hist. and geneal. The Times, Westminster, Md., Friday, Nov. 18, 1932. Newsp. clipp. MHS.
Gist, Col. Joshua. Land grants, from 1791. Md. Geneal. Rec. Com., 1938-39, p. 30. Mss. DAR.
Gist, Joshua, Carroll Co. Copy of will, 1839. Md. Geneal. Rec. Com., 1937-38, p. 34. Mss. MHS.
Gist, Mordecai, S. C. Copy of will, 1792. Md. Geneal. Rec. Com., 1937-38, p. 16. Mss. DAR.
†**Gist, Gen. Mordecai.** Biog. sketches of distinguished Marylanders. Boyle. MHS; DAR.
Sketches of Natl. Portrait Gallery of Distinguished Amer. Longacre and Herring.
†Chronicles of Balto. Scharf. 1874, p. 264. MHS; DAR.
Mordecai Gist and his Amer. progenitors. Katherine W. Blakeslee. Pub. by Mordecai Gist Chapter, D. A. R., Balto., 1923, pamph. MHS; DAR.
*‡Hist. and geneal. B. Gist Lynch. The Times, Westminster, Md., Friday, July 1, 1932. Newsp. clipp. MHS.
*Hist. of Md. Scharf. V. 2, pp. 328-29.
†(1743-92). M. H. Mag., v. 12, p. 219.
Gist, Richard. Patent "Gist Inspection," 1731. Md. Geneal. Rec. Com., 1934-35, p. 285. Mss. DAR.
Gist, Rachel, Balto. Co. Copy of will, 1829. Md. Geneal. Rec. Com., 1937-38, p. 31. Mss. MHS.
Gist, Thomas, Balto. Co. Copy of will, 1807. Md. Geneal. Rec. Com., 1937-38, p. 25. Mss. DAR.
(Father of Gen. Mordecai Gist.) Copy of will, 1787. Md. Geneal. Rec. Com., 1937-38, p. 11. Mss. DAR.
***Gist Family.** Gist family. Charles T. Cockey. Pikesville, 1885. Pamph. MHS.
*Gist family of S. C. and its Md. antecedents. W. Gee. Priv. pr., Charlottesville, Va., 1934. MHS; DAR.
*Graveyard records, Carroll Co., 1804-1877 (earliest birth, 1748). Hist. of West. Md. Scharf. V. 2, p. 921. MHS; DAR.
Graveyard rec., with notes on Gist family. Hist. of West. Md. Scharf. V. 2, pp. 921-23.
Gist Family, Balto. Co. M. H. Mag., 1913, v. 8, pp. 373-91.
Gist-Cockey-Hammond. D. A. R. Mag., v. 70, no. 5, pp. 457-58.
Gittings. Ances. rec. and portraits. Col. Dames of Amer., 1910, v. 2, p. 670. MHS; DAR.
Barroll in Great Britain and Amer. Barroll. P. 73. MHS.
†Biog. cyc. of rep. men of Md. and D. C. Pp. 466, 553. MHS; DAR.
Miss M. S. Brogden chart. MHS.
Cary Geneal. Coll. Ms. MHS.
Col. families of U. S. A. Mackenzie. V. 1, p. 604. MHS; DAR.
Hist. graves of Md. and D. C. Ridgely. MHS.
†Hist. of Balto. City and Co. Scharf. P. 719. MHS.

Gittings. S. G. Hopkins chart. MHS.
Howard-Montague-Warfield geneal. chart. Culver and Marye. MHS.
Rev. Joseph Hull (1595) and some of his descendants. Hull. 1904. MHS.
Lehr chart. MHS.
†Med. Annals Md. Cordell. 1903, p. 411. MHS.
Merryman family. Culver. M. H. Mag., 1915, v. 10, pp. 176, 286.
Pedigree of Francis Joseph Baldwin. Soc. Col. Wars Md. Culver. 1940. MHS; DAR.
Pedigree of Wm. Handy Collins Vickers. Soc. Col. Wars Md. Culver. 1940. MHS; DAR.
Mrs. Pennington chart. MHS.
St. Paul's Parish, Balto. V. 1, 2, 4. Mss. MHS.
Trinity P. E. churchyard, Long Green. Typed ms. MHS; DAR.
†Gittings, J. S. Balto., hist. and biog. Richardson and Bennett. 1871, pp. 289–91. MHS; DAR.
Gittings, Mrs. John Sterett (Rosalie K. May). Chart. Col. Dames, Chap. I. MHS.
Gittings Family. Arch. of Georgetown Univ., Wash., D. C., v. 130, no. 7.
Gittings Line. Mrs. R. Barton, Jr., charts. MHS.
(1760–1881). W. S. G. Williams pedigree chart. Soc. Col. Wars, Md. Johnston. 1905, p. 128. MHS.
Gittings-Parran-Sellman-Smith. Abr. Compend. Amer. Geneal. Virkus. V. 4, p. 210. MHS.
***Givins.** Wicomico Co. families. Tilghman. Ms., p. 96. DAR.
Gladden. Rumsey-Smithson Bible rec. Md. Geneal. Rec. Com., 1932–33, v. 5, pp. 63–142. DAR.
Rumsey-Smithson family rec. bk. Md. Geneal. Rec. Com., 1932, pp. 63–158. DAR.
Smithson-Rumsey rec. bk. Ms. MHS.
†Gladfelter, Reuben. Men of mark in Md. Johnson. V. 4. DAR; Enoch Pratt Lib.
Gladhill. U. B. cemetery, Sabillasville. Young. Natl. Geneal. Soc. Quart., Sept., 1938, v. 26, no. 3, p. 61 (to be contd.)
Gladman. St. Paul's Parish, Balto. V. 1. Mss. MHS.
Gladwin. Chart. Wm. Preston of Newcastle on Tyne, Eng., and Phila., Pa., and allied families. Belsterling. MHS.
Glasgow. Harford Co. Hist. Soc. Mss. Coll. JHU.
†Med. Annals Med. Cordell. 1903, p. 411. MHS.
West Nottingham Cemetery. M. H. Mag., 1923, v. 18, p. 55.
Glassell. Hist. of Caroline Co., Va. Wingfield.
Glassell, Va. Va. geneal. Hayden. MHS; DAR.
Glazier, John, from Conn. to Md. Revolutionary war pention. D. A. R. Mag., v. 63, no. 2, p. 102.
Revolutionary pension. D. A. R. Mag., Feb., 1929, v. 63, no. 2, p. 102.
Gleason Family. Old N. W. Geneal. Soc. Quart., Columbus, Ohio 1903, v. 6. MHS.
Gleibsattler. *See* Klebsattel.
Glen. *See* Glenn.
Glenn. Balto., its hist., its people. Hall. V. 3. MHS; DAR.
Brooks chart. MHS.
Col. and Revolutionary families of Pa. Jordan. 1932, v. 4, p. 78.
Pa. Mag., v. 18, p. 516.
Perin chart. MHS.
St. Paul's Parish, Balto. V. 2, 3. Mss. MHS.
Seagrave chart. MHS.
Smithsons of Harford Co. Md. Geneal. Rec. Com., 1932–33, pp. 158. Mss. DAR.
See Howard-Glenn.
Glenn, Glen. Col. families of U. S. A. Mackenzie. V. 3, p. 181. MHS; DAR.
Pedigree of Coleman Randall Freeman. Soc. Col. Wars Md. Culver. 1940. MHS; DAR.
Glison. Glison-Sellman-Murphy-Cooley Bible rec. Ms. DAR.
John White Bible rec. Ms. MHS.
Glison-Sellman-Murphy-Cooley. Ms. DAR.
Glorius. St. John's R. C. Church cemetery, Montgomery Co. Md. Geneal. Rec. Com., 1926, p. 27. Mss. DAR.
Glossbrenner. Hagerstown tombstone inscriptions. Gruder. Natl. Geneal. Soc. Quart., 1919, v. 8, nos. 1, 2.
Glover. Abr. Compend. Amer. Geneal. Virkus. V. 1, pp. 622–23. DAR.
Anne Arundel Co. Col. families of Amer. Lawrence. V. 6, p. 69. MHS.
Mrs. R. F. Brent chart. MHS.
Cary Geneal. Coll. Ms. MHS.
Col. families of Amer. Lawrence. V. 6, p. 69. MHS.
***Glover, Charles Carroll.** Burke's landed gentry. 1939. MHS.
†Glover, Charles (1780–1827), Washington and Carroll Cos. Rec. Columbia Hist. Soc., v. 31; v. 32, p. 299.
Gnegy Family. Mountain Democrat, Garrett Co., Nov. 8, 1934. Newsp. clipp. MHS; DAR.
***Godard, Goddard.** Wicomico Co. families. Tilghman. Ms, pp. 99, 113, 123. DAR.
Goddard. Abr. Compend. Amer. Geneal. Virkus. V. 1, p. 288. DAR.
Geneal. descendants of Thomas Angell. Angell. Providence, R. I., 1872.
†Hist. printing in Col. Md. Wroth. MHS.
Md. gleanings in Eng. Wills. M. H. Mag., 1907, v. 2, no. 4.
Somerset Co. Court Book. Tilghman. 1937. Ms. DAR.
See Godard.
†Goddard, Henry P. Men of mark in Md. Johnson. V. 2. DAR; Enoch Pratt Lib.
†Goddard, Mary Katharine (Md. Journal, 1773). Ladies of press. Ross. 1936.
†Goddard, William. Hist. of Md. Scharf. V. 2, p. 308. MHS.
Goddard, Godard. St. Paul's Parish, Balto. V. 2. Mss. MHS.
Gode. *See* Goode.
†Godefray. Maximilian Godefray and Eliza, his wife, daughter of Dr. John Crawford; sketches of their lives; with letters. M. H. Mag., 1934, v. 29, pp. 1–20, 175–212.
Godfrey. Mt. Olive M. P. churchyard and, Worcester Co. Md. Geneal. Rec. Com., 1937, Mrs. Lines. Mss. DAR.
Mt. Zion P. E. Churchyard, Worcester Co. Md. Geneal. Rec. Com., 1937, Mrs. Lines. Mss. DAR.
St. Paul's Parish, Balto. V. 1, 2. Mss. MHS.

Sherburne chart. MHS.
*Wicomico Co. families. Tilghman. Ms, p. 86. DAR.
Godfrey, Worcester Co. Md. and Sussex Co., Del., moved to Ohio. Bible rec., 1762–1888. Bible rec. of Dorchester and Somerset Cos. and Del. P. 30. DAR.
Godfrey Family, Md. and Del. Md. Geneal. Rec. Com., 1937. Parran, p. 71. Mss. DAR.
Godman, Stephen Beard and his descendants. Townsend. Ms. MHS.
Thomas McKnew, Prince George Co., and his descendants. Townsend. Ms. MHS.
†Med. Annals Md. Cordell. 1903, pp. 412, 574, 771–79. MHS.
Notes. D. A. R. Mag., v. 72, no. 2, pp. 62–63.
Patriotic Md. Md. Soc. of S. A. R., 1930. MHS; DAR.
Godman, Humphrey. And his descendants. Ms. MHS.
***Godman Family.** Humphrey Godman and his descendants. S. W. Townsend. Ms. MHS.
Godmont. St. Stephens Parish, Cecilton, Md. MHS; DAR.
Godshall. *See* Godshield.
Godshield, Godshall. St. Paul's Parish, Balto. V. 2. Mss. MHS.
Godwin. Rec., Queen Anne's Co., 1776–1905. Md. Geneal. Rec. Com., 1932–33. DAR.
See Childs-Biscoe-Godwin.
Goffe. *See* Gooch.
Gogel. Geneal. of descendants of George and Sarah Smedley. Cope. P. 637. MHS. DAR.
Gold. Zion Reformed Church, Hagerstown. Md. Geneal. Rec. Com., 1934–35. Mss. DAR.
Golder. St. Paul's Parish, Balto. V. 2. Mss. MHS.
Goldesburgh. *See* Goldsborough.
Goldsborough. Abr. Compend. Amer. Geneal. Virkus. V. 1, pp. 33, 625, 921; v. 6, p. 423. DAR.
†Bench and Bar of Md. Sams and Riley. 1901, v. 2, pp. 420, 620. Lib. Cong.; MHS; Peabody Lib.
†Biog. cyc. of rep. men of Md. and D. C. Pp. 254, 476, 664. MHS; DAR.
Brief family rec., 1660-1722, Dorchester and Frederick Cos. Md. O. R. Soc. Bull., no. 1, p. 73.
Chart of Col. John Rodgers. DAR.
(36 stones.) Christ P. E. Church cemetery, Cambridge. Steele. 1936. MHS; DAR.
*Coat of arms. Burke's landed gentry. 1939. MHS.
Col. families of Amer. Lawrence. V. 16, p. 90–91.
Col. families of U. S. A. Mackenzie. V. 1. MHS; DAR.
Descendants of Joran Kyn of New Sweden. Keen. MHS; DAR.
Descendants of Joran Kyn. Pa. Mag., vol. 7, p. 464.
Dobbin chart. MHS.
Dorsey chart. MHS.
Duckett chart. MHS.
See Duvall. Abr. Compend. Amer. Geneal. Virkus. V. 1, p. 282. DAR.
Geneal. Ms. Coll. MHS.
Geneal. notes of Chamberlaine family. MHS.
†G. S. Goldsborough. G. H. Nock. Balto., 1906 (?) MHS.
Griffith geneal. Griffith. MHS; DAR.
Hist. graves of Md. and D. C. Ridgely. MHS.
†Hist. of Frederick Co. Williams. MHS; DAR.
†Hist. of Md. Scharf. V. 2, p. 635. MHS.
Md. families. Culver. Ms. Personal list.
Med. Annals Md. Cordell. 1903, pp. 398, 413–14. MHS.
Patriotic Md. Md. Soc. of S. A. R., 1930. MHS; DAR.
Peale Geneal. Coll. Ms. MHS.
Pedigree of Tilghman Goldsborough Pitts. Soc. Col. Wars Md. Culver. 1940. MHS; DAR.
Portrait and biog. rec. of East. Shore of Md. 1898, pp. 161, 231, 261, 438, 559, 681, 801, 858, 893. MHS; DAR.
Portrait and biog. rec. of Sixth Cong. Dist. of Md. 1898, pp. 416, 591. MHS; DAR.
St. Paul's Parish, Balto. V. 2, 4. Mss. MHS.
Side lights on Md. hist. Richardson. V. 2, p. 109. MHS; DAR.
(22 stones.) Spring Hill Cemetery, Talbot Co. Md. O. R. Soc. Bull., no. 1, pp. 35–41. MHS.
*The Sun, Balto., Sept. 20, 1903.
Thomas family of Talbot Co. Spencer. P. 70. MHS; DAR.
See Henry.
***Goldsborough,** Easton, Md. Lineage Bk. Daughters of Founders and Patriots, v. 17, pp. 84–85. MHS.
Goldsborough, Gov. Charles. Balto., its hist., its people. Hall. V. 3. MHS; DAR.
*Founders of Anne Arundel and Howard Cos. Warfield. P. 260. MHS; DAR.
†Governors of Md. Buchholz. P. 86. MHS.
†**Goldsborough, Hon. Robert.** M. H. Mag., 1915, v. 10, pp. 100–09.
†**Goldsborough, Robt. Henry** (1779–1836). Hist. of Talbot Co. Tilghman. V. 1, p. 408. MHS; DAR.
***Goldsborough Family.** Arch. of Georgetown Univ., Wash., D. C., v. 287.
*Bible. Md. Geneal. Bull., v. 10, no. 2. MHS; DAR.
*Old Kent. Hanson. Pp. 276–96. Chart, presented by Dr. J. Hall Pleasants, p. 282. MHS; DAR.
Patriotic Marylander, v. 1, no. 4, p. 62; v. 3, no. 4, pp. 236–39. MHS; DAR.
***Goldsborough Family,** Toulon, France, and Palermo, Sicily. Coat of arms. Miss L. E. Gouldsbury. 1866, pamph. MHS.
Goldsborough Line. Col. and Revolutionary lineages of Amer. 1939, v. 1, pp. 106–08; v. 2, pp. 197–200. MHS.
Manning family, Mass. Col. and Revolutionary families of Pa. Jordan. 1932, v. 4, p. 642.
Goldsborough-Pascault. Bible rec. Ms. MHS.
***Goldsborough, Goldesburgh.** Hist. Dorchester. Co. Jones. 1925, pp. 316–27. MHS. DAR.
Goldsby, (W. W.)-Bayne-Boswell-Finley-Fowke. Abr. Compend. Amer. Geneal. Virkus. V. 4, pp. 213–14. MHS.
Goldsmith. Blackford chart. MHS.
Geneal. of family of Gideon Gilpin. MHS.
Greenway chart. MHS.
Md. families. Culver. Ms. Personal list.

†**Goldsmith.** Med. Annals Md. Cordell. 1903, p. 414. MHS.
Old Somerset. Torrence. MHS; DAR.
Peale Geneal. Coll. Ms. MHS.
St. Paul's Parish, Balto. V. 1, 2. Mss. MHS.
Somerset Co. Court Book. Tilghman. 1937. Ms. DAR.
Wallis chart. MHS.
Goldthwaite. St. Paul's Parish, Balto. V. 2. Mss. MHS.
Goldwaite. Ancest. rec. and portraits. Col. Dames of Amer., 1910, v. 2, p. 821. MHS; DAR.
Ellicott-Campbell chart. MHS.
***Goll.** Frederick Co. families. Markell. Ms. Personal list.
Patriotic Md. Md. Soc. of S. A. R., 1930. MHS; DAR.
Golley. Naturalizations in Md., 1666–1765; Laws. Bacon. MHS.
Gooch. Ances. rec. and portraits. Col. Dames of Amer., 1910, v. 2, p. 730. MHS; DAR.
Stevenson chart. MHS.
Gooch, Gouge, Goffe, Gough. William and Mary. Quart., 1st series, v. 5, p. 110.
***Goode.** John Goode of Whitley. Francis Collier Goode. 1888. MHS.
***Goode,** Va. Coat of arms. Burke's landed gentry. 1939. MHS.
***Goode, Gode, Family.** Geneal. Va. cousins. Descendants of John of Whitby, Va. 1600. G. Brown Goode. J. W. R. Randolph and English, Richmond, Va., 1887. Pp. 27–428. MHS.
Goodenow, Rufus King, Jr. Pedigree. Soc. Col. Wars Md. Culver. 1940. MHS; DAR.
Goodfellow. St. John's R. C. Church cemetery, Montgomery Co. Md. Geneal. Rec. Com., 1926, p. 27. Mss. DAR.
Goodhart. *See* McCormick-Goodhart.
Gooding. St. Stephens Parish, Cecilton, Md. MHS; DAR.
***Goodloe.** Pennington Papers. Ms. MHS.
Goodson. Abr. Compend. Amer. Geneal. Virkus. V. 4, p. 341. MHS.
Goodwin. H. D. G. Carroll. Ms. Book. In H. F. Thompson Papers. MHS.
Cary Geneal. Coll. Ms. MHS.
S. C. Chew pedigree chart. Soc. Col. Wars, Md. Johnston. 1905, p. 13. MHS.
Col. families of U. S. A. Mackenzie. V. 2, p. 609. MHS; DAR.
Dorsey and allied families. Ms. MHS.
Dorsey chart. MHS.
Goodwin family in Amer. William and Mary Quart., 1st series, supplement to v. 6, no. 2; Balto. Co., p. 122; Carroll Co., p. 120; East. Shore of Md. (fragment), p. 123; St. Mary's Co., pp. 84–91.
Goodwin family in Amer. William and Mary Quart, 1st series, supplement, Oct. 1899, v. 8, no. 2; Balto., pp. 108–14; Kent Co., p. 101; Porter, Md., p. 108; unidentified Goodwins of Md., pp. 102–08.
Ms. MHS.
†Med. Annals Md. Cordell. 1903, p. 415. MHS.
Peale Geneal. Coll. Ms. MHS.
Pedigree of Thomas Murray Maynadier. Soc. Col. Wars Md. Culver. 1940. MHS; DAR.
Ridgely chart. Cary Geneal. Coll.' Ms. MHS.
St. Paul's Parish, Balto. V. 1, 2. Mss. MHS.
Segrave chart. MHS.
Trinity P. E. churchyard, Long Green. Typed ms. MHS; DAR.
See Childs-Biscoe-Goodwin.
***Goodwin,** Va. Lineage Bk., Daughters of Founders and Patriots, v. 18, p. 79. MHS; DAR.
***Goodwin Family.** Goodwin family. Whittet and Shepperson. 1898. MHS.
*Supplement. William and Mary Quart., 1897.
Gootee. Tombstone rec. of Dorchester Co. Jones. DAR.
Gordon. Ances. rec. and portraits. Col. Dames of Amer., 1910, v. 2, p. 753. MHS; DAR.
Ancestry of Mrs. Fulton Ray Gordon, nee Ellen Marjorie Gray. D. C. Geneal. Rec. Com., 1932–34, v. 10, pp. 120–27. Typed bd. DAR.
Balto., its hist., its people. Hall. V. 2. MHS; DAR.
Geneal. rec. of family of Thomas. Thomas. MHS.
†Hist. of Allegany Co. Thomas and Williams. V. 1. MHS; DAR.
Miss Ann Huntly Chart. Col. Dames, Chap. I. MHS.
Mrs. H. F. Johnston chart. MHS.
Lineage Bk., Order of Washington, p. 123. MHS; DAR.
†Med. Annals Md. Cordell. 1903, p. 415. MHS.
Palmer chart. MHS.
Pocahontas and her descendants. Robertson. MHS; DAR.
St. Paul's Parish, Balto. V. 1, 2, 3. Mss. MHS.
St. Stephens Parish, Cecilton, Md. MHS; DAR.
(Scotch line). Dodge family R. I., 1670. Col. and Revolutionary families of Pa. Jordan. 1932, v. 4, p. 334.
Somerset Co. Court Book. Tilghman. 1937. Ms. DAR.
Stevenson chart. MHS.
Times Dispatch, Richmond, Va., Dec. 13, 27, 1903. Newsp. clipp.
See Sprigg-Addison-Cresap-Lamar-Gordon.
Gordon, Del. Mrs. Wm. Graham Bowdoin chart. MHS.
Miss Sidney Price chart. MHS.
Gordon, Va. Balch chart. MHS.
*Gordons of Va., with notes on Gordons of Scotland and Ireland. A. C. Gordon. Hackensach, N. J., W. M. Clemens, 1918.
*The Sun, Balto., May 7, 1905.
Gordon, Mrs. Alexander (Margaret D'Arcy Hilles). Chart. Col. Dames, Chap. I. MHS.
†**Gordon, Charles.** M. H. Mag., V. 12, p. 220.
Gordon, Douglas, Balto. Va. Mag. Hist. and Biog., v. 45, p. 281.
***Gordon, Douglas H.** Burke's landed gentry. 1939. MHS.
†Men of mark in Md. Johnson. V. 2, DAR; Enoch Pratt Lib.
Gordon, Miss Elizabeth S. Chart. Col. Dames, Chap. I. MHS.
Gordon, Miss Sarah Stanley. Chart. Col. Dames, Chap. I. MHS.
***Gordon Family.** Old Kent. Hanson. P. 134. MHS; DAR.
Gordon-Knox-Fitzhugh-Cooke Line, Va. D. H. Thomas pedigree chart, plate 2. Soc. Col. Wars, Md. Johnson. 1905, p. 110. MHS.

Gordy. Mt. Olive M. P. churchyard, Worcester Co. Md. Geneal. Rec. Com., 1937, Mrs. Lines. Mss. DAR.
Wicomico Co. families. Bible rec. Ms. DAR.
*Wicomico Co. families. Tilghman. Ms, pp. 21, 100, 105-06. DAR.
***Gore.** Frederick Co. families. Markell. Ms. Personal list.
Gorman. Founders of Anne Arundel and Howard Cos. Warfield. Pp. 371-73. MHS; DAR.
Monumental City. Howard. MHS; DAR.
†**Gorman, Arthur Pue** (1839-1906). M. H. Mag., v. 12, p. 220.
†Geneal. and mem. encyc. of Md. Spencer. V. 2, p. 347. MHS; DAR.
†**Gorman, Wm. H.** Men of mark in Md. Johnson. V. 4. DAR; Enoch Pratt Lib.
Gorrell. Portrait and biog. rec. of Harford and Cecil Cos. 1897, p. 156. MHS; DAR.
Gorsuch. Barnes chart. Va. Mag. Hist. and Biog., v. 17, p. 292.
Balto. Herald, April 17, 1898. Newsp. clipp. Scrap Book. MHS.
Bible rec. Ms. MHS.
Bond family geneal. Ms. MHS.
Chart, photos., 1 sheet. Cary Geneal. Coll. Ms. MHS.
Deford chart. MHS.
J. T. Dennis pedigree chart, plate 2. Soc. Col. Wars, Md. Johnston. 1905, p. 22. MHS.
Mrs. W. H. Harris, Sr., chart. MHS.
Gorsuch and allied families. (1) Geneal. chart, (2) biog. notes. Gertrude Gorsuch Harrison. Mss. MHS.
†Hist. of Balto. City and Co. Scharf. Pp. 880, 921. MHS.
Md. families. Culver. Ms. Personal list.
†Med. Annals Md. Cordell. 1903, p. 15. MHS.
Merryman family. Culver. M. H. Mag., 1915, v. 10, pp. 176, 286.
Patriotic Marylander, v. 1, no. 1, p. 86. MHS; DAR.
Pedigree of Corbin Braxton Dallam. Soc. Col. Wars Md. Culver. 1940. MHS; DAR.
Pedigree of Charles Thomas Holloway. Soc. Col. Wars Md. Culver. 1940. MHS; DAR.
Pedigree of Wm. Henry Perkins, Jr. Soc. Col. Wars Md. Culver. 1940. MHS; DAR.
Price ancestral data (paternal). Bd. ms. MHS.
St. Paul's Parish, Balto. V. 1, 2, 3, 4. Mss. MHS.
St. Thomas' Parish, Balto. Co. Bd. ms. MHS. Also: Md. Geneal. Rec. Com., 1937, pp. 109-82. Mss. DAR.
Turner Geneal. Coll. Ms. MHS.
See Todd-Gorsuch.
Gorsuch, Balto. Co. J. A. Wilson pedigree chart, plate 1. Soc. Col. Wars, Md. Johnston. 1905, p. 130. MHS.
Gorsuch, Rev. John and Anne (Lovelace). Winston of Va. Torrence. P. 110. MHS; DAR.
Gorsuch, Thomas, Middlesex, Eng. Copy of will, 1819-20. Ms. MHS.
***Gorsuch Family.** Wilson Mss. Coll., no. 4; no. 101. MHS.
Gorsuch Line, Balto. Co. G. N. Mackenzie pedigree chart, plate 3. Soc. Col. Wars, Md. Johnston. 1905, p. 63. MHS.
Gorsuch-Lovelace. Gorsuch-Lovelace families. J. Hall Pleasants. Va. Mag. Hist. and Biol., v. 24, p. 81 (Gorsuch arms); p. 214 (children of Daniel Gorsuch); p. 317 (Richard Gorsuch, Talbot Co.); p. 425 (Anna Gorsuch and Todd family, Va. and Md.); v. 25, p. 85 (Anna Gorsuch and Todd and Baylor families, Va. and Md.); p. 212; pp. 302, 431 (Anna Gorsuch, Todd, Seaton, Moore, Hide and North families, Va. and Md.); v. 26, p. 89 (Anna Gorsuch and Todd, Johnson, Dallam, Gibson families, Md.); p. 207 (children of Rev. John Gorsuch [Daniel], William[1] and wife Anne Lovelace, Elizabeth[4] Gorsuch, Charles[4] Gorsuch, Elizabeth Gorsuch and Powell family, Lancaster Co., Va., and Talbot Co., Md.); p. 325 (Charles Gorsuch, Balto. Co.); p. 421 (Charles[4] Gorsuch, Balto. Co.); v. 28, p. 83 (corrections).
*Wilson Mss. Coll., no. 4. MHS.
Gorswick, St. Paul's Parish, Balto. V. 1. Mss. MHS.
†**Gorter.** Med. Annals Md. Cordell. 1903, p. 415. MHS.
Goslee. Rec. of Stepney Parish. MHS; DAR.
***Goslee, Gosle.** Wicomico Co. families. Tilghman. Ms, pp. 51, 99, 107, 120-21, 124. DAR.
Goslin. Fisher family. Morse. MHS.
Fisher family, Sussex Co., Del., and Md. Ms. MHS.
Gosnell. Mt. Paran Pres. churchyard, Harrisonville, Balto. Co. Typed ms. MHS; DAR.
Talbott of "Poplar Knowle." Shirk. MHS; DAR.
Gosnell-O'Dell-Towson-Worthington, Balto. Co. Tombstone inscriptions. H. P. Gerald. Natl. Geneal. Soc. Quart., v. 25, p. 59; see also p. 61.
Gostwick. St. Paul's Parish, Balto. V. 1. Mss. MHS.
Goswick. St. Paul's Parish, Balto. V. 1. Mss. MHS.
Goteé. Naturalizations in Md., 1666-1765; Laws. Bacon. MHS.
Gott. Darby geneal. Darby. MHS.
†Hist. of West. Md. Scharf. V. 1, p. 730. MHS; DAR.
Pedigree of Maurice Edward Skinner. Soc. Col. Wars Md. Culver. 1940. MHS; DAR.
Pedigree of Mason Locke Weems Williams. Soc. Col. Wars Md. Culver. 1940. MHS; DAR.
Portrait and biog. rec. of Sixth Cong. Dist. of Md. 1898, p. 715. MHS; DAR.
St. Paul's Parish, Balto. V. 1. Mss. MHS.
St. Thomas' Parish, Balto. Co. Bd. ms. MHS. Also: Md. Geneal. Rec. Com., 1937, pp. 109-82. Mss. DAR.
Gott Family, Montgomery Co. Hist. of West. Md. Scharf. V. 1, p. 730.
†**Gottlieb.** Men of mark in Md. Johnson. V. 2. DAR; Enoch Pratt Lib.
Goucher. Balto., its hist., its people. Hall. V. 3. MHS; DAR.
Gouge. *See* Gooch.
Gouges, Armand. Abs. of will. proved Nov. 4, 1797. D. A. R. Mag., Oct., 1927, v. 61, no. 10, p. 784.
Gough. Ancest. rec. and portraits. Col. Dames of Amer., 1910, v. 2, p. 575. MHS; DAR.
Bolton chart. MHS.
H. D. G. Carroll. Ms. Book. In H. F. Thompson Papers. MHS.
Centenary of Catholicity in Ky. Webb. 1884. MHS.

Gough. Col. families of U. S. A. Mackenzie. V. 3, p. 216. MHS.
Dorsey and allied families. Ms. MHS.
*Frederick Co. families. Markell. Ms. Personal list.
Harford Co. Hist. Soc. Mss. Coll. JHU.
Mrs. T. C. Jenkins chart. MHS.
Md. gleanings in Eng. Wills. M. H. Mag., 1907, v. 2, no. 3.
Milligan chart. MHS.
Miss C. Petre chart. MHS.
St. Paul's Parish, Balto. V. 1, 2. Mss. MHS.
See Carroll-Gough.
See Gooch.
Gough, Perry Hall. Cary Geneal. Coll. Ms. MHS.
Gough, Harry Dorsey (1745–1808), Perry Hall, on Gunpowder River. Inventory of estate. Ms. Book. MHS.
Gough Family. Ames Geneal. Coll. Ms. MHS.
Goul. St. Inigoes churchyard, St. Mary's Co. Md. O. R. Soc. Bull., no. 3, p. 58.
Gould. Abr. Compend. Amer. Geneal. Virkus. V. 1, p. 921. DAR.
Mrs. R. Barton, Jr., charts. MHS.
Bible rec., Queen Anne's Co., 1705–1901. Md. Geneal. Rec. Com., 1932–33, pp. 36–38. Mss. DAR.
Howard-Montague-Warfield geneal. chart. Culver and Marye. MHS.
See Hubbard. Abr. Compend. Amer. Geneal. Virkus. V. 4, p. 668. MHS.
Purnell family tree. MHS.
Sweetser chart. MHS.
St. Paul's Parish, Balto. V. 2, 4. Mss. MHS.
***Gould, Lyttleton B.** Burke landed gentry. 1939. MHS.
Goulding. St. Paul's Parish, Balto. V. 2. Mss. MHS.
Gouldsmith. Deford chart. MHS.
Pedigree of Corbin Braxton Dallam. Soc. Col. Wars Md. Culver. 1940. MHS; DAR.
Pedigree of Septimus Davis. Soc. Col. Wars Md. Culver. 1940. MHS; DAR.
***Gouley.** Wilson Mss. Coll., no. 8, B. MHS.
Goutee. Naturalizations in Md., 1666–1765; Laws. Bacon. MHS.
Govane. Brice-Govane-Howard tombstone inscriptions. Ms. MHS.
Howard-Govane-Woodward-Law Bible rec. Ms. MHS.
†**Govens.** Hist. of Frederick Co. Williams. Pp. 1088, 1089. MHS; DAR.
Gover. Cary Geneal. Coll. Ms. MHS.
Col. families of Amer. Lawrence. V. 3, p. 306. MHS.
Col. families of U. S. A. Mackenzie. V. 3. MHS; DAR.
Eldridge chart. MHS.
Hopkins chart. Cary Geneal. Coll. Ms. MHS.
S. Gover Hopkins chart. MHS.
Md. families. Culver. Ms. Personal list.
Patriotic Md. Md. Soc. of S. A. R., 1930. MHS; DAR.
Pedigree of George Webb Constable. Soc. Col. Wars Md. Culver. 1940. MHS; DAR.
Price Family and other Gunpowder Friends. Death notices; photos. of newsp. clipp. MHS.
St. Paul's Parish, Balto. V. 2. Mss. MHS.
Thomas-Chew-Lawrence. Thomas. MHS.
Gowan. St. Paul's Parish, Balto. V. 2. Mss. MHS.
Graf, Groff, Grove. Graf, Groff and Grove Family Rec. Pub. monthly, Balto. V., no. 1, Nov., 1868. MHS.
Rec. Newsp. clipp. from Balto., 1868. MHS.
Graff. St. Paul's Parish, Balto. V. 2. Mss. MHS.
Grafflin. Balto., its hist., its people. Hall. V. 3. MHS; DAR.
Grafton. Pedigree of Andrew Noel Trippe. Soc. Col. Wars Md. Culver. 1940. MHS; DAR.
Rumsey-Smithson Bible rec. Md. Geneal. Rec. Com., 1932–33, v. 5, pp. 63–142. DAR.
Smithson-Rumsey rec. bk. Ms. MHS.
Graham. Ancest. rec. and portraits. Col. Dames of Amer., 1910; v. 2, p. 486. MHS; DAR.
Bailliere chart. MHS.
Sara R. Baldwin chart. MHS.
Balto., its hist., its people. Hall. V. 3. MHS; DAR.
†Bench and bar of Md. Sams and Riley. 1901, v. 2, p. 651. Lib. Cong.; MHS; Peabody Lib.
Mrs. Howard Bruce chart. MHS.
Col. families of U. S. A. Mackenzie. V. 7. MHS; DAR.
Mrs. T. C. Jenkins chart. MHS.
Patriotic Md. Md. Soc. of S. A. R., 1930. MHS; DAR.
St. Paul's Parish, Balto. V. 2, 3, 4. Mss. MHS.
St. Stephens Parish, Cecilton, Md. MHS; DAR.
Trinity Church cemetery, Dorchester Co. Md. O. R. Soc. Bull., no. 3, pp. 42–52.
*Wicomico Co. families. Tilghman. Ms, pp. 101, 125. DAR.
Graham, Prince George Co. Segrave chart. MHS.
†**Grahame.** Hist. of Allegany Co. Thomas and Williams. V. 2. MHS; DAR.
Grainger. St. Paul's Parish, Balto. V. 2. Mss. MHS.
Grammar. Hist. graves of Md. and D. C. Ridgely. MHS.
Grange. Naturalizations in Md., 1666–1765; Laws. Bacon. MHS.
Granger. Md. gleaning in Eng. Wills. M. H. Mag., 1907, v. 2, no. 3.
Grant. Founders of Anne Arundel and Howard Cos. Warfield. P. 475. MHS; DAR.
*Garrett Co. pioneer families. Haye. Newsp. clipp. MHS; DAR.
Hooper family. Col. and Revolutionary families of Pa. Jordan. 1932, v. 4, p. 227.
Md. families. Culver. Ms. Personal list.
Mountain Democrat, Garrett Co. Newsp. clipp. MHS; DAR.
St. Paul's Parish, Balto. V. 1, 2. Mss. MHS.
Grant, J. R. Abr. Compend. Amer. Geneal. Virkus. V. 1, p. 301. DAR.
Grason. Christ P. E. Church cemetery, Cambridge. Steele. 1936. MHS; DAR.
†**Grason, Gov. William.** Founders of Anne Arundel and Howard Cos. Warfield. P. 273. MHS; DAR.
†Buchholz. P. 130. MHS.
Grason Line. Col. and Revolutionary lineages of Amer. 1939, v. 3, p. 286.
Gratiot. Cary Geneal. Coll. Ms. MHS.
Gravatt. Hist. of Caroline Co., Va. Wingfield.

Graves. Md. tombstone rec. Md. Geneal. Rec. Com., 1937, Parran, p. 3. Mss. DAR.
Wathen Prayer Book rec. Ms. MHS.
See Thurman-Graves-Jones.
Gray. Chart of Com. John Rodgers. DAR.
Edmund Beauchamp of East. Shore of Md. D. A. R. Mag., v. 66, no. 4, pp. 234–38.
†Med. Annals Md. Cordell. 1903, p. 416. MHS.
†Papers relating to early hist. of Md. Streeter. 1876. MHS.
*Pennington Papers. Ms. MHS.
St. Paul's Parish, Balto. V. 1, 2, 3, 4. Mss. MHS.
Somerset Co. Court Book. Tilghman. 1937. Ms. DAR.
Talbott of "Poplar Knowle." Shirk. MHS; DAR.
Gray, Somerset Co. Bible rec. Ms. MHS.
Gray, Joseph. Bible rec. Photos., 4 sheets. MHS.
Gray, Robert, Va. Family Bible rec. Photos., 5 sheets. MHS.
***Gray Family.** Md. Geneal. Bull., v. 10, no. 1, pp. 2–3. MHS; DAR.
William and Mary Quart., 1st series, v. 12, p. 267.
Gray Family, Ohio, also Md., 1729–1819. Rec. Natl. Geneal. Soc. Quart., v. 23, no. 3, p. 87.
Gray, Grey. St. Stephens Parish, Cecilton, Md. MHS; DAR.
Graybill, Greybill. Hagerstown tombstone inscriptions. Gruder. Natl. Geneal. Soc. Quart., 1919, v. 8, nos. 1, 2.
Grayson. Col. Grayson and Gen. Smallwood. Tyler's Quart. Mag., v. 8, pp. 119–126.
Elliott chart. MHS.
Hist. sketch of P. F. Eichelberger. Eichelberger.
†Hist. of Washington Co. Williams. 1906, v. 2, p. 1292. MHS; DAR.
Grayson Family, Va. Tyler's Quart. Mag., v. 5, pp. 195–208, 261–68; additions (Va.), v. 6, pp. 201–02; additions (Ga.), v. 7, pp. 54–56; (Va.), v. 12, pp. 181–89.
Green. Bleakley Bible rec. Ms. MHS.
Cemetery Creek, Anne Arundel Co., Tombstone Inscriptions. Founders of Anne Arundel and Howard Cos. Warfield. P. 333. MHS; DAR.
Chart, photos., 1 sheet. Cary Geneal. Coll. Ms. MHS.
Chart. Raskob-Green red. book. Raskob. MHS.
Col. families of U. S. A. Mackenzie. V. 5, p. 267. MHS; DAR.
†Hist. of Frederick Co. Williams. MHS; DAR.
Data. St. Anne's Parish register, Annapolis. Ms. MHS.
Day-Star of Amer. Freedom. Davis. P. 181. MHS; DAR.
Descendants of Thomas Hale of Del. Streets. 1913, pamph. MHS.
Hamilton family of Charles Co. Kelly. P. 69. MHS.
Harwood chart. MHS.
Hist. of printing in Col. Md. Wroth. Chap. 7. MHS.
Lineage Bks., Natl. Soc. of Daughters of Amer. Col., v. 3, p. 11. MHS; DAR.
See Long. Abr. Compend. Amer. Geneal. Virkus. V. 1, p. 800. DAR.
Md. families. Culver. Ms. Personal list.
Naturalizations in Md., 1666–1765; Laws. Bacon. MHS.
Rec. of Stepney Parish. MHS; DAR.
Semmes and allied families. Semmes. P. 149. MHS.
Side lights on Md. hist. Richardson. V. 2, p. 339. MHS; DAR.
*Wicomico Co. families. Tilghman. Ms, p. 113. DAR.
Green, Va. Amer. Clan Gregor Year Book, 1912, pp. 112–14; 1915, p. 74, 1917, p. 67. MHS; DAR.
*The Sun, Balto., Dec. 31, 1905.
†Green, Jonas (1712–67). Hist. of printing in col. Md. Wroth. P. 75.
Green, Robt., Charles Co. Deed, 1703. D. C. Geneal. Rec. Com., 1932–34, v. 10, pp. 158–61. Typed, bd. DAR.
Green, Sam'l E. III. Md. Soc., War of 1812, v. 3, no. 293. Ms. MHS.
Green, T. N. Med. Soc., War of 1812, v. 1, no. 50. Ms. MHS.
Green, Gov. Thomas. McCall-Tidwell families. McCall. P. 486. MHS; DAR.
***Green Family.** Newsp. clipp. in Penning Papers. Ms. MHS.
Del. Bible rec. Md. Geneal. Rec. Com., 1933–34, p. 215. Mss. DAR.
*Semmes Geneal. Coll. Ms. MHS.
*Wilson Mss. Coll., no. 8, A; 8, B. MHS.
Green Family, Va. Newsp. clipp. MHS.
†Green-Rind. Hist. of printing in Col. Md. Wroth. MHS.
Greenberry, Ances. rec. and portraits. Col. Dames of Amer., 1910, v. 1, p. 255. MHS; DAR.
Bailliere chart. MHS.
Britton Scrap Book. V. 1. Ms. MHS.
Col. families of Amer. Lawrence. V. 2, p. 45; v. 16, p. 93. MHS.
Col. mansions of Md. and Del. Hammond. Pp. 86, 270. MHS.
Dobbin chart. MHS.
Dorsey chart. Lib. Cong.; MHS.
Eldridge chart. MHS.
*Founders of Anne Arundel and Howard Cos. Warfield. P. 162–64. MHS; DAR.
Founders of col. families, Ridgly, Dorsey, and Greenberry, Evans. MHS; DAR.
Griffith chart. Cary Geneal. Coll. Ms. MHS.
Griffith geneal. Griffith. MHS; DAR.
Howard-Montague-Warfield geneal. chart. Culver and Marye. MHS.
Md. families. Culver. Ms. Personal list.
†Old brick churches of Md. Ridgly. 1894, p. 86. MHS; DAR.
Peale Geneal. Coll. Ms. MHS.
Pedigree of Duncan Keener Brent. Soc. Col. Wars Md. Culver. 1940. MHS; DAR.
Pedigree of James Dorsey Brown, Jr. Soc. Col. Wars Md. Culver. 1940. MHS; DAR.
Pedigree of Gustavus Warfield Evans. Soc. Col. Wars Md. Culver. 1940. MHS; DAR.
Pedigree of Charles Worthington Hoff. Soc. Col. Wars Md. Culver. 1940. MHS; DAR.
Pedigree of Arthur Lafayette Jones. Soc. Col. Wars Md. Culver. 1940. MHS; DAR.
Pedigree of Thomas Dobbin Penniman. Soc. Col. Wars Md. Culver. 1940. MHS; DAR.
Pedigree of Pleasants Pennington. Soc. Col. Wars Md. Culver. 1940. MHS; DAR.

Greenberry, Pedigree of Tilghman Goldsborough Pitts. Soc. Col. Wars Md. Culver. 1940. MHS; DAR.
Pedigree of Townsend Scott, IV. Soc. Col. Col. Wars Md. Culver. 1940. MHS; DAR.
Pedigree of Levin Gale Shreve. Soc. Col. Wars Md. Culver. 1940. MHS; DAR.
Pedigree of Mark Alexander Herbert Smith. Soc. Col. Wars Md. Culver. 1940. MHS; DAR.
Pedigree of John Ogle Warfield, Jr. Soc. Col. Wars Md. Culver. 1940. MHS; DAR.
Pedigree of Andrew Jackson Young, Jr. Soc. Col. Wars Md. Culver. 1940. MHS; DAR.
Side lights on Md. hist. Richardson. V. 2, p. 330. MHS; DAR.
Welsh-Hyatt and kindred. Welsh. Section. 5, p. 176. MHS; DAR.
Greenberry, Col. Nicholas. Grave of col. officer is moved; an article taken from the Sun, Balto., 1925. DAR.
(1627–1697). R. C. Hoffman pedigree chart. Soc. Col. Wars, Md. Johnston. 1905, pp. 40, 146. MHS.
Greenberry Family. Md. Geneal. Rec. Com., 1933–34, pp. 66–69. Mss. DAR.
Greenberry-Hammond. Chart, photos., 2 sheets. Cary Geneal. Coll. Ms. MHS.
Greenberry-Warfield. Chart, photos., complete in 1 sheet. Cary Geneal. Coll. Ms. MHS.
Greenberry-Watkins. Abr. Compend. Amer. Geneal. Virkus. V. 4, p. 613. MHS.
Greenbury. Col. Nicholas Duvall family Records. Price. Bd.`ms. MHS.
Lineage Bks., Natl. Soc. of Daughters of Amer. Col., v. 4, pp. 7, 13. MHS; DAR.
Pedigree of Howard Hall Macy Lee. Soc. Col. Wars Md. Culver. 1940. MHS; DAR.
Pedigree of Wm. Handy Collins Vickers. Soc. Col. Wars Md. Culver. 1940. MHS; DAR.
Greene. Ances. Rec. and portraits. Col. Dames of Amer. 1910, pp. 108–10. MHS; DAR.
† Papers relating to early hist. of Md. Streeter. 1876. MHS.
St. Paul's Parish, Balto. V. 1, 2, 4. Mss. MHS.
Somerset Co. Court Book. Tilghman. 1937. Ms. DAR.
Greenfield. Beall and Bell families. Beall. MHS.
Cary Geneal. Coll. Ms. MHS.
Graves, Trent Hall on Patuxent. Md. O. R. Soc. Bull., no. 3, pp. 60–61. MHS.
Hist. graves of Md. and D. C. Ridgely. MHS.
St. Paul's Parish, Balto. V. 2. Mss. MHS.
Greenfield-Truman, Trent Hall, on Patuxent, St. Mary's Co. Tombstone inscriptions, 1672. Md. O. R. Soc. Bull., no. 3, pp. 60–61.
Greening. Naturalizations in Md., 1666–1765; Laws. Bacon. MHS.
Greenleaf. Ances. rec. and portraits. Col. Dames of Amer., 1910, p. 264. MHS; DAR.
Greenlee. Harford Co. Hist. Soc. Mss. Coll. JHU.
Greentree, Benj. Revolutionary pension abs. Natl. Geneal. Soc. Quart., v. 23, p. 80.
Greenway. Ances. rec. and portraits. Col. Dames of Amer., 1910, v. 1, p. 255. MHS; DAR.
Col. families of U. S. A. Mackenzie. V. 1, p. 604. MHS; DAR.
Mss. Geneal. Coll. composed of 7 binders and 1 box of loose papers. MHS.
St. Paul's Parish, Balto. V. 3. Mss. MHS.
Greenway, Mrs. Eugene (Frances Davis). Chart. Col. Dames, Chap. I. MHS.
Greenwell. Centenary of Catholicity in Ky. Webb. 1884. MHS.
See Roach-Greenwell-Thompson-Williams.
***Greenwood.** Bible rec. Old Kent Chapter, D. A. R., East. Shore of Md. Md. Geneal. Rec. Com., 1926–27, pp. 7–10. DAR.
St. Paul's P. E. churchyard, Kent Co. Md. O. R. Soc. Bull., no. 2, pp. 54–65.
St. Paul's Parish, Balto. V. 2. Mss. MHS.
St. Steven's graveyard, Cecil Co. Md. Geneal. Rec. Com., 1934–35, pp. 213–14. Mss. DAR.
Greer. St. Paul's Parish, Balto. V. 2. Mss. MHS.
Greetham. St. Paul's Parish, Balto. V. 2. Mss. MHS.
Greeves. *See* Grewes.
Gregg. Md. families. Culver. Ms. Personal list.
*Pennington Papers. Ms. MHS.
St. Paul's Parish, Balto. V. 2. Mss. MHS.
Tombstone rec. of Glendy burying ground (vault). Md. Geneal. Rec. Com., 1933–34, pp. 171–78. Mss. DAR.
Gregg, Maurice. Pedigree. Soc. Col. Wars Md. Culver. 1940. MHS; DAR.
Gregoire. *See* Wilkinson-Brown-Bullitt-Gregoire.
Gregor. *See* Alpine-Gregor-McGregor-Magruder Clan.
Gregory. Ances. rec. and portraits. Col. Dames of Amer., 1910, p. 418. MHS; DAR.
See Beachey. Abr. Compend. Amer. Geneal. Virkus. V. 4, p. 646. MHS.
Geneal. Stone Family Assoc. MHS.
Greville or Gregory book. Balto. Herald, Mar. 29, 1903. Newsp. clipp. MHS.
†Hist. of Frederick Co. Williams. V. 2, p. 1573. MHS; DAR.
Md. tombstone rec. Md. Geneal. Rec. Com., 1937, Parran, p. 3. Mss. DAR.
†Med. Annals Md. Cordell. 1903, p. 417. MHS.
St. Paul's Parish, Balto. V. 1, 2. Mss. MHS.
***Gregory,** Va. The Sun, Balto. Jan. 15, 1905.
Gregory Family. Tercentenary hist. of Md. Andrews. V. 4, p. 408. MHS; DAR.
Greives, Greeves. St. Paul's Parish, Balto. V. 2. Mss. MHS.
Greme. Trap Church burial rec., Harford Co. Md. Geneal. Rec. Com., 1934–35, p. 108. Mss. DAR.
Grenwood. Bible, Dublin, N. H., rec., 1776–1883. Bible in possession of Mr. and Mrs. Frank Skirven, Chestertown, R.R. #2. Md. Geneal. Rec. Com., 1937–38, pp. 127–28. Mss. DAR.
Greville. Greville or Gregory book. Balto. Herald, Mar. 29, 1903. Newsp. clipp. MHS.
***Greville-Brook.** Balto. Herald, Mar. 29, 1903. Newsp. clipp. MHS.
Grewthorp. St. Paul's Parish, Balto. V. 2. Mss. MHS.
Grey. St. Paul's Parish, Balto. V. 1. Mss. MHS.
See Gray.
Greybill. *See* Graybill.
Grice. Hist. graves of Md. and D. C. Ridgely. MHS.

Md. gleanings in Eng. Wills. M. H. Mag., 1907, v. 2, no. 4.
St. Paul's Parish, Balto. V. 2. Mss. MHS.
†**Griener, John E.** Men of mark in Md. Johnson. V. 2. DAR; Enoch Pratt Lib.
Grier. Abr. Compend. Amer. Geneal. Virkus. V. 4, p. 225. MHS.
Bible rec. of Dorchester and Somerset Cos. and Del. P. 42. DAR.
†Hist. of West. Md. Scharf. V. 1, p. 587. MHS; DAR.
*Wicomico Co. families. Tilghman. Ms, p. 11. DAR.
Wicomico Co. families. Bible rec. Ms. DAR.
Griesser, Mary Ridout (Green). Amer. Clan Gregor Year Book, 1915, p. 74. MHS; DAR.
Griest. Maulsby family in Amer. Barnard. DAR; Peabody Lib.
Griffeth. *See* Griffith.
Griffin. Cary Geneal. Coll. Ms. MHS.
Christ P. E. Church cemetery, Cambridge. Steele. 1936. MHS; DAR.
*Descendants of Chisolm Griffin. Clarence Griffin. Spindale, N. C., 1931, mimeog. MHS.
Geneal. of Va. family of Lomax. Lib. Cong.
Patriotic Md. Md. Soc. of S. A. R., 1930. MHS; DAR.
St. Paul's Parish, Balto. V. 1, 2, 4. Mss. MHS.
See Peachey-Griffin.
Griffin, Md. and Kent Co., Del. Some allied families. Streets. 1904, pamph. MHS.
†**Griffin, Edw. H.** Men of mark in Md. Johnson. V. 2. DAR; Enoch Pratt Lib.
***Griffin Family.** Descendants of Samuel Griffin (Planter) of New Castle Co. on Delaware. T. H. Streets. Phila., 1905. MHS; DAR.
Griffith. Abr. Compend. Amer. Geneal. Virkus. V. 1, p. 307. DAR.
Ancest. rec. and portraits. Col. Dames of Amer., 1910, v. 2, p. 629. MHS; DAR.
*Bible rec. of Joseph Griffith (1757–1810), Revolutionary soldier, and his wife Mary Anne Boulware. D. C. Geneal. Rec. Com., 1928–30. DAR.
Botfield and allied families. Ms. DAR.
Chart, photos., 2 sheets. Cary Geneal. Coll. Ms. MHS.
Christ P. E. Church cemetery, Cambridge. Steele. 1936. MHS; DAR.
Col. families of Amer. Lawrence. V. 5, p. 86. MHS.
Col. families of U. S. A. Mackenzie. V. 5, p. 358. MHS.
*Data relative to Lewis Hill, who married Mary E. Griffith. In: Jacob Duckett of Md. Ms. DAR.
Dorsey and allied families. Ms. MHS.
Col. Nicholas Duvall family rec. Price. Bd. ms. MHS.
*Early comers to the Province. Georgians in Anne Arundel Co. Atlanta Jour., Sept. 22, 1906. Newsp. clipp. File case, MHS.
Eldridge chart. MHS.
*Founders of Anne Arundel and Howard Cos. Warfield. Pp. 69, 87, 93, 347–51, 377. MHS; DAR.
*Frederick Co. families. Markell. Ms. Personal list.
*Geneal. of Descendants of George and Sarah Smedley, Cope. MHS; DAR.
*Geneal. of Griffith family. Descendants of William and Sarah Maccubin Griffith of Anne Arundel Co. R. R. Griffith, Jr. Balto., W. K. Voyle & Son, 1892. MHS. Ms. index by E. Hammond. Bd. MHS; DAR.
Geneal. of Henrietta Chauncy Wilson. Upshur. Bk. of photos. MHS.
Greenway chart. MHS.
*Griffith family. Laura Webb-Peploc. 1924, 11 pp., typed. DAR.
Hazelhurst chart. MHS.
Hist. of Allegany Co. Thomas and Williams. V. 1, pp. 556–57; v. 2, p. 881. MHS; DAR.
†Hist. of Frederick Co. Williams. V. 2, p, 1152. MHS; DAR.
Hist. graves of Md. and D. C. Ridgely. MHS.
†Hist. of West. Md. Scharf. V. 1, pp. 604–05, 737. MHS; DAR.
Mrs. R. N. Jackson chart. MHS.
Laytonsville M. E. churchyard, Montgomery Co. Md. Geneal. Rec. Com., 1934–35, p. 69. Mss. DAR.
Miss Cassandra Lee chart. MHS.
*Lineage Bk. Daughters of Amer. Colonists. V. 3, p. 5. MHS; DAR.
Lloyd family hist. of Wales, Pa., and Md. DAR.
Md. families. Culver. Ms. Personal list.
Md. Geneal. Bull., v. 3, p. 30. MHS; DAR.
Matthews-Price chart. MHS.
†Med. Annals. Md. Cordell. 1903, pp. 418–19. MHS.
Monocacy Cemetery, Beallsville, Montgomery Co. Md. Geneal. Rec. Com., 1926–27. Mss. DAR.
Mt. Calvary Church burial ground, Cooksville Pike, Montgomery Co. Md. Geneal. Rec. Com., 1934. Mss. DAR.
Mt. Calvary Church burial ground, Howard Co. Md. Geneal. Rec. Com., 1934–35, pp. 95–99. Mss. DAR.
Patriotic Md. Md. Soc. of S. A. R., 1930. MHS; DAR.
Peale Geneal. Coll. Ms. MHS.
Pedigree of Duncan Keener Brent. Soc. Col. Wars Md. Culver. 1940. MHS; DAR.
Pedigree of James Dorsey Brown, Jr. Soc. Col. Wars Md. Culver. 1940. MHS; DAR.
Pedigree of Septimus Davis. Soc. Col. Wars Md. Culver. 1940. MHS; DAR.
Pedigree of Thomas Dobbin Penniman. Soc. Col. Wars Md. Culver. 1940. MHS; DAR.
Pedigree of Charles Worthington Hoff. Soc. Col. Wars Md. Culver. 1940. MHS; DAR.
Pedigree of Tilghman Goldsborough Pitts. Soc. Col. Wars Md. Culver. 1940. MHS; DAR.
Pedigree of Richard Walker Worthington. Soc. Col. Wars Md. Culver. 1940. MHS; DAR.
Mrs. J. Piper chart. MHS.
Portrait and biog. rec. of Sixth Cong. Dist. of Md. 1898, p. 730. MHS; DAR.
Price ancestral data (paternal). Bd. ms. MHS.
*Quaker rec. of Pa. Wilson Mss. Coll., no. 81. MHS.
Rec. of Nicholas Meriwether of Wales, and descendants in Va. and Md. Griffith. Pp. 151–62.
Revolutionary war pension abs. Natl. Geneal. Soc. Quart., v. 23, no. 2, p. 54.
Riggs of Anne Arundel, Frederick and Montgomery Cos. prior to 1663. Pamph. MHS.
St. Paul's Parish, Balto. V. 1, 2, 3. Mss. MHS.
*The Sun, Balto., Dec. 12, 1905.

Griffith. Tercentenary hist. of Md. Andrews. V. 4, p. 107. MHS; DAR.
Tombstone rec. of Dorchester Co. Jones. DAR.
Turner Geneal. Coll. Ms. MHS.
Warfields of Md. Warfield. MHS.
Welsh-Hyatt and kindred. Welsh. Sec. 4, p. 172. MHS; DAR.
Western Run Parish book. Allen. Bd. ms. MHS.
Whiteley chart. MHS.
Griffith, Montgomery Co. Bible rec., 1727–1880. Natl. Geneal. Soc. Quart., v. 17, no. 3, pp. 51–52.
†**Griffith, Goldsborough S.** Story of great life. Rev. George H. Nock. Balto., H. E. Houck Co., 1906. MHS.
Griffith, L. P. Md. Soc., War of 1812, v. 1, no. 2. Ms. MHS.
Griffith, Samuel. Md. pension. Natl. Geneal. Soc. Quart., v. 23, no. 2, p. 54.
***Griffith, Sam'l.,** Harford Co. Ms., 7 pp. DAR.
***Griffith Family.** Anne Arundel Co. gentry. Newman. Pp. 153–88. MHS; DAR.
*Arch. of Georgetown Univ., Wash., D. C., v. 287.
Data. Md. Geneal. Bull., v. 3, pp. 30–31. MHS; DAR.
*Griffith family. Kate Singer Curry, 1420 Girard St. N.W., Washington, D. C.
*Index (from Mr. Hammond's ms. index in MHS). Md. Geneal. Bull., v. 10, no 2; cont. V. 11, no. 2, p. 21. MHS; DAR.
*Ms. DAR.
Griffith-Garretson. Greenway Mss. Geneal. Coll. Binder's title, Hawkins-Bordley. MHS.
***Griffith-Garrettson.** Rec. Pamph. DAR.
Griffith, Griffeth. St. Stephens Parish, Cecilton, Md. MHS; DAR.
Griffith-Hook-Penniman Families. Focke Geneal. Coll. Ms. MHS.
Griggs. Mrs. H. DeCourcy Wright Thom chart. MHS.
Grigsby. Docura Bible rec. Ms. MHS.
*The Sun, Balto., May 21, 1905; Oct. 6, 1907.
***Grigsby Family.** Geneal. incl. brief sketch of Porter family. Pub. by Wm. H. Grigsby, Dec., 1878; republished by Robert Hall McCormick, Chicago, 1905, pamph. with books. MHS.
Grim. *See* Grimm.
†**Grimes.** Hist. of Frederick Co. Williams. MHS; DAR.
Md. families. Culver. Ms. Personal list.
†Med. Annals. Md. Cordell. 1903, p. 419. MHS.
Mt. Carmel burial ground, Unity, Montgomery Co. Md. Geneal. Rec. Com., 1934–35, p. 85. Mss. DAR.
St. Barnabas P. E. churchyard. Typed ms. MHS; DAR.
St. Paul's Parish, Balto. V. 1, 2, 4. Mss. MHS.
†**Grimm.** Hist. of Washington Co. Williams. 1906, v. 1, p. 585. MHS; DAR.
Grimm, Grim. Catonsville pioneers of Luth. faith. Natl. Geneal. Soc. Quart., v. 9, no. 2, p. 29.
Grimshaw. St. Paul's Parish, Balto. V. 2. Mss. MHS.
Grindall, Charles Sylvester. Pedigree. Soc. Col. Wars Md. Culver. 1940. MHS; DAR.
Md. Soc., War of 1812, v. 3, no. 208. Ms. MHS.
Grineff. Peale Geneal. Coll. Ms. MHS.
Griner. Hagerstown tombstone inscriptions. Gruder. Natl. Geneal. Soc. Quart., 1919, v. 8, nos. 1, 2.
Griswold. Amer. Armory and Blue Bk. Matthews. 1908, p. 244. DAR.
Abr. Compend. Amer. Geneal. Virkus. V. 1, p. 309. DAR.
Balto., its hist., its people. Hall. V. 2. MHS; DAR.
Docura Bible rec. Ms. MHS.
St. Paul's Parish, Balto. V. 2, 4. Mss. MHS.
Griswold, Benjamin Howell. Pedigree charts, plates 1 and 2. Soc. Col. Wars, Md. 1905, pp. 29–30. MHS.
(New Eng. rec.) Pedigree. Soc. Col. Wars Md. Culver. 1940. MHS; DAR. See Pedigree Book, 1905, pp. 29, 30.
Griswold, Robertson. (New Eng. Rec.) Pedigree. Soc. Col. Wars Md. Culver. 1940. MHS; DAR. See Pedigree Book, 1905, pp. 29, 30.
Groeff. St. Paul's Parish, Balto. V. 1. Mss. MHS.
Groff. Peale Geneal. Coll. Ms. MHS.
See Grove.
Groome. Abr. Compend. Amer. Geneal. Virkus. V. 1, p. 631. DAR.
†Bench and bar of Md. Sams and Riley. 1901, v. 2, p. 409. Lib. Cong.; MHS; Peabody Lib.
†Biog. cyc. of rep. men of Md. and D. C. Pp. 248, 289, 313. MHS; DAR.
Cary Geneal. Coll. Ms. MHS.
Founders of Anne Arundel and Howard Cos. Warfield. P. 289. MHS; DAR.
Gov. James Black Groome line. Pedigree of George Webb Constable. Soc. Col. Wars Md. Culver. 1940. MHS; DAR.
McCormick chart. MHS.
Md. families. Culver. Ms. Personal list.
†Med. Annals Md. Cordell. 1903, p. 419. MHS.
Spring Hill cemetery, Easton. Md. O. R. Soc. Bull., no. 1, pp. 35–41.
†**Groome, James Black.** Governors of Md. Buchholz. P. 207. MHS.
***Groome Family.** Old Kent. Hanson. Pp. 180–82. MHS; DAR.
Groomes. Laytonsville M. E. churchyard, Montgomery Co. Md. Geneal. Rec. Com., 1934–35, p. 69. Mss. DAR.
Grose. Scruggs geneal. Dunklin. P. 23.
†**Grosh.** Hist. of West. Md. Scharf. V. 2, pp. 1034–35. MHS; DAR.
Patriotic Md. Md. Soc. of S. A. R., 1930. MHS; DAR.
St. Paul's Parish, Balto. V. 2. Mss. MHS.
Gross-Weiss (or White). Horwitz chart. MHS.
Gross (Grosse)-Weiss (White)-Brandt Families. Ms. MHS.
Grosse. Mrs. R. Barton, Jr., charts. MHS.
Peale Geneal. Coll. Ms. MHS.
See Gross.
Grossman-Peppler Families, from Germany to Balto. Md. Geneal. Rec. Com., 1938–39, pp. 173–81. Mss. DAR.
†**Grossnickle.** Hist. of Frederick Co. Williams. MHS; DAR.
Ground. Zion Reformed Church Hagerstown. Md. Geneal. Rec. Com., 1934–35. Mss. DAR.

Grove. Extracts from hist. of Carrollton Manor, Frederick Co. Wm. J. Grove. D. C. Geneal. Rec. Com., 1932–34, v. 10, pp. 30–31. Typed, bd. DAR.
Forney's Weekly Press, Phila., June 22, 1867. Newsp. clipp. MHS.
Geneal. notes and wills. D. C. Geneal. Rec. Com., 1932–34, v. 10, pp. 138–39, 141–42, 214–15, 251–57. Typed, bd. DAR.
†Hist. of Frederick Co. Williams. MHS; DAR.
†Hist. of Washington Co. Williams. 1906, v. 1, p. 865. MHS; DAR.
Hist. of West. Md. Scharf. V. 1218. MHS.
Md. tombstone rec. Md. Geneal. Rec. Com., 1937, Parran, p. 3. Mss. DAR.
Patriotic Md. Md. Soc. of S. A. R., 1930. MHS; DAR.
See Graf-Groff-Grove.
†Grove, Wm. Jarboe. Men of mark in Md. Johnson. V. 4. DAR; Enoch Pratt Lib.
†Grove, Groff. Hist. of West. Md. Scharf. V. 2, p. 1218. MHS; DAR.
Grover. Note. Md. Geneal. Bull., Apr., 1940. V. 11, no. 2, p. 26. MHS; DAR.
St. Paul's Parish, Balto. V. 2. Mss. MHS.
Talbott of "Poplar Knowle." Shirk. MHS, DAR.
Groverman. Griffith geneal. Griffith. MHS; DAR.
***Groves,** Prince George Co. Alstons of North and South Carolina. Groves. P. 389. MHS.
Grubb. Taney and allied families. Silverson. MHS; DAR.
Gruber. Hagerstown tombstone inscriptions. Gruder. Natl. Geneal. Soc. Quart., 1919, v. 8, nos. 1, 2.
Gruder. Abr. Compend. Amer. Geneal. Virkus. V. 4, p. 316. MHS.
Zion Reformed Church, Hagerstown. Md. Geneal. Rec. Com., 1934–35. Mss. DAR.
Grumbine. *See* Shriner-Grumbine.
Grundy. Ances. rec. and portraits. Col. Dames of Amer., 1910, v. 2, p. 591–93. MHS; DAR.
Mrs. R. Barton, Jr., charts. MHS.
Battee, Brewer, Boteler, etc., family rec. Murray. Photos. MHS.
Md. families. Culver. Ms. Personal list.
Pedigree of Dr. Christopher Johnston, Jr. Soc. Col. Wars Md. Culver. 1940. MHS; DAR.
Pedigree of Gustav Wm. Lurman. Soc. Col. Wars Md. Culver. 1940. MHS; DAR.
Pedigree of Franklin Buchanan Owen. Soc. Col. Wars Md. Culver. 1940. MHS; DAR.
St. Paul's Parish, Balto. V. 1, 2. Mss. MHS.
Tilghman chart. MHS.
Grymes. Cary Geneal. Coll. Ms. MHS.
*The Sun, Balto., Oct. 22 (Va.), 29, 1905.
***Gubenator Family.** Arch. of Georgetown Univ., Wash., D. C., v. 170, no. 9.
Guerny-Baker. Lineage Bks., Natl. Soc. of Daughters of Amer. Col., v. 1, no. 1. MHS; DAR.
Guest. Abr. Compend. Amer. Geneal. Virkus. V. 1, p. 631. DAR.
Bankhead family. William and Mary Quart., 2nd series, v. 9, p. 303.
Mrs. Howard Bruce chart. MHS.
Mulford chart. MHS.
Mrs. Newhall chart. MHS.
Mrs. E. W. Poe chart. MHS.
*Wicomico C. families. Tilghman. Ms., p. 126. DAR.
Guest, Rebecca. Family rec. and journal, 1800–10. Ms. MHS.
Guibert. Naturalizations in Md., 1666–1765; Laws. Bacon. MHS.
Guichard. Naturalizations in Md., 1666–1765; Laws. Bacon. MHS.
†Guilder. Med. Annals Md. Cordell. 1903, p. 20. MHS.
***Guilford.** Geneal. Helen M. Guilford. Minneapolis, Minn. 1918. MHS.
Gull. Patriotic Md. Md. Soc. of S. A. R., 1930. MHS; DAR.
Gullett. Somerset Co. Court Book. Tilghman. 1937. Ms. DAR.
†Gunby. Col. John Gunby of Md. line. A. A. Gunby. Cincinnati, Robert Clarke Co., 1902.
†Med. Annals Md. Cordell. 1903, p. 420. MHS.
†Men of mark in Md. Johnson. V. 3. DAR; Enoch Pratt Lib.
Revolutionary war service of Col. John Gunby. Md. Geneal. Rec. Com., 1932–33. Mss. DAR.
St. Paul's Parish, Balto. V. 1, 2. Mss. MHS.
Somerset Co. Court Book. Tilghman. 1937. Ms. DAR.
Summers-Jones-Gunby-Morris Bible rec. Md. Geneal. Rec. Com., 1937–38, pp. 142–46. Mss. DAR.
*Wicomico Co. families. Tilghman. Ms., pp. 100, 103, 105–06, 125, 128. DAR.
Worcester Co. militia, 1794. Covington. P. 155. MHS.
†Gundry. Med. Annals. Md. Cordell. 1903, pp. 420–21. MHS.
Gupton. Rec. of Stepney Parish. MHS; DAR.
†Gurley. Hist. of Allegany Co. Thomas and Williams. V. 2. MHS; DAR.
***Gustine.** Compendium; arms. Gustine C Weaver (Mrs. Clifford Weaver). Cincinnati, Ohio, Powell & White, 1929. MHS; DAR.
†Guth, W. W. Encyc. of Amer. biog. Amer. Hist. Soc., new series, v. 1, p. 114. MHS; DAR.
***Guthrie.** Amer. Guthrie and allied families. Lineal representatives of the col. representatives of colonial Guthries; Conn., Del., Md., N. C., S. C., Pa. and Va. L. R. Guthrie. 4 bks. Bk. 1, Va., 1652; bk. 2, immigrants from Ulster, 1700–1755; bk. 3, immigrants after Revolutionary war; bk. 4, allied families (64). Chambersburg, Pa., Ker Printing Co., 1933. DAR.
†Guting (present form Keedy). Hist. of Frederick Co. Williams. P. 1403. MHS; DAR.
Guttro. St. Paul's Parish, Balto. V. 2. Mss. MHS.
Guttry. St. Paul's Parish, Balto. V. 2. Mss. MHS.
Guyton, Aaron, Md. Revolutionary soldiers buried in northwest S. C. Natl. Geneal. Soc. Quart., v. 21, no. 2, p. 48.
Guyton-Kirr-Rush-Holland-Conn. Harford Co. Hist. Soc. Mss. Coll. JHU.
Gwathmey. Bird chart. MHS.
Pedigree of James Alfred Merritt. Soc. Col. Wars Md. Culver. 1940. MHS; DAR.
Gwathmey, Va. Pedigree and hist. of Washington family. Welles. P. 204. MHS.
Gwinn. Balto. its hist., its people. Hall. V. 3. MHS; DAR.
Brooks chart. MHS.

Gwinn. Mrs. B. S. Johnston chart. MHS.
†Med. Annals Md. Cordell. 1903, p. 421. MHS.
Patriotic Md. Md. Soc. of S. A. R., 1930. MHS; DAR.
*Pennington Papers. Ms. MHS.
*The Sun, Balto., Nov. 26, 1905.
Gwinn, Gwin. St. Paul's Parish, Balto. V. 2. Mss. MHS.
Gwyn, David. Va. Pedigree of Tilghman Goldsborough Pitts. Soc. Col. Wars Md. Culver. 1940. MHS; DAR.
Gwynn. Mrs. J. G. Brogden chart. MHS.
Hist. graves Md. and D. C. Ridgely. MHS.
Keene family. Jones. MHS; DAR.
Md. families. Culver. Ms. Personal list.
Semmes and allied families. Semmes. MHS.
***Gwynn or Wynnes.** The Sun, Balto., Nov. 12, 19, 1905.
Gwynn Line. Col. and Revolutionary lineages of Amer. 1939, v. 2, p. 65. MHS.

H

***Haacks.** Wicomico Co. families. Tilghman. Ms., p. 116. DAR.
Hack. All Hallow's P. E. churchyard, Snow Hill, Worcester Co. Hudson. Bd. ms. MHS; DAR. Also: Md. Geneal. Rec. Com., 1935-36, p. 24. Mss. DAR.
Balto., its hist., its people. Hall. V. 3. MHS; DAR.
Bower-Hack-Warner Bible rec. Md. Geneal. Com., 1939-40, pp. 178-80. Mss. DAR.
Col. and Revolutionary families of Pa. Amer. Hist. Soc., N. Y., 1934, p. 15.
Naturalizations in Md., 1666-1765; Laws. Bacon. MHS.
St. Stephens Parish, Cecilton, Md. MHS; DAR.
Turner Geneal. Coll. Ms. MHS.
Hack Family, Md. and Va. Tyler's Quart. Mag., v. 7, pp. 253-62; v. 9, pp. 64-65.
†**Hacke.** Hist. sketch of Rev. Nicolas P. Hacke, Greensburg, Pa. (born in Balto.). G. B. Russel. Mercersburg Rev., 1878, v. 25, pp. 579-99.
Hackett. Bible rec. D. A. R. Mag., v. 66, no. 9, p. 605; Oct., 1932, no. 10, pp. 671-72.
D. A. R. Mag., Sept., 1933, v. 67, no. 9, pp. 583-88.
*Hist. Dorchester Co. Jones. 1925, pp. 327-30. MHS; DAR.
Holdens Cemetery, Kent Co. Md. Geneal. Rec. Com., 1932, v. 5, p. 211. Mss. DAR.
See Layton. Abr. Compend. Amer. Geneal. Virkus. V. 6, p. 357. DAR.
Pattison wills. Md. Geneal. Rec. Com., 1929, pp. 7-42; 1930-31. Mss. DAR.
Pedigree of Hope Horsey Barroll. Soc. Col. Wars Md. Culver. 1940. MHS; DAR.
Rec. from Tilghman and Luke Hackett's Bible, Fork Dist., Dorchester Co. D. A. R. Mag., v. 66, no. 9, p. 605; no. 10, p. 671.
Hackett, Fork Dist., Dorchester Co. Bible rec. of Dorchester and Somerset Cos. and Del. P. 31. DAR.
Hackett family tree. Mrs. Mary Turpin Layton, Bridgeville, Del. Printed. MHS.
Hackett Family, Dorchester Co. Seven generations. D. A. R. Mag., April, 1931, v. 65, no. 4, pp. 222-25.
Hackman. St. Paul's Parish, Balto. V. 2. Mss. MHS.
***Hackney.** Burke's landed gentry. 1939. MHS.
Haddaway. Dawson chart. MHS.
***Haddaway Family.** Md. Geneal. Bull., v. 10, no. 2, p. 13. MHS; DAR.
Hadel, A. K., M.D. Md. Soc., War of 1812, v. 1, no. 5. Ms. MHS.
Hadfield. *See* Sterett-Hadfield.
Hafly. *See* Haiffle.
***Hagan.** Frederick Co. families. Markell. Ms. Personal list.
*Semmes Geneal. Coll. Ms. MHS.
St. Joseph's R. C. churchyard. Md. O. R. Soc. Bull., no. 3, p. 64.
Hagar. Ances. rec. and portraits. Col. Dames of Amer., 1910, v. 2, pp. 568-71. MHS; DAR.
Clark chart. MHS.
†Hist. of West. Md. Scharf. V. 2, pp. 1012-16, 1059. MHS; DAR.
†Hist. of Md. Scharf. V. 2, pp. 155-56. MHS.
Manly chart. MHS.
Peale Geneal. Coll. Ms. MHS.
See Hager.
†**Hagar, Jonathan.** Founder. Mary V. Mish. Hagerstown, 1937, pamph., 73 pp. MHS; DAR.
†Founder of Hagerstown. Soc. for Hist. of Germans in Md. 2nd ann. rept, 1888, pp. 17-30.
†Jonathan Hagar. Basil Sollers. MHS.
***Hagar Family.** Wilson Mss. Coll., no. 5, no. 16. MHS.
Hage. St. Paul's Parish, Balto. V. 2. Mss. MHS.
Hager. Md. families. Culver. Ms. Personal list.
Zion Reformed Church, Hagerstown. Md. Geneal. Rec. Com., 1934-35. Mss. DAR.
Hager, Hagar, Heger. Hagerstown tombstone inscriptions. Gruder. Natl. Geneal. Soc. Quart., 1919, v. 8, nos. 1, 2.
†**Hagerty.** Men of mark in Md. Johnson. V. 3. DAR; Enoch Pratt Lib.
Hagmeyer, Hogmire. Hagerstown tombstone inscriptions. Gruder. Natl. Geneal. Soc. Quart., 1919, v. 8, nos. 1, 2.
Hagner. Founders of Anne Arundel and Howard cos. Warfield. P. 119. MHS; DAR.
Portrait and biog. rec. of Sixth Cong. Dist. of Md. 1898, p. 555. MHS; DAR.
†**Hagner, Alexander B.** Men of mark in Md. Johnson. V. 1. DAR; Enoch Pratt Lib.
***Hahn.** Frederick Co. families. Markell. Ms. Personal list.
†Hist. of Frederick Co. Williams. MHS; DAR.
Zion Reformed Church, Hagerstown. Md. Geneal. Rec. Com., 1934-35. Mss. DAR.
Haiffle, Hafly. Baust or Emanuel Reformed churchyard, Carroll Co. Md. Geneal. Rec. Com., 1935-36. Mss. DAR.
Haight. Mt. Paran Pres. churchyard, Harrisonville, Balto. Co. Typed ms. MHS; DAR.
Ruf-Haight-Eddy-Sumner-Hatch and allied families. Ms. MHS.
Haight Family. Ms. MHS.
Haile. St. Paul's Parish, Balto. V. 1, 2. Mss. MHS.
See Hale.
***Haines.** Ancestry of William Haines. Chart. W. F. Cregar. Phila., Patterson & White, 1887. MHS.

Harlan family geneal., Chester Co., Pa. Harlan. P. 295. MHS.
Jackson family gathering. 1878.
Joseph Radcliff and his descendants. Bd. ms. MHS.
Florence Eyster Weaver chart. MHS.
See Husband-Price-Haines.
†**Haines, Oakley P.** Men of mark in Md. Johnson. V. 2. DAR; Enoch Pratt Lib.
Haines, Sam'l (born 1762; died 1833). Oldest stone in Pipe Creek Quaker Cemetery. Hist. of West. Md. Scharf. V. 2, p. 971. MHS; DAR.
Haines-Roberts. Marriage certificate of Nathan Haines and Elizabeth Roberts, 1871, Uniontown, Carroll Co. Md. Geneal. Rec. Com., 1935-36, pp. 213-15. Mss. DAR.
Haise. *See* Hays.
Haldane, now **Stump.** Burke's landed gentry. 1939, p. 3002. MHS.
Haldeman, Pa. Bible rec. Md. Geneal. Rec. Com., 1932, p. 204. DAR.
Hale. Descendants of Thomas Hale of Del., with account of Jamison and Green families, and some allied families of Kent Co., Del. Series 3 and 4. Thomas Hale Streets. Phila., 1913, pamph. MHS.
(Haile.) Revolutionary war pension abs. Natl. Geneal. Soc. Quart., v. 23, no. 2, p. 55.
St. Paul's Parish, Balto. V. 1. Mss. MHS.
*Wicomico Co. families. Tilghman. Ms., p. 96. DAR.
See Douglas-Hale.
Hale (Haile), Amon. Pension rec. Natl. Geneal. Soc. Quart., v. 23, no. 2, p. 55.
***Halfehead.** Letters of administration, 1677. Notes from public rec. Hodges. M. H. Mag., 1915, v. 10, pp. 284-85.
Halfpenny. St. Paul's Parish, Balto. V. 2. Mss. MHS.
Haliburton Family, Va. Data. Mss. DAR.
Haliburton, Halleburton. Peale Geneal. Coll. Ms. MHS.
Hall. Ahrens chart. MHS.
Abr. Compend. Amer. Geneal. Virkus. v. 6, p. 554. DAR.
Ancest. rec. and portraits. Col. Dames of Amer., 1910, v. 2, pp. 610, 628. MHS; DAR.
Ancestry of Mrs. Fulton Ray Gordon, nee Ellen Marjorie Gray. D. C. Geneal. Rec. Com., 1932-34, v. 10, p. 120. Typed bd. DAR.
Mrs. R. Barton, Jr., charts. MHS.
†Bench and bar of Md. Sams and Riley. 1901, v. 1, p. 175. Lib. Cong.; MHS; Peabody Lib.
Bowie-Claggett chart. MHS.
Bromwell geneal. Ms. Lib. Cong.; MHS.
Carey chart. MHS.
Col. families of East. Shore and their descendants. Emory. 1900, pp. 223-26. MHS.
Col. families of U. S. A. Mackenzie. V. 2, p. 315 (see Hill family); v. 5; v. 7, pp. 229-61 (Anne Arundel Co.). MHS; DAR.
Cummings chart. Lib. Cong.; MHS; DAR.
Daughter of Md.; Mother of Texas. Bell. MHS; DAR.
D. C. Geneal. Rec. Com., 1932-34, v. 10, pp. 120-21. Typed, bd. DAR.
Duckett chart. MHS.
Dundas-Hesselius. P. 120. MHS.
Col. Nicholas Duvall family Records. Price. Bd. ms. MHS.
Eldridge chart. MHS.
Ellicott-King chart. MHS.
*Founders of Anne Arundel Cos. Warfield. Pp. 99-100. MHS; DAR.
Gilpin chart. MHS.
Gittings chart. MHS.
Hall family of Calvert Co. Christopher Johnston. M. H. Mag., 1913, v. 8, no. 3, pp. 291-301; no. 4, pp. 381-82.
Mrs. Sarah Ewing Hall, author, born 1761, died 1830, member of Ewing family, Cecil Co. Poets and poetry of Cecil Co.
Harford Co. Hist. Soc. Mss. Coll. JHU.
Hist. graves of Md. and D. C. Ridgely. MHS.
Hist. of Harford Co. Preston. MHS; DAR.
Iglehart chart. MHS.
Howard-Montague-Warfield geneal. chart. Culver and Marye. MHS.
Miss Cassandra Lee chart. MHS.
*Lineage Bk. Daughters of Amer. Colonists. V. 1, p. 23, see White; v. 2, p. 187, see Zoller; v. 5, p. 417, Capt. John Hall. MHS; DAR.
Machen chart. MHS.
Manly chart. MHS.
Md. families. Culver. Ms. Personal list.
Md. Geneal. Rec. Com., 1926-27, v. 2, pp. 51-54. DAR.
Md. gleanings in Eng. Wills. M. H. Mag., 1907, v. 2, no. 2.
†Med. Annals Md. Cordell. 1903, pp. 422-24. MHS.
Morris family of Phila. Moon. V. 3, p. 1039. MHS.
Muford chart. MHS.
See Mullikin-Anderson-Woodward-Hall. DAR.
*Mullikin family Bible rec. Mss., in Binder. DAR.
Neill chart. MHS.
Mrs. Newhall chart. MHS.
*Old Kent. Hanson. Pp. 49, 87. MHS; DAR.
Old Somerset. Torrence. MHS; DAR.
Paca chart. Cary Geneal. Coll. Ms. MHS.
Patriotic Md. Md. Soc. of S. A. R., 1930. MHS; DAR.
Pedigree of W. Wallace McKaig. Soc. Col. Wars Md. Culver. 1940. MHS; DAR.
Pedigree of Tilghman Goldsborough Pitts. Soc. Col. Wars Md. Culver. 1940. MHS; DAR.
Pedigree of Mark Alexander Herbert Smith. Soc. Col. Wars. Md. Culver. 1940. MHS; DAR.
Pedigree of Richard Dennis Steuart. Soc. Col. Wars Md. Culver. 1940. MHS; DAR.
Pedigree of Mason Locke Weems Williams. Soc. Col. Wars Md. Culver. 1940. MHS; DAR.
Pedigree of Richard Walker Worthington. Soc. Col. Wars Md. Culver. 1940. MHS; DAR.
Mrs. M. L. Price chart. MHS.
St. James Parish Rec., Anne Arundel Co. Ms. MHS.
St. Paul's Parish, Balto. V. 1, 2, 4. Mss. MHS.
St. Stephens Parish, Cecilton, Md. MHS; DAR.
Sherburne chart. MHS.
Side lights on Md. hist. Richardson. V. 2, p. 112. MHS; DAR.
Somerset Co. Court Book. Tilghman. 1937. Ms. DAR.
Southern Bapt. Church cemetery, Worcester Co. Md. Geneal. Rec. Com., 1937, Mrs. Lines. Mss. DAR.

***Hall.** The Sun, Balto., Sept. 13, 1903; Sept. 30, Oct. 7, 14, Dec. 23 (letter; Prince George, Co.), 1906.
Turner Geneal. Coll. Ms. MHS.
*Wicomico Co. families. Tilghman. Ms, pp. 11, 96, 117, 119, 125. DAR.
Will of Henry Hall on Gunpowder. Photos. DAR.
See Zoller. Lineage Bks., Natl. Soc. of Daughters of Amer. Col., v. 2, 187. MHS; DAR.
See Carvill-Hall-Matthews.
See Duvall-Hall-Tyler.
Hall, Anne Arundel Co. Boone chart. MHS.
Mrs. A. C. Bruce chart. MHS.
Mrs. G. R. Veazey chart. MHS.
Hall, Calvert Co. Abr. Compend. Amer. Geneal. Virkus. V. 6, p. 711. DAR.
B. B. Browne pedigree chart. Soc. Col. Wars, Md. Johnston. 1905, pp. 8, 146. MHS.
Cary Geneal. Coll. Ms. MHS.
Lineage Bks., Natl. Soc. of Daughters of Amer. Col., v. 3, p. 25. MHS; DAR.
Hall, Cecil Co. Abr. Compend. Amer. Geneal. Virkus. V. 6, p. 740. DAR.
Hall, Frederick Co. Mrs. J. Piper chart. MHS.
†**Hall,** Harford Co. Chesapeake Bay Country. Earle. P. 241. MHS.
Hall, Pa. and Md. Mrs. Pennington chart. MHS.
Bonsal charts. MHS.
Hall, Miss Annie Amelia. Chart. Col. Dames, Chap. I. MHS.
Hall, Aquila and Walter Tolley. Bible rec. Ms. DAR.
Hall, Charles Chauncy. Pedigree. Soc. Col. Wars Md. Culver. 1940. MHS; DAR.
Hall, Clayton C. Balto., its hist., its people. Hall. V. 3. MHS; DAR.
*Encyc. of Amer. biog. Amer. Hist. Soc., N. Y., v. 9, p. 219. MHS.
Eng. and New Eng. Pedigree charts, plates 1 and 2. Soc. Col. Wars, Md. Johnston. 1905, pp. 31-32. MHS.
†(1847-1916.) M. H. Mag., 1916, v. 11, pp. 203-04.
†Men of mark in Md. Johnson. V. 1. DAR; Enoch Pratt Lib.
Md. Soc., War of 1812, v. 3, no. 262. Ms. MHS.
Hall, Mrs. Clayton C. (Camilla Ridgely Morris). Chart. Col. Dames, Chap. I. MHS.
Hall, E. and A. Col. Ms. MHS.
Hall, Mrs. Harry Prescott (Elizabeth Anne Ranson). Chart. (Mostly W. Va. families.) Col. Dames, Chap. I. MHS.
Hall, Henry, on Gunpowder, Balto. Co. Will. Photos. DAR.
Hall, Jacob. Greenway Mss. Geneal. Coll. Binder's title, Taylor, no. 2. MHS.
Jacob Hall, surgeon and educator, 1747-1812. J. Hall Pleasants. M. H. Mag., 1913, v. 8, no. 3, p. 217.
Md. Soc., War of 1812, v. 1, no. 32. Ms. MHS.
Pedigree of Pleasants Pennington. Soc. Col. Wars Md. Culver. 1940. MHS; DAR.
†**Hall, John E.** Hist. of Md. Scharf. V. 3, p. 18. MHS.
Pedigree of Iredell Waddell Iglehart. Soc. Col. Wars. Md. Culver. 1940. MHS; DAR.
Hall, Richard. Garrett Co. families. Charles E. Hoye. Pp. 47-50. In Binder. DAR.
Pedigree of Benedict Henry Hanson, Jr. Soc. Col. Wars Md. Culver. 1940. MHS; DAR.
Pedigree of Raphael Semmes. Soc. Col. Wars Md. Culver. 1940. MHS; DAR.
Pedigree of James Donnel Tilghman. Soc. Col. Wars Md. Culver. 1940. MHS; DAR.
Hall, Richard, Calvert Co. W. Bowie, Jr., pedigree chart. Soc. Col. Wars, Md. Johnston. 1905, pp. 6, 146. MHS.
Hall, Summerfield D. Md. Soc., War of 1812, v. 3, no. 238. Ms. MHS.
Hall, Thomas Randolph (born in 1828; married Clarinda Beecher Phillips of Md., 1860). Mss. DAR.
Family Bible rec. Ms. DAR.
Hall Family. Ames Geneal. Coll. Ms. MHS.
*Anne Arundel Co. gentry. Newman. Pp. 624-30. MHS; DAR.
Christopher Johnston. M. H. Mag., 1913, v. 8, pp. 217-35, 291-301, 381-82.
Descendants of Col. Thomas White. Morris. Pp. 127, 132. MHS.
*Hist. of Cecil Co. Johnston. Pp. 480-85. MHS; DAR.
Hist. of Pocomoke. James Murray. 1883, pp. 71, 77, 134. DAR.
Hist. of Washington Co. Williams. Pp. 281, 282, 284, 286.
Over 700 reference cards to Hall Family. File Case. DAR.
Hall Family, "Cranberry Hall," St. Mary's Co. D. C. Geneal. Rec. Com., v. 36, pp. 145-47. Typed, bd. DAR.
Hall Family, Prince George Co. Bible rec. Md. Geneal. Rec. Com., 1926-27, v. 2, pp. 51-54. DAR.
Marine family and Hall family Bible rec., 1655-1836. Md. Geneal. Rec. Com., 1926-27, v. 2, pp. 41-50. Mss. DAR.
Hall Family, Tacony, Phila. Co., Pa., and Md. William and Mary. Quart., 1st series, v. 22, p. 265.
Hall Line, Balto. Co. (now Harford Co.). Col. and Revolutionary families of Pa. Amer. Hist. Soc., N. Y., 1934, p. 597.
Hall-Bond-Cromwell-Delaport-Harris-Reisinger-Reardon, Harford Co. Hist. Soc. Mss. Coll. JHU.
Hall-Carvill-Mathews. Harford Co. Hist. Soc. Mss. Coll. JHU.
Hall-Collins-Elliott-Tingley Families. With geneal. Mostly Del. rec. J. C. Stow. Balto., 1931. Bd. Ms. MHS.
Hall-Duvall. Marriage, 1683, Anne Arundel Co. Md. Geneal. Rec. Com., 1937-38, p. 134. Mss. DAR.
***Hall-Morris-White.** "Mrs. Robert Morris, nee Mary White." Reunion June 7, 1877. Pa. Mag. Hist. and Biog., v. 2, p. 157.
Hall-Tolley. Family Bible of Aquila Hall and Walter Tolley. DAR.
Family Bible rec. of Aquila Hall, Jr. (born in Balto. Co., 1750) and Anne Tolley (born 1756). Mss. DAR.
Hall-Tucker. Harford Co. Hist. Soc. Mss. Coll. JHU.
Halleburton. *See* Haliburton.
†**Haller.** Hist. of Frederick Co. Williams. MHS; DAR.
Mt. Olivet Cemetery, Frederick. Md. Geneal. Rec. Com., 1934-35, p. 111. Mss. DAR.

Hallett. Md. gleanings in Eng. Wills. M. H. Mag., 1907, v. 2, no. 4.
Halley. *See* Hawley-Halley.
***Halley-Hawley-Pike.** Extracts from Brit. Arch. E. F. McPike. Repr. in Mag. of Hist., N. Y., 1909. MHS.
Halliday. *See* Holliday.
***Hallock.** Hallock family in Amer. Revolution. Dr. L. H. Hallock. 1926. Ms. DAR.
Capt. Wm. Hallock of Continental navy. D. H. Hallock (Dorchester Co.). D. A. R. Mag., Aug., 1932, v. 66, no. 8, pp. 508–11.
Hallock Family, Long Island, N. Y., and Dorchester Co. Natl. Geneal. Soc. Quart., v. 20, no. 3, p. 79.
†**Hallwig, Paul.** Men of mark in Md. V. 2. DAR; Enoch Pratt Lib.
Halpin. St. John's R. C. Church cemetery, Montgomery Co. Md. Geneal. Rec. Com., 1926, p. 27. Mss. DAR.
Halsey. Miss G. Eyre Wright chart. MHS.
Halsey Family. Book of ghosts. H. D. and F. R. Halsey. 1927. MHS.
†**Halstead.** Med. Annals Md. Cordell. 1903, p. 424. MHS.
Halton. Cary Geneal. Coll. Ms. MHS.
*Pennington Papers. Ms. MHS.
*Semmes Geneal. Coll. Ms. MHS.
Ham, Hamm. St. Stephens Parish, Cecilton, Md. MHS; DAR.
Haman. Still Pond Church and cemetery. Md. O. R. Soc. Bull., no. 2, pp. 65–75.
See Hayman.
Hambleton. Amer. Armory and Blue Book. Matthews. 1911–12, p. 247.
Balto., its hist., its people. Hall. V. 2. MHS; DAR.
†Biog. cyc. of rep. men of Md. and D. C. P. 261. MHS; DAR.
Bond chart. MHS.
Col. families of U. S. A. Mackenzie. V. 5, p. 88; v. 6, p. 420. MHS; DAR.
Elliott chart. MHS.
Geneal. and memorial encyc. of Md. Spencer. V. 2, pp. 505–12. MHS; DAR.
†Hist. of Balto. City and Co. Scharf. P. 477. MHS.
Hist. of Talbot Co. Tilghman. V. 1, pp. 455–92. MHS; DAR
Ms. MHS.
Mrs. James McHenry chart. MHS.
Monumental City. Howard. MHS; DAR.
See Ober. Abr. Compend. Amer. Geneal. Virkus. V. 1, p. 750. DAR.
Pedigree of Maurice Edward Skinner. Soc. Col. Wars Md. Culver. 1940. MHS; DAR.
Ringgold-Elliott chart. MHS.
Rolle family rec., Talbot Co. Ms. MHS.
Sherwood charts. 1937. Mss. DAR.
Spring Hill cemetery, Easton. Md. O. R. Soc. Bull., no. 1, pp. 35–41.
Wilcox-Rose Bible rec. Ms. MHS.
See Man-Needles-Hambleton.
Hambleton, Frank Sherwood. Pedigree chart. Soc. Col. Wars, Md. Johnston. 1905, pp. 33, 146. MHS.
†**Hambleton, P. S.** (1777–1851). Hist. of Talbot Co. Tilghman. V. 1, pp. 455–76. MHS; DAR.
Hambleton, Col. Sam'l. (1812–1886). Hist. of Talbot Co. Tilghman. V. 1, pp. 476–92. MHS; DAR.
Hambleton, Thomas Edward. Pedigree. Soc. Col. Wars Md. Culver. 1940. MHS; DAR.
Hamel. St. Paul's Parish, Balto. V. 2. Mss. MHS.
†**Hamill.** Hist. of Balto. City and Co. Scharf. P. 430. MHS.
†Hist. of West. Md. Scharf. V. 2, p. 1520. MHS; DAR.
‡Newsp. clipp. MHS.
Hamill, Miss Mary Baldwin. Chart. Col. Dames, Chap. I. MHS.
Hamill Family. Mountain Democrat, Garrett Co., Nov. 29, 1934. Newsp. clipp. MHS; DAR.
Hamilton. Amer. Clan Gregor Year Book, 1916, pp. 32, 33, 34, 45. MHS; DAR.
†Bench and bar of Md. Sams and Riley. 1901, v. 2, p. 412. Lib. Cong.; MHS; Peabody Lib.
Buck family Bible rec. Md. Geneal. Rec. Com., v. 1, pp. 12–13. DAR.
Centenary of Catholicity in Ky. Webb. 1884. MHS.
Data. Foy and allied families. MHS.
J. T. Dennis pedigree chart, plate 2. Soc. Col. Wars, Md. Johnston. 1905, p. 22. MHS.
Geneal. tables of descendants of John Hamilton of "Locust Hill," Lexington, Va. (Born 1789; died 1872.) Privately printed, 1933. MHS.
*Hamilton family of Charles Co. Mrs. M. L. Hamilton Kelly and Mrs. I. B. Cherault. Houston, Texas, Standard Printing Co., 1930. MHS.
Hilles chart. MHS.
†Med. Annals Md. Cordell. 1903, pp. 424–25. MHS.
O'Daniel-Hamilton ancestry in Md. and Ky. O'Daniel. Pp. 49–71. MHS.
Pedigree of John Ogle Warfield, Jr. Soc. Col. Wars Md. Culver. 1940. MHS; DAR.
St. Barnabas P. E. churchyard. Typed ms. MHS; DAR.
St. Paul's Parish, Balto. V. 1, 2, 3. Mss. MHS.
St. Thomas' Parish, Balto. Co. Bd. ms. MHS. Also: Md. Geneal. Rec. Com., 1937, pp. 109–82. Mss. DAR.
Semmes and allied families. Semmes. MHS.
*Semmes Geneal. Coll. Ms. MHS.
Toy-Hamilton chart. O'Gorman. Ms. DAR.
See O'Daniel-Hamilton.
***Hamilton,** Charles Co. Lineage Bk., Daughters of Amer. Colonists, v. 4, p. 169. MHS; DAR.
Lineage Bk., Daughters of Founders and Patriots, v. 21, p. 34. MHS.
Hamilton, Talbott Co. Abr. Compend. Amer. Geneal. Virkus. V. 1, p. 371. DAR.
Hamilton (Mrs. Gordon Paxton Paine). Americans of gentle birth and their ancestors. Pitman. P. 78. MHS.
Hamilton, Thomas, Somerset Co. Death. Natl. Geneal. Soc. Quart., Sept., 1938, v. 26, no. 3, p. 63.
Hamilton, Mrs. William Howard (Rosalie Braxton Page). Chart. Col. Dames, Chap. I. MHS.
Mrs. Douglas Gordon Lovell chart. MHS.
†**Hamilton, Gov. William T.** Founders of Anne Arundel and Howard Cos. Warfield. P. 292. MHS; DAR.
†Hist. of Md. Scharf. V. 3, p. 745. MHS.
†Governors of Md. Buchholz. P. 221. MHS.

*__Hamilton Family.__ Arch. of Georgetown Univ., Wash., D. C., v. 97, no. 15.
__Hamilton-Trew.__ Bible rec. Upper Penins. East. Shore, p. 212–15. MHS; DAR.
__Hamler.__ St. Paul's Parish, Balto. V. 2. Mss. MHS.
__Hamm.__ Holdens Cemetery, Kent Co. Md. Geneal. Rec. Com., 1932, v. 5, p. 211. Mss. DAR.
See Ham.
__Hammer.__ Hagerstown tombstone inscriptions. Gruder. Natl. Geneal. Soc. Quart., 1919, v. 8, nos. 1, 2.
__Hammersley.__ Trinity Church cemetery, Dorchester Co. Md. O. R. Soc. Bull., no. 3, pp. 42–52.
__Hammond.__ All Hallow's P. E. churchyard, Snow Hill, Worcester Co. Hudson. Bd. ms. MHS; DAR. Also: Md. Geneal. Rec. Com., 1935–36, p. 24. Mss. DAR.
Amer. Armory and Blue Book. Matthews, 1911–12, p. 267.
Abr. Compend. Amer. Geneal. Virkus. V. 1, p. 138. DAR.
Ances. rec. and portraits. Col. Dames of Amer., 1910, v. 1, p. 254; v. 2, p. 608, 629. MHS; DAR.
†Biog. cyc. of rep. men of Md. and D. C. P. 261. MHS; DAR.
Blackwell chart. MHS.
Bonsal charts. MHS.
Mrs. Howard Bruce chart. MHS.
Carlyle family and Carlyle house. Spencer. P. 24. MHS.
Carlyle family. William and Mary Quart., 1st series, v. 18, pp. 201, 278.
Cary Geneal. Coll. Ms. MHS.
W. W. Coleman pedigree chart. Soc. Col. Wars, Md. Johnston. 1905, p. 17. MHS.
Col. families of U. S. A. Mackenzie. V. 4, p. 362; v. 5. MHS; DAR.
Col. mansions of Md. and Del. Hammond. 1914. MHS.
Cox (Cock) family. Leef and Webb. Ms. MHS.
D. A. R. Mag., v. 70, no. 5, pp. 457–58.
Dorsey and allied families. Ms. MHS.
Dorsey chart. Lib. Cong.; MHS.
Dorsey chart. MHS.
*Founders of Anne Arundel and Howard Cos. Warfield. Pp. 178–84. MHS; DAR.
*Frederick Co. families. Markell. Ms. Personal list.
Geneal. notes of Chamberlaine family. MHS.
Griffith chart. Cary Geneal. Coll. Ms. MHS.
Griffith geneal. Griffith. MHS; DAR.
Hist. graves of Md. and D. C. Ridgely. MHS.
†Hist. of Frederick Co. Williams. MHS; DAR.
R. C. Hoffman pedigree chart. Soc. Col. Wars, Md. Johnston. 1905, p. 40. MHS.
Line of descent from Maj. Gen. John Hammond, 1643–1721. Mrs. L. H. Webb-Peploe. Ms. DAR.
*Lineage Bks., Natl. Soc. of Daughters of Amer. Col., v. 1, pp. 13, 41; v. 4, p. 47. MHS; DAR.
Md. families. Culver. Ms. Personal list.
Md. Geneal. Bull., v. 5, p. 3. MHS; DAR.
†Med. Annals Md. Cordell. 1903, pp. 425–26. MHS.
Moale-Croxall-North chart. Cary Geneal. Coll. Ms. MHS.
H. A. Orrick pedigree chart. Soc. Col. Wars, Md. Johnston. 1905, pp. 79, 146. MHS.
Patriotic Md. Md. Soc. of S. A. R., 1930. MHS; DAR.
Pedigree of Francis Joseph Baldwin. Soc. Col. Wars Md. Culver. 1940. MHS; DAR.
Pedigree of James Dorsey Brown, Jr. Soc. Col. Wars Md. Culver. 1940. MHS; DAR.
Pedigree of Gustavus Warfield Evans. Soc. Col. Wars Md. Culver. 1940. MHS; DAR.
Pedigree of Charles Chauncy Hall. Soc. Col. Wars Md. Culver. 1940. MHS; DAR.
Pedigree of Arthur Lafayette Jones. Soc. Col. Wars Md. Culver. 1940. MHS; DAR.
Pedigree of Pleasants Pennington. Soc. Col. Wars Md. Culver. 1940. MHS; DAR.
Pedigree of Tilghman Goldsborough Pitts. Soc. Col. Wars Md. Culver. 1940. MHS; DAR.
Pedigree of Townsend Scott, IV. Soc. Col. Wars Md. Culver. 1940. MHS; DAR.
Pedigree of Levin Gale Shreve. Soc. Col. Wars Md. Culver. 1940. MHS; DAR.
Pedigree of Mark Alexander Herbert Smith. Soc. Col. Wars Md. Culver. 1940. MHS; DAR.
Pedigree of Wm. Handy Collins Vickers. Soc. Col. Wars Md. Culver. 1940. MHS; DAR.
Pedigree of Richard Walker Worthington. Soc. Col. Wars Md. Culver. 1940. MHS; DAR.
Mrs. Pennington chart. MHS.
Mrs. J. Piper, chart. MHS.
Mrs. E. W. Poe chart. MHS.
Posey chart. MHS.
Mrs. G. H. Williams, Jr., chart. MHS.
St. Paul's P. E. churchyard, Berlin, Worcester Co. Hudson. Bd. ms. MHS; DAR. Also: Md. Geneal. Rec. Com., 1937, Mrs. Lines. Mss. DAR.
St. Paul's Parish, Balto. V. 1, 2, 3, 4. Mss. MHS.
St. Thomas' Parish, Balto. Co. Bd. ms. MHS. Also: Md. Geneal. Rec. Com., 1937, pp. 109–82. Mss. DAR.
Spring Hill cemetery, Easton. Md. O. R. Soc. Bull., no. 1, pp. 35–41. MHS.
*The Sun, Balto., Oct. 4, 11, 18, 1903; Feb. 10, 17, 24, 1905. Aug. 13, 1905 (letter; Hammond-Orrick).
Turner family. Forman. P. 53. MHS.
Turner Geneal. Coll. Ms. MHS.
Warfields of Md. Warfield. MHS.
Welsh-Hyatt and kindred. Welsh. Sec. 2, pp. 150–68. MHS; DAR.
*Wilson Mss. Coll., no. 37, A, B, C; no. 81; no. 89. MHS.
Zion Reformed Church, Hagerstown. Md. Geneal. Rec. Com., 1934–35. Mss. DAR.
See Greenberry-Hammond.
See Howard-Hammond.
See Welsh-Hammond-Riggs.
__Hammond,__ Somerset Co. Side lights in Md. Hist. Richardson. V. 2, pp. 115, 346. MHS; DAR.
__Hammond, Edw.__ Md. Soc., War of 1812, v. 4, no. 308. Ms. MHS.
__Hammond, Edward.__ Pedigree. Soc. Col. Wars Md. Culver. 1940. MHS; DAR.
__Hammond, Edward Cuyler.__ Pedigree. Soc. Col. Wars Md. Culver. 1940. MHS; DAR.
__Hammond, Edward Mackubin.__ Pedigree. Soc. Col. Wars Md. Culver. 1940. MHS; DAR.

***Hammond, Frank Lloyd.** Burke's landed gentry. 1939. MHS.
†Hammond, Nicholas III (1758–1830). Hist. of Talbot Co. Tilghman. V. 1, p. 579. MHS; DAR.
***Hammond Family.** Anne Arundel Co. gentry. Newman. Pp. 189–234. MHS; DAR.
Hist. of Hammond family, Anne Arundel Co. Laura Webb-Peploe. 1922, pamph. MHS; DAR.
***Hammond-Cromwell Families.** Amer. Hist. Reg., 1895, v. 2, pp. 867–73. MHS.
Hammond-Dorsey. Bible rec. Ms. MHS.
Hamtranck. Williamson Bible rec. Ms. MHS.
Hana, Hanah, Hanna, Hannah. Marriages, 1779. Md. Geneal. Bull., v. 2, p. 8. MHS; DAR.
Hanah. *See* Hana.
Hance. Mrs. Charles Carter chart. MHS.
Cary Geneal. Coll. Ms. MHS.
Mrs. C. C. Hall chart. MHS.
Jaquett family. Sellers. 1907, p. 167. MHS.
Pedigree of Charles O'Donnell Mackall. Soc. Col. Wars Md. Culver. 1940. MHS; DAR.
Sweetser chart. MHS.
Sweetser family of Md. and Mass. Gardner. Pamph., repr. from M. H. Mag., June, 1932, p. 144. MHS; DAR.
Mrs. G. H. Williams, Jr., chart. MHS.
Hance, Capt. John. G. N. Mackenzie pedigree chart, plate 1. Soc. Col. Wars, Md. Johnston. 1905, pp. 61, 146. MHS.
Hance, Samuel, Calvert Co. (born 1730). D. A. R. Mag., v. 68, no. 5, p. 284.
Hance Family. Geneal. of Mays family. Mays. P. 213. MHS.
Hancock. Patriotic Md. Md. Soc. of S. A. R., 1930. MHS; DAR.
Southern Bapt. Church cemetery, Worcester Co. Md. Geneal. Rec. Com., 1937, Mrs. Lines. Mss. DAR.
St. Paul's Parish, Balto. V. 2. Mss. MHS.
Hancock, J. Eichberger. Md. Soc., War of 1812, v. 3, no. 223. Ms. MHS.
Pedigree. Soc. Col. Wars Md. Culver. 1940. MHS; DAR.
Hancy. Keyser chart. MHS.
Hand. Jennings-Hand Bible rec. Photos. MHS.
Hands. Barroll in Great Britain and Amer. Barroll. Pp. 84–85. MHS.
Hist. graves of Md. and D. C. Ridgely. MHS.
Handy. All Hallow's P. E. churchyard, Snow Hill, Worcester Co. Hudson. Bd. ms. MHS; DAR. Also: Md. Geneal. Rec. Com., 1935–36, p. 24. Mss. DAR.
Amer. Armory and Blue Bk. Matthews. 1908, p. 268. DAR.
Abr. Compend. Amer. Geneal. Virkus. V. 1, p. 141. DAR.
Amer. of gentle birth, and their ancestors. Pittman. V. 1, p. 190. MHS; DAR.
H. T. Barnes Bible rec. Ms. MHS.
*Biog. cyc. of rep. men of Md. and D. C. Pp. 515, 693. MHS; DAR.
Buckingham Pres. churchyard, Worcester Co. Hudson. Bd. ms. MHS; DAR.
Cabells and their kin. Brown. Pp. 506–07. MHS.
†Chesapeake Bay Country. Earle. P. 414. MHS.
Christ P. E. Church cemetery, Cambridge. Steele. 1936. MHS; DAR.
*Handy and their kin. Isaac W. Ker Handy. N. Y., 2 vols.
Hist. Graves of Md. and D. C. Ridgely. MHS.
Hist. Salisbury, Wicomico Co. Truitt. DAR.
Makemie Memorial Pres. churchyard, Snow Hill, Worcester Co. Hudson. Bd. ms. MHS; DAR. Also: Md. Geneal. Rec. Com., Mrs. Lines. Mss. DAR.
Md. families. Culver. Ms. Personal list.
†Med. Annals Md. Cordell. 1903, pp. 426–27. MHS.
Memorial to Thomas Potts, Jr. James. MHS.
See Moss. Abr. Compend. Amer. Geneal. Virkus. V. 1, p. 644. DAR.
John Neill of Lewes, Del., 1739. Pr. for family, Phila., 1875.
†Old Buckingham by the Sea, East. Shore of Md. Page. DAR.
Rec. of Stepney Parish. MHS; DAR.
St. Paul's P. E. churchyard, Kent Co. Md. O. R. Soc. Bull., no. 2, pp. 54–65.
St. Paul's churchyard, Kent Co. Md. O. R. Soc. Bull., no. 2, pp. 54–65. MHS.
St. Paul's Parish, Balto. V. 2, 4. Mss. MHS.
Sketches of John Slemmons Stevenson and Rev. Samuel McMaster. Stevenson. Pp. 19–20. MHS.
Somerset Co. Court Book. Tilghman. 1937. Ms. DAR.
Southern Bapt. Church cemetery, Worcester Co. Md. Geneal. Rec. Com., 1937, Mrs. Lines. Mss. DAR.
Tombs (3), Makemie Memorial Churchyard, Snow Hill, Worcester Co., 1799–1817. Md. O. R. Soc., June 1906, Bull., no. 1, p. 53.
Turner Geneal. Coll. Ms. MHS.
*Wicomico Co. families. Tilghman. Ms., pp. 22, 34, 96–100, 110. DAR.
See O'Carroll. Focke Geneal. Coll. Ms. MHS.
Handy, John Custis. Pedigree. Soc. Col. Wars Md. Culver. 1940. MHS; DAR.
Md. Soc., War of 1812, v. 2, no. 199. Ms. MHS.
Handy-Gillis. Wicomico Co. families. Bible rec. Ms. DAR.
Hane. Frederick Co. tombstone inscriptions. Gruder. Natl. Geneal. Soc. Quart., 1919, v. 8, nos. 1, 2.
Hanenkampe. Zion Reformed Church, Hagerstown. Md. Geneal. Rec. Com., 1934–35. Mss. DAR.
Hanenkampf. Rev. Christian Frederick Post and Peter Humrickhouse. Humrickhouse. P. 23. MHS.
Hanley. Buckingham Pres. churchyard, Worcester Co. Hudson. Bd. ms. MHS; DAR.
†Men of mark in Md. Johnson. V. 4. DAR; Enoch Pratt Lib.
Hann. St. Joseph's R. C. churchyard. Md. O. R. Soc. Bull., no. 3, p. 64.
Hanna. Geneal. of Va. and Ky. Floyd families. Floyd. P. 94. DAR
Glendy churchyard, Balto. Md. Geneal. Rec. Com., 1933–34. Mss. DAR.
†Hist. of Allegany Co. Thomas and Williams. V. 2. MHS; DAR.
See Hana.
Hannah. Harford Co. Hist. Soc. Mss. Coll. JHU.
See Hana.

Hannon, Walter W. Charles Co. Deed, Mar. 2, 1837. D. C. Geneal. Rec. Com., 1937–38, v. 35, pp. 65–68. Typed, bd. DAR.
Hansford. Mrs. Henry Du Pont Baldwin chart. MHS.
Cary Geneal. Coll. Ms. MHS.
Hanshaw. Mt. Olivet Cemetery, Frederick. Md. Geneal. Rec. Com., 1934–35, p. 111. Mss. DAR.
Hanshew. Steiner geneal. Steiner. 1896. MHS.
Hanslap. Chew family. Culver. M. H. Mag., 1935, v. 30, no. 2, pp. 157–75.
Col. families of Amer. Lawrence. V. 2, pp. 39–41. MHS.
Howard-Montague-Warfield geneal. chart. Culver and Marye. MHS.
Side lights on Md. hist. Richardson. V. 2, p. 356. MHS; DAR.
Hanson. Abr. Compend. Amer. Geneal. Virkus. V. 6, pp. 122, 647. DAR.
Amer. of gentle birth, and their ancestors. Pittman. V. 1, p. 16. MHS; DAR.
Ances. rec. and portraits. Col. Dames of Amer., 1910, v. 2, pp. 718, 726–27. MHS; DAR.
Ancestry of Mrs. Fulton Ray Gordan, nee Ellen Marjorie Gray. D. C. Geneal. Rec. Com., 1932–34, p. 127. Typed, bd. DAR.
Balto. Herald, April 12, 1903. Newsp. clipp. MHS.
Bantz geneal. notes. Ms. MHS.
Barber, "Luckland," St. Mary's Co. Bible rec. Natl. Geneal. Soc. Quart., v. 22, no. 4, pp. 89–92.
†Bench and bar of Md. Sams and Riley. 1901, v. 1, p. 215. Lib. Cong.; MHS; Peabody Lib.
Brisko-Brisco-Briscoe and some family connections. Ramey. P. 18. Ms. MHS.
Robert Brooke chart. MHS; DAR.
Chart, photos., complete in 1 sheet. Cary Geneal. Coll. Ms. MHS.
Colston chart. Cary Geneal. Coll. Ms. MHS.
Col. families of U. S. A. Mackenzie. V. 1; v. 2, p. 202 (see Contee); v. 6, p. 367. MHS; DAR.
Col. mansions of Md. and Del. Hammond. 1914. MHS.
Daughter of Md., Mother of Texas. Bell. MHS; DAR.
Dorsey and allied families. Ms. MHS.
Geneal. rec. of family of Thomas. Thomas. MHS.
John Hanson estate, Charles Co. Tombstone inscriptions, 1740–1922. Md. Geneal. Rec. Com., 1932–33. DAR.
†John Hanson, and Inseparable Union. J. A. Nelson. Boston, 1939, 146 pp. (Md. patriot and statesman of Revolutionary period and first President of U. S. in Congress assembled.)
†John Hanson of Mulberry Grove. J. Bruce Kremer. N. Y., 1938, 188 pp. (home of Md. President, near Port Tobacco, Charles Co.) MHS; DAR.
†John Hanson, 1715–83; our first President. Seymour W. Smith. N. Y., Brewer-Warren and Putnam, 1932. MHS.
Hist. graves of Md. and D. C. Ridgely. MHS.
†Hist. of Frederick Co. Williams. MHS; DAR.
Hist. of Waltham family. Md. Geneal. Rec. Com., 1935–36, p. 71. Mss. DAR.
Md. families. Culver. Ms. Personal list.
May-Hanson-Pollard-Philips. Eiler. 1929, pamph. MHS.
†Med. Annals Md. Cordell. 1903, p. 427. MHS.
Naturalizations in Md., 1666–1765; Laws. Bacon. MHS.
Notes, 1707–26. Liber L., no. 2. Natl. Geneal. Soc. Quart., v. 18, p. 31.
Patriotic Md. Md. Soc. of S. A. R., 1930. MHS; DAR.
Pedigree of Garner Wood Denmead. Soc. Col. Wars Md. Culver. 1940. MHS; DAR.
Pedigree of Coleman Randall Freeman. Soc. Col. Wars Md. Culver. 1940. MHS; DAR.
Pedigree of Pleasants Pennington. Soc. Col. Wars Md. Culver. 1940. MHS; DAR.
*Pennington Papers. Ms. MHS.
Portrait and biog. rec. of Sixth Cong. Dist. of Md. 1898, see Veirs p. 721. MHS; DAR.
See Rumsey, B. C. Abr. Compend. Amer. Geneal. Virkus. V. 1, p. 541. DAR.
St. Paul's Parish, Balto. V. 1, 2, 4. Mss. MHS.
Semmes and allied families. Semmes. MHS.
*Side lights on Md. hist. Richardson. V. 2, p. 117. MHS; DAR.
Miss Margaret M. Steele chart. MHS.
Stevenson chart. MHS.
*The Sun, Balto. Feb. 7, 1904; July 29, Aug. 5, 12, 1906.
Thomas-Chew-Lawrence. Thomas. MHS.
†**Hanson Alexander, Contee** (U. S. senator; died April 23, 1918). Hist. of Md. Scharf. V. 2, p. 575; v. 3, p. 3. MHS.
Hanson, Benedict Henry, Jr. Pedigree. Soc. Col. Wars Md. Culver. 1940. MHS; DAR.
†**Hanson, John.** Hist. of Md. Scharf. V. 2, p. 332. MHS.
†(1715–83). M. H. Mag., v. 13, p. 76.
*Semmes Geneal. Coll. Ms. MHS.
Hanson, Hans, of Cecil and Kent Cos. Pedigree of Richard Constable Bernard. Soc. Col. Wars Md. Culver. 1940. MHS; DAR.
Hanson, Col. Hans, Kent Co. (1646–1703). A. L. and S. L. Jenkins pedigree chart. Soc. Col. Wars, Md. Johnson. 1905, pp. 45, 146. MHS.
Hanson Family. Lee of Va., 1642–1892. E. J. Lee. P. 157. Lib. Cong.; MHS.
(1653). Morris family of Phila. Moon. V. 2, p. 622. MHS.
*Old Kent. Hanson. Pp. 110–14, 159–69, 308; arms, p. 111. MHS; DAR.
Hanson Line. Lilburn family. Col. and Revolutionary families of Phila. Jordan. 1933, v. 1, pp. 382–98.
D. H. Thomas pedigree chart, plate 1. Soc. Col. Wars, Md. Johnson. 1905, pp. 109, 146. MHS.
***Hanson-Hutchens.** Ancestors and descendants of S. Elijah Hanson, Revolutionary soldier of Va., and Strangeman Hutchens, Revolutionary soldier of N. C., with some data of allied families Cox, Gardner, Trent and others. M. D. Van Valin. 1938, pamph. DAR.
Harbaugh. Abr. Compend. Amer. Geneal. Virkus. V. 6, p. 420. DAR.
*Annals of Harbaugh family in Amer., 1736–1856. Rev. H. Harbaugh. Chambersburg, Pa., M. Kieffer Co., 1856, 148 pp. MHS.
Hagerstown tombstone inscriptions. Gruder. Natl. Geneal. Soc. Quart., 1919, v. 8, nos. 1, 2.
Harbaugh family notes. Mss. MHS.

*Harbaugh Reformed Church cemetery rec., Rouzervill, Pa.
†Hist. of Frederick Co. Williams. MHS; DAR.
†Hist. of West. Md. Scharf. V. 1, pp. 612–14. MHS; DAR.
Spessard family. Spessard. MHS; DAR.
Tom's Creek M. E. Church cemetery, near Emmitsburg. Md. Geneal. Rec. Com., 1932–33, p. 70. Mss. DAR.

***Harbaugh, Jacob.** Burial ground inscriptions. Ms. MHS.
Cemetery; burial rec. MHS.

Harbaugh Family. Notes. Ms. MHS.

Harbert. Bond family geneal. Ms. MHS.

Harbin. Centenary of Catholicity in Ky. Webb. 1884. MHS.

***Hardcastle.** Bible of John Hardcastle, Castle Hall; Caroline Co. Geneal. Soc. Pa. Pub., 1921–23, v. 8, pp. 289–91.
†Biog. cyc. of rep. men of Md. and D. C. P. 326. MHS; DAR.
†Chesapeake Bay Country. Earle. P. 378. MHS.
Col. families of East. Shore and their descendants. Emory. 1900, p. 26. MHS.
†Med. Annals Md. Cordell. 1903, p. 428. MHS.
Patriotic Md. Md. Soc. of S. A. R., 1930. MHS; DAR.
Portrait and biog. rec. East. Shore of Md. 1898, p. 189. MHS; DAR.
*Rec. from account book of Thomas Hardcastle, Castle Hall, Caroline Co. Geneal. Soc. Pa. Pub., 1921–23, v. 8, p. 292.
See Culbreth-Hardcastle.

Hardcastle, Talbot Co. H. Mullikin pedigree chart, plate 2. Soc. Col. Wars. Md. Johnston. 1905, p. 75. MHS.

†Hardcastle, Hughlett. Men of mark in Md. Johnson. V. 4. DAR; Enoch Pratt Lib.

Hardcastle, John H., "Castle Hall," Caroline Co. Bible rec. and family memoranda, 1739–1874. Pub. Geneal. Soc. Pa., v. 8, no. 3, pp. 289–92.
Of "Castle Hall," Caroline Co. Bible and family rec. from Account Book, p. 292. Ms. MHS.

†Hardcastle, Mrs. S. W. Poets and prose writers of Cecil Co. Johnston.

Harden. Balto., its hist., its people. Hall. V. 3. MHS; DAR.
Dorsey and allied families. Ms. MHS.
Talbott of "Poplar Knowle." Shirk. MHS; DAR.

Hardesty. St. Paul's Parish, Balto. V. 2, 3. Mss. MHS.

Hardidge. Hardwick, Hardidge family, Md. and Va. William and Mary Quart., 2nd series, v. 23, pp. 59–69.

Hardin. Pa. Mag., v. 35, pp. 120–21.

Harding. Col. Nicholas Duvall family rec. Price. Bd. ms. MHS.
St. Barnabas P. E. churchyard. Typed ms. MHS; DAR.
St. Paul's Parish, Balto. V. 2, 4. Mss. MHS.

***Harding Family.** Arch. of Georgetown Univ., Wash., D. C., v. 274, no. 1.

Harding-Drane, Ky. Amer. Clan Gregor Year Book, 1937, p. 78. MHS; DAR.

Hardwick, Hardidge Family, Md. and Va. William and Mary Quart., 2nd series, v. 23, pp. 59–69.

Hardy. Fisher family. Morse. MHS.
Fisher family, Sussex Co., Del., and Md. Ms. MHS.
St. John's R. C. Church cemetery, Montgomery Co. Md. Geneal. Rec. Com., 1926, p. 27. Mss. DAR.
St. Paul's Parish, Balto. V. 1, 2, 3. Mss. MHS.
Somerset Co. Court Book. Tilghman. 1937. Ms. DAR.

Hare. St. Paul's Parish, Balto. V. 2. Mss. MHS.

Harford, Frances Mary (sister of Henry Harford, last proprietor of Md.). Notes and queries. M. H. Mag., Mar., 1940, v. 35, no. 1, pp. 86–87.

†Harford-Wheland. Notes. Hist. of Md. Scharf. V. 2, pp. 137–39. MHS.

Hargarader. *See* Baker-Hargarader-De Hoff.

†Hargett. Hist. of Frederick Co. Williams. MHS; DAR.
†Men of mark in Md. Johnson. V. 4, p. 346. DAR; Enoch Pratt Lib.

Hargett, D. H. Md. Soc., War of 1812, v. 2, no. 148. Ms. MHS.

†Hargett, P. Lilburn. Men of mark in Md. Johnson. V. 4, p. 327. DAR; Enoch Pratt Lib.

Hargis. Makemie Memorial Pres. churchyard, Snow Hill, Worcester Co. Hudson. Bd. ms. MHS; DAR. Also: Md. Geneal. Rec. Com., Mrs. Lines. Mss. DAR.
Pocomoke Pres. churchyard. Bd. ms. MHS; DAR.

Hargrove Line. Col. and Revolutionary lineages of Amer. 1939, v. 3, pp. 403–07. MHS.
*Encyc. Amer. biog. Amer. Hist. Soc., new series, v. 1, p. 171. (Irwin, p. 173.) MHS; DAR.

†Harlan. Bench and bar of Md. Sams and Riley. 1901, v. 2, p. 551. Lib. Cong.; MHS; Peabody Lib.
*Hist. and geneal. of Harlan family; particularly of descendants of George and Michael Harlan, who settled in Chester Co., Pa. (Mostly Quaker rec.) A. H. Harlan. Balto., Lord Baltimore Press, 1914. MHS.
†Hist. of West. Md. Scharf. V. 1, p. 616. MHS; DAR.
†Med. Annals Md. Cordell. 1904, p. 428. MHS.
Portrait and biog. rec. of Harford and Cecil Cos. 1897. Pp. 133, 481, 509. MHS; DAR.
Stump family of Cecil and Harford Cos. Pamph. MHS.

Harlan Family (1687–1912). Ms. MHS.

Harlin. Somerset Co. Court Book. Tilghman. 1937. Ms. DAR.

Harman. Mt. Olivet Cemetery, Frederick. Md. Geneal. Rec. Com., 1934–35, p. 111. Mss. DAR.
St. Paul's Parish, Balto. V. 2. Mss. MHS.

Harmanson. Frances Murray Bowdoin chart. MHS.
Geneal. of Henrietta Chauncy Wilson. Upshur. Bk. of photos. MHS.

Harmon. Notes. Henry and Abell Burton of Va. Ms. File case, DAR.

Harmonson. Buckingham Pres. churchyard, Worcester Co. Hudson. Bd. ms. MHS; DAR.

Harned. Newsp. clipp. MHS.
See Davis-Harned.

Harney, Somerset Co. Abr. Compend. Amer. Geneal. Virkus. V. 6, p. 693. DAR.
†**Harp.** Hist. of Frederick Co. Williams. MHS; DAR.
Harper. Auld chart. MHS.
Bannister studies of Harper, with probable Md. background. Ms. MHS.
†Bench and bar of Md. Sams and Riley. 1901, v. 1, p. 217. Lib. Cong.; MHS; Peabody Lib.
Bible rec. Md. Geneal. Rec. Com., 1926–27, v. 2, p. 61. DAR.
†Med. Annals Md. Cordell. 1904, p. 429. MHS.
*Pennington Papers. Ms. MHS.
St. Paul's Parish, Balto. V. 2. Mss. MHS.
St. Stephens Parish, Cecilton, Md. MHS; DAR.
Somerset Co. Court Book. Tilghman. 1937. Ms. DAR.
Still Pond Church and cemetery. Md. O. R. Soc. Bull., no. 2, pp. 65–75.
*Studies of Banister Harper, Halifax and Wilkes Cos., Va., with probably Md. backgrounds. Ms. MHS.
Turner Geneal. Coll. Ms. MHS.
Harper, Va. and Md. William and Mary Quart., 1st series, v. 3, p. 204.
***Harper, Carl Brown.** Coat of arms. Burke's landed gentry. 1939. MHS.
†**Harper, Robt. Goodloe.** Balto., hist. and biog. Richardson and Bennett. 1871, pp. 293–94. MHS; DAR.
†Chronicles of Balto. Scharf. 1874, p. 418. MHS; DAR.
†Hist. of Md. Scharf. V. 2, p. 613. MHS.
Harratt Family. Hardwick family, Md. and Va. William and Mary Quart., 2nd series, v. 23, p. 69.
Harrett. Somerset Co. Court Book. Tilghman. 1937. Ms. DAR.
Harriman, Harryman. St. Paul's Parish, Balto. V. 1. Mss. MHS.
Harrington. Britton chart. MHS.
Christ P. E. Church cemetery, Cambridge. Steele. 1936. MHS; DAR.
Greensboro old churchyard. Md. Geneal. Rec. Com., 1935–36, p. 168. Mss. DAR.
*Hist. Dorchester Co. Jones. 1925, p. 330. MHS; DAR.
Marriages. Dorchester Co. marriages, 1781–1807. Md. Geneal. Rec. Com., v. 4, p. 80. DAR.
Old churchyard, Greensboro, Caroline Co. Tombstone inscriptions (5 stones). Md. Geneal. Rec. Com., 1935–36, p. 168. DAR.
Old Md. families. Bromwell. MHS; DAR.
St. Paul's Parish, Balto. V. 2, 3. Mss. MHS.
Trinity Church cemetery, Dorchester Co. Md. O. R. Soc. Bull., no. 3, pp. 42–52.
Harriott. Tombstone inscriptions, St. Joseph's churchyard, Emmitsburg. Md. O. R. Soc. Bull., no. 3, pp. 64–66. MHS.
Harris. Ances. rec. and portraits. Col. Dames of Amer., 1910, v. 1, pp. 56, 63, 243; v. 2, p. 604. MHS; DAR.
Balto., its hist., its people. Hall. V. 2. MHS; DAR.
Battee, Brewer, Boteler, etc., family rec. Murray. Photos. MHS.
In Blaine Bible records. Turner Geneal. Coll. Ms. MHS.
Mrs. R. F. Brent chart. MHS.
Britton Scrap. Book. V. 2. Ms. MHS.
Cary Geneal. Coll. Ms. MHS.
*Crittenden-Harris chart. MHS.
Harris Family Assoc. of Md. and Va. M. B. Little, secretary, 1510 Varnum St., Wash., D. C. DAR.
Joseph, Harris, of Ellenborough. George Forbes. M. H. Mag., Dec., 1936, v. 31, no. 4, pp. 333–37.
Hist. graves of Md. and D. C. Ridgely. MHS.
†Hist. of Frederick Co. Williams. MHS; DAR.
Marriage rec. of Frederick Co. Markell. Md. Geneal. Rec. Com., 1938–39. Mss. DAR.
Md. families. Culver. Ms. Personal list.
Maulsby family in Amer. Barnard. DAR; Peabody Lib.
Owings and Harris Bible rec. Ms. MHS.
Pedigree of Duncan Keener Brent. Soc. Col. Wars Md. Culver. 1940. MHS; DAR.
Pedigree of Nicolas Leeke Dashiell. Soc. Col. Wars Md. Culver. 1940. MHS; DAR.
Rec. of Stepney Parish. MHS; DAR.
St. Paul's Parish, Balto. V. 1, 2, 4. Mss. MHS.
*Semmes Geneal. Coll. Ms. MHS.
Somerset Co. Court Book. Tilghman. 1937. Ms. DAR.
Talbott of "Poplar Knowle". Shirk. MHS; DAR.
Tombstone inscriptions at Ellenborough, St, Mary's Co. Md. O. R. Soc. Bull., no. 2. pp. 81–82. MHS.
*Wicomico Co. families. Tilghman. Ms., pp. 62, 118–19, 122–23. DAR.
See Bond-Cromwell-Delaport-Harris-Reisinger-Reardon.
See Laveille-Harris.
See Owings-Dryden-Harris.
See Owings-Harris.
See Travis-Harris-Turner.
Harris, Balto. Abr. Compend. Amer. Geneal. Virkus. V. 1, pp. 157–58. DAR.
Harris, Talbot Co. Mrs. J. Hall Pleasants, Jr., chart. MHS.
†**Harris, Chapin A.** Hist. of dentistry. Lufkin. Enoch Pratt Lib.
Harris, Capt. David. Westminster churchyard. Patriotic Marylander, v. 2, no. 4, pp. 54–60. MHS; DAR.
Harris, Col. David. Revolutionary war heroes. Cole. Bklet. Enoch Pratt Lib.
Harris, Joseph. Ellenborough. Charles Co., 1773–1855. M. H. Mag. 1936. V. 31, pp. 333–37.
†**Harris, J. Morrison.** Biog. cyc. of rep. men of Md. and D. C. P. 645. MHS; DAR.
Harris, Morrison. Descendants of Joran Kyn of New Sweden. Keen. MHS; DAR.
Harris, Nathaniel. Bible rec. Focke Geneal. Coll. Mss. MHS.
Harris, Thomas and Sarah (Offutt). Natl. Geneal. Soc. Quart., v. 12, no. 2, p. 28.
Harris, Wm. Barney. Md. Soc., War of 1812, v. 4, no. 304. Ms. MHS.
Harris, Wm. Barney, Jr. Md. Soc., War of 1812, v. 4, no. 322. Ms. MHS.
Harris, Mrs. W. Hall (Alice Patterson). Chart. Col. Dames, Chap. I. MHS.
Harris, Wm. Hall. Md. Soc., War of 1812, v. 3, no. 242. Ms. MHS.
†Memorial minute. M. H. Mag., June, 1938, v. 33, no. 2, p. 107.

†Men of mark in Md. Johnson. V. 1. DAR; Enoch Pratt Lib.

Harris, Wm. Hall, Jr. Md. Soc., War of 1812, v. 3, no. 283. Ms. MHS.

Harris, Mrs. William Hall, Jr. (Lavinia Hawley Brush). Chart. Col. Dames, Chap. I. MHS.

Harris, William Torrey (1835–1935). MHS.

Harris, Maj. Wm. St. Mary's Co. (1650–1712). W. A. and S. W. Merritt pedigree charts. Soc. Col. Wars, Md. Johnston. 1905, pp. 67, 146. MHS.

***Harris Family.** Assoc. of Md. and Va. DAR.
Sam'l. Evans and others. Harford Co. Hist. Soc. Mss. Coll. JHU.
Md. Geneal. Rec. Com., 1933–34, p. 91. Mss. DAR.

Harris-Atwaters. Harford Co. Hist. Soc. Mss. Coll. JHU.

Harris-Claiborne Line. (11 generations.) Pedigree of John Benj. Thomas, Jr. Soc. Col. Wars Md. Culver. 1940. MHS; DAR.

Harris-Dodd. Rec., Kent Co., 1745–1914. Md. Geneal. Rec. Com., 1938–39, pp. 118–22. Mss. DAR.

Harris - Maddox - Williams - Smith - Powell - Travers. Bible rec., 1773–1856. Bible owned by Mrs. T. A. Smith, Salisbury. Md. Geneal. Rec. Com., 1938–39, pp. 204–06. Mss. DAR.

Harris-McKinney-Stump. Sam'l Evans. Harford Co. Hist. Soc. Mss. Coll. JHU.

Harris-Willson. Thomas Book. Thomas. P. 337. Lib. Cong.; MHS.

***Harrison.** Ancestry of Benjamin Harrison, president of the U. S., 1889–93, showing descendants of William Henry Harrison, 1773–1841. Chart. C. Penrose Keith. Phila. Lippincott. 1893. MHS; DAR; Peabody Lib.
*Aris Sonis Focisque, being memoir of Amer. family, "Harrison's of Skimino." F. B. Harrison. Priv. pr., N. Y., De Vinne Press, 1910. MHS.
Mrs. Frank G. Baldwin chart. MHS.
†Bench and bar of Md. Sams and Riley. 1901, v. 1, p. 211. Lib. Cong.; MHS; Peabody Lib.
Bible rec. Upper Penins. East. Shore. Pp. 9–13, 50–54. MHS; DAR.
Bolton chart. MHS.
Burton ancestry. Ms. MHS.
Carlyle family and Carlyle house. Spencer. P. 29. MHS.
Chew family. Culver. M. H. Mag., 1935, v. 30, no. 2, pp. 157–75.
Christ P. E. Church cemetery, Cambridge. Steele. 1936. MHS; DAR.
Dorchester Co. Ances. rec. and portraits. Col. Dames of Amer., 1910, v. 1, pp. 56, 63, 79, 320. MHS; DAR.
Early Quaker rec., Anne Arundel and Calvert Cos., 1665–1889. Pub. Geneal. Soc. Pa., v. 3, no. 3, pp. 197–200.
*Harrison of Va. and allied families. "Settlers by the long Grey Trail." Contributions to hist. and geneal. of col. families of Rockingham Co., Va. J. H. Harrison. Dayton, Va., 1935, 1 vol. indexed. DAR.
†Hist. of Balto. City and Co. Scharf. P. 891. MHS.
Hist. graves of Md. and D. C. Ridgely. MHS.
†Hist. of Frederick Co. Williams. MHS; DAR
Marshall of Marshall Hall. Natl. Geneal. Soc. Quart., v. 19, no. 1, p. 1; no. 4, pp. 86–96.
Md. families. Culver. Ms. Personal list.
†Med. Annals Md. Cordell. 1904, p. 430. MHS.
Patriotic Md. Md. Soc. of S. A. R., 1930. MHS; DAR.
Pedigree of Leigh Bonsal. Soc. Col. Wars Md. Culver. 1940. MHS; DAR.
Pedigree of Harrison Tilghman. Soc. Col. Wars Md. Culver. 1940. MHS; DAR.
Pocahontas and her descendants. Robertson. MHS; DAR.
Rogers Coll. Ms. MHS.
*Royal ancestry of George Lieb Harrison of Phila. Wm. Welsh Harrison. Edited by Wm. M. Mervine. Printed for priv. circulation, Phila., 1914. MHS.
St. Paul's Parish, Balto. V. 1, 2, 3, 4. Mss. MHS.
*Semmes Geneal. Coll. Ms. MHS.
Some Md. and Va. ancestors. Bell. Natl. Geneal. Soc. Quart., v. 19, no. 4, pp. 86–96.
Somerset Co. Court Book. Tilghman. 1937. Ms. DAR.
There is always tomorrow; story of checkered life. Mrs. Margaret Elton (Baker) Harrison. N. Y., 1935. Peabody Lib.
Thomas-Chew-Lawrence. Thomas. MHS.
Trinity Church cemetery, Dorchester Co. Md. O. R. Soc. Bull., no. 3, pp. 42–52.
Va. families. Du Bellett.
Mrs. G. H. Williams, Jr., chart. MHS.
M. L. W. Williams pedigree chart. Soc. Col. Wars, Md. Johnston. 1905, p. 126. MHS.
See Armistead-Harrison.
See Gibson-Harrison.
See Thomas-Harrison.

Harrison, Carroll Co. Col. families of Amer. Lawrence. V. 6, p. 384. MHS.

Harrison, James River, Va. Pedigree chart. Kate D. Harrison. Lithographed, 1928, 1934. MHS.
Va. Mag. Hist. and Biog., v. 31, p. 361; v. 32, pp. 97, 199, 298, 404; v. 33, pp. 97, 205, 312; v. 34, pp. 84, 183, 285, 384; v. 35; v. 36; v. 37; v. 38.

***Harrison,** Talbot Co. Lineage Bk., Daughters of Amer. Col., v. 2, p. 29. MHS; DAR.

Harrison, Va. See Carr, Dabney. Abr. Compend. Amer. Geneal. Virkus. V. 1, p. 167. DAR.
Geneal. of Page family, Va. Page. MHS; DAR.

***Harrison,** Va. and Md. The Sun, Balto., April 30, 1905; Sept. 2, Dec. 16, 23, 30 (Va.), 1906.

Harrison, Benj. Fletcher. (Born in Charles Co., 1799; died in Calvert Co., 1880.) Copy of will. Ms. MHS.

Harrison, Edmund Pendleton Hunter. Pedigree. Soc. Col. Wars Md. Culver. 1940. MHS; DAR.

***Harrison, Dr. Elisha.** Patriots of Revolutionary period interred in D. C. Balch. Rec. of Columbia Hist. Soc., v. 19, v. 20.

Harrison, Fairfax. Abr. Compend. Amer. Geneal. Virkus. V. 1, p. 646. DAR.

Harrison, George, St. Mary's Co. Pedigree. Soc. Col. Wars Md. Culver. 1940. MHS; DAR.

Harrison, Hartman K. Abr. Compend. Amer. Geneal. Virkus. V. 1, p. 168. DAR.

†**Harrison, James** (1628–87), Md. and Pa. Index to biog. sketches pub. in "The Friend," v. 26, v. 27. Pub. Geneal. Soc. Pa., v. 3, no. 2, pp. 109–34.
†**Harrison, Orlando.** Men of mark in Md. Johnson. V. 3. DAR; Enoch Pratt Lib.
Harrison, Robt. Hanson. Death. Natl. Geneal. Soc. Quart., Sept. 1938, v. 26, no. 3, p. 63.
†Hist. of Md. Scharf. V. 2, p. 560. MHS.
†**Harrison, Saml. A.** (Md., 1822–90). Hist. of Talbot Co. Tilghman. V. 1, p. 1. MHS; DAR.
Harrison, Mrs. Thomas Bullitt (Marguerite Elton Baker). Chart. Col. Dames, Chap. I. MHS.
Harrison, Wm., Charles Co. Will, Mar. 15, 1786. D. C. Geneal. Rec. Com., 1932–34, v. 10, pp. 224–33. Typed, bd. DAR.
Harrison Family. Ames Geneal. Coll. Ms. MHS.
Harrison Family, Charles Co. Hove family. Md. Geneal. Rec. Com., 1932, p. 246. DAR.
Harrison Family, Md. and Va. Marriages, 1742. Geneal., Mag. Amer. Ancestry, N. Y., 1916, v. 7, no. 3.
Harrison Family, North Va. Va. Mag. Hist. and Biog., v. 23, pp. 214, 339, 443; v. 24, pp. 97, 211, 314.
Harrison Line. Encyc. of Amer. biog. Amer. Hist. Soc., new series, v. 1, p. 171. (Irwin, p. 173.) MHS; DAR.
Harrison Line, Anne Arundel Co. Col. and Revolutionary lineages of Amer. 1939, v. 1, pp. 481–84. MHS.
Harrison-Haskins-Caile-Loockerman. Four families of Dorchester Co. Joseph S. Ames. M. H. Mag., 1915, v. 10, no. 4, p. 376; 1916, v. 11, pp. 76–83, 193–202, 295–300.
Harrison-Clements, Caroline Co. Bible rec. 1782–85. M. H. Mag., 1917, v. 12, pp. 386–91.
Harrison (Va.)**-Burwell.** Chart, photos., complete in 1 sheet. Cary Geneal. Coll. Ms. MHS.
***Harrison-Waples.** Harrison-Waples and allied families. Being hist. of George Leib Harrison of Pa. and his wife Sarah Ann Waples. By their son W. W. Harrison. Pr. for priv. circulation, Phila., 1910. MHS.
Harry. Bowies and their kindred. Bowie. MHS; DAR.
Harry, Herry. Hagerstown tombstone inscriptions. Gruder. Natl. Geneal. Soc. Quart., 1919, v. 8, nos. 1, 2.
Harryman. Bond family geneal. Ms. MHS.
Brooks chart. MHS.
Chart, photos., complete in 1 sheet. Cary Geneal. Coll. Ms. MHS.
Hist. graves of Md. and D. C. Ridgely. MHS.
McCormick chart. MHS.
See Harriman.
†**Harshman.** Hist. of Frederick Co. Williams. MHS; DAR.
†**Hart.** Gov. John Hart of Md., 1714–20. Geneal. Soc. Pa. Pub., Jan., 1895, v. 1, no. 1.
†Lucretia Hart, Hagerstown girl who became wife of Henry Clay. R. S. Schwarz. Hagerstown, Stouffer Printing Co., 28 pp. MHS.
Old Somerset. Torrence. MHS; DAR.
Rogers Coll. Ms. MHS.
St. Paul's Parish, Balto. V. 2, 4. Mss. MHS.
Hart, John (Governor of Md. from 1714–20). Geneal. Soc. Pa. and N. J., Pub., 1895, v. 1, no. 1.
Hart Family, Kent Co. Geneal. notes, 1781–1896. Md. Geneal. Rec. Com., 1937. DAR.
Hart-Shehan-Clayton-Meloir. Bible rec., Kent Co. Md. Geneal. Rec. Com., 1937, Parran, pp. 216–18. Mss. DAR.
†**Hartley.** Hist. of Allegany Co. Thomas and Williams. V. 2. MHS; DAR.
†**Hartman.** Med. Annals Md. Cordell. 1904, p. 431. MHS.
***Hartman, Johannes,** Chester Co., Pa. And his descendants. J. M. Hartman. 1937. DAR.
Hartshorne. Sharpless family geneal. Cope. Pp. 774–75. MHS; DAR.
Hartshorne Family. Hist. of Cecil Co. Johnston. Pp. 534–36. MHS; DAR.
Hartsock. Roop geneal. Pamph. MHS.
Harvey. Abr. Compend. Amer. Geneal. Virkus. V. 6, p. 166. DAR.
†Geneal. and mem. encyc. of Md. Spencer. V. 1, p. 316. MHS; DAR.
*Harvey-Beckwith-Linthicum-Claggett-Sollers. Lineage Bk., Daughters of Amer. Colonists, v. 2, p. 207. MHS; DAR.
Lineage Bks., Natl. Soc. of Daughters of Amer. Col., v. 2, p. 207. MHS; DAR.
Merryman family. Culver. M. H. Mag., 1915. V. 10, pp. 176, 286.
Naturalizations in Md., 1666–1765; Laws. Bacon. MHS.
St. Paul's Parish, Balto. V. 1, 2, 4. Mss. MHS.
St. Thomas' Parish, Balto. Co. Bd. ms. MHS. Also: Md. Geneal. Rec. Com., 1937, pp. 109–82. Mss. DAR.
Harvey, Mrs. Wallace Pinkney (Miss Josephine Gilmor). Chart. Col. Dames, Chap. I. MHS.
Harvey-Slye. Bible rec. Ms. MHS.
Harwood. Ancestry of Mrs. Fulton Ray Gordon, nee Ellen Marjorie Gray. D. C. Geneal. Rec. Com., 1932–34, p. 126. Typed bd. DAR.
Anne Arundel Co. tombstone inscriptions. Ms. DAR.
Balto., its hist., its people. Hall. V. 3. MHS; DAR.
Cary Geneal. Coll. Ms. MHS.
Cemetery Creek, Anne Arundel Co., Tombstone Inscriptions. Founders of Anne Arundel and Harford Cos. Warfield. P. 333. MHS; DAR.
Christ P. E. Church cemetery, Cambridge. Steele. 1936. MHS; DAR.
Col. families of U. S. A. Mackenzie. V. 2, p. 701; v. 5, pp. 264–70. MHS; DAR.
Col. mansions of Md. and Del. Hammond. 1914. MHS.
*Founders of Anne Arundel and Howard Cos. Warfield. Pp. 96–99. MHS; DAR.
Geneal. of family of Stockett, 1558–1892. Stockett. Pamph., p. 22. MHS; DAR.
Hist. graves of Md. and D. C. Ridgely. MHS.
Md. families. Culver. Ms. Personal list.
Md. gleanings in Eng. Wills. M. H. Mag., 1909, v. 4, no. 2.
†Med. Annals Md. Cordell. 1904, p. 432. MHS.

Patriotic Md. Md. Soc. of S. A. R., 1930. MHS; DAR.
St. Paul's Parish, Balto. V. 2, 3, 4. Mss. MHS.
Segrave chart. MHS.
*Side lights on Md. Hist. Richardson. V. 2, p. 121. MHS; DAR.
*The Sun, Balto. March 15, 1904.
See Scarsbrook-Scarsbrooke-Harwood-Cary.

Harwood, Thos. Noble. Portrait and biog. rec. of Sixth Cong. Dist. of Md. 1898, p. 335. MHS; DAR.

Harwood Family, Anne Arundel Co. Chart. Dr. H. J. Berkley. 1925. Ms. MHS.

Hasfurt. Somerset Co. Court Book. Tilghman. 1937. Ms. DAR.

Hasfurt, Hossford. Old Somerset. Torrence. MHS; DAR.

Haskell Family, Mass. Col. and Revolutionary families of Pa. Amer. Hist. Soc., N. Y., 1934, pp. 745–52. (Ancestry of Helen Tudor (Haskell) Robinson (Mrs. David Moore), p. 747.)

Haskin Family, Va. Col. men and times. Harp. Pp. 303–28. MHS.

Haskins. Bolton chart. MHS.
Memorial to Thomas Potts, Jr. James. P. 248. MHS.
See Harrison-Haskins-Caile-Loockerman.

Haskins Family. Dupuy family. Dupuy. Pp. 62–68. MHS.

Haslet. Md. families. Culver. Ms. Personal list.
Mrs. N. S. Pendleton, Jr., chart. MHS.

Haslett. Mrs. G. H. Williams, Jr., chart. MHS.

Hassard. Old Somerset. Torrence. MHS; DAR.
Somerset Co. Court Book. Tilghman. 1937. Ms. DAR.

Hasselbach. Machen chart. MHS.

†**Hasselback.** Nicholas Hasselback, printer of first book printed in Balto. Pr. with sketch of Hasselback's life and work. G. W. McCreary. Balto., Kohn & Pollock. MHS.
Hist. printing in Col. Md. Wroth. MHS.

Hasselbaugh. Jenkins-Courtney chart. MHS.

Hassford. *See* Hasfurt.

Haste. Old Somerset. Torrence. MHS; DAR.

Hastings. *See* Prier-Parks-Hastings.
*Wicomico Co. families. Tilghman. Ms, pp. 52, 107, 109–10, 119. DAR.

Hatch. Dent family of Md. Ms. File case, DAR.
Ms. MHS.
Ruf-Haight-Eddy-Sumner-Hatch and allied families. Ms. MHS.

***Hatch-Powell.** Mass. and Md. Lineage Bk., Daughters of Founders and Patriots, v. 16, pp. 98–99. MHS.

Hateley. Somerset Co. Court Book. Tilghman. 1937. Ms. DAR.

Hatrey, Hattrey. St. Stephens Parish, Cecilton, Md. MHS; DAR.

Hatton. Bowie-Claggett chart. MHS.
Robert Brooke chart. MHS; DAR.
Chart, photos., complete in 1 sheet. Cary Geneal. Coll. Ms. MHS.
Daughter of Md.; Mother of Texas. Bell. MHS; DAR.
†Day-Star of Amer. Freedom, Davis. P. 200. MHS; DAR.
Hatton and Johnson families (Md. 1648). Christopher Johnston. William and Mary Quart., 1st series, v. 23, p. 113.
Mrs. T. C. Jenkins chart. MHS.
Md. families. Culver. Ms. Personal list.
Pedigree of W. Wallace McKaig. Soc. Col. Wars Md. Culver. 1940. MHS; DAR.
*Pennington Papers. Ms. MHS.
Semmes and allied families. Semmes. MHS.
*Semmes Geneal. Coll. Ms. MHS.
Side lights on Md. hist. Richardson. V. 2, p. 125. MHS; DAR.
*The Sun, Balto., July 31, 1904.
Mrs. E. Worthington chart. MHS.

Hatton Line. Col. and Revolutionary lineages in Amer. 1939, v. 2, p. 75. MHS.

Hattrey. *See* Hatrey.

Hauer. Frederick Co. tombstone inscriptions. Gruder. Natl. Geneal. Soc. Quart., 1919, v. 8, nos. 1, 2.

Haugh. Haugh's Lutheran Church tombstone rec. Md. Geneal. Rec. Com., 1939–40. Mss. DAR.
†Hist. of Frederick Co. Williams. MHS; DAR.

Haughey. Pedigree of Andrew Jackson Young, Jr. Soc. Col. Wars Md. Culver. 1940. MHS; DAR.

Haughton-Alricks. Lineage Bks., Natl. Soc. of Daughters of Amer. Col., v. 3, p. 9. MHS; DAR.

Haupt. Haupt family in Amer. W. H. Haupt, Charitown, Iowa. Md. Haupts, p. 30. Ms. MHS.

Hause. Beards' Luth. graveyard, Washington Co. Md. Geneal. Rec. Com., 1935–36. Mss. DAR.

Hausil. Family notes. M. H. Mag., 1915, v. 10, pp. 57–58.

Hawken. Hagerstown tombstone inscriptions. Gruder. Natl. Geneal. Soc. Quart., 1919, v. 8, nos. 1, 2.
Rev. Christian Frederick Post and Peter Humrickhouse. Humrickhouse. P. 32. MHS.

Hawkins. Ances. rec. and portraits. Col. Dames of Amer., 1910, v. 2, p. 666–68. MHS; DAR.
Mrs. R. Barton, Jr., charts. MHS.
Bond family geneal. Ms. MHS.
Cary Geneal. Coll. Ms. MHS.
Chart of Com. John Rodgers. DAR.
Col. families of U. S. A. Mackenzie. V. 1, p. 603; v. 4, p. 118. MHS; DAR.
Founders of Anne Arundel and Howard Cos. Warfield. P. 43. MHS; DAR.
*Frederick Co. families. Markell. Ms. Personal list.
*George Donald Riley. Riley. DAR.
Gorsuch chart. Cary Geneal. Coll. Ms. MHS.
Hamilton family of Charles Co. Kelly. MHS.
Hist. graves of Md. and D. C. Ridgely. MHS.
†Hist. of Balto. City and Co. Scharf. P. 877. MHS.
†Hist. of Allegany Co. Thomas and Williams. V. 2. MHS; DAR.
Jenkins-Courtney chart. MHS.
Machen chart. MHS.
Marriage rec., 1781–1892, Harford Co. Md. Geneal. Rec. Com., 1934–35, p. 108. DAR.
Md. families. Culver. Ms. Personal list.
†Med. Annals Md. Cordell. 1904, p. 432. MHS.

Hawkins. Pedigree of Rev. James Mitchell Magruder. Soc. Col. Wars Md. Culver. 1940. MHS; DAR.
*Pennington Papers. Ms. MHS.
St. Paul's Parish, Balto. V. 1, 2. Mss. MHS.
St. Thomas' Parish, Balto. Co. Bd. ms. MHS. Also: Md. Geneal. Rec. Com., 1937, pp. 109–82. Mss. DAR.
*Semmes Geneal. Coll. Ms. MHS.
Miss Eliza Thomas chart. MHS.
J. S. Williams pedigree chart. Soc. Col. Wars, Md. Johnston. 1905, p. 125. MHS.
Hawkins, Harford Co. Wallis chart. MHS.
Hawkins, John. Family rec. from Bible, 1794. MHS.
Hawkins, John, Fells Point, Balto. Bible rec., 1794. Ms. MHS.
Hawkins, Col. John, Queen Anne's Co. (1656–1717). W. S. G. Williams pedigree chart. Soc. Col. Wars, Md. Johnston. 1905, pp. 128, 147. MHS.
***Hawkins, Walter.** Burke's landed gentry. 1939. MHS.
Hawkins Family. Copied from Riley family. Md. Geneal. Rec. Com., 1934–35, p. 433. Mss. DAR.
*Wilson Mss. Coll., no. 10. MHS.
Hawkins Line. Col. and Revolutionary lineages of Amer. 1939, v. 1, p. 480. MHS.
Hawkins-Bordley. Greenway Mss. Geneal. Coll. MHS.
Hawley. Hawley rec. Elias S. Hawley. Buffalo, E. H. Hutchinson & Co., 1890.
Md. gleanings in Eng. Wills. M. H. Mag., 1908, v. 3, no. 2.
†Papers relating to early hist. of Md. Streeter. 1876, p. 104. MHS.
Sydney-Smith and Clagett-Price families. Price. MHS; DAR.
See Halley-Hawley-Pike.
Hawley, N. Y. Mrs. W. H. Harris, Jr., chart. MHS.
‡Hawley, Jerome. Founders of Md. Neill. 1879.
Hawley-Halley. Some unpublished data. M. H. Mag., 1939, v. 34, no. 2, pp. 175–79.
Hawthorn. Hagerstown tombstone inscriptions. Gruder. Natl. Geneal. Soc. Quart., 1919, v. 8, nos. 1, 2.
Hawyard. Hist. graves of Md. and D. C. Ridgely. MHS.
Haxall. Mrs. R. W. Johnson, Jr., chart. MHS.
Haxall, John Triplett. Pedigree. Soc. Col. Wars Md. Culver. 1940. MHS; DAR.
Haxall, Mrs. John Triplett (Rose Stanley Gordon). Chart. Col. Dames, Chap. I. MHS.
Hay, Hayes. Rogers Coll. Ms. MHS.
Hayden. Centenary of Catholicity in Ky. Webb. 1884. MHS.
Founders of Anne Arundel and Howard Cos. Warfield. Pp. 524–25. MHS; DAR.
†Hist. of West. Md. Scharf. V. 2, pp. 955–57. MHS; DAR.
†Med. Annals Md. Cordell. 1904, pp. 432–33. MHS.
St. Paul's Parish, Balto. V. 2. Mss. MHS.
Hayden, Mass. and Md. Col. families of U. S. A. Mackenzie. V. 3. MHS.
†Hayden, Horace H. Hist. of dentistry. Lufkin. Enoch Pratt Lib.
Hayden, William Mozart. Pedigree charts, plates 1 and 2. Soc. Col. Wars, Md. Johnston. 1905, pp. 34–35. MHS.
***Haye.** Paul Haye Soc. Bulletin, 1930. MHS.
Hayes. Balto., its hist., its people. Hall. V. 3. MHS; DAR.
Bible rec. Photos. MHS.
Family burying ground. Ms. MHS.
Mrs. W. H. Harris chart. MHS.
*Henry Hayes, West Chester, Pa., 1705–1905. Bi-Centennial Book. MHS.
St. Paul's Parish, Balto. V. 1, 2. Mss. MHS.
Stansbury chart. Cary Geneal. Coll. Ms. MHS.
See Hay.
See Hays.
Hayes, Kent Co., Del. Posey chart. MHS.
†Hayes, T. G. Geneal. and mem. encyc. of Md. Spencer. V. 1, pp. 58–65. MHS; DAR.
***Hayes Family.** Burying ground, Montgomery Co. Hist. of West Md. Scharf. V. 1, p. 731. MHS; DAR. Also ms. in MHS.
Hayes, Hays, Cecil Co. Col. families of U. S. A. Mackenzie. V. 3, p. 215. MHS; DAR.
Hayman. Ms. MHS.
Mt. Zion P. E. churchyard, Worcester Co. Md. Geneal. Rec. Com., 1937, Mrs. Lines. Mss. DAR.
Old Somerset. Torrence. MHS; DAR.
St. Paul's P. E. churchyard, Berlin, Worcester Co. Hudson. Bd. ms. MHS; DAR. Also: Md. Geneal. Rec. Com., 1937, Mrs. Lines. Mss. DAR.
Turner Geneal. Coll. Ms. MHS.
*Wicomico Co. families. Tilghman. Ms, pp. 39, 44–45, 47, 110. DAR.
Hayman, Haman. Somerset Co. Court Book. Tilghman. 1937. Ms. DAR.
Haymond. Haymond family. Morgantown, Va., Acme Pub. Co., 1903, pamph. MHS.
Newsp. clipp., 1903. MHS.
Hayne. Balto., its hist., its people. Hall. V. 3. MHS; DAR.
†Men of mark in Md. Johnson. V. 2. DAR; Enoch Pratt Lib.
Haynes. Pedigree of Leigh Bonsal. Soc. Col. Wars Md. Culver. 1940. MHS; DAR.
Haynes, Nathan Wm. Pedigree. Soc. Col. Wars Md. Culver. 1940. MHS; DAR.
Haynie. Bible rec., 1793. Ms. MHS.
Done Bible rec. Ms. MHS.
†Med. Annals Md. Cordell. 1904, pp. 433–34. MHS.
Hays. Abr. Compend. Amer. Geneal. Virkus. V. 6, p. 54. DAR.
Myer-Hays-Mordecai family rec. Ms. MHS.
See Hayes.
Hays, David. Tombstone rec. of Glendy burying ground (vault, 1836). Md. Geneal. Rec. Com., 1933–34, pp. 171–78. Mss. DAR.
***Hays, Thomas Archer.** Burke's landed gentry. 1939. MHS.
Hays Family, Harford and Montgomery Cos. Bible rec. Md. Geneal. Bull., v. 1, p. 17; v. 4, p. 5. MHS; DAR.
Hays, Hayes, Hay, Haise, Charles Co. (1678). Md. Geneal. Bull., v. 7, no. 4.
Hayward. All Hallow's P. E. churchyard, Snow Hill, Worcester Co. Hudson. Bd. ms. MHS; DAR. Also: Md. Geneal. Rec. Com., 1935–36, p. 24. Mss. DAR.

Abr. Compend. Amer. Geneal. Virkus. V. 1, p. 330. DAR.
Balto., its hist., its people. Hall. V. 2, pp. 42-54. MHS; DAR.
(10 stones.) Christ P. E. Church cemetery, Cambridge. Steele. 1936. MHS; DAR.
Ellicott-Campbell chart. MHS.
Geneal. notes of Chamberlaine family. MHS.
Geneal. of Henrietta Chauncy Wilson. Upshur. Bk. of photos. MHS.
Haymond family. 1903, pamph. MHS.
Md. families. Culver. Ms. Personal list.
Md. Geneal. Bull., v. 2, p. 28. MHS; DAR.
*Old Kent. Hanson. P. 251. MHS; DAR.
Old Md. families. Bromwell. MHS; DAR.
Patriotic Md. Md. Soc. of S. A. R., 1930. MHS; DAR.
Pedigree of Richard Elliott Marine. Soc. Col. Wars Md. Culver. 1940. MHS; DAR.
St. Mary's P. E. churchyard, Pocomoke, Worcester Co., Hudson. Bd. ms. MHS; DAR.
Spring Hill Cemetery, Talbot Co. Md. O. R. Soc. Bull., no. 1, pp. 35-41. MHS.
Turner Geneal. Coll. Ms. MHS.
*Wicomico Co. families. Tilghman. Ms, p. 124. DAR.

Hazard. Mrs. Frank G. Baldwin chart. MHS.

Hazelhurst. Greenway Mss. Geneal. Coll. Binder's title, Hawkins-Bordley. MHS.
Hazelhurst and allied families. Charts, 3 linen and 5 blue prints. (Incl. McKim charts.) MHS.
Miss E. V. Latrobe chart. MHS.
St. Paul's Parish, Balto. V. 3. Mss. MHS.
St. Stephens Parish, Cecilton, Md. MHS; DAR.

Hazelhurst, Phila. Mrs. A. Randall chart. MHS.

Hazelwood. Md. families. Culver. Ms. Personal list.

Hazlehurst, Mrs. George Blagden (Louisa Morris Gill). Chart. Col. Dames, Chap. I. MHS.

Hazlitt, Rev. Wm. Note. M. H. Mag., 1920, v. 15, pp. 303-04.

Hazzard. Abstracts of wills, in registers' office, Georgetown, Del. Pub. Geneal. Soc. Pa., v. 4, pp. 13-19.

Hazzard Family, of S. C. Stone family. Natl. Geneal. Soc. Quart., April, 1914, to Jan., 1915, v. 3.

Heacock. Lloyd family hist. of Wales, Pa., and Md. DAR.
Trinity P. E. churchyard, Long Green. Typed ms. MHS; DAR.

***Head.** Frederick Co. families. Markell. Ms. Personal list.
St. Paul's Parish, Balto. V. 1. Mss. MHS.
*Wilson Mss. Coll., no. 8, B. MHS.

Headington. Col. family of U. S. A. Mackenzie. V. 3, p. 183. MHS; DAR.
Lineage Bks., Natl. Soc. of Daughters of Amer. Col., v. 1, p. 40. MHS; DAR.

Heald. Griffith geneal. Griffith. MHS; DAR.

Healey. Hazelhurst charts. MHS.

Healfleich, Heilflick, Hoefligh. Hagerstown tombstone inscriptions. Gruder. Natl. Geneal. Soc. Quart., 1919, v. 8, nos. 1, 2.

Heaps. Amer. Armory and Blue Book. Matthews. 1911-12, p. 387.
*Burke's landed gentry. 1939. MHS.

Hearn. Rec. of Stepney Parish. MHS; DAR.
*Wicomico Co. families. Tilghman. Ms, pp. 9, 102, 114-15, 118-19, 123-24, 129. DAR.

***Heath.** Balto. Sun, Nov. 27, Dec. 4 (Va.), 1904.
Edmund Beauchamp of East. Shore of Md. D. A. R. Mag., April, 1932. V. 66, no. 4, pp. 234-38.
*Bible and wills. File case, MHS.
Bible rec. Md. Geneal. Rec. Com., 1937-38, pp. 147-49. Mss. DAR.
Descendants of Col. Thomas White. Morris. MHS.
Hackett Bible rec. Bible rec. of Dorchester and Somerset Cos. and Del. P. 31. DAR.
Hazelhurst charts. MHS.
Heath family. H. Brooks. Ms. MHS.
*Heath family. H. Brooks. N. Dakota Hist. Quart., Jan., 1930, v. 4, no. 2
Rec. and wills. N. Dakota Hist. Quart., Jan., 1930, v. 4, no. 2. MHS.
St. Paul's Parish, Balto. V. 2. Mss. MHS.
Somerset Co. Court Book. Tilghman. 1937. Ms. DAR.
The Sun, Balto., Nov. 27, Dec. 4 (Va.), 1904.
*Wicomico Co. families. Tilghman. Ms, pp. 43, 97, 114, 117, 121, 124. DAR.

***Heath,** Somerset Co. Bible rec. File case A, MHS.
Bible rec. of Dorchester and Somerset Cos. and Del. Pp. 32-34, 35. DAR.

Heath Family. Bible rec. and wills. Ms. MHS.
*Data. MHS.

Heathcote. Md. gleanings in Eng. Wills. M. H. Mag., 1907, v. 2, no. 3.

Heathrington. St. Paul's Parish, Balto. V. 2. Mss. MHS.

Hebb. Hist. graves of Md. and D. C. Ridgely. MHS.
†Med. Annals Md. Cordell. 1903, p. 434. MHS.
Parr chart. MHS.
Porto Bello, St. Mary's Co., tombstone inscriptions. Md. O. R. Soc. Bull., no. 3, p. 55. MHS.
Portrait and biog. rec. of Sixth Cong. Dist. of Md. 1898, p. 147. MHS; DAR.
Raisin chart. MHS.
*Wilson Mss. Coll., no. 8, B. MHS.

†Hebbard. Med. Annals Md. Cordell. 1903, p. 434. MHS.

Heddinger. St. Paul's Parish, Balto. V. 2. Mss. MHS.

Hedges. Col. families of U. S. A. Mackenzie. V. 4. MHS; DAR.
*Frederick Co. families. Markell. Ms. Personal list
†Hist. of Frederick Co. Williams. MHS; DAR.
Md. families. Culver. Ms. Personal list.
Patriotic Md. Md. Soc. of S. A. R., 1930. MHS; DAR.

***Hedges,** Frederick Co., Md., and N. J. Lineage Bk., Daughters of Founders and Patriots, v. 23, p. 108. MHS; DAR.

Hedley. St. Paul's Parish, Balto. V. 2. Mss. MHS.

***Hedrick Family.** Arch. of Georgetown Univ., Wash., D. C., v. 210, no. 12.

Hedricks. St. Paul's Parish, Balto. V. 1. Mss. MHS.

Heffner. M. E. Church, South cemetery, near Poolesville, Montgomery Co. Md. Geneal. Rec. Com., 1926. Mss. DAR.
See Hufner
***Heffur.** Frederick Co. families. Markell. Ms. Personal list.
Heflebower. St. Paul's Parish, Balto. V. 4. Mss. MHS.
Heger. *See* Hager.
Heidelbach. Catonsville pioneers of Luth. faith. Natl. Geneal. Soc. Quart., v. 9, no. 2, p. 29.
Heilflick. *See* Healfleich.
Hein. Abr. Compend. Amer. Geneal. Virkus. V. 1, p. 333. DAR.
Heiner. St. Paul's Parish, Balto. V. 1. Mss. MHS.
***Heintz, Hines, Hindes.** Patriots of Revolutionary period interred in D. C. Balch. Rec. of Columbia Hist. Soc., v. 19, v. 20.
Heise. Mt. Olivet Cemetery, Frederick. Md. Geneal. Rec. Com., 1934-35, p. 111. Mss. DAR.
***Heiskell.** Geneal. of Md. Heiskells. Geneal. Soc. Pa., v. 8, p. 293.
Md. families. Culver. Ms. Personal list.
Heiskell, Va. (1756). Geneal. Pub. Geneal. Soc. Pa., v. 8, no. 3, p. 293.
Heiskill. Children of Alex P. and M. C. Hill. Ms. MHS.
Heister. Zion Reformed Church, Hagerstown. Md. Geneal. Rec. Com., 1934-35. Mss. DAR.
See Hiester.
Heleine. Zion Reformed Church, Hagerstown. Md. Geneal. Rec. Com., 1934-35. Mss. DAR.
Helfenstein. Frederick Co. tombstone inscriptions. Gruder. Natl. Geneal. Soc. Quart., 1919, v. 8, nos. 1, 2.
†**Helfenstein, Rt. Rev. Edward Trail.** Encyc. of Amer. biog. Amer. Hist. Soc., new series, v. 1, p. 186. MHS; DAR.
†**Hellen.** Med. Annals Md. Cordell. 1903, p. 435. MHS.
Monnet family geneal. Monette. Pp. 288, 371, 1116. MHS.
St. Paul's Parish, Balto. V. 2. Mss. MHS.
Hellings. Brooks family and Hellings family. Ms. File case, DAR.
Helm. Sharpless family geneal. Cope. Pp. 352, 1091-92. MHS; DAR.
Helm, Maberry. Westminster churchyard. Patriotic Marylander, v. 2, no. 4, pp. 54-60. MHS; DAR.
Helms. St. Paul's Parish, Balto. V. 1, 2. Mss. MHS.
†**Hemmeter.** Med. Annals Md. Cordell. 1903, p. 435. MHS.
Hemmington. Peale Geneal. Coll. Ms. MHS.
***Hemp.** Frederick Co. families. Markell. Ms. Personal list.
Hemphill. Abr. Compend. Amer. Geneal. Virkus. V. 1, p. 293. DAR.
Hemsley. Dobbin chart. MHS.
Hist. graves of Md. and D. C. Ridgely. MHS.
Md. families. Culver. Ms. Personal list.
†Med. Annals Md. Cordell. 1903, p. 435. MHS.
*Old Kent. Hanson. Pp. 237, 251-52. MHS; DAR.
Pedigree of Ralph Robinson. Soc. Col. Wars Md. Culver. 1940. MHS; DAR.
Side lights on Md. hist. Richardson. V. 2, p. 359. MHS; DAR.
Thomas family of Talbot Co. Spencer. P. 142. MHS; DAR.
Mrs. Emory Whitridge chart. MHS.
Henckel. *See* Henkel.
***Henckel Family.** Assoc. New Market, Va. MHS; DAR.
Assoc. 12 pamph. MHS; DAR.
*News Letter. MHS.
*Rec. Hist. of Henckel family in Europe and Amer., 1635-1717. Nos. 1-6, MHS; Jan., 1935, no. 12, DAR.
***Henderson.** Ancestry and descendants of Lieut. John Henderson, Greenbrier Co., Va., 1650-1900. J. L. Miller. Richmond, Va., 1902. MHS.
Blackford chart. MHS.
Clasping hands with generations past. Lloyd. MHS; DAR.
Geneal. of family of Gideon Gilpin. MHS.
†Hist. of Allegany Co. Thomas and Williams. V. 1; v. 2. MHS; DAR.
Hughes family of Va. Horton. MHS.
†Men of mark in Md. Johnson. V. 3, v. 4. DAR; Enoch Pratt Lib.
Naturalizations in Md., 1666-1765; Laws. Bacon. MHS
Orme geneal. chart. MHS.
Rehobeth P. E. churchyard, Somerset Co. Md. Geneal. Rec. Com., 1937, Mrs. Lines. Mss. DAR.
St. Paul's Parish, Balto. V. 1, 2, 3. Mss. MHS.
St. Stephens Parish, Cecilton, Md. MHS; DAR.
†**Henderson,** Allegany Co. Encyc. of Amer. biog. Amer. Hist. Soc., N. Y., 1928, v. 33, p. 207.
Henderson, C. F. Md. Soc., War of 1812, v. 3, no. 212. Ms. MHS.
Henderson, C. Griffin. Md. Soc., War of 1812, v. 3, no. 296. Ms. MHS.
Henderson, G. Washington. Md. Soc., War of 1812, v. 4, no. 315. Ms. MHS.
Henderson (Cecil Co.)-**Brinckle-Gill-Yoe** (Baltimore Co.). Abr. Compend. Amer. Geneal. Virkus. V. 4, pp. 575-76. MHS.
Hendon. St. Paul's Parish, Balto. V. 1. Mss. MHS.
Hendree. Burton ancestry. Ms. MHS.
†**Hendrick.** Men of mark of Md. Johnson. V. 2. DAR; Enoch Pratt Lib.
Hendrick, Calvin Wheeler. (Va. rec.) Pedigree. Soc. Col. Wars Md. Culver. 1940. MHS; DAR.
Hendrick, Herring de la Porte. (Va. rec.) Pedigree. Soc. Col. Wars Md. Culver. 1940. MHS; DAR.
Hendrick, J. Burford, Jr. Md. Soc., War of 1812, v. 3, no. 252. Ms. MHS.
Hendrickson. Hendrickson farm burying ground, near Millington, Md. Md. Geneal. Rec. Com., 1933-34, pp. 208-09. Mss. DAR
†Hist. of Allegany Co. Thomas & Williams. V. 2, MHS; DAR.
Naturalizations in Md., 1666-1765; Laws. Bacon. MHS.
St. Stephens Parish, Cecilton, Md. MHS; DAR.
Hendrix Family, Del. Bible rec. Md. Geneal. Rec. Com., 1933-34, p. 228. Mss. DAR.

Henkel, Henkle, Henckel, Hinkle. Henkel Family Assoc. Rec., 1637–1717. O. Elon Henkel, editor. No. 1, May, 1926–No. 13, July, 1935. New Market, Va., Henkel Press. MHS; DAR.
Henkle. Md. Geneal. Soc., v. 6, p. 2. MHS; DAR.
Swope family. Swope. MHS.
See Henkel.
Henley, Va. Chart, photos., complete in 1 sheet. Cary Geneal. Coll. Ms. MHS.
Hennick. Md. families. Culver. Ms. Personal list.
Hennighausen. Balto., its hist., its people. Hall. V. 3. MHS; DAR.
†Bench and bar of Md. Sams and Riley. 1901, v. 2, p. 626. Lib. Cong.; MHS; Peabody Lib.
Hennin. St. Paul's Parish, Balto. V. 2. Mss. MHS.
Henning. Birth certificates. Ms. MHS.
Henning, Thomas. Bible rec. Pub. Geneal. Soc. Pa., v. 10, p. 80.
Henry. Abr. Compend. Amer. Geneal. Virkus. V. 1, p. 293. DAR.
Abr. Compend. Amer. Geneal. Virkus. V. 4, p. 263. MHS.
†Biog. cyc. of rep. men of Md. and D. C. P. 186. MHS; DAR.
Buckingham Pres. churchyard, Worcester Co., Hudson. Bd. ms. MHS; DAR.
Christ P. E. Church cemetery, Cambridge. Steele. 1936. MHS; DAR.
Col. families of U. S. A. Mackenzie. V. 1. MHS; DAR.
*Hist. of Dorchester Co. Jones. 1925, pp. 331–41. MHS; DAR.
Hist. graves of Md. and D. C. Ridgely. MHS.
Handy and their kin. Handy.
†Hist. of Md. Scharf. V. 2, p. 598. MHS.
†Med. Annals Md. Cordell. 1903, p. 436. MHS.
Memoir of John Henry. Prepared by his grandson. Balto., Sun Job Printing Co., Feb., 1887, pamph. MHS.
Patriotic Md. Md. Soc. of S. A. R., 1930. MHS; DAR.
Rehobeth P. E. churchyard, Somerset Co. Md. Geneal. Rec. Com., 1937, Mrs. Lines. Mss. DAR.
St. Paul's P. E. churchyard, Berlin, Worcester Co. Hudson. Bd. ms. MHS; DAR. Also: Md. Geneal. Rec. Com., 1937, Mrs. Lines. Mss. DAR.
St. Paul's Parish, Balto. V. 2, 4. Mss. MHS.
Selden chart. MHS
Side lights on Md. hist. Richardson. V. 2, p. 127. MHS; DAR.
*The Sun, Balto., July 10 (Md.), 1904; March, 18, 25 (Va.), 1906.
*Wicomico Co. families. Tilghman. Ms, p. 96. DAR.
Henry, J. Winfield (Dr. A. F.) (Dulin's daughter Louise married Mr. Henry). Balto., Its Hist., Its People. V. 2, p. 357. MHS; DAR.
†**Henry, James.** Balto., hist. and biog. Richardson and Bennett. 1871, pp. 317–19. MHS; DAR.
Henry, John. Death, Jan., 1810; Bethel graveyard, Harford Co. Md. Geneal. Rec. Com. 1933–34, p. 128. Mss. DAR.
†**Henry, Gov. John.** Founders of Anne Arundel and Howard Cos. Warfield. P. 247. MHS; DAR.
*Geneal. and his descendants. Prepared by his grandsons. Baltimore, Feb., 1887. MHS.
†Buchholz. P. 41. MHS.
Henry, Mrs. Morton Rebecca Angelica Morison Jackson. Mrs. R. Barton, Jr., chart. MHS.
Chart. Col. Dames, Chap. I. MHS.
Henry-Steele-Nevitt-Goldsborough. Notes. Turner Geneal. Coll. Ms. MHS.
Hepborn. I. U. Church cemetery. Md. O. R Soc. Bull., no. 2, pp. 76–78.
Still Pond churchyard, Kent Co. Md. O. R Soc., v. 2. MHS.
***Hepbron Family.** Old Kent. Hanson. P. 197. MHS; DAR.
†**Hepburn.** Med. Annals Md. Cordell. 1903, p. 436. MHS.
Neill chart. MHS.
Hepworth. St. Paul's Parish, Balto. V. 2. Mss. MHS.
Herbert. Arnold chart. MHS.
Barroll chart. MHS.
Carlyle family and Carlyle house. Spencer. P. 20. MHS.
Carlyle family. William and Mary Quart., 1st series, v. 18, pp. 201, 278.
Chart of Com. John Rodgers. DAR.
Daughter of Md.; Mother of Texas. Bell. MHS; DAR.
Dryden and allied families. Ms. MHS.
Gentleman's Mag. MHS.
Hist. graves of Md. and D. C. Ridgely. MHS.
†Med. Annals Md. Cordell. 1903, p. 436. MHS.
†Men of mark in Md. Johnson. V. 4. DAR; Enoch Pratt Lib.
Pedigree of Mark Alexander Herbert Smith. Soc. Col. Wars Md. Culver. 1940. MHS; DAR.
St. Paul's Parish, Balto. V. 1, 2. Mss. MHS.
Herbert, Alexandria. Thomas Book. Thomas. Lib. Cong.; MHS.
Herbert, Charles Co. Cary Geneal. Coll. Ms. MHS.
Herbert, Va. Mrs. Lee Barroll chart. MHS.
Herbert Line. Posey chart. MHS.
Herbert Line, Queen Anne's Co. Col. and Revolutionary lineages of Amer. 1939, v. 1, p. 526. MHS.
Herbert-Baker. Harford Co. Hist. Soc. Mss. Coll. JHU.
†**Herdman.** Med. Annals Md. Cordell. 1903, p. 436. MHS.
Hering, Frederick Co., Balto., its hist., its people. Hall. V. 2. MHS; DAR.
Herman. Ancient families of Bohemia Manor; their homes and their graves. C. P. Mallory. Pub. by Hist. Soc. Del., 1888. MHS.
Bohemia Manor, Cecil Co. Mallery. Ms. MHS.
†Chesapeake Bay Country. Earle. P. 305. MHS.
Col. families of Amer. Lawrence. V. 7, p. 392. MHS.
Descendants of Joran Kyn. Pa. Mag., v. 3, p. 451; v. 7, pp. 88 (portrait), 299.
Augustine Herman and Bohemia Manor, Cecil Co. Bibliog. on German settlements in col. N. Amer. Meynen. P. 64. MHS.
†Hist. of Cecil Co. Johnson. MHS; DAR.

Herman. Husband and allied families. P. 16. Ms. MHS.
†Med. Annals Md. Cordell. 1903, pp. 436–37. MHS.
Old Kent. Hanson. P. 80. MHS; DAR.
Pedigree of George Webb Constable. Soc. Col. Wars Md. Culver. 1940. MHS; DAR.
Pedigree of George Washington Williams. Soc. Col. Wars Md. Culver. 1940. MHS; DAR.
Pedigree of Joseph Lee Wickes. Soc. Col. Wars Md. Culver. 1940. MHS; DAR.
*Pennington Papers. Ms. MHS.
Mrs. J. Hall Pleasants, Jr., chart. MHS.
*Side lights on Md. hist. Richardson. V. 2, p. 131. MHS; DAR.
Stump family of Cecil and Harford Cos. Pamph. MHS.
*The Sun, Balto., Sept. 9, 1885, (in ms. on Bohemia Manor, in MHS); Dec. 6, 1903.
See Herrman.

Herman, Augustine (born in Prague; naturalized in Md., 1666), and family, Bohemia Manor, Cecil Co. Naturalizations in Md., 1666–1765; Laws. Bacon. MHS.
Family notes. Hist. of Md. Scharf. V. 1, pp. 413, 429.
*Augustine Herman, founder of Bohemia Manor. (Augustine Herman Stump, I; Augustine Herman Stump, II.) Leaflet. MHS.
Seven pioneers of col. East. Shore. Skirven. M. H. Mag., 1920, v. 15, no. 3, p. 230–50, no. 4, p. 394–419.
Thomas Book. Thomas. P. 343. Lib. Cong.; MHS.

***Herman-Stump.** Geneal. chart. Augustine Herman, founder of Bohemia Manor; Augustine Herman Stump I; Augustine Herman Stump II. MHS.

Hermann. Md. families. Culver. Ms. Personal list.

Heron. St. Paul's Parish, Balto. V. 2. Mss. MHS.

***Herr.** Rev. Hans Herr, 1639 to present time. Theodore W. Herr, geneal. Lancaster, Pa., 1908.

Herring. St. Paul's Parish, Balto. V. 2. Mss. MHS.

†**Herring, Joshua.** Men of mark in Md. Johnson. V. 2. DAR; Enoch Pratt Lib.

Herrington. Harford Co. Hist. Soc. Mss. Coll. JHU.

Herrman. Mt. Olivet Cemetery, Frederick. Md. Geneal. Rec. Com., 1934–35, p. 111. Mss. DAR.
See Herman.

Herrman, Augustine (1605–86). Address by Gen. J. G. Wilson.
†"Bohemia Manor." Biog. sketch of Herrman, with reproduction of his celebrated map and facsimilies of documents, etc. Monograph by Thomas Capek, Prague, 1930. MHS.
"Bohemian Manor." Copy of will, 1684. Pa. Mag. Hist. and Biog., 1891, v. 15. MHS.

Herry. *See* Harry.

Hersh. Haugh's Lutheran Church, Carroll Co., tombstone rec. Md. Geneal. Rec. Com., 1939–40. Mss. DAR.

***Hershberge.** Frederick Co. families. Markell. Ms. Personal list.

Hershey. Hagerstown tombstone inscriptions. Gruder. Natl. Geneal. Soc. Quart., 1919, v. 8, nos. 1, 2.

Hershide. St. Joseph's R.C. churchyard. Md. O.R. Soc. Bul., no 3, p. 64.

Herwick. Cary Geneal. Coll. Ms. MHS.

Heslip. St. Paul's Parish, Balto. V. 2. Mss. MHS.

Heslop-Alricks. Lineage Bks., Natl. Soc. of Daughters of Amer. Col., v. 3, p. 250. MHS; DAR.

Hess. Graves, Fairview Cemetery, Wash. Co. Hist. of West. Md. Scharf. V. 2, p. 1306.
Holdens Cemetery, Kent Co. Md. Geneal. Rec. Com., 1932, v. 5, p. 211. Mss. DAR.

Hesselius. Dundas and Hesselius families, 1600—date. Hist. Pub. Soc., Phila., 1938, pp. 98–122. MHS.
†Earliest painter in Amer. Ms. DAR.
†(1682–1755), from Sweden to Wilmington (was Christiana), Del. May, 12, 1712. Dict. of Amer. Biog.
Naturalizations in Md., 1666–1765; Laws. Bacon. MHS.
†One hundred years ago, or life and times of Walter Dulany Addison. Murray. 1895. MHS.
St. Paul's Parish, Balto. V. 2. Mss. MHS.
See Young-Woodward-Hesselius.

Hesselius, Gustavus. Family notes. Pa. Mag., 1905, v. 29, pp. 129, 367.

Hesson. Englar family. Barnes. MHS; DAR.

†**Hetzel.** Hist. of Allegany Co. Thomas and Williams. V. 1. MHS; DAR.

Hetzer. Md. tombstone rec. Md. Geneal. Rec. Com., 1937, Parran, p. 19. Mss. MHS.

Heuisler. Balto., its hist., its people. Hall. V. 3. MHS; DAR.
†Bench and bar of Md. Sams and Riley. 1901, v. 2, p. 505. Lib. Cong.; MHS; Peabody Lib.

Heuisler-Gardiner. Lineage, showing Royal descent. Col. and Revolutionary lineages of Amer. 1939, v. 2, pp. 62–88. MHS.

Hevener. St. Paul's Parish, Balto. V. 2. Mss. MHS.

Hewith. Pattison wills. Md. Geneal. Rec. Com. 1929, pp. 7–42; 1930–31. Mss. DAR.

Hewes. Portrait and biog. rec. of Sixth Cong. Dist. of Md. 1898, p. 316. MHS; DAR.

Hewes, Family, Balto. Fox-Ellicott-Evans families. Evans. MHS; DAR.

Hewitt. St. Paul's Parish, Balto. V. 2. Mss. MHS.

†**Heyser.** Hist. of West. Md. Scharf. V. 2, pp. 1035–36. MHS; DAR.
Zion Reformed Church, Hagerstown. Md. Geneal. Rec. Com., 1934–35. Mss. DAR.

Heyward. Amer. Armory and Blue Book. Matthews. 1911–12, p. 233.

Hiatt. Family rec. of Richard Williams. Ms. DAR.
Md. families. Culver. Ms. Personal list.

Hibbard. Englar family. Barnes. MHS; DAR.

Hibberd. Matthews-Price chart. MHS.
Sharpless family geneal. Cope. P. 514. MHS; DAR.

Hickey. St. Paul's Parish, Balto. V. 2. Mss. MHS.

†**Hickey, William.** Memoirs, 1749–75. Lib. Cong.

Hickley. Jenkins-Courtney chart. MHS.
St. Paul's Parish, Balto. V. 2. Mss. MHS.

Hickman. See Armstrong, Va. Abr. Compend. Amer. Geneal. Virkus. V. 4, p. 33. MHS.

†Med. Annals Md. Cordell. 1903, p. 437. MHS.
St. Paul's Parish, Balto. V. 2, 4. Mss. MHS.
Hickok, Miss Rebecca Northland. Chart. Col. Dames, Chap. I. MHS.
†**Hicks.** Biog. cyc. of rep. men of Md. and D. C. P. 324. MHS; DAR.
*Hist. Dorchester Co. Jones. 1925, pp. 342–50. MHS; DAR.
Md. families. Culver. Ms. Personal list.
Maulsby family in Amer. Barnard. DAR; Peabody Lib.
St. Paul's Parish, Balto. V. 2. Mss. MHS.
Miss Kate Steele chart. MHS.
*Wicomico Co. families. Tilghman. Ms., p. 74. DAR.
See Hutchins-Hicks.
Hicks, Gov. Thomas Holliday. Founders of Anne Arundel and Howard Cos. Warfield. P. 283. MHS; DAR.
*Burke's landed gentry. 1939. MHS.
†Hist. of Md. Scharf. V. 3, p. 575. MHS.
†Governors of Md. Buchholz. P. 171. MHS.
†(1798–1865). M. H. Mag., v. 12, p. 220.
Hicks - Dennis - Edmondson - Phillips - Travers-White. Wicomico Co. families. Bible rec. Ms. DAR.
Hickson. Frederick Co. tombstone inscriptions. Gruder. Natl. Geneal. Soc. Quart., 1919, v. 8, nos. 1, 2.
Hiester, Heister. Hagerstown tombstone inscriptions. Gruder. Natl. Geneal. Soc. Quart., 1919, v. 8, nos. 1, 2.
Higenbotham. Dew chart. MHS.
Higgins. Cary Geneal. Coll. Ms. MHS.
Christ P. E. Church cemetery, Cambridge. Steele. 1936. MHS; DAR.
Col. families of U. S. A. Mackenzie. V. 7, p. 257. MHS; DAR.
Md. tombstone rec. Md. Geneal. Rec. Com., 1937. Parran. P. 27. Mss. DAR.
See Lucas-Higgins.
Higgins, Talbot Co. H. Mullikin pedigree charts, plate 1. Soc. Col. Wars, Md. Johnston. 1905, p. 74. MHS.
Higgins, Samuel, Prince George Co. Will (copy). Ms. DAR.
†**Highbarger.** Hist. of Washington Co. Williams. 1906, v. 2, p. 1017. MHS; DAR.
***Highland - Earle - Patton.** Highland - Earle-Patton families.* W. Va. S. G. Highland. Repr. from Clarksburg Exponent-Telegram Clarksburg, W. Va., 1929. MHS.
Higinbotham. St. Paul's Parish, Balto. V. 2. Mss. MHS.
Higinbothom. Coll. of Amer. epitaphs and inscriptions. Alden. 1814, v. 1. MHS.
Descendants of Col. Thomas White. Morris. MHS.
Hignett. Old Somerset. Torrence. MHS. DAR.
Somerset Co. Court Book. Tilghman. 1937. Ms. DAR.
Hildt, J. C. Md. Soc., War of 1812, v. 3, no. 218. Ms. MHS.
Hildt, Thomas. Md. Soc., War of 1812, v. 3, no. 219. Ms. MHS.
Hill. Amer. Clan Gregor Year Book, 1917, p. 26; 1921, pp. 28–30 (Wm. Isaac); 1923, p. 35 (Wm. W., II); 1927, pp. 93–96; 1928, pp. 12, 19–21; 1930, p. 54. MHS; DAR.
Ances. rec. and portraits. Col. Dames of Amer., 1910, v. 1, pp. 151, 360. MHS; DAR.
Balto., its hist., its people. Hall. V. 2. MHS; DAR.
Bible rec., 1728–1877. (66 entries). Contrib. by Mrs. R. Groves, Chestertown. Md. Geneal. Rec. Com., 1938–39, pp. 128–33. Mss. DAR.
Bible rec. Pa. Mag. Hist. and Biog., v. 31, p. 374.
†Biog. cyc. of rep. men of Md. and D. C. P. 291. MHS; DAR.
See Brooke. Abr. Compend. Amer. Geneal. Virkus. V. 6, p. 738. DAR.
Mrs. Howard Bruce chart. MHS.
H. D. G. Carroll. Ms. Book. In H. F. Thompson Papers. MHS.
Mrs. Charles Carter chart. MHS.
Cary Geneal. Coll. Ms. MHS.
Centenary of Catholicity in Ky. Webb. 1884. MHS.
Children of Alex P. and M. C. Hill. Ms. MHS.
Col. families of Amer. Lawrence. V. 14, p. 134. MHS.
Col. families of U. S. A. Mackenzie. V. 1; v. 2; v. 4 (N. H. and Md.). MHS; DAR.
Dorsey and allied families. Ms. MHS.
See Fergusson. Abr. Compend. Amer. Geneal. Virkus. V. 4, p. 179. MHS.
Geneal. and memorial encyc. of Md. Spencer. V. 1, p. 170. MHS; DAR.
Geneal. of Henrietta Chauncy Wilson. Upshur. Bk. of photos. MHS.
Hamilton family of Charles Co. Kelly. MHS.
*Hill family of Hourston and Spaxton, Eng., Mass., Md., and New Eng., 1334–1934. Repr. from Colonial Families. Pub. by Amer. Hist. Soc. N. Y. MHS.
John Philip Hill Line. Bowyer pedigree of K. U. C. Hill, 1849–1907. Sir G. B. MHS.
*Thomas Hill and descendants. Charts. J. D. Hill. (Hill family from Md. to Ky.) Louisville, Ky. John P. Morton Co., 1900. MHS.
Hills of Mass. Harford Co. Hist. Soc. Coll. JHU.
Howell Bible rec. Ms. MHS.
Howland chart. MHS.
Mrs. T. C. Jenkins chart. MHS.
Md. families. Culver. Ms. Personal list.
Md. gleanings in Eng. Wills. M. H. Mag., 1908, v. 3, no. 2.
See McMahon. Abr. Compend. Amer. Geneal. Virkus. V. 1, p. 199. DAR.
†Med. Annals Med. Cordell. 1903, pp. 438–39. MHS.
Mrs. E. N. Morison chart. MHS.
Pedigree of Thomas Dobbin Penniman. Soc. Col. Wars Md. Culver. 1940. MHS; DAR.
*Pennington Papers. Ms. MHS.
Repr. from Col. families of Hill family of Hourdston and Spaxton, Eng., and Balto. City and Co. MHS.
St. Paul's Parish, Balto. V. 1, 2, 4. Mss. MHS.
St. Stephens Parish, Cecilton, Md. MHS; DAR.
Shrewsbury churchyard. Md. O. R. Soc. Bull., no. 2, pp. 46–54.
Southerland-Latham and allied families. Voorhees. Bd. ms. MHS.
*The Sun, Balto., Feb. 16, 23, March 1, 8, 15 (Va.), April 12, (Anne Arundel Co.), 1908.

Hill. Warfield of Md. Warfield. MHS.
Wicomico Co. families. Bible rec. Ms. DAR.
*Wicomico Co. families. Tilghman. Ms, pp. 23–24, 101, 109, 111, 113. DAR.
Hill, Mass. Giving Maternal line of John Phillip Hill and Bancroft Hill of Balto. Col. and Revolutionary families of Phila. Jordan. 1933, v. 1, pp. 293–322.
***Hill,** New Eng. and Md. Geneal. and mem. encyc. of Md. Spencer. V. 1, p. 170. MHS; DAR.
Hill, South River. Samuel Carpenter of Phila. Carpenter. P. 256. MHS.
†**Hill, C. Geraldine.** Men of mark of Md. Johnson. V. 4. DAR; Enoch Pratt Lib.
Hill, Clarissa, St. Mary's Co. (born 1780). D. A. R. Mag., v. 65, no. 9, p. 571.
Hill, Clement. See Combs. Abr. Compend. Amer. Geneal. Virkus. V. 1, p. 274. DAR.
"Lord Baltimore plants a colony." Amer. Clan Gregor Year Book, 1937, pp. 114–28. MHS; DAR.
Hill, E. Clayton and John Philip. Abr. Compend Amer. Geneal. Virkus. V. 1, p. 342. DAR.
Hill, Henry. McCall-Tidwell families. McCall. P. 465. MHS; DAR.
†**Hill, J. Thomas.** Men of mark in Md. Johnson. V. 4. DAR; Enoch Pratt Lib.
Hill, John Philip. Amer. Armory and Blue Book. Matthews. 1911–12, p. 195.
Pedigree charts, plates 1, 2 and 3. Soc. Col. Wars, Md. Johnston. 1905, pp. 36-38. MHS.
***Hill, John B. Philip Clayton.** Coat of arms. Burke's landed gentry, 1939. MHS.
Pedigree. Soc. Col. Wars Md. Culver. 1940. MHS; DAR.
Hill, Malcolm Westcott. Pedigree chart. Soc. Col. Wars, Md. Johnston. 1905, p. 39. MHS.
Hill, N. Sluley. Md. Soc., War of 1812, v. 1, no. 90. Ms. MHS.
Hill, Norman Allan. Pedigree. Soc. Col. Wars Md. Culver. 1940. MHS; DAR.
Hill, Capt. Richard, Anne Arundel Co. S. C. Chew pedigree chart. Soc. Col. Wars, Md. Johnston. 1905, pp. 13, 147. MHS.
Hill, S. Emory. Md. Soc., War of 1812, v. 1, no. 81. Ms. MHS.
Hill, Thomas. Md. Soc., War of 1812, v. 1, no. 80. Ms. MHS.
†Men of mark in Md. Johnson. V. 2. DAR; Enoch Pratt Lib.
Hill, Thomas Gardener. Pedigree. Soc. Col. Wars Md. Culver. 1940. MHS; DAR.
Hill Family. Ames Geneal. Coll. Ms. MHS.
Morris family of Phila. Moon. V. 2, p. 425. MHS.
Rec. of South. Md., from 1754. Photos. Ms. MHS.
Hill, John Philip, Line. Hill family of Hourston and Spaxton, Eng., Mass., Md., New Eng., 1334–1934. Pp. 299–304. MHS.
Hill-Custis, Va. (Md. ref.) Va. Mag. Hist. and Biog., v. 3, pp. 319–21.
***Hill-Digges.** Lineage Bk. Daughters of Amer. Colonists. V. 1, p. 81. MHS; DAR.
Hill-Moore. Hill (Dr. Richard)-Moore Marriage, 1758. Merion in Welsh tract. Glenn. P. 348.
Hill-Tucker. Harford Co. Hist. Soc. Mss. Coll. JHU.
Hillary. Autobiography of Summerfield Baldwin. MHS; DAR.
Dorsey Papers. Ms. MHS.
Mrs. R. N. Jackson chart. MHS.
Mrs. D. G. Lovell chart. MHS.
See Hilleary.
Hillary, Hilleary. Cary Geneal. Coll. Ms. MHS.
Md. O. R. Soc. Bull., no. 1, p. 51.
*The Sun, Balto., May 20, 1906.
Hillary, Hilleary Family. Monnet family geneal. Monette. Pp. 1081, 1084–96. MHS.
Hilleary. Anne Arundel Co. tombstone inscriptions. Ms. DAR.
Sara R. Baldwin, chart. MHS.
Bible rec. 1782–1875. Md. O. R. Soc. Bull., no. 1, p. 53. MHS.
Family notes. MHS.
*Frederick Co. families. Markell. Ms. Personal list.
Hamill chart. MHS.
*Hilleary family. Ms. MHS.
†Hist. of Allegany Co. Thomas and Williams. V. 2. MHS; DAR.
†Hist. of Frederick Co. Williams. MHS; DAR.
See Howard, Mrs. G. Abr. Compend. Amer. Geneal. Virkus. V. 1, p. 381. DAR.
†Med. Annals Md. Cordell. 1903, p. 439. MHS.
Orme geneal. chart. MHS.
Mullikins of Md. Baker. MHS; DAR.
Pedigree of Mareen Duvall. Soc. Col. Wars Md. Culver. 1940. MHS; DAR.
Pedigree of Thomas Dobbin Penniman. Soc. Col. Wars Md. Culver. 1940. MHS; DAR.
Pedigree of Wm. Emory Warning, Jr. Soc. Col. Wars Md. Culver. 1940. MHS; DAR.
*Wilson Mss. Coll., no. 25. MHS.
Some Va. families. McIlhany.
See Hillary.
Hilleary Family. Notes. Ms. MHS.
Hilleary, Hillary. Col. families of U. S. A. Mackenzie. V. 2. MHS; DAR.
Hillen. Brice-Howard-Govane tombstone inscriptions. Ms. MHS.
Mrs. J. G. Brogden chart. MHS.
Col. families of U. S. A. Mackenzie. V. 1. MHS; DAR.
Early Quaker rec., Anne Arundel and Calvert Cos., 1665–1889. Pub. Geneal. Soc. Pa., v. 3, no. 3, pp. 197–200.
†Nicholas Hasselback, printer. McCreary. MHS.
Hist. graves of Md. and D. C. Ridgely. MHS.
Jenkins-Courtney chart. MHS.
Macsherry chart. MHS.
Md. families. Culver. Ms. Personal list.
John O'Donnell of Balto. Cook. MHS.
Pedigree of John Edward Harst. Soc. Col. Wars Md. Culver. 1940. MHS; DAR.
Posey chart. MHS.
*The Sun, Balto., Aug. 6, 13, 1905.
Mrs. Sherlock Swann chart. MHS.
St. Paul's Parish, Balto. V. 1. Mss. MHS.
Hillery, Calvert Co. (1689). See Maynard family. Focke Geneal. Coll. Ms. MHS.
Hilles, Harford Co. Abr. Compend. Amer. Geneal. Virkus. V. 1, p. 648. DAR.
Mrs. Alexander Gordon chart. MHS.

Hilles, Mrs. William S. (Bessie Beale Wilson). Chart. Col. Dames, Chap. I. MHS.
Hilliard. Old Somerset Torrence. MHS; DAR. Zion Reformed Church, Hagerstown. Md. Geneal. Rec. Com., 1934-35. Mss. DAR.
***Hillman, Hilman.** Wicomico Co. families. Tilghman. Ms, pp. 96, 98-99, 109-10. DAR.
Hills. Col. families of U. S. A. Mackenzie. V. 4. MHS; DAR.
Hillson. Cummings chart. Lib. Cong.; MHS; DAR.
Hilman. *See* Hillman.
Hilton. Mt. Olivet Cemetery, Frederick. Md. Geneal. Rec. Com., 1934-35, p. 111. Mss. DAR.
St. Paul's Parish, Balto. V. 2. Mss. MHS.
Hilton-Howard. Notes, D. A. R. Mag., v. 72, no. 3, p. 71.
Hinckley. Ances. rec. and portraits. Col. Dames of Amer., 1910, v. 2, p. 694. MHS; DAR.
***Hindacy.** Wicomico Co. families. Tilghman. Ms., p. 108. DAR.
Hinderson. Somerset Co. Court Book. Tilghman. 1937. Ms. DAR.
†Hindman. Bench and bar of Md. Sams and Riley. 1901, v. 1, p. 276. Lib. Cong.; MHS; Peabody Lib.
‡Hist. of Talbot Co. Tilghman. V. 2, p. 95. MHS; DAR.
*Pennington Papers. Ms. MHS.
St. Paul's Parish, Balto. V. 2. Mss. MHS.
Winchester-Owings chart. Cary Geneal. Coll. Ms. MHS.
†Hindman Jacob. Hist. of Md. Scharf. V. 3, p. 55. MHS.
†Hindman, Hon. Wm. Memoir. S. A. Harrison. Fund Publication, no. 14, Balto., 1880. MHS.
Hindman-Gist-Seymour. Amer. Compend. Amer. Geneal. Virkus. V. 4, p. 397.
Hinds. Bible rec. Upper Penins. East. Shore., p. 217.
See Heintz.
†Hines, Kent Co. Med. Annals Md. Cordell. 1903, p. 439. MHS.
See Heintz.
Hines, Christian, Frederick Co. Family notes. Rec. Columbia Hist. Soc., v. 22, p. 36.
Hinkle. Hist. and geneal. account of Levering family. Levering. MHS.
See Henkel.
†Hinkley. Bench and bar of Md. Sams and Riley. 1901, v. 2, p. 517. Lib. Cong.; MHS; Peabody Lib.
†Hinkley, John. Men of mark in Md. Johnson. V. 2, DAR; Enoch Pratt Lib.
Hinson. *See* Hynson.
Hinson, Hynson. Ancest. rec. and portraits. Col. Dames of Amer., 1910; v. 1, p. 144; v. 2, pp. 470, 669. MHS; DAR.
Barroll in Great Britain and Amer. Barroll. Pp. 64-67. MHS.
Col. families of East. Shore and their descendants. Emory. 1900, p. 218. MHS.
*Side lights on Md. Richardson. V. 2, p. 137. MHS; DAR.
†Hintze. Med. Annals Md. Cordell. 1903, p. 439. MHS.
Hipwell. St. Paul's Parish, Balto. V. 2. Mss. MHS.
Hirnberger. Ms. MHS.
Hisca. St. Paul's Parish, Balto. V. 2. Mss. MHS.
Hiser. M. E. Church South cemetery, near Poolesville, Montgomery Co. Md. Geneal. Rec. Com., 1926. Mss. DAR.
Hiskey, T. Foley. Md. Soc., War of 1812, v. 3, no. 232. Ms.
Hisky. Balto., its hist., its people. Hall. V. 2. MHS; DAR.
Hisky, J. Guido. Md. Soc., War of 1812, v. 4, no. 316. Ms. MHS.
Hisky, W. G. Md. Soc., War of 1812, v. 4, no. 317. Ms. MHS.
Hiss. W. W. Coleman chart. Soc. Col. Wars, Md. Johnston. 1905, p. 17. MHS.
Freeborn Garrettson Waters Bible rec. Ms. MHS.
†Hist. reg. Hill. V. 1, p. 66. MHS.
Hissey. St. Paul's Parish, Balto. V. 1, 2. Mss. MHS.
Hitch. Abr. Compend. Amer. Geneal. Virkus. V. 1, p. 359. DAR.
Chart, 1687; few of descendants of Adam Hitch. Ms. Institute of Amer. Geneal., 440 Dearborn St., Chicago.
*Chart. Mrs. R. P. (Daisey Hitch) Davis, Long Island, N. Y. Wicomico Co. families. Tilghman. Ms. DAR.
†Med. Annals Md. Cordell. 1903, p. 440. MHS.
St. Paul's Parish, Balto. V. 2. Mss. MHS.
Hitchens. Portrait and biog. rec. of Sixth Cong. Dist. of Md. 1898, p. 536. MHS. DAR.
Hite. Balto., its hist., its people. Hall. V. 3. MHS; DAR.
Mrs. Wm. T. Howard Jr., chart. MHS.
*The Sun, Balto., July 16, 23 (Va.), 1905.
Hite, Va. Col. families of U. S. A. Mackenzie. V. 4. MHS; DAR.
Hite, Drayton Meade. Md. Soc., War of 1812, v. 3, no. 203. Ms. MHS.
Hite, Col. John, Frederick Co., Va. (1710-1792). G. M. Sharp pedigree chart. Soc. Col. Wars, Md. Johnston. 1905, pp. 91, 147. MHS.
Hite Family. Gravestone rec. Ms. DAR.
Hite Family, Va. Ms. MHS.
Hiteshew. Frederick Co. tombstone inscriptions. Gruder. Natl. Geneal. Soc. Quart., 1919, v. 8, nos. 1, 2.
Hitt. Elbert chart. MHS.
†Hist. of Washington Co. Williams. 1906, v. 2, p. 1301. MHS; DAR.
Hixon. See Beachey. Abr. Compend. Amer. Geneal. Virkus. V. 4, p. 646. MHS.
Hobbs. Abr. Compend. Amer. Geneal. Virkus. V. 6, p. 519. DAR.
See Cissel. Abr. Compend. Amer. Geneal. Virkus. V. 4, p. 676. MHS.
Cummings chart. Lib. Cong.; MHS; DAR.
*Founders of Anne Arundel and Howard Cos. Warfield. Pp. 470-72, 524. MHS; DAR.
Griffith geneal. Griffith. MHS; DAR.
†Hist. of West. Md. Scharf. V. 1, p. 601. MHS; DAR.
Lineage Bks., Natl. Soc. of Daughters of Amer. Col., v. 2, p. 298. MHS; DAR.
†Med. Annals Md. Cordell. 1903, p. 440. MHS.
Mt. Carmel burial ground, Unity, Montgomery Co. Md. Geneal. Rec. Com., 1934-35, p. 85. Mss. DAR.
Old Somerset. Torrence. MHS; DAR.

Hobbs. Patriotic Md. Md. Soc. of S. A. R., 1930. MHS; DAR.
Pedigree of John Ogle Warfield, Jr. Soc. Col. Wars Md. Culver. 1940. MHS; DAR.
St. Paul's Parish, Balto. V. 2. Mss. MHS.
Talbot of "Poplar Knowle." Shirk. MHS; DAR.
Warfield of Md. Warfield. MHS.
Hobson. St. Paul's Parish, Balto. V. 2. Mss. MHS.
Hobson, Thomas. And some of his descendants. (Showing Dickinson, Md.) Tyler's Quart. Mag., v. 8, pp. 127-33.
†**Hocking.** Hist. of Allegany Co. Thomas and Williams. V. 2. MHS; DAR.
Hodgdon. Col. families of U. S. A. Mackenzie. V. 5. MHS; DAR.
Patriotic Md. Md. Soc. of S. A. R., 1930. MHS; DAR.
Hodgdon, Alexander Lewis. Pedigree (Mostly Conn. rec.) Soc. Col. Wars Md. Culver. 1940. MHS; DAR.
Hodgdon, Anderson Dana. Pedigree. (Mostly Conn. rec.) Soc. Col. Wars Md. Culver. 1940. MHS; DAR.
Hodge. Cary Geneal. Coll. Ms. MHS.
Lloyd family hist. of Wales, Pa. and Md. DAR.
Mrs. Talbot T. Speer chart. MHS.
Hodges. Col. families of U. S. A. Mackenzie. V. 2. MHS; DAR.
†Hist. of Balto. City and Co. Scharf. P. 416. MHS.
Monumental City. Howard. MHS; DAR.
St. Paul's P. E. churchyard, Kent. Co. Md. O. R. Soc. Bull., no. 2, pp. 54-65.
St. Paul's Parish, Balto. V. 1, 2, 3, 4. Mss. MHS.
†**Hodges,** Kent Co. Biog. cyc. of rep. men of Md. and D. C. P. 287. MHS; DAR.
***Hodges,** Va. and Md. The Sun, Balto., Oct. 18, 1903.
***Hodges Family.** Old Kent. Hanson. P. 309 (arms). MHS; DAR.
Hodson. Christ P. E. Church cemetery, Cambridge. Steele. 1936. MHS; DAR.
*Wicomico Co. families. Tilghman. Ms, pp. 72, 74. DAR.
See Collison-Hodson-Ball.
See Wight-Hodson-Lloyd-Travers.
Hodson-Collison-Ball-Jones-Lankford, Vienna, Md. Bible rec. of Dorchester and Somerset Cos. and Del. Pp. 36-39. DAR.
Hoefligh. *See* Healfleich.
Hoen. Balto., its hist., its people. Hall. V. 2. MHS; DAR.
†**Hoen, Ernest.** In memoriam. Soc. for Hist. of Germans in Md. 7th ann. rept., 1893.
Hoey. St. Paul's Parish, Balto. V. 2. Mss. MHS.
Hofman. Balto., its hist., its people. Hall. V. 2. MHS; DAR.
See Hoffman.
Hoff. Frederick Co. tombstone inscriptions. Gruder. Natl. Geneal. Soc. Quart., 1919, v. 8, nos. 1, 2.
Hoff, Charles Worthington. Pedigree. Soc. Col. Wars Md. Culver. 1940. MHS; DAR.
Hoff, Mrs. Violet (Brown). Hoff Bible rec. Tocke Geneal. Coll. Ms. MHS.
Hoffman. Aristocratic Monitor, June 10, 1848. Newsp. clipp. MHS.
Balto., its hist., its people. Hall. V. 2, 3. MHS; DAR.
Bible rec., Kent Co. Md. Geneal. Rec. Com., 1937, Parran. Mss. DAR.
Cary Geneal. Coll. Ms. MHS.
Curzon family. Pleasants. MHS.
Deford chart. MHS.
Frederick Co. tombstone inscriptions. Gruder. Natl. Geneal. Soc. Quart., 1919, v. 8, nos. 1, 2.
*Gilmor chart. Ms. MHS.
Robert Gilmor chart. MHS.
Henkel Family Assoc., Jan., 1931, no. 6, p. 253. MHS; DAR.
†Hist. of Allegany Co. Thomas and Williams. V. 1. MHS; DAR.
†Hist. of Frederick Co. Williams. MHS; DAR.
†Hist. of West. Md. Scharf. V. 1, p. 459. MHS; DAR.
Hoffman family. Mss. MHS.
Hoffman Family. Miss T. G. Hoffman. Typed. MHS.
Md. Geneal. Bull., v. 5, p. 10.
Monumental City. Howard. MHS; DAR.
*Pennington Papers. Ms. MHS.
St. Paul's Parish, Balto. V. 2, 3, 4. Mss. MHS.
Zion Reformed Church, Hagerstown. Md. Geneal. Rec. Com., 1934-35. Mss. DAR.
†**Hoffman, Peter.** Balto., hist and biog. Richardson and Bennett. 1871, pp. 295-98. MHS; DAR.
Hoffman, Richard Curzon. Pedigree chart. Soc. Col. Wars, Md. Johnston. 1905, p. 40. MHS.
Hoffman Family, Frederick Co. to Balto., 1745-1850. Ms. MHS.
Geneal., 1657-1899. E. A. Hoffman. (N. Y. rec.) N. Y., Dodd, Mead & Co., 1899. MHS.
Rec., 1719-1904. Rec. copied from ancient diary. Md. Geneal. Rec. Com., 1932-33, pp. 179-83. Mss. DAR.
†**Hoffman, Hofman.** Hist. of Washington Co. Williams. 1906, v. 2, p. 1115. MHS; DAR.
Hogan. Abr. Compend. Amer. Geneal. Virkus. V. 1, p. 362. DAR.
***Hoge.** Va. The Sun, Balto., May 21, 28, 1905.
Hogg. St. Paul's Parish, Balto. V. 3. Mss. MHS.
Hogmire. *See* Hagmeyer.
Hogner. St. Paul's Parish, Balto. V. 2. Mss. MHS.
†**Hoke.** Hist. of Frederick Co. Williams. MHS; DAR.
Holbrook. *See* Holebrook.
Holcombe. Amer. Clan Gregor Year Book, 1916, pp. 31, 45. MHS; DAR.
Holden. Portrait and biog. rec. of Harford and Cecil Cos. 1897. P. 155. MHS; DAR.
Holden, Mrs. Joshua Bennett (Mabel Leigh Bonsal). Chart. Col. Dames, Chap. I. MHS.
Holebrook, Holbrook. St. Paul's Parish, Balto. V. 1, 2. Mss. MHS.
Holeoger. St. Stephens Parish, Cecilton, Md. MHS; DAR.
Holladay. Garrett chart. Cary Geneal. Coll. Ms. MHS.
Va. geneal. Hayden. MHS; DAR.
Holland. Abs. of rec. of West River Monthly Meeting. Ms. MHS.
Balto., its hist., its people. Hall. V. 3, p. 610. MHS; DAR.

Bond chart. MHS.
Cary Geneal. Coll. Ms. MHS.
Gilpin chart. MHS.
Griffith geneal. Griffith. MHS; DAR.
†Hist. of Balto. City and Co. Scharf. P. 368. MHS.
Howard-Montague-Warfield geneal. chart. Culver and Marye. MHS.
Lineage Bks., Natl. Soc. of Daughters of Amer. Col., v. 1, p. 14. MHS; DAR.
Md. families. Culver. Ms. Personal list.
†Med. Annals Md. Cordell. 1903, p. 441. MHS.
Naturalizations in Md., 1666–1765; Laws. Bacon. MHS.
Patriotic Md. Md. Soc. of S. A. R., 1930. MHS; DAR.
Portrait and biog. rec. of East. Shore of Md. 1898, pp. 238, 616, 795. MHS; DAR.
St. Paul's Parish, Balto. V. 1, 2, 4. Mss. MHS.
Side lights on Md. hist. Richardson. V. 2, p. 140. MHS; DAR.
Somerset Co. Court Book. Tilghman. 1937. Ms. DAR.
*The Sun, Balto., Dec. 18, 1904.
*Wicomico Co. families. Tilghman. Ms, p. 98. DAR.
See Guyton-Kirr-Rush-Holland-Conn.

Holland, Anthony. Will, 1702. Md. Geneal. Rec. Com., 1932, p. 189. DAR.

†**Holland, Charles Fisher.** Men of mark in Md. Johnson. V. 3. DAR; Enoch Pratt Lib.

Holland Line, Anne Arundel Co. Col. and Revolutionary lineages of Amer. 1939, v. 1, pp. 484–86. MHS.

Holliday. Amer. Guthrie and allied families. Guthrie. Bk. 4. DAR.
Anne Arundel Co. tombstone inscriptions. Ms. DAR.
Lineage. Ms. MHS.
Papers; containing Holliday or Hollyday and Denwood families. Geneal., 1678–1749. Ms. MHS.
*Semmes Geneal. Coll. Ms. MHS.

Holliday-Ringgold (1650). Morris family of Phila. Moon. V. 1, p. 180; v. 2, pp. 622, 763. MHS.

Holliday, Halliday. Some notable families of south. States. Armstrong. V. 2, pp. 161–73. DAR.

Hollinger. Peale Geneal. Coll. Ms. MHS.

Hollingsworth. Allyn-Foote-Webb-Cooch-Wilkins geneal. Cooch. Bd. ms. MHS; DAR.
Abr. Compend. Amer. Geneal. Virkus. V. 6, pp. 73, 122, 543. DAR.
Carton charts. MHS.
Chart of Com. John Rodgers. DAR.
Chart, photos., complete in 1 sheet. Cary Geneal. Coll. Ms. MHS.
Christ P. E. Church cemetery, Cambridge. Steele. 1936. MHS; DAR.
Col. families of East. Shore and their descendants. Emory. 1900, p. 85. MHS.
Col. families of U. S. A. Mackenzie. V. 7. MHS; DAR.
Cosden family data. Ms. MHS.
Miss M. W. Davis chart. MHS.
De Ford chart. MHS.
*Descendants of Valentine Hollingsworth, Sr. J. A. Stewart. Louisville, Ky., John P. Morton & Co., Inc., added to and corrected, 1925. 208 pp. MHS; DAR.
*Encyc. of Amer. biog. Amer. Hist. Soc., N. Y., v. 9, p. 226. MHS.
*Geneal. memoranda United States, 1682–1884. Descendants of Valentine Hollingsworth, Sr., New Castle, Pa., 1682. W. B. Hollingsworth. Balto., Wm. K. Boyle & Sons, 1884. MHS; DAR.
Mrs. C. C. Hall chart. MHS.
Harford Co. Hist. Soc. Mss. Coll. JHU.
Hist. and geneal. account of Jolliffe family o Va. Jolliffe. DAR.
Hist. graves of Md. and D. C. Ridgely. MHS.
†Hist. of Cecil Co. Johnston. MHS; DAR.
†(No Md. ref.) Hist. reg. Hill. V. 2, p. 48. MHS.
†Hist. of Washington Co. Williams. 1906, v. 2, p. 902. MHS; DAR.
*Hollingsworth geneal. Dr. John Neil. 1869, 1st ed.
Valentine Hollingsworth. Edw. W. Cooch. From Quaker rec. (Valentine Hollingsworth was one of founders of Newark Monthly Meeting, Del.) D. A. R. Mag., v. 70, no. 9, pp.949–58.
See Huidekoper. Abr. Compend. Amer. Geneal. Virkus. V. 4, p. 295. MHS.
Lineage Bks., Natl. Soc. of Daughters of Amer. Col., v. 1, p. 354; v. 4, p. 50. MHS; DAR.
Md. Families. Culver. Ms. Personal list.
Md. Geneal. Bull., v. 6, p. 45. MHS; DAR.
Morris family of Phila. Moon. V. 2, pp. 560–63. MHS.
North-American, Phila., Dec. 15, 1907. MHS.
Papers. Ms. MHS.
Patriotic Md. Md. Soc. of S. A. R., 1930. MHS; DAR.
Pedigree of Charles Morris Howard. Soc. Col. Wars Md. Culver. 1940. MHS; DAR.
St. Paul's Parish, Balto. V. 1, 2, 3. Mss. MHS.
Mrs. Edw. Simpson chart. MHS.
*The Sun, Balto., Feb. 26, 1905; March 25, 1906 (descendants of Valentine Hollingsworth).
Mrs. E. C. Cenable, chart. MHS.
Mrs. G. H. Williams, Jr., chart. MHS.

Hollingsworth, Valentine, Sr. Descendants. M. H. Mag., 1925, v. 20, p. 390.

***Hollingsworth Family.** Additions and corrections. Md. Geneal. Bull., v. 10, no. 3, p. 33. MHS; DAR.
Bible rec., 1767–1844. Ms. MHS.
Descendants of Valentine, Chester Co., Pa. (born 1635). Our kindred. Stern. 1885, pp. 6–11, 56–60.

Hollingsworth Line. Col. and Revolutionary lineages of Amer. 1939, v. 1, pp. 518–24. MHS.

Hollins. Cary Geneal. Coll. Ms. MHS.
Mrs. N. S. Pendleton, Jr., chart. MHS.
Mrs. G. H. Williams, Jr., chart. MHS.
J. G. and M. G. Wilson pedigree chart. Soc. Col. Wars, Md. Johnston. 1905, p. 129. MHS.
St. Paul's Parish, Balto. V. 2. Mss. MHS.
St. Stephens Parish, Cecilton, Md. MHS; DAR.
See McKim-Hollins-Patterson.

†**Hollins, G. N.** Hist. of Md. Scharf. V. 3, p. 452. MHS.

†**Hollins, Commodore George Nicholas** (1799–1878). Autobiography. M. H. Mag., 1939, v. 34, no. 3, pp. 228–43.
Hollins Family. Ames Geneal. Coll. Ms. MHS.
Hollis. Pedigree of Charles Morton Stewart. Soc. Col. Wars Md. Culver. 1940. MHS; DAR.
Mrs. Talbot T. Speer chart. MHS.
Hollis, Amos, Harford Co. Will probated May, 1789, also June, 1824. D. A. R. Mag., v. 65, no. 8, p. 506.
Hollis, Clark or William, Harford Co. Will probated May 17, 1819. D. A. R. Mag., v. 65, no. 8, p. 506.
Hollis, William, Harford Co. Will, 1824. D. A. R. Mag., v. 65, no. 8, p. 506.
Will probated May 9, 1789. D. A. R. Mag., v. 65, no. 8, p. 506.
Holloway. Bible rec., from Bible owned by T. J. Fassitt, Berlin, Md. Md. Geneal. Rec. Com., 1937–38, pp. 150–51. Mss. DAR.
Col. families of U. S. A. Mackenzie. V. 7, p. 301. MHS; DAR.
Geneal. and memorial encyc. of Md. Spencer. V. 2, p. 445. MHS; DAR.
*Geneal. of Holloway families. O. E. Holloway. Knightstown, Ind., 1927. MHS; DAR.
Patriotic Md. Md. Soc. of S. A. R., 1930. MHS; DAR.
Turner Geneal. Coll. Ms. MHS.
*Wicomico Co. families. Tilghman. Ms, p. 25. DAR.
Holloway, Lieut. C. T. Md. Soc., War of 1812, v. 3, no. 279. Ms. MHS.
Holloway, Charles Thomas. Pedigree. Soc. Col. Wars Md. Culver. 1940. MHS; DAR.
***Holloway, Reuben Ross.** Geneal. and mem. encyc. of Md. Spencer. V. 2, pp. 445–50. MHS; DAR.
Md. Soc., War of 1812, v. 1, no. 109. Ms. MHS.
***Holloway Family.** Holloway family in Amer. O. E. Holloway, M.D. Knightstown, Ind. DAR.
Holloway-Hooper. Wicomico Co. families. Bible rec. Ms. DAR.
Hollyday. Abr. Compend. Amer. Geneal. Virkus. V. 1, p. 367; v. 6, p. 302. DAR.
*Bible of Judge George Steuart Hollyday and wife Caroline Carvel Hollyday. 2 vols. MHS.
†Chesapeake Bay Country. Earle. Pp. 329, 366. MHS.
Col. families of U. S. A. Mackenzie. V. 2, pp. 333–42. MHS; DAR.
Col. mansions of Md. and Del. Hammond. 1914. MHS.
Done Bible rec. Ms. MHS.
*Early Hist. of Hollyday family, 1297–1800. H. Hollyday, Easton Md. Balto., J. H Furst Co., 1931, 15 pp. MHS; DAR.
Gale family pedigree, Somerset and Cecil Cos. Ms. MHS.
Geneal. notes of Chamberlaine family. MHS.
Hist. graves of Md. and D. C. Ridgely. MHS.
Hist. of Talbot. Co. Tilghman. V. 1, pp. 46, 64, 614–17. MHS; DAR.
*Hollyday lineage. MHS.
Lineage (arms). Removed from Hollyday Papers. Pamph. MHS.
Miss Katherine Lurman chart. MHS.
Md. families. Culver. Ms. Personal list.
Pedigree of Charles O'Donnell Mackall. Soc. Col. Wars Md. Culver. 1940. MHS; DAR.
Pedigree of Rev. James Mitchell Magruder. Soc. Col. Wars Md. Culver. 1940. MHS; DAR.
Pedigree of Levin Gale Shreve. Soc. Col. Wars Md. Culver. 1940. MHS; DAR.
Pedigree of Harrison Tilghman. Soc. Col. Wars Md. Culver. 1940. MHS; DAR.
*The Sun, Balto., Sept. 6, 1903.
Tilghman chart. MHS.
See Holliday.
***Hollyday,** Talbot Co. Burke's landed gentry. 1939. MHS.
Hollyday, Guy Tilghman Orme. Pedigree. Soc. Col. Wars Md. Culver. 1940. MHS; DAR.
†**Hollyday, James.** Biog. memoirs. G. T. Hollyday. Pa. Mag. Hist. and Biog., 1883, v. 7, pp. 426–47.
†**Hollyday, Hon. James, Jr.** (1722–86). Hist. of Talbot Co. Tilghman. V. 1, pp. 46–66. MHS; DAR.
Hollyday, Hon. Richard Carmichael (1810–85). Hist. of Talbot Co. Tilghman. V. 1, pp. 614–17. MHS; DAR.
Hollyday, Thomas Worthington. Pedigree. Soc. Col. Wars Md. Culver. 1940. MHS; DAR.
Hollyday Family. Bible 1696. Md. Geneal. Bull., v. 1, no. 2, pp. 9–11. MHS; DAR.
*Hollyday Family (1297–1800). Henry Hollyday. Balto., J. H. Furst Co., 15 pp. DAR.
M. H. Mag., 1931, v. 26, no. 2, p. 159–71.
*Old Kent. Hanson. Pp. 246–50. MHS; DAR.
Holman. Ms. MHS.
*Pennington Papers. Ms. MHS.
Holmes. Mrs. R. Barton, Jr., charts. MHS.
Griffith geneal. Griffith. MHS; DAR.
St. Paul's Parish, Balto. V. 1, 2. Mss. MHS.
*Semmes Geneal. Coll. Ms. MHS.
See Purnell.
Holston. Elbert chart. MHS.
Holt. Cary Geneal. Coll. Ms. MHS.
Portrait and biog. rec. of Harford and Cecil Cos. 1897, p. 163. MHS; DAR.
St. Stephens Parish, Cecilton, Md. MHS; DAR.
Wicomico Co. families. Tilghman. Ms, p. 18. DAR.
Holt, H. Abr. Compend. Amer. Geneal. Virkus. V. 1, p. 369. DAR.
Holter. Bible rec., 1776–98. Natl. Geneal. Soc. Quart., v. 23, no. 1, p. 20.
†Hist. of Frederick Co. Williams. MHS; DAR.
†**Holton.** Hist. of Balto. City and Co. Scharf. P. 829. MHS.
St. Stephens Parish, Cecilton, Md. MHS; DAR.
Holtz. Frederick Co. tombstone inscriptions. Gruder. Natl. Geneal. Soc. Quart., 1919, v. 8, nos. 1, 2.
Holvershot. Englar family. Barnes. P. 9. MHS; DAR.
Holyday. St. Stephens Parish, Cecilton, Md. MHS; DAR.
†**Holzshu, J. H.** Men of mark in Md. Johnson. V. 3. DAR; Enoch Pratt Lib.
Homer. Balto., its hist., its people. Hall. V. 2. MHS; DAR.
†Geneal. and mem. encyc. of Md. Spencer. V. 1, pp. 184–88. MHS; DAR.

***Homewood Family.** Anne Arundel Co. gentry. Newman. Pp. 557-66. MHS; DAR.
Hones. Gantt geneal. Ms. MHS.
Honey. Southern Bapt. Church cemetery, Worcester Co. Md. Geneal. Rec. Com., 1937, Mrs. Lines. Mss. DAR.
Honeywell. *See* Marshall-Honeywell.
***Honywood.** Pennington Papers. Ms. MHS.
Hood. Bible rec., including Owings. Md. Geneal. Bull., v. 2, pp. 10-12. MHS; DAR.
Focke Geneal. Coll. Ms. MHS.
*Founders of Anne Arundel and Howard Cos. Warfield. Pp. 469, 472-79. MHS; DAR.
Griffith geneal. Griffith. MHS; DAR.
†Hist. of Frederick Co. Williams. MHS; DAR.
Hist. graves of Md. and D. C. Ridgely. MHS.
†Hist. of West. Md. Scharf. V. 2, pp. 1007-08. MHS; DAR.
*Owings-Gaither-Hood-Thomas Bible rec. Ms. File case, MHS.
Patriotic Md. Md. Soc. of S. A. R., 1930. MHS; DAR.
Pedigree of Andrew Jackson Young, Jr. Soc. Col. Wars Md. Culver. 1940. MHS; DAR.
Portrait and biog. rec. Sixth Cong. Dist. of Md. 1898, p. 415. MHS; DAR.
Hood, John Mifflin. Memoirs. John M. Hood, Jr. Pamph. MHS.
Hood, Sarah Smith. Bible rec. Ms. MHS.
Hood Family. Bible rec. Pamph. MHS.
Hood-Worthington-Owings. Geneal. concerning Hood family. Maj. C. W. Hood. 1870. Ms. MHS.
Hooe. Bible rec. D. C. Geneal. Rec. Com., v. 31, pt. 1, pp. 237-39. DAR.
***Hooe,** Va. and Md. The Sun, Balto., March 22, 1908.
Hooe Family. Md. Geneal. Rec. Com., 1932, p. 246. DAR.
Hooe-Barnes. Va. geneal. Hayden. MHS; DAR.
Hooe-Barnes, Va. and Md. Repr. from Hayden's Va. geneal. Pamph. MHS.
***Hoogs Family.** Arch. of Georgetown Univ., Wash., D. C., v. 274, no. 6.
Hook. Balto., its hist., its people. Hall. V. 2. MHS; DAR.
Md. tombstone rec. Md. Geneal. Rec. Com., 1937, Parran, p. 31. Mss. DAR.
See Miller family. Focke Geneal. Coll. Ms. MHS.
St. Paul's Parish, Balto. V. 1, 2. Mss. MHS.
Hook, Hooke. Abr. Compend. Amer. Geneal. Virkus. V. 4, p. 584. MHS.
*James Hook and Virginia Eller. Family hist. and geneal. J. W. Hook. New Haven, Conn., Tuttle-Morehouse-Taylor Co., 1925. MHS; DAR.
***Hooke.** Humphrey Hooke of Bristol, and his descendants in Eng. and Amer., in 17th-century. Frederick W. Todd (late of Boston, Mass). 1938. MHS.
See Hook.
Hooker. Chart, photos., 1 sheet. Cary Geneal. Coll. Ms. MHS.
Early Quaker rec., Anne Arundel and Calvert Cos., 1665-1889. Pub. Geneal. Soc. Pa., v. 3, no. 3, pp. 197-200.
Md. families. Culver. Ms. Personal list.
St. Paul's Parish, Balto. V. 2. Mss. MHS.
Thomas-Chew-Lawrence. Thomas. MHS.
Hooper. Abr. Compend. Amer. Geneal. Virkus. V. 1, p. 652; v. 3, p. 555. DAR.
Ances. rec. and portraits. Col. Dames of Amer., 1910, v. 1, p. 148; v. 2, p. 682. MHS; DAR.
Balto., its hist., its people. Hall. V. 2. MHS; DAR.
Mrs. Howard Bruce chart. MHS.
†Chesapeake Bay Country. Earle. P. 385. MHS.
Christ P. E. Church cemetery, Cambridge. Steele. 1936. MHS; DAR.
*Arms. Hist. of Dorchester Co. Jones. 1925, pp. 350-67. MHS.
Md. families. Culver. Ms. Personal list.
Notes on hist., v. 1, pp. 37-38. MHS; DAR.
Patriotic Md. Md. Soc. of S. A. R., 1930. MHS; DAR.
See Parrott. Abr. Compend. Amer. Geneal. Virkus. V. 1, p. 757. DAR.
Pattison Bible rec. Ms. MHS.
Pedigree of Franklin Buchanan Owen. Soc. Col. Wars Md. Culver. 1940. MHS; DAR.
Pedigree of Tilghman Goldsborough Pitts. Soc. Col. Wars Md. Culver. 1940. MHS; DAR.
Pedigree of Rev. Sam'l Tagart Steele. Soc. Col. Wars Md. Culver. 1940. MHS; DAR.
Pedigree of Mason Locke Weems Williams. Soc. Col. Wars. Md. Culver. 1940. MHS; DAR.
†11 scrap bks. of Mayor Hooper, Balto. MHS.
St. Paul's Parish, Balto. V. 1, 2. Mss. MHS.
Side lights on Md. hist. Richardson. V. 2, p. 143. MHS; DAR.
Somerset Co. Court Book. Tilghman. 1937. Ms. DAR.
Miss Kate Steele chart. MHS.
*The Sun, Balto., Nov. 13, 1904.
Tombstone rec. of Dorchester Co. Jones. DAR.
*Wicomico Co. families. Tilghman. Ms, pp. 10, 26, 99-01, 103-04. DAR.
See Holloway-Hooper.
Hooper, Amos (Revolutionary soldier). Friends burying ground, Balto. Patriotic Marylander, v. 2, no. 4, p. 54. MHS; DAR.
Hooper, James (veteran). Md. Soc., War of 1812, v. 1, no. 60. Ms. MHS.
Hooper Family. Col. and Revolutionary families of Pa. Jordan. 1932, v. 4, pp. 221-56.
Md. Geneal. Bull., v. 11, no. 2, p. 24. MHS; DAR.
Hooper-Denwood. Ances. rec. and portraits. Col. Dames of Amer., 1910, v. 2, p. 682. MHS; DAR.
Hoopes. Rec. of Cope family. Cope. P. 209. MHS.
Hoover. Amer. Armory and Blue Book. Matthews. 1911-12, p. 146.
Ancestry. Geneal., Jour. Amer. Ancestry, 1922, v. 10, no. 7, pp. 72-73 (Prompton Lake, N. J.).
*Boyd family. Boyd. DAR.
Family register. West Branch Monthly Meeting, Niami Co., Ohio. D. A. R. Mag., 1934, v. 68, no. 10, p. 633.
*Huber-Hoover family. H. W. Hoover. 1928. DAR.
St. Joseph's churchyard, Emmitsburg, Md. O. R. Soc. Bull., no. 3, pp. 64-66. MHS.
St. Joseph's R. C. churchyard. Md. O. R. Soc. Bull., no. 3, p. 64.

Hoover. Spessard family. Spessard. MHS; DAR.
See Huber-Hoover.
Hoover, Carroll Co. Orig. parchment plat of tract of land, home of Andrew Hoover, 1740–60. Autographed by Herbert Hoover in Hist. Soc. of Carroll Co. M. H. Mag., Mar., 1940, v. 35, no. 1, pp. 87–88.
Hoover, Herbert Clark. Abr. Compend. Amer. Geneal. Virkus. V. 1, p. 370. DAR.
Hoover, Mrs. Howard. Abr. Compend. Amer. Geneal. Virkus. V. 4, p. 17. MHS.
Hoover, Theodore Jessie. Col. families of U. S. A. Mackenzie. V. 6. MHS; DAR.
Hoover Family. Col. and Revolutionary lineages of Amer., 1939, v. 3, pp. 426–46. MHS.
Hoover (Huber). Ancestry. Natl. Geneal. Soc. Quart., Dec., 1935, v. 23, no. 4, pp. 110–11.
Hope. Abr. Compend. Amer. Geneal. Virkus. V. 1, p. 924. DAR.
Southern Bapt. Church cemetery, Worcester Co. Md. Geneal. Rec. Com., 1937, Mrs. Lines. Mss. DAR.
Hopewell. Howard-Montague-Warfield geneal. chart. Culver and Marye. MHS.
Pedigree of Culbreth Hopewell Warner. Soc. Col. Wars Md. Culver. 1940. MHS; DAR.
***Hopewell Family.** Bible rec., 1837–73. Ms. MHS.
Hopewell, Capt. Richard, Line, St. Mary's Co. (1688–1872). C. H. Warner pedigree chart. Soc. Col. Wars, Md. Johnston. 1905, pp. 123, 147. MHS.
Hopkins. Abs. of rec. of West River Monthly Meeting. Ms. MHS.
Birthplace of Johns Hopkins. J. H. U. Alumni Mag., v. 23, no. 2, pp. 154–55.
Brief letters of Md. medical student. Dr. Richard Hopkins. M. H. Mag., 1928, v. 23, pp. 279–92; 1929, v. 24, pp. 23–30.
Col. families of Amer. Lawrence. V. 3, p. 307. MHS.
Col. families of U. S. A. Mackenzie. V. 2, v. 7. MHS; DAR.
†Descendants of Hopkins family, Md.; brief sketch. Pa. Academy of Fine Arts, catalogue of memorial exhibition of portraits by Thomas Sully, 2nd ed., 1922, p. 138. Enoch Pratt Lib.
Dorsey and allied families. Ms. MHS.
Eldridge chart. MHS.
Ellicott-King chart. MHS.
Founders of Anne Arundel and Howard Cos. Warfield. P. 318. MHS; DAR.
Geneal. notes of Thomas family. Thomas. MHS; DAR.
Hazelhurst charts. MHS.
Mrs. M. J. Henry chart. MHS.
*Hopkins and allied families, from estate of Hon. George M. Sharp, Sept. 12, 1911. Ms. MHS.
Hopkins and allied families. (Wm. Hopkins of Mt. Air, Harford Co.) Notes on Chew, p. 21; Husband, Newland, Pusey, pp. 175, 229. (From estate of Hon. Geo. M. Sharpe.) Sept. 21, 1911. Bd. ms. MHS.
Howard-Govane-Woodward-Law Bible rec. Ms. MHS.
*Hopkins of Va. and related families. W. L. Hopkins. 1931. DAR.
Husband and allied families. Ms. MHS.
See Janney. Abr. Compend. Amer. Geneal. Virkus. V. 4, pp. 309–10. MHS.
Makemie Memorial Pres. churchyard, Snow Hill, Worcester Co. Hudson. Bd. ms. MHS; DAR. Also: Md. Geneal. Rec. Com., Mrs. Lines. Mss. DAR.
Marriage rec., 1781–1892, Harford Co. Md. Geneal. Rec. Com., 1934–35, p. 108. DAR.
Md. families. Culver. Ms. Personal list.
See Maynard family. Focke Geneal. Coll. Ms. MHS.
†Med. Annals Md. Cordell. 1903, pp. 442–43. MHS.
Pedigree of Benedict Henry Hanson, Jr. Soc. Col. Wars Md. Culver. 1940. MHS; DAR.
Price Family and other Gunpowder Friends. Death notices; photos. of newsp. clipp. MHS.
Purnell family tree. MHS.
Pusey-Hopkins and allied families. G. Cope.
Rec. of Stepney Parish. MHS; DAR.
Mrs. Renshaw chart. MHS.
St. Paul's Parish, Balto. V. 1, 2, 4. Mss. MHS.
Sarah Smith Hood Bible rec. Ms. MHS.
Some col. ancestors of Johns Hopkins. Miles White, Jr. Repr. from Pub. South. Hist. Assoc., Nov., 1900, v. 4, no. 6, pp. 395–442. MHS.
Somerset Co. Court Book. Tilghman. 1937. Ms. DAR.
South. Quakers and slavery. Weeks. 1896. MHS; DAR.
Stump family of Cecil and Harford Cos. Pamph. MHS.
Thomas Book. Thomas. Pp. 346–58. Lib. Cong.; MHS.
Thomas-Chew-Lawrence. Thomas. MHS.
Turner family. Forman. P. 52. MHS.
Mrs. Sara E. White chart. MHS.
See Ford-Hopkins.
Hopkins, Anne Arundel Co., Chart, photos., 1 sheet. Cary Geneal. Coll. Ms. MHS.
S. G. Hopkins chart. MHS.
Hopkins, Miss Elizabeth Corbin. Chart. Col. Dames, Chap. I. MHS.
Mrs. A. H. Renshaw chart. MHS.
Hopkins, Granville Bowdle. Pedigree. Soc. Col. Wars Md. Culver. 1940. MHS; DAR.
†**Hopkins, Johns** (1795–1873). Balto. Amer., June 16, 1883, p. 2, col. 3. Newsp. clipp. Enoch Pratt Lib.
†Balto., hist. and biog. Richardson and Bennett. 1871, pp. 299–304. MHS; DAR.
†Biog. encyc. of rep. men of Md. and D. C., 1879, pp. 682–83.
†Geneal. and mem. encyc. of Md. Spencer. V. 2, pp. 337–41. MHS; DAR.
†Hist. of Balto. City and Co. Scharf. P. 231. MHS.
†Hullabaloo, Johns Hopkins Univ., 1890, pp. 18–20.
Kinsey family; supplementary data on ancestors of Johns Hopkins. South. Hist. Assoc., 1901, v. 5, no. 4, p. 300.
†Natl. cyc. of Amer. biog., v. 5, p. 169.
Phila. Bible rec., 1742–1832. Md. Geneal. Rec. Com., 1929, v. 3, p. 67–68. DAR.
†(Born in Anne Arundel Co., 1795; died in 1873.) Silhouette. Helen Hopkins Thom. 1929. MHS; DAR.

Some col. ancestors. Miles White, Jr. Pub. South. Hist. Assoc., 1900, v. 4, no. 6, pp. 395, 442; 1901, v. 5, p. 300.
*Southern Hist. Assoc., 1900, v. 4.
South. Quakers and slavery. Weeks. 1896. MHS; DAR.
***Hopkins, R. Brooke.** Burke's landed gentry. 1939. MHS.
Hopkins, Samuel Gover. Chart. Gilbert Cope. Photos. MHS.
***Hopkins Family.** Arch. of Georgetown Univ., Wash., D. C., v. 274, no. 6.
*Early marriages in U. S. W. M. Clemens. 1916.
Hopkins-Ford. Abr. Compend. Amer. Geneal. Virkus. V. 4, p. 287. MHS.
Hopkins-Johns. W. deC. Poultney pedigree chart. Soc. Col. Wars, Md. Johnston. 1905. p. 86. MHS.
Hopkins, Husband, Johns, Sharp and Webster families. B. B. Browne. Bd. ms. MHS.
Hopkins-Johns-Kinsey. G. M. Sharp pedigree chart, plate 2. Soc. Col. Wars, Md. Johnston. 1905, p. 92. MHS.
Hopkins-Kinsey-Baker. Hopkins-Kinsey-Baker families of Md. Miles White, Jr. Pub. by S. Hist. Assoc., Nov., 1900–Nov., 1901. MHS.
Hopkinson. St. Paul's Parish, Balto. V. 2, 4. Mss. MHS.
Hopkinson, Phila. Col. and Revolutionary families of Phila. Jordan. 1933, v. 1, pp. 22–86.
†**Hopkinson, Francis.** Biog. sketch. C. R. Hildebarn. Phila., 1878. MHS.
Hopkinson Family. Geneal. of McKean family of Pa. Buchanan. P. 149. MHS.
Hopkinson Family, Phila. Col. and Revolutionary families of Pa. Jordan. 1932, v. 4, pp. 3–49.
Hopper. Cary Geneal. Coll. Ms. MHS.
Geneal. of Henrietta Chauncy Wilson. Upshur. Bk. of photos. MHS.
Hynson chart. Cary Geneal. Coll. Ms. MHS.
Md. families. Culver. Ms. Personal list.
Nicholson-Hynson-Noel chart. Cary Geneal. Coll. Ms. MHS.
Pedigree of John Philemon Paca. Soc. Col. Wars Md. Culver. 1940. MHS; DAR.
Hopper, Col. Wm., Queen Anne Co. W. A. and S. W. Merritt pedigree charts, plate 2. Soc. Col. Wars, Md. Johnston. 1905, pp. 68, 147. MHS.
Hopper Family, East. Shore of Md. Chart. P. G. Skirven. Photos. of mss. MHS.
Hord. Hord family of Va. A. H. Hord. Supplement to Hord family. M. H. Mag., 1915, v. 10, p. 398.
†**Horine.** Hist. of Frederick Co. Williams. MHS; DAR.
Horn. *See* Horne.
Hornberger-Menges-Rahn-Yingling Families. With geneal. C. J. Rahn. 1930. Bd. ms. MHS.
Horne, Horn. St. Paul's Parish, Balto. V. 2. Mss. MHS.
Horner. St. Paul's Parish, Balto. V. 2. Mss. MHS.
Whiting-Little-Horner-Brown. Va. families. MHS.
See Macpherson-Horner.
Horner-Brown Families. Blair-Banister-Braxton families. Horner. Pp. 209–57. MHS.
Horney. Abr. Compend. Amer. Geneal. Virkus. V. 4, p. 638. MHS.
†**Horsay.** Med. Annals Md. Cordell. 1903. P. 443.
Horsefoot. St. Paul's Parish, Balto. V. 2. Mss. MHS.
Horseman. Somerset Co. Court Book. Tilghman. 1937. Ms. DAR.
Horsey. Barroll in Great Britain and Amer Barroll. P. 82. MHS.
Bible rec., 1832–36. Md. Geneal. Rec. Com., 1938–39, p. 217. Mss. DAR.
Col. families of U. S. A. Mackenzie. V. 1. MHS; DAR.
See Munoz. Abr. Compend. Amer. Geneal. Virkus. V. 1, p. 627. DAR.
Old Somerset. Torrence. MHS; DAR.
Pedigree of Wm. Parke Custis Munoz. Soc. Col. Wars Md. Culver. 1940. MHS; DAR.
Pocomoke Pres. churchyard, Worcester Co., Hudson. Bd. ms. MHS; DAR.
Shrewsbury churchyard, Kent Co. Md. O. R. Soc., v. 2, pp. 46–54. MHS.
Somerset Co. Court Book. Tilghman. 1937. Ms. DAR.
*The Sun, Balto., July 23, 30, 1905.
Taliaferro family, Va. Tyler's Quart. Mag., v. 11, pp. 241–51.
Turner Geneal. Coll. Ms. MHS.
Horsey-Keene. Bible rec. Upper Penins. East. Shore, pp. 167–76. MHS; DAR.
Horton. Balto., its hist., its people. Hall. V. 3. MHS; DAR.
†Med. Annals Md. Cordell. 1903, p. 443. MHS.
Horwitz. Chart, family tree or maternal ancestors of Carolyn Norris Horwitz; arms. Printed. MHS.
†Med. Annals Md. Cordell. 1903, p. 443. MHS.
*The Sun, Balto., April 30, 1905.
Horwitz, Caroline Norris. Amer. Armory and Blue Bk. Matthews. 1908, p. 227. DAR.
Hosier, Calvert Co. (1663). Chart, photos., 2 sheets. Cary Geneal. Coll. Ms. MHS.
Hosier, Kent Co. Ellicott-King chart. MHS.
Hosier Line, Kent Co. W. A. and S. W. Merritt pedigree charts, plate 1. Soc. Col. Wars, Md. Johnston. 1905, pp. 67, 147. MHS.
Hoskin, Philip, Conn. Pedigree of Garner Wood Denmead. Soc. Col. Wars Md. Culver. 1940. MHS; DAR.
Hoskins. Children of Alex P. and M. C. Hill. Ms. MHS.
Christ P. E. Church cemetery, Cambridge. Steele. 1936. MHS; DAR.
*Semmes Geneal. Coll. Ms. MHS.
St. Paul's Parish, Balto. V. 2. Mss. MHS.
***Hosmer.** Geneal. G. L. Hosmer. 1928. MHS; DAR.
See Barney-Hosmer.
Hostetter-Dupuy. Chart. Dupuy family. Dupuy. P. 120. MHS.
Hostetter Family, Pa. Dupuy family. Dupuy. Pp. 121–28. MHS.
Hotchkiss. St. Paul's Parish, Balto. V. 2. Mss. MHS.
Houck. Col. families of U. S. A. Mackenzie. V. 7, p. 309. MHS; DAR.

***Houck.** Frederick Co. families. Markell. Ms. Personal list.
Frederick Co. tombstone inscriptions. Gruder. Natl. Geneal. Soc. Quart., 1919, v. 8, nos. 1, 2.
†Med. Annals Md. Cordell. 1903, p. 444. MHS.
Pedigree of Charles Thomas Holloway. Soc. Col. Wars Md. Culver. 1940. MHS; DAR.
Houck, G. Wesley. Md. Soc., War of 1812, v. 4, no. 331. Ms. MHS.
Houck, H. E. Md. Soc., War of 1812, v. 4, no. 332. Ms. MHS.
Houck-Quynn. Lineage Bks., Natl. Soc. of Daughters of Amer. Col., v. 2, p. 186. MHS; DAR.
***Hough.** Boyd family. Boyd. DAR.
Hough family of Bucks Co., Pa. MHS.
Laytonsville M. E. churchyard, Montgomery Co. Md. Geneal. Rec. Com., 1934-35, p. 69. Mss. DAR.
Hough, Frederick Co. Col. families of Amer. Lawrence. V. 15, p. 168. MHS.
Hough, Worcester Co. Ellicott-Campbell chart. MHS.
Hough, J. E. Md. Soc., War of 1812, v. 1, no. 25. Ms. MHS.
Hough, Pliney Miles. Md. Soc., War. of 1812, v. 1, no. 133. Ms. MHS.
***Hough Family.** Early Hough families of Buck's Co., Pa. W. I. Hough. Repr. for author, 1935. MHS.
Hough Family, Bucks Co., Pa. Ms. MHS.
Houghland. St. Paul's Parish, Balto. V. 2. Mss. MHS.
Houghton. Somerset Co. Court Book. Tilghman. 1937. Ms. DAR.
St. Paul's Parish, Balto. V. 2. Mss. MHS
Houghton, Ira Holden. Pedigree. Soc. Col. Wars Md. Culver. 1904. MHS; DAR.
Md. Soc., War of 1812, v. 3, no. 207. Ms. MHS.
Houlston. Lloyd family hist. of Wales, Pa., and Md. DAR.
***House.** Frederick Co. families. Markell. Ms. Personal list.
Frederick Co. tombstone inscriptions. Gruder. Natl. Geneal. Soc. Quart., 1919, v. 8, nos. 1, 2.
***Houseman.** Houseman family of Westmoreland Co., Pa. H. H. Frazier. 1937. DAR.
Houser, West. Md. and through. See Aderton. Abr. Compend. Amer. Geneal. Virkus. V. 1, p. 899. DAR.
Housman. Peale Geneal. Coll. Ms. MHS.
Houston. Butler-Houston-Ellicott family Bibles. DAR.
Cannon - Riley - Truitt - Houston - Kollock - Stow families. Stow. Ms. MHS.
*Editorials. The Sun, Balto. MHS.
*Houston family from Scotland to Somerset Co., Md., 1668. Mrs. Ida M. Shirk. Typed, bd., 10 pp. MHS; DAR.
Patriotic Md. Md. Soc. of S. A. R., 1930. MHS; DAR.
St. Paul's churchyard, Kent Co. Md. O. R. Soc. Bull., no. 2, pp. 54-65. MHS.
Turner Geneal. Coll. Ms. MHS.
See Huston.
Houston, Kent Co. Manning chart. MHS.
Mrs. E. W. Poe chart. MHS.
***Houston,** Monongalia. W. Va. Hist. Mag., v. 3, no. 4, pp. 281-85.
Houston Family. Ms. DAR.
Hist.; from Scotland to Somerset Co. (now Worcester Co.), 1668. Elissa Houston, Springfield, Ohio, and R. R. Sweet, geneal., Wash., D. C. Bd. ms. MHS.
*Old Kent. Hanson. P. 99. MHS; DAR.
Hovington. Rec. of Stepeney Parish. MHS; DAR.
Howard. Amer. Armory and Blue Book. Matthews. 1911-12, p. 200.
†Amer. Biog. Dict. W. Allen. P. 472.
Amer. Clan Gregor Year Book, 1924, p. 26. MHS; DAR.
Abr. Compend. Amer. Geneal. Virkus. V. 4, p. 665, MHS; v. 6, pp. 40, 656. DAR.
†Amer. Cyc. Ripley and Dana. V. 9, p. 19.
Ances. rec. and portraits. Col. Dames of Amer., 1910, v. 2, pp. 495, 630, 776. MHS; DAR.
Bantz geneal. notes. Ms. MHS.
†Bench and bar of Md. Sams and Riley. 1901, v. 2, p. 637. Lib. Cong.; MHS; Peabody Lib.
Bible rec., Rehoboth, East. Shore of Md. Md. Geneal. Bull., v. 2, p. 18. MHS; DAR.
†Biog. cyc. of rep. men of Md. and D. C. Pp. 343, 362 (John Eager Howard). MHS; DAR.
†Biog. Dict. of Amer. Congress, 1774-1903. Engart. P. 607.
†Biog. Dict. of U. S. J. H. Lamb Co., v. 6, p. 184.
Bond chart. MHS.
Brice-Govane Howard tombstone inscriptions. Ms. MHS.
Britton chart. MHS.
Brooks chart. MHS.
H. D. G. Carroll Ms. Book. In H. F. Thompson Papers. MHS.
Carton chart. MHS.
Chart, photos. Cary Geneal. Coll. Ms. MHS.
Col. families of Amer. Lawrence. V. 2, p. 44; v. 5, p. 91; v. 16, pp. 89, 95 (Matthew). MHS.
Col. families of U. S. A. Mackenzie. V. 1, pp. 266-70; v. 7, pp. 55, 60, 175. MHS; DAR.
See Courtenay. Abr. Compend. Amer. Geneal. Virkus. V. 1, p. 568. DAR.
Data. Md. Geneal. Rec. Com., 1933-34, p. 24. Mss. DAR.
Darby geneal. Darby. MHS.
Descendants of Col. Thomas White. Morris. MHS.
Descent of Lottie Repp Caldwell, from William the Conqueror. D. C. Geneal. Rec. Com., v. 34, pp. 30-33. Typed, bd. DAR.
Dorsey and allied families. Ms. MHS.
Dorsey chart. MHS.
Dorsey chart. Lib. Cong.; MHS.
Duckett chart. MHS.
Eldridge chart. MHS.
"Fairview," home of Gov. Oden Bowie, near Bowie, Prince George Co. Private burying ground, 1745-1904. Ms. MHS; DAR.
Family of John Eager Howard. William and Mary Quart., 1st series, v. 9, p. 189.
First families of Md. The Post, Balto., Feb. 2, 3, 4, 6, 7, 8, 1933. Newsp. clipp., bd. MHS.
Ford and other lines. Md. Geneal. Rec. Com., 1932-33, pp. 7-20. Mss. DAR.
*Founders of Anne Arundel and Howard Cos. Warfield. Pp. 67-77, 240 (Gov. John Eager), 267 (Gov. George), 385-89, 410-411, 435-36. MHS; DAR.

*Frederick Co. families. Markell. Ms. Personal list.
Freeman family. Col. and Revolutionary families of Phila. Jordan. 1933, v. 1, pp. 323–28.
Garrison Church. Allen. Pp. 131–34. MHS; DAR.
Geneal. notes. Md. Geneal. Rec. Com., 1937. DAR.
*Gilmor chart. Ms. MHS.
Robert Gilmor chart. MHS.
Gilpin chart. MHS.
Gist chart. Cary Geneal. Coll. Ms. MHS.
Griffith Geneal. Griffith. MHS; DAR.
Matthew Howard Line and Samuel Howard Line. Britton Scrap Book. V. 1, 2. Ms. MHS.
Hist. graves of Md. and D. C. Ridgely. MHS.
†Hist. of Balto. City and Co. Scharf. P. 862. MHS.
Hood family Bible rec. Pamph. MHS.
Howard family. Charles Howard. Ms. MHS.
*John Eager Howard, reprint from Baltimore Gazette, Oct. 15, 1827. The Sun, Balto., 1863, memorial, 8 pp. MHS.
*Howard lineage. G. C. Weaver. Cincinnati, Ohio, Powell & White, 1929. MHS.
Mrs. B. S. Johnston chart. MHS.
Mrs. J. F. Lee chart. MHS.
*Lineage Bk. Daughters of Amer. Colonists., v. 2, pp. 226–27; v. 3, pp. 240–41; v. 4, pp. 97, 304. MHS; DAR.
Lloyd family hist. of Wales, Pa., and Md. DAR.
M. H. Mag., 1939, v. 34, no. 3, p. 304.
Md. families. Culver. Ms. Personal list.
‡Medallic hist. of U. S. Loubat. (Short sketch of John Eager Howard, pp. 10, 48–49; inscription on medal given in Congress Mar. 9, 1781, p. 40.) 1880. MHS.
†Med. Annals Md. Cordell. 1903, pp. 444–45. MHS.
No Name Mag., v. 2, pp. 142–57. MHS.
*Notes. M. H. Mag., Sept., 1936, v. 31, no. 3, p. 254.
Mrs. E. N. Morison chart. MHS.
Owings Bible rec. Ms. MHS.
Patriotic Md. Md. Soc. of S. A. R., 1930. MHS; DAR.
Pedigree of Rev. James Mitchell Magruder. Soc. Col. Wars Md. Culver. 1940. MHS; DAR.
Pedigree of Tilghman Goldsborough Pitts. Soc. Col. Wars Md. Culver. 1940. MHS; DAR.
Pedigree of Andrew Jackson Young, Jr. Soc. Col. Wars Md. Culver. 1940. MHS; DAR.
*Pennington Papers. Ms. MHS.
Poem copied from Balto. Gazette, Oct. 15, 1827, written upon death of Col. John Eager Howard. M. H. Mag., 1934, v. 29, p. 258.
*Progenitors of Howards of Md., John Eager Howard; Joshua Howard, Balto. Co., Margaretta (Peggy) Oswald Chew Howard; Matthew Howard, Anne Arundel Co. Henry Ridgely Evans. Sold by W. H. Lowdermilk & Co., Washington, D. C., 1938, 20 pp. MHS; DAR.
Progenitors of Howards of Md. Evans. 1938. Review in M. H. Mag., June, 1938, v. 33, no. 2, pp. 205–07.
St. Paul's Parish, Balto. V. 1, 2, 3, 4. Mss. MHS.
St. Thomas Parish, Balto. Co. Bd. ms. MHS. Also: Md. Geneal. Rec. Com., 1937, pp. 109–82. Mss. DAR.
Sater geneal. Bd. Ms. MHS.
Semmes and allied families. Semmes. MHS.
*Semmes Geneal. Coll. Ms. MHS.
Side lights on Md. hist. Richardson. V. 2, p. 145. MHS; DAR.
Mrs. Edw. Simpson chart. MHS.
Sarah Smith Hood Bible rec. Ms. MHS.
Sir George Yeardley. Upshur. Pp. 15, 33. MHS.
Some notable families of south. States. Armstrong. V. 1, pp. 100–19. DAR.
Somerset Co. Court Book. Tilghman. 1937. Ms. DAR.
Southern Bapt. Church cemetery, Worcester Co. Md. Geneal. Rec. Com., 1937, Mrs. Lines. Mss. DAR.
Talbott of "Poplar Knowle." Shirk. MHS; DAR.
The Day, Feb. 22, 1883. Newsp. clipp. Scrap Book. MHS.
*The Sun, Balto., Jan. 17, 1904; March 5, (Va.), May 28, June 11, 18, July 30, 1905; Oct. 2, 21 (Va. and Md.), 1906.
Turner Geneal. Coll. Ms. MHS.
Mrs. E. C. Venable chart. MHS.
Warfields of Md. Warfield. MHS.
Welsh-Hyatt and kindred. Welsh. Sec. 1, p. 144. MHS; DAR.
*Wicomico Co. families. Tilghman. Ms., pp. 51, 88–90, 97, 120, 124. DAR.
See Brown-Howard.
See Burchinal-Howard.
See Ford-Dorsey-Hyland, etc.
See Mounts-Howard.
See Phillips-Howard.
See Welsh-Riggs-Howard.
See Wimbrough-Dashiell-Howard.
Howard, Anne Arundel Co. Pedigree of Francis Joseph Baldwin. Soc. Col. Wars Md. Culver. 1940. MHS; DAR.
Howard, Belvidere. Thomas Book. Thomas. Pp. 362–64; Lib. Cong.; MHS.
Howard, Charles Co. and Va. Chart, photos., 2 sheets. Cary Geneal. Coll. Ms. MHS.
Howard, Md. and Va. Md. Geneal. Rec. Com., 1933–34, pp. 73–80. Mss. DAR.
Howard, Pa. and Md. Howard-Montague-Warfield geneal. chart. Culver and Marye. MHS.
Howard, Beale. Will. Will Book, 2. Orphan Court, Alexandria. Mss. DAR.
Howard, Benj. Some notable families of south. States. Armstrong. V. 1, pp. 108–10. DAR.
†**Howard, Benj. Chew.** Appleton's Cyc. Wilson and Fiske. 1888, v. 3, p. 276.
Thomas Book. Thomas. Pp. 362, 364. Lib. Cong.; MHS.
Howard, Charles Morris. Pedigree. Soc. Col. Wars Md. Culver. 1940. MHS; DAR.
Howard, Ernest. Md. Soc., War of 1812, v. 1, no. 22. Ms. MHS.
Howard, Mrs. G. H. (nee Magill). Abr. Compend. Amer. Geneal. Virkus. V. 1, p. 381. DAR.
†**Howard, George.** Governors of Md. Buchholz. P. 114. MHS.
Howard-Glenn. Bible rec. Upper Penins. East. Shore, p. 121–34. MHS; DAR.

Howard, John Duvall. Pedigree. Soc. Col. Wars Md. Culver. 1940. MHS; DAR.
†Howard, Col. John Eager. Appleton's Cyc. 1887, v. 3, p. 277.
†Balto., hist. and biog. Richardson and Bennett. 1871, pp. 305–08. MHS; DAR.
†Chronicles of Balto. Scharf. 1874, p. 423. MHS; DAR.
Clark chart. MHS.
De Ford chart. MHS.
†Governors of Md. Buchholz. P. 26. MHS.
†Hist. of Md. Scharf. V. 2, p. 398. MHS.
†John Eager Howard, Belvedere of Balto. Crocker. D. A. R. Mag., v. 73, no. 10, pp. 48–51.
Life and portrait. Sketches of Natl. Portrait Gallery of Distinguished Amer. Longacre and Herring. V. 2, p. 14.
†Mag. Amer. Hist., v. 7. MHS.
(1752–1827). Line 1665–1904. Md. Geneal. Rec. Com., 1937, pp. 37–39. Mss. DAR.
†M. H. Mag., v. 12, p. 222.
†Memoirs of generals. T. Wyatt. Pp. 70–78. MHS.
†Monumental city. Howard. Pp. 507–10.
Portrait. Chester Hardinge, painter. E. Pruhomme, engraver. MHS.
†Real stories from Balto. Co. Hist. Davidson. 1917.
Rec. of This Gallant Marylander. Newsp. clipp. MHS.
(Revolutionary soldier). St. Paul's P. E. graveyard. Patriotic Marylander, v. 2, no. 4, pp. 54–60. MHS; DAR.
†Sages and heroes of Amer. Revolution. Judson. P. 439.
†(1752–1827). See biog. file in Md. Room, Enoch Pratt Lib.
Sketch and portrait. Monumental City. Howard. Pp. 507–10. MHS; DAR.
†Sketches of "Fermit's Howard" (containing fine view of monument). (John Eager Howard born Belvedere Balto. Co., June 4, 1752; son of Cornelius and Ruth (Eager) Howard; died Oct. 12, 1827; married Margaret Chew, Phila., May 18, 1787.) Address by Daniel Colt Gilman. MHS.
†Sketch with small cut. Biog. Dict. of U. S. Lamb. V. 4, p. 188.
Howard, Joshua. Ances. rec. and portraits. Col. Dames of Amer., 1910, v. 2, p. 495. MHS; DAR.
Howard, Matthew. Some notable families of south. States. Armstrong. V. 1, pp. 103–05. DAR.
Howard, Matthew II. Md. Geneal. Rec. Com., 1933–34, p. 69. Mss. DAR.
Howard, McHenry. Balto., its hist., its people. Hall. V. 3, pp. 508–16. MHS; DAR.
Pedigree chart, plates 1 and 2. Soc. Col. Wars, Md. Johnston. 1905, pp. 41–42. MHS.
Howard, Robert. Glendy churchyard. Patriotic Marylander, v. 2, no. 4, pp. 54–60. MHS; DAR.
***Howard, Thomas.** Brasses of Thomas Howard, Second Duke of Norfolk, and Agnes, his wife, 1524. MHS.
Howard, Thomas Cornelius. Will, Jan. 20, 1801. D. C. Geneal. Rec. Com., 1937–38, v. 35, pp. 14–18. Typed, bd. DAR.
Howard, Capt. Vachel D., Va. and Md. M. H. Mag., 1936, v. 31, no. 3, p. 254.
***Howard, Wm. Ross.** Burke's landed gentry. 1939. P. 3003. MHS.
Howard, Wm. T. Balto., its hist., its people. Hall. V. 2, p. 93. MHS; DAR.
Howard, Wm. Travis. Abr. Compend. Amer. Geneal. Virkus. V. 1, p. 382. DAR.
Howard, Mrs. Wm. Travis. Barton charts. MHS.
(Rebecca Williams). Chart. Col. Dames, Chapt. I. MHS.
Howard, Mrs. Wm. Travis, Jr. (May Cushing Williams). Chart. Col. Dames, Chap. I. MHS.
Howard Family. Ab. of wills, Anne Arundel and Charles Cos. Md. Geneal. Rec. Com., 1934–35, pp. 145–47. Mss. DAR.
*Anne Arundel Co. gentry. Newman. Pp. 237–308. MHS; DAR.
Discovery of coat of arms. F. B. Culver. William and Mary Quart., 1st series, v. 26, p. 125.
The Day, Annapolis, Feb. 22, 1883.
Howard Family, Balto. Co. (1665–1897). Md. Geneal. Rec. Com., 1933–34, p. 185. Mss. DAR.
Howard Family, Charles and Anne Arundel Cos. Abstracts of wills. Md. Geneal. Rec. Com., 1934–35, p. 134. DAR.
***Howard (John Eager) Family.** Old Kent. Hanson. Pp. 40–48. MHS; DAR.
William and Mary Quart., 1901, v. 9. MHS.
Howard (Matthew) Family, Va. and Md. (1630–1891). Md. Geneal. Rec. Com., 1933–34, p. 186. Mss. DAR.
Howard Line. Col. and Revolutionary families of Pa. Amer. Hist. Soc., N. Y., 1934, p. 365.
Howard-Dorsey-Boone. Welsh-Hyatt and kindred. Supplement. Welsh. P. 19. MHS; DAR.
Howard-Govane-Woodward-Law. Bible rec. Ms. MHS.
Howard-Hammond Families, Anne Arundel Co. Armorial seals. F. B. Culver. M. H. Mag., 1917, v. 12, p. 198.
Howard-Hilton. Notes. D. A. R. Mag., v. 72, no. 3, p. 71.
Howard-Montague-Warfield. Geneal. chart. Francis B. Culver and Wm. B. Marye. Ancestral background of Bessie Wallis Warfield Simpson (Duchess of Windsor). Mss. MHS. Also pub. in Southern Spectator, 1937.
Howard-Wood-Baker-Gilmer. William and Mary Quart., 1st series, v. 6, p. 94.
Howe. Abr. Compend. Amer. Geneal. Virkus. V. 4, p. 612. MHS.
†Howell. Biog. cyc. of rep. men of Md. and D. C. P. 172. MHS; DAR.
Jones family, Bible rec. Frederick Co. Ms. MHS.
†Med. Annals Md. Cordell. 1903, pp. 445–46. MHS.
Memorials of Reading, Howell, Yerkes, Latham and Elkins families. Leach.
St. Paul's Parish, Balto. V. 2. Mss. MHS.
Howes. Mt. Carmel burial ground, Unity, Montgomery Co. Md. Geneal. Rec. Com., 1934–35, p. 85. Mss. DAR.
***Howland.** Howland Quart. Pub. by The Pilgrim John Howland Soc. MHS.
Howland, Mrs. Frederick Hoppin (Ellen Swan Dobbin). Chart. Col. Dames, Chap. I. MHS.
Howlett Family. Ms. MHS.

Hoxton. See Randolph. Abr. Compend. Amer. Geneal. Virkus. V. 1, p. 17. DAR.
See Sioussat. Abr. Compend. Amer. Geneal. Virkus. V. 1, p. 828. DAR.
Hoye. Paul Hoye Soc., Jan., 20, 1931. (Md. pioneers, 1700.) 4615 18th St., Los Angeles, Cal. MHS.
*Garrett Co. pioneer families. Hoye. MHS; DAR.
Hoye Family. Mountain Democrat, Garrett Co., Nov. 15, 1935. Newsp. clipp. MHS; DAR.
Hoyle. Bible rec., from Bible in possession of Mrs. H. T. Hoyle, Fairilee RR #2, Chestertown. Md. Geneal. Rec. Com., 1937–38, pp. 121–22. Mss. DAR.
Hrapster. Cummings chart. Lib. Cong.; MHS; DAR.
Hubbard. Balto., its hist., its people. Hall. V. 2, p. 198; v. 3, p. 630. MHS; DAR.
*One thousand years of Hubbard hist., 866–1895. E. W. Day. Hubbard, Md., pp. 347–50. Pub. by H. P. Hubbard, G. W. Rogers & Co., N. Y., 1895. MHS.
Hubbard, Wilbur Ross. Pedigree. Soc. Col. Wars Md. Culver. 1940. MHS; DAR.
Hubbard-Gould. Abr. Compend. Amer. Geneal. Virkus. V. 4, p. 668. MHS.
Hubbell. All Hallow's P. E. churchyard, Snow Hill, Worcester Co. Hudson. Bd. Ms. MHS; DAR. Also: Md. Geneal. Rec. Com., 1935–36, p. 24. Mss. DAR.
*History of Hubbell family and geneal. rec. W. Hubbell. Incl. Hubbell of Md., pp. 337, 419–420. N. Y., J. H. Hubbell Co., 1881, 1st ed. MHS.
Huber. *See* Hoover.
Huber (Hoover). Rec.; origin and ancestry. Natl. Geneal. Soc. Quart., v. 15, no. 1, pp. 2–4; v. 17, no. 1, pp. 6–8, 19–24, 53–56; v. 23, no. 4, p. 110.
Huber-Hoover, Switzerland and Pa. Pub. Geneal. Soc. Pa., v. 12, no. 3, p. 223.
***Huber-Hoover Family.** Hist. H. W. Hoover. 1928. DAR.
†**Hubner, John.** Men of mark in Md. Johnson. V. 4. DAR; Enoch Pratt Lib.
Huchinson. St. Stephens Parish, Cecilton, Md. MHS; DAR.
Huckin, Hukin. St. Stephens Parish, Cecilton, Md. MHS; DAR.
Huddle-Newcomer. Abr. Compend. Amer. Geneal. Virkus. V. 4, p. 294. DAR.
Huddleson, James Howard, Jr. Md. Soc., War of 1812, v. 3, no. 240. Ms. MHS.
Hudgell. St. Thomas' Parish, Balto. Co. Bd. ms. MHS. Also: Md. Geneal. Rec. Com., 1937, pp. 109–82. Mss. DAR.
Hudson. All Hallow's P. E. churchyard, Snow Hill, Worcester Co. Hudson. Bd. Ms. MHS; DAR. Also: Md. Geneal. Rec. Com., 1935–36, p. 24. Mss. DAR.
Lloyd - Pemberton - Hutchinson - Hudson - Parke families. Glenn. MHS; DAR.
Rehobeth P. E. churchyard, Somerset Co. Md. Geneal. Rec. Com., 1937, Mrs. Lines. Mss. DAR.
St. Paul's P. E. churchyard, Berlin, Worcester Co. Hudson. Bd. ms. MHS; DAR. Also: Md. Geneal. Rec. Com., 1937, Mrs. Lines. Mss. DAR.
St. Paul's Parish, Balto. V. 2, 4. Mss. MHS.
St. Thomas' Parish, Balto. Co. Bd. ms. MHS. Also: Md. Geneal. Rec. Com., 1937, pp. 109–82. Mss. DAR.
*The Sun, Balto., Jan. 21, 1906.
See Huttson.
†**Huffer.** Hist. of Frederick Co. Williams. MHS; DAR.
Huffington. Rec. of Stepney Parish. MHS; DAR.
*Wicomico Co. families. Tilghman. Ms., p. 27. DAR.
Wicomico Co. families. Bible rec. Ms. DAR.
Hufner (Heffner)-King. Bible rec., Pa., and Leitersburg, Md. Natl. Geneal. Soc. Quart., v. 24, p. 15.
Hughes. Abr. Compend. Amer. Geneal. Virkus. V. 6, p. 642. DAR.
Armistead family of Va. Appleton. 1899, pamph. Lib. Cong.; MHS.
Balch chart. MHS.
Bible rec. Ms. MHS.
Dorsey and allied families. Ms. MHS.
*Frederick Co. families. Markell. Ms. Personal list.
Geneal. notes of Chamberlaine family. MHS.
Geneal. of family of Gideon Gilpin. MHS.
Harford Co. Hist. Soc. Mss. Coll. JHU.
†Hist. of Frederick Co. Williams. MHS; DAR.
†Hist. of Washington Co. Williams. 1906, v. 1, p. 247. MHS; DAR.
†Hist. of West. Md. Scharf. V. 2, pp. 1011–12. MHS; DAR.
See Hope. Abr. Compend. Amer. Geneal. Virkus. V. 1, p. 924. DAR.
*Hughes family hist., contains Dalton, Henderson, Martin, all originally from Va. and many kindred branches. L. Henderson Horton. Franklin, Tenn., Press of the News, 1922. MHS.
Lehr chart. MHS.
W. T. Manning pedigree chart. Soc. Col. Wars, Md. Johnston. 1905, p. 65. MHS.
Md. families. Culver. Ms. Personal list.
†Med. Annals Md. Cordell. 1903, p. 446. MHS.
†Men of mark in Md. Johnson. V. 4. DAR; Enoch Pratt Lib.
M. E. Church South cemetery, near Poolesville, Montgomery Co. Md. Geneal. Rec. Com., 1926. Mss. DAR.
My family memoirs. T. Hughes. Balto., King Bros., 1st ed. 1880; 2nd ed., 1813; 3rd ed., 1931, MHS; 1931, DAR.
Orme geneal. chart. MHS.
Patriotic Md. Md. Soc. of S. A. R., 1930. MHS; DAR.
Plummer family. A. P. H. Ms. MHS.
Rec. of Stepney Parish. MHS; DAR.
Rehobeth P. E. churchyard, Somerset Co. Md. Geneal. Rec. Com., 1937, Mrs. Lines. Mss. DAR.
St. Mary's churchyard, Tyaskin, Md. Md. Geneal. Rec. Com., 1938–39, pp. 187–92. Mss. DAR.
St. Paul's Parish, Balto. V. 1, 2, 3, 4. Mss. MHS.
St. Stephens Parish, Cecilton, Md. MHS; DAR.
Turner Geneal. Coll. Ms. MHS.
*Wicomico Co. families. Tilghman. Ms., p. 16. DAR.
Mrs. G. H. Williams, Jr., chart. MHS.

Hughes, Adrian. Md. Soc., War of 1812, v. 4, no. 320. Ms. MHS.

†**Hughes, Christopher.** Hist. of Md. Scharf. V. 3, pp. 136–37. MHS.

Hughes, Jane (signed Hughis), Balto. Co. Will probated Oct. 31, 1765. D. A. R. Mag., v. 65, no. 8, p. 506.

Hughes, Thomas, Cecil Co. Abr. Compend. Amer. Geneal. Virkus. V. 1, p. 393. DAR.

Hughes, Wm., Md. Revolutionary soldiers buried in northwest S. C. Natl. Geneal. Soc. Quart., v. 21, no. 2, p. 50.

Hughett, Huyett. Hagerstown tombstone inscriptions. Gruder. Natl. Geneal. Soc. Quart., 1919, v. 8, nos. 1, 2.

Hughlett. Bible rec. Ms. MHS.
*Data. H. Adams. Ms. File case, MHS.
Md. Geneal. Bull., v. 6, p. 28. MHS; DAR.
Spring Hill Cemetery, Md. O. R. Soc. Bull., no. 1, pp. 35–41. MHS.
Turner Geneal. Coll. Ms. MHS.
See Adams-Hughlett.

†**Hughlett, Hughletts.** Hist. of Caroline Co. Noble. MHS.

Hughletts. *See* Hughlett.

Hughs. St. Joseph's R. C. churchyard. Md. O. R. Soc. Bull., no. 3, p. 64.

Hughs, Wm. (tavern keeper), Balto. Co. Will probated Jan. 3, 1748. D. A. R. Mag., v. 65, no. 8, p. 505.

***Huidekoper.** Amer. ancestry of Frederick Louis Huidekoper and Reginald Shippen Huidekoper. F. L. Huidekoper. Wash., D. C., 1930. MHS; DAR.
Amer. ancestry of Frederick Louis Huidekoper and Reginald Shippen Huidekoper. F. L. Huidekoper and R. S. Huidekoper. Repr. from Compendium of Amer. Geneal., Virkus, 1930, v. 4, pp. 295–298. Geneva, Switzerland, May, 1931. MHS; DAR.
Amer. branch; contains Stabler-Huidekoper folding chart. F. L. Huidekoper. Switzerland, April 15, 1928, pamph. MHS; DAR.
*Holland branch, 1730–1924. MHS.
Lukens chart. MHS.
N. Y. Geneal. and Biog. Rec., v. 66, p. 183.

Huidekoper, Pa. Abr. Compend. Amer. Geneal. Virkus. V. 1, pp. 393–94. DAR.

Huidekoper Family (1730–1924). Contains geneal. table of Edgar Huidekoper. Meadville, Pa., priv. pr., Hill Home, 1924, pamph. MHS.

Huidekoper - Galloway - Hollingsworth - Shryock-Wallis. Abr. Compend. Amer. Geneal. Virkus. V. 4, p. 295. MHS.

Huie. Col. families of U. S. A. Mackenzie. V. 5. MHS; DAR.

Hukin. *See* Huckin.

Hull. Ances. rec. and portraits. Col. Dames of Amer., 1910, v. 1, p. 292. MHS; DAR.
*Frederick Co. families. Markell. Ms. Personal list.
Md. tombstone rec. Md. Geneal. Records Com., 1937, Parran, pp. 10, 19, 21. Mss. DAR.
Rec. of Stepney Parish. MHS; DAR.
*Rev. Joseph Hull and some of his descendants. Amy L. E. Hull. Balto., 1904. MHS; DAR.
St. Paul's Parish, Balto. V. 1, 2, 3. Mss. MHS.

Hull, Miss Amy Eleanor. Chart. Col. Dames, Chap. I. MHS.

Hull, John Baker Thompson. Pedigree. Soc. Col. Wars Md. Culver. 1940. MHS; DAR.

Hull, Mrs. John Baker Thompson (Louise G. Merrifield Ranstead). Chart. (Mostly New Eng. and N. Y. families.) Col. Dames, Chapt. I. MHS.

Hull, J. R. Abr. Compend. Amer. Geneal. Virkus. V. 1, p. 396. DAR.

Hulse, Wm. B. Md. Soc., War of 1812, v. 1, no. 108. Ms. MHS.

†**Humbertson.** Hist. of Allegany Co. Thomas and Williams. V. 2. MHS; DAR.

†**Humbird.** Hist. of Allegany Co. Thomas and Williams. V. 2. MHS; DAR.
*Humbird family of Lorraine, Hessen and Md. J. W. Humbird. DAR.

***Hume.** Old Kent. Hanson. P. 267. MHS; DAR.

Hume, E. E. Md. Soc., War of 1812, v. 3, no. 247. Ms. MHS.

Humerickhouse. Zion Reformed Church, Hagerstown. Md. Geneal. Rec. Com., 1934–35. Mss. DAR.

Humphrey. St. Paul's Parish, Balto. V. 2. Mss. MHS.

†**Humphreys.** Med. Annals Md. Cordell. 1903, p. 447. MHS.
Page family Bible rec. Ms. MHS.
With collateral branches. Side lights on Md. hist. V. 2, pp. 362–73. MHS; DAR.
See Humphries.

Humphreys-Parsons. Wicomico Co. families. Bible rec. Ms. DAR.

Humphreys-Riley. Wicomico Co. families. Bible rec. Ms. DAR.

Humphreys, Humpries-Collier. Wicomico Co. families. Bible rec. Ms. DAR.

Humphries. Hist. Salisbury, Wicomico Co. Truitt. DAR.
Patriotic Md. Md. Soc. of S. A. R., 1930, MHS; DAR.
Rec. of Stepney Parish. MHS; DAR.
See Humphreys.

***Humphries, Romilly F.** Burke's landed gentry. 1939. MHS.

***Humphries-Pope-Brock-Parker.** Humphries-Pope-Brock-Parker, descendants of Charles Humphries of Va., Nathaniel Pope of Va., Reuben Brock of Ireland and Aaron Parker of Va. J. D. Humphries. DAR.

***Humphries, Humphreys, Umphreys.** Wicomico Co. families. Tilghman. Ms., pp. 21, 28–33, 98–101, 103–04, 106. DAR.

Humphry. Somerset Co. Court Book. Tilghman. 1937. Ms. DAR.

Humpris. Rec. of Stepney Parish. MHS; DAR.

Humrichouse. Hagerstown tombstone inscriptions. Gruder. Natl. Geneal. Soc. Quart., 1919, v. 8, nos. 1, 2.
†Hist. of West. Md. Scharf. V. 2, pp. 1035, 1037–38. MHS; DAR.
†Med. Annals Md. Cordell. 1903, p. 447. MHS.

Humrickhouse. See Beachey. Abr. Compend. Amer. Geneal. Virkus. V. 4, p. 646. MHS.
Rev. Christian Post-Peter Humrickhouse, and some of latter's family. Harry Humrickhouse. 1913. MHS.
*(Peter Humrickhouse, born in York Co., Pa., Oct., 10, 1753, married Mary Post, only daughter of Rev. Christian Post.) Notes and Queries, Egle, 1898, p. 79.

Humrickhouse, Wash. Co. Rev. Christian Frederick Post and Peter Humrickhouse. Humrickhouse. MHS.

Hungerford. Griffith geneal. Griffith. MHS; DAR.
*Hungerford family. C. Johnston. M. H. Mag., 1910, v. 5, pp. 381–85.
Lineage Bk., Order of Washington, p. 145. MHS; DAR.
Md. families. Culver. Ms. Personal list.

Hungerford, Charles Co. Southerland-Latham and allied families. Voorhees. Bd. Ms. MHS.

Hungerford Family, Charles Co. Ms. MHS.

Hunley. St. Paul's Parish, Balto. V. 2. Mss. MHS.

Hunt. Founders of Anne Arundel and Howard Cos. Warfield. P. 529. MHS; DAR.
Geneal. and memorial encyc. of Md. Spencer. 1909, v. 2, p. 691. MHS; DAR.
Hist. graves of Md. and D. C. Ridgely. MHS.
Lloyd family hist. of Wales, Pa., and Md. DAR.
Matthews-Price chart. MHS.
†Med. Annals Md. Cordell. 1903, p. 447. MHS.
St. Paul's Parish, Balto. V. 1, 2. Mss. MHS.

†Hunt, Jesse. Balto., hist. and biog. Richardson and Bennett. 1871, pp. 309–16. MHS; DAR.

Hunt, Thomas. Revolutionary pension abs. Natl. Geneal. Soc. Quart., v. 24, p. 66.

Hunter. Burton ancestry. Ms. MHS.
Col. families of U. S. A. Mackenzie. V. 1, p. 274. MHS; DAR.
Dorsey chart. MHS.
Hist. graves of Md. and D. C. Ridgely. MHS.
Jenkins-Courtney chart. MHS.
St. John's R. C. Church cemetery, Montgomery Co. Md. Geneal. Rec. Com., 1926, p. 27. Mss. DAR.
St. Paul's Parish, Balto. V. 2. Mss. MHS.
Selden chart. MHS.

***Hunter,** Va. The Sun, Balto., Nov. 11, 18, 1906.

Hunter, John. Bible rec., 1817–1922. Bible now in possession of Mrs. C. C. Baden. D. C. Geneal. Rec. Com., 1932–34, v. 10, pp. 3–8. Typed, bd. DAR.

Hunter, Robt. Wade, Prince George Co. Will. D. C. Geneal. Rec. Com., 1932–34, v. 10, pp. 237–45. Typed, bd. DAR.

***Hunter Family.** Rec. Wm. M. Clemens. Pub. by author, ltd. ed., N. Y., 1914. MHS.

Huntingdon. Taney and allied families. Silverson. MHS; DAR.

Hurd. First superintendent of Johns Hopkins Hospital, Henry Mills Hurd. Thomas S. Cullen. Balto., 1920.
†Med. Annals Md. Cordell. 1903, p. 447. MHS.

Hurley. Pattison wills. Md. Geneal. Rec. Com., 1929, pp. 7–42; 1930–31. Mss. DAR.

Hurlock. Blakiston churchyard, Kent Co., Del., near Millington. Md. Geneal. Rec. Com., 1933–34, pp. 204–07. Mss. DAR.
Holdens Cemetery, Kent Co. Md. Geneal. Rec. Com., 1932, v. 5, p. 211. Mss. DAR.
Morris family of Phila. Moon. V. 3, p. 931. MHS.
Pattison wills. Md. Geneal. Rec. Com., 1929, pp. 7–42; 1930–31. Mss. DAR.

Hurst. Abr. Compend. Amer. Geneal. Virkus. V. 1, p. 404. DAR.
Balto., its hist., its people. Hall. V. 2. MHS; DAR.
*Burke's landed gentry. 1939. MHS.
Joshua Dryden Bible rec. Ms. MHS.
Geneal. and memorial encyc. of Md. Spencer. V. 2, p. 498. MHS; DAR.
Md. families. Culver. Ms. Personal list.
Pedigree of Tilghman Vickers Morgan. Soc. Col. Wars Md. Culver. 1940. MHS; DAR.
Purnell family tree. MHS.
St. Paul's Parish, Balto. V. 1, 2. Mss. MHS.

***Hurst, John E.** Geneal. and mem. encyc. of Md. Spencer. V. 2, pp. 498–504. MHS; DAR.
Pedigree. Soc. Col. Wars Md. Culver. 1940. MHS; DAR.

Hurst, Bishop John Fletcher. Bishop John Fletcher Hurst. A. Osborn. N. J., 1905. MHS.
†(Born in Dorchester Co., 1834; died 1902). Md. authors. Steiner. Ms. list., Md. Room, Enoch Pratt Lib.

Hurst, Mrs. John J. (Miriam Eccleston Poe). Chart. Col. Dames, Chap. I. MHS.
Mrs. Edwin Wingate Poe chart. MHS.
Cary Geneal. Coll. Ms. MHS.
Col. families of Amer. Lawrence. V. 7, p. 391. MHS.
Hopkins, Husband, Johns, Sharp and Webster families. Browne. Bd. ms. MHS.
Husband and allied families, Cecil and Harford Cos. Bd. ms. MHS.
Md. families. Culver. Ms. Personal list.
Pedigree of George Webb Constable. Soc. Col. Wars Md. Culver. 1940. MHS; DAR.
*Pennington Papers. Ms. MHS.
G. M. Sharp pedigree chart, plate 2. Soc. Col. Wars, Md. Johnston. 1905, p. 92. MHS.
Washington ancestry and rec. Hoppin. V. 2. MHS; DAR.
See Veazey-Dormott-Husband.

Husband Family. Mallory and allied families. P. 16. Ms. MHS.
Morris family of Phila. Moon. V. 2, pp. 689–92. MHS.

***Husband Lineage.** Arms. The Sun, Balto. Dec. 24, 1905.

Husband, Husbands. St. Stephens Parish, Cecilton, Md. MHS; DAR.

Husband-Price-Haines. Bible rec. Pa. Mag. Hist. and Biog., v. 10, p. 119.

Hush. St. Paul's Parish, Balto. V. 1, 2. Mss. MHS.

Huss. Somerset Co. Court Book. Tilghman. 1937. Ms. DAR.

Hussey (see Sumner). Amer. Armory and Blue Book. Matthews. 1911–12, p. 404.
Md. families. Ms. Personal list.
Maulsby family in Amer. Barnard. DAR; Peabody Lib.
Robins family tree. MHS.
Southern Bapt. Church cemetery, Worcester Co. Md. Geneal. Rec. Com., 1937, Mrs. Lines. Mss. DAR.

†Huston. Med. Annals Md. Cordell. 1903, p. 448. MHS.

Huston, John. Tombstone rec. of Glendy burying ground (vault, 1837). Md. Geneal. Rec. Com. 1933–34, pp. 171–78. Mss. DAR.

***Huston, Houston.** Wicomico Co. families. Tilghman. Ms., pp. 33, 97–98. DAR.

Hutchens. *See* Hanson-Hutchens.

Hutcheson. Makemie Memorial Pres. churchyard, Snow Hill, Worcester Co. Hudson. Bd. ms. MHS; DAR. Also: Md. Geneal. Rec. Com., Mrs. Lines. Mss. DAR.
See Miller family. Focke Geneal. Coll. Mss. MHS.
Hutcheson, Hutchinson. St. Stephens Parish, Cecilton, Md. MHS; DAR.
Hutchins. Black chart. MHS.
Mrs. Charles Carter chart. MHS.
Chart, photos., complete in 1 sheet. Cary Geneal. Coll. Ms. MHS.
Col. families of U. S. A. Mackenzie. V. 6, p. 367. MHS; DAR.
See Ewen-Chew, etc. Lineage Bks., Natl. Soc. of Daughters of Amer. Col., v. 4, p. 269. MHS; DAR.
Four generations of family of Strangeman Hutchins and his wife Elizabeth Cox. G. W. and E. C. Crider. Pamph. MHS; DAR.
†Hist. of Balto. City and Co. Scharf. P. 916. MHS.
Price family and other Gunpowder Friends. Death notices; photos. of newsp. clipp. MHS.
St. Paul's Parish, Balto. V. 1, 2. Mss. MHS.
Miss Kate Steele chart. MHS.
Taney and allied families. Silverson. MHS; DAR.
Mrs. G. H. Williams, Jr., chart. MHS.
Hutchins, Calvert Co. G. N. Mackenzie, pedigree chart, plate 1. Soc. Col. Wars, Md. Johnston. 1905, pp. 61, 147. MHS.
Hutchins Family. Thomas Book. Thomas. P. 371. Lib. Cong.; MHS.
***Hutchins-Cox.** Four generations of family of Strangeman Hutchins and his wife Elizabeth Cox. Old Va. family. Mrs. G. W. Crider and Edw. C. Crider. Pamph. MHS; DAR.
Hutchins-Hicks. Ances. rec. and portraits. Col. Dames of Amer., 1910, v. 2, p. 679. MHS; DAR.
Hutchinson. Hutchinson family of Eng. and New Eng., and connection with Marburys and Drydens. J. L. Chester. New Eng. Hist. Reg., 1866, v. 20, pp. 355–67. MHS.
Lloyd - Pemberton - Hutchinson - Hudson - Parke families. Glenn. MHS; DAR.
*Pennington Papers. Ms. MHS.
St. Paul's Parish, Balto. V. 1, 2. Mss. MHS.
Sweetser chart. MHS.
See Hutcheson.
***Hutchinson-Scott.** Eng. ancestry of Anne Marbury Hutchinson and Katherine Marbury Scott. M. B. Colket. 1936. DAR.
Hutson. St. Paul's Parish, Balto. V. 2. Mss. MHS.
†Huttner. Med. Annals Md. Cordell. 1903, p. 448. MHS.
Hutton. Jackson family gathering. 1878.
Lanahan chart. MHS.
Mamm-Needles-Hambleton families. Needles. P. 109. MHS; DAR.
Mt. Calvary Church burial ground, Cooksville Pike, Montgomery Co. Md. Geneal. Rec. Com., 1934. Mss. DAR.
Mt. Calvary Church burial ground Howard Co. Md. Geneal. Rec. Com., 1934–35, pp. 95–99. Mss. DAR.
St. Paul's Parish, Balto. V. 2. Mss. MHS.
Stones from Bowie Davis place, Montgomery Co. Md. Geneal. Rec. Com., 1934, p. 61. Mss. DAR.
Talbott of "Poplar Knowle." Shirk. MHS; DAR.
Mrs. J. Whitridge Williams chart 1. MHS.
Hutton, Anne Arundel Co. Mrs. Sherlock Swann chart. MHS.
Huttson. Somerset Co. Court Book. Tilghman. 1937. Ms. DAR.
Huttson, Hudson. Old Somerset. Torrence. MHS; DAR.
†Huyett. Hist. of Washington Co. Williams. 1906, v. 2, p. 1236. MHS; DAR.
See Hughett.
Hyatt. Abr. Compend. Amer. Geneal. Virkus. V. 1, p. 792, See Regester. DAR.
M. E. Church South cemetery, near Poolesville, Montgomery Co. Md. Geneal. Rec. Com., 1926. Mss. DAR.
Pedigree of James Dorsey Brown, Jr. Soc. Col. Wars Md. Culver. 1940. MHS; DAR.
St. Paul's Parish, Balto. V. 2. Mss. MHS.
Welsh and Hyatt kin. Supplement to Ancestral Col. families. Welsh. 1932, pamph. MHS; DAR.
Welsh-Hyatt and kindred. Welsh. P. 2, pp. 102–44. MHS; DAR.
See Reynolds-Hyatt.
Hyatt-Todd-Miller. Welsh-Hyatt and kindred. Supplement. Welsh. P. 12. MHS; DAR.
Hyde. Balto., its hist., its people. Hall. V. 2. MHS; DAR.
Col. families of U. S. A. Mackenzie. V. 1; v. 2. DAR; MHS.
Denison family of Mass. to Harford Co. Ms. DAR.
Patriotic Md. Md. Soc. of S. A. R., 1930. MHS; DAR.
Rodgers Bible rec. Ms. MHS.
Hyde, Enoch Pratt. Abr. Compend. Amer. Geneal. Virkus. V. 1, p. 653. DAR.
Hyder. Family hist. Ella Bean. Taneytown, Md., 1909. MHS.
†Hist. of Frederick Co. Williams. MHS; DAR.
Hyder-Delaplaine. Family hist. of John Hyder (born 1787) and Catherine Delaplaine (born 1788), Taneytown, Carroll Co. Ella Bean. Carroll Record Print, 1909, pamph. MHS.
Hyland. Ances. rec. and portraits. Col. Dames of Amer., 1910, v. 1, p. 167. MHS; DAR.
Britton Scrap Book. V. 1. Ms. MHS.
Ford and other lines. Md. Geneal. Rec. Com., 1932–33, pp. 7–20. Mss. DAR.
Ford chart. MHS.
Hyland chart. MHS.
*Hyland family, Cecil Co. E. Mitchell Hyland. Balto., 1914. Bd. ms. MHS.
*Hyland-Jones family of East. Shore, of Md. Kate Singer Curry, 1420 Girard St., N.W., Wash., D. C.
Md. families. Culver. Ms. Personal list.
Md. Geneal. Rec. Com., 1933–34, p. 25. Mss. DAR.
†Med. Annals Md. Cordell. 1903, p. 448. MHS.
Patriotic Md. Md. Soc. of S. A. R., 1930. MHS; DAR.
Pedigree of Howard Hall Macy Lee. Soc. Col. Wars Md. Culver. 1940. MHS; DAR.
St. Paul's Parish, Balto. V. 2. Mss. MHS.
St. Stephens Parish, Cecilton, Md. MHS; DAR.
*The Sun, Balto., July 19, 1908.

Winchester-Owens-Price families. M. H. Mag., 1930, v. 25, no. 4, p. 385-405.
See Ford-Dorsey-Hyland, etc.
See Tilghman-Hyland-Ford.

Hyland, James. Md. Soc., War of 1812, v. 1, no. 11. Ms. MHS.

***Hyland Family.** Hist. of Cecil Co. Johnston. Pp. 522-24. MHS; DAR.
Portrait and biog. rec. of Harford and Cecil Cos. 1897. P. 504. MHS; DAR.

Hyland Family, Cecil Co. Chart. T. A. Glenn. Edited and corrected by E. Mitchell Hyland, 1914. Ms. MHS.

Hyland Line, Md. from 1695. Dilks, N. J. Col. and Revolutionary families of Phila. Jordan. 1933, v. 1, pp. 11-21.

Hynes. St. Stephens Parish, Cecilton, Md. MHS; DAR.

†**Hynson.** Biog. cyc. of rep. men of Md. and D. C. P. 336. MHS; DAR.
Mrs. R. F. Brent chart. MHS.
Mrs. Howard Bruce chart. MHS.
I. U. Church cemetery. Md. O. R. Soc. Bull., no. 2, pp. 76-78.
Md. families. Culver. Ms. Personal list.
†Men of mark in Md. Johnson. V. 4, pp. 295, 365. DAR; Enoch Pratt Lib.
W. A. and S. W. Merritt pedigree charts, plates 1 and 2. Soc. Col. Wars, Md. Johnston. 1905, pp. 67-68. MHS.
Pedigree of Duncan Keener Brent. Soc. Col. Wars Md. Culver. 1940. MHS; DAR.
Pedigrees (2) of George Webb Constable. Soc. Col. Wars Md. Culver. 1940. MHS; DAR.
Pedigree of Coleman Randall Freeman. Soc. Col. Wars Md. Culver. 1940. MHS; DAR.
Pedigree of Thomas Gardener Hill. Soc. Col. Wars Md. Culver. 1940. MHS; DAR.
Pedigree of Henry Irvine Keyser, II. Soc. Col. Wars Md. Culver. 1940. MHS; DAR.
Pedigree of Franklin Buchanan Owen. Soc. Col. Wars Md. Culver. 1940. MHS; DAR.
Pedigree of John Philemon Paca. Soc. Col. Wars Md. Culver. 1940. MHS; DAR.
Pedigree of Pleasants Pennington. Soc. Col. Wars Md. Culver. 1940. MHS; DAR.
Pedigree of Tilghman Goldsborough Pitts. Soc. Col. Wars Md. Culver. 1940. MHS; DAR.
Pedigree of Wm. Handy Collins Vickers. Soc. Col. Wars Md. Culver. 1940. MHS; DAR.
Pedigree of George Washington Williams. Soc. Col. Wars Md. Culver. 1940. MHS; DAR.
Mrs. J. Hall Pleasants, Jr., chart. MHS.
St. Paul's churchyard, Kent Co. Md. O. R. Soc. Bull., no. 2, pp. 54-65. MHS.
St. Paul's Parish, Balto. V. 2. Mss. MHS.
St. Stephens Parish, Cecilton, Md. MHS; DAR.
Mrs. H. De Courcy Wright Thom chart. MHS.
Mrs. Emory Whitridge chart. MHS.
See Hinson.
See Nicholson-Hynson-Noel.

Hynson, Thomas. M. H. Mag., 1920, v. 15, pp. 230-50, 394-419.
Seven pioneers of col. East. Shore. Skirven. M. H. Mag., v. 15, no. 3, p. 230-50; no. 4, p. 394-419.

Hynson Family. Geneal. Soc. Pa. Mss. Coll.

Hynson Line, Kent Co. Abr. Compend. Amer. Geneal. Virkus. V. 1, p. 407; v. 4, p. 587.
M. W. Hill pedigree chart. Soc. Col. Wars Md. Johnston. 1905, pp. 39, 147, 148. MHS.

†**Hynson-Wright.** Chesapeake Bay Country. Earle. P. 338. MHS.

Hynson, Hinson. Chart, photos., complete in 1 sheet. Cary Geneal. Coll. Ms. MHS.
Col. families of U. S. A. Mackenzie. V. 1. MHS; DAR.
Side lights on Md. hist. Richardson. V. 2, p. 137. MHS; DAR.
*The Sun, Balto., Nov. 6, 1904.

Hynson, Hinson and Smith Families. Christopher Johnston. M. H. Mag., 1923, v. 18, pp. 186-92.

***Hyslop.** Burke's landed gentry. 1939. MHS.

Hyson. *See* Hinson.

***Hyson Family.** Old Kent. Hynson. Pp. 99-102. MHS; DAR.

I

Iams. Zimmerman-Waters and allied families. Allen. MHS; DAR.

Iauman. Catonsville pioneers of Luth. faith. Natl. Geneal. Soc. Quart., v. 9, no. 2, p. 29.

Iglehart. Cemetery Creek, Anne Arundel Co., Tombstone inscriptions. Founders of Anne Arundel and Howard Cos. Warfield. P. 333. MHS; DAR.
Col. families of Amer. Lawrence. V. 10, p. 34. MHS.
Col. families of U. S. A. Mackenzie. V. 5, p. 271. MHS; DAR.
Founders of Anne Arundel and Howard Cos. Warfield. P. 329. MHS; DAR.
Griffith geneal. Griffith. MHS; DAR.
Md. families. Culver. Ms. Personal list.
†Med. Annals Md. Cordell. 1903, pp. 448-49. MHS.
Pedigree of Wm. Winchester Eareckson. Soc. Col. Wars Md. Culver. 1940. MHS; DAR.
St. Paul's Parish, Balto. V. 2. Mss. MHS.

Iglehart, Iredell Waddell. Pedigree. Soc. Col. Wars Md. Culver. 1940. MHS; DAR.

Iglehart, Mrs. Iredell Waddell (Alice Bowie Whitridge). Chart. Col. Dames, Chap. I. MHS.

Iglehart, J. Davidson, M.D. Md. Soc., War of 1812, v. 1, no. 91. Ms. MHS.

Iglehart, James Davidson. Pedigree. Soc. Col. Wars Md. Culver. 1940. MHS; DAR.

Igon, Igone. St. Paul's Parish, Balto. V. 1, 2. Mss. MHS.

Ijams. Ellen Emmerich Mears. Col. and Revolutionary families of Phila. Jordan. 1933, v. 1, pp. 412-15.
Patriotic Md. Md. Soc. of S. A. R., 1930. MHS; DAR.
Pedigree of Mareen Duvall. Soc. Col. Wars Md. Culver. 1940. MHS; DAR.

***Ijams Family.** Anne Arundel Co. gentry. Newman. Pp. 392-422. MHS; DAR.
*Wilson Mss. Coll., no. 86. MHS.

Iiler. *See* Eiler-Boone-Anderson-Scothoron.

Imbert. Naturalizations in Md., 1666-1765; Laws. Bacon. MHS.

Inery. *See* Jnery.

***Ingersol.** Wicomico Co. families. Tilghman. Ms., p. 97. DAR.

***Ingersoll Family.** Geneal. from Wm. Belt Ingersoll. Ms. DAR.

Ingham. Fox-Ellicott-Evans families. Evans. MHS; DAR.

Ingle. Richard Ingle of Md. M. H. Mag., 1906, v. 1, pp. 125–401.
St. Paul's Parish, Balto. V. 2. Mss. MHS.
Ingle, Henry (1764–1822). His ancestry and descendants, 1690–1913. Edward Ingle. (Ingle of Md. pp. 9–25) Pamph. MHS.
†Ingle, Capt. Richard. Md. pirate and rebel, 1642–53. E. Ingle. M. H. S. Fund Pub., no. 19, Balto., 1884. MHS.
English. Somerset Co. Court Book. Tilghman. 1937. Ms. DAR.
Ingraham. John Neill of Lewes, Del., 1739. Pr. for family, Phila., 1875.
St. Paul's Parish, Balto. V. 2. Mss. MHS.
Ingraham Family, Boston, Phila. and Miss. Incl. Coates, Duffield and Maury families. Md. Geneal. Rec. Com., 1938–39, pp. 142–67. Mss. DAR.
Ingram. See Edmondson family. Focke Geneal. Coll. Ms. MHS.
I. U. Church cemetery. Md. O. R. Soc. Bull., no. 2, pp. 76–78.
Somerset Co. Court Book. Tilghman. 1937. ms. DAR.
Ingram Family. Note. Old Somerset. Torrence. MHS; DAR.
†Inloes. Med. Annals Md. Cordell. 1903, p. 449. MHS.
St. Paul's Parish, Balto. V. 2. Mss. MHS.
Wills from Balto. City court house, 1790, 1872 and 1874. Md. Geneal. Rec. Com., 1937, p. 15–19. Mss. DAR.
See Enloes.
Insley. Tombstone rec. of Dorchester Co. Jones. DAR.
*Wicomico Co. families. Tilghman. Ms, p. 119. DAR.
Ireland. Bible rec., Kent Co. Md. Geneal. Rec. Com., 1933–34, p. 216. Mss. DAR.
Descendants of Valentine Hollingsworth, Sr. Stewart. MHS; DAR.
†Med. Annals Md. Cordell. 1903, p. 449. MHS.
St. Paul's Parish, Balto. V. 1, 2, 4. Mss. MHS.
Ireland, Louisa Co., Va., and Williamsburg, Va. Cary Geneal. Coll. Ms. MHS.
†Irons. Med. Annals Md. Cordell. 1903, p. 450. MHS.
Ironshire. Pedigree of Lee Cummins Cary. Soc. Col. Wars Md. Culver. 1940. MHS; DAR.
Purnell family tree, MHS.
Robins family, Va. and Worcester Co., Md., and allied families. Bd. ms. MHS.
Irvin. St. Paul's Parish, Balto. V. 2. Mss. MHS.
Irving. Handy and their kin. Handy.
†Med. Annals. Md. Cordell. 1903, p. 450. MHS.
St. Joseph's R. C. churchyard. Md. O. R. Soc. Bull., no. 3, p. 64.
Wicomico Co. families. Bible rec. Ms. DAR.
*Wicomico Co. families. Tilghman. Ms, pp. 22, 34, 97. DAR
***Irwin.** Frederick Co. families. Markell. Ms. Personal list.
Hagerstown tombstone inscriptions. Gruder. Natl. Geneal. Soc. Quart., 1919, v. 8, nos. 1, 2.
Marriage rec. of Frederick Co. Markell. Md. Geneal. Rec. Com., 1938–39. Mss. DAR.
*The Sun, Balto., Nov. 26, 1905.

Isaac. Autobiography of Summerfield Baldwin. MHS; DAR.
Beall and Bell families. Beall. MHS; DAR.
See Gordon. Abr. Compend. Amer. Geneal. Virkus. V. 1, p. 300. DAR.
Griffith geneal. Griffith. MHS; DAR.
†Hist. of Balto. City and Co. Scharf. P. 893. MHS.
Lineage Bk., Daughters of Amer. Colonists, v. 2, 328. MHS; DAR.
Md. families. Culver. Ms. Personal list.
Mullikins of Md. Baker. P. 43. MHS; DAR.
See Passano. Abr. Compend. Amer. Geneal. Virkus. V. 1, p. 138. DAR.
Pedigree of Charles Gambrill Baldwin. Soc. Col. Wars Md. Culver. 1940. MHS; DAR.
Pedigree of Mareen Duvall. Soc. Col. Wars Md. Culver. 1940. MHS; DAR.
Pedigree of Dr. Christopher Johnston, Jr. Soc. Col. Wars Md. Culver. 1940. MHS; DAR.
Pedigree of Gustav Wm. Lurman. Soc. Col. Wars Md. Culver. 1940. MHS; DAR.
Pedigree of Franklin Buchanan Owen. Soc. Col. Wars Md. Culver. 1940. MHS; DAR.
Pedigree of Edward Boteler Passano. Soc. Col. Wars Md. Culver. 1940. MHS; DAR.
Pedigree of James Donnell Tilghman. Soc. Col. Wars Md. Culver. 1940. MHS; DAR.
Queen Anne's Parish rec., Prince George Co. Ms. MHS.
*The Sun, Balto., March 17, 1907.
See Purnell.
Isaac, Joseph. McCall-Tidwell families. McCall. P. 471. MHS; DAR.
Isaac, Isaack. Ance. rec. and portraits. Col. Dames of Amer., 1910; v. 1, p. 87. MHS; DAR.
Cary Geneal. Coll. Ms. MHS.
Col. families of U. S. A. Mackenzie. V. 1, p. 148, v. 3; v. 6. MHS; DAR.
Rolle family rec., Talbot Co. Ms. MHS.
Isaack. *See* Isaac.
Isaacs. St. Paul's Parish, Balto. V. 2. Mss. MHS.
Iselin. John O'Donnell of Balto. Cook. MHS.
Isham. Bowies and their kindred. Bowie. MHS; DAR.
Israel, Rt. Rev. Rogers. Pedigree. Soc. Col. Wars Md. Culver. 1940. MHS; DAR.
Israello. St. Paul's Parish, Balto. V. 1. Mss. MHS.
Ivery. Old Somerset. Torrence. MHS; DAR.

J

Jacks. Abr. Compend. Amer. Geneal. Virkus. V. 4, p. 587, MHS; v. 6, p. 547. DAR.
***Jacks Family.** Wilson Mss. Coll., no. 72. MHS.
Jackson. Amer. Clan Gregor Year Book, 1926, p. 62. MHS; DAR.
Balto., its hist., its people. Hall. V. 3. MHS; DAR.
Burton ancestry. Ms. MHS.
Christ P. E. Church cemetery, Cambridge. Steele. 1936. MHS; DAR.
Col. family of U. S. A. Mackenzie. V. 6. MHS; DAR.
Founders of Anne Arundel and Howard Cos. Warfield. P. 295 (Elihu). MHS; DAR.
*Hist. of Frederick Co. Williams. MHS; DAR.

Hist. Salisbury, Wicomico Co. Truitt. P. 13. DAR.
†Med. Annals Md. Cordell. 1903, p. 450. MHS.
Patriotic Md. Md. Soc. of S. A. R., 1930. MHS; DAR.
Pedigree of John Hurst Morgan. Soc. Col. Wars Md. Culver. 1940. MHS; DAR.
Rec. of Stepney Parish. MHS; DAR.
Rumsey-Smithson Bible rec. Md. Geneal. Rec. Com., 1932–33, v. 5, pp. 63–142. DAR.
St. Paul's Parish, Balto. V. 1, 2, 3, 4. Mss. MHS.
Side lights on Md. hist. Richardson. V. 2, p. 376. MHS; DAR.
Wicomico Co. families. Bible rec. Ms. DAR.
*Wicomico Co. families. Tilghman. Ms, pp. 35–37, 125. DAR.

Jackson, Fell's Point. Miss Cassandra Lee chart. MHS.

Jackson, Miss Catharine Bond. Chart. Col. Dames, Chap. I. MHS.
Mrs. R. N. Jackson chart. MHS.

†**Jackson, Elihu Emory.** Governors of Md. Buchholz. P. 242. MHS.
†(1837–1907). M. H. Mag., v. 12, p. 222.
†Men of mark in Md. Johnson. V. 3. DAR; Enoch Pratt Lib.

Jackson, Lloyd Lowndes. Pedigree. Soc. Col. Wars Md. Culver. 1940. MHS; DAR.

Jackson, Mrs. Richard Newton (Catharine Wilder Bond). Chart. Col. Dames, Chap. I. MHS.

Jackson, T. Jackson Arnold. Abr. Compend. Amer. Geneal. Virkus. V. 1, p. 190. DAR.

†**Jackson, Wm. P.** Men of mark in Md. Johnson. V. 3. DAR; Enoch Pratt Lib.

Jackson, Wm. Purnell. Abr. Compend. Amer. Geneal. Virkus. V. 1, p. 153. DAR.

***Jackson Family,** East. Shore of Md. Wilson Mss. Coll., no. 8, A. MHS.
*Md. Geneal. Bull., v. 10, no. 2, p. 21. MHS; DAR.
*Proceedings of sesqui centennial gathering of the descendants of Isaac and Anne Jackson, at Harmony Grove, Chester, Pa. Pa. descendants named Bailey, Chalfant, Evans, Gibson, Haines, Hutton, Lewis, Starr, Windel and Woodward traced in Del., Md., and Pa. Phila., 1878.

Jackson Line. Col. and Revolutionary lineages of Amer. 1939, v. 1, pp. 530–31. MHS.

Jacob. Amer. ancestry of Frederick Louis and Reginald Shippen Huidekoper. 1931, pamph., pp. 19–20. MHS; DAR.
Autobiography of Summerfield Baldwin. MHS; DAR.
Sara R. Baldwin chart. MHS.
Carton charts. MHS.
Col. families of U. S. A. Mackenzie. V. 5. MHS; DAR.
Duckett chart. MHS.
Col. Nicholas Duvall family rec. Price. Bd. ms. MHS.
Griffith geneal. Griffith. MHS; DAR.
Hamill chart. MHS.
Pedigree of John Ogle Warfield, Jr. Soc. Col. Wars Md. Culver. 1940. MHS; DAR.
See Ashman.

Jacob, Rev. John J., Anne Arundel Co. Burial rec. (born 1757). Md. Geneal. Rec. Com., 1934–35, p. 2. Mss. MHS.

***Jacob Family.** Anne Arundel Co. gentry. Newman. Pp. 423–54. MHS; DAR.

Jacob Line. Col. and Revolutionary families of Pa. Amer. Hist. Soc., N. Y., 1934, p. 364.

Jacob-Cheney. Chart, photos., complete in 2 sheets. Cary Geneal. Coll. Ms. MHS.

Jacob, Jacobs. St. Paul's Parish, Balto. V. 1, 2, 4. Mss. MHS.

Jacobs. Balto., its hist., its people. Hall. V. 2. MHS; DAR.
Col. families of U. S. A. Mackenzie. V. 3. MHS; DAR.
*Frederick Co. families. Markell. Ms. Personal list.
Frederick Co. tombstone inscriptions. Gruder. Natl. Geneal. Soc. Quart., 1919, v. 8, nos. 1, 2.
Griffith geneal. Griffith. MHS; DAR.
*Hist. of Frederick Co. Williams. MHS; DAR.
Md. families. Culver. Ms. Personal list.
†Med. Annals Md. Cordell. 1903; p. 451. MHS.
Peale Geneal. Coll. Ms. MHS.
St. Stephens Parish, Cecilton, Md. MHS; DAR.
Mrs. E. C. Venable chart. MHS.
See Jacob.

Jacobs, Frederick Co. Abr. Compend. Amer. Geneal. Virkus. V. 4, p. 308. MHS.

***Jacobs, Henry Barton.** Burke's landed gentry. 1939. MHS.
†Men of mark in Md. Johnson. V. 4, DAR; Enoch Pratt Lib.

Jacobs, Henry Barton, M.D., New Eng. Pedigree charts, plates 1 and 2. Soc. Col. Wars, Md. Johnston. 1905, pp. 43–44. MHS.

Jacobs, Mrs. Henry Barton; formerly Mrs. Robert Garret (Mary Sloan Frick). Chart. Col. Dames, Chap. I. MHS.

Jacobson. Naturalizations in Md., 1666–1765; Laws. Bacon. MHS.
†Hist. of West. Md. Scharf. V. 2, pp. 1295, 1297. MHS; DAR.

Jacques. *See* Beachey. Abr. Compend. Amer. Geneal. Virkus. V. 4, p. 646. MHS.

Jacques-Gregory-Hixon. Abr. Compend. Amer. Geneal. Virkus. V. 4, pp. 309–10. MHS.

Jacquett. St. Paul's Parish, Balto. V. 2. Mss. MHS.

Jacquette. Pedigree of Hope Horsey Barroll. Soc. Col. Wars Md. Culver. 1940. MHS; DAR.

Jaffray, James. Westminster churchyard. Patriotic Marylander, v. 2, no. 4, pp. 54–60. MHS; DAR.

Jamar. Ford chart. MHS.
†Med. Annals Md. Cordell. 1903, p. 451. MHS.

Jamar, Jamart Family. Geneal. Ms. MHS.

James. Balto., its hist., its people. Hall. V. 3. MHS; DAR.
Mrs. Wm. Graham. Bowdoin, Jr., chart. MHS.
Centenary of Catholicity in Ky. Webb. 1884. MHS.
Christ P. E. Church cemetery, Cambridge. Steele. 1936. MHS; DAR.
Faith Pres. Church (Glendy graveyard). Mss. MHS.
*Frederick Co. families. Markell. Ms. Personal list.
†Med. Annals Md. Cordell. 1903, p. 452. MHS.

James. Patriotic Md. Md. Soc. of S. A. R., 1930. MHS; DAR.
St. Paul's Parish, Balto. V. 1, 2, 4. Mss. MHS.
*Wicomico Co. families. Tilghman. Ms. pp. 95, 97, 110-13. DAR.
See Cook-James.
James, Cecil Co. Col. families of Amer. Lawrence. V. 10, pp. 35-81. MHS.
James, Mrs. Charles I. (Mary Tasker Ranson). Chart. (Mostly W. Va. families.) Col. Dames, Chap. I. MHS.
***James, Rev. Colin Dew.** Repr. from Jour. Ill. Hist. Soc., Jan., 1917, v. 9, no. 4. MHS.
James, Mrs. Macgill (Bruce Kinsolving). Chart. Col. Dames, Chap. I. MHS.
James, Mrs. Nathaniel Willis (Francis Lowndes Ranson). Chart. (Mostly W. Va. families.) Col. Dames, Chap. I. MHS.
Jameson. Harford Co. Hist. Soc. Mss. Coll. JHU.
Hist. graves of Md. and D. C. Ridgely. MHS.
See Gibson. Amer. Armory and Blue Book. Matthews. 1911-12, p. 339.
†**Jameson, Jamison.** Med. Annals Md. Cordell. 1903, pp. 452-53, 779-95. MHS.
St. Paul's Parish, Balto. V. 1, 2, 3. Mss. MHS.
Jamison. Descendants of Thomas Hale of Del. Streets. 1913, pamph. MHS.
*Frederick Co. families. Markell. Ms. Personal list.
†Hist. of Frederick Co. Williams. MHS; DAR.
Pedigree of Francis Joseph Baldwin. Soc. Col. Wars Md. Culver. 1940. MHS; DAR.
Pedigree of Edwin Austin Baughman. Soc. Col. Wars Md. Culver. 1940. MHS; DAR.
Pedigree of Alfred Jenkins Torney. Soc. Col. Wars Md. Culver. 1940. MHS; DAR.
See Cowden-Ridgely-Jamison.
See Jameson.
***Jamison Family.** Data. Ms. MHS.
Jamison-Wallace Family. Rec., 1748-1847, with copy of will of Joseph Jamison, 1847. Md. Geneal. Rec. Com., 1932-33, p. 43. Mss. DAR.
Tombstone inscriptions and wills, 1748-1847. Md. Geneal. Rec. Com., 1932-33. DAR.
Janes Family. Geneal. and brief hist. of descendants of Wm. Janes, emigrant ancestor, 1637. F. Janes. (Conn. family with early branches in Vt., Va. and Md.) N. Y., 1868. MHS.
Janney. Abr. Compend. Amer. Geneal. Virkus. V. 4, pp. 309-10. MHS.
Chart of Thomas Janney and Margery, his wife, of Cheshire, Eng., who settled in Buck's Co., Pa., 1683. S. M. Janney. DAR.
Geneal. of ancestors and descendants of John and Hannah (Fincher) Russell. Russell. 1887, 1889, pamph. MHS.
Geneal. Miles White, Jr. Pub. South., Hist. Assoc., 1904, v. 8, pp. 119, 197, 275, 744.
Hist. and geneal. account of Jolliffe family of Va. Jolliffe. DAR.
Miss E. C. Hopkins chart. MHS.
Plummer family. A. P. H. Ms. MHS.
Russell family. Russell. 1889, 2nd ed., p. 20. MHS.
St. Paul's Parish, Balto. V. 2. Mss. MHS.
Miss Sara E. White chart. MHS.
See Taylor-Janney.
Janney, Abel, Pa. Pedigree of Malcolm Van Vechten Tyson. Soc. Col. Wars Md. Culver 1940. MHS; DAR.
†**Janney, Samuel** (Quaker minister of Md. and Va.) Memoirs. By Himself. Phila., 1888. MHS.
†**Janney, Stewart S.** Men of mark in Md. Johnson. V. 1. DAR; Enoch Pratt Lib.
Janney, Thomas. Pedigree of Benedict Henry Hanson, Jr. Soc. Col. Wars Md. Culver. 1940. MHS; DAR.
†Provincial councilor. Miles White, Jr. Pa. Mag., Apr. 1903, v. 27, pp. 212-39.
Janney, Thomas, Pa. (1634-1696). T. M. Smith pedigree charts, plate 2. Soc. Col. Wars, Md. Johnston. 1905, pp. 96, 148. MHS.
Janney Line. Encyc. of Amer. biog. Amer. Hist. Soc., new series, v. 1, p. 209. (Miles White family, p. 212.) MHS; DAR.
Janney-Hopkinson-Snowden-Thomas. Abr. Compend. Amer. Geneal. Virkus. V. 6, p. 323. DAR.
Jaquelin. Aylett chart. Cary Geneal. Coll. Ms. MHS.
*Descendants of Edward Jacquelin and allied families, Ambler, Cary, etc. "Some prominent Va. families." Louise Pecquet du Bellet. V. 1, 4. pts. MHS.
***Jaquelin,** Va. The Sun, Balto., Feb. 25, 1906.
Jaquett. Ancestry and descendants of Nancy Allyn (Foote) Webb, etc. Cooch. MHS; DAR.
***Jaquett Family.** Geneal. E. Jaquett Sellers. (Del. families.) Phila., ltd. ed., revised ed., 1907. MHS.
*Supplement to geneal. E. Jaquett Sellers. Phila., 1922. MHS.
Jarbo. Naturalizations in Md., 1666-1765; Laws. Bacon. MHS.
Jarboe. Thomas Hill and descendants. Hill. P. 5. MHS.
Hist. graves of Md. and D. C. Ridgely. MHS.
Taney and allied families. Silverson. MHS; DAR.
Miss Eliza Thomas chart. MHS.
See Contee-Duval-Jarboe.
Jarboe, Col. John. Some early col. Marylanders. M. H. Mag., 1920, v. 15, pp. 312-19.
Jarboe, Lieut-Col. John, St. Mary's Co. (1619-1674). E. A. and F. DeS. Jenkins pedigree Chart. Soc. Col. Wars, Md. Johnston. 1905, pp. 46, 148. MHS.
Jarboe Line. Col. and Revolutionary lineages of Amer. 1939. V. 2, p. 74. MHS.
Jarman. Buckingham Pres. churchyard, Worcester Co., Hudson. Bd. ms. MHS; DAR.
Lloyd family hist. of Wales, Pa., and Md. DAR.
Makemie Memorial Pres. churchyard, Snow Hill, Worcester Co. Hudson. Bd. ms. MHS; DAR. Also: Md. Geneal. Rec. Com. Mrs. Lines. Mss. DAR.
Lineage Bks., Natl. Soc. of Daughters of Amer. Col., v. 4, p. 328. MHS; DAR.
Jarratt. Lineage Bks., Natl. Soc. of Daughters of Amer. Col., v. 4, p. 328. MHS; DAR.
Jarret, Jarrett. St. Paul's Parish, Balto. V. 1. Mss. MHS.
Jarrett. Bond chart. MHS.
Col. families of U. S. A. Mackenzie. V. 3, p. 217. MHS; DAR.

Maulsby family in Amer. Barnard. DAR; Peabody Lib.
Patriotic Md. Md. Soc. of S. A. R., 1930. MHS; DAR.
Tombstones, 1739-1866, on Cranberry Farm, near Aberdeen, Harford Co. Md. Geneal. Rec. Com., 1929, p. 60. Mss. DAR.
See **Jarret.**
***Jarrett,** Harford Co. Lineage Bk., Daughters o Amer. Colonists, v. 4, p. 328. MHS; DAR.
Jarvis. St. Martin's P. E. Church, Worcester Co. Md. Geneal. Rec. Com., 1937, Mrs. Lines. Mss. DAR.
St. Paul's P. E. churchyard, Berlin, Worcester Co. Hudson. Bd. ms. MHS; DAR. Also: Md. Geneal. Rec. Com., 1937, Mrs. Lines. Mss. DAR.
St. Paul's Parish, Balto. V. 1, 2. Mss. MHS.
St. Thomas Parish, Balto. Co. Bd. ms. MHS. Also: Md. Geneal. Rec. Com., 1937, pp. 109-82. Mss. DAR.
Winn-Jarvis geneal. Ms. MHS; DAR.
See Winn-Jarvis.
Jarvis, Stephen, Huntington, Long Island, N. Y. Some descendants, 1635-1885. Md. Geneal. Rec. Com., 1935-36, p. 226. DAR.
†Jay. Med. Annals Md. Cordell. 1903, p. 453. MHS.
Jay, Harford Co. Abr. Compend. Amer. Geneal. Virkus. V. 1, p. 174. DAR.
Jean. *See* Miller-Jean.
See Ousler-Jean-Ridgely.
Jean-Baker-George. Marriages and deaths. Md. Geneal. Rec. Com., 1932-33, p. 44. Mss. DAR.
Jean-Miller. Bible rec., 1760-1845. Md. Geneal. Rec. Com., 1932-33, v. 5. Mss. DAR.
Jeanneret. Turner Geneal. Coll. Ms. MHS.
Jefferies. Peale Geneal. Coll. Ms. MHS.
***Jefferson.** Bible rec. Typed copy. MHS.
Bible rec., New Castle, Del. Upper Penins East. Shore, p. 200. MHS; DAR.
Cary Geneal. Coll. Ms. MHS.
*Frederick Co. families. Markell. Ms. Personal list.
Marvel-Jefferson Bible rec. Ms. MHS.
Trinity Church burial ground, near Cambridge, Md. Md. Geneal. Rec. Com., 1937-38, pp. 93-104. Mss. DAR.
*Wicomico Co. families. Tilghman. Ms., p. 127. DAR.
Jefferson, Del. Data. Md. Geneal. Rec. Com., 1937. Parran. Pp. 64-66. Mss. DAR.
Jefferson, Richard, Sussex Co., Del. (formerly Worcester Co., Md.). Ab. of will. Md. Geneal. Rec. Com., 1937. Parran. Pp. 67-68, 69. Mss. DAR.
Jeffery. Balto., its hist., its people. Hall. V. 3. MHS; DAR.
Jeffery-French. Col. and Revolutionary lineages of Amer. 1939, v. 1, pp. 490-531. MHS.
†Men of mark in Md. Johnson. V. 3. DAR; Enoch Pratt Lib.
†Jeffreys, Edw. M. Men of mark in Md. Johnson. V. 1. DAR; Enoch Pratt Lib.
Jekyll. Balch letters and papers. Pamph., p. 19. MHS.
Jellet. St. Paul's Parish, Balto. V. 2. Mss. MHS.
Jemison. Somerset Co. Court Book. Tilghman. 1937. Ms. DAR.
Jenckes. Ancest. rec. and portraits. Col. Dames of Amer., 1910; v. 2, p. 770. MHS; DAR.
Jencks. de Ghize chart. MHS.
Jencks, Mrs. Elizabeth Platt (Elizabeth Platt). Chart. Col. Dames, Chap. I. MHS.
Jenifer. Bantz geneal. notes. Ms. MHS.
Md. gleanings in Eng. Wills. M. H. Mag., 1907, v. 2, no. 4.
†Med. Annals Md. Cordell. 1903, p. 453. MHS.
***Jenifer, Daniel,** St. Thomas. Queries. M. H. Mag., 1906, v. 1, p. 76.
***Jenifer Family.** Old Kent. Hanson. P. 124. MHS; DAR.
Jenikins. Somerset Co. Court Book. Tilghman. 1937. Ms. DAR.
Jenings. Lee of Va., 1642-1892. E. J. Lee. P. 300. Lib. Cong., MHS.
Jenkins. Abr. Compend. Amer. Geneal. Virkus. V. 1, pp. 45, 656. DAR.
Bailliere chart. MHS.
Balto. Herald, Mar. 22, 1903. Newsp. clipp. MHS.
Balto., its hist., its people. Hall. V. 3. MHS; DAR.
Centenary of Catholicity in Ky. Webb. 1884. MHS.
Coat of arms, *See* Alfred Jenkins Shriver.
Col. families of U. S. A. Mackenzie. V. 1, pp. 284-85; v. 4, pp. 259-63; v. 5. MHS; DAR.
See Devereux. Abr. Compend. Amer. Geneal. Virkus. V. 1, p. 43. DAR.
Done Bible rec. Ms. MHS.
Grandma Stories. Sister Mary Xavier Queen. MHS.
Hist. graves of Md. and D. C. Ridgely. MHS.
Lloyd family hist. of Wales, Pa., and Md. DAR.
Lucketts of Portobacco. Newman. DAR.
Md. families. Culver. Ms. Personal list.
Md. tombstone rec. Md. Geneal. Rec. Com., 1937, Parran, p. 4. Mss. DAR.
†Med. Annals Md. Cordell. 1903, p. 454. MHS.
†Nicholas Hasselback, printer. McCreary. MHS.
Parr chart. MHS.
Patriotic Md. Md. Soc. of S. A. R., 1930. MHS; DAR.
Patriotic Marylander, v. 1, no. 3, p. 60. MHS; DAR.
Peale Geneal. Coll. Ms. MHS.
Pedigree of Austin Jenkins Lilly. Soc. Col. Wars Md. Culver. 1940. MHS; DAR.
Pedigree of Charles O'Donovan. Soc. Col. Wars Md. Culver. 1940. MHS; DAR.
Pedigree of Alfred Jenkins Tormey. Soc. Col. Wars Md. Culver. 1940. MHS; DAR.
Posey chart. MHS.
See Shriver. Abr. Compend. Amer. Geneal. Virkus. V. 1, p. 424. DAR.
Rec. of Stepney Parish. MHS; DAR.
St. Charles R. C. Church graveyard, Indianhead, Charles Co. Md. Geneal. Rec. Com., 1933-34, p. 137. Mss. DAR.
St. Inigoes churchyard, St. Mary's Co. Md. O. R. Soc. Bull., no. 3, p. 58.
St. Paul's Parish, Balto. V. 1, 2, 3, 4. Mss. MHS.
Semmes and allied families. Semmes. MHS.
*Semmes Geneal. Coll. Ms. MHS.

*__Jenkins.__ (Settled in Md., 1670.) St. Thomas Manor, Charles Co. H. A. Brown. Newsp. clipp. Peabody Lib.
Somerset Co. Court Book. Tilghman. 1937. Ms. DAR.
*Southerland Book. Vorhees. P. 83.
Southerland-Latham and allied families. Voorhees. Bd. ms. MHS.
*The Sun, Balto., Feb. 25, March 4, 11, 1906.
*Wicomico Co. families. Tilghman. Ms, p. 59. DAR.
Willcox and allied families. Willcox. P. 87. MHS; DAR.
__Jenkins,__ Talbot Co., and Pa. H. Mullikin pedigree charts, plates 1 and 2. Soc. Col. Wars, Md. Johnston. 1905, pp. 74–75. MHS.
__Jenkins, Austin Lowe,__ and Jenkins, Spalding Lowe. Pedigree chart. Soc. Col. Wars, Md. Johnston. 1905, p. 45. MHS.
__Jenkins, B. Wheeler.__ Md. Soc., War of 1812, v. 3, no. 261. Ms. MHS.
__Jenkins, Benj. Wheeler.__ Pedigree. Soc. Col. Wars Md. Culver. 1940. MHS; DAR.
__Jenkins, E. Austin.__ Md. Soc., War of 1812, v. 1, no. 131. Ms. MHS.
__Jenkins, Edward Austin, and Jenkins, Francis de Sales.__ Pedigree chart. Soc. Col. Wars, Md. Johnston. 1905, p. 46. MHS.
__Jenkins, Francis de Sales.__ Md. Soc., War of 1812, v. 1, no. 130. Ms. MHS.
See Jenkins, Edward Austin and Francis de Sales.
__Jenkins, Mrs. George C. (Mary Catharine Key).__ Chart. Col. Dames, Chap. I. MHS.
Mrs. Ral Parr charts. MHS.
†__Jenkins, Michael.__ Geneal. and mem. encyc. of Md. Spencer. V. 1, p. 111. MHS; DAR.
Md. Soc., War of 1812, v. 3, no. 250. Ms. MHS.
__Jenkins, Spaulding Lowe.__ *See* Jenkins, Austin Lowe and Spaulding Lowe.
__Jenkins, Thomas Courtney.__ Pedigree chart. Soc. Col. Wars, Md. Johnston. 1905, p. 47. MHS.
__Jenkins, Mrs. Thomas Courtenay, (Dorothy Blake Frick).__ Chart. Col. Dames, Chap. I. MHS.
Jacobs chart. MHS.
†__Jenkins, Wm.__ Balto., hist. and biog. Richardson and Bennett. 1871, pp. 321–24. MHS; DAR.
*__Jenkins Family.__ Arch. of Georgetown Univ., Wash., D. C., v. 138, no. 10.
*Chart. File case A, MHS.
Record of Mrs. George C. Jenkins (née Key). Francis B. Culver. Photos. of ms. MHS.
__Jenkins-Courtney.__ Chart; descendants of William Jenkins, son of Ap Jenkins of Wales. Data collected by Mark Jenkins, 1869, continued and compiled by his son. Photos. of negative. Jan. 1, 1877. MHS.
*__Jenkins-Key.__ Chart. In Jenkins folder. MHS.
__Jenks, Wm. Henry,__ Buck Co., Pa., and Md. In memoriam. Pub. Geneal. Soc. Pa., v. 4, no. 1, p. 119.
†__Jennings.__ Bench and bar of Md. Sams and Riley. 1901, v. 1, p. 175. Lib. Cong.; MHS; Peabody Lib.
Cary Geneal. Coll. Ms. MHS.
Corbin chart. Cary Geneal. Coll. Ms. MHS.
Pedigree of John McPherson Dennis. Soc. Col. Wars Md. Culver. 1940. MHS; DAR.
*Edmund Randolph family. Leaflet. MHS.
St. Paul's Parish, Balto. V. 2, 3, 4. Mss. MHS.
See Rutledge-Stump-Jennings.
__Jennings, Edmund.__ Will, March 24, 1756. Va. Mag. Hist. and Biog., v. 12, pp. 306–10.
__Jennings Family.__ Bible. Md. Geneal. Bull., v. 2, p. 9. MHS; DAR.
__Jennings-Hand.__ Bible rec. Photos. MHS.
__Jenson.__ St. Paul's Parish, Balto. V. 2. Mss. MHS.
__Jephenson, John__ (War of 1812). Glendy churchyard. Patriotic Marylander, v. 2, no. 4, pp. 54–60. MHS; DAR.
*__Jerningham.__ Lineage Bk., Daughters of Amer. Col., v. 2, p. 66; v. 5, p. 19. MHS; DAR.
__Jerome.__ Jerome hist. and geneal., and ancestry of Sarah Noble (Mass., 1650). (Timothy Jerome came to Amer. about 1710, settled in Conn.; his descendant John Hanson Thomas Jerome born in Balto., Feb. 26, 1816, was Mayor of Balto., 1850–52.) Typed, bd., 66 pp. MHS.
†__Jessop.__ Hist. of Balto. City and Co. Scharf. P. 925. MHS.
Levi Ferguson and Kezia B. Jessop marriage license. Ms. MHS.
Hist. graves of Md. and D. C. Ridgely. MHS.
Md. families. Culver. Ms. Personal list.
†Med. Annals Md. Cordell. 1903, p. 455. MHS.
Peale Geneal. Coll. Ms. MHS.
St. Paul's Parish, Balto. V. 1. Mss. MHS.
St. Paul's P. E. churchyard, Kent Co. Md. O. R. Soc. Bull., no. 2, pp. 54–65.
__Jessop,__ Balto. Co. Col. families of Amer. Lawrence. V. 3, p. 196; v. 7, p. 202. MHS.
__Jessup.__ Talbott of "Poplar Knowle." Shirk. MHS; DAR.
__Jester.__ Tombstone inscriptions, 1805, Andover Farm, Kent Co. Md. Geneal. Rec. Com., 1932, p. 208. DAR.
Trinity Church burial ground, near Cambridge, Md. Md. Geneal. Rec. Com., 1937–38, pp. 93–104. Mss. DAR.
__Jewell.__ Harford Co. Hist. Soc. Mss. Coll. JHU.
__Jewett.__ Col. families of Amer. Lawrence. V. 7, p. 393. MHS.
Husband and allied families. Ms. MHS.
Monumental City. Howard. MHS; DAR.
*__Jewett, Hugh Judge.__ Coat of arms. Burke's landed gentry. 1939. MHS.
__Jewett Family.__ Harford Co. Hist. Soc. Mss. Coll. JHU.
__Jewett Line.__ Turner family. Forman. P. 58. MHS.
__Jewett-Ashton.__ Harford Co. Hist. Soc. Mss. Coll. JHU.
*__Jewett, Jewitt.__ Hist. of Jewetts of Amer. F. C. Jewett. Jewetts in Mass., 1638, of Md., v. 2, pp. 935–36, 2 vols. N. Y., Grafton Press, 1908, 2 vols. MHS.
__Jewitte.__ *See* Jewett.
__Jnery, Inery.__ Somerset Co. Court Book. Tilghman. 1937. Ms. DAR.
__Job.__ Descendants of Andrew Job, Chester Co., Pa. Mrs. Fannie (Jobe) McGuire. Md. ref. 1928, typed, bd. MHS.
*Hist. of Cecil Co. Johnston. MHS; DAR.
Md. families. Culver. Ms. Personal list.
Sharpless family geneal. Cope. Pp. 527–30. MHS; DAR.

Joce. Pedigree of George Washington Williams. Soc. Col. Wars Md. Culver. 1940. MHS; DAR.
Johnes. *See* Johns.
Johns. Abs. of rec. of West River Monthly Meeting. Ms. MHS.
Beirne chart. MHS.
Black chart. MHS.
Cary Geneal. Coll. Ms. MHS.
Chart of the Welsh ancestry of the Johns family. Col. Dames, Chap. I. MHS.
See Cotten. Abr. Compend. Amer. Geneal. Virkus. V. 1, p. 568. DAR.
Cotton chart. MHS.
Eldridge chart. MHS.
Ellicott-King chart. MHS.
*Geneal. of family of Richard Johns, Dover, Balto. Co., 1753–1863 and his son Richard Johns, 1790–1881. Md. Geneal. Rec. Com., 1934. DAR.
†Hist. of Allegany Co. Thomas and Williams. V. 1. MHS; DAR.
Hopkins chart. Cary Geneal. Coll. Ms. MHS.
S. G. Hopkins chart. MHS.
Hopkins, Husband, Johns, Sharp and Webster families. Browne. Bd. ms. MHS.
Hutchins chart. Cary Geneal. Coll. Ms. MHS.
Johns family. Elias Jones. Democrat and News, Cambridge, Friday, Feb. 26, 1926. Newsp. clipp. MHS.
Marriage of S. S. Johns and Elizabeth G. Skinner, Prince George Co., Oct. 10, 1805. Natl. Geneal. Soc. Quart., June, 1938, v. 26, no. 2, p. 33.
Md. families. Culver. Ms. Personal list.
†Med. Annals Md. Cordell. 1903, p. 455. MHS.
Mrs. Renshaw chart. MHS.
Orme geneal. chart. MHS.
Pedigree of Charles O'Donnell Mackall. Soc. Col. Wars Md. Culver. 1940. MHS; DAR.
Pedigree of Maurice Edward Skinner. Soc. Col. Wars Md. Culver. 1940. MHS; DAR.
Price ancestral data (maternal). Bd. ms. MHS.
Rucker family. Whitley.
See Strain, Mrs. R. J. (nee Canby). Abr. Compend. Amer. Geneal. Virkus. V. 1, p. 535. DAR.
Turner family. Forman. P. 87. MHS.
Miss Sara, E. White chart. MHS.
See Hopkins-Johns.
See Hopkins-Johns-Kinsey.
See Van Dyke-Johns-Montgomery-Manlove.
Johns, Right Rev. John. N. Y. Geneal. and Biog. Rec., v. 8, p. 95.
†**Johns, Kensey.** Appleton's cyc. Wilson and Fiske. 1888, v. 3, p. 436.
†**Johns, Richard** (1645–1717), Md. Index to biog. sketches pub. in "The Friend," v. 26, v. 27. Pub. Geneal. Soc. Pa., v. 3, no. 2, pp. 109–34.
Johns, Richard, Dover, Balto. Co. Family geneal., 1790–1847. Md. Geneal. Rec. Com., 1933–34, pp. 257–58. Mss. DAR.
Johns, Richard H. Geneal. and mem. encyc. of Md. Spencer. V. 2, p. 687. MHS; DAR.
Johns-Hutchins. Thomas Book. Thomas. P. 370. Lib. Cong.; MHS.
Johns-Kinsey. Ances. rec. and portraits. Col. Dames of Amer., 1910, v. 1, p. 218–20, 222, 224. MHS; DAR.
Johns, Johnes. St. Paul's Parish, Balto. V. 1, 2. Mss. MHS.
Johnson. All Hallow's P. E. church yard, Snow Hill, Worcester Co. Hudson. Bd. ms. MHS; DAR. Also: Md. Geneal. Rec. Com., 1935–36, p. 24. Mss. DAR.
*Ancestry of Rosalie Morris Johnson, daughter of George Calvert Morris and Elizabeth Kuhn. Charts and pedigrees. R. W. Johnson. Pr. for priv. circulation, Ferris & Leach. 1905, 1908. MHS; DAR.
Beirne chart. MHS.
†Bench and bar of Md. Sams and Riley. 1901, v. 1, p. 330. Lib. Cong.; MHS; Peabody Lib.
Botfield and allied families. Ms. DAR.
Cary Geneal. Coll. Ms. MHS.
*Frederick Co. families. Markell. Ms. Personal list.
†Founders of Anne Arundel and Howard Cos. Warfield. P. 128 (Reverdy), 224 (Gov. Thomas), 535. MHS; DAR.
Griffith geneal. Griffith. MHS; DAR.
Mrs. C. C. Hall chart. MHS.
Hatton and Johnson families (Md. 1648). Christopher Johnston. William and Mary quart., 1st series, v. 23, p. 113.
†Hist. of Allegany Co. Thomas and Williams. V. 2. MHS; DAR.
*Hist. of Frederick Co. Williams. V. 1, p. 111. MHS; DAR.
†Hist. of Washington Co. Williams. 1906, v. 2, p. 1071. MHS; DAR.
†Hist. of West. Md. Scharf. V. 1, pp. 389–92, 453–54. MHS; DAR.
Holdens Cemetery, Kent Co. Md. Geneal. Rec. Com., 1932, v. 5, p. 211. Mss. DAR.
*Johnson and allied families. R. W. Johnson and L. J. Morris. 1934. DAR.
*Johnsons of Md. (Gov. Thomas Johnson family.) D. A. R. Mag., Oct., 1914, v. 45, p. 173.
†Life of Reverdy Johnson. B. C. Steiner. Balto., 1914. MHS; DAR.
†Life of Thomas Johnson. Edw. S. Delaplaine. N. Y., Grafton Press, 1927, 517 pp. MHS; DAR.
†Life of Thomas Johnson, Edw. S. Delaplaine. M. H. Mag., 1919, v. 14, through v. 20.
Lineage Bks., Natl. Soc. of Daughters of Amer. Col., v. 3, p. 219, v. 4, p. 219. MHS; DAR.
Md. families. Culver. Ms. Personal list.
†Med. Annals Md. Cordell. 1903, pp. 455–58. MHS.
M. E. churchyard, Snow Hill, Worcester Co., Hudson. Bd. ms. MHS; DAR.
Naturalizations in Md., 1666–1765; Laws. Bacon. MHS.
Patriotic Md. Md. Soc. of S. A. R., 1930. MHS; DAR.
Plummer family. A. P. H. Ms. MHS.
Old Somerset. Torrence. MHS; DAR.
Portrait and biog. rec. of Sixth Cong. Dist. of Md. 1898, pp. 87, 195, 207, 834, 857. MHS; DAR.
Rehobeth P. E. churchyard, Somerset Co. Md. Geneal. Rec. Com., 1937, Mrs. Lines. Mss. DAR.

Johnson. St. John's R. C. Church cemetery, Montgomery Co. Md. Geneal. Rec. Com., 1926, p. 27. Mss. DAR.
St. Paul's Parish, Balto. V. 1, 2, 3, 4. Mss. MHS.
St. Stephens Parish, Cecilton, Md. MHS; DAR.
Somerset Co. Court Book. Tilghman. 1937. Ms. DAR.
Taylor Bible rec. Ms. MHS.
Geneal. notes of Thomas family. Thomas. MHS; DAR.
Tombstone rec. of Dorchester Co. Jones. DAR.
Turner Geneal. Coll. Ms. MHS.
Western Run Parish book. Allen. Bd. ms. MHS.
Wicomico Co. families, Bible rec. Ms. DAR.
*Wicomico Co. families. Tilghman. Ms, pp. 38-39, 42, 46-47, 97-98, 100. DAR.
See Love-Johnson.
See Montgomery-Love-Johnson.
Johnson, Balto. Abr. Compend. Amer. Geneal. Virkus. V. 6, p. 685. DAR.
Johnson, Balto. Co. Pedigree of Francis Joseph Baldwin. Soc. Col. Wars Md. Culver. 1940. MHS; DAR.
Johnson, Calvert and Frederick Cos. Col. families of U. S. A. Mackenzie. V. 1, v. 2. MHS; DAR.
***Johnson,** Dorchester Co. Burke's landed gentry. 1939. MHS.
Johnson, Frederick Co. Talbott of "Poplar Knowle." Shirk. MHS; DAR.
Johnson, N. H. Balto., its hist., its people. Hall. V. 3. MHS; DAR.
Johnson, Charles Wm. Leverett. Pedigree. (Mostly New Eng. and N. Y. family rec.) Soc. Col. Wars Md. Culver. 1940. MHS; DAR.
Pedigree charts, plates 1, 2, 3 and 4. Soc. Col. Wars, Md. Johnston. 1905, pp. 49-52. MHS.
Johnson, Daniel. Abr. Compend. Amer. Geneal. Virkus. V. 6, p. 580. DAR.
Johnson, Rev. Elias Henry. Pedigree chart. Soc. Col. Wars, Md. Johnston. 1905, p. 48. MHS.
†**Johnson, Reverdy.** Balto., hist. and biog. Richardson and Bennett. 1871, p. 325. MHS; DAR.
Mrs. Charles Carter chart. MHS.
Geneal. and memorial encyc. of Md. Spencer. V. 2, p. 342. MHS; DAR.
Ghiselin chart. Cary Geneal. Coll. Ms. MHS.
†Hist. of Md. Scharf. V. 3, p. 704. MHS.
Hollingsworth chart. Cary Geneal. Coll. Ms. MHS.
†M. H. Mag., 1920, v. 15, pp. 42-55.
†Men of mark in Md. Johnson. V. 4. DAR; Enoch Pratt Lib.
Mrs. G. H. Williams, Jr., chart. MHS.
Johnson, Mrs. Robert W., Jr. (Rose Stanley Gordon Haxall). Chart. (Mostly Va. families.) Col. Dames, Chap. I. MHS.
†**Johnson, Thomas.** Appleton's cyc. 1887, v. 3, pp. 450-51. MHS.
†Biog. sketches of distinguished Marylanders. Boyle. MHS; DAR.
†M. H. Mag., v. 12, p. 222.
***Johnson, Gov. Thomas.** Ancestry in Eng. Md. Geneal. Bull., v. 10, no. 3, p. 25. MHS; DAR.
†(Son of Thomas and Dorcas (Sedwick) Johnson; born St. Leonard's Creek, Calvert Co., Nov. 4, 1732; married Anne Jennings, daughter of Thomas Jennings, Annapolis, Feb. 16, 1766; elected (first) Governor of Md., Feb. 13, 1777; died at Rose Hill, Frederick, Oct. 26, 1819). Hist. of Md. Scharf. V. 2, pp. 285-88. MHS. See also Md. Hist. Mag., 1919, v. 14: 1920, v. 15.
(First elected Governor of Md.). Geneal. Ms. MHS.
†Thomas Johnson, Governor of Md. Buchholz. P. 1. MHS.
***Johnson Family.** Hist. of Dorchester Co. Jones. 1925, pp. 367-71. MHS; DAR.
*Notes. Ms. File case, MHS.
*Old Kent. Hanson. Pp. 50-59, 283. MHS; DAR.
Thomas Book. Thomas Pp. 372-75. Lib. Cong.; MHS.
Johnson Family, Annapolis. Ms. MHS.
Johnson-Buchanan. Marriage of Thomas Johnson and Susan Buchanan. Natl. Geneal. Soc. Quart., Sept., 1938, v. 26, no. 3, p. 63.
Johnson-Love. D. A. R. Mag., June, 1932, v. 66, no. 6, p. 361.
†**Johnston.** Bench and bar of Md. Sams and Riley. 1901, v. 1, p. 192. Lib. Cong.; MHS; Peabody Lib.
Donaldson family. Donaldson. 1931, pamph. MHS.
*Johnstons of Salisbury, with brief supplement concerning Hancock, Strother, and Preston families. W. Preston Johnston. New Orleans. G. Graham & Son, Ltd., 1897. MHS; DAR.
Life of Richard Malcolm Johnston in Md. 1867-98. F. T. Long. M. H. Mag., Sept., 1940, v. 35, no. 3, pp. 270-86; to be continued.
†Med. Annals Md. Cordell. 1903, pp. 458-59, 750, 835-42. MHS.
St. Andrews P. E. churchyard, Princess Anne, Somerset Co. Md. O. R. Soc. Bull., no. 1, pp. 29-32.
St. Paul's Parish, Balto. V. 1, 2, 4. Mss. MHS.
Whitridge chart. MHS.
***Johnston,** Va. Burke's landed gentry. 1939. MHS.
Johnston, Mrs. Bartlett S. (Caroline Cole Brooks). Chart. Col. Dames, Chap. I. MHS.
Mrs. Wm. G. McCormick chart. MHS.
Johnston, Christopher. Col. families of U. S. A. Mackenzie. V. 4. MHS; DAR.
†Men of mark in Md. Johnson. V. 2. DAR; Enoch Pratt Lib.
Pedigree charts, plates 1 and 2. Soc. Col. Wars, Md. Johnston. 1905, pp. 53-54. MHS.
(1856-1914). Tribute to Christopher Johnston. M. H. Mag., 1914, v. 9, p. 297.
Westminster churchyard. Patriotic Marylander, v. 2, no. 4, pp. 54-60. MHS; DAR.
Johnston, Dr. Christopher, Jr. Pedigree. Soc. Col. Wars Md. Culver. 1940. MHS; DAR.
Johnston, Mrs. Herbert French; formerly **Mrs. Albert Page Boyce (Anne Gordon Thom).** Chart. Col. Dames, Chap. I. MHS.
Johnston, Mrs. J. Edward (Macy Mathilde Manly). Chart. Col. Dames, Chap. I. MHS.
***Johnston, Robt. McClanahan,** Va. Family notes, etc. Ms. File case, MHS.

Johnston, Samuel. Autobiog. Ms. MHS.
Johnston, Johnstone. Geneal., 1569–1888. Typed ms., 6 pp. MHS.
Johnstone. *See* Johnston.
Johnstone, Miss Emma Elliott. Chart. Col. Dames, Chap. I. MHS.
Joice, Joyce. St. Paul's Parish, Balto. V. 1, 2. Mss. MHS.
Joiner. Data. Md. Geneal. Rec. Com., 1937, Parran, pp. 213, 215. Mss. DAR.
See Cannan-Bush-Calder-Joiner-Meeks.
Jolley. Harford Co. Hist. Soc. Mss. Coll. JHU.
***Jolliffe.** Hist. and geneal. account of Jolliffe family of Va., 1652–1693. W. Jolliffe. Phila., J. B. Lippincott, 1893. DAR.
Jolliffee. Geneal. and memorial encyc. of Md. Spencer. V. 1, p. 237. MHS; DAR.
Jolly. St. Paul's Parish, Balto. V. 2. Mss. MHS.
Wallis chart. MHS.
Jolly, Harford Co. Miss C. Petre chart. MHS.
Jones. All Hallow's P. E. churchyard, Snow Hill, Worcester Co. Hudson. Bd. ms. MHS; DAR. Also: Md. Geneal. Rec. Com., 1935–36, p. 24. Mss. DAR.
Auld chart. MHS.
Balto., its hist., its people. Hall. V. 3. MHS; DAR.
†Bench and bar of Md. Sams and Riley. 1901, v. 1, pp. 92, 229. Lib. Cong.; MHS; Peabody Lib.
Bible rec., Kent Co. Md. Geneal. Rec. Com., 1937, Parran, p. 206. Mss. DAR.
Bible rec. M. H. Mag., 1919, v. 14, no. 1, p. 76–79.
*Bible rec. Photos. MHS.
†Biog. cyc. of rep. men of Md. and D. C. P. 44. MHS; DAR.
Botfield and allied families. Ms. DAR.
Darby geneal. Darby. MHS.
Done Bible rec. Ms. MHS.
Family hist. of Peter Jones and John Jones (through their Ohio descendants). Peter Jones, Sr., came to Md. from Wales, 1750. In binder, typed. MHS.
Founders of Anne Arundel and Howard Cos. Warfield. P. 526. MHS; DAR.
*Frederick Co. families. Markell. Ms. Personal list.
Griffith geneal. Griffith. MHS; DAR.
Mrs. T. B. Harrison chart. MHS.
†Hist. of Allegany Co. Thomas and William. V. 1. MHS; DAR.
†Hist. of Balto. City and Co. Scharf. P. 889. MHS.
Hist. graves of Md. and D. C. Ridgely. MHS.
*Hist. of Frederick Co. Williams. MHS; DAR.
†Hist. Printing in Col. Md. Wroth. MHS.
Hyland-Jones family of East. Shore of Md. Curry.
*Jones family of Walnut Grove. "Visit to Patapsco Neck." The American, May 7, 1883. MHS.
Judge Thomas Jones of Patapsco Neck. Basil Sellers. M. H. Mag., 1907, v. 2, pp. 245–59.
Land grants, deeds, patents, from estate of Georgia G. Jones. Ms. MHS.
Lee Mag. of Va., April, 1923. V. 1, no. 2. MHS.
Lloyd family hist. of Wales, Pa., and Md. DAR.
Makemie Memorial Pres. churchyard, Snow Hill, Worcester Co. Hudson. Bd. ms. MHS; DAR. Also: Md. Geneal. Rec. Com., Mrs. Lines. Mss. DAR.
Marriages. Dorchester Co. Marriages, 1781–1807. Md. Geneal. Rec. Com., v. 4, p. 80. DAR.
Marriages of Dorchester Co., 1780–1820. Natl. Geneal. Soc. Quart., Dec., 1931, v. 19, no. 4, pp. 103–04.
Md. families. Culver. Ms. Personal list.
†Med. Annals Md. Cordell. 1903, pp. 459–62. MHS.
M. E. churchyard, Snow Hill, Worcester Co., Hudson. Bd. ms. MHS; DAR.
Mt. Zion P. E. churchyard, Worcester Co. Md. Geneal. Rec. Com., 1937, Mrs. Lines. Mss. DAR.
Old Somerset. Torrence. MHS; DAR.
Patriotic Md. Md. Soc. of S. A. R., 1930. MHS; DAR.
Pedigree of Wm. Winchester Eareckson. Soc. Col. Wars Md. Culver. 1940. MHS; DAR.
Pocomoke Pres. churchyard, Worcester Co., Hudson. Bd. ms. MHS; DAR.
Portrait and biog. rec. of Sixth Cong. Dist. of Md. 1898, pp. 139, 527, 670, 701, 732, 828. MHS; DAR.
Rec. of Stepney Parish. MHS; DAR.
St. Andrews P. E. churchyard, Princess Anne, Somerset Co. Md. O. R. Soc. Bull., no. 1, pp. 29–32.
St. Mary's churchyard, Tyaskin, Md. Md. Geneal. Rec. Com., 1938–39, pp. 187–92. Mss. DAR.
St. Mary's P. E. churchyard, Pocomoke, Worcester Co., Hudson. Bd. ms. MHS; DAR.
St. Paul's P. E. churchyard, Berlin, Worcester Co. Hudson. Bd. ms. MHS; DAR. Also: Md. Geneal. Rec. Com., 1937, Mrs. Lines. Mss. DAR.
St. Paul's Parish, Balto. V. 1, 2, 3, 4. Mss. MHS.
St. Stephens Parish, Cecilton, Md. MHS; DAR.
Shrewsbury churchyard, Kent Co. Md. O. R. Soc., v. 2, pp. 46–54. MHS.
Somerset Co. Court Book. Tilghman. 1937. Ms. DAR.
Southern Bapt. Church cemetery, Worcester Co. Md. Geneal. Rec. Com., 1937, Mrs. Lines. Mss. DAR.
Summers-Jones-Gunby-Morris Bible rec. Md. Geneal. Rec. Com., 1937–38, pp. 142–46. Mss. DAR.
*The Sun, Balto., July 16, 1905; Jan. 7, 1906 (Jones-Lake families).
Talbott of "Poplar Knowle." Shirk. MHS; DAR.
Mrs. H. De Courcy Wright Thom Chart. MHS.
Thomas Book. Thomas. P. 376. Lib. Cong.; MHS.
Tombstone rec. of Dorchester Co. Jones. DAR.
(62 graves.) Trinity Church burial ground, near Cambridge, Md. Md. Geneal. Rec. Com., 1937–38, pp. 93–104. Mss. DAR.
(44 tombstones.) Trinity Church cemetery, Dorchester Co. Md. O. R. Soc. Bull., no. 3, pp. 42–52.
Turner Geneal. Coll. Ms. MHS.
Wicomico Co. families Bible rec. Ms. DAR.
*Wicomico Co. families. Tilghman. Ms, pp. 40, 98, 100, 111, 129. DAR.

Jones. *See* Hodson-Collison-Ball-Jones-Lankford. *See* Thurman-Graves-Jones.
Jones, Anne Arundel Co. Col. families of U. S. A. Mackenzie. V. 2, pp. 396–400; v. 4, pp. 273–75 (Va.); v. 6, p. 421. MHS; DAR.
Lineage Bks., Natl. Soc. of Daughters of Amer. Col., v. 1, p. 188. MHS; DAR.
Tombstone inscriptions. Ms. DAR.
Jones, Baltimore. Mrs. T. R. Brown chart. MHS.
Jones, Corn Field Harbor, St. Michael's Manor, St. Mary's Co. Tombstone inscriptions. (Earliest birth, 1747; first burial, 1800.) Md. O. R. Soc. Bull., no. 3, p. 56.
†**Jones,** Carroll Co. Hist. of West. Md. Scharf. V. 2, pp. 929–30. MHS; DAR.
Jones, Frederick Co. Rec. from three Bibles. Ms. MHS.
***Jones,** Talbot Co. Burke's landed gentry. 1939. MHS.
Jones, Va. Amer. Clan Gregor Year Book, 1912, p. 118; 1915, p. 79. MHS; DAR.
Jones, Arthur Lafayette. Pedigree. Soc. Col. Wars Md. Culver. 1940. MHS; DAR.
Jones, Edward Croxall. Pedigree. Soc. Col. Wars Md. Culver. 1940. MHS; DAR.
Jones, H. Burgess. Md. Soc., War of 1812, v. 1, no. 98. Ms. MHS.
Jones, Isaac D. Memorial to Thomas Potts, Jr. James. P. 307. MHS.
†**Jones, J. Wynne.** Men of mark in Md. Johnson. V. 2. DAR; Enoch Pratt Lib.
†**Jones, John** (died in Md., 1774). Index to biog. sketches pub. in "The Friend," v. 26, v. 27. Pub. Geneal. Soc. Pa., v. 3, no. 2, pp. 109–34.
Jones, Col. John. Revolutionary grave, in yard of oldest church in Md. Md. Geneal. Rec. Com., v. 2, p. 14. Mss. DAR.
***Jones, Peter and Richard.** Geneal. Comp. from orig. sources of Augusta B. Fathergill. Richmond, Va., 1924, 1st ed. MHS.
***Jones, Lieut. Col. Robert Copeland.** Coat of arms. Burke's landed gentry. 1939. MHS.
†**Jones, Robert Morris.** Men of mark in Md. Johnson. V. 3. DAR; Enoch Pratt Lib.
†**Jones, Robley D.** Men of mark in Md. Johnson. V. 4. DAR; Enoch Pratt Lib.
***Jones, Capt. Roger Jones,** London and Va. Some of his antecedents and descendants. Browning.
Jones, Rev. Rowland. Cary Geneal. Coll. Ms. MHS.
†**Jones, Spencer C.** Men of mark in Md. Johnson. V. 1. DAR; Enoch Pratt Lib.
Jones, Thomas. Revolutionary grave in yard of oldest church in Md. Md. Geneal. Rec. Com., v. 2, p. 15. Mss. DAR.
Jones, Washington. Revolutionary grave in yard of oldest church in Md. Md. Geneal. Rec. Com., v. 2, p. 15. Mss. DAR.
Jones, Wm. B. Family Bible rec., 1817–53. Md. Geneal. Rec. Com., 1937–38, p. 152. Mss. DAR.
Jones Family, "Clean Drinking Manor," Montgomery Co. Ms. MHS.
Lee of Va., 1642–1892. E. J. Lee. P. 365. Lib. Cong.; MHS.
*Old Kent. Hanson. 315–17. MHS; DAR.
Jones Family, Kent Co. Births, marriages, deaths, 1876–1929. Md. Geneal. Rec. Com., 1937, p. 206. DAR.
Jones Family, Walnut Grove. Balto. American, May 7, 1883. Newsp. clipp. MHS.
Jones-Foster-Kenedy. Harford Co. Hist. Soc. Mss. Coll. JHU.
Jones-Larmore. Bible rec. (Bible owned by Prof. Lloyd Larmore, Tyaskin, Md.) Md. Geneal. Rec. Com., 1938–39, pp. 215–16. Mss. DAR.
Jonson. St. Stephens Parish, Cecilton, Md. MHS; DAR.
Jopling. Chart of Com. John Rodgers. DAR.
Jordan. Cary Geneal. Coll. Ms. MHS.
Burton ancestry. Ms. MHS.
†Hist. of Balto. City and Co. Scharf. P. 871. MHS.
St. Paul's Parish, Balto. V. 2, 4. Mss. MHS.
St. Thomas' Parish, Balto. Co. Bd. ms. MHS. Also: Md. Geneal. Rec. Com., 1937, pp. 109–82. Mss. DAR.
Wathen Prayer Book rec. Ms. MHS.
Jordan, Balto. Co. Abr. Compend. Amer. Geneal. Virkus. V. 6, p. 334. DAR.
Jordan Family, Va. Chart. A. H. Pugh.
Jourdain. Naturalizations in Md., 1666–1765; Laws. Bacon. MHS.
Jourdan. Portrait and biog. rec. of Sixth Cong. Dist. of Md. 1898, p. 361. MHS; DAR.
†**Jowles.** Bench and bar of Md. Sams and Riley. 1901, v. 1, p. 86. Lib. Cong.; MHS Peabody Lib.
Joyce. Anne Arundel Co. tombstone inscriptions. Ms. DAR.
See Joice.
Joyce, Kent Co. Mrs. J. Hall Pleasants, Jr., chart. MHS.
Joynes, Reuben. Land grant, Va., 1809. Md. Geneal. Rec. Com., 1932–33, p. 1. Mss. DAR.
Judd-Sutton-Boquets. Harford Co. Hist. Soc. Mss. Coll. JHU.
Judik. Balto., its hist., its people. Hall. V. 2. MHS; DAR.
Judrell. Somerset Co. Court Book. Tilghman. 1937. Ms. DAR.
***Judy.** Frederick Co. families. Markell. Ms. Personal list.
Jump. Centreville cemetery. Md. O. R. Soc. Bull., no. 1, pp. 41–47.
Portrait and biog. rec. of East. Shore of Md. 1898. Pp. 396, 791, 874, 918. MHS; DAR.
Junkin-Johnson. Abr. Compend. Amer. Geneal. Virkus. V. 1, p. 663. DAR.
***Justice.** Frederick Co. families. Markell. Ms. Personal list.
Justice, Justis. St. Paul's Parish, Balto. V. 1, 2, 4. Mss. MHS.
See Justice.

K

Kain, Kean, Cain. St. Paul's Parish, Balto. V. 2. Mss. MHS.
Kaminsky. St. Paul's Parish, Balto. V. 2. Mss. MHS.
Kane. Faith Pres. Church (Glendy graveyard). Mss. MHS.
Kane, John W. (War of 1812). Glendy churchyard. Patriotic Marylander, v. 2, no. 4, pp. 54–60. MHS; DAR.
Kankey. Md. families. Culver. Ms. Personal list.
Kanky. Husband and allied families. Ms. MHS.

Kanode. Lehman family in Md. Lehman. 1935, pamph., pp. 31–32, 53. MHS; DAR.
Kapp, Capp. Hagerstown tombstone inscriptions. Gruder. Natl. Geneal. Soc. Quart., 1919, v. 8, nos. 1, 2.
Kaufman. Mt. Olivet Cemetery, Frederick. Md. Geneal. Rec. Com., 1934–35, p. 111. Mss. DAR.
Kaufman, J. W. Md. Soc., War of 1812, v. 2, no. 180. Ms. MHS.
Kausler. Hagerstown tombstone inscriptions. Gruder. Natl. Geneal. Soc. Quart., 1919, v. 8, nos. 1, 2.
Kay. Florence Eyster Weaver chart. MHS.
Kays. St. Paul's Parish, Balto. V. 2. Mss. MHS.
Keagy. Eldridge chart. MHS.
Kealfofer, Hagerstown. Geneal. and mem. encyc. of Md. Spencer. V. 1, p. 305. MHS; DAR.
Kealhofer. Rev. Christian Frederick Post and Peter Humrickhouse. Humrickhouse. P. 23. MHS.
Kean. *See* Kain.
***Kearsley.** Descendants of Jonathan Kearsley, from Scotland, who settled at Carlisle, Pa. Chart. 1900.
Keating. Centreville cemetery. Md. O. R. Soc. Bull., no. 1, pp. 41–47.
St. Paul's Parish, Balto. V. 2. Mss. MHS.
Kee, Cecil Co. Sharpless family geneal. Cope. P. 1165. MHS; DAR.
Keech. Dorsey chart. MHS.
Md. families. Culver. Ms. Personal list.
Patriotic Md. Md. Soc. of S. A. R., 1930. MHS; DAR.
St. Paul's Parish, Balto. V. 2. Mss. MHS.
***Keech Family.** Wilson Mss. Coll., no. 10. MHS.
†**Keedy.** Bench and bar of Md. Sams and Riley. 1901, v. 2, p. 633. Lib. Cong.; MHS; Peabody Lib.
†Hist. of Washington Co. Williams. 1906, v. 2, p. 1259. MHS; DAR.
Taney and allied families. Silverson. MHS; DAR.
†**Keedy, Martin L.** Men of mark in Md. Johnson. V. 1. DAR; Enoch Pratt Lib.
Keefer. Md. tombstone rec. Md. Geneal. Rec. Com., 1937, Parran, pp. 21, 22. Mss. DAR.
Keen. Descendants of Nathaniel Bayless. DAR. *See* Keene.
Keene. Abr. Compend. Amer. Geneal. Virkus. V. 4, p. 436. MHS.
Ances. rec. and portraits. Col. Dames of Amer., 1910, v. 2, p. 451. MHS; DAR.
Balto. Herald, April 9, 1903. Newsp. clipp. Scrap Book. MHS.
Baptisms, births, deaths, marriages and wills. Keene family. Jones. Pp. 265–318. MHS; DAR.
*Burke's landed gentry. 1939. MHS.
Col. families of U. S. A. Mackenzie. V. 6, p. 449. MHS; DAR.
Descendants of Valentine Hollingsworth, Sr. Stewart. MHS; DAR.
*Hist. and geneal. of Keene family. E. Jones. Balto., Kohn & Pollock, 1923. MHS; DAR.
*Hist. of Dorchester Co. Jones, 1925, pp. 372–74. MHS; DAR.
Lineage Bks., Natl. Soc. of Daughters of Amer. Col., v. 3, pp. 76, 262. MHS; DAR.
Md. families. Culver. Ms. Personal list.
†Med. Annals Md. Cordell. 1903, pp. 463–64. MHS.
Patriotic Md. Md. Soc. of S. A. R., 1930. MHS; DAR.
Pedigree of Dorsey Richardson. Soc. Col. Wars Md. Culver. 1940. MHS; DAR.
Somerset Co. Court Book. Tilghman. 1937. Ms. DAR.
Trinity Church burial ground, near Cambridge, Md. Md. Geneal. Rec. Com., 1937–38, pp. 93–104. Mss. DAR.
Trinity Church cemetery, Dorchester Co. Md. O. R. Soc. Bull., no. 3, pp. 42–52.
See Horsey-Keene.
***Keene,** 1657–1722, Dorchester Co. Lineage Bk., Daughters of Amer. Col., v. 3, pp. 76, 262–63. MHS; DAR.
***Keene, John Henry.** Geneal. and mem. encyc. of Md. Spencer. V. 2, p. 708. MHS; DAR.
Keene, Keen. St. Paul's Parish, Balto. V. 2. Mss. MHS.
***Keener.** Md. Geneal. Bull., v. 10, no. 1, p. 1. MHS; DAR.
†Med. Annals Md. Cordell. 1903, p. 464. MHS.
Peale Geneal. Coll. Ms. MHS.
St. Paul's Parish, Balto. V. 2. Mss. MHS.
Keener, Richard, Va. Pedigree of Duncan Keener Brent. Soc. Col. Wars Md. Culver. 1940. MHS; DAR.
Keeports, Capt. George R. Westminster churchyard. Patriotic Marylander, v. 2, no. 4, pp. 54–60. MHS; DAR.
(1718–1814). Revolutionary war heroes. Cole. Bklet. Enoch Pratt Lib.
Keerfort. Ms. (In this is Monius or Monyn family of Waldeshare, Kent, Eng.) Ms. MHS.
†**Keerl.** Hist. of Balto. City and Co. Scharf. P. 773. MHS.
†Med. Annals Md. Cordell. 1903, p. 464. MHS.
Richard Dobbs Spaight of N. C. Wheeler. 1880, pamph., p. 25. MHS.
†**Kefauver.** Hist. of Frederick Co. Williams, MHS; DAR.
Kehler. Frederick Co. tombstone inscriptions. Gruder. Natl. Geneal. Soc. Quart., 1919, v. 8, nos. 1, 2.
†**Keidel, George C.** Autobiog. sketch. Keideliana list pub. of George C. Keidel. Pamph. MHS.
Keighler. St. Paul's Parish, Balto. V. 2. Mss. MHS.
Keim. Index to Keim Geneal. Vols. 1 and 2. Ms. DAR.
Keim and allied families in Amer. and Europe, 1698–1898. De B. Randolph Keim, editor. V. 1, no. 1, Dec., 1898–no. 3, 1899. Harrisburg Pub. Co., Pa. MHS.
*Keim and allied families. Bulletins, 1898, 1899, v. 1, 2, 3. MHS; DAR.
***Keim Family.** Account of Keim family. H. M. Keim. Pr. priv., Reading, Pa., 1874. MHS.
Keire. Joshua Dryden Bible rec. Ms. MHS.
†**Keirle.** Med. Annals Md. Cordell. 1903, pp. 464–65. MHS.
†**Keirn.** Med. Annals Md. Cordell. 1903, p. 465. MHS.
Keisecker, Kiesecker, Kissecker. Hagerstown tombstone inscriptions. Gruder. Natl. Geneal. Soc. Quart., 1919, v. 8, nos. 1, 2.

Keith. Abr. Compend. Amer. Geneal. Virkus. V. 1, p. 665. DAR.
Cary Geneal. Coll. Ms. MHS.
St. Paul's Parish, Balto. V. 2. Mss. MHS.
*The Sun, Balto., Nov. 18, 25, Dec. 2, 1906.
See Fleming-Keith.
Keith Family, Fauquier Co., Va. Md. Geneal. Rec. Com., 1935–36, p. 278. Mss. DAR.
Keith Line. Col. and Revolutionary lineages of Amer. 1939, v. 1, p. 495. MHS.
Kell. Bond chart. MHS.
Hist. of Harford Co. Preston. MHS; DAR.
***Kellam.** Wicomico Co. families. Tilghman. Ms., pp. 19–20. DAR.
Kellenberger. John Swadner and his descendants. Evans. 1919. Typed, bd. MHS.
***Keller.** Descendants of Henry Keller, York Co., Pa., and Fairfield, Co., Ohio. E. S. S. Shumaker, editor; A. Kello, assoc. editor., Z (Lulie) Jones, asst. editor. Pub. by E. S. S. Shumaker, Indianapolis, Ind., 1924. MHS.
*Frederick Co. families. Markell. Ms. Personal list.
Frederick Co. tombstone inscriptions. Gruder. Natl. Geneal. Soc. Quart., 1919, v. 8, nos. 1, 2.
†Hist. of Frederick Co. Williams. MHS; DAR.
†Hist. of West. Md. Scharf. V. 2, p. 1538. MHS; DAR.
†Rev. Ezra Keller, founder and first president of Wittenberg College (born in Frederick Co., 1812). Springfield, O., Ruralist Pub. Co., 1859.
†Med. Annals Md. Cordell. 1903, p. 465: MHS.
Zion Reformed Church, Hagerstown. Md. Geneal. Rec. Com., 1934–35. Mss. DAR.
Kelley. St. Paul's Parish, Balto. V. 1, 2, 4. Mss. MHS.
St. Thomas' Parish, Balto. Co. Bd. ms. MHS. Also: Md. Geneal. Rec. Com., 1937, pp. 109–82. Mss. DAR.
Kelley, James. Church rec. St. Paul's Rec. Bk., no. 1, Balto. (James Kelly married Prudence Logsdon, 1735; Rec. of their children, 1736–81.) Natl. Geneal. Soc. Quart., v. 22, pp. 60–61.
Kelly. Barlow family Bible rec. Photos. DAR.
Kent geneal. Kent. P. 37. MHS.
Meade relations. Prichard. DAR.
†Med. Annals Md. Cordell. 1903, pp. 465–66. MHS.
Patriotic Md. Md. Soc. of S. A. R., 1930. MHS; DAR.
Kelly, Howard A. Abr. Compend. Amer. Geneal. Virkus. V. 1, p. 170. DAR.
†Men of mark in Md. Johnson. V. 2. DAR; Enoch Pratt Lib.
Kelly, Irving Washington. Md. Soc., War of 1812, v. 3, no. 270. Ms. MHS.
†Kelly, John J. Men of mark in Md. Johnson. v. 3. DAR; Enoch Pratt Lib.
Kelly, Capt. William, Richmond, Va., and Balto. (1775–1850). Cary Geneal. Coll. Ms. MHS.
Kelly (Charles Co.)**-Brooke-Hamilton-Spalding-Willson.** Abr. Compend Amer. Geneal. Virkus. V. 4, p. 320. MHS.
Kelso. Geneal. of Augusta Maitland (Carter) Libby, of Denver, Col., 1704–1933. Ms. MHS.
Mrs. G. H. Williams Jr., chart. MHS.
Kelsoe. Kelsoe family. Mrs. G. F. Libby. Ms. MHS.
Kemp. Chart of Kemp of Eng. to Kemp, emigrant of Va. DAR.
Christ P. E. Church cemetery. Cambridge. Steele, 1936, MHS; DAR.
First settlement of Germans in Md. Schultz. 1896, p. 41. MHS.
*Frederick Co. families. Markell. Ms. Personal list.
Geneal., Mag. Amer. Ancestry, N. Y., 1916, v. 3, no. 2.
†Hist. of Frederick Co. Williams. MHS; DAR.
Hist. of Shriver family. Shriver. P. 88. MHS.
Jour. Amer. Ancestry, N. Y., 1913, v. 3, p. 33.
Md. families. Culver. Ms. Personal list.
†Med. Annals Md. Cordell. 1903, p. 466. MHS.
Patriotic Md. Md. Soc. of S. A. R., 1930, MHS; DAR.
Pedigree of Francis Barnum Culver. Soc. Col. Wars Md. Culver. 1940. MHS; DAR.
St. John's R. C. Church cemetery, Montgomery Co. Md. Geneal. Rec. Com., 1926, p. 27. Mss. DAR.
St. Paul's Parish, Balto. V. 3, 4. Mss. MHS.
Segrave chart. MHS.
Kemp, Talbot Co. Culver pedigree chart. MHS.
*Lineage Bk., Daughters of Founders and Patriots, v. 7, pp. 7–8, 10. MHS.
†Kemp, Bishop James. Balto., hist. and biog. Richardson and Bennett. 1871; p. 331. MHS; DAR.
Kemp Line, Talbot Co. H. Mullikin pedigree charts, plate 2. Soc. Col. Wars, Md. Johnston. 1905, p. 75. MHS.
Kemp-Shields. Bible rec., Kent Co. Md. Geneal. Rec. Com., 1933–34, pp. 230–31. Mss. DAR.
Kemp-Troth. Marriage certificate of John Kemp and Sarah P. Troth, Nov. 4, 1790, at Third Haven Monthly Meeting, witnessed by 43 members of congregation. Framed. MHS.
***Kemp-Waters Line** (arms). The Sun, Balto., July 9, 16, 1905.
Kempe. Cary Geneal. Coll. Ms. MHS.
Zimmerman-Waters and allied families. Allen. Pp. 37–44. MHS; DAR.
Kemper. Crain chart. MHS.
Kempton, Samuel Atkinson. Deed and other land rec., 1802–13. Ms. MHS.
Kemptt. St. Paul's Parish, Balto. V. 2. Mss. MHS.
Kendall. Bible rec. Upper Penins. East. Shore., pp. 55–59. MHS; DAR.
Geneal. of Henriette Chauncy Wilson, Upshur. Bk of photos. MHS.
Kendall family journal. (Many Md. ref.) Grafton, W. Va. MHS.
Kendall journal. Norman F. Kendall. Pub. in Grafton, W. Va. MHS.
St. Paul's Parish, Balto. V. 2, 4. Mss. MHS.
Turner Geneal. Coll. Ms. MHS.
Mrs. Morris Whitridge chart. MHS.
Kendig. Eldridge chart. MHS.
Kenedy. Cotton chart. MHS.
*Wicomico Co. families. Tilghman. Ms, p. 16. DAR.
See Jones-Foster-Kenedy.
Kenedy-Foster. Harford Co. Hist. Soc. Mss. Coll. JHU.
†Kenly. Bench and bar of Md. Sams and

Riley. 1910, v. 2, p. 367. Lib. Cong.; MHS; Peabody Lib.
Portrait and biog. rec. of Harford and Cecil Cos. 1897, p. 145. MHS; DAR.
†**Kenly, John Reese** (1822–91). M. H. Mag., v. 12, p. 224.
Kenly, Wm. Watkins. Md. Soc., War of 1812, v. 2, no. 170. Ms. MHS.
Kennard. Abr. Compend. Amer. Geneal. Virkus. V. 6, p. 727. DAR.
Bible rec., 1769–1884. Md. Geneal. Bull., v. 3, p. 17.
Bible rec. Md. Geneal. Rec. Com., 1939–40, pp. 109–11. Mss. DAR.
Bond chart. MHS.
Dorsey and allied families. Ms. MHS.
Hist. graves of Md. and D. C. Ridgely. MHS.
Spring Hill cemetery, Easton. Md. O. R. Soc. Bull., no. 1, pp. 35–41.
Kennedy. Bailliere chart. MHS.
†Bench and bar of Md. Sams and Riley. 1910, v. 1, p. 276. Lib. Cong.; MHS; Peabody Lib.
†Discourse on life and character of John P. Kennedy, 1795–1870, before Md. Hist. Soc. John Murphy. Balto., 1845. MHS.
Fox-Ellicott-Evans families. Evans. MHS; DAR.
Glendy churchyard, Balto. Md. Geneal. Rec. Com., 1933–34. Mss. DAR.
†Hist. of Balto. City and Co. Scharf. P. 653.
†Hist. of West. Md. Scharf. V. 2, pp. 1033, 1225–26. MHS; DAR.
Jenkins-Courtney chart. MHS.
†John Pendleton Kennedy. Edward M. Gwathmey. N. Y., Nelson, 1931. MHS.
†Life of John Pendleton Kennedy. Henry T. Tuckerman. N. Y., G. P. Putman & Sons, 1871. MHS; DAR.
†Med. Annals Md. Cordell. 1903, pp. 466–67. MHS.
Monumental City. Howard. MHS; DAR.
Posey chart. MHS.
Rec. of Stepney Parish. MHS; DAR.
Mrs. C. L. Riggs chart. MHS.
St. Paul's Parish, Balto. V. 2, 3. Mss. MHS.
Selden chart. MHS.
*Will of John Kennedy and his wife. Pennington Papers. Ms. MHS.
See Beall-Kennedy.
See Beedle-Foster-Kennedy-Walker.
Kennedy, Charles Co. Coll. of Amer. epitaphs and inscriptions. Alden. 1814, v. 5. MHS.
†**Kennedy, Edmund Pendleton** (1780–1844). M. H. Mag., v. 12, p. 224.
Kennedy, Capt. John (war of 1812). Glendy churchyard. Patriotic Marylander, v. 2, no. 4, pp. 54–60. MHS; DAR.
†**Kennedy, John P.** Balto., hist. and biog. Richardson and Bennett. 1871, pp. 333–36. MHS; DAR.
†Hist. of Md. Scharf. V. 3, p. 727. MHS.
Kennedy, Stephen Dandridge. Col. families of U. S. A. Mackenzie. V. 1, p. 29. MHS; DAR.
†**Kennedy, Wm.** Balto., hist. and biog. Richardson and Bennett. 1871, pp. 337–38. MHS; DAR.
***Kennedy Family.** Arch. of Georgetown Univ., Wash., D. C., v. 138, no. 10.
Kennerly. Md. Families. Culver. Ms. Personal list.
*Wicomico Co. Families. Tilghman. Ms, pp. 117, 121, 124. DAR.
***Kennon,** Va. The Sun, Balto., June 18, 25, 1905; Oct. 20 (Va.), 1907.
†**Kensett, Thomas.** Balto., hist. and biog. Richardson and Bennett. 1871, pp. 340–42. MHS; DAR.
Kensey. Beirne chart. MHS.
Md. Families. Culver. Ms. Personal list.
Mrs. Renshaw chart. MHS.
Kent. Col. families of U. S. A. Mackenzie. V. 1, p. 438. MHS; DAR.
†Founders of Anne Arundel and Howard Cos. Warfield. P. 264 (Gov. Joseph). MHS; DAR.
*Geneal. A. S. Kent. Kent of Md., pp. 5–6. Priv. pr., 1933. MHS.
Maulsby family in Amer. Barnard. DAR; Peabody Lib.
†Med. Annals Md. Cordell. 1903, p. 467. MHS.
Pedigree of Thomas Carroll Roberts. Soc. Col. Wars Md. Culver. 1940. MHS; DAR.
St. Paul's Parish, Balto. V. 2. Mss. MHS.
See Darumple-Tucker-Kent.
Kent, Calvert Co. Mrs. G. R. Veazey chart. MHS.
†**Kent, Joseph.** Governor of Md. Buchholz. P. 99. MHS.
†Hist. of Md. Scharf. V. 2, p. 635. MHS.
Keplinger, J. B. Md. Soc., War of 1812, v. no. 117. Ms. MHS.
Ker. Handy and their kin. Handy.
*Wicomico Co. families. Tilghman. Ms, pp. 99–104, 115; DAR.
†**Ker, Kerr.** Med. Annals Md. Cordell. 1903, p. 467. MHS.
Kerby, Kirby, York and Elizabeth Cos., Va. William and Mary Quart., 1st series, v. 14, pp. 154–58. (Md. ref., p. 158.)
Kerfoot. Abr. Compend. Amer. Geneal. Virkus. V. 1, p. 667. DAR.
Right Rev. John Barrett Kerfoot. With selections from his diaries. Hall Harrison. N. Y., 1886, 2 vols.
Two ms. note books in box in vault, marked Kerfoot Ms. Geneal. (Much of this is abstracted from Laurence B. Thomas Geneal. Notes, pub., 1877.) MHS.
Kernan, James L. Balto., its hist., its people. Hall. V. 2. MHS; DAR.
Kernes, Kerns. St. Paul's Parish, Balto. V. 2. Mss. MHS.
Kerns. *See* Kernes.
Kerr. Abr. Compend. Amer. Geneal. Virkus. V. 4, p. 325. MHS.
Balto., its hist., its people. Hall. V. 3. MHS; DAR.
†Bench and bar of Md. Sams and Riley. 1910, v. 2, p. 418. Lib. Cong.; MHS; Peabody Lib.
Dobbin chart. MHS.
Done Bible rec. Ms. MHS.
Geneal. notes of Chamberlaine family. MHS.
Hist. graves of Md. and D. C. Ridgely. MHS.
Lanahan chart. MHS.
Pedigree of Levin Gale Shreve. Soc. Col. Wars Md. Culver. 1940. MHS; DAR.
Pedigree of Harrison Tilghman. Soc. Col. Wars Md. Culver. 1940. MHS; DAR.
Mrs. Sherlock Swann chart. MHS.
Tilghman chart. MHS.

Kerr. Thomas family of Talbot Co. Spencer. MHS; DAR.
See Ker.
Kerr, Archibald. Glendy churchyard. Patriotic Marylander, v. 2, no. 4, pp. 54-60. MHS; DAR.
†**Kerr, David** (1749-1814). Hist. of Talbot Co. Tilghman. V. 1, pp. 300-03. MHS; DAR.
†**Kerr, John Bozman** (1809-78). Hist. of Talbot Co. Tilghman. V. 1, pp. 414-23. MHS; DAR.
†**Kerr, Hon. John Leeds** (1780-1844). Hist. of Talbot Co. Tilghman. V. 1, pp. 388-408. MHS; DAR.
†**Kerr, Robert P.** Men of mark in Md. Johnson. V. 2. DAR; Enoch Pratt Lib.
***Kerr Family.** Old Kent. Hanson. Pp. 183, 285. MHS; DAR.
Kerr-Bantz, Frederick Co. Data. D. A. R. Mag., v. 70, no. 5, p. 453.
Kershner, Kirchner. Hagerstown tombstone inscriptions. Gruder. Natl. Geneal. Soc. Quart., 1919, v. 8, nos. 1, 2.
Patriotic Md. Md. Soc. of S. A. R., 1930. MHS; DAR.
Kertchner. Hist. sketch of P. F. Eichelberger. Eichelberger.
Kessinger. Beards' Luth. graveyard, Washington Co. Md. Geneal. Rec. Com., 1935-36. Mss. DAR.
Kessuch. St. Paul's Parish, Balto. V. 2. Mss. MHS.
Kettleman, Kutleman. St. Paul's Parish, Balto. V. 1, 2. Mss. MHS.
Kettlewell. Hickok chart. MHS.
Mrs. James McHenry chart. MHS.
Mrs. Lancaster Williams chart. MHS.
Key. Ances. rec. and portraits. Col. Dames of Amer., 1910, v. 1, p. 352. MHS; DAR.
Ancestry of Rosalie Morris Johnson. Johnson. 1905. MHS; DAR.
Application for membership in Natl. Soc., Col. Dames of Amer. Ms. MHS.
Balto., its hist., its people. Hall. V. 2 (Key line); v. 3, p. 512. MHS; DAR.
Bantz geneal. notes. Ms. MHS.
†Bench and bar of Md. Sams and Riley. 1910, v. 1, pp. 176, 292. Lib. Cong.; MHS; Peabody Lib.
Cary Geneal. Coll. Ms. MHS.
Cemetery Creek, Anne Arundel Co., tombstone inscriptions. Founders of Anne Arundel and Howard Cos. Warfield. P. 334. MHS; DAR.
*Chart. Mary Chatherine Key and George Cromwell Key. Ms. MHS.
Col. families of Amer. Lawrence. V. 9, p. 135. MHS.
Col. families of U. S. A. Mackenzie. V. 1, pp. 299-304. MHS; DAR.
See Daingerfield. Abr. Compend. Amer. Geneal. Virkus. V. 1, p. 45. DAR.
DeFord chart. MHS.
Descendants of Col. Thomas White. Morris. MHS.
Dorsey and allied families. Ms. MHS.
Founders of Anne Arundel and Howard Cos. Warfield. P. 154. MHS; DAR.
Hist. graves of Md. and D. C. Ridgely. MHS.
†Hist. of Frederick Co. Williams. V. 1, pp. 313-16. MHS; DAR.
†Hist. of West. Md. Scharf. V. 2, p. 898. MHS; DAR.
McH. Howard pedigree chart, plate 2. Soc. Col. Wars, Md. Johnston. 1905, p. 42. MHS.
Howland chart. MHS.
Mrs. George C. Jenkins chart. MHS.
*Jenkins-Key chart. In Jenkins folder. MHS.
*Key and allied families. Mrs. J. C. Lane. Macon, Ga. J. W. Blake Co., 1931. DAR.
Key family. Christopher Johnston. M. H. Mag., 1910, v. 5, pp. 194-200.
Francis Scott Key as churchman. C. C. Wroth. M. H. Mag., 1909, v. 4, pp. 154-70.
*Francis Scott Key, author of Star-Spangled Banner; what else he was and who he was. F. S. Key-Smith. 1911.
Francis Scott Key, the man. Patriotic Marylander, v. 1, no. 1, pp. 26-28, 86. MHS; DAR.
†Life and times of Francis Scott Key; man, patriot, poet. E. S. Delaplaine. Pub. by Biog. Press. Brooklyn, N. Y., 1937, 480 pp. Lib. Cong.; MHS; DAR.
Sir John Zouch and his descendants. Va. Mag. Hist. and Biog., v. 12, pp. 429-32.
†Spangled Banner. Life of Francis Scott Key. V. Weybright. 1935. DAR.
Md. families. Culver. Ms. Personal list.
Memorial to Thomas Potts, Jr. James. P. 270. MHS.
*Old Kent. Hanson. Pp. 36-39. MHS; DAR.
Parr chart. MHS.
Patriotic Md. Md. Soc. of S. A. R., 1930. MHS; DAR.
Pedigree of Charles Morris Howard. Soc. Col. Wars Md. Culver. 1940. MHS; DAR.
Raisin chart. MHS.
*Side lights on Md. hist. Richardson. V. 2, p. 149. MHS; DAR.
Some notable families of south. States. Armstrong. V. 1, pp. 120-23. DAR.
Some old Eng. letters. M. H. Mag., 1914, v. 9, no. 2, pp. 107-56.
*The Sun, Balto., Sept. 11, 1904. Also Jan. 13, 1843, in MHS.
Mrs. E. C. Venable chart. MHS.
Va. geneal. Hayden. MHS; DAR.
*Will of Philip Barton Key. Printed. MHS.
Wolseley chart. Cary Geneal. Coll. Ms. MHS.
Key, Edward. Pedigree. Soc. Col. Wars Md. Culver. 1940. MHS; DAR.
Key, Francis Scott. Analectic Mag., 1814, v. 4, p. 433. Containing first printing (except for newspaper) of Star Spangled Banner.
*Author of "The Star Spangled Banner." Md. O. R. Soc., v. 2, pp. 4-21.
Biog. sketches of distinguished Marylanders. Boyle. P. 236. MHS; DAR.
Biog. sketch; with glimpse of his ancestors. F. S. Key Smith. Rec. Columbia Hist. Soc., v. 12, pp. 71-88.
Birth. M. H. Mag., 1907, v. 2, no. 2, pp. 137-40.
†Cavalcade of Amer. D. R. Fox, editor. A. M. Schlesinger. V. 2.
†(Composer of Star Spangled Banner, on night of Sept. 13, 1814; born in Frederick Co., Aug. 1, 1779; graduated from St. John's College, Annapolis, 1796; died in Balto., Jan. 11, 1843; buried in Mount Olivet Cemetery, Frederick.

Hist. of Md. Scharf. V. 3, pp. 117–20. MHS.
Life and times. E. S. Delaplaine. DAR.
†(1779–1843). M. H. Mag., v. 12, p. 255.
Portrait and biog. rec. of Sixth Cong. Dist. of Md. 1898, p. 277. MHS; DAR.

Key, Hon. Philip (1696–1764). T. C. Jenkins pedigree chart. Soc. Col. Wars, Md. Johnston. 1905, pp. 47, 148. MHS.
†Hist. of Md. Scharf. V. 2, pp. 572, 602. MHS.

***Key, Philip Barton.** Bible, with family data. MHS.

Key Family. Geneal. and descendants. Md. O. R. Soc. June, 1910, Bull., no. 2, pp. 4–21.

Key-Evans. Key-Evans duel, 1792. M. H. Mag., 1911, v. 6, p. 274.

***Key-Sewell.** Key-Sewell family data. Ms, 1 vol. MHS.

Keyes. Bible rec. Natl. Geneal. Soc. Quart., March, 1939, v. 27, no. 1, p. 32.
See Keys.

Keys. Greenway Mss. Geneal. Coll. Binder's title, Taylor, no. 2. MHS.
Pedigree of John Philemon Paca. Soc. Col. Wars Md. Culver. 1940. MHS; DAR.
Polk family. Polk. P. 7. MHS; DAR.

Keys, Keyes. Griffith geneal. Griffith. MHS; DAR.

Keyser. Ances. rec. and portraits. Col. Dames of Amer., 1910, v. 2, p. 572. MHS; DAR.
Beall and Bell families. Beall. MHS.
*Bicentennial reunion of Keyser family, 1688–1888. Descendants of Dirck Keyser of Amsterdam. C. S. Keyser. Keyser geneal., pp. 121–56; Keyser-Fort, Balto. Co., p. 129. Phila., Wm. Fell Co., 1889, 161 pp. MHS; DAR.
Clark chart. MHS.
Gary chart. MHS.
Geneal. and memorial encyc. of Md. Spencer. 1909, v. 2, p. 486. MHS; DAR.
Hist. and geneal. account of Levering family. Levering. MHS.
†Hist. of Allegany Co. Thomas and Williams. V. 2. MHS; DAR.
Horwitz chart. MHS.
Mrs. J. E. Johnson chart. MHS.
Manly chart. MHS.
Mead relations, Prichard. DAR.
Mt. Paran Pres. churchyard, Harrisonville, Balto. Co. Typed ms. MHS; DAR.
Pedigree and hist. of Washington family. Welles. P. 261. MHS.
Robins family tree. MHS.
Mrs. H. De Courcy Wright Thom chart. MHS.

Keyser, Henry Irvine, II. Pedigree. (Rec. of Ashton, Aylett, Ball and Corbin, of Va.) Soc. Col. Wars Md. Culver. 1940. MHS; DAR.

Keyser, Mrs. Henry Irvine (Mary Anne Washington). Chart. Col. Dames, Chap. I. MHS.

Keyser, Robert Brent. Pedigree charts, plates 1 and 2. Soc. Col. Wars, Md. Johnston. 1905, pp. 55–56. MHS.

***Keyser, Wm.** Geneal. and mem. encyc. of Md. Spencer. V. 2, pp. 487–97. MHS; DAR.
†Men of mark in Md. Johnson. V. 1. DAR; Enoch Pratt Lib.

Keyser, Mrs. Wm. Keyser, Jr. (Jean Hancy). Chart. Col. Dames, Chap. I. MHS.

Keyser-Wyman. Balto., its hist., its people. Hall. V. 2, pp. 289–95. MHS; DAR.

Khler. Mt. Olivet Cemetery, Frederick. Md. Geneal. Rec. Com., 1934–35, p. 111. Mss. DAR.

Kibble. Rec. of Stepney Parish. MHS; DAR.
Wicomico Co. families. Bible. rec. Ms. DAR.

***Kibble, Cibble.** Wicomico Co. families. Tilghman. Ms, pp. 50, 61. DAR.

Kible-Whayland. Bible rec. Md. Geneal. Rec. Com., 1937–38, pp. 153–54. Mss. DAR.

Kidd. Harford Co. Hist. Soc. Mss. Coll. JHU.

Kidwell. Md. tombstone rec. Md. Geneal. Rec. Com., 1937, Parran, p. 4. Mss. DAR.

***Kidwell, James** (born in Engl. about 1675; died in Charles Co. about 1740). James Kidwell. Pierre E. Haynes, 3345 Guilford Ave., Indianapolis Ind. In preparation.

Kiefer. Mt. Olivet Cemetery, Frederick. Md. Geneal. Rec. Com., 1934–35, p. 111. Mss. DAR.

Kiesecker. *See* Keisecker.

Kilboarn. *See* Kilbourne.

Kilbourne, Kilboarn. St. Paul's Parish, Balto. V. 2. Mss. MHS.

Kilbourne, Ruple. Glendy churchyard. Patriotic Marylander, v. 2, no. 4, pp. 54–60. MHS; DAR.

Kilbraith. St. Paul's Parish, Balto. V. 2. Mss. MHS.

Kilby (Dorchester Co.)**-Thompson.** Americans of gentle birth and their ancestors. Pitman. P. 139. MHS.

Kilgore. Abr. Compend. Amer. Geneal. Virkus. V. 4, p. 326. MHS.

Kilgour. Portrait and biog. rec. of Sixth Cong. Dist. of Md. 1898, p. 758, 775. MHS; DAR.

Kilgour, Charles Co. Some Va. families. McIlhany.

Killan. Rec. of Stepney Parish. MHS; DAR.

Killen. Cotton chart. MHS.

Kilty. Ances. rec. and portraits. Col. Dames of Amer., 1910, v. 2, p. 517. MHS; DAR.
Mrs. J. G Brogden chart. MHS.
†Bench and bar of Md. Sams and Riley. 1901, v. 1, p. 275. Lib. Cong.; MHS; Peabody Lib.
Kilty family of Md., and notes on Rear Admiral Augustus Kilty. Ms. MHS.

†Kilty, Augustus H. Appleton's Cyc. Wilson and Fiske. 1888, v. 3, p. 535.

†Kilty, Augustus Henry (1807–79). M. H. Mag., v. 12, p. 225.

†Kilty, Wm., M.D. (born in Md., 1758; died 1821; surgeon in Revolutionary war). Md. authors. Steiner. Ms list, Md. Room, Enoch Pratt Lib.
†Hist. of Md. Scharf. V. 2, p. 622. MHS.
M. H. Mag., 1918, v. 13, pp. 103–07.

Kimball. St. Paul's Parish, Balto. V. 2, 4. Mss. MHS.
St. Stephens Parish, Cecilton, Md. MHS; DAR.

Kimber. St. Stephens Parish, Cecilton, Md. MHS; DAR.
See Carey-Kimber.

†Kimble, J. Haines. Men of mark in Md. Johnson. V. 3. DAR; Enoch Pratt Lib.

***Kimble, Kemble.** Lineage Bk. Daughters of Founders and Patriots, v. 16, pp. 136–37; v. 17, p. 43. MHS.

***Kincheloe.** The Sun, Balto., Dec. 29, 1907.

King. Abr. Compend. Amer. Geneal. Virkus. V. 4, p. 327. MHS.
Ances. rec. and portraits. Col. Dames of Amer., 1910, v. 2, p. 810. MHS; DAR.
Autobiography of Summerfield Baldwin. MHS; DAR.
Mrs. Wm. Graham Bowdoin, Jr., chart. MHS.
Mrs. J. G. Brogden chart. MHS.
†Chesapeake Bay Country. Earle. P. 426. MHS.
Crain chart. MHS.
Death of Susan, 1875, daughter of Dr. and Mrs. John King. J. F. Barnes Bible rec. Ms. MHS.
Ellicott-King chart. MHS.
Fox-Ellicott-Evans families. Evans. MHS; DAR.
Griffith geneal. Griffith. MHS; DAR.
Hagerstown tombstone inscriptions. Gruder. Natl. Geneal. Soc. Quart., 1919, v. 8, nos. 1, 2.
Hamill chart. MHS.
†Hist. of Allegany Co. Thomas and Williams. V. 2. MHS; DAR.
Md. families. Culver. Ms. Personal list.
Mrs. J. L. McLane chart. MHS.
†Med. Annals. Md. Cordell. 1903, p. 468. MHS.
Monocacy Cemetery, Beallsville, Montgomery Co. Md. Geneal. Rec. Com., 1926–27. Mss. DAR.
Mullikins of Md. Baker. MHS; DAR.
See O'Carroll. Focke Geneal. Coll. Ms. MHS.
*Pennington Papers. Ms. MHS.
Rec. of Stepney Parish. MHS; DAR.
St. Mary's P. E. churchyard, Pocomoke, Worcester Co., Hudson. Bd. ms. MHS; DAR.
St. Paul's Parish, Balto. V. 1, 2, 3, 4. Mss. MHS.
St. Stephens Parish, Cecilton, Md. MHS; DAR.
Side lights on Md. hist. Richardson. V. 2, p. 154. MHS; DAR.
Somerset Co. Court Book. Tilghman. 1937. Ms. DAR.
*The Sun, Balto., Feb. 21, 1904.
*Wicomico Co. families. Tilghman. Ms, pp. 92, 96, 100, 106. DAR.
See Hufner-King.

King, Prince George Co. Sara R. Baldwin chart. MHS.

King, Somerset Co., N. Y. and Va. Cary Geneal. Coll. Ms. MHS.

King, C. A. Ely, U.S.N. Md. Soc., War of 1812, v. 1, no. 127. Ms. MHS.

King, John, and children. Will. Md. Geneal. Rec. Com., 1937. DAR.

King, John of Thomas. Will, 1875, Balto. Court House. Md. Geneal. Rec. Com., 1937, p. 21. Mss. DAR.

King, Thomson. Pedigree. Soc. Col. Wars Md. Culver. 1940. MHS; DAR.

King Family. Notes. Old Somerset. Torrence. MHS; DAR.
Thomas Book. Thomas. Pp. 379–81. Lib. Cong.; MHS.

King-Carroll. Chart, photos., 2 sheets. Cary Geneal. Coll. Ms. MHS.

Kingla. St. John's R. C. Church cemetery, Montgomery Co. Md. Geneal. Rec. Com., 1926, p. 27. Mss. DAR.

Kinkee. Naturalizations in Md., 1666–1765; Laws. Bacon. MHS.

Kinkle. Hist. sketch of P. F. Eichelberger. Eichelberger.

†Kinnemon. Med. Annals Md. Cordell. 1903, p. 468. MHS.

Kinsey. Black chart. MHS.
Cotton chart. MHS.
Eldridge chart. MHS.
Ellicott-King chart. MHS.
See Ewen-Chew, etc. Lineage Bks., Natl. Soc. of Daughters of Amer. Col., v. 4, p. 269. MHS; DAR.
Hopkins chart. Cary Geneal. Coll. Ms. MHS.
Hutchins chart. Cary Geneal. Coll. Ms. MHS.
Kinsey family; supplementary data on ancestors of Johns Hopkins. South. Hist. Assoc., 1901, v. 5, no. 4, p. 300.
Matthews-Price chart. MHS.
Mt. Calvary Church burial ground, Cooksville Pike, Montgomery Co. Md. Geneal. Rec. Com., 1934–35, pp. 95–99. Mss. DAR.
Mt. Carmel burial ground, Unity, Montgomery Co. Md. Geneal. Rec. Com., 1934–35, p. 85. Mss. DAR.
Turner family. Forman. P. 52. MHS.
Van Dyke-Johns-Montgomery-Manlove chart. Cary Geneal. Coll. Ms. MHS.
See Hopkins-Johns-Kinsey.
See Hopkins-Kinsey-Baker.
See Johns-Kinsey.

Kinsey, Jacob. And his descendants. Ms. MHS.

Kinsey Family. Supplement to ancestors of Johns Hopkins. Pub. South. Hist. Assoc., v. 4, p. 433; v. 5, p. 300 through v. 6.

***Kinsey, Kintzey.** Hist. of Jacob Kinsey, and his descendants. Wm. Kinsey. (Mostly Pa. rec.; few Md. ref.) Union Bridge, Md., The Pilot Pub. Co., 1934.

Kinsolving. Balto., its hist., its people. Hall. V. 3. MHS; DAR.
*Geneal. and early hist. of Va. and Md. Seven centuries of lines. Studies in pre-Amer. and early Amer. col. times. W. L. Kinsolving, 2107 North Ave., Richmond. 1935. DAR.
James chart. MHS.
Some Va. families. McIlhany.

†Kinsolving, Arthur B. Men of mark in Md. Johnson. V. 2. DAR; Enoch Pratt Lib.

Kintzey. *See* Kinsey.

***Kipp-Shryler-Shroyer-Stow Families.** Kipp-Shryler-Shroyer-Stow families. John Carroll Stow. March, 1936. Ms. MHS.

Kipshaven Family, Del. Allied families of Delaware. Sellers. MHS.

Kirby. Barroll chart. MHS.
Hist. graves of Md. and D. C. Ridgely. MHS.
My family memoirs. Hughes. 1931, p. 59. MHS; DAR.
St. Paul's Parish, Balto. V. 1, 4. Mss. MHS.
See Kerby.

***Kirby Family.** Founders of Anne Arundel and Howard Cos. Warfield. Pp. 143–45, 143 (Kirbys in the War of the Revolution). MHS; DAR.

Kirchner. *See* Kershner.

Kirk. Ancestry of Wm Haines. Cregar. MHS.
†Chesapeake Bay Country. Earle. P. 389. MHS.
Fisher family. Morse. MHS.

Fisher family, Sussex Co., Del., and Md. Ms. MHS.
Geneal. and memorial encyc. of Md. Spencer. 1909, v. 1. MHS; DAR.
Harlan family geneal., Chester Co., Pa. Harlan. MHS.
Nann-Needles-Hambleton families. Needles. Pp. 120-21. MHS; DAR.
Trinity P. E. churchyard, St. Mary's City. Md. O. R. Soc. Bull., no. 3, p. 59.
White Geneal. Tree. MHS.
***Kirk, Sam'l.** Geneal. and mem. encyc. of Md. Spencer. V. 1, pp. 274-85. MHS; DAR.
***Kirk Family,** Darby, Pa. Descendants of John Kirk, born 1660, at Alfreston, Derbyshire, Eng.; died 1705, in Darby Township, Chester (now Del.) Co., Pa. M. S. Roberts. 1912-13. Geneal. Bd. ms. MHS.
†**Kirkland.** Balto., hist. and biog. Richardson and Bennett. 1871, pp. 344-48. MHS; DAR.
Mrs. T. R. Brown chart. MHS.
Kirkland, Miss A. P. Barton chart. MHS.
Kirkman. Cary Geneal. Coll. Ms. MHS.
St. Paul's Parish, Balto. V. 2. Mss. MHS.
***Kirkpatrick-Howat.** Burke's landed gentry. 1939. MHS.
Kirkwood. St. Paul's Parish, Balto. V. 2. Mss. MHS.
Kirr. *See* Guyton-Kirr-Rush-Holland-Conn.
Kirtley. St. Stephens Parish, Cecilton, Md. MHS; DAR.
***Kirwan.** Hist. Dorchester Co. Jones. 1925, pp. 375-77. MHS; DAR.
Kissecker. *See* Keisecker.
Kitchin. Naturalizations in Md., 1666-1765; Laws. Bacon. MHS.
Kizer. Hagerstown tombstone inscriptions. Gruder. Natl. Geneal. Soc. Quart., 1919, v. 8, nos. 1, 2.
Klay. Mt. Olivet Cemetery, Frederick. Md. Geneal. Rec. Com., 1934-35, p. 111. Mss. DAR.
Klebsadler. *See* Klebsattel.
Klebsattel, Klebsadler, Gleibsattler. Hagerstown tombstone inscriptions. Gruder. Natl. Geneal. Soc. Quart., 1919, v. 8, nos. 1, 2.
†**Klees.** Hist. of Balto. City and Co. Scharf. Pp. 404-05. MHS.
Klein, Kline. Hagerstown tombstone inscriptions. Gruder. Natl. Geneal. Soc. Quart., 1919, v. 8, nos. 1, 2.
Kleinard. Frederick Co. tombstone inscriptions. Gruder. Natl. Geneal. Soc. Quart., 1919, v. 8, nos. 1, 2.
Kline. Frederick Co. tombstone inscriptions. Gruder. Natl. Geneal. Soc. Quart., 1919, v. 8, nos. 1, 2.
†Hist. of Frederick Co. Williams. MHS; DAR.
See Klein.
Klunk, L. W. Md. Soc., War of 1812, v. 3, no. 280. Ms. MHS.
†**Knabe, Wm.** Balto., hist. and biog. Richardson and Bennett. 1871, pp. 349-52. MHS; DAR.
Knapp. Balto, its hist., its people. Hall. V. 3. MHS; DAR.
Beirne chart. MHS.
†Men of mark in Md. Johnson. V. 4. DAR; Enoch Pratt Lib.
Mrs. N. S. Pendleton, Jr., chart. MHS.
***Knauff.** Frederick Co. families. Ms. Personal list.
Knickl. Zion Reformed Church, Hagerstown. Md. Geneal. Rec. Com., 1934-35. Mss. DAR.
Knight. Hist. of Byberry and Moreland. Martindale. MHS.
Howard-Montague-Warfield geneal. chart. Culver and Marye. MHS.
Lloyd family hist. of Wales, Pa., and Md. DAR.
†Med. Annals Md. Cordell. 1903, pp. 469-70. MHS.
Pedigree of George Ross Veazey. Soc. Col. Wars Md. Culver. 1940. MHS; DAR.
St. Paul's Parish, Balto. V. 1, 2. Mss. MHS.
St. Stephens Parish, Cecilton, Md. MHS; DAR.
Tombstone rec. of Kitty Knight. Md. Geneal. Rec. Com., v. 4, p. 79. DAR.
Wathen Prayer Book rec. Ms. MHS.
White geneal. tree. MHS.
‡**Knight, Elizabeth.** Two Md. heroines. M. H. Mag., 1908, v. 3, pp. 133-37.
Knighton. Md. gleanings in Eng. Wills. M. H. Mag., 1907, v. 2, no. 3.
Knipe. Mrs. G. C. Jenkins chart. MHS.
***Knode.** Frederick Co. families. Markell. Ms. Personal list.
Zion Reformed Church, Hagerstown. Md. Geneal. Rec. Com., 1934-35. Mss. DAR.
Knodle. Hagerstown tombstone inscriptions. Gruder. Natl. Geneal. Soc. Quart., 1919, v. 8, nos. 1, 2.
Knodt. St. Paul's Parish, Balto. V. 2. Mss. MHS.
Knorr. Mrs. H. De Courcy Wright Thom chart. MHS.
Knott. Balto., its hist., its people. Hall. V. 3. MHS; DAR.
†Bench and bar of Md. Sams and Riley. 1901, v. 2, p. 439. Lib. Cong.; MHS; Peabody Lib.
†Biog. cyc. of rep. men of Md. and D. C. Pp. 258-61. MHS; DAR.
Cummings chart. Lib. Cong.; MHS; DAR.
Geneal. and memorial encyc. of Md. Spencer. V. 2, p. 519. MHS; DAR.
†Hist. of Balto. City and Co. Scharf. P. 720. MHS.
Patriotic Md. Md. Soc. of S. A. R., 1930. MHS; DAR.
Side lights on Md. hist. Richardson. V. 2, p. 382. MHS; DAR.
***Knott, A. Leo.** Geneal. and mem. encyc. of Md. Spencer. V. 2, pp. 519-34. MHS; DAR.
Md. Soc., War of 1812, v. 1, no. 134. Ms. MHS.
Knott, Leo Aloysius. Pedigree chart. Soc. Col. Wars, Md. Johnston. 1905, p. 57. MHS.
†**Knowles.** Biog. cyc. of rep. men of Md. and D. C. P. 161. MHS; DAR.
Lloyd family hist. of Wales, Pa., and Md. DAR.
Warfields of Md. Warfield. MHS.
*Wicomico Co. families. Tilghman. Ms, pp. 96, 110. DAR.
Knowles Family. Thomas Book. Thomas. P. 385. Lib. Cong.; MHS.
Knox. Balch chart. MHS.
Geneal. rec. of family of Thomas. Thomas. MHS.
Mrs. M. L. Price chart. MHS.
St. Paul's Parish, Balto. V. 2, 4. Mss. MHS.
See Fitzhugh-Knox.
See Gordon-Knox-Fitzhugh-Cooke.

†**Knox, J. H. M., Jr.** Men of mark in Md. Johnson. V. 2. DAR; Enoch Pratt Lib.
Knox, Mrs. J. Mason (Marion Gordon Bowdoin). Chart. Col. Dames, Chap. I. MHS.
Mrs. Howard Bruce chart. MHS.
Mrs. Wm. Graham Bowdoin chart. MHS.
Knox, Rev. Sam'l. Notes. M. H. Mag., 1907, v. 2, pp. 285–86; 1909, v. 4, pp. 276–79.
***Knox Family.** Old Kent. Hanson. P. 134. MHS; DAR.
Knupling. Catonsville pioneers of Luth. faith. Natl. Geneal. Soc. Quart., v. 9, no. 2, p. 29.
Koch. Hagerstown tombstone inscriptions. Gruder. Natl. Geneal. Soc. Quart., 1919, v. 8, nos. 1, 2.
See Cook.
†**Koechling.** Med. Annals Md. Cordell. 1903, p. 470. MHS.
Kolb. Catonsville pioneers of Luth. faith. Natl. Geneal. Soc. Quart., v. 9, no. 2, p. 29.
*Frederick Co. families. Markell. Ms. Personal list.
†Med. Annals Md. Cordell. 1903, p. 470. MHS.
Mt. Olivet Cemetery, Frederick. Md. Geneal. Rec. Com., 1934–35, p. 111. Mss. DAR.
Kollenberg. *See* Kollengers.
***Kollengers** or **Kollenberg.** Frederick Co. families. Markell. Ms. Personal list.
Kollock. Cannon-Riley-Truitt-Houston-Kollock. Stow. Ms. MHS.
***Kollock,** Sussex Co., Del. N. Y. Geneal. and Biog. Rec., v. 8, p. 184.
Kollock, Col. Jacob, Sussex Co., Del. (1692–1772). J. L. Minis pedigree chart. Soc. Col. Wars, Md. Johnston. 1905, pp. 71, 148. MHS.
***Kollock Family,** Sussex Co., Del. Geneal., 1657–1897. E. J. Sellers. Phila., 1897. MHS.
***Konable.** Frederick Co. families. Markell. Ms. Personal list.
†**Koogle.** Hist. of Frederick Co. Williams. MHS; DAR.
†Hist. of Washington Co. Williams. 1906, v. 2, p. 825. MHS; DAR.
Koontz. Frederick Co. tombstone inscriptions. Gruder. Natl. Geneal. Soc. Quart., 1919, v. 8, nos. 1, 2.
†Hist. of Frederick Co. Williams. MHS; DAR.
Hist. sketch of P. F. Eichelberger. Eichelberger.
Koppenhaven. *See* Copenhaven.
Krafft. St. Paul's Parish, Balto. V. 2. Mss. MHS.
Kramer. *See* Cramer.
***Krebs.** Bible rec. of George Warner and Maria Krebs, Balto., 1847. File case, MHS.
Bible rec., 1808–76. Typed, 4 pp. MHS.
Chart. Geneal. tables of descendants of John Hamilton, Va. MHS.
Pedigree of Culbreth Hopewell Warner. Soc. Col. Wars Md. Culver. 1940. MHS; DAR.
St. Paul's Parish, Balto. V. 2. Mss. MHS.
See Warner-Krebs.
Krebs Line. Geneal. tables of descendants of John Hamilton. MHS.
Kreiger-Gilmor-White. Abr. Compend. Amer. Geneal. Virkus.. V. 4, p. 331. MHS.
Kreiss. *See* Crise.
Krepp. Mt. Olivet Cemetery, Frederick. Md. Geneal. Rec. Com., 1934–35, p. 111. Mss. DAR.
Kreuss. *See* Crise.
Krick. *See* Creek.
Kriech. Hagerstown tombstone inscriptions. Gruder. Natl. Geneal. Soc. Quart., 1919, v. 8, nos. 1, 2.
†Men of mark in Md. Johnson. V. 2. DAR; Enoch Pratt Lib.
Krieger. Abr. Compend. Amer. Geneal. Virkus. V. 1, p. 672. DAR.
Kries. *See* Crise.
Krise. Biggs family. Ms. DAR.
Family association, held June 9, 1940, at Mt. Tabor Park, Frederick Co. President, Mrs. Ethel Close Buckey, 1815 Park Ave., Balto. Rec. DAR.
Md. Geneal. Bull., v. 4, p. 26; v. 6, p. 12. MHS.
Tom's Creek M. E. Church cemetery, near Emmitsburg. Md. Geneal. Rec. Com., 1932–33, p. 70. Mss. DAR.
See Crise.
Krise, Solomon. Bible rec., 1795–1917. Md. Geneal. Rec. Com., 1932–33, pp. 62–63. Mss. DAR.
Krouse. Beards' Luth. graveyard, Washington Co. Md. Geneal. Rec. Com., 1935–36. Mss. DAR.
Krumbach. *See* Crumbaugh.
Krumbein. *See* Shriner-Grumbine.
Krumbine. *See* Shriner-Grumbine.
†**Kuhn.** Justus Engelhardt Kuhn, early eighteenth century portrait painter. J. Hall Pleasants. Worcester, Mass., repr. from Amer. Antiquarian Soc. Proc., Oct., 1936, 40 pp. MHS; Enoch Pratt Lib.
Kuhn, Justus Engelhart. Early eighteenth century Md. portrait painter. J. Hall Pleasants. (Notes on some of families he painted: Carroll, Darnall and Digges.(Repr. from Proc. of Amer. Antiquarin Soc., Worcester, Mass., Oct., 1936, pub. by Society, 1937, pamph. MHS.
Kuhns. *See* Wagoner-Kuhns.
†**Kunkel.** Hist. of West. Md. Scharf. V. 1, pp. 554, 629. MHS; DAR.
Kuntz. Hagerstown tombstone inscriptions. Gruder. Natl. Geneal. Soc. Quart., 1919, v. 8, nos. 1, 2.
Kurtz. Coll. of Amer. epitaphs and inscriptions. Alden. 1814, v. 5. MHS.
*Frederick Co. families. Markell. Ms. Personal list.
Hagerstown tombstone inscriptions. Gruder. Natl. Geneal. Soc. Quart., 1919, v. 8, nos. 1, 2.
St. Paul's Parish, Balto. V. 2. Mss. MHS.
Kutleman. *See* Kettleman.
***Kyn.** Descendants of Joran Kyn of New Sweden. G. B. Keen. Pub. by Swedish Col. Soc., Phila., 1913. MHS; DAR.
Miss C. Petre chart. MHS.
Kyn, Joran. Descendants. Founder of Upland. G. B. Keen. Pa. Mag. Hist. Biog. 1878, v. 2; 1879, v. 3; 1880, v. 4; 1881, v. 5; 1882, v. 6; 1883, v. 7.
Pa. Mag., v. 6, pp. 106, 207, 329, 453; corrections, p. 494; v. 7.
Kyper. Hagerstown tombstone inscriptions. Gruder. Natl. Geneal. Soc. Quart., 1919, v. 8, nos. 1, 2.

L

Lacey. Peale Geneal. Coll. Ms. MHS.
Lacy. Roll of house of Lacy. Pedigrees, military

memoirs, etc., with memoir of Brownes (Md. family). Balto., 1928.
***Lacy-Hoge, Va.** The Sun, Balto., May 28, 1905.
***Ladson.** Pennington Papers. Ms. MHS.
†Lafayette. Lafayette in Harford Co. Memorial monograph, 1781–1931. DAR.
Lafferty. St. Paul's Parish, Balto. V. 2. Mss. MHS.
Laine. *See* Lane.
Laird. Abr. Compend. Amer. Geneal. Virkus. V. 6, p. 423. DAR.
Balto., its hist., its people. Hall. V. 3. MHS; DAR.
Christ P. E. Church cemetery, Cambridge. Steele. 1936. MHS; DAR.
*Hist. of Dorchester Co. Jones. 1902, p. 341. MHS; DAR.
See Bordley-Abbott-Laird-Winder.
*Wicomico Co. families. Tilghman. Ms, p. 102. DAR.
***Laird Family.** Descendants of Rev. James Laird, 1771–1816. Md. O. R. Soc. Bull., no. 2, pp. 42–45.
Laird Family, Pa. and Somerset Co. Md. O. R. Soc. Bull., no. 2, pp. 42–45.
Laird Line. Col. and Revolutionary lineages of Amer. 1939, v. 1, pp. 90–95. MHS.
***Lake.** Arms. Hist. of Dorchester Co. Jones. 1925, p. 377. MHS; DAR.
Cary Geneal. Coll. Ms. MHS.
Christ P. E. Church cemetery, Cambridge. Steele. 1936. MHS; DAR.
Md. O. R. Soc. Bull., no. 3, p. 53.
*Side lights on Md. hist. Richardson. V. 2, p. 157. MHS; DAR.
Somerset Co. Court Book. Tilghman. 1937. Ms. DAR.
*The Sun, Balto., April 10, 1904. See also Jan. 7, 1906 (Jones-Lake families).
Trinity P. E. churchyard, Long Green. Typed ms. MHS; DAR.
Lake, R. Pinkney. Md. Soc., War of 1812, v. 2, no. 157. Ms. MHS.
Lake-Bird Family. Monnet family geneal. Monette. Pp. 1117–18. MHS.
Lamar. Abr. Compend. Amer. Geneal. Virkus. V. 1, p. 674. DAR.
Cummings chart. Lib. Cong.; MHS; DAR.
*Formerly Kerr, of Talbot Co. Burke's landed gentry. 1939. MHS.
†Hist. of Allegany Co. Thomas and Williams. V. 1. MHS; DAR.
†Hist. of Frederick Co. Williams. MHS; DAR.
M. families. Culver. Ms. Personal list.
*Notes. M. H. Mag., v. 34, no. 3, p. 304.
Patriotic Md. Md. Soc. of S. A. R., 1930. MHS; DAR.
*The Sun, Balto., Oct. 22, 29, Dec. 3 (D. C.), 1905.
See Sprigg-Addison-Cresap-Lamar-Gordon.
Lamar, Allegany Co. Hist. of West. Md. Scharf. V. 2, p. 1495.
Lamar, Thomas. And some of his descendants. Pub. South. Hist. Assoc., 1897, v. 1, pp. 203–10.
Lamb. *See* Armstrong, Va. Abr. Compend. Amer. Geneal. Virkus. V. 4, p. 33. MHS.
Bible rec., 1772–1935. Md. Geneal. Rec. Com., Parran, 1937, pp. 199–200. DAR.
(Giving name of wife of Nicholas Watkins.) Cary Geneal. Coll. Ms. MHS.
Matthews-Price chart. MHS.
†Men of mark in Md. Johnson. V. 3. DAR; Enoch Pratt Lib.
***Lamb Family.** Early marriages in U. S. W. M. Clemens. 1916.
Lambdin, East. Shore. Chart. Col. Wm. McK. Lambdin, U.S.A. Blue print. MHS.
S. G. Hopkins chart. MHS.
Lambert. Frederick Co. tombstone inscriptions. Gruder. Natl. Geneal. Soc. Quart., 1919, v. 8, nos. 1, 2.
St. Paul's Parish, Balto. V. 2. Mss. MHS.
Lambertson. Southern Bapt. Church cemetery, Worcester Co. Md. Geneal. Rec. Com., 1937, Mrs. Lines. Mss. DAR.
Lamden. Holdens Cemetery, Kent Co. Md. Geneal. Rec. Com., 1932, v. 5, p. 211. Mss. DAR.
Lamée. Naturalizations in Md., 1666–1765; Laws. Bacon. MHS.
Lammot. Hazelhurst charts. MHS.
Lamping, Wm. Md. Soc., War of 1812, v. 1, no. 7. Ms. MHS.
Lampton Family (1708). Geneal., Mag. Amer. Ancestry, N. Y., 1916, v. 4, no. 4; v. 4, no. 5 (Lampton marriages in Md.).
(1654–1726). Md. Geneal. Bull., v. 3, p. 23. MHS; DAR.
Lanahan. Balto., its hist., its people. Hall. V. 2. MHS; DAR.
Col. families of U. S. A. Mackenzie. V. 1, p. 494. MHS; DAR.
Lanahan, C. Wallace. Md. Soc., War of 1812, v. 4, no. 335. Ms. MHS.
Lanahan, William. Appreciation of career and account of his funeral. Priv. pr., 1912. MHS.
Lanahan, Mrs. Wm. Wallace (Eleanor Addison Williams). Chart. Col. Dames, Chap. I. MHS.
Mrs. R. Barton, Jr., chart. MHS.
Lancaster. Dorsey Papers. Ms. MHS.
Harford Co. Hist. Soc. Mss. Coll. JHU.
Manly chart. MHS.
†Med. Annals Md. Cordell. 1903, p. 471. MHS.
*Semmes Geneal. Coll. Ms. MHS.
Lancaster, H. C. Abr. Compend. Amer. Geneal. Virkus. V. 1, pp. 186–87. DAR.
Land. Cary Geneal. Coll. Ms. MHS.
Pedigree of Leigh Bonsal. Soc. Col. Wars Md. Culver. 1940. MHS; DAR.
Landen. Md. gleanings in Eng. Wills. M. H. Mag., 1907, v. 2, no. 3.
Landerman. St. Paul's Parish, Balto. V. 2. Mss. MHS.
Landers, Scotland to Middleburg, Md. Bible rec., 1796–1927. Md. Geneal. Rec. Com., 1932–33, p. 60. Mss. DAR.
Landis. Cummings chart. Lib. Cong.; MHS; DAR.
***Landis Family.** Twenty-fourth reunion of Landis family, Landisville Pa., Aug. 3, 1939. Pamph. MHS.
Landstreet, John. Md. Soc., War of 1812, v. 2, no. 182. Ms. MHS.
†Lane. Bench and bar of Md. Sams and Riley. 1901, v. 2, pp. 368, 549. Lib. Cong.; MHS; Peabody Lib.
*Frederick Co. families. Markell. Ms. Personal list.
†Hist. of Washington Co. Williams. 1906, v. 2, p. 1020. MHS; DAR.

Lane. Holdens Cemetery Kent Co. Md. Geneal. Rec. Com., 1932, v. 5, p. 211. Mss. DAR.
Lineage Bks., Natl. Soc. of Daughters of Amer. Col., v. 4, p. 137. MHS; DAR.
Old Somerset. Torrence. MHS; DAR.
Somerset Co. Court Book. Tilghman. 1937. Ms. DAR.
***Lane,** Anne Arundel Co. Lineage Bk. Daughters of Founders and Patriots. V. 16, pp. 134–35. MHS.
Lane, Western Md. Geneal. and mem. encyc. of Md. Spencer. V. 1, pp. 43–47. MHS; DAR.
***Lane Family.** Notes. J. Kendall, Jeffersonville, Md. Photos. MHS.
***Lane-Dawson-Hawkins.** Lineage Bk., Daughters of Amer. Colonists, v. 1, p. 51; v. 5, p. 161. MHS; DAR.
Lane-Smith. Lane family, 1663, and Smith family, 1698, in Calvert Co.; also Lane family in Balto., Cecil, Dorchester, Somerset, Talbot and Worcester Cos., contains notes on Henry Sater, and membership of Sater's Bapt. Church, Balto. Co., 1742. Photos. MHS.
***Lane-Smith Families.** Photos. MHS.
Lane, Laine. St. Paul's Parish, Balto. V. 1, 2. Mss. MHS.
Lang. Balto., its hist., its people. Hall. V. 3. MHS; DAR.
Langford, John. Ms. MHS.
†**Langhammer.** Geneal. and mem. encyc. of Md. Spencer. V. 2, p. 681. MHS; DAR.
Langhorn. Md. gleanings in Eng. Wills. M. H. Mag., 1907, v. 2, no. 4.
Langhorne. Cary Geneal. Coll. Ms. MHS.
See Brent-Langhorne.
Langhorne, Va. Col. families of U. S. A. Mackenzie. V. 2. MHS; DAR.
*The Sun, Balto., Dec. 25, 1904.
Langhorne, C. McIndoe. Md. Soc., War of 1812, v. 2, no. 186. Ms. MHS.
Langley. Md. gleanings in Eng. Wills. M. H. Mag., 1907, v. 2, no. 2.
St. Paul's Parish, Balto. V. 1, 2. Mss. MHS.
Langsdale. Wicomico Co. families. Bible rec. Ms. DAR.
*Wicomico Co. families. Tilghman. Ms, p. 96. DAR.
Lanham, Thomas. Revolutionary pension abs. Natl. Geneal. Soc. Quart., v. 23, p. 96.
Lanier. Burton ancestry. Ms. MHS.
Dedicated to Sidney Lanier. Southern Literary Messenger, Jan., 1940. 109 E. Cary St., Richmond, Va.
Pedigree and hist. of Washington family. Welles. P. 261. MHS.
†**Lanier, Sidney.** Sidney Lanier. A. H. Starke. Pub. by Univ. of N. C. Press.
†Sidney Lanier. E. Mims. 1905.
†Sidney Lanier, "Familiar Citizen of the Town." J. S. Short Portrait. M. H. Mag., June, 1940, v. 35, no. 2, pp. 121–46.
†Pub. Southern Hist. Assoc., v. 3, p. 190.
Lankford. Rec. of Stepney Parish. MHS; DAR.
St. Mary's churchyard, Tyaskin, Md. Md. Geneal. Rec. Com., 1938–39, pp. 187–92 Mss. DAR.
St. Mary's P. E. churchyard, Pocomoke, Worcester Co., Hudson. Bd. ms. MHS; DAR.
Turner Geneal. Coll. Ms. MHS.
*Wicomico Co. families. Tilghman. Ms, pp. 111, 114. DAR.
See Hodson-Collison-Ball-Jones-Lankford.

Lanman. Mrs. A. R. Riggs chart. MHS.
Lanmany. St. Paul's Parish, Balto. V. 2. Mss. MHS.
Lansdale. Abs. of will. D. A. R. Mag., June, 1927, v. 61, no. 6, p. 469.
Md. families. Culver. Ms. Personal list.
†Med. Annals. Md. Cordell. 1903, p. 472. MHS.
Mt. Calvary Church burial ground, Cooksville Pike, Howard Co. Md. Geneal. Rec. Com., 1934–35, pp. 95–99. Mss. DAR.
Lansdale, Thomas, Prince George Co. Will proved Jan. 27, 1803. D. A. R. Mag., v. 61, no. 6, p. 469.
Lantz. Beards' Luth. graveyard, Washington Co. Md. Geneal. Rec. Com., 1935–36. Mss. DAR.
Descendants of John, Lancaster Co., Pa., 1740. Notes and queries. Egle. 1896, series 3, pp. 123–24. MHS.
Geneal. MHS.
***Lantz Family.** Rec.; being brief account of Lantz family in Amer. J. W. Lantz. Voluminous ref. to Lantz family in Balto., p. 60; Frederick Co., p. 139; Leitersburg District, Md., from Pa., 1775, p. 23; Wash. Co., p. 73. Cedar Springs, Va., 1931. MHS.
Lapage. St. Stephens Parish, Cecilton, Md. MHS; DAR.
Laramore, Laremore. Somerset Co. Court Book. Tilghman. 1937. Ms. DAR.
Laremore. *See* Larramore.
Large Family. Thomas Book. Thomas. P. 386. Lib. Cong.; MHS.
Large Family, Pa.-Poultney, Balto. and Mifflin, N. J. Morris family of Phila. Moon. V. 2, p. 616. MHS.
Larkin. Blackwell chart. MHS.
Mrs. Howard Bruce chart. MHS.
Cary Geneal. Coll. Ms. MHS.
Eldridge chart. MHS.
Lineage Bks., Natl. Soc. of Daughters of Amer. Col., v. 1, p. 14. MHS; DAR.
Maccubin-Lusby chart. Cary Geneal. Coll. Ms. MHS.
Notes and marriages. Md. Geneal. Bull., v. 6, p. 23. MHS; DAR.
See Gassaway-Larkin.
Tompkins chart. MHS.
Larkin Line. Col. and Revolutionary lineages of Amer. 1939, v. 1, p. 487. MHS.
Larmore. Rec. of Stepney Parish. MHS; DAR.
*Wicomico Co. families. Tilghman. Ms, p. 80. DAR.
See Jones-Larmore.
Larmour. St. Mary's churchyard, Tyaskin, Md. Md. Geneal. Rec. Com., 1938–39, pp. 187–92. Mss. DAR.
Larned. Hist. graves of Md. and D. C. Ridgely. MHS.
†Med. Annals Md. Cordell. 1903, p. 472. MHS.
Larned, Charles Willis. Pedigree. Soc. Col. Wars Md. Culver. 1940. MHS; DAR.
†**Laroque.** Med. Annals Md. Cordell. 1903, p. 472. MHS.
Larramore, Laramore. St. Stephens Parish, Cecilton, Md. MHS; DAR.
Larrimore. Centreville cemetery. Md. O. R. Soc. Bull., no. 1, pp. 41–47.
†**Larsh.** Med. Annals Md. Cordell. 1903, p. 473. MHS.

Larzelere Family, Pa. and Cecil Co. Md. Geneal. Rec. Com., 1937–38, pp. 46–51. Mss. DAR.
†**Lashley.** Hist. of Allegany Co. Thomas and Williams. V. 2. MHS; DAR.
Lassells, Lassell. St. Stephenson Parish, Cecilton, Md. MHS; DAR.
Latane. Capt. Roger Jones of London and Va. Browning.
Latané, Henry Holladay. Pedigree. Soc. Col. Wars Md. Culver. 1940. MHS; DAR.
Late. Frederick Co. tombstone inscriptions. Gruder. Natl. Geneal. Soc. Quart., 1919, v. 8, nos. 1, 2.
Laterman. St. Paul's Parish, Balto. V. 2. Mss. MHS.
Latham. Memorials of Reading, Howell, Yerkes, Watts, Latham and Elkins families. Leach.
*Southerland, Latham and allied families. Register of ancestors of Imogen Southerland. E. K. Voorhees. Pr. for priv. circulation, Atlanta, Ga., 1931. MHS; DAR.
St. Stephens Parish, Cecilton, Md. MHS; DAR.
***Latimer.** Bartow geneal. Bartow. Pp. 132–35. Lib. Cong.; MHS.
†Med. Annals Md. Cordell. 1903, p. 473. MHS.
St. Paul's Parish, Balto. V. 2. Mss. MHS.
†**Latimer, Elizabeth Wormeley.** Biog. dict. of U. S. J. H. Lamb Co., v. 1.
Latimer, Wm. Geddes. Geneal. of George Small, etc. Small. MHS.
Latour. St. Paul's Parish, Balto. V. 2. Mss. MHS.
La Tremville Family. Gift of Mrs. Reginald Petre. MHS.
Latrobe. Abr. Compend. Amer. Geneal. Virkus. V. 1, p. 676. DAR.
Balto., its hist., its people. Hall. V. 2. MHS; DAR.
†Bench and bar of Md. Sams and Riley, 1910, v. 2, pp. 376, 533, 578. Lib. Cong.; MHS; Peabody Lib.
Dukehart and collateral lines. Ms. MHS.
†Geneal. and mem. encyc. of Md. Spencer. V. 2, p. 561. MHS; DAR.
Hazelhurst charts. MHS.
†John H. B. Latrobe and his times, 1803–91. John E. Semmes. Balto., Waverly Press, 1917. MHS; DAR.
†Life and times of Henry Antes. McMinn. P. 284. MHS; DAR.
Monumental City. Howard. MHS; DAR.
†Proc. of Md. Hist. Soc. in commemoration of Hon. J. H. B. Latrobe. M. H. S. Fund Pub. MHS; Enoch Pratt Lib.
†**Latrobe, Benjamin H.** Benjamin H. Latrobe and classical influence of his work. W. S. Rusk. (Latrobe Bibliog. p. 151.) M. H. Mag., 1936, v. 31, pp. 126–54.
†Descent and Works. T. C. Latrobe, II. M. H. Mag., Sept., 1938, v. 33, no. 3, p. 247.
Latrobe, Miss Ellen Virginia. Chart. Col. Dames, Chap. I. MHS.
†**Latrobe, F. C.** Men of mark in Md. Johnson. V. 1. DAR; Enoch Pratt Lib.
†**Latrobe, J. H. B.** Rept. of Latrobes literary life. M. H. Mag., 1910, v. 5, pp. 375–77.
Lattamus, Lattamos. St. Stephens Parish, Cecilton, Md. MHS; DAR.
***Laucks (Loucks) Family,** Pa. (Contains book in Laucks family.) Wilson Mss. Coll., no. 44; no. 46. MHS.
Laugharne. Maulsby family in Amer. Barnard. DAR; Peabody Lib.
***Laughborough** Bible rec. from Bible in possession of Margaret C. (Mrs. James H.) Laughborough, Bethesda, Md. D. A. R. Mag., v. 45, no. 6, pp. 345–47.
Laughlin, G. M., III. Abr. Compend. Amer. Geneal. Virkus. V. 1, p. 148. DAR.
Laughter, Wm. Hunt. Md. Soc., War of 1812, v. 1, no. 61. Ms. MHS.
Laurenson. Col. families of U. S. A. Mackenzie. V. 1, p. 67. MHS; DAR.
Laveille. Bible rec., 1820–1922, Westminster, Md. (Presented by C. C. Clemson.) Typed, 4 pp. MHS.
***Laveille Family.** Notes and tombstone inscriptions. Ms. MHS.
Laveille-Harris. Inscriptions on tombstones in lot on Laveille Place, Calvert Co., 1800–82 (3 stones). Md. Geneal. Rec. Com., 1938–39, p. 20. Mss. DAR.
Lavender. St. Paul's Parish, Balto. V. 2. Mss. MHS.
Lavielle. Naturalizations in Md., 1666–1765; Laws. Bacon. MHS.
†**Law.** Biog. sketch of Maj. James O. Law. Discourse by Rev. G. W. Musgrave, pastor of Third Presbyterian Church, by request of Independent Greys. Sherwood Co., Balto., 1847. Enoch Pratt Lib.
Cannon- Riley- Truitt- Houston- Kollock. Stow. Ms. MHS.
Law, James. Glendy churchyard. Patriotic Marylander, v. 2, no. 4, pp. 54–60. MHS; DAR.
Law-Carter Families. Col. and Revolutionary families of Pa. Jordan. 1932, v. 4, pp. 560–66.
Law-Davies. Bible rec. Ms. MHS.
Howard-Govane-Woodward-Law Bible rec. Ms. MHS.
See Collins-Law-Polk.
Wicomico Co. families. Bible rec. Ms. DAR.
***Law, Laws.** Wicomico Co. families. Tilghman. Ms., pp. 12–13, 87. DAR.
Lawes. Old Somerset. Torrence. MHS; DAR.
Lawrason. Hist. and geneal. account of Levering family. Levering. MHS.
Neill chart. MHS.
Riggs of Anne Arundel, Frederick and Montgomery Cos. prior to 1663. Pamph. MHS.
Lawrason-Levering Line. Geneal. and mem. encyc. of Md. Spencer. V. 2, pp. 614–19. MHS; DAR.
Lawrence. Ances. rec. and portraits. Col. Dames of Amer., 1910, v. 2, p. 566. MHS; DAR.
Cary Geneal. Coll. Ms. MHS.
Cummings chart, Lib. Cong.; MHS; DAR.
*Founders of Anne Arundel and Howard Cos. Warfield. Pp. 434–35, 487–88. MHS; DAR.
Geneal. memoir of family of John Lawrence of Watertown, 1636. 1847, pamph. MHS.
Geneal. notes of Thomas family. Thomas. MHS; DAR.
Hagerstown tombstone inscriptions. Gruder. Natl. Geneal. Soc. Quart., 1919, v. 8, nos. 1, 2.
†Hist. of West. Md. Scharf. V. 2, p. 1012. MHS; DAR.
Hist. sketch of Lawrence family. R. M. Lawrence. Boston, 1888. MHS.

Lawrence. See Kerfoot. Abr. Compend. Amer. Geneal. Virkus. V. 1, p. 667. DAR.
Lineage Bks., Natl. Soc. of Daughters of Amer. Col., v. 1, p. 42; v. 2, p. 298. MHS; DAR.
Manly chart. MHS.
†Med. Annals Md. Cordell. 1903, p. 474. MHS.
St. Paul's Parish, Balto. V. 1, 2, 4. Mss. MHS.
St. Thomas' Parish, Balto. Co. Bd. ms. MHS. Also: Md. Geneal. Rec. Com., 1937, pp. 109–82. Mss. DAR.
Talbott of "Poplar Knowle." Shirk. MHS; DAR.
Thomas-Chew-Lawrence. Thomas. MHS.
Zion Reformed Church, Hagerstown. Md. Geneal. Rec. Com., 1934–35. Mss. DAR.
See Lucas-Belt-Lawrence-West.
Lawrence, Calvert Co. Thomas Book. Thomas. Pp. 387–89. Lib. Cong.; MHS.
Lawrence, Hagerstown and Balto. Clark chart. MHS.
***Lawrence-Chase-Townley.** Estate. "The Mystery Solved." F. A. Hill. Boston, Rand Avery Co., 1888, 1st ed. MHS.
***Lawrence-Townley and Chase-Townley.** Estates in Eng. With copious hist. and geneal notes on Chase, Lawrence and Townley families. J. Usher. N. Y., 1883. Lib. Cong.; MHS.
Laws. Bible rec. Bible now owned by Victor H. Laws, Wango, Md. Md. Geneal. Rec. Com., 1937–38, p. 155. Mss. DAR.
Md. Geneal. Bull., v. 6, pp. 13, 25. MHS; DAR.
Somerset Co. Court Book. Tilghman. 1937. Ms. DAR.
See Hall-Collins-Elliott-Laws-Tingley.
See Law.
Lawson. Beall and Bell families. Beall. MHS.
Md. families. Culver. Ms. Personal list.
Md. gleanings in Eng. Wills. M. H. Mag., 1907, v. 2, nos. 3, 4.
Public parks of Balto. Ann. Rept., no. 3. MHS; DAR.
St. Paul's Parish, Balto. V. 1, 2. Mss. MHS.
*The Sun, Balto., Aug. 20, 1903.
Mrs. Wm. L. Watson chart. MHS.
Lawson, Balto. Hardwick family, Md. and Va. William and Mary Quart., 2nd series, v. 23, pp. 67–69.
***Lawson, John.** (Courts and marries Mary Hermen.) Hist. of Cecil Co. Johnston. Pp. 174, 176, 177 (his will), 180. MHS; DAR.
***Lawson Family.** Old Kent. Hanson. Pp. 173–75. MHS; DAR.
Lawton. Somerset Co. Court Book. Tilghman. 1937. Ms. DAR.
***Lawyan.** Wicomico Co. families. Tilghman. Ms., p. 53. DAR.
Lay, Rt. Rev. Henry Champlin, D.D. (1823–85). Hist. of Talbot Co. Tilghman. V. 1, pp. 600–06. MHS; DAR.
Layburn. St. Paul's Parish, Balto. V. 2. Mss. MHS.
Layfield. Mt. Zion P. E. churchyard, Worcester Co. Md. Geneal. Rec. Com., 1937, Mrs. Lines. Mss. DAR.
Old Somerset Torrence. MHS; DAR.
*Wicomico Co. families. Tilghman. Ms., p. 116. DAR.
†**Layman.** Hist. of Allegany Co. Thomas and Williams. V. 2. MHS; DAR.
Layton. Bible rec. D. A. R. Mag., Oct., 1932, v. 66, no. 10, pp. 672–74.
Bible rec. D. C. Geneal. Rec. Com., v. 32, p. 55. Typed, bd. DAR.
D. A. R. Mag., Sept., 1933, v. 67, no. 9, pp. 583–88.
*Hackett family of Dorchester Co. D. A. R. Mag., v. 65, no. 4, p. 223.
Hackett family tree. Layton. MHS.
Lineage Bks., Natl. Soc. of Daughters of Amer. Col., v. 4, p. 309. MHS; DAR.
Somerset Co. Court Book. Tilghman. 1937. Ms. DAR.
Wm. Turpin, Dorchester Co., Bible rec. D. A. R. Mag., v. 66, no. 10, p. 672.
Layton, Sussex and Bridgeville, Del. Bible rec. of Dorchester and Somerset Cos. and Del. Pp. 40–46. DAR.
Layton, Tilghman. Bible rec. D. A. R. Mag., v. 66, no. 10, p. 674.
Layton, Tilghman, Jr., Sussex Co., Del. Bible rec., 1820–1928. D. A. R. Mag., v. 66, no. 11, p. 733.
***Layton-Turpin-Douglas.** Lineage Bk., Daughters of Amer. Col., v. 4, p. 309. MHS; DAR.
Layton-Turpin-Hackett-Adams. Abr. Compend. Amer. Geneal. Virkus. V. 6, p. 357. DAR.
†**LaZear.** Med. Annals Md. Cordell. 1903, p. 474. MHS.
Naturalizations in Md., 1666–1765; Laws. Bacon. MHS.
Lazenby. Family data, particularly of Jos. L. Lawson of N. C. Ms. MHS.
*Pamph. DAR.
Lea. Dobbin chart. MHS.
Fox-Ellicott-Evans families. Evans. MHS; DAR.
Winchester-Owens-Price families. M. H. Mag., 1930, v. 25, no. 4, p. 385–405.
Leab. Frederick Co. tombstone inscriptions. Gruder. Natl. Geneal. Soc. Quart., 1919, v. 8, nos. 1, 2.
Leach. Abr. Compend. Amer. Geneal. Virkus. V. 6, p. 290. DAR.
Leaf. Western Run Parish book. Allen. Bd. ms. MHS.
See Leef.
See Lief.
League. Bleakley Bible rec. Ms. MHS.
Leak. Somerset Co. Court Book. Tilghman. 1937. Ms. DAR.
Leake. Scruggs geneal. Dunklin. M. H. Mag., 1914, v. 9, p. 88.
St. Paul's Parish, Balto. V. 2. Mss. MHS.
Leakin. Dorsey and allied families. Ms. MHS.
See Sioussat. Abr. Compend. Amer. Geneal. Virkus. V. 1, p. 828. DAR.
St. Paul's Parish, Balto. V. 2. Mss. MHS.
Leapard. Hagerstown tombstone inscriptions. Gruder. Natl. Geneal. Soc. Quart., 1919, v. 8, nos. 1, 2.
Leaphard. Hagerstown tombstone inscriptions. Gruder. Natl. Geneal. Soc. Quart., 1919, v. 8, nos. 1, 2.
Leapley. M. E. Church South cemetery, near Poolesville, Montgomery Co. Md. Geneal. Rec. Com., 1926. Mss. DAR.
†**Lear, Wm. W.** M. H. Mag., v. 12, p. 226.
Leary. Pedigree of Wm. Emory Waring, Jr. Soc. Col. Wars Md. Culver. 1940. MHS; DAR.
St. Paul's Parish, Balto. V. 1, 2. Mss. MHS.

†**Leary, Peter, Jr.** Men of mark in Md. Johnson. V. 2. DAR; Enoch Partt Lib.
Md. Soc., War of 1812, v. 2, no. 137. Ms. MHS.
†**Leary, Richard P.** M. H. Mag., v. 12, p. 227.
Leary, Rudolph Williams. Md. Soc., War of 1812, v. 4, no. 328. Ms. MHS.
Lease. Frederick Co. tombstone inscriptions. Gruder. Natl. Geneal. Soc. Quart., 1919, v. 8, nos. 1, 2.
Leatherbury. Rec. of Stepney Parish. MHS; DAR.
†**Leatherman.** Hist. of Frederick Co. Williams. MHS; DAR.
Leathers. Cummings chart. Lib. Cong.; MHS; DAR.
Somerset Co. Court Book. Tilghman. 1937. Ms. DAR.
Leaverton. Bible rec., Kent Co., 1808–68. Md. Geneal. Rec. Com., 1932–33, pp. 311–14. Mss. DAR.
Leckron. Spessard family. Spessard. MHS; DAR.
Le Compt. St. Paul's P. E. churchyard, Kent Co. Md. O. R. Soc. Bull., no. 2, pp. 54–65. MHS.
Le Compte. Abr. Compend. Amer. Geneal. Virkus. V. 6, p. 359. DAR.
*Arms. Hist. of Dorchester Co. Jones. 1925, pp. 396–413. MHS; DAR.
Col. families of U. S. A. Mackenzie. V. 6, p. 419. MHS; DAR.
(13 stones.) Christ P. E. Church cemetery, Cambridge. Steele. 1936. MHS; DAR.
Keene family. Jones. MHS; DAR.
Le Compte family. F. B. Culver. M. H. Mag., 1917, v. 12, no. 1, pp. 46–58.
*Lineage Bk., Daughters of Founders and Patriots, v. 16, p. 123. MHS.
Md. families. Culver. Ms. Personal list.
Patriotic Md. Md. Soc. of S. A. R., 1930. MHS; DAR.
M. E. churchyard, Snow Hill, Worcester Co., Hudson. Bd. ms. MHS; DAR.
Pattison wills. Md. Geneal. Rec. Com., 1929, pp. 7–42; 1930–31. Mss. DAR.
Le Compte Family-Col. Taylor-Lee Webster. Harford Co. Hist. Soc. Mss. Coll. JHU.
Le Conte. Col. families of U. S. A. Mackenzie. V. 2. MHS; DAR.
Lecount. Naturalizations in Md., 1666–1765; Laws. Bacon. MHS.
Lederer. Naturalizations in Md., 1666–1765; Laws. Bacon. MHS.
***Lednum.** Wicomico Co. families. Tilghman. Ms., p. 126. DAR.
See Callahan-Lednum-Willis-Wright.
Lee. Amer. Armory and Blue Book. Matthews. Pt. 3.
Ances. rec. and portraits. Col. Dames of Amer., 1910, v. 1, p. 192; v. 2, p. 773. MHS; DAR.
*Ancestry and posterity of John Lea of Wiltshire, Eng., and Pa., 1503–1906. J. H. and G. H. Lea. 1906.
Arnold chart. MHS.
Bible rec. owned by Ralph Lee, Spencerville, Md., 1818–1915. D. C. Geneal. Rec. Com., 1936–37, v. 31, pt. 2, pp. 446–48. DAR.
†Biog. of Robert E. Lee. D. S. Freeman.
Mrs. A. C. Bruce chart. MHS.
*Chronicles of Little, Lee and Albert Buckingham families. MHS.
Col. families of Amer. Lawrence. V. 3, p. 303. MHS.
Col. families of U. S. A. Mackenzie. V. 1, pp. 266–70, 313 (Fenner Lee); v. 2, pp. 435–37 (Lee, Md.); v. 5, p. 536 (Fenner Lee); v. 7. MHS; DAR.
Col. Nicholas Duvall family rec. Price. Bd. ms. MHS.
Eldridge chart. MHS.
First families of Md. The Post, Balto., Feb. 2, 3, 4, 6, 7, 8, 1933. Newsp. clipp., bd. MHS.
*Geneal. hist. of Lee family of Va. and Md., 1300–1866. Coats of arms. E. C. Mead. N. Y., 1871. Lib. Cong.
Gilpin chart. MHS.
Hagerstown tombstone inscriptions. Gruder. Natl. Geneal. Soc. Quart., 1919, v. 8, nos. 1, 2.
*Hist. of Dorchester Co. Jones. 1902, pp. 295–97. MHS; DAR.
†Hist. of Frederick Co. Williams. MHS; DAR.
†Hist. of West. Md. Scharf. V. 1, p. 460; v. 2, p. 871. MHS; DAR.
*Lees of Va. Biog. of family from 1640 forward. B. J. Hendrick. 1935. MHS; DAR.
Little-Lee-Albert Buckingham families. Millie A. Little. 1936. MHS.
Mag. of Soc. of Lees of Va. V. 1, no. 1, Dec., 1922, to v. 3, 1925. (Md. list of members of Soc. of Lees of Va., v. 2, no. 2, Nov., 1924, pp. 84, 188.) MHS.
Md. families. Culver. Ms. Personal list.
†Med. Annals Md. Cordell. 1903, p. 475. MHS.
See Miller, Mrs. T. G. Abr. Compend. Amer. Geneal. Virkus. V. 1, p. 728. DAR.
Obituaries of John R. Lee (died Mar. 16, 1877). Two newsp. clipp. Filing case A, MHS.
John O'Donnell of Balto. Cook. MHS.
Patriotic Md. Md. Soc. of S. A. R., 1930. MHS; DAR.
*Pedigree; from orig. vellum roll in possession of Rev. Dr. F. G. Lee. Coat of arms. Genealogist, London, April 24, 1876, pp. 177–80. Lib. Cong.
Pedigree of James Donnell Tilghman. Soc. Col. Wars Md. Culver. 1940. MHS; DAR.
Mrs. A. Randall chart. MHS.
*Rec. of descendants of Col. Richard Lee of Va. C. F. Lee, Jr., and J. Packard, Jr. Repr. Boston, 1872. Lib. Cong.
†Robert E. Lee. Gen. Fitzhugh Lee.
Rumsey-Smithson Bible rec. Md. Geneal. Rec. Com., 1932–33, v. 5, pp. 63–142. DAR.
Rumsey-Smithson family rec. bk. Md. Geneal. Rec. Com., 1932, pp. 63–158. DAR.
St. Barnabas P. E. churchyard. Typed ms. MHS; DAR.
St. Paul's Parish, Balto. V. 1, 2, 3, 4. Mss. MHS.
Selden chart. MHS.
*Semmes Geneal. Coll. Ms. MHS.
*Side lights on Md. hist. Richardson. V. 20, p. 160. MHS; DAR.
Smithson-Rumsey rec. Bk. Ms. MHS.
†Son of Light Horse Harry. J. Barnes.
Stratford Hall and Lees connected with its hist. Biog., Geneal. and hist. Coat of arms. F. W. Alexander. Oak Grove, Va., 1912.
Stump family of Cecil and Harford Cos. Pamph. MHS.
*Typed copy of notes made by John Wesley Lee. MHS.

Lee. Va. families. Du Bellett.
Wathen Prayer Book rec. Ms. MHS.
See Le Compte Family-Col. Taylor-Lee-Webster.
See Sewall-Darnall-Brooke-Calvert-Lee.
See Webster-Lee.
***Lee,** Charles Co. Cary Geneal. Coll. Ms. MHS.
***Lee,** Harford Co. Cary Geneal. Coll. Ms. MHS.
Lee, Md. and Va. Amer. of gentle birth, and their ancestors. Pittman. V. 1, p. 13. MHS; DAR.
*Burke's landed gentry. 1939. MHS.
***Lee,** Va. (1642–1892). Biog. and geneal. sketches of descendants of Col. Richard Lee. Coat of Arms. Edmond Jenings Lee. Phila., 1895. Lib. Cong.; MHS.
*Geneal. notes proving error of previously accepted pedigree. J. H. Lea. Repr. Boston, 1892. Lib. Cong.; MHS.
(1641.) Md. Geneal. Rec. Com., 1935–36, p. 282. Mss. DAR.
*New Eng. Hist. and Geneal. Reg., v. 44, pp. 103–11. (Pedigree chart, p. 110.)
Pedigree of Charles Lee Packard. Soc. Col. Wars Md. Culver. 1940. MHS; DAR.
*The Sun, Balto., Oct. 25, 1905.
Lee, Miss Cassandra. Chart. Col. Dames, Chap. I. MHS.
Lee, Elizabeth Collins. Abr. Compend. Amer. Geneal. Virkus. V. 1, p. 327. DAR.
Notes. MHS.
Lee, Fenner. Mrs. M. L. Price chart. MHS.
***Lee, Grace.** Typed notes, 1862–1928. MHS.
Lee, Hillyard Cameron, and Lee, Julian Henry. Pedigree charts, plates 1, 2 and 3. Soc. Col. Wars, Md. Johnston. 1905, pp. 58–60. MHS.
Lee, Howard Hall Macy. Md. Soc., War of 1812, v. 1, no. 111. Ms. MHS.
Pedigree. Soc. Col. Wars Md. Culver. 1940. MHS; DAR.
Lee, James, Charles Co. (1658). Col. families of Amer. Lawrence. V. 3, pp. 303–09. MHS.
Lee, Mrs. James Fenner (Mary Cornelia Read). Chart. Col. Dames, Chap. I. MHS.
***Lee, Mrs. John Wesley (Lucinda Green Fowler)** (1827–1920). Typed notes. MHS.
†**Lee, John W. M.** John W. M. Lee, 1848–96. Ruth Lee Briscoe. M. H. Mag., 1937, v. 32, pp. 1–9.
Lee, Julian Henry. *See* Lee, Hillyard Cameron and Julian Henry.
Lee, Otho Scott. Miss Cassandra Lee chart. MHS.
***Lee, Richard,** Blenheim, Md. Private burial ground rec. Ms. File case, MHS.
Lee, Col. Richard, Eng. and "Stratford Hall," Va. (1641). Md. Geneal. Rec. Com., 1935–36, v. 8, p. 282. DAR.
†**Lee, Robert E.** Biog. G. Carleton Lee. 1905.
Lee, Mrs. Stephen (Mrs. Sarah Fenner Mallet). Chart. Col. Dames, Chap. I. MHS.
Lee, Thomas Sim (1745–1819). Dict. of Amer. Biog., v. 11, p. 132.
†Governors of Md. Buchholz. P. 9. MHS.
†Hist. of Md. Scharf. V. 2, p. 488. MHS.
†Founders of Anne Arundel and Howard Cos. Warfield. Pp. 226–35. MHS; DAR.
(1745–1819). Lee of Va., 1642–1892. E. J. Lee. P. 306. Lib. Cong.; MHS.
Lee Family. Notes. Ms. MHS.
*South. Md. graves, on property of John Matthews. Blue pr. MHS.
Lee Family, Harford Co. War rec. Ms. MHS.
Lee (Harford Co. and Va.)-**Wilson,** (Anne Arundel Co.) Chart, photos., 1 sheet. Cary Geneal. Coll. Ms. MHS.
***Lee, Leigh.** John Lee of Agawan, Ipswich, Mass., 1634–17—?. Geneal. notes and biog. sketches of all his descendants. W. M. Lee. Ref. to other Lee families in Conn., Me., N. Y., and Md. Albany, N. Y., 1888. Lib. Cong.
Leech, Tobias, Pa. Pedigree of George Thornburgh Macauly Gibson. Soc. Col. Wars Md. Culver. 1940. MHS; DAR.
Pedigree of Maurice Falconer Rodgers. Soc. Col. Wars Md. Culver. 1940. MHS; DAR.
Pedigree of Anthony Morris Tyson. Soc. Col. Wars Md. Culver. 1940. MHS; DAR.
Leeds. Barroll in Great Britain and Amer. Barroll. P. 77. MHS.
Dobbin chart. MHS.
Hist. of Talbot Co. Tilghman. V. 1, p. 376. MHS; DAR.
Peale Geneal. Coll. Ms. MHS.
Pedigree of Levin Gale Shreve. Soc. Col. Wars Md. Culver. 1940. MHS; DAR.
Pedigree of Harrison Tilghman. Soc. Col. Wars Md. Culver. 1940. MHS; DAR.
Thomas family of Talbot Co. Spencer. P. 58. MHS; DAR.
Leeds Family. Ames Geneal Coll. Ms. MHS.
Leef, Leif, Lief, Leaf. Rec. from Bell Bible. Md. Geneal. Rec. Com., 1937, pp. 20–21. Mss. DAR.
Leek. Centenary of Catholicity in Ky. Webb. 1884. MHS.
Leeke. Patriotic Md. Md. Soc. of S. A. R., 1930. MHS; DAR.
Pedigree of Nicholas Leeke Dashiell. Soc. Col. Wars Md. Culver. 1940. MHS; DAR.
Pedigree of James Etchberger Hancock. Soc. Col. Wars Md. Culver. 1940. MHS; DAR.
St. Paul's Parish, Balto. V. 2. Mss. MHS.
Leeper. West. Nottingham Cemetery. M. H. Mag., 1923, v. 18, p. 55.
†**Lefever.** Hist. of West. Md. Scharf. V. 2, p. 916. MHS; DAR.
Leffler. *See* Rice-Leffler.
Leftwich. Balto., its hist., its people. Hall. V. 3. MHS; DAR.
†Memorial service held in First Presbyterian Church, Balto., March 3, 1897; James Turner Leftwick, pastor 1879–93 (born 1837). Enoch Pratt Lib.
***Leftwich,** Va., The Sun, Balto., Aug. 13, 20, 1905.
***Leftwich-Turner.** Leftwich-Turner families of Va., and their connections. Coat of arms. W. L. Hopkins. 1931. DAR.
Le Gendre, Mrs. William. Mrs. James Piper chart. MHS.
(Sophia Norris Pitts.) Chart. (Maternal line, N. C. families.) Col. Dames, Chap. I. MHS.
†**Legg.** Biog. cyc. of rep. men of Md. and D. C. P. 499. MHS; DAR.
St. Paul's Parish. Balto. V. 2. Mss. MHS.
*The Sun, Balto., Sunday, Jan. 4, 1914.
***Legg-Washington families.** By E. C. Legg. The Sun, Balto., Dec. 4, 1914.
Legge. Legge-Washington families. Etta Legge Galloway. Ms. MHS.

Legge Family, Eng. to Kent Island. Geneal. Md. Geneal. Rec. Com., 1924–25, v. 1. Pp. 55–67. DAR.
***Le Gore.** Frederick Co. families. Ms. Personal list.
***Lehman.** Frederick Co. families. Markell. Ms. Personal list.
†Hist. of Washington Co. Williams. 1906, v. 2, p. 1274. MHS; DAR.
Lehman family in Md. Samuel A. Lehman. 1935. MHS.
Short hist. of Lehman family in Md. S. A. Lehman. Pamph. 1935. DAR.
Short hist. of Lehman family in Md. S. A. Lehman. Balto., Hess Printing Co., 1935, pamph. MHS; DAR.
Lehman Family. Ms. MHS.
Lehr. Balto., its hist., its people. Hall. V. 3. MHS; DAR.
Lehr, Mrs. Louis (Eleanor Addison Moale). Chart. Col. Dames, Chap. I. MHS.
Leicht. Hagerstown tombstone inscriptions. Gruder. Natl. geneal. Soc. Quart., 1919, v. 8, nos. 1, 2.
Leif. *See* Leef.
See Lief.
Leigh. Geneal. notes of Chamberlaine family. MHS.
Manly chart. MHS.
Pedigree of Leigh. Bonsal. Soc. Col. Wars Md. Culver. 1940. MHS; DAR.
St. Inigoes churchyard, St. Mary's Co. Md. O. R. Soc. Bull., no. 3, p. 58.
Mrs. J. G. Thomas chart. MHS.
Thomas family of Talbot Co. Spencer. P. 64. MHS; DAR.
See Lee.
Leigh, John. John Leigh, Agawan (Ipswich), Mass. (1634–71), and his descendants of name of Lee. Wm. Lee. (54 pp. on other Lee families, Conn., Me., N. Y. and Md.) Albany, 1888.
Leighs. Ances. rec. and portraits. Col. Dames of Amer., 1910, v. 2, p. 781. MHS; DAR.
Leightheiser. *See* Borroway-Leightheiser.
Leimbach. Catonsville pioneers of Luth. faith. Natl. Geneal. Soc. Quart., v. 9, no. 2, p. 29.
Leiper, Pa. Miss Eliza Thomas chart. MHS.
Thomas Book. Thomas. Pp. 435–41. Lib. Cong.; MHS.
†**Leitch, John Wm.** Men of mark in Md. Johnson. V. 4. DAR; Enoch Pratt Lib.
Leiter. Steiner geneal. Steiner. 1896. MHS.
***Le Loilais Family.** Arch. of Georgetown Univ., Wash., D. C., v. 124, no. 6.
Le Master Family (as connected with Hayes, Hay, Haise family). Md. Geneal. Bull., v. 8, no. 4, p. 46. MHS; DAR.
†**Lemmon.** Med. Annals Md. Cordell. 1903, p. 475. MHS.
Morris family of Phila. Moon. V. 2, p. 726. MHS.
St. Paul's Parish, Balto. V. 1, 2. Mss. MHS.
Lemmonier. St. Paul's Parish, Balto. V. 2. Mss. MHS.
Lemon. Dorsey and allied families. Ms. MHS.
Griffith geneal. Griffith. MHS; DAR.
See Lemmon.
Le Moyne. Abr. Compend. Amer. Geneal. Virkus. V. 1, p. 507. DAR.
McLanahan chart. MHS.
Mrs. A. G. Ober chart. MHS.
Le Neve. Md. gleanings in Eng. Wills. M. H. Mag., 1907, v. 2, no. 3.
Lenox. St. Paul's Parish, Balto. V. 1. Mss. MHS.
Leonard. Balto., its hist., its people. Hall. V. 2. MHS; DAR.
†Hist. of Allegany Co. Thomas and Williams. V. 2. MHS; DAR.
See Koster, New Eng. Abr. Compend. Amer. Geneal. Virkus. V. 1, p. 672. DAR.
†Med. Annals Md. Cordell. 1903, p. 476. MHS.
*Wicomico Co. families. Tilghman. Ms., pp. 35–37, 41, 82, 96–98, 111–12, 115, 129. DAR.
***Leslie Family.** Hist. of Cecil Co. Johnston. P. 520. MHS; DAR.
***Lester Family.** Quaker rec. of Pa. Wilson Mss. Coll., no. 81. MHS.
†**Letherbury.** Med. Annals Md. Cordell. 1903, p. 476. MHS.
Lett. St. Paul's Parish, Balto. V. 1. Mss. MHS.
Letter. St. Paul's Parish, Balto. V. 2. Mss. MHS.
***Leuther.** Frederick Co. families. Markell. Ms. Personal list.
Leveille. Hist. graves of Md. and D. C. Ridgely. MHS.
Levering. Abr. Compend. Amer. Geneal. Virkus. V. 1, p. 685. DAR.
Bailiere chart. MHS.
†Biog. cyc. of rep. men of Md. and D. C. P. 139. MHS; DAR.
*Hist. and geneal. account of Levering family. Col. John Levering. W. B. Burford, pub. by the Levering Hist. Assoc., Indianapolis, Ind., 1897. MHS.
Monumental City. Howard. MHS; DAR.
Neill chart. MHS.
Proc. of Levering family reunion, held at Levering, Knox Co., Ohio. Pub. by order of Assoc. of Columbus, Ohio. J. L. Trauger, 1892, pp. 1–120.
Robins family tree. MHS.
Sater geneal. Bd. ms. MHS.
Stump family of Cecil and Harford Cos. Pamph. MHS.
*The Sun, Balto., Jan. 8, 1905.
See Lawrason Levering Line.
***Levering, Eugene.** Amer. Armory and Blue Bk. Matthews. 1908, p. 8. DAR.
†Men of mark in Md. Johnson. V. 1. DAR; Enoch Pratt Lib.
†**Levering, Joshua.** Men of mark in Md. Johnson. V. 2. DAR; Enoch Pratt Lib.
***Levering Family.** Or geneal. of Wigard and Gerhard Levering, two of pioneer settlers of Roxborough Township, Phila. Co., Pa., and their descendants. H. G. Jones. Pr. for author, Phila., King & Baird, 1858. MHS.
Levering-Lawrason Line. Geneal. and memorial encyc. of Md. Spencer. V. 2, p. 614. MHS; DAR.
Leverton. Notes. D. A. R. Mag., Sept., 1932, v. 66, no. 9, p. 604.
Leverton, Arthur, Caroline Co. (married Margaret A. Turpin, March 21, 1832). Bible rec., also signers of marriage certificate. D. A. R. Mag., v. 66, no. 9, p. 604.
Leverton Family, Kent Co. Bible rec. Md. Geneal. Rec. Com., 1932–33, v. 5. Mss. DAR.

Levett. Md. gleanings in Eng. Wills. M. H. Mag., 1907, v. 2, no. 2.
Le Viness, Charles Thabor, III. Pedigree. Soc. Soc. Col. Wars Md. Culver. 1940. MHS; DAR.
Levis. Winchester-Owens-Price families. M. H. Mag., 1930, v. 25, no. 4, p. 385–405.
Levy. Frederick Co. tombstone inscriptions. Gruder. Natl. Geneal. Soc. Quart., 1919, v. 8, nos. 1, 2.
St. Paul's Parish, Balto. V. 1, 2. Mss. MHS.
See Pearce-Levy.
Lewes. Somerset Co. Court Book. Tilghman. 1937. Ms. DAR.
†Lewger. Papers relating to early hist. of Md. Streeter. 1876. MHS.
†Lewger, John. Bench and bar of Md. Sams and Riley. 1901, v. 1, p. 9. Lib. Cong.; MHS; Peabody Lib.
Lewin. Hazelhurst chart. MHS.
Mary E. Jenkins Surratt, maternal line. Md. Geneal. Bull., v. 1, pp. 1–3.
***Lewin Family.** Old Kent. Hanson. P. 320. MHS; DAR.
Lewis. Samuel Carpenter of Phila. Carpenter. P. 179. MHS.
Fox-Ellicott-Evans families. Evans. MHS; DAR.
*Geneal. of Lewis and kindred families of Va. J. M. McAllister, Atlanta, Ga., and L. B. Tandy, Columbia, Mo. 1906.
Hagerstown tombstone inscriptions. Gruder. Natl. Geneal. Soc. Quart., 1919, v. 8, nos. 1, 2.
Husband and allied families. P. 95. Ms. MHS.
Jackson family gathering. 1878.
Capt. Roger Jones of London and Va. Browning.
*Lewis family in Amer. W. T. Lewis. 1893. DAR.
*Lewis of Warner Hall. M. E. Sorley. (Va. rec.) 1935. DAR.
*Lewises, Meriwethers and their kin. Sarah T. L. (Scott) Anderson (1847–1926). Richmond, Va., Dietz Pub. Co. 1938, 652 pp.
See Linthicum family. Focke Geneal. Coll. Ms. MHS.
Md. Geneal. Bull., v. 4, p. 6. MHS; DAR.
McCormick chart. MHS.
Mt. Paran Pres. churchyard, Harrisonville, Balto. Co. Typed ms. MHS; DAR.
(58 rec.) St. Paul's Parish, Balto. V. 1, 2, 4. Mss. MHS.
Va. geneal. Hayden. MHS; DAR.
*Wicomico Co. families. Tilghman. Ms., p. 91. DAR.
Williamson Bible rec. Ms. MHS.
See Warner-Lewis.
See Washington-Marshall-Lewis.
See Wimbrow-Lewis-Tubbs.
†Lewis, Frederick Co. Hist. of West. Md. Scharf. V. 1, p. 572. MHS; DAR.
Lewis, Kent Co. Manning chart. MHS.
Lewis, Va. Ances. rec. and portraits. Col. Dames of Amer., 1910, v. 1, pp. 129–34. MHS; DAR.
Bird chart. MHS.
*The Sun, Balto., June 4, Jan. 22, Aug. 27, 1905.
†Lewis, David. Men of mark in Md. Johnson. V. 4. DAR; Enoch Pratt Lib.
Lewis, Fielding. Pedigree of Francis Fielding Reid. Soc. Col. Wars Md. Culver. 1940. MHS; DAR.
Lewis Family, "Warner Hall," Va. William and Mary Quart., 1st series, v. 9, pp. 191, 259–65 (showing Addison, Bowles, Brooke and Tasker connections, p. 265); v. 10; v. 11.
*Giving royal descent, and allied families Bronaugh, Carter, Dale, Fowke Martiau, Mason, Reade, Warner, Washington, Windebanke. Col. and Revolutionary lineages of Amer. 1939, v. 3, pp. 100–41. MHS.
Lewis-Spencer. Rumsey-Smithson family rec. bk. Md. Geneal. Rec. Com., 1932, pp. 136–37. DAR.
Leyburn, Rev. John. Monumental City. Howard. MHS; DAR.
Leypold. Greenway chart. MHS.
Cassanda Lee chart. MHS.
Lidster. Somerset Co. Court Book. Tilghman. 1937. Ms. DAR.
Liebhart, Liphart. Hagerstown tombstone inscriptions. Gruder. Natl. Geneal. Soc. Quart., 1919, v. 8, nos. 1, 2.
Lief. *See* Leef.
Lief, John (born 1758; married 1781; died 1836). Copy of will. Md. Geneal. Rec. Com., 1937. DAR.
Lief, Leif, Leaf. Bible rec. from Bell Bible, 1782–83. Md. Geneal. Rec. Com., 1937. DAR.
†Ligan, Gen. James Maccubin. Hist. of Md. Scharf. V. 3, p. 17. MHS.
†Light. Hist. of Allegany Co. Thomas and Williams. V. 2. MHS; DAR.
Lightfoot. Cary Geneal. Coll. Ms. MHS.
Lighthall. St. Paul's Parish Balto. V. 2. Mss. MHS.
Lightner. Family hist. of John Hyder and Catherine Delaplaine. Beam. 1909, pamph. MHS.
St. Paul's Parish, Balto. V. 2. Mss. MHS.
Lightner, John M. (Revolutionary soldier). Loudon Park cemetery, Balto., Patriotic Marylander, v. 2, no. 4, pp. 54–60. MHS; DAR.
Ligon. John Price, emigrant, Jamestown Col., 1620. Price. MHS.
Proc., in two sections, of Ligon Family Kinsmen Assoc. Section 1, constitution. Section 2, first reunion. Wm. D. Ligon, Jr., editor. Pub. by Ligon Family Assoc., N. Y. V. 1, no. 1, Oct., 1937. MHS; DAR.
***Ligon,** Va. Pedigrees 1, 2, 3. Coat of arms. Burke's landed gentry. 1939. MHS.
†Ligon, Gov. Thomas Watkins. Founders of Anne Arundel and Howard Cos. Warfield. P. 281. MHS; DAR.
†Governors of Md. Buchholz. P. 165. MHS.
***Ligon Family.** Ligon family. Wm. D. Ligon, Jr., N. Y. City. V. 1, no. 1. MHS.
Lilburn. Col. and Revolutionary families of Phila. Jordan. 1933, v. 1, pp. 382–98.
Trinity P. E. churchyard, St. Mary's City. Md. O. R. Soc. Bull., no. 3, p. 59.
†Lilburn, J. G. H. Men of mark in Md. Johnson. V. 4. DAR; Enoch Pratt Lib.
***Lillard.** Family of col. Va., 1415–1928. J. E. S. Lillard. Richmond, Va., Williams Printing Co., 1928. MHS.
*Marriages. Ms. DAR.
Lillard Family. Ms. MHS.
Lillingston. Ancestry of Rosalie Morris Johnson. Johnson. 1905. MHS; DAR.
Lilly. Mrs. J. G. Brogden chart. MHS.
Cary Geneal. Coll. Ms. MHS.

Centenary of Catholicity in Ky. Webb. 1884. MHS.
Jenkins-Courtney chart. MHS.
*Lilly family of Md. Kate Singer Curry, 1420 Girard St., N.W., Wash., D. C.
Lilly, Mass. and Balto. A. L. Thomsen, H. I. Thomsen and J. J. Thomsen pedigree chart. Soc. Col. Wars, Md. Johnston. 1905, p. 112. MHS.
Lilly, Austin Jenkins. Pedigree. Soc. Col. Wars Md. Culver. 1940. MHS; DAR.
Lilly Family, Sweden, France and Amer. Ms. MHS.
Linch. Focke Geneal. Coll. Mss. MHS.
Linch, Lynch. St. Paul's Parish, Balto. V. 1, 2. Mss. MHS.
***Lind.** Frederick Co. families. Markell. Ms. Personal list.
Lindenberger. St. Paul's Parish, Balto. V. 2. Mss. MHS.
Lindersmith. Lineage Bks., Natl. Soc. of Daughters of Amer. Col., v. 3, p. 238. MHS; DAR.
***Lindesmith,** Hagerstown, Md. Lineage Bk., Daughters of Amer. Colo., v. 3, p. 238. MHS; DAR.
Lindsay. Cary Geneal. Coll. Ms. MHS.
Geneal. of Va. family of Lomax. Lib. Cong.
†Hist. of Balto. City and Co. Scharf. P. 762. MHS.
Lindsay Family Assoc. of Amer. Organized Feb. 16, 1904. 9th Annual Year Book, 1912. Mrs. James Lindsay Atkinson, editor. MHS.
*Pennington Papers. Ms. MHS.
St. Paul's Parish, Balto. V. 2. Mss. MHS.
*Scotland to Va. The Sun, Balto., May 5, 1905; April 14, 21, 28, 1907.
Selden chart. MHS.
Turner Geneal. Coll. Ms. MHS.
*Wicomico Co. families. Tilghman. Ms., p. 83. DAR.
See White-Lindsay.
***Lindsay Family.** Reports, 1904–1912. MHS.
Lindsey. Somerset Co. Court Book. Tilghman. 1937. Ms. DAR.
Ling. St. Paul's Parish, Balto. V. 2. Mss. MHS.
Lingan. Ances. rec. and portraits. Col. Dames of Amer., 1910, v. 2, p. 596. MHS; DAR.
Battee, Brewer, Boteler, etc., family rec. Murray. Photos. MHS.
Chew family. Culver. M. H. Mag., 1935, v. 30, no. 2, pp. 157–75.
Coll. of Amer. epitaphs and inscriptions. Alden. 1814, v. 5. MHS.
Pedigree of Edward Boteler Passano. Soc. Col. Wars Md. Culver. 1940. MHS; DAR.
Rock Creek Cemetery interments. (Maj. Thomas Lingan, rec. no. 1.) Natl. Geneal. Soc. Quart., v. 7, no. 3, p. 41.
St. Paul's Parish, Balto. V. 2. Mss. MHS.
Lingan, Gen. James Maccubin (1751–) Marking grave of hero. E. C. Tulloch. Amer. Monthly Mag., v. 23, p. 268. DAR.
†Biograph. sketch. Ella M. Dorsey. Rec. Columbia Hist. Soc., v. 13, pp. 1–48.
*Patriots of Revolutionary period interred in D. C. Balch. Rec. of Columbia Hist. Soc., v. 19, v. 20.
S. M. Ely. Repr. from Columbia Hist. Soc. Rec., v. 21, pp. 134–35. DAR.
Lingan Family. E. G. R. Calvert. Harford Co. Hist. Soc. Mss. Coll. JHU.
E. L. Davey. Harford Co. Hist. Soc. Mss. Coll. JHU.
***Lingan-Boteler.** The Sun, Balto. June 18, 1905.
Lininger. Hist. of Allegany Co. Thomas and Williams. V. 2, pp. 955–56. MHS; DAR.
***Link.** Frederick Co. families. Markell. Ms. Personal list.
Linthicum. Abr. Compend. Amer. Geneal. Virkus. V. 6, p. 422. DAR.
Chart, photos., 3 sheets. Cary Geneal. Coll. Ms. MHS.
Col. and Revolutionary families of Pa. Amer. Hist. Soc., N. Y., 1934, pp. 640–65.
Copy of orig. grant made by Lord Baltimore to Thomas Linthicum. Ms. MHS.
Dorsey-Linthicum Bible rec. Ms. MHS.
(1658). Focke Geneal. Coll. Mss. MHS.
*Geneal. of Linthicum and allied families. M. P. Badger. 1934. Mimeog. DAR.
†Hist. of Frederick Co. Williams. V. 2, p. 1227. MHS; DAR.
*Lineage Bk., Daughters of Amer. Col., v. 3, p. 180. MHS; DAR.
Md. families. Culver. Ms. Personal list.
Md. Geneal. Bull., v. 4, p. 14, 23. MHS; DAR.
†Med. Annals Md. Cordell. 1903, p. 477. MHS.
Old Md. families. Bromwell. MHS; DAR.
Portrait and biog. rec. of Sixth Cong. Dist. of Md. 1898. P. 601. MHS; DAR.
Stewart chart. Cary Geneal. Coll. Ms. MHS.
Sweetser chart. MHS.
Tercentenary hist of Md. Andrews. V. 2, pp. 265, 563. MHS; DAR.
Trinity Church burial ground, near Cambridge, Md. Md. Geneal. Rec. Com., 1937–38, pp. 93–104. Mss. DAR.
Trinity Church cemetery, Dorchester Co. Md. O. R. Soc. Bull., no. 3, pp. 42–52.
See Disney-Linthicum.
See Stewart.
†Linthicum, J. Charles. J. Charles, Linthicum. late representative from Md. Memorial address in Congress. Wash., U. S. Gov. Print. Office., 1893. Enoch Pratt Lib.
Linthicum, Lot. Bible rec. Ms. DAR.
***Linthicum Family.** Anne Arundel Co. gentry. Newman. Pp. 455–76. MHS; DAR.
Linthicum family. M. P. J. Badger. Balto., 1936. (Two typed leaves of Wills family, inserted after p. 138 and four leaves of correction at end. 189 pp. Lib. Cong.; DAR.
Linthicum Family, Anne Arundel Co. And branches. M. H. Mag., 1930, v. 25, no. 3, p. 275–84 corrections, no. 4, p. 406–9.
Linthicum-Pattison. Bible rec. Typed. DAR.
Linton. Marriage rec. of Frederick Co. Markell. Md. Geneal. Rec. Com., 1938–39. Mss. DAR.
Linton (Elijah) Family, Md. and Va. Data. Ms. DAR.
Linville. Bible rec., 1755–1873. Md. Geneal. Rec. Com., 1932–33, p. 54. Mss. DAR.
Bond chart. MHS.
St. Paul's Parish, Balto. V. 2. Mss. MHS.
Linville, C. Hardesty. Md. Soc., War of 1812, v. 3, no. 295. Ms. MHS.
Liphart. *See* Liebhart.
Lippincott. Trinity P. E. churchyard, Long Green. Typed ms. MHS; DAR.

Lippincott. Florence Eyster Weaver chart. MHS.
Lippold. Hist. of Allegany Co. Thomas and Williams. V. 2, p. 958. MHS; DAR.
†**Lipps, Christopher.** In memoriam. Soc. for Hist. of Germans in Md. 6th ann. rept., 1892.
Lisboa. Col. families of Md. Emory. P. 139. MHS; DAR.
Lister. Edmund Beauchamp of East. Shore of Md. D. A. R. Mag., v. 66, no. 4, pp. 234–38.
*Frederick Co. families. Markell. Ms. Personal list.
Litchfield. Ances. rec. and portraits. Col. Dames of Amer., 1910, p. 693. MHS; DAR.
Tercentenary hist. of Md. Andrews. V. 4, p. 257. MHS; DAR.
***Litchfield Family.** Assoc., pt. 1, no. 1, 1901–no. 5, 1906. MHS.
Littig. Bond chart. MHS.
†Med. Annals Md. Cordell. 1903, p. 478. MHS.
Tercentenary hist. of Md. Andrews. V. 3, p. 277. MHS; DAR.
Little. Balch chart. MHS.
Brown-Little families, Carroll and Frederick Cos. Ms. File case, DAR.
*Chronicles of Little, Lee, and Albert Buckingham families. MHS.
Elliott chart. MHS.
Hagerstown tombstone inscriptions. Gruder. Natl. Geneal. Soc. Quart., 1919, v. 8, nos. 1, 2.
Hist. of Allegany Co. Thomas and Williams. V. 2, pp. 958–59. MHS; DAR.
Md. tombstone rec. Md. Geneal. Rec. Com., 1937, Parran, p. 31. Mss. DAR.
St. Paul's Parish, Balto. V. 1, 2. Mss. MHS.
Tercentenary hist. of Md. Andrews. V. 2, p. 333; v. 4, pp. 487, 908. MHS; DAR.
Whiting-Little-Horner-Brown. Va. families. MHS.
Little, Pa. and Carroll Co. Data. D. A. R. Mag., v. 62, no. 1, p. 55.
†**Little, Henry.** M. H. Mag., v. 12, p. 227.
†**Little, John Mays.** Men of mark in Md. Johnson. V. 4. DAR; Enoch Pratt Lib.
†**Little, Col. Peter.** Hist. of Md. Scharf. V. 2, p. 635. MHS.
***Little-Lee-Albert Buckingham Families.** Chronicles. M. A. Little. Westminster, Md., 1936. With books, MHS.
Littlejohn. St. Paul's Parish, Balto. V. 2. Mss. MHS.
Littlepage. Va. geneal. Hayden. MHS; DAR.
***Littlepage Family,** Va. Hist. Mrs. Paul T. Maslin. 1937. Address Mrs. Paul T. Maslin, 708 Edgewood St., Balto., Md.
Littleton. Mrs. Henry Du Pont. Baldwin chart. MHS.
Col. families of U. S. A. Mackenzie. V. 4, p. 126. MHS; DAR.
Littleton Family of Va. Repr. from New Eng. Hist. and Geneal. Reg., Oct., 1887, v. 41, pp. 364–68.
See Waters, Littleton.
Littleton, Accomac Co., Va. Ancestry. William and Mary Quart., 1900, v. 8, p. 230; 1901, v. 9, p. 62.
Littleton, Va. Col. families of Amer. Lawrence. V. 10, pp. 33, 57. MHS.
Pedigree of John Custis Handy. Soc. Col. Wars Md. Culver. 1940. MHS; DAR.
Littleton, Nathaniel, Va. Pedigree of Lee Cummins Cary. Soc. Col. Wars Md. Culver. 1940. MHS; DAR.
Littleton, Col. Southey, Va. (1645–1679). J. T. Dennis pedigree chart. Soc. Col. Wars, Md. Johnston. 1905, pp. 21, 149. MHS.
Pedigree of Sam'l King Dennis. Soc. Col. Wars Md. Culver. 1940. MHS; DAR.
***Littleton Family.** Va. Mag. Hist. and Biog., v. 18, p. 20; v. 46, no. 2, pp. 171–72.
***Littleton Family,** Va. Tentative pedigree. Robt. P. Robins. Boston, 1887.
Littleton Line. Geneal. tables of paternal lines of Dennis family. Dennis. Pp. 46–59. MHS.
Littleton or **Lyttleton.** Geneal. of Henrietta Chauncy Wilson. Upshur. Bk. of photos. MHS.
Litzinger, Henry. Revolutionary pension abs. Natl. Geneal. Soc. Quart., v. 23, p. 5.
Livers. Centenary of Catholicity in Ky. Webb. 1884. MHS.
Lineage Bks., Natl. Soc. of Daughters of Amer. Col., v. 2, pp. 22, 95. MHS; DAR.
Naturalizations in Md., 1666–1765; Laws. Bacon. MHS.
Pedigree of Francis Joseph Baldwin. Soc. Col. Wars Md. Culver. 1940. MHS; DAR.
***Livers-Elder.** Lineage Bk., Daughters of Amer. Col. V. 2, p. 22. MHS; DAR.
Livezey. Balto., its Hist., its people. Hall. V. 2. MHS; DAR.
Mrs. T. B. Harrison chart. MHS.
Rumsey-Smithson Bible rec. Md. Geneal. Rec. Com., 1932–33, pp. 63–142. DAR.
Rumsey-Smithson family rec. bk. Md. Geneal. Rec. Com., 1932, pp. 63–158. DAR.
Smithson-Rumsey rec. bk. Ms. MHS.
***Livingston.** Wicomico Co. families. Tilghman. Ms, p. 99. DAR.
Lloyd. Abs. of Va. land patents. Va. Mag. Hist. and Biog., v. 3, p. 187.
All of Pa. Col. and Revolutionary families of Pa. Jordan. 1932, v. 4, p. 66.
Ances. rec. and portraits. Col. Dames of Amer., 1910, v. 1, p. 354. MHS; DAR.
Bantz geneal. notes. Ms. MHS.
†Biog. cyc. of rep. men of Md. and D. C. Pp. 522–23. MHS; DAR.
Britton Scrap Book. V. 2. Ms. MHS.
Cadwalder family. Col. and Revolutionary families of Pa. Jordan. 1932, v. 4.
Cary Geneal. Coll. Ms. MHS.
†Chesapeake Bay Country. Earle. P. 351. MHS.
Chew family. Culver. M. H. Mag., 1935, v. 30, no. 2, pp. 157–75.
Christ P. E. Church cemetery, Cambridge. Steele. 1936. MHS; DAR.
Col. families of Amer. Lawrence. V. 9, p. 139. MHS.
Col. mansions of Md. and Del. Hammond. 1914. MHS.
De Ford chart. MHS.
Descendants of Joran Kyn of New Sweden. Keen. MHS; DAR.
Early hist. of Hollyday family. Hollyday. MHS; DAR.
*Family hist. of Wales, Pa., and Md. Welsh rec. from coll. of late Howard W. Lloyd. Lancaster, Pa., 1912. DAR.
†Founders of Anne Arundel and Howard Cos.

Warfield. Pp. 255 (Gov. Edward), 294 (Gov. Henry). MHS; DAR.
Geneal notes of Chamberlaine family. MHS.
Gittings chart. MHS.
*Graveyard, Wye House. Inscriptions from 1684. McHenry Howard. M. H. Mag., 1922, v. 17, pp. 20–33, (corrections) 226.
Hist. graves of Md. and D. C. Ridgely. MHS.
Hist. of Talbot Co. Tilghman. V. 1, pp. 132–228. MHS; DAR.
Howland chart. MHS.
Inscriptions on tombstones at "Wye House." Geneal. notes of Chamberlaine family. P. 34. MHS.
Lloyd family. Christopher Johnston. M. H. Mag., 1912, v. 7, pp. 420–30; 1913, v. 8, pp. 85–87, 202–03.
*Lloyd family. Oswald. Tilghman. M. H. Mag., June 1913, v. 8, no. 2, p. 202.
Lloyds of Wye House, Talbot Co. Howard McHenry. M. H. Mag., 1923, v. 18, pp. 293–99. Also Md. O. R. Soc. Bull. no. 1, pp. 11–17.
Miss Katherine Lurman chart. MHS.
*Lloyds of Wye House. Md. O. R. Soc., v. 1, pp. 11–17.
Md. families. Culver. Ms. Personal list.
*McGarth, Lloyd and other families. M. H. Mag., 1929, v. 24, pp. 291–324.
W. A. and S. W. Merritt pedigree charts, plate 2. Soc. Col. Wars, Md. Johnston. 1905, p. 68. MHS.
Milligan chart. MHS.
J. P. Paca pedigree chart. Soc. Col. Wars, Md. Johnston. 1905, pp. 80, 149. MHS.
Patriotic Md. Md. Soc. of S. A. R., 1930. MHS; DAR.
Pedigree. Geneal. of McKean family of Pa. Buchanan. Pp. 180–83. MHS.
Pedigree of Edward Hammond. Soc. Col. Wars Md. Culver. 1940. MHS; DAR.
Pedigree of Charles Morris Howard. Soc. Col. Wars Md. Culver. 1940. MHS; DAR.
Pedigree of Dr. Christopher Johnston, Jr. Soc. Col. Wars Md. Culver. 1940. MHS; DAR.
Pedigree of Gustav Wm. Lurman. Soc. Col. Wars Md. Culver. 1940. MHS; DAR.
Pedigree of Franklin Buchanan Owen. Soc. Col. Wars Md. Culver. 1940. MHS; DAR.
Pedigree of John Philemon Paca. Soc. Col. Wars Md. Culver. 1940. MHS; DAR.
Pedigree of Pleasants Pennington. Soc. Col. Wars Md. Culver. 1940. MHS; DAR.
Pedigree of Tilghman Golbsborough Pitts. Soc. Col. Wars Md. Culver. 1940. MHS; DAR.
Pedigree of Ralph Robinson. Soc. Col. Wars Md. Culver. 1940. MHS; DAR.
Pedigree of Levin Gale Shreve. Soc. Col. Wars Md. Culver. 1940. MHS; DAR.
Pedigree of Harrison Tilghman. Soc. Col. Wars Md. Culver. 1940. MHS; DAR.
Pedigree of James Donnell Tilghman. Soc. Col. Wars Md. Culver. 1940. MHS; DAR.
*Pennington Papers. Ms. MHS.
St. Paul's Parish, Balto. V. 2, 4. Mss. MHS.
*Side lights on Md. Hist. Richardson. P. 163. MHS; DAR.
*The Sun, Balto., July 19, 1903.
Tilghman chart. MHS.
Mrs. E. C. Venable chart. MHS.
Mrs. Emory Whitridge chart. MHS.
Wye Island. Bordley, Lloyd and Paca families. Lippincott Mag., v. 19.
See Bordley-Lloyd-Paca.
See Buchanan-Lloyd.
See Francis-Watkins-Lloyd.
See Moore-Lloyd.
See Wight-Hodson-Lloyd-Travers.

Lloyd, Talbot Co. McH. Howard pedigree chart. plate 2. Soc. Col. Wars, Md. Johnston. 1905, pp. 42, 149. MHS.

Lloyd, Mrs. Charles. 2 charts. Col. Dames, Chap. I. MHS.

***Lloyd, Mrs. Charles Howard (Mary Chesley Donnell).** Chart. Col. Dames Amer., Chap. I. MHS.

†Lloyd, Daniel Boone. Men of mark in Md. Johnson. V. 3. DAR; Enoch Pratt Lib.

***Lloyd, Edward.** Burke's landed gentry. 1939. MHS.
†Governors of Md. Buchholz. P. 70. MHS.
Edw. Lloyd, Gov. of Md., 1709–14. G. McCall. Pa. Soc. of Col. Gov., v. 1. MHS.
†(1826–1907). M. H. Mag., v. 12, p. 227.

†Lloyd, Henry. Governors of Md. Buchholz. P. 235. MHS.

Lloyd, Wm. Henry. Pedigree. (Mostly Mass. families.) Soc. Col. Wars Md. Culver. 1940. MHS; DAR.

***Lloyd Family.** Old Kent. Hanson. Pp. 28–36. MHS; DAR.
*Wilson Mss. Coll., no. 107, MHS.

Lloyd Line. Balto., its hist., its people. Hall. V. 3, p. 513. MHS; DAR.
Manning family, Mass. Col. and Revolutionary families of Pa. Jordan. 1932, v. 4, p. 643.

***Lloyd - Pemberton - Hutchinson - Hudson - Parke Families.** Geneal. notes. T. A. Glenn. Phila. J. P. Parke, 1898. MHS; DAR.

Lloyd-Preston. Col. families of Amer. Lawrence. V. 15, p. 152. MHS.

Lloyd, Loyd. Col. families of U. S. A. Mackenzie. V. 1, p. 363; v. 2, p. 463 (Pa. and Md.). MHS; DAR.
*Wicomico Co. families. Tilghman. Ms, pp. 72, 74. DAR.

†Lloyds, Wye. Hist. of Talbot. Co. Tilghman. V. 1, pp. 132–228. MHS; DAR.

Lluelen, Lluellin. Somerset Co. Court Book. Tilghman. 1937. Ms. DAR.

Lluellin. *See* Lluelen.

Lobdell. Abr. Compend. Amer. Geneal. Virkus. V. 1, p. 938. DAR.

Loch. St. James Parish rec., Anne Arundel Co. Ms. MHS.

Lock. Chew family. Culver. M. H. Mag., 1935, v. 30, no. 2, pp. 157–75.
*Frederick Co. families. Markell. Ms. Personal list.

Lockard Family. Graveyard, formerly Beaver graveyard, 3 miles east of Westminster on Reisterstown Rd., Balto. Co. Md. Geneal. Rec. Com., 1935–36, P. 50. Mss. DAR.

†Locke. Med. Annals of Md. Cordell. 1903, p. 478. MHS.
Pedigree of Mason Locke Weems Williams. Soc. Col. Wars Md. Culver. 1940. MHS; DAR.

Lockeman, Loockerman. Bolton chart. MHS.

Lockerman. Ances. rec. and portraits. Col. Dames of Amer., 1910, v. 1, pp. 59, 321. MHS; DAR.
Christ P. E. Church cemetery, Cambridge. Steele. 1936. MHS; DAR.

Lockerman. Hist. graves of Md. and D. C. Ridgely. MHS.
Huguenot Bartholomew Dupuy. Dupuy.
Naturalizations in Md., 1666–1765; Laws. Bacon. MHS.
Pattison wills. Md. Geneal. Rec. Com., 1929, pp. 7–42; 1930–31. Mss. DAR.
St. Paul's Parish, Balto. V. 2. Mss. MHS.
Turner Geneal. Coll. Ms. MHS.
Lockerman, Loockerman. Col. mansions of Md. and Del. Hammond. 1914. MHS.
Lockey. Cary Geneal. Coll. Ms. MHS.
Lockhart. St. Paul's Parish, Balto. V. 2. Mss. MHS.
Lockwood, G. R. Abr. Compend. Amer. Geneal. Virkus. V. 1, p. 694. DAR.
Lockwood, J. A., Worcester Co. Abr. Compend. Amer. Geneal. Virkus. V. 1, p. 192. DAR.
†Lodge. Story of Rev. H. C. Lodge. 1919. DAR.
Lodman. Elbert chart. MHS.
Loe. *See* Lowes.
Loehr. Mt. Olivet Cemetery, Frederick. Md. Geneal. Rec. Com., 1934–35, p. 111. Mss. DAR.
Loftis. St. Stephens Parish, Cecilton, Md. MHS; DAR.
Logan. *See* Cresap-Logan.
See De Sincay. Abr. Compend. Amer. Geneal. Virkus. V. 1, p. 582. DAR.
†Logan and Cresap. Tah-Gah-Jute. Col. Brantz Mayer. 1867. MHS.
***Logsdon** (?). Frederick Co. families. Markell. Ms. Personal list.
Logue. St. Paul's Parish, Balto. V. 2. Mss. MHS.
Loker. Pedigree. of Duncan Keener Brent. Soc. Col. Wars Md. Culver. 1940. MHS; DAR.
***Lokey.** Wicomico Co. families. Tilghman. Ms, p. 56. DAR.
See Morris-Lokey.
Lomas. Md. gleannings in Eng. Wills. M. H. Mag., 1909, v. 4, no. 2.
***Lomax.** Geneal. of Va. family of Lomax. (Prominent Va. and Md. families.) Chicago, 1913. Lib. Cong.
London. Old Somerset. Torrence. MHS; DAR.
Loneridge. Somerset Co. Court Book. Tilghman. 1937. Ms. DAR.
Loney. Barroll in Great Britain and Amer. Barroll. P. 94. MHS.
Md. families. Culver. Ms. Personal list.
St. Paul's Parish, Balto. V. 1, 2. Mss. MHS.
Loney - Boyce - Day - Garrett - Ross - Stansbury. Harford Co. Hist. Soc. Mss. Coll. JHU.
Long. Carne and allied family notes. Coues. Ms. MHS.
Coll. of Amer. epitaphs and inscriptions. Alden. 1814, v. 5, p. 125. MHS.
*Daughter of Md.; Mother of Texas, Mrs. Jane Herbert (Wilkinson) Long. A. H. Bell. 142 pp. MHS; DAR.
†Hist. of Frederick Co. Williams. MHS; DAR.
Lineage Bks., Natl. Soc. of Daughters of Amer. Col., v. 2, p. 289. MHS; DAR.
Md. families. Culver. Ms. Personal list.
St. Paul's Parish, Balto. V. 1, 2. Mss. MHS.
Sketches of John Slemmons Stevenson and Rev. Samuel McMaster. Stevenson. P. 17. MHS.
Somerset Co. Court Book. Tilghman. 1937. Ms. DAR
Trinity P. E. churchyard, Long Green. Typed ms. MHS; DAR.
Turner Geneal. Coll. Ms. MHS.
Wicomico Co. families. Bible rec. Ms. DAR.
*Wicomico Co. families. Tilghman. Ms, pp. 4, 12. DAR.
See Chaille-Long.
Long, Talbot Co. H. Mullikin pedigree charts, plate 1. Soc. Col. Wars, Md. Johnston. 1905, p. 74. MHS.
†Long, C. Chaille. Men of mark in Md. Johnson. V. 2. DAR; Enoch Pratt Lib.
Long, John Dudley. Pedigree. Soc. Col. Wars Md. Culver. 1940. MHS; DAR.
Long, S. Burkett. Md. Soc., War of 1812. V. 1, no. 26. Ms. MHS.
Long, Wm. F. Md. Soc., War of 1812, v. 1, no. 19. Ms. MHS.
Long Family. Old Somerset. Torrence. MHS. DAR.
Long Family, Worcester Co. Bible rec. MHS.
***Long-Addams-Crew.** M. H. Mag., 1927, v. 22, p. 304.
Longenecker. Peale Geneal. Coll. Ms. MHS.
Longnecker. Hagerstown tombstone inscriptions. Gruder. Natl. Geneal. Soc. Quart., 1919, v. 8, nos. 1, 2.
Loockerman. N. Y. Geneal. and Biog. Rec., 1877, v. 8. Pp. 11, 91, 94, 141.
See Harrison-Haskins-Caile-Loockerman.
See Lockeman.
See Lockerman.
Loockerman Family. Dupuy family. Dupuy. Pp. 107–20. MHS.
Lookerman. Townley geneal. chart. MHS.
***Loomis Family,** Ohio. Chart. Photos. DAR.
Looton. Naturalizations in Md., 1666–1765; Laws. Bacon. MHS.
Lord. Lineage Bks., Natl. Soc. of Daughters of Amer. Col., v. 4, p. 10. MHS; DAR.
†Med. Annals Md. Cordell. 1903, p. 479. MHS.
Lord, Me. and Md. Giving Pope line of Mass. and Md. Col. and Revolutionary families of Phila. Jordan. 1933, v. 1, pp. 361–70.
Lord, Jere W. Balto., its hist., its people. Hall. V. 3. MHS; DAR.
Lord-Pope. Marriage certificate of Jere Williams Lord and Evelyn Pope, 1898. Md. Geneal. Rec. Com., 1935–36, pp. 219–23. Mss. DAR.
Lord-Williams. Marriage certificate of John D. Lord and Jannet Williams, 1861. Md. Geneal. Rec. Com., 1935–36, p. 224. Mss. DAR.
Lorman. Glendy churchyard, Balto. Md. Geneal. Rec. Com., 1933–34. Mss. DAR.
Lorsbaugh. Hagerstown tombstone inscriptions. Gruder. Natl. Geneal. Soc. Quart., 1919, v. 8, nos. 1, 2.
Loton. Harford Co. Hist. Soc. Mss. Coll. JHU.
Loucks. *See* Laucks.
Love. Amer. Guthrie and allied families. Guthrie. Bk. 4. DAR.
Geneal. Copied from Love Bible. Md. Geneal. Rec. Com., 1933–34 pp. 261–68. Mss. DAR.
*Geneal. Thomas Love, the Elder, 1720–1830; Dr. Thomas Love, Cecil Co., 1753–1888; Thomas Love, the younger, 1803–1910; Christopher Austin Love, Balto. Co., 1809–

1856; Robert Horace Love, Balto. Co., 1812–1879; Rufus King Love, Balto. Co., 1815–1888. Md. Geneal. Rec. Com., 1934. DAR.
Lee Mag. of Va., April, 1923, v. 1, no. 2, p. 67. MHS.
Martin family, 1680–1934. Porcher. P. 37. DAR.
Md. families. Culver. Ms. Personal list.
McSpadden-Love-Meigs-Clendinen-Von Bibber-Pope chart, MHS.
†Med. Annals Md. Cordell. 1903, p. 479. MHS.
St. Paul's Parish, Balto. V. 1, 2, 4. Mss. MHS.
See Montgomery-Love-Johnson.
Love, Christopher Austin, Balto. Co. (Born April 13, 1809; married Sarah Weems Worthington, Jan. 6, 1812.) Md. Geneal. Rec. Com., 1933–34, p. 267. Mss. DAR.
Love, Robert Horace, Balto. Co. (Born 1812; Married March 4, 1835, Polly Worthington Johns.) Md. Geneal. Rec. Com., 1933–34, p. 268. Mss. DAR.
Love, Rufus King, Balto. Co. (Married Mary Brown in Phila., July 7, 1853.) Md. Geneal. Rec. Com., 1933–34, p. 267. Mss. DAR.
Love, Dr. Thomas, Cecil Co. (1753–1821). Geneal. Md. Geneal. Rec. Com., 1933–34, p. 263. Mss. DAR.
Love, Thomas, the Younger, Balto. Co. (Born Aug. 27, 1803; married Fanny Presbury, 1817). Md. Geneal. Rec. Com., 1933–34, pp. 266. Mss. DAR.
Love, Thomas, the Elder. Bible rec. Md. Geneal. Rec. Com., 1934–35, v. 7 DAR.
(1720–84). Geneal. Md. Geneal. Rec. Com., 1933–34, p. 261. Mss. DAR.
***Love, Dr. Wm. Samuel.** Burke's landed gentry. 1939. MHS.
Love Family. Harford Co. Hist. Soc. Mss. Coll. JHU.
Love-Johnson, Cecil and Harford Cos. Notes. D. A. R. Mag., June, 1932. V. 66, no. 6, p. 361.
Lovejoy. Abr. Compend. Amer. Geneal. Virkus. V. 1, p. 697. DAR.
*Family of John Lovejoy, 1622–1917. A. G. Jackson. 1917. DAR.
See Duvall-Lovejoy-Sprigg.
Lovejoy, Prince George Co., 1698. Coat of arms. Burke's landed gentry. 1939. MHS.
Lovelace. Barnes chart. Va. Mag. Hist. and Biog., v. 17, p. 292.
Bible rec. Ms. MHS.
Chart, photos., complete in 2 sheets. Cary Geneal. Coll. Ms. MHS.
Col. families of U. S. A. Mackenzie. V. 7, p. 306. MHS; DAR.
Gorsuch chart. Cary Geneal. Coll. Ms. MHS.
Lineage through eight generations 1367–1658. Comp. by Gertrude Gorsuch Harrison. Md. Geneal. Rec. Com. 1937–38, pp. 222–31. Mss. DAR.
Lovelace family and connections. J. Hall Pleasants. Va. Mag. Hist. and Biog., v. 17, pp. 288–93; v. 24, p. 81; v. 25; v. 26; v. 27; v. 28; v. 29.
Francis Lovelace, 1668–73. J. Hall Pleasants. N. Y. Geneal. and Biog. Rec., July, 1920, v. 51, no. 3, pp. 175–94.
Md. families. Culver. Ms. Personal list.
Pedigree of Corbin Braxton Dallam. Soc. Col. Wars Md. Culver. 1940. MHS; DAR.
*Pennington Papers. Ms. MHS.
See Gorsuch-Lovelace.
Lovelace, Anne. Chart. Winston of Va. Torrence. MHS; DAR.
***Lovelace, Sir Wm.** Va. Lineage Bk., Daughters of Amer. Col. V. 3, p. 327. MHS; DAR.
***Lovelace-Gorsuch.** Wilson Mss. Coll., no. 4. MHS.
Lovelace-Todd-Gorsuch Line. Deford chart. MHS.
Mrs. W. H. Harris, Sr., chart. MHS.
Loveless. Beall and Bell families. Beall. MHS.
Lovell. St. Paul's Parish, Balto. V. 2. Mss. MHS.
Lovell, Mrs. Douglas Gordon (Virginia Dandridge Page). Chart. Col. Dames, Chap. I. MHS.
Lovell, Mrs. John Quitman Anne Campbell Gordon). Chart. (Mostly Va. families.) Col. Dames, Chap. I. MHS.
Loviet. St. Paul's Parish, Balto. V. 2. Mss. MHS.
Low. Md. Geneal. Bull., v. 7, p. 15. MHS; DAR.
*Wicomico Co. families. Tilghman. Ms, p. 115. DAR.
See Lowes.
Low, Henry. Revolutionary war pension. D A. R. Mag., Sept., 1937, v. 71, no. 9, pp. 848–49.
***Lowber.** Old Kent. Hanson. Pp. 188–89. MHS; DAR.
Lowdermilk Family. Mountain Democrat, Garrett Co., Nov. 22, 1934. Newsp. clipp. MHS; DAR.
Lowe. Andrews' Scrap Book. MHS.
Bible rec.; incl. Faw. Ms. MHS.
Chart, photos., complete in 1 piece. Cary Geneal. Coll. Ms. MHS.
Col. families of U. S. A. Mackenzie. V. 2; v. 4, p. 118. MHS; DAR.
Dobbin chart. MHS.
†Founders of Anne Arundel and Howard Cos. Warfield. P. 280. MHS; DAR.
Frederick Co. tombstone inscriptions. Gruder. Natl. Geneal. Soc. Quart., 1919, v. 8, nos. 1, 2.
Gittings chart. MHS.
Graves, Fenwick Manor. Md. O. R. Soc. Bull., no. 3, p. 61. MHS.
†Hist. of Balto. City and Co. Scharf. P. 866. MHS.
†Hist. of Frederick Co. Williams. MHS; DAR.
Hist. of Talbot Co. Tilghman. V. 1, p. 378. MHS; DAR.
S. G. Hopkins chart. MHS.
Mrs. G. C. Jenkins chart. MHS.
See Jenkins. Abr. Compend. Amer. Geneal. Virkus. V. 1, p. 656. DAR.
Lambdin chart. MHS.
*Lineage Bk., Daughters of Amer. Col., v. 1, pp. 81, 82; v. 5, pp. 182, 202, 207. MHS; DAR.
*Lineage Bk., Daughters of Founders and Patriots, v. 22, pp. 142–43. MHS; DAR.
Md. families. Culver. Ms. Personal list.
Md. gleannings in Eng. Wills. M. H. Mag., 1907, v. 2, nos. 2, 3.
Neale family of Md. The Times, Balto., Sunday. Dec. 27, 1885. Scrap Book, no. 7 MHS.
Old Md. families. Bromwell. MHS; DAR.
Peale Geneal. Coll. Ms. MHS.
*Pennington Papers. Ms. MHS.

Lowe. St. Paul's Parish, Balto. V. 1, 2. Mss. MHS.
*Semmes Geneal. Coll. Ms. MHS.
*Side lights on Md. hist. Richardson. V. 2, p. 174. MHS; DAR.
Some old Eng. letters. M. H. Mag., 1914, v. 9, no. 2, pp. 107-56.
*The Sun, Balto., Nov. 15, 1903.
Thomas family of Talbot Co. Spencer. P. 53. MHS; DAR.
Tilghman chart. MHS.
Wathen Prayer Book rec. Ms. MHS.
Wolseley chart. Cary Geneal. Coll. Ms. MHS.
See Low.
Lowe, Enoch L. Amer. Clan Gregor Year Book, 1909-10, p. 45. MHS; DAR.
†Governors of Md. Buchholz. P. 158. MHS.
Lowe, Lieut.-Col. Henry. B. B. Browne pedigree chart. Soc. Col. Wars, Md. Johnston. 1905, pp. 8, 149. MHS.
***Lowe Family.** Old Kent. Hanson. P. 194. MHS; DAR.
Rec. Ms. MHS.
Lowe Line. A. L. and S. L. Jenkins pedigree chart. Soc. Col. Wars, Md. Johnston. 1905, pp. 45, 149. MHS.
Lowery. Lambdin chart. MHS.
Lowes, Loe, Low. Rec. of Stepney Parish. MHS; DAR.
Lowmaster. Lowmaster family, York Co., Pa., and Ohio. Natl. Geneal. Soc. Quart., Mar., 1939, v. 27, no. 1, pp. 16-17.
Lowndes. Bowie-Claggett chart. MHS.
Col. families of U. S. A. Mackenzie. V. 3. MHS; DAR.
*Eng. pedigree. M. H. Mag., 1907, v. 2, pp. 276-79.
†Hist. of West. Md. Scharf. V. 2, pp. 1448-50. MHS; DAR.
*Lowndes family. Christopher Johnston. M. H. Mag., Sept. 1907, v. 2, no. 3, pp. 276-79.
Portrait and biog. rec. of East. Shore of Md. 1898, p. 208. MHS; DAR.
*The Sun, Balto., Sept. 15, 22, 29, Oct. 6, 13, 1907.
†Lowndes, Gov. Lloyd. Founders of Anne Arundel and Howard Cos. Warfield. P. 297. MHS.
†(1845-1905). M. H. Mag., v. 12, p. 228.
†Governors of Md. Buchholz. P. 255. MHS.
Lowndes-Frame, ances. rec. and portraits. Col. Dames of Amer., 1910, v. 1, p. 287. MHS; DAR.
Lowry. Gary chart. MHS.
Mrs. J. Whitridge Williams chart 1. MHS.
St. Paul's Parish, Balto. V. 2. Mss. MHS.
Lowry, N. Parks. Md. Soc., War of 1812, v. 1, no. 36. Ms. MHS.
Lowry, R. Kelly. Md. Soc., War of 1812, v. 1 no. 40. Ms. MHS.
Lowther. Md. Geneal. Bull., v. 4, p. 12. MHS; DAR.
Loyd. *See* Lloyd.
***Lucas.** Frederick Co. families. Markell. Ms. Personal list.
Md. families. Culver. Ms. Personal list.
St. Paul's Parish, Balto. V. 2. Mss. MHS.
Turner Geneal. Coll. Ms. MHS.
Lucas, Prince George Co. Cary Geneal. Coll. Ms. MHS.
Lucas, Basil, Prince George Co. Pedigree of Morris Gregg. Soc. Col. Wars Md. Culver. 1940. MHS; DAR.
Lucas Family. Bible rec. Ms. MHS.
Lucas-Belt-Lawrence-West. Chart, photos., complete in 3 sheets. Cary Geneal. Coll. Ms. MHS.
Lucas-Higgins. Chart, photos., complete in 1 sheet. Cary Geneal. Coll. Ms. MHS.
***Lucas-Powell Line.** The Sun, Balto. March 3, 1907.
***Luckens.** Ancestry and descendants of John and Sarah Luckens, of Phila., 1683-1900. Chart. Theodore Cooper. N. Y., Oct., 1900. MHS.
Luckett. Centenary of Catholicity in Ky. Webb. 1884. MHS.
Cummings chart, Lib. Cong.; MHS; DAR.
*Frederick Co. families. Markell. Ms. Personal list.
Luckett and allied families. Md. Geneal. Rec. Com., v. 2, pp. 2-11. DAR.
*Lucketts of Portobello, Charles Co. H. W. Newman. 108 pp. Wash. D. C. 1938. DAR.
*Semmes Geneal. Coll. Ms. MHS.
Talbott of "Poplar Knowle." Shirk. MHS; DAR.
See McClellan-Luckett.
Luckett, William, Frederick Co. Will dated Oct. 1, 1817. D. A. R. Mag., v. 62, no. 12, p. 773.
Luckey. Bible rec., 1789-1883. (Rev. George Luckey, Pastor Bethel Presbyterian Church, Harford Co., 1784-1825.) Md. Geneal. Rec. Com., 1935-36, pp. 273-75. Mss. DAR.
See Arnold-Luckey.
Luckey, George (pastor of Bethel Presbyterian Church, Harford Co.) Bible rec., 1784-1825. Md. Geneal. Rec. Com., 1935-36, v. 8. DAR.
Ludlow. Miss C. Petre chart. MHS.
Pedigree of Corbin Braxton Dallam. Soc. Col. Wars Md. Culver. 1940. MHS; DAR.
Ludwell. Cary Geneal. Coll. Ms. MHS.
Lukens. Chart; descendants of John Lukens (born in Germany, 1683; settled in Phila.). Contains chart of Samuel Wallis I and Arthur Young, Members of Patuxent Meeting, Friends, Calvert Co. (Samuel Wallis II and family moved to Deer Creek, Harford Co., 1735.) Theo. Cooper. Printed New York. 1900. Book form. MHS.
***Lukin.** Frederick Co. families. Markell. Ms. Personal list.
Lum. *See* Lunn.
***Lum (Sylvanus) Family.** Lum family, 1307-1930. E. D. Lum. Mostly New Eng. families, Bean, Fuller, Gray, Paine, Riggs, Van de Bogurt and others. Pamph. 1933. MHS.
***Lum Family.** Lum family. E. H. Lum. 1927. DAR.
Lumberson, John (veteran). Md. Soc., War of 1812, v. 1, no. 120. Ms. MHS.
Lume. *See* Lunn.
Lumsdon. Copy of Bible rec. of Rachel Pottenger Lumsdon (nee Magruder), 1738-1837. Md. Geneal. Rec. Com., 1935-36, v. 8, p. 272. Mss. DAR.
Lun. *See* Lunn.
Lunn, Lum, Lun, Lunne, family. Note. Old Somerset. Torrence. MHS; DAR.
Lurman. Mrs. Talbot T. Speer chart. MHS.
Sir George Yeardley. Upshur. P. 36. MHS.
St. Paul's Parish, Balto. V. 3. Mss. MHS.

Lurman, Miss Frances Donnell. Chart. Col. Dames, Chap. I. MHS.
Lurman, Gustav Wilhelm. Pedigree. Soc. Col. Wars Md. Culver. 1940. MHS; DAR.
Lurman, Miss Katherine. Chart. Col. Dames, Chap. I. MHS.
Lurman, Miss Minna. Chart. Col. Dames, Chap. I. MHS.
Lurman, Richard Lloyd Tilghman. Pedigree. Soc. Col. Wars Md. Culver. 1940. MHS; DAR.
Lurman, Theodor Gerhard. Pedigree. Soc. Col. Wars Md. Culver. 1940. MHS; DAR.
Lurman Line. Col. and Revolutionary lineages in Amer. 1939, v. 2, p. 113. MHS.
Lusby. Anne Arundel Co. tombstone inscriptions. Ms. DAR.
Cary Geneal. Coll. Ms. MHS.
Mrs. Charles Carter chart. MHS.
Mrs. C. C. Hall chart. MHS.
Mrs. J. Piper chart. MHS.
*George Donald Riley. Riley. DAR.
St. Stephens Parish, Cecilton, Md. MHS; DAR.
Mrs. G. H. Williams, Jr., chart. MHS.
See Maccubin-Lusby.
Luther. Hagerstown tombstone inscriptions. Gruder. Natl. Geneal. Soc. Quart., 1919, v. 8, nos. 1, 2.
Luttrell. *See* Read-Corbin-Luttrell-Bywaters.
Lutz, John, Georgetown, D. C. Bible rec. D. C. Geneal. Rec. Com., v. 32, pp. 190-92. Typed, bd. DAR.
Lux. Bolton chart. MHS.
Cary Geneal. Coll. Ms. MHS.
Col. families of East. Shore and their descendants. Emory. 1900, p. 32. MHS.
Darby Geneal. Darby. MHS.
Dorsey chart. MHS.
McCormick chart. MHS.
Patriotic Md. Md. Soc. of S. A. R., 1930. MHS; DAR.
Pedigree of Eustis Thompson. Soc. Col. Wars Md. Culver. 1940. MHS; DAR.
Pedigree of John McPherson Dennis. Soc. Col. Wars Md. Culver. 1940. MHS; DAR.
Rogers Bible rec. Ms. MHS.
*Russell-Lux Bible rec. Photos. MHS.
St. Paul's Parish, Balto. V. 1, 2. Mss. MHS.
See Cottman-Lux-Detrick.
Lux, Darby. J. G. and M. G. Wilson pedigree chart. Soc. Col. Wars, Md. Johnston. 1905, pp. 129, 149. MHS.
Patriotic Marylander, v. 1, no. 4, p. 45. MHS; DAR.
Lux Family. Ames Geneal Coll. Ms. MHS.
Lux-Stewart-Wilson Family. Ms. MHS.
***Lycett.** Burke's landed gentry. 1939. MHS.
Lyde. Dorsey and allied families. Ms. MHS.
Pedigree of Thomas Murray Maynadier. Soc. Col. Wars Md. Culver. 1940. MHS; DAR.
Lyeth. St. Paul's Parish, Balto. V. 2. Mss. MHS.
Lyles. See Robinson, C. B. Abr. Compend. Amer. Geneal. Virkus. V. 1, p. 802. DAR.
Pedigree of Richard Dennis Steuart. Soc. Col. Wars Md. Culver. 1940. MHS; DAR.
Lyman Family, New Eng., (1580-1932). 11 generations; 303 records. Md. Geneal. Rec. Com., 1932-33, pp. 226-41. Mss. DAR.
†Lynch. Bench and bar of Md. Sams and Riley, 1901, v. 2, p. 610. Lib. Cong.; MHS; Peabody Lib.
Dorsey and allied families. Ms. MHS.
†Hist. of Frederick Co. Williams. MHS; DAR.
Lehr chart. MHS.
Md. families. Culver. Ms. Personal list.
†Med. Annals Md. Cordell. 1903, p. 480. MHS.
Mt. Paran Pres. churchyard, Harrisville, Balto. Co. Typed ms. MHS; DAR.
Mrs. C. L. Riggs chart. MHS.
Rogers Coll. Ms. MHS.
St. Stephens Parish, Cecilton, Md. MHS; DAR.
Mrs. Morris Whitridge chart. MHS.
*Wilson Mss. Coll., no. 8, B. MHS.
See Linch.
See Stansbury-Rogers-Lynch.
Lynch, Balto. Co. W. A. Moale pedigree chart, plate 2. Soc. Col. Wars, Md. Johnston. 1905, p. 73. MHS.
Lynch-Owings. Tombstone rec., from burial ground, near Randallstown, Balto. Co. Ms. MHS.
Lynch-Roberts, Lynchburg, Va. Bible rec., 1789-1812. Md. Geneal. Rec. Com., 1924-25, v. 1, p. 70. DAR.
***Lynn.** Frederick Co. families. Markell. Ms. Personal list.
†Hist. of Allegany Co. Thomas and Williams. V. 1. MHS; DAR.
†Med. Annals Md. Cordell. 1903, p. 481. MHS.
Patriotic Md. Md. Soc. of S. A. R., 1930. MHS; DAR.
Lyon. Gillett-Miller families. Ms. MHS.
†Med. Annals Md. Cordell. 1903, p. 481. MHS.
St. Paul's Parish, Balto. V. 2. Mss. MHS.
Taney and allied families. Silverson. MHS; DAR.
Lyon Family. Garrison Church. Allen. P. 145. MHS; DAR.
Lyons. St. John's R. C. Church cemetery, Montgomery Co. Md. Geneal. Rec. Com., 1926, p. 27. Mss. DAR.
***Lytle.** Chart; revised May 28, 1921, prepared for Leonard Lytle, Detroit, Mich. MHS.
Lyttleton. Mrs. Morris Whitridge chart. MHS.
See Littleton.

M

Mabrey. Blakiston churchyard, Kent Co., Del., near Millington. Md. Geneal. Rec. Com., 1933-34, pp. 204-07. Mss. DAR.
Macalister. *See* Mc Allister.
MacAlpin. *See* Alpin.
†Macauley. Med. Annals Md. Cordell. 1903, p. 481. MHS.
St. Paul's Parish, Balto. V. 2. Mss. MHS.
Macceney. *See* Maccenne.
Maccenne. Maccenne, Macseney, Mackeney, Macceney, Mc Ceney, 1666-1915. Md. Geneal. Rec. Com., 1932, v. 5, pp. 24-48. DAR.
MacComas. Pedigree of Anthony Morris Tyson. Soc. Col. Wars Md. Culver. 1940. MHS; DAR.
Maccrah. *See* Mackrah.
Maccubbin. A. L. and S. L. Jenkins pedigree chart. Soc. Col. Wars, Md. Johnston. 1905, p. 45. MHS.

Maccubin. Ances. rec. and portraits. Col. Dames of Amer., 1910, v. 2, p. 605. MHS; DAR.
Battee, Brewer, Boteler, etc., family rec. Murray. Photos. MHS.
Bolton chart. MHS.
*Burke's landed gentry. 1939. MHS.
*Founders of Anne Arundel and Howard Cos. Warfield. Pp. 177–78. MHS; DAR.
Griffith geneal. Griffith. MHS; DAR.
Hist. graves of Md. and D. C. Ridgely. MHS.
Mrs. T. C. Jenkins chart. MHS.
Milligan chart. MHS.
Ms. MHS.
Md. families. Culver. Ms. Personal list.
Pedigree of Edward Hammond. Soc. Col. Wars Md. Culver. 1940. MHS; DAR.
Pedigree of Thomas Dobbin Penniman. Soc. Col. Wars Md. Culver. 1940. MHS; DAR.
Miss C. Petre chart. MHS.
Raisin chart. MHS.
*The Sun, Balto., June 10, 17, 1906.
Welsh-Hyatt and kindred. Welsh. Sec. 3, p. 168. MHS; DAR.
Mrs. G. H. Williams, Jr., chart. MHS.
See Baldwin-Brewer-Disney-Maccubin.
See Carroll-Maccubin.

Maccubin Line. Col. and Revolutionary lineages in Amer. 1939, v. 2, pp. 123–25. MHS.

Maccubin-Lusby. Chart, photos., complete in 3 cheets. Cary Geneal. Coll. Ms. MHS.

Maccubin, Mackubin. Col. families of U. S. A. Mackenzie. V. 4, p. 350. MHS; DAR.

Maccubin, McCubbin H. D. G. Carroll. Ms. Book. In H. F. Thompson Papers. MHS.
*Pennington Papers. Ms. MHS.

MacDonald, New Castle, Del. Greenway Mss. Geneal. Coll. Binder's title, Greenway-MacDonald. MHS.

MacDonnell, Austin MacCarthy. Pedigree. Soc. Col. Wars Md. Culver. 1940. MHS; DAR.

MacDonnell, Edward Orrick. Pedigree. Soc. Col. Wars Md. Culver. 1940. MHS; DAR.

Mace. Hagerstown tombstone inscriptions. Gruder. Natl. Geneal. Soc. Quart., 1919, v. 8, nos. 1, 2.
†Med. Annals Md. Cordell. 1903, p. 482. MHS.
Primitive or Old School Bapt. Church cemetery. Milton. Md. O. R. Soc. Bull., no. 3, p. 54.
Trinity Church cemetery, Dorchester Co. Md. O. R. Soc. Bull., no. 3, pp. 42–52.

Macfarland. Donaldson family. Donaldson. 1931, pamph. MHS.

Macgill. Griffith geneal. Griffith. MHS; DAR.
Hist. graves of Md. and D. C. Ridgely. MHS.
†Hist. of West. Md. Scharf. V. 2, pp. 1138–39. MHS; DAR.
See Howard. Abr. Compend. Amer. Geneal. Virkus. V. 1, p. 381. DAR.
†Med. Annals Md. Cordell. 1903, pp. 482–83. MHS.
Pedigree of Charles O'Donnell Mackall. Soc. Col. Wars Md. Culver. 1940. MHS;DAR.
See Mc Gill.

Macglamery. Rec. of Stepney Parish. MHS; DAR.

MacGregor. Amer. Clan Gregor Year Book, 1909–10, p. 22 (war cry, badge, motto); 1917, p. 63; 1919, pp. 99–101 (MacGregor-Bowie); 1934, p. 73. MHS; DAR.
See Alpin.

***MacGregor, Macgregor.** The Sun, Balto. Oct. 2, Dec. 25, 1904; Oct. 23, Nov. 5, 1907.

Machdowele. St. Stephens Parish, Cecilton, Md. MHS; DAR.

Machen. Burton ancestry. Ms. MHS.
Geneal. and memorial encyc. of Md. Spencer. V. 2. MHS; DAR.
†Letters of Arthur W. Machen; with biog. sketch. A. W. Machen, Jr. Priv. pr., Balto., 1917. Enoch Pratt Lib.

Machen, Mrs. Arthur Webster, Jr. (Helen Chase Woods). Chart. Col. Dames, Chap. I. MHS.
*Geneal. and mem. encyc. of Md. Spencer. V. 2, p. 577. MHS; DAR.

Machen, Mrs. Thomas Gresham (Cornelia Paine Wallace Burton). Chart. Col. Dames, Chap. I. MHS.

Mackal. *See* Mackall.

Mackal, Mackall. Taylor Bible rec. Ms. MHS.

Mackall. Abr. Compend. Amer. Geneal. Virkus. V. 1, pp. 191, 708–09; v. 6, p. 657. DAR.
Beall and Bell families. Beall. MHS; DAR.
†Bench and bar of Md. Sams and Riley. 1901, v. 1, p. 229. Lib. Cong.; MHS; Peabody Lib.
Brisko-Brisco-Briscoe and some family connections. Ramey. P. 40. Ms. MHS.
Mrs. Charles Carter chart. MHS.
†Character sketch of Leonard Mackall. W. W. Mackall. (Born in Balto.; died 1937). 1938. Enoch Pratt Lib.
Chew family. Culver. M. H. Mag., 1935, v. 30, no. 2, pp. 157–75.
"Fairview," home of Gov. Oden Bowie, near Bowie, Prince George Co. Private burying ground, 1745–1904. Ms. MHS; DAR.
Graveyard near site of first Episcopal Church, St. Mary's Co. Md. O. R. Soc. Bull., no. 3, p. 95. MHS.
Mrs. C. C. Hall chart. MHS.
†Mackall Square. Rec. Columbia Hist. Soc., v. 18, pp. 92–94.
Male descent of Col. John Mackall, James Mackall and Benjamin Mackall, sons of pioneer James Mackall of Md. Chart. DAR.
†Med. Annals Md. Cordell. 1903, pp. 483–84. MHS.
Patriotic Md. Md. Soc. of S. A. R., 1930. MHS; DAR.
Pedigree of Walter Ireland Dawkins. Soc. Col. Wars Md. Culver. 1940. MHS; DAR.
Taylor, Calvert Co., Bible rec. Md. Geneal. Rec. Com., v. 1, pp. 94–99. DAR.
Mrs. G. H. Williams, Jr., chart. MHS.
See Mackal.

Mackall, Calvert Co. Pedigrees. Mss., in Folder. MHS.

Mackall, Benj., Calvert Co. Will proved Nov. 1, 1804. D. A. R. Mag., v. 61, no. 8, p. 607.

Mackall, Benjamin H., IV, Calvert Co. Will. Ms. MHS.

Mackall, Charles O'Donnell. Pedigree. Soc. Col. Wars Md. Culver. 1940. MHS; DAR.

Mackall, Robert McGill. Pedigree. Soc. Col. Wars Md. Culver. 1940. MHS; DAR.

Mackall Line. G. N. Mackenzie pedigree chart, plate 1. Soc. Col. Wars, Md. Johnston. 1905, pp. 61, 149. MHS.

Mackall, Mackal. Col. families of U. S. A. Mackenzie. V. 1; v. 4, p. 119. MHS; DAR.
Monnet family geneal. Monette. MHS.
Mackall, Mackal Family, Calvert Co. Wills, with ref. to Potts family. Ms. MHS.
Mackeele Family, Dorchester Co. Md. Geneal. Rec. Com., 1932, v. 5, p. 51. DAR.
†**Mackelfresh.** Med. Annals Md. Cordell. 1903, p. 484. MHS.
Mackeney. *See* Maccenne.
Mackenzie. Amer. Armory and Blue Book. Matthews. 1911–12, p. 277.
†Chesapeake Bay Country. Earle. P. 172. MHS.
Heraldry of Clan Mackenzie. Register of arms. Alexander W. Mackenzie. Columbus, Ohio, 1907, pamph. 100 copies. MHS.
Lineage Bk., Order of Washington, p. 170. MHS; DAR.
†Med. Annals Md. Cordell. 1903, pp. 484–85. MHS.
Old, N. W. Geneal. Soc. Quart., Columbus, Ohio, 1905, v. 8, p. 33; 1907, v. 10, pp. 167–74. MHS.
Pedigree of Charles O'Donnell. Mackall. Soc. Col. Wars Md. Culver. 1940. MHS; DAR.
Tabb family of Va. William and Mary Quart., 1st series, v. 13, p. 172.
Whitridge chart. MHS.
Mackenzie, Colin. Glendy churchyard. Patriotic Marylander, v. 2, no. 4, pp. 54–60. MHS; DAR.
Mackenzie, G. Norbury. Md. Soc., War of 1812, v. 1, no. 35. Ms. MHS.
†Men of mark in Md. Johnson. DAR; Enoch Pratt Lib.
Mackenzie, George Norbury, 2nd. Pedigree charts. plates 1, 2 and 3. Soc. Col. Wars, Md. Johnston. 1905, pp. 61–63. MHS.
Mackenzie, George Norbury, 3rd. Pedigree chart. Soc. Col. Wars, Md. Johnston. 1905, p. 64. MHS.
Mackenzie, McKenzie. Col. families of U. S. A. Mackenzie. V. 1; v. 2. MHS; DAR.
***Mackenzie, McKenzie,** Calvert Co., 1746. The Sun, Balto., June 25, July 2, 1905.
Mackey. Abr. Compend. Amer. Geneal. Virkus. V. 1, p. 651. DAR.
Md. families. Culver. Ms. Personal list.
See Mackie.
Mackie. Md. gleanings in Eng. Wills. M. H. Mag., 1907, v. 2, no. 4.
Mackie, Mackey. St. Paul's Parish, Balto. V. 1, 2, 4. Mss. MHS.
†**Macklin.** Chesapeake Bay Country. Earle. P. 344. MHS.
Mackrah, Macrah. Somerset Co. Court Book. Tilghman. 1937. Ms. DAR.
†**Mackrill.** Med. Annals Md. Cordell. 1903, p. 485. MHS.
Mackubin. Abr. Compend. Amer. Geneal. Virkus. V. 1, p. 192. DAR.
Ancestry of Rosalie Morris Johnson. Johnson. 1905. MHS; DAR.
See Maccubin.
***MacMaster, McMaster.** Hist. of MacMaster family. FitzHugh McMaster. Md. MacMasters, pp. 60–63. Columbia, S. C., State Co., 1926. MHS.
Turner Geneal. Coll. Ms. MHS.
†**Machoughty.** Med. Annals Md. Cordell. 1903, p. 485. MHS.
Macomb. Chart of Com. John Rodgers. DAR.
Macpherson-Buchanan -Cooke -Neale -Sewall. Abr. Compend Amer. Geneal. Virkus. V. 4, p. 184. MHS.
Macpherson-Horner. Col. families of U. S. A. Mackenzie. V. 4. MHS.
MacPike. Abr. Compend. Amer. Geneal. Virkus. V. 4, p. 675. DAR.
***MacQueen.** The Mac Queens of Scotland and Va. (near Garrett Co. line, Md.). J. A. Nydegger. Balto., Myer & Thalheimer, 1928. MHS; DAR.
Macseney. *See* Maccenne.
Macsherry. Balto., its hist., its people. Hall. V. 3. MHS; DAR.
MacSherry. John O'Donnell of Balto. Cook. MHS.
Macsherry, Mrs. Allan (Emily Hillen). Chart. Col. Dames, Chap. I. MHS.
MacSherry, McSherry. Ances. rec. and portraits. Col. Dames of Amer., 1910, v. 2, p. 518. MHS; DAR.
***MacTarnaghan.** Wallis family of Md. chart. MHS.
MacTavish. *See* Mc Tavish.
Mactier. Deford chart. MHS.
***Macy-Polk Family.** Chart. Ella F. O'Gorman. Ms. MHS; DAR.
Madden. St. Paul's Parish, Balto. V. 2. Mss. MHS.
***Maddison.** Wicomico Co. families. Tilghman. Ms, p. 127. DAR.
Maddock. Hist. graves of Md. and D. C. Ridgely. MHS.
†Hist. of Washington Co. Williams. 1906, v. 1, p. 586. MHS; DAR.
*Semmes Geneal. Coll. Ms. MHS.
***Maddock,** St. Mary's Co. The Sun, Balto., Dec. 3, 1905.
Maddok, John, St. Mary's Co. Will, April 12, 1811. D. A. R. Mag. v. 62, no. 12, p. 773.
Maddouxe. *See* Madox.
Maddox. Col. and Revolutionary families of Phila. Jordan. 1933, v. 1, pp. 401–02.
†Hist. of West. Md. Scharf. V. 2, p. 1141. MHS; DAR.
Lucketts of Portobacco. Newman. DAR.
Old Somerset. Torrence. MHS; DAR.
Portrait and biog. rec. of Sixth Cong. Dist. of Md. 1898, p. 724. MHS; DAR.
*Wicomico Co. families. Tilghman. Ms, pp. 49, 100, 109–10, 129. DAR.
See Harris-Maddox-Williams-Smith-Powell-Travers.
See Parsons-Maddox-Travers.
Maddox, Mattocks, Va. and Md. Side lights on Md. Hist. Richardson. V. 2, p. 391. MHS; DAR.
†**Maddux.** Med. Annals Md. Cordell. 1903, p. 485. MHS.
Rec. of Stepney Parish. MHS; DAR.
See Madox.
Maddux, St. Mary's Co. Abr. Compend. Amer. Geneal. Virkus. V. 1, p. 178. DAR.
Madeira. Abr. Compend. Amer. Geneal. Virkus. V. 1, p. 711. DAR.
Maden. Robinson chart. MHS.
Madira. *See* Medeira.
***Madison.** Photo of 2 miniatures by Peale. Pennington Papers. Ms. MHS.
*The Sun, Balto., March 17, July 9 (Va.), 1905.
Madox, Maddouxe, Maddux. Somerset Co. Court Book. Tilghman. 1937. Ms. DAR.

Magdalene. Hist. sketch of P. F. Eichelberger. Eichelberger.
Magee. Deford chart. MHS.
Somerset Co. Court Book. Tilghman. 1937. Ms. DAR.
St. Paul's Parish, Balto. V. 2. Mss. MHS.
***Magill.** Magill family rec. Robt. M. Magill, Richmond, Va., 1907.
***Maglemery.** *See* Mc Glammery.
†**Magraw.** Med. Annals Md. Cordell. 1903, p. 485. MHS.
Magruder. Abs. of will of Haswell and Wm. Magruder, Prince George Co. Ms. DAR.
Amer. Armory and Blue Book. Matthews. 1911–12, pp. 204, 287.
Amer. Clan Gregor Year Book, 1925, pp. 92–95 (Ninian Offutt, 1744–1803, Md. and Ga., signed the Patriotic Oath, Montgomery Co., 1778); 1926–27, p. 97 (Ninian, pioneer, Frederick Co.); 1926–27, pp. 133–35 (Ninian Offutt); 1931, pp. 69–71 (Ninian, Bible record, 1772–1900). MHS; DAR.
Abr. Compend. Amer. Geneal. Virkus. V. 6, pp. 276, 684. DAR.
Ances. rec. and portraits. Col. Dames of Amer., 1910, p. 718. MHS; DAR.
Ancestral beginnings in Amer. of McGregor, Magruder, Beall, Price, Phillips, Bland, McKisick, Young and related families. Caroline B. Price. 1928. DAR.
Bankhead family. William and Mary Quart., 2nd series, v. 9, p. 303.
See Barrickman, Ky. Abr. Compend. Amer. Geneal. Virkus. V. 4, p. 46. MHS.
Beall and Bell families. Beall. MHS; DAR.
Beall chart. Cary Geneal. Coll. Ms. MHS.
Bible rec. D. C. Geneal. Rec. Com., v. 32, pp. 43–45. Typed, bd. DAR.
Births, baptisms and marriages, St. John's P. E. Church, Piscataway Parish, Prince George Co., 1701–1805. Amer. Clan Gregor Year Book, 1916, p. 86. MHS; DAR.
Births, and marriages, St. Barnabus P. E. Church, Queen Anne's Parish, Prince George Co., 1705–73. Amer. Clan Gregor Year Book, 1916, p. 87. MHS; DAR.
Births, St. Paul's P. E. Church, Prince George's Parish, formerly in Prince George's Co., subsequently in Frederick and Montgomery Cos., and now District of Columbia, 1726–1829. Amer. Clan Gregor Year Book, 1916, pp. 87–88. MHS; DAR.
Bowies and their kindred. Bowie. MHS; DAR.
Robt. Brooke geneal. Stabler. Ms. MHS.
*Burke's landed gentry. 1939. MHS.
Col. families of Amer. Lawrence. V. 16, pp. 74–79. MHS.
Col. families of U. S. A. Mackenzie. V. 1; v. 2. MHS; DAR.
*Dent-Magruder-Trueman family notes. Natl. Geneal. Soc. Quart., Dec., 1937, v. 25, no. 4, pp. 104–13.
*Descendants of Aquilla Magruder (born in Md., 1773; died in Ky., 1825). Ms. DAR.
Descendants of Isaac Magruder, Revolutionary Soldier. C. C. Magruder. Reprint from Amer. Clan Year Book. DAR.
Descendants of Revolutionary soldiers from Montgomery Co. Amer. Clan Gregor Year Book, 1926–27, pp. 123–31 (pt. 1); 1928, p. 18 (pt. 2); 1929, p. 26 (pt. 3); 1930, pp. 11–26 (pt. 4); 1931, p. 25 (pt. 5); p. 71 (corrections); 1934, p. 62 (pt. 6); 1935, p. 34 (pt. 7); 1936, p. 56 (pt. 5 contd.). MHS; DAR.
Descendants of the daughters of George Magruder of Ga. Amer. Clan Gregor Year Book, 1937, p. 37. MHS; DAR.
Col. Nicholas Duvall family rec. Price. Bd. ms. MHS.
*Encyc. of Amer. biog. Amer. Hist. Soc., N. Y., 1928, v. 33, p. 231.
*Family rec. of George Fraser Magruder and his wife Eleanor Bowie, Dec., 1763. DAR.
Frazier burial ground. Md. Geneal. Rec. Com., 1938–39, p. 21. Mss. DAR.
*Genealogies from Alpin, MacAchaia, crowned King of the Scotts, 833 A.D. Amer. Clan Gregor Year Book, 1923, pt. 2, p. 17. MHS; DAR.
Graduates of the U. S. Military Academy, 1827–1923. Amer. Clan Gregor Year Book, 1926–27, p. 106. MHS; DAR.
Griffith geneal. Griffith. MHS; DAR.
Hist. graves of Md. and D. C. Ridgely. MHS.
†Hist. of Frederick Co. Williams. V. 2, p. 1510. MHS; DAR.
Hist. of West. Md. Scharf. V. 1, pp. 686, 729, 769, 780, 785; v. 2, p. 1455. MHS; DAR.
A. L. and S. L. Jenkins pedigree chart. Soc. Col. Wars, Md. Johnston. 1905, pp. 45, 149. MHS.
*Lineage Bk., Daughters of Amer. Col., v. 2, p. 174. MHS (pencil correction); DAR.
*Lineage Bk., Daughters of Founders and Patriots, v. 3, p. 52; v. 6, p. 46. MHS.
John Magruder of Dumblaine, 1694–1750. C. C. Magruder. Repr. from Year Book of Amer. Clan Gregor Soc., 1913. Balto., Waverly Press, 1913, pamph. MHS.
Nathan Magruder, of Knaves Dispute. C. C. Magruder. Repr. from Year Book of Amer. Clan Gregor Soc., 1915. Charlottsville, Va., Michie Co., 1915, pamph.
Nathaniel Magruder of Dumblaine. C. C. Magruder. Repr. from Year Book of Amer. Clan Gregor Soc., 1916. Richmond, Va., Appeals Press Inc., 1917, pamph. MHS.
Marriage licenses. Amer. Clan Gregor Year Book, 1919, p. 105 (1777–1851, Baltimore City); 1916, pp. 88–89 (Dec. 1811–Sept. 1, 1854, and 1934), pp. 80–82 (June 16, 1870–Jan., 1935, District of Columbia); 1911–12, p. 23 (1778–1912, Frederick Co.); 1913, pp. 16, 24, 32, 55, 59, 64–65 (1798–1913, Montgomery Co.); 1911–12, p. 98 (1777–99), p. 102 (1800–39), p. 114, (1840–1912, Prince George Co.); 1916, p. 90 (1799–1904, Washington Co.). MHS; DAR.
†Med. Annals Md. Cordell. 1903, p. 486. MHS.
Mt. Lubentia, old Magruder home, in Prince George Co. Amer. Clan Gregor Year Book, 1932, p. 10; 1936, p. 52. MHS; DAR.
Oaths of fidelity. Natl. Geneal. Soc. Quart., April, July, 1917, pp. 1–24.
Old Kent. Hanson. P. 131. MHS; DAR.
Patriotic Md. Md. Soc. of S. A. R., 1930. MHS; DAR.
Pedigree of Mareen Duvall. Soc. Col. Wars. Md. Culver. 1940. MHS; DAR.
Pedigree of Edward Boteler Passano. Soc. Col. Wars Md. Culver. 1940. MHS; DAR.

Price ancestral data (maternal). Bd. Ms. MHS.
Revolutionary rec. of Md. Brumbaugh and Hodges. 1924. MHS; DAR.
St. Paul's Parish, Balto. V. 2, 3. Mss. MHS.
Settlers in Ga. after Revolutionary war. Amer. Clan Gregor Year Book, 1909-10, p. 50. MHS; DAR.
*Side lights on Md. hist. Richardson. V. 2, p. 178. MHS.
Soldiers and sailors of the Spanish American War and Philippine Insurrection. Amer. Clan Gregor Year Book, 1930, pp. 28-31. MHS; DAR.
Soldiers and sailors between the States, 1861-65. Amer. Clan Gregor Year Book, 1935, pp. 38-41. MHS; DAR.
Students, at leading educational institutions in U. S. Amer. Clan Gregor Year Book, 1921, pp. 36-42; 1922, pp. 62-65. MHS; DAR.
Talbott of "Poplar Knowle." Shirk. MHS; DAR.
*The Sun, Balto., Dec. 25, 1904.
Warfields of Md. Warfields. P. 22. MHS.
Zimmerman-Waters and allied families. Allen. Pp. 126-33. MHS; DAR.
See Alpine-Gregor-Mc Gregor-Magruder Clan.
See Pottenger.

Magruder, "Old Orchard," Prince George Co. Cemetery records, 1790-1903. Amer. Clan Gregor Year Book, 1916, pp. 47-48. MHS; DAR.

Magruder, Acquila, Md. and Ky. Bible records, 1773-1859. Amer. Clan Gregor Year Book, 1916, pp. 79-80. MHS; DAR.

Magruder, Alexander (emigrant). Amer. Clan Gregor Year Book, 1909-10, p. 20; 1911-12, p. 29; 1929, p. 81; 1935, pp. 42-45. MHS; DAR.
Bible rec. Natl. Geneal. Soc. Quart., Dec., 1938, v. 26, p. 135.

Magruder, Alexander Leonard Covington, Miss. Amer. Clan Gregor Year Book, 1925, p. 102. MHS; DAR.

Magruder, Archibald (born in Md. 1751; died in Ky., after 1832). Amer. Clan Gregor Year Book, 1926-27, pp. 123-28; 136-37. MHS; DAR.

Magruder, Benjamin Drake, Miss. Amer. Clan Gregor Year Book, 1911-12, p. 38. MHS DAR.

Magruder, Benjamin H. Amer. Clan Gregor Year Book, 1921, pp. 49-58. MHS; DAR.

Magruder, Caleb Clarke, First. Amer. Clan Gregor Year Book, 1919, pp. 71-80. MHS; DAR.

Magruder, C. C., Jr. Md. Soc., War of 1812, v. 3, no. 263. Ms. MHS.

Magruder, Catharine Fleming, Montgomery Co. Will probated Dec. 11, 1821. D. A. R. Mag., v. 61, no. 10, p. 785.

Magruder, Catharine Waring, Montgomery Co. Copy of will. Ms. DAR.

Magruder, Cephas Bailey, Ga. Amer. Clan Gregor Year Book, 1926-27, p. 75. MHS; DAR.

Magruder, Dr. Daniel (born in Frederick Co., 1763). Amer. Clan Gregor Year Book, 1926-27, p. 129. MHS; DAR.

Magruder, Daniel Randall (1835-1915). Amer. Clan Gregor Year Book, 1915, pp. 42-46. MHS; DAR.

Magruder, Gen. David Lynn, Frederick Co. Amer. Clan Gregor Year Book, 1914, p. 66. MHS; DAR.

Magruder, Fielder Montgomery. Amer. Clan Gregor Year Book, 1917, pp. 19-20. MHS; DAR.

Magruder, Franklin Minor, Va. Amer. Clan Gregor Year Book, 1913, p. 60. MHS; DAR.

Magruder, George Fraser. Amer. Clan Gregor Year Book, 1929, p. 83; 1936, pp. 60-65. MHS; DAR.

Magruder, Dr. George Lloyd, Wash., D. C. (1848-1914). Amer. Clan Gregor Year Book, 1914, p. 79. MHS; DAR.

Magruder, George Milton, Ga. Amer. Clan Gregor Year Book, 1928, p. 38. MHS; DAR.

Magruder, Henry Minor, Va. Amer. Clan Gregor Year Book, 1920, p. 37. MHS; DAR.

Magruder, Herbert Staley, Ky. Amer. Clan Gregor Year Book, 1928, p. 64. MHS; DAR.

***Magruder, Horatio Erskine**, Va. Amer. Clan Gregor Year Book, 1924, pp. 32-34. MHS; DAR.

Magruder, Isaac, "Arthur's Seat," Montgomery Co. Amer. Clan Gregor Year Book, 1917, pp. 21-30. MHS; DAR.

Magruder, James, Frederick Co. (born 1758 or 1760). Amer. Clan Gregor Year Book, 1929, pp. 18-26. MHS; DAR.

Magruder, James Bailey, Ga. Amer. Clan Gregor Year Book, 1926-27, p. 112. MHS; DAR.

Magruder, Rev. James Mitchell, D.D. Pedigree. Soc. Col. Wars Md. Culver. 1940. MHS; DAR.

Magruder, Capt. James Truman. Amer. Clan Gregor Year Book, 1911-12, p. 62. MHS; DAR.

Magruder, James Wm., Ohio. Amer. Clan Gregor Year Book, 1926-27, pp. 43-45. MHS; DAR.

Magruder, Dr. Jeffrey (1762-1805) "Knave's Dispute," Frederick Co. Amer. Clan Gregor Year Book, 1914, p. 62; 1934, pp. 62-66; 1935, p. 34-37 (with corrections). MHS; DAR.

Magruder, John. Mounted newsp. article, taken from Wash. Star. DAR.

Magruder, John, "Dumblane." Amer. Clan Gregor Year Book, 1911-12, pp. 82-95. MHS; DAR.

Magruder, John Archibald, Ga. Amer. Clan Gregor Year Book, 1928, p. 42. MHS; DAR.

Magruder, John Beall (born Frederick Co.). Amer. Clan Gregor Year Book, 1926-27, p. 132 (Revolutionary soldier); 1930, pp. 61-63. MHS; DAR.

Magruder, Gen. John Bankhead. Amer. Clan Gregor Year Book, 1913, p. 35; 1926-27, p. 106; 1930, p. 32; 1932, p. 44. MHS; DAR.

Magruder, Col. John Bowie, Va. Amer. Clan Gregor Year Book, 1909-10, p. 40. MHS; DAR.

Magruder, John Holmes, Wash. Amer. Clan Gregor Year Book, 1926-27, p. 12. MHS; DAR.

Magruder, John Reed, Annapolis. Amer. Clan Gregor Year Book, 1916, p. 68. MHS; DAR.

Magruder, Capt. Joseph. Will, 1793. DAR.

Magruder, Dr. Julian. Amer. Clan Gregor Year Book, 1917, pp. 32-38; 1925, p. 96 (Julian, Jr.). MHS; DAR.

Magruder, Katherine Fleming, Montgomery Co. Abs. of will. D. A. R. Mag., Oct., 1927, v. 61, no. 10, p. 785.
Magruder, Levin, Ky. Bible records, 1796–1898). Amer. Clan Gregor Year Book, 1934, pp. 82–83. MHS; DAR.
Magruder, Lloyd, Montgomery Co. Amer. Clan Gregor Year Book, 1914, pp. 80–81 (Bible records, 1781–1836); 1917, pp. 51–54. MHS; DAR.
Magruder, Nathan. "Dumblane." C. C. Magruder, Jr. Richmond, Va., Appeals Press, 1917. Reprint from Amer. Clan Gregor Year Book, 1916. DAR.
Magruder, Nathan, "Knave's Dispute." Amer. Clan Gregor Year Book, 1914, pp. 55–65. MHS; DAR.
C. C. Magruder. 11 pp. excerpt in Binder. DAR.
Magruder, Nathaniel. Amer. Clan Gregor Year Book, 1911–12, p. 29; 1916, pp. 20–46 (Nathaniel of "Dunblane"). MHS; DAR.
Magruder, Ninian Beall. Amer. Clan Gregor Year Book, 1926–27, pp. 67–74, 132 (Prince George Co., moved to Ga. after Revolutionary war); 1931, pp. 69–71 (Bible records, 1772–1900). MHS; DAR.
Magruder, Norman Bruce (born in Frederick Co., 1754; Revolutionary soldier, Montgomery Co., died in Ind., 1836). Amer. Clan Gregor Year Book, 1926–27, p. 132. MHS; DAR.
Magruder, Patrick. Amer. Clan Gregor Year Book, 1917, p. 53; 1920, p. 25; 1936, p. 56. MHS; DAR.
Magruder, Paul Klienpeter, La. Amer. Clan Gregor Year Book, 1924–25, p. 91. MHS; DAR.
Magruder, Robert Walter, Miss. (son of Dr. Thomas Baldwin Magruder; born in Prince George Co., 1800). Amer. Clan Gregor Year Book, 1929, pp. 68–73. MHS; DAR.
Magruder, Samuel, 1st. Will. Amer. Clan Gregor Year Book, 1929 (appears as an insert). MHS; DAR.
Magruder, Samuel, III (1708–86). Amer. Clan Gregor Year Book, 1926–27, p. 61. MHS; DAR.
Magruder, Samuel Brewer (1744–1818). Amer. Clan Gregor Year Book, 1929, pp. 27–39; 1930, p. 11. MHS; DAR.
Magruder, Samuel Sprague (U.S.N.R., 1917; from Miss.) Amer. Clan Gregor Year Book, 1920, p. 45. MHS; DAR.
Magruder, Samuel Wade (1728–92). "Locust Grove" and old Md. homes and those who lived in them. Amer. Clan Gregor Year Book, 1917, pp. 51–54; 1925, p. 86; 1931, pp. 25–32. MHS; DAR.
Magruder, Sarah (widow of Samuel, 1st.) Will. Amer. Clan Gregor Year Book, 1929, p. 89. MHS; DAR.
Magruder, Thomas. Amer. Clan Gregor Year Book, 1917, p. 27, (born 1779; died 1830; married Mary Clarke, 1800); 1929, p. 67. MHS; DAR.
Magruder, Thomas, "The Forest" (1779–1830). Amer. Clan Gregor Year Book, 1926–27, pp. 16–23. MHS; DAR.
Magruder, Dr. Thomas Baldwin (1800–1885). Amer. Clan Gregor Year Book, 1922, p. 32. MHS; DAR.
Magruder, Thomas Jefferson. Amer. Clan Gregor Year Book, 1920, p. 19; 1928, pp. 29–37 (son of Ninian, Va.); 1935, p. 90 (Bible records, 1826–71). MHS; DAR.
Magruder, Warren Keach. Pedigree. (See pedigree of Edward B. Passano.) Soc. Col. Wars Md. Culver. 1940. MHS; DAR.
Magruder, William (died 1765). Amer. Clan Gregor Year Book, 1929, p. 83. MHS; DAR.
†**Magruder, Dr. William B.** Rec. Columbia Hist. Soc., v. 19, p. 150.
Magruder, Dr. Wm. Bowie (son of Zadok). Amer. Clan Gregor Year Book, 1911–12, pp. 24–29. MHS; DAR.
Magruder, Wm. Hezekiah Nathaniel, Miss. (1815–1900). Amer. Clan Gregor Year Book, 1911–12, p. 61. MHS; DAR.
Magruder, Wm. Howard, Miss. (1837–1913). Amer. Clan Gregor Year Book, 1914, pp. 27–33. MHS; DAR.
Magruder, Wm. Reardon, Ga. Amer. Clan Gregor Year Book, 1926–27, p. 115. MHS; DAR.
Magruder, Zadock, Md. and Ga. Amer. Clan Gregor Year Book, 1926–27, pp. 54–57, 115. MHS; DAR.
Magruder Chapter, D. A. R. Organized Feb. 5, 1911. List of charter members. Amer. Clan Gregor Year Book, 1909–10, p. 39. MHS; DAR.
Magruder Family (3rd and 4th generations). Amer. Clan Gregor Year Book, 1936, p. 61. MHS; DAR.
*Robert Smith Chew and his ancestors in Md. and Va. Pollock. Pp. 98–101. Typed, in Binder. DAR.
Columbia Hist. Soc. Rec., v. 16, p. 150; v. 22, p. 222.
Day-Star, Davis, 1885, p. 83. MHS; DAR.
Hist. of Albemarle Co., Va. Edgar Woods. 1901, p. 260. DAR.
Hist. of Coshocton Co., Ohio. N. N. Hill, Jr. 1881, p. 742. DAR.
Hist. of Champaign Co., Ohio. Beers & Co., 1881, p. 891. DAR.
Hist. of Chamgaign Co., Ohio. E. P. Middleton. 1917, v. 2, p. 771. DAR.
Hist. of Fairfield and Perry Cos., Ohio. A. A. Graham. 1883, pt. 6, p. 475. DAR.
Hist. of Orange Co., Va. W. W. Scott. 1907, p. 156. DAR.
Hist. of Shenandoah Co., Va. J. W. Wayland. 1927, pp. 542, 548. DAR.
Line of Alexander Magruder of Md. Natl. Geneal. Soc. Quart., Dec., 1938, v. 26, no. 4, p. 135.
Md. Geneal. Rec. Com., 1934, pp. 287–92. DAR.
Pictures of City of Wash. S. C. Busey. 1898, p. 175. DAR.
Tercentenary Hist. of Md. Andrews. V. 3, p. 329; v. 4, pp. 556, 827. MHS; DAR.
Tyler's Quart. Mag., v. 19, p. 97. MHS; DAR.
Magruder Line. Beck, Pa. Col. and Revolutionary families of Phila. Jordan. 1933, v. 1, pp. 329–39.
Braithwaite family of Md., 1636. 2 charts. Ms. File case, DAR.
Magruder-Brewer. Proof of marriage of Ninian Magruder and Elizabeth Brewer. Amer. Clan Gregor Year Book, 1928, p. 57. MHS; DAR.
Magruder-Washington. Abr. Compend. Amer. Geneal. Virkus. V. 4, p. 374. MHS.

***Maguire.** Hist. of Dorchester Co. Jones. 1925, p. 413. MHS; DAR.
†Med. Annals Md. Cordell. 1903, p. 486. MHS.
Patriotic Md. Md. Soc. of S. A. R., 1930. MHS; DAR.
Maguns. St. Paul's Parish, Balto. V. 2. Mss. MHS.
Mahan (Mayon), with Md. background. Rec. of families of Calif. pioneers. Pub. by Calif. State Com. on Geneal. Research, D. A. R. V. 2, p. 99. MHS; DAR.
See Ball-Mahan-Pullen-Wright.
Mahon. St. Paul's Parish, Balto. V. 2. Mss. MHS.
Mahoney. St. Paul's Parish, Balto. V. 1. Mss. MHS.
Mahool. Glendy churchyard, Balto. Md. Geneal. Rec. Com., 1933–34. Mss. DAR.
Mahool, J. Barry. Md. Soc., War of 1812, v. 2, no. 194. Ms. MHS.
Mainwaring. Ances. rec. and portraits. Col. Dames of Amer., 1910, v. 2, p. 561. MHS; DAR.
Balto. Herald, May 10, 1903. Newsp. clipp. MHS.
Robt. Brooke geneal. Stabler. Ms. MHS.
Pedigree of Duncan Keener Brent. Soc. Col. Wars Md. Culver. 1940. MHS; DAR.
Zimmerman-Waters and allied families. Allen. MHS; DAR.
Maisack. Hagerstown tombstone inscriptions. Gruder. Natl. Geneal. Soc. Quart., 1919, v. 8, nos. 1, 2.
Maisel. Catonsville pioneers of Luth. faith. Natl. Geneal. Soc. Quart., v. 9, no. 2, p. 29.
Maitland. St. Paul's Parish, Balto. V. 3. Mss. MHS.
***Major.** Frederick Co. families. Markell. Ms. Personal list.
***Majors.** Majors and their marriages. J. Branch Cabell. (Allied families, Aston, Ballard, Christian, Dancy, Hartwell, Hubbard, Macon, Marable, Mason, Patterson, Piersey, Seawell, Stephens, Waddell, etc. Richmond, Va., W C. Hall Printing Co. MHS.
†Malcolm. Geneal. and mem. encyc. of Md. Spencer. V. 2, p. 403. MHS; DAR.
***Malcomb.** Wicomico Co., families. Tilghman. Ms, pp. 57–58; 61. DAR.
***Malemains, Malmaynes.** Pennington Papers. Ms. MHS.
***Malhide Family.** Arch. of Georgetown Univ., Wash., D. C., v. 353, no. 12.
Malin. Col. families of U. S. A. Mackenzie. V. 7, p. 293. MHS; DAR.
Mallalieu. *See* Adams-Mallalieu.
***Mallet.** John Mallet. Huguenot, and his descendants. Anna S. Mallet. Harrisburg, Pa., Harrisburg Pub. Co., 1895. MHS.
***Mallone.** Founders of Anne Arundel and Howard Cos. Warfield. Pp. 142–43. MHS; DAR.
Rec. of Stepney Parish. MHS; DAR.
Mallory. Mallory and allied families of Bohemia Manor. MHS.
Balto., its hist., its people. Hall. V. 2. MHS; DAR.
†Mallory, Dwight D. Men of mark in Md. Johnson. V. 3. DAR; Enoch Pratt Lib.
Malmaynes. *See* Malemains.
†Malone. Med. Annals Md. Cordell. 1903, p. 487. MHS.
Parrish family. Boyd. MHS; DAR.
Wicomico Co. families. Bible rec. Ms. DAR.
*Wicomico Co. families. Tilghman. Ms, pp. 5, 19, 101. DAR.
See Blyden-Malone.
Malone-Disharoon-Stanford. Bible rec., 1812–64. (Bible owned by Miss Pauline White Insley.) Md. Geneal. Rec. Com., 1938–39, p. 210. Mss. DAR.
Maloney, J. A. Md. Soc., War of 1812, v. 1, no. 86. Ms. MHS.
Malott. Hagerstown tombstone inscriptions. Gruder. Natl. Geneal. Soc. Quart., 1919, v. 8, nos. 1, 2.
Md. Geneal. Bull., v. 4, p. 21. MHS; DAR.
Maloy. Balto., its hist., its people. Hall. V. 3. MHS; DAR.
St. Paul's Parish, Balto. V. 2. Mss. MHS.
Malster. Monumental City. Howard. MHS; DAR.
Maltbie, Wm. H. Md. Soc., War of 1812, v. 3, no. 221. Ms. MHS.
Maltby-Dorsey-Frisby-Howard. Abr. Compend. Amer. Geneal. Virkus. V. 4, p. 379. MHS.
Maltby (Maulsby). Early hist. Md. Geneal. Rec. Com., 1937–38, pp. 171–80. Mss. DAR.
Man or **Marr, R. E. L.** Md. Soc., War of 1812, v. 1, no. 55. Ms. MHS.
Man or **Marr, Wm. G.** Md. Soc., War of 1812, v. 1, no. 54. Ms. MHS.
***Man (Mann)-Needles (Nedels)-Hambleton (Hampleton) Families.** With others affiliated thereunto (1495-1876 ms.). Revised, enlarged and modern rec. corrected. S. Hambleton Needles. (Mostly Talbot Co. families.) Printed for subscribers by E. Deacon, Phila., 1876. MHS; DAR.
Manard Family. Focke Geneal. Coll. Ms. MHS.
Mankin. Brandt chart. MHS.
Mrs. H. H. Wrenn chart. MHS.
Mankin, Charles Co. de Ghize chart. MHS.
Manley. Balch chart. MHS.
St. Paul's Parish, Balto. V. 2. Mss. MHS.
Manlove. Cotton chart. MHS.
Fisher family. Morse. MHS.
Fisher family, Sussex Co., Del., and Md. Ms. MHS.
Old Somerset. Torrence. MHS; DAR.
Polk family. Polk. Pp. 469–70, 474–78. MHS; DAR.
St. Steven's graveyard, Cecil Co. Md. Geneal. Rec. Com., 1934–35, pp. 213–14. Mss. DAR.
W. M. Hayden pedigree chart, plate 1. Soc. Col. Wars, Md. Johnston. 1905, p. 34. MHS.
See Van Dyke-Johns-Montgomery-Manlove.
Manlove, Kent Co., Del. Middendorf chart. MHS.
Manlow. Somerset Co. Court Book. Tilghman. 1937. Ms. DAR.
Manly. Abr. Compend. Amer. Geneal. Virkus. V. 6, p. 719. DAR.
Balto., its hist., its people. Hall. V. 3. MHS; DAR.
Mrs. J. Edward Johnston chart.
Manly chart. MHS.
Manly, Mrs. Wm. M. (Mathilde Lawrence Keyser). 3 charts. Col. Dames, Chap. I. MHS.

Mann. Dryden and allied families. Ms. MHS. *See* Man.
St. Paul's Parish, Balto. V. 2, 4. Mss. MHS.
†**Mann, George Washington.** M. H. Mag., v. 12, p. 229.
Mannadoe. Naturalizations in Md., 1666–1765; Laws. Bacon. MHS.
†**Manners.** Day-Star of Amer. Freedom. Davis. P. 231. MHS; DAR.
***Manning.** Semmes Geneal. Coll. Ms. MHS.
Turner Geneal. Coll. Ms. MHS.
Manning, C. P. Abr. Compend. Amer. Geneal. Virkus. V. 1, p. 942. DAR.
Manning, Mrs. James Russell (Miriam Shoemaker Donaldson). Chart. Col. Dames, Chap. I. MHS.
Manning, William Thurston, Mass. Pedigree chart. Soc. Col. Wars, Md. Johnston. 1905, p. 65. MHS.
Manning Family, Mass. Col. and Revolutionary families of Pa. Jordan. 1932, v. 4, pp. 640–46.
†**Manro.** Hist. of West. Md. Scharf. V. 2, pp. 875–76. MHS; DAR.
†Med. Annals Md. Cordell. 1903, p. 487. MHS.
Mans. Naturalizations in Md., 1666–1765; Laws. Bacon. MHS.
***Mansell.** Samuel Mansell, Sr. (1715–79), Anne Arundel Co. C. P. Hopkins. Ms. DAR.
Talbott of "Poplar Knowle." Shirk. MHS; DAR.
†**Mansfield.** Med. Annals Md. Cordell. 1903, pp. 487–88. MHS.
Wallis chart. MHS.
St. Paul's Parish, Balto. V. 2. Mss. MHS.
Mantz. Frederick Co. tombstone inscriptions. Gruder. Natl. Geneal. Soc. Quart., 1919, v. 8, nos. 1, 2.
Patriotic Md. Md. Soc. of S. A. R., 1930. MHS; DAR.
***Mao.** Founders of Anne Arundel and Howard Cos. Warfield. P. 323. MHS; DAR.
Mapey. *See* Massey.
Mapy. *See* Massey.
Marburg. Balto., its hist., its people. Hall. V. 3. MHS; DAR.
Bowies and their kindred. Bowie. MHS; DAR.
Col. families of U. S. A. Mackenzie. V. 2. MHS; DAR.
Col. and Revolutionary families of Pa. Amer. Hist. Soc., N. Y., 1934, p. 10.
Dent family of Md. Ms. File case, DAR.
†**Marburg, Theodore.** Men of mark in Md. Johnson. V. 2. DAR; Enoch Pratt Lib.
Marbury, Wm. Luke. Pedigree. (Marshall and Randolph rec. of Va.) Soc. Col. Wars Md. Culver. 1940. MHS; DAR.
March. Abr. Compend. Amer. Geneal. Virkus. V. 1, p. 713. DAR.
Marchand. Griffith geneal. Griffith. MHS; DAR.
Marchant. St. Paul's Parish, Balto. V. 1. Mss. MHS.
Marchland. Abr. Compend. Amer. Geneal. Virkus. V. 4, p. 221. MHS.
Marcum. Old Somerset. Torrence. MHS; DAR.
Mareen. Col. Nicholas Duvall family rec. Price. Bd. ms. MHS.
Margetty. Hist. graves of Md. and D. C. Ridgely. MHS.
Mariarti. Lineage Bks., Natl. Soc. of Daughters of Amer. Col., v. 1, p. 42; v. 2, p. 298. MHS; DAR.
Monnet family geneal. Monnet. Pp. 1099–1101. MHS.
Marine. Abr. Compend. Amer. Geneal. Virkus. V. 1, p. 202. DAR.
Balto., its hist., its people. Hall. V. 2. MHS; DAR.
Col. families of U. S. A. Mackenzie. V. 7. MHS; DAR.
Duckett chart. MHS.
*Hist. of Dorchester Co. Jones. 1925, pp. 415–25. MHS; DAR.
Marine, Madison. Md. Soc., War of 1812, v. 2, no. 169. Ms. MHS.
Marine, R. Ellicott. Md. Soc., War of 1812, v. 2, no. 168. Ms. MHS.
Marine, Richard Elliott. Pedigree. Soc. Col. Wars Md. Culver. 1940. MHS; DAR.
Marine, W. M. Md. Soc., War of 1812, v. 1, no. 123. Ms. MHS.
Marine Family. Md. Geneal. Rec. Com., v. 2, pp. 40–57. DAR.
Notes. Spirit of Md. Lantz. P. 257.
Marine (De Marin), Md. and Del., **and Hall Family,** Prince George Co. Bible rec., 1655–1836. Md. Geneal. Rec. Com., 1926–27, v. 2, pp. 41–50. Mss. DAR.
†**Maris.** Med. Annals Md. Cordell. 1903, p. 488. MHS.
Maritt, Marrett. Somerset Co. Court Book. Tilghman. 1937. Ms. DAR.
Mark. *See* Marks.
***Markell.** Frederick Co. families. Markell. Ms. Personal list.
Frederick Co. tombstone inscriptions. Gruder. Natl. Geneal. Soc. Quart., 1919, v. 8, nos. 1, 2.
†Hist. of Frederick Co. Williams. MHS; DAR.
Markey. Hist. of Frederick Co. Williams. V. 2, p. 772. MHS; DAR.
Roop geneal. Pamph. MHS.
Markham. Pochahontas and her descendants, Robertson. MHS; DAR.
***Markle.** Boyd family. Boyd. DAR.
Markoe. Thomas family of Talbot Co. Spencer. P. 132. MHS; DAR.
Marks, Mark. St. Paul's Parish, Balto. V. 2. Mss. MHS.
Marple Family. Marriage certificate and Bible rec., 1796–1928. Md. Geneal. Rec. Com., 1933–34, pp. 150–51. Mss. DAR.
***Marquette Family.** Arch. of Georgetown Univ., Wash., D. C., v. 98, no. 11.
Marr or **Man, R. E. L.** Md. Soc., War of 1812, v. 1, no. 55. Ms. MHS.
Marr or **Man, Wm. G.** Md. Soc., War of 1812, v. 1, no. 54. Ms. MHS.
Marr Family. Notes. Md. Geneal. Bull., v. 2, p. 27. MHS; DAR.
Marrett. *See* Maritt.
Marriott. Abr. Compend. Amer. Geneal. Virkus. V. 1, p. 627. DAR.
*Founders of Anne Arundel and Howard Cos. Warfield. Pp. 132–33, 488. MHS; DAR.
Geneal. and mem. encyc. of Md. Spencer. V. 1, p. 266. MHS; DAR.
Hazelhurst charts. MHS.
Md. families. Culver. Ms. Personal list.
Mrs. C. L. Riggs chart. MHS.
Pedigree of Charles Gambrill Baldwin. Soc. Col. Wars Md. Culver. 1940. MHS; DAR.

Pedigree of Mark Alexander Herbert Smith. Soc. Col. Wars Md. Culver. 1940. MHS; DAR.
Posey chart. MHS.
Townley geneal. chart. MHS.
Marriott, Mrs. Aline (Bracco). Obituary. The Sun, Balto., Mar. 30, 1939, p. 19.
†**Marriott, James C.** M. H. Mag., v. 12, p. 229.
Marsden-Rawlings. Lineage Bks., Natl. Soc. of Daughters of Amer. Col., v. 3, p. 250. MHS; DAR.
Marsh. Founders of Anne Arundel and Howard Cos. Warfield. P. 42. MHS; DAR.
†Hist. of Balto. City and Co. Scharf. P. 905. MHS.
Hist. graves of Md. and D. C. Ridgely. MHS.
*Lineage Bk., Daughters of Amer. Col., v. 3, p. 133. MHS; DAR.
†Med. Annals Md. Cordell. 1903, pp. 488–89. MHS.
Pedigree of Joseph Lee Wickes. Soc. Col. Wars Md. Culver. 1940. MHS; DAR.
St. Paul's Parish, Balto. V. 1, 2. Mss. MHS.
Somerset Co. Court Book. Tilghman. 1937. Ms. DAR.
Trinity P. E. churchyard, Long Green. Typed ms. MHS; DAR.
See Athey-Marsh.
***Marsh, Thomas.** Four gentlemen of name Thomas Marsh. Chart. E. B. Roberts. M. H. Mag., June, 1940, v. 35, no. 2, pp. 190–99.
Marsh, William, Balto. (moved to Ky.; born 1735; married Patience Lemons about 1762). D. A. R. Mag., v. 66, no. 2, p. 120.
Marsh-Athey. Lineage Bks., Natl. Soc. of Daughters of Amer. Col., v. 3, p. 133. MHS; DAR.
Marshall. All Hallow's P. E. churchyard, Snow Hill, Worcester Co. Hudson. Bd. ms. MHS; DAR. Also: Md. Geneal. Rec. Com., 1935–36, p. 24. Mss. DAR.
Bible rec. D. C. Geneal. Rec. Com., v. 32, pp. 160–63. Typed, bd. DAR.
Chart of Marshall and allied families. Md. Geneal. Rec. Com., 1939–40, pp. 97–101. Mss. DAR.
Col. families of Amer. Lawrence. V. 3, p. 195; v. 7, pp. 188–209 (Md. p. 201). MHS.
Daughter of Md.; Mother of Texas. Bell. MHS; DAR.
Family data. Alexander H. Bell. D. C. Geneal. Rec. Com., v. 34, pp. 110–28. Typed, bd. DAR.
*Frederick Co. families. Markell. Ms. Personal list.
Geneal. Marshall Hall and Potomac points, in story and picture. Minnie Kendall-Lowther. Pamph., pp. 16–24. MHS; DAR.
†Hist. of Allegany Co. Thomas and Williams. V. 1; v. 2. MHS; DAR.
Marshall and Taney, statesmen of law. Ben W. Palmer. Minneapolis, Univ. of Minn. Press, 1939, 281 pp. MHS.
*Marshall family. Louise Pecquet du Bellet.
*Marshall family, Westmoreland Co., Va. Paxton. 2 vols.
"Marshall Hall." Bible rec. Geneal. Soc. Quart., Sept., 1927, v. 15, no. 3.
Marshall of Marshall Hall, and Dent family notes, Md. and Va. Natl. Geneal. Soc. Quart., v. 19, no. 1, p. 1; no. 4, pp. 86–96.
*Marshall Hall burying ground, Marshall Hall, Md. M. H. Mag., 1929, v. 24, pp. 172–76.
Md. families. Culver. Ms. Personal list.
M. E. churchyard, Snow Hill, Worcester Co., Hudson. Bd. ms. MHS; DAR.
Papers relating to Marshall, Marshall Hall, Charles Co. MHS.
St. Paul's P. E. churchyard, Berlin, Worcester Co. Hudson. Bd. ms. MHS; DAR. Also: Md. Geneal. Rec. Com., 1937, Mrs. Lines. Mss. DAR.
St. Paul's Parish, Balto. V. 1, 2, 3, 4. Mss. MHS.
*Semmes Geneal. Coll. Ms. MHS.
Some Md. and Va. ancestors. Bell. Natl. Geneal. Soc. Quart., v. 19, no. 4, pp. 86–96.
Southern Bapt. Church cemetery, Worcester Co. Md. Geneal. Rec. Com., 1937, Mrs. Lines. Mss. DAR.
Miss Margaret M. Steele chart. MHS.
Stevenson chart. MHS.
Trinity P. E. churchyard, Long Green. Typed ms. MHS; DAR.
Turner Geneal. Coll. Ms. MHS.
See Washington-Marshall-Lewis.
Marshall, Charles Co. Ancestry of Mrs. Fulton Ray Gordon, nee Ellen Majorie Gray. D. C. Geneal. Rec. Com., 1932–34, v. 10, p. 125. Typed bd. DAR.
***Marshall,** Ky., Md., N. C., S. C. and Va. Two lines of descent, Smith and Martin. The Sun, Balto., Oct. 13, 1907.
†**Marshall,** Prince George Co. Med. Annals. Md. Cordell. 1903, p. 489. MHS.
Marshall, Va. Balto., its hist., its people. Hall. V. 3. MHS; DAR.
*Lineage Bk., Daughters of Founders and Patriots, v. 6, pp. 32, 33. MHS.
Westmoreland Co., Va. Cary Geneal. Coll. Ms. MHS.
Marshall, James, Frederick Co. Abs. of will, 1803. D. A. R. Mag., June, 1927, v. 61, no. 6, p. 471.
Marshall, John, Va. Pedigree of Carlyle Barton. Soc. Col. Wars Md. Culver. 1940. MHS; DAR.
Pedigree of Henry Lee Smith, Sr. Soc. Col. Wars Md. Culver. 1940. MHS; DAR.
Marshall, John Drummond. Prayer book rec. Ms. MHS.
***Marshall Family.** Old Kent. Hanson. P. 132. MHS; DAR.
Marshall Family, Balto. Ms. MHS.
Marshall Family, Balto. Co. Letter, Jan. 25, 1925. MHS.
***Marshall Family,** Lewes, Del. Geneal. Pa. Mag. Hist. and Biog., 1905, v. 29. MHS.
Marshall Family, "Marshall Hall," Charles Co. No. 48022 with Mss. Coll. In vault, DAR.
*With Ms. Coll., in Vault. MHS.
Marshall Family, Va., Lee of Va., 1642–1892. E. J. Lee. P. 512. Lib. Cong.; MHS.
Tombstone inscriptions. Md. Geneal. Rec. Com., v. 1, pp. 78–85. DAR.
Marshall-Dent. Family notes. Natl. Geneal. Soc. Quart., Mar., 1931, v. 19, no. 1, pp. 1–4. MHS; DAR.
Marshall-Honeywell. Bible rec., 1792–1878. Md. Geneal. Rec. Com., 1935–36, pp. 172–74. Mss. DAR.

Marshall-Honeywell, N. Y. and Balto. Bible rec., 1792–1878. Md. Geneal. Rec. Com., 1935–36, v. 8, p. 1. DAR.
Marshall-Parrish. Morris family of Phila. Moon. V. 2, p. 577. MHS.
Marsham. Col. families of U. S. A. Mackenzie. V. 4, p. 441. MHS; DAR.
Lineage Bks., Natl. Soc. of Daughters of Amer. Col., v. 2, p. 66. MHS; DAR.
Taney and allied families. Silverson. MHS; DAR.
Marsham Line. Col. and Revolutionary lineages in Amer. 1939, v. 2, p. 74. MHS.
***Marstellers.** Seven Marstellers and their lineal descendants. J. A. Thompson. Fincastle, Va., Jan., 1938. MHS.
Marston. Col. families of U. S. A. Mackenzie. V. 3. MHS; DAR.
Marston, Peirce. Abr. Compend. Amer. Geneal. Virkus. V. 1, p. 714. DAR.
Marteney. Hagerstown tombstone inscriptions. Gruder. Natl. Geneal. Soc. Quart., 1919, v. 8, nos. 1, 2.
†**Martiau, Nicholas.** Adventurous Huguenot, military engineer and earliest Amer. ancestor of George Washington (Yorktown, Va.). J. B. Stoudt. N. Y., Huguenot Memorial Assoc., 1932. DAR.
†**Martin.** Bench and bar of Md. Sams and Riley. 1901, v. 1, p. 224. Lib. Cong.; MHS; Peabody Lib.
Bible rec. Natl. Geneal. Soc. Quart., v. 19, no. 3, pp. 76–79.
Mrs. Howard Bruce chart. MHS.
†Chesapeake Bay Country. Earle. P. 372. MHS.
Christ P. E. Church cemetery, Cambridge. Steele. 1936. MHS; DAR.
Col. families of U. S. A. Mackenzie. V. 2. MHS; DAR.
Descendants of Joran Kyn. Pa. Mag., v. 7, p. 464.
Dobbin chart. MHS.
Early Martin and Spencer tombs. Md. O. R. Soc. Bull., no. 1, p. 47. MHS.
Ellicott-Campbell chart. MHS.
Freeborn Garrettson Waters Bible rec. Ms. MHS.
Robert Gilmor chart. MHS.
†Hist. of Allegany Co. Thomas and Williams. V. 1. MHS; DAR.
†Hist. of Balto. City and Co. Scharf. P. 749. MHS.
Hist. graves of Md. and D. C. Ridgely. MHS.
†Hist. of Frederick Co. Williams. MHS; DAR.
†Hist. of West. Md. Scharf. V. 2, p. 1459. MHS; DAR.
Hughes family of Va. Horton. MHS.
†Influence of Luther Martin in making Constitution of U. S. (Federal convention, 1787). E. D. Obrecht. M. H. Mag., 1932, v. 27, pp. 173–90, 280–96.
Jour. Amer. Hist., v. 24, p. 209. MHS.
†Luther Martin in Md. Natl. politics. Essary. 1915.
Makemie Memorial Pres. churchyard, Snow Hill, Worcester Co. Hudson. Bd. ms. MHS; DAR. Also: Md. Geneal. Rec. Com., Mrs. Lines. Mss. DAR.
*Martin family (1680–1934). (Mostly Va. rec.) Mrs. C. G. Porcher. Mimeog. Bd. 1935. MHS.
†Med. Annals. Md. Cordell. 1903, pp. 254, 489–91, 752–57. MHS.
John Neill of Lewes, Del., 1739. Pr. for family, Phila., 1875.
Porcher chart. MHS.
Revolutionary war pension abs. Natl. Geneal. Soc. Quart., v. 18, no. 3, p. 61.
St. Paul's Parish, Balto. V. 1, 2, 3, 4. Mss. MHS.
See Shaw. Abr. Compend. Amer. Geneal. Virkus. V. 1, p. 824. DAR.
Shrewsbury churchyard. Md. O. R. Soc. Bull., no. 2, pp. 46–54.
Smithson-Rumsey rec. bk. Ms. MHS.
Somerset Co. Court Book. Tilghman. 1937. Ms. DAR.
Spring Hill cemetery, Easton. Md. O. R. Soc. Bull., no. 1, pp. 35–41.
Miss Kate Steele chart. MHS.
Thomas family of Talbot Co. Spencer. P. 98. MHS; DAR.
Turner Geneal. Coll. Ms. MHS.
Whiteley chart. MHS.
Martin, Calvert Co. Deford chart. MHS.
***Martin,** Talbot Co., in 1663. The Sun, Balto., April 15, 22, 29, 1906.
Martin, Benson Blake. Abr. Compend. Amer. Geneal. Virkus. V. 1, p. 206. DAR.
Martin, Gov. Daniel. Founders of Anne Arundel and Howard Cos. Warfield. P. 265. MHS; DAR.
†(1780–1831). Hist. of Talbot Co. Tilghman. V. 1, pp. 228–31. MHS; DAR.
†Governors of Md. Buchholz. P. 104. MHS.
Martin, Dr. Ennalls (1758–1834). Hist. of Talbot Co. Tilghman. V. 1, pp. 257–71. MHS; DAR.
†**Martin, Dr. Frank.** Men of mark in Md. Johnson. V. 4. DAR; Enoch Pratt Lib.
Martin, H. Culner. Md. Soc., War of 1812, v. 1, no. 121. Ms. MHS.
Martin, James Lloyd (1815–72). Hist. of Talbot Co. Tilghman. V. 1, pp. 617–22. MHS; DAR.
Martin, John and Barbara Ann (Funfrock), Frederick Co. Revolutionary war pension. Natl. Geneal. Soc. Quart., Sept., 1930, v. 18, no. 3, p. 61.
†**Martin, Luther.** Balto., hist and biog. Richardson and Bennett. 1871, pp. 353–55 MHS; DAR.
†Eight great Amer. lawyers. Hagan. 1923. MHS.
†Federal bull-dog. H. P. Goddard. M. H. S. Fund Pub., no. 24. Balto., 1887. MHS; Enoch Pratt Lib.
†Hist. of Md. Scharf. V. 2, p. 540. MHS.
***Martin Family.** Geneal.; proof sheets from Amer. Family Antiquity. MHS.
Martin-Spencer, Talbot Co. Tombstone inscriptions, 1676–1836. Md. O. R. Soc. Bull., no. 1, pp. 47–48.
Martindale. Hist. of Byberry and Moreland. Martindale. MHS.
Martindale, Caroline Co. Col. families of Amer. Lawrence. V. 10, p. 319. MHS.
Martz. Mt. Olivet Cemetery, Frederick. Md. Geneal. Rec. Com., 1934–35, p. 111. Mss. DAR.

Marvel. Abr. Compend. Amer. Geneal. Virkus. V. 1, p. 154, DAR; v. 4, p. 379. MHS.
Marvel, Joseph. Family rec. Md. Geneal. Rec. Com., 1937, Parran, p. 70. Mss. DAR.
Marvel-Jefferson. Bible rec. Ms. MHS.
Marvin. Mrs. Lee Barroll chart. MHS.
Cary Geneal. Coll. Ms. MHS.
Maslin. Done Bible rec. Ms. MHS.
Mason. All Hallow's churchyard, Snow Hill. Md. Geneal. Rec. Com., 1935-36, pp. 24-32. Mss. DAR.
Balto., its hist., its people. Hall. V. 2, 3. MHS; DAR.
Bible rec. Contrib. by Mrs. W. C. Newman, Chestertown. Md. Geneal. Rec. Com., 1938-39, pp. 112-13. Mss. DAR.
Geneal. of Henrietta Chauncy Wilson. Upshur. Bk. of photos. MHS.
Hazelhurst charts. MHS.
†Hist. of Balto. City and Co. Scharf. P. 396. MHS.
†Life and times of Stevens Thomson Mason (of Va.), "Boy Governor" of Mich. L. T. Hermans. Michigan Hist. Soc., 1920.
Mason family cemetery, Gunston Hall, Va. Natl. Geneal. Soc. Quart., Dec., 1938, v. 26, no. 4, pp. 118-19.
M. E. Church cemetery, Hillsboro, Caroline Co. Md. O. R. Soc. Bull., no. 1, p. 50.
†Narrative of R. L. Mason in Pioneer West, 1819. (Dr. Mason was native of Md.) N. Y., 1915. MHS.
*Old Kent. Hanson. P. 269. MHS; DAR.
St. Paul's Parish, Balto. V. 1, 2, 3. Mss. MHS.
St. Thomas' Parish, Balto. Co. Bd. ms. MHS. Also: Md. Geneal. Rec. Com., 1937, pp. 109-82. Mss. DAR.
Selden chart. MHS.
Turner family. Forman. P. 52. MHS.
Turner Geneal. Coll. Ms. MHS.
Mason, Cecil Co. Md. gleanings in Eng. Wills. M. H. Mag., 1907, v. 2, no. 2.
Mason, Norfolk, Va. Ances. rec. and portraits. Col. Dames of Amer., 1910, v. 2, pp. 789-90. MHS; DAR.
***Mason,** Va. The Sun, Balto., April 9, Sept. 3, 10, 1905; Oct. 14, 1906.
***Mason, Archibald Dale** (born in Snow Hill, Md., Feb. 23, 1786). His life, ancestry and descendants. H. D. Mason. Priv. pr. Pittsburg, Pa., 1921, ltd. ed. MHS.
Mason, George. Pedigree of Frederick Morgan Colston. Soc. Col. Wars Md. Culver. 1940. MHS; DAR.
Mason, Hon. Col. George, Gunston Hall. Pedigree of Francis Joseph Baldwin. Soc. Col. Wars. Md. Culver. 1940. MHS; DAR.
Mason, Rev. Henry M. Hist. of Talbot Co. Tilghman. V. 1, p. 606. MHS; DAR.
Mason Family, Va. Lee of Va., 1642-1892. E. J. Lee. P. 410. Lib. Cong.; MHS.
Mason Family, Norfolk, Va. (1651). Stevens Thomson Mason. Chart, coat of arms. Balto., 1907. Ms. MHS.
***Mason-Steuart Line,** Va. The Sun, Balto., April 9, Sept 3, 10, 1905; Oct. 14, 1906.
Mass. St. Paul's Parish, Balto. V. 2. Mss. MHS.
Massey. Bible rec., Kent Co. Md. Geneal. Rec. Com., 1937, Parran, pp. 187-94. Mss. DAR.
Bible rec. Upper Penins. East. Shore. Pp. 128, 203-09, 241-43. MHS; DAR.
Buckingham Pres. churchyard, Worcester Co., Hudson. Bd. ms. MHS; DAR.
Descendants of Joran Kyn. Pa. Mag., v. 7, p. 464.
Graves. Hendrickson farm burying ground, near Millington, Md. Md. Geneal. Rec. Com., 1933-34, pp. 208-09. Mss. DAR.
Holdens Cemetery, Kent Co. Md. Geneal. Rec. Com., 1932, v. 5, p. 211. Mss. DAR.
Machen chart. MHS.
Portraits and biog. rec. of East. Shore of Md. 1898, p. 240. MHS; DAR.
***Massey,** Md., Pa., and Del. Coat of arms. Burke's landed gentry. 1939. MHS.
***Massey, Augustine Herman.** Tilghman-Hyland-Ford charts (9). Md. Geneal. Rec. Com., 1934-35, p. 7. Mss. DAR.
Massey Family. Rec. Family of Mrs. Herman Biddle Massey and Mrs. Robert Lewis Mitchell, 1066-1921. Md. Geneal. Rec. Com., 1924-25, pp. 30-45. DAR.
Massey Family, Kent Co. Rec. of births, marriages and deaths, 1714-1858. Md. Geneal. Rec. Com., 1937, pp. 187-94. DAR.
*Wicomico Co. families. Tilghman, Ms, p. 95. DAR.
Massie. Mrs. H. F. Johnston chart. MHS.
Massie Family, Va. William and Mary Quart., 1st series, v. 13; v. 15 (showing Gordon of Balto., p. 128).
Masson, Stafford Co., Va. Ances. rec. and portraits. Col. Dames of Amer., 1910, v. 2, pp. 805-07. MHS; DAR.
Massy. St. Paul's Parish, Balto. V. 2. Mss. MHS.
Masten. Still Pond Church and cemetery. Md. O. R. Soc. Bull., no. 2, pp. 65-75.
Master, Leigh (died Mar. 22, 1796, aged 79 years; oldest tombstone in Ascension P. E. Church cemetery, Westminster, Md.). Hist. of West. Md. Scharf. V. 2, p. 941.
Masters, Margaret, Montgomery Co. Abs. of will, Aug. 2, 1806. D. A. R. Mag., Aug., 1927, v. 61, no. 8, p. 607.
†**Mathews.** Biog. cyc. of rep. men of Md. and D. C. P. 538. MHS; DAR.
Founders of Anne Arundel and Howard Cos. Warfield. P. 448. MHS; DAR.
Miss Cassandra Lee chart. MHS.
Lineage Bks., Natl. Soc. of Daughters of Amer. Col., v. 2, p. 55. MHS; DAR.
*Mathews family. K. R. Greenfield. 1927, pamph. DAR.
†Med. Annals Md. Cordell. 1903, p. 492. MHS.
Somerset Co. Court Book. Tilghman. 1937. Ms. DAR.
Southern Bapt. Church cemetery, Worcester Co. Md. Geneal. Rec. Com., 1937, Mrs. Lines. Mss. DAR.
See Matthews.
Mathews, Edward Bennett. Pedigree. (Gov. Wm. Bradford of Plymouth and James Fitch of Conn.) Soc. Col. Wars Md. Culver. 1940. MHS; DAR.
Mathews, R. Stockett. Balto., its hist., its people. Hall. V. 2. MHS; DAR.
Mathews, Matthews. Griffith geneal. Griffith. MHS; DAR.

Mathiason. St. Stephens Parish, Cecilton, Md. MHS; DAR.
Matson. Naturalizations in Md., 1666–1765; Laws. Bacon. MHS.
Priest Bible rec. Md. Geneal. Rec. Com., 1938–39. Mss. DAR.
Matthai. Balto., its hist., its people. Hall. V. 2. MHS; DAR.
Matthew. Boarman geneal. Thomas. 1935. MHS; DAR.
Matthews. Abr. Compend. Amer. Geneal. Virkus. V. 1, p. 413. DAR.
Dallam family. Dallam. 1929, p. 24. MHS.
Hist. and geneal. account of Levering family. Levering. MHS.
Hist. graves of Md. and D. C. Ridgely. MHS.
†Hist. of Balto City and Co. Scharf. Pp. 883, 911. MHS.
*Matthews; from estate of Hon. George M. Sharp. Sept 21, 1911. Ms. MHS.
Luke Matthews, Brunswick Co., Va., 1739–88, and his descendants. Wm. K. Matthews. Kobe, Japan, H. Kodama. MHS.
M. E. churchyard, Snow Hill, Worcester Co., Hudson. Bd. ms. MHS; DAR.
Naturalizations in Md., 1666–1765; Laws. Bacon. MHS.
Peale Geneal. Coll. Ms. MHS.
Price family and other Gunpowder Friends. Death notices; photos. of newsp. clipp. MHS.
St. Paul's Parish, Balto. V. 1, 2, 4. Mss. MHS.
St. Stephens Parish, Cecilton, Md. MHS; DAR.
Semmes and allied families. Semmes. P. 274. MHS.
*Semmes Geneal. Coll. Ms. DAR.
Trinity P. E. churchyard, Long Green. Typed ms. MHS; DAR.
See Carvill-Hall-Matthews.
See Mathews.
†**Matthews, Francis Brooke.** Men of mark in Md. Johnson. V. 4. DAR; Enoch Pratt Lib.
***Matthews Clan,** Va. The Sun, Balto., June 9, 16, 23, 30, 1907.
Matthews Family. Bd. ms. MHS.
Rec., owned by Mrs. H. Fowler, Chestertown. Md. Geneal. Rec. Com., 1938–39, pp. 115–16. Mss. DAR.
Matthews Family, Westminster, Carroll Co. Bible rec. Md. Geneal. Rec. Com., 1939–40, pp. 181–85. Mss. DAR.
Matthews Line, Balto. Co. G. M. Sharp pedigree chart, plate 2. Soc. Col. Wars, Md. Johnston. 1905, p. 92. MHS.
Matthews-Price. Chart. (Mostly Quaker records of Balto. Co.) Thomas H. Matthews. Presented by A. Russell Slagle. Ms. MHS.
Matthews, Mathews. Col. families of U. S. A. Maynadier. V. 5, p. 359. MHS; DAR.
Matthiason, alias **Freeman.** Naturalizations in Md., 1666–1765; Laws. Bacon. MHS.
Mattingly. Centenary of Catholicity in Ky. Webb. 1884. MHS.
Mattison. Mrs. T. R. Brown chart. MHS.
Maugridge. Burton ancestry. Ms. MHS.
Maulden. Van Dyke-Johns-Montgomery-Manlove chart. Cary Geneal. Coll. Ms. MHS.
Maulden, Cecil Co. Cotton chart. MHS.
Mauldin. Cary Geneal. Coll. Ms. MHS.
*The Sun, Balto., Dec. 11, 1904.
Mauldin Family, Cecil Co. Geneal. notes. Md. Geneal. Rec. Com., 1924–25, p. 87. DAR.
Hist. of Cecil Co. Johnston. P. 510. MHS; DAR.
***Mauldin Family,** of Wales and Cecil Co. Geneal. notes, 1684. Md. Geneal. Rec. Com., 1930–31, v. 4, pp. 68–69. DAR.
Maule. Steiner geneal. Steiner. 1896. MHS.
***Maulsby, Maltby.** Maulsby, Maltby family in Amer. Descendants of William and Mary Maltby of Nottinghamshire, Eng., to Pa. Ella K. Barnard. Balto., 1909. DAR; Peabody Lib.
See Maltby.
Maulsby Family. Geneal., 1538–1844. Md. Geneal. Rec. Com., 1937–38, pp. 181–200. Mss. DAR.
†**Maunsell.** Day Star Amer. Freedom. Davis. P. 237. MHS; DAR.
Maupin, Va. Va. Mag., Hist. and Biog. 1901, v. 8, p. 216.
Maury. Mrs. Wm. T. Howard, Jr., chart. MHS.
Ingraham family. Md. Geneal. Rec. Com., 1938–39, pp. 142–67. Mss. DAR.
***Maus.** Frederick Co. families. Markell. Ms. Personal list.
Maxey. Abr. Compend. Amer. Geneal. Virkus. V. 4, p. 385. MHS.
Maxfield. St. Paul's Parish, Balto. V. 1. Mss. MHS.
Maxwell. Ances. rec. and portraits. Col. Dames of Amer., 1910, v. 1, p. 332. MHS; DAR.
Cary Geneal. Coll. Ms. MHS.
Descendants of Joran Kyn. Pa. Mag., v. 7, p. 299.
Howland chart. MHS.
Jacobs chart. MHS.
†Med. Annals. Md. Cordell. 1903, p. 492. MHS.
Pedigree of John Milton Reifsnider. Soc. Col. Wars Md. Culver. 1940. MHS; DAR.
Shrewsbury churchyard. Md. O. R. Soc. Bull., no. 2, pp. 46–54.
Wallis chart. MHS.
Maxwell, Charles Co. Mrs. Wm. L. Watson chart. MHS.
May. Amer. Armory and Blue Book. Matthews. 1911–12, pp. 262, 359.
Ances. rec. and portraits. Col. Dames of Amer. 1910, v. 2, p. 665. MHS; DAR.
Mrs. R. Barton, Jr., charts. MHS.
Col. families of U. S. A. Maynadier. V. 1, p. 602. MHS; DAR.
Gittings chart. MHS.
Hagerstown tombstone inscriptions. Gruder. Natl. Geneal. Soc. Quart., 1919, v. 8, nos. 1, 2.
Md. Geneal. Bull., v. 4, p. 13. MHS; DAR.
May-Hanson-Pollard-Philips families. Our ancestors. H. Eiler. Kansas, 1929, pamph. MHS.
W. S. G. Williams pedigree chart. Soc. Col. Wars, Md. Johnston. 1905, p. 128. MHS.
†**May,** Washington, D. C. Med. Annals. Md. Cordell. 1903, p. 492. MHS.
*Burke's landed gentry. 1939. MHS.
†**May, Dr. John Frederick.** Rec. Columbia Hist. Soc., v. 13, p. 49; v. 29–30, p. 341; v.31–32, p. 307.
May-Hanson-Pollard-Philips. Our ancestors; rec. of these families. Homer Eiler. Grenola, Kansas, James S. Dancy, 1929, pamph. MHS.

Mayberry. Blakiston churchyard, Kent Co., Del., near Millington. Md. Geneal. Rec. Com., 1933–34, pp. 204–07. Mss. DAR.
Mayer. Amer. Armory and Blue Book. Matthews. 1911–12, p. 219.
†Bench and bar of Md. Sams and Riley. 1901, v. 1, p. 318. Lib. Cong.; MHS; Peabody Lib.
†Hist. of Balto. City and Co. Scharf. Pp. 388–89, 463, 650. MHS.
†Hist. of West. Md. Scharf. V. 2, p. 1443. MHS; DAR.
Keim and allied families in Amer. and Europe, 1698–1898. Keim. Feb., 1899, v. 1, no. 3, p. 81. MHS.
*Mayer family, 1604–1911. Charts. Harriet Hyatt Mayer. Supplement to Mayer family, by Brantz Mayer. Annisquam, Mass., 1911, bd. ms., 8 pp. MHS; photos. copy of same, DAR.
*Memoir and geneal. of Md. and Pa. family of Mayer, 1495–1878, which originated in Free Imperial City of Ulm, Wurtemburg. Brantz Mayer. (Some of the families into which they intermarried, Atkins, Bryan, Cottrell, Dannenberg, Dinkle, Ernst, Fahnestock, Houseal, Keim, Millholand, Randolph, Shepherd, Steinman, Thomas, Wetherill.) Priv. pr. for family, W. K. Boyle & Son, Balto., 1878, 179 pp. MHS; DAR.
†Memorial to Charles F. Mayer (died 1904). Bklet. Enoch Pratt Lib.
Monumental City. Howard. MHS; DAR.
St. Paul's Parish, Balto. V. 3. Mss. MHS.
†**Mayer, Brantz** (1809–79). Appleton's cyc. of Amer. biog., v. 4, p. 273.
†Balto., hist. and biog. Richardson and Bennett. 1871, pp. 357–60. MHS; DAR.
†Sketch of his life. B. C. Steiner. M. H. Mag., 1910, v. 5, pp. 1–21.
†(son of Christian and Anne Katharine (Baum) Mayer, who emigrated from Ulm to Balto.) M. H. Mag., 1910, v. 5, no. 1, pp. 1–22.
Mayer, Christian. Miscellaneous family papers going back to migration to Balto., 1784. Ms. MHS.
***Mayer Family.** Notes and Queries, Egle, 1898, pp. 129–30.
Maynadier. Abr. Compend. Amer. Geneal. Virkus. V. 6, pp. 31–437. DAR.
Ances. rec. and portraits. Col. Dames of Amer., 1910, v. 1, p. 146; v. 2, p. 680. MHS; DAR.
Balto., its hist., its people. Hall. V. 3. MHS; DAR.
Bond chart. MHS.
Mrs. Howard Bruce chart. MHS.
Cemetery Creek, Anne Arundel Co., tombstone inscriptions. Founders of Anne Arundel and Howard Cos. Warfield. P. 334. MHS; DAR.
Col. families of U. S. A. Maynadier. V. 1, pp. 361–72. MHS; DAR.
Hist. graves of Md. and D. C. Ridgely. MHS.
Md. families. Culver. Ms. Personal list.
†Med. Annals Md. Cordell. 1903, p. 492. MHS.
Naturalizations in Md., 1666–1765; Laws. Bacon. MHS.
Pedigree of Franklin Buchanan Owen. Soc. Col. Wars Md. Culver. 1940. MHS; DAR.
Pedigree of Tilghman Goldsborough Pitts. Soc. Col. Wars Md. Culver. 1940. MHS; DAR.
Pedigree of Rev. Sam'l Tagart Steele. Soc. Col. Wars Md. Culver. 1940. MHS; DAR.
Mrs. E. W. Poe chart. MHS.
Some old Eng. letters. M. H. Mag., 1914, v. 9, no. 2, pp. 107–56.
Miss Kate Steele chart. MHS.
Maynadier, Thomas Murray. Pedigree. Soc. Col. Wars Md. Culver. 1940. MHS; DAR.
Md. Soc., War of 1812, v. 3, no. 217. Ms. MHS.
***Maynadier Family.** Wilson Mss. Coll., no. 4. MHS.
Maynard. Peale Geneal. Coll. Ms. MHS.
*Side lights on Md. hist. Richardson. V. 2, p. 181. MHS; DAR.
*The Sun, Balto., Sept. 18, 1904.
See Owens-Claytor-Maynard-Rutter-Welsh.
Hist. graves of Md. and D. C. Ridgely. MHS.
Mayo, Va. Col. families of U. S. A. Mackenzie. V. 2. MHS; DAR.
Mrs. H. F. Johnston chart. MHS.
*The Sun, Balto., June 11, Aug. 6, 1905.
†**Mayo, Isaac.** M. H. Mag., v. 12, p. 230.
***Mayo, Robert Bainbridge.** Burke's landed gentry. 1939. MHS.
Mayo, Wm. Bainbridge. Pedigree. Soc. Col. Wars Md. Culver. 1940. MHS; DAR.
Mayo-Poythress-Bland-Bennett Line, Va. W. H. DeC. W. Thom pedigree charts, plate 1. Soc. Col. Wars, Md. Johnston. 1905, p. 107. MHS.
Mayo-Tabb Line, Va. W. H. DeC. W. Thom pedigree charts, plate 1. Soc. Col. Wars, Md. Johnston. 1905, p. 107. MHS.
Mayon. *See* Mahan.
Mayor (name changed from **Mayer** in 1918). Abr. Compend. Amer. Geneal. Virkus. V. 1, p. 721.
Mays. Abr. Compend. Amer. Geneal. Virkus. V. 1, p. 722. DAR.
*Geneal. of Mays family and related families. S. E. Mays. Plant City Enterprise, Florida. 1929, 288 pp. MHS.
McAdow. Harford Co. Hist. Soc. Mss. Coll. JHU.
McAllister. Md. tombstone rec. Md. Geneal. Rec. Com., 1937, Parran, p. 20. Mss. DAR.
Orme geneal. chart. MHS.
St. Paul's Parish, Balto. V. 2. Mss. MHS.
***McAllister,** Pa. and Va. Family register. J. G. McAllister.
McAllister or **Macalister.** Hopper family chart. Skirven. MHS.
McAtee. Centenary of Catholicity in Ky. Webb. 1884. MHS.
O'Daniel-Hamilton ancestry in Md. and Ky. O'Daniel. Pp. 49–71. MHS.
Originally Macketee. Side lights on Md. hist. Richardson. V. 2, p. 386. MHS; DAR.
McAvoy. Md. tombstone rec. Md. Geneal. Rec. Com., 1937, Parran, p. 32. Mss. DAR.
McBeath. Whiteley chart. MHS.
McBlair. Col. families of U. S. A. Mackenzie. V. 2, p. 611. MHS; DAR.
***McBreity.** Wicomico Co. families. Tilghman. Ms, pp. 100, 105. DAR.
McBride. Pedigree of Philip Livingston Poe. Soc. Col. Wars Md. Culver. 1940. MHS; DAR.

McBride. Somerset Co. Court Book. Tilghman. 1937. Ms. DAR.
Taney and allied families. Silverson. MHS; DAR.
***McBride, McBryde.** Wicomico Co. families. Tilghman. Ms, pp. 26, 56, 98, 127. DAR.
McBryde. *See* McBride.
McCabe. Rec. of Stepney Parish. MHS; DAR.
McCain. Clasping hands with generations past. Lloyd. MHS; DAR.
McCall. Descendants of Joran Kyn. Pa. Mag., v. 6, p. 207.
*Mrs. Utie (Headington) McCall. Lineage Bk., Daughters of Amer. Col., v. 1, pp. 39, 46; v. 5, pp. 109, 128–29, 197–201. MHS; DAR.
Sherburne chart. MHS.
St. Paul's Parish, Balto. V. 2. Mss. MHS.
McCall, George, Pa. Pedigree of Iredell Waddell Iglehart. Soc. Col. Wars Md. Culver. 1940. MHS; DAR.
***McCall-Tidwell.** McCall-Tidwell and allied families. Mrs. E. Tidwell McCall. Atlanta, Ga., pub. by author, 1931. MHS; DAR.
McCallmont. Descendants of Joran Kyn. Pa. Mag., v. 7, p. 464.
McCammon. Zion Reformed Church, Hagerstown. Md. Geneal. Rec. Com., 1934–35. Mss. DAR.
St. Paul's Parish, Balto. V. 2. Mss. MHS.
†**McCardell.** Men of mark in Md. Johnson. V. 4. DAR; Enoch Pratt Lib.
Zion Reformed Church, Hagerstown. Md. Geneal. Rec. Com., 1934–35. Mss. DAR.
McCarteney - McKenny - Cragin Families, Georgetown, D. C., and Eng. Bible rec., 1750–1892. D. C. Geneal. Rec. Com., v. 31, pt. 1, pp. 117–22. Typed, bd. DAR.
***McCarthy.** McCarthys in early Amer. hist. M. J. O'Brien. Md. McCarthys, chap. 4, pp. 107–15. N. Y., Dodd, Mead & Co., 1921. MHS.
St. Paul's Parish, Balto. V. 2. Mss. MHS.
McCarty. Ances. rec. and portraits. Col. Dames of Amer., 1910, v. 2, p. 817. MHS; DAR.
***McCarty,** Va. and Md. The Sun, Balto., April 16, 1905.
McCauley. U. B. cemetery, Sabillasville. Young. Natl. Geneal. Soc. Quart., Sept., 1938, v. 26, no. 3, p. 61 (to be contd.)
†**McCauley, James.** Poets and poetry of Cecil Co. Johnston.
†Poets and verse writers of Md. Perine.
McCausland. Col. Nicholas Duvall family rec. Price. Bd. ms. MHS.
St. Paul's Parish, Balto. V. 2. Mss. MHS.
McCay. West. Nottingham Cemetery. M. H. Mag., 1923, v. 18, p. 55.
St. Stephens Parish, Cecilton, Md. MHS; DAR.
McCay, Cecil Co. Balto., its hist., its people. Hall. V. 2. MHS; DAR.
McCeney. *See* McKenzee.
See Maccenne.
McClain. U. B. cemetery, Sabillasville. Young. Natl. Geneal. Soc. Quart., Sept., 1938, v. 26, no. 3, p. 61 (to be contd.)
***McClanahan, Robt.,** Va. And some descendants. W. W. Causey. 1933. File case, MHS.
***McClary.** McClary family, 1726–1869. Pamph. DAR.
McClary Family. Ms. MHS.

McClatchy. Bible rec. Md. Geneal. Rec. Com., 1932–33, p. 56. Mss. DAR.
McClatchy-Sewell. Bible and gravestone rec., 1805-1906. Md. Geneal. Rec. Com., 1932–33, v. 5. Mss. DAR.
McCleary. St. Stephens Parish, Cecilton, Md. MHS; DAR.
†**McCleave.** Hist. of Allegany Co. Thomas and Williams. V. 2. MHS; DAR.
McClellan. Chart; list of descendants of Col. David and Janet (Buchanan) McClellan of Marsh Creek, Pa., and Balto. Printed, 1887. MHS.
*Chart of Wm. McClellan III, Marsh Creek, Pa. Pr. MHS.
*Descendants of Wm. McClellan III, Marsh Creek, Cumberland Township, now Adams Co., Pa. Photos. DAR.
McClellan, Col. David. Westminster churchyard. Patriotic Marylander, v. 2, no. 4, pp. 54–60. MHS; DAR.
McClellan, John (1738–1820). Revolutionary war heroes. Cole. Bklet. Enoch Pratt Lib.
McClellan, Capt. John. Westminster churchyard. Patriotic Marylander, v. 2, no. 4, pp. 54–60. MHS; DAR.
McClellan-Luckett. McClellan-Luckett and allied families. Md. Geneal. Rec. Com., 1926–27, p. 9. Mss. DAR.
***McClellan-McKeen.** Bible rec. Ms. File case A, MHS.
†**McClenahan.** Biog. cyc. of rep. men of Md. and D. C. P. 268. MHS; DAR.
Morris family of Phila. Moon. V. 3, p. 937. MHS.
McClester. Rec. of Stepney Parish. MHS; DAR.
McClintock. Culver pedigree chart. MHS.
McCloy. St. Paul's Parish, Balto. V. 2. Mss. MHS.
McClure. Clasping hands with generations past. Lloyd. MHS; DAR.
*McClure clan. Mabel B. McClure. Okla., 1934. MHS.
*McClure family. J. A. McClure. MHS.
***McClure Family.** Rec. Wm. M. Clemens. N. Y., Wm. M. Clemens, 1914, ltd. ed. MHS.
McClurre, Lieut. John. Westminster churchyard. Patriotic Marylander, v. 2, no. 4, pp. 54–60. MHS; DAR.
McClyment. Lambdin chart. MHS.
McColgan, Edw. Md. Soc., War of 1812, v. 4, no. 336. Ms. MHS.
McColl. *See* Dorsett.
McCollister, Queen Anne Co. Hopper family chart. Skirven. MHS.
McComas. Abr. Compend. Amer. Geneal. Virkus. V. 1, p. 180. DAR.
Ellicott-Campbell chart. MHS.
Lanahan chart. MHS.
†Med. Annals Md. Cordell. 1903, p. 493. MHS.
Mrs. Pennington chart. MHS.
Pedigree of John Edward Hurst. Soc. Col. Wars Md. Culver. 1940. MHS; DAR.
Smithsons of Harford Co. Md. Geneal. Rec. Com., 1932–33, pp. 159. Mss. DAR.
Mrs. Sherlock Swann chart. MHS.
McComas, Henry Angle. Md. Soc., War of 1812, v. 3, no. 226. Ms. MHS.
McComas, Rev. J. Patton, D.D. Md. Soc., War of 1812, v. 3, no. 284. Ms. MHS.

†**McComas, Lewis Emory** (1846–1907). M. H. Mag., v. 12, p. 228.
McComb. Mrs. T. R. Brown chart. MHS.
Harvey chart. MHS.
*Rodgers Bible rec. (family of Com. John Rodgers, U.S.N.). Ms. File case, MHS.
McConachie. Balto., its hist., its people. Hall. V. 2. MHS; DAR.
†**McConachie, Alexander D.** Men of mark in Md. Johnson. V. 2. DAR; Enoch Pratt Lib.
McConkey. St. Paul's Parish, Balto. V. 2. Mss. MHS.
McConky. Pedigree of Andrew Noel Trippe. Soc. Col. Wars Md. Culver. 1940. MHS; DAR.
McConnell. Maulsby family in Amer. Barnard. DAR; Peabody Lib.
***McCormick.** Bible rec. Ms. File case, MHS.
Chart; antecedents and collateral families, related to the children of Dr. Thomas Pugh McCormick and his wife Agnes Lewis Selden. Rev. Robert Wilson. Blue print, 1918. MHS.
Deaths, 1862–86. Md. Geneal. Rec. Com., 1932–33, p. 340. Mss. DAR.
*Geneal. tables of descendants of Robert McCormick, "Walnut Grove," Rockbridge Co., Va., 1780–1846. Folding chart. L. McCormick-Goodhart. 1934. MHS.
Md. tombstone rec. Md. Geneal. Rec. Com., 1937, Parran, p. 32. Mss. DAR.
McCormick family trees accompanying the genealogy of the McCormick family. Leander J. McCormick. Chicago, Ill., 1896. MHS.
St. Paul's Parish, Balto. V. 2. Mss. MHS.
†**McCormick, Alexander H.** Men of mark in Md. Johnson. V. 3. DAR; Enoch Pratt Lib.
McCormick, Chauncey Brooks. Abr. Compend. Amer. Geneal. Virkus. V. 1, pp. 705–06. DAR.
McCormick, John Pleasants. Copy of baptismal, 1842. Md. Geneal. Rec. Com., 1932–33. Mss. DAR.
Marriage, 1830. Md. Geneal. Rec. Com., 1932–33. Mss. DAR.
McCormick, Mrs. Wm. Grigsby (Eleanor Brooks). Chart. Col. Dames, Chap. I. MHS.
Mrs. Bartlett S. Johnson chart. MHS.
McCormick Family, Pa. and Va. Pa. geneal. Egle. Pp. 384–425. MHS.
McCormick Line. Geneal. tables of descendants of John Hamilton. MHS.
McCormick-Goodhart. Chart. Geneal. tables of descendants of John Hamilton, Va. MHS.
*Hands across the sea. H. L. McCormick-Goodhart. 1921. DAR.
†**McCosker.** Geneal. and mem. encyc. of Md. Spencer. V. 2, pp. 671–74. MHS; DAR.
†**McCosker, Thomas.** Men of mark in Md. Johnson. V. 1. DAR; Enoch Pratt Lib.
McCoy. Gillingham family. Gillingham. P. 79. MHS; DAR.
Hagerstown tombstone inscriptions. Gruder. Natl. Geneal. Soc. Quart., 1919, v. 8, nos. 1, 2.
†Hist. of Balto. City and Co. Scharf. P. 406. MHS.
Md. families. Culver. Ms. Personal list.
McCracken. Whiteley chart. MHS.
McCrackin. Abr. Compend. Amer. Geneal. Virkus. V. 1, p. 603. DAR.
†**McCreary, George W.** Men of mark in Md. Johnson. V. 2. DAR; Enoch Pratt Lib.
***McCree.** Wicomico Co. families. Tilghman. Ms, p. 26. DAR.
***McCubbin.** Early Comers to the Province. Georgians in Anne Arundel Co. Atlanta Jour., Sept. 22, 1906. Newsp. clipp. File case, MHS.
Peale Geneal. Coll. Ms. MHS.
St. Paul's Parish, Balto. V. 1, 2. Mss. MHS.
See Maccubin.
McCullah. St. Stephens Parish, Cecilton, Md. MHS; DAR.
McCulloch. Miss M. S. Brogden chart. MHS.
†Hist. of Balto. City and Co. Scharf. Pp. 46, 923. MHS.
McCulloch, C. C., Jr. Abr. Compend. Amer. Geneal. Virkus. V. 1, p. 706. DAR.
McCulloh. Mrs. R. N. Jackson chart. MHS.
†**McCullough.** Med. Annals Md. Cordell. 1903, pp. 494–95. MHS.
McCullough, Hiram, Cecil Co. Notes. Ms. File case, MHS.
McCurley, Felix, Com. U.S.N. Md. Soc., War of 1812, v. 1, no. 51. Ms. MHS.
McCurley, J. Wallace. Md. Soc., War of 1812, v. 1, no. 53. Ms. MHS.
McCusker. Md. tombstone rec. Md. Geneal. Rec. Com., 1937, Parran, p. 32. Mss. MHS.
***McDade.** Frederick Co. families. Markell. Ms. Personal list.
McDaniel. Wallis chart. MHS.
*Wicomico Co. families. Tilghman. Ms, p. 126. DAR.
McDonald. Mt. Olivet Cemetery, Frederick. Md. Geneal. Rec. Com., 1934–35, p. 111. Mss. DAR.
St. John's R. C. Church cemetery, Montgomery Co. Md. Geneal. Rec. Com., 1926, p. 27. Mss. DAR.
St. Paul's Parish, Balto. V. 1, 2, 4. Mss. MHS.
McDonald, J. Stuart. Md. Soc., War of 1812, v. 2, no. 188. Ms. MHS.
McDonald, Gen. Wm. (War of 1812). Glendy churchyard. Patriotic Marylander, v. 2, no. 4, pp. 54–60. MHS; DAR.
Tombstone rec. of Glendy burying ground (vault, 1855). Md. Geneal. Rec. Com., 1933–34, pp. 171–78. Mss. DAR.
McDonald, Wm. B. Md. Soc., War of 1812, v. 2, no. 179. Ms. MHS.
McDonnald-Elliott. Bible rec. Ms. MHS.
McDonnell. Abr. Compend. Amer. Geneal. Virkus. V. 6, pp. 278–79. DAR.
St. Paul's Parish, Balto. V. 1, 2. Mss. MHS.
†**McDonogh.** Life and work of John McDonogh, by W. Allen. Sketch of McDonogh School, by J. Johnson, Jr. Pub. by trustees. Baltimore, Isaac Friedenwald Co. Enoch Pratt Lib.
Lineage Bks., Natl. Soc. of Daughters of Amer. Col., v. 3, p. 239. MHS; DAR.
†**McDonogh, John.** His life and work. W. T. Childs. Baltimore, Meyer & Thalheimer, 1939, 255 pp. MHS.
McDonough, John. Westminster churchyard. Patriotic Marylander, v. 2, no. 4, pp. 54–60. MHS; DAR.
***McDougle.** Frederick Co. families. Markell. Ms. Personal list.

†**McDowell.** Med. Annals Md. Cordell. 1903, p. 496. MHS.
McElderry. Glendy churchyard. Patriotic Marylander, v. 2, no. 4, pp. 54–60. MHS; DAR.
Miss Margaret M. Steele chart. MHS.
Mrs. J. Whitridge Williams chart 1. MHS.
McElderry, Thomas. Glendy churchyard. Patriotic Marylander, v. 2, no. 4, pp. 54–60. MHS; DAR.
†**McElfish.** Hist. of Allegany Co. Thomas and Williams. V. 2. MHS; DAR.
McElfresh. Cummings chart. Lib. Cong.; MHS; DAR.
Griffith geneal. Griffith. MHS; DAR.
†Hist. of Frederick Co. Williams. MHS; DAR.
†Hist. of West. Md. Scharf. V. 1, p. 415. MHS; DAR.
†Med. Annals Md. Cordell. 1903, p. 496. MHS.
McElheny. St. Paul's Parish, Balto. V. 2. Mss. MHS.
McElroy. Abr. Compend. Amer. Geneal. Virkus. V. 1, p. 707. DAR.
Cummings chart. Lib. Cong.; MHS; DAR.
St. Paul's Parish, Balto. V. 2, 3. Mss. MHS.
McEvoy. Balto., its hist., its people. Hall. V. 3. MHS; DAR.
*Burke's landed gentry. 1939. MHS.
Some Va. families. McIlhany.
St. Paul's Parish, Balto. V. 2. Mss. MHS.
***McGarth.** McGarth, Lloyd and other families. M. H. Mag., 1929, v. 24, pp. 291–324.
McGary. Centenary of Catholicity in Ky. Webb. 1884. MHS.
McGaughy. St. Paul's Parish, Balto. V. 2. Mss. MHS.
McGaw. Balto., its hist., its people. Hall. V. 3. MHS; DAR.
McGaw, G. Keen. Md. Soc., War of 1812, v. 3, no. 233. Ms. MHS.
***McGee.** Wicomico Co. families. Tilghman. Ms, p. 25. DAR.
†**McGill.** Hist. of Frederick Co. Williams. MHS; DAR.
James Hook and Virginia Eller. Hook. MHS; DAR.
Mrs. D. G. Lovell chart. MHS.
†Md. Annals Md. Cordell. 1903, pp. 496–97. MHS.
McGill, MacGill. St. Paul's Parish, Balto. V. 2. Mss. MHS.
***McGlammery.** Wicomico Co. families. Tilghman. Ms, pp. 96–97. DAR.
McGlaughlin. St. Paul's Parish, Balto. V. 2. Mss. MHS.
***McGlawin.** Wicomico Co. families. Tilghman. Ms, p. 12. DAR.
McGowman. St. Paul's Parish, Balto. V. 2. Mss. MHS.
McGraw, Mrs. M. A. (nee **Warden**). Amer. Armory and Blue Book. Matthews. 1911–12, p. 378.
McGregor. Amer. Clan Gregor Year Book, 1916, pp. 36–40. MHS; DAR.
Abr. Compend. Amer. Geneal. Virkus. V. 6, p. 732. DAR.
Ancestral beginnings in Amer. of McGregor, Magruder, Beall, Price, Phillips, Bland, McKisick, Young and related families. Caroline B. Price. 80 pp. Austin, Texas. 1928. DAR.
See Alpine-Gregor-McGregor-Magruder Clan.
McGregor-Fassit. Bible rec., 1774–1878. Bible owned by Miss McGregor, Berlin, Md. Md. Geneal. Rec. Com., 1937–38, pp. 140–41. Mss. DAR.
***McGrew.** Boyd family. Boyd. DAR.
McGuire. Patriotic Md. Md. Soc. of S. A. R., 1930. MHS; DAR.
McHaffey. Jenkins-Courtney chart. MHS.
McHaffie. Mrs. J. G. Brogden chart. MHS.
Macsherry chart. MHS.
McHenry. Balto., its hist., its people. Hall. V. 3. MHS; DAR.
†Bench and bar of Md. Sams and Riley. 1901, v. 2, pp. 535, 616. Lib. Cong.; MHS; Peabody Lib.
Clark chart. MHS.
Descendants of Col. Thomas White. Morris. MHS.
*Garrett Co. pioneer families. Haye. Newsp. clipp. MHS; DAR.
†Hist. of Md. Scharf. V. 2, pp. 435–39. MHS.
†Life and correspondence of James McHenry, 1753–1816. Burrows Bros. Co. Enoch Pratt. Lib.
†Life and correspondence of James McHenry, Sec. of War, under Washington. B. C. Steiner. 1907. MHS; DAR.
†Med. Annals Md. Cordell. 1903, p. 497. MHS.
Mountain Democrat, Garrett Co. Newsp. clipp. MHS; DAR.
St. Paul's Parish, Balto. V. 2, 4. Mss. MHS.
Sketch of life of Dr. James McHenry, aide-de-camp to Gen. Washington, aide-de-camp to Marquis de Lafayette, Sec. of War, 1796–1800. M. H. S. Fund Pub., no. 10. Balto., 1877. MHS.
†**McHenry, James.** Memoir. Tunstall Smith. Balto., 1916. MHS.
Westminster churchyard. Patriotic Marylander, v. 2, no. 4, pp. 54–60. MHS; DAR.
McHenry, Col. James. Revolutionary war heroes. Cole. Bklet. Enoch Pratt Lib.
McHenry, Mrs. James; formerly Mrs. Wm. McHenry Keyser (Majorie Hambleton Ober). Chart. Col. Dames, Chap. I. MHS.
McHenry (James Howard) - Cary. Chart. photos., complete in 1 sheet. Cary Geneal. Coll. Ms. MHS.
***McHenry Family.** Wilson Mss. Coll., no. 98. MHS.
McIlhenny. Abr. Compend. Amer. Geneal. Virkus. V. 1, p. 708, DAR; v. 4, p. 367. MHS.
McIlvain. McIlvain. F. W. Leach. North Amer., Phila., June 16, 1912.
McIlvain family. A. J. Justice.
McIlvaine Lineage, Pa. Torrence and allied families. Torrence. Pp. 395–447. MHS; DAR.
McIntire. Balto., its hist., its people. Hall. V. 3. MHS; DAR.
McIntire, McIntyre. St. Paul's Parish, Balto. V. 2, 4. Mss. MHS.
†**McIntosh.** Bench and bar of Md. Sams and Riley. 1901, v. 2, p. 458. Lib. Cong.; MHS; Peabody Lib.
†Hist. of Balto. City and Co. Scharf. P. 896. MHS.

*Scotland to Norfolk, Va. The Sun, Balto., Feb. 9, 1908.
St. Paul's Parish, Balto. V. 2. Mss. MHS.
***McIntyre.** Wicomico Co. families. Tilghman. Ms, pp. 96–97, 129. DAR.
See McIntire.
†McJilton, John Nelson (born in Balto. 1806; died in N. Y. City, 1875). M. H. Mag., 1937, v. 32, no. 4, pp. 301–31.
†McKaig. Hist. of Allegany Co. Thomas and Williams. V. 2. MHS; DAR.
†Hist. of Balto. City and Co. Scharf. P. 724. MHS.
†Hist. of West. Md. Scharf. V. 2, p. 1398. MHS; DAR.
McKaig, W. Wallace. Pedigree. Soc. Col. Wars Md. Culver. 1940. MHS; DAR.
McKalvey. Md. tombstone rec. Md. Geneal. Rec. Com., 1937, Parran, p. 27. Mss. DAR.
McKay. Dulaney churchyard, near Massey, Kent Co. Md. Geneal. Rec. Com., 1933–34, pp. 210–12. Mss. DAR.
*Family of Richard McKay. 1934, pamph., revised ed. MHS; DAR.
†Hist. of Allegany Co. Thomas and Williams. V. 1. MHS; DAR.
Sketch of family of Richard McKay. Oscar Reed McKay. Indianapolis, Ind., rev. ed., 1934, pamph. MHS; DAR.
McKay-Brown. Abr. Compend. Amer. Geneal. Virkus. V. 4, p. 370. MHS.
McKean. Dundas-Hesselius. P. 40. MHS.
*Geneal. of McKean family of Pa. Life of Thomas McKean. R. Buchanan. Lancaster, Pa., Inquirer Printing Co., 1890. MHS.
*Hist. notes. F. G. McKean. Wash., D. C., Scottish Records, 1906. MHS.
Pedigree of Franklin Buchanan Owen. Soc. Col. Wars Md. Culver. 1940. MHS; DAR.
See McKeen.
McKean, McKeen. Clasping hands with generations past. Lloyd. MHS; DAR.
McKeen. McClellan-McKeen Bible rec. Ms. File case A, MHS.
See McKean.
McKeldir. Glendy churchyard, Balto. Md. Geneal. Rec. Com., 1933–34. Mss. DAR.
McKendree. Lambdin chart. MHS.
McKenny. *See* McCarteney-McKenny-Cragin.
McKenzee, McCeney. McKenzee, McCeney and allied families. Md. Geneal. Rec. Com., 1932, p. 23. DAR.
McKenzie. Newsp. clipp. Andrews Scrap Book. MHS.
St. Paul's Parish, Balto. V. 1, 2. Mss. MHS.
See Mackenzie.
McKenzie, Mackenzie. Col. families of U. S. A. Mackenzie. V. 1. MHS; DAR.
McKeown. Faith Pres. Church (Glendy graveyard). Mss. MHS.
McKesson-Reed. (McKesson, Adams Co., Pa.; Reed, Powell's Creek, Lancaster Co. (now Dauphin Co.), Pa.; from Ireland, 1730). Greenway Mss. Geneal. Coll. MHS.
†McKew. Med. Annals. Md. Cordell. 1903, p. 498. MHS.
McKey. St. Stephens Parish, Cecilton, Md. MHS; DAR.
McKim. Ances. rec. and portraits. Col. Dames of Amer., 1910, v. 2, p. 636. MHS; DAR.
Balto., its hist., its people. Hall. V. 3. MHS; DAR.
Charts; in Hazelhurst charts. MHS.
Col. families of U. S. A. Mackenzie. V. 1. MHS; DAR.
*Geneal. and mem. encyc. of Md. Spencer. V. 1, pp. 161–65. MHS; DAR.
Greenway Mss. Geneal. Coll. Binder's title, Hawkins-Bordley. MHS.
Mrs. C. C. Hall chart. MHS.
Mrs. W. H. Harris chart. MHS.
†Hist. of Balto. City and Co. Scharf. P. 476. MHS.
Pedigree of George Ross Veazey. Soc. Col. Wars Md. Culver. 1940. MHS; DAR.
Mrs. N. S. Pendleton, Jr., chart. MHS.
St. Paul's Parish, Balto. V. 2. Mss. MHS.
D. Veazey pedigree chart, plate 2. Soc. Col. Wars, Md. Johnston. 1905, p. 122. MHS.
See Smith (Samuel)-McKim-Spear-Brown.
McKim, Mrs. Hollins (?) (Lydia Hollingsworth Morris). Chart. Col. Dames, Chap. I. MHS.
Mrs. G. H. Williams, Jr., chart. MHS.
McKim, S. Hollins. Abr. Compend. Amer. Geneal. Virkus. V. 1, p. 710. DAR.
McKim, W. P. Abr. Compend. Amer. Geneal. Virkus. V. 1, p. 191. DAR.
***McKim, Wm.** Balto., hist and biog. Richardson and Bennett. 1871, pp. 391–95. MHS; DAR.
McKim-Hollins-Patterson. Charts (2), photos. Cary Geneal. Coll. Ms. MHS.
McKinley. Md. tombstone rec. Md. Geneal. Rec. Com., 1937, Parran, p. 5. Mss. DAR.
St. Paul's Parish, Balto. V. 1, 2, 3. Mss. MHS.
McKinnell, Wm. Wendell Bollman. Md. Soc., War of 1812, v. 4, no. 344. Ms. MHS.
McKinney. *See* Harris-McKinney-Stump.
McKinstry. Englar family. Barnes. MHS; DAR.
McKisick. Ancestral beginnings in Amer. of McGregor, Magruder, Beall, Price, Phillips, Bland, McKisick, Young and related families. Caroline B. Price. 1928. DAR.
McKnew. Stephen Beard and his descendants. Townsend. Ms. MHS.
*McKnew and descendants. S. W. Townsend. Ms. MHS.
Thomas McKnew, Prince George Co., and his descendants. S. W. Townsend. Ms. MHS.
McKnown. St. Paul's Parish, Balto. V. 2. Mss. MHS.
McLanahan, Mrs. Austin (Romaine Le Moyne). Chart. Col. Dames, Chap. I. MHS.
†McLane. Bench and bar of Md. Sams and Riley. 1901, v. 2, pp. 368, 570. Lib. Cong.; MHS; Peabody Lib.
Mrs. Wm. Graham Bowdoin, Jr., chart. MHS.
Cary Geneal. Coll. Ms. MHS.
Curzon family. Pleasants. MHS.
†Med. Annals Md. Cordell. 1903, p. 498. MHS.
St. Paul's Parish, Balto. V. 2, 4. Mss. MHS.
Tompkins chart. MHS.
McLane, Allan. Abr. Compend. Amer. Geneal. Virkus. V. 1, p. 194. DAR.
*Burke's landed gentry. 1939. MHS.
†Men of mark in Md. Johnson. V. 2. DAR; Enoch Pratt Lib.
McLane, Mrs. James Latimer (Fanny King). Chart. (Mostly N. E. and N. Y. families.) Col. Dames, Chap. I. MHS.

†McLane, Gov. Robert Milligan. 1815–1898. Governors of Md. Buchholz. P. 228. MHS.
†Balto., hist and biog. Richardson and Bennett. 1871, pp. 361–69. MHS; DAR.
Founders of Anne Arundel and Howard Cos. Warfield. P. 293. MHS; DAR.
†McLaughlin. Hist. of Allegany Co. Thomas and Williams. V. 2. MHS; DAR.
St. John's R. C. Church cemetery, Montgomery Co. Md. Geneal. Rec. Com., 1926, p. 27. Mss. DAR.
St. Paul's Parish, Balto. V. 2. Mss. MHS.
McLean. Christ P. E. Church cemetery, Cambridge. Steele. 1936. MHS; DAR.
†Geneal. and mem. encyc. of Md. Spencer. V. 2, p. 466. MHS; DAR.
St. Paul's Parish, Balto. V. 1. Mss. MHS.
McLean, Ritchie. Americans of gentle birth and their ancestors. Pitman. P. 103. MHS.
McLeod. M. E. Church South cemetery, near Poolesville, Montgomery Co. Md. Geneal. Rec. Com., 1926. Mss. DAR.
McLeod, Robert. Md. pensioner on Miss. pension rolls. D. A. R. Mag., v. 69, no. 11, p. 685.
McMahan (Daniel) Family, Pa. and N. C. McCall-Tidwell families. McCall. Pp. 454–56. MHS; DAR.
†McMahon. Bench and bar of Md. Sams and Riley. 1901, v. 1, p. 310. Lib. Cong.; MHS; Peabody Lib.
†Life of John Van Lear McMahon. J. T. Mason; completed and revised by his son J. T. Mason. (John McMahon, born in Cumberland, Md., 1800; compiler of hist. of Md.; died 1871.) Balto., 1879. MHS; Enoch Pratt Lib.
Monumental City. Howard. MHS; DAR.
***McManis.** Wicomico Co. families. Tilghman. Ms, p. 92. DAR.
†McMaster. Biog. cyc. of rep. men of Md. and D. C. P. 241. MHS; DAR.
†Med. Annals Md. Cordell. 1903, p. 499. MHS.
Pocomoke Pres. churchyard, Worcester Co., Hudson. Bd. ms. MHS; DAR.
Sketches of John Slemmons Stevenson and Rev. Samuel McMaster. Stevenson. P. 29. MHS.
*Sketch of Rev. Samuel McMaster, 1744–1811. Jersey City, N. J., A. J. Doan, 1900, 42 pp. MHS.
See MacMaster.
McMaster, Hugh. Will, 1787. Md. Geneal. Rec. Com., 1924–25, v. 1, p. 73–76. DAR.
McMaster Family. Hist. Ms. MHS.
†McMechen. Bench and bar of Md. Sams and Riley. 1901, v. 1, p. 214. Lib. Cong.; MHS; Peabody Lib.
Crittenden-McMechen chart. MHS.
St. Paul's Parish, Balto. V. 2. Mss. MHS.
McMillan. Descendants of Joran Kyn. Pa. Mag., v. 7, p. 464.
McMillan, Va. Some notable families of south. States. Armstrong. V. 1. DAR.
†McMurray. Hist. of Balto. City and Co. Scharf. P. 775. MHS.
†Hist. of West. Md. Scharf. V. 1, pp. 491–92. MHS; DAR.
St. Paul's Parish, Balto. V. 2. Mss. MHS.
McNabb. Bible rec., Natl. Geneal. Soc. Quart., v. 24, p. 46. See Preston Bible rec., v. 24, p. 29.
†McNair. Andrew McNair and Liberty Bell, 1776. Mary D. Alexander. 1929.
St. Paul's Parish, Balto. V. 2. Mss. MHS.
***McNair-McNear-McNeir.** Geneal. (Supplement 1928). J. B. McNair. Md. McNairs, pp. 105–06; 1923 ed., p. 83. Chicago, 1929, 340 pp. MHS.
McNamara. Christ P. E. Church cemetery, Cambridge. Steele. 1936. MHS; DAR.
Tombstone rec. of Dorchester Co. Jones. DAR.
***McNary.** McNary family; with trees and hist. T. A. McNary. DAR.
McNeal, J. Vansant. Md. Soc., War of 1812, v. 2, no. 142. Ms. MHS.
McNeale. St. Paul's Parish, Balto. V. 2. Mss. MHS.
McNear. *See* McNair.
McNeil, James (War of 1812). Glendy churchyard. Patriotic Marylander, v. 2, no. 4, pp. 54–60. MHS; DAR.
McNeir. Abr. Compend. Amer. Geneal. Virkus. V. 6, p. 384. DAR.
*Burke's landed gentry. 1939. MHS.
*Lineage Bk., Daughters of Amer. Col., v. 4, p. 79, 310. MHS; DAR.
See McNair.
McNeir Line. Col. and Revolutionary lineages in Amer. 1939, v. 2, pp. 122–23. MHS.
†McNemara. Bench and bar of Md. Sams and Riley. 1901, v. 1, p. 83. Lib Cong.; MHS; Peabody Lib.
St. Paul's Parish, Balto. V. 1. Mss. MHS.
McNew-Prather-Turner. Tombstone inscriptions, from private burying ground, Beltsville, Prince George Co. Natl. Geneal. Soc. Quart., v. 9, p. 39.
†McPhail, Daniel H. M. H. Mag., v. 12, p. 228.
McPherson. See Clarkson, N. Y., 1690. Ms. File case, DAR.
†Hist. of Frederick Co. Williams. MHS; DAR.
†Hist. of West. Md. Scharf. V. 1, p. 459. MHS; DAR.
*Lineage Bk., Daughters Amer. Col. V. 1, p. 46. MHS; DAR.
†Med. Annals. Md. Cordell. 1903, p. 499. MHS.
Pedigree of John McPherson Dennis. Soc. Col. Wars Md. Culver. 1940. MHS; DAR.
Rehobeth P. E. churchyard, Somerset Co. Md. Geneal. Rec. Com., 1937, Mrs. Lines. Mss. DAR.
Revolutionary war pension abs. Natl. Geneal. Soc. Quart., 1931, v. 19, no. 3, p. 74, no. 4, p. 110. MHS; DAR.
St. Paul's Parish, Balto. V. 3. Mss. MHS.
Miss Sara E. White chart. MHS.
See Bruce-McPherson.
McPike Family. Notes. Pamph. MHS.
McRoberts. Tombstone rec. of Glendy burying ground. Md. Geneal. Rec. Com., 1933–34, pp. 171–78. Mss. DAR.
†McShane. Med. Annals Md. Cordell. 1903, p. 499. MHS.
†McSherry. Bench and bar of Md. Sams and Riley. 1901, v. 2, p. 542. Lib. Cong.; MHS; Peabody Lib.
†Hist. of West. Md. Scharf. V. 1, pp. 412–13. MHS; DAR.
†Med. Annals Md. Cordell. 1903, pp. 499–500. MHS.

Portrait and biog. rec. of Sixth Cong. Dist. of Md. 1898, pp. 129, 650. MHS; DAR.
See MacSherry.
†**McSherry, James** (1842–1907). M. H. Mag., v. 12, p. 229.
McSpadden-Love-Meigs-Clendinen-Von Bibber-Pope. Chart, photos., 1906. MHS.
McTavish. Caton chart. Cary Geneal. Coll. Ms. MHS.
Robert Gilmor chart. MHS.
***McTavish, MacTavish.** Pennington Papers. Ms. MHS.
McVeigh. Some Va. families. McIlhany.
McWhorter. Blakiston churchyard, Kent Co., Del., near Millington. Md. Geneal. Rec. Com., 1933–34, pp. 204–07. Mss. DAR.
McWilliams. Sacred Heart R. C. churchyard, Bushwood, St. Mary's Co. Md. Geneal. Rec. Com., 1929. Mss. DAR.
***Mead.** Mead relations. A. M. Prichard. (Mostly Va. and Ky. rec.; Brown, Keyser, Mead and Powell families.) Staunton, Va., McClure Co., 1933, 250 pp. DAR.
Mead, Wm., Cecil Co. D. A. R. Mag., v. 65, no. 9, p. 569.
Meade. Cary Geneal. Coll. Ms. MHS.
*Andrew Meade of Ireland and Va.; his ancestors and descendants. Meade tables. H. Baskreville. (Related families of Everhard, Hardaway, Overton, Pettus, Segar and others.) Richmond, Va., Old Dominion Press, 1921. MHS.
*The Sun, Balto., Aug. 21, 1904; March 24, 31, April 7, 1907 (Va.).
Times Dispatch, Richmond, Va., Feb. 4, 1906. Newsp. clipp.
Meade, Va. Ancestors and descendants of Col. David Funsten. Randolph. MHS.
†**Meade, Right Rev. W., D.D.** Memoirs. Rev. John Johns. Balto., 1867.
Meakins. St. Stephens Parish, Cecilton, Md. MHS; DAR.
†**Mealey.** Hist. of West. Md. Scharf. V. 2, p. 1041. MHS; DAR.
Mealy. Bible rec. Md. Geneal. Rec. Com., 1937–38, p. 158. Mss. DAR.
***Means Family.** Old Kent. Hanson. P. 171. MHS; DAR.
Mears. Lineage Bks., Natl. Soc. of Daughters of Amer. Col., v. 3, p. 280. MHS; DAR.
Mears, Adelbert W. Md. Soc., War of 1812, v. 4, no. 350. Ms. MHS.
Mears, Ellen Emmerich. Col. and Revolutionary families of Phila. Jordan. 1933, v. 1, pp. 412–15.
***Mears Family.** Old Kent. Hanson. P. 316. MHS; DAR.
Meccelpin. Rec. of Stepney Parish. MHS; DAR.
Medairy, G. R. Md. Soc., War of 1812, v. 1, no. 46. Ms. MHS.
Medairy, J. R. Md. Soc., War of 1812, v. 1, no. 47. Ms. MHS.
†**Medders.** Med. Annals Md. Cordell. 1903, p. 500. MHS.
Medeira, Madira. St. Paul's Parish, Balto. V. 1, 2. Mss. MHS.
Medford. Descendants of Joran Kyn. Pa. Mag., v. 5, p. 334.
See Andrews-Bonner-Carroll-Corkran-Medford.
Medford Family. Records. Photos. Andrews' Scrap Book. MHS.
Medford Family, Dorchester Co. Ms. MHS.
Medford - Bonner - Carroll - Corkran - Stevens. Bible rec. of Dorchester and Somerset Cos. and Del. Pp. 47–48, 51–56. DAR.
Meeds. Sarah Smith Hood Bible rec. Ms. MHS.
***Meehhuch.** Frederick Co. families. Markell. Ms. Personal list.
Meek. Autobiography of Summerfield Baldwin. MHS; DAR.
Bowie-Claggett chart. MHS.
Cary Geneal. Coll. Ms. MHS.
*Lineage Bk., Daughters of Amer. Col., v. 4, p. 289. MHS; DAR.
Ms. MHS.
Md. families. Culver. Ms. Personal list.
Pedigree of Charles Gambrill Baldwin. Soc. Col. Wars Md. Culver. 1940. MHS; DAR.
Pedigree of Mark Alexander Herbert Smith. Soc. Col. Wars. Md. Culver. 1940. MHS; DAR.
West. Nottingham Cemetery. M. H. Mag., 1923, v. 18, p. 55.
Meek, Meeke, Anne Arundel Co. Posey chart. MHS.
Meeke. *See* Meek.
Meeker, Richards Carson. Pedigree chart. Soc. Col. Wars, Md. Johnston. 1905, p. 66. MHS.
Meeker, Wm. Painter. Pedigree. Soc. Col. Wars Md. Culver. 1940. MHS; DAR.
Meekin. Trinity Church burial ground, near Cambridge, Md. Md. Geneal. Rec. Com., 1937–38, pp. 93–104. Mss. DAR.
Meekins. Keene family. Jones. MHS; DAR.
Tombstone rec. of Dorchester Co. Jones. DAR.
Meeks. Bible rec., Kent Co. Md. Geneal. Rec. Com., 1933–34, p. 239. Mss. DAR.
St. Paul's churchyard, Kent Co. Md. O. R. Soc. Bull., no. 2, pp. 54–65. MHS.
See Cannan-Bush-Calder-Joiner-Meeks.
Meeks, Kent Co. Md. Geneal. Rec. Com., 1937, Parran, p. 213. Mss. DAR.
Meeks-Shawhan. Data. M. H. Mag., 1939, v. 34, no. 2, p. 204.
†**Meeteer.** Med. Annals. Md. Cordell. 1903, p. 500. MHS.
Meginnis. Holden's Cemetery, Kent Co. Md. Geneal. Rec. Com., 1932, v. 5, p. 211. Mss. DAR.
Meguiness. Meguiness graves, near Massey, Kent Co. Bible rec. Upper Penins. East. Shore. Pp. 101–02. MHS; DAR.
†**Mehring.** Hist. of Frederick Co. Williams. MHS; DAR.
Meiere. Geneal. of McKean family of Pa. Buchanan. P. 214. MHS.
Meigs. Balto., its hist., its people. Hall. V. 3. MHS; DAR.
Chart. of Com. John Rodgers. DAR.
Col. families of U. S. A. Mackenzie. V. 2. MHS; DAR.
McSpadden-Love-Meigs-Clendinen-Von Bibber-Pope chart. MHS.
Rodgers Bible rec. Ms. MHS.
Meigs, H. B. Md. Soc., War of 1812, v. 2, no. 165. Ms. MHS.
†Men of mark in Md. Johnson. V. 4. DAR; Enoch Pratt Lib.
Melbourne. Turner Geneal. Coll. Ms. MHS.
Melcher. St. Paul's Parish, Balto. V. 2. Mss. MHS.

Mellon, E. P. Abr. Compend. Amer. Geneal. Virkus. V. 1, p. 724. DAR.
Meloir. *See* Hart-Shehan-Clayton-Meloir.
Melton. Centenary of Catholicity in Ky. Webb. 1884. MHS.
***Melvin.** Bible of Solomon Melvin, Caroline Co. Geneal. Soc. Pa. Pub., v. 8, p. 298.
Col. and Revolutionary families of Phila. Jordan. 1933, v. 1, p. 447.
St. Mary's P. E. churchyard, Pocomoke, Worcester Co., Hudson. Bd. ms. MHS; DAR.
Melvin, Brumwell and Wm. Bishop. Bible rec. Ms. MHS.
†**Melvin, George T.** Men of mark in Md. Johnson. V. 3. DAR; Enoch Pratt Lib.
Melvin, Solomon, Caroline Co. Bible rec. Ms. MHS.
Melvin Family. Ms. MHS.
Menchey. Mt. Olivet Cemetery, Frederick. Md. Geneal. Rec. Com., 1934-35, p. 111. Mss. DAR.
†**Mencken.** Happy days, 1880-92. H. L. Mencken. Memoirs of boyhood in Balto. 324 pp. Knopf. N. Y. 1940. MHS.
Modern encyc. McDannald. 1933.
†Tales of wayward inn. Frank Case, proprietor of Algonquin Hotel. Enoch Pratt Lib.
Mencken, H. L. Contemporary Amer. authors. Fred B. Millett.
Mendenhall. Harlan family geneal., Chester Co., Pa. Harlan. P. 299. MHS.
Menges. Rahn and allied families. Ms. MHS. *See* Hornberger-Menges-Rahn-Yingling.
Mentzer, Conrad, Washington Co. Will, 1845. D. C. Geneal. Rec. Com., 1932-34, v. 10, pp. 205-07. Typed, bd. DAR.
Merceir. *See* Wilson-Merceir.
***Merceir Family.** Wilson Mss. Coll., no. 72. MHS.
Mercer. Ancestry of Susannah Mercer, wife of Robert Porter. Md. Geneal. Rec. Com., 1934-35, pp. 276-81. Mss. DAR.
†Bench and bar of Md. Sams and Riley. 1901, v. 1, p. 269. Lib. Cong.; MHS; Peabody Lib.
Col. families of U. S. A. Mackenzie. V. 3. MHS; DAR.
Garnett-Mercer families. Garnett. MHS.
Hooper family. Col. and Revolutionary families of Pa. Jordan. 1932, v. 4, p. 239.
*Old Kent. Hanson. P. 271. MHS; DAR.
St. Paul's Parish, Balto. V. 2. Mss. MHS.
St. Stephens Parish, Cecilton, Md. MHS; DAR.
Side lights on Md. hist. Richardson. V. 2, p. 183. MHS; DAR.
Talbott of "Poplar Knowle." Shirk. MHS; DAR.
***Mercer,** Va. and Md. The Sun, Balto., Sept. 17, 24, 1905.
Mercer, John. Copy of will. Md. Geneal. Rec. Com., 1934-35, p. 296. Mss. DAR.
Mercer, Gov. John Francis. Founders of Anne Arundel and Howard Cos. Warfield. P. 250. MHS; DAR.
†Governors of Md. Buchholz. P. 51. MHS.
J. Mercer Garnett son of Robert and Ann (Roy) Mercer; born, Stafford Co., Va., May 17, 1759; married Sophia Sprigg, Anne Arundel Co., Feb. 3, 1785; died in Phila., 1821. M. H. Mag., 1907, v. 2, no. 3, pp. 191-213.
†Hist. of Md. Scharf. V. 2, p. 607. MHS.
Mercer Family, Va. and Md. William and Mary Quart., 1st series, v. 17, pp. 85, 204-23.
Mercier. Abr. Compend. Amer. Geneal. Virkus. V. 6, p. 547. DAR.
Lineage Bks., Natl. Soc. of Daughters of Amer. Col., v. 2, p. 48. MHS; DAR.
Merdl. Makemie Memorial Pres. churchyard, Snow Hill, Worcester Co. Hudson. Bd. ms. MHS; DAR. Also: Md. Geneal. Rec. Com., Mrs. Lines. Mss. DAR.
Meredith. Abr. Compend. Amer. Geneal. Virkus. V. 1, p. 725. DAR.
Burton ancestry. Ms. MHS.
Lineage Bk., Order of Washington, p. 181. MHS; DAR.
*Pennington Papers. Ms. MHS.
St. Paul's Parish, Balto. V. 1, 2. Mss. MHS.
†**Meredith, Jonathan.** Balto., hist. and biog. Richardson and Bennett. 1871, p. 371. MHS; DAR.
†**Mergenthaler.** Geneal. and mem. encyc. of Md. Spencer. V. 2, p. 567. MHS; DAR.
†**Mergenthaler, Ottmar,** Balto. from Germany, 1872. Our foreign-born citizens. Annie E. S. Beard. 1939. Enoch Pratt Lib.
Balto., its hist., its people. Hall. V. 2. MHS; DAR.
Merikin, D. Willis. Md. Soc., War of 1812, v. 1, no. 16. Ms. MHS.
***Merrill (Morrell) Family.** Wilson Mss. Coll., no. 10. MHS.
Merritt. Shrewsbury churchyard, Kent Co. Md. O. R. Soc., v. 2, pp. 46-54. MHS.
Meriweather. Griffith geneal. Griffith. MHS; DAR.
Patriotic Md. Md. Soc. of S. A. R., 1930. MHS; DAR.
Meriwether. Capt. Roger Jones of London and Va. Browning.
Lewises, Meriwethers and their kin. Anderson.
*Lineage of Meriwethers and Minors. Minor Meriwether. St. Louis, Mo., 1895.
*Meriwethers and their connections. Louisa H. A. Minor. Albany, N. Y., Joel Musell's Sons, 1892, 1st ed. MHS.
Pedigree of Edward Hammond. Soc. Col. Wars Md. Culver. 1940. MHS; DAR.
*Rec. of Nicholas Meriwether of Wales and descendants in Va. and Md. Wm. Ridgely Griffith. St. Louis, Mo., 1899, ltd. ed.
***Meroney.** Frederick Co. families. Markell. Ms. Personal list.
†**Merrick.** Bench and bar of Md. Sams and Riley. 1901, v. 2, p. 418. Lib. Cong.; MHS; Peabody Lib.
†Med. Annals Md. Cordell. 1903, p. 501. MHS.
St. Paul's Parish, Balto. V. 1. Mss. MHS.
Merriken. Md. gleanings in Eng. Wills. M. H. Mag., 1907, v. 2, no. 4.
St. Paul's Parish, Balto. V. 2. Mss. MHS.
Merrill. Pocomoke Pres. churchyard, Worcester Co., Hudson. Bd. ms. MHS; DAR.
Merriman. *See* Merryman.
Merrit. St. Stephens Parish, Cecilton, Md. MHS; DAR.
Merritt. Chestertown cemetery. Md. O. R. Soc. Bull., no. 1, pp. 18-29.
*Coat of arms. Burke's landed gentry. 1939. MHS.
Col. families of U. S. A. Mackenzie. V. 1. MHS; DAR.
Patriotic Md. Md. Soc. of S. A. R., 1930. MHS; DAR.

Revised Merritt rec. D. Merritt. (Merritts of Mass., N. Y., N. J. and Md.) N. Y., 1916.
Shrewsbury churchyard. Md. O. R. Soc. Bull., no. 2, pp. 46–54.
Merritt, Kent Co. Data. Md. Geneal. Rec. Com., 1937, Parran, p. 204. Mss. DAR.
Merritt, J. Black, III. Md. Soc., War of 1812, v. 2, no. 171. Ms. MHS.
Merritt, James Alfred. Pedigree. Soc. Col. Wars Md. Culver. 1940. MHS; DAR.
Merritt, Paymaster Wm. Alfred. Pedigree. Soc. Col. Wars Md. Culver. 1940. MHS; DAR.
Merritt, Paymaster William Alfred Merritt, and Dr. Simon Wickes Merritt. Pedigree charts, plates 1 and 2. Soc. Col. Wars, Md. Johnston. 1905, pp. 67–68. MHS.
Merritt, Dr. Simon Wickes. *See* Merritt, Wm. Alfred and Simon Wickes.
***Merritt Family.** Old Kent. Hanson. P. 184. MHS; DAR.
Merritt Family, Kent Co. Births, 1799–1819. Md. Geneal. Rec. Com., 1937. DAR.
Merriweather. Dorsey chart. MHS.
See Merryweather.
***Merriweather, Meriweather.** The Sun, Balto., Oct. 27, Nov. 3 (Boyd-Buchanan-Smith, western branch), 1907.
Merry. Coll. of Amer. epitaphs and inscriptions. Alden. 1814, v. 5. MHS.
†**Merryman.** Biog. cyc. of rep. men of Md. and D. C. P. 312. MHS; DAR.
†Hist. of Balto. City and Co. Scharf. P. 884. MHS.
*Lineage Bk., Daughters of Amer. Col., v. 1, p. 70; v. 3, p. 201; v. 5, p. 216. MHS; DAR.
Md. families. Culver. Ms. Personal list.
†Med. Annals Md. Cordell. 1903, p. 501. MHS.
Merryman family, additional data from Old Frisby Family Bible. M. H. Mag. 1916, v. 11, p. 85.
Merryman family. F. B. Culver. M. H. Mag. 1915. V. 10, pp. 176, 286.
Monumental City. Howard. MHS; DAR.
Newsp. clipp. R. H. Spencer Scrap Book. MHS.
Parrish family. Boyd. MHS; DAR.
Talbott of "Poplar Knowle." Shirk. MHS; DAR.
See Bosley-Bowen-Merryman.
***Merryman,** Baltimore Co. The Sun, Balto. Dec. 26, 29, 1909; Jan. 2 (by F. B. Culver), 1910.
Merryman, Charles. Pedigree of Wm. Henry Perkins, Jr. Soc. Col. Wars Md. Culver. 1940. MHS; DAR.
***Merryman Family.** Wilson Mss. Coll., no. 4. MHS.
Merryman, Merriman. St. Paul's Parish, Balto. V. 1, 2. Mss. MHS.
***Merryweather** or **Merriweather.** Pennington Papers. Ms. MHS.
Mesick Family. Ms. MHS.
Messick. Md. Geneal. Bull., v. 5, p. 21; v. 6, p. 33. MHS; DAR.
See Mezick.
Messick, Baptist. Glendy churchyard. Patriotic Marylander, v. 2, no. 4, pp. 54–60. MHS; DAR.
Messick Family. Md. Geneal. Bull., Hayes, July, 1934, v. 5, no. 3, pp. 21–24; no. 4, pp. 33–34.
Messick Family, Bridgeville, Del. Bible rec. of Dorchester and Somerset Cos. and Del. Pp. 57–60. DAR.
Messix. Rec. of Stepney Parish. MHS; DAR.
Metcalf. Harford Co. Hist. Soc. Mss. Coll. JHU.
***Metcalfe.** Wicomico Co. families. Tilghman. Ms, p. 30. DAR.
St. Thomas' Parish, Balto. Co. Bd. ms. MHS. Also: Md. Geneal. Rec. Com., 1937, pp. 109–82. Mss. DAR.
Metzger. Frederick Co. tombstone inscriptions. Gruder. Natl. Geneal. Soc. Quart., 1919, v. 8, nos. 1, 2.
***Mewer.** Wicomico Co. families. Tilghman. Ms, p. 126. DAR.
Meyerheffer. Frederick Co. tombstone inscriptions. Gruder. Natl. Geneal. Soc. Quart., 1919, v. 8, nos. 1, 2.
Mezick. Bible rec., 1788–1863. Records were copied from old sheets taken from old Bible, in order to be kept in safe deposit box, owned by Glenn Mesick, Quantico Rd., Salisbury. Md. Geneal. Rec. Com., 1938–39, pp. 213–14. Mss. DAR.
Rec. of Stepney Parish. MHS; DAR.
***Mezick, Messick.** Wicomico Co. families. Tilghman. Ms, pp. 9, 38, 75, 80, 84, 101. DAR.
Mezwick. Bible rec., 1761. Md. Geneal. Rec. Com., 1926–27, v. 2, p. 47. DAR.
***Michael.** Frederick Co. families. Markell. Ms. Personal list.
Geneal. of Henrietta Chauncy Wilson. Upshur. Bk. of photos. MHS.
†Med. Annals Md. Cordell. 1903, p. 502. MHS.
Portrait and biog. rec. of Harford and Cecil Cos. 1897. P. 148. MHS; DAR.
Michael Family. 3 pts. Md. Geneal. Bull., v. 8, no. 4, p. 43. MHS; DAR.
***Michell.** Semmes Geneal. Coll. Ms. MHS.
Mickle. Monumental City. Howard. MHS; DAR.
Middendorf, Mrs. Henry Stump (Sarah Kennedy Boone). Chart. Col. Dames, Chap. I. MHS.
Neill chart. MHS.
Posey chart. MHS.
Middlekauff. Zion Reformed Church, Hagerstown. Md. Geneal. Rec. Com., 1934–35. Mss. DAR.
Middlekauff, Mittelkauff. Hagerstown tombstone inscriptions. Gruder. Natl. Geneal. Soc. Quart., 1919, v. 8, nos. 1, 2.
Middlemore. Dallam family. Dallam. 1929, p. 23. MHS.
Md. families. Culver. Ms. Personal list.
Tombstones, 1739–1866, on Cranberry Farm, near Aberdeen, Harford Co. Md. Geneal. Rec. Com., 1929, p. 60. Mss. DAR.
Middleton. Cary Geneal. Coll. Ms. MHS.
Col. families of U. S. A. Mackenzie. V. 3. MHS; DAR.
†Med. Annals Md. Cordell. 1903, p. 503. MHS.
Peale Geneal. Coll. Ms. MHS.
Pedigree of St. George Leakin Sioussat. Soc. Col. Wars Md. Culver. 1940. MHS; DAR.
Semmes and allied families. Semmes. P. 184. MHS.
*Semmes Geneal. Coll. Ms. MHS.

Middleton, Harvey. Pedigree charts., plates 1 and 2. Soc. Col. Wars, Md. Johnston. 1905, pp. 69-70. MHS.
Middleton, Nathan Atherton. Pedigree. (Rec. of Harrison, Pemberton families of Pa.) Soc. Col. Wars Md. Culver. 1940. MHS; DAR.
Mihill. Cary Geneal. Coll. Ms. MHS.
Milborne. All Hallow's P. E. churchyard, Snow Hill, Worcester Co. Hudson. Bd. ms. MHS; DAR. Also: Md. Geneal. Rec. Com., 1935-36, p. 24. Mss. DAR.
Miles. Balto., its hist., its people. Hall. V. 3. MHS; DAR.
Cary Geneal. Coll. Ms. MHS.
Centenary of Catholicity in Ky. Webb. 1884. MHS.
Dorsey Papers. Ms. MHS.
Humphrey Cissel farm, Montgomery Co. Md. Geneal. Rec. Com., 1926-27, p. 75. Mss. DAR.
Thomas Hill and descendants, Hill. P. 3. MHS.
Md. tombstone rec. Md. Geneal. Rec. Com., 1937, Parran, p. 12. Mss. DAR.
†Med. Annals Md. Cordell. 1903, p. 503. MHS.
Plummer family. A. P. H. Ms. MHS.
St. Paul's Parish, Balto. V. 1, 2, 4. Mss. MHS.
Somerset Co. Court Book. Tilghman. 1937. Ms. DAR.
Southern Bapt. Church cemetery, Worcester Co. Md. Geneal. Rec. Com., 1937, Mrs. Lines. Mss. DAR.
The Beckwiths. Pp. 30, 331.
Turner Geneal. Coll. Ms. MHS.
Miles, Balto. Pedigree of Francis Joseph Baldwin. Soc. Col. Wars. Md. Culver. 1940. MHS; DAR.
†**Miles, George H.** Biog. sketches of distinguished Marylanders. Boyle. MHS; DAR.
Miles, Mrs. Robert Mickle (Serena Chestnut Williams). Chart. (Mostly N. C. and S. C. families.) Col. Dames, Chap. I. MHS.
Millanges. *See* Millingas.
Millard. St. Paul's Parish, Balto. V. 2. Mss. MHS.
Miller. See Albee. Abr. Compend. Amer. Geneal. Virkus. V. 4, p. 675. MHS.
Ances. rec. and portraits. Col. Dames of Amer., 1910, v. 2, p. 669. MHS; DAR.
Anne Arundel Co. tombstone inscriptions. Ms. DAR.
†Bench and bar of Md. Sams and Riley. 1901, v. 2, p. 414. Lib. Cong.; MHS; Peabody Lib.
Bible rec. Ms. MHS.
Dr. J. J. Caldwell. Md. Geneal. Rec. Com., 1933-34, pp. 269-70. Mss. DAR.
Carton chart. MHS.
Dorsey and allied families. Ms. MHS.
See Edmundson family. Focke Geneal. Coll. Ms. MHS.
*Everhart-Miller and allied families. A. E. Miller. 1931. DAR.
*Frederick Co. families. Markell. Ms. Personal list.
Geneal. Ms. MHS.
Gillett-Miller families, 1755-1859. Ms. MHS.
Hagerstown tombstone inscriptions. Gruder. Natl. Geneal. Soc. Quart., 1919, v. 8, nos. 1, 2.
Hazelhurst charts. MHS.
†Hist. of Balto. City and Co. Scharf. P. 411. MHS.
†(204 ref.) Hist. of Frederick Co. Williams. MHS; DAR.
Md. families. Culver. Ms. Personal list.
Md. tombstone rec. Md. Geneal. Rec. Com., 1937, Parran, pp. 12, 22. Mss. DAR.
†Med. Annals Md. Cordell. 1903, pp. 504-05. MHS.
Monumental City. Howard. MHS; DAR.
Mt. Olivet Cemetery, Frederick. Md. Geneal. Rec. Com., 1934-35, p. 111. Mss. DAR.
Mt. Paran Pres. churchyard, Harrisonville, Balto. Co. Typed ms. MHS; DAR.
Page family Bible rec. Ms. MHS.
Pedigree of Duncan Keener Brent. Soc. Col. Wars Md. Culver. 1940. MHS; DAR.
Roop geneal. Pamph. MHS.
St. Paul's P. E. churchyard, Berlin, Worcester Co. Hudson. Bd. ms. MHS; DAR. Also: Md. Geneal. Rec. Com., 1937, Mrs. Lines. Mss. DAR.
St. Paul's P. E. churchyard, Kent Co. Md. O. R. Soc. Bull., no. 2, pp. 54-65.
St. Paul's Parish, Balto. V. 1, 2, 3, 4. Mss. MHS.
St. Stephens Parish. Cecilton, Md. MHS; DAR.
St. Thomas' Parish, Balto. Co. Bd. ms. MHS. Also: Md. Geneal. Rec. Com., 1937, pp. 109-82. Mss. DAR.
Somerset Co. Court Book. Tilghman. 1937. Ms. DAR.
U. B. cemetery, Sabillasville. Young. Natl. Geneal. Soc. Quart., Sept., 1938, v. 26, no. 3, p. 61 (to be contd.).
Zion Reformed Church, Hagerstown. Md. Geneal. Rec. Com., 1934-35. Mss. DAR.
See Bradford-Miller.
See Hyatt-Todd-Miller.
Miller, Kent Co. Abr. Compend. Amer. Geneal. Virkus. V. 1, pp. 729, 944. DAR.
Balto., its hist., its people. Hall. V. 2. MHS; DAR.
Mrs. R. Barton, Jr., charts. MHS.
Miller, Va. Balto., its hist., its people. Hall. V. 2. MHS; DAR.
Miller, Andrew. Geneal. data. D. A. R. Mag., Sept., 1935, v. 69, no. 9, p. 566.
Miller, Andrew, Washington Co. Data. D. A. R. Mag., Sept., 1935, v. 69, no. 9, p. 566.
Miller, C. R. Md. Soc., War of 1812, v. 4, no. 329. Ms. MHS.
†**Miller, C. Wilbur.** Men of mark in Md. Johnson. V. 4. DAR; Enoch Pratt Lib.
†**Miller, Daniel.** Balto., hist. and biog. Richardson and Bennett. 1871, pp. 373-76. MHS; DAR.
*Geneal. and mem. encyc. of Md. Spencer. V. 2, pp. 535-36. MHS; DAR.
Miller, George (War of 1812). Glendy churchyard. Patriotic Marylander, v. 2, no. 4, pp. 54-60. MHS; DAR.
Miller, J. H. Md. Soc., War of 1812, v. 3, no. 229. Ms. MHS.
Miller, Jacob, Pa. Cary Geneal. Coll. Ms. MHS.
Miller, L. H. Md. Soc., War of 1812, v. 1, no. 4. Ms. MHS.
†**Miller, Lewis.** Biog. essay. E. Hendrick. (Miller of Md., German origin, pp. 5-19.) N. Y., 1925. MHS.

Miller, Michael, Kent Co. W. A. and S. W. Merritt pedigree charts. Soc. Col. Wars, Md. Johnston. 1905, pp. 67, 150. MHS.
Miller, Mrs. Robert Talbott, Jr. (Mary Edes Hooper). Chart. (Mostly Mass. families.) Col. Dames, Chap. I. MHS.
Miller, Theodore. Ms. MHS.
†**Miller, Theodore K.** Men of mark in Md. Johnson. V. 1. DAR; Enoch Pratt Lib.
Miller Family (1790). Focke Geneal. Coll. Ms. MHS.
Miller Line. Col. and Revolutionary lineages of Amer. 1939, v. 1, pp. 527-29. MHS.
Miller-Jean. Bible rec., Balto. Co., 1760-1845. Md. Geneal. Rec. Com., 1932-33, p. 42. Mss. DAR.
*__Miller-Stabler.__ Chart. DAR.
*__Miller, Mueller.__ Miller or Mueller family and their kin. W. Va. Hist. Mag., v. 2, no. 2, pp. 38-53.
†**Millholland.** Med. Annals Md. Cordell. 1903, pp. 503-04. MHS.
Memoir and geneal. of Md. and Pa. family of Mayer. Mayer. P. 101. MHS; DAR.
Millican. *See* Millingas.
Milligan. Amer. Armory and Blue Book. Matthews. 1911-12, p. 344.
Mrs. Wm. Graham Bowdoin, Jr., chart. MHS.
Cary Geneal. Coll. Ms. MHS.
Dorsey chart. MHS.
Hist. graves of Md. and D. C. Ridgely. MHS.
Millikin and Milligan family chart. Mrs. Charles E. Smith. 1921. DAR.
St. Paul's Parish, Balto. V. 1, 2, 3. Mss. MHS.
St. Stephens Parish, Cecilton, Md. MHS; DAR.
Tompkins chart. MHS.
Turner Geneal. Coll. Ms. MHS.
See Millingas.
Milligan, Miss Sophia Carroll. Chart. Col. Dames, Chap. I. MHS.
Milliken. *See* Millingas.
Millikin. Balto., its hist., its people. Hall. V. 2. MHS; DAR.
*Millikin and Milligan family chart. Mrs. Charles E. Smith. Ohio, 1921. DAR.
Geneal. of Augusta Maitland (Carter) Libby, of Denver, Col., 1704-1933. Ms. MHS.
*__Millingas.__ Hist. of Millingas and Millanges of Saxony and Normandy; comprising geneal. and biog. of their posterity surnamed Milliken, Millikin, Millican, Milligan, Mulliken, Mullikin, 800-1905. 30,000 names. G. T. Ridlon, Sr. Maine, 1907.
Mills. Beauchamp chart. DAR.
Edmund Beauchamp of East. Shore of Md. D. A. R. Mag., April, 1932. V. 66, no. 4, pp. 234-38.
Bible rec., 1832-74, from Bible owned by Amelia J. Collins Truitt (Mrs. Charles R.), Salisbury. Md. Geneal. Rec. Com., 1937-38, p. 157. Mss. DAR.
Dent family of Md. Ms. File case. DAR.
Dorsey and allied families. Ms. MHS.
Makemie Memorial Pres. churchyard, Snow Hill, Worcester Co. Hudson. Bd. ms. MHS; DAR. Also: Md. Geneal. Rec. Com., Mrs. Lines. Mss. DAR.
Md. tombstone rec. Md. Geneal. Rec. Com., 1937, Parran, pp. 19, 22. Mss. DAR.
*Peter Mills and Mary Shirtcliffe Mills, St. Mary's Co., 1635-1935. J. Abell Mills. Elizabeth, N. J., 1936, ltd. ed. MHS; DAR.
Naturalizations in Md., 1666-1765; Laws. Bacon. MHS.
Pocomoke Pres. churchyard, Worcester Co., Hudson. Bd. ms. MHS; DAR.
Rec. of Stepney Parish. MHS; DAR.
St. Mary's P. E. churchyard, Pocomoke, Worcester Co., Hudson. Bd. ms. MHS; DAR.
St. Paul's Parish, Balto. V. 1, 2, 3, 4. Mss. MHS.
*The Sun, Balto., Oct. 16, Dec. 4, 1904.
*Wicomico Co. families. Tilghman. Ms, pp. 97-98, 100-01. DAR.
See Bradley-Mills.
Mills, Ezekiel, Jr. Md. Soc., War of 1812, v. 1, no. 21. Ms. MHS.
Mills, G. A. Md. Soc., War of 1812, v. 1, no. 33. Ms. MHS.
†**Mills, Robert.** (Architect of Natl. Wash. monument.) Daily Monument, Balto., 1816. M. H. Mag., 1935, v. 30, pp. 257-71.
Mills, Roland Yearly. Md. Soc., War of 1812, v. 3, no. 297. Ms. MHS.
*__Mills Family.__ Early marriages in U. S. W. M. Clemens. 1916.
†**Miltenberger.** Balto., hist. and biog. Richardson and Bennett. 1871, pp. 377-80. MHS; DAR.
†Med. Annals Md. Cordell. 1903, p. 505. MHS.
Monumental City. Howard. MHS; DAR.
Milton, Va. Col. families of U. S. A. Mackenzie. V. 2. MHS; DAR.
Mince. *See* Shaw-Mince.
Minis. Col. Nicholas Duvall family rec. Price. Bd. ms. MHS.
Minis, John Livingston. Pedigree chart. Soc. Col. Wars, Md. Johnston. 1905, p. 71. MHS.
Minor. Cary Geneal. Coll. Ms. MHS.
Pedigree of Duncan Keener Brent. Soc. Col. Wars Md. Culver. 1940. MHS; DAR.
*Pennington Papers. Ms. MHS.
*__Minor,__ Va. The Sun, Balto., April 23, 1905.
Minors. Lineage of Meriwethers and Minors. Minor Meriwether. St. Louis, Mo., 1895.
Minshall. Old Somerset. Torrence. MHS; DAR.
Somerset Co. Court Book. Tilghman. 1937. Ms. DAR.
Minton. Hazelhurst charts. MHS.
Mirch. *See* Murch.
See Newman-Mirch.
†**Mish, Frank W.** Men of mark in Md. Johnson. V. 2. DAR; Enoch Pratt Lib.
Mister. Tombstone rec. of Dorchester Co. Jones. DAR.
Mitchel. *See* Mitchell.
Mitchel, Mitchell. Mitchel, Mitchell Family in Md., 1684. H. H. Simms. 4 ms. bks. MHS.
Mitchell. Geneal., Mag. Amer. Ancestry, N. Y., 1916, v. 7, no. 6.
Geneal. of Augusta Maitland (Carter) Libby of Denver, Col., 1704-1933. Ms. MHS.
Graveyard on late Henry Mitchell's plantation, near Bowie, Prince George Co. Md. O. R. Soc. Bull., no. 1, p. 52.
†Hist. of Balto. City and Co. Scharf. P. 901. MHS.

Mitchell. Marriage rec., 1781–1892, Harford Co. Md. Geneal. Rec. Com., 1934–35, p. 108. DAR.
Md. families. Culver. Ms. Personal list.
Md. Geneal. Rec. Com., 1932–33, pp. 208–09. Mss. DAR.
†Med. Annals Md. Cordell. 1903, pp. 506–07. MHS.
Mitchell family. Mrs. G. F. Libby. Ms. MHS.
Old Somerset. Torrence. MHS; DAR.
Patriotic Md. Md. Soc. of S. A. R., 1930. MHS; DAR.
St. Barnabas P. E. churchyard. Typed ms. MHS; DAR.
St. Paul's Parish, Balto. V. 1, 2, 3, 4. Mss. MHS.
Stump family of Cecil and Harford Cos. Pamph. MHS.
Somerset Co. Court Book. Tilghman. 1937. Ms. DAR.
William and Mary Quart., 1st series, v. 27, p. 299.
See Mitchel.
See Tipton Murray-Mitchell.
†**Mitchell,** Charles Co. Chesapeake Bay Country. Earle. P. 116. MHS.
†**Mitchell, Dr. Abram,** Cecil Co. Md. Geneal. Rec. Com., 1937–38, p. 44. Mss. DAR.
Mitchell, Nicholas, Prince George Co. Will proved Aug. 13, 1808. D. A. R. Mag., Aug. 1927, v. 61, no. 8, p. 607.
Mitchell, R. Levis, M.D. Md. Soc., War of 1812, v. 3, no. 297. Ms. MHS.
Mitchell Family. Hist. of Cecil Co. Johnston. P. 495. MHS; DAR.
*Old Kent. Hanson. P. 119. MHS; DAR.
Mitchell-Smith-Fowke Families, Md., Va. and Ky. With geneal. Gerard Fowke. Bd. Ms., 442 pp. MHS.
Mitchell, Mitchel. Col. families of U. S. A. Mackenzie. V. 6, p. 60. MHS; DAR.
*See Woodruff. Semmes Geneal. Coll. Ms. MHS.
***Mitchell, Mitchel, Family.** Hist. of Cecil Co. Johnston. Pp. 495–507. MHS; DAR.
Mitcheson. St. Paul's Parish, Balto. V. 1. Mss. MHS.
Mittag. Hagerstown tombstone inscriptions. Gruder. Natl. Geneal. Soc. Quart., 1919, v. 8, nos. 1, 2.
Zion Reformed Church, Hagerstown. Md. Geneal. Rec. Com., 1934–35. Mss. DAR.
Mittelkauff. *See* Middlekauff.
Moale. Barroll in Great Britain and Amer. Barroll. MHS.
*Bartow geneal. Bartow. P. 145. Lib. Cong.; MHS.
Bible rec. Ms. MHS.
†Biog. cyc. of rep. men of Md. and D. C. P. 277. MHS; DAR.
Curzon family. Pleasants. MHS.
Deford chart. MHS.
Descendants of Valentine Hollingsworth, Sr. Stewart. MHS; DAR.
†Garrison Church. Allen. P. 144. MHS; DAR.
Greenway Mss. Geneal. Coll. Binder's titles. Taylor, nos. 1 and 2. MHS.
Hist. Graves of Md. and D. C. Ridgely. MHS.
R. C. Hoffman pedigree chart. Soc. Col. Wars, Md. Johnston. 1905, p. 40. MHS.
In rural churchyard. Day, Aug. 13, 1882. Newsp. clipp. MHS.
Lehr chart. MHS.
Moale family. J. H. Moale. Va. Mag. Hist. and Biog., v. 25, p. 444.
No Name Mag., v. 2, pp. 129–44. MHS.
Rogers Coll. Ms. MHS.
Pedigree of Francis Joseph Baldwin. Soc. Col. Wars Md. Culver. 1940. MHS; DAR.
Pedigree of Wm. Winchester Eareckson. Soc. Col. Wars Md. Culver. 1940. MHS; DAR.
Pedigree of Arthur Lafayette Jones. Soc. Col. Wars Md. Culver. 1940. MHS; DAR.
Pedigree of Wm. Handy Collins Vickers. Soc. Col. Wars Md. Culver. 1940. MHS; DAR.
W. de C. Poultney pedigree chart. Soc. Col. Wars, Md. Johnston. 1905, p. 86. MHS.
St. Paul's Parish, Balto. V. 1, 2, 3, 4. Mss. MHS.
Townley geneal. chart. MHS.
Moale, William Armistead. Pedigree charts, plates 1 and 2. Soc. Col. Wars, Md. Johnston. 1905, pp. 72–73, 150. MHS.
Moale Family (1739). Focke Geneal. Coll. Mss. MHS.
Moale-Croxall-North. Chart photos., complete in 2 sheets. Cary Geneal. Coll. Ms. MHS.
***Mobberly.** Frederick Co. families. Markell. Ms. Personal list.
†**Moberbley.** Med. Annals Md. Cordell. 1903, p. 508. MHS.
Mobley. M. E. Church burial ground, Laytonsville, Montgomery Co. Md. Geneal. Rec. Com., 1934–35, pp. 69–82. Mss. DAR.
Mobray. Trinity Church cemetery, Dorchester Co. Md. O. R. Soc. Bull., no. 3, pp. 42–52.
†**Moffat.** Men of mark in Md. Johnson. V. 2. DAR; Enoch Pratt Lib.
See Moffit.
***Moffet Family.** Hist. and rec. E. R. Moffett and C. A. Melvin. DAR.
Moffett. Bible rec., Kent Co., 1769–1865. Md. Geneal. Rec. Com., 1932–33, pp. 323–24. Mss. DAR.
Bible rec. Upper Penins. East. Shore. Pp. 102, 232–33. MHS; DAR.
Still Pond cemetery, Kent Co. Md. O. R. Soc., v. 2. MHS.
Moffett Family. Moffett family. Ellen R. Moffett, Chestertown, Md., and Cora A. Melvin, Newport News, Va. Mss. Bk; DAR.
Moffit. Md. tombstone rec. Md. Geneal. Rec. Com., 1937, Parran, p. 4. Mss. DAR.
Moffitt, Moffat. St. Paul's Parish, Balto. V. 2, 4. Mss. MHS.
Mohler, Isaac Wimbert, Jr. Md. Soc., War of 1812, v. 3, no. 257. Ms. MHS.
†**Mohlhenrick.** Men of mark in Md. Johnson. V. 3. DAR; Enoch Pratt Lib.
***Mohr Family,** East Shore of Md. Wilson Mss. Coll., no. 52. MHS.
Mohun. Dorsey chart. MHS.
Moizne. Naturalizations in Md., 1666–1765; Laws. Bacon. MHS.
***Moles.** Wicomico Co. families. Tilghman. Ms., p. 32. DAR.
Moleston. Van Dyke-Johns-Montgomery-Manlove chart. Cary Geneal. Coll. Ms. MHS.
Mollihorne. Centenary of Catholicity in Ky. Webb. 1884. MHS.
Moncure. Gillett-Miller families. Ms. MHS.
Va. geneal. Hayden. MHS; DAR.

Monette. Amer. Armory and Blue Book. Matthews. 1911–12, pp. 14, 45.
Lineage Bk. Order of Washington, p. 184. MHS; DAR.
Lineage Bks., Natl. Soc. of Daughters of Amer. Col. v. 3, p. 223; v. 4, p. 145. MHS; DAR.
See Monette.
See Monnet.
Monette, Monnet. Col. families of U. S. A. Mackenzie. V. 3; v. 4. MHS; DAR.
Monette, Monnette. Abr. Compend. Amer. Geneal. Virkus. V. 3, p. 619. DAR; v. 4, p. 604. MHS.
Money. Monnet family geneal. Monette. P. 394. MHS.
St. Stephens Parish, Cecilton, Md. MHS; DAR.
Mong. Diffenderfer family, arrived in Phila., 1727. Ms. File case, DAR.
***Monius** or **Monyn.** Pennington Papers. Ms. MHS.
Monius, Monyn, Waldesharre, Kent, Eng. Pedigree. Ms. MHS.
†**Monkur.** Med. Annals Md. Cordell. 1903, p. 508. MHS.
†**Monmonier.** Med. Annals Md. Cordell. 1903, p. 508. MHS.
Monnet. N. Y. Geneal. and Biog. Rec., July, 1915, v. 46, no. 3, p. 304.
***Monnet, Monnette** (sometimes spelled **Money**). Family geneal.; emphasis of noble Huguenot heritage. O. E. Monette. Los Angeles, C. E. Bireley Co., 1911. MHS.
Monnett. Amer. families. Geneal. and heraldic. Amer. Hist. Soc., N. Y., pp. 388–96. DAR.
*Lineage Bk., Daughters of Amer. Col., v. 3, p. 223. MHS; DAR.
Monnette, M. J. Abr. Compend. Amer. Geneal. Virkus. V. 1, p. 397. DAR.
***Monroe.** Burke's landed gentry. 1939. MHS.
Md. ancestry of James Monroe. Monroe Johnson. M. H. Mag., 1928, v. 23, pp. 193–95.
†Med. Annals Md. Cordell. 1903, p. 509. MHS.
†Monroe family. Letter to Mary Mason from Sarah Monroe. M. H. Mag., 1934, v. 29, pp. 245–52.
Monroe, Annapolis. Abr. Compend. Amer. Geneal. Virkus. V. 1, p. 31.
Monroe, James. William and Mary Quart., 1st series, v. 4, p. 272.
***Montague.** Geneal. of Peter Montague of Nansemond Co., Va., and his descendants. 1621–1893. G. W. Montague. (Incl. Md. Montagues.) Amherst, Mass., 1904. Lib. Cong.
Warfield and Montague; pedigree of Bessie Wallis Warfield Simpson. F. B. Culver and W. B. Marye. 1937. Ms. MHS.
Montague, Va. Howard-Montague-Warfield geneal. chart. Culver and Marye. MHS.
***Montell.** Bartow geneal. Bartow. P. 154 Lib. Cong.; MHS.
St. Paul's Parish, Balto. V. 3. Mss. MHS.
Montgomery. Amer. Armory and Blue Book. Matthews. 1911–12, p. 114.
*Ancestors of James Montgomery and descendants of James and Lydia Montgomery. J. M. Riddell. 1938, pamph., MHS; DAR.
Ances. rec. and portraits. Col. Dames of Amer., 1910, v. 1, p. 240. MHS; DAR.
Chart of Com. John Rodgers. DAR.
Descendants of James and Lydia Montgomery. J. F. Montgomery. 1933, pamph. MHS.
*Frederick Co. families. Markell. Ms. Personal list.
†Med. Annals Md. Cordell. 1903, p. 509. MHS.
Montgomery Family Mag. Wm. M. Clemens, publisher, N. Y., 1915. MHS.
Naturalizations in Md., 1666–1765; Laws. Bacon. MHS.
O'Daniel-Hamilton ancestry in Md. and Ky. O'Daniel. Pp. 37–48. MHS.
St. Paul's Parish, Balto. V. 2, 3, 4. Mss. MHS.
Sherburne chart. MHS.
*The Sun, Balto , Aug. 16, 1903.
Williamson Bible rec. Ms. MHS.
See Van Dyke-Johns-Montgomery-Manlove.
Montgomery, Pa. Cary Geneal. Coll. Ms. MHS.
Cotton chart. MHS.
***Montgomery Family.** Geneal. N. Y., Jan. 27, 1912, v. 1, no. 4. MHS.
Montgomery-Love-Johnson. Harford Co. Hist. Soc. Mss. Coll. JHU.
Monyn. *See* Monius.
Moody. Mt. Carmel burial ground, Unity, Montgomery Co. Md. Geneal. Rec. Com., 1934–35, pp. 85, 221–22. Mss. DAR.
Port. and biog. rec. of Sixth Cong. Dist. of Md. P. 609.
St. Paul's Parish, Balto. V. 2. Mss. MHS.
Moody-Woodall. Bible rec., Kent Co. Md. Geneal. Rec. Com., 1933–34, p. 221. Mss. DAR.
Moolson. Somerset Co. Court Book. Tilghman. 1937. Ms. DAR.
Moon. Harford Co. Hist. Soc. Mss. Coll. JHU.
***Moon Family,** East. Shore of Md. Wilson Mss. Coll., no. 52; no. 81; no. 126. MHS.
***Mooney.** Old Kent. Hanson. P. 277. MHS; DAR.
Moor. Rec. of Stepney Parish. MHS; DAR.
West. Nottingham Cemetery. M. H. Mag., 1923, v. 18, p. 55.
See More.
Moore. All Hallow's P. E. churchyard, Snow Hill, Worcester Co. Hudson. Bd. Ms. MHS; DAR. Also: Md. Geneal. Rec. Com., 1935–36, p. 24. Mss. DAR.
Amer. Armory and Blue Book. Matthews. 1911–12, p. 131.
Ances. rec. and portraits. Col. Dames of Amer., 1910, p. 396. MHS; DAR.
*Ancestors and descendants of Andrew Moore. J. A. M. Passmore. Phila., 1897.
Bond chart. MHS.
Bowie-Claggett chart. MHS.
Col. families of U. S. A. Mackenzie. V. 3. MHS; DAR.
*Frederick Co. families. Markell. Ms. Personal list.
Griffith geneal. Griffith. MHS; DAR.
Hist. of Montgomery Co. Boyd. P. 90. DAR.
Hist. of west. Md. Scharf. V. 1, p. 681; v. 2, p. 967. MHS; DAR.
Hudson-Lloyd-Hutchinson-Hudson-Parke families. Glenn. Pp. 13, 15, 16. MHS; DAR.
Jenkins-Courtney chart. MHS.
Lineage Bks., Natl. Soc. of Daughters of Amer. Col., v. 1, p. 83. MHS; DAR.

Moore. Makemie Memorial Pres. churchyard, Snow Hill, Worcester Co. Hudson. Bd. ms. MHS; DAR. Also: Md. Geneal. Rec. Com., Mrs. Lines. Mss. DAR.
Md. gleanings in Eng. Wills. M. H. Mag., 1908, v. 3, no. 2.
McClellan chart. MHS.
†Med. Annals Md. Cordell. 1903, p. 509. MHS.
M. E. churchyard, Snow Hill, Worcester Co. Hudson. Bd. ms. MHS; DAR.
*Wm. Henry Moore and his ancestry, with accounts of Moore family in Amer. Col., 1620–1730. L. E. and Anne L. de Forest. Henry Moore, Charles Co., pp. 247–48; Mordecai Moore, Anne Arundel Co., pp. 366–68. N. Y., De Forest Pub. Co., 1934, ltd. ed. MHS.
Orme geneal. chart. MHS.
Patriotic Md. Md. Soc. of S. A. R., 1930. MHS; DAR.
Patriotic Marylander, 1914, v. 3, no. 1, p. 225. MHS; DAR.
*Pennington Papers. Ms. MHS.
Portrait and biog. rec. of Harford and Cecil Cos. 1897, pp. 198, 294, 510. MHS; DAR.
Price ancestral data (maternal). Bd. Ms. MHS.
Side lights on Md. hist. Richardson. V. 2, p. 397. MHS; DAR.
St. Paul's Parish, Balto. V. 1, 2, 3, 4. Mss. MHS.
Somerset Co. Court Book. Tilghman. 1937. Ms. DAR.
*The Sun, Balto., Feb. 19, 1905; May 27 (Va.), 1906.
Thomas-Chew-Lawrence. Thomas. MHS.
Turner Geneal. Coll. Ms. MHS.
U. B. cemetery, Sabillasville. Young. Natl. Geneal. Soc. Quart., Sept., 1938, v. 26, no. 3, p. 61 (to be contd.).
*Wilson Mss. Coll., no. 52; no. 126. MHS.
See Hill-Moore.
See More.
See Riall-Rider-Moore.

Moore, Anne Arundel Co. Col. families of Amer. Lawrence. V. 15, p. 169. MHS.

Moore, Sandy Springs. See Appleton, W. Hyde. Abr. Compend. Amer. Geneal. Virkus. V. 1, p. 346. DAR.

Moore, Cecil Co. Sharpless family geneal. Cope. P. 1190. MHS; DAR.

***Moore,** Charles Co. Burke's landed gentry. 1939. MHS.

Moore, Md. and Va. Provincial Councillors of Pa. Keith. 1883, p. 74. DAR.

Moore, Prince George Co. Morris family of Phila. Moon. V. 2, p. 426. MHS.

Moore, Daniel, Washington Co. Will, dated 1792. DAR.

Moore, Henry. Abr. Compend. Amer. Geneal. Virkus. V. 1, p. 500. DAR.

Moore, John. Marriage contract of John Moore and Hannah Hibberd of Frederick Co., dated 1796. DAR.

***Moore, Mordecai.** Married Deborah Lloyd, Sept. 12, 1704, p. 15. [Hill, p. 20.] Geneal. Lloyd-Pemberton-Hutchinson-Hudson-Parke. DAR.

Moore, Dr. Mordecai, Anne Arundel Co. Col. families of Amer. Lawrence. V. 15, p. 150. MHS.
Side lights on Md. hist. Richardson. V. 2, p. 397. MHS; DAR.

Moore, Nicholas Ruxton. Patriotic Marylander, v. 3, no. 4, pp. 225–29. MHS; DAR.

Moore, Robert. Glendy churchyard. Patriotic Marylander, v. 2, no. 4, pp. 54–60. MHS; DAR.

Moore, Scott (War of 1812). Glendy churchyard. Patriotic Marylander, v. 2, no. 4, pp. 54–60. MHS; DAR.

Moore, Capt. Thomas (1746–1820). D. C. Geneal. Rec. Com., 1937, v. 35, pp. 128–30. Typed, bd. DAR.

Moore, Lieut. Zedekiah (Md. line). Last bloodshed of Revolution. Culver. M. H. Mag., 1910, v. 5, pp. 329–38.

Moore-Belt. Bible rec. Md. Geneal. Rec. Com., 1926–27, v. 2, p. 23. DAR.

Moore-Lloyd. Moore (Dr. Mordecai) Lloyd marriage, 1704. Merion in Welsh tract. Glenn. P. 351.

Moore-Orrick. Graves in Old St. Paul's P. E. cemetery, Balto.

***Moore, More.** Wicomico Co. families. Tilghman. Ms., pp. 54–55, 88, 96–97, 101, 108–09, 112, 120, 124. DAR.

Moorehead. Col. families of U. S. A. Mackenzie. V. 4, p. 385. MHS; DAR.
U. B. cemetery, Sabillasville. Young. Natl. Geneal. Soc. Quart., Sept., 1938, v. 26, no. 3, p. 61 (to be contd.).

†Moores. Med. Annals Md. Cordell. 1903, pp. 509–10. MHS.

Moores, Harford Co. Col. families of U. S. A. Mackenzie. V. 2, p. 440. MHS; DAR.

†Moran. Med. Annals Md. Cordell. 1903, p. 510. MHS.

†Morawetz. Med. Annals Md. Cordell. 1903, p. 510. MHS.

Mordecai. Myer-Hays-Mordecai family rec. Ms. MHS.
Rogers Coll. Ms. MHS.

Mordical. St. Paul's Parish, Balto. V. 2. Mss. MHS.

More. Rec. of Stepney Parish. MHS; DAR.
See Moore.

More, Moor, Moore. St. Stephens Parish, Cecilton, Md. MHS; DAR.

Morehead. Southerland-Latham and allied families. Voorhees. Bd. Ms. MHS.
See Cox-Morehead.

Morelock. Babylon family. Duttera. P. 34. Ms. MHS.

Morfit. Samuel Carpenter of Phila. Carpenter. P. 232. MHS.
See Bender-Fisk-Morfit.

Morgain. St. Stephens Parish, Cecilton, Md. MHS; DAR.

Morgan, Anne Arundel Co. tombstone inscriptions. Ms. DAR.
Brooks chart. MHS.
Frederick Co. tombstone inscriptions. Gruder. Natl. Geneal. Soc. Quart., 1919, v. 8, nos. 1, 2.
Hist. of Harford Co. Preston. MHS; DAR.
Mrs. J. F. Lee chart. MHS.
Lee-Wilson chart. Cary Geneal. Coll. Ms. MHS.
Md. families. Culver. Ms. Personal list.
†Med. Annals Md. Cordell. 1903, p. 511. MHS.
†Men of mark in Md. Johnson. V. 1; v. 4. DAR; Enoch Pratt Lib.

*Francis Morgan, early Va. Burgess, and some of his descendants. A. Noble Sines; from notes of Wm. Owen N. Scott. Savannah, Ga., Braid & Hutton, Inc., March, 1920. MHS.
Dr. James Dudley Morgan memorial. Columbia Hist. Soc. Rec., 1920, v. 23, p. 215.
Patriotic Md. Md. Soc. of S. A. R., 1930. MHS; DAR.
Pedigree of Pleasants Pennington. Soc. Col. Wars Md. Culver. 1940. MHS; DAR.
*Pennington Papers. Ms. MHS.
Portrait and biog. rec. of East. Shore of Md. 1898, p. 880. MHS.
St. Paul's Parish, Balto. V. 1, 2. Mss. MHS.
St. Stephens Parish, Cecilton, Md. MHS; DAR.
See Pope-Morgan.
Morgan, Balto. Co. De Ford chart. MHS.
Morgan, Cecil Co. Bible rec. Upper Penins. East. Shore., p. 186–91. MHS; DAR.
Morgan, Kent Co. McH. Howard pedigree chart. Soc. Col. Wars, Md. Johnston. 1905, pp. 42, 150. MHS.
Morgan, Pa. and W. Va. Md. Geneal. Rec. Com., v. 3, pp. 52–55. DAR.
Morgan, John Hurst. Pedigree. Soc. Col. Wars Md. Culver. 1940. MHS; DAR.
Md. Soc., War of 1812, v. 1, no. 106. Ms. MHS.
Morgan, Philip Sidney. Pedigree. Soc. Col. Wars Md. Culver. 1940. MHS; DAR.
Morgan, Tilghman Vickers. Pedigree. Soc. Col. Wars Md. Culver. 1940. MHS; DAR.
***Morgan Family.** M. H. Mag., 1907, v. 2, pp. 372–74.
Morgan Line. Col. and Revolutionary lineages of Amer. 1939, v. 1, p. 501. MHS.
Morison. Barton-Morison chart. MHS.
*Family of Nathaniel and Mary Ann (Hopkins) Morison. Leaflet. MHS.
†Med. Annals Md. Cordell. 1903, p. 511. MHS.
†Memorial to Nathaniel Holmes Morison, first provost of Peabody Institute. (Born in N. H., 1815; died in Balto., 1890.) Balto., Isaac Friedenwald Co. Enoch Pratt Lib.
Mrs. A. R. Rogers chart. MHS.
†Morison, N. H. Balto., hist. and biog. Richardson and Bennett. 1871. Pp. 381–85. MHS; DAR.
Morison, Mrs. Ernest N. (Priscilla Ridgely White). Chart. Col. Dames, Chap. I. MHS.
Morison, Mrs. Robert Brown (Elizabeth Hawkins Williams). Chart. Col. Dames, Chap. I. MHS.
Mrs. R. Barton, Jr., chart. MHS.
Morison, Sidney Buchanan. Chart. Col. Dames, Chap. I. MHS.
Mrs. R. Barton, Jr., chart. MHS.
Morison Line. Mrs. R. Barton, Jr., charts. MHS.
Morley Line. Gaither, Va. and Md. Col. and Revolutionary families of Phila. Jordan. 1933, v. 1, pp. 144–67.
Morling, F. L. Md. Soc., War of 1812, v. 1, no. 14. Ms. MHS.
Morningstar. Lehman family in Md. Lehman. 1935, pamph., pp. 25, 43. MHS; DAR.
Morphet, Kent Co. Data. D. A. R. Mag., v. 71, no. 11, pp. 102–04.
Morray. Mrs. J. F. Lee chart. MHS.
Mrs. E. C. Venable chart. MHS.
See Murray.
***Morrel.** Wicomico Co. families. Tilghman. Ms., p. 116. DAR.
Morrell. Lambdin chart. MHS.
See Merrill.
Morrice. St. Paul's Parish, Balto. V. 1. Mss. MHS.
Morris. Ancestry of Rosalie Morris Johnson. Johnson. 1905. MHS; DAR.
Balto., its hist., its people. Hall. V. 3. MHS; DAR.
†Bench and bar of Md. Sams and Riley. 1901, v. 2, p. 555. Lib. Cong.; MHS; Peabody Lib.
Bible rec. from Bible in possession of Mrs. John E. Morris, Chestertown. Md. Geneal. Rec. Com., 1937–38, p. 119. Mss. DAR.
Bible rec. Upper Penins. East. Shore, pp. 222–29. MHS; DAR.
Mrs. Howard Bruce chart. MHS.
Cary Geneal. Coll. Ms. MHS.
Coale chart. MHS.
Miss M. W. Davis chart. MHS.
De Ford chart. MHS.
Descendants of Valentine Hollingsworth, Sr. Stewart. MHS; DAR.
Extracts from Parish register, Bardados. Morris family of Phila. Moon. V. 5, p. 307. MHS.
†Geneal. and mem. encyc. of Md. Spencer. V. 1, pp. 71–74. MHS; DAR.
Mrs. C. C. Hall chart. MHS.
Husband and allied families. Ms. MHS.
†In memorian, Thomas J. Morris, 1837–1912, sometime U. S. Dist. Judge for Dist. of Md. Balto., Norman T. A. Munder & Co. Enoch Pratt Lib.
†Life and reminiscences of old Luthern minister. Rev. John G. Morris, (born in York, Pa., 1803; died in Lutherville, Md., 1895; pastor of First Lutheran Church, Balto., 1827–60). Phila., Lutheran Pub. Soc., 1896. Enoch Pratt Lib.
Lineage Bks., Natl. Soc. of Daughters of Amer. Col., v. 3, p. 58. MHS; DAR.
Md. families. Culver. Ms. Personal list.
†Med. Annals Md. Cordell. 1903, pp. 511–12. MHS.
*Morris family of Phila.; descendants of Anthony Morris, 1654–1721. R. C. Moon. 5 vols. Index of names for v. 1, 2, 3, see v. 3, p. 1133; v. 4, 5, see v. 5, p. 431. Phila., 1898, 1908, 1909. MHS.
Pedigree of Morris Gregg. Soc. Col. Wars Md. Culver. 1940. MHS; DAR.
Pedigree of Charles Morris Howard. Soc. Col. Wars Md. Culver. 1940. MHS; DAR.
Mrs. E. W. Poe chart. MHS.
Rec. of Stepney Parish. MHS; DAR.
St. Paul's Parish, Balto. V. 1, 2, 3. Mss. MHS.
Samuel Carpenter of Phila. Carpenter. P. 158. MHS.
Selden chart. MHS.
Somerset Co. Court Book. Tilghman. 1937. Ms. DAR.
†Story of Robert Morris (1734–1806). Md. O. R. Soc., v. 3, p. 120.
Summers-Jones-Gunby-Morris Bible rec. Md. Geneal. Rec. Com., 1937–38, pp. 142–46. Mss. DAR.
*The Sun, Balto. Dec. 10, 17, 1905.
Mrs. E. C. Venable chart. MHS.
Whitehead chart. MHS.

***Morris.** Wicomico Co. families. Tilghman. Ms., pp. 38, 40, 42–45, 56, 86, 98–99, 101–06. DAR.
Mrs. G. H. Williams, Jr., chart. MHS.
Worcester Co. militia, 1794. Covington. P. 156. MHS.
See Hall-Morris-White.
†Morris, Frederick Co. Biog. cyc. of rep. men of Md. and D. C. P. 649. MHS; DAR.
***Morris,** Oxford, Md. Lineage Bk., Daughters of Amer. Col., v. 3, p. 59. MHS; DAR.
Morris, Pa. Abr. Compend. Amer. Geneal. Virkus. V. 1, pp. 267–69. DAR.
***Morris,** Phila. Pedigree 1, 2, 3. Coat of arms. Burke's landed gentry. 1939. MHS.
Morris, Worcester Co. Cary Geneal. Coll. Ms. MHS.
Round chart. Cary Geneal. Coll. Ms. MHS.
Morris, Anthony, Pa. Pedigree of Lee Cummins Cary. Soc. Col. Wars Md. Culver. 1940. MHS; DAR.
Pedigree of Anthony Morris Tyson. Soc. Col. Wars Md. Culver. 1940. MHS; DAR.
Morris, Isaac (born in Balto., 1797). Notes. D. A. R. Mag., v. 71, no. 8, p. 763.
†Morris, John B. Balto., hist. and biog. Richardson and Bennett. 1871, pp. 387–89. MHS; DAR.
†Morris, John Gottlieb. Men of mark in Md. Johnson. V. 4. DAR; Enoch Pratt Lib.
Morris, Robert. Finances of Amer. Revolution. C. H. Hart. Phila., 1877.
†Morris, Robt. (1711–50). Hist. of Talbot Co. Tilghman. V. 1, pp. 66–83. MHS; DAR.
†Morris, T. Hollingsworth. Men of mark in Md. Johnson. V. 4. DAR; Enoch Pratt Lib.
***Morris Family,** Snow Hill, Md. Encyc. of Amer. biog. Amer. Hist. Soc., N. Y., v. 9, p. 224. MHS.
Morris Line. A. M. and M. S. Tyson pedigree chart. Soc. Col. Wars Md. Johnston. 1905, p. 116. MHS.
Morris Lineage. Descendants of Col. Thomas White. Morris. Pp. 76, 178. MHS.
Morris-Lokey. Wicomico Co. families. Bible rec. Ms. DAR.
Morris-Nixon. Geneal. reg. Mervine. Pp. 28–38. MHS.
Morrison. Bible rec., 1843-1913. Md. Geneal. Rec. Com., 1932–33, v. 5. DAR.
Bond chart. MHS.
†Hist. of Balto. City and Co. Scharf. P. 665. MHS.
†Med. Annals Md. Cordell. 1903, p. 512. MHS.
St. Paul's Parish, Balto. V. 1, 2, 4. Mss. MHS.
Morrison, Iowa. Col. families of U. S. A. Mackenzie. V. 6, pp. 360–68 (showing maternal line Burgess, Md.). MHS.
†Morrison, George C. Men of mark in Md. Johnson. V. 2. DAR; Enoch Pratt Lib.
Morrison-Bruce. Bible rec., 1843–1913. Md. Geneal. Rec. Com., 1932–33, p. 68. Mss. DAR.
Morrison-Morris. Morris family of Phila. Moon. V. 2, pp. 648, 814. MHS.
Morriss. Wicomico Co. families. Bible rec. Ms. DAR.
†Morrow. Geneal. and mem. encyc. of Md. Spencer. V. 1, p. 179. MHS; DAR.
St. Paul's Parish, Balto. V. 1, 2, 3. Mss. MHS.
†Morse. Life of Samuel F. B. Morse, 1791–1872. S. J. Prime. (Morse, inventor of telegraph; first message sent over line from Balto., to Wash., D. C., May 24, 1844.) 1875. MHS.
Letter, 1843. M. H. Mag., 1939; v. 34, p. 40.
Morsell. Lambdin chart. MHS.
Plummer family. A. P. H. Ms. MHS.
Talbott of "Poplar Knowle." Shirk. MHS; DAR.
Morson-Scott-Payne, Va. William and Mary Quart., 1st series, v. 2, p. 87.
Mortimer. See Maynard family. Focke Geneal. Coll. Mss. MHS.
Morton. Carne and allied family notes. Coues. Ms. MHS.
Data. Daniel Morton. St. Joseph, Mo., pamph. MHS.
Done Bible rec. Ms. MHS.
*Family tree of Daniel Morton, M.D., St. Joseph, Mo. Chart and Ms. by author. 1920. MHS.
*Frederick Co. families. Markell. Ms. Personal list.
*Mortons and their kin. Geneal. and source book. 2 vols. D. Morton, M.D. V. 1, the Mortons; v. 2, the Mortons' kin (43 families). St. Joseph, Mo., 1920. 1 copy, Lib. Cong.; 1copy, New berry Lib., Chicago; 1 copy, to be placed in Public Lib., Kansas City.
Mrs. Talbot T. Speer chart. MHS.
St. Paul's Parish, Balto. V. 2. 4. Mss. MHS.
Morton, Va. Family tree of Daniel Morton, M.D., St. Joseph, Mo. 1920. Chart and Mss. MHS.
Morton, John Stewart. Pedigree. (Aston and Cocke rec. of Va.) Soc. Col. Wars Md. Culver. 1940. MHS; DAR.
Morton, Sam'l. Packwood, Jr. Pedigree. (Aston and Cocke rec. of Va.) Soc. Col. Wars Md. Culver. 1940. MHS; DAR.
Moseley. Balto., its hist., its people. Hall. V. 3. MHS; DAR.
***Moseley,** of Va., Lineage Bk., Daughters of Founders and Patriots, v. 18, pp. 135–36. MHS; DAR.
***Mosely.** Wicomico Co. families. Tilghman. Ms., p. 100. DAR.
Moser. U. B. cemetery, Sabillasville. Young. Natl. Geneal. Soc. Quart., Sept., 1938, v. 26, no. 3, p. 61 (to be contd.).
Young Bible rec. Ms. MHS.
†Mosher. Med. Annals Md. 1903, p. 513. MHS.
St. John's R. C. Church cemetery, Montgomery Co. Md. Geneal. Rec. Com., 1926, p. 27. Mss. DAR.
†Mossman. Med. Annals Md. Cordell. 1903, p. 513. MHS.
†Motter. Bench and bar of Md. Sams and Riley. 1901, v. 2, p. 622. Lib. Cong.; MHS; Peabody Lib.
Hagerstown tombstone inscriptions. Gruder. Natl. Geneal. Soc. Quart., 1919, v. 8, nos. 1, 2.
Hist. sketch of P. F. Eichelberger. Eichelberger.
†Hist. of Frederick Co. Williams. MHS; DAR.
†Med. Annals Md. Cordell. 1903, p. 513. MHS.
Mrs. Sherlock Swann chart. MHS.
Mottingly. Dorsey papers. Ms. MHS.

Mounce. St. Stephens Parish, Cecilton, Md. MHS; DAR.
Mt. Lubentia. *See* Magruder.
Mountain. *See* Evans-Mountain.
Mounts. Data. M. H. Mag., 1939, v. 34, no. 2, p. 204.
Naturalizations in Md., 1666–1765; Laws. Bacon. MHS.
Mounts-Howard. M. H. Mag., 1939, v. 34, no. 3, p. 304.
†**Mountz.** Med. Annals Md. Cordell. 1903, p. 513. MHS.
***Mowbray.** Frederick Co. families. Markell. Ms. Personal list.
Pattison wills. Md. Geneal. Rec. Com., 1929, pp. 7–42; 1930–31. Mss. DAR.
†**Mowell.** Hist. of Balto. City and Co. Scharf. P. 879. MHS.
Mowton. St. Paul's Parish, Balto. V. 2. Mss. MHS.
Moxley. Data. D. A. R. Mag., Nov. 1935, v. 69, no. 11, p. 681.
Mudd. Centenary of Catholicity in Ky. Webb. 1884. MHS.
Col. families of U. S. A. Mackenzie. V. 2. MHS; DAR.
†Life of Dr. Samuel A. Mudd. By daughter Nettie Mudd. (It was at his home, near Bryantown, Charles Co., that Dr. Mudd set the leg of John Wilkes Booth, night he assasinated President Lincoln, in Ford's Theater, Wash., D. C.; 1865.) N. Y. & Wash.; Neale Pub. Co., 1906. MHS; Enoch Pratt Lib.
Pedigree of Edwin Austin Baughman. Soc. Col. Wars Md. Culver. 1940. MHS; DAR.
***Mudd,** Charles Co. Burke's landed gentry. 1939. MHS.
Mudd, St. Mary's Co. Abr. Compend. Amer. Geneal. Virkus. V. 1, p. 737. DAR.
Mueller. *See* Miller.
Mugenbourg. Naturalizations in Md., 1666–1765; Laws. Bacon. MHS.
Muir. Christ P. E. Church cemetery, Cambridge. Steele. 1936. MHS; DAR.
Mulford, Mrs. Roland Jessup (Margaret Biddle Guest). Chart. Col. Dames, Chap. I. MHS.
Mull. St. Paul's Parish, Balto. V. 1, 2. Mss. MHS.
Mullan. Patriotic Md. Md. Soc. of S. A. R., 1930. MHS; DAR.
Williamson Bible rec. Ms. MHS.
†**Mullan, Dennis W.** M. H. Mag., v. 12, p. 230.
†Men of mark in Md. Johnson. V. 1. DAR; Enoch Pratt Lib.
Muller. St. Paul's Parish, Balto. V. 2. Mss. MHS.
Mulliken. Col. Nicholas Duvall family rec. Price. Bd. ms. MHS.
Gantt geneal. Ms. MHS.
Mrs. M. L. Price chart. MHS.
Mullikin. Bowie-Claggett chart. MHS.
Mrs. Charles Carter chart. MHS.
Col. families of U. S. A. Mackenzie. V. 3, p. 336. MHS; DAR.
"Fairview," home of Gov. Oden Bowie, near Bowie, Prince George Co. Private burying ground, 1745–1904. Ms. MHS; DAR.
Greenway chart. MHS.
*Lineage Bk., Daughters of Amer. Col., v. 1, p. 124. MHS; DAR.
*Mullikins of Md., descendants of James Mullikin of West. Shore of Md. E. H. Baker. State College, 1932. MHS; DAR.
Pedigree of Mareen Duvall. Soc. Col. Wars Md. Culver. 1940. MHS; DAR.
Pedigree of Granville Bowdle Hopkins. Soc. Col. Wars Md. Culver. 1940. MHS; DAR.
Pedigree of John Ogle Warfield, Jr. Soc. Col. Wars Md. Culver. 1940. MHS; DAR.
St. Barnabas P. E. churchyard. Typed ms. MHS; DAR.
Mrs. G. R. Veazey chart. MHS.
Mrs. G. H. Williams, Jr., chart. MHS.
See Millingas.
Mullikin, Howard. Pedigree chart, plates 1 and 2. (Mostly Talbot Co. records.) Soc. Col. Wars, Md. Johnston. 1905, pp. 74–75. MHS.
Mullikin-Anderson-Woodward-Hall. Bible and court rec. Binder titled Mullikin, file case, DAR.
Mullins. Quisenberry family. Quisenberry. MHS.
Mullock, alias Poulson. Naturalizations in Md., 1666–1765; Laws. Bacon. MHS.
Mumma. Hagerstown tombstone inscriptions. Gruder. Natl. Geneal. Soc. Quart., 1919, v. 8, nos. 1, 2.
Trinity P. E. churchyard, Long Green. Typed ms. MHS; DAR.
Muncaster. Col. families of U. S. A. Mackenzie. V. 1, p. 350. MHS; DAR.
†Hist. of Allegany Co. Thomas and Williams. V. 2. MHS; DAR.
Lineage Bk., Order of Washington, p. 186. MHS; DAR.
Muncastor, Wm. E. Amer. Clan Gregor Year Book, 1922, p. 35. MHS; DAR.
Munn. St. Paul's Parish, Balto. V. 2. Mss. MHS.
Munnichuyden. St. Paul's Parish, Balto. V. 2. Mss. MHS.
Munnikhuysen. Balto., its hist., its people. Hall. V. 2. MHS; DAR.
Col. families of U. S. A. Mackenzie. V. 2, p. 443. MHS; DAR.
Gilpin chart. MHS.
Munnikuysen. Bond chart. MHS.
Geneal. and memorial encyc. of Md. Spencer. V. 2, p. 399. MHS; DAR.
Munoz. Abr. Compend. Amer. Geneal. Virkus. V. 1, p. 627. DAR.
Munoz, Wm. Parke Custis. Pedigree. Soc. Col. Wars Md. Culver. 1940. MHS; DAR.
***Munro.** Hist. of Munros of Fowlis with geneal. of principal families of name. A. Mackenzie. Amer. Munros, pp. 559–632; all of Mass., except Md., pp. 608–09, and N. H., p. 615. Inverness, Scotland, 1898. 647 pp.
St. Paul's Parish, Balto. V. 2. Mss. MHS.
†**Munroe.** Bench and bar of Md. Sams and Riley. 1901, v. 2, p. 663. Lib. Cong., MHS; Peabody Lib.
Cemetery Creek, Anne Arundel Co., tombstone inscriptions. Founders of Anne Arundel and Howard Cos. Warfield. P. 333. MHS; DAR.
Murch. Bible rec. Upper. Penins. East. Shore, p. 148–54.
See Downs-Murch-Mirch.
Murdoch. Chart, photos., 2 sheets. Cary Geneal. Coll. Ms. MHS.

***Murdoch.** Geneal. of Murdoch family, Va., 1640–1934. J. D. Leslie and F. C. Symonds. DAR.
King and Queen Cos., Va.; hist. and geneal. Bagby. 1908.
†Med. Annals Md. Cordell. 1903, p. 514. MHS.
Patriotic Md. Md. Soc. of S. A. R., 1930. MHS; DAR.

†Murdoch, Alexander F. Geneal. and mem. encyc. of Md. Spencer. V. 2, p. 725. MHS; DAR.

Murdoch Family. Geneal., 1640–1934. J. B. Leslie and T. C. Symonds. Pamph. DAR.

Murdock. Ances. rec. and portraits. Col. Dames of Amer., 1910, v. 2, p. 687. MHS; DAR.
Howard-Govane-Woodward-Law Bible rec. Ms. MHS.
Pedigree of Rev. Sam'l Tagart Steele. Soc. Col. Wars Md. Culver. 1940. MHS; DAR.
Miss Kate Steele chart. MHS.
*The Sun, Balto., Dec. 17, 1905.

***Murdock Family.** Murdock family (1640–1934). Rev. J. D. Lewis. Rev. T. C. Symonds. Pamph. DAR.

Murdock Family, Md. and Va. M. H. Mag., 1930, v. 25, no. 3, p. 262–70.

Murphy. Dukehart and collateral lines. Ms. MHS.
Glison-Sellman-Murphy-Cooley Bible rec. Ms. DAR.
†Med. Annals Md. Cordell. 1903, p. 514. MHS.
Rec. of Stepney Parish. MHS; DAR.
St. Paul's Parish, Balto. V. 2, 4. Mss. MHS.
John White Bible rec. Ms. MHS.
Wicomico Co. families. Bible rec. Ms. DAR.
*Wicomico Co. families. Tilghman. Ms. pp. 40, 115–16. DAR.

Murphy-Hall. Lineage Bks., Natl. Soc. of Daughters of Amer. Col., v. 2, p. 187. MHS; DAR.

Murrain. St. Stephens Parish, Cecilton, Md. MHS; DAR.

Murray. Abr. Compend. Amer. Geneal. Virkus. V. 6, pp. 31, 437. DAR.
Ances. rec. and portraits. Col. Dames of Amer., 1910, v. 1, p. 145, 147; v. 2, p. 681. MHS; DAR.
Ancestry of Rosalie Morris Johnson. Johnson. 1905. MHS; DAR.
†Bench and bar of Md. Sams and Riley. 1901, v. 1, p. 223. Lib. Cong.; MHS; Peabody Lib.
Mrs. Henry Johns Bowdoin chart. MHS.
Mrs. Howard Bruce chart. MHS.
Cemetery Creek, Anne Arundel Co., Tombstone Inscriptions. Founders of Anne Arundel and Howard Cos. Warfield. Pp. 334–35. MHS; DAR.
(8 stones.) Christ P. E. Church cemetery, Cambridge. Steele. 1936. MHS; DAR.
Col. families of Amer. Lawrence. V. 5, p. 93. MHS.
Dorsey and allied families. Ms. MHS.
Dorsey chart. MHS.
*Frederick Co. families. Markell. Ms. Personal list.
Geneal. reg. Mervine. Pp. 227–35. MHS.
Hist. graves of Md. and D. C. Ridgely. MHS.
Hynson chart. Cary Geneal. Coll. Ms. MHS.
Md. tombstone rec. Md. Geneal. Rec. Com., 1937, Parran, p. 32. Mss. MHS.
McLanahan chart. MHS.
†Med. Annals Md. Cordell. 1903, p. 515. MHS.
Morris family of Phila. Moon. V. 2, p. 726. MHS.
Mrs. A. G. Ober chart. MHS.
Pedigree of Franklin Buchanan Owen. Soc. Col. Wars Md. Culver. 1940. MHS; DAR.
Pedigree of Tilghman Goldsborough Pitts. Soc. Col. Wars Md. Culver. 1940. MHS; DAR.
*Pennington Papers. Ms. MHS.
Mrs. E. W. Poe chart. MHS.
Purnell family tree. MHS.
Pocahontas and her descendants. Robertson. MHS; DAR.
St. John's R. C. Church cemetery, Montgomery Co. Md. Geneal. Rec. Com., 1926, p. 27. Mss. DAR.
St. Paul's Parish, Balto. V. 1, 2, 3, 4. Mss. MHS.
*Wicomico Co. families. Tilghman. Ms, pp. 96–97, DAR.
See Tipton-Murray-Mitchell.

Murray, Dorchester Co. Miss Kate Steele chart. MHS.

***Murray,** Scotland to Md. The Sun, Balto. April 7, 14, 21, 1907.

†Murray, Daniel, Lieut., Amer. Navy. Letter, 1842. (Letter from Hon. Francis S. Key, written at time of his death.) M. H. Mag., 1925, v. 20, pp. 200–04.
†U. S. N. (1778–1842). M. H. Mag., 1925, v. 20, no. 2, p. 200.

†Murray, Frances Key. M. H. Mag., v. 12, p. 231.

†Murray, Rt. Rev. John G. Encyc. of Amer. biog. Amer. Hist. Soc., new series, v. 1, p. 187. MHS; DAR.
Hist. of Frederick Co. Williams. V. 2, pp. 773–74. MHS; DAR.

†Murray, Osgar G. Men of mark in Md. Johnson. V. 2. DAR; Enoch Pratt Lib.

†Murray, Wm. Vans, 1762–1803. (Author of Constitutions and Laws of U. S.; born Glasgow, near Cambridge, Dorchester Co.). Hist. of Md. Scharf. V. 2, p. 601. MHS.
South. Hist. Assoc., 1901, v. 5, pp. 151–58.

***Murray Family.** Old Kent. Hanson. Pp. 267–70. MHS; DAR.

Murray, Morray. Col. families of U. S. A. Mackenzie. V. 1, pp. 100, 361, 478, 503; v. 2. MHS; DAR.

†Murrow. Med. Annals Md. Cordell. 1903, p. 576. MHS.

Murry, James. Photos. copy of will, 1704. Md. Geneal. Rec. Com., 1938–39. Mss. DAR.

Muschamp. Md. gleanings in Eng. Wills. M. H. Mag., v. 2, 1907, no. 3.

Muschett. Md. Geneal. Rec. Com., 1932–33, pp. 208–09. Mss. DAR.

***Muschett Family.** Old Kent. Hanson. P. 120. MHS; DAR.

Muse. (20 stones.) Christ P. E. Church cemetery, Cambridge. Steele. 1936. MHS; DAR.

***Muse-Reed-Washington Families,** Va. The Sun, Balto., July 5, 1906.

Musgrove. Mt. Carmel burial ground, Unity, Montgomery Co. Md. Geneal. Rec. Com., 1934–35, p. 85. Mss. DAR.

†Muth, J. C. Encyc. of Amer. biog. Amer. Hist. Soc., N. Y., 1928, v. 33, p. 204.

†**Myer.** Hist. of Balto. City and Co. Scharf. P. 395. MHS.
Myer-Hays-Mordecai Families. Rec. Ms. MHS.
Myer, Myers. St. Paul's Parish, Balto. V. 1, 2, 3, 4. Mss. MHS.
***Myers.** Frederick Co. families. Markell. Ms. Personal list.
Frederick Co. tombstone inscriptions. Gruder. Natl. Geneal. Soc. Quart., 1919, v. 8, nos. 1, 2.
Faith Pres. Church (Glendy Graveyard). Mss. MHS.
†Hist. of Frederick. Co. Williams. MHS; DAR.
Md. tombstone rec. Md. Geneal. Rec. Com., 1927, Parran, pp. 10, 11, 22. Mss. DAR.
†Med. Annals Md. Cordell. 1903, p. 516. MHS.
Norris-Myers chart. MHS.
Patriotic Md. Md. Soc. of S. A. R., 1930. MHS; DAR.
Stirling chart. MHS.
See Myer.
See Norris-Myers.
Myers, near Balto. Mrs. J. P. Thom chart. MHS.
Myers, J. A. Md. Soc., War of 1812, v. 1, no. 62. Ms. MHS.
Myers, William Starr. Pedigree chart. Soc. Col. Wars, Md. Johnston. 1905, p. 76. MHS.
***Myers Family,** Hagerstown. Wilson Mss. Coll., no. 59. MHS.
Mynn. Chart, photos. from orig. Negative. MHS.
Mynskie. Naturalizations in Md., 1666–1765; Laws. Bacon. MHS.

N

Nagely. Branch of Philip Adams family of Md. Adams. MHS.
†**Nairn.** Med. Annals Md. Cordell. 1903, p. 516. MHS.
*Wicomico Co. families. Tilghman. Ms, p. 99. DAR.
Nairne. All Hallow's P. E. churchyard, Snow Hill, Worcester Co. Hudson. Bd. ms. MHS; DAR. Also: Md. Geneal. Rec. Com., 1935–36, p. 24. Mss. DAR.
***Nash.** Oberholtzer and Nash family hist. Fritz.
St. Paul's Parish, Balto. V. 1, 2, 3. Mss. MHS.
See Ober-Nash-Clark.
Nash, C. W. Md. Soc., War of 1812, v. 1, no. 41. Ms. MHS.
Naudine. Bible rec. Upper Penins. East. Shore, p. 152. MHS.
†**Naylor.** Med. Annals Md. Cordell. 1903, p. 516. MHS.
*The Sun, Balto., March 12, 1905.
Neal. Graves. Hendrickson farm burying ground, near Millington, Md. Md. Geneal. Rec. Com., 1933–34, pp. 208–09. Mss. DAR.
Neal, Sussex Co., Del. Revolutionary service, wills, Bible rec. Md. Geneal. Rec. Com., v. 4, pp. 83–86. DAR.
Neal, George. Bible rec. Md. Geneal. Rec. Com., 1932, p. 216. DAR.
Neal Family, Caroline Co. Md. Geneal. Rec. Com., 1930–31, pp. 83–86, 88–89. DAR.
Neal, O'Neale. Rec. of Stepney Parish. MHS; DAR.
Neale. Ances. rec. and portraits. Col. Dames of Amer., 1910, v. 2, pp. 548–51. MHS; DAR.
Boarman geneal. Thomas. 1935. MHS; DAR.
Bowie-Claggett chart. MHS.
J. L. Brent pedigree chart. Soc. Col. Wars, Md. Johnston. 1905, p. 7. MHS.
B. B. Browne pedigree chart. Soc. Col. Wars, Md. Johnston. 1905, pp. 8, 150. MHS.
Browne-Cochrane-Brooke-Neale-Bennett chart. File case, MHS.
Col. families of East. Shore and their descendants. Emory. 1900, pp. 221–23. MHS.
Dorsey Papers. Ms. MHS.
Geneal. notes of Chamberlaine family. MHS.
Gittings chart. MHS.
Hazelhurst chart. MHS.
Mrs. G. C. Jenkins chart. MHS.
R. B. Keyser pedigree chart, plate 2. Soc. Col. Wars, Md. Johnston. 1905, p. 56. MHS.
*Lineage Bk., Daughters of Amer. Col., v. 2, p. 54. MHS; DAR.
Manly chart. MHS.
Md. families. Culver. Ms. Personal list.
†Med. Annals Md. Cordell. 1903, p. 517. MHS.
Naturalizations in Md., 1666–1765; Laws. Bacon. MHS.
*Neale family of Md. Incl. Bennett, Brooke, Darnall and Lowe families. The Times, Balto., Sunday, Dec. 27, 1885. Scrap Book, no. 7. MHS.
*Old Kent. Hanson. P. 29. MHS; DAR.
Pedigree of Duncan Keener Brent. Soc. Col. Wars Md. Culver. 1940. MHS; DAR.
Pedigree of Coleman Randall Freeman. Soc. Col. Wars Md. Culver. 1940. MHS; DAR.
Pedigree of Edward Hammond. Soc. Col. Wars Md. Culver. 1940. MHS; DAR.
Pedigree of Charles Morris Howard. Soc. Col. Wars Md. Culver. 1940. MHS; DAR.
Pedigree of Dr. Christopher Johnston, Jr. Soc. Col. Wars Md. Culver. 1940. MHS; DAR.
Pedigree of Gustav Wm. Lurman. Soc. Col. Wars Md. Culver. 1940. MHS; DAR.
Pedigree of Franklin Buchanan Owen. Soc. Col. Wars Md. Culver. 1940. MHS; DAR.
Pedigree of John Philemon Paca. Soc. Col. Wars Md. Culver. 1940. MHS; DAR.
Pedigree. of Pleasants Pennington. Soc. Col. Wars Md. Culver. 1940. MHS; DAR.
Pedigree of Levin Gale Shreve. Soc. Col. Wars Md. Culver. 1940. MHS; DAR.
Pedigree of Alfred Jenkins Tormey. Soc. Col. Wars Md. Culver. 1940. MHS; DAR.
*Pennington Papers. Ms. MHS.
Sacred Heart R. C. churchyard, Bushwood, St. Mary's Co. Md. Geneal. Rec. Com., 1929. Mss. DAR.
St. John's R. C. Church cemetery, Montgomery Co. Md. Geneal. Rec. Com., 1926, p. 27. Mss. DAR.
St. Paul's Parish, Balto. V. 2, 3, 4. Mss. MHS.
Semmes and allied families. Semmes. P. 239. MHS.
*Side lights on Md. hist. Richardson. V. 2, p. 184. MHS; DAR.
Taney and allied families. Silverson. MHS; DAR.

***Neale.** The Sun, Balto., May 17, 1903; Aug. 6, 1905.
Tilghman chart. MHS.
Sir George Yeardley. Upshur. P. 29. MHS.
Zimmerman-Waters and allied families. Allen. Pp. 134–38. MHS; DAR.
See Brown-Cochrane-Brooke-Neale-Bennett.
Neale, Anthony, Charles Co. Pedigree of Charles Sylvester Grindall. Soc. Col. Wars Md. Culver. 1940. MHS; DAR.
*Semmes Geneal. Coll. Ms. MHS.
Neale Family, Charles Co. C. Johnston. M. H. Mag., 1912, v. 7, pp. 201–08.
Neale Line, St. Mary's Co. L. A. Knott pedigree chart. Soc. Col. Wars, Md. Johnston. 1905, p. 57. MHS.
Neall. Neall notes, 1698–1706. Md. Geneal. Rec. Com., 1939–40, p. 114. Mss. DAR.
Nedels. *See* Man-Needles-Hambleton.
See Needles.
Nedles. *See* Needles.
Needles. Abr. Compend. Amer. Geneal. Virkus. V. 6, p. 581. DAR.
Matthews-Price chart. MHS.
See Man-Needles-Hambleton.
Needles, Nedels, Nedles. Note. D. A. R. Mag., v. 70, no. 4, p. 353.
Neely, Henry. Family Bible rec. Ms. DAR.
Neff. Hagerstown tombstone inscriptions. Gruder. Natl. Geneal. Soc. Quart., 1919, v. 8, nos. 1, 2.
*Meaning of name of Neff. Elizabeth C. Neff. Cleveland, Ohio, 1899. DAR.
†Med. Annals Md. Cordell. 1903, p. 517. MHS.
Peale Geneal. Coll. Ms. MHS.
Neff, Peter. Pedigree chart. Soc. Col. Wars, Md. Johnston. 1905, p. 77. MHS.
†Negley. Hist. of West. Md. Scharf. V. 2, pp. 1145–46. MHS; DAR.
Neil-Booth-Reynolds. Notes. D. A. R. Mag., v. 70, no. 4, p. 359.
†Neill. Hist. of West. Md. Scharf. V. 2, pp. 1042–43. MHS; DAR.
Hist. and geneal. account of Jolliffe family of Va. Jolliffe. DAR.
Miss E. C. Hopkins chart. MHS.
†Md. Annals Md. Cordell. 1903, p. 517. MHS.
Memorial to Thomas Potts, Jr. James. MHS.
*John Neill of Lewes, Del., 1739, and his descendants. Incl. Duffield, Handy, Humphreys, Martin, Neill, Potts, Rutter, Savage; mostly Phila. families, with many intermarriages into Bishop, Duffield, Franklin, Handy, Ingram, Martin and Wilson families of Worcester Co. Pr. for family, Phila., 1875.
Neill, Mrs. William, Jr. (Alice L. Buckler). Chart. Col. Dames. Chap. I. MHS.
Buckler chart. MHS.
Middendorf chart. MHS.
Posey chart. MHS.
Neilson. Manning chart. MHS.
†Men of mark in Md. Johnson. V. 4. DAR; Enoch Pratt Lib.
Mrs. E. W. Poe chart. MHS.
St. Paul's Parish, Balto. V. 2. Mss. MHS.
Neilson, Oliver H. (War of 1812). Glendy churchyard. Patriotic Marylander, v. 2, no. 4, pp. 54–60. MHS; DAR.
Neilson, R. Musgrave. Md. Soc., War of 1812, v. 2, no. 141. Ms. MHS.
***Nelmes.** Wicomico Co. families. Tilghman. Ms, pp. 95, 97. DAR.
Nelson. Ances. rec. and portraits. Col. Dames of Amer., 1910, v. 2, p. 683. MHS; DAR.
Mrs. Henry DuPont Baldwin chart. MHS.
Balto., its hist., its people. Hall. V. 2. MHS; DAR.
†Bench and bar of Md. Sams and Riley. 1901, v. 1, p. 338. Lib. Cong.; MHS; Peabody Lib.
Blackford chart. MHS.
Cary Geneal. Coll. Ms. MHS.
Cummings chart. Lib. Cong.; MHS; DAR.
Dorsey chart. MHS.
Fox-Ring-Prosser-Nelson families. Bible rec. Ms. DAR.
*Frederick Co. families. Markell. Ms. Personal list.
†Hist. of Allegany Co. Thomas and Williams. V. 1. MHS; DAR.
†Hist. of Frederick Co. Williams. MHS; DAR.
Maulsby family in Amer. Barnard. DAR; Peabody Lib.
†Med. Annals Md. Cordell. 1903, p. 518. MHS.
M. E. churchyard, Snow Hill, Worcester Co., Hudson. Bd. ms. MHS; DAR.
Naturalizations in Md., 1666–1765; Laws. Bacon. MHS.
Patriotic Md. Md. Soc. of S. A. R., 1930. MHS; DAR.
Pedigree and hist. of Washington family. Welles. P. 171. MHS.
Pedigree of Rev. Sam'l Tagart Steele. Soc. Col. Wars, Md. Culver. 1940. MHS; DAR.
Mrs. N. S. Pendleton, Jr., chart. MHS.
Portrait and biog. rec. of Sixth Cong. Dist. of Md. 1898, pp. 302, 307, 743. MHS; DAR.
St. Paul's Parish, Balto. Vol. 1, 2, 4. Mss. MHS.
Turner family, Va. Va. Mag. Hist. and Biog., v. 21, p. 315.
Turner Geneal. Coll. Ms. MHS.
Nelson, Frederick Co. Ancestors and descendants of Col. David Funsten. Randolph. P. 65. MHS.
†Hist. of West. Md. Scharf. V. 1, pp. 405–08. MHS; DAR.
Nelson, Va. Va. council journals. Va. Mag. Hist. and Biog., v. 33, pp. 188–93.
***Nelson,** Va. and Md. The Sun, Balto., May 6, 13, 1906.
Nelson, George Peabody. Md. Soc., War of 1812, v. 2, no. 156. Ms. MHS.
Nelson, Wm. Marbury. Amer. Armory and Blue Bk. Matthews. 1908, p. 259. DAR.
Nelson, William, Cecil Co. (died in Balto. Co., May 14, 1772). D. A. R. Mag., v. 70, no. 1, p. 56.
Nelson Family. Geneal. of Page family, Va. Page. Pp. 150–94. MHS; DAR.
Nelson Family, Va. Tyler's Quart. Mag., v. 13, pp. 185–87.
Nelson Line, Frederick Co. Miss Kate Steele chart. MHS.
Nelson-Worthington. Bible rec., 1749–1923. D. C. Geneal. Rec. Com., v. 31, pt. 1, pp. 112–16. Typed, bd. DAR.
Nelson, Nellson Family. Note. Old Somerset. Torrence. MHS; DAR.
Nellson. Rec. of Stepney Parish. MHS; DAR.
See Nelson.

Nengfinger. Naturalization in Md., 1666–1765; Laws. Bacon. MHS.
Nesbett. Rec., Bible in possession of Mrs. Madeline M. Hurlock. Bible rec. of Dorchester and Somerset Cos. and Del. Pp. 61–62. DAR.
Nesbit. T. C. Jenkins chart. MHS.
*Nesbit, Ross, Porter and Taggart families of Pa. Geneal. B. T. Hartman. 1929. DAR.
Mrs. E. Worthington chart. MHS.
Neuschwanger. Md. Geneal. Bull., v. 6, pp. 32, 39. MHS; DAR.
Nevett. Pedigree of Rev. Sam'l Tagart Steele. Soc. Col. Wars Md. Culver. 1940. MHS; DAR.
Miss Kate Steele chart. MHS.
Nevett-Maynadier. Ances. rec. and portraits. Col. Dames of Amer., 1910, v. 2, p. 680. MHS; DAR.
Neville. Col. families of U. S. A. Mackenzie. V. 7, p. 209. MHS; DAR.
Nevitt. Christ P. E. Church cemetery, Cambridge. Steele. 1936. MHS; DAR.
Md. families. Culver. Ms. Personal list.
See Henry.
***Newbold.** Geneal. and mem. encyc. of Md. Spencer. V. 1, pp. 320–25. MHS; DAR.
Newbold, Michael, N. J. Pedigree of Townsend Scott, IV. Soc. Col. Wars Md. Culver. 1940. MHS; DAR.
†Newburn. Med. Annals Md. Cordell. 1903, p. 502. MHS.
Newby. Miss Sara E. White chart. MHS.
Newcomb. Col. Families of U. S. A. Mackenzie. V. 1. MHS; DAR.
*Geneal. memoir of Newcomb family. Containing rec. of nearly every person of name in Amer., 1635–1874, also first generation of children, descended from females, who lost their name by marriage. J. B. Newcomb. Chicago, 1874. MHS.
†Men of mark in Md. Johnson. V. 4. DAR; Enoch Pratt Lib.
Newcomer. Abstracts from journal of Bishop Christian Newcomer (1795–1830). N. H. Betts. 16 pp., in Binder. DAR.
Balto., its hist., its people. Hall. V. 2. MHS; DAR.
†Biog. sketch of Benjamin Franklin Newcomer. Waldo Newcomer, N. Y. Grafton Press, 1902. Enoch Pratt Lib.
†Geneal. and mem. encyc. of Md. Spencer. V. 2, p. 378. MHS; DAR.
†Hist. of Balto. City and Co. Scharf. P. 478. MHS.
†Hist. of Washington Co. Williams. 1906, v. 2, p. 1222. MHS; DAR.
†Hist. of West. Md. Scharf. V. 2, pp. 1037–40. MHS; DAR.
See Huddle. Abr. Compend. Amer. Geneal. Virkus. V. 4, p. 294. MHS.
*Life and journal of Rev. Christian Newcomer, late bishop of Church of United Brethren in Christ. Written by himself. Containing his travels and labours from 1795–1830, with 110 rec. of marriages and burials in Frederick and Washington Cos., Md., Ohio and Va. Hagerstown. F. G. W. Kapp, 1834. MHS.
†Men of mark in Md. Johnson. V. 1, pp. 266, 274. DAR; Enoch Pratt Lib.
Newhall, Mrs. Thomas. Ancestral line. Mrs. Roland J. Mulford. MHS.
(Honora Bankhead Guest). Chart. Col. Dames, Chap. I. MHS.
Newland. Hopkins and allied families. Bd. ms. MHS.
Ms. MHS.
Newman. Hist. graves of Md. and D. C. Ridgely. MHS.
Lloyd family hist. of Wales, Pa., and Md. DAR.
St. Paul's Parish, Balto. V. 1, 2, 3. Mss. MHS.
St. Stephens Parish, Cecilton, Md. MHS; DAR.
*Wicomico Co. families. Tilghman. Ms, p. 16. DAR.
Zion Reformed Church, Hagerstown. Md. Geneal. Rec. Com., 1934–35. Mss. DAR.
Newman, Balto. Co. Md. gleanings in Eng. Wills. M. H. Mag., 1907, v. 2, no. 2.
Newman, Francis, Charles Co. Will. Mss. DAR.
Newman Family. Bible rec. of Dorchester and Somerset Cos. and Del. Pp. 63–65. DAR.
Newman (Queen Anne Co.)**-Mirch** (New Castle, Del.). Md. Geneal. Rec. Com., 1937–38, pp. 76–77. Mss. DAR.
Newport. St. Paul's Parish, Balto. V. 3. Mss. MHS.
Newton. Cary Geneal. Coll. Ms. MHS.
Md. gleanings in Eng. Wills. M. H. Mag., 1907, v. 2, no. 3.
Notes. Ms. MHS.
St. Paul's Parish. Balto. V. 2. Mss. MHS.
See Stanard. Abr. Compend. Amer. Geneal. Virkus. V. 1, p. 951. DAR.
*The Sun, Balto., March 29, 1908.
Nicholas. Cary Geneal. Coll. Ms. MHS.
St. Paul's Parish, Balto. V. 2, 3. Mss. MHS.
*The Sun, Balto., Sept. 25, 1904; April 2, 1905 (Va.)
Nicholas, James, (Born in Scotland, 1803; came to Talbot Co.). Md. Geneal. Rec. Com., 1937. DAR.
†Nicholas, Hon. Thomas. Sketch. R. H. Spencer. M. H. Mag., 1911, v. 6, pp. 145–63.
Nicholison. *See* Nichols.
Nicholls. Talbott of "Poplar Knowle." Shirk. MHS; DAR.
Nicholls-Smith Family (1607–1925). Md. Geneal. Rec. Com., 1932–33, pp. 167–75. Mss. DAR.
Nichols. Christ P. E. Church cemetery, Cambridge. Steele. 1936. MHS; DAR.
*Frederick Co. families. Markell. Ms. Personal list.
Hist. graves of Md. and D. C. Ridgely. MHS.
*Old Kent. Hanson. MHS; DAR.
Rec. of Stepney Parish. MHS; DAR.
St. Paul's churchyard, Kent Co. Md. O. R. Soc. Bull., no. 2, pp. 54–65. MHS.
St. Paul's Parish, Balto. V. 3, 4. Mss. MHS.
See Porter-Nichols.
***Nichols, Nicholison.** Wicomico Co. families. Tilghman. Ms, pp. 20, 95, 111–12. DAR.
Nicholson. Balto., its hist., its people. Hall. V. 2. MHS; DAR.
Beall and Bell families. Beall. MHS; DAR.
†Bench and bar of Md. Sams and Riley. 1901, v. 1, pp. 270, 293. Lib. Cong.; MHS; Peabody Lib.
Mrs. R. F. Brent chart. MHS.
Chestertown cemetery. Md. O. R. Soc. Bull., no. 1, pp. 18–29.

Nicholson. Col. families of Amer. Lawrence. V. 12, p. 289-91. MHS.
Dorsey and allied families. Ms. MHS.
Dorsey chart. MHS.
Elbert chart. MHS.
Griffin family. Streets. P. 117. DAR.
Hist. graves of Md. and D. C. Ridgely. MHS.
Hynson chart. Cary Geneal. Coll. Ms. MHS.
Mrs. T. C. Jenkins chart. MHS.
Md. gleanings in Eng. Wills. M. H. Mag., 1907, v. 2, no. 2.
W. A. and S. W. Merritt pedigree charts, plate 2. Soc. Col. Wars, Md. Johnston. 1905, p. 68. MHS.
Morris family of Phila. Moon. V. 1, p. 180; v. 2, p. 631. MHS.
*Old Kent. Hanson. P. 31. MHS; DAR.
Old Somerset. Torrence. MHS; DAR.
J. P. Paca pedigree chart. Soc. Col. Wars, Md. Johnston. 1905, p. 80. MHS.
Pedigree of John Philemon Paca. Soc. Col. Wars Md. Culver. 1940. MHS; DAR.
Rec. of Stepney Parish. MHS; DAR.
St. Paul's Parish, Balto. V. 1, 2, 3. Mss. MHS.
St. Stephens Parish, Cecilton, Md. MHS; DAR.
*Side lights on Md. hist. Richardson. V. 2, p. 187. MHS; DAR.
Somerset Co. Court Book. Tilghman. 1937. Ms. DAR.
*Stevens of New Eng., Gallatin of N. Y. and Nicholson of Md. P. K. Stevens. Pp. 26-36. Pub. Natl. Americana Soc., N. Y., 1911. MHS.
*The Sun, Balto. Sept. 25, 1904.

†**Nicholson, Benj.** Hist. of Md. Scharf. V. 3, p. 52. MHS.

†**Nicholson, Capt. James.** Hist. of Md. Scharf. V. 2, p. 203. MHS.

†**Nicholson, Joseph Hopper.** Hist. of Md. Scharf. V. 2, p. 607. MHS.

Nicholson, Gov. Thomas. Early career of Gov. Thomas Nicholson. C. W. Sommerville. M. H. Mag., 1909. V. 4, pp. 101-04, 201-20.

Nicholson Family. Ancestry of Albert Gallatin, (1761-1849), born in Geneva, Switzerland, and of Hannah Nicholson (1766-1849), with a list of their descendants. (Nicholson ancestry is of Va. and Md.) N. Y.

Nicholson-Hynson-Noel. Chart, Nicholson crests (3), photos. Cary Geneal. Coll. Ms. MHS.

Nicholson-Witter. Griffin family. Streets. P. 117. MHS.

Nickerson. Holdens Cemetery, Kent Co. Md. Geneal. Rec. Com., 1932, v. 5, p. 211. Mss. DAR.

Nicklin, Pa. Col. families of U. S. A. Mackenzie. V. 4, p. 391. MHS; DAR.

Nicklin, Benj. Patten. Pedigree. (Va. rec.) Soc. Col. Wars Md. Culver. 1940. MHS; DAR.

Nicklin, J. B., III. Abr. Compend. Amer. Geneal. Virkus. V. 1, p. 743. DAR.

Nicklin, John Bailey, Jr. Pedigree. (Va. rec.) Soc. Col. Wars Md. Culver. 1940. MHS; DAR.

Nicklin-Calvert. Abr. Compend. Amer. Geneal. Virkus. V. 4, pp. 409-10. MHS.

Nicodemus. Englar family. Barnes. MHS; DAR.
†Hist. of Frederick Co. Williams. MHS; DAR.
†Hist. of West. Md. Scharf. V. 2, pp. 1260-61. MHS; DAR.
†Men of mark in Md. Johnson. V. 3; v. 4. DAR; Enoch Pratt Lib.
Patriotic Md. Md. Soc. of S. A. R., 1930. MHS; DAR.
Roop geneal. Pamph. MHS.

***Nicolai.** Geneal. and mem. encyc. of Md. Spencer. V. 2, p. 539, MHS; DAR.

Nicolas, Magruder. Descendants of Brig. Gen. Lewis Nicolas, member of Militia of Pa., 1772-77, Continental Army to close of Revolutionary war. Amer. Clan Gregor Year Book, 1937, pp. 88-107. MHS; DAR.

Nicoll, B. B. Md. Soc., War of 1812, v. 1, no. 30. Ms. MHS.

Nicols. Geneal. notes of Chamberlaine family. MHS.
Gittings chart. MHS.
St. Paul's Parish, Balto. V. 1, 2. Mss. MHS.
W. A. and S. W. Merritt pedigree charts, plate 2. Soc. Col. Wars, Md. Johnston. 1905, p. 68. MHS.

Nicols Family. Nicols family of Md. K. N. Grove. DAR.

Nicols Family, Queen Anne's Co. Nichols-Wright Bible rec., 1832-1925. D. C. Geneal. Rec. Com., v. 31, pp. 124-27. Typed, bd. DAR.

Nield. Trinity Church burial ground, near Cambridge, Md. Md. Geneal. Rec. Com., 1937-38, pp. 93-104. Mss. DAR.
Trinity Church cemetery, Dorchester Co. Md. O. R. Soc. Bull., no. 3, pp. 42-52.
Handy and their kin. Handy.

†**Niemeyer.** Light in darkness; autobiog. of Mary A. Niemeyer. Revised by Sara S. Rice. (Mary A. Neimeyer, born in Deisel, Germany; lived in Middletown, Frederick Co.) James Young. Balto., 1873. Enoch Pratt Lib.

Niles. Freeborn Garrettson Waters Bible rec. Ms. MHS.

†**Niles, Hezekiah.** Niles as economist. R. G. Stone. Series 51, no. 2, 1933. Johns Hopkins Univ. Press. MHS; Enoch Pratt Lib.

Nimmo. Antiquary; Lower Norfolk Co., Va. V. 1. MHS.
Mt. Paran Pres. churchyard, Harrisonville, Balto. Co. Typed ms. MHS; DAR.

Nimmo-Ball-Dorsey-Howard. Abr. Compend. Amer. Geneal. Virkus. V. 4, p. 418. MHS.

Ninde. St. Paul's Parish, Balto. V. 2. Mss. MHS.

Nisbet. Arnold chart. MHS.
Coll. of Amer. epitaphs and inscriptions. Alden. 1814, v. 5, p. 215. MHS.
Hist. graves of Md. and D. C. Ridgely. MHS.

Nissley (in Amer). 5 generations. DAR.

Nivison, Va. Mrs. J. Hall Pleasants, Jr., chart. MHS.

***Nixon.** Unbroken line from 1416. The Sun, Balto., Nov. 24, Dec. 1, 1907.
Van Dyke-Johns-Montgomery-Manlove chart. Cary Geneal. Coll. Ms. MHS.
See Morris-Nixon.

Nixon, Del. Cotton chart. MHS.

Noble. Geneal. of family of Stockett, 1558-1892. Stockett. Pamph., p. 20. MHS; DAR.
Keene family. Jones. MHS; DAR.
Md. families. Culver. Ms. Personal list.
Rec. of Stepney Parish. MHS; DAR.
St. Paul's Parish, Balto. V. 2. Mss. MHS.

Somerset Co. Court Book. Tilghman. 1937. Ms. DAR.
Noble, Talbot Co. Wills, 1682–1837. Md. Geneal. Rec. Com., v. 1, pp. 91–92. DAR.
Noble, Robert, Talbot Co., will probated May 16, 1733. D. A. R. Mag., v. 67, no. 6, p. 385.
***Noblit.** Geneal. coll. relating to families of Noblit. J. H. Noblit. Noblit families, N.C., N. J., N. Y., Pa. and Tenn. Pr. for priv. circulation, Ferris-Leach, 1906. MHS.
Nock. Makemie Memorial Pres. churchyard, Snow Hill, Worcester Co. Hudson. Bd. ms. MHS; DAR. Also: Md. Geneal. Rec. Com., Mrs. Lines. Mss. DAR.
Rehobeth P. E. churchyard, Somerset Co. Md. Geneal. Rec. Com., 1937, Mrs. Lines. Mss. DAR.
Noel. Balto., its hist., its people. Hall. V. 2. MHS; DAR.
Christ P. E. Church cemetery, Cambridge. Steele. 1936. MHS; DAR.
Md. tombstone rec. Md. Geneal. Rec. Com., 1937, Parran. Mss. DAR.
†Med. Annals Md. Cordell. 1903, p. 519. MHS.
St. Paul's Parish, Balto. V. 1, 2, 3. Mss. MHS.
See Nicholson-Hynson-Noel.
Noel, Caroline Co. Bible Rec. of Dorchester and Somerset Cos. and Del. P. 68. DAR.
Noel, Dorchester Co. Segrave chart. MHS.
Noel, J. E. Md. Soc., War of 1812, v. 1, no. 124. Ms. MHS.
Nokes. Chart of Com. John Rodgers. DAR.
Noland. St. John's R. C. Church cemetery, Montgomery Co. Md. Geneal. Rec. Com., 1926, p. 27. Mss. DAR.
Noland, Daniel (born in Md., 1766). D. A. R. Mag., v. 70, no. 7, p. 709.
***Noles.** *See* Knowles.
Nomers. Naturalizations in Md., 1666–1765; Laws. Bacon. MHS.
Noonan. Geneal. and mem. encyc. of Md. Spencer. V. 2, p. 689. MHS; DAR.
Norbury. Col. Families of U. S. A. Mackenzie. V. 1. MHS; DAR.
Norman. Focke Geneal. Coll. Ms. MHS.
Mrs. A. Randall chart. MHS.
Southerland-Latham and allied families. Voorhees. Bd. ms. MHS.
St. Paul's Parish, Balto. V. 2. Mss. MHS.
Norris. Balto., its hist., its people. Hall. V. 2. MHS; DAR.
Bonsal charts. MHS.
Col. families of Amer. Lawrence. V. 5, pp. 82–95. MHS.
Ellicott-Campbell chart. MHS.
*Frederick Co. families. Markell. Ms. Personal list.
Hist. of Harford Co. Preston. MHS; DAR.
Md. families. Culver. Ms. Personal list.
†Med.Annals Md. Cordell. 1903, p. 520. MHS.
*Norris family of Md., 1642. T. M. Myers. W. M. Clemens, 1916, ltd. ed. MHS; Peabody Lib.
Pedigree of Pleasants Pennington. Soc. Col. Wars Md. Culver. 1940. MHS; DAR.
Mrs. Pennington chart. MHS.
Riggs of Anne Arundel, Frederick and Montgomery Cos. prior to 1663. Pamph. MHS.
St. Paul's Parish, Balto. V. 2, 3. Mss. MHS.
See Calder-Norris.
Norris, St. James Parish, Balto. Co. Chart, photos., 2 sheets. Cary Geneal. Coll. Ms. MHS.
Norris, Bennet Biscoe. Pedigree. Soc. Col. Wars Md. Culver. 1940. MHS; DAR.
†**Norris, W. I.** Public parks, Balto., ann. rept., no. 3. MHS; DAR.
Norris-Dixon-Amoss. Abr. Compend. Amer. Geneal. Virkus. V. 1, p. 214. DAR.
Norris-Myers Family. Chart. T. M. Myers. Printed. MHS.
Chart. MHS.
North. Col. families of East. Shore and their descendants. Emory. 1900, p. 84. MHS.
Deford chart. MHS.
Hist. graves of Md. and D. C. Ridgely. MHS.
Lehr chart. MHS.
W. A. Moale pedigree charts, plate 1. Soc. Col. Wars, Md. Johnston. 1905, p. 72. MHS.
St. Paul's Parish, Balto. V. 1, Mss. MHS.
*Wicomico Co. families. Tilghman. Ms, p. 127. DAR.
See Moale-Croxall-North.
North, Ellin (1741–1826). Portrait. Va. Mag. Hist. and Biog., v. 25, p. 442.
R. C. Hoffman pedigree chart. Soc. Col. Wars, Md. Johnston. 1905, p. 40. MHS.
North Family. Burial ground, on farm on "Flat Land Road," 3 miles from Chestertown, Kent Co. Md. Geneal. Rec. Com., 1934–35. Mss. DAR.
***Northcroft,** Frederick Co. families. Markell. Ms. Personal list.
Norton. St. John's R. C. Church cemetery, Montgomery Co. Md. Geneal. Rec. Com., 1926, p. 27. Mss. DAR.
Norwood. Burton ancestry. Ms. MHS.
*Early comers to the Province. Georgians in Anne Arundel Co. Atlanta Jour., Sept. 22, 1906. Newsp. clipp. File case, MHS.
Founders of Anne Arundel and Howard Cos. Warfield. P. 161. MHS. DAR.
Lineage Bks., Natl. Soc. of Daughters of Amer. Col., v. 1, p. 42. MHS; DAR.
Norwood in Worcester Co., 1650. L. D. Scisco. M. H. Mag., 1923, v. 18, pp. 130–34.
Patriotic Md. Md. Soc. of S. A. R., 1930. MHS; DAR.
Pedigree of Maurice Falconer Rodgers. Soc. Col. Wars Md. Culver. 1940. MHS; DAR.
St. Paul's Parish, Balto., v. 1, 2. Mss. MHS.
Norwood, Randolph, Maj., U.S.A. Md. Soc., War of 1812, v. 1, no. 65. Ms. MHS.
Notley. Cary Geneal. Coll. Ms. MHS.
Md. families. Culver. Ms. Personal list.
Nourse. Abr. Compend. Amer. Geneal. Virkus. V. 4, p. 285. MHS.
Obituaries. D. C. Geneal. Rec. Com., 1932–34, v. 10, p. 164. Typed, bd. DAR.
Portrait and biog. rec. of Sixth Cong. Dist. of Md. 1898, p. 794. MHS; DAR.
See Dempsey-Nourse-Bond.
Nourse, Prof. Joseph. Obituary, Oct. 8, 1889. D. C. Geneal. Rec. Com., 1932–34, v. 10, pp. 164–66. Typed, bd. DAR.
Nourse, Michael, Washington Co. Will. D. C. Geneal. Rec. Com., 1932–34, v. 10, pp. 234–36. Typed, bd. DAR.
Nowland. Bible rec. Upper Penins. East. Shore. Pp. 68–86. MHS; DAR.
St. Stephens Parish, Cecilton, Md. MHS; DAR.

Nufer, Nuffer. Beards' Luth. graveyard, Washington Co. Md. Geneal. Rec. Com., 1935-36. Mss. DAR.
Nuffer. *See* Nufer.
Nugent, Wm. Standard-bearer of Md. (Calvert Papers.) M. H. Mag., 1908, v. 3, pp. 277-79.
Numbers. St. Stephens Parish, Cecilton, Md. MHS; DAR.
†**Nusbaum.** Hist. of Frederick Co. Williams. MHS; DAR.
Nussbaum. Babylon family. Duttera. Ms. MHS.
Nusz. Mt. Olivet Cemetery, Frederick. Md. Geneal. Rec. Com., 1934-35, p. 111. Mss. DAR.
Nuthall. Ancestry of Mrs. Fulton Ray Gordon, nee Ellen Marjorie Gray. D. C. Geneal. Rec. Com., 1932-34, p. 127. Typed bd. DAR.
Ances. rec. and portraits. Col. Dames of Amer., 1910, v. 1, p. 92. MHS; DAR.
Autobiography of Summerfield. Baldwin. MHS; DAR.
Sara R. Baldwin chart. MHS.
Md. families. Culver. Ms. Personal list.
Monnet family geneal. Monette. Pp. 1067-69. MHS.
Nuthall Line. Mullikins of Md. Baker. Pp. 160-62. MHS; DAR.
†**Nuthead.** Hist. of printing in Col. Md. Wroth. MHS.
(First printer in Col.) Liber C. B., 1693-94 (orig.), pp. 33-34. Hall of Records, Annapolis.
Nuttall. Cary Geneal. Coll. Ms. MHS.
Murdoch chart. Cary Geneal. Coll. Ms. MHS.
Nutter. Bible rec. of Dorchester and Somerset Cos. and Del. P. 69. DAR.
Old Somerset. Torrence. MHS; DAR.
Purnell family tree. MHS.
Rec. of Stepney Parish. MHS; DAR.
Somerset Co. Court Book. Tilghman. 1937. Ms. DAR.
Talbott of "Poplar Knowle." Shirk. MHS; DAR.
*Wicomico Co. families. Tilghman. Ms, p. 15. DAR.
Nutter-Taylor-Parsons-Adkins. Wicomico Co. families. Bible rec. Ms. DAR.
Nye. Pedigree and hist. of Washington family. Welles. P. 226. MHS.

O

Oates. St. Paul's Parish, Balto. V. 1, Mss. MHS.
Ober. Abr. Compend. Amer. Geneal. Virkus. V. 1, p. 750. DAR.
Griffith geneal. Griffith. MHS; DAR.
Hickok chart. MHS.
†Hist. of Balto. City and Co. Scharf. P. 400. MHS.
Mrs. James McHenry chart. MHS.
Mrs. R. Lancaster Williams chart. MHS.
See Ober-Nash-Clark.
Ober, Mrs. Albert Graham (Katharine Le Moyne Fisher). Chart. Col. Dames, Chap. I. MHS.
Ober, Gustavus. Pedigree chart. (Mostly Mass. rec.) Soc. Col. Wars, Md. Johnston. 1905, p. 78. MHS.
Ober Family, Wash, D. C. Bible rec., 1827-1920. D. C. Geneal. Rec. Com., v. 31, pt. 1, pp. 143-44. Typed, bd. DAR.
Ober-Nash-Clark Families, Md. Bible rec., 1805-1921. D. C. Geneal. Rec. Com., v. 31, pt. 1, pp. 140-42. Typed, bd. DAR.
***Oberholtzer.** Oberholtzer and Nash family history. Fritz.
*Some account of Jacob Oberholtzer, who settled, about 1719, in Montgomery Co., Pa., and some of his descendants in Amer. E. S. Loomis. 1931.
St. Joseph's R. C. churchyard. Md. O. R. Soc. Bull., no. 3, p. 64.
O'Brian, *See* O'Bryan.
O'Brien. Cummings chart. Lib. Cong.; MHS; DAR.
†Med. Annals Md. Cordell. 1903, p. 521. MHS.
O'Bryan, O'Brian. O'Daniel-Hamilton ancestry in Md. and Ky. O'Daniel. Pp. 72-85. MHS.
***O'Bryon Family.** Wilson Mss. Coll., no. 59. MHS.
O'Carroll. Brooks chart. MHS.
*See Carroll. The Sun, Balto., Feb. 19, 1905.
De Ford chart. MHS.
Pedigree of Francis Joseph Baldwin. Soc. Col. Wars Md. Culver. 1940. MHS; DAR.
O'Carroll, Carroll, Henry, St. Mary's Co. (1702). And allied families Barnes and Handy and King of Somerset Co. Focke Geneal. Coll. Mss. MHS.
O'Connell. Abr. Compend. Amer. Geneal. V rkus. V. 6, p. 467. DAR.
†**O'Conner.** Med. Annals Md. Cordell. 1903, p. 521. MHS.
***O'Daniel-Hamilton.** O'Daniel-Hamilton and allied ancestry and hist. in Md. and Ky. Victor F. O'Daniel, native of Ky. Somerset, Ohio, The Rosary Press, 1933. MHS.
Odber. Old Somerset. Torrence. MHS; DAR.
***Odell.** Geneal., U. S. and Canada, 1635-1935. Ten generations in Amer. in direct line. M. L. Pool. 1935. DAR.
Mrs. D. G. Lovell chart. MHS.
St. Paul's Parish, Balto. V. 2. Mss. MHS.
O'dell. Biog. and geneal. rec. of Fite families in U. S.
O'dell pedigree of the United States and Canada, 1639-1894. Six lines of descent, traced by Rufus King. New York, 1894. MHS.
Peale Geneal. Coll. Ms. MHS.
O'Dell. Mt. Paran Pres. churchyard, Harrisonville, Balto. Co. Typed ms. MHS; DAR.
See Gosnell-O'Dell-Towson-Worthington.
Odell Family. Burying ground. Natl. Geneal. Soc. Quart., June, 1937, v. 25, no. 2, p. 61.
Oden. Mrs. A. C. Bruce chart. MHS.
Col. Nicholas Duvall family rec. Price. Bd. ms. MHS.
Iglehart chart. MHS.
Mrs. G. R. Veazey chart. MHS.
Odenbaugh. My family memoirs. Hughes. 1931, p. 57. MHS; DAR.
O'Donnell. Abr. Compend. Amer. Geneal. Virkus. V. 6, p. 422. DAR.
Mrs. J. G. Brogden chart. MHS.
First families of Md. The Post, Balto., Feb. 2, 3, 4, 6, 7, 8, 1933. Newsp. clipp., bd. MHS.
See Iselin. Abr. Compend. Amer. Geneal. Virkus. V. 1, p. 148. DAR.
Jenkins-Courtney chart. MHS.
John O'Donnell of Balto.; his forbears and descendants. E. T. Cook. Incl. geneal. trees

1 and 2 of Carroll, Findley, Hillen, Iselin, Lee, O'Donnell, and Tyson families. London, Favil Press, Ltd., 1934. MHS.
Macsherry chart. MHS.
†Med. Annals Md. Cordell. 1903, p. 521. MHS.
St. Paul's Parish, Balto. V. 2. Mss. MHS.
See Donnell.
†O'Donnell, Columbus. Balto., hist. and biog. Richardson and Bennett. 1871, pp. 397-99. MHS; DAR.
O'Donnell, John Charles. Amer. Armory and Blue Bk. Matthews. 1908. DAR.
†O'Donovan. Med. Annals Md. Cordell. 1903, p. 521. MHS.
O'Donovan, Charles. Pedigree. Soc. Col. Wars Md. Culver. 1940. MHS; DAR.
Oelrichs. Mrs. Talbot T. Speer chart. MHS.
Oeth. Naturalizations in Md., 1666-1765; Laws. Bacon: MHS.
Offley. Col. families of U. S. A. Mackenzie. V. 7. MHS; DAR.
*Mrs. Charles Howard Lloyd chart. Col. Dames Amer., Chap. 1. MHS.
*(Md. descendants of Robert). The Sun, Balto., July 28, Aug. 4, 1907.
Mason chart. MHS.
Wallis chart. MHS.
Offley, Va. Rec. Harrison-Waples and allied families. Harrison. MHS.
Offley Family, Va. Va. Mag. Hist. and Biog., v. 12, p. 201.
Offutt. Abr. Compend. Amer. Geneal. Virkus. V. 1, p. 750. DAR.
Col. families of U. S. A. Mackenzie. V. 2, p. 95. MHS; DAR.
Lucketts of Portobacco. Newman. DAR.
†Med. Annals Md. Cordell. 1903, p. 522. MHS.
Patriotic Md. Md. Soc. of S. A. R., 1930. MHS; DAR.
*The Sun, Balto., Dec. 30, 1906.
Offutt, Reuben Ford, Ky. Amer. Clan Gregor Year Book, 1929, p. 54. MHS; DAR.
Offutt-Clagett. Bible records, 1721-1861. Amer. Clan Gregor Year Book, 1914, p. 91. MHS; DAR.
***O'Gallagher, Gallagher, Gallaher.** The Sun, Balto., Jan. 29, Feb. 12, 1905; Oct. 28, Nov. 4, 1906.
O'Gallaher. *See* Gallaher.
Ogg. Blackford chart. MHS.
St. Paul's Parish, Balto. V. 1. Mss. MHS.
St. Thomas' Parish, Balto. Co. Bd. ms. MHS. Also: Md. Geneal. Rec. Com., 1937, pp. 109-82. Mss. DAR.
Ogle. Col. families of U. S. A. Mackenzie. V. 1, p. 515; v. 3. MHS; DAR.
Daily News, Frederick, April 2, 1914. Newsp. clipp. Scrap Book. MHS.
Hist. graves of Md. and D. C. Ridgely. MHS.
Hist. of Frederick Co. Williams. V. 2, pp. 1584, 1585, 1586, 1587. MHS; DAR.
Md. families. Culver. Ms. Personal list.
†Med. Annals Md. Cordell. 1903, p. 522. MHS.
Pedigree of John Ogle Warfield, Jr. Soc. Col. Wars Md. Culver. 1940. MHS; DAR.
St. Paul's Parish, Balto. V. 2. Mss. MHS.
Side lights on Md. hist. Richardson. V. 2, p. 190. MHS; DAR.
*The Sun, Balto., Dec. 25, 1904; March 15, 1906.
†Ogle, Benjamin. Governors of Md. Buchholz. P. 46. MHS.
Founders of Anne Arundel and Howard Cos. Warfield. P. 248. MHS; DAR.
***Ogle Family.** Old Kent. Hanson. P. 244. MHS; DAR.
Ohl. Cummings chart. Lib. Cong.; MHS; DAR.
†Ohr. Hist. of Allegany Co. Thomas and Williams. V. 1. MHS; DAR.
†Med. Annals Md. Cordell. 1903, p. 522. MHS.
Ohrendorf. Ances. rec. and portraits. Col. Dames of Amer., 1910, v. 2, p. 571. MHS; DAR.
Manly chart. MHS.
Ohrendorff. Hagerstown tombstone inscriptions. Gruder. Natl. Geneal. Soc. Quart., 1919, v. 8, nos. 1, 2.
Oke. Somerset Co. Court Book. Tilghman. 1937. Ms. DAR.
Oke, Okee, Okey. Old Somerset. Torrence. MHS; DAR.
Olanman. Somerset Co. Court Book. Tilghman. 1937. Ms. DAR.
***Old, Olds, Ould.** Old, Olds, Ould families in Eng. and Amer. Amer. geneal. E. B. Olds Eng. pedigree. Miss S. S. G. Old. Comp. and Pub. by Edson B. Olds, Wash., D. C. 1915, 359 pp. Lib. Cong.; DAR.
Olden. St. Paul's Parish, Balto. V. 2. Mss. MHS.
Oldfield. St. Paul's Parish, Balto. V. 2. Mss. MHS.
Oldham. Bohemia Manor. Mallory. P. 24. MHS.
Sweetser family of Md. and Mass. Gardner. Pamph., repr. from M. H. Mag., June, 1932, p. 142. MHS; DAR.
†Med. Annals Md. Cordell. 1903, p. 523. MHS.
See Ensor-Oldham.
Oldham, Col. Edward. (Revolutionary soldier, died Nov. 4, 1798, aged 42 yrs.; buried St. Augustine cemetery, Cecil Co.) Md. Geneal. Rec. Com., 1933-34, p. 232. Mss. DAR.
Oldman. Chart. Wm. Preston of Newcastle on Tyne, Eng., and Phila., Pa., and allied families. Belsterling. MHS.
Olds. *See* Old.
Oldson. Naturalizations in Md., 1666-1765; Laws. Bacon. MHS.
Oler. Balto., its hist., its people. Hall. V. 3. MHS; DAR.
***Oley.** Lineage Bk., Daughters of Amer. Col., v. 3, pp. 163, 220. MHS; DAR.
Naturalizations in Md., 1666-1765; Laws. Bacon. MHS.
Oliphant. Rec. of Stepney Parish. MHS; DAR.
Olive, Miss. and Ga. Amer. Clan Gregor Year Book, 1928, pp. 46, 47. MHS; DAR.
Oliver. Balto., its hist., its people. Hall. V. 3. MHS; DAR.
Bible rec., 1826-73. (Presented by estate of H. Oliver Thompson.) Typed, 3 pp. MHS.
Foursquare; story of fourfold life. John Rathborne Oliver. N. Y., Macmillan Co., 1929. Enoch Pratt Lib.
Fowler chart. MHS.
St. Paul's Parish, Balto. V. 2. Mss. MHS.
St. Stephens Parish, Cecilton, Md. MHS; DAR.
Turner Geneal. Coll. Ms. MHS.

Oliver, Hancock, Md. Md. tombstone rec. Md. Geneal. Rec. Com., 1937, Parran, p. 13. Mss. DAR.
Onderdonk. Hazelhurst charts. MHS.
†Hist. of Washington Co. Williams. 1906, v. 2, p. 1286. MHS; DAR.
*Onderdonk family in Amer. Elmer Onderdonk. With revisions, addenda and appendix, by A. J. Onderdonk. 1910. N. Y. DAR.
Rehobeth P. E. churchyard, Somerset Co. Md. Geneal. Rec. Com., 1937, Mrs. Lines. Mss. DAR.
O'Neale. *See* Neal.
†**O'Neill, John.** Hist. of Md. Scharf. V. 3, p. 43. MHS.
†**O'Neill, Mathilda.** Two Md. heroines. M. H. Mag., 1908, v. 3, pp. 133–41.
†**Onion.** Hist. of Balto. City and Co. Scharf. Pp. 391, 922. MHS.
Pedigree of Maurice Falconer Rodgers. Soc. Col. Wars Md. Culver. 1940. MHS; DAR.
Rumsey-Smithson Bible rec. Md. Geneal. Rec. Com., 1932–33, v. 5, pp. 63–142. DAR.
Rumsey-Smithson family rec. bk. Md. Geneal. Rec. Com., 1932, pp. 139, 140. DAR.
Smithson-Rumsey rec. bk. Ms. MHS.
See Colgate-Onion-Bond-Waters.
†**Opie.** Med. Annals Md. Cordell. 1903, p. 523. MHS.
Oram. St. Paul's Parish, Balto. V. 1. Mss. MHS.
Ord. Gen. Edward O. Cresap, 1818–83. Cresap Soc. Bull., no. 8. MHS.
†Hist. of Allegany Co. Thomas and Williams. V. 1. MHS; DAR.
Orem. Coale chart. MHS.
Col. families of U. S. A. Mackenzie. V. 2. MHS; DAR.
*Hist. of Dorchester Co. Jones. 1925, p. 427. MHS; DAR.
Trinity Church cemetery, Dorchester Co. Md. O. R. Soc. Bull., no. 3, pp. 42–52.
Zimmerman-Waters and allied families. Allen. MHS; DAR.
***Orem,** Talbot Co., in 1679. The Sun, Balto., Dec. 22, 1907.
Orem, J. H., Jr. Md. Soc., War of 1812, v. 3, no. 228. Ms. MHS.
Orem-Edmondstone. Ances. rec. and portraits. Col. Dames of Amer., 1910, v. 2, p. 468. MHS; DAR.
***Orendorff.** Geneal. Incl. Christopher Orendorff, born in Md., 1770. M. Custer. Bloomington, Ill., 1919.
Patriotic Md. Md. Soc. of S. A. R., 1930. MHS; DAR.
Organ. St. Thomas' Parish, Balto. Co. Bd. ms. MHS. Also: Md. Geneal. Rec. Com., 1937, pp. 109–82. Mss. DAR.
Orm. St. Paul's Parish, Balto. V. 2, Mss. MHS.
Orme. Abr. Compend. Amer. Geneal. Virkus. V. 6, pp. 426–27. DAR.
Beall and Bell families. Beall. MHS; DAR.
Beall chart. Cary Geneal. Coll. Ms. MHS.
Echoes of the lives of Magruder matrons. Amer. Clan Gregor Year Book, 1915, pp. 29–33. MHS; DAR.
Genealogical chart; descendants of the Rev. John Orme (born 1691; will probated in Prince George Co., 1758) and connected families. Printed. Book form. MHS.
Lineage Bks., Natl. Soc. of Daughters of Amer. Col., v. 1, p. 83. MHS; DAR.
Pedigree of Coleman Randall Freeman. Soc. Col. Wars Md. Culver. 1940. MHS; DAR.
Pedigree of Henry Irvine Keyser II. Soc. Col. Wars Md. Culver. 1940. MHS; DAR.
Mrs. H. De Courcy Wright Thom chart. MHS.
***Ormonde-Dunboyne-Butler,** Pa. The Sun, Balto., March 27, 1904.
Ormsby. Faith Pres. Church (Glendy graveyard). Mss. MHS.
†**Orndorff.** From mill wheel to plowshare. Julia A. Drake and J. R. Orndorff. (Christian Orndorff settled in West. Md., 1762; soldier of Revolution.) MHS.
Review of above by Francis B. Culver. M. H. Mag., 1939, v. 34, no. 2, p. 200; correction, no. 3, p. 399.
***Orndorff Family,** Hagerstown. Wilson Mss. Coll., no. 16. MHS.
Orne. St. Paul's Parish, Balto. V. 2. Mss. MHS.
***Orrendorff.** Frederick Co. families. Markell. Ms. Personal list.
Orrick. Amer. families. Geneal. and heraldic. Amer. Hist. Soc., N. Y., pp. 322–27. DAR.
Baldwin-Woodward chart. Cary Geneal. Coll. Ms. MHS.
†Hist. of Allegany Co. Thomas and Williams. V. 1. MHS; DAR.
Lineage Bks., Natl. Soc. of Daughters of Amer. Col., v. 1, p. 13. MHS; DAR.
Md. families. Culver. Ms. Personal list.
Md. tombstone rec. Md. Geneal. Rec. Com., 1937, Parran, p. 27. Mss. DAR.
†Med. Annals Md. Cordell. 1903, p. 523. MHS.
†Men of mark in Md. Johnson. V. 3. DAR; Enoch Pratt Lib.
St. Paul's Parish. Balto. V. 1, 2. Mss. MHS.
Semmes and allied families. Semmes. MHS.
G. M. Sharp pedigree chart, plate 2. Soc. Col. Wars, Md. Johnston. 1905, p. 92. MHS.
See Moore-Orrick.
See Pendleton-Orrick-Strother-Calvert.
Orrick, Anne Arundel Co. Blackwell chart. MHS.
Orrick, Henry Albert. Pedigree chart. Soc. Col. Wars, Md. Johnston. 1905, pp. 79 150. MHS.
Orrick, Orrock. Balto., its hist., its people. Hall. V. 3. MHS; DAR.
Cary Geneal. Coll. Ms. MHS.
***Orrick, Orrock,** Anne Arundel Co., 1665. The Sun, Balto., Feb. 10, 17, 24, 1907.
See Orrick.
Orsler (**Oursler-Owens** (**Owings**). Natl. Geneal. Soc. Quart., Apr., 1917, v. 6, no. 1, p. 32.
***Osborn.** Lineage Bk., Daughters of Founders and Patriots, v. 3, p. 99; v. 6, pp. 85–86, 88. MHS.
See Farmer Family; Harford Co. Hist. Soc. Mss. Coll. JHU.
St. Paul's Parish, Balto. V. 1, 2. Mss. MHS.
See Robertson-Osborn.
Osborn, Cyrus, Harford Co. Will probated Dec. 10, 1798. D. A. R. Mag., v. 65, no. 8, p. 507.
Osborn, Jane, Harford Co. Will probated Nov. 26, 1787. D. A. R. Mag., v. 65, no. 8, p. 506.

Osborn, Lawrence, Harford Co. (died Feb. 20, 1789). Will Book A. J., no. 2, p. 504. All to Phrisby Dorsey. D. A. R. Mag., v. 65, no. 8, p. 507.
Osborne. Sara R. Baldwin chart. MHS.
Monnet family geneal. Monette. P. 1111. MHS.
Osborne, Va. Chart. Geneal. tables of descendants of John Hamilton, Va. MHS.
Osbourn. Somerset Co. Court Book. Tilghman. 1937. Ms. DAR.
†**Osler.** Great physician; short life of Sir William Osler. Edith Gettings Reid. London, N. Y., Toronto, Oxford Univ. Press, 1931. Enoch Pratt Lib.
†Life of Sir William Osler. Harvey W. Cushings. 2 v. Oxford, Clarendon Press, 1925, 2 vols. MHS; Enoch Pratt Lib.
†Med. Annals Md. Cordell. 1903, pp. 523–24. MHS.
†**Osler, Sir William, Bart.** Brief tributes to his personality, influence and his public service. Johns Hopkins Univ. Press, 1920. Enoch Pratt Lib.
†Canadian Med. Assoc. Jour., memorial number. July, 1920. Enoch Pratt Lib.
Oswald. Chew family. Culver. M. H. Mag., 1935, v. 30, no. 2, pp. 157–75.
De Ford chart. MHS.
†Hist. of Washington Co. Williams. 1906, v. 2, p. 986. MHS; DAR.
Mrs. J. F. Lee chart. MHS.
†Men of mark in Md. Johnson. V. 1. DAR; Enoch Pratt Lib.
Mrs. E. C. Venable chart. MHS.
Oswald, Jonathan, D.D. Memoir. Quart. Rev. of Evangelical Luth. Church, Gettysburg, 1892, v. 22, pp. 341–53.
Othoson. Naturalizations in Md., 1666–1765; Laws. Bacon. MHS.
St. Stephens Parish, Cecilton, Md. MHS; DAR.
Ott. Frederick Co. tombstone inscriptions. Gruder. Natl. Geneal. Soc. Quart., 1919, v. 8, nos. 1, 2.
Hagerstown tombstone inscriptions. Gruder. Natl. Geneal. Soc. Quart., 1919, v. 8, nos. 1, 2.
†**Otterbein.** Life of Rev. Philip Wm. Otterbein, founder of Church of United Brethren in Christ. Rev. A. W. Drury. (Born in Germany, 1726; died in Md., 1813.) Dayton, Ohio, United Brethren Pub. House, 1884, 1913 MHS; Enoch Pratt Lib.
U. B. cemetery, Harbaugh Valley. Burial rec. MHS.
‡**Otterbein, Philip William.** Otterbein and Reformed Church. W. J. Hinke. Presbyterian and Reformed Rev., 1901, v. 12, pp. 437–52.
†**Otto.** Med. Annals of Md. Cordell. 1903, p. 524. MHS.
Ould. Geneal. and memorial encyc. of Md. Spencer. V. 1, p. 250. MHS; DAR.
See Old.
***Oursler.** Burke's landed gentry. 1939. MHS.
*Lineage Bk., Daughters of Amer. Col., v. 1, pp. 31–32. MHS; DAR.
Mt. Paran Pres. churchyard, Harrisonville, Balto. Co. Typed ms. MHS; DAR.
St. Thomas' Parish, Balto. Co. Bd. ms. MHS. Also: Md. Geneal. Rec. Com., 1937, pp. 109–82. Mss. DAR.
See Orsler.
Ousler. Beall and Bell families. Beall. MHS; DAR.
Ousler-Jean-Ridgely. Bible rec. Focke Geneal. Coll. Ms. MHS.
Outen. Somerset Co. Court Book. Tilghman. 1937. Ms. DAR.
Outten. Turner Geneal. Coll. Ms. MHS.
Overall. Orme geneal. chart. MHS.
Owen. Anne Arundel Co. tombstone inscriptions. Ms. DAR.
Beall and Bell families. Beall. MHS; DAR.
Matthews-Price chart. MHS.
Patriotic Md. Md. Soc. of S. A. R., 1930. MHS; DAR.
Pedigree of Dr. Christopher Johnston, Jr. Soc. Col. Wars Md. Culver. 1940. MHS; DAR.
Pedigree of Gustav Wm. Lurman. Soc. Col. Wars Md. Culver. 1940. MHS; DAR.
Pedigree of James Donnell Tilghman. Soc. Col. Wars Md. Culver. 1940. MHS; DAR.
St. Paul's Parish, Balto. V. 2. Mss. MHS.
Somerset Co. Court Book. Tilghman. 1937. Ms. DAR.
Tiernan families. Tiernan. 1901. MHS; DAR.
See Anderson-Owen-Beall.
See Owens.
Owen, Frederick Co. C. B. Tiernan pedigree chart. Soc. Col. Wars, Md. Johnston. 1905, p. 113. MHS.
Owen, Franklin Buchanan. Pedigree. Soc. Col. Wars Md. Culver. 1940. MHS; DAR.
Owen, Richard, Wales. See Maynard family. Focke Geneal. Coll. Ms. MHS.
†**Owen, Owens, Owings.** Med. Annals Md. Cordell. 1903, pp. 524–25. MHS.
Wills. Rogers Coll. Ms. MHS.
Owen, Owens, Owings, Balto. Co. Focke Geneal. Coll. Ms. MHS.
Owens. Bible rec. Anne Arundel Co. Natl. Geneal. Soc. Quart. 1931. V. 19, no. 4, p. 109.
*Bible rec. M. H. Mag., Mar. 1935, v. 30, no. 1, pp. 42–45.
†Hist. of Balto. City and Co. Scharf. P. 295. MHS.
Richard Owens and Rachel Beall. Ms. DAR.
Patriotic Md. Md. Soc. of S. A. R., 1930. MHS; DAR.
Rec. from Bible owned by Mrs. A. B. Owens. Ms. MHS.
White geneal. tree. MHS.
Winchester-Owens-Owings-Price and allied families. M. H. Mag., 1930, v. 25, no. 4, p. 385–405.
See Orsler-Owens.
See Owen.
See Owings.
***Owens, Albert S.** Encyc. of Amer. biog. Amer. Hist. Soc., new series, v. 1, p. 215. MHS; DAR.
Owens, E. Burneston. Md. Soc., War of 1812, v. 2, no. 138. Ms. MHS.
Owens, E. Burneston, Jr. Md. Soc., War of 1812, v. 4, no. 333. Ms. MHS.
Owens, Franklin Buchanan. Md. Soc., War of 1812, v. 4, no. 305. Ms. MHS.
Owens, Isaac Burneston. Bible rec. Ms. MHS.
Owens, James, Anne Arundel Co. Family data. Ms. MHS.

†**Owens, John E.** Memoirs of professional and social life. By his wife. Balto., 1892. MHS.
Owens, Thomas and Elizabeth. Bible rec. Ms. MHS.
Owens - Claytor - Maynard - Rutter - Welsh. Bible rec., 1791–1909. Focke Geneal. Coll. Ms. MHS.
Owens, Owen, Prince George Co. Col. families of U. S. A. Mackenzie. V. 4. MHS.
Owens, Owen, Owings. Dorsey and allied families. Ms. MHS.
Families. 5500 indexes. Focke Geneal. Coll. Ms. MHS.
***Owens, Owins.** Wicomico Co. families. Tilghman. Ms, pp. 109, 115. DAR.
Owerard. Naturalizations in Md., 1666–1765; Laws. Bacon. MHS.
Owing. *See* Owen.
Owings. Arnold chart. MHS.
Bailliere chart. MHS.
Beall and Bell families. Beall. MHS. DAR.
Bible rec. Ms. MHS.
Bible rec. Md. Geneal. Bull., v. 2, pp. 10–12. MHS; DAR.
Cary Geneal. Coll. Ms. MHS.
Cemetery Creek, Anne Arundel Co., tombstone inscriptions. Founders of Anne Arundel and Howard Cos. Warfield. P. 334. MHS; DAR.
Data. D. A. R. Mag., v. 70, no. 2, p. 130.
*Dryden family Bible. File case, MHS.
Family note from estate of Mrs. Wilson Burns Trundle. MHS.
Founders of Anne Arundel and Howard Cos. Warfield. Pp. 389–90. MHS; DAR.
*Garrison Church. Allen. Pp. 134–38. MHS; DAR.
Griffith geneal. Griffith. MHS; DAR.
†Hist. of Balto. City and Co. Scharf. P. 862. MHS.
†Hist. of Frederick Co. Williams. MHS; DAR.
Hood family Bible rec. Pamph. MHS.
*Hood-Worthington-Owings. Ms. MHS.
Jennings-Hand Bible rec. Photos. MHS.
Joshua Dryden Bible rec. Ms. MHS.
Lehr chart. MHS.
*Lineage Bk., Daughters of Founders and Patriots, v. 15, pp. 120–21. MHS.
Lineage Bks., Natl. Soc. of Daughters of Amer. Col., v. 1, pp. 42, 309; v. 2, pp. 95, 297. MHS; DAR.
Marriages of Frederick and St. Mary's Co. Focke Geneal. Coll. Ms. MHS.
Md. families. Culver. Ms. Personal list.
*Owings-Gaither-Hood-Thomas Bible rec. Ms. File case, MHS.
*Old Md. Bibles, family rec. M. H. Mag., v. 29, p. 322.
Patriotic Md. Md. Soc. of S. A. R., 1930. MHS; DAR.
Pedigree of Charles Worthington Hoff. Soc. Col. Wars Md. Culver. 1940. MHS; DAR.
Pedigree of Charles O'Donovan. Soc. Col. Wars Md. Culver. 1940. MHS; DAR.
Pedigree of Richard Walker Worthington. Soc. Col. Wars Md. Culver. 1940. MHS; DAR.
Mrs. C. L. Riggs chart. MHS.
St. Paul's Parish, Balto. V. 1, 2. Mss. MHS.
St. Thomas' Parish, Balto. Co. Bd. ms. MHS. Also: Md. Geneal. Rec. Com., 1937, pp. 109–82. Mss. DAR.
Sarah Smith Hood Bible rec. Ms. MHS.
Talbott of "Poplar Knowle." Shirk. MHS; DAR.
*Wethered-Owings Bible rec. from Wethered Bible. File case, MHS.
Wills of Balto. and Montgomery Cos. Focke Geneal. Coll. Ms. MHS.
Winchester-Owens-Owings-Price and allied families. M. H. Mag., 1930, v. 25, no. 4, p. 385–405.
See Fite-Owings-Stinchcomb.
See Hood-Worthington-Owings.
See Lynch-Owings.
See Orsler-Owens (Owings).
See Owen.
See Owens.
See Wethered-Owings.
See Winchester-Owings.
***Owings,** Balto. Co. and Frost, Howard Co. Notes. M. H. Mag., 1939, v. 34, no. 3, p. 304.
Owings, Caleb. Bible rec. Natl. Geneal. Soc. Quart., v. 5, no. 4, p. 63.
Owings, James Winchester (1775–1837). Old Md. Bibles. M. H. Mag., 1934, v. 29, no. 4, pp. 322–30.
Owings, John Cockey. Bible rec., 1772-1918. Ms. Filing case A, MHS.
Owings, Richard. Copy of will. Ms. MHS.
Owings, Richard Munro. Graveyard, Morgan Valley, Westminster, Carroll Co. Ms. MHS.
Owings, Samuel and **Ruth Cockey** (1791–1861). Old Md. Bibles. M. H. Mag., v. 29, no. 4, pp. 322–30.
Owings, Samuel. Geneal. (complete) and allied families Cromwell, Moale, Randall, Winchester and twenty others. Focke Geneal. Coll. Ms. MHS.
Owings, Samuel, Balto. Co. W. A. Moale pedigree charts, plate 2. Soc. Col. Wars, Md. Johnston. 1905, pp. 73, 150. MHS.
Owings, Thomas. Copy of will. Ms. MHS.
***Owings, Thomas Deye** (1776–1853). Soldier and pioneer of West. M. H. Mag., Mar., 1935, v. 30, no. 1, p. 39.
Owings, Urath Randall (1707–56). Old Md. Bibles. M. H. Mag., 1934. V. 29, no. 4, pp. 322–30.
Owings, W. M. Bible rec., 1777–1840. Natl. Geneal. Soc. Quart., v. 18, no. 3, p. 68; v. 19, no. 4, p. 109.
Owings Family. Bible. Md. Geneal. Bull., v. 2, p. 9; v. 3, p. 18; v. 6, pp. 1, 46. MHS; DAR.
Charts (60) from 1692–1890. Focke Geneal. Coll. Ms. MHS.
Geneal. Soc. Pa., Mss. Coll.
Natl. Geneal. Soc. Quart., v. 4, no. 4, p. 62. MHS; DAR.
Origin and chart of Richard Owen, 1470–1673. Focke Geneal. Coll. Ms. MHS.
Rec., copied from data in possession of Miss Alice E. Owings, Reistertown, Md. Ms. MHS.
Wills; Thomas, 1863; Richard, 1818. Ruth Owings estate. File case A, MHS.
Owings-Dryden-Harris. Bible rec., 1699–1875. Focke Geneal. Coll. Ms. MHS.
Owings-Harris. Bible rec. Focke Geneal. Coll. Ms. MHS.
Owings-Reister. Bible rec., 1765–1894. Focke Geneal. Coll. Ms. MHS.

Owings, Owens. Owings and Owens of Md. Geneal., Mag. Amer. Ancestry, N. Y., 1916, v. 3, no. 5.
Tombstone rec. from burial ground on farm of Mr. Ward, 1 mile north of Randallstown; few stones in Granite Presbyterian Church Cemetery, Baltimore Co.; also inscriptions on farm called "Rotchester" near Westminster, Carroll Co. Focke Geneal. Coll. Ms. MHS.
Owins. *See* Owens.
Ozey. St. Stephens Parish, Cecilton, Md. MHS; DAR.
Ozier. St. Stephens Parish, Cecilton, Md. MHS; DAR.

P

Paca. Abr. Compend. Amer. Geneal. Virkus. V. 6, p. 429. DAR.
Bantz geneal. notes. Ms. MHS.
†Bench and bar of Md. Sams and Riley. 1901, v. 1, p. 160. Lib. Cong.; MHS; Peabody Lib.
†Biog. cyc. of rep. men of Md. and D. C. P. 310. MHS; DAR.
Chart, photos., complete in 2 sheets. Cary Geneal. Coll. Ms. MHS.
Col. families of U. S. A. Mackenzie. V. 1. MHS; DAR.
Col. mansions of Md. and Del. Hammond. 1914. MHS.
Cotton chart. MHS.
Dallam family. Dallam. 1929, p. 26. MHS.
Descendants of Col. Thomas White. Morris. MHS.
Gantz family geneal. Ms. MHS.
*Gantz geneal. notes. File case A, MHS.
Hist. of Harford Co. Preston. MHS; DAR.
†Hist. of Talbot Co. Tilghman. V. 2, p. 550. MHS; DAR.
Lineage Bks., Natl. Soc. of Daughters of Amer. Col., v. 2, p. 94. MHS; DAR.
Modern encyc. McDannald. 1933.
Patriotic Md. Md. Soc. of S. A. R., 1930. MHS; DAR.
*Pennington Papers. Ms. MHS.
Side lights on Md. hist. Richardson. V. 2, p. 194. MHS; DAR.
*The Sun, Balto., July 3, 24, 1904.
Wye Island. Bordley, Lloyd and Paca families. Lippincott Mag., v. 19.
See Bordley-Lloyd-Paca.
See Carmichael-Paca-Tilghman-Veazey.
See Carroll-Chase-Paca-Stone.
See Taylor-Robertson-Standiford.
Paca, James Philemon Davidson. (7 generations.) Pedigree. Soc. Col. Wars Md. Culver. 1940. MHS; DAR.
Paca, John Philemon. Pedigree. Soc. Col. Wars Md. Culver. 1940. MHS; DAR.
Pedigree chart. Soc. Col. Wars, Md. Johnston. 1905, pp. 80, 150, 151. MHS.
Paca, John Philemon V. Pedigree. Soc. Col. Wars Md. Culver. 1940. MHS; DAR.
Paca, Wm. Biog. of signers of Declaration of Independence. Joseph M. Sanderson. 1820–27, v. 8, pp. 173–78.
†**Paca, Gov. William.** Founders of Anne Arundel and Howard Cos. Warfield. P. 235. MHS; DAR.
†Governors of Md. Buchholz. P. 14. MHS.
†(1740–99). M. H. Mag., v. 12, p. 231.
†Hist. of Md. Scharf. V. 2, p. 225. MHS.
***Paca Family.** Arch. of Georgetown Univ., Wash., D. C., v. 287.
Data. Times, Phila., 1879. Newsp. clipp. MHS.
Paca-Quinan. Harford Co. Hist Soc. Mss. Coll. JHU.
Paca-Smithson-Forwood. (1904) G. N. Mackenzie on Patterson. Harford Co. Hist. Soc. Mss. Coll. JHU.
Pack, William, Frederick Co. D. A. R. Mag., v. 71, no. 12, p. 1110.
†**Packard.** In memoriam of Joseph Packard, lawyer and layman (died in Balto., 1923). Pamph. Enoch Pratt Lib.
†Men of mark in Md. Johnson. V. 2. DAR; Enoch Pratt Lib.
Packard, Charles Lee. Pedigree. Soc. Col. Wars, Md. Culver. 1940. MHS; DAR.
Packard, Joseph. Pedgiree. Soc. Col. Wars Md. Culver. 1940. MHS; DAR.
Packard Family. Lee of Va., 1642–1892. E. J. Lee. P. 369. Lib. Cong.; MHS.
Packet. Naturalizations in Md., 1666–1765; Laws. Bacon. MHS.
Pacquet. Naturalizations in Md., 1666–1765; Laws. Bacon. MHS.
†**Page.** Bench and bar of Md. Sams and Riley. 1901, v. 2, p. 648. Lib. Cong.; MHS; Peabody Lib.
Christ P. E. Church cemetery, Cambridge. Steele. 1936. MHS; DAR.
*Geneal. of Page family in Va. and other distinguished families in Va. Coat of arms. R. C. M. Page. N. Y., Press Publishers Printing Co., 1893. MHS; DAR.
Mrs. D. G. Lovell chart. MHS.
†Med. Annals Md. Cordell. 1903, pp. 525–26. MHS.
*Pennington Papers. Ms. MHS.
St. Paul's Parish, Balto. V. 1, 2. Mss. MHS.
Selden chart. MHS.
***Page,** Middlesex Co., Va. Burke's landed gentry. 1939. MHS.
Page, Louis Rodman. Pedigree chart. Soc. Col. Wars, Md. Johnston. 1905, p. 81. MHS.
Page Family. Bible rec. (John Page, 1790.) Ms. MHS.
***Page Family,** Va. By E. C. Meade. The Sun, Balto., July 3, 24, 31, 1904; Jan. 20, 27, Feb. 3, 10, 1907.
Lee of Va., 1642–1892. E. J. Lee. P. 482. Lib. Cong.; MHS.
Page-Wickes-Wroth. Bible rec., Kent Co. Md. Geneal. Rec. Com., 1933–34, pp. 223–27. Mss. DAR.
Paget. Naturalizations in Md., 1666–1765; Laws. Bacon. MHS.
†**Pagett.** Med. Annals Md. Cordell. 1903, p. 526. MHS.
Somerset Co. Court Book. Tilghman. 1937. Ms. DAR.
Pagues. *See* Peagus.
Paine. Balto., its hist., its people. Hall. V. 3. MHS; DAR.
Burton ancestry. Ms. MHS.
*Geneal. of Ipswich branch. Albert W. Paine. 1881.
Hist. of Balto. Lewis Pub. Co., 1912, v. 3, pp. 926–27. DAR.
Painter. Geneal. of family of Gideon Gilpin. MHS.

Painter. Harlan family geneal., Chester Co., Pa. Harlan. P. 682. MHS.
William Painter and his father Dr. Edward Painter. O. C. Painter. Balto., 1914. MHS; DAR; Enoch Pratt Lib.
***Painter Family** (1699-1903). Samuel Painter, who came from Eng. about 1699, settled in Chester Co., Pa. O. C. Painter. Balto., John S. Bridges Co., 1903. MHS; DAR.
Paiver. Ring's End private burying ground, Queen Anne's Co. Md. Geneal. Rec. Com., 1933-34, p. 208. Mss. DAR.
Palmer. Centerville cemetery. Md. O. R. Soc. Bull., no. 1, pp. 41-47.
Geneal. of family of Gideon Gilpin. MHS.
†Hist. of Frederick Co. Williams. MHS; DAR.
Hist. of West. Md. Scharf. V. 1, pp. 412, 778.
Howell Bible rec. Ms. MHS.
†Med. Annals Md. Cordell. 1903, p. 527. MHS.
St. Paul's Parish, Balto. V. 1, 2. Mss. MHS.
***Palmer,** Delaware Co., Pa. Geneal. L. Palmer. 1875.
Palmer, Montgomery Co. Sharpless family geneal. Cope. Pp. 1173-74. MHS; DAR.
Port. and biog. rec. of Sixth Cong. Dist. P. 745. MHS; DAR.
***Palmer, Edw. Livingston.** Geneal. and mem. encyc. of Md. Spencer. V. 2, pp. 712-17. MHS; DAR.
Palmer, Mrs. Howard Keppel (Virginia Southall Gordon). Chart. Col. Dames, Chap. I. MHS.
Palmer Family. Mss. DAR.
Palmer-Brown. Abr. Compend. Amer. Geneal. Virkus. V. 1, p. 756. DAR.
***Palton.** Frederick Co. families. Markell. Ms. Personal list.
Pamphilion. St. Paul's Parish, Balto. V. 1, 2. Mss. MHS.
Pancoast. Florence Eyster Weaver chart. MHS.
Gilpin chart. MHS.
Sharpless family geneal. Cope. P. 908. MHS; DAR.
Talbott of "Poplar Knowle." Shirk. MHS; DAR.
Pangborn. Balto., its hist., its people. Hall. V. 2. MHS; DAR.
Hist. of Balto. Lewis Pub. Co., 1912, v. 2, p. 209. DAR.
Paramour. Somerset Co. Court Book. Tilghman. 1937. Ms. DAR.
Parandier. Naturalizations in Md., 1666-1765; Laws. Bacon. MHS.
†**Pardee.** Geneal. and mem. encyc. of Md. Spencer. V. 2, p. 685. MHS; DAR.
†**Paret.** Reminiscences by Rt. Rev. William Paret, D.D., L.L.D., sixth Bishop of Md. Phila., George W. Jacobs & Co., 1911. MHS; Enoch Pratt Lib.
†**Paret, Bishop Wm.** Men of mark in Md. Johnson. V. 4, p. 94. DAR; Enoch Pratt Lib.
Parish. Cary Geneal. Coll. Ms. MHS.
The North-American, Phila., Dec. 24, 1911. Newsp. clipp. R. H. Spencer Scrap Book. MHS.
R. H. Spencer Scrap Book. MHS.
*The Sun, Balto., Jan. 22, 1905.
Parish Family. North American, Phila., Dec. 24, 1911, p. 91. MHS.
Parish, Parrish. St. Paul's Parish, Balto. V. 1, 2, 4. Mss. MHS.
Park. Burton ancestry. Ms. MHS.
Cummings chart. Lib. Cong.; MHS; DAR.
See Avery-Fairchild-Park Families.
Park, Charles McKnew. Pedigree. Soc. Col. Wars Md. Culver. 1940. MHS; DAR.
Parke. Arthur Parke of Pa. and some of his descendants. Frank Sylvester Parks. (Parke, Md., p. 13.) Washington, D. C., 1922, pamph. MHS.
†Hist. of West. Md. Scharf. V. 2, pp. 944-45. MHS; DAR.
Lloyd - Pemberton - Hutchinson - Hudson - Parke families. Glenn. MHS; DAR.
***Parke Family.** Arch. of Georgetown Univ., Wash., D. C., v. 287.
Parker. All Hallow's P. E. churchyard, Snow Hill, Worcester Co. Hudson. Bd. ms. MHS; DAR. Also: Md. Geneal. Rec. Com., 1935-36, p. 24. Mss. DAR.
Abr. Compend. Amer. Geneal. Virkus. V. 1, p. 756. DAR.
Ances. rec. and portraits. Col. Dames of Amer., 1910, pp. 227, 234, 576. MHS; DAR.
Balto., its hist., its people. Hall. V. 2. MHS; DAR.
Bible rec., 1777-1869. Bible now in possession of E. A. Marriner, Indiantown, Md. Md. Geneal. Rec. Com., 1937-38, pp. 161-62. Mss. DAR.
Britton Scrap Book. V. 1. Ms. MHS.
Hist. of Balto. Lewis *Pub. Co., 1912, v. 2, p. 334. DAR.
Hist. of Kent Co. Usilton. Pp. 43-44. DAR.
Howard-Montague-Warfield geneal. chart. Culver and Marye. MHS.
Md. Geneal. Rec. Com., 1937-38, pp. 158-62. Mss. DAR.
†Med. Annals Md. Cordell. 1903, pp. 527-28. MHS.
M. E. churchyard, Snow Hill, Worcester Co., Hudson. Bd. ms. MHS; DAR.
Parker family of Northampton and Accomac Cos., Va. (also Md.). Va. Mag. Hist. and Biog., v. 6, pp. 412-18.
Rec. of Stepney Parish. MHS; DAR.
St. Barnabas P. E. churchyard. Typed ms. MHS; DAR.
St. Paul's Parish, Balto. V. 2, 4. Mss. MHS.
Taylor Bible rec. Ms. MHS.
Trinity Church cemetery, Dorchester Co. Md. O. R. Soc. Bull., no. 3, pp. 42-52.
Turner Geneal. Coll. Ms. MHS.
*Wicomico Co. families. Tilghman. Ms, pp. 17, 41, 95. DAR.
See Humphries-Pope-Brock-Parker.
Parker, Northern Neck, Va. Cary Geneal. Coll. Ms. MHS.
Parker, Va. Miss G. Eyre Wright chart. MHS.
***Parker, George.** D. C. Geneal. Rec. Com., 1933-34, v. 12, p. 104. Typed, bd. DAR.
***Parker, Sumner A.** Burke's landed gentry. 1939. MHS.
***Parker Family,** Va. By E. C. Meade. The Sun, Balto., Nov. 13, Dec. 4, 1904.
Parker Family, Va., Md. and Ga. D. A. R. Mag., Dec., 1934, v. 68, no. 12, pp. 728-30.
(Parker and Furner families sailed from Balto. to Ga., 1790.) D. A. R. Mag., v. 68, no. 12, pp. 728-30.

Parker-Brittingham. Bible rec., from Bible owned by John Parker Minus, of John of John, Pittsville, Wicomico Co. Md. Geneal. Rec. Com., 1937–38, pp. 158–60. Mss. DAR.
Parkinson. Patriotic Md. Md. Soc. of S. A. R., 1930. MHS; DAR.
†**Parks.** Hist. of printing in Col. Md. Wroth. MHS.
Lehr chart. MHS.
Mrs. A. G. Obert chart. MHS.
Pedigree and hist. of Washington family. Welles. Pp. 182, 212, 214. MHS.
Miss Margaret M. Steele chart. MHS.
St. Paul's Parish, Balto. V. 1, 2. Mss. MHS.
Still Pond Church and cemetery. Md. O. R. Soc. Bull., no. 2, pp. 65–75. MHS.
*Wicomico Co. families. Tilghman. Ms., p. 52. DAR.
Mrs. J. Whitridge Williams chart. MHS.
See Prier-Parks-Hastings.
†**Parks, Wm.** Hist. of Md. Scharf. V. 1, p. 394. MHS.
†Printer and journalist of Eng. and col. Amer. L. C. Wroth. William Parks Club Pub.,no.3. Richmond, Va., Appeals Press, Inc., 1926. MHS; Enoch Pratt Lib.
Parlett. St. Paul's Parish, Balto. V. 1. Mss. MHS.
Trinity P. E. churchyard, Long Green. Typed ms. MHS; DAR.
Parnell. St. Paul's Parish, Balto. V. 2. Mss. MHS.
Parnham. Ances. rec. and portraits. Col. Dames of Amer., 1910, v. 2, p. 535. MHS; DAR.
J. L. Brent pedigree chart. Soc. Col. Wars, Md. Johnston. 1905, p. 7. MHS.
Manly chart. MHS.
†Med. Annals Md. Cordell. 1903, p. 528. MHS.
Pedigree of Duncan Keener Brent. Soc. Col. Wars Md. Culver. 1940. MHS; DAR.
*Wills. Semmes Geneal. Coll. Ms. MHS.
Parr. Balto., its hist., its people. Hall. V. 3. MHS; DAR.
Hist. of Balto. Lewis Pub. Co. V. 3, p. 644. DAR.
Maulsby family in Amer. Barnard. DAR; Peabody Lib.
Parr, Mrs. Ral (Laura Sewall Jenkins). 2 charts, showing the royal lineage of Mrs. Parr. Col. Dames, Chap. I. MHS.
Parramore. Rec. of Stepney Parish. MHS; DAR.
Parran. Col. families of U. S. A. Mackenzie. V. 5, p. 169. MHS; DAR.
Geneal. and mem. encyc. of Md. Spencer. V. 2, p. 420. MHS; DAR.
†Med. Annals Md. Cordell. 1903, p. 528. MHS.
Parran papers of Calvert Co. Photos. (4 papers). Will of Alex Parran, 1764; also land rec. (2), 1655, 1659. Ms. MHS.
Pedigree of Walter Ireland Dawkins. Soc. Col. Wars Md. Culver. 1940. MHS; DAR.
Taylor Bible rec. Ms. MHS.
Parran, Dalrymple. Pedigree. Soc. Col. Wars Md. Culver. 1940. MHS; DAR.
Parran, Francis Joseph. Pedigree. Soc. Col. Wars Md. Culver. 1940. MHS; DAR.
Parreymore. Rec. of Stepney Parish. MHS; DAR.
Parrine-Edmundson Family. Focke Geneal. Coll. Mss. MHS.
Parrish. Abr. Compend. Amer. Geneal. Virkus. V. 6, p. 675. DAR.
*Boyd family. Boyd. DAR.
Griffith geneal. Griffith. MHS; DAR.
Hist. of west. Md. Scharf. V. 1, p. 631.
Md. families. Culver. Ms. Personal list.
See Parish.
Parrish, J. Hagerty. Md. Soc., War of 1812, v. 1, no. 83. Ms. MHS.
Parrish, W. Trippet. Md. Soc., War of 1812, v. 1, no. 84. Ms. MHS.
Parrish Family. Marriages in Md., 1782–1849. Parrish family. Boyd. MHS; DAR.
*Parrish family. Scott Lee Boyd, Santa Barbara, Cal. Geneal., Katherine Cox Gottschalk. (Many Quaker family rec. from Balto. Meeting and Gunpowder Meeting in Balto. Co.) 1935. MHS; DAR.
Parrish-Marshall. Morris family of Phila. Moon. V. 2, p. 577. MHS.
Parrott. Mrs. G. H. Williams, Jr., chart. MHS.
Parrott, H. E. Abr. Compend. Amer. Geneal. Virkus. V. 1, p. 757. DAR.
Parrott, Wm. Pedigree of Granville Bowdle Hopkins. Soc. Col. Wars Md. Culver. 1940. MHS; DAR.
Parrott Family. Port. and biog. rec. of Sixth Cong. Dist. of Md. P. 487. MHS; DAR.
Parrott Line, Talbot Co. H. Mullikin pedigree charts, plates 1 and 2. Soc. Col. Wars, Md. Johnston. 1905, pp. 74–75, 151. MHS.
Parry. Turner Geneal. Coll. Ms. MHS.
Parsley. Graves. Lay Hill burial ground, Montgomery Co. Md. Geneal. Rec. Com., 1934–35, pp. 66–67. Mss. DAR.
Parsley, Parsly. St. Stephens Parish, Cecilton, Md. MHS; DAR.
Parson. Geneal. and mem. encyc. of Md. Spencer. V. 2, pp. 650–52. MHS; DAR.
Parsons. Chestertown cemetery. Md. O. R. Soc. Bull., no. 1, pp. 18–29.
Price family and other Gunpowder Friends. Death notices; photos. of newsp. clipp. MHS.
Rec. of Stepney Parish. MHS; DAR.
St. Stephens Parish, Cecilton, Md. MHS; DAR.
Somerset Co. Court Book. Tilghman. 1937. Ms. DAR.
*Wicomico Co. families. Tilghman. Ms., pp. 30, 46–50, 116, 121, 124. DAR.
See Humphreys-Parsons.
See Nutter-Taylor-Parsons-Adkins.
Parsons, Charles Lathrop, Jr. Pedigree. (New Eng. families, Plymouth colony.) Soc Col. Wars Md. Culver. 1940. MHS; DAR.
Parsons, Thomas, Anne Arundel Co. Will, 1683. Md. Geneal. Rec. Com., 1932, p. 188. DAR.
Parsons Family. Notes of Stepney Parish, Somerset Co., 1702–1807. Md. Geneal. Bull., v. 6, pp. 16–17. MHS; DAR.
David and Charles Parsons of Charles Co. Data. Ms. DAR.
Rec. of John of Harford Co.; also Waltham and Kelly family data. Ms. DAR.
Parsons-Maddox-Travers. Wicomico Co. families. Bible rec. Ms. DAR.
Parsons-Price-Tipton. Parrish family. Boyd. MHS; DAR.

Partridge. Bond chart. MHS.
Bond family geneal. Ms. MHS.
Miss C. Petre chart. MHS.
St. Paul's Parish, Balto. V. 2. Mss. MHS.
Somerset Co. Court Book. Tilghman. 1937. Ms. DAR.
Taney and allied families. Silverson. MHS; DAR.
Parvin. Andrews' Scrap Book. MHS.
Newsp. clipp. Andrews Scrap Book. MHS.
Pascault. Mrs. J. G. Brogden chart. MHS.
Goldsborough-Pascault Bible rec. Ms. MHS.
Spring Hill cemetery, Easton. Md. O. R. Soc. Bull., no. 1, pp. 35–41.
Paschall. Lloyd family hist. of Wales, Pa., and Md. DAR.
Paschall, Chester Co., Pa. H. Mullikin pedigree charts, plate 2. Soc. Col. Wars, Md. Johnston. 1905, p. 75. MHS.
Passano. Abr. Compend. Amer. Geneal. Virkus. V. 1, p. 138. DAR.
***Passano, Edward Boteler.** See Magruder. Burke's landed gentry. 1939. MHS.
Amer. Armory and Blue Book. Matthews. 1911–12, p. 265.
*Encyc. of Amer. biog. Amer. Hist. Soc., N. Y., 1928, v. 33, p. 230.
Pedigree. Soc. Col. Wars Md. Culver. 1940. MHS; DAR.
Passano, Edward Magruder. Pedigree. Soc. Col. Wars Md. Culver. 1940. MHS; DAR.
Passmore. Sharpless family geneal. Cope. P. 298. MHS; DAR.
St. Paul's Parish, Balto. V. 2. Mss. MHS.
Passwater. *See* Robinson-Passwater-Smith-Wiatt.
Paterson. *See* Patterson.
Patrick. Patriotic Md. Md. Soc. of S. A. R., 1930. MHS; DAR.
*Wicomico Co. families. Tilghman. Ms., p. 95. DAR.
Patten. Descendants of Joran Kyn. Pa. Mag., v. 7, p. 299.
Patten, Mrs. J. M. C. Abr. Compend. Amer. Geneal. Virkus. V. 1, p. 760. DAR.
Patterson. Bible rec., 1803–22. Md. Geneal. Rec. Com., 1932–33, v. 5, p. 20. DAR.
*Frederick Co. families. Markell. Ms. Personal list.
Funeral services of George Patterson, Jr., son of George and Prudence A. Patterson of Springfield, Carroll Co., who died Dec. 21, 1845. Thomas J. Shepherd. Balto., John D. Toy, 1850. Enoch Pratt Lib.
Greenway Mss. Geneal. Coll. Binder's title, Hawkins-Bordley. MHS.
Geneal. and mem. encyc. of Md. Spencer. V. 1, p. 86. MHS; DAR.
Mrs. W. H. Harris chart. MHS.
†Hist. of Allegany Co. Thomas and Williams. V. 1, pp. 611–12. MHS; DAR.
†Hist. of West. Md. Scharf. V. 2, p. 874. MHS; DAR.
Md. families. Culver. Ms. Personal list.
†Med. Annals Md. Cordell. 1903, p. 529. MHS.
*Old Kent. Hanson. P. 333. MHS; DAR.
Peale Geneal. Coll. Ms. MHS.
†Public parks of Balto. No. 2, p. 6. MHS.
Patterson family of Pa. Wilson Mss. Coll., no. 97. MHS.
*Personal Ms. Coll., under Patterson. MHS.
Price family and other Gunpowder Friends. Death notices; photos. of newsp. clipp. MHS.
Turner family, Va. Va. Mag. Hist. and Biog., v. 21, p. 315.
*Wicomico Co. families. Tilghman. Ms, p. 9. DAR.
West. Nottingham Cemetery. M. H. Mag., 1923, v. 18, p. 55.
See Bonaparte-Patterson.
See Taylor-Roberts-Standiford-Patterson-Reardon-Baker-Reisinger-Scharf.
See McKim-Hollins-Patterson.
†Patterson, Phila. and Allegany Co. Encyc. of Amer. biog. Amer. Hist. Soc., N. Y., 1928, v. 33, p. 209.
†Patterson, George. Balto., hist. and biog. Richardson and Bennett. 1871, p. 405. MHS; DAR.
Patterson, James Wilson. Pedigree chart. Soc. Col. Wars, Md. Johnston. 1905, p. 82. MHS.
Patterson, Mrs. T. H. H., Phila. Abr. Compend. Amer. Geneal. Virkus. V. 1, p. 601. DAR.
†Patterson, Wm. Balto. hist. and biog. Richardson and Bennett. 1871, pp. 402–04. MHS; DAR.
†Hist. of Md. Scharf. V. 2, p. 207. MHS.
Patterson-Lamar. Bible rec. of Patterson, Buchs Co., Pa., and Lamar, Georgetown, D. C. Md. Geneal. Rec. Com., 1932, p. 20.DAR.
Patterson, Paterson. St. Paul's Parish, Balto. V. 1, 2, 3, 4. Mss. MHS.
Patteson. Rogers Coll. Ms. MHS.
Pattison. Bible. Md. Geneal. Bull., v. 4, p. 13. MHS; DAR.
Christ P. E. Church cemetery, Cambridge. Steele. 1936. MHS; DAR.
*Hist. Dorchester Co. Jones. 1925, pp. 429–36. MHS; DAR.
Keene family. Jones. MHS; DAR.
Linthicum-Pattison Bible rec. Typed. DAR.
Md. families. Culver. Ms. Personal list.
Wills. Md. Geneal. Rec. Com. 1930–1931, v. 4, pp. 1–7. DAR.
Wills; also Extracts; 1747, 1776, 1797, 1814, 1836, 1873. Md. Geneal. Rec. Com.,1929, pp. 7–42; also 1930–31. Mss. DAR.
***Pattison,** Cambridge, Md. Lineage Bk., Daughters of Founders and Patriots, v.17, pp. 104–05. MHS.
***Pattison,** Dorchester Co. Burke's landed gentry. 1939. MHS.
Pattison Family. Wills. 1747–1875. Md. Geneal. Rec. Com., v. 3, pp. 7–25. DAR.
Patton. *See* Highland-Earle-Patton.
Patton, Somerset Co. Lineage Bks., Natl. Soc. of Daughters of Amer. Col., v. 4, p. 196. MHS; DAR.
Paul. Abr. Compend. Amer. Geneal. Virkus. V. 1, p. 328. DAR.
†Hist. of West. Md. Scharf. V. 2, pp. 1488–89. MHS; DAR.
Lloyd family hist. of Wales, Pa., and Md. DAR.
St. Paul's Parish, Balto. V. 2. Mss. MHS.
Paull. West. Nottingham Cemetery. M. H. Mag., 1923, v. 18, p. 55.
Paulus. Beards' Luth. graveyard, Washington Co. Md. Geneal. Rec. Com., 1935–36. Mss. DAR.
Pawson. Bible rec. Ms. MHS.
Paxton. Hist. of west. Md. Scharf. V. 1, p. 586.

Payne. Bible rec. Md. Geneal. Bull., v. 2, pp. 13-14. MHS; DAR.
Col. families of U. S. A. Mackenzie. V. 1. MHS; DAR.
Paynes ledger, 1758-61. List of names (some Md.) in ledger of Daniel Payne, merchant of Dumfries, Prince William Co., Va. William and Mary Quart., 2nd series, v. 4, pp. 99–117.
*Paynes of Va. B. Payne. 1937. DAR.
St. Paul's Parish, Balto. V. 2, 4. Mss. MHS.
Turner Geneal. Coll. Ms. MHS.
See Morson-Scott-Payne.
Payne, Mrs. G. H. Abr. Compend. Amer. Geneal. Virkus. V. 1, p. 404. DAR.
Payne, George Houson, Jr. Pedigree. (Alexander, Edmunds and Hooe rec. of Va.) Soc. Col. Wars Md. Culver. 1940. MHS; DAR.
†**Peabody.** Biog. sketch of George Peabody of London. Repr. from Hunt's Merchant Mag., Apr. 1857, N. Y., Baker & Godwin, 1857. Enoch Pratt Lib.
†Discourse and life and character of George Peabody. Severn Teackle Wallis. Pub. by the Peabody Institute, John Murphy & Co., Balto., 1870. Enoch Pratt Lib.
†Eulogy pronounced at funeral of George Peabody at Peabody, Mass., Feb. 8, 1870. Robt. Winthrop. Boston, John Wilson & Son, 1870. Enoch Pratt Lib.
George Peabody and his services to State. M. H. Mag., 1910, v. 5, pp. 326–29.
†(1795–1869). M. H. Mag., v. 12, p. 231.
†**Peabody, George** (1795–1870). Life. Phebe A. Hanaford. Boston, B. B. Russell, 1870. Enoch Pratt Lib.
†Modern encyc. McDannald. 1933.
Peachey-Griffin. Chart. Cary Geneal. Coll. Ms. MHS.
Peachy. St. Paul's Parish, Balto. V. 2. Mss. MHS.
Peacock Family. Bible rec., 1779–1931, of Thomas, son of Richard and Editha Hacket. Mss. DAR.
Rec. Md. Geneal. Rec. Com., 1934-35, pp. 196–200. Mss. DAR.
Pead. Somerset Co. Court Book. Tilghman. 1937. Ms. DAR.
Peagus, Pagues. Cary Geneal. Coll. Ms. MHS.
†**Peake.** Day-Star of Amer. Freedom. Davis. P. 247. MHS.
Peale. Ames Geneal. Coll. Ms. MHS.
Ances. rec. and portraits. Col. Dames of Amer., 1910, v. 2, p. 600. MHS; DAR.
Battee, Brewer, Boteler, etc., family rec. Murray. Photos. MHS.
Descendants of Col. Thomas White. Morris. MHS.
Edithweston Rectors. Ms. File case, MHS.
*Geneal. coll. of Dr. Charles Peale, geneal. of Washington, D. C. Most of Dr. Peale's mss. are of families of Lancaster, Pa., but many are from Md. and Va. 67 families in index; ref. to 280 families. MHS.
Geneal. reg. Mervine. Pp. 274–92. MHS.
*George Donald Riley. Riley. DAR.
Hist. of Kent Co. Usilton. P. 146. DAR.
List of Peale portraits. Pa. Mag. Hist. and Biog., 1904, v. 28. MHS.
Md. gleanings in Eng. Wills. M. H. Mag., 1907, v. 2, no. 3.
Mrs. E. N. Morison chart. MHS.
Old Kent. Hanson. Pp. 331–34.
See Sellers, Chester, Pa. Abr. Compend. Amer. Geneal. Virkus. V. 1, p. 822. DAR.
St. Paul's Parish, Balto. V. 1. Mss. MHS.
Peale, Angelica. Descendants of Alexander Robinson and Angelica Peale. Hall. Lib. Cong.
†**Peale, Charles Willson.** America's old masters. Flexner.
†(1741–1827). Artist of Revolution. Early life of Charles Willson Peale. C. C. Sellers. Conn., 293 pp. MHS.
†Artist, soldier. Pa. Mag. Hist. and Biog., port., July, 1914, v. 38, pp. 257–80.
Biog. sketches of distinguished Marylanders. Boyle. MHS; DAR.
Public services during Amer. Revolution. Amer. Monthly Mag., v. 14, pp. 197–208, 371–91.
†Vallye Forge. H. E. Wildes.
†**Peale, Rembrant.** Modern encyc. McDannald. 1933.
***Peale (Charles Wilson) Family.** Old Kent. Hanson. Pp. 333–34. MHS; DAR.
Peale Line. Mrs. A. R. Rogers chart. MHS.
Peale-Brewer-Ridgely. Lineage Bks., Natl. Soc. of Daughters of Amer Col., v. 2, p. 201. MHS; DAR.
Peane. Naturalizations in Md., 1666–1765; Laws. Bacon. MHS.
†**Pearce.** Bench and bar of Md. Sams and Riley. 1901, v. 1, p. 329; v. 2, p. 559. Lib. Cong.; MHS; Peabody Lib.
†Hist. of Balto. City and Co. Scharf. P. 907. MHS.
Hist. graves of Md. and D. C. Ridgely. MHS.
†Hist. of Frederick Co. Williams. P. 511. MHS; DAR.
Hist. of Kent Co. Usilton. P. 141. DAR.
Lineage Bks., Natl. Soc. of Daughters of Amer. Col., v. 4, p. 57. MHS; DAR.
Md. Geneal. Rec. Com., 1934. Mss. DAR.
†Med. Annals Md. Cordell. 1903, p. 530. MHS.
†Men of mark in Md. Johnson. V. 1, pp. 281, 284. DAR; Enoch Pratt Lib.
*Old Kent. Hanson. Pp. 160–63, 182. MHS; DAR.
Rogers Coll. Ms. MHS.
St. Paul's Parish, Balto. V. 1, 2. Mss. MHS.
St. Stephens Parish, Cecilton, Md. MHS; DAR.
Pearce, Balto. Co. Balto., its hist., its people. Hall. V. 3. MHS; DAR.
Pearce, Kent Co. Milligan chart. MHS.
†**Pearce, James Alfred.** James Alfred Pearce. B. C. Steiner. M. H. Mag., 1921, v. 16, pp. 3 19–39; v. 17; v. 18; v. 19.
Pearce, Joseph, Balto. Co. Will, dated 1829. See Wyle, Luke. Ms. DAR.
Pearce-Levy. Bible rec., 1719–98, from Bibles belonging to Judge Moses. M. H. Mag., 1926, v. 21, pp. 201–06.
Pearcy. Somerset Co. Court Book. Tilghman. 1937. Ms. DAR.
Pearle. Somerset Co. Court Book. Tilghman. 1937. Ms. DAR.
†**Pearre.** Hist. of Allegany Co. Thomas and Williams. V. 1, pp. 300, 320–21. MHS; DAR.
Hist. of Frederick Co. Williams. V. 2, pp. 763, 895, 944.
Pearson. Burton ancestry. Ms. MHS.
Cary Geneal. Coll. Ms. MHS.
Lloyd family hist. of Wales, Pa., and Md. DAR.

Pearson. Port. and biog. rec. of Sixth Cong. Dist. of Md. P. 152. MHS; DAR.
St. Paul's Parish, Balto. V. 2. Mss. MHS.
***Pearson Family,** Ohio. Notes. Natl. Geneal. Soc. Quart., March, 1938, v. 26, no. 1, pp. 14–22.
Pechin. Wm. Pechin (1773–1849); his ancestry and descendants, 1591–1914. MHS.
Pechin, Christopher (1737–79). His ancestry and descendants, 1706–1914. Pamph. MHS.
Pechin Family (1706–1914). Christopher Pechin (1737–79); his ancestry and descendants. MHS.
Peck. Peck family of Va. and Sharpesburg. (Showing Carper family of Md.) William and Mary Quart., 2nd series, v. 13, pp. 273–76.
St. Paul's Parish, Balto. V. 1, 2. Mss. MHS.
Peckham. Ances. rec. and portraits. Col. Dames of Amer., 1910, pp. 105, 123. MHS; DAR.
Peddenton, Peddington Family. Note. Old Somerset. Torrence. MHS; DAR.
Peddicord. Hist. of Frederick Co. Williams. V. 2, p. 1066. MHS; DAR.
Hist. of Md. Scharf. V. 2, p. 1539. MHS.
†Hist. of West. Md. V. 2, p. 1540. MHS; DAR.
Peddington. *See* Peddenton.
Peele. Md. gleanings in Eng. Wills. M. H. Mag., 1907, v. 2, no. 4.
†**Peerce.** Hist. of Balto. City and Co. Scharf. P. 912. MHS.
***Peery, Perry.** Wicomico Co. families. Tilghman. Ms., p. 128. DAR.
Pegram. Miss Margaret M. Steele chart. MHS.
Peirce. Jenkins-Courtney chart. MHS.
St. Stephens Parish, Cecilton, Md. MHS; DAR.
Peirce, Montgomery Co. Col. families of U. S. A. Mackenzie. V. 1, pp. 403–08. MHS; DAR.
Peirce, Wm. Henry. Pedigree. (Shapleigh rec. of New Eng.) Soc. Col. Wars Md. Culver. 1940. MHS; DAR.
Pemberton. Bonsal charts. MHS.
Lloyd - Pemberton - Hutchinson - Hudson - Parke families. Glenn. Pp. 41–68. MHS; DAR.
***Pemberton,** Buck Co., Pa. Burke's landed gentry. 1939. MHS.
Pemberton, John and James (sons of James Pemberton of Boston, Mass., who came over with Gov. Winthrop, 1630). Ms. MHS.
Pemberton Family, Pa. and Md. Bible rec. Pub. Geneal. Soc. Pa., v. 10, p. 70.
Pemberton Family, Talbot Co. Ms. MHS.
Pendleton. Greenway Mss. Geneal. Coll. Binder's title, Hawkins-Bordley. MHS.
Pendleton, Va. Col. families of Amer. Lawrence. V. 9, pp. 125–44. MHS.
Col. families of U. S. A. Mackenzie. V. 4. MHS; DAR.
Families. Du Bellett.
Southerland-Latham and allied families. Voorhees. Bd. ms. MHS.
*The Sun, Balto., March 12, 1905.
Whitehead chart. MHS.
Pendleton, Mrs. Nathan Smith, Jr. (Elise Vorhees Steele). Chart. Col. Dames, Chap. I. MHS.
Miss Kate Steele chart. MHS.
Pendleton Family, Va. Geneal. Va. Mag. Hist. and Biog., v. 40, pp. 81, 179, 293, 383; v. 41, pp. 80, 166, 362; v. 42, pp. 83, 181, 268, 366. MHS.
Geneal. of Page family, Va. Page. Pp. 239–46. MHS; DAR.
Pendleton-Orrick-Strother-Calvert Families, Va. and Tenn. Natl. Geneal. Soc. Quart., 1931, v. 19, no. 1, pp. 16–19.
Pennington. *See* Pennington.
Peninton. *See* Pennington.
Penn. Cary Geneal. Coll. Ms. MHS.
Laytonsville M. E. churchyard, Montgomery Co. Md. Geneal. Rec. Com., 1934–35, p. 69. Mss. DAR.
Md. families. Culver. Ms. Personal list.
Patriotic Md. Md. Soc. of S. A. R., 1930. MHS; DAR.
*Pennington Papers. Ms. MHS.
St. Paul's Parish, Balto. V. 1, 2. Mss. MHS.
***Penn,** Pa. The Sun, Balto., June 9, 16, 1907.
Penn, Benj. Revolutionary pension rec. D. A. R. Mag., v. 71, no. 1, p. 88.
Penn Family. Md. data. Mss. DAR.
***Penn Family,** Va. Chronolog. rec. N. Y., Wm. M. Clemens, 1915, ltd. ed. MHS.
Pennell. Lloyd family hist. of Wales, Pa., and Md. DAR.
Mt. Zion P. E. churchyard, Worcester Co. Md. Geneal. Rec. Com., 1937, Mrs. Lines. Mss. DAR.
Penniman. Dorsey and allied families. Ms. MHS.
Dorsey chart. MHS.
Gantt geneal. Ms. MHS.
Griffith geneal. Griffith. MHS; DAR.
Mrs. R. N. Jackson chart. MHS.
Pedigree of Duncan Keener Brent. Soc. Col. Wars Md. Culver. 1940. MHS; DAR.
St. Paul's Parish, Balto. V. 3. Mss. MHS.
Mrs. J. Whitridge Williams chart 2. MHS.
See Griffith-Hook-Penniman.
Penniman, Nicholas Griffith, III. Pedigree of Thomas Dobbin Penniman. Soc. Col. Wars Md. Culver. 1940. MHS; DAR.
Penniman, Thomas Dobbin. Pedigree. (Incl. New Eng. rec.), Soc. Col. Wars Md. Culver. 1940. MHS; DAR.
†**Penning.** Med. Annals Md. Cordell. 1903, p. 531. MHS.
Pennington. Col. families of U. S. A. Mackenzie. V. 3. MHS; DAR.
Md. families. Culver. Ms. Personal list.
See Haile. Abr. Compend. Amer. Geneal. Virkus. V. 1, p. 633. DAR.
†Med. Annals Md. Cordell. 1903, p. 531. MHS.
Patriotic Md. Md. Soc. of S. A. R., 1930. MHS; DAR.
*Pedigree of Sir Josslyn Pennington. Joseph Foster. Priv. pr., London, Chiswick Press, 1878. MHS.
*Pennington Papers. Geneal. Coll. Mss. MHS.
St. Paul's Parish, Balto. V. 1, 2, 3, 4. Mss. MHS.
Pennington, Josias. Md. Soc., War of 1812, v. 3, no. 230. Ms. MHS.
Pennington, Mrs. Josias (Margaret Riggs Pleasants). Chart. Col. Dames, Chap. I. MHS.
Pennington, Pleasants. Pedigree. (Incl. Harrison, Kirkbride and Pemberton of Pa.) Soc. Col. Wars Md. Culver. 1940. MHS; DAR.

Pennington, William Clapham. Pedigree chart. Soc. Col. Wars, Md. Johnston. 1905, p. 83. MHS.
Pennington, Penington, Peninton. (80 rec.) St. Stephens Parish, Cecilton, Md. MHS; DAR.
Pennock. Ms. MHS.
Winchester-Owens-Price families. M. H. Mag., 1930, v. 25, no. 4, p. 385–405.
Penny. St. Charles R. C. Church graveyard, Indianhead, Charles Co. Md. Geneal. Rec. Com., 1933–34, p. 137. Mss. DAR.
St. Paul's Parish, Balto. V. 1, 2. Mss. MHS.
Pennypacker, I. A. Abr. Compend. Amer. Geneal. Virkus. V. 1, p. 630. DAR.
Penrice. St. Paul's Parish, Balto. V. 2. Mss. MHS.
†**Penrose.** Hist. of West. Md. Scharf. V. 2, p. 964. MHS; DAR.
Col. families of Md. and their descendants. Emory. 1900, p. 189. MHS; DAR.
Pedigree of George Thornburgh Macauly Gibson. Soc. Col. Wars Md. Culver. 1940. MHS; DAR.
Pedigree of Anthony Morris Tyson. Soc. Col. Wars Md. Culver. 1940. MHS; DAR.
Penrose, Pa. Abr. Compend. Amer. Geneal. Virkus. V. 1, p. 23. DAR.
†**Penrose, Clement A.** Men of mark in Md. Johnson. V. 2. DAR; Enoch Pratt Lib.
Penrose Family. Thomas Book. Thomas. P. 462. Lib. Cong.; MHS.
Penruddock. Md. gleanings in Eng. Wills. M. H. Mag., 1909. V. 4, no. 2.
Pentz, Franklin Eldridge. Md. Soc., War of 1812, v. 2, no. 158. Ms. MHS.
Pentz, Wm. Fletcher. Md. Soc., War of 1812, v. 2, no. 159. Ms. MHS.
***Pepple.** Frederick Co. families. Markell. Ms. Personal list.
Peppler. *See* Grossman-Peppler.
†**Perdew.** Hist. of Allegany Co. Thomas and Williams. V. 1, v. 2, pp. 1026–27. MHS; DAR.
Perdue. Mt. Olive M. P. churchyard, Worcester Co. Md. Geneal. Rec. Com., 1937, Mrs. Lines. Mss. DAR.
†**Peregoy.** Hist. of Balto. City and Co. Scharf. P. 887. MHS.
Perigo. *See* Perregoy.
Perin. Balto., its hist., its people. Hall. V. 2. MHS; DAR.
Perin, Bradford. (10 generations.) Pedigree. Soc. Col. Wars Md. Culver. 1940. MHS; DAR.
Perin, Mrs. Lawrence (Eliza Washington Perine). Chart. Col. Dames, Chap. I. MHS.
Mrs. H. I. Keyser chart. MHS.
Perin, Nelson. Pedigree chart. Soc. Col. Wars, Md. Johnston. 1905, p. 84. MHS.
Perin, Perine, Perrine. St. Paul's Parish, Balto. V. 2. Mss. MHS.
Perine. Amer. Armory and Blue Book. Matthews. 1911–12, p. 291.
Col. families of U. S. A. Mackenzie. V. 1, p. 415. MHS; DAR.
Pedigree and hist. of Washington family. Welles. P. 262. MHS.
Pedigree of Coleman Randall Freeman. Soc. Col. Wars Md. Culver. 1940. MHS; DAR.
Sharar-Perine-Day Bible rec. Ms. MHS.
See Washington Col. families of U. S. A. Mackenzie. V. 2, pp. 740–46. MHS; DAR.
See Perin.
***Perine,** Washington. Burke's landed gentry. 1939. MHS.
Perine Line. Perin chart. MHS.
Perkins. Ances. rec. and portraits, Col. Dames of Amer., 1910, v. 1, p. 225. MHS; DAR.
Bible rec. Md. Geneal. Rec. Com., 1926–27, v. 2, p. 55–57. DAR.
Cary Geneal. Coll. Ms. MHS.
Chestertown cemetery. Md. O. R. Soc. Bull., no. 1, pp. 18–29.
Cotton chart. MHS.
See Dashiell. Abr. Compend. Amer. Geneal. Virkus. V. 1, p. 202. DAR.
Dobbin chart. MHS.
*Geneal. Perkins family in U. S. in 1790. D. W. Perkins. With ref. to Perkins family in Eng., Del., Md., Mass., N. J. and Va. Utica, N. Y., 1911.
†Med. Annals Md. Cordell. 1903, p. 532. MHS.
St. Paul's Parish, Balto. V. 3, 4. Mss. MHS.
Somerset Co. Court Book. Tilghman. 1937. Ms. DAR.
Van Dyke-Johns-Montgomery-Manlove chart. Cary Geneal. Coll. Ms. MHS.
Wallis chart. MHS.
White House Farm burial ground, Kent Co. Bible rec. Upper Penins. East. Shore. P. 97; see also pp. 102, 103. MHS; DAR.
Perkins, Kent Co. A. L. and S. L. Jenkins pedigree chart. Soc. Col. Wars, Md. Johnston. 1905, p. 45. MHS.
Perkins, Wm. Henry, Jr. Md. Soc., War of 1812, v. 3, no. 237. Ms. MHS.
Pedigree. Soc. Col. Wars Md. Culver. 1940. MHS; DAR.
Perkins Family (1650–1932), Chestertown, Kent Co. (9 generations) Md. Geneal. Rec. Com., 1939–40, pp. 124–47. Ms. DAR.
***Perkins Family.** Old Kent. Hanson. Pp. 189–96, 261. MHS; DAR.
Perregoy, Perigo, Perrigo. St. Paul's Parish, Balto. V. 1. Mss. MHS.
Perrey. St. Stephens Parish, Cecilton, Md. MHS; DAR.
Perrie. *See* Wolfe-Perrie-Wailes.
Perrigo. *See* Perregoy.
Perrin. Abr. Compend. Amer. Geneal. Virkus. V. 6, p. 339. DAR.
†Hist. of Allegany Co. Thomas and Williams. V. 1, v. 2, pp. 1023–24, 1120–21. MHS; DAR.
Kent geneal. Kent. P. 37. MHS.
Md. gleanings in Eng. Wills. M. H. Mag., 1910, v. 5.
Perrine. Beall and Bell families. Beall. MHS; DAR.
See Perin.
***Perrine Family.** Leaflet. MHS.
***Perry.** Ancestors and descendants of James Perry, who came to Del. about 1730. Lynn Perry. (Some Wicomico Co. families.) 1931. DAR.
Bible rec., 1793–1859. Md. Geneal. Rec. Com., 1933–34, p. 129. Mss. DAR.
Black chart. MHS.
*Boyd family. Boyd. DAR.
See Brooke. Abr. Compend. Amer. Geneal. Virkus. V. 6, p. 738. DAR.
Chart of Com. John Rodgers. DAR.

Perry. Dobbin chart. MHS.
Englar family. Barnes. MHS; DAR.
Chart of Com. John Rodgers. DAR.
Dobbin chart. MHS.
Englar family. Barnes. MHS; DAR.
†Hist. of Allegany Co. Thomas and Williams. V. 1. MHS; DAR.
Hist. of Frederick Co. Williams. V. 2, pp. 758, 1539. MHS; DAR.
Hist. of West. Md. Scharf. V. 1, p. 682. MHS; DAR.
Md. families. Culver. Ms. Personal list.
Md. Geneal. Bull., v. 3, p. 11. MHS; DAR.
†Med. Annals Md. Cordell. 1903, p. 532. MHS.
Patriotic Md. Md. Soc. of S. A. R., 1930. MHS; DAR.
Rogers Coll. Ms. MHS.
St. Paul's Parish, Balto. V. 1, 2, 4. Mss. MHS.
Turner Geneal. Coll. Ms. MHS.
See Peery.
†**Perry, Hon. Wm.** (1746–99). Hist. of Talbot Co. Tilghman. V. 1, pp. 444–49. MHS; DAR.
Perryman. Miss C. Petre chart. MHS.
Peter. Amer. Clan Gregor Year Book, 1916, p. 84; 1932, p. 30. MHS; DAR.
Ancestry of Rosalie Morris Johnson. Johnson. 1905. MHS; DAR.
†Hist. of West. Md. Scharf. V. 1, p. 732. MHS; DAR.
Portrait and biog. rec. of Sixth Cong. Dist. of Md. 1898, p. 639. MHS.
†**Peter, George.** Hist. of Md. Scharf. V. 3, p. 83. MHS.
*__Peter, Robert.__ Patriots of Revolutionary period interred in D. C. Balch. Rec. of Columbia Hist. Soc., v. 19, v. 20.
Peterkin. St. Paul's Parish, Balto. V. 2. Mss. MHS.
Peters. Chart of Com. John Rodgers. DAR.
Hist. of Frederick Co. Williams. V. 2, pp. 762, 763. MHS; DAR.
Holdens Cemetery, Kent Co. Md. Geneal. Rec. Com., 1932, v. 5, p. 211. Mss. DAR.
Men of mark in Md. Johnson. V. 4, p. 172. DAR.
Naturalizations in Md., 1666–1765; Laws. Bacon. MHS.
St. Paul's Parish, Balto. V. 2, 4. Mss. MHS.
†**Peters, C. Massey.** Men of mark in Md. Johnson. V. 4. DAR; Enoch Pratt Lib.
Peters, Winfield. Md. Soc., War of 1812, v. 1, no. 101. Ms. MHS.
Peterson. Naturalizations in Md., 1666–1765; Laws. Bacon. MHS.
St. Paul's Parish, Balto. V. 2. Mss. MHS.
Petery. Hagerstown tombstone inscriptions. Gruder. Natl. Geneal. Soc. Quart., 1919, v. 8, nos. 1, 2.
†**Petherbridge.** Med. Annals Md. Cordell. 1903, p. 533. MHS.
Petre (Eng. pedigree). Miss C. Petre chart. MHS.
Stettinuis chart. MHS.
Petre, Miss Constance. Chart. (Maternal line.) Col. Dames, Chap. I. MHS.
Pettingall. Mt. Olivet Cemetery, Frederick. Md. Geneal. Rec. Com., 1934–35, p. 111. Mss. DAR.
*__Pettit.__ Pettit family in Amer. A. H. Pettit. Md., pp. 172–73. Portland, Oregon, 1906. MHS.
Peverley. Lambdin chart. MHS.
Peyton. Newsp. clipp. Scrap Book. MHS.
*The Sun, Balto., June 17, 24, July 1 (Va.), 1906.
Va. geneal. Hayden. MHS; DAR.
Peyton Family, Va. Ms. MHS; DAR.
†**Phelps.** Almira Hart Lincoln Phelps. Almira Phelps King. MHS.
†Almira Hart Lincoln Phelps; her life and works. Emma L. Bolzau. (General Assembly of Md. passed Act for female seminary at Ellicott's Mills; Patapsco Institute Jan. 18, 1834; Mrs. Phelps was its head mistress for many years.) Lancaster, Pa., The Science Press Print Co., 1936. Enoch Pratt Lib.
Christ P. E. Church cemetery, Cambridge. Steele. 1936. MHS; DAR.
*Frederick Co. families. Markell. Ms. Personal list.
*Hist. Dorchester Co. Jones. 1925, p. 436. MHS; DAR.
Mrs. B. S. Johnston chart. MHS.
Md. families. Culver. Ms. Personal list.
†Med. Annals Md. Cordell. 1903, p. 533. MHS.
†Sketch of life of Almira Hart Phelps. Forrest.
*Late Rear Admiral Wm. Woodward. Burke's landed gentry. 1939. P. 3008. MHS.
Phelps, W. W. Abr. Compend. Amer. Geneal. Virkus. V. 1, p. 636. DAR.
Phifer, R. S., Jr. Md. Soc., War of 1812, v. 2, no. 178. Ms. MHS.
Philips. May-Hanson-Pollard-Philips. Eiler. 1929, pamph. MHS.
Phillips. Ancestral beginnings in Amer. of McGregor, Magruder, Beall, Price, Phillips, Bland, McKisick, Young and related families. Caroline B. Price. 1928. DAR.
Bible rec., 1799–1866. (Bible owned by Emory L. Phillips, Delmar, Md.) Md. Geneal. Rec. Com., 1938–39, pp. 195–97. Mss. DAR.
Bible rec. Md. Geneal. Rec. Com., 1926–27, v. 2, pp. 42. DAR.
*Frederick Co. families. Markell. Ms. Personal list.
*Hist. of Dorchester Co. Jones. 1925, p. 437. MHS; DAR.
Hist. of Harford Co. Preston. 1901, p. 42. MHS; DAR.
Marriage rec. of Frederick Co. Markell. Md. Geneal. Rec. Com., 1938–39. Mss. DAR.
Md. families. Culver. Ms. Personal list.
Mt. Olive M. P. churchyard, Worcester Co. Md. Geneal. Rec. Com., 1937, Mrs. Lines. Mss. DAR.
Mt. Paran Pres. churchyard, Harrisonville, Balto. Co. Typed ms. MHS; DAR.
Old Balto., 1791, on Bush River, Harford Co. Tombstone inscriptions, 1744–1812. Md. Geneal. Rec. Com., 1929, p. 60. DAR.
Patriotic Md. Md. Soc. of S. A. R., 1930. MHS; DAR.
Portrait and biog. rec. of East. Shore of Md. 1898, pp. 186, 450, 633, 649, 735, 905. MHS; DAR.
Rec. of Stepney Parish. MHS; DAR.
St. Paul's Parish, Balto. V. 2, 4. Mss. MHS.
Sketch of ancestry of Thruston Phillips families. D. A. R. Mag., v. 65, no. 3.

Somerset Co. Court Book. Tilghman. 1937. Ms. DAR.
*Wicomico Co. families. Tilghman. Ms., pp. 51, 73, 75–76, 99, 117–18, 121–25. DAR.
See Hicks-Dennis-Edmondson-Phillips-Travers-White.
See Sargent-Phillips.
Phillips, Calvert Co. Price chart. MHS.
†**Phillips,** Frederick Co. Hist. of West. Md. Scharf. V. 1, pp. 615–16. MHS; DAR.
Phillips, G. T. Md. Soc., War of 1812, v. 3, no. 246. Ms. MHS.
***Phillips, George.** Geneal. of Barlow family. Barlow. MHS.
Phillips, John Fowler. Pedigree. Soc. Col. Wars Md. Culver. 1940. MHS; DAR.
Phillips, Levi Benj. Md. Soc., War of 1812, v. 4, no. 309. MHS.
Phillips-Howard. Wicomico Co. families. Bible rec. Ms. DAR.
Phillipse, Frederick, N. Y. Pedigree of James Mather Sill. Soc. Col. Wars Md. Culver. 1940. MHS; DAR.
Phillpot. Somerset Co. Court Book. Tilghman. 1937. Ms. DAR.
Philpot. Abr. Compend. Amer. Geneal. Virkus. V. 1, p. 938. DAR.
Garrison Church. Allen. Pp. 75–76. MHS; DAR.
Beirne chart. MHS.
†Hist. of Balto. City and Co. Scharf. P. 863. MHS.
Patriotic Md. Md. Soc. of S. A. R., 1930. MHS; DAR.
St. Paul's Parish, Balto. V. 3, 4. Mss. MHS.
Mrs. Talbot T. Speer chart. MHS.
Western Run Parish book. Allen. Bd. ms. MHS.
†**Philpott.** Papers relating to early hist. of Md. Streeter. 1876. MHS.
***Phippin.** Wicomico Co. families. Tilghman. Ms., pp. 121–122. DAR.
Phipps. Rec. of Stepney Parish. MHS; DAR.
St. Paul's Parish, Balto. V. 2, 3. Mss. MHS.
Phleeger Family. Hist. of Frederick Co. Williams. V. 2, p. 1307. MHS; DAR.
Portrait and biog. rec. of Sixth Cong. Dist. of Md. 1898, p. 1307. MHS; DAR.
Phoeniz. St. Paul's Parish, Balto. V. 2. Mss. MHS.
Piatt. *See* Andrew-Piatt.
Pick. Bleakley Bible rec. Ms. MHS.
Pickersgill. Md. families. Culver. Ms. Personal list.
Young Bible rec. Ms. MHS.
Pidgeon. St. Paul's Parish, Balto. V. 2. Mss. MHS.
Piel. Catonsville pioneers of Luth. faith. Natl. Geneal. Soc. Quart., v. 9, no. 2, p. 29.
Pielert. Catonsville pioneers of Luth. faith. Natl. Geneal. Soc. Quart., v. 9, no. 2, p. 29.
***Pierce.** Rec. of births, deaths and marriages of first seven generations in Amer. H. C. Pierce. 1936. DAR.
St. Stephens Parish, Cecilton, Md. MHS; DAR.
†**Pierce Family.** Historic Rock Creek. L. P. Shoemaker. Rec. Columbia Hist. Soc., v. 12, pp. 38–52.
***Pierce Family,** Pa. to Montgomery Co. The Sun, Balto., May 27, June 3, 1906.
Pierpont. Bonsal charts. MHS.
Md. families. Culver. Ms. Personal list.
Neill chart. MHS.
G. M. Sharp pedigree chart, plate 1. Soc. Col. Wars, Md. Johnston. 1905, p. 91. MHS.
St. Paul's Parish, Balto. V. 2, 4. Mss. MHS.
Pierpont Line. Gaither, Va. and Md. Col. and Revolutionary families of Phila. Jordan. 1933, v. 1, pp. 144–67.
Piersey. Cary Geneal. Coll. Ms. MHS.
Pierson. Sharpless family geneal. Cope. P. 1207. MHS; DAR.
†**Piggott.** Med. Annals Md. Cordell. 1903, pp. 533–34. MHS.
†**Pigman.** Hist. of Allegany Co. Thomas and Williams. V. 1. MHS; DAR.
See Shriver. Col. families of U. S. A. Mackenzie. V. 2, p. 670. MHS; DAR.
†**Pigot.** Hist. of West. Md. Scharf. V. 2, p. 881. MHS; DAR.
Pike. *See* Halley-Hawley-Pike.
Pilch. St. Paul's Parish, Balto. V. 2. Mss. MHS.
Pile. Ances. rec. and portraits. Col. Dames of Amer., 1910, v. 2, p. 535. MHS; DAR.
Cary Geneal. Coll. Ms. MHS.
†Day-Star of Amer. Freedom. Davis. P. 186. MHS.
*Semmes Geneal. Coll. Ms. MHS.
Pile, Capt. John, St. Mary's Co. R. B. Keyser pedigree chart. Soc. Col. Wars, Md. Johnston. 1905, pp. 56, 151. MHS.
Piles. Lineage Bks., Natl. Soc. of Daughters of Amer. Col., v. 1, p. 9. MHS; DAR.
Pilkinton. St. Paul's Parish, Balto. V. 2. Mss. MHS.
Pim. Burton ancestry. Ms. MHS.
Pinchin. All Hallow's P. E. churchyard, Snow Hill, Worcester Co. Hudson. Bd. Ms. MHS; DAR. Also: Md. Geneal. Rec. Com., 1935–36, p. 24. Mss. DAR.
Pinckerton. St. Paul's Parish, Balto. V. 2. Mss. MHS.
†**Pinckney.** Med. Annals Md. Cordell. 1903, p. 534. MHS.
†**Pinckney, William.** Chronicles of Balto. Scharf. 1874, p. 400. MHS; DAR.
Pincoffs, Mrs. Maurice Charles. Beirne chart. MHS.
(**Susan Katharine Randall.**) Chart. Col. Dames, Chap. I. MHS.
Pindel. Md. families. Culver. Ms. Personal list.
Maulsby family in Amer. Barnard. DAR; Peabody Lib.
†Med. Annals Md. Cordell. 1903, p. 534. MHS.
Rogers Coll. Ms. MHS.
†Some letters, 1781–1817. Militant surgeon of Revolution. M. H. Mag., 1923, v. 18, pp. 309–23.
Pindell. St. Paul's Parish, Balto. V. 2. Mss. MHS.
St. Thomas Parish, Balto. Co. Bd. ms. MHS. Also: Md. Geneal. Rec. Com., 1937, pp. 109–82. Mss. DAR.
Pine. St. Paul's Parish, Balto. V. 2. Mss. MHS.
***Pinkerton.** Boyd family. Boyd. DAR.
†**Pinkney.** Bench and bar of Md. Sams and Riley. 1901, v. 1, p. 271. Lib. Cong.; MHS; Peabody Lib.

Pinkney. Carton chart. MHS.
Cemetery Creek, Anne Arundel Co. tombstone inscriptions. Founders of Anne Arundel and Howard Cos. Warfield. P. 333. MHS; DAR.
Chart of Com. John Rodgers. DAR.
Col. mansions of Md. and Del. Hammond. 1914. MHS.
Founders of Anne Arundel and Howard Cos. Warfield. P. 127. MHS; DAR.
†Hist. of Balto. City and Co. Scharf. Pp. 644–45. MHS.
†Life of Right Rev. William Pinkney, fifth Bishop of Md., 1810–83. Orlando Hutton. Wash., D. C., Gibson Bros., 1890. MHS; Enoch Pratt Lib.
†Life of William Pinkney. By his nephew Rev. William Pinkney. N. Y., Appleton Co., 1853. MHS; DAR; Enoch Pratt Lib.
Marriage of Ninian Pinkney and Mrs. Amelia Hobbs, May 1, 1806. Natl. Geneal. Soc. Quart., June, 1938, v. 26, p. 34.
Maulsby family in Amer. Barnard. DAR; Peabody Lib.
See Maynard family. Focke Geneal. Coll. Ms. MHS.
†Rev. of life of William Pinkney, fifth Bishop of Md., of Hutton's biography. Hall Harrison. Balto., Cushing Co., 1891. MHS; Enoch Pratt Lib.
†Some account of life, writings and speeches of William Pinkney, 1764–1822. Henry Wheaton. N. Y., J. W. Palmer Co., 1826. Enoch Pratt Lib.
St. Paul's Parish, Balto. V. 2. Mss. MHS.
†**Pinkney, Edward Coate.** Biog. sketches of distinguished Marylanders. Boyle. MHS; DAR.
†Hist. of Md. Scharf. V. 2, p. 620. MHS.
†Poets and verse writers of Md.
†**Pinkney, Frederick.** Biog. sketches of distinguished Marylanders. Boyle. MHS; DAR.
†**Pinkney, Ninian.** M. H. Mag., v. 12, p. 233.
†**Pinkney, William.** Biog. sketches of distinguished Marylanders. Boyle. MHS; DAR.
†Eight great Amer. lawyers. Hagan. 1923. MHS.
Hist. Md. Scharf. V. 2, p. 619. MHS.
U.S.N. (died 1822). Men interred in Congressional Cemetery, who may have been in Revolutionary war. Natl. Geneal. Soc. Quart., v. 7, no. 3, p. 40.
†**Pinkney, Wm.** Balto., hist. and biog. Richardson and Bennett. 1871, pp. 409–14. MHS; DAR.
Pinner. Lineage Bks., Natl. Soc. of Daughters of Amer. Col., v. 4, p. 38. MHS; DAR.
†**Piper.** Hist. of Allegany Co. Thomas and Williams. V. 1. MHS; DAR.
†Hist. of Balto. City and Co. Scharf. P. 899. MHS.
†Hist. of West. Md. Scharf. V. 2, pp. 1468–69. MHS; DAR.
†Med. Annals Md. Cordell. 1903, pp. 534–35. MHS.
Somerset Co. Court Book. Tilghman. 1937. Ms. DAR.
Piper, Jacob. Will, 1792; also of Daniel Piper, 1856, Washington Co. Ms. DAR.
†**Piper, James.** M. H. Mag., v. 12, p. 233
Piper, Mrs. James (Alice Dickinson Pitts). Chart. Col. Dames, Chap. I. MHS.
Pitcher. Gantt geneal. Ms. MHS.
†**Pitsnogle.** Med. Annals Md. Cordell. 1903, p. 535. MHS.
Pitt. Faris-Pitt Bible rec. Ms. MHS.
Robert Gilmor chart. MHS.
Monumental City. Howard. MHS; DAR.
St. Paul's Parish, Balto. V. 2. Mss. MHS.
†**Pittinger.** Hist. of Frederick Co. Williams. MHS; DAR.
Pittman. Md. tombstone rec. Md. Geneal. Rec. Com., 1937, Parran, p. 16. Mss. DAR.
Pitts. Ances. rec. and portraits. Col. Dames of Amer., 1910, v. 2, p. 628. MHS; DAR.
Buckingham Presbyterian churchyard, Worcester Co. Hudson. Bd. ms. MHS; DAR.
*Burke's landed gentry. 1939. MHS.
*Early comers to the Province. Georgians of Anne Arundel Co. Atlanta Jour., Sept. 22, 1906. Newsp. clipp. File case, MHS.
Founders of Anne Arundel and Howard Cos. Warfield. Pp. 142, 160. MHS; DAR.
Griffith geneal. Griffith. MHS; DAR.
Le Gendre chart. MHS.
Marriages, 1778–1856. Parrish family. Boyd. MHS; DAR.
Md. families. Culver. Ms. Personal list.
†Med. Annals Md. Cordell. 1903, p. 535. MHS.
†Men of mark in Md. Johnson. V. 4. DAR; Enoch Pratt Lib.
Mrs. J. Piper chart. MHS.
Turner Geneal. Coll. Ms. MHS.
†**Pitts, Sullivan.** Geneal. and mem. encyc. of Md. Spencer. V. 2, pp. 659–60. MHS; DAR.
***Pitts, Tilghman Goldsborough.** Burke's landed gentry. 1939, p. 3009. MHS.
Pedigree. Soc. Col. Wars Md. Culver. 1940. MHS; DAR.
Pitts-Besson-Gassaway.... Amer. Compend. Amer. Geneal. Virkus. V. 4, p. 613. MHS.
Plaine. Carroll Co. Newsp. clipp., bd. MHS.
Planner. Old Somerset. Torrence. MHS; DAR.
Plaskitt. Worthington-Plaskitt families. J. Plaskitt Lamar. Pamph. with other Balto. families and additional ms. data. 1886. MHS.
See Worthington-Plaskitt.
Plater. Abr. Compend. Amer. Geneal. Virkus. V. 1, pp. 773–74. DAR.
†Bench and bar of Md. Sams and Riley. 1901, v. 1, p. 212. Lib. Cong.; MHS; Peabody Lib.
Col. mansions of Md. and Del. 1914, p. 237. MHS; DAR.
De Ford chart. MHS.
Geneal. of Va. family of Lomax. Lib. Cong.
Hist. of Balto. Lewis Pub. Co., 1912, v. 3, p. 834. DAR.
Md. families. Culver. Ms. Personal list.
McH. Howard pedigree chart, plate 2. Soc. Col. Wars, Md. Johnston. 1905, pp. 42, 151. MHS.
Parr chart. MHS.
Pedigree of Charles Morris Howard. Soc. Col. Wars Md. Culver. 1940. MHS; DAR.
Pedigree of Pleasants Pennington. Soc. Col. Wars Md. Culver. 1940. MHS; DAR.
Pedigree of Tilghman Goldsborough Pitts. Soc. Col. Wars Md. Culver. 1940. MHS; DAR.
Plater family. Christopher Johnston. M. H. Mag., 1907, v. 2, pp. 370–72. Corrections, 1908, v. 3, pp. 188–90.

Portraits and biog. rec. of Sixth Cong. Dist. of Md. 1898, p. 846. MHS; DAR.
Raisin chart. MHS.
Side lights on Md. hist. Richardson. V. 2, p. 200. MHS; DAR.
*The Sun, Balto., Nov. 22, 1903.
Tasker chart. Cary Geneal. Coll. Ms. MHS.
Mrs. E. C. Venable chart. MHS.
Sir John Zouch and his descendants. Va. Mag., v. 12, pp. 429–32.
See Bowles-Plater.

†Plater, George. Governor of Md. Buchholz. P. 32. MHS.
†Hist. of Md. Scharf. V. 2, p. 542. MHS.
*Founders of Anne Arundel and Howard Cos. Warfield. P. 243. MHS; DAR.
Three George Platers. Some early col. Marylanders. M. H. Mag., 1920, v. 15, p. 168.

Plater Family. Brief notes. Joseph Forrest, Esq., Wash. Ms. MHS.

Plater Line. Balto., its hist., its people. Hall. V. 3, p. 834. MHS; DAR.

Platt. Col. families of U. S. A. Mackenzie. V. 1, p. 415. MHS; DAR.
de Ghize chart. MHS.
†Men of mark in Md. Johnson. V. 2. DAR; Enoch Pratt Lib.
Mt. Olivet Cemetery, Frederick. Md. Geneal. Rec. Com., 1934–35, p. 111. Mss. DAR.

Platt, Walter Brewster. Pedigree chart. (Mostly New Eng. records.) Soc. Col. Wars, Md. Johnston. 1905, p. 85. MHS.

Pleasanton Family. Rec. of Pleasanton-Lewis-Laws families, relating to Stephen Lewis (about 1744, in Kent Co., Del.; died, 1811). Binder's title Stephen Lewis, Del. Ms. DAR.

Pleasants. Ances. rec. and portraits. Col. Dames of Amer., 1910, v. 2, p. 610. MHS; DAR.
Bonsal charts. MHS.
Cary Geneal. Coll. Ms. MHS.
Curzon family. Pleasants. P. 150. MHS.
Eng. descent of John Pleasants, 1645–68, of Henrico Co., Va. J. Hall Pleasants. Va. Mag., v. 16, p. 218; v. 17; v. 18.
Mrs. H. F. Johnston chart. MHS.
Lloyd-Pemberton-Hutchinson Hudson-Parke families. Glenn. MHS; DAR.
Mrs. Pennington chart. MHS.
St. Paul's Parish, Balto. V. 2, 3. Mss. MHS.

Pleasants, Mrs. J. Hall, Jr. (Delia Tudor Wilmer). Chart. Col. Dames, Chap. I. MHS.

Pleasants, Mrs. John (Mary C. Frick). Chart. Col. Dames, Chap. I. MHS.
Mrs. H. B. Jacobs chart. MHS.

Plestoo. Md. gleanings in Eng. Wills. M. H. Mag., 1908, v. 3, no. 2.

***Ploughe.** Wicomico Co. families. Tilghman. Ms., p. 92. DAR.

Plowden. Arms. William Hickey, Greenvale, p. 112. Rec. Columbia Hist. Soc., v. 35; v. 36, pp. 109–23.
Balto. Herald, Mar. 22, 1903. Newsp. clipp. Scrap Book. MHS.
Boarman geneal. Thomas. 1935. MHS; DAR.
Grandma stories. Sister Mary Xavier Queen. MHS.
One branch of Plowdens of Md. and their ancestors. N.d. Peabody Lib.
Patriotic Md. Md. Soc. of S. A. R., 1930. MHS; DAR.
Side lights on Md. hist. Richardson. V. 2, p. 203. MHS; DAR.
*The Sun, Balto. June 12, 19, 1904.
See Ford-Plowden.

Plowden, Sir Edmund. E. A. and F De Sales Jenkins pedigree chart. Soc. Col. Wars, Md. Johnston. 1905, pp. 46, 151. MHS.
†Pa. Mag., 1881, v. 5, p. 206.

Plowman. Court, family, Revolutionary rec. of Jonathan Plowman and wife, Rebecca, of Balto. Co. Ms. DAR.
St. Thomas' Parish, Balto. Co. Bd. ms. MHS. Also: Md. Geneal. Rec. Com., 1937, pp. 109–82. Mss. DAR.

Plowman Family, Md. Particularly those members who immigrated to Ohio, Illinois and Kansas, etc. Henrietta Plowman Meek. Typed, 7 pp. DAR.

Plumer. Pamph. (with geneal.) of Newbury, Mass. MHS.

Plummer. Barber, "Luckland," St. Mary's Co. Bible rec. Natl. Geneal. Soc. Quart., v. 22, no. 4, pp. 89–92.
Chestertown cemetery. Md. O. R. Soc. Bull., no. 1, pp. 18–29.
†Hist. of West. Md. Scharf. V. 1, pp. 606–08. MHS; DAR.
Plummer family. A. P. H. Ms. MHS.
Talbott of "Poplar Knowle." Shirk. MHS; DAR.
Thomas-Chew-Lawrence. Thomas. MHS.

Plummer, Samuel, Md. and Ky. Born, 1754; died, 1850. Ms. DAR.

***Plummer Family.** Notes. Gift of Miss L. D. Plummer. MHS.

Plunkett. *See* Brooke-Plunkett.

Plunkett Family. Gilmor papers. Ms. MHS.

Pocock. St. Paul's Parish, Balto. V. 1, 2. Mss. MHS.

Pocock Family. Harford Co. Hist. Soc. Mss. Coll. JHU.
Notes. Edwin Kinsey Voorhees. Atlanta, Ga., rev., 1930, typed. MHS; DAR.

***Pocock Family,** Balto. Co. Wilson Mss. Coll., no. 4. MHS.

***Pocohontas.** Pocohontas and her descendants through her marriage at Jamestown, Va., April, 1614, with John Rolfe, gentleman. W. Robertson. Biog. sketch and hist. notes by R. A. Brock. Richmond, Va., W. Randolph and English, 1887, 1932. MHS; DAR.
Lineage Bks., Natl. Soc. of Daughters of Amer. Col., v. 3, p. 313. MHS; DAR.

Poe. Balto; its hist., its people. Hall. V. 3. MHS; DAR.
Bible rec. Md. Geneal. Rec. Com., 1934–35, p. 63. Mss. DAR.
Complete poems of Edgar Allan Poe; with memoir. J. H. Whitty. Houghton-Mifflin Co., 1911. MHS.
Complete work of Edgar Allan Poe. J. A. Harrison. N. Y., 1902. Peabody Lib.
Data. D. A. R. Mag., v. 67, no. 9, p. 541.
Edgar Allan Poe; life and letters. J. A. Harrison. N. Y., 1903. Peabody Lib.
†Edgar Allan Poe: the man, the master, the martyr. Oliver Leigh. Chicago, Frank M. Martin Co., 1906, 78 pp.
Geneal. and mem. encyc. of Md. Spencer. V. 1, pp. 193–201. MHS; DAR.

†**Poe.** Hist. of Frederick Co. Williams. MHS; DAR.
Hurst chart. MHS.
*Lineage Bk., Daughters of Amer. Col., v. 5, pp. 144-45. MHS; DAR.
Music and Edgar Allan Poe. May Garretson Evans. 93 pp. J. H. Press. Enoch Pratt Lib.
New glimpses of Edgar Allan Poe, 1809-49. J. A. Harrison. N. Y., 1901. Peabody Lib.
Notes. Gulf State Mag., Jan., 1903. MHS.
*Origin and early hist. of family of Poe, with full pedigrees of Irish branch of family, and discussion of true ancestry of Edgar Allen Poe. 3 charts. Sir E. T. Bewley. Dublin, Ponsonby & Gibbs, 1906.
Patriotic Md. Md. Soc. of S. A. R., 1930. MHS; DAR.
†Poe's literary Balto. J. G. French. (Poe's life in Balto., 1831-35.) M. H. Mag., 1937, v. 32, pp. 101-12.
St. Paul's Parish, Balto. V. 3, 4. Mss. MHS.
Samuel Carpenter of Phila. Carpenter. P. 158. MHS.
True ancestry of Edgar Allen Poe. Sir Edmund T. Bewley. N. Y. Geneal. and Biog. Rec., Jan., 1907, v. 38, no. 1, p. 55.
See Shultz-Clemm-Poe.

Poe, Gen. David. Westminster churchyard. Patriotic Marylander, v. 2, no. 4, pp. 54-60. MHS; DAR.

†**Poe, Edgar Allan.** Balto., hist. and biog. Richardson and Bennett. 1871, pp. 415-19. MHS; DAR.
Life and poems of Edgar Allan Poe. E. L. Didier. (Poe was born in Boston, 1809; died in Balto., 1849; buried in Westminster Presbyterian churchyard, Balto.) N. Y., 1877.
†Men of mark in Md. Johnson. V. 2, p. 177. DAR; Enoch Pratt Lib.
†Poems and essays; with biog. sketch. N. H. Dole.
Selected or select works, poetical and prose; with a new memoir. R. H. Stoddard. N. Y., 1880, 1896.
†Sketch. F. W. H. Myers. Warner's library of world's best literature.

Poe, Mrs. Edwin Wingate (Augusta Eccleston Murray). Chart. Col. Dames, Chap. I. MHS.

†**Poe, John Prentiss** (1836-1909). M. H. Mag., v. 12, p. 233.
†Men of mark in Md. Johnson. V. 2. DAR; Enoch Pratt Lib.

Poe, Philip Livingston. Pedigree. Soc. Col. Wars Md. Culver. 1940. MHS; DAR.

Poe Family, Va. and S. C. Geneal. of Mays family. Mays. P. 228. MHS.

Poffenbarger, George. Abr. Compend. Amer. Geneal. Virkus. V. 1, p. 775. DAR.

†**Poffenberger.** Hist. of Frederick Co. Williams. MHS; DAR.

Poist. Portraits and biog. rec. of Harford and Cecil Cos. 1897, pp. 348-51. MHS; DAR.

†**Poits.** Med. Annals Md. Cordell. 1903, p. 535. MHS.

†**Pole.** Med. Annals Md. Cordell. 1903, p. 536. MHS.

Polfrey. Arnold chart. MHS.

Polk. N. P. Barnes Bible rec. Ms. MHS.
†Biog. cyc. of rep. men of Md. and D. C. P. 223. MHS; DAR.
Col. families of U. S. A. Mackenzie. V. 6, p. 100 (see Brooke family). MHS; DAR.
Geneal. and memorial encyc. of Md. Spencer. V. 2, p. 422. MHS; DAR.
Handy and their kin. Handy
Haynie Bible rec. Ms. MHS.
*Index to Polk family and kinsmen. W. H. Polk. 1936. Ms. DAR.
Macy-Polk chart. MHS.
Macy-Polk chart. Ella F. O'Gorman. Ms. DAR.
Md. Geneal. Bull., v. 6, pp. 13, 25. MHS; DAR.
Peale Geneal. Coll. Ms. MHS.
Pedigree of Dr. Christopher Johnston, Jr. Soc. Col. Wars Md. Culver. 1940. MHS; DAR.
Pedigree of Gustav Wm. Lurman. Soc. Col. Wars Md. Culver. 1940. MHS; DAR.
Pedigree of Franklin Buchanan Owen. Soc. Col. Wars Md. Culver. 1940. MHS; DAR.
Pedigree of James Donnell Tilghman. Soc. Col. Wars Md. Culver. 1940. MHS; DAR.
Pedigree of Malcolm Van Vechten Tyson. Soc. Col. Wars Md. Culver. 1940. MHS; DAR.
Pocomoke Pres. churchyard; Worcester Co. Hudson. Bd. ms. MHS; DAR.
*Polk family and kinsmen. W. H. Polk. (Old Somerset Co. families.) Louisville, Ky., Press of Bradley Gilbert, 1912. MHS; DAR.
Posey chart. MHS.
St. Paul's Parish, Balto. V. 2. Mss. MHS.
*Side lights on Md. Hist. Richardson. V. 2, p. 204. MHS; DAR.
*The Sun, Balto., Sept. 4, 1904.
Some notable families of south. States. Armstrong. V. 1, pp. 173-79. DAR.
*Wicomico Co. families. Tilghman. Ms., pp. 97, 100, 128. DAR.
Samuel White and his father, Judge Thomas White. Conrad. 1903, pamph. MHS.
See Collins-Law-Polk.
See Pollok.

Polk, David, Dorchester Co. Will, dated 1773; also will of Sarah Houston Collins, 2nd wife of John Collins, dated 1835. Ms. DAR.

***Polk, W. S.** Geneal. and mem. encyc. of Md. Spencer. V. 2, pp. 422-27. MHS; DAR.

Polk Family. Md. Geneal. Rec. Com., 1934, p. 119. Typed, bd. DAR.
*Old Kent. Hanson. P. 194. MHS; DAR.

Polk Line. M. Van V. Tyson pedigree chart, plate 4. Soc. Col. Wars, Md. Johnston. 1905, p. 120. MHS.

Polk Line, Somerset Co. A. L. and S. L. Jenkins pedigree chart. Soc. Col. Wars Md. Johnston. 1905, p. 45. MHS.

Polk, Pollock. Carey chart. MHS.

Pollard. Mrs. R. N. Jackson chart. MHS.
May-Hanson-Pollard-Philips. Eiler. 1929, pamph. MHS.
St. Paul's Parish, Balto. V. 2. Mss. MHS.
Pollett. Somerset Co. Court Book. Tilghman. 1937. Ms. DAR.

Pollitt. Sketches of John Slemmons Stevenson and Rev. Samuel McMaster. Stevenson. Pp. 17, 21. MHS.
Wicomico Co. families. Bible rec. Ms. DAR.
*Wicomico Co. families. Tilghman. Ms., pp. 38-39, 43-45, 81, 98, 100, 102-03, 105. DAR.

Pollock. Boyd family, Md. and Va. Ms. DAR.
Carey chart. MHS.
Peale Geneal. Coll. Ms. MHS.
St. Paul's Parish, Balto. V. 1, 2. Mss. MHS.

Pollock, Dorchester Co., Polk family. Polk. P. 41. MHS; DAR.
***Pollock, David,** Westmoreland Co., Pa. And his descendants. E. T. Pollock and H. C. Griffith. DAR.
Pollock, Edwin T. Robert Smith Chew and his ancestors. 2 pts. Wash., D. C. Part 1: Hist. of ancestors in Md. and Va.; 1938. Part 2: Hist. of ancestors in Mass. and Conn.; 1939. DAR.
***Pollok, Polk.** Pedigree, 1075–1896. Mary Winder Garrett. Amer. Hist. Mag., Nashville, Tenn., v. 1, pp. 154–71; v. 2, pp. 46–65, 124; v. 3, p. 376. MHS.
†**Polmyer, Frederick.** In memoriam. Soc. for Hist. of Germans in Md. 6th ann. rept., 1892.
Pomeroy. Col. families of U. S. A. Mackenzie. V. 2. MHS; DAR.
Pomroy. Hagerstown tombstone inscriptions. Gruder. Natl. Geneal. Soc. Quart., 1919, v. 8, nos. 1, 2.
Ponsonby. Miss Kate Steele chart. MHS.
Pool. *See* Poole.
Poole. Balto., its hist., its people. Hall. V. 2. MHS; DAR.
Col. families of Amer. Lawrence. V. 5, p. 82. MHS.
*Geneal. and hist. of Coleman Poole and allied families. G. W. L. and L. C. Meeker. 1937. DAR.
†Hist of Frederick Co. Williams. MHS; DAR.
Lineage Bks., Natl. Soc. of Daughters of Amer. Col., v. 1, p. 8. MHS; DAR.
Monocacy Cemetery, Beallsville, Montgomery Co. Md. Geneal. Rec. Com., 1926–27. Pp. 70–73. Mss. DAR.
Mt. Olivet Cemetery, Frederick Md. Geneal. Rec. Com., 1934–35, p. 111. Mss. DAR.
Notes on Hist., v. 1, pp. 15–19. MHS; DAR.
Somerset Co. Court Book. Tilghman. 1937. Ms. DAR.
†**Poole, George.** Men of mark in Md. Johnson. V. 4. DAR; Enoch Pratt Lib.
Poole, Pool. Old Somerset. Torrence. MHS; DAR.
Pooly. St. Stephens Parish, Cecilton, Md. MHS; DAR.
Poor, C. L. Jr. Abr. Compend. Amer. Geneal. Virkus. V. 1, p. 623. DAR.
Pope. Ances. rec. and portraits. Col. Dames of Amer., 1910, v. 2, p. 438. MHS; DAR.
Beirne chart. MHS.
Few abs. from will book at Annapolis. William and Mary Quart., 1st series, v. 13, p. 27.
Lee Mag. of Va., May, 1925, v. 3, no. 1, p. 11. MHS.
*Lineage Bk., Daughters of Amer. Col., v. 4, pp. 10, 48. MHS; DAR.
McSpadden-Love-Meigs-Clendinen-Von Bibber-Pope chart. MHS.
Pedigree of Lloyd Bankson Whitham. Soc. Col. Wars Md. Culver. 1940. MHS; DAR.
*Pope family of Mass., 1634–1888. C. H. Pope. 1888. DAR.
Rumsey-Smithson Bible records. Md. Geneal. Rec. Com., 1932–33, v. 5, pp. 63–142. DAR.
St. Stephens Parish, Cecilton, Md. MHS; DAR.
Smithson-Rumsey rec. bk. Ms. MHS.
See Humphries-Pope-Brock-Parker.
See Lord-Pope.
***Pope,** Va. and Md. Burke's landed gentry. 1939. MHS.
Pope, G. A. Geneal. and mem. encyc. of Md. Spencer. V. 2, p. 721. MHS; DAR.
Pope, Nathaniel, Va. Pedigree of Francis Fielding Reid. Soc. Col. Wars Md. Culver. 1940. MHS; DAR.
Pope, Lieut. Col. Nathaniel, Md. and Va. Washington ancestry and rec. Hoppin. V. 1. MHS; DAR.
Pope Family. William and Mary Quart., 1st series, v. 4 (Va.); v. 12, p. 192 (Md.); v. 13.
Pope Line. Lord, Mass. and Md. Col. and Revolutionary families of Phila. Jordan. 1933, v. 1, pp. 361–70.
Pope-Morgan. Rumsey-Smithson family rec. bk. Md. Geneal. Rec. Com., 1932, p. 136. DAR.
Pope-Riley. Marriage certificate of David S. Pope and Sarah Riley, 1827. Md. Geneal. Rec. Com., 1935–36, pp. 216–18. Mss. DAR.
Porcher Family. Chart, including number of southern Huguenot families. Revised 1936. MHS.
***Porter.** Allied families of Delaware. Sellers. Pp. 26–29. MHS.
Ancestry and some descendants of James Porter from Lower Norfolk Co., Va., who settled at Susquehanna Manor, Cecil Co., Md. Md. Geneal. Rec. Com., 1934–35, pp. 267–74. Mss. DAR.
Antiquary. Lower Norfolk Co., Va., Antiquary, v. 3, pp. 50–51; v. 4, pp. 36, 79; v. 5, p. 147. MHS.
Clasping hands with generations past. Lloyd. MHS; DAR.
Clay family of Pa. Ms. File case, DAR.
*Grigsby family geneal, including sketch of Porter family. Pamph. with books. MHS.
†Hist. of Allegany Co. Thomas and Williams. V. 2. MHS; DAR.
†Hist. of West. Md. Scharf. V. 2, pp. 1477, 1504–05. MHS; DAR.
†Med. Annals Md. Cordell. 1903, p. 536. MHS.
Patriotic Md. Md. Soc. of S. A. R., 1930. MHS; DAR.
Portrait and biog. rec. of Sixth Cong. Dist. of Md. 1898, p. 517. MHS.
Rec. of Stepney Parish. MHS; DAR.
‡Reply to review of Judge Advocate of Gen. Hart, of proceedings, findings and sentence of General Court Marshall, in case of Maj-Gen. Fitz John Porter, and vindication of that officer. Reverdy Johnson. Balto., John Murphy Co., 1863, pamph. Enoch Pratt Lib.
St. Paul's Parish, Balto. V. 1, 2, 4. Mss. MHS.
St. Stephen's Parish register, Cecil Co. Ms. MHS; DAR.
Side lights on Md. hist. Richardson. V. 2, p. 207. MHS; DAR.
Somerset Co. Court Book. Tilghman. 1937. Ms. DAR.
South. Quakers and slavery. Weeks. 1896. MHS; DAR.
Susquehanna Manor. Lineage Bk., Daughters of Founders and Patriots, v. 16, pp. 59–60; v. 17, p. 13. MHS.
Taney and allied families. Silverson. MHS; DAR.
Turner Geneal. Coll. Ms. MHS.
*Wicomico Co. families. Tilghman. Ms., pp. 96, 98. DAR.

Porter. *See* Barcus-Porter.
See Grigsby family.
Porter, Somerset Co. Hooper family. Col. and Revolutionary families of Pa. Jordan. 1932, v. 4, p. 237.
Porter, Worcester Co. Bible rec. Md. Geneal. Bull., v. 2, p. 18. MHS; DAR.
Porter, David (1754–1808). Revolutionary war heroes. Cole. Bklet. Enoch Pratt Lib.
Porter, Capt. David. Westminster churchyard. Patriotic Marylander, v. 2, no. 4, pp. 54–60. MHS; DAR.
Porter, John. Will probated at Easton court house, 1798; family data, 1798–1930. Md. Geneal. Rec. Com., 1937, pp. 22–31. DAR.
***Porter Capt. Robert** (Md. battalion) **and Susannah (Mercer).** Natl. Geneal. Soc. Quart., March, 1938, v. 26, no. 1, p. 27.
Porter, Wm. David. Abr. Compend. Amer. Geneal. Virkus. V. 1, p. 779. DAR.
†**Porter, Wm. F.** Men of mark in Md. Johnson. DAR; Enoch Pratt Lib.
Porter-Nichols Families, Talbot Co. (1798–1930). Md. Geneal. Rec. Com., 1937, pp. 22–36. Mss. DAR.
Portzman. Hagerstown tombstone inscriptions. Gruder. Natl. Geneal. Soc. Quart., 1919, v. 8, nos. 1, 2.
***Posey.** Col. and Revolutionary families in Pa. Jordan. New series, v. 4. MHS.
Hist. of Frederick Co. Williams. V. 2. p. 1472. MHS; DAR.
Md. families. Culver. Ms. Personal list.
†Tercentenary hist. of Md. Andrews. V. 3, p. 917. MHS; DAR.
Posey, Charles Co. Note. D. A. R. Mag., v. 67, no. 8, p. 512.
Posey, St. Mary's Co. (1640). Col. and Revolutionary families of Pa. Jordan. 1932, v. 4, pp. 494–519.
Posey, Mrs. Charles P. (Carlyle Boone). Chart. Col. Dames, Chap. I. MHS.
Middendorf chart. MHS.
Neill chart. MHS.
Post. Rec., 1710–85. Humrickhouse; some of later family. 1913, 51 pp. Ms. DAR.
***Post-Humrickhouse.** Rev. Christian Frederick Post and Peter Humrickhouse and some of latter's family. H. H. Humrickhouse. 1913, 51 pp. MHS.
Postlethwaite. Cummings chart. Lib. Cong.; MHS; DAR.
†**Postley.** Med. Annals Md. Cordell. 1903, p. 537. MHS.
†Old Buckingham by the Sea, East. Shore of Md. Page. DAR.
Postley, Postly. Turner. Geneal. Coll. Ms. MHS.
Postly. C. H. B. Turner's Geneal. Coll. Mss. no. 78. MHS.
See Postley.
†**Potee.** Tercentenary hist. of Md. Andrews. V. 3, p. 740. MHS; DAR.
Poteet. Rumsey-Smithson Bible rec. Md. Geneal. Rec. Com., 1932–33, v. 5, pp. 63–142. DAR.
Rumsey-Smithson family rec. bk. Md. Geneal. Rec. Com., 1932, p. 97. DAR.
Smithson-Rumsey rec. bk. Ms. MHS.
Pott. Lloyd family hist. of Wales, Pa., and Md. DAR.
Pottenger. Abr. Compend. Amer. Geneal. Virkus. V. 1, p. 106, v. 6, pp. 479, 701 (Ohio). DAR.
Autobiography of Summerfield Baldwin. MHS; DAR.
*Burke's landed gentry. 1939. MHS.
Mullikins of Md. Baker. MHS; DAR.
St. John's P. E. Parish, Hagerstown. Md. Geneal. Rec. Com., 1939–40. Mss. DAR.
Pottenger, John. McCall-Tidwell families. McCall. P. 470. MHS; DAR.
Pottenger Family. Col. families of Amer. Lawrence. V. 15, pp. 170–83; v. 16, pp. 83–84. MHS.
***Pottenger-Magruder-Wade.** The Sun, Balto., March 10, 17, 24, 31, 1907.
Pottenger, Pottinger. Col. families of U. S. A. Mackenzie. V. 2. MHS.
†**Potter.** Hist. of Caroline Co. Noble. MHS.
McClellan chart. MHS.
†Med. Annals Md. Cordell. 1903, p. 537. MHS.
Rec. of Stepney Parish. MHS; DAR.
St. Paul's Parish, Balto. V. 2, 3, 4. Mss. MHS.
†**Potter,** Caroline Co. Chesapeake Bay Country. Earle. P. 381. MHS.
Potter, Cedric. Abr. Compend. Amer. Geneal. Virkus. V. 1, p. 422. DAR.
Potterf. Revolutionary war pension abs. Natl. Geneal. Soc. Quart., v. 23, no. 3, p. 88.
See Batdorf.
Pottinger. Beall and Bell families. Beall. MHS; DAR.
Bowie-Claggett chart. MHS.
Md. families. Culver. Ms. Personal list.
†Med. Annals Md. Cordell. 1903, p. 537. MHS.
See Pottenger.
†**Potts.** Bench and bar of Md. Sams and Riley. 1901, v. 1, p. 291. Lib. Cong.; MHS; Peabody Lib.
†Hist. of Allegany Co. Thomas and Williams V. 1. MHS; DAR.
†Hist. of Frederick Co. Williams. MHS; DAR.
Mackall family, Calvert Co. Ms. MHS.
†Med. Annals Md. Cordell. 1903, pp. 537–38. MHS.
Memoir of Hon. Richard Potts. L. H. Steiner. File case, MHS.
†Memoir of Hon. Richard Potts. M. H. Mag., 1910, v. 5, no. 1, p. 63.
*Memorial to Thomas Potts, Jr. Mrs. T. Potts James. Incl. eight generations of Potts family in Pa., with notes on Md. families. Priv. pr., Cambridge, 1874. MHS.
Orme geneal. chart. MHS.
*Our family ancestors. T. M. Potts. Canonsburg, Pa., 1895. Lib. Cong.; DAR.
St. Paul's Parish, Balto. V. 2. Mss. MHS.
*Short biog. sketch of Maj. James Potts (1752–1822). Ancestral charts. T. M. Potts. 85 pp. Peabody Lib.
†**Potts,** Prince George Co. Hist. of West. Md. Scharf. V. 1, p. 392. MHS; DAR.
†**Potts, Hon. Richard.** Memoir. L. H. Steiner. Ms. MHS. Also: M. H. Mag., 1910, v. 5, pp. 63–68.
***Potts Family.** Old Kent. Hanson. Pp. 56, 68–69. MHS; DAR.
Poulson, Alias **Mullock.** Naturalizations in Md., 1666–1765; Laws. Bacon. MHS.

Poultney. Balto., its hist., its people. Hall. V. 2. MHS; DAR.
Col. families of U. S. A. Mackenzie. V. 5, p. 61. MHS.
Curzon family. Pleasants. MHS.
Fox-Ellicott-Evans families. Evans. MHS; DAR.
Hist. of Balto. Lewis Hist. Pub. Co., Balto., 1912, v. 2, p. 1479. DAR.
Lineage and arms. Copied from Balto. Sun, Feb. 5, 1905. Md. Geneal. Rec. Com., 1934–35, pp. 368–76. Mss. DAR.
Lloyd - Pemberton - Hutchinson - Hudson - Parke families. Glenn. MHS; DAR.
Morris family of Phila. Moon. V. 2, p. 616. MHS.
Plummer family. A. P. H. Ms. MHS.
St. Paul's Parish, Balto. V. 3, 4. Mss. MHS.
Thomas Book. Thomas. Pp. 465–68. Lib. Cong.; MHS.
To Amer., 1736; to Md., 1815. The Sun, Balto. Feb. 5, 1905.
Poultney, Walter de Curzon. Pedigree chart. Soc. Col. Wars, Md. Johnston. 1905, p. 86. MHS.
Poundstone, Mrs. H. (Lenita Brandt). Chart. Col. Dames, Chap. I. MHS.
***Pountney Family.** Account of descendants of William Pountney of Birmingham. E. Pountney Davis. Annapolis, Capital Gazette Press, 1933.
Powel. Greenway Mss. Geneal. Coll. Binder's title, Hawkins-Bordley. MHS.
Powell. Abr. Compend. Amer. Geneal. Virkus. V. 6, pp. 302, 735. DAR.
Buckingham Pres. churchyard, Worcester Co., Hudson. Bd. ms. MHS; DAR.
Col. families of U. S. A. Mackenzie. V. 1. MHS; DAR.
Geneal. of Henrietta Chauncy Wilson. Upshur. Bk. of photos. MHS.
Hist. of Allegany Co. Thomas and Williams. V. 2, p. 1037. MHS; DAR.
†Hist. of Frederick Co. Williams. V. 2, p. 1238. MHS; DAR.
Mead relations. Prichard. DAR.
†Med. Annals Md. Cordell. 1903, p. 538. MHS.
M. E. churchyard, Snow Hill, Worcester Co., Hudson. Bd. ms. MHS; DAR.
Mt. Zion P. E. churchyard, Worcester Co. Md. Geneal. Rec. Com., 1937, Mrs. Lines. Mss. DAR.
See Riely. Abr. Compend. Amer. Geneal. Virkus. V. 1, p. 367. DAR.
St. Paul's P. E. churchyard, Berlin, Worcester Co. Hudson. Bd. ms. MHS; DAR. Also: Md. Geneal. Rec. Com., 1937, Mrs. Lines. Mss. DAR.
St. Paul's Parish, Balto. V. 1, 2. Mss. MHS.
St. Stephens Parish, Cecilton, Md. MHS; DAR.
Side lights on Md. hist. Richardson. V. 2, pp. 403, 413 (Nicholas, Va.), 416 (Old Thomas and Goodie). MHS; DAR.
Somerset Co. Court Book. Tilghman. 1937. Ms. DAR.
†Tercentenary hist. of Md. Andrews. V. 3, p. 758; v. 4, p. 389. MHS; DAR.
Third Haven Friends Meeting House, Easton. Vital rec. MHS. Also: Natl. Geneal. Soc. Quart., v. 11, no. 1, pp. 9–14.
See Tucker. Abr. Compend. Amer. Geneal. Virkus. V. 1, p. 864. DAR.
Turner Geneal. Coll. Ms. MHS.
*Wicomico Co. families. Tilghman. Ms., p. 55. DAR.
See Hatch-Powell.
See Harris - Maddox - Williams - Smith - Powell-Travers.
***Powell,** Balto. Co. Rec. Pub. Geneal. Soc. Pa., 1921–23, v. 8, p. 163.
***Powell,** Somerset Co. Encyc. Amer. biog. Amer. Hist. Soc., new series, v. 1, p. 291. MHS; DAR.
Powell, Va. A. E. Hull chart. MHS.
Powell Family. Chart; genealogy of the Powells of Castle Madoe, S. Wales and Cadet Branch of Phila.; coat of arms. W. B. Powell. Printed, 1895. MHS.
***Powell-Lucas,** Va. The Sun, Balto., Oct. 2, 1904; March 3, 1907.
†Power. Med. Annals Md. Cordell. 1903, p. 538. MHS.
*Wills. Semmes Geneal. Coll. Ms. MHS.
Power, James. Revolutionary war pension. Natl. Geneal. Soc. Quart., Sept., 1938, v. 26, no. 3, p. 44.
Power, J. Leonard. Md. Soc., War of 1812, v. 4, No. 313. Ms. MHS.
Powers. St. Paul's Parish, Balto. V. 2. Mss. MHS.
Powles. Zion Reformed Church, Hagerstown. Md. Geneal. Rec. Com., 1934–35. Mss. DAR.
Poythress. Miss E. K. Thom chart. MHS.
See Mayo-Poythress-Bland-Bennett.
Prater. Md. families. Culver. Ms. Personal list.
Prather. Abr. Compend. Amer. Geneal. Virkus. V. 4, p. 457. MHS.
Autobiography of Summerfield Baldwin. MHS; DAR.
*Frederick Co. families. Markell. Ms. Personal list.
*Lineage Bk., Daughters of Amer. Col. V. 5, p. 429. MHS; DAR.
Marriage rec. of Frederick Co. Markell. Md. Geneal. Rec. Com., 1938–39. Mss. DAR.
Monnet family geneal. Monette. P. 1081. MHS.
Mullikins of Md. Baker. MHS; DAR.
See Sprigg. Col. families of U. S. A. Mackenzie. V. 2, p. 695. MHS; DAR.
*Wills. Semmes Geneal. Coll. Ms. MHS.
See McNew-Prather-Turner.
Prather, Beltsville. Private burying ground. Natl. Geneal. Soc. Quart., v. 9, no. 3, p. 39.
Prather, Thomas. Revolutionary war pension. Natl. Geneal. Soc. Quart., Sept., 1938, v. 26, no. 3, p. 45.
***Prather Family.** D. A. R. Mag., Mar. 1939, v. 73, no. 3, p. 87.
Lillard, family of col. Va. Lillard. Pp. 245–49 MHS.
*Rec. D. A. R. Mag., v. 73, no. 3, p. 87.
†Pratt. Bench and bar of Md. Sams and Riley. 1901, v. 1, p. 320. Lib. Cong.; MHS; Peabody Lib.
†Biog. sketch of Isaac Pratt, Enoch Pratt and Isaac Pratt, Jr. Natives of Middleboro, Mass. Repr. from hist. of Plymouth Co., Mass, 1884. Phila. J. W. Lewis Co. Enoch Pratt Lib.

Pratt Family. Blakiston churchyard, Kent Co., Del., near Millington. Md. Geneal. Rec. Com., 1933-34, pp. 204-07. Mss. DAR.
Mrs. D. G. Lovell chart. MHS.
†Med. Annals Md. Cordell. 1903, p. 538. MHS.
Sacred Heart R. C. churchyard, Bushwood, St. Mary's Co. Md. Geneal. Rec. Com., 1929. Mss. DAR.
St. Paul's Parish, Balto. V. 1, 2. Mss. MHS.
†**Pratt, Enoch.** Biog. cyc. of rep. men of Md. and D. C. P. 493. MHS; DAR.
†(1808-96). M. H. Mag., v. 12, p. 234.
†Story of plain man. Richard H. Hart. Fiftieth anniversary Pub. of Enoch Pratt Free Lib., Balto., 1935.
Pratt, Gov. Thomas George. Founders of Anne Arundel and Howard Cos. Warfield. P. 278. MHS; DAR.
(Governor of Md., 1845-48). Amer. Clan Gregor Year Book, 1911, pp. 43-49. MHS; DAR.
†Governors of Md. Buchholz. P. 144. MHS.
Prentice. Somerset Co. Court Book. Tilghman. 1937. Ms. DAR.
Prentice, Mrs. William Kelly (Maria Woodward Baldwin). Chart. Col. Dames, Chap. I. MHS.
***Prentis.** Burke's landed gentry. 1939. MHS.
St. Paul's Parish, Balto. V. 2. Mss. MHS.
†**Prentiss.** Med. Annals Md. Cordell. 1903, p. 539. MHS.
Presbury. Descendants of Col. Thomas White. Morris. MHS.
Greenway chart. MHS.
Harford Co. Hist. Soc. Mss. Coll. JHU.
Hist. of Harford Co. Preston. MHS; DAR.
Howard-Montague-Warfield geneal. chart. Culver and Marye. MHS.
Pedigree of Septimus Davis. Soc. Col. Wars Md. Culver. 1940. MHS; DAR.
St. Paul's Parish, Balto. V. 2. Mss. MHS.
Preshur. St. Paul's Parish, Balto. V. 2. Mss. MHS.
†**Presstman, Stephen Wilson.** Hist. of Md. Scharf. V. 3, p. 29. MHS.
Preston. Amer. Armory and Blue Book. Matthews. 1911-12, p. 271.
Balto., its hist., its people. Hall. V. 3. MHS; DAR.
Bible rec. Natl. Geneal. Soc. Quart., v. 24, p. 29.
Bond chart. MHS.
*Descent of Carpenter branch, from Samuel Preston. Some col. mansions and those who lived in them. Glenn. 2nd series, 1900, v. 2, pp. 376-88. MHS.
Dorsey chart. MHS.
Few abs. from will book at Annapolis. William and Mary Quart., 1st series, v. 13, p. 27.
‡Founders of Md. Neill. 1879.
Geneal. David C. Preston. N. Y., Stivers Printing Co., 1913, pamph. MHS.
*Geneal. of Orange Co. branch, and life sketch of compiler. Coat of arms, 3 geneal. charts. D. C. Preston. Pub. by author, Middletown, N. Y., 1913.
Harford Co. Hist. Soc. Mss. Coll. JHU.
Md. families. Culver. Ms. Personal list.
†Med. Annals Md. Cordell. 1903, p. 539. MHS.
Peale Geneal. Coll. Ms. MHS.
Pedigree of Maurice Edward Skinner. Soc. Col. Wars Md. Culver. 1940. MHS; DAR.
Miss C. Petre chart. MHS.
*Preston at Patuxent. Some col. mansions and those who lived in them. 2nd series, 1900, v. 2, p. 369. MHS. Also: Pamph. repr. from above. MHS.
Preston-on-the-Patuxent. Home of Richard Preston, 1652-60, became Provincial Court, Meeting of Assembly and repository of official rec., 1654-60. Geneal., pp. 377-94. Repr. from Col. Mansions, 2nd series. Pamph. MHS.
*William Preston of Newcastle upon Tyne, Eng., and Phila., Pa., and allied families. C. S. Belsterling. (Armorial Bearings, pedigree charts.) Pr. for priv. distribution, Dolphin Press, 1934. MHS.
St. Paul's Parish, Balto. V. 3, 4. Mss. MHS.
See Lloyd-Preston.
Preston, Harford Co. Abr. Compend. Amer. Geneal. Virkus. V. 1, p. 493. DAR.
Preston, New Castle upon Tyne, and Phila. Pub. Geneal. Soc. Pa., v. 11, pp. 103-26. (Preston, Md., p. 109.)
Preston, Patuxent. Founders of Anne Arundel and Howard Cos. Warfield. P. 112. MHS; DAR.
†**Preston, James.** Geneal. and mem. encyc. of Md. Spencer. V. 1, p. 313. MHS; DAR.
Preston, Richard. Charles' gift. Footner.
†**Preston, Richard, Sr.** (Puritan Quaker of Md., grandfather of Samuel Preston, Mayor of Phila.) S. Troth. Pa. Mag. Hist. and Biog., 1892, v. 16, p. 207.
Preston, Sarah-Ford, Wm. Marriage certificate, 1670. Notes from public rec. Hodges. M. H. Mag., 1915, v. 10, pp. 284-85.
***Preston Family.** Old Kent. Hanson. P. 169. MHS; DAR.
***Preston Family,** Va. By E. C. Meade. The Sun, Balto., Oct. 16, 1904; July 8, 15, 22, 1906.
Preston Line. Col. and Revolutionary lineages of Amer. 1939, v. 1, pp. 231. MHS.
Prettyman. Hist. graves of Md. and D. C. Ridgely. MHS.
†Men of mark in Md. Johnson. V. 1. DAR; Enoch Pratt Lib.
Pretzman. Zion Reformed Church, Hagerstown. Md. Geneal. Rec. Com., 1934-35. Mss. DAR.
Prevett. Boydstun family. Weaver. P. 51. MHS; DAR.
***Prewitt, Pruitt.** Wicomico Co. families. Tilghman. Ms, p. 125. DAR.
Price. Amer. Clan Gregor Year Book, 1934, p. 71. MHS; DAR.
Ancestral beginnings in Amer. of McGregor, Magruder, Beall, Price, Phillips, Bland, McKisick, Young and related families. Caroline B. Price. 1928. DAR.
*Price ancestral data, concerning Eldridge C. Price and his mother Martha Ann Cowman. Bd. ms. MHS.
Ances. rec. and portraits, Col. Dames of Amer., 1910, v. 1, pp. 167, 168, 186; v. 2, p. 487. MHS; DAR.
†Biog. cyc. of rep. men. of Md. and D. C. Pp. 377, 443 (Queen Anne Co.) MHS; DAR.
Black chart. MHS.
Mrs. Howard Bruce chart. MHS.

Centreville cemetery. Md. O. R. Soc. Bull., no. 1, pp. 41–47.
Chart of Com. John Rodgers. DAR.
Chart, photos., 1 sheet. Cary Geneal. Coll. Ms. MHS.
Col. families of U. S. A. Mackenzie. V. 3; v. 5, p. 359. MHS; DAR.
†Day-Star of Amer. Freedom. Davis. P. 183. MHS.
Dorsey and allied families. Ms. MHS.
Col. Nicholas Duvall family rec. Price. Bd. ms. MHS.
Emory-Price family. M. H. Mag., 1931, v. 26, pp. 198–201.
†Hist. of Allegany Co. Thomas and Williams. V. 2. MHS; DAR.
†Hist. of Balto. City and Co. Scharf. Pp. 756, 883. MHS.
†Hist. of Frederick Co. Williams. MHS; DAR.
Marriages, 1778–1856. Parrish family. Boyd. MHS; DAR.
Md. families. Culver. Ms. Personal list.
Md. gleanings in Eng. Wills. M. H. Mag., 1907, v. 2, no. 3.
*Matthews-Price chart. T. A. Matthews. M.H.S.
†Med. Annals Md. Cordell. 1903, pp. 539–40. MHS.
†Memoir of Hannah A. Price, 1814–87, late of Fallston, Md. Morgan R. Wills. Norristown Pa., 1889. Enoch Pratt Lib.
†Men of mark in Md. Johnson. V. 3, V. 4. DAR., Enoch Pratt Lib.
†Papers relating to early hist. of Md. Streeter. 1876. MHS.
Patriotic Md. Md. Soc. of S. A. R., 1930. MHS; DAR.
Portrait and biog. rec. of Sixth Cong. Dist. of Md. 1898, pp. 211, 721. MHS.
Price and Emory families. Additions and corrections. M. H. Mag., 1931, v. 26, no. 2, p. 198.
Price family and other Gunpowder Friends, Baltimore Co. Death notices. Photos. of Newsp. clipp. MHS.
*John Price, emigrant, Jamestown Col., 1620, and some of his descendants. B. L. Price, minister First Pres. Church, Alexandria, Louisiana. Incl. notes on Dorsey, Ligon and Watkins families in Md., pp. 61–62. 1910. MHS.
St. Paul's Parish, Balto. V. 1, 2, 3, 4. Mss. MHS.
St. Stephens Parish, Cecilton, Md. MHS; DAR.
*Scruggs geneal. MHS.
Sydney-Smith and Clagett-Price families. Price. MHS; DAR.
Wicomico Co. families. Bible rec. Ms. DAR.
*Wicomico Co. families. Tilghman. Ms., pp. 53, 69, 77, 112. DAR.
Winchester-Owens-Owings-Price and allied families. M. H. Mag., 1930, v. 25, no. 4, p. 385–405.
See Cole-Price.
See Husband-Price-Haines.
See Matthews-Price.
Price, Cecil Co. Abr. Compend. Amer. Geneal. Virkus. V. 4, p. 183.
Price, Del. Mrs. Wm. Graham Bowdoin chart. MHS.
Price, Md. and Del. Miss Sidney Price chart. MHS.
Price, Eldridge C. Ancestral data. Paternal rec., Cooper, Gill, Gorsuch, Griffith and Rogers families; maternal rec., Beall, Brooke, Cowman, Edmondston, Galloway, Hopkins, Johns, and Magruder families. Typed in folder, 215 pp., ms. MHS.
Price, Mrs. Marshall L. (Henrietta Cowman George). Chart. Col. Dames, Chap. I. MHS.
Price, Miss Sidney. Chart. Col. Dames, Chap. I. MHS.
Price, Col. Thomas, Frederick Co. C. Johnston pedigree chart. Soc. Col. Wars, Md. Johnston. 1905, pp. 54, 151. MHS.
Price Family. Note. Old Somerset. Torrence. MHS; DAR.
*Rec. MHS.
Price Family, Charles Co. Dryden and allied families. Ms. MHS.
Price Family, Gunpowder River, Balto. Co. (Md. in 1634). Chart. Blue print. MHS.
Price Line. Taylor family, Balto. Co. Col. and Revolutionary families of Phila. Jordan. 1933, v. 1, pp. 260–67.
Price (Texas)-**Beall-Magruder.** Abr. Compend. Amer. Geneal. Virkus. V. 4, p. 437. MHS.
Prichard. Mead relations. Prichard. DAR.
Prichett. Rec. of Stepney Parish. MHS; DAR.
†**Prideaux.** Old Buckingham by the Sea, East. Shore of Md. Page. DAR.
Prier. *See* Pryor.
Prier-Parks-Hastings. Wicomico Co. families. Bible rec. Ms. DAR.
***Priest.** Descent on Matson side of family. Ms. DAR.
Old family Bible. Priest descent on Matson side of family (early Swedish settlers), 1638 to date. Md. Geneal. Rec. Com., 1938–39. Mss. DAR.
St. Paul's Parish, Balto. V. 2. Mss. MHS.
Priestley. Orme geneal. chart. MHS.
†**Prigg.** Med. Annals Md. Cordell. 1903, p. 540. MHS.
See Rogers-Ely-Prigg.
Primrose, S. Fletcher. Md. Soc., War of 1812, v. 1, no. 17. Ms. MHS.
***Prince.** The Sun, Balto., Sept. 30, 1906.
Pringle. Rogers Bible rec. Ms. MHS.
Russell-Lux Bible rec. Photos. MHS.
St. Paul's Parish, Balto. V. 2. Mss. MHS.
Prior. *See* Pryor.
Prise. Somerset Co. Court Book. Tilghman. 1937. Ms. DAR.
Pritchard. Lineage of Sarah Elizabeth Pritchard, wife of Rear Admiral Arthur John Pritchard, U. S. N. With Eccleston data. 1929, typed, bd. MHS.
Pritchard, A. J. Md. Soc., War of 1812, v. 3, no. 215. Ms. MHS.
***Pritchard Family.** Wilson Mss. Coll., no. 8, A. MHS.
Pritchett. Fisher family. Morse. MHS.
Fisher family, Sussex Co., Del., and Md. Ms. MHS.
Tombstone rec. of Dorchester Co. Jones. DAR.
Pritchett Family. Pritchett Family. H. D. Cranor. M. H. Mag., 1911, v. 6, pp. 70–75.
*Wilson Mss. Coll., no. 8, A. MHS.

Proctor. Still Pond Church and cemetery. Md. O. R. Soc. Bull., no. 2, pp. 65–75.
St. Paul's Parish, Balto. V. 2. Mss. MHS.
Prosser. Fox-Nelson-Prosser-Ring families. Va. Bible rec. Ms. DAR.
St. Paul's Parish, Balto. V. 2. Mss. MHS.
Protzman. Beards' Luth. graveyard, Washington Co. Md. Geneal. Rec. Com., 1935–36. Mss. DAR.
Proud. Bible rec. Ms. MHS.
St. Paul's Parish, Balto. V. 2. Mss. MHS.
Provoost. Abr. Compend. Amer. Geneal. Virkus. V. 1, p. 785. DAR.
Pruitt. *See* Prewitt.
Pry. Portrait and biog. rec. of Sixth Cong. Dist. of Md. 1898, pp. 859, 862. MHS; DAR.
†**Pryor.** Med. Annals Md. Cordell. 1903, p. 541. MHS.
Patriotic Md. Md. Soc. of S. A. R., 1930. MHS; DAR.
Pedigree of Thomas Wilson Williamson. Soc. Col. Wars Md. Culver. 1940. MHS; DAR.
*Side lights on Md. hist. Richardson. V. 2, p. 210. MHS; DAR.
Wicomico Co. families. Bible rec. Ms. DAR.
***Pryor, Prior, Prier.** Wicomico Co. families. Tilghman. Ms., pp. 5, 52, 80, 99, 114. DAR.
Pue. Cary Geneal. Coll. Ms. MHS.
H. D. G. Carroll Ms. Book. In H. F. Thompson Papers. MHS.
Howland chart. MHS.
Mrs. T. C. Jenkins chart. MHS.
†Med. Annals Md. Cordell. 1903, p. 541. MHS.
Milligan chart. MHS.
Portrait and biog. rec. of Harford and Cecil Cos. 1897, p. 153. MHS; DAR.
St. Paul's Parish, Balto. V. 2. Mss. DAR.
Warfields of Md. Warfield. MHS.
See Dorsey-Pue.
See Pugh.
Pue-Dorsey. Bible rec., 1760–1924. Md. Geneal. Rec. Com., 1935–36. Pp. 175–95. Mss. DAR.
Pue-Ridgely. Descendants of Dr. Wm. Shippen. Pa. Mag. Hist. and Biog., v. 1, pp. 109–11.
Pue-Rutter. Ances. rec. and portraits. Col. Dames of Amer., 1910, v. 1, p. 360. MHS; DAR.
Pugh. McCormick chart. MHS.
Pugh, Pue. Dorsey and allied families. Ms. MHS.
Pullen. *See* Ball-Mahan-Pullen-Wright.
Pumphrey. *See* Boone-Talbott-Pumphrey.
Purden. St. Paul's Parish, Balto. V. 2. Mss. MHS.
Purnell. All Hallow's P. E. churchyard, Snow Hill, Worcester Co. Hudson. Bd. ms. MHS; DAR. Also: Md. Geneal. Rec. Com., 1935–36, p. 24. Mss. DAR.
Buckingham Pres. churchyard, Worcester Co., Hudson. Bd. ms. MHS; DAR.
†Chesapeake Bay Country. Earle. P. 443. MHS.
Col. families of U. S. A. Mackenzie. V. 4, p. 127. MHS; DAR.
†Hist. of Allegany Co. Thomas and Williams. V. 2. MHS; DAR.
†Hist. of Caroline Co. Noble. MHS.
Hist. Salisbury, Wicomico Co. Truitt. DAR.
See Hurst, John. Abr. Compend. Amer. Geneal. Virkus. V. 1, p. 921. DAR.
Lineage Bk., Daughters of Founders and Patriots, v. 14, p. 107; v. 15, p. 53. MHS.
Makemie Memorial Pres. churchyard, Snow Hill, Worcester Co. Hudson. Bd. ms. MHS; DAR. Also: Md. Geneal. Rec. Com., Mrs. Lines. Mss. DAR.
John Drummond Marshall prayer book rec. Ms. MHS.
See McDougal. Abr. Compend. Amer. Geneal. Virkus. V. 1, p. 185. DAR.
†Med. Annals Md. Cordell. 1903, pp. 541–42. MHS.
Pedigree of Lee Cummins Cary. Soc. Col. Wars Md. Culver. 1940. MHS; DAR.
Polk family. Polk. P. 470. MHS; DAR.
Purnell Family Tree. (After original tree by Capt. John Purnell.) Printed; Big. Zol. Print; Reg. Al. Zoll Service. MHS.
Robins family, Va. and Worcester Co., Md. and allied families. Bd. ms. MHS.
St. Martin's P. E. Church, Worcester Co. Md Geneal. Rec. Com., 1937, Mrs. Lines. Mss. DAR.
St. Paul's Parish, Balto. V. 2. Mss. MHS.
(34 tombs, 1776–1906.) St. Paul's P. E. churchyard, Berlin, Worcester Co. Hudson. Bd. ms. MHS; DAR. Also: Md. Geneal. Rec. Com., 1937, Mrs. Lines. Mss. DAR.
Turner Geneal. Coll. Ms. MHS.
Purnell, Somerset Co. A. L. and S. L. Jenkins pedigree chart. Soc. Col. Wars, Md. Johnston. 1905, pp. 45, 152. MHS.
†**Purnell, Clayton.** Men of mark in Md. Johnson. V. 1. DAR; Enoch Pratt Lib.
Purnell Family. Notes. Natl. Geneal. Soc. Quart., v. 21, pp. 105–08.
***Purnell-Ball-Bowie-Holmes-Isaac.** The Sun, Balto., March 25, 1906. See also Gardiner Envelope, p. 2, in MHS.
Purner. Andrews Scrap Book. MHS.
White geneal. tree. MHS.
Purse. St. Paul's Parish, Balto. V. 2. Mss. MHS.
†**Purviance.** Balto., hist. and biog. Richardson and Bennett. 1871, pp. 421–22. MHS; DAR.
†Biog. cyc. of rep. men of Md. and D. C. P. 96. MHS; DAR.
Cary Geneal. Coll. Ms. MHS.
Coll. of Amer. epitaphs and inscriptions. Alden. 1814, v. 5. MHS.
Death of Robert Purviance and biog. sketch, April 6, 1858. Newsp. Clipp. MHS.
Miss E. V. Latrobe chart. MHS.
Monumental City. Howard. P. 601. MHS; DAR.
Patriotic Md. Md. Soc. of S. A. R., 1930. MHS; DAR.
Peale Geneal. Coll. Ms. MHS.
Pedigree of Leigh Bonsal. Soc. Col. Wars Md. Culver. 1940. MHS; DAR.
†M. H. Mag., v. 12, p. 235
St. Paul's Parish, Balto. V. 2. Mss. MHS.
Purviance, Robert (1733–1806). Revolutionary War Heroes. Cole. Bklet. Enoch Pratt Lib.
Westminster churchyard. Patriotic Marylander, v. 2, no. 4, pp. 54–60. MHS; DAR.
†**Purviance, Saml.** Hist. of Md. Scharf. V. 2, p. 504. MHS.
Pusey. Col. families of Amer. Lawrence. V. 7, p. 392. MHS.

Hopkins and allied families. Pp. 175, 229. Bd. ms. MHS.
*Pusey-Hopkins and allied families. G. Cope.
*Wicomico Co. families. Tilghman. Ms, pp. 35-36. DAR.
***Putman.** Brief hist. of Andrew Putman, Christian Wyandt and Adam Snyder, Wash. Co. E. C. Wyand. Hagerstown, Bookbinding and Publishing Co., 1909.
*Frederick Co. families. Markell. M., Personal list.
†Hist. of Frederick Co. Williams. MHS., DAR.
Pye. Md. gleanings in Eng. Wills. M. H. Mag., 1907, v. 2, no. 3.
Pedigree of Alfred Jenkins Tormey. Soc. Col. Wars Md. Culver. 1940. MHS; DAR.
St. Charles R. C. Church graveyard, Indianhead, Charles Co. Md. Geneal. Rec. Com., 1933-34, p. 137. Mss. DAR.
Semmes and allied families. Semmes. MHS.
*Semmes Geneal. Coll. Ms. MHS.
Pyfer. Frederick Co. tombstone inscriptions. Gruder. Natl. Geneal. Soc. Quart., 1919, v. 8, nos. 1, 2.
Pyle. Lloyd family hist. of Wales, Pa., and Md. DAR.
Ms. MHS.
Rec. of Cope family. Cope. Pp. 70, 151-52. MHS.

Q

Quail. Mrs. T. R. Brown chart. MHS.
Quarles, James. Will. MHS.
Quay. St. Paul's Parish, Balto. V. 2. Mss. MHS.
Queen. Abr. Compend. Amer. Geneal. Virkus. V. 1, p. 788; v. 6, p. 738. DAR.
Boarman geneal. Thomas. 1935. MHS; DAR.
Col. families of U. S. A. Mackenzie. V. 4. MHS; DAR.
Col. Joseph Belt. Hist. papers of Soc. Col. Wars. Magruder. 1909. MHS; DAR.
†Med. Annals Md. Cordell. 1903, p. 542. MHS.
Sacred Heart R. C. churchyard, Bushwood, St. Mary's Co. Md. Geneal. Rec. Com., 1929. Mss. DAR.
Semmes and allied families. Semmes. MHS.
Sweetser chart. MHS.
Quick. St. Paul's Parish, Balto. V. 2. Mss. MHS.
Quillaine. Somerset Co. Court Book. Tilghman. 1937. Ms. DAR.
Old Somerset. Torrence. MHS; DAR.
†Med. Annals Md. Cordell. 1903, p. 543. MHS.
See Paca-Quinan.
Quinby. Rev. Joseph Hull (1595) and some of his descendants. Hull. 1904. MHS.
Quincey. St. Paul's Parish, Balto. V. 2. Mss. MHS.
†**Quincy, Walter Cottrell.** Men of mark in Md. Johnson. V. 4. DAR; Enoch Pratt Lib.
Quinn. St. Paul's Parish, Balto. V. 2. Mss. MHS.
Turner Geneal. Coll. Ms. MHS.
Quisenberry. Col. families of U. S. A. Mackenzie V. 1, p. 230; v. 4. MHS; DAR.
*Geneal. memoranda of Quisenberry family and other families. A. C. Quisenberry. Wash., D. C., 1897. MHS.
*Memorials of Quisenberry family in Germany, Eng. and Amer. Coat of arms. A. A. C. Quisenberry. Wash., D. C., 1900, 137 pp.
Quisenbury, John, Va. Will. Ms. DAR.
†**Quynn.** Hist. of Frederick Co. Williams. MHS; DAR.
Patriotic Md. Md. Soc. of S. A. R., 1930. MHS; DAR.
Quynn-Houck. Lineage Bks., Natl. Soc. of Daughters of Amer. Col., v. 2, p. 186. MHS; DAR.

R

Rabbit. St. John's R. C. Church cemetery, Montgomery Co. Md. Geneal. Rec. Com., 1926, p. 27. Mss. DAR.
Raberg. Peale Geneal. Coll. Ms. MHS.
Raborg, Christopher. Westminster churchyard. Patriotic Marylander, v. 2, no. 4, pp. 54-60. MHS; DAR.
Raborg, E. Livingston. Md. Soc., War of 1812, v. 3, no. 264. Ms. MHS.
Rackliffe, Sarah, Worcester Co. Abs. of will, 1801. D. A. R. Mag., June, 1927, v. 61, no. 6, p. 471.
Radcliff. John Swadner and his descendants. Evans. 1919. Typed, bd. MHS.
Joseph Radcliff and his descendants, 1802-1924. Grace Radcliff Evans. Decatur, Ill., 1924. MHS.
Radcliffe. Geneal. and mem. encyc. of Md. Spencer. V. 1, p. 257. MHS; DAR.
Hazelhurst charts. MHS.
Lands of James Radcliffe in Talbot Co., 1760. Md. Geneal. Bull., v. 1, p. 3. MHS; DAR.
†Med. Annals Md. Cordell. 1903, p. 543. MHS.
Radish. Rec. of Stepney Parish. MHS; DAR.
See Reddish.
Rae. *See* Ray.
Ragan. Hagerstown tombstone inscriptions. Gruder. Natl. Geneal. Soc. Quart., 1919, v. 8, nos. 1, 2.
Ragland. Burton ancestry. Ms. MHS.
Rahauser. Zion Reformed Church, Hagerstown. Md. Geneal. Rec. Com., 1934-35. Mss. DAR.
***Rahn.** Hornberger-Menges-Rahn-Yingling families. C. J. Rahn. 1930. MHS.
Rahn and allied families. Ms. MHS.
See Hornberger-Menges-Rahn-Yingling.
***Railford.** Boone-Railford, 1763-1834. Ms. DAR.
Raine. Balto., its hist., its people. Hall. V. 3. MHS; DAR.
†Hist. of Balto. City and Co. Scharf. P. 625. MHS.
St. Paul's Parish, Balto. V. 2. Mss. MHS.
†**Raine, Frederick.** In memoriam. Soc. for Hist. of Germans in Md. 7th ann. rept., 1893.
Raisin. Elliott chart. MHS.
Raisin, Mrs. Carroll W. Mrs. Charles Carter chart. MHS.
(Katherine Sewall Daingerfield). Chart. Col. Dames, Chap. I. MHS.
***Raisin Family.** Old Kent. Hanson. P. 186. MHS; DAR.
Raisin, Reasin. Ringgold-Elliott chart. MHS.

Raisin (Reasin)-Claypoole Line. Balto., its hist., its people. Hall. V. 3, p. 765. MHS; DAR.
Raley. Wathen Prayer Book rec. Ms. MHS.
Rallings. *See* Rawlings.
Ralph. Rec. of Stepney Parish. MHS; DAR.
*Wicomico Co. families. Tilghman. Ms, pp. 120, 124. DAR.
Ramsay. Balto., its hist., its people. Hall. V. 2. MHS; DAR.
Descendants of Col. Thomas White. Morris. MHS.
Mrs. T. C. Jenkins chart. MHS.
Peale Geneal. Coll. Ms. MHS.
St. Paul's Parish, Balto. V. 1. Mss. MHS.
Ramsay, I. Tombstone rec. of Glendy burying ground (vault). Md. Geneal. Rec. Com. 1933–34, pp. 171–78. Mss. DAR. ,
Ramsay, James. Glendy churchyard. Patriotic Marylander, v. 2, no. 4, pp. 54–60. MHS; DAR.
†**Ramsay, Margaret Jane.** Biog. sketches of distinguished Marylanders. Boyle. MHS; DAR.
***Ramsay, Col. Nathaniel.** Sketch. Hist. of Cecil Co. Johnston. Pp. 537–48. MHS; DAR.
(1741–1817). Revolutionary war heroes. Cole. Bklet. Enoch Pratt Lib.
†Life and character. W. F. Brand. M. H. S. Fund Pub., no. 24, pt. 2, Balto., 1887. MHS.
Ramsburg. Brisko-Brisco-Briscoe and some family connections. Ramey. Ms. MHS.
*Frederick Co. families. Markell. Ms. Personal list.
†Hist. of Frederick Co. Williams. MHS; DAR.
Steiner geneal. Steiner. 1896. MHS.
Thomas geneal.; descendants of Gabriel, John, Valentine and Christian Thomas and George Ramsburg. Thomas. Pp. 15–19. MHS.
Ramsburgh. Abr. Compend. Amer. Geneal. Virkus. V. 1, p. 789. DAR.
Frederick Co. tombstone inscriptions. Gruder. Natl. Geneal. Soc. Quart., 1919, v. 8, nos. 1, 2.
Geneal. of descendants of Gabriel, John, Valentine and Christian Thomas and George Ramsburgh. Prof. Cyrus Thomas. Wash., D. C., 1902–05, pamph. MHS.
Randall. Balto., its hist., its people. Hall. V. 2. MHS; DAR.
Beall and Bell families. Beall. MHS; DAR.
Bible rec. Photos. MHS.
Cemetery Creek, Anne Arundel Co., tombstone inscriptions. Founders of Anne Arundel and Howard Cos. Warfield. P. 333. MHS; DAR.
*Founders of Anne Arundel and Howard Cos. Warfield. Pp. 116–21, 129. MHS; DAR.
Lehman family in Md. Lehman. 1935, pamph., p. 54. MHS; DAR.
Lehr chart. MHS.
Lineage Bks., Natl. Soc. of Daughters of Amer. Col., v. 1, p. 42; v. 2, p. 298. MHS; DAR.
†Med. Annals Md. Cordell. 1903, p. 543. MHS.
See Samuel Owings geneal. Focke Geneal. Coll. Mss. MHS.
Patriotic Md. Md. Soc. of S. A. R., 1930. MHS; DAR.
Pedigree of Coleman Randall Freeman. Soc. Col. Wars Md. Culver. 1940. MHS; DAR.
Mrs. N. S. Pendleton, Jr., chart. MHS.
Mrs. C. L. Riggs chart. MHS.
Rogers Coll. Ms. MHS.
St. Paul's Parish, Balto. V. 1, 2, 4. Mss. MHS.
St. Thomas' Parish, Balto. Co. Bd. ms. MHS. Also: Md. Geneal. Rec. Com., 1937, pp. 109–82. Mss. DAR.
Side lights in Md. hist. Richardson. V. 2, p. 418. MHS; DAR.
Slack chart. MHS.
Turner Geneal. Coll. Ms. MHS.
Wallis chart. MHS.
Winchester-Owens-Price families. M. H. Mag., 1930, v. 25, no. 4, p. 385–405.
Randall, Balto. Co. W. A. Moale pedigree chart, plate 2. Soc. Col. Wars. Johnston. 1905, p. 73. MHS.
Talbott of "Poplar Knowle." Shirk. MHS; DAR.
Randall, Mrs. Alexander (Aurora Eustis Carter). Chart, with appendix. Wm. B. Marye, 1926. Col. Dames, Chap. I. MHS.
Randall, Daniel Richard. Pedigree. Soc. Col. Wars Md. Culver. 1940. MHS; DAR.
Randall, Mrs. Daniel Richard (Elizabeth Winson Harding). Chart. (Mostly N. Y. and Mass. families.) Col. Dames, Chap. I. MHS.
Randall, Miss Elizabeth Harding. Chart. Col. Dames, Chap. I. MHS.
Randall, Miss Emily Brune. Chart. Col. Dames, Chap. I. MHS.
†**Randall, James Ryder** (1839-1908). M. H. Mag., v. 12, p. 235.
"Maryland, My Maryland," war song, in "South songs." De Leon. James Ryder Randall, born in Balto., 1839; died 1908; his poems have been collected and pub.; "My Maryland," first pub. in 1861; orig. mss. MHS.
Randall, Richard Harding. Pedigree. Soc. Col. Wars Md. Culver. 1940. MHS; DAR.
Randall, Watson Beale. Md. Soc., War of 1812. V. 1, no. 94. Ms. MHS.
Randall Family. Geneal. of branch of D. Randall family, 1666–1879. Book of photos. File case, MHS.
Randall Line. Beirne chart. MHS.
Miss E. H. and Miss E. B. Randall charts MHS.
Randalleon. Turner Geneal. Coll. Ms. MHS.
Randolph. Abr. Compend. Amer. Geneal. Virkus. V. 1, pp. 17–18. DAR.
Cary Geneal. Coll. Ms. MHS.
†Med. Annals Md. Cordell. 1903, p. 544. MHS.
Pocohontas and her descendants. Robertson. MHS; DAR.
*Randolph family, Va. John Randolph. 15 pp.
Randolph of Tuckahoe. Charts. Blue print. In folder marked Ames charts. MHS.
Tuckahoe (Va.) and Tuchahoe Randolphs. Va. Mag. Hist. and Biog., v. 45, pp. 55–86, 392–405.
***Randolph,** Va. By E. C. Meade. The Sun, Balto., March 19, 1905.
W. M. Cary pedigree chart. Soc. Col. Wars, Md. 1905, pp. 11, 152. MHS.
Clark chart. MHS.
Va. families. Du Bellett.
Randolph, Va. and Md. Col. families of U. S. A. Mackenzie. V. 5, p. 426. MHS; DAR.

Randolph, Francis F. Pedigree. Soc. Col. Wars Md. Culver. 1940. MHS; DAR.
Randolph, George F. Pedigree. Soc. Col. Wars Md. Culver. 1940. MHS; DAR.
†**Randolph, John.** Balto., hist. and biog. Richardson and Bennett. 1871, pp. 424-27. MHS; DAR.
Randolph, R. F., Va. (born Feb. 2, 1811; married Alice Weems, Md.). D. A. R. Mag., v. 70, no. 2, p. 136.
†**Randolph, R. Lee.** Men of mark in Md. Johnson. V. 2. DAR; Enoch Pratt Lib.
Randolph Family. Thomas Book. Thomas. Pp. 343-45. Lib. Cong.; MHS.
Randolph Family, Va. Chart. K. D. Harrison. Lithograph, 1928. MHS.
Geneal. of Page family, Va. Page. Pp. 251-72. MHS; DAR.
Lee of Va., 1642-1892. E. J. Lee. P. 406. Lib. Cong.; MHS.
*__Randolph (Edmund) Family.__ Leaflet. MHS.
*__Rankin.__ Frederick Co. families. Markell. Ms. Personal list.
†Old Buckingham by the Sea, East. Shore of Md. Page. DAR.
*Rankin and Wharton family. S. M. Rankin. DAR.
Ranson. Ances. rec. and portraits. Col. Dames of Amer., 1910, v. 1, p. 285. MHS; DAR.
Rasboon. Naturalizations in Md., 1666-1765; Laws. Bacon. MHS.
†**Rasin.** Biog. cyc. of rep. men of Md. and D. C. Pp. 158-60. MHS; DAR.
Family notes from Cecil Meeting. Md. Geneal. Rec. Com., 1939-40, pp. 115-16. Mss. DAR.
†Hist. of Balto. City and Co. Scharf. Pp. 397-98. MHS.
Morris family of Phila. Moon. V. 1, p. 180; v. 2, pp. 621 (family), 763-64; v. 3, pp. 929-31, 1060; v. 5, p. 295. MHS.
Still Pond Church and cemetery. Md. O. R. Soc. Bull., no. 2, pp. 65-75.
Wallis chart. MHS.
Rasin-Claypool. Ms. MHS.
Rasin-Claypool Line. Balto.: its hist., its people. C. C. Hall. V. 3, p. 765. MHS.
Rasin, Reasin. Family rec. (From New Testament, N. Y., to Md., in 1821.) Ms. MHS.
*__Raskob-Green.__ Rec. book. John J. Raskob. Contains charts of Green, Thomas and Wheeler families, 1634-1919. Archmere, Claymont, Del., Franklin Printing Co., 1921. MHS.
Ratcliff. Purnell family tree. MHS.
Ratford. Marine officers of Amer. Revolution. McClellan. D. A. R. Mag., Sept., 1932, v. 66, no. 9, pp. 560-68.
Rattenbury. Blackwell chart. MHS.
Rauleigh. Pattison wills. Md. Geneal. Rec. Com., 1929, pp. 7-42; 1930-31. Mss. DAR.
Raven. Cary Geneal. Coll. Ms. MHS.
Greenway chart. MHS.
Mrs. W. H. Harris chart. MHS.
Jenkins-Courtney chart. MHS.
Macsherry chart. MHS.
Md. families. Culver. Ms. Personal list.
Posey chart. MHS.
Mrs. Sherlock Swann chart. MHS.
Rawley. Somerset Co. Court Book. Tilghman. 1937. Ms. DAR.
Rawlings. Anne Arundel Co. Tombstone inscriptions. Ms. DAR.
Cary Geneal. Coll. Ms. MHS.
Duckett chart. MHS.
*Founders of Anne Arundel and Howard Cos. Warfield. Pp. 134-35. MHS; DAR.
†Hist. of Allegany Co. Thomas and Williams. V. 2. MHS; DAR.
†Hist. of West. Md. Scharf. V. 2, p. 1462. MHS; DAR.
*Lineage Bk., Daughters of Amer. Col. V. 3, p. 250. MHS; DAR.
Lineage Bk., Daughters of Founders and Patriots. V. 21, pp. 53-54; V. 23, 97-98. MHS; DAR.
*Lineage of Rawlings; old homestead in Anne Arundel Co. Emily E. Lantz. Balto., 1915. MHS.
Md. families. Culver. Ms. Personal list.
†Med. Annals Md. Cordell. 1903, p. 544. MHS.
Patriotic Md. Md. Soc. of S. A. R., 1930. MHS; DAR.
Pedigree of Charles Gambrill Baldwin. Soc. Col. Wars Md. Culver. 1940. MHS; DAR.
Mrs. C. L. Riggs chart. MHS.
St. Paul's Parish, Balto. V. 1, 2. Mss. MHS.
†**Rawlings, Moses.** Hist. of Md. Scharf. V. 2, p. 583. MHS.
*__Rawlings Family and Old Homestead.__ The Sun, Balto., May 14, June 11, 1905.
Rawlings-Marsden. Lineage Bks., Natl. Soc. of Daughters of Amer. Col., v. 3, p. 250. MHS; DAR.
Rawlings, Rallings, Rawlins. Col. families of U. S. A. Mackenzie. V. 3. MHS; DAR.
Rawlins. *See* Rawlings.
Rawlins Family. Skeltons of Paxton, Powhatan Co., Va. Baskerville. MHS.
Ray. Botfield and allied families. Ms. DAR.
Darby geneal. Darby. MHS.
Lineage Bk., Order of Washington, p. 195. MHS; DAR.
Md. families. Culver. Ms. Personal list.
Patriotic Md. Md. Soc. of S. A. R., 1930. MHS; DAR.
Ray, Rae, Rea. St. Paul's Parish, Balto. V. 2. Mss. MHS.
Rayman. Naturalizations in Md., 1666-1765; Laws. Bacon. MHS.
Raymond. Bond chart. MHS.
Gantz family geneal. Ms. MHS.
Pedigree of Lee Cummins Cary. Soc. Col. Wars Md. Culver. 1940. MHS; DAR.
Rayne. Buckingham Pres. churchyard, Worcester Co., Hudson. Bd. ms. MHS; DAR.
†**Rayner.** Bench and bar of Md. Sams and Riley. 1901, v. 2, p. 470. Lib. Cong.; MHS; Peabody Lib.
Sweetser chart. MHS.
†**Rayner, Isidore** (1850-1912). M. H. Mag., v. 12, p. 235.
†**Raynor.** Memorial address on life and character of Isidor Raynor (senator from Md.). Wash., D. C., 1914. Enoch Pratt Lib.
Razolini. Naturalizations in Md., 1666-1765; Laws. Bacon. MHS.
Rea. *See* Ray.
†**Read.** Bench and bar of Md. Sams and Riley. 1901, v. 1, p. 301. Lib. Cong.; MHS; Peabody Lib.
Blackford chart. MHS.
Descendants of Joran Kyn. Pa. Mag., v. 6, p. 207.
Mrs. J. F. Lee chart. MHS.

†**Read.** Med. Annals Md. Cordell. 1903, p. 544. MHS.
Patriotic Md. Md. Soc. of S. A. R., 1930. MHS; DAR.
St. Paul's Parish, Balto. V. 1, 2. Mss. MHS.
*The Sun, Balto., Jan. 17, 1904.
See Dale-Read.
Read, Va. Bible rec. (Showing Magruder.) Va. Mag. Hist. and Biog., v. 21, pp. 326–27.
†**Read, Wm. G.** Balto., hist. and biog. Richardson and Bennett. 1871, pp. 429–33. MHS; DAR.
***Read-Corbin-Luttrell-Bywaters.** Read-Corbin-Luttrell-Bywaters and allied families. A. M. Prichard. Staunton, Va., 1930. DAR.
Reade. *See* Bernard-Reade-Throckmorton.
***Reade,** Va. The Sun, Balto., Nov. 10, 1904; Sept. 15, 22, 29, Oct. 6, 1907.
Reade Family, Va. and Md. William and Mary Quart., 1st series, v. 14, pp. 117–26. (See Magruder, p. 121.)
†**Readell.** Med. Annals Md. Cordell. 1903, p. 544. MHS.
Reades, Va. Chart, photos., complete in 2 sheets. Cary Geneal. Coll. Ms. MHS.
Reading. Harvey chart. MHS.
†Hist. printing in Col. Md. Wroth. MHS.
*Memorials of Reading, Howell, Yerkes, Watts, Latham and Elkins families. J. G. Leach. Phila., J. P. Lippincott Co., 1898.
Reamer. Frederick Co. tombstone inscriptions. Gruder. Natl. Geneal. Soc. Quart., 1919, v. 8, nos. 1, 2.
Reaney. St. Paul's Parish, Balto. V. 2, 4. Mss. MHS.
Reaney Family. Ms. MHS.
†**Reardon.** Med. Annals Md. Cordell. 1903, p. 545. MHS.
See Bond-Cromwell-Delaport-Harris-Reisinger-Reardon.
See Hall-Bond-Cromwell.
See Taylor-Roberts-Standiford-Patterson-Reardon-Baker-Reisinger-Scharf.
Reasin. *See* Raisin.
See Rasin.
†**Reckord.** Hist. of Balto. City and Co. Scharf. P. 925. MHS.
†**Redden.** Men of mark in Md. Johnson. V. 3. DAR; Enoch Pratt Lib.
***Reddish, Radish.** Wicomico Co. families. Tilghman. Ms, pp. 96–97, 110, 112. DAR.
***Reddy.** Revolutionary ancestors of A. W. Reddy, W. Va. 1930. DAR.
Redgrave. S. G. Hopkins chart. MHS.
Mrs. Pennington chart. MHS.
Redman. Md. Geneal. Bull., v. 4, p. 29. MHS; DAR.
Redmond. St. Paul's Parish, Balto. V. 2. Mss. MHS.
Redue. Bible rec. Upper Penins. East. Shore, p. 109–12. MHS; DAR.
Redwood Family, Balto. See Chowning family, Lancaster Co., Va. Ms. File case, DAR.
Ree. Miss M. W. Davis chart. MHS.
Mrs. G. H. Williams, Jr.; chart. MHS.
Reed. Frederick Co. tombstone inscriptions. Gruder. Natl. Geneal. Soc. Quart., 1919, v. 8, nos. 1, 2.
Geneal. and memorial encyc. of Md. Spencer. V. 1, p. 118. MHS; DAR.
*Geneal. J. L. Reed. Balto., 1901.
I. U. Church cemetery. Md. O. R. Soc. Bull., no. 2, pp. 76–78.
Lloyd family hist. of Wales, Pa., and Md. DAR.
M. E. Church South cemetery, near Poolesville, Montgomery Co. Md. Geneal. Rec. Com., 1926. Mss. DAR.
Pedigree and hist. of Washington family. Welles. P. 232. MHS.
Portrait and biog. rec. of Harford and Cecil Cos. 1897, pp. 152, 243, 470. MHS; DAR.
Rec., Kent Co. Md. Geneal. Rec. Com., 1934–35, p. 185. Mss. DAR.
*Gen. Philip Reed, warrior and statesman and Caulk's Field: Ceremonies attending unveiling of stone to mark Caulk's Field, battle ground, Kent Co., Oct. 18, 1902, and slab at Gen. Reed's grave. Reed tombstones in I. U. Cemetery, pp. 88–89. Pamph. Enoch Pratt Lib.
*Wicomico Co. families. Tilghman. Ms, p. 64. DAR.
See Baker-Reed-Young-Wroth.
See McKesson-Reed.
See Muse.
Reed, John Loduvicus. Md. Soc., War of 1812. V. 1, no. 103. Ms. MHS.
Pedigree charts, plates 1 and 2. Soc. Col. Wars, Md. Johnston. 1905, pp. 87–88. MHS.
Reed, Gen. Philip (1760–1829). (Wars of 1776 and 1812; hero of Caulk's field; U. S. senator; buried in I. U. cemetery. Md. Geneal. Rec. Com., 1933–34, p. 232. Mss. DAR.
†Hist. of Md. Scharf. V. 3, p. 93. MHS.
***Reed, Wm.** Geneal. and mem. encyc. of Md. Spencer. V. 1, pp. 118–31. MHS; DAR.
Reed-Schrack-Hardin. Pa. Mag., v. 35, pp. 120–21.
Reeder. Descendants of Col. Thomas White. Morris. MHS.
Hist. graves of Md. and D. C. Ridgely. MHS.
Monumental City. Howard. MHS; DAR.
Tombstone inscriptions at Ellenborough, St. Mary's Co. Md. O. R. Soc. Bull., no. 2, pp. 81–82. MHS.
Reeder, C. H. Md. Soc., War of 1812, v. 4, no. 337. Ms. MHS.
Reeder, C. L. Md. Soc., War of 1812, v. 4, no. 338. Ms. MHS.
Reeder, C. Merrick. Md. Soc., War of 1812, v. 4, no. 334. Ms. MHS.
†**Reeder, Charles.** Balto., hist. and biog. Richardson and Bennett. 1871, pp. 435–47. MHS; DAR.
Reeder, Clarence. Md. Soc., War of 1812, v. 4, no. 347. Ms. MHS.
Reeder, J. Dawson. Md. Soc., War of 1812, v. 4, no. 339. Ms. MHS.
Reeder, L. B. Md. Soc., War of 1812, v. 4, no. 340. Ms. MHS.
Reeder, M. Lanahan. Md. Soc., War of 1812, v. 4, no. 341. Ms. MHS.
Rees. Descendants of Joran Kyn. Pa. Mag., v. 7, p. 299.
Rees, Md. and Kent Co., Del. Some allied families. Streets. 1904, pamph. MHS.
†**Rees, Reese.** Med. Annals Md. Cordell. 1903, p. 545. MHS.
Reese. Abr. Compend. Amer. Geneal. Virkus. V. 1, p. 792. DAR.
Dedicated to Joel Chandler Harris. Lizette Woodworth Reese and Stephens Collins Foster. Southern Literary Messenger, Feb., 1940. 109 E. Cary St., Richmond, Va.

Englar family. Barnes. MHS; DAR.
*Encyc. of Amer. biog. Amer. Hist. Soc., new series, v. 1, p. 318. MHS; DAR.
†Men of mark in Md. Johnson. V. 2; v. 3. DAR; Enoch Pratt Lib.
Mt. Olivet Cemetery, Frederick. Md. Geneal. Rec. Com., 1934–35, p. 111. Mss. DAR.
Parrish family. Boyd. MHS; DAR.
Patriotic Md. Md. Soc. of S. A. R., 1930. MHS; DAR.
Roop geneal. Pamph. MHS.
Rumsey-Smithson family rec. bk. Md. Geneal. Rec. Com., 1932, p. 138. DAR.
St. Paul's Parish, Balto. V. 1, 2, 4. Mss. MHS.
Smithson-Rumsey rec. bk. Ms. MHS.
See Rees.

Reese, Howard Hopkins. Md. Soc., War of 1812, v. 3, no. 216. Ms. MHS.

Reese, Lizette Woodworth. Contemporary Amer. authors. Fred B. Millett.
(1856–1935). Worleys; introduction by John Farrar. 1936. Enoch Pratt Lib.
†Living authors. N. Y., 1931, p. 333.

Reese Family. Thomas Book. Thomas. P. 469. Lib. Cong.; MHS.

Reeves. See Blue family. 24 mss. File case, DAR.
Miss Eliza Thomas chart. MHS.
St. Paul's Parish, Balto. V. 1, 2. Mss. MHS.

Reeves, Va. Southerland-Latham and allied families. Voorhees. Bd. ms. MHS.

Reeves-Clotworthy. Samuel Carpenter of Phila. Carpenter. P. 253. MHS.

Regester. Abr. Compend. Amer. Geneal. Virkus. V. 1, p. 792. DAR.
*Wilson Mss. Coll., no. 79. MHS.

***Register.** Burke's landed gentry. 1939. MHS.

***Register Family.** Wilson Mss. Coll., no. 63. MHS.

Reich. Catonsville pioneers of Luth. faith. Natl. Geneal. Soc. Quart., v. 9, no. 2, p. 29.

Reich Family, Frederick Co. Bible rec., 1755–79. D. C. Geneal. Rec. Com. Typed, bd. DAR.

†Reichard. Hist. of Washington Co. Williams. 1906, v. 1, pp. 429, 573; v. 2, p. 965. MHS; DAR.

***Reichart.** Frederick Co. families. Markell. Ms. Personal list.

Reid. Christ P. E. Church cemetery, Cambridge. Steele. 1936. MHS; DAR.
Col. families of U. S. A. Mackenzie. V. 7. MHS; DAR.

Reid, Andrew. Bird chart. MHS.

Reid, Francis Fielding. Pedigree. Soc. Col. Wars Md. Culver. 1940. MHS; DAR.

Reid, John. Geneal. rec. of George Small, etc. Small. MHS.

Reidenauer. Dorsey and allied families. Ms. MHS.
Howland chart. MHS.

***Reifsnider, John Milton** (1865–1920). Encyc. of Amer. biog. Amer. Hist. Soc., N. Y., v. 9, p. 125. MHS.
Md. Soc., War of 1812, v. 3, no. 241. Ms. MHS.
Pedigree. Soc. Col. Wars Md. Culver. 1940. MHS; DAR.

Reiley. St. Paul's Parish, Balto. V. 2. Mss. MHS.

Reineck, Wm. K. R. Certificate of membership in Sons of Temperance, 1847. Ms. MHS.

†Reinhard. Hist. of Allegany Co. Thomas and Williams. V. 2. MHS; DAR.

†Reinhart. Med. Annals Md. Cordell. 1903, p. 547. MHS.

Reinhoff, Mrs. Wm. Francis, Jr. Mrs. Bennett Crain chart. MHS.

Reip. Jenkins-Courtney chart. MHS.
St. Paul's Parish, Balto. V. 2. Mss. MHS.

Reip, A. H. Md. Soc., War of 1812, v. 1, no. 1. Ms. MHS.

Reip, T. H. Md. Soc., War of 1812, v. 1, no. 23. Ms. MHS.

***Reisher.** Frederick Co. families. Markell. Ms. Personal list.

Reisinger. *See* Bond-Cromwell-Delaport-Harris-Reisinger-Reardon.
See Taylor-Roberts-Standiford-Patterson-Reardon-Baker-Reisinger-Scharf.

Reister. Bible rec., 1759. Focke Geneal. Coll. Ms. MHS.

Reitenauer. Pedigree of Thomas Dobbin Penniman. Soc. Col. Wars Md. Culver. 1940. MHS; DAR.
Rec. of Hill Church, Berks Co., Pa. Hist. Soc. Pa.

Reitenauer, Pa. German pioneers. Strassburger-Hinke. 1934.

Reitenauer, Ridenour. Hagerstown tombstone inscriptions. Gruder. Natl. Geneal. Soc. Quart., 1919, v. 8, nos. 1, 2.

Reitenaur (Ritenour). Baptismal rec., 1755-96, St. John's Evan. Church, Hagerstown. Natl. Geneal. Soc. Quart., v. 22, no. 4, pp. 105–06.

Reitmeyer. Frederick Co. tombstone inscriptions. Gruder. Natl. Geneal. Soc. Quart., 1919, v. 8, nos. 1, 2.

***Remey Family.** Hist. sketch. Ms. MHS.

†Remsen, Ira. Biog. dict. of U. S. J. H. Lamb. Co., v. 1.
Life of Ira Remsen. Frederick H. Getman. Enoch Pratt Lib.

Rench. Hist. of West. Md. Scharf. V. 2, pp. 1308–09. MHS; DAR.
Md. families. Culver. Ms. Personal list.
Zion Reformed Church, Hagerstown. Md. Geneal. Rec. Com., 1934–35. Mss. DAR.

Rench, Hagerstown. Lineage Bks., Natl. Soc. of Daughters of Amer. Col., v. 1, p. 198. MHS; DAR.

Rencher. Pedigree of Nicholas Leeke Dashiell. Soc. Col. Wars Md. Culver. 1940. MHS; DAR.
Rec. of Stepney Parish. MHS; DAR.

Rennert. Balto., its hist., its people. Hall. V. 2. MHS; DAR.

†Rennolds. Med. Annals Md. Cordell. 1913, p. 547. MHS.

Renshaw. Somerset Co. Court Book. Tilghman. 1937. Ms. DAR.

Renshaw, Mrs. Alfred Howard (Lucy Braxton Hopkins). Chart. Col. Dames, Chap. I. MHS.
Miss E. C. Hopkins chart. MHS.

Rentch. Zion Reformed Church, Hagerstown. Md. Geneal. Rec. Com., 1934–35. Mss. DAR.

Rentz. Catonsville pioneers of Luth. faith. Natl. Geneal. Soc. Quart., v. 9, no. 2, p. 29.

Repold. Coll. of Amer. epitaphs and inscriptions. Alden. 1814, v. 5. MHS.

Repose. St. Stephens Parish, Cecilton, Md. MHS; DAR.

Requeadt. See Miller family. Focke Geneal. Coll. Ms. MHS.
Resh. Hagerstown tombstone inscriptions. Gruder. Natl. Geneal. Soc. Quart., 1919, v. 8, nos. 1, 2.
Resley. Md. tombstone rec. Md. Geneal. Rec. Com., 1937, Parran, p. 5. Mss. DAR.
Reuling. Balto., its hist., its people. Hall. V. 3. MHS; DAR.
†Med. Annals Md. Cordell. 1903, p. 547. MHS.
†Reuling, George. Biog. sketch. MHS.
Reutenauer. *See* Ridenour.
Revell. Geneal. of Henrietta Chauncy Wilson. Upshur. Bk. of photos. MHS.
Md. families. Culver. Ms. Personal list.
Old Somerset. Torrence. MHS; DAR.
Pedigree of Sam'l King Dennis. Soc. Col. Wars Md. Culver. 1940. MHS; DAR.
Pedigree of Wm. Parke Custis Munoz. Soc. Col. Wars Md. Culver. 1940. MHS; DAR.
Revell, Randall. J. T. Dennis pedigree chart. Soc. Col. Wars, Md. Johnston. 1905, pp. 21, 152. MHS.
Revercomb. *See* Rubincam-Revercomb.
Reyburn. St. Paul's Parish, Balto. V. 2. Mss. MHS.
Reynell. Cary Geneal. Coll. Ms. MHS.
***Reyner Family.** Old Kent. Hanson. P. 190. MHS; DAR.
†Reynold. Med. Annals Md. Cordell. 1903, p. 548. MHS.
Reynold Family Assoc., 1632, 1928. Wash. Co. line, v. 31, pp. 202–23; v. 37, pp. 44, 64; v. 39; v. 40, p. 16 (births). Cecil Co., marriages, 1777–1840, v. 38, p. 32. Del. rec., v. 39; v. 40, pp. 60–62. MHS; DAR.
Reynolds. Ancestry of Wm. Haines. Cregar. MHS.
Balto., its hist., its people. Hall. V. 3. MHS; DAR.
†Biog. cyc. of rep. men of Md. and D. C. P. 242. MHS; DAR.
Chart of Com. John Rodgers. DAR.
Wm. Conway of Md. and Pa. Ms. File case, DAR.
Dupuy family. Dupuy. P. 83. MHS.
†Hist. of Washington Co. Williams. 1906, v. 2, p. 1304. MHS; DAR.
Patriotic Md. Md. Soc. of S. A. R., 1930. MHS; DAR.
Mrs. J. Piper chart. MHS.
Reynolds, Tewelles, Walls and kindred families. Geneal. sketches. Winston-Salem, N. C., Commercial Printers, Inc., 1928, pamph. MHS.
St. Paul's Parish, Balto. V. 2, 4. Mss. MHS.
St. Stephens Parish, Cecilton, Md. MHS; DAR.
Spessard family. Spessard. MHS; DAR.
Trinity P. E. churchyard, Long Green. Typed ms. MHS; DAR.
White geneal. tree. MHS.
See Neil-Booth-Reynolds.
Reynolds, C. Ambrose, Col. U.S.A. Md. Soc., War of 1812, v. 1, no. 69. Ms. MHS.
Reynolds, Joseph. Abr. Compend. Amer. Geneal. Virkus. V. 1, p. 794. DAR.
Reynolds, Wm. B., Capt. U.S.A. Md. Soc., War of 1812, v. 1, no. 126. Ms. MHS.
***Reynolds-Hyatt.** Robert and Mary Reynolds and Hyatt descendants. M. H. Reynolds. 1928. DAR.
***Reysurder.** Frederick Co. families. Markell. Ms. Personal list.
***Rhea.** Lineage Bk., Daughters of Amer. Col., v. 1, p. 111. MHS; DAR.
Rheam. Haugh's Lutheran Church. Md. Geneal. Rec. Com., 1939-40. Mss. DAR.
Rhees. Lukens chart. MHS.
***Rhett.** Pennington Papers. Ms. MHS.
†Rhind. Hist. of West. Md. Scharf. V. 2, pp. 1394–95. MHS; DAR.
Rhoades. Somerset Co. Court Books. Tilghman. 1937. Ms. DAR.
See Rhodes.
Rhodes. Blackford chart. MHS.
Centenary of Catholicity in Ky. Webb. 1884. MHS.
Rhodes Family in Amer. V. 1, no. 1, June, 1919. Pub. 3 times a year. Nelson Osgood Rhoades, 1208 Merchants Natl. Bank Bldg., Los Angeles, Calif. MHS.
Somerset Co. Court Book. Tilghman. 1937. Ms. DAR.
Sweetser chart. MHS.
*Wicomico Co. families. Tilghman. Ms, p. 122. DAR.
Rhodes, Rhoades, Roads. Old Somerset. Torrence. MHS; DAR.
Riall. St. Mary's churchyard, Tyaskin Md. Md. Geneal. Rec. Com., 1938–39, pp. 187–92. Mss. DAR.
*Wicomico Co. families. Tilghman. Ms, p. 80. DAR.
Riall-Rider-Moore. Wicomico Co. families. Bible rec. Ms. DAR.
Ricaud. Cotton chart. MHS.
*Geneal. Ms. File case, MHS.
St. Paul's churchyard, Kent Co. Md. O. R. Soc. Bull., no. 2, pp. 54–65. MHS.
***Ricaud Family.** Old Kent. Hanson. P. 87. MHS; DAR.
†Rice. Hist. of Allegany Co. Thomas and Williams. V. 2. MHS; DAR.
Old Somerset. Torrence. MHS; DAR.
St. Stephens Parish, Cecilton, Md. MHS; DAR.
Rice Family, Hagerstown. Bromwell geneal. Bromwell. Pp. 177–99. MHS.
Rice-Leffler. Bromwell geneal. Ms. Lib. Cong.; MHS.
Rich. Col. families of U. S. A. Mackenzie. V. 1, p. 581. MHS; DAR.
†Med. Annals Md. Cordell. 1903, p. 548. MHS.
Naturalizations in Md., 1666–1765; Laws. Bacon. MHS.
St. Paul's Parish, Balto. V. 3. Mss. MHS.
Whiteley chart. MHS.
Rich, Dorchester Co. Mrs. G. H. Williams, Jr., chart. MHS.
Rich, Riche. Peale Geneal. Coll. Ms. MHS.
Richard. Naturalizations in Md., 1666–1765; Laws. Bacon. MHS.
Richards. Christ P. E. Church cemetery, Cambridge. Steele. 1936. MHS; DAR.
Geneal. of descendants of George and Sarah Smedley. Cope. P. 284. MHS; DAR.
Harlan family geneal., Chester Co., Pa. Harlan. P. 162. MHS.
†Hist. of Allegany Co. Thomas and Williams. V. 2. MHS; DAR.

Mt. Zion P. E. churchyard, Worcester Co. Md. Geneal. Rec. Com., 1937, Mrs. Lines. Mss. DAR.
Old Somerset. Torrence. MHS; DAR.
Rec. of Stepney Parish. MHS; DAR.
St. Paul's Parish, Balto. V. 1, 2, 3. Mss. MHS.
Mrs. H. DeCourcy Wright Thom chart. MHS.

Richardson. Bible rec. Md. Geneal. Bull., v. 11, no. 2, p. 16. MHS; DAR.
Col. families of U. S. A. Mackenzie. V. 6, p. 367. MHS; DAR.
*Early comers to the Province. Georgians in Anne Arundel Co. Atlanta Jour., Sept. 22, 1906. Newsp. clipp. File case, MHS.
Early Quaker rec., Anne Arundel and Calvert Cos., 1665–1889. Pub. Geneal. Soc., Pa., v. 3, no. 3, pp. 197–200.
*Frederick Co. families. Markell. Ms. Personal list.
Freeborn Garrettson Waters. Bible rec. Ms. MHS.
†Hist. of Caroline Co. Noble. MHS.
*Hist. Dorchester Co. Jones. 1925, p. 439. MHS; DAR.
Makemie Memorial Pres. churchyard, Snow Hill, Worcester Co. Hudson. Bd. ms. MHS; DAR. Also: Md. Geneal. Rec. Com., Mrs. Lines. Mss. DAR.
Md. Geneal. Bull., v. 3, p. 2. MHS. DAR.
M. E. churchyard, Snow Hill, Worcester Co. Hudson. Bd. ms. MHS; DAR.
Patriotic Md. Md. Soc. of S. A. R., 1930. MHS; DAR.
Pedigree of Leigh Bonsal. Soc. Col. Wars Md. Culver. 1940. MHS; DAR.
Pedigree of Duncan Keener Brent. Soc. Col. Wars Md. Culver. 1940. MHS; DAR.
Rec. of Stepney Parish. MHS; DAR.
See Robertson. Abr. Compend. Amer. Geneal. Virkus. V. 1, p. 802. DAR.
Rolle family rec., Talbot Co. Ms. MHS.
St. Paul's Parish, Balto. V. 1, 2, 4. Mss. MHS.
Side lights on Md. hist. Richardson. V. 2, p. 426. MHS; DAR.
Smithsons of Harford Co. Md. Geneal. Rec. Com., 1932–33, pp. 156. Mss. DAR.
Somerset Co. Court Book. Tilghman. 1937. Ms. DAR.
Talbott of "Poplar Knowle." Shirk. MHS; DAR.
Thomas-Chew-Lawrence. Thomas. MHS.
Tombstone inscriptions of branch of Richardson family, Dorchester Co., 1789–1890. Md. O. R. Soc. Bull., no. 3, pp. 62–3.
Trinity Church burial ground, near Cambridge, Md. Md. Geneal. Rec. Com., 1937–38, pp. 93–104. Mss. DAR.
Trinity Church cemetery, Dorchester Co. Md. O. R. Soc. Bull., no. 3, pp. 42–52.
Turner Geneal. Coll. Ms. MHS.
*Wicomico Co. families. Tilghman. Ms, pp. 97, 109, 114. DAR.

***Richardson,** West River. Founders of Anne Arundel and Howard Cos. Warfield. Pp. 174–77. MHS; DAR.

†**Richardson, B. H.** Balto., hist. and biog. Richardson and Bennett. 1871, pp. 439–43. MHS; DAR.

Richardson, Dorsey. Pedigree. Soc. Col. Wars Md. Culver. 1940. MHS; DAR.

Richardson, Joel. Geneal. rec. of George Small, etc. Small. MHS.

Richardson, John, Frederick Co. Lineage Bk., Daughters of Founders and Patriots, v. 12, p. 52. MHS.

Richardson Family. Thomas Book. Thomas. Pp. 477–79. Lib. Cong.; MHS.

Richardson Family, Va. Ms. MHS.

Richardson Line, Anne Arundel Co. G. M. Sharp pedigree chart, plate 1. Soc. Col. Wars, Md. Johnston. 1905, pp. 91, 152. MHS.

Riche. *See* Rich.

Richerds. Mt. Olivet Cemetery, Frederick. Md. Geneal. Rec. Com., 1934–35, p. 111. Mss. DAR.

†**Richmond,** Bench and bar of Md. Sams and Riley. 1901, v. 2, p. 537. Lib. Cong.; MHS; Peabody Lib.

***Richmond Family.** H. Richmond. Rec. of Ireland and Somerset, also Md., New Eng. and Va. 3 v. 1933, 1936, 1938. MHS.

Rickenbaugh. Zion Reformed Church, Hagerstown. Md. Geneal. Rec. Com., 1934–35. Mss. DAR.

Rickets. *See* Ricketts.

Ricketts. Md. families. Culver. Ms. Personal list.

Ricketts, Rickets. St. Stephens Parish, Cecilton, Md. MHS; DAR.

Riddel. St. Paul's Parish, Balto. V. 1, 2. Mss. MHS.

Riddell. Dobbin chart. MHS.
Pedigree of Dr. Christopher Johnston, Jr. Soc. Col. Wars Md. Culver. 1940. MHS; DAR.
Pedigree of James Donnell Tilghman. Soc. Col. Wars Md. Culver. 1940. MHS; DAR.
Thomas family of Talbot Co. Spencer. P. 47. MHS; DAR.

Riddle. Cummings chart. Lib. Cong.; MHS; DAR.

Riddle Family, Balto. Co. Bible rec. Gorsuch and allied families. Harrison. Mss. MHS.
*Frederick Co. families. Markell. Ms. Personal list.
Mt. Paran Pres. churchyard, Harrisonville, Balto. Co. Typed ms. MHS; DAR.

Riddlemoser. St. Joseph's R. C. churchyard. Md. O. R. Soc. Bull., no. 3, p. 64.

Ridely. Mt. Carmel burial ground, Montgomery Co. Md. Geneal. Rec. Com., 1934, p. 85. Mss. DAR.

†**Ridemour.** Hist. of Frederick Co. Williams. MHS; DAR.
Md. families. Culver. Ms. Personal list.
See Reitenauer.

Ridenour, Reutenauer. Chart, photos. complete. Cary Geneal. Coll. Ms. MHS.

Rider. Bible rec., from old Noah Rider Bible, 1752–1863, now owned by descendant, Mrs. A. J. (Margaret Rider Jackson) Vander Bogart, Tony Tank, Md. Md. Geneal. Rec. Com., 1938–39, pp. 201–03. Mss. DAR.
Christ P. E. Church cemetery, Cambridge. Steele. 1936. MHS; DAR.
Jackson chart. MHS.
Pedigree of Rev. Sam'l. Tagart Steele. Soc. Col. Wars Md. Culver. 1940. MHS; DAR.
St. Joseph's R. C. churchyard. Md. O. R. Soc. Bull., no. 3, p. 64.
St. Paul's Parish, Balto. V. 1, 2, 3, 4. Mss. MHS.
St. Stephens Parish, Cecilton, Md. MHS; DAR.

Rider. Miss Kate Steele chart. MHS.
Turner Geneal. Coll. Ms. MHS.
*Wicomico Co. families. Tilghman. Ms., pp. 54-55, 95-96, 115, 124. DAR.
See Riall-Rider-Moore.
See Walker-Rider-Fletcher.
Rider, Somerset Co., side lights on Md. hist. Richardson. V. 2, p. 431. MHS; DAR.
Ridgate, T. Howe. Md. Soc., War of 1812, v. 1, no. 128. Ms. MHS.
Ridge. St. Stephens Parish, Cecilton, Md. MHS; DAR.
Ridgely. Amer. Armory and Blue Bk. Matthews. 1908, p. 240. DAR.
Abr. Compend. Amer. Geneal. Virkus. V. 6, p. 744. DAR.
Ames Geneal. Coll. Ms. MHS.
Ances. rec. and portraits. Col. Dames of Amer. 1910. V. 1, pp. 86, 249-50, 255; v. 2, pp. 603, 607, 615, 674. MHS; DAR.
Anne Arundel Co. gentry. Newman. MHS; DAR.
Autobiography of Summerfield Baldwin. MHS; DAR.
Bailliere chart. MHS.
Sara R. Baldwin chart. MHS.
Balto. Herald, April 17, 1898. Newsp. clipp. Scrap Book. MHS.
Mrs. Lee Barroll chart. MHS.
Mrs. R. Barton, Jr., charts. MHS.
Battee, Brewer, Boteler, etc., family rec. Murray. Photos. MHS.
†Bench and bar of Md. Sams and Riley. 1901, v. 1, pp. 75, 302. Lib. Cong.; MHS; Peabody Lib.
Bolton chart. MHS.
Boone chart. MHS.
Botfield and allied families. Ms. DAR.
See Brewer-Ridgely-Peale. Lineage Bks., Natl. Soc. of Daughters of Amer. Col., v. 2, p. 201; v. 3, p. 236. MHS; DAR.
Britton Scrap Book. V. 2. Ms. MHS.
Carnan chart. Cary Geneal. Coll. Ms. MHS.
H. D. G. Carroll Ms. Book. In H. F. Thompson Papers. MHS.
Chart, photos., 3 sheets. Cary Geneal. Coll. Ms. MHS.
Col. families of Amer. Lawrence. V. 2, p. 44; v. 3, p. 291; v. 5, p. 89; v. 14, p. 134; v. 16, p. 88. MHS.
Col. families of U. S. A. Mackenzie. V. 2, pp. 608-18; v. 7, pp. 49, 51, 59. MHS; DAR.
Col. mansions of Md. and Del. Hammond. 1914. MHS.
Descendants of Joran Kyn. Pa. Mag., v. 7, p. 464.
Descendants of Valentine Hollingsworth, Sr. Stewart. MHS; DAR.
Dorsey and allied families. Ms. MHS.
Dorsey chart. Lib. Cong.; MHS.
Col. Nicholas Duvall family. Records. Price. Bd. ms. MHS.
Eldridge chart. MHS.
Ford and other lines. Md. Geneal. Rec. Com., 1932-33, pp. 7-20. Mss. DAR.
*Founders of Anne Arundel and Howard Cos. Warfield. Pp. 77-83, 259-60 (Gov. Charles Carnan Ridgely), 351-53, 379-80, 416-18, 428-31. MHS; DAR.
*Frederick Co. families. Markell. Ms. Personal list.
Geneal. of family of Edward Ridgely, 1775-1820. Md. Geneal. Rec. Com., 1934. DAR.
Griffith chart. Cary Geneal. Coll. Ms. MHS.
Griffith geneal. Griffith. MHS; DAR.
Hamill chart. MHS.
Hist. graves of Md. and D. C. Ridgely. MHS.
Hist. sketch of P. F. Eichelberger. Eichelberger.
Howard-Montague-Warfield geneal. chart. Culver and Marye. MHS.
Mrs. R. N. Jackson chart. MHS.
Mrs. T. C. Jenkins chart. MHS.
Lehr chart. MHS.
*Lineage Bk., Daughters of Amer. Col., v. 4, pp. 210, 341. MHS; DAR.
Mrs. M. D. Lovell chart. MHS.
Md. families. Culver. Ms. Personal list.
†Med. Annals Md. Cordell. 1903, p. 549. MHS.
Milligan chart. MHS.
Mrs. E. N. Morison chart. MHS.
Neill chart. MHS.
Nicholson-Hynson-Noel chart. Cary Geneal. Coll. Ms. MHS.
Patriotic Md. Md. Soc. of S. A. R., 1930. MHS; DAR.
Peale Geneal. Coll. Ms. MHS.
Pedigree of Charles Gambrill Baldwin. Soc. Col. Wars Md. Culver. 1940. MHS; DAR.
Pedigree of Francis Joseph Baldwin. Soc. Col. Wars Md. Culver. 1940. MHS; DAR.
Pedigree of Duncan Keener Brent. Soc. Col. Wars Md. Culver. 1940. MHS; DAR.
Pedigree of Gustavus Warfield Evans. Soc. Col. Wars Md. Culver. 1940. MHS; DAR.
Pedigree of John Ridgely Fisher. Soc. Col. Wars Md. Culver. 1940. MHS; DAR.
Pedigree of Thomas Murray Maynadier. Soc. Col. Wars Md. Culver. 1940. MHS; DAR.
Pedigree of Pleasants Pennington. Soc. Col. Wars Md. Culver. 1940. MHS; DAR.
Pedigree of Thomas Dobbin Penniman. Soc. Col. Wars Md. Culver. 1940. MHS; DAR.
Pedigree of Tilghman Goldsborough Pitts. Soc. Col. Wars Md. Culver. 1940. MHS; DAR.
Pedigree of Townsend Scott, IV. Soc. Col. Wars Md. Culver. 1940. MHS; DAR.
Pedigree of Mark Alexander Herbert Smith. Soc. Col. Wars Md. Culver. 1940. MHS; DAR.
Pedigree of John Ogle Warfield, Jr. Soc. Col. Wars Md. Culver. 1940. MHS; DAR.
Pedigree of Andrew Jackson Young, Jr. Soc. Col. Wars Md. Culver. 1940. MHS; DAR.
*Pennington Papers. Ms. MHS.
Miss C. Petre chart. MHS.
Prentice chart. MHS.
Mrs. A. Randall chart. MHS.
Ridgely family to Md., 1659. Emily E. Lantz. The Sun, Balto., March 1, 8, 15, 1908.
St. Paul's Parish, Balto. V. 1, 2, 3, 4. Mss. MHS.
Side lights on Md. hist. Richardson. V. 2, p. 437 (Anne Arundel Co.), 211 (Baltimore Co.). MHS; DAR.
Mrs. Edw. Simpson chart. MHS.
Talbott of "Poplar Knowle." Shirk. MHS; DAR.
*The Sun, Balto., May 24, 1903 (Hampton); Feb. 23, March 1, 8, 15, 22, 1908.
Thomas family of Talbot Co. Spencer. P. 148. MHS; DAR.
Warfields of Md. Warfield. MHS.
Mrs. J. Whitridge Williams chart 2. MHS.

W. S. G. Williams pedigree chart. Soc. Col. Wars Md. Johnston. 1905, pp. 128, 152. MHS.
*Wilson Mss. Coll., no. 42. MHS.
See Cowden-Ridgely-Jamison.
See Ford-Dorsey-Hyland, etc.
See Oussler-Jean-Ridgely.
See Pue-Ridgely.
Ridgely, Del. and Md. Amer. Armory and Blue Book. Matthews. 1911-12, pp. 144, 299.
†**Ridgely, Charles, Jr.** Seafaring in time of war, 1756-63. Mrs. Helen W. Ridgely. M. H. Mag., 1915, v. 10, pp. 1-15.
†**Ridgely, Charles Carnan.** Governor of Md. Buchholz. P. 81. MHS.
†**Ridgely, Charles G.** (1784-1848). M. H. Mag., v. 12, p. 235.
Ridgely, Henry. Patent "Small Land," 1748. Md. Geneal. Rec. Com., 1935-36, pp. 201-03. Mss. DAR.
Ridgely, Col. Henry. J. P. Hill pedigree chart, Soc. Col. Wars Md. Johnston. 1905, pp. 37. 152. MHS.
Pedigree of John B. Philip C. Hill. Soc. Col. Wars Md. Culver. 1940. MHS; DAR.
***Ridgely, Henry,** of Dover, Delaware. Burke's landed gentry. 1939, p. 3012. MHS.
***Ridgely, John,** of Hampton. Coat of arms. Burke's landed gentry. 1939. MHS.
Ridgely, Julian White. Pedigree. Soc. Col. Wars Md. Culver. 1940. MHS; DAR.
†**Ridgely, Randolph.** Hist. of Md. Scharf. V. 3, p. 228. MHS.
†M. H. Mag., v. 12, p. 236.
Ridgely, Wm. McCall-Tidwell families. McCall. Pp. 468-70. MHS; DAR.
Ridgely Family. Bible rec., 1764-1849. M. H. Mag., 1916, v. 11, pp. 376-78.
Copied from Riley family. Md. Geneal. Rec. Com., 1934-35, pp. 383-86, 395. Mss. DAR. Ms. MHS.
To Md., 1659. Md. Geneal. Rec. Com., 1933-34, pp. 27, 81-86, 262, 272-86. Mss. DAR.
Ridgely Family, Hampton, Md. Papers and plantation account bk., 1723. Mss. MHS.
Ridgely Line. Col. and Revolutionary lineages of Amer. 1939, v. 1, pp. 290-313. MHS.
***Ridgely-Dorsey-Evans.** Founders of col. families. H. R. Evans. Wash., D. C., 1935, 45 pp. MHS.
***Ridgely-Dorsey-Greenberry.** Founders of col. families of Ridgely, Dorsey and Greenberry of Md. H. Ridgely Evans. Wash., D. C., sold by W. H. Lowdermilk & Co., 1935. MHS; DAR.
***Ridout.** Founders of Anne Arundel Cos. Warfield. P. 100. MHS; DAR.
†Med. Annals Md. Cordell. 1903, p. 549. MHS.
Reminiscences of Thomas Ridout. M. H. Mag., 1925, v. 20, pp. 215-35.
Ridout, from "Whitehall". Anne Arundel Co. tombstone inscriptions. Ms. DAR.
†**Ridout, Thomas.** Reminiscences of 1754-1829. Memoranda of his experiences written 1786. M. H. Mag., 1925, v. 20, pp. 215-35.
Ridout Family. Ten years in upper Canada. Lady Matilda Edgar. MHS.
Ridouts. Col. mansions of Md. and Del. Hammond. 1914. MHS.
†**Rieman.** Hist. of Balto. City and Co. Scharf. P. 419. MHS.
See Holliday. Abr. Compend. Amer. Geneal. Virkus. V. 1, p. 650. DAR.
Rieman, Charles Ellet. Abr. Compend. Amer. Geneal. Virkus. V. 1, p. 296. DAR.
Rienhoff, Mrs. Wm. Francis, Jr. (Frances Kemper Young). Chart. Col. Dames, Chap. I. MHS.
Whitehead chart. MHS.
Rigbey. *See* Rigby.
Rigbie. Deford chart. MHS.
Rigbie-Stewart. Notes and Queries from Cary-Hall on the Hall Kin. Harford Co. Hist. Soc. Mss. Coll. JHU.
Rigbie, Rigby, Lineage. Turner family. Forman. P. 42. MHS.
Rigby. Done Bible rec. Ms. MHS.
Lambdin chart. MHS.
See Rigbie.
Rigby, Rigbey. St. Paul's Parish, Balto. V. 2. Mss. MHS.
Riggen, Rigon Somerset Co. Court Book. Tilghman. 1937. Ms. DAR.
Riggin. Makemie Memoria Pres. churchyard, Snow Hill, Worcester Co. Hudson. Bd. ms. MHS; DAR. Also: Md. Geneal. Rec. Com., Mrs. Lines. Mss. DAR
†Med. Annals Md. Cordell. 1903, p. 549. MHS.
*Wicomico Co. families. Tilghman. Ms., p. 99. DAR.
Riggs. Abr. Compend. Amer. Geneal. Virkus. V. 1, pp. 324-25. DAR.
Ances. rec. and portraits. Col. Dames of Amer., 1910, v. 1, p. 253; v. 2, p. 607. MHS; DAR.
Bailliere chart. MHS.
Bonsal charts. MHS.
*Frederick Co. families. Markell. Ms. Personal list.
Geneal. of Riggs and allied families. John Beverley Riggs, Brookeville, Md. To be pub.
Griffith geneal. Griffith. MHS; DAR.
Hist. and geneal. account of Levering family. Levering. MHS.
Md. families. Culver. Ms. Personal list.
†Med. Annals Md. Cordell. 1903, pp. 549-50. MHS.
Neill chart. MHS.
Patriotic Md. Md. Soc. of S. A. R., 1930. MHS; DAR.
Pedigree of Pleasants Pennington. Soc. Col. Wars Md. Culver. 1940. MHS; DAR.
Mrs. Pennington chart. MHS.
Riggs, Anne Arundel, Frederick and Montgomery Cos. 1 vol. DAR.
Riggs farm burial ground rec., Montgomery Co., 1817-1905. Md. Geneal. Rec. Com., 1932-33, p. 206. Mss. DAR.
Riggs family of Md. J. B. Riggs. Balto., Author, 1939, 534 pp. MHS.
Riggs of Anne Arundel, Frederick and Montgomery Cos. prior to 1663. Pamph. MHS.
St. Paul's Parish, Balto. V. 2. Mss. MHS.
Stones from Bowie Davis place, Montgomery Co. Md. Geneal. Rec. Com., 1934, p. 61. Mss. DAR.
Warfields of Md. Warfield. MHS.
See Dorsey-Riggs.
See Welsh-Hammond-Riggs.
Riggs, Mrs. Alfred Randolph (Laura Theresa Lanman). Chart. (Conn. and Mass. families.) Col. Dames, Chap. I. MHS.

†**Riggs, Clinton L.** Men of mark in Md. Johnson. V. 2. DAR; Enoch Pratt Lib.
Riggs, Clinton Levering. Md. Soc., War of 1812, v. 3, no. 243. Ms. MHS.
Riggs, Mrs. Clinton Levering (Mary Kennedy Cromwell). Chart. Col. Dames, Chap. I. MHS.
***Riggs, Elisha.** Geneal. and mem. encyc. of Md. Spencer. V. 2, pp. 599-619. MHS; DAR.
Riggs, James. Revolutionary soldier, of Montgomery Co. 1936. Ms. DAR.
Riggs Family. Geneal. and memorial encyc. of Md. Spencer. V. 2, pp. 599-605. MHS; DAR.
***Riggs Family,** Anne Arundel, Frederick and Montgomery Cos., 1722-1875. Founders of Anne Arundel and Howard Cos. Warfield. Pp. 354-61. MHS; DAR.
Riggs Line. Gaither, Va. and Md. Col. and Revolutionary families of Phila. Jordan. 1933, v. 1, pp. 144-67.
Rigon. *See* Riggen.
Riley. Cannon-Riley-Truitt-Houston-Kollock. Stow. Ms. MHS.
Geneal. of George Donald Riley. Elihu S. Riley. Copy. Md. Geneal. Rec. Com., 1934-35, pp. 378-435. Mss. DAR.
Makemie Memorial Pres. churchyard, Snow Hill, Worcester Co. Hudson. Bd. ms. MHS; DAR. Also: Md. Geneal. Rec. Com., Mrs. Lines. Mss. DAR.
†Med. Annals Md. Cordell. 1903, p. 550. MHS.
St. Joseph's R. C. churchyard. Md. O. R. Soc. Bull., no. 3, p. 64.
St. Paul's Parish, Balto. V. 2. Mss. MHS.
Turner Geneal. Coll. Ms. MHS.
*Wicomico Co. families. Tilghman. Ms, p. 29. DAR.
See Humphreys-Riley.
See Pope-Riley.
†**Riley, Bennet** (1786-1853). M. H. Mag., v. 12, p. 236.
Riley, Elihu E. Founders of Anne Arundel and Howard Cos. Warfield. P. 325. MHS; DAR.
Riley, Elihu S. Death. Anne Arundel Advertiser, Annapolis, July, 1883. Newsp. clipp. DAR.
†Men of mark in Md. Johnson. V. 3. DAR; Enoch Pratt Lib.
***Riley, George Donald.** Geneal. Elihu S. Riley. Annapolis, July 27, 1917. DAR.
Rind. *See* Green.
Rinehard. Baust or Emanuel Reformed churchyard, Carroll Co. Md. Geneal. Rec. Com., 1935-36. Mss. DAR.
Rinehart. Englar family. Barnes. MHS; DAR.
Family hist. of John Hyder and Catherine Delaplaine. Beam. 1909, pamph. MHS.
Graves, Fairview Cemetery, Wash. Co. Hist. of West. Md. Scharf. V. 2, p. 1306.
Hagerstown tombstone inscriptions. Gruder. Natl. Geneal. Soc. Quart., 1919, v. 8, nos. 1, 2
†Hist. of West. Md. Scharf. V. 2, pp. 791, 860, 1256. MHS; DAR.
Md. tombstone rec. Md. Geneal. Rec. Com., 1937, Parran, p. 33. Mss. DAR.
Mt. Olivet Cemetery, Frederick. Md. Geneal. Rec. Com., 1934-35, p. 111. Mss. DAR.
†Notes on life of William Henry Rinehart, sculptor, with tentative list of his work. M. H. Mag., 1924, v. 19, no. 4, pp. 309-38; 1925, v. 20, pp. 380-83.
Roop geneal. Pamph. MHS.
Rinehart, E. Urner. Md. Soc., War of 1812, v. 2, no. 190. Ms. MHS.
Rinehart, T. Warden. Md. Soc., War. of 1812, v. 2, no. 189. Ms. MHS.
†**Rinehart, Wm. H.** (sculptor). Biog. cyc. of rep. men of Md. and D. C. P. 473. MHS; DAR.
†Biog. sketches of distinguished Marylanders. Boyle. MHS; DAR.
†Distinguished Amer. artist. Wm. S. Rusk. Balto., Oct., 1939, ltd. ed., 180 pp.
†Sculptor. Notes on life; with tentative list of his works. W. S. Rusk. M. H. Mag., 1924, v. 19, pp. 309-38.
†Soc. for Hist. of Germans in Md. 6th ann. rept., 1892.
Rinehart Family. Mountain Democrat, Garrett Co., Jan. 31, 1935. Newsp. clipp. MHS; DAR.
Ring. Fox-Ring-Prosser-Nelson families, Va. Bible rec. Ms. DAR.
Naturalizations in Md., 1666-1765; Laws. Bacon. MHS.
Ringgold. Bantz geneal. notes. Ms. MHS.
Barroll in Great Britain and Amer. Barroll. Pp. 54-57, 70-73. MHS.
Bible rec. Ms. MHS.
†Biog. Dict. Gardiner.
B. B. Browne pedigree chart. Soc. Col. Wars, Md. Johnston. 1905, pp. 8, 152. MHS.
Dobbin chart. MHS.
Elliott chart. MHS.
†Hist. of Balto. City and Co. Scharf. P. 395. MHS.
Hist. graves of Md. and D. C. Ridgely. MHS.
Md. families. Culver. Ms. Personal list.
†Memoir of Maj. Samuel Ringgold, of U. S. Army, 1800-46. James Wynne, M.D. (Read before the Md. Hist. Soc., Apr. 1, 1847.) Balto., John Murphy, 1847. MHS; Enoch Pratt Lib.
P. Neff pedigree chart. Soc. Col. Wars, Md. Johnston. 1905, p. 77. MHS.
Pedigree of Richard Constable Bernard. Soc. Col. Wars Md. Culver. 1940. MHS; DAR.
Pedigree of Coleman Randall Freeman. Soc. Col. Wars Md. Culver. 1940. MHS; DAR.
Pedigree of Henry Irvine Keyser, II. Soc. Col. Wars Md. Culver. 1940. MHS; DAR.
Pedigree of George Ross Veazey. Soc. Col. Wars Md. Culver. 1940. MHS; DAR.
Mrs. J. Hall Pleasants, Jr., chart. MHS.
St. Paul's churchyard, Kent Co. Md. O. R. Soc. Bull., no. 2, pp. 54-65. MHS.
St. Paul's P. E. churchyard, Kent Co. Md. O. R. Soc. Bull., no. 2, pp. 54-65.
St. Paul's Parish, Balto. V. 2, 3. Mss. MHS.
Mrs. H. DeCourcy Wright Thom chart. MHS.
Tree. Horwitz chart. MHS.
M. Van V. Tyson pedigree charts, plate 4. Soc. Col. Wars, Md. Johnston. 1905, p. 120. MHS.
Mrs. Emory Whitridge chart. MHS.
See Holliday-Ringgold.
†**Ringgold, Cadwalder** (1802-67). M. H. Mag., v. 12, p. 237.
Ringgold, James. Seven pioneers of col. East. Shore. Skirven. M. H. Mag., 1920, v. 15, no. 3, p. 230-50. No. 4, p. 394-419.

†**Ringgold, Major.** Hist. of Md. Scharf. V. 3, pp. 221–22. MHS.
Ringgold, Rebecca, consort of Edward Ringgold. (Died Sept. 30, 1857, in 81st yr.) Grave, Chestertown. Md. Geneal. Rec. Com., 1933–34, p. 232. Mss. DAR.
Ringgold, Rebecca, Ellendale, Eastern Neck, Kent Co., Md. Tombstone inscription; died 1750, aged 55 years. Md. Geneal. Rec. Com., 1937. DAR.
†**Ringgold, Sam'l** (1800–46). M. H. Mag., v. 12, p. 238.
***Ringgold Family.** Old Kent. Hanson. Pp. 60–69, 308. MHS; DAR.
Thomas Book. Thomas. Pp. 480–81. Lib. Cong.; MHS.
Ringgold Family, Wash. Co. Hist. of West. Md. Scharf. V. 2, p. 1023.
Ringgold-Elliott. Chart, photos. (2). MHS.
Ringgold-Wilmer. Ances. rec. and portraits. Col. Dames of Amer., 1910, v. 2, p. 474–75. MHS; DAR.
Rippin. St. Stephens Parish, Cecilton, Md. MHS; DAR.
Rippon. Mrs. E. W. Poe chart. MHS.
Rippon, Kent Co. Manning chart. MHS.
†**Risley.** Hist. of Washington Co. Williams. 1906, no. 2, p. 1150. MHS; DAR.
Risteau. Hist. graves of Md. and D. C. Ridgely. MHS.
†Hist. of Balto. City and Co. Scharf. Pp. 863, 921. MHS.
St. Paul's Parish, Balto. V. 1. Mss. MHS.
St. Thomas' Parish, Balto. Co. Bd. ms. MHS. Also: Md. Geneal. Rec. Com., 1937, pp. 109–82. Mss. DAR.
Risteau, Balto. Co. Pedigree of Francis Joseph Baldwin. Soc. Col. Wars Md. Culver. 1940. MHS; DAR.
Risteau, Capt. John. Garrison Church. Allen. P; 142. MHS; DAR.
Ristone. St. Paul's Parish, Balto. V. 1. Mss. MHS.
Ristrum. Plummer family. A. P. H. Ms. MHS.
Ritchey. Mt. Olivet Cemetery, Frederick. Md. Geneal. Rec. Com., 1934–35, p. 111. Mss. DAR.
Ritchie. Geneal. and memorial encyc. of Md. Spencer. V. 1. MHS; DAR.
†Hist. of West. Md. Scharf. V. 1, pp. 413–14. MHS; DAR.
†Med. Annals Md. Cordell. 1903, p. 550. MHS.
Portrait and biog. rec. of Sixth Cong. Dist. o Md. 1898, p. 175. MHS; DAR.
***Ritchie, Albert.** Geneal. and mem. encyc. of Md. Spencer. V. 1, p. 89–95. MHS; DAR.
In memoriam. M. H. S. Ann. rept., 1903, Balto., 1904, p. 281. MHS.
†Men of mark in Md. Johnson. V. 1. DAR; Enoch Pratt Lib.
Personal recollections of Gov. Albert C. Ritchie. Stuart S. Janney. MHS.
†Sketch. Md. Manual, 1933. (Born Aug. 9, 1876; son of Albert and Elizabeth Caskie (Cabell) Ritchie).
Ritchie, Mrs. Albert (Elizabeth Caskie Cabell). Chart. (Va. families.) Col. Dames, Chap. I. MHS.
Ritenhaur, Reidenauer, Ritenhauer. Howland chart. MHS.
Ritenour. *See* Reitenaur.
†**Ritter.** Hist. of Allegany Co. Thomas and Williams. V. 2. MHS; DAR.
†Hist. of West. Md. Scharf. V. 2, p. 872. MHS; DAR.
Rixon. Somerset Co. Court Book. Tilghman. 1937. Ms. DAR.
†**Rizer.** Hist. of Allegany Co. Thomas and Williams. V. 2. MHS; DAR.
†**Roach.** Med. Annals Md. Cordell. 1903, p. 550. MHS.
Old Somerset. Torrence. MHS; DAR.
*Wicomico Co. families. Tilghman. Ms, p. 106. DAR.
Roach, Del. Abr. Compend. Amer. Geneal. Virkus. V. 1, p. 800. DAR.
Roach-Greenwell-Thompson-Williams. Bible rec., 1765–1820. Md. Geneal. Rec. Com., 1929, v. 3, pp. 43–44. DAR.
Roach, Roch. Somerset Co. Court Book. Tilghman. 1937. Ms. DAR.
Roache. St. Paul's Parish, Balto. V. 2. Mss. MHS.
Roacre. All Hallow's P. E. churchyard, Snow Hill, Worcester Co. Hudson. Bd. ms. MHS; DAR. Also: Md. Geneal. Rec. Com., 1935–36, p. 24. Mss. DAR.
Roades. Md. gleanings in Eng. Wills. M. H. Mag., 1907, v. 2, no. 3.
Roades, Roads, Rodes. Maulsby family in Amer. Barnard. DAR; Peabody Lib.
Roads. *See* Rhodes.
***Roberdeau.** Geneal. of Roberdeau family. Coat of arms. J. Buchanan. Wash., D. C. Joseph L. Pearson, 1876. DAR.
Robert. Naturalizations in Md., 1666–1765; Laws. Bacon. MHS.
Roberts. Ancestry of Rosalie Morris Johnson. Johnson. 1905. MHS; DAR.
Christ P. E. Church cemetery, Cambridge. Steele. 1936. MHS; DAR.
Gantt geneal. Ms. MHS.
†Med. Annals Md. Cordell. 1903, p. 551. MHS.
Patriotic Md. Md. Soc. of S. A. R., 1930. MHS; DAR.
Rec. of Stepney Parish. MHS; DAR.
*Roberts family. Emerson Roberts.
St. Paul's Parish, Balto. V. 1, 2, 3, 4. Mss. MHS.
St. Stephens Parish, Cecilton, Md. MHS; DAR.
Somerset Co. Court Book. Tilghman. 1937. Ms. DAR.
*The Sun, Balto., May 31, 1903; April 10, 1908 (letter).
Uhler Bible rec. Md. Geneal. Rec. Com., v. 2. DAR.
*Wicomico Co. families. Tilghman. Ms, p. 128. DAR.
See Denny-Roberts.
See Haines-Roberts.
See Lynch-Roberts.
See Taylor-Roberts-Standiford-Patterson-Reardon-Baker-Reisinger-Scharf.
Roberts, Calvert Co. Col. families of U. S. A. Mackenzie. V. 1, pp. 434–42. MHS; DAR.
Roberts, James. Revolutionary pension abs. Natl. Geneal. Soc. Quart., v. 24, p. 102.
Roberts, Josiah and Lydia, N. J. (1849). Md. Geneal. Rec. Com., 1935–36, pp. 210–22. Mss. DAR.

Roberts, Thomas Carroll. Pedigree. Soc. Col. Wars Md. Culver. 1940. MHS; DAR.
Roberts Line, Calvert Co. Mrs. G. R. Veazey chart. MHS.
Robertson. Balto., its hist., its people. Hall. V. 3. MHS; DAR.
Christ P. E. Church cemetery, Cambridge. Steele. 1936. MHS; DAR.
J. T. Dennis pedigree chart, plate 1. Soc. Col. Wars, Md. Johnston. 1905, p. 21. MHS.
*Frederick Co. families. Markell. Ms. Personal list.
†Med. Annals Md. Cordell. 1903, pp. 551–52. MHS.
Pedigree of John McPherson Dennis. Soc. Col. Wars Md. Culver. 1940. MHS; DAR.
Rehobeth P. E. churchyard, Somerset Co. Md. Geneal. Rec. Com., 1937, Mrs. Lines. Mss. DAR.
Rec. of Stepney Parish. MHS; DAR.
St. Paul's Parish, Balto. V. 2, 3, 4. Mss. MHS.
Thomas-Chew-Lawrence. Thomas. MHS.
Tiernan families. Tiernan. 1901. MHS; DAR.
Turner Geneal. Coll. Ms. MHS.
*Wicomico Co. families. Tilghman. Ms, pp. 9, 129. DAR.
See Addams-Robertson-Wright.
See Barnes-Robertson.
Robertson, George Sadtler. Md. Soc., War of 1812, v. 3, no. 245. Ms. MHS.
***Robertson Family.** Old Kent. Hanson. P. 118. MHS; DAR.
Robertson Line. Col. and Revolutionary lineages of Amer. 1939, v. 1, p. 496. MHS.
Robertson Line, Va. C. B. Tiernan pedigree chart. Soc. Col. Wars, Md. Johnston. 1905, p. 113. MHS.
Robertson-Cooke. Amer. Clan Gregor Year Book, 1919, pp. 44–54. MHS; DAR.
Robertson-Osborn. Family Charts. Harford Co. Hist. Soc. Mss. Coll. JHU.
†**Robinette.** Hist. of Allegany Co. Thomas and Williams. V. 2. MHS; DAR.
Robinette, Pa. and Md. Col. and Revolutionary families of Pa. Jordan. 1932, v. 4, pp. 125–29.
Robins. All Hallow's P. E. churchyard, Snow Hill, Worcester Co. Hudson. Bd. ms. MHS; DAR. Also: Md. Geneal. Rec. Com., 1935–36, p. 24. Mss. DAR.
Col. families of Amer. Lawrence. V. 10, p. 56. MHS.
Early hist. of Hollyday family. Hollyday. MHS; DAR.
Geneal. notes of Chamberlame family. MHS.
Geneal. of Henrietta Chauncy Wilson. Upshur. Bk. of photos. MHS.
*Old Kent. Hanson. Pp. 245–46, 251. MHS; DAR.
Patriotic Md. Md. Soc. of S. A. R., 1930. MHS; DAR.
Pedigree of Lee Cummins Cary. Soc. Col. Wars Md. Culver. 1940. MHS; DAR.
Pedigree of Levin Gale Shreve. Soc. Col. Wars Md. Culver. 1940. MHS; DAR.
Pedigree of Harrison Tilghman. Soc. Col. Wars Md. Culver. 1940. MHS; DAR.
Robins family, Va. and Worcester Co., Md., and allied families. Typed, bd. MHS.
Robins family tree. MHS.
Purnell family tree. MHS.
St. Paul's P. E. churchyard, Berlin, Worcester Co. Hudson. Bd. ms. MHS; DAR. Also: Md. Geneal. Rec. Com., 1937, Mrs. Lines. Mss. DAR.
St. Paul's Parish, Balto. V. 2, 4. Mss. MHS.
Sketches of John Slemons Stevenson and Rev. Samuel McMaster. Stevenson. P. 16. MHS.
Tilghman chart. MHS.
Turner Geneal. Coll. Ms. MHS.
Mrs. Morris Whitridge chart. MHS.
Worcester Co. militia, 1794. Covington. P. 166. MHS.
***Robins,** Md. and Va. Burke's landed gentry. 1939. MHS.
Robins Family. Mss., 7 pp. MHS.
Robins Line. Col. and Revolutionary lineages in Amer. 1939, v. 2, p. 128. MHS.
Robins Line, Gaither, Va. and Md. Col. and Revolutionary families of Phila. Jordan. 1933, v. 1, pp. 144–67.
Robinson. Abr. Compend. Amer. Geneal. Virkus. V. 1, p. 802. DAR.
Ames Geneal. Coll. Ms. MHS.
Ances. rec. and portraits. Col. Dames of Amer., 1910, v. 2, p. 598. MHS; DAR.
Battee, Brewer, Boteler, etc., family rec. Murray. Photos. MHS.
†Bench and bar of Md. Sams and Riley. 1901, v. 2, p. 411. Lib. Cong.; MHS; Peabody Lib.
Col. families of U. S. A. Mackenzie. V. 2; v. 5. MHS; DAR.
*Descendants of Alexander Robinson and Angelica Peale. Wm. Carvel Hall. Wash., D. C., 1896, Autographed from typewritten copy. Lib. Cong.
Greenway chart. MHS.
Mrs. M. J. Henry chart. MHS.
Md. Geneal. Bull., v. 4, p. 15. MHS; DAR.
†Med. Annals Md. Cordell. 1903, p. 552. MHS.
Mrs. E. N. Morison chart. MHS.
Patriotic Md. Md. Soc. of S. A. R., 1930. MHS; DAR.
Rumsey-Smithson Bible rec. Md. Geneal. Rec. Com., 1932–33, v. 5, pp. 63–142. DAR.
St. Paul's Parish, Balto. V. 1, 2, 3, 4. Mss. MHS.
St. Stephens Parish, Cecilton, Md. MHS; DAR.
Somerset Co. Court Book. Tilghman. 1937. Ms. DAR.
Smithson-Rumsey rec. bk. Ms. MHS.
*The Sun, Balto., Aug. 26, 1906.
Tombstone rec. of Dorchester Co. Jones. DAR.
Helen Tudor (Haskell) Robinson (New Eng. rec.) Lineage Bk., Daughters of Founders and Patriots, v. 17, p. 141. MHS.
Turner Geneal. Coll. Ms. MHS.
Robinson, Anne Arundel Co. Chart, photos., complete in 1 sheet. Cary Geneal. Coll. Ms. MHS.
Robinson, Kent Co., Del., and Balto. W. M. Hayden pedigree chart, plate 1. Soc. Col. Wars, Md. Johnston. 1905, p. 34. MHS.
Robinson, Md. and Va. Col. and Revolutionary lineages of Amer. 1939, v. 1, pp. 235–40. MHS.
Robinson, York Co., Va. Chart, photos., complete in 1 sheet. Cary Geneal. Coll. Ms. MHS.
Robinson, Alexander. Johnstons of Salisbury. Johnston. Pp. 128–29. MHS; DAR.

Robinson, C. B., Jr. Abr. Compend. Amer. Geneal. Virkus. V. 1, p. 803. DAR.
Robinson, David Moore. Abr. Compend. Amer. Geneal. Virkus. V. 6, p. 479.
Robinson, George D. F., Jr. Pedigree. Soc. Col. Wars Md. Culver. 1940. MHS; DAR.
†**Robinson, Katharine,** (1663–1746); (daughter of Valentine Hollingsworth). Index to biog. sketches pub. in "The Friend," v. 26, v. 27. Pub. Geneal. Soc. Pa., v. 3, no. 2, pp. 109–34.
Robinson, Ralph. Pedigree. Soc. Col. Wars Md. Culver. 1940. MHS; DAR.
Robinson, Robert. Patent "Double Trouble," 1670, Balto. Co. Md. Geneal. Rec. Com., 1934–35, pp. 282–84. Mss. DAR.
Robinson, Mrs. W. Champlin (Bettie Campbell Clark). 2 charts. Col. Dames, Chap. I. MHS.
Robinson (old Del. family)-**Passwater-Smith-Wiatt.** Bible rec. of Dorchester and Somerset Cos. and Del. Pp. 70–72. DAR.
Robison. St. Paul's Parish, Balto. V. 1, 4. Mss. MHS.
Robosson, Allegheny Co. Amer. Clan Gregor Year Book, 1930, p. 13. MHS; DAR.
Robson. Md. families. Culver. Ms. Personal list.
†**Roby.** Med. Annals Md. Cordell. 1903, p. 553. MHS.
Roch. *See* Roach.
Roche. Jenkins-Courtney chart. MHS.
Naturalizations in Md., 1666–1765; Laws. Bacon. MHS.
Patriotic Md. Md. Soc. of S. A. R., 1930. MHS; DAR.
Rochester. Bible rec. Upper Penins East. Shore, pp. 88–93; 139–40. MHS; DAR.
†Hist. of West. Md. Scharf. V. 2, pp. 1017–18. MHS; DAR.
Rock (Rouch), Allegany Co. (1799). D. A. R. Mag., v. 70, no. 2, p. 135.
Rockhold. Mrs. Howard Bruce chart. MHS.
Rockholds of early Md. N. B. Nimmo. M. H. Mag., v. 32, no. 4, p. 371.
Rockland. Lineage Bks., Natl. Soc. of Daughters of Amer. Col., v. 1, p. 42, MHS; DAR.
Rodes. *See* Roades.
Rodgers. Bible rec. of family of Commander John Rodgers, U.S.N. Ms. MHS.
†Biog. of Commodore John Rodgers. C. O. Paullin. (Commodore John Rodgers, 1773–1838, Captain, Commodore and Senior Officer of Amer. Navy.) Cleveland, Ohio, Arthur H. Clark Co, 1910. DAR.
Chew family. Culver. M. H. Mag., 1935, v. 30, no. 2, pp. 157–75.
*Geneal. chart of Commodore John Rodgers. Original chart owned by J. Alexis Shriver, "Olney Farm," Joppa, Md. Photos. copy. DAR.
Md. families. Culver. Ms. Personal list.
Rodgers and allied families of Harford Co., 1580–1905. Md. Geneal. Rec. Com., 1929, v. 3 pp. 108–10. DAR.
†**Rodgers,** Frederick. Men of mark in Md. Johnson. V. 1. DAR; Enoch Pratt Lib.
†**Rodgers, George Washington** (1787–1832). M. H. Mag., v. 12, p. 238.
†**Rodgers, John** (1771–1838). M. H. Mag., v. 12, p. 239.
†**Rodgers, John Leonard.** Amer. Clan Gregor Year Book, 1919, pp. 34–36. MHS; DAR.
Rodgers, Col. John. Carton chart. MHS.
*Col. John Rodgers (1726–94; born in Scotland). Chart. DAR.
Rodgers, Col. John, Havre de Grace. Col. families of Amer. Lawrence. V. 9, pp. 97–111. MHS.
†**Rodgers, Com. John.** Biog. cyc. of rep. men of Md. and D. C. P. 702. MHS; DAR.
*Burke's landed gentry. 1939. MHS.
Family Bible. MHS.
Rodgers, Maurice Falconer. Pedigree. Soc. Col. Wars Md. Culver. 1940. MHS; DAR.
Rodman. Mrs. Frank G. Baldwin chart. MHS.
Sara Rodman Baldwin chart. MHS.
Hamill chart. MHS.
Prentice chart. MHS.
Roe. St. Paul's Parish, Balto. V. 1, 2. Mss. MHS.
Roeder. Shrewsbury churchyard. Md. O. R. Soc. Bull., no. 2, pp. 46–54.
Shrewsbury churchyard. Kent Co. Md. O. R Soc., v. 2, pp. 46–54. MHS.
Still Pond Church and cemetery. Md. O. R. Soc. Bull., no. 2, pp. 65–75.
Roelands. Naturalizations in Md., 1666–1765; Laws. Bacon. MHS.
Roger. Epitaphs of Roger family, Druid Hill Park, Balto., 1753–1895. Md. Geneal. Rec. Com., 1932–33, pp. 51–52. Mss. DAR.
Rogers. Ances. rec. and portraits. Col. Dames of Amer., 1910, v. 2, p. 674. MHS; DAR.
Balto., its hist., its people. Hall. V. 3, p. 382. MHS; DAR.
Mrs. R. Barton, Jr., charts. MHS.
Bible rec. Ms. MHS.
Miss M. S. Brogden chart. MHS.
Burial ground, Druid Hill Park, Balto. City, 1753–1896. Md. Geneal. Rec. Com., 1932–33. Mss. DAR.
Mrs. Charles Carter chart. MHS.
Cary Geneal. Coll. Ms. MHS.
W. W. Coleman pedigree chart. Soc. Col. Wars, Md. Johnston. 1905, p. 17. MHS.
Col. families of U. S. A. Mackenzie. V. 6, p. 367. MHS; DAR.
Joshua Dryden Bible rec. Ms. MHS.
*Founders of Anne Arundel and Howard Cos. Warfield. P. 527. MHS; DAR.
Hist. graves of Md. and D. C. Ridgely. MHS.
†Hist. of Balto. City and Co. Scharf. Pp. 723, 834. MHS.
Howell Bible rec. Ms. MHS.
Md. families. Culver. Ms. Personal list.
Mrs. James McHenry chart. MHS.
†Med. Annals Md. Cordell. 1903, pp. 553–54. MHS.
Pedigree of Franklin Buchanan Owen. Soc. Col. Wars Md. Culver. 1940. MHS; DAR.
Price ancestral data (paternal). Bd. ms. MHS.
Public parks of Balto. No. 3. MHS.
*Rogers Mss. Coll. (Mostly Balto. Co. families.) MHS.
St. Paul's Parish, Balto. V. 1, 2, 3. Mss. MHS.
Sweetser family of Md. and Mass. Gardner. Pamph., repr. from M. H. Mag., June, 1932, p. 144. MHS; DAR.
Torrence and allied families. Torrence. Pp. 449–74. MHS; DAR.
Turner Geneal. Coll. Ms. MHS.
Western Run Parish book. Allen. Bd. ms. MHS.

Rogers. W. S. G. Williams pedigree chart. Soc. Col. Wars, Md. Johnston. 1905, p. 128. MHS. *See* Stansbury-Rogers-Lynch.
Rogers, "Druid Hill." Pedigree of Francis Joseph Baldwin. Soc. Col. Wars Md. Culver. 1940. MHS; DAR.
Rogers, A. C. Abr. Compend. Amer. Geneal. Virkus. V. 1, p. 804. DAR.
Rogers, Mrs. Arthur Raleigh. Mrs. M. J. Henry chart. MHS.
Mrs. R. Barton, Jr., chart. MHS.
(Sidney Brown Morison.) Chart. Col. Dames, Chap. I. MHS.
†**Rogers, John.** Hist. of Md. Scharf. V. 2, pp. 206, 560. MHS.
Lineage Bks., Natl. Soc. of Daughters of Amer. Col., v. 2, p. 117. MHS; DAR.
Rogers, Com. John. Butler chart. Cary Geneal. Coll. Ms. MHS.
Rogers Line. Gaither, Va. and Md. Col. and Revolutionary families of Phila. Jordan. 1933, v. 1, pp. 144–67.
Rogers - Gassaway - Howard - Worthington. Abr. Compend. Amer. Geneal. Virkus. V. 4, p. 688. MHS.
Rogers-Elys-Priggs Families, Harford Co., Bible rec., 1748–1892. Md. Geneal. Rec., Com. 1929, v. 3, p. 69–71. DAR.
Rogerson, Pa. Cotton chart. MHS.
Roher. Hagerstown tombstone inscriptions. Gruder. Natl. Geneal. Soc. Quart., 1919, v. 8, nos. 1, 2.
Rohr. Frederick Co. tombstone inscriptions. Gruder. Natl. Geneal. Soc. Quart., 1919, v. 8, nos. 1, 2.
†**Rohrback.** Men of mark in Md. Johnson. V. 1. DAR; Enoch Pratt Lib.
†**Rohrer.** Hist. of Washington Co. Williams. 1906, v. 2, pp. 963, 1121. MHS; DAR.
Roland. Hagerstown tombstone inscriptions. Gruder. Natl. Geneal. Soc. Quart., 1919, v. 8, nos. 1, 2.
Rolfe. *See* Bolling.
***Rolfe-Bolling,** Va. The Sun, Balto., Nov. 5, 1905.
Rolle. Md. gleanings in Eng. Wills. M. H. Mag., 1909, v. 4, no. 2.
Roop geneal. Pamph. MHS.
Rolle Family, Talbot Co. Rec. Ms. MHS.
†**Rollins, Thornton.** Men of mark in Md. Johnson. V. 2. DAR; Enoch Pratt Lib.
Rollke. Frederick Co. tombstone inscriptions. Gruder. Natl. Geneal. Soc. Quart., 1919, v. 8. nos. 1, 2.
Rolph. Bible rec., Kent Co. Md. Geneal. Rec. Com., 1933–34, p. 233. Mss. DAR.
Roman. Monumental City. Howard. MHS; DAR.
Roop. Englar family. Barnes. MHS; DAR.
*Roop geneal.; descendants of Christian Roop, 1733–1810. Press of Times Printing Co., Westminster, Carroll Co. Pamph. MHS.
***Ropp.** Descendants of Christian Ropp, 1733–1810. Pr. at Westminster, Md. MHS; DAR.
Roscoe. *See* Rouse.
Rose. Bernard family, Va. P. 184. William and Mary Quart., 1st series, v. 5, pp. 62, 181.
Burton ancestry. Ms. MHS.
†Hist. of Frederick Co. Williams. Pp. 1335, 1471. MHS; DAR.
Ms. MHS.
Pedigree of Wm. Winchester Eareckson. Soc. Col. Wars Md. Culver. 1940. MHS; DAR.
Plummer family. A. P. H. Ms. MHS.
Portrait and biog. rec. of Harford and Cecil Cos. 1897, p. 154. MHS; DAR.
St. Stephens Parish, Cecilton, Md. MHS; DAR.
Wilcox-Rose Bible rec. Ms. MHS.
Rose, Cecil Co. Gillingham family. Gillingham. Pp. 85–88. MHS; DAR.
Rose, J. Carter. Abr. Compend. Amer. Geneal. Virkus. V. 1, p. 807. DAR.
Rose, John Carter. Pedigree chart. (Mostly New Eng. records.) Soc. Col. Wars, Md. Johnston. 1905, p. 89. MHS.
Roseberry. Still Pond churchyard, Kent Co. Md. O. R. Soc. Bull., v. 2. MHS.
***Roseberry Family.** Old Kent. Hanson. P. 199. MHS; DAR.
†**Rosenau.** Men of mark in Md. Johnson. V. 2. DAR; Enoch Pratt Lib.
Rosewell. *See* Roswell.
Ross. Bantz geneal. notes. Ms. MHS.
†Betsy Ross, Quaker rebel. E. S. Parry. 1930. DAR.
Christ P. E. Church cemetery, Cambridge. Steele. 1936. MHS; DAR.
Col. families of Amer. Lawrence. V. 3, p. 367; v. 6, p. 274; v. 9, p. 137. MHS.
DeFord chart. MHS.
*Founders of Anne Arundel and Howard Cos. Warfield. P. 154. MHS; DAR.
*Frederick Co. families. Markell. Ms. Personal list.
Griffith geneal. Griffith. MHS; DAR.
†Hist of Frederick Co. Williams. V. 2, pp. 185–86.
*Old Kent. Hanson. P. 55. MHS; DAR.
Parr chart. MHS.
Pedigree of Charles Worthington Hoff. Soc. Col. Wars Md. Culver. 1940. MHS; DAR.
Pedigree of George Ross Veazey. Soc. Col. Wars Md. Culver. 1940. MHS; DAR.
Raisin chart. MHS.
St. Paul's Parish, Balto. V. 1, 2, 3, 4. Mss. MHS.
Some old Eng. letters. M. H. Mag., 1914, v. 9, no. 2, pp. 107–56.
Southern Bapt. Church cemetery, Worcester Co. Md. Geneal. Rec. Com., 1937, Mrs. Lines. Mss. DAR.
Mrs. E. C. Venable chart. MHS.
Will of John Ross, Annapolis. M. H. Mag., 1916, v. 11, p. 378.
Sir John Zouch and his descendants. Va. Mag., v. 12, pp. 429–32.
See Cochran-Beard-Carr-Ross-Wassan.
See Davenport-Sabritt-Doss-Bowen.
See Loney-Boyce-Day-Garrett-Ross-Stansbury.
***Ross Family.** Rec. MHS.
Ross, John Annapolis. Will, 1766. M. H. Mag., 1916, v. 11, pp. 378–82.
Rosse. Turner Geneal. Coll. Ms. MHS.
†**Rosse,** Worcester Co. Med. Annals Md. Cordell. 1903, p. 555. MHS.
Roswell. Manly chart. MHS.
Roswell, Rosewell. Ances. rec. and portraits. Col. Dames of Amer., 1910, v. 2, p. 551. MHS; DAR.
Rothrock, Pa. and Md. Moravian Church of York, Pa., regester of 1780. Pub. Geneal. Soc. Pa., v. 4, p. 332.
Rouch. *See* Rock.

***Roudebush.** Frederick Co. families. Markell. Ms. Personal list.
Patriotic Md. Md. Soc. of S. A. R., 1930. MHS; DAR.
†Roulette. Men of mark in Md. Johnson. V. 3. DAR; Enoch Pratt Lib.
Round. Makemie Memorial Pres. churchyard, Snow Hill, Worcester Co. Hudson. Bd. ms. MHS; DAR. Also: Md. Geneal. Rec. Com., Mrs. Lines. Mss. DAR.
Pattison Bible. Md. Geneal. Bull., v. 4, p. 13. DAR.
Pattison Bible rec. Ms. MHS.
Turner Geneal. Coll. Ms. MHS.
White chart. Cary Geneal. Coll. Ms. MHS.
Mrs. G. H. Williams, Jr., chart. MHS.
Round, Somerset Co. (as early as 1686–1688). Chart, photos., complete in 1 sheet. Cary Geneal. Coll. Ms. MHS.
Rounds. De Ford chart. MHS.
Mrs. E. C. Venable chart. MHS.
Rosby. Ances. and portraits. Col. Dames of Amer., 1910, v. 1, p. 357. MHS; DAR.
†Bench and bar of Md. Sams and Riley. 1901, v. 1, p. 82. Lib. Cong.; MHS; Peabody Lib.
Chart, photos., complete in 1 sheet. Cary Geneal. Coll. Ms. MHS.
Daughter of Md.; Mother of Texas. Bell. MHS; DAR.
Md. gleanings in Eng. Wills. M. H. Mag., 1907, v. 2, no. 4.
Parr chart. MHS.
Pedigree of Charles Morris Howard. Soc. Col. Wars Md. Culver. 1940. MHS; DAR.
Pedigree of Franklin Buchanan Owen. Soc. Col. Wars Md. Culver. 1940. MHS; DAR.
Pedigree of Pleasants Pennington. Soc. Col. Wars Md. Culver. 1940. MHS; DAR.
Pedigree of Tilghman Goldsborough Pitts. Soc. Col. Wars Md. Culver. 1940. MHS; DAR.
Raisin chart. MHS.
Side lights on Md. hist. Richardson. V. 2, p. 214. MHS; DAR.
Susquehanna, St. Mary's Co. Tombstone inscriptions. Md. O. R. Soc. Bull., no. 3, pp. 59–60.
*The Sun, Balto., June 12, 1904.
Tombs, Susquehanna on Patuxent. Md. O. R. Soc. Bull., no. 3, p. 59. MHS.
Mrs. E. C. Venable chart. MHS.
Rousby, Calvert Co. McH. Howard pedigree chart. Soc. Col. Wars, Md. Johnston. 1905, pp. 42, 153. MHS.
Rousby, Christopher John. Some early col. Marylanders. M. H. Mag., 1920, v. 15, p. 292.
***Rouse.** Clasping hands with generations past. Rouse (or Roscoe)-Zimmerman-Tanner families. Emma Rouse Lloyd. Priv. pr., Cincinnati, Ohio, Wilson Hart Press, 1932. MHS; DAR.
†Rousset. Med. Annals Md. Cordell. 1903, p. 555. MHS.
†Routsahn, Routzen. (90 ref.), Hist. of Frederick Co. Williams. MHS; DAR.
†Rouzer. Hist. of West. Md. Scharf. V. 1, p. 630. MHS; DAR.
Zion Reformed Church, Hagerstown. Md. Geneal. Rec. Com., 1934–35. Mss. DAR.
***Rowan.** The Sun, Balto., Sept. 24, 1904.
Rowe. Portrait and biog. rec. of East. Shore of Md. 1898, p. 435. MHS; DAR.
Rowell. Somerset Co. Court Book. Tilghman. 1937. Ms. DAR.
Rowland. Balto., its hist., its people. Hall. V. 3. MHS; DAR.
Hagerstown tombstone inscriptions. Gruder. Natl. Geneal. Soc. Quart., 1919, v. 8, nos. 1, 2.
Md. tombstone rec. Md. Geneal. Rec. Com., 1937, Parran, p. 5. Mss. DAR.
†Med. Annals Md. Cordell. 1903, p. 556. MHS.
West. Nottingham Cemetery. M. H. Mag., 1923, v. 18, p. 55.
Rowland, Charles Ranson. Pedigree. Soc. Col. Wars Md. Culver. 1940. MHS; DAR.
†Rowland, Sam'l. Men of mark in Md. Johnson. V. 2. DAR; Enoch Pratt Lib.
Rowland, Sam'l Carson. Pedigree. Soc. Col. Wars Md. Culver. 1940. MHS; DAR.
Rowles. St. Paul's Parish, Balto. V. 1, 2. Mss. MHS.
White geneal. tree. MHS.
Rowlington. St. Paul's Parish, Balto. V. 2. Mss. MHS.
Rownd. Miss M. W. Davis chart. MHS.
Mrs. C. C. Hall chart. MHS.
Roxburgh. Hist. Salisbury, Wicomico Co. Fruitt. Pp. 41–42. DAR.
*Wicomico Co. families. Tilghman. Ms, p. 127. DAR.
***Roy.** Roy family, Va. and Ky. N. R. Roy. 1935. DAR.
St. Paul's Parish, Balto. V. 2. Mss. MHS.
Royce, Rev. Alfred Lee. Pedigree chart. Soc. Col. Wars, Md. Johnston. 1905, p. 90. MHS.
Royer. Laytonsville M. E. churchyard, Montgomery Co. Md. Geneal. Rec. Com., 1934–35, p. 69. Mss. DAR.
Roop geneal. Pamph. MHS.
Royle. St. Paul's Parish, Balto. V. 2. Mss. MHS.
Royston. Hist. graves of Md. and D. C. Ridgely. MHS.
Rozer. Cary Geneal. Coll. Mss., B. 78. MHS.
Laws of Md., 1787. Hanson. Chap. 19. MHS.
Md. families. Culver. Ms. Personal list.
Rozier. Mrs. Charles Carter chart. MHS.
Centreville Record, Feb. 4, 1893. Newsp. clipp. Scrap Book. MHS.
Columbia Hist. Mag., v. 21, p. 2. MHS.
Gittings chart. MHS.
***Ruark.** Wicomico Co. families. Tilghman. Ms, p. 128. DAR.
Rubincam-Revercomb Family, Pa. and Va. Revolutionary reg. Milton Rubicam. Ms. DAR.
†Ruby. Hist. of Balto. City and Co. Scharf. P. 900. MHS.
Rucker. Rucker family and their descendants. E. J. R. Whitley. 1927.
***Rucker Family.** Geneal.; with their ancestors, descendants and connections. Sudie Rucker Wood. Richmond, 1932.
Rudasili. Hagerstown tombstone inscriptions. Gruder. Natl. Geneal. Soc. Quart., 1919, v. 8, nos. 1, 2.
Rudd. Centenary of Catholicity in Ky. Webb. 1884. MHS.
Md. gleanings in Eng. Wills. M. H. Mag., 1907, v. 2, no. 4.

†**Rudolph, Zebulon,** Cecil Co. Poets and verse writers of Md.
***Rudolph Family.** Hist. of Cecil Co. Johnston. Pp. 513–20. MHS; DAR.
†**Rudy.** Hist. of Frederick Co. Williams. MHS; DAR.
Ruf. Ruf-Haight-Eddy-Sumner-Hatch and allied families. Ms. MHS.
Ruff. Catonsville pioneers of Luth. faith. Natl. Geneal. Soc. Quart., v. 9, no. 2, p. 29.
***Ruffin.** Ruffin and other geneal. R. D. Henry. Pr. chart, containing Bland, Bolling, Shippen, Skipwith, Willing, etc.
Ruffner. Jenkins-Courtney chart. MHS.
Ruke. Rec. of Stepney Parish. MHS; DAR.
Rule. Dobbin chart. MHS.
Geneal. of Augusta Maitland (Carter) Libby, of Denver, Col., 1704–1933. Ms. MHS.
Ruley. Autobiography of Summerfield Baldwin. MHS; DAR.
Baldwin-Woodward chart. Cary Geneal. Coll. Ms. MHS.
Cary Geneal. Coll. Ms. MHS.
Hamill chart. MHS.
Pedigree of Charles Gambrill Baldwin. Soc. Col. Wars Md. Culver. 1940. MHS; DAR.
Ruley, Rully. St. Stephens Parish, Cecilton, Md. MHS; DAR.
Rumbold. One thousand years of Hubbard hist. Day. P. 348. MHS.
Rumsey. Abr. Compend. Amer. Geneal. Virkus. V. 1, p. 541. DAR.
†Bench and bar of Md. Sams and Riley. 1901, v. 1, p. 230. Lib. Cong.; MHS; Peabody Lib.
Patriotic Md. Md. Soc. of S. A. R., 1930. MHS; DAR.
St. Stephens Parish, Cecilton, Md. MHS; DAR.
*Smithson-Rumsey rec. bk. Unpub. rec., Harford Co. Typed bd. ms., 76 pp. MHS.
*W. Va. Hist. Mag., v. 3, no. 3, pp. 187–88.
***Rumsey,** Cecil Co. The Sun, Balto., June 5, 1904.
Rumsey, Charles Leslie. Pedigree. Soc. Col. Wars Md. Culver. 1940. MHS; DAR.
Rumsey (James) Family. W. Va. Hist. Mag., July, 1903, v. 3, no. 3.
†Ingenious mechanic and international genius. M. P. Andrews. W. Va. Hist., 1st issue (R. Bird Cook, editor), 1939. Enoch Pratt Lib.
†Inventor of steamboat. G. M. Beltzhoover.
†Pioneer in steam navigation. Ella M. Turner. (James Rumsey, mechanical engineer; born "Bohemia Manor," Cecil Co., 1743; first to apply steam in navigation, 1786.) Scottsdale, Pa., Mennonite Pub. House, 1930. Enoch Pratt Lib.
Rumsey Family. Hist. of Cecil Co. Johnston. P. 508. MHS; DAR.
***Rumsey-Smithson Family.** Rec. bk. Unpub. rec., Harford Co. Copied by Iola M. E. Smithson, 1931. Md. Geneal. Rec. Com., 1932, pp. 63–158. DAR.
Harford Co. Bible rec. from 1682. Md. Geneal. Rec. Com., 1932–33, v. 5, pp. 63–142. DAR.
†**Runkle.** Med. Annals Md. Cordell. 1903, p. 556. MHS.
***Rupp.** Brief biog. memorial of Joh Jonas Rupp, Pa., and complete geneal. family register of his lineal descendants, 1756–1875. With appendix. J. D. Rupp. Phila., 1875.
Ruse. Balto., its hist., its people. Hall. V. 3. MHS; DAR.
Rush. *See* Guyton-Kirr-Rush-Holland-Conn.
***Rush,** Pa. Burke's Landed Gentry, Amer. Families. 1939. MHS.
Pedigree of Henry Hurd Dunton. Soc. Col. Wars Md. Culver. 1940. MHS; DAR.
Rusk. Patriotic Md. Md. Soc. of S. A. R., 1930. MHS; DAR.
Rusk, J. Krebs. Md. Soc., War of 1812, v. 2, No. 145. Ms. MHS.
Russel. *See* Russell.
Russell. Bible rec. contributed by Mrs. J. N. Wheatley, Chestertown. Md. Geneal. Rec. Com., 1939–40, pp. 118–20. Mss. DAR.
Englar family. Barnes. MHS; DAR.
Geneal. comprising some ancestors and all descendants of John and Hannah (Fincher) Russell. Isaac S. Russell. New Market, Md., 1887, 1889, pamph. MHS.
Matthews-Price chart. MHS.
Price family and other gunpowder Friends. Death notices; photos. of newsp. clipp. MHS.
Rec. of Stepney Parish. MHS; DAR.
Rogers Bible rec. Ms. MHS.
*Some geneal. of Russell family, giving some of ancestors and all of descendants of John and Hanna (Fincher) Russell. Isaac S. Russell. New Market, Md., 1st ed. 1887, 2nd ed. 1889. MHS.
Wathen Prayer Book rec. Ms. MHS.
Whiteley chart. MHS.
*Wicomico Co. families. Tilghman. Ms, pp. 97, 112. DAR.
†**Russell, John H.** M. H. Mag., v. 12, p. 240.
Russell and Sewall. Thomas Book. Thomas. P. 482. Lib. Cong.; MHS.
***Russell-Lux.** Bible rec. Photos. MHS.
Russell, Russel. St. Paul's Parish, Balto. V. 1, 2, 4. Mss. MHS.
Russum. Atkinson family (Somerset Co.) Bible rec. Ms. MHS.
†Med. Annals Md. Cordell. 1903, p. 557. MHS.
*Complete hist. Wilson Mss. Coll., no. 100. MHS.
***Rutan.** Garrett Co. pioneer families. Hoye. MHS; DAR.
Mountain Democrat, Garrett Co. Newsp. clipp. MHS; DAR.
Ruth. Bible rec., Kent Co. Md. Geneal. Rec. Com., 1933–34, p. 217. Mss. DAR.
Rutherford. Hist. sketch of P. F. Eichelberger. Eichelberger.
Geneal. notes of Thomas family. Thomas. MHS; DAR.
St. Paul's Parish, Balto. V. 2. Mss. MHS.
***Rutherford,** Va. The Sun, Balto., Sept. 11, 18, 1904.
Rutherford Family. Thomas Book. Thomas. Pp. 483–84. Lib. Cong.; MHS.
Rutland. Cary Geneal. Coll. Ms. MHS.
Founders of Anne Arundel and Howard Cos. Warfield. P. 129. MHS; DAR.
Md. families. Culver. Ms. Personal list.
Rutland Family. Thomas Book. Thomas. Pp. 485–86. Lib. Cong.; MHS.
†**Rutledge.** Hist. of Balto. City and Co. Scharf. P. 873. MHS.
Rutledge-Stump-Jennings. Geneal. charts, showing ancestors of Annie Hope and Minnie

Belle Cairnes, Belair. 10 pp. Md. Geneal. Rec. Com., 1938–39, p. 50. Mss. DAR.

Rutter. Dorsey and allied families. Ms. MHS.
Howland chart. MHS.
Md. families. Culver. Ms. Personal list.
†Med. Annals Md. Cordell. 1903, p. 557. MHS.
Pedigree of Thomas Dobbin Penniman. Soc. Col. Wars Md. Culver. 1940. MHS; DAR.
*Pennington Papers. Ms. MHS.
St. Paul's Parish, Balto. V. 1, 2. Mss. MHS.
See Owens-Claytor-Maynard-Rutter-Welsh.
See Pue-Rutter.

Ryan. White Geneal. Tree. MHS.

Ryan Family. Ms. MHS.

Ryder. Hist. Salisbury, Wicomico Co. Truitt. P. 13. DAR.

Rye. St. Stephens Parish, Cecilton, Md. MHS; DAR.

Ryland. Patriotic Md. Md. Soc. of S. A. R., 1930. MHS; DAR.
St. Paul's Parish, Balto. V. 1, 2. Mss. MHS.
St. Stephens Parish, Cecilton, Md. MHS; DAR.

***Ryland Family,** Cecil Co. Wilson. Mss. Coll., no. 47. MHS.

S

Sabritt. *See* Davenport-Sabritt-Ross-Bowen.

Sackett. Cary Geneal. Coll. Ms. MHS.

Sackett Family. Bible rec., 1762–1902. Md. Geneal. Rec. Com., 1933–34, pp. 132–33. Mss. DAR.

Sadler. Mrs. Alexander Gordon chart. MHS.
St. Paul's Parish, Balto. V. 2, 4. Mss. MHS.

Sadtler. Geneal. and memorial encyc. of Md. Spencer. V. 2. MHS; DAR.

Sadtler, C. C. Md. Soc., War of 1812, v. 1, no. 64. Ms. MHS.

Sadtler, C. E. Md. Soc., War of 1812, v. 2, no. 155. Ms. MHS.

Sadtler, C. H. Md. Soc., War of 1812, v. 1, no. 37. Ms. MHS.

Sadtler, G. W. Geneal. and mem. encyc. of Md. Spencer. V. 2, p. 718. MHS; DAR.

Sadtler, Howard Plitt. Md. Soc., War of 1812, v. 1, no. 29. Ms. MHS.

Sadtler, J. P. B. Md. Soc., War of 1812, v. 1, no. 75. Ms. MHS.

Sagle. Md. tombstone rec. Md. Geneal. Rec. Com., 1937, Parran, p. 5. Mss. DAR.

Sailor. Hagerstown tombstone inscriptions. Gruder. Natl. Geneal. Soc. Quart., 1919, v. 8, nos. 1, 2.
See Saylor.

St. Clair-Edwards, Mercersburg, Pa., and Md. Data. D. A. R. Mag., v. 70, no. 1, p. 55.

St. Clair, Sinclair. Turner family. Forman. Pp. 47, 77. MHS.

Salmon. Coll. of Amer. epitaphs and inscriptions. Alden. 1814, v. 5. MHS.
Frederick Co. tombstone inscriptions. Gruder. Natl. Geneal. Soc. Quart., 1919, v. 8, nos. 1, 2.
Getzendanner family of Frederick Co. 1890, pamph. MHS; DAR.
Marriage rec. of Frederick Co. Markell. Md. Geneal. Rec. Com., 1938–39. Mss. DAR.

Salmon, Thomas, Cecil Co. Copy of will, 1675. Md. Geneal. Rec. Com., 1932–33, p. 165. Mss. DAR.
Will dated June 24, 1675; first official document recorded at Elkton. Spirit of Md. Lantz. P. 74.

Sample, Wm. M. Md. Soc., War of 1812, v. 4, no. 321. Ms. MHS.

Sampson. Geneal. of family of Gideon Gilpin. MHS.
St. Paul's Parish, Balto. V. 1. Mss. MHS.
Williamson Bible rec. Ms. MHS.
See Foster-Ford-Sampson.

Sampson, Richard (married Jane M. Heath), Somerset and Worcester Cos. and Ohio. Bible rec. of Dorchester and Somerset Cos. and Del. Pp. 73–76. DAR.

***Sampson Family.** Charts. Lilla B. Sampson. Md. Sampsons, pp. 197–201. Balto., Williams & Wilkins Co., 1914. MHS.

Sams. Balto., its hist., its people. Hall. V. 3, p. 573. MHS; DAR.

Samuel. *See* Samuell.

Samuell, Samuel. Somerset Co. Court Book. Tilghman. 1937. Ms. DAR.

Samuels. Rec. of Stepney Parish. MHS; DAR.

Sanborn. See Anson-Sanborn chart. DAR.

Sanderlaine. Ames Geneal. Coll. Ms. MHS.

Sanders. Semmes and allied families. Semmes. P. 200. MHS.
*Semmes Geneal. Coll. Ms. MHS.
See Saunders.

Sanderson. Balch chart. MHS.
Md. families. Culver. Ms. Personal list.
Med. Annals Md. Cordell. 1903, p. 557. MHS.

Sandford. Md. gleanings in Eng. Wills. M. H. Mag., 1910, v. 5.

Sands. Abr. Compend. Amer. Geneal. Virkus. V. 1, p. 816. DAR.
†Med. Annals Md. Cordell. 1903, p. 558. MHS.

Sanford. Mrs. Sam'l. K. Abr. Compend. Amer. Geneal. Virkus. V. 1, p. 816. DAR.
(Harriet Williams.) Chart. Col. Dames, Chap. I. MHS.

Sanford-Iglehart. Abr. Compend. Amer. Geneal. Virkus. V. 4, p. 455. MHS.

Sanford-Williams. Encyc. of Amer. biog. Amer. Hist. Soc., N. Y., 1928, v. 33, p. 212.

Sank. St. Paul's Parish, Balto. V. 2. Mss. MHS.

Sapenton. *See* Sapington.

Sapington, Sapenton, Sapinton. St. Stephens Parish, Cecilton, Md. MHS; DAR.

Sapinton. *See* Sapington.

***Sapp.** Hist. of Sapp family. J. G. Sapp and H. W. Stanley. Sapps, West. Md., pp. 11–14. 1910. MHS.
St. Paul's Parish, Balto. V. 2. Mss. MHS.

Sappington. Bible rec., 1855–1924. D. C. Geneal. Rec. Com., 1936–37, v. 31, pt. 2, p. 466. DAR.
Col. Nicholas Duvall family rec. Price. Bd. ms. MHS.
Correction of Sappington records, and will of Nathaniel Sappington, Cecil Co. Md. Geneal. Rec. Com. Mss. DAR.
D. A. R. Mag., Sept., 1926, v. 60, no. 9, p. 568.
*Founders of Anne Arundel and Howard Cos. Warfield. Pp. 129, 378. MHS; DAR.
Great West. Edward. St. Louis, 1860, p. 85.
†Hist. of Frederick Co. Williams. MHS; DAR.
*Lineage Bk., Daughters of Amer. Col., v. 2, p. 35; v. 4, p. 139; v. 5, p. 426. MHS, DAR.
Md. families. Culver. Ms. Personal list.
†Med. Annals Md. Cordell. 1903, pp. 558–59. MHS.

Sappington. Notes. D. A. R. Mag., v. 60, no. 9, p. 568.
Pedigree of Charles Gambrill Baldwin. Soc. Col. Wars Md. Culver. 1940. MHS; DAR.
St. Paul's P. E. churchyard, Kent Co. Md. O. R. Soc. Bull., no. 2, pp. 54–65.
Sappington, John, Sr., Anne Arundel Co. Will probated Sept. 17, 1816. D. A. R. Mag., Sept. 1928, v. 62, no. 9, p. 583.
Sappington-Willson. Bible rec. Md. Geneal. Rec. Com., 1937–38, pp. 123–24. Mss. DAR.
Sargeant. H. D. G. Carroll Ms. Book. In H. F. Thompson Papers. MHS.
Col. families of East. Shore and their descendants. Emory. 1900, p. 19. MHS.
Col. families of U. S. A. Mackenzie. V. 3. MHS; DAR.
St. Paul's Parish, Balto. V. 1. Mss. MHS.
Sargeant Family. Rec. Ms. MHS.
Sargent. Abr. Compend. Amer. Geneal. Virkus. V. 6, p. 42. DAR.
*Bartow geneal. Bartow. Pp. 137–40. Lib. Cong.; MHS.
See Van Ness.
Sargent-Phillips Family. Notes. Natl. Geneal. Soc. Quart., v. 23, no. 1, p. 20.
Sarson. Early Quaker rec., Anne Arundel and Calvert Cos., 1665–1889. Pub. Geneal. Soc. Pa., v. 3, no. 3, pp. 197–200.
Satchell Family. Rec. H. M. H. Smith. Ms. MHS.
Satchell Family, Dorchester Co. William and Mary Quart., 2nd series, v. 12, p. 143.
Satchell-Wilson. Satchell-Wilson families. E. S. Lane. Ms. MHS.
Sater. Col. families of Amer. Lawrence. V. 15, pp. 180–83. MHS.
Geneal. Henry Sater (1690–1754) and Sater's Bapt. Meeting House, Balto. Co., with list of pastors, 1742–1897. Contains also family geneal. Typed. Bd. MHS.
Hist. graves of Md. and D. C. Ridgely. MHS.
Lane-Smith families, Calvert Co. (Contains notes on Henry Sater, and membership of Sater's Bapt. Church, Balto. Co., 1742. Photos. MHS.
*(1690–1754). Lineage Bk., Daughters of Amer. Col., v. 4, p. 274. MHS; DAR.
*The Sun, Balto., Jan. 14, 21, May 20, 1906.
Sater, Henry. Some notable families of south. States. Armstrong. V. 1, pp. 105–08. DAR.
Satterfield. Spring Hill cemetery, Easton. Md. O. R. Soc. Bull., no. 1, pp. 35–41.
Satterthwaite. McClellan chart. MHS.
Saulsbury. Pedigree of Maurice Edward Skinner. Soc. Col. Wars Md. Culver. 1940. MHS; DAR.
Saunders. Ames Geneal. Coll. Ms. MHS.
Cary Geneal. Ms. MHS.
Jenkins-Courtney chart. MHS.
McCormick chart. MHS.
Naturalizations in Md., 1666–1765; Laws. Bacon. MHS.
Pedigree of John McPherson Dennis. Soc. Col. Wars Md. Culver. 1940. MHS; DAR.
Pedigree of Eustis Thompson. Soc. Col. Wars Md. Culver. 1940. MHS; DAR.
Trinity Church cemetery, Dorchester Co. Md. O. R. Soc. Bull., no. 3, pp. 42–52.
Trinity Church burial ground, near Cambridge, Md. Md. Geneal. Rec. Com., 1937–38, pp. 93–104. Mss. DAR.
Saunders, Anne Arundel Co. J. G. and M. G. Wilson pedigree chart. Soc. Col. Wars, Md. Johnston. 1905, pp. 129, 153. MHS.
†**Saunders, John Selden** (1836–1904). M. H. Mag., v. 12, p. 240.
Saunders, Sanders. St. Paul's Parish, Balto. V. 1, 2, 4. Mss. MHS.
Saurman. Hist. of Byberry and Moreland. Martindale. MHS.
Savage. Cosden family data. Ms. MHS.
*Garrett Co. pioneer families. Hoye. Newsp. clipp. MHS; DAR.
Geneal. of Henrietta Chauncy Wilson. Upshur. Bk. of photos. MHS.
Geneal. of Va. family of Lomax. Lib. Cong.
St. Joseph's R. C. churchyard. Md. O. R. Soc. Bull., no. 3, p. 64.
St. Paul's Parish, Balto. V. 1. Mss. MHS.
Whiteley chart. MHS.
Mrs. Morris Whitridge chart. MHS.
Savage, Va. Miss G. Eyre Wright chart. MHS.
*The Sun, Balto., Dec. 18, 1904.
Savage Family. Mountain Democrat, Garrett Co., Dec. 20, 1934. Newsp. clipp. MHS; DAR.
Savin. St. Stephens Parish, Cecilton, Md. MHS; DAR.
Savory, Wm. Patent. "Gist's Addition," 1747. Md. Geneal. Rec. Com., 1934–35, p. 288. Mss. DAR.
Sawser. Somerset Co. Court Book. Tilghman. 1937. Ms. DAR.
Saxon. Serton or Saxon family, Monmouth, N. J. Md. Geneal. Rec. Com., v. 2, pp. 17–22. DAR.
Saxton. Robins family tree. MHS.
***Sayler Family.** Hist. and coll. of geneal. notes, relative to Daniel Sayler, Frederick Co., who came to Amer. about 1725–30, and his descendants. J. L. Sayler. Albany, N. Y., Joel Munsell's Sons, 1898.
Saylor, Sailor. Zion Reformed Church, Hagerstown. Md. Geneal. Rec. Com., 1934–35. Mss. DAR.
Sayre. Col. families of U. S. A. Mackenzie. V. 1. MHS; DAR.
Scamper. Naturalizations in Md., 1666–1765; Laws. Bacon. MHS.
†**Scanlon.** Med. Annals Md. Cordell. 1903, p. 560. MHS.
Scarborough. All Hallow's P. E. churchyard, Snow Hill, Worcester Co. Hudson. Bd. ms. MHS; DAR. Also: Md. Geneal. Rec. Com., 1935–36, p. 24. Mss. DAR.
Mrs. Henry Du Pont Baldwin chart. MHS.
Rec. (complete). Pa. Hist. Soc.
Mrs. Wm. L. Watson chart. MHS.
Scarborough, Pa., Md. and Eng. Old Md. families. Bromwell. MHS; DAR.
***Scarborough,** Va. The Sun, Balto., March 26, June 11, 1905.
Scarborough, Edmund, Va. Pedigree of Gustave Wm. Lurman. Soc. Col. Wars Md. Culver. 1940. MHS; DAR.
Scarburgh, Va. Rec. Harrison-Waples and allied families. Harrison. P. 126. MHS.
Scarf, Scharfe. Patriotic Md. Md. Soc. of S. A. R., 1930. MHS; DAR.
Scarfe. *See* Scarf.

†**Scarff.** Hist. of Balto. City and Co. Scharf. P. 755. MHS.
Rumsey-Smithson family rec. bk. Md. Geneal. Rec. Com., 1932, p. 97. DAR.
Smithson-Rumsey rec. bk. Ms. MHS.
Scarff, Harford Co. Biog. cyc. of rep. men of Md. and D. C. P. 219. MHS; DAR.
Scarlett. Balto., its hist., its people. Hall. V. 3. MHS; DAR.
Scarsbrook, Scarsbrooke-Harwood-Cary. Chart, photos., complete in 1 sheet. Cary Geneal. Coll. Ms. MHS.
Schach. Hagerstown tombstone inscriptions. Gruder. Natl. Geneal. Soc. Quart., 1919, v. 8, nos. 1, 2.
Schaefer. Trinity P. E. churchyard, Long Green. Typed ms. MHS; DAR.
Schaeffer. Frederick Co. tombstone inscriptions. Gruder. Natl. Geneal. Soc. Quart., 1919, v. 8, nos. 1, 2.
†**Schaeffer, Charles William.** In memorian. H. E. Jacobs. Phila., Luth. Church Rev., 1896, v. 20, p. 369.
†**Schaffer, Schespschel, Rev. Dr.** Twenty-five years activity in cause of orthodox Judaism, 1893–1918. Balto., Shearith Israel Congregation. Enoch Pratt Lib.
Schaffer Family. Chart. ("A Rebel of 61.") J. R. Stonebraker. MHS.
Schaible. Catonsville pioneers of Luth. faith. Natl. Geneal. Soc. Quart., v. 9, no. 2, p. 29.
Schank, Pa. and Md. Moravian Church of York, Pa., register of 1780. Pub. Geneal. Soc. Pa., v. 4, p. 345.
†**Scharf.** Biog. cyc. of rep. men of Md. and D. C. P. 123. MHS; DAR.
See Taylor-Roberts-Standiford-Patterson-Reardon-Baker-Reisinger-Scharf.
Schaub. Catonsville pioneers of Luth. faith. Natl. Geneal. Soc. Quart., v. 9, no. 2, p. 29.
Schee. Naturalizations in Md., 1666–1765; Laws. Bacon. MHS.
Scheib, S. H. Md. Soc., War of 1812, v. 2, no. 181. Ms. MHS.
***Schenck. Rev. William Schenck;** his ancestry and his descendants. A. D. Schenck. Wash., D. C., Rufus H. Darby, 1883. MHS; DAR.
***Schenking.** Pennington Papers. Ms. MHS.
Schiaffino. Balto., its hist., its people. V. 2. MHS; DAR.
Schieffelin. Geneal. notes of Thomas family. Thomas. MHS; DAR.
Schieffelin Family. Thomas Book. Thomas. Pp. 487–95. Lib. Cong.; MHS.
Schiels. St. Stephens Parish, Cecilton, Md. MHS; DAR.
Schindel. Hagerstown tombstone inscriptions. Gruder. Natl. Geneal. Soc. Quart., 1919, v. 8, nos. 1, 2.
†**Schindel, Schindell.** Hist. of Washington Co. Williams. 1906, v. 2, p. 1140. MHS; DAR.
Schindell. Lineage Bk., Order of Washington, p. 204. MHS; DAR.
See Schindel.
Schissler. Frederick Co. tombstone inscriptions. Gruder. Natl. Geneal. Soc. Quart., 1919, v. 8, nos. 1, 2.
Schlatter. Life of Rev. Michael Schlatter, with full account of his travels and labors among Germans in Pa., N. J., Md., and Va.; incl. his services as chaplain in French and Indian and Revolutionary wars (1716–1790). H. Harbaugh. Lindsay and Blackiston, 1857, xxxi, 27–375. Rev. of above by E. V. Gerhart. Mercersburg Quart. Rev., Chambersberg, Pa., 1857, v. 9, pp. 460–85.
Schlegel. *See* Slagle.
Schlegle. *See* Slagle.
Schleigh. Zion Reformed Church, Hagerstown, Md. Geneal. Rec. Com., 1934–35. Mss. DAR.
†**Schley.** Bench and bar of Md. Sams and Riley. 1901, v. 2, pp. 634, 636. Lib. Cong.; MHS; Peabody Lib.
Col. families of U. S. A. Mackenzie. V. 2. MHS; DAR.
Frederick Co. tombstone inscriptions. Gruder. Natl. Geneal. Soc. Quart., 1919, v. 8, nos. 1, 2.
Geneal. and memorial encyc. of Md. Spencer. V. 2, p. 356. MHS; DAR.
†(108 ref.) Hist. of Frederick Co. Williams.
†Hist. of West. Md. Scharf. V. 1, pp. 408, 448–49; v. 2, pp. 1127–29. MHS; DAR.
Hist. of Shriver family. Shriver. Pp. 123–27, 128–31. MHS.
†Med. Annals Md. Cordell. 1903, p. 560. MHS.
*Old Kent. Hanson. P. 164. MHS; DAR.
Patriotic Md. Md. Soc. of S. A. R., 1930. MHS; DAR.
Pedigree of John Ogle Warfield, Jr. Soc. Col. Wars Md. Culver. 1940. MHS; DAR.
Portrait and biog. rec. of Sixth Cong. Dist. of Md. 1898, p. 155. MHS; DAR.
Rogers Coll. Ms. MHS.
See Shoemaker, M. M. Abr. Compend. Amer. Geneal. Virkus. V. 1, p. 827. DAR.
Steiner geneal. Steiner. 1896. MHS.
Schley, Frederick Co. Abr. Compend. Amer. Geneal. Virkus. V. 1, p. 245; v. 6, p. 688. DAR.
†**Schley, Wm.** Balto., hist. and biog. Richardson and Bennett. 1871, pp. 445–48. MHS; DAR.
†**Schley, Winfield Scott.** Geneal. and mem. encyc. of Md. Spencer. V. 2, p. 356–58. MHS; DAR.
†(1839–1911). M. H. Mag., v. 12, p. 241.
†Men of mark in Md. Johnson. V. 1. DAR; Enoch Pratt Lib.
Schley Family. Geneal. notes. Signed by G. Ernest Bantz. Ms. MHS.
Schmahl. *See* Small.
Schmid, John, Frederick Co. Naturalization, 1761. D. C. Geneal. Rec. Com., v. 34, pp. 34–35. Typed, bd. DAR.
Schmidt. *See* Smith.
***Schmidt Family.** Arch. of Georgetown Univ., Wash., D. C., v. 274, no. 2.
Schminke, F. W. Md. Soc., War of 1812, v. 1, no. 7. Ms. MHS.
†**Schmuck, Jacob.** M. H. Mag., v. 12, p. 243.
Schmucker. Balto., its hist., its people. Hall. V. 3. MHS; DAR.
Schmucker, Dr. S. S. (born in Hagerstown, 1799). Quart. Rev. of Evangelical Luth. Church, Gettysburg, new series, 1874, v. 4, pp. 1–15.
Schnebley. Zion Reformed Church, Hagerstown. Md. Geneal. Rec. Com., 1934–35. Mss. DAR.
†**Schnebly.** Hist. of West. Md. Scharf. V. 2, p. 1036. MHS; DAR.

Schnebly. Hagerstown tombstone inscriptions. Gruder. Natl. Geneal. Soc. Quart., 1919, v. 8, nos. 1, 2.
Schneck. Dorsey chart. MHS.
Schnelby. Md. Families. Culver. Ms. Personal list.
†**Schnively.** Med. Annals Md. Cordell. 1903, p. 560. MHS.
Schockley. Mt. Olive M. P. churchyard, Worcester Co. Md. Geneal. Rec. Com., 1937, Mrs. Lines. Mss. DAR.
Rec. of Stepney Parish. MHS; DAR.
Somerset Co. Court Book. Tilghman. 1937. Ms. DAR.
Schoenfeld. Abr. Compend. Amer. Geneal. Virkus. V. 4, p. 623. MHS.
***Scholl.** Boyd family. Boyd. DAR.
***Scholl, Sholl, Shull.** Scholl, Sholl, Shull family. J. W. Scholl. Scholls, Frederick Co., 1751, p. 782. N. Y., Grafton Press, 1930. MHS; DAR.
Scholtz, Shultz Family. Schwenkfelder families. Brecht. Pp. 88–130. MHS.
***Schoofield.** The Sun, Balto., July 8, 1906.
Schoolfield Family, Somerset Co. Bible rec. of Dorchester and Somerset Cos. and Del. Pp. 77–78. DAR.
***Schott.** Frederick Schott of Derry Township, Lancaster, Pa., and his descendants. Kate Singer Curry. Wash., D. C., 1933.
Schott Family. K. S. Curry. Ms. MHS.
Schrack. Pa. Mag., v. 35, pp. 120–21.
Schreiber. *See* Shriver.
Schreiner. Baust or Emanuel Reformed churchyard, Carroll Co. Md. Geneal. Rec. Com., 1935–36. Mss. DAR.
See Shriner.
Schreyack. *See* Shryock.
†**Schriver, Ja.** In memoriam. Soc. for Hist. of Germans in Md. 6th ann. rept., 1892.
Schroeder. Coll. of Amer. epitaphs and inscriptions. Alden. 1814, v. 5. MHS.
†Men of mark in Md. Johnson. V. 2. DAR; Enoch Pratt Lib.
St. Paul's Parish, Balto. V. 2. Mss. MHS.
***Schryock.** Frederick Co. families. Markell. Ms. Personal list.
Schultz. Frederick Co. tombstone inscriptions. Gruder. Natl. Geneal. Soc. Quart., 1919, v. 8, nos. 1, 2.
†**Schultz, Edw. T.** Men of mark in Md. Johnson. V. 1. DAR; Enoch Pratt Lib.
†**Schumacher.** Balto., hist. and biog. Richardson and Bennett. 1871, pp. 449–52. MHS; DAR.
†**Schumucker.** Bench and bar of Md. Sams and Riley. 1901, v. 2, p. 554. Lib. Cong.; MHS; Peabody Lib.
Schwartz. Hagerstown tombstone inscriptions. Gruder. Natl. Geneal. Soc. Quart., 1919, v. 8, nos. 1, 2.
†**Schwartze.** Med. Annals Md. Cordell. 1903, p. 561. MHS.
†**Schwatka.** Med. Annals Md. Cordell. 1903, p. 561. MHS.
†**Schwatka, J. Bushrod.** Men of mark in Md. Johnson. V. 3. DAR; Enoch Pratt Lib.
Schwedtner. *See* Swadner.
***Schwenkfelder.** Geneal. rec. of Schwenkfelder families. S. K. Brecht. N. Y., Rand, McNally Co., 1923. MHS.
Scindall. St. Paul's Parish, Balto. V. 1, 2. Mss. MHS.
Scoffield. St. Paul's Parish, Balto. V. 2. Mss. MHS.
Scofield. Mrs. Renshaw chart. MHS.
***Scothoron.** Boone-Anderson-Scothoron. Homer Eiler. Topeka, Kans., 1929. MHS.
See Eiler-Boone-Anderson-Scothoron.
***Scott.** Account book of Solomon Scott, 1800. Death notices posted. Ms. MHS.
Bantz geneal. notes. Ms. MHS.
Mrs. J. G. Brogden chart. MHS.
Burton ancestry. Ms. MHS.
Cemetery Creek, Anne Arundel Co., tombstone inscriptions. Founders of Anne Arundel and Howard Cos. Warfield. P. 334. MHS; DAR.
Cummings chart. Lib. Cong.; MHS; DAR.
Dorsey and allied families. Ms. MHS.
Dorsey chart. MHS.
Eng. ancestry of Anne Marbury Hutchinson and Katherine Marbury Scott. Colket. DAR.
*Frederick Co. families. Markell. Ms. Personal list.
Hist. of Harford Co. Preston. MHS; DAR.
Land grants (2); patent (1); Balt. Co., 1754, 1770, 1792. Photos. Md. Geneal. Rec. Com., 1932–33. Mss. DAR.
Lineage Bks., Natl. Soc. of Daughters of Amer. Col., v. 4, p. 270. MHS; DAR.
Macsherry chart. MHS.
Md. families. Culver. Ms. Personal list.
Md. gleanings in Eng. Wills. M. H. Mag., 1909, v. 4, no. 2; 1910, v. 5.
Matthews-Price chart. MHS.
Mrs. James McHenry chart. MHS.
†Med. Annals Md. Cordell. 1903, pp. 62, 561–63, 738–46. MHS.
Pedigree of T. Edward Hambleton. Soc. Col. Wars Md. Culver. 1940. MHS; DAR.
Pedigree of John Edward Hurst. Soc. Col. Wars Md. Culver. 1940. MHS; DAR.
Pedigree of Pleasants Pennington. Soc. Col. Wars Md. Culver. 1940. MHS; DAR.
Mrs. Pennington chart. MHS.
Posey chart. MHS.
Rec. of Stepney Parish. MHS; DAR.
St. Paul's Parish, Balto. V. 2, 4. Mss. MHS.
St. Stephens Parish, Cecilton, Md. MHS; DAR.
Somerset Co. Court Book. Tilghman. 1937. Ms. DAR.
See Morson-Scott-Payne.
Scott, Balto. Co. E. A. and F. De Sales Jenkins pedigree chart. Soc. Col. Wars, Md. Johnston. 1905, pp. 46, 153. MHS.
Mrs. Sherlock Swann chart. MHS.
Scott, Daniel. Pedigree of Charles Chauncy Hall. Soc. Col. Wars Md. Culver. 1940. MHS; DAR.
Pedigree of Benj. Wheeler Jenkins. Soc. Col. Wars Md. Culver. 1940. MHS; DAR.
Pedigree of Charles O'Donovan. Soc. Col. Wars Md. Culver. 1940. MHS; DAR.
Pedigree of Maurice Falconer Rodgers. Soc. Col. Wars Md. Culver. 1940. MHS; DAR.
Pedigree of Alfred Jenkins Tormey. Soc. Col. Wars Md. Culver. 1940. MHS; DAR.
Scott, Gustavus, Washington Co. Will. D. C. Geneal. Rec. Com., 1932–34, v. 10, pp. 189–93. Typed, bd. DAR.
Scott, Margaret of George. Will, 1799. D. A. R. Mag., v. 61, no. 8, p. 607.

†**Scott, Norman Bruce, Jr.** Men of mark in Md. Johnson. V. 4. DAR; Enoch Pratt Lib.

Scott, Townsend, IV. Pedigree. Soc. Col. Wars Md. Culver. 1940. MHS; DAR.

Scott-Kimberly. Abr. Compend. Amer. Geneal. Virkus. V. 4, p. 624. MHS.

Scrivener. Md. gleanings in Eng. Wills. M. H. Mag., 1907, v. 2, no. 2.

***Scroggin.** Wicomico Co. families. Tilghman. Ms, p. 96. DAR.
See Scrogin.

Scrogin. Tyler-Polk. William and Mary Quart., 1st series, v. 21, p. 21.

Scrogin, Scroggin. Col. families of U. S. A. Mackenzie. V. 7, p. 477. MHS; DAR.

***Scruggs.** Geneal. Ethel H. Scruggs Dunklin. N. Y., Laplante & Dunklin, 1912.
Scruggs geneal. E. H. Scruggs Dunklin. M. H. Mag., 1914, v. 9, p. 88.
*Geneal.; with brief hist. of allied families, Biscoe, Dial, Dunkin, Leake and Price. N. Y., 1912. MHS.

Scull. Balto., its hist., its people. Hall. V. 3. MHS; DAR.

Scull, Skull. Focke Geneal. Coll. Ms. MHS.

Scurrey. St. Stephens Parish, Cecilton, Md. MHS; DAR.

Seabrease. Geneal. reg. Mervine. P. 139. MHS.

Seabrook. Harvey chart. MHS.

Seabrooke. Mrs. T. R. Brown chart. MHS.

Seaman. Md. gleanings in Eng. Wills. M. H. Mag., 1907, v. 2, no. 3.

Sear, Sears. Hezekiah Wilson's Diary, Montgomery Co. Natl. Geneal. Soc. Quart., 1917, v. 6, no. 1, pp. 27–31.

Searight. Searight family, Uniontown, Pa. Richmond, Ind., M. Cullaton & Co., 1893. MHS.

Sears. Geneal. ms. coll. of Dr. Thomas E. Sears. Ms. MHS.
*Dr. Thomas E. Sears Geneal. Coll. MHS.
St. Paul's Parish, Balto. V. 2. Mss. MHS.

Sears, Mrs. F. E. Abr. Compend. Amer. Geneal. Virkus. V. 1, p. 950. DAR.

Seccombe. St. Paul's Parish, Balto. V. 2. Mss. MHS.

Seckel. Jenkins-Courtney chart. MHS.

Seddon. St. Paul's Parish, Balto. V. 1, Mss. MHS.

Sedgeley Family. Ms. MHS.

***Sedgewick.** Frederick Co. families. Markell. Ms. Personal list.

Sedgley. Burbank family. Sedgley. MHS.

***Sedgwick Family.** Wilson Mss. Coll., no. 43. MHS.

Sedwick. Plummer family. A. P. H. Ms. MHS.
See Wilson-Sedwick-Williams.

Seekamp. Williamson Bible rec. Ms. MHS.

Sefferson, Severson. St. Stephens Parish, Cecilton, Md. MHS; DAR.

Sefton, John, London Town, Md. Will probated Jan. 4, 1800. D. A. R. Mag., v. 62, no. 11, p. 714.

Segrave, Mrs. Charles M. (Mary Lucy Harwood). Chart. Col. Dames, Chap. I. MHS.

Seicke. Catonsville pioneers of Luth. faith. Natl. Geneal. Soc. Quart., v. 9, no. 2, p. 29.

†**Seidenstricker.** Hist. of Balto. City and Co. Scharf. Pp. 485–87. MHS.

†**Seiss, Rev. J. A.,** Frederick Co. (1823–1904). Bibliog. Md. authors. Steiner. Ms. list, Md. Room, Enoch Pratt Lib.

Seitz. Descendants of John Seitz; born in Germany; died in Pa. Bd. Ms. MHS.
Zion Reformed Church, Hagerstown. Md. Geneal. Rec. Com., 1934–35. Mss. DAR.

Seitz, John and Eva Stabler, Shrewsbury Township, York Co., Pa. Ms. MHS.

Seitz Family. Ms. notes in copy of descendants of Henry Keller, York Co., Pa., and Fairfield, Ohio. Shumaker, editor, 1924. MHS.

Seitz Family, York Co., Pa. Descendants of John and Eva (Stabler) Seitz, Shrewsbury Township, York Co., Pa. Wm. Clinton Seitz, Glenrock, Pa. Copied by Mary Albright Seitz, Towson, Md. Mss. MHS.

Seitz, Sitze. Hagerstown tombstone inscriptions. Gruder. Natl. Geneal. Soc. Quart., 1919, v. 8, nos. 1, 2.

Selby. All Hallow's P. E. churchyard, Snow Hill, Worcester Co. Hudson. Bd. ms. MHS; DAR. Also: Md. Geneal. Rec. Com., 1935–36, p. 4. Mss. DAR.
Bible rec. Md. Geneal. Bull., v. 3, no. 4, p. 26. MHS; DAR.
Gillett-Miller families. Ms. MHS.
Marriage rec. of Frederick Co. Markell. Md. Geneal. Rec. Com., 1938–39. Mss. DAR.
Md. families. Culver. Ms. Personal list.
†Med. Annals Md. Cordell. 1903, p. 563. MHS.
M. E. churchyard, Snow Hill, Worcester Co. Hudson. Bd. ms. MHS; DAR.
(1852–89). Old Md. Bibles. M. H. Mag., 1934, v. 29, no. 4, pp. 322–30.
Pedigree of James Etchberger Hancock. Soc. Col. Wars Md. Culver. 1940. MHS; DAR.
Purnell family tree. MHS.
Somerset Co. Court Book. Tilghman. 1937. Ms. DAR.
St. Paul's P. E. churchyard, Berlin, Worcester Co. Hudson. Bd. ms. MHS; DAR. Also: Md. Geneal. Rec. Com., 1937, Mrs. Lines. Mss. DAR.
Turner Geneal. Coll. Ms. MHS.
See Wilson-Selby.

***Selby Family.** Notes. Charles L. Stewart. Bement, Ill., 1929, mimeog. MHS.
Notes. Charles L. Stewart. (Worcester Co., Md., p. 6). Typed. MHS.

***Selden.** Ancestry. E. Van D. Selden. 1931. DAR.
Col. families of U. S. A. Mackenzie. V. 1. MHS; DAR.
Duckett chart. MHS.
McCormick chart. MHS.
*Seldens of Va. and allied families. Coat of arms. M. S. Kennedy. N. Y., 1911.

Selden, Va. Chart; 29 coats of arms. A. A. Selden, Balto. Photos. MHS.

Selden-Duckett. Bible rec. Ms. MHS.

Sellers. Burial ground near Hillsboro, Caroline Co. (Charlotte Sellers married Bishop John Emory.) Md. Geneal. Rec. Com., 1935–36, p. 169. Mss. DAR.
Lloyd family hist. of Wales, Pa., and Md. DAR.
St. Paul's Parish, Balto. V. 2. Mss. MHS.
*Sellers family of Pa. E. J. Sellers. Phila., ltd. ed. MHS.
See Sollars.

Sellers, Paul. Data, mostly Pa. D. A. R. Mag., v. 67, no. 3, p. 144.
Sellers Family, Phila. (from 1600). Contains photos. copy of chart of Lloyd family. Photos. copy of chart, Col. services of Blanston-Paschall-Lloyd. Revolutionary services of Nicholas Dieh and Col. Hugh Lloyd. 18 rec., 375 items, 20 pp. Md. Geneal. Rec. Com., 1935-36. Mss. DAR.
***Sellers-Wampole Families.** Sellers-Wampole families. E. J. Sellers. Pr. for priv. circulation, J. B. Lippincott Co., 1930. MHS.
Sellman. Anne Arundel Co. tombstone inscriptions. Ms. DAR.
Catonsville pioneers of Luth. faith. Natl. Geneal. Soc. Quart., v. 9, no. 2, p. 29.
Col. families of U. S. A. Mackenzie. V. 7, p. 238. MHS; DAR.
*Early comers to the Province. Georgians in Anne Arundel Co. Atlanta Jour., Sept. 22, 1906. Newsp. clipp. File case, MHS.
*Founders of Anne Arundel and Howard Cos. Warfield. P. 479. MHS; DAR.
Glison-Sellman-Murphy-Cooley Bible rec. Ms. DAR.
Hazelhurst chart. MHS.
Hist. graves of Md. and D. C. Ridgely. MHS.
†Med. Annals Md. Cordell. 1903, p. 563. MHS.
Patriotic Md. Md. Soc. of S. A. R., 1930. MHS; DAR.
St. Paul's Parish, Balto. V. 1, 2. Mss. MHS.
John White Bible rec. Ms. MHS.
***Sellman Family.** Wilson Mss. Coll., no. 3, B. MHS.
Semmes. Abr. Compend. Amer. Geneal. Virkus. V. 1, p. 822. DAR.
Balto., its hist., its people. Hall. V. 2. MHS; DAR.
See Freeman. Abr. Compend. Amer. Geneal. Virkus. V. 1, p. 920. DAR.
Freeman family. Col. and Revolutionary families of Phila. Jordan. 1933, v. 1, pp. 323-28.
†Hist. of Allegany Co. Thomas & Williams. V. 2. MHS; DAR.
Lucketts of Portobacco. Newman. DAR.
Md. families. Culver. Ms. Personal list.
†Med. Annals Md. Cordell. 1903, p. 564. MHS.
St. Paul's Parish, Balto. V. 4. Mss. MHS.
‡Semmes of "Alabama." W. A. Roberts. (Civil War sea exploits.) 1938. Enoch Pratt Lib.
*Semmes and allied families. R. T. Semmes. Balto., Sun & Job Printing Co., 1918. MHS.
*Semmes Geneal. Coll. Bequest of Raphael Semmes. 1917. Ms. MHS.
Western Run Parish book. Allen. Bd. ms. MHS.
See Simms.
***Semmes, Anthony.** Descendants of Anthony: James Semmes; John Semmes; Marmaduke Semmes. Semmes Geneal. Coll. Ms. MHS.
Semmes, John E. (1851-1925). In memoriam. The Sun, May 18, 1925; Evening Sun, May 18, 1925; memorial services held by Supreme Bench, Balto. City, June 18, 1925. Enoch Pratt Lib.
†**Semmes, Raphael** (1809-77). M. H. Mag., v. 12, p. 243.
Pedigree. Soc. Col. Wars Md. Culver. 1940. MHS; DAR.
†Raphael Semmes (1809-77). B. Colyer Meriwether. Phila., Geo. W. Jacobs and Co., 1913.
Semmes Family. Harford Co. Hist. Soc. Mss. Coll. JHU.
Semmes, Simms. Pedigree of Coleman Randall Freeman. Soc. Col. Wars Md. Culver. 1940. MHS; DAR.
Sensel. Md. tombstone rec. Md. Geneal. Rec. Com., 1937, Parran, pp. 5, 33. Mss. DAR.
Senseney. Englar family. Barnes. MHS; DAR.
Senseney, Carroll Co. Newsp. clipp., bd. MHS.
Serman. *See* Sherman.
Serman-Stevens. Wicomico Co. families Bible rec. Ms. DAR.
Sermon, Sherman, Shirman. Rec. of Stepney Parish. MHS; DAR.
Serton. Serton or Saxon family, Monmouth, N. J. Md. Geneal. Rec. Com., v. 2, pp. 17-22. DAR.
Seth. Dawson chart. MHS.
†Med. Annals Md. Cordell. 1903, p. 564. MHS.
†Men of mark in Md. Johnson. V. 1. DAR; Enoch Pratt Lib.
Naturalizations in Md., 1666-1765; Laws. Bacon. MHS.
Patriotic Md. Md. Soc. of S. A. R., 1930. MHS; DAR.
†Recollections of long life on East. Shore of Md. J. B. Seth. DAR.
Seth, Talbot Co. Amer. Armory and Blue Book. Matthews. 1911-12, p. 364.
Seth Family, Talbot Co. Bible rec. Ms. MHS.
Seton. Letters to Mother Seton from Mrs. Julianna Scott. Edited by Rev. Joseph B. Code. Emmitsburg, Md., 1935. Enoch Pratt Lib.
Soul of Elizabeth Seton (foundress of Daughters of Charity in North Amer.). Spiritual autobiog., culled from Mother Seton's writings and memoirs. By Daughter of Charity of St. Vincent de Paul, St. Joseph's College, Emmitsburg, Md. Benziger Bros., 1936. Enoch Pratt Lib.
St. Paul's Parish, Balto. V. 2. Mss. MHS.
Seton, Elizabeth. Elizabeth Seton. Madame De Barberey. N. Y., McMillan Co., 1927. Enoch Pratt Lib.
Severson. Still Pond Church and cemetery. Md. O. R. Soc. Bull., no. 2, pp. 65-75.
See Sefferson.
Sevier. Some notable families of south. States. Armstrong. V. 1, pp. 180-206. (Md. ref.) DAR.
Sewall. Britton Scrap Book. V. 2. Ms. MHS.
Col. families of Amer. Lawrence. V. 3, p. 308. MHS.
Dawson chart. MHS.
Freeborn Garrettson Waters Bible rec. Ms. MHS.
C. Johnston pedigree chart. Soc. Col. Wars, Md. Johnston. 905, p. 54. MHS.
Miss Katherine Lurman chart. MHS.
W. A. and S. W. Merritt pedigree charts, plate 2. Soc. Col. Wars, Md. Johnston. 1905, p. 68. MHS.
Milligan chart. MHS.
Parr chart. MHS.
Pedigree of Duncan Keener Brent. Soc. Col. Wars Md. Culver. 1940. MHS; DAR.

Pedigree of W. Wallace McKaig. Soc. Col. Wars Md. Culver. 1940. MHS; DAR.
Pedigree of John Philemon Paca. Soc. Col. Wars Md. Culver. 1940. MHS; DAR.
Pedigree of Pleasants Pennington. Soc. Col. Wars Md. Culver. 1940. MHS; DAR.
Pedigree of Levin Gale Shreve. Soc. Col. Wars Md. Culver. 1940. MHS; DAR.
Pedigree of St. George Leakin Sioussat. Soc. Col. Wars Md. Culver. 1940. MHS; DAR.
Pedigree of Harrison Tilghman. Soc. Col. Wars Md. Culver. 1940. MHS; DAR.
Pedigree of Mason Locke Weems Williams. Soc. Col. Wars Md. Culver. 1940. MHS; DAR.
Mrs. E. W. Poe chart. MHS.
Raisin chart. MHS.
Side lights on Md. hist. Richardson. V. 2, p. 219. MHS; DAR.
Some old Eng. letters. M. H. Mag., 1914, v. 9, no. 2, pp. 107–56.
*The Sun, Balto., Dec. 27, 1903; May 7, 1905.
See Sewell.

Sewall, Cecil Co. Manning chart. MHS.

Sewall Family. Thomas Book. Thomas. P. 482. Lib. Cong.; MHS.

***Sewall Family,** Va. and Severn, Md., with Sewall Revolutionary Muster Roll. Founders of Anne Arundel and Howard Cos. Warfield. Pp. 135–40. MHS.

Sewall Line. T. C. Jenkins pedigree chart. Soc. Col. Wars, Md. Johnston. 1905, pp. 47, 153. MHS.

Sewall (or **Sewell) - Brooke - Darnall - Beall.** Chart. Complete negatives. Cary Geneal. Coll. Ms. MHS.

Sewall-Darnall-Brooke-Calvert-Lee (Va.). Chart. Cary Geneal. Coll. Ms. MHS.

Sewall, Sewell. Ances. rec. and portraits. Col. Dames of Amer., 1910, v. 2, pp. 513,533. MHS; DAR.
Col. families of U. S. A. Mackenzie. V. 1, p. 290. MHS; DAR.
Hist. graves of Md. and D. C. Ridgely. MHS.
Md. families. Culver. Ms. Personal list.
*Pennington Papers. Ms. MHS.
Sewall, Sewell family. Christopher Johnston. M. H. Mag., 1909, v. 4, no. 3, p. 290–95.
St. Stephens Parish, Cecilton, Md. MHS; DAR.

Sewell. Anne Arundel Co. tombstone inscriptions. Ms. DAR.
Eldridge chart. MHS.
Few abs. from will book at Annapolis. William and Mary Quart., 1st series, v. 13, p. 27.
*Key-Sewell family data. Ms., 1 vol. MHS.
Pedigree of Charles Gambrill Baldwin. Soc. Col. Wars Md. Culver. 1940. MHS; DAR.
Pedigree of Franklin Buchanan Owen. Soc. Col. Wars Md. Culver. 1940. MHS; DAR.
St. Paul's Parish, Balto. V. 2, 4. Mss. MHS.
Tombstone rec., 1725–1873, Anne Arundel Co. Founders of Anne Arundel and Howard Cos. Warfield. P. 140.
Mrs. G. H. Williams, Jr., chart. MHS.
See McClatchy-Sewell.
See Sewall.

Sewell Family. Harford Co. Hist. Soc. Mss. Coll. JHU.

Sewell-McClatchy. Bible and gravestone rec., 1805–1906. Md. Geneal. Rec. Com., 1932–33, v. 5. Mss. DAR.

Sexton. Balto., its hist., its people. Hall. V. 2. MHS; DAR.

Seymour. Md. gleanings in Eng. Wills. M. H. Mag., 1907, v. 2, no. 2.
Newsp. clipp. MHS.

†**Shaaff.** Med. Annals Md. Cordell. 1903, p. 564. MHS.

Shackleford. Md. Geneal. Rec. Com., 1932–33, pp. 208–09. Mss. DAR.
Times Dispatch, Richmond, Va., May 7, 1905. Newsp. clipp. MHS.

Shackleford Family, Va. Ms. MHS.

Shafer. Founders of Anne Arundel and Howard Cos. Warfield. P. 319. MHS; DAR.
†Hist. of Washington Co. Williams. 1906, v. 2, p. 884. MHS; DAR.
†Hist. of West. Md. Scharf. V. 2, p. 1267. MHS; DAR.
Price family and other Gunpowder Friends. Death notices; photos. of newsp. clipp. MHS.

†**Shafer, Shaffer.** Hist. of Frederick Co. Williams. MHS; DAR.

Shahan. Blakiston churchyard, Kent Co., Del., near Millington. Md. Geneal. Rec. Com., 1933–34, pp. 204–07. Mss. DAR.
Shahan farm, Millington, Kent Co. Tombstone inscriptions. Ms. DAR.

Shallcross. Still Pond Church and cemetery. Md. O. R. Soc. Bull., no. 2, pp. 65–75.

†**Shane.** Med. Annals Md. Cordell. 1903, p. 564. MHS.
St. Paul's Parish, Balto. V. 2, 4. Mss. MHS.

Shank. Hagerstown tombstone inscriptions. Gruder. Natl. Geneal. Soc. Quart., 1919, v. 8, nos. 1, 2.
Spessard family. Spessard. MHS; DAR.

Shanley. Amer. Clan Gregor Year Book, 1916, p. 28. MHS; DAR.

Shanly, J. D. Abs. of will. D. A. R. Mag., Sept., 1927, v. 61, no. 9, p. 704.

Shannahan. Patriotic Md. Md. Soc. of S. A. R., 1930. MHS; DAR.

Shannon. Descendants of Joran Kyn. Pa. Mag., v. 7, pp. 299, 464.
St. Paul's Parish, Balto. V. 2. Mss. MHS.

Sharar-Perine-Day. Bible rec. Ms. MHS.

Sharkly. Tombstone inscriptions of Princess Anne and Snow Hill. Turner Geneal. Coll. Ms. MHS.

Sharp. Cary Geneal. Coll. Ms. MHS.
Lee-Wilson chart. Cary Geneal. Coll. Ms. MHS.
Hopkins, Husband, Johns, Sharp and Webster families. Browne. Bd. ms. MHS.
*Sharp family. From estate of Hon. George M. Sharp, Sept. 21, 1911. Ms. MHS.
*Sharps of Chester Co., Pa., and abstracts of rec. in Great Britain. W. C. Sharpe. Seymour, Conn., 1903. MHS.
*Wicomico Co. families. Tilghman. Ms., p. 97. DAR.

Sharp, A. Ellicott. Md. Soc., War of 1812, v. 3, no. 254. Ms. MHS.

Sharp, Hon. George Matthews. Pedigree chart, plates 1 and 2. Soc. Col. Wars, Md. Johnston. 1905, pp. 91–92. MHS.

Sharp Family. Entries in Friends Register, Eng. Ms. MHS.

Sharp Family, Cecil Co. Will of Thomas Sharp, 1749; Will of Thomas Sharp Jr., 1785; Indenture of Thomas Sharp, 1799. Md. Geneal. Rec. Com., 1929. V. 3. Pp. 1–4. DAR.

Sharp Family, Chester Co., Pa. (Quaker rec.) Bd. ms. MHS.

Sharpe. Mrs. Wm. Graham Bowdoin chart. MHS.
*Family bulletins, 1893–96. MHS.
*Geneal. and miscellany. W. C. Sharpe. Seymour, Conn., Record Print, 1880. MHS.
‡Gilmor Papers. Misc. papers of Robert Gilmor, relating to administration of Gov. Sharp. Ms. MHS.
‡Gov. Horatio Sharpe and hist. of Md. government. M. H. Mag., 1937, v. 32, no. 2, p. 156.
†Gov. Horatio Sharpe retires, 1768. P. H. Giddens. M. H. Mag., 1936, v. 31, pp. 215–25.
‡Md. career of Gov. Horatio Sharpe of Md., 1753–69. Lady Matilda Edgar. N. Y., 1912. MHS.
*Sharpe family in N. J. MHS.
The Sharpes, monthly, Bull. 1, Jan., 1893–Bull. 32, 1896. W. C. Sharpe, ed. Seymour, Conn. John, Md. and N. C., Bull. 1, p. 21; Thomas I, Bull. 4, p. 18; Thomas II, Bull. 11, pp. 92, 96, 150; Dr. Peter, Bull. 11, pp. 92, 109. MHS.

Sharpe, Rev. Charles. Family Bible rec. Md. Geneal. Rec. Com., 1934–35, v. 7, p. 6. DAR.

Sharpe, George M. Coll. of letters. Md. geneal. Mss. MHS.

***Sharpe, Mary-Sterns, Wm.** Marriage certificate, 1670. Note from public rec. Hodges M. H. Mag., 1915, v. 10, pp. 284–85.

***Sharples.** Wicomico Co. families. Tilghman. Ms., p. 126. DAR.
See Sharpless.

Sharples, Sharpless, Pa. Burke's landed gentry. 1939. MHS.

Sharpless. Mass. Hist. Soc. Pro., 2nd series, 1881–87, v. 13. MHS.

***Sharpless, Sharples Family.** Geneal.; descendants of John and Jane Sharples, settlers near Chester, Pa., 1682–1882. G. Cope. Phila., 1887. MHS; DAR.

Sharpley. C. H. B. Turner Geneal. Coll. Mss. MHS.

Shaw. Abr. Compend. Amer. Geneal. Virkus. V. 1, p. 608. DAR.
Bible rec., 1766–1929. Md. Geneal. Rec. Com., 1932–33, pp. 64–67. Mss. DAR.
Col. Nicholas Duvall family rec. Price. Bd. ms. MHS.
See Harrold. Abr. Compend. Amer. Geneal. Virkus. V. 1, p. 646. DAR.
Hist. graves of Md. and D. C. Ridgely. MHS.
†Hist. of Allegany Co. Thomas and Williams. V. 1. MHS. DAR.
†Hist. of Frederick Co. Williams. MHS; DAR.
†Hist. of West. Md. Scharf. V. 2, pp. 1466–68. MHS; DAR.
McCormick chart. MHS.
†Med. Annals Md. Cordell. 1903, p. 565. MHS.
St. Paul's Parish, Balto. V. 1, 2. Mss. MHS.

Shaw, R. M. Abr. Compend. Amer. Geneal. Virkus. V. 1, p. 824. DAR.

Shaw, W. Checkley. Capt. John Frazier. Leach. P. 99. MHS.

Shaw-Mince Families, Balto. Co. (1799–1906). With ref. to Joseph Mince's will. Md. Geneal. Rec. Com., 1933–34, p. 153. Mss. DAR.

***Shawey.** Frederick Co. families. Markell. Ms. Personal list.

Shawhan. Data. M. H. Mag., 1939, v. 34, no. 2, p. 204.

Shawn, Frederick. Revolutionary pension abs. Natl. Geneal. Soc. Quart., v. 23, p. 16.

†**Shaws.** Hist. of Allegany Co. Thomas and Williams. V. 2. MHS; DAR.

Shearer. Hist. of Byberry and Moreland. Martindale. MHS.

Shehan. *See* Hart-Shehan-Clayton-Meloir.

Sheib, Sam'l Henry. Pedigree. Soc. Col. Wars Md. Culver. 1940. MHS; DAR.

Sheild. Culver pedigree chart. MHS.
Pedigree of Francis Barnum Culver. Soc. Col. Wars Md. Culver. 1940. MHS; DAR.

Sheilles. Somerset Co. Court Book. Tilghman. 1937. Ms. DAR.

Shelby. Col. families of U. S. A. Mackenzie. V. 2. MHS; DAR.
*Frederick Co. families. Markell. Ms. Personal list.
Geneal. of Va. and Ky. Floyd families. Floyd. P. 12. DAR.
Md. families. Culver. Ms. Personal list.
Report of first three generations of Shelby family in U. S. (Md. and Pa., 1735). 1922, pamph. MHS.
†Col. Isaas Shelby and other Md. heroes of Battle of King's Mountain, Oct. 7, 1780. H. J. Berkley. M. H. Mag., 1932, v. 27, pp. 128–29.

†**Shelby, Isaac** (1750–1826). M. H. Mag., v. 2, p. 244.

Shelby Family. And John Duncan, N. C. McCall-Tidwell families. McCall. MHS; DAR.
Mountain Democrat, Garrett Co., Feb. 14, 1935. Newsp. clipp. MHS; DAR.

***Shell.** Frederick Co. families. Markell. Ms. Personal list.

Shelley. Matthews-Price chart. MHS.

Shellman. Md. families. Culver. Ms. Personal list.

Shelton. Dulaney churchyard, near Massey, Kent Co. Md. Geneal. Rec. Com., 1933–34, pp. 210–12. Mss. DAR.
See Ellis-Shelton.

***Shenton.** Hist. of Dorchester Co. Jones. 1925, pp. 442–45. MHS; DAR.

Shepard. *See* Duke-Shepard-Van Meter.

Sheperd. Portrait and biog. rec. of East. Shore of Md. 1898, p. 735. MHS; DAR.

Sheperd Family. Lee of Va., 1642–1892. E. J. Lee. P. 470. Lib. Cong.; MHS.

†**Shepherd.** Biog. cyc. of rep. men of Md. and D. C. Pp. 91, 264. MHS; DAR.
Christ P. E. Church cemetery, Cambridge. Steele. 1936. MHS; DAR.
Ellen Emmerich Mears. Col. and Revolutionary families of Phila. Jordan, 1933, v. 1, pp. 412–15.
*Hist. Dorchester Co. Jones. 1925, p. 446. MHS.
†Hist. of West. Md. Scharf. V. 2, p. 972. MHS; DAR.
*Shepherd family. Partial list of chapters: Amer. origins; (1) Louis Du Bois, (2) Jan Joosten Van Meter, (3) the Hite Grant, (4) will of John Van Meter, (5) descendants of John Van Meter of Pa., Md. and Va.
See Duke-Shepherd-Van Metre.
See Elting-Shepherd.

Shepherd, Moses. Monumental City. Howard. MHS; DAR.

Shepherd, Col. Moses, Shepherdstown, W. Va. (1776–1867). W. Va. Hist. Mag., v. 3, no. 3, pp. 190, 209.
Shepherd, Sheppard. St. Paul's Parish, Balto. V. 1, 2, 4. Mss. MHS.
Sheppard. Crumpton graveyard. Md. Geneal. Rec. Com., 1933–34, pp. 193–203. Mss. DAR.
Dawson family of Md. Ms. File case, DAR.
Gittings chart. MHS.
Hagerstown tombstone inscriptions. Gruder. Natl. Geneal. Soc. Quart., 1919, v. 8, nos. 1, 2.
Md. tombstone rec. Md. Geneal. Rec. Com., 1937, Parran, pp. 12, 13. Mss. DAR.
Pedigree of Maurice Falconer Rodgers. Soc. Col. Wars Md. Culver. 1940. MHS; DAR.
Portrait and biog. rec. of East. Shore of Md. 1898, p. 881. MHS; DAR.
Mrs. Wm. L. Watson chart. MHS.
White geneal. tree. MHS.
See Shepherd.
Sheppard, Talbot Co. W. H. De C. W. Thom pedigree charts, plate 2. Soc. Col. Wars, Md. Johnston. 1905, p. 108. MHS.
†**Sheppard, Moses.** Biog. notice of late Moses Sheppard. J. S. Norris.
*The Sun, Balto., May 19, 1913.
Sherburne, Mrs. John Henry (Mary Patterson Harris). Chart. Col. Dames, Chap. I. MHS.
(Maternal line.) Mrs. W. Hall Harris chart. MHS.
Shercliffe. Hamilton family of Charles Co Kelly. Pp. 14, 62–63, 69. MHS.
Sheredine. Cary Geneal. Coll. Ms. MHS.
Chew family. Culver. M. H. Mag., 1935, v. 30, no. 2, pp. 157–75.
†Hist. of West. Md. Scharf. V. 1, p. 456. MHS; DAR.
Manning chart. MHS.
Mrs. E. W. Poe chart. MHS.
St. Paul's Parish, Balto. V. 1. Mss. MHS.
Sheriff. Abr. Compend. Amer. Geneal. Virkus. V. 1, p. 825. DAR.
Amer. Clan Gregor Year Book, 1922, pp. 55–59; 1928, p. 11. MHS; DAR.
Beall and Bell families. Beall. MHS; DAR.
Sweetser chart. MHS.
Sherlock. Wm. Conway of Md. and Pa. Ms. File case, DAR.
Robert Gilmor chart. MHS.
St. Paul's Parish, Balto. V. 2. Mss. MHS.
Sherman. *See* Sermon.
***Sherman, Serman, Sirman.** Wicomico Co. Families. Tilghman. Ms., pp. 47, 58–60, 62, 97–98, 115, 122. DAR.
Sherwood. Balto., its hist., its people. Hall. V. 3. MHS; DAR.
Charts (12), Talbot Co. Md. Geneal. Rec. Com., 1937, pp. 59–62. Mss. DAR.
Chart, typed. Md. Geneal. Rec. Com., Mrs. Paran, 1937. Mss. DAR.
*Hist. of Dorchester Co. Jones. 1925, p. 293. MHS; DAR.
*Hist. of Sherwood family, Talbot Co. Ms. DAR.
Mann-Needles-Hambleton families. Needles. MHS; DAR.
Old Md. families. Bromwell. MHS; DAR.
Pedigree of T. Edward Hambleton. Soc. Col. Wars Md. Culver. 1940. MHS; DAR.
Pedigree of Maurice Edward Skinner. Soc. Col. Wars Md. Culver. 1940. MHS; DAR.
Pedigree of Harrison Tilghman. Soc. Col. Wars Md. Culver. 1940. MHS; DAR.
Rec. Natl. Geneal. Soc. Quart., v. 12, no. 2, p. 27.
Rolle family rec., Talbot Co. Ms. MHS.
St. Paul's Parish, Balto. V. 2. Mss. MHS.
Third Haven Friends Meeting House, Easton. Vital rec. MHS. Also: Natl. Geneal. Soc. Quart., v. 11, no. 1, pp. 9–14.
Turner family. Forman. P. 85. MHS.
***Sherwood,** Talbot Co. Burke's landed gentry. 1939. MHS.
F. S. Hambleton pedigree chart. Soc. Col. Wars, Md. Johnston. 1905, pp. 33, 153. MHS.
*Lineage Bk., Daughters of Founders and Patriots, v. 15, p. 37. MHS.
Shiall. Old Somerset. Torrence. MHS; DAR.
Shidel. Frederick Co. tombstone inscriptions. Gruder. Natl. Geneal. Soc. Quart., 1919, v. 8, nos. 1, 2.
Shield. Patriotic Md. Md. Soc. of S. A. R., 1930. MHS; DAR.
Shields. Bible rec. D. C. Geneal. Rec. Com., v. 32, pp. 16–27. Typed, bd. DAR.
Mrs. W. H. Harris chart. MHS.
†Med. Annals Md. Cordell. 1903, p. 566. MHS.
J. G. and M. G. Wilson pedigree chart. Soc. Col. Wars, Md. Johnston. 1905, p. 129. MHS.
St. Paul's Parish, Balto. V. 2. Mss. MHS.
See Kemp-Shields.
Shiess. Beards' Luth. graveyard, Washington Co. Md. Geneal. Rec. Com., 1935–36. Mss. DAR.
Shiles, Worcester Co. Geneal. reg. Mervine. P. 139. MHS.
Shilletto. Somerset Co. Court Book. Tilghman. 1937. Ms. DAR.
Shipley. A Md. Royal and Baronial Scrap Book. Britton. V. 2. Mss. MHS.
Abr. Compend. Amer. Geneal. Virkus. V. 1, p. 826; v. 6, p. 358. DAR.
Britton chart. MHS.
See Britton-Shipley. Abr. Compend. Amer. Geneal. Virkus. V. 6, p. 91. DAR.
Data. Md. Geneal. Rec. Com., 1933–34, p. 23. Mss. DAR.
Founders of Anne Arundel and Howard Cos. Warfield. Pp. 485–86. MHS; DAR.
Griffith geneal. Griffith. MHS; DAR.
†Hist. of Frederick Co. Williams. MHS; DAR.
*Index to "Shipley of Md." Ms. DAR.
Md. Geneal. Bull., v. 5, p. 3. MHS; DAR.
Pedigree of Richard Walker Worthington. Soc. Col. Wars Md. Culver. 1940. MHS; DAR.
Rogers Coll. Ms. MHS.
St. Paul's Parish, Balto. V. 1, 2, 4. Mss. MHS.
St. Thomas' Parish, Balto. Co. Bd. ms. MHS. Also: Md. Geneal. Rec. Com., 1937, pp. 109–82. Mss. DAR.
*Shipleys of Md. Geneal. study. B. Committee appointed at Shipley reunion at College Park, Md., Aug., 1937. MHS; DAR.
*Wicomico Co. families. Tilghman. Ms., p. 101. DAR.
*Wilson Mss. Coll., no. 66. MHS.
See Welsh-Shipley.
***Shipley, Dr. Arthur M.** Burke's landed gentry. 1939. MHS.

Shipley, Benjamin, Anne Arundel Co. Will, Nov. 19, 1827. D. A. R. Mag., v. 62, no. 11, p. 713.
***Shipley, Joseph W.** Burke's landed gentry. 1939. MHS.
Shipley Family. Rec., 1668–1918. Md. Geneal. Rec. Com., 1932–33, v. 5. DAR.
Jerome hist. and geneal., and ancestry of Sarah Noble. P. 62. Mss. MHS.
Shippen. Amer. ancestry of Frederick Louis and Reginald Shippen Huidekoper. 1931, pamph., p. 16. MHS; DAR.
Ancestry of Rosalie Morris Johnson. Johnson. 1905. MHS; DAR.
Balch letters and papers. Pamph., p. 19. MHS.
Col. families of U. S. A. Mackenzie. V. 2. MHS; DAR.
*Geneal. of descendants of Dr. William Shippen, the Elder, Phila. R. Buchanan. Priv. pr., Joseph L. Pearson, Wash., D. C., 1877. MHS.
Lee of Va., 1642–1892. E. J. Lee. Lib. Cong.; MHS.
Lukens chart. MHS.
Peale Geneal. Coll. Ms. MHS.
Ruffin and other geneal. Pr. chart. Henry.
Dr. William Shippen, the Elder. Roberdeau Buchanan. Wash., D. C., Joseph L. Pearson, 1877, pamph. MHS.
Shippen, R. L. Ms. MHS.
Shippen, Dr. Wm. Descendants. Pa. Mag. Hist. and Biog., v. 1, pp. 109–11.
***Shippen Family.** Old Kent. Hanson. Pp. 331–33. MHS; DAR.
Shippen Family, Pa. N. Y. Geneal. and Biog. Rec., April, 1924, v. 55, no. 2, pp. 131–42.
Shirk. Balto., its hist., its people. Hall. V. 3. MHS; DAR.
Shirman. *See* Sermon.
Shives. Md. tombstone rec. Md. Geneal. Rec. Com., 1937, Parran, pp. 6, 16, 20, 23. Mss. DAR.
Shock. Howland chart. MHS.
Shockley. Mt. Zion P. E. churchyard, Worcester Co. Md. Geneal. Rec. Com., 1937, Mrs. Lines. Mss. DAR.
*Wicomico Co. families. Tilghman. Ms., pp. 39, 83. DAR.
Shocky, Christopher, Frederick Co. Will, June 8, 1773. D. A. R. Mag., v. 62, no. 11, p. 712.
Shoemaker. Abr. Compend. Amer. Geneal. Virkus. V. 1, p. 827. DAR.
†Balto., hist. and biog. Richardson and Bennett. 1871, pp. 453–56. MHS; DAR.
Col. families of U. S. A. Mackenzie. V. 1, pp. 478–80. MHS; DAR.
*Frederick Co. families. Markell. Ms. Personal list.
*Geneal. of Shoemaker family of Cheltenham, Pa. 1903.
†Hist. of Balto. City and Co. Scharf. Pp. 359–60. MHS.
Manning chart. MHS.
Md. tombstone rec. Md. Geneal. Rec. Com., 1937, Parran, p. 23. Mss. DAR.
Pedigree of Anthony Morris Tyson. Soc. Col. Wars Md. Culver. 1940. MHS; DAR.
Mrs. E. W. Poe chart. MHS.
*Shoemaker - Wheeler-Ownings - Brawner - Livers. Lineage Bk., Daughters of Amer. Colonists. V. 2, pp. 95–96. MHS; DAR.
Whitridge chart. MHS.
Shoemaker, Germany, Pa., and Montgomery Co. Encyc. of Amer. biog. Amer. Hist. Soc., new series, v. 1, pp. 55–57. MHS; DAR.
Shoemaker, M. Myers. Md. Soc., War of 1812, v. 1, no. 110. Ms. MHS.
Shoemaker-Turnbull. Col. and Revolutionary families of Pa. Amer. Hist. Soc., N. Y., 1934, p. 592.
Sholl. *See* Scholl.
Shooman. *See* Shuman.
***Shorp or Shupe.** Frederick Co. families. Markell. Ms. Personal list.
†**Short,** Balto. Lydia Darragh of Revolution. Pa. Mag. Hist. and Biog., v. 23, pp. 90–91.
Shoup. Roop geneal. Pamph. MHS.
Shouse, Jouett. Abr. Compend. Amer. Geneal. Virkus. V. 1, p. 827. DAR.
Showell. St. Martin's P. E. Church, Worcester Co. Md. Geneal. Rec. Com., 1937, Mrs. Lines. Mss. DAR.
St. Paul's P. E. churchyard, Berlin, Worcester Co. Hudson. Bd. ms. MHS; DAR. Also: Md. Geneal. Rec. Com., 1937, Mrs. Lines. Mss. DAR.
Worcester Co. militia, 1794. Covington. P. 165. MHS.
†**Shower.** Med. Annals Md. Cordell. 1903, p. 566. MHS.
Shower Family. Hist. of Everhart and Shower family. Everhart. 1883.
Shreeves Family. Ms. MHS.
Shreve. Gale family pedigree, Somerset and Cecil Cos. Ms. MHS.
Hist. graves of Md. and D. C. Ridgely. MHS.
Talbott of "Poplar Knowle." Shirk. MHS; DAR.
Tilghman chart. MHS.
***Shreve, Col. Arthur Lee.** Burke's landed gentry. 1939. MHS.
Shreve, Levin Gale. Pedigree. Soc. Col. Wars Md. Culver. 1940. MHS; DAR.
Shriner. Englar family. Barnes. MHS; DAR.
†Hist. of West. Md. Scharf. V. 1, p. 624. MHS; DAR.
Roop geneal. Pamph. MHS.
Scholl, Sholl, Shull family. Scholl. P. 787. MHS; DAR.
Shriner, Carroll Co. Newsp. clipp., bd. MHS.
Shriner-Getzendanner-Stierner (Stoner). Lineage Bks., Natl. Soc. of Daughters of Amer. Col., v. 3, p. 121. MHS; DAR.
Shriner (Schreiner, Shryner)-Grumbine (Krumbein, Krumbine). Abr. Compend. Amer. Geneal. Virkus. V. 4, p. 624.
Shriver. Babylon family. Duttera. Ms. MHS.
Col. families of U. S. A. Mackenzie. V. 2. MHS; DAR.
Englar family. Barnes. MHS; DAR.
Geneal. and memorial encyc. of Md. Spencer. V. 2, p. 661. MHS; DAR.
†Hist. of Allegany Co. Thomas and Williams. 4. 1; v. 2. MHS; DAR.
Letters of old homestead, Union Mills, 1822–98. In binder, MHS.
Lineage Bks., Natl. Soc. of Daughters of Amer. Col., v. 3, p. 212. MHS; DAR.
Md. families. Culver. Ms. Personal list.
Pedigree of Charles O'Donovan. Soc. Col. Wars Md. Culver. 1940. MHS; DAR.
Patriotic Md. Md. Soc. of S. A. R., 1930. MHS; DAR.
Swope family. Swope. MHS.

Zion Reformed Church, Hagerstown. Md. Geneal. Rec. Com., 1934-35. Mss. DAR.
***Shriver**, Frederick Co. Lineage Bk., Daughters of Amer. Col., v. 3, p. 212. MHS; DAR.
Shriver, Alfred J. Balto., its hist., its people. Hall. V. 3. MHS; DAR.
Shriver, Alfred Jenkins. Abr. Compend. Amer. Geneal. Virkus. V. 1, p. 424. DAR.
*Burke's landed gentry. 1939. MHS.
Md. Soc., War of 1812, v. 3, no. 260. Ms. MHS.
†Men of mark in Md. Johnson. V. 4. DAR; Enoch Pratt Lib.
Pedigree. Soc. Col. Wars Md. Culver. 1940. MHS; DAR.
Shriver, Edward Jenkins. Pedigree. Soc. Col. Wars Md. Culver. 1940. MHS; DAR.
***Shriver, H. T.** Geneal. and mem. encyc. of Md. Spencer. V. 2, pp. 661-67. MHS; DAR.
Shriver, J. Alexis. Abr. Compend. Amer. Geneal. Virkus. V. 1, p. 424. DAR.
Shriver, Robert Hickley. Pedigree. Soc. Col. Wars Md. Culver. 1940. MHS; DAR.
***Shriver, Schreiber.** Hist. of West. Md. Scharf. V. 1, p. 527 (burying ground, Carroll Co., 1771-1863); v. 2, pp. 864, 915, 917. MHS; DAR.
*Hist. of Shriver family and their connections, 1684-1888. Charts. S. S. Shriver. Pub. by members of family Guggenheimer, Weil Co., Balto., 1888. MHS.
Western Run Parish book. Allen. Bd. ms. MHS.
Shroyer. Kipp-Shryer-Stow families. Ms. MHS.
Shryack. St. Paul's Parish, Balto. V. 2. Mss. MHS.
Shryer. Kipp-Shryer-Stow families. Ms. MHS.
Shryler. *See* Kipp-Shryler-Shroyer-Stow.
Shryner. *See* Shriner.
Shryock. Balto., its hist., its people. Hall. V. 2. MHS; DAR.
*Geneal. and mem. encyc. of Md. Spencer. V. 2, pp. 555-60. MHS; DAR.
*Geneal. J. G. Shryock. Phila., 1930. Ms. MHS.
See Huidekoper. Abr. Compend. Amer. Geneal. Virkus. V. 4, p. 295. MHS.
Patriotic Md. Md. Soc. of S. A. R., 1930. MHS; DAR.
Pedigree. N. Y. Geneal. and Biog. Rec., Oct., 1930, v. 61, no. 4, p. 410.
Shryock, Schreyack. Family chart. J. G. Shryock. Phila., 1930. Blue pr., corrected. MHS.
Shryrock. Abr. Compend. Amer. Geneal. Virkus. V. 4, p. 625. MHS.
†**Shuck.** Hist. of Allegany Co. Thomas and Williams. V. 2. MHS; DAR.
Shuey. Bible rec. MHS.
*Frederick Co. families. Markell. Ms. Personal list.
Shuey, Carroll Co. Bible rec. Ms. MHS.
Shuey-Owings, Carroll Co. Bible rec., 1820-1904. Focke Geneal. Coll. Ms. MHS.
Shull. *See* Scholl.
Shultz. Pedigree of Alfred Jenkins Shriver. Soc. Col. Wars Md. Culver.1940.. MHS; DAR.
Mrs. E. W. Poe chart. MHS.
See Scholtz.
Shultz-Clemm-Poe. Hist. of Shriver family. Shriver. MHS.
†**Shuman.** Med. Annals Md. Cordell. 1903, p. 566. MHS.
Shuman, Shooman. Hagerstown tombstone inscriptions. Gruder. Natl. Geneal. Soc. Quart., 1919, v. 8, nos. 1, 2.
Shunk. Ancestry of Benjamin Harrison. Keith. Pp. 59-60. MHS; DAR.
Shupe. *See* Shorp.
Shupp. Spessard family. Spessard. MHS; DAR.
Shure. St. Paul's Parish, Balto. V. 2. Mss. MHS.
Shute. St. Paul's Parish, Balto. V. 2. Mss. MHS.
Shuttleworth. Somerset Co. Court Book. Tilghman. 1937. Ms. DAR.
Shuyter Family. Bohemia Manor. Mallory. MHS.
†**Shyrock.** Hist. of Allegany Co. Thomas and Williams. V. 2. MHS; DAR.
Sidener. Family data. O. C. Geneal. Rec. Com., v. 33, pp. 118-34. Typed, bd. DAR.
*Frederick Co. families. Markell. Ms. Personal list.
Siegelen. Wallis family chart. MHS.
*Wallis family of Md. chart. MHS.
Siess. Graves, 1749. Hist. of West. Md. Scharf. V. 1, p. 634. MHS; DAR.
Signaigo. Auld chart. MHS.
Sill, Howard. Pedigree charts, plates 1 and 2. Soc. Col. Wars, Md. Johnston. 1905, pp. 93-94. MHS.
Sill, James Mather. Pedigree. Soc. Col. Wars Md. Culver. 1940. MHS; DAR.
†**Silver.** Biog. cyc. of rep. men of Md. and D. C. P. 280. MHS; DAR.
Col. families of U. S. A. Mackenzie. V. 2. MHS; DAR.
Marriage rec., 1781-1892, Harford Co. Md. Geneal. Rec. Com., 1934-35, p. 108. DAR.
Trap Church burial rec., Harford Co. Md. Geneal. Rec. Com., 1934-35, p. 108. Mss. DAR.
Silver Family. Harford Co. Hist. Soc. Mss. Coll. JHU.
Silverson. Taney and allied families. Silverson. MHS; DAR.
Silverson-Tanney. Lineage Bks., Natl. Soc. of Daughters of Amer. Col., v. 4, p. 44. MHS; DAR.
†**Silvester.** Men of mark in Md. Johnson. V. 3. DAR; Enoch Pratt Lib.
Sim. Ances. rec. and portraits. Col. Dames of Amer., 1910, v. 2, p. 685. MHS; DAR.
Md. families. Culver. Ms. Personal list.
†Med. Annals Md. Cordell. 1903, pp. 566-67. MHS.
See Ramsburg. Abr. Compend. Amer. Geneal. Virkus. V. 1, p. 789. DAR.
Miss Kate Steele chart. MHS.
St. Paul's Parish, Balto. V. 1. Mss. MHS.
Simkin. St. Thomas' Parish, Balto. Co. Bd. ms. MHS. Also: Md. Geneal. Rec. Com., 1937, pp. 109-82. Mss. DAR.
Simm. *See* Simons.
Simmers, Summers. Trinity P. E. churchyard, Long Green. Typed ms. MHS; DAR.
***Simmes.** Semmes Geneal. Coll. Ms. MHS.

Simmonds. Bible rec. Upper Penins. East. Shore, pp. 192. MHS; DAR.
Rec. of births, marriages and deaths, 1700–1838, from register of St. James P. E. Parish, Anne Arundel Co. Md. Geneal. Rec. Com., 1939–40, pp. 168–72. Mss. DAR.
*Rec. Eight family Bibles. MHS.
See Buck-Simmonds-Trew.
Simmons. Amer. of gentle birth and their ancestors. Pittman. 1903, v. 1, p. 244. MHS; DAR.
Bible rec. Ms. File case, MHS.
Bond chart. MHS.
*Frederick Co. families. Markell. Ms. Personal list.
Haugh's Lutheran Church tombstone rec. Md. Geneal. Rec. Com., 1939–40. Mss. DAR.
†Med. Annals Md. Cordell. 1903, p. 567. MHS.
St. Paul's Parish, Balto. V. 3, 4. Mss. MHS.
See Drury-Simmons.
Simmons, William, Chestertown, Kent Co. Revolutionary pension rec. D. A. R. Mag. v. 72, no. 3, p. 79.
Simmons Line. Col. and Revolutionary lineages of Amer. 1939, v. 1, p. 486. MHS.
Simmons-Torrence-Dorsey. Old Md. families. Geneal. Mag. of Amer. Ancestry, 1916, v. 3, no. 7.
Simmons, Simons. St. Stephens Parish, Cecilton, Md. MHS; DAR.
Simms. Abr. Compend. Amer. Geneal. Virkus. V. 4, p. 27. MHS.
Semmes and allied families. Semmes. MHS.
See Semmes.
Simms, Harold H. Geneal. coll. (4 ms. bks. and 7 boxes of miscellaneous rec.). Ms. MHS.
***Simms, Semmes.** Lineage Bk., Daughters of Founders and Patriots, v. 15, p. 69. MHS.
†Simon. Men of mark in Md. Johnson. V. 3. DAR; Enoch Pratt Lib.
Simons. *See* Simmons.
Simons, Simm, Simmons. St. Paul's Parish, Balto. V. 2. Mss. MHS.
Simonson Family, Pa. and Balto. Md. Geneal. Bull., v. 2, p. 26. MHS; DAR.
†Simpers. Med. Annals Md. Cordell. 1903, p. 567. MHS.
Portrait and biog. rec. of Harford and Cecil Cos. 1897, pp. 158, 256. MHS; DAR.
White geneal. tree. MHS.
Simpson. Centenary of Catholicity in Ky. Webb. 1884. MHS.
Col. families of U. S. A. Mackenzie. V. 3. MHS; DAR.
St. Mary's Co. See Hein. Abr. Compend. Amer. Geneal. Virkus. V. 1, p. 333. DAR.
†Hist. of Frederick Co. Williams. MHS; DAR.
McCall-Tidwell families, McCall. P. 485. MHS; DAR.
St. Paul's Parish, Balto. V. 2, 4. Mss. MHS.
Semmes and allied families. Semmes. P. 145. MHS.
*Semmes Geneal. Coll. Ms. MHS.
Simpson, Edward Ridgely. Burke's landed gentry. 1939. MHS.
Simpson, Mrs. Edward (Camilla Morris Ridgely). Chart. Col. Dames, Chap. I. MHS.
(Maternal line.) Mrs. G. H. Williams, Jr., chart. MHS.

Sims. Semmes and allied families. Semmes. MHS.
***Sinclair.** Sinclairs of Eng. Ludgate Hill, London, Trubner & Co., 1887. MHS.
St. Stephens Parish, Cecilton, Md. MHS; DAR.
See St. Clair.
Sindall. St. Paul's Parish, Balto. V. 2. Mss. MHS.
Sines Family. Mountain Democrat, Garrett Co., Sept. 20, 1934. Newsp. clipp. MHS; DAR.
Singleton. Abr. Compend. Amer. Geneal. Virkus. V. 1, p. 402. DAR.
Griffith geneal. Griffith. MHS; DAR.
Hist. graves of Md. and D. C. Ridgely. MHS.
St. Paul's Parish, Balto. V. 3. Mss. MHS.
Singleton, Jacob. Copy of will, 1834. Md. Geneal. Rec. Com., 1933–34. Mss. DAR.
Sink. St. Paul's Parish, Balto. V. 2. Mss. MHS.
Sinn. Frederick Co. tombstone inscriptions. Gruder. Natl. Geneal. Soc. Quart., 1919, v. 8, nos. 1, 2.
†Sinnott. Med. Annals Md. Cordell. 1903, p. 567. MHS.
Sinton. Balto., its hist., its people. Hall. V. 2. MHS; DAR.
Sioussat. Abr. Compend. Amer. Geneal. Virkus. V. 1, p. 828. DAR.
Sioussat, St. George Leakin. Pedigree. Soc. Col. Wars Md. Culver. 1940. MHS; DAR.
Md. Soc., War of 1812, no. 265. Ms. MHS.
Sipes. *See* Fite, Sipes and Stinchcomb.
Sipes, Joshua. Bible rec., 1756. Focke Geneal. Coll. Ms. MHS.
Sirman. *See* Sherman.
†Sisk. Men of mark in Md. Johnson. V. 3. DAR; Enoch Pratt Lib.
†Sisson. Hist. of Balto. City and Co. Scharf. P. 421. MHS.
St. Paul's Parish, Balto. V. 2, 4. Mss. MHS.
Sitze. *See* Seitz.
***Skelly.** Wicomico Co. families. Tilghman. Ms., p. 99. DAR.
Skelton. Capt. Roger Jones of London and Va. Browning.
*Skeltons of Paxton, Powhatan Co., Va. Charts. P. H. Baskerville. Richmond, Va., Old Dominion Press, 1922. MHS.
Skidmor. Bond chart. MHS.
Skinner. Abr. Compend. Amer. Geneal. Virkus. V. 6, p. 732. DAR.
Abs. of will, 1814. D. A. R. Mag., June, 1927, v. 61, no. 6, p. 470.
Andrew Skinner book, 1801. In envelope under Skinner, with personal Mss. Coll. Notes (few) on Skinner-Tilghman families. MHS.
*Arms. Hist. of Dorchester Co. Jones. 1925, pp. 447–55. MHS; DAR.
Balto., its hist., its people. Hall. V. 3. MHS; DAR.
Bible rec. Ms. MHS.
Mrs. Charles Carter chart. MHS.
Col. families of U. S. A. Mackenzie. V. 6, pp. 418–24. MHS; DAR.
Lambdin chart. MHS.
*Lineage Bk., Daughters of Amer. Col., v. 1, p. 32. MHS; DAR.
*Lineage Bk., Daughters of Founders and Patriots, v. 21, p. 133. MHS.
†Med. Annals Md. Cordell. 1903, p. 568. MHS.

†Men of mark in Md. Johnson. V. 1. DAR; Enoch Pratt Lib.
Natl. Geneal. Soc. Quart., v. 7, no. 3, pp. 45–48.
Pedigree of Granville Bowdle Hopkins. Soc. Col. Wars Md. Culver. 1940. MHS; DAR.
Pedigree of Rev. James Mitchell Magruder. Soc. Col. Wars Md. Culver. 1940. MHS; DAR.
St. Paul's Parish, Balto. V. 23. Mss. MHS.
*Skinner, sporting family of South. Five generations, starting with John Stuart Skinner, 1788, and ending with his great-great-grandson, 1936. Harry Worcester Smith and Frederick G. Skinner. Albany, N. Y., J. B. Lyon Co., 1936. Enoch Pratt Lib.
*The Sun, Balto., Oct. 13, 27 (letter), Nov. 24 1907.
Skinner, James, Calvert Co. Will dated Sept. 19, March 11, 13, 1807. D. A. R. Mag., v. 61, no. 6, p. 470.
Skinner, Col. John Stewart. Patriotic Marylander, v. 1, no. 4, p. 49. MHS; DAR.
†Skinner, John Stuart. Biog. sketch. Ben Perley Poore. Repr. from The Plough, The Loom and The Anvil, 1854, John L. O'Conner. Enoch Pratt Lib.
Skinner, Maurice Edward. Pedigree. Soc. Col. Wars Md. Culver. 1940. MHS; DAR.
Skinner, William. Bible rec. Ms. MHS.
Skinner, Wm. Howser. Pedigree. Soc. Col. Wars Md. Culver. 1940. MHS; DAR.
Skinner, Zachariah. Bible rec. Ms. MHS.
Skinner Family. Natl. Geneal. Soc. Quart., v. 24, p. 104.
Skipwith. Early Quaker rec., Anne Arundel and Calvert Cos., 1665–1889. Pub. Geneal. Soc. Pa., v. 3, no. 3, pp. 197–200.
Pedigree of Maurice Edward Skinner. Soc. Col. Wars Md. Culver. 1940. MHS; DAR.
Ruffin and other geneal. Pr. chart. Henry.
See Skipworth. Cary Geneal. Coll. Ms. MHS.
Thomas-Chew-Lawrence. Thomas. MHS.
Skipwith, Va. Mrs. J. Hall Pleasants, Jr., chart. MHS.
Skipwith, Skipworth. Col. families of U. S. A. Mackenzie. V. 3. MHS; DAR.
Skipworth. Skipwith, in Cary Geneal. Coll. Ms. MHS.
See Skipwith.
Skirven. Bible rec., Kent Co., 1772–1866. Md. Geneal. Rec. Com., 1937–38, pp. 125–26. Mss. DAR.
†Chesapeake Bay Country. Earle. P. 316. MHS.
Patriotic Md. Md. Soc. of S. A. R., 1930. MHS; DAR.
St. Paul's churchyard, Kent Co. Md. O. R. Soc. Bull., no. 2, pp. 54–65. MHS.
Skull. *See* Scull.
†Skyles. Hist. of Allegany Co. Thomas and Williams. V. 2. MHS; DAR.
Slack, Mrs. Henry Richmond, Jr. Beirne chart. MHS.
(Elizabeth Blanchard Randall.) Chart. Col. Dames, Chap. I. MHS.
Slacombe. *See* Slaycomb.
Slacum. Trinity Church cemetery, Dorchester Co. Md. O. R. Soc. Bull., no. 3, pp. 42–52.
Slade. Arnold chart. MHS.
Blackwell chart. MHS.
Md. Families. Ms. Personal list.
Slagel. Md. tombstone rec. Md. Geneal. Rec. Com., 1937, Parran, p. 12. Mss. DAR.
St. Joseph's R. C. churchyard. Md. O. R. Soc. Bull., no. 3, p. 64.
Slagle. Col. families of U. S. A. Mackenzie. V. 4. MHS; DAR.
Matthews-Price chart. MHS.
Price family and other Gunpowder Friends. Death notices; photos. of newsp. clipp. MHS.
Florence Eyster Weaver chart. MHS.
Slagle, Schlegel, Schlegle. Monnet family geneal. Monette. Pp. 1126–30. MHS.
Slater. St. Paul's Parish, Balto. V. 1, 2. Mss. MHS.
Slater, Sarah Contee. Bible rec. Md. Geneal. Rec. Com., 1938–39, p. 230. Mss. DAR.
†Slaughter. Encyc. of Amer. biog. Amer. Hist. Soc., new series, v. 1, p. 63. MHS; DAR.
St. Paul's Parish, Balto. V. 2. Mss. MHS.
***Slaughter,** Va. The Sun, Balto., Feb. 11, 18, March 25, 1906.
***Slaycomb, Slacombe.** Notes. Hist. of Dorchester Co. Jones. 1902, p. 346. 1925, pp. 382–96. MHS.
Slayter. Naturalizations in Md., 1666–1765; Laws. Bacon. MHS.
Slecombe. Naturalizations in Md., 1666–1765; Laws. Bacon. MHS.
Sleeper. St. Paul's Parish, Balto. V. 2. Mss. MHS.
***Slemmons.** Wicomico Co. families. Tilghman. Ms., pp. 56, 97, 99, 100–01, 104–05. DAR.
Slemmons, Slemons. Data regarding descendants of Rev. John Slemmons. Ms. MHS.
Slemons. Ferguson Papers. Mss. MHS.
Notes. Ferguson papers. Ms. MHS.
Wicomico Co. families. Bible rec. Ms. DAR.
See Slemmons.
†Slemons, Somerset Co. Med. Annals. Md. Cordell. 1903, p. 568. MHS.
Slemons, James Wm. Pedigree. Soc. Col. Wars Md. Culver. 1940. MHS; DAR.
Slemons Family (British). Data; Maine, Pa., and Wicomico and Carroll Cos., Md. Repr. from Geneal. Quart., Sept., 1932. London, Fudge & Co., Ltd., pamph. MHS.
*Data. J. A. Slemons. (Wicomico Co. families.) Leaflet. MHS.
Sley. Monnet family geneal. Monette. MHS.
†Slicer, Henry. Balto., hist. and biog. Richardson and Bennett. 1871, p. 457. MHS; DAR.
†Slifer. Med. Annals Md. Cordell. 1903, p. 568. MHS.
†Slingluff. Bench and bar of Md. Sams and Riley. 1901, v. 2, p. 575. Lib. Cong.; MHS; Peabody Lib.
Englar family. Barnes. MHS; DAR.
F. S. Hambleton pedigree chart. Soc. Col. Wars, Md. Johnston. 1905, p. 33. MHS.
†Hist. of Balto. City and Co. Scharf. P. 852. MHS.
†Hist. of West. Md. Scharf. V. 2, pp. 904–05. MHS; DAR.
Mrs. James McHenry chart. MHS.
Pedigree of T. Edward Hambleton. Soc. Col. Wars Md. Culver. 1940. MHS; DAR.
Slingluff Family. Pa.-German, Lebanon, Pa., 1906, v. 7, pp. 341–44.
Sloan. Jacobs chart. MHS.
Neill chart. MHS.
Mrs. J. Pleasants chart. MHS.
See Sloane.

Sloan, C. W. Md. Soc., War of 1812, v. 3, no. 268. Ms. MHS.
Sloan, Francis Burns. Pedigree. (Daniel Cushing, Mass., 9 generations.) Soc. Col. Wars Md. Culver. 1940. MHS; DAR.
Sloan, Francis Eugene. Pedigree. Soc. Col. Wars Md. Culver. 1940. MHS; DAR.
Sloan, George Frederick. Pedigree. Soc. Col. Wars Md. Culver. 1940. MHS; DAR.
†**Sloan, Dr. Martin Francis.** Beloved physician; Native of Texas; superintendent of Eudowood. Anne Martin. Balto., St. Mary's Industrial School Press, 1935. Enoch Pratt Lib.
Sloan, Sloane. Col. families of U. S. A. Mackenzie. V. 7. MHS; DAR.
†Nicholas Hasselback, printer. McCreary. MHS.
†**Sloane.** Hist. of Allegany Co. Thomas and Williams. V. 1. MHS; DAR.
See Sloan.
Sloane, Sloan. Portrait and biog. rec. of Sixth Cong. Dist. of Md. 1898, pp. 140, 156. MHS; DAR.
***Slomaker.** Wilson Mss. Coll., no. 8, A. MHS.
Slothower, Henry. Md. Soc., War of 1812, v. 4, no 323. Ms. MHS.
Sluyter. Cotton chart. MHS.
Naturalizations in Md., 1666-1765; Laws. Bacon. MHS.
St. Stephens Parish, Cecilton, Md. MHS; DAR.
Sly. *See* Slye.
Slye. "Bushwood," St. Mary's Co. Ances. Rec. and Portraits, Col. Dames of Amer.1910, v. 2, p. 547. MHS; DAR.
Grandma Stories. Sister Mary Xavier Queen. MHS.
Harvey-Slye Bible rec. Ms. MHS.
Harvey-Slye family data. Ms. MHS.
Macsherry chart. MHS.
Pedigree of Duncan Keener Brent. Soc. Col. Wars Md. Culver. 1940. MHS; DAR.
Will of Capt. Robert Slye of Md., 1670; with notes in Eng. New Eng., Hist. Reg., 1896, v. 50, pp. 354-56.
Slye, St. Mary's Co. E. A. and F. De SalesJenkins pedigree chart. Soc. Col. Wars, Md. Johnston. 1905, pp. 46, 154. MHS.
Slye, Sly. Monnet family geneal. Monette. P. 370. MHS.
Small. Mt. Olivet Cemetery, Frederick. Md. Geneal. Rec. Com., 1934-35, p. 111. Mss. DAR.
St. Paul's Parish, Balto. V. 3, 4. Mss. MHS.
Small, Jacob. Coll. of Amer. epitaphs and inscriptions. Alden. 1814, v. 5, p. 128. MHS.
Small Line. Col. and Revolutionary lineages in Amer. 1939, v. 2, pp. 104-07. MHS.
***Small, Schmahl.** Geneal. rec. of George Small, Philip Albright, Johann Daniel Dunckle, William Geddes Latimer, Thomas Bartow, John Reid, Daniel Benezet, Jean Crommelin, Joel Richardson. Sam'l Small, Jr., York, Pa. Pr. for priv. distribution, J. B. Lippincott Co., Phila., 1905. MHS.
Smallwood. Amer. ancestry of Gen. Wm. Smallwood, Revolutionary hero. Assembled by H. J. Berkley. Md. Geneal. Rec. .Com., 1934-35, pp. 249-53. Mss. DAR.
‡Ceremonies at unveiling of monument over remains of Maj. Gen. William Smallwood. By Md. Soc. S. A. R., July 4, 1898. (William Smallwood born Kent Co., 1732; son of Bayne and Priscilla (Heabred) Smallwood; died Mattawoman, Charles Co., Feb. 14, 1792.) Enoch Pratt Lib.
Chancery abs. of Gen. Smallwood, 1735-99. Md. Geneal. Rec. Com., 1932-33. Mss. DAR.
Col. Grayson and Gen. Smallwood. Tyler's Quart. Mag., v. 8, pp. 119-26.
Hist. graves of Md. and D. C. Ridgely. MHS.
Md. families. Culver. Ms. Personal list.
Pedigree of John Dudley Long. Soc. Col. Wars Md. Culver. 1940. MHS; DAR.
St. Paul's Parish, Balto. V. 2, 4. Mss. MHS.
†**Smallwood, Sam'l Nicholls,** Charles Co. Rec. Columbia Hist. Soc., v. 28, pp. 23-61.
†**Smallwood, William.** Chronicles of Balto. Scharf. 1874, p. 265. MHS; DAR.
†(1732-92). M. H. Mag., v. 12, p. 244.
Smallwood, Gen. William. Chancery rec., showing next of kin. Md. Geneal. Rec. Com., 1938-39, pp. 44-48. Mss. DAR.
†M. H. Mag., 1924, v. 19, pp. 304-06.
†**Smallwood, Gov. William.** Founders of Anne Arundel and Howard Cos. Warfield. P. 237. MHS; DAR.
†Governors of Md. Buchholz. P. 20. MHS.
Smallwood Family. Md. Geneal. Bull., v. 4, p. 1. MHS; DAR.
*Smallwood family of Charles Co. A. L. Keith. M. H. Mag., 1927, v. 22, p. 139.
Smallwood-Ball. Family notes. Ms. MHS.
Smart. Geneal. of Henrietta Chauncy Wilson. Upshur. Bk. of photos. MHS.
†Med. Annals Md. Cordell. 1903, p. 568. MHS.
St. Stephens Parish, Cecilton, Md. MHS; DAR.
Smart, Va. Rec. Harrison-Waples and allied families. Harrison. MHS.
***Smedley.** Geneal. of descendants of George and Sarah Smedley, settlers in Chester Co., Pa. Coat of arms. G. Cope. Lancaster, Pa., Wickersham Printing Co., 1901. MHS; DAR.
Sharpless family geneal. Cope. P. 910. MHS; DAR.
Smith. All Hallow's P. E. churchyard, Snow Hill, Worcester Co. Hudson. Bd. ms. MHS; DAR. Also: Md. Geneal. Rec. Com., 1935-36, p. 24. Mss. DAR.
Ames Geneal. Coll. Ms. MHS.
Ances. rec. and portraits. Col. Dames of Amer., 1910, v. 1, pp. 143, 288; v. 2, pp. 617-22, 672, 691. MHS; DAR.
Aylett chart. Cary Geneal. Coll. Ms. MHS.
Barroll chart. MHS.
†Bench and bar of Md. Sams and Riley. 1901, v. 1, pp. 89, 213; v. 2, p. 480. Lib. Cong.; MHS; Peabody Lib.
Bible rec. of Dorchester and Somerset Cos. and Del. P. 78. DAR.
Bible rec., Kent Co., 1809-72. Md. Geneal. Rec. Com., 1932-33, pp. 316-17. Mss. DAR.
See Brice family of Md. Ms. File case, DAR.
Capt. John Smith, Frederick Co., of Revolution, and some of his ancestors. Francis F. Smith. Amer. Catholic Hist. Soc. of Phila. Rec., 1898, v. 9.
Clark chart. MHS.
Col. families of Amer. Lawrence. V. 16, p. 82. MHS.
Dallam family. Dallam. 1929, pp. 25-26. MHS.

Dorsey and allied families. Ms. MHS.
*formerly **Fairfax.** Burke's landed gentry. 1939. MHS.
*Frederick Co. families. Markell. Ms. Personal list.
Fox-Ellicott-Evans families. Evans. MHS; DAR.
Geneal. and mem. encyc. of Md. Spencer. V. 1, pp. 207, 283. MHS; DAR.
Geneal. of family of Gideon Gilpin. MHS.
Hackett family tree. Layton. MHS.
Hagerstown tombstone inscriptions. Gruder. Natl. Geneal. Soc. Quart., 1919, v. 8, nos. 1, 2.
*Hist. of Dorchester Co. Jones. 1925, p. 455. MHS; DAR.
Hist. graves of Md. and D. C. Ridgely. MHS.
†Hist. of Allegany Co. Thomas and Williams. V. 2. MHS.
†(320 ref). Hist. of Frederick Co., Williams. MHS; DAR.
Jenkins-Courtney chart. MHS.
*Lane-Smith families. Photos. MHS.
Lehr chart. MHS.
Lineage Bks., Natl. Soc. of Daughters of Amer. Col., v. 2, p. 94 (Baltimore Co.); v. 3, p. 25 (Calvert Co.). MHS; DAR.
Lloyd family hist. of Wales, Pa., and Md. DAR.
Md. families. Culver. Ms. Personal list.
Md. gleanings in Eng. Wills. M. H. Mag., 1907, v. 2, no. 3.
†Med. Annals Md. Cordell. 1903, pp. 569-75, 630, 818-35. MHS.
†Men of mark in Md. Johnson. V. 1; v. 3; v. 4. DAR; Enoch Pratt Lib.
Natl. Geneal. Soc. Quart., 1914, v. 3.
Old Md. families. Bromwell. MHS; DAR.
Patriotic Md. Md. Soc. of S. A. R., 1930. MHS; DAR.
Pedigree of Edwin Austin Baughman. Soc. Col. Wars Md. Culver. 1940. MHS; DAR.
Pedigree of Walter Ireland Dawkins. Soc. Col. Wars. Md. Culver. 1940. MHS; DAR.
Pedigree of W. Wallace McKaig. Soc. Col. Wars Md. Culver. 1940. MHS; DAR.
Pedigree of Franklin Buchanan Owen. Soc. Col. Wars Md. Culver. 1940. MHS; DAR.
Pedigree of John Philemon Paca. Soc. Col. Wars Md. Culver. 1940. MHS; DAR.
Pedigree of Pleasants Pennington. Soc. Col. Wars Md. Culver. 1940. MHS; DAR.
Pedigree of Mason Locke Weems Williams. Soc. Col. Wars Md. Culver. 1940. MHS; DAR.
Mrs. N. S. Pendleton, Jr., chart. MHS.
Mrs. Pennington chart. MHS.
*Pennington Papers. Ms. MHS.
Private burial ground, 1760, Anne Arundel Co. Md. Geneal. Bull., v. 4, p. 7. MHS; DAR. Also Ms., MHS.
Revolutionary purveyor, Wm. Smith (1728-1814), Merchant of Balto. M. H. Mag., 1912, v. 7, pp. 304-06.
St. Stephens Parish, Cecilton, Md. MHS; DAR.
Samuel Carpenter of Phila. Carpenter. Pp. 112, 179. MHS.
Sherburne chart. MHS.
*Smith, family, Calvert Co. The Times, Jan., 1886. MHS.
*Smith family, Pa. and N. Y. S. G. Highland. Repr. from Clarksburg exponent, Clarksburg, W. Va., Saturday morning, Dec. 25, 1926. MHS.
*Smith family, Pa.; Johann Frederich Schmidt, 1746-1812. J. Bennett Nolan. DAR.
Smith graveyard, Anne Arundel Co. Ms. MHS.
*Smith, (Va.)-Gatch-Bailey. Lineage Bk., Daughters of Amer. Col., v. 2, pp. 150, 233. MHS; DAR.
Somerset Co. Court Book. Tilghman. 1937. Ms. DAR.
Miss Margaret M. Steele chart. MHS.
Sydney-Smith and Clagett-Price families. Price. MHS; DAR.
*The Sun, Balto., Feb. 25, March 4, 11, 1906 (Va.); Jan. 27, Feb. 3 (Richard) Oct. 27 (Elizabeth) 1907 (Calvert Co. Md.)
U. B. cemetery, Sabillasville. Young. Natl. Geneal. Soc. Quart., Sept., 1938, v. 26, no. 3, p. 61 (to be contd.).
Wicomico Co. families. Tilghman. Ms., pp. 57-60, 62, 96-97, 110, 114, 125. DAR.
Wills, births and deaths rec. of John Samuel and Margaret Spear Smith families. Md. Geneal. Rec. Com., 1934-35, pp. 134-44. Mss. DAR.
Sir George Yeardley. Upshur. Pp. 29-32, 35. MHS.
See Abell-Smith-Winsatt.
See Briscoe-Smith.
See Brown-Smith.
See Harris-Maddox-Williams-Smith-Powell-Travers.
See Mitchell-Smith-Fowke.
See Nicholls-Smith.
See Robinson-Passwater-Smith-Wiatt.
See Smythe.
See Watts-Smith-Willis.
Smith, Accomac Co., Va. Howland chart. MHS.
†**Smith,** Allegany Co. Hist. of West. Md. Scharf. V. 2, pp. 1403-04. MHS; DAR.
Smith, Balto. Gilpin chart. MHS.
†Hist. and biog. Richardson and Bennett. 1871, pp. 463-71. MHS; DAR.
Smith, Frederick Co. Bible rec. D. C. Geneal. Rec. Com., v. 36, pp. 133-37. Typed, bd. DAR.
Smith, Calvert Co. Abr. Compend. Amer. Geneal. Virkus. V. 6, p. 136. DAR.
Mrs. R. Barton, Jr., charts. MHS.
Beirne chart. MHS.
B. B. Browne pedigree chart. Soc. Col. Wars, Md. Johnston. 1905, pp. 8, 154. MHS.
Mrs. Charles Carter chart. MHS.
Bowie-Claggett chart. MHS.
C. Johnston pedigree chart, plate 2. Soc. Col. Wars, Md. Johnston. 1905, p. 54. MHS.
Semmes and allied families. Semmes. MHS.
Smith, Cecil Co. Portrait and biog. rec. of Harford and Celil Cos. 1897, pp. 161, 191, 295, 308, 393, 540, 571. MHS; DAR.
Smith, Charles Co. Southerland-Latham and allied families. Voorhees. P. 76. Bd. ms. MHS.
Smith, Kent Co. Cary Geneal. Coll. Ms. MHS.
Mrs. A. G. Ober chart. MHS.
Smith, Northampton Co., Va. Cary Geneal. Coll. Ms. MHS.
Smith, Queen Anne Co. Bible rec. Upper Penins. East. Shore, p. 60-67. MHS; DAR.
Smith, A. Crawford. Greenway Mss. Geneal. Coll. Binder's title, Taylor, no. 2. MHS.
Smith, Asa H. Md. Soc., War of 1812, v. 1, no. 34. Ms. MHS.

Smith, Bayard. Cary Geneal. Coll. Ms. MHS.
Smith, Francis Hopkinson (born in Balto., 1838). Md. authors. Steiner. Ms. list, Md. Room, Enoch Pratt Lib.
Smith, Francis Scott Key. Md. Soc., War of 1812, v. 4, no. 330. Ms. MHS.
Smith, G. Long. Md. Soc., War of 1812, v. 3, no. 251. Ms. MHS.
Smith, Hannah, wife of Wm. Smith. (Died June 21, 1851, in 72nd yr., Chestertown.) Md. Geneal. Rec. Com., 1933-34, p. 233. Mss. DAR.
***Smith, Henry Lee.** Burke's landed gentry. 1939. MHS.
Smith, Henry Lee, Jr. Pedigree. Soc. Col. Wars Md. Culver. 1940. MHS; DAR.
Smith, Henry Lee, Sr. Pedigree. Soc. Col. Wars Md. Culver. 1940. MHS; DAR.
Smith, James, Kent Co. W. A. and S. W. Merritt pedigree charts. Soc. Col. Wars Md. Johnston. 1905, pp. 68, 154. MHS.
Smith, John. Westminster churchyard. Patriotic Marylander, v. 2, no. 4, pp. 54-60. MHS; DAR.
Smith, John, Balto. W. M. Cary pedigree chart. Soc. Col. Wars Md. Johnston. 1905, pp. 12, 154. MHS.
Smith, John, Warwick. Cary Geneal. Coll. Ms. MHS.
†Smith, Capt. John. Hist. of Md. Scharf. V. 2, p. 420. MHS.
†Smith, Gen. John Spear. Gen. John Spear Smith (1786-1866), first president of Md. Hist. Soc. B. C. Steiner. M. H. Mag., 1924, v. 19, pp. 213-20.
†Smith, John Walter. Governors of Md. Buchholz. P. 261. MHS.
†Founders of Anne Arundel and Howard Cos. Warfield. P. 298. MHS; DAR.
Makemie Memorial Pres. churchyard, Snow Hill, Worcester Co. Hudson. Bd. ms. MHS; DAR. Also: Md. Geneal. Rec. Com., Mrs. Lines. Mss. DAR.
Smith, Joseph. Westminster churchyard. Patriotic Marylander, v. 2, no. 4, pp. 54-60. MHS; DAR.
Smith, Josephine Fairfax (Mrs. Tunstall). Abr. Compend. Amer. Geneal. Virkus. V. 6, p. 744. DAR.
Smith, Miss Louise Tunstall. Mrs. Lee Barroll chart. MHS.
Chart, with appendix. Culver. Col. Dames, Chap. I. MHS.
Smith, Mark Alexander Herbert. Pedigree. Soc. Col. Wars Md. Culver. 1940. MHS; DAR. (See pedigree of Henry Lee Smith.)
Smith, Mary Ellet. *See* Thomas-Smith.
Smith, Nathan Ryno. Mrs. J. Whitridge Williams chart 2. MHS.
Smith, Maj. Nathaniel. Westminster churchyard. Patriotic Marylander, v. 2, no. 4, pp. 54-60. MHS; DAR.
Smith, R. Taylor. Md. Soc., War of 1812, v. 1, no. 7. Ms. MHS.
Smith, Richard (came to Md., 1649). M. L. W. Williams pedigree chart. Soc. Col. Wars, Md. Johnston. 1905, pp. 126, 154. MHS.
Pedigree of Raphael Semmes. Soc. Col. Wars Md. Culver. 1940. MHS; DAR.
Pedigree of Dalrymple Smith. Soc. Col. Wars Md. Culver. 1940. MHS; DAR.
Pedigree of James Donnell Tilghman. Soc. Col. Wars Md. Culver. 1940. MHS; DAR.
†Smith, Robert. Hist. of Md. Scharf. V. 2, p. 561. MHS.
(1758-1842). Revolutionary war heroes. Cole. Bklet. Enoch Pratt Lib.
†(Second Secretary of Navy.) M. H. Mag., 1919, v. 14, pp. 385.
Westminster churchyard. Patriotic Marylander, v. 2, no. 4, pp. 54-60. MHS; DAR.
Smith, Robert Lee. Pedigree. Soc. Col. Wars Md. Culver. 1940. MHS; DAR.
Smith, Robert White. Pedigree. (Marshall and Randolph rec. of Va.) Soc. Col. Wars Md. Culver. 1940. MHS; DAR.
Smith, Samuel. Mrs. G. H. Williams, Jr., chart. MHS.
†Smith, Maj. Gen. Sam'l. Biog. cyc. of rep. men of Md. and D. C. P. 237. MHS; DAR.
†Chronicles of Balto. Scharf. 1874, p. 497. MHS; DAR.
†Hist. of Md. Scharf. V. 3, pp. 106-07. MHS.
(1752-1839.) Revolutionary war heroes. Cole. Bklet. Enoch Pratt Lib.
Torrence and allied families. Torrence. P. 490. MHS; DAR.
Westminster churchyard. Patriotic Marylander, v. 2, no. 4, pp. 54-60. MHS; DAR.
Smith, Thomas, Mass. Cary Geneal. Coll. Ms. MHS.
Smith, Thomas Marsh. Pedigree charts, plates 1 and 2. Soc. Col. Wars, Md. Johnston. 1905, pp. 95-96. MHS.
Smith, Thomas Marshall. Pedigree. (Marshall and Randolph rec. of Va.) Soc. Col. Wars Md. Culver. 1940. MHS; DAR.
Smith, Mrs. Tunstull. Mrs. Lee Barroll chart. MHS.
(Josephine Fairfax.) Chart, with appendix. Col. Dames, Chap. I. MHS.
Smith, Mrs. Walter Prescott. Barton charts. MHS.
(Charlotte Williams.) Chart. Col. Dames, Chap. I. MHS.
Morison chart. MHS.
Smith, William (1728-1814). Ames Geneal. Coll. Ms. MHS.
†Hist. of Md. Scharf. V. 2, p. 343. MHS.
(1728-1814.) Revolutionary war heroes. Cole. Bklet. Enoch Pratt Lib.
Westminster churchyard. Patriotic Marylander, v. 2, no. 4, pp. 54-60. MHS; DAR.
Smith Family. Hist. Washington Co. Williams. 1906. V. 2, p. 1302. MHS; DAR.
Md. Geneal. Rec. Com., 1938-39, p. 87. Mss. DAR.
M. H. Mag., 1923, v. 18, p. 186.
Note. Old Somerset. Torrence. MHS; DAR.
Smith Family, Calvert Co. Dandridge family of Va. William and Mary Quart., 1st series, v. 5, pp. 30, 81.
Lane-Smith families, Calvert Co. Photos. MHS.
C. Johnston. M. H. Mag., 1908, v. 3, pp. 66-78, 384-85; 1909, v. 4, pp. 65-69.
The Times, Sunday, Jan. 17, 1886. Newsp. clipp. Scrapbook, no. 7, p. 4. MHS.
Smith Family, Fork Dist., Dorchester Co. Bible rec. of Dorchester and Somerset Cos. and Del. Pp. 80-82. DAR.

Smith Family, Kent Co. Bible rec. Md. Geneal. Rec. Com., 1932–33, v. 5. DAR.
Smith Line, mostly Va. Mrs. Lee Barroll chart. MHS.
(1649–1848). W. S. G. Williams pedigree chart. Soc. Col. Wars Md. Johnston. 1905, p. 128. MHS.
Smith-Addison. Ances. rec. and portraits. Col. Dames of Amer., 1910, p. 687. MHS; DAR.
Smith-Crouth. Wicomico Co. families. Bible Ms. DAR.
***Smith-Davison Lineage,** Va. The Sun, Balto., March 4, 1906.
Smith (Samuel) - McKim - Spear - Brown. Chart, photos., 2 sheets. Cary Geneal. Coll. Ms. MHS.
Smith, Schmidt. Lineage Bks., Natl. Soc. of Daughters of Amer. Col., v. 2, p. 224. MHS; DAR.
Smith, Smithe, Smythe. (249 rec.) St. Paul's Parish, Balto. V. 1, 2, 3, 4. Mss. MHS.
Smithe. *See* Smith.
Smithers. Miss Cassandra Lee chart. MHS.
Md. families. Culver. Ms. Personal list.
Naturalizations in Md., 1666–1765; Laws. Bacon. MHS.
Smithson. Hist. of Harford. Co. Preston. MHS; DAR.
Md. families. Culver. Ms. Personal list.
Rumsey-Smithson families, Harford Co., Bible rec. from 1682. Md. Geneal. Rec. Com., 1932–33, v. 5, pp. 63–142. DAR.
*Rumsey-Smithson family rec. bk. Unpub. rec., Harford Co. Copied by Iola M. E. Smithson, 1931. Md. Geneal. Rec. Com., 1932, pp. 63–158. DAR.
***Smithson,** Harford Co. (1723–1930). (With Amoss, Barton, Beale, Galloway, Glenn, McComas, Richardson, Stansbury, Taylor and Wright families.) Md. Geneal. Rec. Com., 1932–33, pp. 148–62. Mss. DAR.
See Paca-Smithson-Forwood.
Smithson, Thomas, Balto. Co. Will probated March 8, 1732. D. A. R. Mag., v. 65, no. 8, p. 506.
Smithson, William, Harford Co. Will, 1805. Md. Geneal. Rec. Com., 1933–34, pp. 125–27. Mss. DAR.
Smithson Line. Geneal. tables of descendants of John Hamilton. MHS.
***Smithson-Rumsey.** Rec. bk. Unpub. rec., Harford Co. Typed, bd. Ms., MHS.
Smocke. Md. gleanings in Eng. Wills. M. H. Mag., 1907, v. 2, no. 4.
Smoot. Abr. Compend. Amer. Geneal. Virkus. V. 6, p. 357. DAR.
Bible rec. D. A. R. Mag., Oct., 1932, v. 66, no. 10, pp. 672–74.
*Lineage Bk., Daughters of Amer. Col., v. 2, p. 224. MHS; DAR.
Pedigree of James Davidson Iglehart. Soc. Col. Wars Md. Culver. 1940. MHS; DAR.
Trinity P. E. churchyard, St. Mary's City. Md. O. R. Soc. Bull., no. 3, p. 59.
Wm. Turpin, Dorchester Co., Bible rec. D. A. R. Mag., v. 66, no. 10, p. 672.
Wills; extracts from La Plata, Charles Co. Natl. Geneal. Soc. Quart., April and July, 1919, v. 8.
See Beauchamp - Smoot - Turpin - White - Willis - Wilson.
See Douglas-Smoot.
See Ford-Smoot.
See Smoote.
†**Smoot, Joseph.** M. H. Mag., v. 2, p. 245.
Smoot (or Smoote)-Briscoe. Chart, photos., complete in 2 pieces. Cary Geneal. Coll. Ms. MHS.
Smoote. *See* Smoot.
Smoote, Smoot. Family data. Mrs. W. H. Smoot. Ms. MHS.
Smoote, Smott. Utah Geneal. and Hist. Mag., v. 24, p. 104. MHS.
***Smoots.** Smoots, Md. and Va. H. W. Newman. Wash., D. C., 1936, ltd. ed. DAR; SAR.
Smott. Lineage Bks., Natl. Soc. of Daughters of Amer. Col., v. 2, p. 224. MHS; DAR.
See Smoote.
†**Smouse.** Hist. of Allegany Co. Thomas and Williams. V. 2. MHS; DAR.
Smull. Faith Pres. Church (Glendy Graveyard.) Mss. MHS.
*John Augustus Smull, Pa. Lane E. Hart, State Printer, Harrisburg, Pa., 1881. MHS.
Smull, David Burke. Bible rec. MHS.
Smull, Jacob and David Burke. Bible rec. Focke Geneal. Coll. Ms. MHS.
***Smullin.** Wicomico Co. families. Tilghman. Ms., p. 112. DAR.
Smyser. Balto., its hist., its people. Hall. V. 2. MHS; DAR.
*Hist. of Smyser family in Amer., Sept., 1731–Sept., 1931. A. L. L. Xanders. York, Pa., York Printing Co., 1931. DAR.
Hist. sketch of P. F. Eichelberger. Eichelberger.
Florence Eyster Weaver chart. MHS.
***Smysers,** York Co., Pa. Notes and queries, Egle, v. 1, pp. 154–55.
Smyth, Del. Abr. Compend. Amer. Geneal. Virkus. V. 6, pp. 528–29. DAR.
See Smythe.
Smythe. B. B. Browne pedigree chart. Soc. Col. Wars, Md. Johnston. 1905, pp. 8, 154. MHS.
Hamilton family of Charles Co. Kelly. MHS.
†Med. Annals Md. Cordell. 1903, p. 575. MHS.
P. Neff pedigree chart. Soc. Col. Wars Md. Johnston. 1905, p. 77. MHS.
Thompson-Smythe papers. Ms. MHS.
See Smith.
***Smythe,** Kent Co. (1694). Geneal. notes and 2 Peale miniatures. Amer. Hist. Reg., 1895, v. 1, pp. 231–38. MHS.
Smythe, Maj. Thomas. Typed. File case, MHS.
Smythe-Tilghman-Willson, Trumpington, near Chesapeake Bay. Tombstone inscriptions, 1819–76. Md. Geneal. Rec. Com., 1937, Parran, p. 203. Mss. DAR.
Snader. Englar family. Barnes. MHS; DAR.
Snavely. Abr. Compend. Amer. Geneal. Virkus. V. 6, p. 529. DAR.
Hagerstown tombstone inscriptions. Gruder. Natl. Geneal. Soc. Quart., 1919, v. 8, nos. 1, 2.
Md. families. Culver. Ms. Personal list.
Sneckenberger. Beards' Luth. graveyard, Washington Co. Md. Geneal. Rec. Com., 1935–36. Mss. DAR.
Snelson. Md. gleanings in Eng. Wills. M. H. Mag., 1908, v. 3, no. 2.
Snider. Hagerstown tombstone inscriptions. Gruder. Natl. Geneal. Soc. Quart., 1919, v. 8, nos. 1, 2.

Snively. Md. tombstone rec. Md. Geneal. Rec. Com., 1937, Parran, p. 6. Mss. DAR.
Snively Family. Hist. Washington Co. Williams. 1906, v. 2, p. 1243. MHS; DAR.
†**Snook.** Hist. of Frederick Co. Williams. Pp. 745, 1399. MHS; DAR.
Snouffer. Carrollton Manor. Grove. 1921, pp. 4, 57, 62. DAR.
Hist. of Carrollton Manor, Frederick Co. 1928, p. 171. DAR.
Hist. of Frederick Co. Williams. V. 2, p. 1322. MHS; DAR.
Snow. Makemie Memorial Pres. churchyard, Snow Hill, Worcester Co. Hudson. Bd. ms. MHS; DAR. Also: Md. Geneal. Rec. Com., Mrs. Lines. Mss. DAR.
†Papers relating to early hist. of Md. Streeter. 1876. MHS.
Turner Geneal. Coll. Ms. MHS.
Wicomico Co. families. Bible rec. Ms. DAR.
*Wicomico Co. families. Tilghman. Ms., p. 68. DAR.
*Wilson Mss. Coll., no. 8, B. MHS.
Snow, Henry. Md. Soc., War of 1812, v. 4, no. 349. Ms. MHS.
Snowden. Abr. Compend. Amer. Geneal. Virkus. V. 1, p. 835. DAR.
Abs. of rec. of West River monthly meeting. Ms. MHS.
Balto., its hist., its people. Hall. V. 2. MHS; DAR.
Mrs. Lee Barroll chart. MHS.
Boone chart. MHS.
Carlyle family and Carlyle house. Spencer. P. 20. MHS.
Chart, photos., complete in 5 sheets. Cary Geneal. Coll. Ms. MHS.
Col. and Revolutionary families of Pa. Amer. Hist. Soc., N. Y., 1934, p. 881.
Col. families of Amer. Lawrence. V. 3, pp. 291–302. MHS.
Col. mansions of Md. and Del. Hammond. 1914. MHS.
Eldridge chart. MHS.
Ellicott-King chart. MHS.
*Founders of Anne Arundel and Howard Cos. Warfield. Pp. 361–64. MHS; DAR.
Geneal. and memorial encyc. of Md. Spencer. V. 1, p. 102. MHS; DAR.
Geneal. notes of Thomas family. Thomas. MHS; DAR.
Hist. graves of Md. and D. C. Ridgely. MHS.
†Hist. of Balto. City and Co. Scharf. Pp. 669–722. MHS.
See Janney. Abr. Compend. Amer. Geneal. Virkus. V. 4, pp. 309–10. MHS.
Jenkins-Courtney chart. MHS.
Marriages. Ms. MHS.
†Med. Annals Md. Cordell. 1903, p. 576. MHS.
Patriotic Md. Md. Soc. of S. A. R., 1930. MHS; DAR.
Pedigree of Francis Joseph Baldwin. Soc. Col. Wars Md. Culver. 1940. MHS; DAR.
Pedigree of Mark Alexander Herbert Smith. Soc. Col. Wars Md. Culver. 1940. MHS; DAR.
Posey chart. MHS.
W. de C. Poultney pedigree chart. Soc. Col. Wars, Md. Johnston. 1905, p. 86. MHS.
Mrs. M. L. Price chart. MHS.
Mrs. Renshaw chart. MHS.
St. Paul's Parish, Balto. V. 2. Mss. MHS.
See Smith. Abr. Compend. Amer. Geneal. Virkus. V. 6, p. 744. DAR.
T. M. Smith pedigree charts, plate 2. Soc. Col. Wars Md. Johnston. 1905, pp. 96, 154. MHS.
*The Sun, Balto., Jan. 29, 1905.
Talbott of "Poplar Knowle." Shirk. MHS; DAR.
Thomas Book. Thomas. Pp. 507–18. Lib. Cong.; MHS.
Warfields of Md. Warfield. MHS.
Miss Sara E. White chart. MHS.
Snowden, Lieut. Jonathan. Md. notes from Va. rec. M. H. Mag., 1936, v. 31, no. 3, p. 254.
Snowden, Wilton. Col. families of U. S. A. Mackenzie. V. 1, p. 491. MHS; DAR.
†Men of mark in Md. Johnson. V. 1. DAR; Enoch Pratt Lib.
***Snowden Family.** Geneal. and mem. encyc. of Md. Spencer. V. 1, pp. 102–10. MHS; DAR.
*Wilson Mss. Coll., no. 10. MHS.
Snyder. Bible rec. Natl. Geneal. Soc. Quart., v. 24, pp. 15–17.
Brief hist. of Andrew Putman, Christian Wyandt and Adam Snyder, Wash. Co. E. C. Wyand. Hagerstown Bookbinding and Publishing Co., 1909.
†Hist. of Frederick Co. Williams. Pp. 917, 1308. MHS; DAR.
†Med. Annals Md. Cordell. 1903, p. 576. MHS.
Md. tombstone rec. Md. Geneal. Rec. Com., 1937, Parran, pp. 23, 24. Mss. DAR.
Portraits and biog. rec. of Sixth Cong. Dist. of Md. 1898, p. 510. MHS; DAR.
See Putman-Wyandt-Snyder.
Snyder, Carroll Co. Md. Geneal. Bull., v. 5, p. 4. MHS; DAR.
Snyder, Jacob. Annals of Harbaugh family. Harbaugh. P. 119.
Solemon. St. Paul's Parish, Balto. V. 2. Mss. MHS.
Sollars, Sellers. Sollars, Sellers (1651), Va., and Anne Arundel Co. Md. Geneal. Rec. Com., 1932, v. 5, pp. 33–48. DAR.
Sollers. Lineage Bks., Natl. Soc. of Daughters of Amer. Col., v. 2, p. 207. MHS; DAR.
Md. families. Culver. Ms. Personal list.
Patriotic Md. Md. Soc. of S. A. R., 1930. MHS; DAR.
Plummer family. A. P. H. Ms. MHS.
St. Paul's Parish, Balto. V. 1, 2. Mss. MHS.
Talbott of "Poplar Knowle." Shirk. MHS; DAR.
Tomey and allied families. Silverson. MHS; DAR.
***Solomon.** Wilson Mss. Coll., no. 8, A. MHS.
Somers. Hist. Salisbury, Wicomico Co. Truitt. DAR.
†Med. Annals Md. Cordell. 1903, p. 576. MHS.
See Summers.
Somers, Summers. Children of Alex P. and M. C. Hill. Ms. MHS.
Somersall. Zimmerman-Waters and allied families. Allen. MHS; DAR.
Somervell, Somerville. Col. families of U. S. A. Mackenzie. V. 2; v. 3. MHS; DAR.
Md. families. Culver. Ms. Personal list.

Patriotic Md. Md. Soc. of S. A. R., 1930. MHS; DAR.
See Somerville.
Hist. graves of Md. and D. C. Ridgely. MHS.
Tiernan families. Tiernan. 1901. MHS; DAR.
Somervill - Erskine - Skinner - Stuart - Thornton-Waite. Natl. Geneal. Soc. Quart., v. 7, no. 3, pp. 45–48.
†**Somerville.** Med. Annals Md. Cordell. 1903, p. 576. MHS.
See Somervell.
Somerville, Somervell. Bleakley Bible rec. Ms. MHS.
*The Sun, Balto., July 26, 1903; Aug. 25, Sept. 1, 8, 1907.
Somford, J. Lowry. Md. Soc., War of 1812, v. 3, no. 287. Ms. MHS.
***Sorthoron Family.** Wilson Mss. Coll., no. 10. MHS.
Sotheron. Md. families. Culver. Ms. Personal list.
Sothoron. Eiler - Anderson - Boon - Sothoron - Witten. Eiler. 1929, pamph. MHS.
†Med. Annals Md. Cordell. 1903, pp. 576–77. MHS.
Soulsby. St. Paul's Parish, Balto. V. 2. Mss. MHS.
Southall. Southalls of Va. Va. Mag., v. 45, pp. 277–302. (Douglas Gordon, Balto., p. 281.)
†**Southby, Wm.** (died after 1717), Pa. and Md. Index to biog. sketches pub. in "The Friend," v. 26, v. 27. Pub. Geneal Soc. Pa., v. 3, no. 2, pp. 109–34.
***Southerland.** Southerland, Latham and allied families. Register of ancestors of Imogen Southerland Voorhees. E. K. Voorhees. Pr. for priv. circulation, Atlanta, Ga., 1931. MHS; DAR.
Southern. Old Somerset. Torrence. MHS; DAR.
***Southeron.** Wilson Mss. Coll., no. 58. MHS.
Southgate. Col. families of U. S. A. Mackenzie. V. 7. MHS; DAR.
Morris family of Phila. Moon. V. 2, p. 913. MHS.
Southley. Geneal. of Henrietta Chauncy Wilson. Upshur. Bk. of photos. MHS.
Sower. Col. families of Amer. Lawrence. V. 2, p. 51. MHS.
†**Sowers.** Hist. of Allegany Co. Thomas and Williams. V. 2. MHS; DAR.
***Spach.** Descendants of Adam Spach. H. W. Foltz. Transl. from German rec. of Adelaide L. Fries, archivist of Moravian Church, Southern Province. Pub. by Wachovia Hist. Soc., Winston-Salem, N. C., 1924. MHS.
†**Spach, Adam.** Meynen's bibliog. on German settlements in col. North Amer. 1937, p. 566.
Spaight. Richard Dobbs Spaight of N. C. John H. Wheeler. Balto., William K. Boyle, 1880, pamph. MHS.
*Sketch of life of Richard Dobbs Spaight. J. W. Wheeler Spaight. N. C., Wm. K. Boyle, 1880. MHS.
Spalding. Abr. Compend. Amer. Geneal. Virkus. V. 6, p. 608. DAR.
Centenary of Catholicity in Ky. Webb. 1884. MHS.
Col. families of U. S. A. Mackenzie. V. 1, p. 285. MHS; DAR.
Hamilton family of Charles Co. Kelly. MHS.
Jenkins-Courtney chart. MHS.
†Life of Archbishop Spalding, Most Rev. M. J. Archbishop of Balto. J. L. Spalding. N. Y. Catholic Pub. Soc.; Balto., John Murphy & Co., 1873.
†Med. Annals Md. Cordell. 1903, p. 577. MHS.
O'Daniel-Hamilton ancestry in Md. and Ky. O'Daniel. Pp. 72–85. MHS.
Pedigree of Francis Joseph Baldwin. Soc. Col. Wars Md. Culver. 1940. MHS; DAR.
Pedigree of Alfred Jenkins Shriver. Soc. Col. Wars Md. Culver. 1940. MHS; DAR.
St. Paul's Parish, Balto. V. 2. Mss. MHS.
†**Spalding, Archbishop.** Balto., hist. and Biog., Richardson and Bennett. 1871, pp. 473–80. MHS; DAR.
Spalding Line. Origins of Clements-Spalding families of Md. and Ky. Clements. Pp. 52–65. MHS.
Spamers. Trinity P. E. churchyard, Long Green. Typed ms. MHS; DAR.
Spangler. Hist. of Shriver family. Shriver. MHS.
***Spangler Family.** Spangler family. E. W. Spangler. York, Pa.
Spangler Family, Md. and W. Va. Md. Geneal. Rec. Com., 1937, pp. 1–14. Mss. DAR.
Spanks. St. Inigoes churchyard, St. Mary's Co. Md. O. R. Soc. Bull., no. 3, p. 58.
Sparks. Bible rec. Upper Penins. East. Shore, pp. 177–86. MHS; DAR.
Crumpton graveyard. Md. Geneal. Rec. Com., 1933–34, pp. 193–203. Mss. DAR.
†Hist. of Balto. City and Co. Scharf. P. 915. MHS.
†In memorian of Jareb Sparks, LL.D. (Born in Conn., 1789; pastor of Unitarian Church in Balto., 1819.) March 14, 1866. Enoch Pratt Lib.
†Med. Annals Md. Cordell. 1903, p. 577. MHS.
†Memoir of Jared Sparks, LL.D. Brantz Mayer. Balto., John Murphy, 1867. Enoch Pratt Lib.
Jared Sparks and Alexis de Tocqueville. H. B. Adams. J. H. Univ. Studies, series 16, Balto., 1898.
St. Paul's Parish, Balto. V. 2. Mss. MHS.
Sparks, Jared. Memoir. Brantz Mayer. Balto., 1867. MHS.
Sparrow. Ellicott-King chart. MHS.
†Hist. of printing in Col. Md. Wroth. MHS.
Miss E. C. Hopkins chart. MHS.
Pedigree of Mason Locke Weems Williams. Soc. Col. Wars Md. Culver. 1940. MHS; DAR.
South. Hist. Assoc., v. 4, pp. 421–31.
Spaulding. Dorsey Papers. Ms. MHS.
Wathen Prayer Book rec. Ms. MHS.
†**Speake.** Med. Annals Md. Cordell. 1903, p. 597. MHS.
Speake, Charles Co. and Va. M. H. Mag., 1936, v. 31, no. 3, p. 256.
***Speake, Lieut. Joseph.** Notes. M. H. Mag., Sept., 1936, v. 31, no. 3, p. 256.
Spear. Photos. Cary Geneal. Coll. Ms. MHS.
Gantz family geneal. Ms. MHS.
Mrs. W. H. Harris chart. MHS.
Torrence and allied families. Torrence. P. 490. MHS; DAR.
See Smith (Samuel)-McKim-Spear-Brown.

Spear, John. Westminster churchyard. Patriotic Marylander, v. 2, no. 4, pp. 54–60. MHS; DAR.
Spedden. Portrait and biog. rec. of East. Shore of Md. 1898, p. 699. MHS; DAR.
Rumsey-Smithson Bible rec. Md. Geneal. Rec. Com., 1932–33, v. 5, pp. 63–142. DAR.
***Speed.** Pennington Papers. Ms. MHS.
Speer. Somerset Co. Court Book. Tilghman. 1937. Ms. DAR.
***Speer, Talbot Taylor.** Burke's landed gentry. 1939. MHS.
Speer, Mrs. Talbot Taylor (Mary Washington Stewart). Chart. Col. Dames, Chap. I. MHS.
Speight. Lambdin chart. MHS.
Spence. Bible rec., from Bible in possession of Mrs. J. W. Lynch, Elkton. Md. Geneal. Rec. Com., 1937–38, pp. 52–54. Mss. DAR.
Hazelhurst chart. MHS.
Makemie Memorial Pres. churchyard, Snow Hill, Worcester Co. Hudson. Bd. ms. MHS; DAR. Also: Md. Geneal. Rec. Com., Mrs. Lines. Mss. DAR.
Old Somerset. Torrence. MHS; DAR.
Robins family, Va. and Worcester Co., Md., and allied families. Bd. ms. MHS.
St. Paul's Parish, Balto. V. 2. Mss. MHS.
Somerset Co. Court Book. Tilghman. 1937. Ms. DAR.
Somerset Parish. Abs. of rec. Turner Geneal. Coll. Ms. MHS.
*Wicomico Co. families. Tilghman. Ms., p. 33. DAR.
Turner Geneal. Coll. Ms. MHS.
†**Spence,** Worcester Co. Med. Annals Md. Cordell. 1903, p. 577. MHS.
†**Spence, Wm. H.** Men of mark in Md. Johnson. V. 1. DAR; Enoch Pratt Lib.
Spence, Mrs. Wm. Wallace (Harriet McCrum Wade). Chart. (Mostly Va. families.) Col. Dames, Chap. I. MHS.
***Spence Family,** Dorchester Co. The American, Nov. 13, 1880. MHS.
***Spence Family.** Old Kent. Hanson. P. 151. MHS; DAR.
Spence Family, Worcester Co. Balto. American, Nov. 13, 1880. Newsp. clipp. MHS.
Spencer. Balto., its hist., its people. Hall. V. 3. MHS; DAR.
Carlyle family. William and Mary Quart., 1st series, v. 18, pp. 201, 278.
Cary Geneal. Coll. Ms. MHS.
Chestertown cemetery. Md. O. R. Soc. Bull., no. 1, pp. 18–29.
Col. families of East. Shore and their descendants. Emory. 1900, p. 164. MHS.
Geneal. and memorial encyc. of Md. Spencer. V. 1, p. 154. MHS; DAR.
Geneal. rec. of family of Thomas. Thomas. MHS.
Hist. graves of Md. and D. C. Ridgely. MHS.
Md. O. R. Soc. Bull., no. 1, p. 67.
†Med. Annals Md. Cordell. 1903, p. 578. MHS.
Morris family of Phil. Moon. V. 2, p. 765; v. 3, p. 933. MHS.
*Notes of descendants of James Spencer, Jr., "Spencer Hall," Talbot Co. T. F. Jewell. Newport, R. I., 1892. MHS.
Pedigree of Harrison Tilghman. Soc. Col. Wars Md. Culver. 1940. MHS; DAR.
Rumsey-Smithson Bible rec. Md. Geneal. Rec. Com., 1932–33, v. 5, pp. 63–142. DAR.
St. Paul's Parish, Balto. V. 1, 2. Mss. MHS.
Shrewsbury churchyard, Kent Co. Md. O. R. Soc., v. 2, pp. 46–54. MHS.
*Side lights on Md. hist. Richardson. V. 2, p. 222. MHS; DAR.
Smithson-Rumsey rec. bk. Ms. MHS.
R. H. Spencer Scrap Book. MHS.
*The Sun, Balto., April 24, 1904.
Thomas family of Talbot Co. Spencer. MHS; DAR.
See Lewis-Spencer.
See Martin-Spencer.
See Washington-Spencer.
***Spencer,** Talbot Co. Burke's landed gentry. 1939. MHS.
Spencer, James, Jr., Spencer Hall, Talbot Co. Descendants. T. F. Jewell. Newport, R. I., Jan. 1, 1892, pamph. MHS.
Spencer, Jervis. Williamson Bible rec. Ms. MHS.
***Spencer, Mrs. Julia Spencer Ardery** (Wm. Breckenridge). Revolutionary chart. (23 Rev. ancestors of Va.) D. A. R. Mag., May, 1939, v. 73, no. 5, pp. 86–87.
Spencer, Zachariah. D. A. R. Mag., v. 70, no. 4, p. 352.
***Spencer Family.** Old Kent. Hanson. Pp. 95–96, 187–88. MHS; DAR.
Rec. from Bible owned by Mrs. J. A. Powell. Ms. MHS.
Spencer Family, Worcester and Somerset Cos. Bible rec. Ms. File case, MHS.
†**Sperry.** Hist. of Allegany Co. Thomas and Williams. V. 2. MHS; DAR.
St. Paul's Parish, Balto. V. 2. Mss. MHS.
***Spessard.** Brief hist. of Spessard family, and complete family register. H. L. Spessard. (Hagerstown, Washington Co., Md., Tenn., Va. and W. Va.) Hagerstown, Hagerstown Bookbinding Co., 1930. MHS; DAR.
†Hist. of Washington Co. Williams. 1906, v. 2, p. 904. MHS; DAR.
Spicer. Dorsey and allied families. Ms. MHS.
Keene family. Jones. MHS; DAR.
Md. families. Culver. Ms. Personal list.
Md. tombstone rec. Md. Geneal. Rec. Com., 1937, Parran, p. 33. Mss. DAR.
†Med. Annals Md. Cordell. 1903, p. 578. MHS.
Pedigree of Thomas Dobbin Penniman. Soc. Col. Wars Md. Culver. 1940. MHS; DAR.
Pedigree of Pleasants Pennington. Soc. Col. Wars Md. Culver. 1940. MHS; DAR.
Rumsey-Smithson Bible rec. Md. Geneal. Rec. Com., 1932–33, v. 5, pp. 63–142. DAR.
Smithson-Rumsey rec. bk. Ms. MHS.
†**Spidden.** Med. Annals Md. Cordell. 1903, p. 578. MHS.
Spielman. Zion Reformed Church, Hagerstown. Md. Geneal. Rec. Com., 1934–35. Mss. DAR.
Sponseller. Patriotic Md. Md. Soc. of S. A. R., 1930. MHS; DAR.
Spooner, Miss Ellen Otis. Chart. (Mostly Mass. families.) Col. Dames, Chap. I. MHS.
Spooner, Miss Mary Torry. Chart. Col. Dames, Chap. I. MHS.
Spotswood. Goode family. Va. cousins. Goode. MHS.

Lineage Bks., Natl. Soc. of Daughters of Amer. Col., v. 1, p. 188; v. 2, p. 223. MHS; DAR.
Selden chart. MHS.
*Spotswood family of Scotland and Va. C. Campbell. 1868.
***Spottswood,** Va. The Sun, Balto., Jan. 28, Feb. 4, 1906.
Sprague. Sweetser chart. MHS.
Sprangler. Portrait and biog. rec. of Sixth Cong. Dist. of Md. 1898, p. 699. MHS; DAR.
Sprangler Family, Md. and W. Va. Geneal., 1757-1929. Md. Geneal. Rec. Com., 1937, pp. 1-14. DAR.
†Sprecher. Portraiture of life of Samuel Sprecher, D.D., L.L.D. P. G. Bell. Pub. by author. Lutheran Pub. Soc., 1907, v. 8, p. 146.
Sprigg. Abr. Compend. Amer. Geneal. Virkus. V. 6, p. 269. DAR.
Ances. rec. and portraits. Col. Dames of Amer., 1910, v. 1, p. 89-92. MHS; DAR.
Ancestry of Mrs. Fulton Ray Gordon, nee Ellen Marjorie Gray. D. C. Geneal. Rec. Com., 1932-34, pp. 124-25. Typed bd. DAR.
Autobiography of Summerfield Baldwin. MHS; DAR.
Sara R. Baldwin chart. MHS.
Beall and Bell families. Beall. MHS; DAR.
Col. Joseph Belt. Hist. papers of Soc. Col. Wars. Magruder. 1909. MHS; DAR.
Bowie chart. Cary Geneal. Coll. Ms. MHS.
*Burke's landed gentry. 1939. MHS.
Mrs. Charles Carter chart. MHS.
Cary Geneal. Coll. Ms. MHS.
Col. families of U. S. A. Mackenzie. V. 2. MHS; DAR.
Dorsey and allied families. Ms. MHS.
Hamill chart. MHS.
Hazelhurst charts. MHS.
Hist. graves of Md. and D. C. Ridgely. MHS.
†Hist. of Allegany Co. Thomas and Williams. V. 1. MHS; DAR.
Lineage Bks., Natl. Soc. of Daughters of Amer. Col., v. 1, p. 173. MHS; DAR.
*Mrs. Charles Howard Lloyd chart. Col. Dames Amer., Chap. I. MHS.
Mason chart. MHS.
Md. families. Culver. Ms. Personal list.
Neill chart. MHS.
*Old Kent. Hanson. P. 271. MHS; DAR.
Patriotic Md. Md. Soc. of S. A. R., 1930. MHS; DAR.
Pedigree of Charles Gambrill Baldwin. Soc. Col. Wars Md. Culver. 1940. MHS; DAR.
Pedigree of Leigh Bonsal. Soc. Col. Wars Md. Culver. 1940. MHS; DAR.
Pedigree of Mareen Duvall. Soc. Col. Wars Md. Culver. 1940. MHS; DAR.
Pedigree of Charles O'Donnell Mackall. Soc. Col. Wars Md. Culver. 1940. MHS; DAR.
Pedigree of James Mather Sill. Soc. Col. Wars Md. Culver. 1940. MHS; DAR.
Pedigree of James Donnell Tilghman. Soc. Col. Wars Md. Culver. 1940. MHS; DAR.
Segrave chart. MHS.
Sprigg family. Christopher Johnston. M. H. Mag., 1913, v. 8, no. 1, pp. 74-84.
*The Sun, Balto., Feb. 11, 18, 25, May 6, 27, June 3, 17, July 8, 15, Sept. 30, 1906; July 7, 1907.
Talbott of "Poplar Knowle." Shirk. MHS; DAR.
Thomas Book. Thomas. P. 510. Lib. Cong.; MHS.
Thomas-Chew-Lawrence. Thomas. MHS.
Mrs. G. H. Williams, Jr., chart. MHS.
Wolseley chart. Cary Geneal. Coll. Ms. MHS.
See Yarnall, **Z. Sprigg.** Abr. Compend. Amer. Geneal. Virkus. V. 1, p. 898. DAR.
See Duvall-Lovejoy-Sprigg.
Sprigg, Gov. Samuel. Founders of Anne Arundel and Howard Cos. Warfield. P. 261. MHS.
†Governor of Md. Buchholz. P. 92. MHS.
Sprigg Family. Monnet family geneal. Monette. Pp. 388, 1070-83. MHS.
Sprigg Line. Mullikins of Md. Baker. Pp. 163-72. MHS; DAR.
Sprigg-Addison-Cresap-Lamar-Gordan families (1634-1812). Brief supplementary details of col. and revolutionary ancestry. Md. Geneal. Rec. Com., 1933-34, pp. 9-18. Mss. DAR.
Springer. Zion Reformed Church, Hagerstown. Md. Geneal. Rec. Com., 1934-35. Mss. DAR.
†Sproston. Med. Annals Md. Cordell. 1903, p. 578. MHS.
Spry. Lambdin chart. MHS.
Shrewsbury churchyard, Kent Co. Md. O. R. Soc., v. 2, pp. 46-54. MHS.
Spurrier. Makemie Memorial Pres. churchyard, Snow Hill, Worcester Co. Hudson. Bd. ms. MHS; DAR. Also: Md. Geneal. Rec. Com., Mrs. Lines. Mss. DAR.
St. Paul's Parish, Balto. V. 2. Mss. MHS.
Squires, W. H. T., Md. and Va. Abr. Compend. Amer. Geneal. Virkus. V. 1, p. 838. DAR.
***Stabler.** Ancestry of Caleb and Anne (Moore) Stabler, Sandy Springs, Md.
Balto., its hist., its people. Hall. V. 3. MHS; DAR.
Geneal. of ancestors and descendants of John and Hannah (Fincher) Russell. Russell. 1887, 1889, pamph. MHS.
Geneal. and memorial encyc. of Md. Spencer. V. 1, p. 81. MHS; DAR.
Geneal. of family of Gideon Gilpin. MHS.
Golden wedding of Edward and Ann R. Stabler, Sandy Springs, Md., Dec. 24, 1878. Balto., Sun Printing Co., 1874. Enoch Pratt Lib.
†Med. Annals Md. Cordell. 1903, p. 578. MHS.
Miller-Stabler chart. DAR.
*Stabler family, Pa., Md., and Ill. Ms. MHS.
*Stabler family of Pa. and Md. F. H. Frey. Illus., typed, with bd. books. (1938?) MHS.
Thomas Book. Thomas. P. 519. Lib. Cong.; MHS.
Stabler-Huidekoper. Chart; Amer. branch. Huidekoper. 1928, pamph. MHS; DAR.
Stachell. Stachell family rec. Mss. MHS.
†Stafford. Med. Annals Md. Cordell. 1903, p. 578. MHS.
St. Paul's Parish, Balto. V. 2. Mss. MHS.
Stahl. Hagerstown tombstone inscriptions. Gruder. Natl. Geneal. Soc. Quart., 1919, v. 8, nos. 1, 2.
Zoin Reformed Church, Hagerstown. Md. Geneal. Rec. Com., 1934-35. Mss. DAR.
Stake. Marriage rec., 1781-1892, Harford Co. Md. Geneal. Rec. Com., 1934-35, p. 108. DAR.

†**Staley.** Hist. of West. Md. Scharf. V. 1, p. 557. MHS; DAR.
†Med. Annals Md. Cordell. 1903, p. 579. MHS.

Stall. St. Paul's Parish, Balto. V. 2. Mss. MHS.

†**Stallings.** Hist. of Allegany Co. Thomas and Williams. V. 2. MHS; DAR.

Stamm. Catonsville pioneers of Luth. faith. Natl. Geneal. Soc. Quart., v. 9, no. 2, p. 29.

Standford. Somerset Co. Court Book. Tilghman. 1937. Ms. DAR.

†**Standiford.** Hist. of Balto. City and Co. Scharf. P. 874. MHS.
See Taylor-Roberts-Standiford-Patterson-Reardon-Baker-Reisinger-Scharf.

Standiford Family. See Paca-Smithson-Forwood Harford Co. Hist. Soc. Mss. Coll. JHU.
See Taylor-Roberts-Standiford.

Standish, Cary Geneal. Coll. Ms. MHS.

Standish, Miles, of Plymouth colony. Pedigree of Julian White Ridgely. Soc. Col. Wars Md. Culver. 1940. MHS; DAR.

Standridge. Somerset Co. Court Book. Tilghman. 1937. Ms. DAR.

Stanfield. Talbot of "Poplar Knowle." Shirk. MHS; DAR.

Stanford. Atkinson family (Somerset Co.) Bible rec. Ms. MHS.
Certain comeovers. Crapo. P. 809.
Wicomico Co. families. Bible rec. Ms. DAR.
*Wicomico Co. families. Tilghman. Ms. Pp. 19, 43–44, 46, 63–66, 71, 97–100. DAR.
See Malone-Disharoon-Stanford.

Stanley. Col. families of U. S. A. Mackenzie. V. 1, p. 489. MHS; DAR.
Geneal. and mem. encyc. of Md. Spencer. V. 1, p. 245. MHS; DAR.
Still Pond Church and cemetery. Md. O. R. Soc. Bull., no. 2, pp. 65–75.

†**Stanley, Charles H.** Men of mark in Md. Johnson. V. 1. DAR; Enoch Pratt Lib.

Stanley, James Gordon, Talbot Co., Pedigree chart. Soc. Col. Wars, Md. Johnston. 1905, p. 97. MHS.

Stanley, Stanly. St. Stephens Parish, Cecilton, Md. MHS; DAR.

Stanly. *See* Stanley.

Stannesby. Md. gleannings in Eng. Wills. M. H. Mag., 1907, v. 2, no. 3.

†**Stansbury.** Biog. cyc. of rep. men of Md. and D. C. Pp. 181–82. MHS; DAR.
Bond family geneal. Ms. MHS.
Buck family Bible rec. Md. Geneal. Rec. Com., v. 1, pp. 12–13. DAR.
†Chesapeake Bay Country. Earle. P. 236. MHS.
Custis-Teakle chart. Cary Geneal. Coll. Ms. MHS.
J. T. Dennis pedigree chart, plate 2. Soc. Col. Wars, Md. Johnston. 1905, p. 22. MHS.
Descendants of Col. Thomas White. Morris. MHS.
Dorsey and allied families. Ms. MHS.
Mrs. W. H. Harris chart. MHS.
Hilles chart. MHS.
Hist. graves of Md. and D. C. Ridgely. MHS.
†Hist. of Bapt. Church in Md. Weishampel. 1885.
Mrs. R. N. Jackson chart. MHS.
†Life and times of Hon. Elijah Stansbury. Rev. A. Hawkins. (An old defender, 1st Regiment of Md., Artillery of Md. Militia, War of 1812, p. 24; together with early reminiscences dating from 1662, embracing period of 212 years.) Balto., 1874. MHS; DAR; Enoch Pratt Lib.
Md. families. Culver. Ms. Personal list.
Monumental City. Howard. MHS; DAR.
Pedigree of T. Edward Hambleton. Soc. Col. Wars Md. Culver. 1940. MHS; DAR.
Pedigree of Maurice Edward Skinner. Soc. Col. Wars Md. Culver. 1940. MHS; DAR.
Pedigree of Philip Bartley Watts. Soc. Col. Wars Md. Culver. 1940. MHS; DAR.
Later geneal. Bd. Ms. MHS.
(94 rec.) St. Paul's Parish, Balto. V. 1, 2, 3. Mss. MHS.
St. Thomas Parish, Balto. Co. Bd. ms. MHS. Also: Md. Geneal. Rec. Com., 1937, pp. 109–82. Mss. DAR.
Smithsons of Harford Co. Md. Geneal. Rec. Com., 1932–33, pp. 155. Mss. DAR.

Stansbury, Balto. Co. Marriages. Md. Geneal. Bull., v. 3, p. 1; v. 5, p. 5. MHS; DAR.

Stansbury, James, Harford Co. Will. Md. Geneal. Rec. Com., 1932, p. 164. DAR.
†Hist. of Md. Scharf. V. 3, p. 25. MHS.

Stansbury, John. Children as mentioned in his will. Ms. MHS.
Data from M. E. Skinner. Ms. MHS.

Stansbury, Tobias, Family. *See* Stirling Family. Harford Co. Hist. Soc. Mss. Coll. JHU.

Stansbury, Gen. Tobias Emerson (1757–1849). Chart. MHS.

***Stansbury Family.** Complete hist. Wilson Mss. Coll., no. 45. MHS.
F. B. Culver, M. H. Mag., 1914, v. 9, no. 1, pp. 72–88; corrections, 1915, v. 10, no. 1, p. 62–3.
Notes. Ms. MHS.

Stansbury Line, Balto. Co., Md. F. S. Hambleton pedigree chart. Soc. Col. Wars Md. Johnston. 1905, p. 33.
(1652–1798). J. A. Wilson pedigree chart, plate 1. Soc. Col. Wars, Md. Johnston. 1905, pp. 130, 155. MHS.

***Stansbury-Dew Family.** Chart. MHS.

Stansbury-Rogers-Lynch. Bible rec., Kent Co. Md. Geneal. Rec. Com., 1933–34, pp. 234–35. Mss. DAR.

Stansbury, Steniberg, Stemberg. Chart, photos., complete in 1 sheet. Cary Geneal. Coll. Ms. MHS.
See Loney-Boyce-Day-Garret-Ross-Stansbury.

Stansfield. Mt. Paran Pres. churchyard, Harrisonville, Balto. Co. Typed ms. MHS; DAR.

***Stanton.** Garrett Co. Pioneer Families. Haye. MHS; DAR.
†Hist. of Allegany Co. Thomas and Williams. V. 1. MHS; DAR.
St. Barnabas P. E. churchyard. Typed ms. MHS; DAR.
*Wicomico Co. families. Tilghman. Ms., p. 16. DAR.

†**Stanton,** Garrett Co. Hist. of West. Md. Scharf. V. 2, p. 1528. MHS; DAR.

***Stanton, Hon. Robert Field.** Burke's landed gentry. 1939. MHS.
Pedigree. (Mostly Conn. and Mass. rec.) Soc. Col. Wars Md. Culver. 1940. MHS; DAR.

Stanton Family. (8 gener.) Mountain Democrat, Garret Co., Dec. 27, 1934. Newsp. clipp. MHS; DAR.

***Stanyarne.** Pennington Papers. Ms. MHS.
***Staplefort.** Hist. of Dorchester Co. Jones. 1925, p. 457. MHS; DAR.
Staples. Bible rec. Upper. Penins. East. Shore. Pp. 68–86. MHS; DAR.
Starkweather. Mrs. Lee Barroll chart.
Starling, Anne Arundel Co. Col. families of U. S. A. Mackenzie. V. 1, p. 556. MHS; DAR.
Starr. Jackson family gathering. 1878.
†Med. Annals Md. Cordell. 1903, p. 579. MHS.
St. Thomas Parish, Balto. Co. Bd. ms. MHS. Also: Med. Geneal. Rec. Com., 1937, pp. 109–82. Mss. DAR.
Starr Line (1658–1894). W. S. Myers pedigree charts. Soc. Col. Wars, Md. Johnston. 1905, p. 76. MHS.
Startt. Bible rec., Kent Co. Md. Geneal. Rec. Com., 1933–34, p. 238. Mss. DAR.
Startzman, Stertzman, Stertsman, Stertsmaennen. Hagerstown tombstone inscriptions. Gruder. Natl. Geneal. Soc. Quart., 1919, v. 8, nos. 1, 2.
Staton. Makemie Memorial Pres. churchyard, Snow Hill, Worcester Co. Hudson. Bd. ms. MHS; DAR. Also: Md. Geneal. Rec. Com., Mrs. Lines. Mss. DAR.
St. Paul's P. E. churchyard, Berlin, Worcester Co. Hudson. Bd. ms. MHS; DAR. Also: Md. General. Rec. Com., 1937, Mrs. Lines. Mss. DAR.
Stauffer. Englar family. Barnes. MHS; DAR.
*Geneal. in Amer. E. N. Stauffer. 1917. DAR.
†Hist. of Frederick Co. Williams. V. 2, pp. 1205, 1259. MHS; DAR.
Hist. Washington Co. Williams. 1906, v. 1, v. 2. MHS; DAR.
Pedigree of John Ogle Warfield, Jr. Soc. Col. Wars Md. Culver. 1940. MHS; DAR.
Joseph Radcliff and his descendants. Bd. ms. MHS.
Stauffer, Pa. Col. families of Amer. Lawrence. V. 15, p. 164. MHS.
†Staup. Hist. of Allegany Co. Thomas and Williams. V. 2. MHS; DAR.
Staveley. I. U. Church cemetery. Md. O. R. Soc. Bull., no. 2, pp. 76–78.
***Stavely Family.** Old Kent. Hanson. Pp. 190–91. MHS; DAR.
Steal. *See* Steele.
***Stear, Steer, Steir.** Stear family of Pa. Wilson. Mss. Coll., no. 5. MHS.
***Stebbins Family.** Geneal. Pr. by Ebenezer Watson, Hartford, Conn. Copy no. 53. MHS; DAR.
Steel. St. Paul's Parish, Balto. V. 2. Mss. MHS.
See Steele.
Steele. Ances. rec. and portraits. Col. Dames of Amer., 1910, v. 2, p. 676–78. MHS; DAR.
Ancestry of Rosalie Morris Johnson. Johnson. 1905. MHS; DAR.
Andre and Mary Steele Bible rec., 1768–1888, Del., Co., Pa. Md. Geneal. Rec. Com., v. 3, pp. 50–51. DAR.
*Arms. Hist. of Dorchester Co. Jones. 1925, pp. 458–67. MHS; DAR.
Bantz geneal. notes. Ms. MHS.
†Bench and bar of Md. Sams and Riley. 1901, v. 2, pp. 413, 642. Lib. Cong.; M.H.S; Peabody Lib.
Cemetery Creek, Anne Arundel Co., Tombstone Inscriptions Founders of Anne Arundel and Howard Cos. Warfield. P. 334. MHS; DAR.
(7 stones.) Christ P. E. Church cemetery, Cambridge. Steele. 1936. MHS; DAR.
Col. families of U. S. A. Mackenzie. V. 1, p. 362. MHS; DAR.
*Frederick Co. families. Markell. Ms. Personal list.
Hazelhurst charts. MHS.
Hist. graves of Md. and D. C. Ridgely. MHS.
†Hist. of Balto. City and Co. Scharf. P. 715. MHS.
†Hist. of West. Md. Scharf. V. 2, p. 877. MHS; DAR.
Last will of James Steele, Phila. Md. Geneal. Rec. Com., 1937, pp. 91–94. Mss. DAR.
*Old Kent. Hanson. P. 37. MHS; DAR.
See Henry.
†Steele, I. Nevett. Balto., hist. and biog. Richardson and Bennett. 1871, pp. 481–86. MHS; DAR.
Steele, Miss Kate. Chart. Col. Dames, Chap. I. MHS.
Steele, Miss Margaret Mary. Chart. Col. Dames, Chap. I. MHS.
***Steele, Richard.** Data. Ms. MHS.
Steele, Miss Rosa Nelson. Miss Kate Steele chart. MHS.
Chart. Col. Dames, Chap. I. MHS.
Steele, Rev. Sam'l Tagart. Pedigree. Soc. Col. Wars Md. Culver. 1940. MHS; DAR.
Steele, Thomas, Chester Co., Pa. Bible rec. Md. Geneal. Rec. Com., 1934–35, p. 110. Mss. DAR.
Steele Family. Will of James Steele of Phila. Md. Geneal. Rec. Com., 1937. DAR.
Steele Line. Miss Kate Steele chart. MHS.
Steele, Steel, Steal. St. Stephens Parish, Cecilton, Md. MHS; DAR.
Steelman. Naturalizations in Md., 1666–1765; Laws. Bacon. MHS.
Steer. *See* Stear.
Steidinger. Hagerstown tombstone inscriptions. Gruder. Natl. Geneal. Soc. Quart., 1919, v. 8, nos. 1, 2.
Md. families. Culver. Ms. Personal list.
Steiger. Hist. of Shriver family. Shriver. Pp. 94–96. MHS.
Steinbeck. Gen. Tobias Emerson Stansbury chart. MHS.
Steiner. Col. families of U. S. A. Mackenzie. V. 1, pp. 503–06. MHS; DAR.
Frederick Co. tombstone inscriptions. Gruder. Natl. Geneal. Soc. Quart. 1919, v. 8, nos. 1, 2.
Geneal.; especially descendants of Jacob Steiner of Frederick Co. Bernard C. Steiner and Lewis H. Steiner. Balto., Friedenwald Co., 1896, pamph. MHS.
†Hist. of West. Md. Scharf. V. 1, p. 488. MHS; DAR.
†Med. Annals Md. Cordell. 1903, p. 579. MHS.
Memoir; sketch of Steiner family, 1311–1878. Cincinnati, Robert Clarke & Co., 1880, pamph. MHS.
Patriotic Md. Md. Soc. of S. A. R., 1930. MHS; DAR.

†**Steiner.** Lewis Henry Steiner and his son Bernard Christian Steiner. Richard H. Hart. 1936, mimeog. Enoch Pratt Lib.
See Stoner.
Steiner, B. C. Abr. Compend. Amer. Geneal. Virkus. V. 1, p. 840. DAR.
Steiner Family. Geneal. Lewis H. Steiner and Bernard C. Steiner. Balto., 1896. MHS.
***Steiner-Stoner.** Frederick Co. families. Markell. Ms. Personal list.
*Lineage Bk., Daughters of Amer. Col., v. 3, p. 121. MHS; DAR.
Steir. *See* Stear.
†**Stellman.** Hist. of Balto. City and Co. Scharf. P. 417. MHS.
Stem. Geneal. of ancestors and descendants of John and Hannah (Fincher) Russell. Russell. 1887, 1889, pamph. MHS.
Stemberg. *See* Stansbury.
Stemple. Hagerstown tombstone inscriptions. Gruder. Natl. Geneal. Soc. Quart., 1919, v. 8, nos. 1, 2.
Steniberg. *See* Stansbury.
Stephens. Md. tombstone rec. Md. Geneal. Rec. Com., 1937, Parran, p. 6. Mss. DAR.
†Med. Annals Md. Cordell. 1903, p. 580. MHS.
St. Paul's churchyard, Kent Co. Md. O. R. Soc. Bull., no. 2, pp. 54–65. MHS.
St. Stevens graveyard. Cecil Co. Md. Geneal. Rec. Com., 1934–35, pp. 213–14, Mss. DAR.
See Stevens.
***Stephenson.** Rec. Mrs. E. M. S. Fite. N. Y. MHS.
St. Paul's Parish, Balto. V. 1. Mss. MHS.
***Steptoe,** Va. The Sun, Balto., Oct. 15, 1905.
Steptoe Family, Lancaster Co., Va. Md. Geneal. Rec. Com., 1935–36, pp. 283–85. Mss. DAR.
Steptoe Family, Va. Geneal. and arms. Md. Geneal. Rec. Com., 1935–36, p. 284. DAR.
Newsp. clipp. Scrap Book. MHS.
Sterett. Ames Geneal. Coll. Ms. MHS.
Bible rec., 1789–1850. Ms. MHS.
Lehr chart. MHS.
Pedigree of Francis Joseph Baldwin. Soc. Col. Wars Md. Culver. 1940. MHS; DAR.
Mrs. Edward Simpson chart. MHS.
Sterett, Capt. John. Westminster churchyard. Patriotic Marylander, v. 2, no. 4, pp. 54–60. MHS; DAR.
Sterett, Maj. Samuel. Westminster churchyard. Patriotic Marylander, v. 2, no. 4, pp. 54–60. MHS; DAR.
Sterett-Hadfield. Sterett-Hadfield duel, 1791. Expeditive Archives. M. H. Mag., 1911, v. 6, pp. 79–85, 274–75.
Sterling. Cary Geneal. Coll. Ms. MHS.
†Med. Annals Md. Cordell. 1903, p. 580. MHS.
*Sterling geneal. A. M. Sterling. (From Scotland to La., Ky., Md., (p. 73) and Va.) 1909.
***Sterns, Wm.-Sharpe, Mary.** Marriage certificate, 1670. Note from public rec. Hodges. M. H. Mag., 1915, v. 10, pp. 284–85.
Sterret. St. Paul's Parish, Balto. V. 2. Mss. MHS.
Sterrett. Amer. Guthrie and allied families. Guthrie. Bk. 4. DAR.
Mrs. R. Barton, Jr., charts. MHS.
Miss M. S. Brogden chart. MHS.
Peale Geneal. Coll. Ms. MHS.
Portrait and biog. rec. of Harford and Cecil Cos. 1897, pp. 162, 205, 232. MHS; DAR.
Spessard family. Spessard. MHS; DAR.
W. S. G. Williams pedigree chart. Soc. Col. Wars Md. Johnston. 1905, p. 128. MHS.
Sterrett, Andrew (1760–1807). M. H. Mag., v. 12, p. 246.
†**Sterrett, Isaac S.** M. H. Mag., v. 12, p. 246.
Sterrett, James, Balto. Co. (father-in-law of Gen. Mordecai Gist). Copy of will, 1792. Md. Geneal. Rec. Com., 1937–38, p. 19. Mss. MHS.
Sterrett, Maj. Samuel (1756–1833). Revolutionary War Heroes. Cole. Bklet. Enoch Pratt Lib.
Stertsmaennen. *See* Startzman.
Stertsman. *See* Startzman.
Stertzman. *See* Startzman.
Stettinuis, Mrs. Wm. Carrington (Achsah Petre). Chart. Col. Dames, Chap. I. MHS.
Miss Constance Petre chart. MHS.
Steuart. Ancestry of Rosalie Morris Johnson. Johnson. 1905. MHS; DAR.
*Bartow geneal. Bartow. P. 145. Lib. Cong.; MHS.
See Davis. Abr. Compend. Amer. Geneal. Virkus. V. 1, p. 106. DAR.
†Med. Annals Md. Cordell. 1903, pp. 580–81. MHS.
St. Paul's Parish, Balto. V. 3. Mss. MHS.
Side lights on Md. hist. Richardson. V. 2, p. 225. MHS; DAR.
Talbott of "Poplar Knowle." Shirk. MHS; DAR.
Tilghman chart. MHS.
See Mason.
See Stewart.
See Stuart.
***Steuart,** Anne Arundel Co. Entire membership, 1742–1904. The Sun, Balto., April 17, 1904.
Steuart, Ambler J. Md. Soc., War of 1812, v. 2, no. 192. Ms. MHS.
Steuart, J. Edmondson. Md. Soc., War of 1812. V. 1, no. 125. Ms. MHS.
Steuart, Richard Dennis. Pedigree. Soc. Col. Wars Md. Culver. 1940. MHS; DAR.
†**Steuart, R. S.** Balto., hist. and biog. Richardson and Bennett. 1871, pp. 487–92. MHS; DAR.
***Steuart Family,** Old Kent. Hanson. Pp. 193, 267, 273–75. MHS; DAR.
Records. Photos. Scrap Book. MHS.
Steuart, Stewart Line. Hamilton family of Charles Co. Kelly. MHS.
Stevens. Blakiston churchyard, Kent Co., Del., near Millington. Md. Geneal. Rec. Com., 1933–34, pp. 204–07. Mss. DAR.
Crumpton graveyard. Md. Geneal. Rec. Com., 1933–34, pp. 193–203. Mss. DAR.
Elliott chart. MHS.
*Hist. Dorchester Co. Jones. 1925, p. 467. MHS; DAR.
Md. families. Culver. Ms. Personal list.
†Med. Annals Md. Cordell. 1903, p. 581. MHS.
Memorial to Thomas Potts, Jr. James. MHS.
†Men of mark in Md. Johnson. V. 1. DAR; Enoch Pratt Lib.
Monumental City. Howard. MHS; DAR.
Old Buckingham by the Sea, East. Shore of Md. Page. DAR.

Old Somerset. Torrence. MHS; DAR.
*Pennington Papers. Ms. MHS.
Photos. Andrews' Scrap Book. MHS.
Ringgold-Elliott chart. MHS.
Newsp. clipp. Scrap Book. MHS.
St. Paul's Parish, Balto. V. 1, 2, 4. Mss. MHS.
Side lights on Md. hist. Richardson. V. 2, p. 441. MHS; DAR.
Somerset Co. Court Book. Tilghman. 1937. Ms. DAR.
Somerset Parish. Abs. of rec. Turner Geneal. Coll. Ms. MHS.
Turner Geneal. Coll. Ms. MHS.
Whiteley chart. MHS.
See Medford-Bonner-Carroll-Corkran-Stevens.
See Serman-Stevens.
See Townley-Stevens.

Stevens, S. C. and Md. Col. families of Amer. Lawrence. V. 16, pp. 41–96. MHS.

†**Stevens, Elizabeth Johns,** Md. and Pa. Index to biog. sketches pub. in "The Friend," v. 26, v. 27. Pub. Geneal. Soc. Pa., v. 3, no. 2, pp. 109–34.

Stevens, Gov. Samuel. Founders of Anne Arundel and Howard Cos. Warfield. P. 262. MHS; DAR.
†Governor of Md. Buchholz. P. 95. MHS.
(1778–1860). Hist. of Talbot Co. Tilghman. V. 1, ppl 622–24. MHS; DAR.

Stevens, William, Rehobeth, Somerset Co., 1649. Ms. MHS.
†(died in 1687; aged 57 years). Rehoboth by the River. Bischof. DAR.

Stevens, Stephens. Lawrence-Chase-Townley estate. Hill. MHS.
*Wicomico Co. families. Tilghman. Ms., pp. 62, 97–99, 113–14. DAR.

Stevenson. Abr. Compend. Amer. Geneal. Virkus. V. 4, p. 654. MHS.
Ancestral pilgrimage. (Book.)
Miss M. S. Brogden chart. MHS.
Cary Geneal. Coll. Ms. MHS.
Makemie Memorial Pres. churchyard, Snow Hill, Worcester Co. Hudson. Bd. ms. MHS; DAR. Also: Md. Geneal. Rec. Com., Mrs. Lines. Mss. DAR.
Md. families. Culver. Ms. Personal list.
†Med. Annals Md. Cordell. 1903; pp. 30, 581–82. MHS.
Pedigree of George Webb Constable Soc. Col. Wars Md. Culver. 1940. MHS; DAR.
*Pennington Papers. Ms. MHS.
Pocomoke Pres. churchyard, Worcester Co. Hudson. Bd. ms. MHS; DAR.
St. Paul's Parish, Balto. V. 1, 2, 4. Mss. MHS.
Some Va. families. McIlhany.
Somerset Parish. Abs. of rec. Turner Geneal. Coll. Ms. MHS.
Turner Geneal. Coll. Ms. MHS.
*Wicomico Co. families. Tilghman. Ms., pp. 67, 98. DAR.
See Field-Williamson-Stevenson.
See Ford-Stevenson.
See Stinson (Stevenson).

Stevenson, Dr. John (died Mar. 23, aged 67 years). Death. Md. Journal, Mar., 25, 1785, p. 1, col. 3. Will and public sale, p. 2, col. 3.

Stevenson, Mrs. Robert H., Jr. (Alice Lee Whitridge Thomas). Chart. Col. Dames, Chap. I. MHS.

Stevenson Family. Data of John (from Peabody Lib.). Ms. MHS.
*Old Kent. Hanson. Pp. 84–88. MHS; DAR.

***Stevenson-McMaster.** Sketch of John Slemmons Stevenson, 1807–1867, of Somerset Co., Md., and Mo. Sketch of Rev. Samuel McMaster, 1774–1811. J. Stevenson McMaster. Jersey City, N. J., A. J. Doan Printer, prepared in 1895, revised 1900, 1902. MHS.

Steward. Abr. Compend. Amer. Geneal. Virkus. V. 4, p. 196. MHS.

Steward, Steuart. (52 rec.) St. Paul's Parish, Balto. V. 2. Mss. MHS.
St. Stephens Parish, Cecilton, Md. MHS; DAR.

Stewart. Ames Geneal. Coll. Ms. MHS.
Arson of Peggy Stewart. Newsp. clipp. MHS.
H. F. Barnes Bible rec. Ms. MHS.
Bolton chart. MHS.
Mrs. J. G. Brogden chart. MHS.
Cemetery Creek, Anne Arundel Co., Tombstone Inscriptions, Founders of Anne Arundel and Howard Cos. Warfield. Pp. 334. MHS; DAR.
(11 stones.) Christ P. E. Church cemetery, Cambridge. Steele. 1936. MHS; DAR.
Col. families of U. S. A. Mackenzie. V. 7, p. 299. MHS; DAR.
Done Bible rec. Ms. MHS.
Col. Nicholas Duvall family rec. Price. Bd. ms. MHS.
*Frederick Co. families. Markell. Ms. Personal list.
Robert Gilmor chart. MHS.
See Harrold. Abr. Compend. Amer. Geneal. Virkus. V. 1, p. 646. DAR.
†Hist. of Allegany Co. Thomas and Williams. V. 2. MHS; DAR.
*Hist. Dorchester Co. Jones. 1925, p. 469. MHS; DAR.
Lux-Stewart-Wilson family. Ms. MHS.
John Drummond Marshall prayer book rec. Ms. MHS.
†Med. Annals Md. Cordell. 1903, pp. 582–83, 606. MHS.
W. A. and S. W. Merritt pedigree charts, plate 1. Soc. Col. Wars Md. Johnston. 1905, p. 67. MHS.
*Old Kent. Hanson. P. 265. See Stewart. MHS; DAR.
Patriotic Md. Md. Soc. of S. A. R., 1930. MHS; DAR.
Peale Geneal. Coll. Ms. MHS.
Russell-Lux Bible rec. Photos. MHS.
Charles Morton Stewart—Josephine Lurman Stewart, "Cliffeholme," Baltimore Co. Memoir. Days gone by. Ellinor Stewart Heiser. Balto., 1940.
St. Paul's Parish, Balto. V. 1, 2, 3, 4. Mss. MHS.
Stewart Clan Mag., v. 1, nos. 1–12. MHS.
*Stewart Clan Mag., David Stewart, Anne Arundel Co. From compilations of late Wilson Miles Cary. Ms. Coll., Nov., 1930–31, v. 9, no. 5. Beatrice, Nebraska. MHS.
†Redmond C. Stewart, foxhunter and gentleman of Md. Gordon Grand. N. Y. Scribner's, 1938, 198 pp. MHS.
Trinity Church cemetery, Dorchester Co. Md. O. R. Soc. Bull., no. 3, pp. 42–52.
*Wicomico Co. families. Tilghman. Ms., pp. 104, 123. DAR.

Stewart. Sir George Yeardley. Upshur. Pp. 18, 36. MHS.
See Steuart.
Stewart, Anne Arundel Co. Chart, photos., 2 sheets. Cary Geneal. Coll. Ms. MHS.
***Stewart,** East. Shore of Md. Wilson Mss. Coll., no. 8, A. MHS.
Stewart, Kent Co. Bible rec. M. H. Mag., v. 12, no. 4, pp. 386–91.
Stewart, Worcester Co. Pedigree of Lewis Warrington Cottman. Soc. Col. Wars Md. Culver. 1940. MHS; DAR.
Stewart, Charles Morton. Pedigree. Soc. Col. Wars Md. Culver. 1940. MHS; DAR.
Stewart, David. Capt. John Frazier. Leach. Pp. 96–99. MHS.
Westminster churchyard. Patriotic Marylander, v. 2, no. 4, pp. 54–60, MHS; DAR.
Stewart, David, Anne Arundel Co. Stewart Clan Monthly Mag., Nov., 1930–31, v. 9, no. 5. MHS.
†**Stewart, Hyland Price.** Men of mark in Md. Johnson. V. 4. DAR; Enoch Pratt Lib.
†**Stewart, James E.** M. H. Mag., v. 12, p. 246.
†**Stewart, John.** M. H. Mag., v. 12, p. 246.
Stewart, Redmond C. Col. and Revolutionary lineages. 1939, v. 2, pp. 100–20. MHS.
***Stewart Family,** Balto. Some account of Capt. John Frazier and his descendants. DAR.
Stewart Family, Kent Co. Notes. M. H. Mag., Dec. 1917, v. 12, no. 4, p. 390.
Stewart Line. Mrs. Talbot T. Speer chart. MHS.
Stewart-Wilson Family. Ms. MHS.
Stewart, Stuart. Stewart Clan Monthly Mag. Geneal. rec. George T. Edson, editor, High St., Beatrice, Neb. MHS.
†**Steyer.** Hist. of West. Md. Scharf. V. 2, p. 1477. MHS; DAR.
Stick-Fair-Fitchett. Abr. Compend. Amer. Geneal. Virkus. V. 4, p. 629. MHS.
Stickney. Monumental City. Howard. MHS; DAR.
Stickney, George H. Md. Soc., War of 1812, v. 1, no. 7. Ms. MHS.
Pedigree chart. Soc. Col. Wars Md. Johnston. 1905, p. 98. MHS.
Stickney, George Lewis. Pedigree. Soc. Col. Wars Md. Culver. 1940. MHS; DAR.
Stidham Family, Del. Allied families o Delaware. Sellers. MHS.
Stiefel-Brooke-Calvert. . . . Abr. Compend. Amer. Geneal. Virkus. V. 4, pp. 488–89. MHS.
Stier. Frances Murray Bowdoin chart. MHS.
Mrs. A. C. Bruce chart. MHS.
Ellicott-Campbell chart. MHS.
*Frederick Co. families. Markell. Ms. Personal list.
Iglehart chart. MHS.
Mrs. E. W. Poe chart. MHS.
Mrs. A. Randall chart. MHS.
Mrs. G. R. Veazey chart. MHS.
Stierner, Stoner. Lineage Bks., Natl. Soc. of daughters of Amer. Col., v. 3, p. 121. MHS; DAR.
Stiles. Faith Pres. Church (Glendy Graveyard). Mss. MHS.
*Stiles family geneal., from Stiles hist. of ancient Windsor. Stiles. MHS.
Stiles Family. Index to Stiles family in Amer. Mary Stiles P. Guild. 1938. Mss. DAR.
Stiles-Braxton (Carter). Lineage Bks., Natl. Soc. of Daughters of Amer. Col., v. 3, p. 305. MHS; DAR.
***Stille.** Frederick Co. families. Markell. Ms. Personal list.
Naturalizations in Md., 1666–1765; Laws. Bacon. MHS.
Stimmel, Frederick Co. Abr. Compend. Amer. Geneal. Virkus. V. 6, p. 545. DAR.
Stinchcomb. Epitaphs. Natl. Geneal. Soc. Quart., v. 20, no. 2, p. 69.
St. Paul's Parish, Balto. V. 1. Mss. MHS.
See Fite-Owings-Stinchcomb.
See Fite, Sipes and Stinchcomb.
Stine. Md. tombstone rec. Md. Geneal. Rec. Com., 1937, Parran, pp. 16, 17. Mss. DAR.
†**Stinnecker.** Med. Annals Md. Cordell. 1903, p. 583. MHS.
Stinson. Dorsey and allied families. Ms. MHS.
Stinson (Stevenson). Revolutionary pension abs. Natl. Geneal. Soc. Quart., v. 24, p. 125.
Stirling. Ances. rec. and portraits. Col. Dames of Amer., 1910, v. 2, p. 698. MHS; DAR.
†Hist. of Balto. City and Co. Scharf. P. 718. MHS.
Jaquett family. Sellers. 1907, p. 147. MHS.
Monumental City. Howard. MHS; DAR.
St. Paul's Parish, Balto. V. 3. Mss. MHS.
Mrs. J. P. Thom chart. MHS.
***Stirling, Campbell Lloyd.** Burke's landed gentry. 1939. MHS.
Stirling, Miss Helen. Chart. Col. Dames, Chap. I. MHS.
Pedigree (Eng.) chart of Mrs. J. Pembroke Thom and Miss Helen Stirling. Col. Dames, Chap. I. MHS.
Stirling, James. Westminster churchyard. Patriotic Marylander, v. 2, no. 4, pp. 54–60. MHS; DAR.
†**Stirling, Yates.** Men of mark in Md. Johnson. V. 2. DAR; Enoch Pratt Lib.
Stirling Family. Harford Co. Hist. Soc. Mss. Coll. JHU.
†**Stirrat.** In love and grateful remembrance, Balto. Commandry, no. 2, does dedicate this memorial, to Sir Knight James Stirrat. (Born in Scotland, 1814; died in Va., 1864; lived in Balto., 1833–55, 1864.) Balto., John Y. Slater, 1865. Enoch Pratt Lib.
Stith. Stith family of Va., with Johnston, Drury, etc., connections. Christopher Johnston. William and Mary. Quart., 1st series, v. 21; v. 22; v. 23.
Stith, Va. C. Johnston pedigree chart. Soc. Col. Wars Md. Johnston. 1905, pp. 53, 155. MHS.
†**Stockbridge, Henry.** Men of mark in Md. Johnson. V. 2. DAR; Enoch Pratt Lib.
Stockbridge, Hon. Henry, and Stockbridge, Hon. Henry, Jr. Pedigree charts, plates 1, 2 and 3. (New Eng. records.) Soc. Col. Wars Md. Johnston. 1905, pp. 99–101. MHS.
Stockbridge, Henry, III. Pedigree. Soc. Col. Wars Md. Culver. 1940. MHS; DAR. (See Pedigree Book, 1905, pp. 100, 101.)
Stockett. Anne Arundel Co. tombstone inscriptions. Ms. DAR.
Cary Geneal. Coll. Ms. MHS.
Col. families of U. S. A. Mackenzie. V. 5, p. 270; v. 7, p. 237. MHS; DAR.

*Founders of Anne Arundel and Howard Cos. Warfield. Pp. 93-96. MHS; DAR.
Geneal. of family, 1558-1892. Frank H. Stockett. Balto., Wm. H. Boyle and Son. MHS.
Harwood chart. MHS.
Mrs. D. G. Lovell chart. MHS.
Md. families. Culver. Ms. Personal list.
Md. Geneal. Bull., v. 4, p. 31. MHS; DAR.
†Med. Annals Md. Cordell. 1903, pp. 583-84. MHS.
Patriotic Md. Md. Soc. of S. A. R., 1930. MHS; DAR.
Pedigree of Mareen Duvall. Soc. Col. Wars Md. Culver. 1940. MHS; DAR.
Pedigree of John B. Philip C. Hall. Soc. Col. Wars Md. Culver. 1940. MHS; DAR.
*George Donald Riley. Riley. DAR.
St. Paul's Parish, Balto. V. 1, 2, 3. Mss. MHS.
Stockett arms. D. A. R. Mag., 1940, v. 74, no. 2, p. 45.
*Stockett family in Md. W. F. Boogher. Phila., 1884.
See Duvall-Stockett.
***Stockett,** Scotland to Md., 1766. The Sun, Balto., Aug. 23, 1903.
Stockett, Joseph, Balto. Co. Will probated April 2, 1795. D. A. R. Mag., v. 65, no. 8, p. 505.
Stockett, Capt. Thomas. J. P. Hill pedigree chart, plate 2. Soc. Col. Wars, Md. Johnston. 1905, pp. 37, 155. MHS.
Stockett Family. Chart. Frank H. Stockett. MHS.
Rec. Ms. MHS.
Stockett-Duvall. Bible rec. Ms. MHS.
Stockley. J. T. Dennis pedigree chart, plate 2. Soc. Col. Wars, Md. Johnston. 1905, p. 22. MHS.
*Geneal. Leaflet. MHS.
Stockley Family Line. With geneal. County Court Note Book. Ljungstedt. MHS; DAR.
Stockton. Geneal. notes of Chamberlaine family. MHS.
St. Stephens Parish, Cecilton, Md. MHS; DAR.
Stockton, Richard, N. J. Pedigree of Townsend Scott, N. Soc. Col. Wars Md. Culver. 1940. MHS; DAR.
Stoddert. Col. families of U. S. A. Mackenzie. V. 5, p. 204. MHS; DAR.
Daughter of Md.; Mother of Texas. Bell MHS; DAR.
Lineage Bks., Natl. Soc. of Daughters of Amer. Col., v. 3, p. 36. MHS; DAR.
***Stoddert,** Charles Co., Lineage Bk., Daughters of Amer. Col., v. 3, p. 316. MHS; DAR.
†Stoddert, Benjamin (first secretary of U. S. Navy). Memoirs. H. S. Stoddert Turner. Rec. Columbia Hist. Soc., v, 20, pp. 141-66.
†Hist. of Md. Scharf. V. 2, p. 437. MHS.
Stokes. Wm. Conway of Md. and Pa. Ms. File case, DAR.
*Frederick Co. families. Markell. Ms. Personal list.
Geneal. of family of Gideon Gilpin. MHS.
†Med. Annals Md. Cordell. 1903, pp. 584-85. MHS.
Stokes Family, Md., Va., S. C., and Ala. Tylers Quart. Mag., v. 10, pp. 44-50.
†Stonbraker. Hist. of West. Md. Scharf. V. 2, pp. 1179, 1203. MHS; DAR.
Stone. Abr. Compend. Amer. Geneal. Virkus. V. 1, p. 680; v. 6, pp. 388, 647. DAR.
Abs. of Va. land patents. Va. Mag. Hist. and Biog., v. 3, pp. 272-73.
Ames Geneal. Coll. Ms. MHS.
Bantz geneal. notes. Ms. MHS.
†Bench and bar of Md. Sams and Riley. 1901, v. 1, pp. 174, 210. Lib. Cong.; MHS; Peabody Lib.
Brisko-Brisco-Briscoe and some family connections. Ramey. P. 24. Ms. MHS.
Chart, photos., complete in 2 sheets. Cary Geneal. Coll. Ms. MHS.
Col. and revolutionary families of Pa. Amer. Hist. Soc., N. Y., 1934, p. 9.
Daughter of Md., Mother of Texas. Bell. MHS; DAR.
†Day-Star of Amer. Freedom. Davies. P. 175. MHS.
*Family Assoc. Bulletins. MHS.
Geneal., descendants of John Stone, Port Tobacco, Md. Nat'l Geneal. Soc. Quart. 1913, v. 2. April, July, Oct. and Jan.; 1914. V. 3. April, July and Jan.
Gov. Wm. Stone. Some notable families of south. States. Armstrong. V. 1, pp. 217-20. DAR.
Hist. Salisbury, Wicomico Co. Truitt. DAR.
*Lineage Bk., Daughters of Founders and Patriots, v. 23, pp. 28-29. MHS; DAR.
Lineage Bks., Natl. Soc. of Daughters of Amer. Col., v. 2, p. 197. MHS; DAR.
†Men of mark in Md. Johnson. V. 1. DAR; Enoch Pratt Lib.
*Notes concerning Stone family in Md. and Va. E. A. Stone. Chicago, Ill.
Patriotic Md. Md. Soc. of S. A. R., 1930. MHS; DAR.
St. Paul's Parish, Balto. V. 1, 2. Mss. MHS.
Stone Family Assoc. Gregory-Simon Stone geneal. MHS.
Stone family of Md. Mrs. Ida Skirk. Natl. Geneal. Soc. Quart., v. 2, no. 1, p. 1; no. 2, p. 34; v. 3, nos. 1, 2, 4; Stone-Marshall notes, v. 21, no. 3, pp. 86-88; Stone family cemetery, "Habre De Venture," v. 21, no. 4, p. 126.
See March, T. Stone. Abr. Compend. Amer. Geneal. Virkus. V. 1, p. 713. DAR.
Stones of Poynton Manor. Harry Wright Newman.
*The Sun, Balto., Nov. 8, 1903.
*Wicomico Co. families. Tilghman. Ms., pp. 26, 123, 127. DAR.
See Carroll-Chase-Paca-Stone.
*Semmes Geneal. Coll. Ms. MHS.
Stone, Balto. Whitely chart. MHS.
†Stone, Charles Co. Biog. cyc. of rep. men of Md. and D. C. P. 358. MHS; DAR.
Stone, Va. and Md. Origin of Stone family. (William Stone came to Md. 1648.) Va. Mag. Hist. and Biog., v. 28, p. 65.
Stone, John, Calvert Co. Will 1693. D. A. R. Mag., v. 66, no. 11, p. 732.
Stone, Gov. John Hoskins. Founders of Anne Arundel and Howard Cos. Warfield. P. 246. MHS; DAR.
†Governor of Md. Buchholz. P. 36. MHS.
†(Born Charles Co., 1745; son of David and Elizabeth (Jenifer Stone); died Oct. 5, 1804, at Annapolis). Hist. of Md. Scharf. V. 2, p. 571. MHS.

†**Stone, John Theodore** (1859–1920). Memorial. Pr. by Md. Casualty Co., Balto., 1920. Enoch Pratt Lib.
†**Stone, Michael Jenifer.** Hist. of Md. Scharf. V. 2, p. 573. MHS.
Stone, Thomas. Biog. of signers' of Declaration of Independence. Joseph M. Sanderson. 1820–27, v. 9, pp. 151–69.
*(1743–87). D. A. R. Mag., Dec., 1914, v. 45, p. 323.
†Hist. of Md. Scharf. V. 2, pp. 235–37. MHS.
†(1743–87). M. H. Mag., v. 12, p. 247.
Stone, William. Abr. Compend. Amer. Geneal. Virkus. V. 6, p. 546. DAR.
Stone, Gov. William. D. A. R. Mag., v. 66, no. 11, p. 734.
***Stone Family.** Natl. Geneal. Soc. Quart., April, 1913, v. 2, no. 2, p. 13, to Jan., 1914, incl.
Notes. Old Northwest. Geneal. Soc. Quart., Columbus, Ohio, 1901, v. 4.
*Old Kent. Hanson. P. 114. MHS; DAR.
Worcester Soc. Antiquity, Worcester, Mass., 1902, v. 8.
Stone Family, Va. Bible rec. D. A. R. Mag., July, 1935, v. 69, no. 7, pp. 428–30.
Stone Line. Hooper family. Col. and Revolutionary families of Pa. Jordan. 1932, v. 4, pp. 232–35.
Lilburn family. Col. and Revolutionary families of Phila. Jordan. 1933, v. 1, pp. 382–98.
***Stone-Dawson.** Lineage Bk., Daughters of Amer. Col., v. 2, p. 197. MHS; DAR.
Stonebraker. Steiner geneal. Steiner. 1896. MHS.
Zion Reformed Church, Hagerstown. Md. Geneal. Rec. Com., 1934–35. Mss. DAR.
Stonebreaker. Abr. Compend. Amer. Geneal. Virkus. V. 6, p. 325. DAR.
Stoner. Abr. Compend. Amer. Geneal. Virkus. V. 4, p. 490. MHS.
Englar family. Barnes. MHS; DAR.
Frederick Co. tombstone inscriptions. Gruder. Natl. Geneal. Soc. Quart., 1919, v. 8, nos. 1, 2.
Roop geneal. Pamph. MHS.
Steiner geneal. Steiner. 1896. MHS.
See Stierner.
Stoner, Steiner. Babylon family. Duttera. P. 35. Ms. MHS.
*Frederick Co. families. Markell. Ms. Personal list.
Patriotic Md. Md. Soc. of S. A. R., 1930. MHS; DAR.
†**Stonestreet.** Med. Annals Md. Cordell. 1903, p. 585. MHS.
Stookes, Cecil Co. Lineage Bks., Natl. Soc. of Daughters of Amer. Col., v. 4, p. 130. MHS; DAR.
Stoop, Stoops. St. Stephens Parish, Cecilton, Md. MHS; DAR.
***Stoops Family,** southern Md. Wilson Mss. Coll., no. 93. MHS.
See Stoop.
Storey. *See* Story.
Stork. Abr. Compend. Amer. Geneal. Virkus. V. 4, p. 491. MHS.
Ancestry of Lieut. and Mrs. Wm. B. Stork; with geneal. of Boteler, Eaton, Ellis, Stork and Warner. Ms. MHS.
Storm. Patriotic Md. Md. Soc. of S. A. R., 1930. MHS; DAR.
Storm, Leonard, Frederick Co. Will probated July 26, 1819. D. A. R. Mag., v. 62, no. 4, p. 247.
Story. Cary Geneal. Coll. Ms. MHS.
†Med. Annals Md. Cordell. 1903, p. 585. MHS.
Story, Col. Walter, Charles Co. (1666–1726). D. H. Thomas pedigree chart. Soc. Col. Wars, Md. Johnston. 1905, pp. 109, 155. MHS.
Story, Storey. St. Paul's Parish, Balto. V. 2, 4. Mss. MHS.
Stotelmyer. U. B. cemetery, Sabillasville. Young. Natl. Geneal. Soc. Quart., Sept., 1938, v. 26, no. 3, p. 61 (to be contd.).
Stotlemyer. Md. tombstone rec. Md. Geneal. Rec. Com., 1937, Parran, p. 17. Mss. DAR.
†**Stottlemyer.** Hist. of Frederick Co. Williams. V. 2; pp. 748. MHS; DAR.
Stouffer. Beards' Luth. graveyard, Washington Co. Md. Geneal. Rec. Com., 1935–36. Mss. DAR.
†(Capt. of ship Antarctic). M. H. Mag., v. 12, p. 247.
Clark chart. MHS.
Englar family. Barnes. MHS; DAR.
*Geneal. memorands, 1630–1903. Comp. and arranged by (Miss) Kate S. Snively. Hagerstown, Md., 1903. Lib. Cong.
Manly chart. MHS.
Pedigree of Henry Irvine Keyser, II. Soc. Col. Wars Md. Culver. 1940. MHS; DAR.
Roop geneal. Pamph. MHS.
Spessard family. Spessard. MHS; DAR.
Mrs. H. DeCourcy Wright Thom chart. MHS.
Stover. Hagerstown tombstone inscriptions. Gruder. Natl. Geneal. Soc. Quart., 1919, v. 8, nos. 1, 2.
Stow. Cannon-Riley-Truitt-Houston-Kollock. Stow. Ms. MHS.
Hall-Collins-Elliott-Laws-Tingley families. J. C. Stow. Bd. ms. MHS.
Kipp-Shryer-Stow families. Ms. MHS.
Rec. from two Bibles, 1774. Ms. MHS.
See Kipp-Shryler-Shroyer-Stow.
Stow Family. Stow family. J. C. S. Stow. 1932. Bd. ms. MHS.
Straebel, A. Perrigo. Md. Soc., War of 1812, v. 1, no. 82. Ms. MHS.
Straffer. Mt. Olivet Cemetery, Frederick. Md. Geneal. Rec. Com., 1934–35, p. 111. Mss. DAR.
Stran. Balto., its hist., its people. Hall. V. 2. MHS; DAR.
St. Paul's Parish, Balto. V. 1. Mss. MHS.
Strasbaugh. Portrait and biog. rec. of Harford and Cecil Cos. 1897, p. 147. MHS; DAR.
***Strassburger.** Strassburger family and allied families. R. B. Strassburger. Pr. for priv. circulation, Gwynedd Valley, Pa., 1922. MHS.
Stratton. Geneal. of Henrietta Chauncy Wilson. Upshur. Bk. of photos. MHS.
†**Straughn.** Med. Annals Md. Cordell. 1903, p. 586. MHS.
Strause. Hagerstown tombstone inscriptions. Gruder. Natl. Geneal. Soc. Quart., 1919, v. 8, nos. 1, 2.
†**Strawbridge.** Hist. of West. Md. Scharf. V. 2, pp. 902–04. MHS; DAR.

†**Strawbridge, Robert.** Hist. of Md. Scharf. V. 2, p. 554. MHS.
Street. Bond chart. MHS.
†Hist. of Allegany Co. Thomas and Williams. V. 1. MHS; DAR.
Hist. of Harford Co. Preston. MHS; DAR.
St. Paul's Parish, Balto. V. 1. Mss. MHS.
***Street Family.** Wilson Mss. Coll., no. 4. MHS.
Street, Streett. Balto., its hist., its people. Hall. V. 2. MHS; DAR.
Col. families of U. S. A. Mackenzie. V. 1, pp. 367–70. MHS; DAR.
†**Streeter, Sebastin Ferris** (1810–65; recording secretary of Md. Hist. Soc.). New Eng. Hist. and Biog. Reg., 1865, v. 19, p. 91.
†**Streett.** Med. Annals Md. Cordell. 1903, p. 586. MHS.
†Men of mark in Md. Johnson. V. 2. DAR; Enoch Pratt Lib.
See Street.
Stretcher Family, Del. Allied families of Delaware. Sellers. MHS.
Stribling. Abr. Compend. Amer. Geneal. Virkus. V. 6, p. 529. DAR.
Stricker. Biog. of Gen. John Stricker, 1759–1825. John Stricker, Jr. M. H. Mag., 1914, v. 9, no. 3, pp. 209–18.
Mrs. R. F. Brent chart. MHS.
Cary Geneal. Coll. Ms. MHS.
†Hist. of West. Md. Scharf. V. 1, pp. 445–46. MHS; DAR.
Md. families. Culver. Ms. Personal list.
†**Stricker, Gen. John.** Hist. of Md. Scharf. V. 3, p. 108. MHS.
(1758–1825). Revolutionary war heroes. Cole. Bklet. Enoch Pratt Lib.
†(1759–1825). Sketch of his military life. M. H. Mag., 1914, v. 9, pp. 209.
Westminster churchyard. Patriotic Marylander, v. 2, no. 4, pp. 54–60. MHS; DAR.
***Strider.** The Sun, Balto., Oct. 15, Dec. 3 (letters), 1905.
Stringer. Frances Murray Bowdoin chart. MHS.
Strobel, J. Wm. Md. Soc., War of 1812, v. 3, no. 214. Ms. MHS.
Stroller. Baust or Emanuel Reformed churchyard, Carroll Co. Md. Geneal. Rec. Co., 1935–36. Mss. DAR.
Strong. See Albee. Abr. Compend. Amer. Geneal. Virkus. V. 4, p. 675. MHS.
Bible rec.; Bible owned by Mrs. Walter Strong, Chestertown. Md. Geneal. Rec. Com., 1937, Parran, pp. 219–22. Mss. DAR.
*Leaflets with geneal. MHS.
Strong, Balto. French chart. MHS.
Strong, Frederick Steele. Pedigree. Soc. Col. Wars Md. Culver. 1940. MHS; DAR. (See Pedigree Book, 1905, p. 102.)
Strong, Lieut.-Col. Richard Polk, U.S.A. Pedigree charts, plates 1, 2 and 3. Soc. Col. Wars, Md. Johnston. 1905, pp. 102–104. MHS.
***Strong Family.** Arch. of Georgetown Univ., Wash., D. C., v. 274, no. 6.
***Strother.** William Strother of Va. and his descendants.
See Pendleton-Orrick-Strother-Calvert.
***Strother,** Va. The Sun, Balto., Nov. 26, Dec. 10, 1905.
Strouble. Md. tombstone rec. Md. Geneal. Rec. Com., 1937, Parran, p. 33. Mss. DAR.
Struman. Abr. Compend. Amer. Geneal, Virkus. V. 4, p. 336. MHS.
Stuart. See Guthrie. Abr. Compend. Amer. Geneal. Virkus. V. 1, p. 314. DAR.
Hagerstown tombstone inscriptions. Gruder. Natl. Geneal. Soc. Quart., 1919, v. 8, nos. 1, 2.
Natl. Geneal. Soc. Quart., v. 7, no. 3, pp. 45–48.
St. Paul's Parish, Balto. V. 1. Mss. MHS.
See Stewart.
Stuart, Somerset Co. Bible rec., 1779–1805. Typed, 2 pp. MHS.
***Stuart,** Va. The Sun, Balto., April 5, July 29, Aug. 5, 12, Oct. 14, 1906.
Stuart, Steuart. Bible rec. Upper Penins. East. Shore, pp. 135, 141, 148. MHS.
Stuart, Stewart. Bible rec. Upper Penins. East Shore. Pp.135–47. Mss. MHS; DAR.
Stubbs. St. John's R. C. Church cemetery. Montgomery Co. Md. Geneal. Rec. Com., 1926, p. 27. Mss. DAR.
St. Paul's Parish, Balto. V. 1, 4. Mss. MHS.
Stubbs, Herbert R., Balto. New Eng. Hist. and Geneal. Reg., v. 86, p. 103.
***Studer.** Frederick Co. families. Markell. Ms. Personal list.
***Stull.** Frederick Co. families. Markell. Ms. Personal list.
Lineage Bks., Natl. Soc. of Daughters of Amer. Col., v. 2, p. 92. MHS; DAR.
***Stull,** Washington Co. Lineage Bk., Daughters of Amer. Col., v. 2, p. 92. MHS; DAR.
***Stump.** Augustine Herman, founder of Bohemia Manor. Leaflet. MHS.
*Chart. H. A. Stump. Jan. 18, 1926. MHS.
†Chesapeake Bay Country. Earle. P. 299. MHS.
Geneal. and memorial encyc. of Md. Spencer. V. 2, p. 643. MHS; DAR.
Herman-Stump geneal. chart. MHS.
Hist. of Harford Co. Preston. MHS; DAR.
Husband and allied families. Ms. MHS.
*John Stump of Cecil Co. H. A. Stump. Balto., 1923. Written additions in copy in MHS.
Miss Cassandra Lee chart. MHS.
Md. families. Culver. Ms. Personal list.
Peale Geneal. Coll. Ms. MHS.
Pedigree of George Webb Constable. Soc. Col. Wars Md. Culver. 1940. MHS; DAR.
*Rec. of Stump family in Md. With geneal. A. P. Silver and H. W. Archer. 1891, pamph. MHS.
St. Paul's Parish, Balto. V. 1, 2. Mss. MHS.
Florence Eyster Weaver chart. MHS.
See Wilson, Mrs. Calvin. Abr. Compend. Amer. Geneal. Virkus. V. 1, p. 894. DAR.
See Haldane.
See Harris-McKinney-Stump.
See Rutledge-Stump-Jennings.
†**Stump, Herman.** Men of mark in Md. Johnson. V. 1. DAR; Enoch Pratt Lib.
*With geneal. Folder. MHS.
***Stump, Col. Herman.** Geneal. and mem. encyc. of Md. Spencer. V. 2, pp. 643–49. MHS; DAR.
Stump, Stumpf. Stump, Stumpf family of Cecil and Harford Cos. Pamph. MHS.
Stumpf. *See* Stump.
***Stunmell** (?). Frederick Co. families. Markell. Ms. Personal list.

Stup. Mt. Olivet Cemetery, Frederick. Md. Geneal. Rec. Com., 1934-35, p. 111. Mss. DAR.

Sturges. All Hallow's P. E. churchyard, Snow Hill, Worcester Co. Hudson. Bd. ms. MHS; DAR. Also: Md. Geneal. Rec. Com., 1935-36, p. 24. Mss. DAR.
Turner Geneal. Coll. Ms. MHS.

Sturges, Somerset Parish. Abst. of rec. Turner Geneal. Coll. Ms. MHS.

Sturgis. Makemie Memorial Pres. churchyard, Snow Hill, Worcester Co. Hudson. Bd. ms. MHS; DAR. Also: Md. Geneal. Rec. Com., Mrs. Lines. Mss. DAR.
*Wicomico Co. families. Tilghman. Ms., p. 26. DAR.

†**Sudler.** Biog. cyc. of rep. men of Md. and D. C. P. 392. MHS; DAR.
Lineage Bks., Natl. Soc. of Daughters of Amer. Col., v. 2, p. 206. MHS; DAR.
Quaker Cemetery, Millington. Md. Geneal. Rec. Com., 1932-33, p. 209. Mss. DAR.
Turner Geneal. Coll. Ms. MHS.
*Queen Anne Co. Lineage Bk., Daughters of Amer., Col., v. 2, p. 206. MHS; DAR.
Somerset Parish. Abs. of rec. Turner Geneal. Coll. Ms. MHS.

Sudler, C. H. Abr. Compend. Amer. Geneal. Virkus. V. 1, p. 848. DAR.

Sudler-Emory. Bible rec., Kent Co. Md. Geneal. Rec. Com., 1933-34, pp. 236-38. Mss. DAR.

Sulivane. See Hemphill. Abr. Compend. Amer. Geneal. Virkus. V. 1, p. 293. DAR.

***Sullivan.** Family of John Sullivan of Berwick. MHS.
Geneal. of family of Gideon Gilpin. MHS.
Geneal. of McKean family of Pa. Buchanan. P. 215. MHS.
Griffith geneal. Griffith. MHS; DAR.
†Med. Annals. Md. Cordell. 1903, p. 586. MHS.
St. Paul's Parish, Balto. V. 1, 2, 3, 4. Mss. MHS.
St. Stephens Parish, Cecilton, Md. MHS; DAR.

Sullivane. (10 stones.) Christ P. E. Church cemetery, Cambridge. Steele. 1936. MHS; DAR.

***Sulmon.** Frederick Co. families. Markell. Ms. Personal list.

Summer. Old Somerset. Torrence. MHS; DAR.

Summers. The Beckwiths. Beckwith.
†Experience and labors of Rev. George D. Summers, man who was born blind. (Born in Montgomery Co., 1793.) Rev. J. S. Inskip. Balto., Armstrong & Berry, Woods Print, 1838. Enoch Pratt Lib.
Graveyard. Md. Geneal. Rec. Com., 1937, Parran, p. 11. Mss. DAR.
†Hist. of Frederick Co. Williams. V. 2, pp. 739, 964, 983, 1340, 1473, 1571, 1578. MHS; DAR.
†Med. Annals Md. Cordell. 1903, p. 587. MHS.
St. Paul's Parish, Balto. V. 1, 2. Mss. MHS.
See Simmers.
See Somers.

Summers, Walter B. Md. Soc., War of 1812, v. 3, no. 206. Ms. MHS.

Summers-Jones-Gunby-Morris. Bible rec., from Bible owned by L. W. Gunby, Salisbury. Md. Geneal. Rec. Com., 1937-38, pp. 142-46. Mss. DAR.

Summers, Somers. Family notes. Ms. MHS.

Summerville. St. Paul's Parish, Balto. V. 2. Mss. MHS.

Summerwell. Christ P. E. Church cemetery, Cambridge. Steele. 1936. MHS; DAR.

Sumner. Amer. Armory and Blue Book. Matthews. Pt. 1.
Ruf-Haight-Eddy-Sumner-Hatch and allied families. Ms. MHS.
Somerset Co. Court Book. Tilghman. 1937. Ms. DAR.

Sumner, Wm. H. Md. Soc., War of 1812, v. 2, no. 163. Ms. MHS.

Sumner Family. Ms. MHS.

***Sunderland.** Noble life of Sarah Broadhead Sunderland. Family geneal., 1745-1914. J. Sunderland and J. T. Sunderland. Geneal. letter by L. T. Sunderland. Kansas City, Mo., 1914. MHS.

Supplee. Bible rec. Md. Geneal. Rec. Com., 1939-40, pp. 12-14. Mss. DAR.

Surman. Somerset Co. Court Book. Tilghman. 1937. Ms. DAR.
Old Somerset. Torrence. MHS; DAR.

Surratt, Mary E. Jenkins. Maternal line. Md. Geneal. Bull., v. 1, pp. 1-3.

Suter. Hagerstown tombstone inscriptions. Gruder. Natl. Geneal. Soc. Quart., 1919, v. 8, nos. 1, 2.
Patterson-Lamar Bible rec. Md. Geneal. Rec. Com., 1932, p. 20. DAR.

Sutliff. St. Paul's Parish, Balto. V. 2. Mss. MHS.

Sutton. Balto., its hist., its people. Hall. V. 2. MHS; DAR.
Cummings chart. Lib. Cong.; MHS; DAR.
St. Paul's Parish, Balto. V. 1. Mss. MHS.
Shrewsbury churchyard, Kent Co. Md. O. R. Soc., v. 2, pp. 46-54. MHS.
Still Pond church and cemetery. Md. O. R. Soc. Bull., no. 2, pp. 65-75.
Still Pond cemetery, Kent Co. Md. O. R. Soc., v. 2. MHS.
*The Sun, Balto., Sept. 18, 1904.
See Judd-Sutton-Boquets.

Sutton, Eben, Mass. and Md. Pedigree. Soc. Col. Wars Md. Culver. 1940. MHS; DAR.

***Sutton-Rutherford,** Va. The Sun, Balto., Sept. 4, 18, 1904.

***Swadner.** John Swadner and his descendants, Frederick Co. (Died 1790.) Grace R. Evans. Decatur, Ill., 1919, mimeog. MHS; DAR.

Swaine. Castle geneal. and chart. MHS.

Swan. Ances. rec. and portraits. Col. Dames of Amer., 1910, v. 1, pp. 330, 335, 361. MHS; DAR.
Bantz geneal. notes. Ms. MHS.
"Fairview," home of Gov. Oden Bowie, near Bowie, Prince George Co. Private burying ground, 1745-1904. Ms. MHS; DAR.
See Frick. Abr. Compend. Amer. Geneal. Virkus. V. 1, p. 919. DAR.
Howland chart. MHS.
Jacobs chart. MHS.
Patriotic Md. Md. Soc. of S. A. R., 1930. MHS; DAR.
Samuel Carpenter of Phila. Carpenter. P. 207. MHS.

*The Sun, Balto., April 23, 1905.
Mrs. Wm. L. Watson chart. MHS.
Swan, Miss Isabel Alexander. Chart. Col. Dames, Chap. I. MHS.
Mrs. Wm. L. Watson chart. MHS.
Swan, Gen. John. Westminster churchyard. Patriotic Marylander, v. 2, no. 4, pp. 54-60. MHS; DAR.
Swan, Matthew (1743-95). Revolutionary War Heroes. Cole. Bklet. Enoch Pratt Lib.
Westminster churchyard. Patriotic Marylander v. 2, no. 4, pp. 54-60. MHS; DAR.
†**Swan, Robt.** M. H. Mag., v. 12, p. 248.
Swan, Samuel. Glendy churchyard. Patriotic Marylander, v. 2, no. 4, pp. 54-60. MHS; DAR.
†**Swan, Thomas.** Governor of Md. Buchholz. P. 184. MHS.
Swan, Wm. Glendy churchyard. Patriotic Marylander, v. 2, no. 4, pp. 54-60. MHS; DAR.
Swan Family. Ms. MHS.
Swan Family, Allegany Co. Land patents, 1790-1836. Ms. MHS.
Swan, Swann. Balto., its hist., its people. Hall. V. 2. MHS; DAR.
Cary Geneal. Coll. Ms. MHS.
St. Paul's Parish, Balto. V. 1, 2, 3, 4. Mss. MHS.
Swann. Mason chart. MHS.
St. Charles R. C. Church graveyard, Indianhead, Charles Co. Md. Geneal. Rec. Com., 1933-34, p. 137. Mss. DAR.
Turner family, Va. Va. Mag. Hist. and Biog., v. 21, p. 315.
See Swan.
Swann, Mrs. Sherlock (Edith R. Deford). Chart. Col. Dames, Chap. I. MHS.
†**Swann, Thomas.** Balto., hist. and biog. Richardson and Bennett. 1871, pp. 493-98. MHS; DAR.
Swann, Gov. Thomas. Founders of Anne Arundel and Howard Cos. Warfield. P. 285. MHS; DAR.
***Swayne.** Descendants of Francis Swayne and others. N. W. Swayne. Pr. for priv. circulation, J. B. Lippincott Co., Phila., 1921, ltd. ed. MHS.
***Sweadner.** Frederick Co. families. Markell. Ms. Personal list.
See Swadner.
Swearingen. Founders of Anne Arundel and Howard Cos. Warfield. P. 320. MHS; DAR.
†Med. Annals Md. Cordell. 1903, p. 587. MHS.
Tiernan families. Tiernan. 1901. MHS; DAR.
See Van Swearingen. Lineage Bks., Natl. Soc. of Daughters of Amer. Col., v. 2, 155; v. 3, pp. 148, 318. MHS; DAR.
Swearingen, Sweringer, Van Swearingen. Abr. Compend. Amer. Geneal. Virkus. V. 6, p. 495.
Col. families of U. S. A. Mackenzie. V. 7, p. 220. MHS; DAR.
Sweat (Sweatman), George Noble. Will probated Jan. 16, 1777. D. A. R. Mag., July, 1933, v. 67, no. 7, p. 441.
Sweatman. Cary Geneal. Coll. Ms. MHS.
Sweeney. Geneal. and mem. encyc. of Md. Spencer. V. 1, p. 303. MHS; DAR.
Peale Geneal. Coll. Ms. MHS.
Sweeting. St. Paul's Parish, Balto. V. 1, Mss. MHS.
Sweetser. Sweetser family of Md. and Mass. Lester D. Gardner. Pamph., repr. from M. H. Mag., June, 1932, v. 27, no. 2. MHS; DAR.
Chart. Ms. MHS.
Sweetser, Seth, Annapolis and Balto. Chart. Pamph. MHS.
Sweetser Line. Col. and Revolutionary families of Pa. Amer. Hist. Soc., N. Y., 1934, p. 363.
***Sweringen.** Family register of Gerret van Sweringen and descendants, 1657-1884. Comp. by member of family. Wash., D. C., C. W. Brown, 2nd ed., 1894. MHS; DAR.
Ms. MHS.
*Register of Gerret van Sweringen II. Wash., D. C., 1904. MHS; DAR.
See Swearingen.
***Sweringen, Van Swearingen.** The Sun, Balto., March 6, 1904.
Swift. St. Paul's Parish, Balto. V. 2. Mss. MHS.
Swindell. Col. families of U. S. A. Mackenzie. V. 1, p. 405. MHS; DAR.
Toy-Swindell chart. O'Gorman. Ms. DAR.
Swineyard. Naturalizations in Md., 1666-1765; Laws. Bacon. MHS.
Swingate-Calvert. Notes and queries. M. H. Mag., Sept., 1940, v. 35, no. 3, p. 310.
Swinton. Joshua Dryden Bible rec. Ms. MHS.
†**Swope.** Med. Annals Md. Cordell. 1903, p. 587. MHS.
*Swope family, 1676-1896. G. E. Swope. Lancaster, Pa., T. B. & H. B. Cochran, 1896. MHS.
Swornstead. Naturalizations in Md., 1666-1765; Laws. Bacon. MHS.
†**Syckes.** Hist. of Allegany Co. Thomas and Williams. V. 2. MHS; DAR.
Mt. Paran Pres. churchyard, Harrisonville, Balto. Co. Typed ms. MHS; DAR.
Sydemon, Jack. See Crumbaugh family. Ms. File case, DAR.
***Sydney-Smith.** Sydney-Smith and Clagett-Price, and allied families. Geneal. Lucy M. S. Price. Strasburg, Va., Shenandoah Pub. House, 1927. MHS; DAR.
†**Syester.** Hist. of Allegany Co. Thomas and Williams. V. 1. MHS; DAR.
Sykes. Chart. Wm. Preston of Newcastle on Tyne, Eng., and Phila., Pa., and allied families. Belsterling. MHS.
Descendants of Joran Kyn. Pa. Mag., v. 7, p. 464.
Miss C. Petre chart. MHS.
Syle. Ances. rec. and portraits. Col. Dames of Amer., 1910, v. 2, p. 547. MHS; DAR.
Symington. Ancestry of Rosalie Morris Johnson. Johnson. 1905. MHS; DAR.
†**Symington, Hon. W. Stuart.** Encyc. of Amer. biog. Amer. Hist. Soc., N. Y., 1928, v. 33, p. 190.
Syserson. Naturalizations in Md., 1666-1765; Laws. Bacon. MHS.
†**Syster.** Bench and bar of Md. Sams and Riley. 1901, v. 2, p. 623. Lib. Cong.; MHS; Peabody Lib.

T

Tabb. Done Bible rec. Ms. MHS.
Geneal. and memorial encyc. of Md. Spencer. V. 2, p. 594. MHS; DAR.
Mrs. H. F. Johnston chart. MHS.
See Mayo-Tabb.
Tabb, Va. See Perrin, Mrs. J. T. Abr. Compend. Amer. Geneal. Virkus. V. 1, p. 192. DAR.
†Tabb, J. Bannister. Men of mark in Md. Johnson. V. 3. DAR; Enoch Pratt Lib.
Tabb Family. Lee of Va., 1642–1892. E. J. Lee. P. 382. Lib. Cong.; MHS.
Tabb Family, Va. William and Mary Quart., 1st series, v. 13, pp. 168–73.
†Tabbs. Md. Annals Md. Cordell. 1903, p. 588. MHS.
***Tabler.** Frederick Co. families. Markell. Ms. Personal list.
Taggart. Md. families. Culver. Ms. Personal list.
St. Paul's Parish, Balto. V. 2. Mss. MHS.
***Taggert.** Russell-Lux Bible rec. Photos. MHS.
Tahy. St. John's R. C. Church cemetery, Montgomery Co. Md. Geneal. Rec. Com., 1926, p. 27. Mss. DAR.
***Tailer.** Pennington Papers. Ms. MHS.
†Talbot. Col. Joseph Belt. Hist. papers of Magruder. Soc. Col. Wars. 1909. MHS; DAR.
Cary Geneal. Coll. Ms. MHS.
Chart of descendants of Richard Talbot, Anne Arundel Co., 1649, showing nine generations, 40 names. Md. Geneal. Rec. Com., 1937–38; filed separately; folder. DAR.
*Lineage Bk., Daughters of Founders and Patriots, v. 9, p. 11. MHS.
Manly chart. MHS.
Md. families. Culver. Ms. Personal list.
Plummer family. A. P. H. Ms. MHS.
William and Mary Quart., 1st series, v. 9, p. 257.
See Darnall-Talbot.
See Talbott.
†Talbot, George. Hist. of Cecil Co. Johnston. MHS; DAR.
†Talbot, Hattersly W. Men of mark in Md. Johnson. V. 1. DAR; Enoch Pratt Lib.
***Talbot Family.** Bit of geneal. of branch of Talbot family. H. A. Talbot. De Pere, Wis., 1897. MHS.
Talbot, Talbott. Balto., its hist., its people. Hall. V. 3. MHS; DAR.
Talbott. Abr. Compend. Amer. Geneal. Virkus. V. 6, pp. 290, 522, 554, 720. DAR.
D. A. R. Mag., July, 1934, v. 68, no. 7, p. 442.
Early Quaker rec., Anne Arundel and Calvert Cos., 1665–1889. Pub. Geneal. Soc. Pa., v. 3, no. 3, pp. 197–200.
Focke Geneal. Coll. Ms. MHS.
*Founders of Anne Arundel and Howard Cos. Warfield. P. 530. MHS; DAR.
Hist. graves of Md. and D. C. Ridgely. MHS.
See Houk, R. T., Jr. Abr. Compend. Amer. Geneal. Virkus. V. 1, p. 376. DAR.
Lineage Bks., Natl. Soc. of Daughters of Amer. Col., v. 1, pp. 6, 42; v. 2, pp. 61, 298. MHS; DAR.
†Memorial address on life and character of J. Fred C. Talbott, representative of Md. Wash., D. C., 1919. Enoch Pratt Lib.
Monocacy Cemetery, Beallsville, Montgomery Co. Md. Geneal. Rec. Com., 1926–27, pp. 70–73. Mss. DAR.
Patriotic Md. Md. Soc. of S. A. R., 1930. MHS; DAR.
Pedigree of Morris Gregg. Soc. Col. Wars Md. Culver. 1940. MHS; DAR.
(8 generations.) Pedigree of Thomas Carroll Roberts. Soc. Col. Wars Md. Culver. 1940. MHS; DAR.
*Pennington Papers. Ms. MHS.
*Plummer family. A. P. H. Mss. File case, MHS.
Thomas-Chew-Lawrence. Thomas. MHS.
St. Paul's Parish, Balto. V. 1, 2, 4. Mss. MHS.
See Boone-Talbott-Pumphrey.
See Talbot.
***Talbott, Adam.** Geneal. notes. Mss. File case, MHS.
Talbott, Hattersley Worthington. Md. Soc., War of 1812, v. 2, no. 139. Ms. MHS.
Talbott, Hattersley Worthington, Jr. Md. Soc., War of 1812, v. 2, no. 160. Ms. MHS.
Talbott, Otho Holland Williams. Md. Soc., War of 1812, v. 2, no. 161. Ms. MHS.
***Talbott Family.** Geneal. chart. M. C. W. Westerman. Mss. MHS.
Rec. gathered by Ida M. M. Shirk. Feb., 1931. Bd. ms., 100 pp. MHS.
Thomas Book. Thomas. P. 527. Lib. Cong.; MHS.
Talbott, Talbot. Col. families of U. S. A. Mackenzie. V. 3. MHS; DAR.
*Descendants of Richard and Elizabeth (Ewen) Talbott of "Poplar Knowle," West River, Anne Arundel Co., 1650. Mrs. I. M. M. Shirk. Balto., Day Printing Co., 1927. MHS; DAR.
Talcott. Pedigree of Septimus Davis. Soc. Col. Wars Md. Culver. 1940. MHS; DAR.
Taliaferro. Chart of descendants of Robert Taliaferro of Va. Ms. Compiled by W. B. McGroaty, Falls Church, Va., 1927; corrections in Wm. and Mary Quart., v. 12, series 2, p. 306.
Family reg. of Nicholas Taliaferro, with notes. W. B. McGroarty. William and Mary Quart., 2nd series, v. 1, no. 3, p. 145; corrections, v. 2, no. 2, p. 134.
Hist. of Caroline Co., Va. Wingfield.
Rucker family. Whitley.
Va. families. Du Bellett.
Zimmerman-Waters and allied families. Allen. Pp. 29–35. MHS; DAR.
***Taliaferro,** Va. The Sun, Balto., July 30, Aug. 6, 1905.
Taliaferro Family. William and Mary Quart., 2nd series, v. 4, no. 3, p. 191.
Taliaferro Family, Va. Tyler's Quart. Mag., v. 11, pp. 51, 179, 241.
†Tall. Med. Annals Md. Cordell. 1903, p. 588. MHS.
Trinity Church cemetery, Dorchester Co. Md. O. R. Soc. Bull., no. 3, pp. 42–52.
Tallmade. Cresap Soc. Bull., no. 4. MHS.
Taney. Abr. Compend. Amer. Geneal. Virkus. V. 1, p. 960. DAR.
Ances. rec. and portraits. Col. Dames of Amer., 1910, v. 2, p. 552. MHS; DAR.
†Bench and bar of Md. Sams and Riley. 1901, v. 1, p. 278. Lib. Cong.; MHS; Peabody Lib.

J. L. Brent pedigree chart. Soc. Col. Wars, Md. Johnston. 1905, p. 7. MHS.
*Chart. MHS.
†Chief Justice Roger B. Taney: His career at Frederick Bar, 1799–1823. Edw. S. Delaplaine. M. H. Mag., 1918, v. 13, pp. 109–42.
†Chief Justice Taney. J. A. Shauch. (Chief Justice 1836–64.) The Green Bag, Dec., 1902. Enoch Pratt Lib.
†Founder of Taneytown. G. A. Taney. M. H. Mag., 1916, v. 11, no. 1, pp. 74–75.
†Hist. of Frederick Co. Williams. V 1. MHS; DAR.
†Hist. of West. Md. Scharf. V. 1, pp. 394–98. MHS; DAR.
Judicial rec. of late Chief Justice Taney. Mss. DAR.
R. B. Keyser pedigree chart, plate 2. Soc. Col. Wars, Md. Johnston. 1905, p. 56. MHS.
†Life of Roger Brooke Taney, Chief Justice of Supreme Court of U. S. Bernard Steiner. Balto., Williams & Wilkins Co., 1922. MHS; Enoch Pratt Lib.
*Lineage Bk., Daughters of Founders and Patriots, v. 22, p. 10. MHS; DAR.
Manly chart. MHS.
Marshall and Taney, statesmen of law. Ben W. Palmer. Minneapolis, Univ. of Minn. Press, 1939, 281 pp. MHS.
Md. tombstone rec. Md. Geneal. Rec. Com., 1937, Parran, p. 33. Mss. DAR.
†Med. Annals Md. Cordell. 1903, p. 588. MHS.
*Memoirs of Roger Brooke Taney, with some data on Brooke family. S. Tyler. Balto., 1872. MHS.
Monumental City. Howard. MHS; DAR.
Pedigree of Duncan Keener Brent. Soc. Col. Wars Md. Culver. 1940. MHS; DAR.
*Pedigree. McHenry Howard. Ms. MHS.
†Proc. of Bench and Bar of Balto., upon death of Roger B. Taney, Chief Justice of Supreme Court of U. S. Balto., John Murphy Co., 1864; Wash., D. C., 1865. Enoch Pratt Lib.
†Roger B. Taney and Mr. Biddle's bank. C. W. Smith, Jr. M. H. Mag., 1936, v. 31, pp. 1–6.
†(Roger Brooke Taney was born "Taney Place," Calvert Co., 1777; died in Wash., 1864). Biog. sketches of eminent Amer. patriots. Taggert. 1907.
St. Joseph's R. C. churchyard. Md. O. R. Soc. Bull., no. 3, p. 64.
Some old Eng. letters. M. H. Mag., 1914, v. 9, no. 2, pp. 107–56.
*Taney and allied families. Geneal. study with brief notes. Katherine T. Silverson. Comp. and priv. pr. for Katherine T. Silverson. Amer. Hist. Soc. Inc., N. Y., 1935. MHS; DAR.
Sir John Zouch and his descendants. Va. Mag. Hist. and Biog., v. 12, pp. 429–32.

Taney, Roger Brooke. And tenets of democracy. Carl B. Swisher. M. H. Mag., Sept., 1939, v. 34, no. 3, p. 207.
†Balto., hist. and biog. Richardson and Bennett. 1871, pp. 499–501. MHS; DAR.
†Biog. sketches of eminent Amer. patriots. Taggart. Pp. 122–70. MHS.
Brief sketch. McHenry Howard. 1921. Ms. MHS.
†Chief Justice Taney. Address by S. Teackle Wallis, Dec. 10, 1872. With reply of His Excellency Governor Whyte. Balto., John Murphy, 1872. Enoch Pratt Lib.
Founders of Anne Arundel and Howard Cos. Warfield. P. 321. MHS; DAR.
†Jacksonian jurist. C. W. Smith, Jr. Chapel Hill Univ. N. C. Press, 1936. MHS; Enoch Pratt Lib.
†(1777–1864). M. H. Mag., v. 12, p. 248.
Marshall and Taney, statesmen of law. Palmer. Enoch Pratt Lib.
†M. H. Mag., v. 34, no. 3, p. 207.
†Memoir. Samuel Tyler. (Notes on Brooke family. Balto., John Murphy Co., 1872. Autobiog. brought down to 1801, which forms an introduction of Tyler's memoir. (Samuel Tyler was born in Prince George Co., 1809; died in Wash., D. C., 1878.)
Reappraisal. Monroe Johnson. Amer. Law Rev., Sept., 1932, v. 66, p. 487.
Roger Brooke Taney. F. R. Jones. The Green Bag, Jan., 1902, v. 14, no. 1. Boston. Enoch Pratt Lib.
†Roger Brooke Taney. C. B. Swisher. N. Y., Macmillan Co., 1935. MHS; DAR; Enoch Pratt Lib.

Taney, Tanney. Bantz geneal. notes. Ms. MHS.

†Taneyhill. Geneal. and mem. encyc. of Md. Spencer. V. 1, p. 149. MHS; DAR.

†Taneyhill, Pa. Med. Annals Md. Cordell. 1903, p. 588. MHS.

***Tannehill.** Frederick Co. families. Markell. Ms. Personal list.

Tanner. Clasping hands with generations past. Lloyd. MHS; DAR.

Tanney. Miss Sara E. White chart. MHS.
*Semmes Geneal. Coll. Ms. MHS.
Roger Brooke Tanney. Mary F. Taney. Amer. Catholic Hist. Soc. of Phila. Rec., 1900, v. 11.
See Taney.

Tanney-Silverson. Lineage Bks., Natl. Soc. of Daughters of Amer. Col., v. 4, p. 44. MHS; DAR.

***Tant or Taut.** Semmes Geneal. Coll. Ms. MHS.

Tapscott. Rev. Joseph Hull (1595) and some of his descendants. Hull. 1904, p. 19. MHS.
Pedigree of John Baker Thompson Hull. Soc. Col. Wars Md. Culver. 1940. MHS; DAR.

Tapscott, Va. A. E. Hull chart. MHS.

Tapscott, John Shurman. Pedigree chart. Soc. Col. Wars, Md. Johnston. 1905, p. 106. MHS.

***Tar.** Wicomico Co. families. Tilghman. Ms, p. 23. DAR.

Tarbutton. Tarbutton-Battis families. Bible rec. Md. Geneal. Rec. Com., 1939–40, pp. 144–47. Mss. DAR.

Tarleton. Centenary of Catholicity in Ky. Webb. 1884. MHS.

***Tarleton,** St. Mary's Co. Col. families of Amer. Lawrence. V. 140. MHS.

Tarlton. St. Paul's Parish, Balto. V. 2. Mss. MHS.

Tarr, F. Crey. Md. Soc., War of 1812, v. 2, no. 193. Ms. MHS.

Tasker. Ames Geneal. Coll. Ms. MHS.
Ances. rec. and portraits. Col. Dames of Amer., 1910, v. 1, p. 286; v. 2, p. 671. MHS; DAR.
Balch chart. MHS.
Mrs. R. Barton, Jr., charts. MHS.
Bolton chart. MHS.

Tasker. Bowie-Claggett chart. MHS.
See Carter of Nomini Hall, Va. New Eng. Hist. and Geneal. Register.
Chart, photos., complete in 2 sheets. Cary Geneal. Coll. Ms. MHS.
Col. families of U. S. A. Mackenzie. V. 4, p. 278. MHS; DAR.
De Ford chart. MHS.
Geneal. of Va. family of Lomax. Lib. Cong.
McH. Howard pedigree chart, plate 2. Soc. Col. Wars, Md. Johnston. 1905, pp. 42, 155. MHS.
Mrs. G. C. Jenkins chart. MHS.
Pedigree of Charles Morris Howard. Soc. Col. Wars Md. Culver. 1940. MHS; DAR.
Pedigree of Dr. Christopher Johnston, Jr. Soc. Col. Wars Md. Culver. 1940. MHS; DAR.
Pedigree of Franklin Buchanan Owen. Soc. Col. Wars Md. Culver. 1940. MHS; DAR.
Pedigree of Pleasants Pennington. Soc. Col. Wars Md. Culver. 1940. MHS; DAR.
Pedigree of Raphael Semmes. Soc. Col. Wars Md. Culver. 1940. MHS; DAR.
St. Ann's churchyard, Annapolis. Md. O. R. S. Bull., no. 3, pp. 55-56.
Tasker family. Christopher Johnston. M. H. Mag., 1909, v. 4, no. 2, pp. 191-92.
The Times, Balto., Jan. 31, 1886. Newsp. clipp. MHS.
See Barnes-Tasker.

Tasker, St. Anne's, Annapolis. Anne Arundel Co. tombstone inscriptions. Ms. DAR.

Tasker, Benj. Inventory (complete). Ms., 4 pp. MHS.

Tasker, Capt. Thomas. Some early col. Marylanders. M. H. Mag., 1921, v. 16, p. 179.

Tate. St. Paul's churchyard, Kent Co. Md. O. R. Soc. Bull., no. 2, pp. 54-65. MHS.
St. Paul's Parish, Balto. V. 2. Mss. MHS.

Tatnall, Del. Mrs. Wm. Graham Bowdoin chart. MHS.

***Tatum.** Narrative, 1626-1925. R. P. Tatum. Phila., 1925. MHS.

***Tatum-Winslow.** Tatum-Winslow families (1626-1927). In Bermuda from 1626 to 1689. R. Tatum. Phila., 1927.

Taut. Frederick Co. tombstone inscriptions. Gruder. Natl. Geneal. Soc. Quart., 1919, v. 8, nos. 1, 2.
See Tant.

Tavert. Naturalizations in Md., 1666-1765; Laws. Bacon. MHS.

Tawney. Babylon family. Duttera. Ms. MHS.

Tayler. Somerset Parish. Abs. of rec. Turner Geneal. Coll. Ms. MHS.
See Taylor.

Tayler, Taylor. Turner Geneal. Coll. Ms. MHS.

Tayloe. Balto., its hist., its people. Hall. V. 3, p. 514. MHS; DAR.
Col. families of Amer. Lawrence. V. 9, pp. 141-42. MHS.
Col. families of U. S. A. Mackenzie. V. 1, p. 514. MHS; DAR.
Corbin chart. Cary Geneal. Coll. Ms. MHS.
DeFord chart. MHS.
Geneal. of Va. family of Lomax. Lib. Cong.
Howland chart. MHS.
Lee of Va., 1642-1892. E. J. Lee. P. 217. Lib. Cong.; MHS.
Some notes from "memorial to Benjamin Ogle Tayloe," comp. in 1872 (rare book). Winslow M. Watson. Tyler's Quart. Mag., v. 2, p. 80.
John Tayloe, II, and his children (married Rebecca Plater of "Sotterley," Md.). Va. Mag., Hist. and Biog., v. 25, pp. 191-92.
Mrs. E. C. Venable chart. MHS.

***Tayloe, John, II,** Va. (married Rebecca Plater, 1747, daughter of George and Rebecca (Bowles) Plater, "Sotterly," Md.). Col. families of Amer. Lawrence. V. 9. MHS.

Tayloe Line, Va. McH. Howard pedigree chart, plate 2. Soc. Col. Wars, Md. Johnston. 1905, pp. 42, 155. MHS.

Taylor. All Hallow's P. E. churchyard, Snow Hill, Worcester Co. Hudson. Bd. ms. MHS DAR. Also: Md. Geneal. Rec. Com., 1935-36, p. 24. Mss. DAR.
Balto., its hist., its people. Hall. V. 3. MHS; DAR.
Bantz geneal. notes. Ms. MHS.
Bible rec. Ms. MHS.
Mrs. T. R. Brown chart. MHS.
Buckingham Pres. churchyard, Worcester Co., Hudson. Bd. ms. MHS; DAR.
Capt. Philip Taylor and some of his descendants. (Born 1610; of Accomac, Va. and Md.; with Wm. Claiborn, on Kent Island, Aug. 17, 1634; died prior 1649.) E. B. Roberts. M. H. Mag., Sept., 1938, v. 33, no. 3, p. 280-93. (Chart, p. 293).
Chart of Com. John Rodgers. DAR.
*Descendants of Robert Taylor. A. R. Justice. Tayler of Frederick Co., p. 44. Pub. by A. R. Justice and J. W. Taylor, Phila., 1925, ltd. ed. MHS.
*Geneal. chart. A. A. E. Taylor. Columbus, Ohio. MHS.
Geneal. of descendants of George and Sarah Smedley. Cope. P. 524. MHS; DAR.
Harvey chart. MHS.
†Hist. of Allegany Co. Thomas and Williams. V. 2. MHS; DAR.
†Hist. of Balto. City and Co. Scharf. P. 923. MHS.
Hist. graves of Md. and D. C. Ridgely. MHS.
Hist. Salisbury, Wicomico Co. Truitt. DAR.
Md. families. Culver. Ms. Personal list.
Md. gleanings in Eng. Wills. M. H. Mag., 1907, v. 2, nos. 3, 4.
†Med. Annals Md. Cordell. 1903, pp. 589-90. MHS.
M. E. churchyard, Snow Hill, Worcester Co., Hudson. Bd. ms. MHS; DAR.
Patriotic Md. Md. Soc. of S. A. R., 1930. MHS; DAR.
Miss C. Petre chart. MHS.
Portrait and biog. rec. of Harford and Cecil Cos. 1897, pp. 63, 155, 265. MHS; DAR.
Rec. of Stepney Parish. MHS; DAR.
(Over 50 rec.) St. Paul's Parish, Balto. V. 1, 2, 3, 4. Mss. MHS.
St. Stephens Parish, Cecilton, Md. MHS; DAR.
St. Paul's P. E. churchyard, Berlin, Worcester Co. Hudson. Bd. ms. MHS; DAR. Also: Md. Geneal. Rec. Com., 1937, Mrs. Lines. Mss. DAR.
Selden chart. MHS.
Smithsons of Harford Co. Md. Geneal. Rec. Com., 1932-33, pp. 150. Mss. DAR.
Somerset Co. Court Book. Tilghman. 1937. Ms. DAR.

Taylor family of Taylor's Mount, Balto. Co. Bible rec. Gorsuch and allied families. Harrison. Mss. MHS.
*Wicomico Co. families. Tilghman. Ms., pp. 15, 105–06. DAR.
See Brooke-Taylor.
See Nutter-Taylor-Parsons-Adkins.
See Paca-Smithson-Forwood. Harford Co. Hist. Soc. Mss. Coll. JHU.
See Tayler.
See Weems-Taylor.
Taylor, Balto. Co. Mrs. C. L. Riggs chart. MHS.
Taylor, Calvert Co. Bible rec. Md. Geneal. Rec. Com., v. 1, pp. 94–99. DAR.
Taylor, Norfolk, Va. Miss G. Eyre Wright chart. MHS.
Taylor, St. Mary's Co. Cary Geneal. Coll. Ms. MHS.
Taylor, Va. Mrs. Henry Du Pont Baldwin chart. MHS.
Geneal. Hayden. MHS; DAR.
*The Sun, Balto., Feb. 5, 1905; Aug. 11, 18, 1907.
Taylor, Col. *See* LeCompte Family-Col. Taylor-Lee-Webster.
Taylor, B. F. Md. Soc., War of 1812, v. 2, no. 175. Ms. MHS.
Taylor, Clifford. Md. Soc., War of 1812, v. 1, no. 9. Ms. MHS.
†**Taylor, J. Kirkbride.** Men of mark in Md. Johnson. V. 3. DAR; Enoch Pratt Lib.
***Taylor, Capt. Phillip.** And some of his descendants. M. H. Mag., Sept., 1938, v. 33, no. 3, p. 280.
Taylor, T. Loockerman, Col. U.S.A. Md. Soc., War of 1812, v. 3, p. 286. Ms. MHS.
Taylor, Mrs. Wm. R. K. (Sarah Anson Hard). Chart. (Mostly N. Y. families.) Col. Dames, Chap. I. MHS.
Taylor, Wm. W. Westminster churchyard. Patriotic Marylander, v. 2, no. 4, pp. 54–60. MHS; DAR.
Taylor Family. Lee of Va., 1642–1892. E. J. Lee. P. 530. Lib. Cong.; MHS.
Taylor Family, Balto. Co. Col. and Revolutionary families of Phila. Jordan. 1933, v. 1, pp. 260–67.
Taylor Family, Pa. and Md. Greenway Mss. Geneal. Coll. Binder's title, Taylor, nos. 1 and 2. MHS.
Taylor Family, York Co., Eng., to Calvert Co. Geneal. notes. Md. Geneal. Rec. Com., 1924–25, p. 95. DAR.
Taylor-De Courcy. Royal lineage of Mrs. W. H. De Courcy Wright and Miss Margaret Eyre Taylor. Chart. Col. Dames, Chap. I. MHS.
***Taylor-Janney.** Rec. from 1794. D. C. Geneal. Rec. Com., 1936–37, v. 31, pt. 2, pp. 327–31. DAR.
Taylor - Roberts - Standiford - Patterson - Reardon-Baker-Reisinger-Scharf. Harford Co. Hist. Soc. Mss. Coll. JHU.
Tazewell. Mrs. Henry Du Pont Baldwin chart. MHS.
Tazwell. Pocahontas and her descendants. Robertson. MHS; DAR.
Teackle. Mrs. Henry Du Pont Baldwin chart. MHS.
Mrs. Howard Bruce chart. MHS.
*Burke's landed gentry. 1939. MHS.
Col. families of U. S. A. Mackenzie. V. 4, p. 128. MHS; DAR.
J. T. Dennis pedigree chart, plate 2. Soc. Col. Wars, Md. Johnston. 1905, p. 22. MHS.
Geneal. of Henrietta Chauncy Wilson. Upshur. Bk. of photos. MHS.
Harvey chart. MHS.
Hist. graves of Md. and D. C. Ridgely. MHS.
*Mrs. Charles Howard Lloyd chart. Col. Dames Amer., Chap. I. MHS.
Miss Minna Lurman chart. MHS.
†Med. Annals Md. Cordell. 1903, p. 590. MHS.
Pedigree of Wallis Giffin. Soc. Col. Wars Md. Culver. 1940. MHS; DAR.
Pedigree of James Donnell Tilghman. Soc. Col. Wars Md. Culver. 1940. MHS; DAR.
Rogers Coll. Ms. MHS.
Mrs. Wm. L. Watson chart. MHS.
Whiteley chart. MHS.
Mrs. Morris Whitridge chart. MHS.
Miss G. Eyre Wright chart. MHS.
See Custis-Teakle.
***Teackle Family.** Old Kent. Hanson. Pp. 311–13. MHS; DAR.
***Teackle Line.** Col. and Revolutionary lineages in Amer. 1939, v. 2, p. 114. MHS.
Geneal. tables of paternal lines of Dennis family. Dennis. Pp. 60–61. MHS.
Teackle Line, Va. W. H. Gill pedigree chart. Soc. Col. Wars, Md. Johnston. 1905, p. 26. MHS.
Teague. Somerset Co. Court Book. Tilghman. 1937. Ms. DAR.
Teakle. Howland chart. MHS.
Wallis chart. MHS.
Teakle-Custis. Jacobs chart. MHS.
Teal. Rumsey-Smithson family rec. bk. Md. Geneal. Rec. Com., 1932, pp. 63–158. DAR.
St. Paul's Parish, Balto. V. 1. Mss. MHS.
Teale, E. Edw. Md. Soc., War of 1812, v. 2, no. 152. Ms. MHS.
Tear. St. Paul's Parish, Balto. V. 2. Mss. MHS.
Tearson. Lineage Bks., Natl. Soc. of Daughters of Amer. Col., v. 1, p. 31. MHS; DAR.
***Teays.** Frederick Co. families. Markell. Ms. Personal list.
Temperly. St. Paul's Parish, Balto. V. 2. Mss. MHS.
Temple. Rumsey-Smithson Bible rec. Md. Geneal. Rec. Com., 1932–33, v. 5, pp. 63–142. DAR.
†**Temple,** Va. Med. Annals Md. Cordell. 1903, p. 590. MHS.
*The Sun, Balto., April 1, 1906.
Tenant. St. Paul's Parish, Balto. V. 2. Mss. MHS.
Tennent. Buckingham Pres. churchyard, Worcester Co., Hudson. Bd. ms. MHS; DAR.
***Terree.** George Donald Riley. Riley. DAR.
Terry. Faith Pres. Church (Glendy Graveyard). Mss. MHS.
St. Stephens Parish, Cecilton, Md. MHS; DAR.
***Tevis Family,** Balto. Co. (Complete.) Wilson Mss. Coll., no. 72. MHS.
Thayer. Geneall. of Wm. Turpin Thayer of Bellingham. MHS.
†Life and convictions of William S. Thayer, physician. Edith Gittings Reed. London, N. Y., Toronto, Oxford Univ. Press, 1936. Enoch Pratt Lib.

†**Thayer.** Med. Annals Md. Cordell. 1903, p. 591. MHS.
Pedigree of Duncan Keener Brent. Soc. Col. Wars Md. Culver. 1940. MHS; DAR.
Theobald. Amer. Armory and Blue Book. Matthews. 1911–12, p. 295.
Ances. rec. and portraits. Col. Dames of Amer., 1910, v. 2, p. 611–14, 617, 627. MHS; DAR.
See Barrickman, Miss. Abr. Compend. Amer. Geneal. Virkus. V. 4, p. 46. MHS.
†Med. Annals Md. Cordell. 1903, p. 591. MHS.
*Pennington Papers. Ms. MHS.
*Semmes Geneal. Coll. Ms. DAR.
Mrs. J. Whitridge Williams chart 2. MHS.
Theobald, Mrs. Samuel. Chart. (Mostly R. I. families.) Col. Dames, Chap. I. MHS.
Theobald Family. Col. and Revolutionary lineages of Amer. 1939, v. 3, pp. 389–99. MHS.
Thom. Abr. Compend. Amer. Geneal. Virkus. V. 1, p. 621. DAR.
Balto., its hist., its people. Hall. V. 2. MHS; DAR.
Geneal. and memorial encyc. of Md. Spencer. V. 2, p. 587. MHS; DAR.
†**Thom, De Courcy.** Men of mark in Md. Johnson. V. 2. DAR; Enoch Pratt Lib.
Thom, Miss Elizabeth Keyser. Chart. Col. Dames, Chap. I. MHS.
Thom, Mrs. Henry De Courcy Wright; formerly **Mrs. John Stewart (Mary Washington Keyser).** Chart. Col. Dames, Chap. I. MHS.
***Thom, J. Pembroke.** Geneal. and mem. encyc. of Md. Spencer. V. 2, pp. 587–98. MHS; DAR.
Thom, Mrs. J. Pembroke (Margaret Yates Stirling). Chart. Col. Dames, Chap. I. MHS.
Thom, Wm. Henry De Courcy Wright. Pedigree charts, plates 1 and 2. Soc. Col. Wars, Md. Johnston. 1905, pp. 107–08. MHS.
Thom Line. Mrs. H. F. Johnston chart. MHS.
Thom-Keyser Families. Col. and Revolutionary lineages of Amer. 1939, v. 3, pp. 228–52. MHS.
Thom-Stirling. Pedigree (Eng.) chart of Mrs. J. Pembroke Thom and Miss Helen Stirling. Col. Dames. Chap. I. MHS.
Thom-Wright Line. Geneal. and memorial encyc. of Md. Spencer. V. 2, p. 596. MHS; DAR.
Thomas. Abr. Compend. Amer. Geneal. Virkus. V. 6, p. 567. DAR.
Abs. of rec. of West River Monthly Meeting. Ms. MHS.
Amer. Armory and Blue Book. Matthews. Pt. 1.
Amer. families. Geneal. and heraldic. Amer. Hist. Soc., N. Y., pp. 149–53. DAR.
Ances. rec. and portraits. Col. Dames of Amer., 1910, v. 2, p. 714–18, 728, 752, 759. MHS; DAR.
Balto., its hist., its people. Hall. V. 3. MHS; DAR.
†Bench and bar of Md. Sams and Riley. 1901, v. 1, p. 322. Lib. Cong.; MHS; Peabody Lib.
Bible rec. Upper Penins. East. Shore, pp. 14–17, 97. MHS; DAR.
Boarman geneal. Thomas. 1935. MHS; DAR.
Robert Brooke chart. MHS; DAR.
Chart. Raskob-Green rec. book. Raskob. MHS.
*Col. families of Amer. Lawrence. V. 3, p. 294; v. 10, p. 207; v. 16, p. 82. MHS.
Col. families of U. S. A. Mackenzie. V. 1 (West River; also D. H. Thomas); v. 4, p. 352; v. 6, p. 367; v. 7. MHS; DAR.
Col. Mansions of Md. and Del. Hammond. 1914. MHS.
Descendants of Joran Kyn. Pa. Mag., v. 7, p. 464.
Ellicott-King chart. MHS.
Founders of Anne Arundel and Howard Cos. Warfield. Pp. 46, 268 (Gov. James), 275 (Gov. Francis), 279 (Gov. Philip Francis). MHS; DAR.
Frederick Co. tombstone inscriptions. Gruder. Natl. Geneal. Soc. Quart., 1919, v. 8, nos. 1, 2.
*Geneal. and mem. encyc. of Md. Spencer. V. 1, pp. 96, 142, 190, 240. MHS; DAR.
*Geneal., descendants of Gabriel, John, Valentine and Christian Thomas and George Ramsburg. C. Thomas. Wash., D. C., 1902–05. Pamph. MHS.
*Geneal. rec. of family of Thomas, from papers in possession of J. Hanson Thomas. Douglas H. Thomas. Balto., C. Harvey Co., 1875. MHS.
Geneal. of Thomas family, 1652–1911 (Pa.). Pamph. DAR.
Graves, "Deep Falls." Md. O. R. Soc. Bull., no. 3. MHS.
Harlan family geneal., Chester Co., Pa. Harlan. P. 291. MHS.
†Hist. of Allegany Co. Thomas and Williams. V. 1. MHS; DAR.
†Hist. of Frederick Co. Williams. V. 1, v. 2. MHS; DAR.
†Hist. of West. Md. Scharf. V. 1, pp. 403, 459. MHS; DAR.
Miss E. C. Hopkins chart. MHS.
See Janney. Abr. Compend. Amer. Geneal. Virkus. V. 4, pp. 309–10. MHS.
Lambdin chart. MHS.
Lineage Bks., Natl. Soc. of Daughters of Amer. Col., v. 2, p. 61; v. 3, p. 187. MHS; DAR
Lloyd family hist. of Wales, Pa., and Md. DAR.
Md. families. Culver. Ms. Personal list.
Md. tombstone rec. Md. Geneal. Rec. Com., 1937, pp. 6, 28. Mss. DAR.
Med. Annals Md. Cordell. 1903, pp. 591–94. MHS.
Monumental City. Howard. MHS; DAR.
*Owings-Gaither-Hood-Thomas Bible rec. Ms. File case, MHS.
†The Parson of the Islands; biog. of Late Rev. Joshua Thomas. Origin of Methodism of Islands of Chesapeake and East. Shore of Md. and Va. Adam Wallace. (Rev. Joshua Thomas born in Somerset Co., Aug. 30, 1776.) Pub. by Office of Methodist Journal, Phila., 1872. MHS; Enoch Pratt Lib.
Patriotic Md. Md. Soc. of S. A. R., 1930. MHS; DAR.
Pedigree of Mark Alexander Herbert Smith. Soc. Col. Wars Md. Culver. 1940. MHS; DAR.
Pedigree of John Ogle Warfield, Jr. Soc. Col. Wars Md. Culver. 1940. MHS; DAR.

Portrait and biog. rec. of Sixth Cong. Dist. of Md. 1898. Pp. 238, 278, 280, 340, 365, 511, see Veirs, p. 721. MHS; DAR.
W. de C. Poultney pedigree chart. Soc. Col. Wars, Md. Johnston. 1905, p. 86. MHS.
(40 rec.) St. Paul's Parish, Balto. V. 1, 2, 3, 4. Mss. MHS.
Scholl, Sholl, Shull family. Scholl. P. 786. MHS; DAR.
Semmens and allied families. Semmes. MHS.
*Semmes Geneal. Coll. Ms. MHS.
Side lights on Md. hist. Richardson. V. 2, p. 229 (Kent Co.), 443 (Talbot Co.). MHS; DAR.
Somerset Co. Court Book. Tilghman. 1937. Ms. DAR.
Sweetser family of Md. and Mass. Gardner. Pamph., repr. from M. H. Mag., June, 1932, p. 145. MHS; DAR.
Talbott of "Poplar Knowle." Shirk. MHS; DAR.
*The Sun, Balto., Oct. 23, 1904; Aug. 20, 1905; March 24, 1907.
*Thomas book; giving ten generations of Sir Rhys ap. Thomas k.g. and family descended from him and allied families. 100 coats of arms. L. B. Thomas. N. Y., Henry T. Thomas Co., 1896. Lib. Cong.; MHS.
*Thomas family of Talbot Co. and allied families. R. H. Spencer. Balto., Williams & Wilkins Co., 1914. MHS; DAR.
Hon. Nicholas Thomas. R. H. Spencer. M. H. Mag., June, 1911, v. 6, no. 2, pp. 145-63.
*Thomas family of Frederick and Washington Cos. Wilson Mss. Coll., no. 127. MHS.
Trinity Church cemetery, Dorchester Co. Md. O. R. Soc. Bull., no. 3, pp. 42-52.
Trinity P. E. churchyard, St. Mary's City. Md. O. R. Soc. Bull., no. 3, p. 59.
Miss Sara E. White chart. MHS.
Whitridge chart. MHS.
Zimmerman-Waters and allied families. Allen. MHS; DAR.
See Boarman-Thomas.
See Chew-Thomas-Worthington.
See Ewen-Chew, etc. Lineage Bks., Natl. Soc. of Daughters of Amer. Col., v. 4, p. 269. MHS; DAR.
Thomas, Charles Co. Chart, complete in 1 piece. Cary Geneal. Coll. Ms. MHS.
Thomas, Deep Falls, St. Mary's Co. Tombstone inscriptions, 1795-1870. Md. O. R. Soc. Bull., no. 3, pp. 61-62.
†**Thomas,** Pa. to Md. Hist. of Balto. City and Co. Scharf. P. 498. MHS.
Thomas, Queen Anne Co., Samuel Carpenter of Phila. Carpenter. P. 112. MHS.
***Thomas,** 1625-1671, St. Mary's Co. Lineage Bk., Daughters of Amer. Col., v. 3, p. 187. MHS; DAR.
***Thomas, Christopher,** Kent Co. Lineage Bk., Daughters of Founders and Patriots, v. 23, pp. 55-56. MHS; DAR.
Pedigree of Granville Bowdle Hopkins. Soc. Col. Wars Md. Culver. 1940. MHS; DAR.
Pedigree of Thomas Wilson Williamson. Soc. Col. Wars Md. Culver. 1940. MHS; DAR.
†**Thomas, D. H.** Biog. cyc. of rep. men of Md. and D. C. P. 344. MHS; DAR.
†Men of mark in Md. Johnson. V. 1, DAR; Enoch Pratt Lib.
Thomas, Douglas H. Amer. of gentle birth and their ancestors. Pittman. V. 1, p. 281. MHS; DAR.
Pedigree charts, plates. 1 and 2. Soc. Col. Wars Md. Johnston. 1905, pp. 109-10. MHS.
Thomas, Douglas Hamilton, Jr. Pedigree chart. Soc. Col. Wars Md. Johnson. 1905, p. 111. MHS.
Thomas, Mrs. Douglas Hamilton (Alice Lee Whitridge). Chart. Col. Dames, Chap. I. MHS.
Thomas, Miss Eliza Snowden. Chart. Col. Dames, Chap. I. MHS.
Thomas, Elizabeth, St. Mary's Co. Abs. of will, 1808. D. A. R. Mag., Aug., 1927, v. 61, no. 8, p. 608.
†**Thomas, Francis.** Governor of Md. Buchholz P. 136. MHS.
†**Thomas, G. P.** Balto., hist. and biog. Richardson and Bennett. 1871, pp. 503-06. MHS; DAR.
Thomas, Howell Harris. Pedigree. Soc. Col. Wars Md. Culver. 1940. MHS; DAR.
†**Thomas, James.** Governor of Md. Buchholz. P. 119. MHS.
†**Thomas, James Sewall.** Men of mark in Md. Johnson. V. 4. DAR; Enoch Pratt Lib.
†**Thomas, James Walter.** Men of mark in Md. Johnson. V. 4. DAR; Enoch Pratt Lib.
†**Thomas, J. Walter.** Encyc. of Amer. biog. Amer. Hist. Soc., N. Y., 1928, v. 33, p. 185.
†**Thomas, John B.** Men of mark in Md. Johnson. V. 2. DAR; Enoch Pratt Lib.
Thomas, John Benjamin, Jr. Pedigree. Soc. Col. Wars Md. Culver. 1940. MHS; DAR.
Thomas, Mrs. John Gregg (Frances Leigh Brooks). Chart. Col. Dames, Chap. I. MHS.
Paternal line. Mrs. B. S. Johnston chart. MHS.
Paternal line. Mrs. McCormick chart. MHS.
Thomas, John Hanson. Colston chart. Cary Geneal. Coll. Ms. MHS.
†Hist. of Md. Scharf. V. 2, p. 611. MHS.
Thomas, Notley W. His marriages. Arch. of Georgetown Univ., Wash., D. C., v. 90, no. 1.
Thomas, Philip. Pedigree of Mareen Duvall. Soc. Col. Wars Md. Culver. 1940. MHS; DAR.
†**Thomas, Philip Francis.** Governor of Md. Buchholz. P. 150. MHS.
(1810-90). Hist. of Talbot Co. Tilghman. V. 1, pp. 583-87. MHS; DAR.
Thomas, T. R. Abr. Compend. Amer. Geneal. Virkus. V. 1, p. 855. DAR.
†**Thomas, T. Rowland.** Men of mark in Md. Johnson. V. 4. DAR; Enoch Pratt Lib.
†**Thomas, Dr. Tristram** (1769-1847). Hist. of Talbot Co. Tilghman. V. 1, pp. 432-44. MHS; DAR.
Thomas, W. H. Abr. Compend. Amer. Geneal. Virkus. V. 1, p. 856. DAR.
***Thomas Family.** Arms. Old Kent. Hanson. Pp. 130-34. MHS; DAR.
Darby Meeting rec., Pa. D. A. R. Mag., Oct., 1933, v. 67, no. 10, pp. 643-45.
*Geneal. notes. L. B. Thomas. Balto., 1877. MHS; DAR.
Memoir and geneal. of Md. and Pa. family of Mayer. Mayer. Pp. 142-45. MHS; DAR.

†**Thomas Family.** Quaker childhood (spent in Balto.). Helen (Thomas) Flexner (Mrs. Simon Flexner). 1940. Enoch Pratt Lib.
*Printed page from unknown book (probably Eng.) about Thomas family. From L. B. Thomas Coll. MHS.
*Thomas family as descended from David and Anna Noble Thomas. W. T. Lyle. Phila., 1907. MHS.
*Thomas family of Kent Co., Md., and Marlboro Co., S. C. Folder, 2 pp. MHS.
*Thomas family of Talbot Co. and allied families. R. H. Spencer. 1914. MHS; DAR.
Thomas Family, Balto. Fox-Ellicott-Evans families. Evans. MHS; DAR.
Thomas Family, Talbot Co. Bible rec. from 1779. D. C. Geneal. Rec. Com., v. 31, pp. 107–09. Typed, bd. DAR.
Ms. MHS.
Thomas Line. Col. and Revolutionary lineages of Amer. 1939, v. 1, p. 233. MHS.
Lilburn family. Col. and Revolutionary families of Phila. Jordan. 1933, v. 1, pp. 382–98.
Thomas Line, Anne Arundel Co. W. M. Ellicott pedigree chart. Soc. Col. Wars, Md. Johnston. 1905, pp. 24, 155. MHS.
***Thomas - Chew - Lawrence.** Thomas-Chew-Lawrence; West River register. Geneal. notes of families in Calvert and Anne Arundel Cos. 1655–1882. L. B. Thomas. (Quaker families.) N. Y., Thomas Whittaker Co., 1883. MHS. See also Geneal. Soc. Pa., v. 3, no. 3, pp. 197–200.
Thomas-Douglas Line. Stevenson chart. MHS.
Thomas-Harrison. Bible rec. Focke Geneal. Coll. Ms. MHS.
Thomas-Smith. Richard Thomas, Queen Anne Co. and Mary Ellet Smith; marriage. Merion in Welsh tract. Glenn. P. 348.
Thompson. Amer. Armory and Blue Book. 1911–12, p. 187.
Ames Geneal. Coll. Ms. MHS.
*Edward Ridgely Thompson and Eliza Enlow, his wife. Pr. for their grandchildren, 1913. MHS.
Mrs. Frank G. Baldwin chart. MHS.
Bible rec., 1800–95. (Presented by estate of H. Oliver Thompson.) Typed, 6 pp. MHS.
Bohemia Manor. Mallory. Pp. 26–27. MHS.
Bolton chart. MHS.
Dorsey papers. Ms. MHS.
*Frederick Co. families. Markell. Ms. Personal list.
A. E. Hull chart. MHS.
Md. Geneal. Bull., v. 6, p. 24. MHS; DAR.
†Med. Annals Md. Cordell. 1903, pp. 594–95. MHS.
M. E. Church South cemetery, near Poolesville, Montgomery Co. Md. Geneal. Rec. Com., 1926. Mss. DAR.
*Old Kent. Hanson. P. 181. MHS; DAR.
Pedigree of Rev. Sam'l. Tagart Steele. Soc. Col. Wars Md. Culver. 1940. MHS; DAR.
Pedigree of George Washington Williams. Soc. Col. Wars Md. Culver. 1940. MHS; DAR.
Pedigree of Joseph Lee Wickes. Soc. Col. Wars Md. Culver. 1940. MHS; DAR.
(60 records.) St. Paul's Parish, Balto. V. 1, 2, 3, 4. Mss. MHS.
St. Stephens Parish, Cecilton, Md. MHS; DAR.
Semmes and allied families. Semmes. MHS.
*Semmes. Geneal. Coll. Ms. MHS.
Wathen Prayer Book rec. Ms. MHS.
See Kilby-Thompson.
See Roach-Greenwell-Thompson-Williams.
Thompson, Cecil Co. Mrs. J. Hall Pleasants, Jr., chart. MHS.
Thompson, Dorchester Co. Abr. Compend. Amer. Geneal. Virkus. V. 1, p. 857. DAR.
Thompson, Eustis. Pedigree. Soc. Col. Wars Md. Culver. 1940. MHS; DAR.
Thompson, H. D. Geneal. and mem. encyc. of Md. Spencer. V. 2, p. 727. MHS; DAR.
***Thompson, Henry Anthony.** Bible rec. Ms. File case, MHS.
Monumental City. Howard. MHS; DAR.
†**Thompson, Henry F.** Men of mark in Md. Johnson. V. 2. DAR; Enoch Pratt Lib.
Pedigree. Soc. Col. Wars Md. Culver. 1940. MHS; DAR.
Thompson, Henry Oliver. Md. Soc., War of 1812, no. 285. Ms. MHS.
Thompson, R. Webb. Md. Soc., War of 1812, v. 3, no. 271. Ms. MHS.
***Thompson Family.** Arch. of Georgetown Univ., Wash., D. C., v. 274, no. 6.
Harford Co. Hist. Soc. Mss. Coll. JHU.
Thompson Family, Vienna, Dorchester Co. Bible rec. of Dorchester and Somerset Cos. and Del. P. 83. DAR.
Thompson-Enlow. Edward Ridgely Thompson and Eliza Enlow, his wife. Pr. for their grandchildren, 1913, pamph. MHS.
Thompson-Smythe (Smith). Papers. Ms. MHS.
Thompson, Thomson. Cary Geneal. Coll. Ms. MHS.
Hist. graves of Md. and D. C. Ridgely. MHS.
*Hylald family, Cecil Co. Ms. MHS.
Thomsen, Alonzo Lilly, Thomsen, Herman Ivah, and Thomsen, John Jacob. Pedigree chart. (Balto. and New Eng. records.) Soc. Col. Wars, Md. Johnston. 1905, p. 112. MHS.
Thomsen, Herman Ivah. *See* Thomsen, Alonzo Lilly, Herman Ivah and John Jacob.
Thomsen, John Jacob. *See* Thomsen, Alonzo Lilly, Herman Ivah and John Jacob.
Thomsen, Rozel Cathcart. Md. Soc., War of 1812, v. 4, no. 310. Ms. MHS.
Thomson. Pedigree of George Ross Veazey. Soc. Col. Wars Md. Culver. 1940. MHS; DAR.
See Thompson.
Thornbery. *See* Thornbury.
†**Thornborough.** Day-Star of Amer. Freedom. Davis. P. 242. MHS.
See Thornbury.
Thornburgh. Hagerstown tombstone inscriptions. Gruder. Natl. Geneal. Soc. Quart., 1919, v. 8, nos. 1, 2.
Soc. of Friends in Md. Thornbury. M. H. Mag., 1934, v. 29, no. 2, p. 101.
Rowland, Thornburgh, Baltimore Co. (1696). Delmar L. Thornbury. Jan. 15, 1934. Ms. MHS.
St. Paul's Parish, Balto. V. 1. Mss. MHS.
See Thornbury.
Thornbury. St. Paul's Parish, Balto. V. 1. Mss. MHS.
Thornbury, Rowland, Balto. Co. Copy of will. 1696. MHS.
Thornbury, Thornburgh, Thornborough, Thornbery. Old St. Mary's City and

Thomas Thornburgh 1642–50; Thornbury family in Balto. Co., 1696–1934. Geneal. Delmar L. Thornbury. Jan., 1934. Typed bd., with photos. MHS.
Thorne. Old Somerset. Torrence. MHS. DAR.
White geneal. tree. MHS.
Thornley Family, Va. Rec. (Md. ref.) Natl. Geneal. Soc. Quart., v. 22, no. 4, pp. 96–101.
Thornton. Hist. of Byberry and Moreland. Martindale. MHS.
Natl. Geneal. Soc. Quart., v. 7, no. 3, pp. 45–48.
Thornton, Francis, Va. Pedigree of Lloyd Bankson Whitham. Soc. Col. Wars Md. Culver. 1940. MHS; DAR.
Thorogood. Dorsey Papers. Ms. MHS.
*Mrs. Charles Howard Lloyd chart. Col. Dames Amer., Chap. I. MHS.
Thorogood, Va. Rec. Harrison-Waples and allied families. Harrison. MHS.
Thoroughgood. Mrs. Lee Barroll chart. MHS.
Thoroughgood-Chandler Family, Va. Va. Mag. Hist. and Biog., v. 3, pp. 91, 321.
Thorowgood. Cary Geneal. Coll. Ms. MHS.
Crain chart. MHS.
*The Sun, Balto., July 21, Oct. 13, 20, 31, Nov. 3, 1907.
Thorowgoode. Geneal. of Henrietta Chauncy Wilson. Bk. of photos. MHS.
Thorpe. St. Paul's Parish, Balto. V. 1, 2. Mss. MHS.
Thouron. Chart of Com. John Rodgers. DAR.
Thrasher. James Hook and Virginia Eller. Hook. MHS; DAR.
Threlkeld. Lineage Bks., Natl. Soc. of Daughters of Amer. Col., v. 1, p. 83. MHS; DAR.
Thrift. Branch of the Md. Magruder family tree. Amer. Clan Gregor Year Book, 1935, pp. 80–90. MHS; DAR.
***Throckmorton.** Geneal.; in Eng. and U. S.; with brief notes on some of allied families. C. Wycliffe Throckmorton. 503 pp. Richmond, Va. 1930. MHS.
*Pedigree chart. Joseph Gardiner. Ms. DAR.
See Bernard-Reade-Throckmorton.
Throckmorton, Va. Balch chart. MHS.
*The Sun, Balto., Oct. 13, 20, 27, Nov. 3, 1907.
Throckmorton, C. Woodson. Md. Soc., War of 1812, v. 2, no. 198. Ms. MHS.
***Throckmorton Family.** Hist. of Throckmorton family in U. S., with cognate branches. F. G. Sitherwood. Incl. family in Salem, Mass., 1630, and Gloucester Co., Va., 1660. 1930.
*Throckmorton family in Eng. and U. S. C. W. Throckmorton. 1930. DAR.
***Thurman-Graves-Jones.** Descendants of John Thurman of Va., William Graves of Va. and James Jones of S. C. J. D. Humphries. 1938. DAR.
Thurmer. Md. gleanings in Eng. Wills. M. H. Mag., 1908, v. 3, no. 2.
Thurston. Col. families of U. S. A. Mackenzie. V. 4. MHS; DAR.
†Hist. of Allegany Co. Thomas and Williams. V. 1. MHS; DAR.
*The Sun, Balto., May 21, 1905.
St. Paul's Parish, Balto. V. 2. Mss. MHS.
Thurston Family, Va. William and Mary Quart., 1st series, v. 4; v. 7 (showing Hughes of Md., p. 130).
Tice. See Alter, Pa. Abr. Compend. Amer. Geneal. Virkus. V. 1, p. 899. DAR.
Hagerstown tombstone inscriptions. Gruder. Natl. Geneal. Soc. Quart., 1919, v. 8, nos. 1, 2.
†Hist. of West. Md. Scharf. V. 2, p. 1160. MHS; DAR.
Tick. Naturalizations in Md., 1666–1765; Laws. Bacon. MHS.
Tidball. Md. tombstone rec. Md. Geneal. Rec. Com., 1937, Parran, p. 8. Mss. DAR.
Tidmarsh. Miss E. K. Thom chart. MHS.
Miss G. Eyre Wright chart. MHS.
Tidwell. *See* McCall-Tidwell.
Tierman. Amer. Armory and Blue Book. Matthews. Pt. 2.
Portrait and biog. rec. of Sixth Cong. Dist. of Md. 1898, see Brien p. 306. MHS; DAR.
*Tiernan and other families in Md. C. B. Tiernan. Balto., Wm. J. Gallery Co., 1898. Revised ed., 1901. MHS; DAR.
*Tiernan family in Md. C. B. Tiernan. 1901. MHS; DAR.
†Hist. of West. Md. Scharf. V. 2, p. 1040. MHS; DAR.
*The Sun, Balto., Jan. 1, 1905.
Williamson Bible rec. Ms. MHS.
***Tiernan, C. B.** Amer. armory and blue bk. Matthews. 1908, p. 97. DAR.
Tiernan, Charles Bernard. Pedigree chart. Soc. Col. Wars, Md. Johnston. 1905, p. 113. MHS.
Tiers. Samuel Carpenter of Phila. Carpenter. P. 247. MHS.
†**Tiffany.** Med. Annals Md. Cordell. 1903, p. 596. MHS.
Monumental City. Howard. P. 467. MHS; DAR.
St. Paul's Parish, Balto. V. 3, 4. Mss. MHS.
†**Tiffany, O. C.** Balto., hist. and biog. Richardson and Bennett. 1871, pp. 507–10. MHS; DAR.
Mrs. R. Barton, Jr., charts. MHS.
Tilden. Ford and other lines. Md. Geneal. Rec. Com., 1932–33, pp. 7–20. Mss. DAR.
Hyland chart. MHS.
Md. families. Culver. Ms. Personal list.
†Med. Annals Md. Cordell. 1903, p. 596. MHS.
Pedigree of Duncan Keener Brent. Soc. Col. Wars Md. Culver. 1940. MHS; DAR.
Pedigree of Howard Hall Macy Lee. Soc. Col. Wars Md. Culver. 1940. MHS; DAR.
Side lights on Md. hist. Richardson. V. 2, p. 235. MHS; DAR.
*The Sun, Balto., Dec. 11, 1904.
See Ford-Dorsey-Hyland, etc.
See Tylden.
Tilden, E. Jane (wife of Charles Tilden, daughter of Edward Ringgold; died Oct. 3, 1856, aged 39 yrs.). Grave, Chestertown. Md. Geneal. Rec. Com., 1933–34, p. 232. Mss. DAR.
Tilden, Tylden. Ford chart. MHS.
*Hyland family, Cecil Co. Ms. MHS.
M. H. Mag., 1906, v. 1, no. 1, p. 75 (from Hanson's Old Kent).
Notes. Ms. MHS.
*Old Kent. Hanson. Pp. 302–08, 313–17; arms, p. 303. MHS; DAR.
Tilghman. Abr. Compend. Amer. Geneal. Virkus. V. 1, p. 860; v. 6, pp. 301, 573. DAR.
Ances. rec. and portraits. Col. Dames of Amer., 1910, v. 2, p. 514. MHS; DAR.

Tilghman. Bantz geneal. notes. Ms. MHS.
Britton chart. MHS.
Britton Scrap Book. V. 2. Ms. MHS.
Chart. Gale Shreve. Photostat of ms., 1929. MHS.
*Charts showing descent of Tilghman, Hyland, Ford and Augustine Herman Massey families of Md. (1) Descent from Charlemagne; (2) Royal Saxon lines from Rolls of Normandy; (3) Clare, Earls of Hertford; (4) Beaumont, Earls of Leicester (2 charts); (5) Neville Lords of Roby of Westmorland. Md. Geneal. Rec. Com., 1934–35, p. 63. Mss. DAR.
†Chesapeake Bay Country. Earle. P. 339. MHS.
Col. families of East. Shore, and their descendants. Emory. 1900, p. 25. MHS.
Data. Md. Geneal. Rec. Com., 1933–34, p. 25. Mss. DAR.
Deford chart. MHS.
*Descendants of John and Mary Truitt Tilghman, to July 24, 1931. Mrs. Rosa Lee Morris. Pamph. 1931. MHS; DAR.
Dobbin chart. MHS.
Early hist. of Hollyday family. Hollyday. MHS; DAR.
Elbert chart. MHS.
†Eulogium upon Hon. William Tilghman, late Chief Justice of Pa. H. Binney. (Born in Talbot Co., 1756; died in 1827.) Philip H. Macklin, Law Bookseller, Miffin & Perry, 1827. Enoch Pratt Lib.
Geneal. notes of Chamberlaine family. MHS.
Hist. graves of Md. and D. C. Ridgely. MHS.
†Hist. of West. Md. Scharf. V. 2, pp. 1016–17. MHS; DAR.
Hist. Salisbury, Wicomico Co. Truitt. P. 12. DAR.
See Hope. Abr. Compend. Amer. Geneal. Virkus. V. 1, p. 924.
Letters between Eng. and Amer. branches of Tilghman families (1697–1764). Edited by Harrison Tilghman. M. H. Mag., June, 1938, v. 33, no. 2, pp. 148–75.
Miss Katherine Lurman chart. MHS.
Md. families. Culver. Ms. Personal list.
†Med. Annals Md. Cordell. 1903, pp. 596–97. MHS.
†Memoir of Lieut. Col. Tench Tilghman (secretary and aide to Washington), together with Revolutionary journal and letters, 1775. (Born in Talbot Co., 1744.) Oswald Tilghman. Albany, Munsell, 1876. MHS; Enoch Pratt Lib.
Mt. Zion P. E. churchyard, Worcester Co. Md. Geneal. Rec. Com., 1937, Mrs. Lines. Mss. DAR.
Pedigree of Duncan Keener Brent. Soc. Col. Wars Md. Culver. 1940. MHS; DAR.
Pedigree of Corbin Braxton Dallam. Soc. Col. Wars Md. Culver. 1940. MHS; DAR.
Pedigree of Dr. Christopher Johnston, Jr. Soc. Col. Wars Md. Culver. 1940. MHS; DAR.
Pedigree of Howard Hall Macy Lee. Soc. Col. Wars Md. Culver. 1940. MHS; DAR.
Pedigree of Gustav Wm. Lurman. Soc. Col. Wars Md. Culver. 1940. MHS; DAR.
Pedigree of Franklin Buchanan Owen. Soc. Col. Wars Md. Culver. 1940. MHS; DAR.
Pedigree of John Philemon Paca. Soc. Col. Wars Md. Culver. 1940. MHS; DAR.
Pedigree of Pleasants Pennington. Soc. Col. Wars Md. Culver. 1940. MHS; DAR.
Pedigree of Tilghman Goldsborough Pitts. Soc. Col. Wars Md. Culver. 1940. MHS; DAR.
Pedigree of Ralph Robinson. Soc. Col. Wars Md. Culver. 1940. MHS; DAR.
Pedigree of Levin Gale Shreve. Soc. Col. Wars Md. Culver. 1940. MHS; DAR.
Mrs. J. Hall Pleasants, Jr., chart. MHS.
Portrait and biog. rec. of East. Shore of Md. 1898, pp. 280, 521. MHS; DAR.
St. Paul's P. E. churchyard, Kent Co. Md. O. R. Soc. Bull., no. 2, pp. 54–65.
St. Paul's Parish, Balto. V. 2, 3. Mss. MHS.
Side lights on Md. hist. Richardson. V. 2, p. 236. MHS; DAR.
Tilghman family. Christopher Johnston. M. H. Mag., 1906. V. 1, pp. 161–84, 280–84, 290, 369–76.
Tilghman notes. Md. Geneal. Rec. Com., v. 1, p. 101. DAR.
*The Sun, Balto., Aug. 9, 1903.
*Tombstone records. Pennington Papers. Ms. MHS.
Wicomico Co. families. Bible rec. Ms. DAR.
Mrs. H. De'Courcy Wright Thom chart. MHS.
Mrs. Emory Whitridge chart. MHS.
Samuel White and his father, Judge Thomas White. Conrad. 1903, pamph. MHS.
See Carmichael-Paca-Tilghman-Veazey.
See Smyth-Tilghman-Willson.
See Tillman.

***Tilghman,** Holloway Court. Pedigrees 1, 2, 3. Burke's landed gentry. 1939. MHS.

Tilghman, Harrison. Pedigree. Soc. Col. Wars Md. Culver. 1940. MHS; DAR.

Tilghman, James Donnell. Pedigree. Soc. Col. Wars Md. Culver. 1940. MHS; DAR.

Tilghman, Gen. Lloyd, of Confederate Army (1816–63). Hist. of Talbot Co. Tilghman. V. 1, pp. 450–55. MHS; DAR.

†**Tilghman, Hon. Matthew** (1718–90). Hist. of Talbot Co. Tilghman. V. 1, pp. 423–32. MHS; DAR.
†Hist. of Md. Scharf. V. 2, p. 157. MHS.
†(1718–90). M. H. Mag., v. 12, p. 249.

†**Tilghman, Oswald.** Men of mark in Md. Johnson. V. 1. DAR; Enoch Pratt Lib.
*Will, 1628. M. H. Mag., 1907, v. 2, p. 65.

†**Tilghman, R. Lloyd.** Men of mark in Md. Johnson. V. 4. DAR; Enoch Pratt Lib.

Tilghman, Richard. Amer. at Eton in col. days. Va. Mag. Hist. and Biog., v. 13, p. 212.
Seven pioneers of col. East. Shore. Skirven. M. H. Mag., 1920, v. 15, no. 3, p. 230–50; no. 4, p. 394–419.

Tilghman, Sam'l. Commission; Admiral of Md. Calvert papers. M. H. Mag., 1908, v. 3, p. 277.

†**Tilghman, Col. Tench.** Hist. of Md. Scharf. V. 2, pp. 253–57. MHS.
†(1744–86). Hist. of Talbot Co. Tilghman. V. 1, pp. 4–46. MHS; DAR.
(Revolutionary soldier.) St. Paul's P. E. graveyard. Patriotic Marylander, v. 2, no. 4, pp. 54–59. MHS; DAR.

†**Tilghman, Gen. Tench** (1810–74). Hist. of Talbot Co. Tilghman. Pp. 625–26. MHS; DAR.

†**Tilghman, Wm.** (1736–1827). Hist. of Talbot Co. Tilghman. V. 1, pp. 368–75, 423–32. MHS; DAR.

†**Tilghman, Wm. Beauchamp.** Men of mark in Md. Johnson. V. 4. DAR; Enoch Pratt Lib.
Tilghman Family. 43 mss., letters and miscellaneous. Ms. MHS.
*Old Kent. Hanson. Pp. 230–32, 238–45, 252–62. MHS; DAR.
Rec., 1702 (Wicomico and Worcester Cos.). Mrs. Rosa Lee Morris. 1931, pamph. MHS.
Rec., with geneal. Mrs. Rosa Lee Morris. Bd. ms. MHS.
Thomas Book. Thomas. Pp. 528–30. Lib. Cong.; MHS.
Tilghman Line. Col. and Revolutionary lineages of Amer. 1939, v. 1, pp. 108–10. MHS.
J. P. Paca pedigree chart. Soc. Col. Wars Md. Johnston. 1905, pp. 80, 156. MHS.
***Tilghman-Hyland-Ford.** 9 charts, showing descent of Augustine Herman Massey. Md. Geneal. Rec. Com., 1934–35, p. 7. Mss. DAR.
Tilghman-Whetenhall Family. Notes. M. H. Mag., Sept., 1906, v. 1, no. 3, p. 290.
Tilghman, Tillman. Col. families of U. S. A. Mackenzie. V. 4, p. 407; v. 6. MHS; DAR.
*Wicomico Co. families. Tilghman. Ms., pp. 20, 115, 128. DAR.
Till. Lloyd family hist. of Wales, Pa., and Md. DAR.
Tillard, Balto. Co., (1676–1776). Md. Geneal. Rec. Com., 1932, v. 5. DAR.
Tillings. St. Barnabas P. E. churchyard. Typed ms. MHS; DAR.
Tillman. Old Somerset. Torrence. MHS; DAR.
Somerset Co. Court Book. Tilghman. 1937. Ms. DAR.
See Tilghman.
***Tillman, Tilghman.** Tillman-Tilghman family. S. E. Tillman. 1930. DAR.
Tillman, Tilghman, Somerset Co. Side lights on Md. hist. Richardson. V. 2, p. 448. MHS; DAR.
Tillotson. Abr. Compend. Amer. Geneal. Virkus. V. 4, p. 672. MHS
Col. families of East. Shore and their descendants. Emory. 1900, p. 8. MHS.
Hist. graves of Md. and D. C. Ridgely. MHS.
Tombs (3), Hillsboro, Caroline Co. Md. O. R. Soc., Bull., no. 1, p. 50.
Tilyard. Rogers Coll. Ms. MHS.
***Timanus.** The Sun. Balto., March 5, 1905.
Timmanus. Rumsey-Smithson Bible rec. Md. Geneal. Rec. Com., 1932–33, v. 5, pp. 63–142. DAR.
Rumsey-Smithson family rec. bk. Md. Geneal. Rec. Com., 1932, p. 139. DAR.
Smithson-Rumsey rec. bk. Ms. MHS.
Timmons. Makemie Memorial Pres. churchyard, Snow Hill, Worcester Co. Hudson. Bd. ms. MHS; DAR. Also: Md. Geneal. Rec. Com., Mrs. Lines. Mss. DAR.
M. E. churchyard, Snow Hill, Worcester Co. Hudson. Bd. ms. MHS; DAR.
Mt. Zion P. E. churchyard, Worcester Co. Md. Geneal. Rec. Com., 1937, Mrs. Lines. Mss. DAR.
Tindall. St. Paul's Parish, Balto. V. 2. Mss. MHS.
Tingle. Buckingham Pres. churchyard, Worcester Co., Hudson. Bd. ms. MHS; DAR.
Makemie Memorial Pres. churchyard, Snow Hill, Worcester Co. Hudson. Bd. ms. MHS; DAR. Also: Md. Geneal. Rec. Com., Mrs. Lines. Mss. DAR.
Notes. D. A. R. Mag., v. 65, no. 9, p. 570.
Sketches of John Slemmons Stevenson and Rev. Samuel McMaster. Stevenson. P. 15. MHS.
St. Paul's P. E. churchyard, Berlin, Worcester Co. Hudson. Bd. ms. MHS; DAR. Also: Md. Geneal. Rec. Com., 1937, Mrs. Lines. Mss. DAR.
Somerset Co. Court Book. Tilghman. 1937. Ms. DAR.
Tingley. Cannon - Riley - Truitt - Houston - Kollock. Stow. Ms. MHS.
See Hall-Collins-Elliott-Laws-Tingley.
***Tingley Family.** Tingley family. R. M. Tingley. 1910. MHS.
***Tinker Family,** Pa. Baptisms; geneal. N. Y., Dec., 1912, v. 2, no. 19. MHS.
Tinsley. Burton ancestry. Ms. MHS.
Tinsley, Thomas Garland. Pedigree. Soc. Col. Wars Md. Culver. 1940. MHS; DAR.
Tippett. Balto., its hist., its people. Hall. V. 3. MHS; DAR.
***Tippin.** Ancestry of Sanford Lathadeus Tippin family of Henderson Co., Ky. James Jackson Tippin. (Wm. Tippin came to Talbot Co., 1664; died in Queen Anne's Co., 1714.) Louisiana, 1940, pamph. MHS.
Tipton. Marriages, 1693–1795. Parrish family. Boyd. MHS; DAR.
Md. families. Culver. Ms. Personal list.
Rumsey-Smithsons' family rec. bk. Md. Geneal. Rec. Com., 1932, p. 97. DAR.
St. Paul's Parish, Balto. V. 1. Mss. MHS.
Tipton Family. Harford Co. Hist. Soc. Mss. Coll. JHU.
Tipton-Murray-Mitchell. Harford Co. Hist. Soc. Mss. Coll. JHU.
Tisdale. Somerset Co. Court Book. Tilghman. 1937. Ms. DAR.
Tivers. St. Inigoes churchyard, St. Mary's Co. Md. O. R. Soc. Bull., no. 3, p. 58.
Tives. St. Thomas' Parish, Balto. Co. Bd. ms. MHS. Also: Md. Geneal. Rec. Com., 1937, pp. 109–82. Mss. DAR.
†**Toadvin.** Men of mark in Md. Johnson. V. 1. DAR; Enoch Pratt Lib.
Side lights on Md. hist. Richardson. V. 2, p. 453. MHS; DAR.
Somerset Co. Court Book. Tilghman. 1937. Ms. DAR.
Toadvin Family. Tercentenary hist. of Md. Andrews. V. 4, p. 495.
Toadvin-Brown. Bible rec. Md. Geneal. Rec. Com., 1937–38, p. 137. Mss. DAR.
Toadvin, Toadvine. Hist. Salisbury, Wicomico Co. Truitt. P. 10. DAR.
Toadvine. Rec. of Stepney Parish. MHS; DAR.
***Toadvine, Todvine.** Wicomico Co. families. Tilghman. Ms., pp. 98–100, 104, 106, 121. DAR.
Tobias. St. Stephens Parish, Cecilton, Md. MHS; DAR.
Todd. Amer. biog. directories of D. C. Macfarland. 1908, p. 474. DAR.
Barnes chart. Va. Mag., v. 17, p. 292.
Mrs. A. C. Bruce chart. MHS.
Mrs. Howard Bruce chart. MHS.

Todd. Cary Geneal. Coll. Ms. MHS.
Col. families of U. S. A. Mackenzie. V. 7, p. 307. MHS; DAR.
†Columbia Hist. Soc. Rec., v. 5, p. 165; v. 7, p. 166. MHS; DAR.
Deford chart. MHS.
Dorsey and allied families. Ms. MHS.
Founders of Anne Arundel and Howard Cos. Warfield. Pp. 48–49, 67. MHS; DAR.
Geneal. and mem. encyc. of Md. Spencer. V. 2, pp. 447–50. MHS; DAR.
Geneal. of James and Elizabeth Todd. Garlough family. Mss. DAR.
Gorsuch chart. Cary Geneal. Coll. Ms. MHS.
Gorsuch-Lovelace families. Va. Mag. Hist. and Biog., 1916, v. 24, p. 81; contd. in vols. 25, 26, 27.
Mrs. W. H. Harris, Sr., chart. MHS.
Hist. graves of Md. and D. C. Ridgely. MHS.
Hist. of Todd family, starting with John Todd of Md., who had four sons. Mss. DAR.
Hist. of West Md. Scharf. V. 1, p. 639. MHS; DAR.
R. C. Hoffman pedigree chart. Soc. Col. Wars Md. Johnston. 1905, pp. 40, 156. MHS.
Iglehart chart. MHS.
Lineage Bks., Natl. Soc. of Daughters of Amer. Col., v. 1, p. 42. MHS; DAR.
Md. families. Culver. Ms. Personal list.
†Med. Annals Md. Cordell. 1903, p. 597. MHS.
Note. M. H. Mag., Dec., 1936, v. 31, no. 4, p. 357.
Pedigree of Corbin Braxton Dallam. Soc. Col. Wars Md. Culver. 1940. MHS; DAR.
Pedigree of Charles Thomas Holloway. Soc. Col. Wars Md. Culver. 1940. MHS; DAR.
Pedigree of Thomas Dobbin Penniman. Soc. Col. Wars Md. Culver. 1940. MHS; DAR.
See Peter. Abr. Compend. Amer. Geneal. Virkus. V. 1, p. 770. DAR.
Mrs. E. W. Poe chart. MHS.
St. Paul's Parish, Balto. V. 1, 2. Mss. MHS.
Talbott of "Poplar Knowle." Shirk. MHS; DAR.
†Tercentenary hist. of Md. Andrews. V. 3, p. 464; v. 4, p. 420. MHS; DAR.
*B. Todd's heirs. Thirtieth Congress, first session. Report no. 255, House of Representatives. DAR.
Todd family. W. G. Standard. Va. Mag. Hist. and Biog., v. 3, p. 79.
Todds of East. Shore of Md. J. R. Witcraft. Phila., Frankford Dispatch Pub. House, 1912, pamph. MHS. DAR.
Todds of Va. J. R. Witcraft. Phila., Frankford Dispatch Pub. House, 1913, pamph. MHS.
Tombstone rec. of Dorchester Co. Jones. DAR.
Wicomico Co. families. Bible rec. Ms. DAR.
Wicomico Co. families. Tilghman. Ms., pp. 67–68, 88, 98, 100–05. DAR.
See Hyatt-Todd-Miller.
Todd, King and Queen Cos., Va. Hist. and geneal. Bagby. 1908.
Todd, Thomas and Anne (Gorsuch), Gloucester Co., Va., and Balto. Co. Pedigree chart. Va. Mag. Hist. and Biog., v. 3, pp. 79–83.
†Todd Family. Hist. of Del. W. L. Bevan. 1929, v. 4, p. 338. MHS.
Chart. Winston of Va. Torrence. Pp. 91–105; chart, p. 92. MHS; DAR.
J. L. Vallandigham. Hist. of Pencader Pres. Church, Glasgow, Del., 1899. D. C. Geneal. Rec. Com., 1929, v. 4, p. 9. Typed, bd. DAR.
Todd Family, Anne Arundel Co. M. H. Mag., 1914, v. 9, no. 3, p. 298–305.
Todd-Gorsuch. Americans of gentle birth and their ancestors. Pitman. P. 127. MHS.
Todvine. *See* Toadvine.
†Toelle. Med. Annals Md. Cordell. 1903, p. 598. MHS.
Togler. *See* Vogler.
Toler. Mead relations. Prichard. DAR.
Tolley. Ances. rec. and portraits. Col. Dames of Amer., 1910, v. 1, p. 254. MHS; DAR.
Ancestral rec. Grafton Press, 1910, p. 254. MHS; DAR.
Bible rec.; Bible owned by Col. Oscar Kemp Tolley, Balto. Co. Mss. MHS.
*Col. families of Amer. Lawrence. V. 5, p. 288. MHS.
†Hist. of Balto. City and Co. Scharf. Pp. 864, 920. MHS.
Howard-Montague-Warfield geneal. chart. Culver and Marye. MHS.
See Hall-Tolley.
Tolly Family. Family bible rec. of Walter Tolley and Nancy Garrettson in 1728. Mss. DAR.
Tolson. Elliott chart. MHS.
Ringgold-Elliott chart. MHS.
†Tome, Jacob (1810–89). M. H. Mag., v. 12, p. 249.
Monumental City. Howard. MHS; DAR.
†Tome Family. Tercentenary hist. of Md. Andrews. V. 2, p. 96. MHS; DAR.
Tomlenson. Hagerstown tombstone inscriptions. Gruder. Natl. Geneal. Soc. Quart., 1919, v. 8, nos. 1, 2.
Tomlinson. Hist. of Byberry and Moreland. Martindale. MHS.
†Hist. of Washington Co. Williams. 1906, v. 1, p. 102. MHS; DAR.
Tomlinson, Benj. (Born and died in Md.). Rec. Ms. DAR.
Tomlinson Family. Ancestral rec. Grafton Press Pub., 1910, p. 123. MHS; DAR.
†Hist. of Allegany Co. Thomas and Williams. V. 1, p. 139. MHS; DAR.
†Hist. of West. Md. Thomas and Williams. V. 2, p. 1527. MHS; DAR.
Tompkins. Mrs. Morris Whitridge chart. MHS.
Tompkins, Mrs. John A. (Frederica Gore McLane). Chart. Col. Dames, Chap. I. MHS.
†Toms. Hist. of Frederick Co. Williams. V. 2, pp. 746, 903, 955, 958, 1028, 1521, 1523. MHS; DAR.
Taney and allied families. Silverson. MHS; DAR.
Miss Sara E. White chart. MHS.
†Toms Family. Tercentenary hist. of Md. Andrews. V. 4, p. 88. MHS; DAR.
Tongue. Hist. graves of Md. and D. C. Ridgely. MHS.
†Med. Annals Md. Cordell. 1903, p. 598. MHS.
Tonstall. Md. gleanings in Eng. Wills. M. H. Mag., 1907, v. 2, no. 4.

Toole. McSpadden - Love - Meigs - Clendinen - Von Bibber-Pope chart. MHS.
Torch. Balto., its hist., its people. Hall. V. 3. MHS; DAR.
†Geneal. and mem. encyc. of Md. Spencer. V. 2, p. 458. MHS; DAR.
Tormey, Alfred Jenkins. Pedigree. Soc. Col. Wars Md. Culver. 1940. MHS; DAR.
Torrance, James. And his descendants. Torrence and allied families. Torrence. Pp. 120–40. MHS.
Torrance Family. Bible. MHS.
***Torrence.** Coat of arms. Burke's landed gentry. 1939. MHS.
*Torrence and allied families. Robert M. Torrence. Under auspices of Geneal. Soc. of Pa. Phila., Wickersham Press, 1938. MHS.
See Simmons-Torrence-Dorsey.
†**Torrey.** Memoir of Rev. Charles T. Torrey, who died in penitentiary of Md., where he was confined for showing mercy to poor. (Born in 1813.) Boston, John P. Jewett Co., 1847. Enoch Pratt Lib.
†**Tottle.** Geneal. and mem. encyc. of Md. Spencer. V. 2, p. 451. MHS; DAR.
Toulson. Naturalizations in Md., 1666–1765; Laws. Bacon. MHS.
Tout. Frederick Co. tombstone inscriptions. Gruder. Natl. Geneal. Soc. Quart., 1919, v. 8, nos. 1, 2.
Tovey, Kent Co. Mrs. J. Hall Pleasants, Jr., Chart. MHS.
***Towles.** Henry Towles, Accomac Co., Va. H. I. Kirk. April, 1929. Bd. ms., pp. 335. MHS.
Towles Family, Va. Henry I. Kirk, Balto. Bound ms., 335 pp. MHS.
Towles, Va. (Md. ref.) Va. Mag. Hist. and Biog., v. 8; v. 9, p. 434.
Townley. Genealogical chart, showing Townley family in Great Britain and pedigrees of those families, who in seventeenth and eighteenth centuries, emigrated to United States and settled in Elizabethtown, New Jersey, and Annapolis, Md. Frank Alden Hill. Boston, 1888. MHS.
Lawrence-Chase-Townley estate. Hill. MHS.
Lawrence-Townley and Chase-Townley estates in Eng. Usher. Lib. Con.; MHS.
See Chase-Townley.
Townley, Margaret (commonly called Lady Mary Townley, of Annapolis). Townley geneal. chart. MHS.
Townley-Stevens. Genealogical chart of Robert Townley and Mary Stevens of Canterbury, Conn. (Both charts removed from "The Lawrence, Chase, Townley Estate.) Frank Alden Hill, 1888. MHS.
Townsend. All Hallow's P. E. churchyard, Snow Hill, Worcester Co. Hudson. Bd. ms. MHS; DAR. Also: Md. Geneal. Rec. Com., 1935-36, p. 24. Mss. DAR.
†Biog. of George Alfred Townsend, in MHS. The Sun, Balto., Dec. 13, 1925.
Dorsey and allied families. Ms. MHS.
Hist. of Byberry and Moreland. Martindale. MHS.
Makemie Memorial Pres. churchyard, Snow Hill, Worcester Co. Hudson. Bd. ms. MHS; DAR. Also: Md. Geneal. Rec. Com., Mrs. Lines. Mss. DAR.
†Men of mark in Md. Johnson. V. 3. DAR; Enoch Pratt Lib.
M. E. churchyard, Snow Hill, Worcester Co. Hudson. Bd. ms. MHS; DAR.
Mt. Carmel burial ground, Unity, Montgomery Co. Md. Geneal. Rec. Com., 1934–35, p. 85. Mss. DAR.
Old Somerset. Torrence. MHS; DAR.
Rec. of Stepney Parish. MHS; DAR.
St. Paul's Parish, Balto. V. 1, 2. Mss. MHS.
Somerset Co. Court Book. Tilghman. 1937. Ms. DAR.
Somerset Parish. Abs. of rec. Turner Geneal. Coll. Ms. MHS.
Turner Geneal. Coll. Ms. MHS.
*Wicomico Co. families. Tilghman. Ms., p. 95. DAR.
Townsend Family, Garrett and Prince George Cos. Mountain Democrat, Garrett Co., Oct. 18, 1934. Newsp. clipp. MHS; DAR.
Towson. Bible rec. MHS.
Data. Old Towsontown. Mary Osborn Odell. The Club Courant, Mar., 1940. MHS.
†Hist. of Balto. City and Co. Scharf. P. 895. MHS.
†Memoir of Gen. Nathan Towson (1784–). MHS.
Mt. Paran Pres. churchyard, Harrisonville, Balto. Co. Typed ms. MHS; DAR.
St. Paul's Parish, Balto. V. 1, 2, 3, 4. Mss. MHS.
St. Thomas' Parish, Balto. Co. Bd. ms. MHS. Also: Md. Geneal. Rec. Com., 1937, pp. 109–82. Mss. DAR.
*Tombstone inscriptions of Balto. Co. (Mt. Paran). Natl. Geneal. Soc. Quart., June, 1937, v. 25, p. 59.
See Ashman.
See Gosnell-O'Dell-Towson-Worthington.
Towson, Washington Co. Bible rec., 1783–1913. New Eng. Hist. and Geneal. Reg., 1925, v. 79, pp. 327–29.
†**Towson, Nathan.** Hist. of Md. Scharf. V. 3, pp. 26–27. MHS.
†(1784–1854). M. H. Mag., v. 12, p. 250.
***Toy-Hamilton.** Family chart. Ella F. O'Gorman. Ms. DAR.
***Toy-Swindell.** Family chart. Ella F. O'Gorman. Ms. DAR.
Traband. Elliott chart. MHS.
Tracy. St. Paul's Parish, Balto. V. 1. Mss. MHS.
Trader. Somerset Parish. Abs. of rec. Turner Geneal. Coll. Ms. MHS.
Turner Geneal. Coll. Ms. MHS.
†**Trail.** Hist. of Frederick Co. Williams. V. 2, pp. 720, 1298. MHS; DAR.
†Hist. of West. Md. Scharf. V. 1, p. 540. MHS; DAR.
†Memorial of Ariana McElfresh Trail. By her daughter Florence Trail. (Born in Frederick Co., 1828; died in 1892.) Boston, 1929. Enoch Pratt Lib.
†**Trail, Charles Bayard.** Men of mark in Md. Johnson. V. 3. DAR; Enoch Pratt Lib.
†**Trail, Charles E.** Men of mark in Md. Johnson. V. 3. DAR; Enoch Pratt Lib.
†**Trapnell.** Med. Annals Md. Cordell. 1903, p. 599. MHS.
Portrait and biog. rec. of Sixth Cong. Dist. of Md. 1898, pp. 751; 756. MHS; DAR.

Traux, Hagerstown. D. A. R. Mag., Aug., 1927, v. 61, no. 8, p. 609.
Travers. Ances. rec. and portraits. Col. Dames of Amer., 1910, v. 2, p. 731. MHS; DAR.
†Biog. cyc. of rep. men of Md. and D. C. P. 200. MHS; DAR.
Geneal. and mem. encyc. of Md. Spencer. V. 1, p. 262. MHS; DAR.
*Hist. of Dorchester Co. Jones. 1925, p. 472. MHS; DAR.
Keene family. Jones. MHS; DAR.
St. Paul's Parish, Balto. V. 1, 3, 4. Mss. MHS.
Whiteley chart. MHS.
See Harris - Maddox - Williams - Smith - Powell - Travers.
See Hicks - Dennis - Edmondson - Phillips - Travers-White.
See Parsons-Maddox-Travers.
See Travis.
See Wight-Hodson-Lloyd-Travers.
***Travers, Travis.** Wicomico Co. families. Tilghman. Ms., pp. 49, 49, 72. DAR.
Travis, Travers-Harris-Turner. Wicomico Co. families. Bible rec. Ms. DAR.
***Treadway.** Edward Treadway and his descendants, 1784–1859. O. G. Treadway. (Treadway family in Harford Co., 1700-1816.) Chicago, Ill. MHS.
Edward Treadway and his descendants. News Letter, 1–4. Oswell Garland Treadway, Suite 4000, 1 N. La Salle St., Chicago, Ill. MHS.
***Treadway Family.** Edward Treadway and his descendants, 1784–1859. O. G. Treadway. Chicago, Ill. News Letter, nos. 1–6. MHS.
***Treakle.** Wicomico Co. families. Tilghman. Ms., pp. 41, 126. DAR.
Tredway. Harford Co. Hist. Soc. Mss. Coll. JHU.
*Treadway family. W. T. Treadway, 1112 Park Bldg., Pittsburg, Pa. 1930.
Trego. Harford Co. Hist. Soc. Mss. Coll. JHU.
*Hist. account of Trego family. A. Trego Shertzer. (Trego family in Pa. and Balto.) Balto., Isaac Friedenwald, 1884. MHS.
Price family and other Gunpowder Friends. Death notices; photos. of newsp. clipp. MHS.
Trehearn. *See* Ashman.
Trehern. Edmund Beauchamp of East. Shore of Md. D. A. R. Mag., v. 66, no. 4, pp. 234–38.
Trew. Bible rec. Upper Penins. East. Shore., p. 212–15. MHS; DAR.
Cary Geneal. Coll. Ms. MHS.
*Rec. Eight family Bibles. MHS.
See Buck-Simmonds-Trew.
Trice. Somerset Co. Court Book. Tilghman. 1937. Ms. DAR.
Trice Family. Photos. MHS.
Trimble. Harford Co. Hist. Soc. Mss. Coll. JHU.
†Med. Annals Md. Cordell. 1903, p. 599. MHS.
Triner, John. Md. pensioner on Miss. pension rolls. D. A. R. Mag., v. 69, no. 11, p. 685.
Triplett, Va. Mrs. H. F. Johnston chart. MHS.
Triplett Family. William and Mary Quart., 1st series, v. 10, p. 136, v. 21, pp. 115–34.
Trippe. Ames Geneal. Coll. Ms. MHS.
Ances. rec. and portraits. Col. Dames of Amer., 1910, v. 1, p. 334. MHS; DAR.
*Arms. Hist. of Dorchester Co. Jones. 1925, p. 473. MHS; DAR.
Balto., its hist., its people. Hall. V. 3. MHS; DAR.
*Burke's landed gentry. 1939. MHS.
Col. families of U. S. A. Mackenzie. V. 1; v. 6. MHS; DAR.
*Geneal. and mem. encyc. of Md. Spencer. V. 1, pp. 53–57. MHS; DAR.
Howland chart. MHS.
Jacobs chart. MHS.
†Med. Annals Md. Cordell. 1903, p. 599. MHS.
Portrait and biog. rec. of East. Shore of Md. 1898, pp. 776–867. MHS; DAR.
Segrave chart. MHS.
Thomas family of Talbot Co. Spencer. P. 137. MHS; DAR.
Mrs. Wm. L. Watson chart. MHS.
Trippe, Andrew Cross, and Trippe, James McConky, Dorchester Co. Pedigree chart. Soc. Col. Wars, Md. Johnson. 1905, pp. 114, 156. MHS.
Trippe, Andrew Noel. Pedigree. Soc. Col. Wars Md. Culver. 1940. MHS; DAR.
Trippe, James McConky. *See* Trippe, Andrew Cross and James McConky.
†**Trippe, John.** M. H. Mag., v. 12, pp. 250, 384–85.
Coll. of Amer. epitaphs and inscriptions. Alden. 1814, v. 6. MHS.
Trippe Family. Col. and Revolutionary lineages of Amer. 1939, v. 2, pp. 187–91. MHS.
Trisler. Frederick Co. tombstone inscriptions. Gruder. Natl. Geneal. Soc. Quart., 1919, v. 8, nos. 1, 2.
Troth. See Coates, W. M. Abr. Compend. Amer. Geneal. Virkus. V. 1, p. 394. DAR.
Cox (Cock) family. Leef and Webb. Ms. MHS.
Hist. of Talbot Co. Tilghman. V. 1, pp. 35–39. MHS; DAR.
Man-Needles-Hambleton families. Needles. MHS; DAR.
Pedigree of Maurice Edward Skinner. Soc. Col. Wars Md. Culver. 1940. MHS; DAR.
Preston at Patuxent. MHS.
*Some col. mansions and those who lived in them. Glenn. 2nd series, 1900, v. 2, pp. 389, 390, 392, 393. MHS. Also: Preston at Patuxent. Pamph. repr. from above. MHS.
Third Haven Friends Meeting House, Easton. Vital rec. MHS. Also: Natl. Geneal. Soc. Quart., v. 11, no. 1, pp. 9–14.
Trinity Church cemetery, Dorchester Co. Md. O. R. Soc. Bull., no. 3, pp. 42–52.
†Henry Troth, Sept. 4, 1794–May 22, 1842. S. Troth. (Troth in Md., 1669.) Priv. pr., Phila., 1903. MHS; DAR.
See Berry-Bruff-Dixon-Troth.
See Kemp-Troth.
Troth, Talbot Co. H. Mullikin pedigree charts, plate 2. Soc. Col. Wars, Md. Johnston. 1905, p. 75. MHS.
Trotten, Trotton. St. Paul's Parish, Balto. V. 1. Mss. MHS.
Trotton. *See* Trotten.
Troup. Christ P. E. Church cemetery, Cambridge. Steele. 1936. MHS; DAR.
Troup-Davidge. Ames Geneal. Coll. Ms. MHS.

†Med. Annals Md. Cordell. 1903, p. 599. MHS.
Williamson Bible rec. Ms. MHS.
See Davidge-Troup.
Trovinger. Hagerstown tombstone inscriptions. Gruder. Natl. Geneal. Soc. Quart., 1919, v. 8, nos. 1, 2.
Troxall. Md. families. Culver. Ms. Personal list.
†**Troxell.** Hist. of West. Md. Scharf. V. 1, p. 583. MHS; DAR.
Trubshawe. Somerset Co. Court Book. Tilghman. 1937. Ms. DAR.
True. Cary Geneal. Coll. Ms. MHS.
***Trueman.** Dent-Magruder-Trueman family notes. Natl. Geneal. Soc. Quart., Dec., 1937, v. 25, no. 4, pp. 104–13.
Early hist. of Hollyday family. Hollyday. MHS; DAR.
Truit. Turner Geneal. Coll. Ms. MHS.
Truitt. All Hallow's P. E. churchyard, Snow Hill, Worcester Co. Hudson. Bd. ms. MHS; DAR. Also: Md. Geneal. Rec. Com., 1935–36, p. 24. Mss. DAR.
Bible rec., Wicomico Co. Md. Geneal. Rec. Com., 1937–38, p. 163. Mss. DAR.
Cannon - Riley - Truitt - Houston - Kollock - Stow families. Stow. MHS.
M. E. churchyard, Snow Hill, Worcester Co. Hudson. Bd. ms. MHS; DAR.
St. Mary's P. E. churchyard, Pocomoke, Worcester Co. Hudson. Bd. ms. MHS; DAR.
St. Paul's P. E. churchyard, Berlin, Worcester Co. Hudson. Bd. ms. MHS; DAR. Also: Md. Geneal. Rec. Com., 1937, Mrs. Lines. Mss. DAR.
Somerset Parish. Abs. of rec. Turner Geneal. Coll. Ms. MHS.
Wicomico Co. families. Bible rec. Ms. DAR.
*Wicomico Co. families. Tilghman. Ms, pp. 71, 116, 128. DAR.
Truman. Graves, Trent Hall on Patuxent. Md. O. R. Soc. Bull., no. 3, pp. 60–61. MHS.
Hist. graves of Md. and D. C. Ridgely. MHS.
See Greenfield-Truman.
Trumbo. Mead relations. Prichard. DAR.
St. Paul's Parish, Balto. V. 1. Mss. MHS.
Trump. Man-Needles-Hambleton families. Needles. Pp. 117, 119. MHS; DAR.
Trundle. Col. families of U. S. A. Mackenzie. V. 2. MHS; DAR.
*Geneal. and mem. encyc. of Md. Spencer. V. 1, pp. 26–33. MHS; DAR.
Hist. graves of Md. and D. C. Ridgely. MHS.
Humphrey Cissel farm, Montgomery Co. Md. Geneal. Rec. Com., 1926–27, p. 75. Mss. DAR.
Patriotic Md. Md. Soc. of S. A. R., 1930. MHS; DAR.
Priv. cemetery on Humphrey Cissel's farm near Poolesville. Md. Geneal. Rec. Com., v. 2, p. 75. Mss. DAR.
Truxel. Md. tombstone rec. Md. Geneal. Rec. Com., 1937, Parran, p. 28. Mss. DAR.
Tschudi, S. Werner. Md. Soc., War of 1812, v. 3, no. 299. Ms. MHS.
***Tubbs.** Wicomico Co. families. Tilghman. Ms, pp. 86, 91. DAR.
See Wimbrow-Lewis-Tubbs.
Tubman. Col. families of U. S. A. Mackenzie. V. 6, pp. 448–51. MHS; DAR.
*Hist. of Dorchester Co. Jones. 1902. MHS.
*Hist. Dorchester Co. Jones. 1925, pp. 475–84. MHS; DAR.
Keene family. Jones. MHS; DAR.
Pattison Bible rec. Ms. MHS.
Miss Eliza Thomas chart. MHS.
Thomas chart. Cary Geneal. Coll. Ms. MHS.
Tuchudi, Howard. Md. Soc., War of 1812, v. 4, no. 312. Ms. MHS.
Tuck. Balto., its hist., its people. Hall. V. 3, p. 771. MHS; DAR.
†Geneal. and mem. encyc. of Md. Spencer. V. 1, p. 77. MHS; DAR.
Mullikins of Md. Baker. MHS; DAR.
Tuck, Philemon Hallam. Pedigree chart. Soc. Col. Wars Md. Johnston. 1905, p. 115. MHS.
***Tucker.** Account of Tucker family of Bermuda. T. A. Emmert. N. Y., Bradstreet Press, 1898.
Centreville cemetery. Md. O. R. Soc. Bull., no. 1, pp. 41–47.
*Frederick Co. families. Markell. Ms. Personal list.
†Geneal. and mem. encyc. of Md. Spencer. V. 2, p. 679. MHS; DAR.
I. U. Church cemetery. Md. O. R. Soc. Bull., no. 2, pp. 76–78.
Rec. of Cope family. Cope. P. 131. MHS.
St. Paul's Parish, Balto. V. 3, 4. Mss. MHS.
Tucker Family Tree. Edward Tucker. Bermuda.
†Thomas Tudor Tucker, M.D. (1744–1828), Treas. of U. S., Continental soldier. Caldwell Woodruff. Linthicum Heights, Md. Ms. MHS.
See Darumple-Tucker-Kent.
See Hill-Tucker.
Tucker, H. St. G., Va. Abr. Compend. Amer. Geneal. Virkus. V. 1, p. 864. DAR.
Tucker, J. Armstrong Owings. Md. Soc., War of 1812. V. 1, no. 96. Ms. MHS.
Tucker, Thomas, (Revolutionary soldier; lived on Severn River, near Annapolis). D. A. R. Mag., v. 67, no. 1, p. 43.
Tucker Family. *See* Beedle-Foster-Kennedy-Walter.
See Hall-Tucker.
***Tucker Family,** Va. By E. C. Meade. The Sun, Balto., Aug. 14, 1904.
Tucker-Cockey. Notes. D. A. R. Mag., v. 68, no. 9, p. 550.
***Tuckerman Family.** Arch. of Georgetown Univ., Wash., D. C., v. 274, no. 1.
Tull. Machen chart. MHS.
Makemie Memorial Pres. churchyard, Snow Hill, Worcester Co. Hudson. Bd. ms. MHS; DAR. Also: Md. Geneal. Rec. Com., Mrs. Lines. Mss. DAR.
Old Somerset. Torrence. MHS; DAR.
Rehobeth P. E. churchyard, Somerset Co. Md. Geneal. Rec. Com., 1937, Mrs. Lines. Mss. DAR.
Somerset Co. Court Book. Tilghman. 1937. Ms. DAR.
Somerset Parish. Abs. of rec. Turner. Geneal. Coll. Ms. MHS.
Turner Geneal. Coll. Ms. MHS.
***Tull Family.** D. C. Geneal. Rec. Com., 1936–37, v. 31, pt. 2, p. 456. DAR.

Tull-Hall. Bible rec., 1771–1850. Md. Geneal. Rec. Com., 1939–40, pp. 162–63. Mss. DAR.
Tulley. Rec. of Stepney Parish. MHS; DAR.
Tully. See Clement. Col. families of U. S. A. Mackenzie. V. 1, pp. 97–100. MHS; DAR.
Tune. St. Paul's Parish, Balto. V. 1. Mss. MHS.
Turbervell Family. Lee of Va., 1642–1892. E. J. Lee. P. 93. Lib. Cong.; MHS.
Turbut. Mt. Olivet Cemetery, Frederick. Md. Geneal. Rec. Com., 1934–35, p. 111. Mss. DAR.
Turbutt. Col. families of East. Shore and their descendants. Emory. 1900, p. 3. MHS.
Dobbin chart. MHS.
Geneal. reg. Mervine. P. 69. MHS.
Md. families. Culver. Ms. Personal list.
Pedigree of Levin Gale Shreve. Soc. Col. Wars Md. Culver. 1940. MHS; DAR.
Pedigree of Harrison Tilghman. Soc. Col. Wars Md. Culver. 1940. MHS; DAR.
***Turbutt Family.** Old Kent. Hanson. Pp. 287, 292. MHS; DAR.
Turbutt-Edmondson. Ames Geneal. Coll. Ms. MHS.
Turnbaugh. Trinity P. E. churchyard, Long Green. Typed ms. MHS; DAR.
***Turnbull.** Burke's landed gentry. 1939. MHS.
Col. families of U. S. A. Mackenzie. V. 5, p. 542. MHS; DAR.
Mrs. T. C. Jenkins chart. MHS.
†Men of mark in Md. Johnson. V. 2. DAR; Enoch Pratt Lib.
Whitridge chart. MHS.
Mrs. E. Worthington chart. MHS.
See Shoemaker-Turnbull.
Turnbull, John Grason. Col. and Revolutionary lineages of Amer. 1939, v. 3, pp. 284–88. MHS.
Turnbull, William. William Turnbull (1751–1822), with some account of those coming after. A. D. Turnbull. Turnbull of "Auburn," Balto. Co., p. 105. Priv. pr. 1933. MHS, F. 153, T. 94.
Turner. Abr. Compend. Amer. Geneal. Virkus. V. 1, p. 866. DAR.
Bantz geneal. notes. Ms. MHS.
Dr. J. J. Caldwell. Md. Geneal. Rec. Com., 1933–34, pp. 269–70. Mss. DAR.
Chart. Rev. Charles Turner. 1800. MHS.
Col. families of U. S. A. Mackenzie. V. 2 (Del.), p. 724, v. 5 (Md.) MHS; DAR.
Cox (Cock) family. Leef and Webb. Ms. MHS.
Fisher family. Morse. MHS.
Fisher family, Sussex Co., Del., and Md. Ms. MHS.
†Hist. of Allegany Co. Thomas and Williams. V. 1. MHS; DAR.
†Hist. of Balto. City and Co. Scharf. P. 872. MHS.
Leftwich-Turner families of Va. Hopkins. DAR.
Lineage Bks., Natl. Soc. of Daughters of Amer. Col., v. 1, p. 382. MHS; DAR.
Md. Geneal. Rec. Com., 1932–33, pp. 208–09. Mss. DAR.
Md. tombstone rec. Md. Geneal. Rec. Com., 1937, Parran, p. 7. Mss. DAR.
Thomas McKnew, Prince George Co., and his descendants. Townsend. Ms. MHS.
†Med. Annals Md. Cordell. 1903, p. 600. MHS.
Naturalizations in Md., 1666–1765; Laws. Bacon. MHS.
Old cemetery, Denton, Caroline Co. Md. Geneal. Rec. Com., 1935–36, p. 168. Mss. DAR.
*Old Kent. Hanson. P. 49. MHS; DAR.
Pedigree of Mareen Duvall. Soc. Col. Wars Md. Culver. 1940. MHS; DAR.
Pedigree of Maurice Edward Skinner. Soc. Col. Wars Md. Culver. 1940. MHS; DAR.
St. Paul's Parish, Balto. V. 1, 2, 3, 4. Mss. MHS.
Southerland-Latham and allied families. Voorhees. Bd. ms. MHS.
*The Sun, Balto., Jan. 22, 1905, Aug. 25, Sept. 15 (Va.), 1907.
*C. H. B. Turner Geneal. Coll. Mss. MHS.
*Turner family of "Hebron" and "Betterton." H. Chandlee Forman. (Families of East. Shore of Md.) Balto., Waverly Press, Inc., 1933. MHS.
Wicomico Co. families. Bible rec. Ms. DAR.
*Wicomico Co. families. Tilghman. Ms, pp. 69–70, 72–73, 76, 122. DAR.
See McNew-Prather-Turner.
See Travis-Harris-Turner.
Turner, Balto. Rev. William Schenck; his ancestry and his descendants. Schenck. Pp. 125–27. Chart, p. 125. MHS; DAR.
Turner, St. Mary's Co. (8 generations.) Pedigree of George Harrison. Soc. Col. Wars Md. Culver. 1940. MHS; DAR.
Turner, Arthur Gordon. Pedigree. Soc. Col. Wars Md. Culver. 1940. MHS; DAR.
†**Turner, C. Y.** (1850–1918). Modern encyc. McDonnald. 1933.
Turner, Edward Raymond. Pedigree. Soc. Col. Wars Md. Culver. 1940. MHS; DAR.
Turner, Mrs. Frank G. (Edith Conant Brandt). Chart. Col. Dames, Chap. I. MHS;
Miss Miriam Brandt chart. MHS.
Turner, James Flynn. Pedigree. Soc. Col. Wars Md. Culver. 1940. MHS; DAR.
Turner Family, Va. Va. Mag. Hist. and Biog., v. 21, pp. 106, 211, 421; v. 22, p. 103.
Turpin. Bailliere chart. MHS.
Beauchamp chart. DAR.
Edmund Beauchamp. Eastern Shore. D. A. R. Mag., April, 1932, v. 66, no. 4, p. 234–38.
Christ P. E. Church cemetery, Cambridge. Steele. 1936. MHS; DAR.
D. A. R. Mag., Sept., 1933, v. 67, no. 9, pp. 583–88.
*Hackett family of Dorchester Co. D. A. R. Mag., v. 65, no. 4, p. 223.
Hackett family tree. Layton. MHS.
Hist. Salisbury, Wicomico Co. Truitt. DAR.
See Layton. Abr. Compend. Amer. Geneal. Virkus. V. 6, p. 357. DAR.
M. E. churchyard, Snow Hill, Worcester Co., Hudson. Bd. ms. MHS; DAR.
Patriotic Md. Md. Soc. of S. A. R., 1930. MHS; DAR.
Pedigree of Nicholas Leeke Dashiell. Soc. Col. Wars Md. Culver. 1940. MHS; DAR.
Rec. of Stepney Parish. MHS; DAR.
Somerset Co. Court Book. Tilghman. 1937. Ms. DAR.

See Beauchamp-Smoot-Turpin-White-Willis-Wilson.
Turpin, Beauchamp, Dorchester Co. Will probated March 15, 1769. D. A. R. Mag., v. 62, no. 12, p. 773.
Turpin, Francis, Dorchester Co. Bible rec. Ms. File case, MHS.
Turpin, Major Francis, Dorchester Co. D. A. R. Mag., v. 66, no. 10, p. 673.
Turpin, William, Dorchester Co. Bible rec. D. A. R. Mag., v. 66, no. 10, p. 672.
Turpin Family, Kingston, Somerset Co. Bible rec. of Dorchester and Somerset Cos. and Del. P. 84. DAR.
Turpin Family, Rehobeth, Del. Bible rec. of Dorchester and Somerset Cos. and Del. Pp. 85-86. DAR.
Turpin - Adams - Douglas - Hackett - Layton - Smoot, Dorchester Co. Bible rec. D. A. R. Mag., Oct., 1932, v. 66, no. 10, pp. 672-74.
Tutt. Whitehead chart. MHS.
Tuttle Family, Va. Ms. MHS.
Newsp. clipp. MHS.
Tutwiler. Hagerstown tombstone inscriptions. Gruder. Natl. Geneal. Soc. Quart., 1919, v. 8, nos. 1, 2.
Tutwiler, Edw. Magruder, Va. (1846-1925). Amer. Clan Gregor Year Book, 1926-27, p. 58. MHS; DAR.
***Twiford.** Wicomico Co. families. Tilghman. Ms, p. 35. DAR.
†**Twigg.** Hist. of Allegany Co. Thomas and Williams. V. 2. MHS; DAR.
***Twilley.** Wicomico Co. families. Tilghman. Ms, p. 66. DAR.
Tydings. Col. Joseph Belt. Hist. papers of Soc. Col. Wars. Magruder. 1909. MHS; DAR.
Britton Scrap Book. V. 2. Ms. MHS.
Bowie-Claggett chart. MHS.
Tylden. Pedigree of Thomas Gardener Hill. Soc. Col. Wars Md. Culver. 1940. MHS; DAR.
*The Sun, Balto., Dec. 11, 1904.
See Tilden.
***Tylden Family.** See Tilden. Old Kent. Hanson. P. 302. MHS; DAR.
Tylden, Tilden. Ances. rec. and portraits. Col. Dames of Amer., 1910, v. 2, p. 692. MHS; DAR.
Tyler. Abr. Compend. Amer. Geneal. Virkus. V. 4, pp. 471, 646. MHS.
Beall and Bell families. Beall. MHS.
Castle geneal. and chart. MHS.
Col. families of Amer. Lawrence. V. 15, p. 172. MHS.
Col. Nicholas Duvall family rec. Price. Bd. ms. MHS.
Hist. of Frederick Co. Williams. V. 1, pp. 563-595; v. 2, p. 1398. MHS; DAR.
Mrs. D. G. Lovell chart. MHS.
Md. families. Culver. Ms. Personal list.
†Med. Annals Md. Cordell. 1903, pp. 601-02. MHS.
†Men of mark in Md. Johnson. V. 1. DAR; Enoch Pratt Lib.
Naturalizations in Md., 1666-1765; Laws. Bacon. MHS.
Patriotic Md. Md. Soc. of S. A. R., 1930. MHS; DAR.
Pedigree of James Mather Sill. Soc. Col. Wars Md. Culver. 1940. MHS; DAR.
St. Paul's Parish, Balto. V. 2, 4. Mss. MHS.
Somerset Co. Court Book. Tilghman. 1937. Ms. DAR.
Tombstone rec. of Dorchester Co. Jones. DAR.
See Duvall-Hall-Tyler.
***Tyler, F. Stansbury.** Burke's landed gentry. 1939. MHS.
Tyler-Brown. Americans of gentle birth and their ancestors. Pitman. P. 21. MHS.
Tynes-Bowie-Catlett-Pendleton . . ., Md. and Va. Abr. Compend. Amer. Geneal. Virkus. V. 4, pp. 112-13.
Tyrar. Somerset Co. Court Book. Tilghman. 1937. Ms. DAR.
Tyre. Somerset Co. Court Book. Tilghman. 1937. Ms. DAR.
***Tyrrell.** Burke's landed gentry. 1939. MHS.
Tyson. Amer. Armory and Blue Book. Matthews. 1911-12, p. 263.
*(Baltimore line). The Sun, Balto., Jan. 22, 1905.
Geneal. and memorial encyc. of Md. Spencer. v. 1, p. 221. MHS; DAR.
Geneal. notes of Thomas family. Thomas. MHS; DAR.
*Gilmor chart. Ms. MHS.
†Hist. of Balto. City and Co. Scharf. P. 771. MHS.
†Life of Elisha Tyson. J. S. Tyson. 1825. DAR; Enoch Pratt Lib.
Md. families. Culver. Ms. Personal list.
†Med. Annals Md. Cordell. 1903, p. 602. MHS.
John O'Donnell of Balto. Cook. MHS.
Pedigree of George Thornburgh Macauly Gibson. Soc. Col. Wars Md. Culver. 1940. MHS; DAR.
St. Joseph's R. C. churchyard. Md. O. R. Soc Bull., no. 3, p. 64.
Tyson, Pa. and Md. Col. families of U. S. A. Mackenzie. V. 2. MHS; DAR.
Tyson, Anthony Morris. Pedigree. Soc. Col. Wars Md. Culver. 1940. MHS; DAR. (See Pedigree Book, 1905. Pp. 95, 96, 116.)
Tyson, Anthony Morris, and Tyson, Matthew Smith. Pedigree chart. Soc. Col. Wars Md. Johnston. 1905, p. 116. MHS.
***Tyson, J. Ellicott.** Geneal. and mem. encyc. of Md. Spencer. V. 1, pp. 221-39. MHS; DAR.
Tyson, Malcolm Van Vechten. Pedigree charts, plates 1, 2, 3 and 4. Soc. Col. Wars, Md. Johnston. 1905, pp. 117-20, 156. MHS.
Pedigree. Soc. Col. Wars Md. Culver. 1940. MHS; DAR. (See Pedigree Book, 1905, pp. 117-20, plates 1-4.)
Tyson, Matthew Smith. *See* Tyson, Anthony Morris and Matthew Smith.
Tyson Family. Thomas Book. Thomas. Pp. 531-37. Lib. Cong.; MHS.
Tyson Family, Balto. Fox-Ellicott-Evans families. Evans. MHS; DAR.
Tyson Line. T. M. Smith pedigree charts, plate 2. Soc. Col. Wars Md. Johnston. 1905, p. 96. MHS.

U

Uhhorn, Rev. John. Quart. Rev. of Evangelical Luth. Church, Gettysburg, 1891, v. 21, pp. 197-205.

Uhler. Bible rec. Md. Geneal. Rec. Com., v. 2. DAR.
Bible rec. Ms. MHS.
Chart. Md. Geneal. Rec. Com., 1932–33. Mss. DAR.
*Genealogy and chart of Uhler family. C. H. Uhler. 1932. DAR.
†Med. Annals Md. Cordell. 1903, p. 602. MHS.
St. Paul's Parish, Balto. V. 2, 4. Mss. MHS.
*Uhler family of Pa. 1901. 35 pp.
***Uhler Family.** Chart. C. H. Uhler. 1932 Coll. 4, photos. DAR.
Geneal. C. H. Uhler. 1932, pamph. DAR.
Uhler-Anderson-Burgess-Galloway. Bible rec., 1751–1912. Md. Geneal. Rec. Com., 1926–27, v. 2, p. 64–68. DAR.
Uhthoff. Price family and other Gunpowder Friends. Death notices; photos. of newsp. clipp. MHS.
Uling. Hist. sketch of P. F. Eichelberger. Eichelberger.
‡**Ulman,** Judge takes the stand. Judge Ulman here relates some of his experiences on Bench of Balto. J. N. Ulman. 1933. MHS.
Ulrich. Hagerstown tombstone inscriptions. Gruder. Natl. Geneal. Soc. Quart., 1919, v. 8, nos. 1, 2.
***Umphreys.** *See* Humphries.
***Umstead.** Wicomico Co. families. Tilghman. Ms, pp. 109–10. DAR.
Umsted, Frederick Co. Lineage Bk., Order of Washington, p. 27. MHS; DAR.
Underhill. Cary Geneal. Coll. Ms. MHS.
Harlan family geneal., Chester Co., Pa. Harlan. P. 43. MHS.
Rev. Joseph Hull (1595) and some of his descendants. Hull. 1904. MHS.
Turner family. Forman. Pp. 56–57, 91–93. MHS.
Underhill, Capt. John. Ms. MHS.
†**Underwood, Alexander** (1688–1767) Del., Md., and York Co., Pa. Index to biog. sketches pub. in "The Friend," v. 26, 27. Pub. Geneal. Soc. Pa., v. 3. No. 2, pp. 109–34.
***Unsult, George Frederick,** (born Aug. 6, 1737; baptised Aug. 22, 1737, by Rev. Mr. Wolf—1st baptismal rec. of Monocacy Congregation), Frederick Co. Ms. MHS.
†**Updegraff.** Hist. of West. Md. Scharf. V. 2, p. 1176. MHS; DAR.
Zion Reformed Church, Hagerstown. Md. Geneal. Rec. Com., 1934–35. Mss. DAR.
Upgate. Miss Eliza Thomas chart. MHS.
Upshur. All Hallow's P. E. churchyard, Snow Hill, Worcester Co. Hudson. Bd. ms. MHS; DAR. Also: Md. Geneal. Rec. Com., 1935–36, p. 24. Mss. DAR.
Ancestry of Rosalie Morris Johnson. Johnson. 1905. MHS; DAR.
†Biog. cyc. of rep. men of Md. and D. C. P. 270. MHS; DAR.
Mrs. Howard Bruce chart. MHS.
Cemetery Creek, Anne Arundel Co., Tombstone Inscriptions. Founders of Anne Arundel. and Howard Cos. Warfield. P. 334. MHS; DAR.
Christ P. E. Church cemetery, Cambridge. Steele. 1936. MHS; DAR.
Custis-Teakle chart. Cary Geneal. Coll. Ms. MHS.
*J. I. Dennis pedigree chart, plates 1 and 2. Soc. Col. Wars, Md. Johnston. 1905, pp. 21–22. MHS.
Geneal. of Henrietta Chauncey Wilson. Upshur. Bk. of photos. MHS.
Harrison-Waples and allied families. Harrison. MHS.
Harvey chart. MHS.
Miss Minna Lurman chart. MHS.
Makemie Memorial Pres. churchyard, Snow Hill, Worcester Co. Hudson. Bd. ms. MHS; DAR. Also: Md. Geneal. Rec. Com., Mrs. Lines. Mss. DAR.
Pedigree of Sam'l King Dennis. Soc. Col. Wars Md. Culver. 1940. MHS; DAR.
Pedigree of James Donnell Tilghman. Soc. Col. Wars Md. Culver. 1940. MHS; DAR.
Somerset Co. Court Book. Tilghman. 1937. Ms. DAR.
Somerset Parish. Abs. of rec. Turner Geneal. Coll. Ms. MHS.
Turner Geneal. Coll. Ms. MHS.
Mrs. Wm. L. Watson chart. MHS.
Mrs. Morris Whitridge chart. MHS.
*Wicomico Co. families. Tilghman. Ms, p. 22. DAR.
William and Mary Quart., 1st series, v. 3, p. 260.
Sir George Yeardley. Upshur. Pp. 18, 29, 30. MHS.
Upshur, Essex Co. Va. Wills (9), 1720–1810. D. A. R. Mag., v. 61, no. 12, pp. 908–09.
Upshur Line. Col. and Revolutionary lineages of Amer. 1939, v. 2, p. 116. MHS.
Geneal. tables of paternal lines of Dennis family. Dennis. Pp. 33–45. MHS.
Urie. Portrait and biog. rec. of East. Shore of Md. 1898, pp. 256, 852. MHS.
St. Paul's Parish, Balto. V. 2. Mss. MHS.
Urner. Englar family. Barnes. MHS; DAR.
Ury. Naturalizations in Md., 1666–1765; Laws. Bacon. MHS.
Usher. Brice-Govane-Howard tombstone inscriptions. Ms. MHS.
St. Paul's Parish, Balto. V. 1, 2, 3. Mss. MHS.
Usilton Family, Kent Co., 1791–1856. Rec. Md. Geneal. Rec. Com., 1937–38, pp. 80–81. Mss. DAR.
Utie. Howard-Montague-Warfield geneal. chart. Culver and Marye. MHS.
Md. families. Culver. Ms. Personal list.
Virginians and Marylanders at Harvard College in 17th century. William and Mary Quart., 2nd series, v. 13, no. 1, p. 1.
†**Utie, Nathaniel.** Sketch. Hist. of Cecil Co. Johnston. P. 28. MHS; DAR.
Utie Family. The Times, Belair, July 23, 1886.
William and Mary Quart., 1st series, v. 4, pp. 52–57.
Utye. *See* Collett-Utye.
Utye-Collett. M. H. Mag., June, 1913, v. 8, no. 2, p. 203.
***Utz-Campbell.** Wilson Mss. Coll., no. 29. MHS.

V

Vagha. Naturalizations in Md., 1666–1765; Laws. Bacon. MHS.
Vale Family, Pa. Col. and Revolutionary families of Phila. Jordan. 1933, v. 1, pp. 168–86.
Valentine. Elliott chart. MHS.

Valentine, Milton, Carroll Co. Quart. Rev. of Evangelical Luth. Church, Gettysburg, 1907, v. 37, pp. 1–17.
Valiant, Talbott Co. Sweetser chart. MHS.
Vallandigham, Lieut. Col. George. Pa. Mag. Hist. and Biog., v. 53, p. 159.
†**Vallandignhan, Clement L.** Life. Rev. James L. Vallandingham. Balto., Turnbull Bros., 1872. MHS.
Van Bebber. St. Stephens Parish, Cecilton, Md. MHS; DAR.
Vanbeeck. Naturalizations in Md., 1666–1765; Laws. Bacon. MHS.
Vanbibber. Naturalizations in Md., 1666–1765; Laws. Bacon. MHS.
Van Bibber. Henry Baker and some of his descendants. White. Pamph., 1901, pp. 28–29. MHS.
†Biog. cyc. of rep. men of Md. and D. C. P. 597. MHS; DAR.
Col. families of U. S. A. Mackenzie. V. 1, p. 538; v. 2, p. 26; v. 5, p. 461. MHS; DAR.
*Hist. of Cecil Co. Johnston. MHS; DAR.
†Med. Annals Md. Cordell. 1903, pp. 602–03. MHS.
Van Bibber, Dr. Abraham. Westminster churchyard. Patriotic Marylander, v. 2, no. 4, pp. 54–60. MHS; DAR.
†**Van Bibber, T. Emory** (1812–81). Poets and verse writers of Md. Perine.
***Van Bibber Family.** W. Va. Hist. Mag., v. 3, no. 3, p. 213.
Van Bibber, Vanbibber. St. Paul's Parish, Balto. V. 1, 2. Mss. MHS.
Van Bibber, von Bibber. McSpadden-Love-Meigs - Clendinen- Van Bibber - Pope chart. MHS.
Vanburkeloe. St. Stephens Parish, Cecilton, Md. MHS; DAR.
Vance. Cummings chart. Lib. Cong.; MHS; DAR.
Rec. of Stepney Parish. MHS; DAR.
*Wicomico Co. families. Tilghman. Ms, pp. 95, 97, 110. DAR.
Vandegrift. Marriage rec., 1781–1892, Harford Co. Md. Geneal. Rec. Com., 1934–35, p. 108. DAR.
***Vanderburg (Walter) Family.** Rec. (In German.) Ms. MHS.
Vanderford. Patriotic Md. Md. Soc. of S. A. R., 1930. MHS; DAR.
†**Vanderford, Henry** (born in Caroline Co., 1811). Poets and verse writers of Md. Perine.
Vandergrift. St. Stephen: Parish, Cecilton, Md. MHS; DAR.
Vandergrift-Aspril. Vandergrift-Aspril and allied families. Orig. from New Castle, Del., numerous descendants in Md., particularly Balto. Births, marriages and deaths (over 2000). Md. Geneal. Rec. Com., 1935–36. Pp. 79–155. DAR.
Vanderheyden. Balch letters and papers. Pamph., p. 19. MHS.
Bordley family of Md. Gibson. P. 21. MHS.
Naturalizations in Md., 1666–1765; Laws. Bacon. MHS.
Pedigree of George Webb Constable. Soc. Col. Wars Md. Culver. 1940. MHS; DAR.
Vander Horst, S. C. and Balto. Abr. Compend. Amer. Geneal. Virkus. V. 1, p. 867. DAR.
***Vanderleyden.** Old Kent. Hayden. Pp. 80–81. MHS; DAR.
Vandervoort. St. Paul's Parish, Balto. V. 1. Mss. MHS.
***Vandevanter.** Bible rec., Va. and Md. Natl. Geneal. Soc. Quart., Sept., 1937, v. 25, no. 3, p. 90.
Vandeventer. St. Paul's Parish, Balto. V. 2. Mss. MHS.
Van Dyke. Cotton chart. MHS.
Van Dyke, Del. Some notable families of south. States. Armstrong. V. 1. DAR.
Van Dyke - Johns - Montgomery - Manlove. Chart, photos., complete in 1 sheet. Cary Geneal. Coll. Ms. MHS.
***Van Hecke.** Van Hecke and allied ancestry. E. J. Sellers. MHS.
Vanhorn. *See* Vanhorne.
Van Horn. Beall and Bell families. Beall. MHS; DAR.
Lay Hill burial ground, Montgomery Co. Md. Geneal. Rec. Com., 1934–35, pp. 66–67. Mss. DAR.
Pedigree of James Mather Sill. Soc. Col. Wars Md. Culver. 1940. MHS; DAR.
Van Horn, Arthur. Md. Soc., War of 1812, v. 3, no. 253. Ms. MHS.
Vanhorne, Vanhorn. St. Stephens Parish, Cecilton, Md. MHS; DAR.
Van Lear. Ancestry of Benjamin Harrison. Keith. P. 57. MHS; DAR.
Black chart. MHS.
†Hist. of West. Md. Scharf. V. 2, pp. 1234–37. MHS; DAR.
***Van Meter.** Geneal. and sketches of some old families of Va. and Ky. B. F. Van Meter. Louisville, 1901. DAR. Index to "Genealogies and Sketches of Some Old Families. B. F. Van Meter. 1901." M. R. McCabe. Ms. DAR. Additional Index of above. B. C. C. Brumbaugh. 1936. Ms. DAR.
†Hist. of Allegany Co. Thomas and Williams. V. 2. MHS; DAR.
See Duke-Shepard-Van Meter.
***Van Metre.** Origin and descent of Amer. Van Metre. Coll. from civil, church, military and family rec. S. Gordon Smythe. Priv. pr., 1923.
Vanneman. Florence Eyster Weaver chart. MHS.
Van Ness. Hist. graves of Md. and D. C. Ridgely. MHS.
†Med. Annals Md. Cordell. 1903, p. 604. MHS.
†**Van Ness, Gen. Peter Van Ness** (mayor of City of Washington). His wife Marcia and her father David Burns. Rec. Columbia Hist. Soc., v. 22, p. 125; see also v. 23, p. 1.
Van Ness-Sargent Line. Balto., its hist., its people. Hall. V. 3. MHS; DAR.
Vannort. Bible rec., Kent Co. Md. Geneal. Rec. Com., 1937, Parran, pp. 208–09. Mss. DAR.
Chestertown cemetery. Md. O. R. Soc. Bull., no. 1, pp. 18–29.
Vannort Family, Kent Co. Births, marriages, deaths, 1812–74. Md. Geneal. Rec. Com., 1937. DAR.
Van Pradallis, Benedict. Focke Geneal. Coll. Ms. MHS.
Van Rensselaer. McCormick chart. MHS.

Van Rensselaer-Taylor. Abr. Compend. Amer. Geneal. Virkus. V. 4, p. 516. MHS.
Vansandt. *See* Vansant.
Vansant. Quaker cemetery, Millington, Kent Co., 1802–1906. Md. Geneal. Rec. Com., 1932–33, v. 5. Mss. DAR.
Vansant, Vansandt. St. Stephens Parish, Cecilton, Md. MHS; DAR.
†Van Sickle. Men of mark in Md. Johnson. V. 1. DAR; Enoch Pratt Lib.
***Vans Murray.** Hist. of Dorchester Co. Jones. 1925, p. 426. MHS; DAR.
Van Swearingen. Abr. Compend. Amer. Geneal. Virkus. V. 6, pp. 166, 495. DAR.
Chart, photos., complete in 1 sheet. Cary Geneal. Coll. Ms. MHS.
Col. families U. S. Mackenzie. V. 7, p. 220. MHS; DAR.
Lineage Bks., natl. Soc. of Daughters of Amer. Col., v. 2, p. 155; v. 3, pp. 148, 318. MHS; DAR.
Patriotic Md. Md. Soc. of S. A. R., 1930. MHS; DAR.
Pedigree of James Dorsey Brown, Jr. Soc. Col. Wars Md. Culver. 1940. MHS; DAR.
Pedigree of Dr. Christopher Johnston, Jr. Soc. Col. Wars Md. Culver. 1940. MHS; DAR.
Pedigree of Gustav Wm. Lurman. Soc. Col. Wars Md. Culver. 1940. MHS; DAR.
Pedigree of Franklin Buchanan Owen. Soc. Col. Wars Md. Culver. 1940. MHS; DAR.
Pedigree of James Donnell Tilghman. Soc. Col. Wars Md. Culver. 1940. MHS; DAR.
Tasker chart. Cary Geneal. Coll. Ms. MHS.
C. B. Tiernan pedigree chart. Soc. Col. Wars Md. Johnston. 1905, pp. 113, 156. MHS.
See Sweringen. Ms. MHS.
Vanswerlngen. Naturalizations in Md., 1666–1765; Laws. Bacon. MHS.
Van Sweringen. Americans of gentle birth and their ancestors. Pittman. P. 148. MHS.
Side lights on Md. hist. Richardson. V. 2, p. 240. MHS; DAR.
Welsh-Hyatt and kindred. Welsh. Sec. 7, p. 190. MHS; DAR.
**See* Sweringen.
Van Twiller. McCormick chart. MHS.
Van Wyck. St. Paul's Parish, Balto. V. 2. Mss. MHS.
Varlet, Verlett. "Bohemia Manor." Col. and Revolutionary families of Pa. Amer. Hist. Soc., N. Y., 1934, p. 16.
Varleth. Descendants of Joram Kyn. Pa. Mag., v. 6, p. 208.
†Vaugh. Day-Star of Amer. Freedom. Davis. P. 190. MHS; DAR.
Fisher family, Sussex Co., Del., and Md. Ms. MHS.
Vaugh, Robert. Seven pioneers of col. East. Shore. Skirven. M. H. Mag., 1920, v. 15, no. 3, pp. 230–50, no. 4, pp. 394–491.
Vaughan. Elliott chart. MHS.
Lloyd family hist. of Wales, Pa., and Md. DAR.
Tilghman chart. MHS.
M. Van V. Tyson pedigree chart. Soc. Col. Wars, Md. Johnston. 1905, pp. 120, 156. MHS.
See Awbrey-Vaughan.
†Vaughn. Biog. cyc. of rep. men of Md. and D. C. P. 240. MHS; DAR.
Fisher family. Morse. MHS.
***Veasey.** Burke's landed gentry. 1939. MHS.
Veasey, Isaac. Amer. Armory and Blue Bk. Matthews. 1908, p. 188. DAR.
Veatch. Abr. Compend. Amer. Geneal. Virkus. V. 6, p. 593. DAR.
Abstracts of wills (9) of Veatches in Md., Frederick, Montgomery and Prince George Cos., 1705–1819. D. A. R. Mag., July, 1937, v. 71, no. 7, p. 678.
*Coat of arms. Burke's landed gentry. 1939. MHS.
Veazey. Abr. Compend. Amer. Geneal. Virkus. V. 1, p. 871. DAR.
Ames Geneal. Coll. Ms. MHS.
Balto., its hist., its people. Hall. V. 3. MHS; DAR.
Blackford chart. MHS.
Col. families of U. S. A. Mackenzie. V. 1, pp. 542–45. MHS; DAR.
Harvey chart. MHS.
†Hist. of Cecil Co. Johnston. MHS; DAR.
†Med. Annals Md. Cordell. 1903, p. 604. MHS.
Pedigree of J. Henry Ferguson. Soc. Col. Wars Md. Culver. 1940. MHS; DAR.
St. Stephens Parish, Cecilton, Md. MHS; DAR.
†Capt. Edward Veazey (1813), Commander, privateer, "Tartar." Balto. MHS.
See Carmichael-Paca-Tilghman-Veazey.
Veazey, Duncan. Amer. Armory and Blue Bk. Matthews. 1908, p. 72. DAR.
Pedigree charts, plates 1 and 2. Soc. Col. Wars, Md. Johnston. 1905, pp. 121–22, 156. MHS.
Veazey, George Ross. Pedigree. Soc. Col. Wars Md. Culver. 1940. MHS; DAR.
Veazey, Mrs. George Ross. (Miss Grace Rogers Roberts). Chart. Col. Dames, Chap. I. MHS.
***Veazey, Gov. Thomas Ward.** Founders of Anne Arundel and Howard Cos. Warfield. P. 270. MHS; DAR.
†Governors of Md. Buchholz. P. 124. MHS.
†Hist. of Md. Scharf. V. 3, p. 25. MHS.
***Veazey Family.** Old Kent. Hanson. Pp. 176–79. MHS; DAR.
Veazey-Dormott-Husband, Cecil Co., Md., and N. C. Washington ancestry and rec. Hoppin. V. 2. MHS; DAR.
Venable. Col. families of U. S. A. Mackenzie. V. 6. MHS; DAR.
*Venables of Va. E. Marshall Venable. Pr. exclusively for family, by J. J. Little & Ives, N. Y., 1925.
***Venable,** Va. The Sun, Balto., Dec. 25, 1904.
Venable, Mrs. Edward Carrington (Nancy Hollingsworth De Ford). Chart. Col. Dames, Chap. I. MHS.
Venable, Miss Helen Skipwith Wilmer. Chart. Col. Dames, Chap. I. MHS.
Mrs. J. Hall Pleasants, Jr., chart. MHS.
Venables. Rec. of Stepney Parish. MHS; DAR.
*Wicomico Co. families. Tilghman. Ms, pp. 97–98. DAR.
Verbrack. Naturalizations in Md., 1666–1765; Laws. Bacon. MHS.
Verlett. *See* Varlet.
Vernay, Peter. Bible rec. Ms. MHS.
*Family rec. from Bible. MHS.
†Vernon. Admiral Vernon; his Marylanders and his Medals. L. McCormick Goodhart. M. H. Mag., 1935, v. 30, pp. 240–57.

Md. gleanings in Eng. Wills. M. H. Mag., 1907, v. 2, no. 2.
†Men of mark in Md. Johnson. V. 1. DAR; Enoch Pratt Lib.
†**Vethake.** Med. Annals Md. Cordell. 1903, p. 604. MHS.
Vickars, Del. Bible rec. Md. Geneal. Rec. Com., 1937. DAR.
Vickars, Anthony S. Rec.; his New Testament. Md. Geneal. Rec. Com., 1937, Parran, p. 64. Mss. DAR.
Vickers. Balto., its hist., its people. Hall. V. 2. MHS; DAR.
Bible rec. of Dorchester and Somerset Cos. and Del. Pp. 87–91. DAR.
Chestertown cemetery. Md. O. R. Soc. Bull., no. 1, pp. 18–29.
Trinity Church cemetery, Dorchester Co. Md. O. R. Soc. Bull., no. 3, pp. 42–52.
Vickers, Wm. Handy Collins. Md. Soc., War of 1812, v. 2, no. 136. Ms. MHS.
Pedigree. Soc. Col. Wars Md. Culver. 1940. MHS; DAR.
***Vickers Family.** Old Kent. Hanson. Pp. 334–37. MHS; DAR.
***Vickers Family,** Mass. Prior to 1637, to Md. about 1730. The Sun, Balto., June 23, 30, 1907.
Victor. All Hallow's P. E. churchyard, Snow Hill, Worcester Co. Hudson. Bd. ms. MHS; DAR. Also: Md. Geneal. Rec. Com., 1935–36, p. 24. Mss. DAR.
Naturalizations in Md., 1666–1765; Laws. Bacon. MHS.
Viers. Humphrey Cissel farm, Montgomery Co. Md. Geneal. Rec. Com., 1926–27, p. 75. Mss. DAR.
M. E. Church, South, cemetery near Poolesville (now abandoned). Md. Geneal. Rec. Com., v. 2. Mss. DAR.
Portrait and biog. rec. of Sixth Cong. Dist. of Md. 1898, p. 721. MHS; DAR.
Viley. Americans of gentle birth and their ancestors. Pitman. P. 169. MHS.
Vincent. Makemie Memorial Pres. churchyard, Snow Hill, Worcester Co. Hudson. Bd. ms. MHS; DAR. Also: Md. Geneal. Rec. Com., Mrs. Lines. Mss. DAR.
*Wicomico Co. families. Tilghman. Ms, pp. 97, 99, 101. DAR.
Vincent, Snow Hill. Md. Bible rec. Md. Geneal. Rec. Com., 1935–36, v. 8, p. 34. DAR.
Vincent Family. Rec., Snow Hill, Md. Md. Geneal. Rec. Com., 1935–36, p. 34. Mss. DAR.
Vinson. Rec. of Stepney Parish. MHS; DAR.
Vinton. Hazelhurst charts. MHS.
†**Virdin.** Med. Annals Md. Cordell. 1903, p. 604. MHS.
***Vivian.** Pennington Papers. Ms. MHS.
Vogler, Togler. Frederick Co. tombstone inscriptions. Gruder. Natl. Geneal. Soc. Quart., 1919, v. 8, nos. 1, 2.
Vogulum. Patriotic Md. Md. Soc. of S. A. R., 1930. MHS; DAR.
Volck, Adalbert. Dr. Adalbert Volck, caricaturist and his family. Ms. MHS.
†**Vollenweider.** Men of mark in Md. Johnson. V. 4. DAR; Enoch Pratt Lib.
Von Bibber. *See* Van Bibber.
von der Becke. Mrs. Talbot T. Speer chart. MHS.
***Vonder Burg.** Walter Vanderburg family rec. (In German.) Ms. MHS.
von Kapff. Bible rec. Ms. MHS.
Sir Geroge Yeardley. Upshur. P. 35. MHS.
St. Paul's Parish, Balto. Mss. MHS.
Von Lingen. Balto., its hist., its people. Hall. V. 2. MHS; DAR.
Von Trevenfeld. Rogers Coll. Ms. MHS.
Voorhees. Mrs. N. S. Pendleton, Jr., chart. MHS.
Voorheess-Allison-Ford-Turner. Abr. Compend. Amer. Geneal. Virkus. V. 4, p. 517. MHS.
Voshell. St. Paul's P. E. churchyard, Kent Co. Md. O. R. Soc. Bull., no. 2, pp. 54–65.
***Vrints.** Rogers Coll. Ms. MHS.
Vrints von Trevenfeld. Chart. Rogers Coll. Ms. MHS.

W

†**Wachtel.** Hist. of Frederick Co. Williams. V. 2, p. 959. MHS; DAR.
†**Wachter.** Hist. of Frederick Co. Williams. V. 2, pp. 724, 1131–32, 1225, 1226, 1283, 1489, 1593. MHS; DAR.
Mt. Olivet Cemetery, Frederick. Md. Geneal. Rec. Com., 1934–35, p. 111. Mss. DAR.
†Tercentenary hist. of Md. Andrews. V. 4, p. 638. MHS; DAR.
†**Waddell.** Med. Annals Md. Cordell. 1903, p. 605. MHS.
St. Paul's Parish, Balto. V. 2. Mss. MHS.
†**Wade.** Balto. Lewis Hist. Pub. Co., 1912, v. 2, p. 258. DAR.
Balto., its hist., its people. Hall. V. 2. MHS; DAR.
Md. gleanings in Eng. Wills. M. H. Mag., 1907, v. 2, no. 3.
Pedigree of Warren Keach Magruder. Soc. Col. Wars Md. Culver. 1940. MHS; DAR.
St. Paul's Parish, Balto. V. 2. Mss. MHS.
See Pottenger.
Wade, Anne. Will, Nov. 9, 1804. D. C. Geneal. Rec. Com., 1937–38, v. 35, pp. 86–88. Typed, bd. DAR.
Wade, Ichabod, Mass. Md. Geneal. Rec. Com., 1934–35, pp. 8–9. Mss. DAR.
Wade, Levi and Dr. Samuel. Amer. Clan Gregor Year Book, 1914, p. 34. MHS; DAR.
Wade, Sam'l H. Md. Soc., War of 1812, v. 1, no. 89. Ms. MHS.
Wade Family. Hist. of Balto. Lewis Hist. Pub. Co., 1912, v. 2, p. 580. DAR.
†**Wagaman.** Hist. of Frederick Co. Williams. V. 2, p. 717. MHS; DAR.
†Tercentenary hist. of Md. Andrews. V. 2, p. 664; v. 3, p. 846. MHS; DAR.
†**Wager.** Tercentenary hist. of Md. Andrews. V. 2, p. 136. MHS; DAR.
Wages. Abr. Compend. Amer. Geneal. Virkus. V. 6, p. 547. DAR.
Waggaman. Christ P. E. Church cemetery, Cambridge. Steele. 1936. MHS; DAR.
Hist. graves of Md. and D. C. Ridgely. MHS.
†Med. Annals Md. Cordell. 1903, p. 605. MHS.
Rec. of Stepney Parish. MHS; DAR.
See Ennalls-Waggaman.
***Waggaman Family.** Letters and wills. Mss. MHS.

Waggaman-Elliott Families. William and Mary Quart., 1st series, v. 17, p. 300.
Waggaman-Ennalls Families, Somerset Co. William and Mary Quart., 1st series, v. 2, pp. 99–105, 135.
†**Wagne.** Port. and biog. rec. of Sixth Cong. Dist. of Md. P. 445. MHS; DAR.
***Wagner.** Memorial, 1722–1881. (Wagner re-interment, Oct. 20, 1881.) MHS.
Patriotic Md. Md. Soc. of S. A. R., 1930. MHS; DAR.
Sunday Times, Jan. 31, 1886. Scrap Book, no. 7. MHS.
***Wagner, Michael, Jr.** Family rec. File case, DAR.
Wagner, Philip, Balto. (married Violet Vaughn Jan. 18, 1807). D. A. R., Mag., v. 71, no. 6, p. 558.
***Wagner Family.** The Times, Jan. 31, 1886. MHS.
Wagner Family, Carroll Co. The Times, Balto., Jan. 31, 1886. Newsp. clipp. MHS.
Wagner-Clingman. Rec. of John and Mary (Crouse) Wagner and Wm. A. and Adelia (de Lourier) Clingman. Ms. DAR.
Wagner, Wagoner. Hagerstown tombstone inscriptions. Gruder. Natl. Geneal. Soc. Quart., 1919, v. 8, nos. 1, 2.
Wagoner. Americans of gentle birth and their ancestors. Pitman. P. 156. MHS.
Hist. of West. Md. Scharf. V. 2, p. 1033. MHS; DAR.
Zion Reformed Church, Hagerstown. Md. Geneal. Rec. Com., 1934–35. Mss. DAR.
See Wagner.
***Wagoner-Kuhns.** Wagoner-Kuhns family, 1681–1931. J. W. Miller. Pa., 1931, pamph. DAR.
Waid-Biddle-Williams. Abr. Compend. Amer. Geneal. Virkus. V. 4, p. 518. MHS.
Wailes. Md. families. Culver. Ms. Personal list.
†Med. Annals Md. Cordell. 1903, p. 605. MHS.
Miss. Geneal. Rec. Com., Misc., 1924, p. 1. Typed. Loose leaf binder, DAR.
Patriotic Md. Md. Soc. of S. A. R., 1930. MHS; DAR.
†Tercentenary hist. of Md. Andrews. V. 2, p. 516. MHS; DAR.
Wicomico Co. families. Bible rec. Ms. DAR.
*Wicomico Co. families. Tilghman. Ms, pp. 22, 82, 103, 105. DAR.
See Wolfe-Perrie-Wailes.
†**Wailes. Benjamin L. C.** Gentleman of Old Natchez Region. Dr. C. S. Sydnor. (B. L. C. Wailes, 1797–1862, with Md. background.) Enoch Pratt Lib.
Wainright. Samuel Carpenter of Phila. Carpenter. P. 65. MHS.
†**Wainwright,** Kent Co. Med. Annals Md. Cordell. 1903, p. 606. MHS.
Waite. Natl. Geneal. Soc. Quart., v. 7, no. 3, pp. 45–48.
***Wakefield.** Frederick Co. families. Markell. Ms. Personal list.
Wakeman, Conn. Pedigree of Valentine Sherman Duke. Soc. Col. Wars Md. Culver. 1940. MHS; DAR.
Walckman. *See* Waltman.
Wale. Somerset Co. Court Book. Tilghman. 1937. Ms. DAR.
Wale, Whaley; Whale, later **Whaley.** Old Somerset. Torrence. MHS; DAR.
Wales. Bible rec. Upper Penins. East. Shore. Pp. 68–86. MHS; DAR.
Walford. Somerset Co. Court Book. Tilghman. 1937. Ms. DAR.
Walke. Mrs. Lee Barroll chart. MHS.
Pocahontas and her descendants. Robertson. MHS; DAR.
Walker. Balch chart. MHS.
Cary Geneal. Coll. Ms. MHS.
*Frederick Co. families. Markell. Ms. Personal list.
Garrison Church. Allen. MHS; DAR.
†Hist. of Balto. City and Co. Scharf. P. 862. MHS.
Hist. graves of Md. and D. C. Ridgely. MHS.
Capt. Roger Jones of London and Va. Browning.
Mrs. D. G. Lovell chart. MHS.
Marriage rec. of Frederick Co. Markell. Md. Geneal. Rec. Com., 1938–39. Mss. DAR.
†Med. Annals Md. Cordell. 1903, p. 606. MHS.
Patriotic Md. Md. Soc. of S. A. R., 1930. MHS; DAR.
Pedigree of Richard Walker Worthington. Soc. Col. Wars Md. Culver. 1940. MHS; DAR.
Pedigree of Andrew Jackson Young, Jr. Soc. Col. Wars Md. Culver. 1940. MHS; DAR.
Sater geneal. Bd. ms. MHS.
(Over 40 rec.) St. Paul's Parish, Balto. V. 1, 3, 4. Mss. MHS.
St. Thomas' Parish, Balto. Co. Bd. ms. MHS. Also: Md. Geneal Rec. Com., 1937, pp. 109–82. Mss. DAR.
Somerset Co. Court Book. Tilghman. 1937. Ms. DAR.
Torrence and allied families. Torrence. P. 467. MHS; DAR.
Turner Geneal. Coll. Ms. MHS.
*Walker family of Toaping Castle, Md. S. H. Walker. Wash., D. C., 1883, 24 pp. MHS.
*Walker family of Va. 1902, 722 pp.
*Wicomico Co. families. Tilghman. Ms, p. 109. DAR.
See Beedle-Foster-Kennedy-Walker.
Walker, N. C. and Md. Col. families of U. S. A. Mackenzie. V. 5. MHS.
Walker, Somerset Co. Side lights on Md. hist. Richardson. V. 2, p. 459. MHS; DAR.
***Walker,** Talbot Co. Lineage Bks., Daughters of Founders and Patriots, v. 3, p. 42; v. 10, p. 41. MHS.
***Walker,** Va. The Sun, Balto., March 3, 10, 17, 1907.
Walker, Henry, Balto. Co. Copy of will. Ms. MHS.
Walker, John Moseley. Pedigree. Soc. Col. Wars Md. Culver. 1940. MHS; DAR.
†**Walker, Lieut. Noah Dixon.** M. H. Mag., 1935, v. 30, pp. 363–67.
†**Walker, Saml. Hamilton.** Hist. of Md. Scharf. V. 3, p. 228. MHS.
Walker, Wm. S. Crittenden. Md. Soc., War of 1812, v. 3, no. 272. Ms. MHS.
Walker Family. Geneal. of Page family, Va. Page. Pp. 195–234. MHS; DAR.
*Old Kent. Hanson. P. 87. MHS; DAR.
Walker-Mercer-Davis. Amer. of gentle birth, and their ancestors. Pittman. V. 1, pp. 312–16. MHS; DAR.

Walker-Rider-Fletcher. Somerset Parish. Abs. of rec. Turner Geneal. Coll. Ms. MHS.
Wall. Thomas McKnew, Prince George Co., and his descendants. Townsend. Ms. MHS.
Wall, A. V. Md. Soc., War of 1812, v. 2, no. 153. Ms. MHS.
Wall, John (born in Md., 1744; died in Spartanburg, S. C., 1836). D. A. R. Mag., v. 71, no. 2, p. 162.
Wallace. Griffith geneal. Griffith. MHS; DAR.
*Hist. of Dorchester Co. Jones. 1925, p. 484. MHS; DAR.
Hist. graves of Md. and D. C. Ridgely. MHS.
Pedigree of George Webb Constable. Soc. Col. Wars Md. Culver. 1940. MHS; DAR.
Pedigree of Andrew Noel Trippe. Soc. Col. Wars Md. Culver. 1940. MHS; DAR.
St. Paul's Parish, Balto. V. 2. Mss. MHS.
St. Stephens Parish, Cecilton, Md. MHS; DAR.
Selden chart. MHS.
Shrewsbury churchyard, Kent Co. Md. O. R. Soc., v. 2, pp. 46–54. MHS.
Tombstone rec. of Dorchester Co. Jones. DAR.
Va. geneal. Hayden. MHS; DAR.
*Wallace family. N. Y., Wm. M. Clemens, 1902, pamph., 27 pp. MHS.
Wallace family of Amer., 1790. J. A. Phelps. (Wallace of Md., pp. 6, 24.) N. Y., Wm. M. Clemens, 1914, pamph. MHS.
*Wicomico Co. families. Tilghman. Ms., p. 97. DAR.
See Jamison-Wallace.
Wallace, Va. Amer. Clan Gregor Year Book, 1927, p. 15. MHS; DAR.
***Wallace Family.** Old Kent. Hanson. Pp. 176, 179. MHS; DAR.
***Wallace-Bruce.** Wallace-Bruce and related families. J. Wallace. 1930. DAR.
***Wallen-Walling.** Wallen-Walling family of Frederick Co. Ms. DAR.
Waller. Old Somerset. Torrence. MHS; DAR.
Rec. of Stepney Parish. MHS; DAR.
Somerset Co. Court Book. Tilghman. 1937. Ms. DAR.
Wicomico Co. families. Bible rec. Ms. DAR.
*Wicomico Co. families. Tilghman. Ms., pp. 40, 51, 99, 110, 122–25. DAR.
Waller Family, Va. Ms. MHS.
Newsp. clipp. Scrap Book. MHS.
Walley. Old Somerset. Torrence. MHS; DAR.
Walley, Whalley. Edward Walley the Regicide. Pa. Mag. Hist. and Biog., v. 4, p. 258.
Walling. Wallen-Walling family. Ms. DAR.
Wallingford. Southern Wallingfords. (Md. ref.) Natl. Geneal. Soc. Quart., v. 23, p. 41.
Wallis. Amer. ancestry of Frederick Louis and Reginald Shippen Huidekoper. 1931, pamph., p. 18. MHS; DAR.
†Bench and bar of Md. Sams and Riley. 1901, v. 2, p. 372. Lib. Cong.; MHS; Peabody Lib.
Greenway Mss. Geneal. Coll. Binder's title, Hawkins-Bordley. MHS.
See Huidekoper. Abr. Compend. Amer. Geneal. Virkus. V. 4, p. 295. MHS.
St. Paul's Parish, Balto. V. 2. Mss. MHS.
Shrewsbury churchyard, Kent Co. Md. O. R. Soc., v. 2, pp. 46–54. MHS.
Talbott of "Poplar Knowle." Shirk. MHS; DAR.
*Wallis family of Md. Chart. MHS.
***Wallis,** Talbot Co. Lineage Bks., Daughters of Founders and Patriots, v. 14, p. 39. MHS.
Wallis, Samuel. Lukens chart. MHS.
Wallis, Severn Teakle (born Sept. 8, 1816). Wallis chart. MHS.
Geneal. and memorial encyc. of Md. Spencer. V. 2, p. 349. MHS; DAR.
†Hist. of Md. Scharf. V. 3, pp. 366–67. MHS.
†Memorial. Balto., 1896. MHS.
Wallis, Wm. Queen Anne Co. Will. D. C. Geneal. Rec. Com., v. 33, pp. 26–27. Typed, bd. DAR.
Wallis Family (to Md. from Eng., 1650). Chart. Blue print, 1902. MHS.
Walls. Crumpton graveyard. Md. Geneal. Rec. Com., 1933–34, pp. 193–203. Mss. DAR.
†Med. Annals Md. Cordell. 1903, pp. 606–07. MHS.
Line of Md. Reynolds, Tewelles, Walls and kindred families. 1928, pamph., p. 31. MHS.
Walmsley. Hist. of Byberry and Moreland. Martindale. MHS.
Walmsley, Wamsly. St. Stephens Parish, Cecilton, Md. MHS; DAR.
Walraven. Bible rec. Upper Penins. East. Shore. Pp. 155–63. MHS; DAR.
Walsh. Amer. Guthrie and allied families. Guthrie. Bk. 4. DAR.
†Bench and bar of Md. Sams and Riley. 1901, v. 2, pp. 417, 419. Lib. Cong.; MHS; Peabody Lib.
†Hist. of West. Md. Scharf. V. 2, pp. 1396–98. MHS; DAR.
St. Paul's Parish, Balto. V. 2. Mss. MHS.
Stirling chart. MHS.
Mrs. J. P. Thom chart. MHS.
Walston. Somerset Co. Court Book. Tilghman. 1937. Ms. DAR.
Walter. Abr. Compend. Amer. Geneal. Virkus. V. 6, p. 602. DAR.
St. Mary's churchyard, Tyaskin, Md. Md. Geneal. Rec. Com., 1938–39, pp. 187–92. Mss. DAR.
*Wicomico Co. families. Tilghman. Ms., pp. 124–25. DAR.
†**Walters.** Hist. of Balto. City and Co. Scharf. P. 675. MHS.
Mrs. C. L. Riggs chart. MHS.
St. Paul's Parish, Balto. V. 2, 4. Mss. MHS.
†**Walters, Wm.** Balto., hist. and biog. Richardson and Bennett. 1871, pp. 512–16. MHS; DAR.
†**Walters, Wm. T.** Biog. cyc. of rep. men of Md. and D. C. P. 519. MHS; DAR.
Monumental City. Howard. MHS; DAR.
Waltham. *See* Adams-Waltham.
Waltham Family. Hist. Md. Geneal. Rec. Com., 1935–36, pp. 71–77. Mss. DAR.
***Waltman.** House of Waltman, and its allied families. Lora S. La Mance. Waltman of Frederick Co., p. 103. St. Augustine, Fla., Record Co., 1928. MHS.
Waltman, Walckman. Revolutionary pension abs. Natl. Geneal. Soc. Quart., v. 23, p. 103.
Walton. Hist. of Byberry and Moreland. Martindale. MHS.
†Med. Annals Md. Cordell. 1903, p. 607. MHS.
St. Paul's Parish, Balto. V. 2. Mss. MHS.
†Tercentenary hist. of Md. Andrews. V. 3, p. 518; v. 4, p. 18 . MHS; DAR.

***Walton.** Walton family of Va. Mrs. K. Cox Gottschalk. Pamph. DAR.
***Walton,** Snow Hill, Md. (1675). Lineage Bk. Daughters of Founders and Patriots, v. 18, p. 71. MHS; DAR.
***Walton,** Va. The Sun, Balto., Nov. 20, 1904.
Walton, Capt. Tilman, N. C. Revolutionary service. Md. Geneal. Rec. Com., 1929, p. 56. DAR.
Walton Family, Del. and Md. Natl. Geneal. Soc. Quart., v. 25, no. 3, p. 98.
†Waltz. Hist. of Frederick Co. Williams. V. 2, p. 1273. MHS; DAR.
†Med. Annals Md. Cordell. 1903, p. 607. MHS.
See Woltz.
Wampler. Englar family. Barnes. MHS; DAR.
Roop geneal. Pamph. MHS.
Wampler Family. Bible. Md. Geneal. Bull., v. 2, p. 18. MHS. DAR.
Wampole. *See* Sellers-Wampole.
Wamsly. *See* Walmsley.
Wantz. Zion Reformed Church, Hagerstown. Md. Geneal. Rec. Com., 1934-35. Mss. DAR.
Waples. Fisher family. Morse. MHS.
Fisher family, Sussex Co., Del., and Md. Ms. MHS.
Somerset Parish. Abs. of rec. Turner Geneal. Coll. Ms. MHS.
Turner Geneal. Coll. Ms. MHS.
See Harrison-Waples.
Ward. Ames Geneal. Coll. Ms. MHS.
Ances. rec. and portraits. Col. Dames of Amer., 1910, v. 1, p. 214, 269, 290, 362. MHS; DAR.
Samuel Carpenter of Phila. Carpenter. P. 145. MHS.
Cary Geneal. Coll. Ms. MHS.
Harvey chart. MHS.
†Hist. of West. Md. Scharf. V. 2, pp. 933, 1475-76. MHS; DAR.
Md. families. Culver. Ms. Personal list.
Md. tombstone rec. Md. Geneal. Rec. Com., 1937, Parran, p. 9. Mss. DAR.
†Med. Annals Md. Cordell. 1903, pp. 607-08. MHS.
†Old Kent. Hanson. Pp. 176-78, 231. MHS; DAR.
Old Somerset. Torrence. MHS; DAR.
Patriotic Md. Md. Soc. of S. A. R., 1930. MHS; DAR.
Pedigree of J. Henry Ferguson. Soc. Col. Wars Md. Culver. 1940. MHS; DAR.
Pedigree of George Ross Veazey. Soc. Col. Wars Md. Culver. 1940. MHS; DAR.
Revolutionary war pension abs. Natl. Geneal. Soc. Quart., v. 23, no. 3, p. 104.
(30 rec.) St. Paul's Parish, Balto. V. 1, 3, 4. Mss. MHS.
St. Stephens Parish, Cecilton, Md. MHS; DAR.
St. Steven's graveyard, Cecil Co. Md. Geneal. Rec. Com., 1934-35, pp. 213-14. Mss. DAR.
Somerset Co. Court Book. Tilghman. 1937. Ms. DAR.
†Tercentenary hist. of Md. Andrews. V. 2, pp. 656, 784; v. 3, p. 527.
See Veazey. Abr. Compend. Amer. Geneal. Virkus. V. 1, p. 871. DAR.
*Wicomico Co. families. Tilghman. Ms., pp. 52, 82, 91-92. DAR.
See Coe-Ward.
Ward, Baltimore Co. Talbott of "Poplar Knowle." Shirk. MHS; DAR.
Marriages. Md. Geneal. Bull., v. 5, pp. 6-7. MHS; DAR.
Ward, Cecil Co. Blackford chart. MHS.
Col. families of U. S. A. Mackenzie. V. 1, p. 543. MHS; DAR.
Ward, Somerset Co. Taliaferro family, Va. Tyler's Quart. Mag., v. 11, pp. 51-61, 179-82.
†Ward, Wash. Co. Portraits and biog. rec. of Sixth Cong. Dist. P. 498. MHS; DAR.
Ward, Edward. Revolutionary pensioner of Md. Natl. Geneal. Soc. Quart., v. 23, no. 3, p. 104.
***Ward, Henry DeCourcy.** Burke's landed gentry. 1939. MHS.
***Ward Family.** Old Kent. Hanson. Pp. 176-78. MHS; DAR.
Ward Line, Cecil Co. D. Veazey pedigree chart, plate 1. Soc. Col. Wars Md. Johnston. 1905, p. 121, 157. MHS.
Warder. Miss Sara E. White chart. MHS.
Wardrop, Calvert Co. Md. gleanings in Eng. Wills. M. H. Mag., 1909, v. 4, no. 2.
Ware. Burton ancestry. Ms. MHS.
†Sketches of life and travels of Rev. Thomas Ware, who has been itinerant Meth. preacher for more than fifty years. Written by himself (Born 1758; Balto. in 1784; also Kent Circuit, East. Shore of Md.) N. Y., 1839. Enoch Pratt Lib.
***Warfel.** Boyd family. Boyd. DAR.
Trinity P. E. churchyard, Long Green. Typed ms. MHS; DAR.
Warfield. Abr. Compend. Amer. Geneal. Virkus. V. 6, p. 744. DAR.
Alexander and Azel Warfield. Correction. M. H. Mag., v. 34, no. 3, p. 303.
Ances. rec. and portraits. Col. Dames of Amer., 1910, v. 1, pp. 82, 151; v. 2, p. 614. MHS; DAR.
Autobiography of Summerfield Baldwin. MHS; DAR.
Sara R. Baldwin chart. MHS.
Balto., its hist., its people. Hall. V. 2. MHS; DAR.
Mrs. Lee Barroll chart. MHS.
Mrs. R. Barton, Jr., charts. MHS.
Britton Scrap Book. V. 1. Ms. MHS.
Mrs. Howard Bruce chart. MHS.
Cabells and their kin. Brown.
Cary Geneal. Coll. Ms. MHS.
*Chart of Mrs. Wallis Warfield Simpson. Southern Spectator, March, 1937, v. 3, no. 2. MHS.
Col. families of Amer. Lawrence. V. 2, p. 43; v. 3, p. 299. MHS.
Col. families of U. S. A. Mackenzie. V. 1; v. 6; v. 7, pp. 48, 49, 50. MHS; DAR.
*Data on Mrs. Wallis Warfield Simpson. Ancestry. Edward L. Worthington. April, 1937. Ms. MHS.
Darby geneal. Darby. MHS.
Descendants of Capt. Richard Warfield. (Corrections and additions.) Francis C. Culver. To be pub. in 1941.
Dorsey and allied families. Ms. MHS.
Dorsey chart. MHS.
Eldridge chart. MHS.
Ford and other lines. Md. Geneal. Rec. Com., 1932-33, pp. 7-20. Mss. DAR.
*Founders of Anne Arundel and Howard Cos. Warfield. Pp. 83-91, 301 (Gov. Edwin War-

field) 365–68, 374–76, 444–48, 451–62, 465–68, 529, 531–32, 541–43 (New York descendants of Md. Warfields). MHS; DAR.
Geneal. and memorial encyc. of Md. Spencer. V. 1. MHS; DAR.
Griffith chart. Cary Geneal. Coll. Ms. MHS.
Griffith geneal. Griffith. MHS; DAR.
Hamill chart. MHS.
†Her name was Wallis Warfield. Life story of Mrs. Ernest Simpson. Edwina H. Wilson. N. Y., E. P. Dutton & Co., 1936. Enoch Pratt Lib.
†Hist. of West. Md. Scharf. V. 2, p. 881. MHS; DAR.
Howland chart. MHS.
Howard-Montague-Warfield geneal. chart. Culver and Marye. MHS.
Mrs. R. N. Jackson chart. MHS.
Lineage Bks., Daughters of Amer. Col. V. 2, pp. 116–17; v. 3, p. 320; v. 5, p. 149. MHS; DAR.
Md. families. Culver. Ms. Personal list.
M. H. Mag., 1939, v. 34, no. 3, p. 303.
†Med. Annals Md. Cordell. 1903, pp. 203, 608–09. MHS.
Milligan chart. MHS.
Mrs. E. N. Morison chart. MHS.
Patriotic Md. Md. Soc. of S. A. R., 1930. MHS; DAR.
Peale Geneal. Coll. Ms. MHS.
Pedigree of Charles Gambrill Baldwin. Soc. Col. Wars Md. Culver. 1940. MHS; DAR.
Pedigree of Francis Joseph Baldwin. Soc. Col. Wars Md. Culver. 1940. MHS; DAR.
Pedigree of Duncan Keener Brent. Soc. Col. Wars Md. Culver. 1940. MHS; DAR.
Pedigree of James Dorsey Brown, Jr. Soc. Col. Wars Md. Culver. 1940. MHS; DAR.
Pedigree of Mareen Duvall. Soc. Col. Wars Md. Culver. 1940. MHS; DAR.
Pedigree of Wm. Winchester Eareckson. Soc. Col. Wars Md. Culver. 1940. MHS; DAR.
Pedigree of Gustavus Warfield Evans. Soc. Col. Wars Md. Culver. 1940. MHS; DAR.
Pedigree of Edward Hambleton. Soc. Col. Wars Md. Culver. 1940. MHS; DAR.
Pedigree of Thomas Murray Maynadier. Soc. Col. Wars Md. Culver. 1940. MHS; DAR
Pedigree of Thomas Dobbin Penniman. Soc. Col. Wars Md. Culver. 1940. MHS; DAR.
Pedigree of Pleasants Pennington. Soc. Col. Wars Md. Culver. 1940. MHS; DAR.
Pedigree of Levin Gale Shreve. Soc. Col. Wars Md. Culver. 1940. MHS; DAR.
Pedigree of Andrew Jackson Young, Jr. Soc. Col. Wars Md. Culver. 1940. MHS; DAR.
Prentice chart. MHS.
Proof of descent of Alice C. Warfield from Richard Warfield, 1st. Ms. MHS.
Mrs. A. Randall chart. MHS.
Riggs of Anne Arundel, Frederick and Montgomery Cos. prior to 1663. Pamph. MHS.
St. Paul's Parish, Balto. V. 2, 4. Mss. MHS.
Side lights on Md. hist. Richardson. V. 2, p. 246. MHS; DAR.
Talbott of "Poplar Knowle." Shirk. MHS DAR.
*The Sun, Balto., Jan. 10, 1904.
*Warfield and Montague; pedigree of Bessie Wallis Warfield Simpson. F. B. Culver and W. B. Marye. 1937. Ms. MHS.
*Warfields of Md. J. Dorsey Warfield. Incl. col. families whose descendants are entitled to enroll in D. A. R. and S. A. R. Balto., Daily Record Co., 1898. MHS.
*Warfield - Burgess - Rogers - Davidge - Gaither - Chew. Lineage Bk., Daughters of Amer. Col., v. 2, pp. 116–17. MHS.
Welsh-Hyatt and kindred. Welsh. Sec. 10, p. 203. MHS; DAR.
Mrs. J. Whitridge Williams chart 2. MHS.
See Ford-Dorsey-Hyland, etc.
See Greenberry-Warfield.
See Welsh-Warfield.
See Waters-Warfield.
***Warfield,** Cumberland. Hist. of Allegany Co. Thomas and Williams. V. 2. MHS; DAR.
†**Warfield, Charles Alexander** (1751–1813). Biography. Ms. MHS.
†**Warfield, Edward.** Governor of Md. Buchholz. P. 268. MHS.
***Warfield, Edwin.** Geneal. and mem. encyc. of Md. Spencer. V. 1, pp. 212–20. MHS; DAR.
†(1848–1920). M. H. Mag., 1920, v. 15, pp. 203–07.
Md. Soc., War of 1812, v. 1, no. 88. Ms. MHS.
†Men of mark in Md. Johnson. V. 1. DAR; Enoch Pratt Lib.
†**Warfield, Elisha Griffith.** Men of mark in Md. Johnson. V. 4. DAR; Enoch Pratt Lib.
Warfield, Frederick Howard. Pedigree. Soc. Col. Wars Md. Culver. 1940. MHS; DAR. (See pedigree of John Ogle Warfield, Jr.)
Warfield, John Ogle, Jr. Pedigree. (Aston, Bolling, Cocke, Mayo, Stith, Tabb and others of Va.) Soc. Col. Wars Md. Culver. 1940. MHS; DAR.
***Warfield, Capt. Richard.** Hist. and descendants. Francis B. Culver, 1226 N. Calvert St., Balto., Md. To be pub.
†**Warfield, S. Davies.** Men of mark in Md. Johnson. V. 3. DAR; Enoch Pratt Lib.
***Warfield Family.** Arch. of Georgetown Univ., Wash., D. C., v. 287.
Bible rec. Natl. Geneal. Soc. Quart., Dec., 1938, v. 26, p. 135.
Hist. of West. Md. Scharf. V. 2, p. 881.
Natl. Geneal. Soc. Quart., Dec., 1938, v. 26, no. 4, p. 135.
Thomas Book. Thomas. Pp. 543–46. Lib. Cong.; MHS.
Warfield Line. Col. and Revolutionary lineages of Amer. 1939, v. 1, pp. 277–82. MHS.
Gaither, Va. and Md. Col. and Revolutionary families of Phila. Jordan. 1933, v. 1, pp. 144–67.
Waring. Anne Arundel Co. tombstone inscriptions. Ms. DAR.
Balto; its hist., its people. Hall. V. 3. MHS; DAR.
Bowies and their kindred. Bowie. MHS; DAR.
Children of Alex P. and M. C. Hill. Ms. MHS.
Duckett chart. MHS.
Gantt geneal. Ms. MHS.
Patriotic Md. Md. Soc. of S. A. R., 1930. MHS; DAR.
Pedigree of Mareen Duvall. Soc. Col. Wars Md. Culver. 1940. MHS; DAR.
Mrs. M. L. Price chart. MHS.
St. Paul's Parish, Balto. V. 2. Mss. MHS.

Waring, Calvert Co. Col. families of U. S. A. Mackenzie. V. 1, pp. 553-57. MHS; DAR.
Waring, Wm. Emory, Jr. Pedigree. Soc. Col. Wars Md. Culver. 1940. MHS; DAR.
Waring Line. Col. and Revolutionary lineages of Amer. 1939, v. 2, p. 195. MHS.
Waring, Warring. Balto. Herald, April 26, 1903. Newsp. clipp. MHS.
Waringe. Balto. Herald, April 26, 1903. Newsp. clipp. MHS.
*The Sun, Balto., Jan. 3, 1904.
Waringe Family. Visitation of Shorpshire. Harleian Soc. Pub., v. 29, p. 485. MHS.
Waringe, Warring. Chart, Md. and Eng. pedigree, visitation of Shropshire, 1623, photos., complete in 1 sheet. Cary Geneal. Coll.Ms. MHS.
Warner. Ancestry of Lieut. and Mrs. Wm. B. Stork. Ms. MHS.
Bower-Hack-Warner bible rec. Md. Geneal. Rec. Com., 1939-40, pp. 178-80. Mss. DAR.
Britton Scrap Book. V. 2. Ms. MHS.
Dobbin chart. MHS.
Fox-Ellicott-Evans families. Evans. MHS; DAR.
Graves. Greensboro churchyard. Md. Geneal. Rec. Com., 1935-36, p. 168. Mss. DAR.
†Hist. of West. Md. Scharf. V. 2, 890. MHS; DAR.
Jenkins-Courtney chart. MHS.
Lineage Bks., Natl. Soc. of Daughters of Amer. Col., v. 1, p. 83. MHS; DAR.
Md. gleanings in Eng. Wills. M. H. Mag., 1909, v. 4, no. 2.
McCormack chart. MHS.
†Med. Annals Md. Cordell. 1903, p. 610. MHS.
Mrs. E. W. Poe chart. MHS.
†Portraits and biog. rec. of Harford and Cecil Cos., 1897. P. 346. MHS; DAR.
*The Sun, Balto., June 25, 1907.
†Tercentenary hist. of Md. Andrews. V. 1, p. 143; v. 2, p. 41; v. 4, pp. 356, 728. MHS; DAR.
*David Warner family rec. See Michael Wagner, Jr. File case, DAR.
*Warner family. H. W. Osler. (Pa. with Md. ref.) 1935, pamph. MHS.
Warner, Pa. to Harford Co., 1770. Hist. Harold W. Osler. Pamph. MHS.
Warner, Phila. Mrs. H. F. Johnston chart. MHS.
Warner, Va. and Md. Ances. rec. and portraits, Col. Dames of Amer., 1910, pp. 103, 439, 604. MHS; DAR.
Warner, C. Hopewell. Md. Soc., War of 1812, v. 1, no. 68. Ms. MHS.
Warner, Culbreth Hopewell. Pedigree. Soc. Col. Wars Md. Culver. 1940. MHS; DAR. (See Pedigree Book, 1905, p. 123, revised.)
Pedigree chart. Soc. Col. Wars, Md. Johnston. 1905, p. 123. MHS.
Warner, G. C. Md. Soc., War of 1812, v. 1, no. 39. Ms. MHS.
Warner, J. E. Md. Soc., War of 1812, v. 1, no. 15. Ms. MHS.
Warner Family. Harford Co. Hist. Soc. Mss. Coll. JHU.
Md. Geneal. Rec. Com., 1933-34, pp. 87-91. Mss. DAR.
Warner-Krebs Line, Phila. C. H. Warner pedigree chart. Soc. Col. Wars, Md. Johnston. 1905, p. 123. MHS.
Warner-Lewis, Gloucester Co., Va. Tombstone inscriptions. Md. Geneal. Rec. Com., v. 1, pp. 103-04. DAR.
†**Warren.** Doctor's experiences in three continents. Edward Warren. Balto., Cushing and Bailey, 1885. Enoch Pratt Lib.
*Semmes Geneal. Coll. Ms. MHS.
Southerland-Latham and allied families. Voorhees. Bd. ms. MHS.
***Warren,** Md. and Del. Lineage Bks., Daughters of Founders and Patriots, v. 23, pp. 98-99. MHS; DAR.
Warren Family, Charles Co. Ms. MHS.
Warren Family, Va. and Md. Va. Mag. Hist. and Biog., v. 6, pp. 200-03.
†**Warrinbuer.** Hist. of West. Md. Scharf. V. 2, p. 917. MHS; DAR.
Warring. *See* Waring.
See Waringe.
Warring, B. H., Jr. Md. Soc., War of 1812, v. 2, no. 173. Ms. MHS.
Warring, Wm. Emory, Jr. Md. Soc., War of 1812, v. 2, no. 172. Ms. MHS.
Washburn. Sweetser chart. MHS.
Washington. Ances. rec. and portraits. Col. Dames of Amer., 1910, v. 2, p. 407. MHS; DAR.
*Arms and birthplace. Misunderstanding exists regarding proper quartering. C. A. Hoppin. New York Times, Sunday, April 14, 1929. MHS.
Barroll in Great Britain and Amer. Barroll. Pp. 97-100. MHS.
Beall and Bell families. Beall. MHS; DAR.
Beall chart. Cary Geneal. Coll. Ms. MHS.
Britton Scrap Book. V. 1, 2. Ms. MHS.
Brooke family of Whitchurch, etc. Balch. P. 59. MHS; DAR.
Chart (from Charlemagne, 768 A.D.), photos. MHS.
Eng. ancestry. New Eng. Hist. and Geneal. Reg., v. 43, pp. 379-424 (chart, p. 420); v. 44; v. 45.
Geneal. of Page family, Va. Page. P. 214. MHS; DAR.
†Hist. of Frederick Co. Williams. MHS; DAR.
†Hist. of life and death, virtues or exploits of Gen. George Washington. Mason L. Weems. Phila., 1918, 288 pp. DAR.
Horwitz chart. MHS.
Lee of Va., 1642-1892. E. J. Lee. Lib. Cong.; MHS.
Legge-Washington families. Galloway. Ms. MHS.
†Life of George Washington, with curious anecdotes. Phila., 1869, 244 pp. DAR.
N. Y. Geneal. and Biog. Rec., v. 47, p. 6.
Orme geneal. chart. MHS.
*Pedigree and hist. of Washington family from 70 B.C. to George Washington. A. Welles. N. Y., Society Library, 1879. MHS.
Pedigree and hist. of Washington family. A. Welles. 1879. Enoch Pratt Lib.
Pedigree of Coleman Randall Freeman. Soc. Col. Wars Md. Culver. 1940. MHS; DAR.
Pedigree of Henry Irvine Keyser, II. Soc. Col. Wars Md. Culver. 1940. MHS; DAR.
Pedigree of Lloyd Bankson Whitham. Soc. Col. Wars Md. Culver. 1940. MHS; DAR.

Pedigree. Pa. Mag., v. 45, pp. 320–63; v. 47, p. 58.
*"Rockefeller assures re-rocking of Washington's cradle." Boston Transcript, Feb. 19, 1929. MHS.
Royal descent of George Washington. Natl. Geneal. Soc. Quart., April, 1914, to Jan., 1915 incl., v. 3.
St. Paul's Parish, Balto. V. 3. Mss. MHS.
Selden chart. MHS.
*Some time of Salgrave Manor and formerly of Mt. Vernon. Coat of arms. Burke's landed gentry. 1939. MHS.
Times Dispatch, Richmond, Va., Feb. 12, 1904. Newsp. clipp.
Va. families. Du Bellett.
*Washington. J. D. Sawyer. 2 vols. V. 1, ancestry and chart. N. Y., Macmillian Co. DAR.
*Washington ancestry and rec. of McLain, Johnson and forty other col. Amer. families. Charts. Prepared for Edward Lee McClain, Greenfield, Ohio, by Charles A. Hoppin. 3 vols. Index, p. 1575. Priv. pr., Yale University Press, 1932, ltd. ed. MHS; DAR. Reviewed in N. Y. Geneal. Biog. Rec., v. 63, p. 310.
Washington and his neighbors, Baldridge, Bernard, Gerrard, Lee, Pope. William and Mary Quart., 1st series, v. 4, pp. 28–43, 75–89. (Md. ref.)
‡Washingtons and their col. homes in W. Va. M. Thurston. Pamph. MHS.
*Washington's birthplace. C. A. Hoppin. Washington Post, April 10, 1929. MHS.
Edward Washington and his kin, 1675. Cordelia Jackson. Wash., D. C., 1934, bklet., mimeog. MHS; DAR.
*Washington family. W. C. Ford. N. Y., 1893.
†George Washington. Shelby Little. 1929, 481 pp.
†George Washington, leader by destiny, man and patriot. Jeanettee Eatin. N. Y., 1938. DAR.
†George Washington. N. Stephenson and W. Dunn. Oxford, 1939, 2 vols.
†Washington, man and Mason. C. H. Callahan. 1913. DAR.
Washington wills. Md. Geneal. Rec. Com., 1932–33, pp. 248–58. Mss. DAR.
See Legg.
See Muse.

Washington, Eng. and Surry Co., Va. Md. Geneal. Rec. Com., 1933-34, p. 29. Mss. DAR.

Washington, Va. Abr. Compend. Amer. Geneal. Virkus. V. 1, p. 17; v. 6, p. 311. DAR.

Washington, Va. and Md. Col. families of U. S. A. Mackenzie. V. 2, pp. 740–46. MHS; DAR.

Washington, George. Ancestry. New Eng. Hist. and Geneal. Reg., v. 21, pp. 25–35 (pedigree chart, p. 35).
†George Washington. Nathaniel W. Stephenson and Waldo H. Dunn. 1940, 2 vols.

Washington, Henry, Albemarle Co., Va. Will. MHS.

Washington, John, King George Co., Va. Will. MHS.
Pedigree of Francis Fielding Reid. Soc. Col. Wars Md. Culver. 1940. MHS; DAR.
William and Mary Quart., 1st series, April, 1893, v. 1, no. 4, p. 181; v. 2, p. 38.

Washington Family. Ms. MHS.

Washington Line. Mrs. H. De Courcy Wright Thom chart. MHS.

Washington-Marshall-Lewis. Geneal. notes. Md. Geneal. Rec. Com., 1924–25, p. 79. DAR.

Washington - Spencer. Washington - Spencer families. Balto. American, Feb. 14, 1909, pt. 2, p. 10. MHS.

Washington-Wright. Connections and some descendants of Major Frances and Anne (Washington) Wright, Va. (Md. connections.) Tyler's Quart. Mag., v. 4, pp. 153, 314.

Waskey Family. Harford Co. Hist. Soc. Mss. Coll. JHU.

Wassan. *See* Cochran-Beard-Carr-Ross-Wassan.

Waters. Amer. Armory and Blue Book. Matthews. 1911–12, p. 327.
Amer. Clan Gregor Year Book, 1915, p. 77; 1929, p. 57; 1931, p. 27. MHS; DAR.
Ancestry of Md. Md. Geneal. Rec. Com., 1933–34, pp. 130–33. Mss. DAR.
Anne Arundel Co. gentry. Newman. 1933, pp. 477–527. MHS; DAR.
†Balto. Lewis Hist. Pub. Co., 1912, v. 2, p. 355; v. 3, pp. 662, 821. MHS; DAR.
Balto., its hist., its people. Hall. MHS; DAR.
†Chesapeake Bay Country. Earle. P. 442. MHS.
Col. families of U. S. A. Mackenzie. V. 1, p. 369; v. 4, p. 128. MHS; DAR.
Done Bible rec. Ms. MHS.
Elzey-Waters, geneal. notes. Ms. MHS.
†Hist. of Frederick Co. Williams. V. 1, p. 596; v. 2, pp. 896, 913, 1128. MHS; DAR.
†Hist. of Montgomery Co. Boyd. Pp. 101, 102. DAR.
Humphrey Cissel farm, Montgomery Co. Md. Geneal. Rec. Com., 1926–27, p. 75. Mss. DAR.
Index to "Waters and kindred families," by P. B. Waters and H. M. Milam. A. B. and A. T. Coons. Ms. DAR.
Md. families. Culver. Ms. Personal list.
Md. gleanings in Eng. Wills. M. H. Mag., 1908, v. 3, no. 2.
†Med. Annals Md. Cordell. 1903, pp. 610–12. MHS.
†Men of mark in Md. Johnson. V. 2; v. 3, p. 205; v. 4, p. 388. DAR. Enoch Pratt Lib.
Mrs. E. N. Morison chart. MHS.
Patriotic Md. Md. Soc. of S. A. R., 1930. MHS; DAR.
Pedigree of John McPherson Dennis. Soc. Col. Wars Md. Culver. 1940. MHS; DAR.
Pedigree of Mareen Duvall. Soc. Col. Wars Md. Culver. 1940. MHS; DAR.
Pedigree of Edward Hammond. Soc. Col. Wars Md. Culver. 1940. MHS; DAR.
Pedigree of George Harrison. Soc. Col. Wars Md. Culver. 1940. MHS; DAR.
*Pedigree of Francis Edward Waters, Balto. T. T. Upshur. Nassawadox, Va., 1906. Ms. MHS.
Portraits and biog. rec. of Sixth Cong. Dist. Pp. 502, 704, 766. MHS; DAR.
*Rec. of Richard Waters, 1759–60–1810. File case, DAR.
Mrs. A. R. Rogers chart. MHS.
Rogers Coll. Ms. MHS.

Waters. (40 rec.) St. Paul's Parish, Balto. V. 1, 2, 3, 4. Mss. MHS.
Somerset Parish. Abs. of rec. Turner Geneal. Coll. Ms. MHS.
Spirit of Md. Lantz. P. 269. DAR.
Talbott of "Poplar Knowle." Shirk. MHS; DAR.
Miss Rosa Nelson Steele chart. MHS.
*The Sun, Balto., Nov. 6, 20, 1904; Dec. 31, 1905; Jan. 7, 28, 1906.
†Tercentenary hist. of Md. Andrews. V. 2, pp. 140, 322, 494, 690, 995; v. 4, pp. 305, 704. MHS; DAR.
*Waters and kindred families. P. B. Waters and H. M. Milam. 1903. DAR.
*Wilson Mss. Coll., no. 96. MHS.
Zimmerman-Waters and allied families. Allen. Pp. 45-75. MHS; DAR.
See Atwater.
See Colgate Onion-Bond-Waters.
See Duvall-Farmer-Waters.
See Kemp.
Waters, Elzey, Notes. Ms. MHS.
Waters, Francis Edward, Balto., Pedigree. Bd. Mss. MHS.
Waters, Freeborn Garrettson. Bible rec., 1795-1858. Ms. MHS.
Waters, John Seymour Taliaferro. Pedigree. (Rec. of Alexander, Cave, Fowke, Hooe, Taliaferro, Thorogood and Townsend of Va.) Soc. Col. Wars Md. Culver. 1940. MHS; DAR.
Waters, Richard, Somerset Co. Revolutionary pension rec.; with geneal. notes. D. A. R. Mag., Feb., 1937, v. 71, no. 2, p. 167.
***Waters, Wm.** (1740-1804), Somerset Co. Family rec. File case, DAR.
***Waters Family.** Anne Arundel Co. gentry. Newman. Pp. 477-527. MHS; DAR.
***Waters-Warfield.** Waters and Warfields of Md. Smith J. Philemon. File case, DAR.
Waters, Atwater. Turner Geneal. Coll. Ms. MHS.
Waters, Littleton, Va. Somerset Co. Va. Mag. Hist. and Biog., v. 1, pp. 92-93.
Wathen. Abr. Compend. Amer. Geneal. Virkus. V. 6, p. 608. DAR.
Wathen Prayer Book rec. Ms. MHS.
***Wathen,** St. Mary's City, 1647. Lineage Bks., Daughters of Founders and Patriots, v. 23, p. 159. MHS; DAR.
Watkins. Bible rec., Kent Co., 1778-1917. Md. Geneal. Rec. Com., 1932-33, pp. 318-20. Mss. DAR.
Bible rec. D. C. Geneal. Rec. Com., 1930-32, v. 5, pp. 4-7. Typed, bd. DAR.
Bible rec. of Jeremiah Watkins and his wife Elizabeth Wough, Montgomery Co., 1762. File case, DAR.
Britton Scrap Book. V. 2. Ms. MHS.
Cary Geneal. Coll. Ms. MHS.
Dorsey chart. MHS.
Ford and other lines. Md. Geneal. Rec. Com., 1932-33, pp. 7-20. Mss. DAR.
*Founders of Anne Arundel and Howard Cos. Warfield. Pp. 95, 158, 411-16, 520. MHS; DAR.
Geneal. and mem. encyc. of Md. Spencer. V. 1, p. 217. MHS; DAR.
Geneal. of family of Stockett, 1558-1892. Stockett. Pamph. MHS; DAR.
Griffith geneal. Griffith. MHS; DAR.
Md. families. Culver. Ms. Personal list.
†Med. Annals Md. Cordell. 1903, p. 612. MHS.
Patriotic Md. Md. Soc. of S. A. R., 1930. MHS; DAR.
Mrs. J. Piper chart. MHS.
John Price, emigrant, Jamestown Col., 1620. Price. MHS.
St. Paul's Parish, Balto. V. 1, 4. Mss. MHS.
St. Stephens Parish, Cecilton, Md. MHS; DAR.
†Tercentenary hist. of Md. Andrews. V. 2, pp. 723, 919; v. 3, p. 727. MHS; DAR.
See Ford-Dorsey-Hyland, etc.
See Francis-Watkins-Lloyd.
***Watkins,** Anne Arundel Co. Lineage Bks., Daughters of Founders and Patriots, v. 10, p. 106; v. 11, p. 30. MHS.
Watkins, Va. and Md. Md. Geneal. Rec. Com., 1933-34, pp. 111-24. Mss. DAR.
***Watkins,** "Walnut Grove." Lineage Bks., Daughters of Founders and Patriots, v. 12, p. 18. MHS.
Watkins, Nicholas. Proof of name of his wife. Ms. MHS.
Watkins, Samuel, Balto. Co. Will probated Aug. 22, 1743. D. A. R. Mag., v. 65, no. 8, p. 505.
Watkins, Samuel Brewer. Amer. Clan Gregor Year Book, 1913, p. 56. MHS; DAR.
Watkins, Wm., Balto. Co. (planter). Will probated, June 10, 1754. D. A. R. Mag., v. 65, no. 8, p. 505.
Watkins Family, Kent Co. Bible rec. Md. Geneal. Rec. Com., 1932-33, v. 5. DAR.
Watkins Line. Balto., its hist., its people. Hall. V. 2, p. 344. MHS; DAR.
Watkins-Griffith. Abr. Compend. Amer. Geneal. Virkus. V. 4, p. 636. MHS.
Watkinson, Va. Md. Geneal. Rec. Com., 1933-34, pp. 108-10. Mss. DAR.
Watson. The Beckwiths. Beckwith.
Geneal. and mem. encyc. of Md. Spencer. V. 2, pp. 513-18. MHS; DAR.
†Hist. of Allegany Co. Thomas and Williams. V. 2, pp. 1104-06. MHS; DAR.
Hist. of Frederick Co. Williams. V. 2, pp. 78, 1565. MHS; DAR.
†Memoirs of volunteer in war with Mexico. Kenly. MHS.
†Men of mark in Md. Johnson. V. 4. DAR; Enoch Pratt Lib.
St. Paul's Parish, Balto. V. 1, 2. Mss. MHS.
†**Watson, Col. W. H.** Geneal. and men. encyc. of Md. Spencer. V. 2, p. 513. MHS; DAR.
†Hist. of Md. Scharf. V. 3, p. 227. MHS.
†**Watson, Wm. H.** (1808-46; killed at Battle of Monterey, Sept. 12, 1846.) M. H. Mag., v. 12, p. 251.
Watson, Mrs. Wm. L. (Ellen Swan). Chart. Col. Dames, Chap. I. MHS.
Watters. Balto., its hist., its people. Hall. V. 2. MHS; DAR.
Col. families of U. S. A. Mackenzie. V. 3, p. 215. MHS; DAR.
†First Amer. itinerant of Methodism, William Watters. (Born in Harford Co., 1751; died in 1827.) Rev. D. A. Watters. Cincinnati, Curtis & Jennings, 1898.
Tombstone rec. of Rev. Wm. Watters of Md. Natl. Geneal. Soc. Quart., Sept. 1939, v. 27, no. 3, p. 95.
***Watters, Robinson C.** Burke's landed gentry. 1939. P. 3018. MHS.

Watters Family, Thomas' Run, Harford Co. Bible rec., 1792–1875. Md. Geneal. Rec. Com., 1929, v. 3, p. 61. DAR.
Watterson. Amer. Clan Gregor Year Book, 1916, pp. 29–31, 33, 45–46. MHS; DAR.
Watts. Cary Geneal. Coll. Ms. MHS.
Memorials of Reading, Howell, Yerkes, Watts, Latham and Elkins families. Leach.
St. Paul's Parish, Balto. V. 1, 2. Mss. MHS.
St. Stephens Parish, Cecilton, Md. MHS; DAR..
Uhler Bible rec. Md. Geneal. Rec. Com., v. 2. DAR.
*Wilson Mss. Coll., no. 8, B. MHS.
Watts, B. Md. Soc., War of 1812, v. 1, no. 24. Ms. MHS.
Watts, Philip Bartley. Pedigree. Soc. Col. Wars Md. Culver. 1940. MHS; DAR.
Watts-Smith-Willis Families, Va. (migrated into Ala., Ky., Md. and S. C.). D. A. R. Mag., v. 66, no. 1, pp. 57–58.
Wattson. St. Stephens Parish, Cecilton, Md. MHS; DAR.
Wattson, Elkton. Bible rec., 1783. Pub. Geneal Soc. Pa., v. 10, p. 180–83.
Waugh. Beatty family. Pa. geneal. Egle. Pp. 79–80. MHS.
Waugh, Rev. (?). Monumental City. Howard. MHS; DAR.
Waughop. Coutanceau and Waughop families, St. Mary's Co., Md., and Va. Christopher Johnston. William & Mary Quart., 1st series, v. 22, p. 271.
Way, Cecil Co. Sharpless family geneal. Cope. P. 1188. MHS; DAR.
Wayland-Wilhoit Families. Monnet family geneal. Monette. Pp. 470–71. MHS.
Wayman. Pedigree of Andrew Jackson Young, Jr. Soc. Col. Wars Md. Culver. 1940. MHS; DAR.
***Wayne.** Wayne ancestry. E. J. Sellers. Phila., 1927. MHS.
†**Ways.** Geneal. and mem. encyc. of Md. Spencer. V. 1, p. 326. MHS; DAR.
†**Wayson.** Med. Annals Md. Cordell. 1903, p. 613. MHS.
Weakley. Trinity P. E. churchyard, Long Green. Typed ms. MHS; DAR.
Weary. St. Paul's Parish, Balto. V. 2. Mss. MHS.
Weaser, Wiese. Catonsville pioneers of Luth. faith. Natl. Geneal. Soc. Quart., v. 9, no. 2, p. 29.
Weast. Hagerstown tombstone inscriptions. Gruder. Natl. Geneal. Soc. Quart., 1919, v. 8, nos. 1, 2.
See Wiest.
Weatherburn. St. Paul's Parish, Balto. V. 2. Mss. MHS.
Weatherle. Somerset Co. Court Book. Tilghman. 1937. Ms. DAR.
Weatherly. Rec. of Stepney Parish. MHS; DAR.
*Wicomico Co. families. Tilghman. Ms., p. 3. DAR.
Weaver. Lineage Bks., Natl. Soc. of Daughters of Amer. Col., v. 3, p. 4. MHS; DAR.
Md. gleanings in Eng. Wills. M. H. Mag., 1907, v. 2, no. 3.
†Med. Annals Md. Cordell. 1903, p. 613. MHS.
Mt. Olivet Cemetery, Frederick. Md. Geneal. Rec. Com., 1934–35, p. 111. Mss. DAR.
St. Paul's Parish, Balto. V. 2. Mss. MHS.
Weaver, Florence Eyster. Table of descent, 1638–1893. Jacob J. Weaver. Md., Mass., New Jersey, Pa. Photos. of ms., 1936. MHS.
***Weaver Family.** Marriages, 1628–1868, in U. S. W. M. Clemens. 1916.
Weaver Family, Frederick Co. Hist. of Everhart and Shower family. Everhart. 1883.
Webb. Amer. Clan Gregor Year Book, 1917, 27–28. MHS; DAR.
*Ancestry and descendants of Nancy Allyn (Foote) Webb, etc. Cooch. MHS; DAR.
Anne Arundel Co. tombstone inscriptions. Ms. DAR.
Centenary of Catholicity in Ky. Webb. 1884. MHS.
County Court Note Book. Ljungstedt. MHS; DAR.
†Hist. of Allegany Co. Thomas and Williams, v. 2. MHS; DAR.
Mrs. J. F. Lee chart. MHS.
†Med. Annals Md. Cordell. 1903, p. 613. MHS.
†Men of mark in Md. Johnson. V. 3. DAR; Enoch Pratt Lib.
Newsp. clipp. Scrap Book. MHS.
(20 rec.) St. Paul's Parish, Balto. V. 1, 2, 4. Mss. MHS.
Somerset Co. Court Book. Tilghman. 1937. Ms. DAR.
Turner family. Forman. P. 86. MHS.
See Allyn-Foote-Webb-Coach-Wilkins.
Webb, Talbot Co. Culver pedigree chart. MHS.
Webb, E. J., Jr. Md. Soc., War of 1812, v. 4, no. 314. Ms. MHS.
Webb, Rev. Williams Rollins. Md. Soc., War 1812, v. 4, no. 342. Ms. MHS.
Pedigree. Soc. Col. Wars Md. Culver. 1940. MHS; DAR.
Webb Family, Va. Newsp. clipp. MHS.
***Webdah.** Wicomico Co. families. Tilghman. Ms., p. 114. DAR.
Weber. Hagerstown tombstone inscriptions. Gruder. Natl. Geneal. Soc. Quart., 1919, v. 8, nos. 1, 2.
†Hist. of Allegany Co. Thomas and Williams. V. 1, p. 370; v. 2, pp. 1008–10, 1167–68. MHS; DAR.
Webster. Cary Geneal. Coll. Ms. MHS.
†Hist. of Frederick Co. Williams. V. 2, p. 1287. MHS; DAR.
†Hist. of Harford Co. Preston. Pp. 230–31, 237–39, 350. MHS; DAR.
Hopkins, Husband, Johns, Sharp and Webster families. Browne. Bd. ms. MHS.
Ms. MHS.
†Med. Annals Md. Cordell. 1903, p. 614. MHS.
Pedigree of Edmund Pendleton Hunter Harrison. Soc. Col. Wars Md. Culver. 1940. MHS; DAR.
†Port. and biog. rec. of Harford and Cecil Cos. 1897, pp. 148, 167–68, 171, 173–74, 182–84, 213–14, 215–16, 221, 345, 375–76, 575. MHS; DAR.
H. H. Simms maternal line of Mrs. Surratt-Webster family. Md. Geneal. Bull., v. 5, pp. 1–3. MHS; DAR.
Stump family of Cecil and Harford Cos. Pamph. MHS.

Webster. Mary E. Jenkins Surratt, maternal line. Md. Geneal. Bull., v. 1, pp. 1-3.
†Tercentenary hist. of Md. Andrews. V. 3, pp. 774, 775. MHS; DAR.
See Wilson, Mrs. Calvin. Abr. Compend. Amer. Geneal. Virkus. V. 1, p. 894. DAR.
Webster, Va. and Harford Co. Col. families of Amer. Lawrence. V. 7, p. 395. MHS.
†**Webster, Edwin H.** Hist. of Md. Scharf. V. 3, p. 692. MHS.
†**Webster, John Adams** (1787-1876). M. H. Mag., v. 12, p. 251.
†**Webster, Capt. John A.,** Harford Co. Patriotic Marylander, v. 1, no. 2, p. 37. MHS; DAR.
***Webster, Jone.** Note on his death, April 12, 1753. From Md. Gazette. M. H. Mag., 1924, v. 19, p. 211.
Webster-Lee. Harford Co. Hist. Soc. Mss. Coll. JHU.
Wedge-Engler. Lineage Bks., Natl. Soc. of Daughters of Amer. Col., v. 4, pp. 47, 61. MHS; DAR.
Weedon. Few abs. from will book at Annapolis. William and Mary Quart., 1st series, v. 13, p. 27.
†Med. Annals Md. Cordell. 1903, p. 614. MHS.
Somerset Co. Court Book. Tilghman. 1937. Ms. DAR.
Weeks Family. Harford Co. Hist. Soc. Mss. Coll. JHU.
Weem Family. Md. Gazette, Annapolis, Dec. 1, 1927. Newsp. clipp. MHS.
***Weems.** Ancestors and descendants of John Weems (born about 1768). File case, DAR.
Bible (orig.). Enoch Pratt Lib.
*Bibliog. Enoch Pratt Lib.
†Biog. cyc. of rep. men of Md. and D. C. P. 607. MHS; DAR.
Bowie chart. Cary Geneal. Coll. Ms. MHS.
Chew family. Culver. M. H. Mag., v. 30, no. 2, p. 157.
*D. C. Geneal. Rec. Com., 1932-34, v. 13, pp. 71-93. Typed, bd. DAR.
Gantt geneal. Ms. MHS.
Geneal. 1779-1852, from bible original property of Gustavus Weems, of "Marsh Seat," Anne Arundel Co. James W. Foster. M. H. Mag., 1935, v. 28, no. 3, p. 265-71.
Md. families. Culver. Ms. Personal list.
†Med. Annals Md. Cordell. 1903, p. 614. MHS.
Patriotic Md. Md. Soc. of S. A. R., 1930. MHS; DAR.
Pedigree of Mason Locke Weems Williams. Soc. Col. Wars Md. Culver. 1940. MHS; DAR.
Mason Locke Weems: his works and ways. P. L. Ford and Emily F. Skeel. Priv. pr., 3 vols. Norwood, Mass., Plimpton Press. MHS.
†Parson Weems. L. C. Wroth. Balto., Eichelberger Book Co., 1911, 104 pp. MHS; DAR; Enoch Pratt Lib.
†Parson Weems of cherry tree; first biographer o George Washington. (Born in Anne Arundel Co., Md., 1759; died 1825.) H. Kellock. N. Y. and London, Century Co., 1928. Enoch Pratt Lib.
*Weems family. E. C. Williams. Md. Gazette, Annapolis, Dec. 1, 1927. Clipping. MHS.
*Weems family. P. V. H. Weems. Annapolis, mimeog. MHS.
*William Locke Weems, Prince George Co., data, 1735-82. File case, DAR.
See Williams, M. L. Weems. Abr. Compend. Amer. Geneal. Virkus. V. 1, pp. 891-92. DAR.
**See* Henry Williams.
Weems, Calvert Co. Mrs. G. R. Veazey chart. MHS.
Weems Family. Bible rec. Typed copy, 12 pp. MHS.
Weems Line. M. L. W. Williams, pedigree chart. Soc. Col. Wars Md. Johnston. 1905, p. 126. MHS.
Weems-Taylor. Marriage of Capt. Wm. Weems and Sally K. Taylor, 1807. Natl. Geneal. Soc. Quart., Sept., 1938, v. 26, no. 3, p. 64.
Weer. Still Pond Churchyard and cemetery. Md. O. R. Soc. Bull., no. 2, pp. 65-75.
Weessels. Naturalizations in Md., 1666-1765; Laws. Bacon. MHS.
Wehland. Catonsville pioneers of Luth. faith. Natl. Geneal. Soc. Quart., v. 9, no. 2, p. 29.
Weigand, Wm. Edw. Md. Soc., War of 1812, v. 4, no. 303. Ms. MHS.
Weigand, Wm. Green. Md. Soc., War of 1812, v. 4, no. 324. Ms. MHS.
***Weikert Family.** Hist., 1735-1930. E. L. Weikert, Jr. Weikert family in Pa., 1753. Harrisburg, Pa., Telegraph Press, 1930. MHS.
Weinmiller. Frederick Co. tombstone inscriptions. Gruder. Natl. Geneal. Soc. Quart., 1919, v. 8, nos. 1, 2.
Weire, John. Copy of will. Ms. MHS.
†**Weis.** Men of mark in Md. Johnson. V. 4. DAR; Enoch Pratt Lib.
Weise, Wise. Patriotic Md. Md. Soc. of S. A. R., 1930. MHS; DAR.
Weise (Wise), Adam. Revolutionary pension abs. Natl. Geneal. Soc. Quart., v. 25, p. 12.
Weisel. Cummings chart. Lib. Cong.; MHS; DAR.
†Hist. of Allegany Co. Thomas and Williams. V. 1. MHS; DAR.
†Med. Annals Md. Cordell. 1903, p. 615. MHS.
Weiser. Harford Co. Hist. Soc. Mss. Coll. JHU.
Weiss. See Gross-Weiss-Brandt families. Ms. MHS.
Weitzel. Hist. and geneal. of descendants of Paul Weitzel, Lancaster Co., Pa., 1740. Edwin Hayden. Wilkes Barre, Pa., 1883, pamph. MHS.
Welborn. *See* Wilburn.
Welborne. Turner Geneal. Coll. Ms. MHS.
Welbourne. Somerset Parish. Abs. of rec. Turner Geneal. Coll. Ms. MHS.
See Wilburn.
Welby. Balch chart. MHS.
†**Welby, Amelia B.** Biog. sketches of distinguished Marylanders. Boyles. MHS; DAR.
***Welch.** Lineage Bk., Daughters of Amer. Col., v. 2, p. 212. MHS; DAR.
See Welsh.
Welch, William Henry. Papers and addresses. Balto., J. H. Press, 1920, 3 vols.
†In honor of William H. Welch. April 2, 1910, pamph. Enoch Pratt Lib.
†Memorial meeting in honor of William Henry Welch. Pub. by University Club, Balto., 1935. Enoch Pratt Lib.

†William Henry Welch at eighty. Pub. by Committee on celebration of Eightieth Birthday of Dr. Welch. N. Y., Milbank Memorial Fund, 1930. Enoch Pratt Lib.
†William Henry Welch. Memorial in Continental Hall, Wash., D. C. Enoch Pratt Lib.
Welcome. Burbank family. Sedgley. MHS.
***Welday.** Boyd family. Boyd. DAR.
†**Welfley.** Hist. of Allegany Co. Thomas and Williams. V. 1. MHS; DAR.
†Hist. of West. Md. Scharf. V. 2, p. 1405. MHS; DAR.
Wellcome Family. Ms. MHS.
Weller. Christ P. E. Church cemetery, Cambridge. Steele. 1936. MHS; DAR.
Marriage rec. of Frederick Co. Markell. Md. Geneal. Rec. Com., 1938–39. Mss. DAR.
Md. tombstone rec. Md. Geneal. Rec. Com., 1937, Parran, pp. 9, 24. Mss. DAR.
Weller, Fred, Frederick Co. (born July 5, 1761; died Sept. 18, 1829; Revolutionary soldier; grave in Brant's Private Burying Ground, near Ligonier, Westmoreland Co., Pa.). Natl. Geneal. Soc. Quart., v. 22, p. 25.
***Welling.** Founders of Anne Arundel and Howard Cos. Warfield. P. 418. MHS; DAR.
†**Wellington.** Hist. of Allegany Co. Thomas and Williams. V. 2. MHS; DAR.
†**Wellington, George L.** Men of mark in Md. Johnson. V. 3. DAR; Enoch Pratt Lib.
Wells. Blackford chart. MHS.
Ellen Emmerich Mears. Col. and Revolutionary families of Phila. Jordan. 1933, v. 1, pp. 412–15.
Founders of Anne Arundel and Howard Cos. Warfield. Pp. 327–28. MHS; DAR.
*Frederick Co. families. Markell. Ms. Personal list.
Griffith geneal. Griffith. MHS; DAR.
Hist. graves of Md. and D. C. Ridgely. MHS.
Md. families. Culver. Ms. Personal list.
*Mss. MHS.
†Med. Annals Md. Cordell. 1903, pp. 615–16. MHS.
Notes. Focke Geneal. Coll. Mss. MHS.
Pedigree of Benedict Henry Hanson, Jr. Soc. Col. Wars Md. Culver. 1940. MHS; DAR.
*George Donald Riley. Riley. DAR.
St. Paul's Parish, Balto. V. 1, 2. Mss. MHS.
St. Thomas Parish, Balto. Co. Bd. ms. MHS. Also: Md. Geneal. Rec. Com., 1937, pp. 109–82. Mss. DAR.
See Butler-Wells-White.
Wells, Kent Co. Tompkins chart. MHS.
Wells, Richard. Pedigree of John B. Philip C. Hall. Soc. Col. Wars Md. Culver. 1940. MHS; DAR.
***Wells Family.** Anne Arundel Co. gentry. Newman. Pp. 631–37. MHS; DAR.
(1892). See Brown. Pp. 39–49. MHS.
Notes and birth rec., 1767–1809. Ms. MHS.
Welsh. Abr. Compend. Amer. Geneal. Virkus. V. 6, p. 642. DAR.
Bonsal charts. MHS.
Bowie-Claggett chart. MHS.
Burbank family. Sedgley. MHS.
Cummings chart. Lib. Cong.; MHS; DAR.
Duvall chart. MHS; DAR.
*Founders of Anne Arundel and Howard Cos. Warfield. Pp. 91–93, 462. MHS; DAR.
Griffith geneal. Griffith. MHS; DAR.
Hazelhurst charts. MHS.
†Hist. of Allegany Co. Thomas and Williams. V. 2. MHS; DAR.
Hist. sketch of P. F. Eichelberger. Eichelberger.
Jenkins-Courtney chart. MHS.
Lineage Bks., Natl. Soc. of Daughters of Amer. Col., v. 2, p. 212; v. 3, p. 59. MHS; DAR.
Thomas McKnew, Prince George Co., and his descendants. Townsend. Ms. MHS.
†Med. Annals Md. Cordell. 1903, p. 616. MHS.
Pedigree of James Dorsey Brown, Jr. Soc. Col. Wars Md. Culver. 1940. MHS; DAR.
Pedigree of Edward Hammond. Soc. Col. Wars Md. Culver. 1940. MHS; DAR.
Pedigree of Howard Hall Macy Lee. Soc. Col. Wars Md. Culver. 1940. MHS; DAR.
Mrs. Pennington chart. MHS.
†Reminiscences of thirty years in Balto. Lilian Welsh, M.D., LL.D. Balto., Norman Remington, 1925. Enoch Pratt Lib.
St. Paul's Parish, Balto. V. 1, 2, 3. Mss. MHS.
Shrewsbury churchyard, Kent Co. Md. O. R. Soc., v. 2, pp. 46–54. MHS.
Welsh and allied families. G. C. Weaver. (Mrs. Clifford Weaver.) Cincinnati, Ohio, Powell & White, 1932. MHS; DAR.
Welsh and Hyatt kin. Supplement to Ancestral col. families. L. W. Welsh. 1932, pamph. MHS; DAR.
See Owens-Claytor-Maynard-Rutter-Welsh.
***Welsh,** Anne Arundel Co. Wilson Mss. Coll., no. 3, A; no. 37. MHS.
Welsh, Adam. Copy of will, 1841. In folder of E. and A. Hall Col. Ms. MHS.
Welsh, John, Anne Arundel Co. Copy of will. Md. Geneal. Rec. Com., 1934–35, pp. 102–05. Mss. DAR.
Welsh, Wm. (veteran). Md. Soc., War of 1812, v. 1, no. 74. Ms. MHS.
†**Welsh, Wm. H.** Men of mark in Md. Johnson. V. 4. DAR; Enoch Pratt Lib.
Welsh-Hammond-Riggs Line. Welsh-Hyatt and kindred. Supplement. Welsh. P. 11. MHS; DAR.
***Welsh-Hyatt.** Welsh-Hyatt and kindred. Supplement. L. W. Welsh. 1932. MHS; DAR.
*Welsh-Hyatt and kindred. Geneal. of Welsh and Hyatt families in Md. and their kin. L. W. Welsh. 3 pts., 11 sections. Independence, Mo., Lambert-Moon Co., 1928. MHS; DAR.
Welsh - Nowland - Staples - Wales - Gerritson. Bible rec. Upper Penins. East. Shore. Pp. 68–86. MHS; DAR.
Welsh-Riggs-Howard Line. Welsh-Hyatt and kindred. Supplement. Welsh. P. 11. MHS; DAR.
Welsh-Shipley Line. Welsh-Hyatt and kindred. Supplement. Welsh. P. 8. MHS; DAR.
Welsh-Warfield Line. Welsh-Hyatt and kindred. Supplement. Welsh. P. 6. MHS; DAR.
***Welsh, Welch.** George Donald Riley. Riley. DAR.
Welty. St. Joseph's churchyard, Emmitsburg. Md. O. R. Soc. Bull., no. 3, pp. 64–66. MHS.
Zion Reformed Church, Hagerstown.. Md. Geneal. Rec. Com., 1934–35. Mss. DAR.
Weltzheimer. Frederick Co. tombstone inscriptions. Gruder. Natl. Geneal. Soc. Quart., 1919, v. 8, nos. 1, 2.
Steiner geneal. Steiner. 1896. MHS.

Wendel. Gen. Tobias Emerson Stansbury chart. MHS.
Wengert, Wingart. Hagerstown tombstone inscriptions. Gruder. Natl. Geneal. Soc. Quart., 1919, v. 8, nos. 1, 2.
***Wenlock.** The Sun, Balto., Jan. 21, 1906.
†**Wenschoff.** Med. Annals Md. Cordell. 1903, p. 616. MHS.
Wentz. Hist. and geneal. account of Levering family. Levering. MHS.
Wertz. Cummings chart. Lib. Cong.; MHS; DAR.
Revolutionary war pension abs. Natl. Geneal. Soc. Quart., v. 23, no. 4, p. 130.
West. Bible rec. of West family of Va. Md. Geneal. Rec. Com., v. 1, p. 106. DAR.
Cary Geneal. Coll. Ms. MHS.
Clark chart. MHS.
Dorsey and allied families. Ms. MHS.
Capt. John Frazier. Leach. MHS.
Garrison Church. Allen. MHS; DAR.
Mrs. D. G. Lovell chart. MHS.
Manly chart. MHS.
Marriage rec. of Frederick Co. Markell. Md. Geneal. Rec. Com., 1938–39. Mss. DAR.
Md. families. Culver. Ms. Personal list.
†Med. Annals Md. Cordell. 1903, p. 616. MHS.
Plummer family. A. P. H. Ms. MHS.
Rec. from Bible of Rev. William West. Ms. MHS.
St. Paul's Parish, Balto. V. 1, 2, 3. Mss. MHS.
Somerset Co. Court Book. Tilghman. 1937. Ms. DAR.
Mrs. Talbot T. Speer chart. MHS.
Trinity Church cemetery, Dorchester Co. Md. O. R. Soc. Bull., no. 3, pp. 42–52.
Mrs. Wm. L. Watson chart. MHS.
See Lucas-Belt-Lawrence-West.
See Yeardley.
West, Anne Arundel Co. Iglehart chart. MHS.
West, Prince George Co. Mrs. A. C. Bruce chart. MHS.
***West Family.** Register, 1326–1928. 2 maps; 4 pedigree charts. Letta Brock Stone, granddaughter five times removed of Joseph West of Prince George Co. (died 1731). Wash., D. C., W. F. Roberts, Inc., 1928.
West Family, Sussex Co., Del. Pub. Geneal. Soc. Pa., v. 3, no. 2, p. 139.
West Family, Va. Md. Geneal. Rec. Com., 1924–25, p. 106. DAR.
1707–1820. Some Old Bible rec. Culver. M. H. Mag., 1916, v. 11, pp. 278–81.
Westall. Sara R. Baldwin chart. MHS.
Cary Geneal. Coll. Ms. MHS.
Md. families. Culver. Ms. Personal list.
***Westbrook Family.** Data. Pr. sheet. MHS.
***Westcott.** Old Kent. Hanson. Pp. 314–15. MHS; DAR.
St. Paul's P. E. churchyard, Kent Co. Md. O. R. Soc. Bull., no. 2, pp. 54–65.
Shrewsbury churchyard, Kent Co. Md. O. R. Soc., v. 2, pp. 46–54. MHS.
Westlake. Md. gleanings in Eng. Wills. M. H. Mag., 1907. V. 2, no. 4.
See Westlock.
Westlock, Westlake. Old Somerset. Torrence. MHS; DAR.
Weston. Geneal. of Henrietta Chauncy Wilson. Upshur. Bk. of photos. MHS.
Hazelhurst charts. MHS.
Life and times of Henry Antes. McMinn. P. 284. MHS; DAR.
*Thomas Weston and his family. Christopher Johnson. Balto., 1896. MHS.
Thomas Weston and his family; extracts from rec. of Provincial Court of Md., 1640. Liber. W. R. C., no. 1, folio 354–56. New Eng. Hist. and Geneal. Reg., 1896, v. 50, pp. 201–06.
Wetenhall. Some old Eng. letters. M. H. Mag., 1914, v. 9, no. 2, pp. 107–56.
Wetherall. Chart of Com. John Rodgers. DAR.
†Hist. of Balto. City and Co. Scharf. P. 425. MHS.
†Med. Annals Md. Cordell. 1903, p. 616. MHS.
Wethered. Descendants of Joran Kyn. Pa. Mag., v. 5, p. 217; v. 7, p. 464.
Fox-Ellicott-Evans families. Evans. MHS; DAR.
(1660). Morris family of Phila. Moon. V. 2, p. 766; v. 3, p. 1062. MHS.
*Old Kent. Hanson. Pp. 317–20. MHS; DAR.
Miss C. Petre chart. MHS.
Shrewsbury churchyard, Kent Co. Md. O. R. Soc., v. 2, pp. 46–54. MHS.
***Wethered-Owings.** Bible rec. from Wethered Bible. File case, MHS.
Bible. Rogers Geneal. Coll. Ms. MHS.
Wetter, J. King, Md. Soc., War of 1812, v. 3, no. 276. Ms. MHS.
Wevill, George. Bible records. Amer. Clan. Gregor Year Book, 1937, pp. 108–09. MHS; DAR.
Weybridght. Englar family. Barnes. Pp. 5–7. MHS; DAR.
Weybright. Roop geneal. Pamph. MHS.
†**Whaland.** Biog. cyc. of rep. men of Md. and D. C. P. 417. MHS; DAR.
Whale. *See* Wale.
Whaley. Somerset Parish. Abs. of rec. Turner Geneal. Coll. Ms. MHS.
Turner Geneal. Coll. Ms. MHS.
Whaley, Wale, Whale. Old Somerset. Torrence. MHS; DAR.
†**Whalley.** Edward Whalley, regicide. Pa. Mag. Hist. and Biog., v. 1, pp. 55–56, 359–60.
Wharton. Ances. rec. and portraits. Col. Dames of Amer., 1910, v. 2. MHS; DAR.
Buckingham Pres. churchyard, Worcester Co. Hudson. Bd. ms. MHS; DAR.
Hamilton family of Charles Co. Kelly. MHS.
Hazelhurst charts. MHS.
†Hist. of West. Md. Scharf. V. 2, pp. 1139–40. MHS; DAR.
Makemie Memorial Pres. churchyard, Snow Hill, Worcester Co. Hudson. Bd. ms. MHS; DAR. Also: Md. Geneal. Rec. Com., Mrs. Lines. Mss. DAR.
Ms. MHS.
Pedigree of Duncan Keener Brent. Soc. Col. Wars Md. Culver. 1940. MHS; DAR.
Rankin and Wharton family. S. M. Rankin. DAR.
Somerset Co. Court Book. Tilghman. 1937. Ms. DAR.
Somerset Parish. Abs. of rec. Turner Geneal. Coll. Ms. MHS.
Turner Geneal. Coll. Ms. MHS.
Va. Mag. Hist. and Biog., v. 20, p. 433.

Wharton, Gov. Jesse. J. L. Brent pedigree chart. Soc. Col. Wars, Md. Johnston. 1905, pp. 7, 157. MHS.
Whayland-Kible. Bible rec. Md. Geneal. Rec. Com., 1937–38, pp. 153–54. Mss. DAR.
Whedbee. Abr. Compend. Amer. Geneal. Virkus. V. 6, p. 719. DAR.
Wheeler. Balto., its hist., its people. Hall. V. 3, p. 634. MHS; DAR.
Boarman geneal. Thomas. 1935. MHS; DAR.
Mrs. J. G. Brogden chart. MHS.
Chart. Raskob-Green rec. book. Raskob. MHS.
W. W. Coleman pedigree chart. Soc. Col. Wars, Md. Johnston. 1905, p. 17. MHS.
Gravestone rec. from Grace M. E. Church, Hamstead, Md., 1698–1803. Md. Geneal. Rec. Com., 1932–33, p. 371. Mss. DAR.
Hist. of Harford Co. Preston. MHS; DAR.
Jenkins-Courtney chart. MHS.
Lineage Bks., Natl. Soc. of Daughters of Amer. Col., v. 2, p. 95. MHS; DAR.
MacSherry chart. MHS.
Md. families. Culver. Ms. Personal list.
Parr chart. MHS.
Patriotic Md. Md. Soc. of S. A. R., 1930. MHS; DAR.
Pedigree of Benj. Wheeler Jenkins. Soc. Col. Wars Md. Culver. 1940. MHS; DAR.
Pedigree of Austin Jenkins Lilly. Soc. Col. Wars Md. Culver. 1940. MHS; DAR.
Pedigree of Charles O'Donovan. Soc. Col. Wars Md. Culver. 1940. MHS; DAR.
Pedigree of Alfred Jenkins Tormey. Soc. Col. Wars Md. Culver. 1940. MHS; DAR.
St. Paul's Parish, Balto. V. 1, 2, 3, 4. Mss. MHS.
Semmes and allied families. Semmes. P. 176. MHS.
*Semmes Geneal. Coll. Ms. MHS.
Somerset Co. Court Book. Tilghman. 1937. Ms. DAR.
Tombstone inscriptions, 1698–1803, from Grace M. E. Church, Hampstead, Balto. Co. Md. Geneal. Rec. Com., 1932–33. DAR.
Western Run Parish book. Allen. Bd. ms. MHS.
Wheeler family of Md. Photos. DAR.
Young Bible rec. Ms. MHS.
Wheeler, Balto. Co. Posey chart. MHS.
Wheeler, Calvert Co. Mrs. G. R. Veazey chart. MHS.
***Wheeler,** Charles Co. (1630–93). Lineage Bk., Daughters of Amer. Col., v. 2, p. 342. MHS; DAR.
Wheeler, Benjamin. Will, 1769, and additional inventory. Ms. MHS.
Wheeler, Benjamin, Balto. Co. Abs. of will, 1806. D. A. R. Mag., June, 1928, v. 62, no. 6, p. 387.
Will dated Jan. 25, 1806. D. A. R. Mag., v. 62, no. 7, p. 456.
Wheeler, Mrs. Everett P. (Alice Gilman). Chart. (Mostly New Eng. and N. Y. Families.) Col. Dames, Chap. I. MHS.
Wheeler, Col. Ignatius of Revolution; buried 1793 in St. Ignatius R. C. churchyard, Harford Co.
†**Wheeler, James R.** Men of mark in Md. Johnson. V. 1. DAR; Enoch Pratt Lib.
Wheeler, Maj. John, Charles Co. E. A. and F. de S. Jenkins pedigree chart. Soc. Col. Wars, Md. Johnston. 1905, pp. 46, 157. MHS.
Wheeler, Jonathan, late of Balto. Co.; at time of his death, Watertown, Mass. Will, Oct. 5, 1809. Ms. MHS.
***Wheeler Family.** Arch. of Georgetown Univ., Wash., D. C., v. 353, no. 11.
Ms. MHS.
***Wheeler Family,** Deer Creek, Harford Co. Arch. of Georgetown Univ., Wash., D. C., v. 130, no. 2.
†**Wheelwright, Jere H.** Men of mark in Md. Johnson. V. 1. DAR; Enoch Pratt Lib.
Whelan. Graves. See St. John's R. C. Church, Forest Glen, Montgomery Co. Ms. MHS.
†Hist. of West. Md. Scharf. V. 1, p. 759. MHS; DAR.
St. John's R. C. Church cemetery, Montgomery Co. Md. Geneal. Rec. Com., 1926, p. 27. Mss. DAR.
Wheland. Centenary of Catholicity in Ky. Webb. 1884. MHS.
See Harford-Wheland.
Whetenhall. Britton Scrap Book. V. 2. Ms. MHS.
Mrs. Charles Carter chart. MHS.
See Tilghman-Whetenhall.
Whetherd Family. Thomas Book. Thomas. Pp. 547–50. Lib. Cong.; MHS.
Whetherell. Memoir and geneal. of Md. and Pa. family of Mayer. Mayer. P. 104. MHS; DAR.
Whips. St. Thomas' Parish, Balto. Co. Bd. ms. MHS. Also: Md. Geneal. Rec. Com., 1937, pp. 109–82. Mss. DAR.
***Whitaker.** Copied from journal written by A. M. Whitaker. E. W. Teemer. 1920. MHS.
Descendants of Col. Thomas White. Morris. MHS.
Dorsey and allied families. Ms. MHS.
Harford Co. Hist. Soc. Mss. Coll. JHU.
Lineage Bks., Natl. Soc. of Daughters of Amer. Col., v. 1, p. 102. MHS; DAR.
Maulsby family in Amer. Barnard. DAR; Peabody Lib.
Newsp. clipp. Scrap Book. MHS.
*Whitaker family, 1431–1926. Mrs. C. R. Whitaker. Southern Pines, N. C. Dixie Printing Co., 1926.
Whitaker Family, Pa. to Md. in 1767. Typed, 8 pp. MHS.
White. Abr. Compend. Amer. Geneal. Virkus. V. 6, p. 124. DAR.
*Account of meeting of descendants of Col. Thomas White of Md., held at Sophia's Dairy, on Bush River, near Perryman, Harford Co., June 7, 1877, on occasion of reinterment of remains of Col. Thomas White. Mrs. Mary (White) Morris. Coat of arms, W. W. Bronson. Phila., 1879. MHS.
Ames Geneal. Coll. Ms. MHS.
*Ancestry of children of James William White. W. F. Cregar. Phila., 1888. MHS.
Balto., its hist., its people. Hall. V. 2. MHS; DAR.
*Bartow geneal. Bartow. Pp. 144–52. Lib. Cong.; MHS.
Beall and Bell families. Beall. MHS; DAR.
Beauchamp chart. DAR.

White. H. D. G. Carroll. Ms. Book. In H. F. Thompson Papers. MHS.
Chart of Milton White, about 1850. MHS.
Christ P. E. Church cemetery, Cambridge. Steele. 1936. MHS; DAR.
Col. families of U. S. A. Mackenzie. V. 1; v. 2 (Dorchester Co.); v. 3; v. 6. MHS; DAR.
Descendants of Henry and Sallie White. 1937, pamph. DAR.
Edmund Beauchamp of East. Shore of Md. D. A. R. Mag., v. 66, no. 4, pp. 234–38.
*Encyc. of Amer. biog. Amer. Hist. Soc., new series, v. 1, pp. 209, 213. MHS; DAR.
Eng. pedigree chart. Descendants of Col. Thomas White. Morris. P. 124. MHS.
*Frederick Co. families. Markell. Ms. Personal list.
Harford Co. Hist. Soc. Mss. Coll. JHU.
Mrs. M. J. Henry chart. MHS.
Hist. and geneal. rec. of descendants of Paul Weitzel. Hayden. 1883, pamph. MHS.
Hist. graves of Md. and D. C. Ridgely. MHS.
†Hist. of Allegany Co. Thomas and Williams. V. 2. MHS; DAR.
†Hist. of Frederick Co. Williams. V. 1, p. 596. MHS; DAR.
Hist. of Harford Co. Preston. MHS; DAR.
Hist. Salisbury, Wicomico Co. Truitt. P. 12. DAR.
Hist. sketch of P. F. Eichelberger. Eichelberger.
Lineage Bks., Natl. Soc. of Daughters of Amer. Col., v. 1, p. 264; v. 2, p. 298. MHS; DAR.
Makemie Memorial Pres. churchyard, Snow Hill, Worcester Co. Hudson. Bd. ms. MHS; DAR. Also: Md. Geneal. Rec. Com., Mrs. Lines. Mss. DAR.
Marriage rec. of Frederick Co. Markell. Md. Geneal. Rec. Com., 1938–39. Mss. DAR.
†Med. Annals Md. Cordell. 1903, pp. 617–18. MHS.
Mrs. E. N. Morison chart. MHS.
Mt. Paran Pres. churchyard, Harrisonville, Balto. Co. Typed ms. MHS; DAR.
Mt. Zion P. E. churchyard, Worcester Co. Md. Geneal. Rec. Com., 1937, Mrs. Lines. Mss. DAR.
Newsp. clipp. Scrap Book. MHS.
Old Somerset. Torrence. MHS; DAR.
Patriotic Md. Md. Soc. of S. A. R., 1930. MHS; DAR.
Pattison wills. Md. Geneal. Rec. Com., 1929, pp. 7–42; 1930–31. Mss. DAR.
Pedigree of Rev. Sam'l Tagart Steele. Soc. Col. Wars Md. Culver. 1940. MHS; DAR.
Pedigree of James Donnell Tilghman. Soc. Col. Wars Md. Culver. 1940. MHS; DAR.
Polk family. Polk. P. 697. MHS; DAR.
Price ancestral data (paternal). Bd. ms. MHS.
Rec. of Stepney Parish. MHS; DAR.
(40 rec.) St. Paul's Parish, Balto. V. 1, 2, 3, 4. Mss. MHS.
St. Stephens Parish, Cecilton, Md. MHS; DAR.
Somerset Co. Court Book. Tilghman. 1937. Ms. DAR.
‡Story of Father Andrew White, S.J. (Born in London, 1579; died in London, 1657; sailed with the Ark and the Dove from Cowes, Isle of Wight, for Md., Nov. 22, 1633, St. Cecilia's Day.) Map. Chicago, Answorth & Co., 1906, pamph. Enoch Pratt Lib.
White Genealogical Tree. With charts; descendants of Thomas White, John White (1650), and Milton White (about 1850). Photos. MHS.
*John Barker White, 1847–1923. N. T. Grove. Repr. from Annals of Kansas City of Missouri Valley Hist. Soc., Dec., 1923. MHS.
Col. Thomas White of Md. W. W. Wiltbank. Pa. Mag. Hist. and Biog., 1877, v. 1. MHS.
Mary White (Mrs. Robert Morris). C. H. Hart. Pa. Mag. Hist. and Biog., 1878, v. 2. MHS.
Zion Reformed Church, Hagerstown. Md. Geneal. Rec. Com., 1934–35. Mss. DAR.
See Beauchamp - Smoot - Turpin - White - Willis - Wilson.
See Butler-Wells-White.
See Gross-Weiss (White)-Brandt families. Ms. MHS.
See Hall-Morris-White.
See Hicks-Dennis-Edmondson-Phillips-Travers-White.
See Whyte.
See Wight.

White, Talbot Co. H. Mullikin pedigree charts, plate 1. Soc. Col. Wars, Md. Johnston. 1905, p. 74. MHS.

***White, Allen Kirby.** Burke's landed gentry. 1939. MHS.

†**White, Father Andrew.** Lives of Cath. Heroes. Murray. 1882.

White, Charles Ridgely. Greenway Mss. Geneal. Coll. Binder's title, Hawkins-Bordley. MHS.

†**White, Francis A.** Men of mark in Md. Johnson. V. 1. DAR; MHS.

White, John. Bible rec. Ms. MHS.
Bible rec., Calvert and Cecil Cos. Natl. Geneal. Soc. Quart., Apr., 1913, v. 2, no. 1, p. 6.
With Glison-Sellman-Murphy-Cooley Bible rec. Ms. DAR.

White, Joseph. Deed Mar. 24, 1837. D. C. Geneal. Rec. Com., 1937-36, v. 35, p. 69. Typed, bd. DAR.

***White, Mary (Mrs. Robert Morris).** Address delivered, by request at Sophia's Dairy, near Perryman, Harford Co., June 7, 1877, on occasion of reinterment of remains of Col. Thomas White, before reunion of his descendants, the Halls, Morrises and Whites. C. H. Hart. Repr. from Pa. Mag. Hist. and Biog., Phila., 1878. MHS.

***White, Miles.** Balto., hist. and biog. Richardson and Bennett. 1871, pp. 517–19. MHS; DAR.

White, Miles, Jr., Line. Miss Sara E. White chart. MHS.

***White, Samuel White,** 1770–1809. And his father Judge Thomas White of Del. H. C. Conrad. Hist. Soc. Del., Wilmington, 1903. Papers Hist. Soc. Del., no. 21.

White, Miss Sara Elizabeth. Chart. Col. Dames, Chap. I. MHS.
Mrs. Josias Pennington chart. MHS.
Mrs. J. G. Thomas chart. MHS.
Mrs. Josias Pennington chart. MHS.
Miss Sara E. White chart. MHS.
(Virginia Purviance Bonsal). Chart. Col. Dames, Chap. I. MHS.

White, Col. Thomas, St. George's Church (Spesutiae) and Sophia's Dairy, near Perryman, Harford Co. Meeting of descendants, June 7, 1877. Wm. White Bronson. Pa. Mag.

Hist. and Biog., 1877, v. 1, p. 263; see also p. 420.
White Family. Ms. MHS.
Natl. Geneal. Soc. Quart., v. 3, Oct. 1914, no. 3, p. 3.
Photos. of ms. in German (very little). MHS.
Turner Geneal. Coll. Ms. MHS.
***White Family,** Balto. Family of Nathaniel and Mary Ann (Hopkins) Morison. Leaflet. MHS.
White Family, S. C. Dr. Joseph S. Ames. Ms. Coll. MHS.
White Line, Somerset Co. Geneal. and mem. encyc. of Md. Spencer. V. 1, p. 29. MHS; DAR.
H. L. Duer pedigree chart. Soc. Col. Wars, Md. Johnston. 1905, pp. 23, 157. MHS.
White-Collins. Somerset Parish. Abs. of rec. Turner Geneal. Coll. Ms. MHS.
White-Lindsay. Wicomico Co. families. Bible rec. Ms. DAR.
White, Whyte, Somerset Co. Chart, photos., complete in 2 sheets. Cary Geneal. Coll. Ms. MHS.
***White, Wight.** Wicomico Co. families. Tilghman. Ms, pp. 11, 72, 77–84, 101, 112, 115, 117, 123, 128. DAR.
***Whitefield.** Wicomico Co. families. Tilghman. Ms, p. 95. DAR.
†**Whiteford.** Med. Annals Md. Cordell. 1903, p. 619. MHS.
†Portraits and biog. rec. of Harford and Cecil Cos., 1897. Pp. 201–02, 286. MHS; DAR.
†**Whitehead.** Tercentenary hist. of Md. Andrews. V. 4, p. 647. MHS; DAR.
Whitehead, Mrs. John B. (Mary Ellen Colston). Chart. Col. Dames, Chap. I. MHS.
***Whiteley.** Hist. Dorchester Co. Jones. 1902, p. 398. MHS; DAR.
†Med. Annals Md. Cordell. 1903, p. 619. MHS.
Patriotic Md. Md. Soc. of S. A. R., 1930. MHS; DAR.
See Wooford.
†*See* Woolford-Whiteley.
Whiteley, Dorchester Co. (1676). Col. families of U. S. A. Mackenzie. V. 1, p. 581; v. 4; v. 5, p. 564. MHS; DAR.
Whiteley, Miss Mabel. Chart. Col. Dames, Chap. I. MHS.
Whiteley Family. Chart. Arthur Whiteley, Dorchester Co., 1676. Ms. MHS.
Whitelock. Abr. Compend. Amer. Geneal. Virkus. V. 1, p. 885; v. 6, pp. 628–29. DAR.
Balto., its hist., its people. Hall. V. 3. MHS; DAR.
†Bench and bar of Md. Sams and Riley. 1901, v. 2, p. 605. Lib. Cong.; MHS; Peabody Lib.
See Huse. Abr. Compend. Amer. Geneal. Virkus. V. 1, p. 405. DAR.
†**Whitelock, George.** Men of mark in Md. Johnson. V. 2. DAR; Enoch Pratt Lib.
Whitely. Geneal. of Henrietta Chauncy Wilson. Upshur. Bk. of photos. MHS.
Whitely, J. G. Amer. Armory and Blue Bk. Matthews. 1908, p. 265. DAR.
Whiteside. St. Paul's Parish, Balto. V. 2. Mss. MHS.
***Whitham.** Burke's landed gentry. 1939. MHS.
Pedigree of George Washington Williams. Soc. Col. Wars Md. Culver. 1940. MHS; DAR.
Whitham, Cecil Co. (born in 1725). Notes D. A. R. Mag., v. 70, no. 12, p. 1267.
Whitham, Lloyd Bankson. Pedigree. Soc. Col. Wars Md. Culver. 1940. MHS; DAR.
Whiting. Balch chart. MHS.
Carlyle family and Carlyle house. Spencer. P. 30. MHS.
Carlyle family. William and Mary Quart., 1st series, v. 18, pp. 201, 278.
†Hist. of Allegany Co. Thomas and Williams. V. 2, pp. 1171–72. MHS; DAR.
***Whiting-Little-Horner-Brown.** Va. families. MHS.
†**Whitman.** Tercentenary hist. of Md. Andrews. V. 2, p. 366. MHS; DAR.
Whitman, Ezra. Monumental City. Howard. MHS; DAR.
Whitmire. McCall-Tidwell families. McCall. Pp. 457–61. MHS; DAR.
†**Whitmore.** Hist. of Frederick Co. Williams. V. 2, pp. 891, 995, 1619. MHS; DAR.
Whitney. Balto., its hist., its people. Hall. V. 2. MHS; DAR.
St. Paul's Parish, Balto. V. 2, 4. Mss. MHS.
Whitridge. Ances. rec. and portraits. Col. Dames of Amer., 1910, v. 2. MHS; DAR.
Balto., its hist., its people. Hall. V. 2. MHS; DAR.
Blackford chart. MHS.
Mrs. A. C. Bruce chart. MHS.
Mrs. Wm. T. Howard, Jr., chart. MHS.
Iglehart chart. MHS.
†Med. Annals Md. Cordell. 1903, p. 620. MHS.
Pedigree chart, photos. from printed chart. MHS.
Stevenson chart. MHS.
Mrs. Douglas Hamilton Thomas chart. MHS.
See Cushing.
Whitridge, Mass. and Balto. Abr. Compend. Amer. Geneal. Virkus. V. 1, p. 891. DAR.
Whitridge, Mrs. Emory; was **Mrs. Horatio L. Whitridge (Matilda Bache Emory).** Chart. Col. Dames, Chap. I. MHS.
Whitridge, Mrs. Horatio L. (Anne Winslow Williams). Chart. Col. Dames, Chap. I. MHS.
***Whitridge, Morris.** Encyc. of Amer. biog. Amer. Hist. Soc., N. Y., 1928, v. 33, p. 200; p. 230 (Whitridge line).
Whitridge, Mrs. Morris (Susan Wilson Mackenzie). Chart. Col. Dames, Chap. I. MHS.
Whitridge, William, M.D. Pedigree chart. Soc. Col. Wars, Md. Johnston. 1905, p. 124. MHS.
Whitridge Line, Mass. and Balto. Col. and Revolutionary families of Pa. Amer. Hist. Soc., N. Y., 1934, p. 593.
Whitridge, Whittridge. Col. families of U. S. A. Mackenzie. V. 5, pp. 540–48. MHS; DAR.
†**Whitson.** Hist. of West. Md. Scharf. V. 2, p. 1293. MHS; DAR.
Rumsey-Smithson Bible rec. Md. Geneal. Rec. Com., 1932–33, v. 5, pp. 63–142. DAR.
Rumsey-Smithson family rec. bk. Md. Geneal. Rec. Com., 1932, pp. 133, 134, 135. DAR.
Smithson-Rumsey rec. bk. Ms. MHS.
Whittaker. Folder. Ms. MHS.
Whittaker-Bradford Families, S. C. Ms. MHS.

Whittam. Patriotic Md. Md. Soc. of S. A. R., 1930. MHS; DAR.
St. Stephens Parish, Cecilton, Md. MHS; DAR.
†**Whitter.** Hist. of Washington Co. Williams. 1906, v. 2, p. 1056. MHS; DAR.
Whitting. Atkinson family (Somerset Co.) Bible rec. Ms. MHS.
†**Whittingham.** Med. Annals Md. Cordell. 1903, p. 621. MHS.
†The Life of William Rollison Whittingham, fourth Bishop of Md. Portrait and facsimilies, 2nd ed., with additions. M. F. Brand. (Born in N. Y., 1805.) N.Y., E. & J. B. Young Co., 1886. Enoch Pratt Lib.
†**Whittingham, Bishop.** Balto., hist. and biog. Richardson and Bennett. 1871, pp. 521–23. MHS; DAR.
Whittington. Frances Murray Bowdoin chart. MHS.
Geneal. of Henrietta Chauncy Wilson. Upshur. Bk. of photos. MHS.
Harrison-Waples and allied families. Harrison. P. 124. MHS.
Makemie Memorial Pres. churchyard, Snow Hill, Worcester Co. Hudson. Bd. ms. MHS; DAR. Also: Md. Geneal. Rec. Com., Mrs. Lines. Mss. DAR.
Lineage Bks., Natl. Soc. of Daughters of Amer. Col., v. 1, p. 263. MHS; DAR.
Md. families. Culver. Ms. Personal list.
†Med. Annals Md. Cordell. 1903, p. 621. MHS.
†Old Buckingham by the Sea, East. Shore of Md. Page. DAR.
Old Somerset. Torrence. P. 379. MHS. DAR.
Pedigree of Howard Hall Macy Lee. Soc. Col. Wars Md. Culver. 1940. MHS; DAR.
Pedigree of Gustav Wm. Lurman. Soc. Col. Wars Md. Culver. 1940. MHS; DAR.
Pedigree of James Donnell Tilghman. Soc. Col. Wars Md. Culver. 1940. MHS; DAR.
Polk family. Polk. P. 235. MHS; DAR.
St. Paul's Parish, Balto. V. 3. Mss. MHS.
Somerset Parish. Abs. of rec. Turner Geneal. Coll. Ms. MHS.
Somerset Co. Court Book. Tilghman. 1937. Ms. DAR.
Turner Geneal. Coll. Ms. MHS.
*Wicomico Co. families. Tilghman. Ms, pp. 55, 97. DAR.
Worcester Co. Militia, 1794. Covington. P. 168. MHS.
***Whittle,** Va. The Sun, Balto. July 7, 1907.
Whittmore. Haugh's Lutheran Church tombstone rec. Md. Geneal. Rec. Com., 1939–40. Mss. DAR.
Whittridge. *See* Whitridge.
Whitty. Old Somerset. Torrence. MHS; DAR.
Whyte. Carton charts. MHS.
Chart of Com. John Rodgers. DAR.
Descendants of Valentine Hollingsworth, Sr. Stewart. MHS; DAR.
Hollingsworth chart. Cary Geneal. Coll. Ms. MHS.
See White.
Whyte, White. Dorsey and allied families. Ms. MHS.
*Gilmor chart. Ms. MHS.
†**Whyte, Wm. Pinkney.** Balto., hist. and biog. Richardson and Bennett. 1871, pp. 525–28. MHS; DAR.
Founders of Anne Arundel and Howard Cos. Warfield. P. 288. MHS; DAR.
†Governors of Md. Buchholz. P. 198. MHS.
†(1824–1908). M. H. Mag., v. 12, p. 252.
†Memorial address in Senate of U. S., Jan. 16, 1909. Gov. Printing Office, Wash., 1909. Enoch Pratt Lib.
Whyte, Wm. Pinkney, Jr. Md. Soc., War of 1812, v. 1, no. 44. Ms. MHS.
Wiatt. *See* Robinson-Passwater-Smith-Wiatt.
Wickes, Kent Co. Bible rec. Md. Geneal. Rec. Com., 1938–39, pp. 90–93. Mss. DAR.
†Biog. cyc. of rep. men of Md. and D. C. P. 420. MHS; DAR.
Family notes, 1821–39. Ms. MHS.
Hynson chart. Cary Geneal. Coll. Ms. MHS.
Md. families. Culver. Ms. Personal list.
†Men of mark in Md. Johnson. V. 4, DAR; Enoch Pratt Lib.
Page family Bible rec. Ms. MHS.
Patriotic Md. Md. Soc. of S. A. R., 1930. MHS; DAR.
Pedigree of Duncan Keener Brent. Soc. Col. Wars Md. Culver. 1940. MHS; DAR.
Pedigree of James Alfred Merritt. Soc. Col. Wars Md. Culver. 1940. MHS; DAR.
St. Paul's churchyard, Kent Co. Md. O. R. Soc. Bull., no. 2, pp. 54–65. MHS.
†Lambert Wickes, sea raider and diplomat; Story of Naval captains of Revolution. W. B. Clark. (Born in Kent Co., 1742.) New Haven, Univ. Press, 1932. MHS; Enoch Pratt Lib.
See Page-Wickes-Wroth.
Wickes, Joseph. Seven pioneers of col. East. Shore. Skirven. M. H. Mag., 1920, v. 15, no. 3, pp. 230–50; no. 4, pp. 394–419.
Wickes, Joseph Lee. Pedigree. Soc. Col. Wars Md. Culver. 1940. MHS; DAR.
†**Wickes, Capt. Lambert.** His rec. during Revolution. DeCourcy W. Thom. M. H. Mag., 1932, v. 27, pp. 1–17.
***Wickes Family.** Old Kent. Hanson. Pp. 89–99. MHS; DAR.
Wickes Line, Kent Co. W. A. and S. W. Merritt pedigree charts, plate 1. Soc. Col. Wars, Md. Johnston. 1905, pp. 67, 157. MHS.
Wickes, Wicks. Portrait and biog. rec. of East. Shore of Md., 1898. Pp. 426, 491, 516, 630, 631. MHS; DAR.
Wickes, Wicks Family. M. H. Mag., Sept. 1920, v. 15, p. 236.
Wickliffe, David (first child born of Protestant parents in Md). William and Mary Quart., 1st series, v. 10, p. 175. MHS.
Wicks. *See* Wickes.
Widerick. Mt. Olivet Cemetery, Frederick. Md. Geneal. Rec. Com., 1934–35, p. 111. Mss. DAR.
Widmer, Pa. Abr. Compend. Amer. Geneal. Virkus. V. 1, p. 887. DAR.
Widmyer. Md. tombstone rec. Md. Geneal. Rec. Com., 1937, Parran, v. 8. Mss. DAR.
Wieber. Joseph Radcliff and his descendants. Bd. ms. MHS.
Wiese. *See* Weaser.
Wiesel. Hist. of Allegany Co. Thomas and Williams. V. 1, pp. 642–46. MHS; DAR.

†**Wiesenthal.** Med. Annals Md. Cordell. 1903, pp. 16, 18, 86, 621. MHS.
Patriotic Md. Md. Soc. of S. A. R., 1930. MHS; DAR.
Tercentenary hist. of Md. Andrews. V. 4, p. 34. MHS; DAR.
Wiest. Tercentenary hist. of Md. Andrews. V. 3, p. 906. MHS; DAR.
Wiest, Weast. Frederick Co. tombstone inscriptions. Gruder. Natl. Geneal. Soc. Quart., 1919, v. 8, nos. 1, 2.
Wigfall. Mrs. G. Eyre Wright chart. MHS.
Wigglesworth. Sweetser chart. MHS.
Wight. Md. families. Culver. Ms. Personal list.
†Men of mark in Md. Johnson. V. 1, p. 402; v. 4. DAR; Enoch Pratt Lib.
Origins of Clements-Spalding families of Md. and Ky. Clements. Pp. 34–41. MHS.
Origin of Wight family in Amer. Ms. MHS.
Ref., in diary of Charles Copeland. William and Mary Quart., 1st series, v. 14, p. 44.
See White.
Wight-White-Hodson-Lloyd-Travers. Wicomico Co. families. Bible rec. Ms. DAR.
Wilburn, Welbourne, Welborn. Abr. Compend. Amer. Geneal. Virkus. V. 6, p. 541. DAR.
Wilcox Line, Talbot Co. Col. and Revolutionary lineages of Amer. 1939, v. 1, pp. 510–18. MHS.
Wilcox-Rose. Bible rec. Ms. MHS.
Wilcox, Willcox. St. Paul's Parish, Balto. V. 2, 4. Mss. MHS.
Wilcoxen. Griffith geneal. Griffith. MHS; DAR.
†**Wilcoxon.** Hist. of Frederick Co. Williams. V. 2, p. 1222. MHS; DAR.
Portrait and biog. rec. of Sixth Cong. Dist. of Md. 1898, p. 338. MHS; DAR.
Wilcoxon Family, Montgomery Co. Bible rec. Ms. DAR.
Land grants. Ms. DAR.
***Wild.** Burke's landed gentry. 1939. MHS.
Wildbore. Wildbores in Amer.; family tree from 1616. John R. Wilbor, president, 3821 Barrington Rd., Balto. 2nd edition, 1925. MHS.
Wilderman Family. Rec. of Jacob Wilderman of Balto. (born 1720; died 1787). Ms. DAR.
†**Wildey, Thomas.** Hist. of Md. Scharf. V. 3, p. 145. MHS.
†**Wiles.** Hist. of Frederick Co. Williams. V. 2, pp. 722, 1387. MHS; DAR.
Wiley. Ances. rec. and portraits. Col. Dames of Amer., 1910, pp. 127, 128. MHS; DAR.
†Hist. of Allegany Co. Thomas and Williams. V. 1, pp. 643–44. MHS; DAR.
†Hist. of West. Md. Scharf. V. 2, p. 1520. MHS; DAR.
One thousand years of Hubbard Hist. Day. P. 349. MHS.
Tercentenary hist. of Md. Andrews. V. 3, p. 33; v. 4, p. 380. MHS; DAR.
Wiley, Cecil Co. (born March 16, 1757). Data. D. A. R. Mag., v. 70, no. 7, p. 706.
†Med. Annals Md. Cordell. 1903, p. 621. MHS.
***Wiley Family.** (Complete.) Wilson. Mss. Coll., no. 10; no. 76; no. 81. MHS.
†**Wilhelm,** St. Mary's Co. Med. Annals Md. Cordell. 1903, p. 621. MHS.
†**Wilhide.** Hist. of Frederick Co. Williams. V. 2, pp. 729, 1457. MHS; DAR.
***Wilhite.** The Sun, Balto., Dec. 15, 1907.
Wilhoit. Monnet family geneal. Monette. Pp. 470–71. MHS.
Wilkerson, C. M. Md. Soc., War of 1812, v. 4, no. 314. Ms. MHS.
***Wilkins.** Ancestry and descendants of Nancy Allyn (Foote) Webb, etc. Cooch. MHS; DAR.
Bible rec., Kent Co., 1753–1884. Md. Geneal. Rec. Com., 1932–33, pp. 276–82. Mss. DAR.
†Biog. cyc. of rep. men of Md. and D. C. P. 459. MHS; DAR.
Chart of Com. John Rodgers. DAR.
Death of Col. Edw. Wilkins, Dec. 31, 1878; born 1813; with family data. Md. Geneal. Rec. Com., 1937–38, pp. 74–75. Mss. DAR.
Dorsey and allied families. Ms. MHS.
Maccubin-Lusby chart. Cary Geneal. Coll. Ms. MHS.
†Med. Annals Md. Cordell. 1903, p. 622. MHS.
*Old Kent. Hanson. Pp. 343–44. MHS; DAR.
Rehobeth P. E. churchyard, Somerset Co. Md. Geneal. Rec. Com., 1937, Mrs. Lines. Mss. DAR.
St. Paul's Parish, Balto. V. 2, 4. Mss. MHS.
Segrave chart. MHS.
Somerset Parish. Abs. of rec. Turner Geneal. Coll. Ms. MHS.
Tercentenary hist. of Md. Andrews. V. 3, p. 1024. MHS; DAR.
Wallis chart. MHS.
Mrs. G. H. Williams, Jr., chart. MHS.
See Allyn-Foote-Webb-Cooch-Wilkins.
Wilkins Family. Md. Geneal. Rec. Com., 1932–33, pp. 276–78. DAR.
Ms. MHS.
Wilkins Family, Kent Co. Bible rec. Md. Geneal. Rec. Com., 1932–33, v. 5. DAR.
Wilkins (Edward) Family. Md. Geneal. Rec. Com., 1937–38, pp. 74–75. DAR.
Wilkinson. Brooks chart. MHS.
Cary Geneal. Coll. Ms. MHS.
Geneal. of Va. family of Lomax. Lib. Cong.
Col. families of Md. Emory. 1900, p. 154. MHS; DAR.
Hist. of Allegany Co. Thomas and Williams. V. 2, p. 1264. MHS; DAR.
Hist. of Pocomoke City. Murray. P. 141. DAR.
Mrs. B. S. Johnston chart. MHS.
Marshall of Marshall Hall. Natl. Geneal. Soc. Quart., v, 19, no. 1, p. 1; no. 4, pp. 86–96.
Md. families. Culver. Ms. Personal list.
Pedigree of Coleman Randall Freeman. Soc. Col. Wars Md. Culver. 1940. MHS; DAR.
Pedigree of W. Wallace McKaig. Soc. Col. Wars Md. Culver. 1940. MHS; DAR.
Pedigree of James Donnell Tilghman. Soc. Col. Wars Md. Culver. 1940. MHS; DAR.
Portrait and biog. rec. of Harford and Cecil Cos. 1897, p. 162. MHS; DAR.
St. Paul's Parish, Balto. V. 1, 4. Mss. MHS.
Some Md. and Va. ancestors. Bell. Natl. Geneal. Soc. Quart., v. 19, no. 4, pp. 86–96.
Miss Margaret M. Steele chart. MHS.
Tercentenary hist. of Md. Andrews. V. 4, pp. 233, 670. MHS; DAR.

Wilkinson. Wills of Wm. Wilkinson, Prince George Co., 1754; Wm. Wilkinson, of Charles Co., 1798, and James Briscoe, of Charles Co., 1779. Mss. DAR.
Wilkinson-Brann-Boon family of Balto. Photos. DAR.
*Wilkinson family of Harrison Co., W. Va. K. C. Gottschalk. DAR.
Wilkinson, Charles Co. Daughter of Md.; Mother of Texas. Bell. MHS; DAR.
†**Wilkinson, Gen. James.** Hist. of Md. Scharf. V. 2, p. 290. MHS.
†Wilkinson, "Tarnished Warrior." (Born near Hunting Creek, Calvert Co., 1757; brigadier in Revolutionary war; commander of Amer. forces in war of 1812.) Maj. J. R. Jacobs. N. Y., Macmillan, 380 pp. DAR; Enoch Pratt Lib.
Wilkinson, Rev. Wm. (1612–63). Some early col. Marylanders. M. H. mag., 1919, v. 14, pp. 384–99.
Wilkinson Family, Va. Family Bible. DAR. Ms. DAR.
Wilkinson-Brown-Bullitt-Gregoire. Bible rec. Natl. Geneal. Soc. Quart., v. 10, no. 2, pp. 94–96.
†**Willard.** Hist. of Frederick Co. Williams. V. 1, p. 596; v. 2, pp. 1093, 1407, 1408, 1453. MHS; DAR.
Patriotic Md. Md. Soc. of S. A. R., 1930. MHS; DAR.
†(President of B. & O. RR.) Daniel Willard rides the line. Edward Hungerford. Putman, 1938, 310 pp. Enoch Pratt Lib.
See Williard.
***Willcox.** Memoir of Mrs. Mary B. Willcox. Supplement. Phila., 1917. DAR.
*Willcox and allied families, Ivy Mills, Del. Co., Pa., 1729–1866. J. Willcox. Priv. pr., Lucas Bros., Balto., 1911. MHS; DAR.
Willcox Paper Mill (Ivy Mills) 1729–1866. Joseph Willcox. Amer. Catholic Hist. Soc. of Phila. Rec. V. 8, 1897.
See Wilcox.
Willcox, Ivy Mills, Pa. (1796–1866). Amer. Catholic Hist. Soc. of Phila. Rec., 1896, v. 7.
Willcoxon, Wilcoxen. Rec. Natl. Geneal. Soc. Quart., July, 1917, v. 6, no. 2, p. 44.
Willet. Ances. rec. and portraits. Col. Dames of Amer., 1910, p. 78. MHS; DAR.
Beall and Bell families. Beall. MHS; DAR.
Price family and other Gunpowder Friends. Death notices; photos. of newsp. clipp. MHS.
***Willett.** Bartow geneal. Bartow. Lib. Cong.; MHS.
*Lineage Bk., Daughters of Amer. Col., v. 1, p. 375. MHS; DAR.
†**Willes.** Med. Annals Md. Cordell. 1903, p. 624. MHS.
Willey. Balto., its hist., its people. Hall. V. 3. MHS; DAR.
Tercentenary hist. of Md. Andrews. V. 2, p. 838. MHS; DAR.
Williams. Abr. Compend. Amer. Geneal. Virkus. V. 1, p. 891. DAR.
All Hallow's P. E. churchyard, Snow Hill, Worcester Co. Hudson. Bd. ms. MHS; DAR. Also: Md. Geneal. Rec. Com., 1935–36, p. 24. Mss. DAR.
Ances. Rec. and Portraits. Col Dames of Amer., 1910, pp. 6, 22, 38, 55, 88, 257, 474, 584, 661–63, 664, 666, 669. MHS; DAR.
Balto., its hist., its people. Hall. V. 2, pp. 238, 287; v. 3, pp. 539, 568. MHS; DAR.
Mrs. Lee Barroll chart. MHS.
The Beckwiths. Beckwith.
†Biog. sketches of distinguished Marylanders. Boyle. MHS.
*Boyd family. Boyd. DAR.
Mrs. A. C. Bruce chart. MHS.
Cabrillo Chapter, D. A. R. (Calif.), in its hist. of Md., 1913–28, p. 233. DAR.
Col. families of Md. Emory. 1900, pp. 22–23, 25. MHS; DAR.
Col. families of U. S. A. Mackenzie. V. 1, pp. 596–605; v. 2; v. 3; v. 4; v. 5, p. 564. MHS; DAR.
Day-Star, Davis, 1855, p. 264. DAR.
Duckett chart. MHS.
Col. Nicholas Duvall family rec. Price. Bd. ms. MHS.
Family rec. of Richard Williams (born in Md., 1726; died in N. C., 1781); with Hiatt data. Ms. DAR.
*Frederick Co. families. Markell. Ms. Personal list.
Gantt geneal. Ms. MHS.
See Gore; See Marriott. Abr. Compend. Amer. Geneal. Virkus. V. 1, p. 627. DAR.
Graves in Williamsport Cemetery, Wash. Co. Hist. of West. Md. Scharf. V. 2, p. 1221.
Graves. Greensboro churchyard. Md. Geneal. Rec. Com., 1935–36, p. 168. Mss. DAR.
Hagerstown tombstone inscriptions. Gruder. Natl. Geneal. Soc. Quart., 1919, v. 8, nos. 1, 2.
Hamill chart. MHS.
†Hist. of Allegany Co. Thomas and Williams. V. 1, pp. 49, 304. MHS; DAR.
Hist of Balto. Lewis Pub. Co., 1912, v. 2, pp. 238, 287; v. 3, pp. 539, 568. DAR.
†Hist. of Balto. City and Co. Scharf. P. 717. MHS.
Hist. of Chelsea, Mass. Mellen Chamberlain. V. 1, pp. 363–64.
†Hist. of Frederick Co. Williams. V. 1, pp. 37, 89, 125; v. 2, p. 710. MHS; DAR.
†Hist. of Washington Co. Williams. 1906, v. 1, pp. 76, 78–9, 128, 163, 191, 417, 452, 588–89. MHS; DAR.
†Hist. of West. Md. Scharf. V. 1, pp. 456, 607, 679, 724; v. 2, pp. 1150, 1220, 1221, 1232, 1259, 1509. MHS; DAR.
Mrs. Wm. T. Howard chart. MHS.
Howell Bible rec. Ms. MHS.
Lloyd family hist. of Wales, Pa., and Md. DAR.
Maddox family. Col. and Revolutionary families of Phila. Jordan. 1933, v. 1, pp. 401–02.
Md. families. Culver. Ms. Personal list.
†Med. Annals Md. Cordell. 1903, pp. 622–24. MHS.
†Men of mark in Md. Johnson. V. 2; v. 3; v. 4. DAR; Enoch Pratt Lib.
Mrs. R. M. Miles chart. MHS.
Monnet family geneal. Monnette. Pp. 369, 1109–10. MHS.
Mrs. R. B. Morison chart. MHS.
Mullikins of Md. Baker. MHS; DAR.
Old Kent. Hanson. P. 193. MHS; DAR.
Old Somerset. Torrence. MHS; DAR.
Orme geneal. chart. MHS.
Patriotic Md. Md. Soc. of S. A. R., 1930. MHS; DAR.
Pedigree of Charles Gambrill Baldwin. Soc. Col. Wars Md. Culver. 1940. MHS; DAR.

Pedigree of Mareen Duvall. Soc. Col. Wars Md. Culver. 1940. MHS; DAR.
Photos. Scrap Book. MHS.
Portrait and biog. rec. of Sixth Cong. Dist. of Md., 1898. Pp. 641, 680. MHS; DAR.
Rumsey-Smithson family rec. bk. Md. Geneal. Rec. Com., 1932, p. 102. DAR.
St. Inigoes churchyard, St. Mary's Co. Md. O. R. Soc. Bull., no. 3, p. 58.
St. Paul's P. E. churchyard, Berlin, Worcester Co. Hudson. Bd. ms. MHS; DAR. Also: Md. Geneal. Rec. Com., 1937, Mrs. Lines. Mss. DAR.
(100 rec.) St. Paul's Parish, Balto. V. 1, 2, 3, 4. Mss. MHS.
St. Stephens Parish, Cecilton, Md. MHS; DAR.
Sanford chart. MHS.
See Sanford. Encyc. of Amer. biog. Amer. Hist. Soc., N. Y., 1928, v. 33, p. 212.
See Sanford, Mrs. S. K. Abr. Compend. Amer. Geneal. Virkus. V. 1, p. 816. DAR.
Sketches of John Slemmons Stevenson and Rev. Samuel McMaster. Stevenson. MHS.
†Sketch of life and services of Otho H. Williams. Osmond Tiffaney. Balto., John Murphy, 1851. MHS.
Smithson-Rumsey rec. bk. Ms. MHS.
Society Hill, S. C. J. S. Ames. Columbia S. C., 1910, 20 pp. DAR.
Somerset Co. Court Book. Tilghman. 1937. Ms. DAR.
Somerset Parish. Abs. of rec. Turner Geneal. Coll. Ms. MHS.
Stump family of Cecil and Harford Cos. Pamph. MHS.
*Surnames and coat of arms of Robert Williams of Roxbury. A. D. French. Priv. pr. Boston, Mass. MHS.
Tercentenary hist. of Md. Andrews. V. 2, pp. 311, 751; v. 3, pp. 174, 826; v. 4, pp. 321, 430. MHS; DAR.
Trinity Church cemetery, Dorchester Co. Md. O. R. Soc. Bull., no. 3, pp. 42–52.
Trinity P. E. churchyard, Long Green. Typed ms. MHS; DAR.
Turner Geneal. Coll. Ms. MHS.
Mrs. Walter P. Smith chart. MHS.
*Wicomico Co. families. Tilghman. Ms, pp. 13, 49, 62, 95, 99–101, 104–05. DAR.
*Williams family in Amer. More particularly descendants of Robert Williams of Roxbury. S. W. Williams. Williams of Md., pp. 336–46. Greenfield, Merriman & Mirick, 1847. MHS.
Williams family of Society Hill, S. C. J. S. Ames. (Md. ref.) Issued by Pee Dee Hist. Assoc., Columbia, S. C., The State Co., 1910, pamph. MHS.
See Harris - Maddox - Williams - Smith - Powell - Travers.
See Lord-Williams.
See Roach-Greenwell-Thompson-Williams.
See Wilson-Sedwick-Williams.
Williams, Anne Arundel Co. Cary Geneal. Coll. Ms. MHS.
Prentice chart. MHS.
Williams, Calvert Co. Autobiography of Summerfield Baldwin. Pp. 63–66. MHS; DAR.
Cary Geneal. Coll. Ms. MHS.
Mrs. G. R. Veazey chart. MHS.
Williams, Charles Co. Abr. Compend. Amer. Geneal. Virkus. V. 4, p. 320. MHS.
Williams, Conn. Cary Geneal. Coll. Ms. MHS.
Williams. Greensboro old churchyard. Md. Geneal. Rec. Com., 1935–36, p. 168. Mss. DAR.
Williams, Prince George Co. Sara R. Baldwin chart. MHS.
Williams, Charles, St. Mary's Co. War pension issued June 19, 1818. D. A. R. Mag., July, 1938, v. 62, no. 7.
***Williams, Daniel and Mary (Jackson).** Early Ky. pioneers, 1752–1898. J. M. Kelley. Pamph. DAR.
†**Williams, George Huntington.** Memorial of friends for friends. (Born in N. Y., 1856; died 1894.) Priv. pr., 1896. Enoch Pratt Lib.
Williams, Mrs. George Huntington, Jr. (Mary Camilla McKim). Chart. Col. Dames, Chap. I. MHS.
Williams, Mrs. George Huntington (Mary Clifton Wood). Chart. (Mostly Mass. and Conn. families.) Col. Dames, Chap. I. MHS.
Williams, George Washington. Md. Soc., War of 1812, v. 4, no. 325. Ms. MHS.
Pedigree. Soc. Col. Wars Md. Culver. 1940. MHS; DAR.
***Williams, Henry.** Burke's landed gentry. 1939. MHS.
*Geneal. and mem. encyc. of Md. Spencer. V. 1, pp. 308–12. MHS; DAR.
Williams, J. T. Geneal. and mem. encyc. of Md. Spencer. V. 2, pp. 552–54. MHS; DAR.
Williams, John Savage. Pedigree chart. Soc. Col. Wars, Md. Johnston. 1905, p. 125. MHS.
†**Williams, John Whitridge.** Academic aspects and biog. J. M. Slemons. (Born in Balto., 1866; died 1931.) Balto., Johns Hopkins Univ. Press, 1935. MHS; Enoch Pratt Lib.
Williams, Mrs. John Whitridge (Margaretta Stewart Brown). Chart 1. Col. Dames, Chap. I. MHS.
Williams, Mrs. John Whitridge; formerly **Mrs. Robert Goodloe Harper Pennington (Caroline DeWolf Theobald).** Chart 2. Col. Dames, Chap. I. MHS.
Williams, Mrs. John Winslow (Kainlani Sewall). Chart. Col. Dames, Chap. I. MHS.
Williams, Joseph, St. Mary's Co. Will, Feb. 17, 1780. Other Joseph Williams, will, March 29, 1815. Both copies. Ms. MHS.
Williams, Lilburn. Dundas-Hesselius. P. 120. MHS.
Williams, Mason Locke Weems. Pedigree chart. Soc. Col. Wars, Md. Johnston. 1905, p. 126. MHS.
Pedigree. Soc. Col. Wars Md. Culver. MHS; DAR. (See Pedigree Book, 1905, p. 126, revised.)
Williams, Mrs. N. Winslow (Anne Tyler Foster). Chart. (Mostly Conn. families.) Col. Dames, Chap. I. MHS.
Williams, Nathan Winslow. Pedigree chart. Soc. Col. Wars, Md. Johnston. 1905, p. 127. MHS.
†**Williams, Gen. Otho Holland** (1749–94). Balto., hist. and biog. Richardson and Bennett. 1871, pp. 529–31. MHS; DAR.

†**Williams, Gen. Otho Holland** (1749–94). Biog. Sketches of Distinguished Marylanders. Boyle. MHS; DAR.
†Chronicles of Balto. Scharf. 1874, p. 275. MHS; DAR.
Coll. of Amer. epitaphs and inscriptions. Alden. 1814, v. 5. MHS.
†Hist. of Md. Scharf. V. 2, pp. 330–35. MHS.
*The Sun, Balto., April 2, 1905.
Williams, Mrs. Robert Lancaster (Rebecca Gustavia Watkins). Chart. Col. Dames, Chap. I. MHS.
Williams, Miss Susanna. Family register from Bible. Ms. DAR.
Williams, Wm. Smith Gittings. Pedigree chart. Soc. Col. Wars, Md. Johnston. 1905, p. 128. MHS.
Williams Family. Bible rec. Ms. MHS.
Williams Family, Md. and Va. County Court Note Book. Ljimgstedt. MHS; DAR.
Williams Family, Pomfret, Conn., and Rockbury. Greenway Mss. Geneal. Coll. MHS.
Williams Family, Wash. Co. Hist. of West. Md. Scharf. V. 2, p. 1022.
Williams Line. Barton charts. MHS.
***Williams Line,** Va. and Md. Encyc. of Amer. biog. Amer. Hist. Soc., N. Y., 1928, v. 33, p. 229.
Williams-Derrickson. Somerset Parish. Abs. of rec. Turner Geneal. Coll. Ms. MHS.
Williams-Gott. Abr. Compend. Amer. Geneal. Virkus. V. 4, p. 641. MHS.
Williamson. Barroll in Great Britain and Amer. Barroll. Pp. 53, 54, 68, 69, 119. MHS.
*Bible rec. Ms. MHS.
Dobbin chart. MHS.
†Hist. of Frederick Co. Williams. V. 2, p. 1550. MHS; DAR.
Makemie Memorial Pres. churchyard, Snow Hill, Worcester Co. Hudson. Bd. ms. MHS; DAR. Also: Md. Geneal. Rec. Com., Mrs. Lines. Mss. DAR.
*Old Kent. Hanson. P. 327. MHS; DAR.
Pedigree of Coleman Randall Freeman. Soc. Col. Wars Md. Culver. 1940. MHS;DAR
Pedigree of Henry Irvine Keyser, II. Soc. Col. Wars Md. Culver. 1940. MHS; DAR.
Pedigree of Wm. Handy Collins Vickers. Soc. Col. Wars Md. Culver. 1940. MHS; DAR.
St. Stephens Parish, Cecilton, Md. MHS; DAR.
Side lights on Md. hist. Richardson. V. 2, p. 253. MHS; DAR.
Tercentenary hist. of Md. Andrews. V. 3, pp. 119, 995. MHS; DAR.
Mrs. H. DeCourcy Wright Thom chart. MHS.
Tree of Anne Williamson. Horwitz chart. MHS.
Mrs. Emory Whitridge chart. MHS.
Zion Reformed Church, Hagerstown. Md. Geneal. Rec. Com., 1934–35. Mss. DAR.
See Field-Williamson-Stevenson.
Williamson, John Laughlin. Pedigree. (New Eng. rec.) Soc. Col. Wars Md. Culver. 1940. MHS; DAR.
Williamson, Thomas Wilson. Md. Soc., War of 1812, v. 2, no. 195. Ms. MHS.
Pedigree. Soc. Col. Wars Md. Culver. 1940. MHS; DAR.
Williar. U. B. cemetery, Sabillasville. Young. Natl. Geneal. Soc. Quart., Sept., 1938, v. 26, no. 3, p. 61 (to be contd.).
Williard. U. B. cemetery, Sabillasville. Young. Natl. Geneal. Soc. Quart., Sept., 1938, v. 26, no. 3, p. 61 (to be contd.).
See Willard.
Williard, Mass. and Conn. D. A. R. Mag., v. 69, no. 7, p. 434; v. 70, no. 2, p. 130.
†**Williard, Daniel.** Men of mark in Md. Johnson. V. 4. DAR; Enoch Pratt Lib.
***Willie.** Abbott-Denison-Willie families, early ancestors, of Bishops, Stratford Co., Herts, Eng. Pamph. MHS.
*Abbott-Denison-Willie families. Spencer Miller. Repr. from N. Y. Geneal. and Biog. Rec., Jan., 1936. MHS.
Willing. Ancestry of Rosalie Morris Johnson. Johnson. 1905. MHS; DAR.
Mrs. Howard Bruce chart. MHS.
Mrs. E. W. Poe chart. MHS.
Ruffin and other geneal. Pr. chart. Henry.
St. Mary's churchyard, Tyaskin, Md. Md. Geneal. Rec. Com., 1938–39, pp. 187–92. Mss. DAR.
Willing, Pa. Ances. reç. and portraits. Col. Dames of Amer., 1910, v. 1, p. 155. MHS; DAR.
Willis. Balto., its hist., its people. Hall. V. 2, p. 196. MHS; DAR.
Bible rec. D. C. Geneal. Rec. Com., v. 31, pt. 1, pp. 283–87; v. 31, pt. 2, p. 461. Typed, bd. DAR.
Bible rec. Ga. Geneal. Rec. Com., 1933, pt. 1, p. 5. Typed, bd. DAR.
Bond chart. MHS.
D. A. R. Mag., Sept., 1933, v. 67, no. 9, pp. 583–88.
Hist. of Balto. Lewis Pub. Co., 1912, v. 2, p. 196. DAR.
†Hist. of Frederick Co. Williams. V. 2, pp. 1024, 1089. MHS; DAR.
†Hist. of West. Md. Scharf. V. 2, p. 904. MHS; DAR.
Patriotic Md. Md. Soc. of S. A. R., 1930. MHS; DAR.
St. Paul's Parish, Balto. V. 2. Mss. MHS.
Somerset Co. Court Book. Tilghman. 1937. Ms. DAR.
Tercentenary hist. of Md. Andrews. V. 2, pp. 212, 691; v. 4, p. 568. MHS; DAR.
Trinity Church burial ground, near Cambridge, Md. Md. Geneal. Rec. Com., 1937–38, pp. 93–104. Mss. DAR.
Trinity Church cemetery, Dorchester Co. Md. O. R. Soc. Bull., no. 3, pp. 42–52.
*Wicomico Co. families. Tilghman. Ms, pp. 8, 113. DAR.
*Willis family of Va. B. C. Willis and R. H. Willis. Incl. Va. families of Ambler, Bassett, Burrell, Byrd, Carter, Champe, Daingerfield, Lewis, Madison, Reade, Smith, Taliaferro, Tayloe, Thornton, Warner, etc. Richmond, Va., Whittet & Shepperson. MHS; DAR.
See Beauchamp - Smoot - Turpin - White - Willis - Wilson.
See Callahan-Lednum-Willis-Wright.
See Watts-Smith-Willis.
***Willis,** Va. The Sun, Balto., Aug. 26, Sept. 2, 9, 1906.
Willis, Wm. N. Md. Soc., War of 1812, v. 2, no. 164. Ms. MHS.
Willison, Allegany Co. See Thomas Conway, Va. and Pa. Ms. File case, DAR.

Willmott. Patriotic Marylander, v. 1, no. 3, p. 44. MHS; DAR.
Willmott, Md. and Ky. Tombstone inscriptions of Robt. C. Willmott and his wife, Priscilla Willmott. Ms. DAR.
Willoughby. Ances. rec. and portraits. Col. Dames of Amer., 1910, p. 744. MHS; DAR.
Chart, photos. 1 sheet. Cary Geneal. Coll. Ms. MHS.
Christ P. E. Church cemetery, Cambridge. Steele. 1936. MHS; DAR.
Willoughby Family. Marriages, Caroline Co. Geneal. Mag., v. 8, p. 36. DAR.
†**Wills.** Med. Annals Md. Cordell. 1903, p. 624. MHS.
Willson. Amer. Clan Gregor Year Book, 1931, pp. 25–27. MHS; DAR.
Children of Alex P. and M. C. Hill. Ms. MHS.
Col. families of Amer. Lawrence. V. 16, p. 84. MHS.
†Hist. of Allegany Co. Thomas and Williams. V. 2. MHS; DAR.
†Hist. of West. Md. Scharf. V. 1, p. 729. MHS; DAR.
Rachel Pottinger (Magruder) Lumsdon Bible rec. Md. Geneal. Rec. Com., 1935–36, v. 8, p. 272. Mss. DAR.
†Med. Annals Md. Cordell. 1903, p. 625. MHS.
Portrait and biog. rec. of East. Shore of Md. 1898, pp. 333, 413. MHS; DAR.
St. Paul's Parish, Balto. V. 1. Mss. MHS.
Somerset Co. Court Book. Tilghman. 1937. Ms. DAR.
See Smyth-Tilghman-Willson.
See Wilson.
Willson, Kent Co. Hamilton family of Charles Co. Kelly. MHS.
†**Willson, Charles Carroll.** Men of mark in Md. Johnson. V. 3. DAR; Enoch Pratt Lib.
Willson, Jonathan. Bible rec. Ms. DAR.
Willson Family. Thomas Book. Thomas. P. 337. Lib. Cong.; MHS.
Montgomery Co. Ms. MHS.
Willson-Sappington. Bible rec., from Bible in possession of Mrs. B. N. Willson, Chestertown, RR #2. Md. Geneal. Rec. Com., 1937–38, pp. 123–24. Mss. DAR.
Wilmer. Ancest. Rec. and Portraits. Col. Dames of Amer., 1910, v. 2, p. 475. MHS; DAR.
Bantz geneal. notes. Ms. MHS.
Barroll in Great Britain and Amer. Barroll. P. 72. MHS.
†Bench and bar of Md. Sams and Riley. 1901, v. 2, p. 507. Lib. Cong.; MHS; Peabody Lib.
†Biog. cyc. of rep. men of Md. and D. C. Pp. 484–85. MHS; DAR.
Bond chart. MHS.
Britton Scrap Book. V. 2. Ms. MHS.
Clay family of Pa. Ms. File case, DAR.
†Defense of Simon Wilmer. Pr. for author by Cole & Hewes, Balto., 1805. MHS.
Deford chart. MHS.
Dobbin chart. MHS.
Ford chart. MHS.
See Hope. Abr. Compend. Amer. Geneal. Virkus. V. 1, p. 924. DAR.
Hyland chart. MHS.
Hyland family, Cecil Co. Ms. MHS.
Md. families. Culver. Ms. Personal list.
Memoirs of Rev. James Jones Wilmer, Kent Co. J. Hall Pleasants. M. H. Mag., Sept. 1924, v. 19, no. 3, pp. 220–46.
Morris family of Phila. Moon. V. 3, p. 937. MHS.
*Notes. Md. Geneal. Rec. Com., v. 1, pp. 111–12.
Pedigree of Duncan Keener Brent. Soc. Col. Wars Md. Culver. 1940. MHS; DAR.
Pedigree of Corbin Braxton Dallam. Soc. Col. Wars Md. Culver. 1940. MHS; DAR.
Pedigree of Howard Hall Macy Lee. Soc. Col. Wars Md. Culver. 1940. MHS; DAR.
Pedigree of Wm. Handy Collins Vickers. Soc. Col. Wars Md. Culver. 1940. MHS; DAR.
See Ringgold-Wilmer. Ances. Rec. and Portraits. Col. Dames of Amer., 1910, v. 2, pp. 474–75. MHS; DAR.
St. Paul's P. E. churchyard, Kent Co. Md. O. R. Soc. Bull., no. 2, pp. 54–65. MHS.
St. Paul's Parish, Balto. V. 2. Mss. MHS.
Wilmer, Rev. James Jones. Memoirs. (Copied from pamph. written by Rev. James Jones Wilmer, pub. in Balto., 1792.) M. H. Mag., 1924, v. 19, pp. 220–46.
Wilmer, Simon, Kent Co. W. A. and S. W. Merritt pedigree charts. Soc. Col. Wars, Md. Johnston. 1905, pp. 67, 158. MHS.
Seven pioneers of East. Shore. Skirven. M. H. Mag., 1920, v. 15, no. 3, pp. 230–50; no. 4, p. 394–419.
***Wilmer Family.** Old Kent. Hanson. Pp. 325–31. MHS; DAR.
Wilmer Line. Mrs. J. Hall Pleasants, Jr., chart. MHS.
***Wilmer-Moore,** Va. The Sun, Balto., Feb. 19, 1905.
Wilmot. Bonsal charts. MHS.
Chenoweth-Cromwell, geneal. and charts. MHS.
Gen. Sullivan's descent upon British on Staten Island; escape of William Wilmot. F. B. Culver. M. H. Mag., June, 1911, v. 6, no. 2, pp. 138–44.
Pedigree of Pleasants Pennington. Soc. Col. Wars Md. Culver. 1940. MHS; DAR.
Mrs. Pennington chart. MHS.
Tombstone rec. from non-Moravians buried in Strangers Row, Old Cemetery, Bethlehem, Pa. Md. Geneal. Bull., v. 6, p. 17.
See Wilmott.
***Wilmot, Capt.,** (Md. line; born in Balto. Co., 1752; killed in action Nov. 14, 1782). Last bloodshed of Revolution. Culver. M. H. Mag., 1910, v. 5, pp. 329–38.
†**Wilmot, John** (1778–1858). M. H. Mag., v. 12, p. 252.
Wilmot, Wilmott. Notes, 1694. Focke Geneal. Coll. Ms. MHS.
*The Sun, Balto., Aug. 11, 18, 1907.
Wilmott. Chart. Geneal. and chart of Chenoweth and Cromwell families of Md. and Va. Chenoweth. MHS.
Md. families. Culver. Ms. Personal list.
Monument erected to memory of Col. Robert Wilmott (1757–1837) and wife, Priscilla Ridgely Dorsey. Photos. DAR.
See Wilmot.
Wilmott, Wilmot. Cary Geneal. Coll. Ms. MHS.

Wilson. All Hallow's P. E. churchyard, Snow Hill, Worcester Co. Hudson. Bd. ms. MHS; DAR. Also: Md. Geneal. Rec. Com., 1935-36, p. 24. Mss. DAR.
See Andrews, Mo. Abr. Compend. Amer. Geneal. Virkus. V. 4, p. 543. MHS.
†Bench and bar of Md. Sams and Riley. 1901, v. 2, p. 407. Lib. Cong.; MHS; Peabody Lib.
Bond chart. MHS.
Mrs. J. G. Brogden chart. MHS.
Chart of Com. John Rodgers. DAR.
Christ P. E. Church cemetery, Cambridge. Steele. 1936. MHS; DAR.
Col. families of U. S. A. Mackenzie. V. 2. MHS; DAR.
D. A. R. Mag., Sept., 1933, v. 67, no. 9, pp. 583-88.
†Day that is done. Story of author's mother, bride in Hagerstown, 1859. Lenore Hamilton Wilson. Repr. from Atlantic Monthly, 1931-32. Enoch Pratt Lib.
J. T. Dennis pedigree chart, plate 2. Soc. Col. Wars, Md. Johnston. 1905, p. 22. MHS.
*Descendants of Ephraim Wilson. J. Breckenridge Handy. (Wilsons of Somerset and Worcester Cos.) Nov., 1897.
Dulaney churchyard, near Massey, Kent Co. Md. Geneal. Rec. Com., 1933-34, pp. 210-12. Mss. DAR.
Fisher family. Morse. MHS.
Fisher family, Sussex Co., Del., and Md. Ms. MHS.
*Geneal. of Henrietta Chauncy Wilson, wife of James Stone Whitely of Balto. Thomas Upshur. Book of photos. 1904. MHS.
Greenway Mss. Geneal. Coll. Binder's title, Hawkins-Bordley. MHS.
Mrs. Alexander Gordon chart. MHS.
Mrs. W. H. Harris chart. MHS.
Hazelhurts charts. MHS.
Hilles chart. MHS.
Hist. and geneal. account of Levering family. Levering. MHS.
†Hist. of Allegany Co. Thomas and Williams. V. 2. MHS; DAR.
†Hist. of Balto. City and Co. Scharf. Pp. 743, 769. MHS.
Hist. of Frederick Co. Williams. V. 2, pp. 725, 1243, 1556. MHS; DAR.
Hist. Salisbury, Wicomico Co. Truitt. P. 195. DAR.
S. G. Hopkins chart. MHS.
Mrs. T. C. Jenkins chart. MHS.
Jenkins-Courtney chart. MHS.
Miss Cassandra Lee chart. MHS.
Leverton family, Kent Co., Bible rec. Md. Geneal. Rec. Com., 1932-33, v. 5. Mss. DAR.
Lux-Stewart-Wilson family. Ms. MHS.
Makemie Memorial Pres. churchyard, Snow Hill, Worcester Co. Hudson. Bd. ms. MHS; DAR. Also: Md. Geneal. Rec. Com., Mrs. Lines. Mss. DAR.
McClellan chart. MHS.
†Med. Annals Md. Cordell. 1903, pp. 625-26. MHS.
Patriotic Md. Md. Soc. of S. A. R., 1930. MHS; DAR.
J. W. Patterson pedigree chart. Soc. Col. Wars, Md. Johnston. 1905, p. 82. MHS.
Portrait and biog. rec. of East. Shore of Md. 1898, pp. 221, 234, 413, 467, 468, 489, 585, 662. MHS; DAR.
(68 rec.) St. Paul's Parish, Balto. V. 1, 2, 3, 4. Mss. MHS.
Somerset Co. Court Book. Tilghman. 1937. Ms. DAR.
Third Haven Friends Meeting House, Easton. Vital rec. MHS. Also: Natl. Geneal. Soc. Quart., v. 11, no. 1, pp. 9-14.
*The Sun, Balto., Oct. 28, 1906; Oct. 27 (letter), 1907.
Trinity P. E. churchyard, Long Green. Typed ms. MHS; DAR.
*Wicomico Co. families. Tilghman. Ms, pp. 22, 56, 68, 113-14, 124, 128. DAR.
Mrs. J. Whitridge Williams chart 1. MHS.
*Henrietta Chauncy Wilson, wife of James Stone Whiteley. T. T. Upshur. 1904. Photos. MHS.
Worcester Co. militia, 1794. Covington. P. 164. MHS.
See Beauchamp - Smoot - Turpin - White - Willis - Wilson.
See Lee-Wilson.
See Satchell-Wilson.
See Worthington-Wilson.
Wilson, Anne Arundel Co. Cary Geneal. Coll. Ms. MHS.
***Wilson,** Calvert Co. Lineage Bks., Daughters of Founders and Patriots, v. 7, pp. 6-7, 45; v. 21, p. 110. MHS.
Wilson, Harford Co. Mrs. R. F. Brent chart. MHS.
Wilson, Richmond Co., Va. Cary Geneal. Coll. Ms. MHS.
Wilson, Somerset Co. Mrs. Morris Whitridge chart. MHS.
†**Wilson,** Somerset and Worcester Cos. Biog. cyc. of rep. men of Md. and D. C. Pp. 511, 515-16. MHS; DAR.
†**Wilson, Alpheus W.** Prince in Israel. (Born in Balto., 1834.) Carlton D. Harris. Board of Church Extension, M. E. Church, South Louisville, Ky. Enoch Pratt Lib.
Wilson, Mrs. Calvin (nee Webster), Harford Co. Abr. Compend. Amer. Geneal. Virkus. V. 1, p. 894. DAR.
Wilson, Ezra, Allegany Co. (born 1802). D. A. R. Mag., v. 66, no. 4, p. 251.
†**Wilson, Rev. Franklin** (Bapt.). Life story as told by himself, in his journals. (Born in Balto., 1822; died in Balto., 1896.) Portrait. Balto., 1897. Enoch Pratt Lib.
Wilson, Henrietta Chauncy. Whiteley chart. MHS.
Wilson, Henry, Harford Co. ("Fighting Quaker"). Pedigree of George Webb Constable. Soc. Col. Wars Md. Culver. 1940. MHS; DAR.
Wilson, Hezekiah, Montgomery Co. Diary. Natl. Geneal. Soc. Quart., 1917, v. 6, no. 1, p. 27-31.
Wilson, J. Appleton. Md. Soc., War of 1812, v. 1, no. 67. Ms. MHS.
Abr. Compend. Amer. Geneal. Virkus. V. 1, p. 732. DAR.
Wilson, John Appleton. Pedigree charts, plates 1, 2, 3, 4 and 5. Soc. Col. Wars, Md. Johnston. 1905, pp. 130-34. MHS.
Wilson, J. J. Md. Soc., War of 1812, v. 1, no. 99. Ms. MHS.

Wilson, James Gulian, and Wilson, Marshall Gulian, Balto. Pedigree chart. Soc. Col. Wars, Md. Johnston. 1904, p. 129. MHS.
Wilson, John Sandford. Md. Soc., War of 1812, v. 1, no. 122. Ms. MHS.
Wilson, Marshall Gulian. *See* Wilson, James Gulian and Marshall Gulian.
Wilson, Robert (died 1746). Oldest tombstone inscription legible of old Broad Creek graveyard, near Stevensville, Kent Island.
†**Wilson, Thomas.** Balto., hist. and biog. Richardson and Bennett. 1871, pp. 533–37. MHS; DAR.
†**Wilson, Wm.** Balto., hist. and biog. Richardson and Bennett. 1871, pp. 539–40. MHS; DAR.
Wilson, William Bowly. Pedigree chart. Soc. Col. Wars, Md. Johnston. 1905, p. 135. MHS.
Wilson, Mrs. Wm. Thomas (Eliza Waller Beale). Chart. Col. Dames, Chap. I. MHS.
Wilson, William Thomas. Pedigree chart. Soc. Col. Wars, Md. Johnston. 1905, p. 136. MHS.
***Wilson Family.** Old Kent. Hanson. Pp. 184–89. MHS; DAR.
Note. Old Somerset. Torrence. MHS; DAR.
Wilson Family, Kent Co. (1700). Morris family of Phila. Moon. V. 2, pp. 502, 622, 764–65. MHS.
Wilson Family, Worcester Co. John Neill of Lewes, Del., 1739. Pr. for family, Phila., 1875.
***Wilson-Merceir.** Lineage Bk., Daughters of Amer. Col., v. 2, p. 48. MHS; DAR.
Wilson-Sedwick-Williams Families, Calvert Co. Bible rec. Mss., in Binder. DAR.
Wilson-Selby, Balto. Notes. D. A. R. Mag., v. 71, no. 7, p. 673.
Wilson, Willson. Cook Bible rec. Ms. MHS.
Wilt. Md. Geneal. Bull., v. 6, p. 10. MHS; DAR.
Wiltbank. Robins family, Va. and Worcester Co., Md., and allied families. Bd. ms. MHS.
Wimbor. *See* Wimborough.
***Wimborough, Wimbrow, Wimbor.** Wicomico Co. families. Tilghman. Ms, pp. 85–87, 91–94. DAR.
Wimbrough, Wimbrow - Dashiell - Howard. Wicomico Co. families. Bible rec. Ms. DAR.
Wimbrow. *See* Wimborough.
See Wimbrough.
Wimbrow-Lewis-Tubbs. Wicomico Co. families. Bible rec. Ms. DAR.
†**Winans.** Geneal. and mem. encyc. of Md. Spencer. V. 2, p. 354. MHS; DAR.
***Winans Family.** "Wynants-Winans." Geneal. Presented to MHS Dec. 12, 1932, by Tom Winans, Southampton, Eng., through courtesy of Ferdinand C. Latrobe. Typed, 37 pp. MHS.
Winants, Mrs. Garet Ellis (Frances Leigh Bonsal). Chart. Col. Dames, Chap. I. MHS.
Mrs. Josias Pennington chart. MHS.
Winchester. Col. families of U. S. A. Mackenzie. V. 1; v. 7. MHS; DAR.
Donaldson family. Donaldson. 1931, pamph. MHS.
(Founder of Westminster, Md.) W. A. Moale pedigree charts, plate 2. Soc. Col. Wars, Md. Johnston. 1905, p. 73. MHS.
Geneal. (Ref. to Winchesters of Md.) Mrs. Fanny Winchester Hotchkiss. New Haven, Conn., Tuttle, Morehouse, Taylor Co.
Lehr chart. MHS.
Md. families. Culver. Ms. Personal list.
See Samuel Owings geneal. Focke, Geneal. Coll. Mss. MHS.
Patriotic Md. Md. Soc. of S. A. R., 1930. MHS; DAR.
(40 rec.) St. Paul's Parish, Balto. V. 1, 2, 3. Mss. MHS.
Talbott of "Poplar Knowle." Shirk. MHS; DAR.
Tombstone rec. Rogers Coll. Ms. MHS.
Winchester - Owens - Owings - Price and allied families. (With biog. of Wm. Winchester, founders of Westminster and his two sons, 1764.) M. H. Mag., 1930, v. 25, no. 4, pp. 385–405.
Winchester, Carroll Co. Boddie and allied families. Boddie. MHS.
Winchester, Kent Island. S. G. Hopkins chart. MHS.
Winchester, Wm. Pedigree. Soc. Col. Wars Md. Culver. 1940. MHS; DAR.
Winchester Family, Carroll Co. Focke Geneal. Coll. Mss. MHS.
Winchester-Owings. Chart, photos., 2 sheets. Cary Geneal. Coll. Ms. MHS.
Windel. Jackson family gathering. 1878.
Winder. H. F. Barnes Bible rec. Ms. MHS.
Carey chart. MHS.
Cary Geneal. Coll. Ms. MHS.
Miss M. W. Davis chart. MHS.
De Ford chart. MHS.
*Frederick Co. families. Markell. Ms. Personal list.
Mrs. C. C. Hall chart. MHS.
Handy and their kin. Handy.
Hist. graves of Md. and D. C. Ridgely. MHS.
Hist. Salisbury, Wicomico Co. Truitt. DAR.
†M. H. Mag., v. 12, p. 253.
†Med. Annals Md. Cordell. 1903, p. 627. MHS.
Old Somerset. Torrence. MHS; DAR.
Patriotic Md. Md. Soc. of S. A. R., 1930. MHS; DAR.
Peale Geneal. Coll. Ms. MHS.
Pedigree of Duncan Keener Brent. Soc. Col. Wars Md. Culver. 1940. MHS; DAR.
Pedigree of Charles Morris Howard. Soc. Col. Wars Md. Culver. 1940. MHS; DAR.
Pedigree of Ralph Robinson. Soc. Col. Wars Md. Culver. 1940. MHS; DAR.
Pedigree of James Wm. Slemons. Soc. Col. Wars Md. Culver. 1940. MHS; DAR.
Pedigree of Winder family in Md. and other states in Amer. Chart. F. A. Winder. 1894. DAR.
Polk family. Polk. P. 54. MHS; DAR.
Rec. of Stepney Parish. MHS; DAR.
Round chart. Cary Geneal. Coll. Ms. MHS.
St. Paul's Parish, Balto. V. 2. Mss. MHS.
Somerset Co. Court Book. Tilghman. 1937. Ms. DAR.
Mrs. E. C. Venable chart. MHS.
*Wicomico Co. families. Tilghman. Ms. pp. 56 97. DAR.

Winder. Mrs. G. H. Williams, Jr., chart. MHS.
*Winders of Amer.; John Winder, N. Y., 1674–75; Thomas Winder, N. J., 1703–34; John Winder, Md., 1665–98. R. Winder Johnson. Phila., Lippincott, 1902. MHS.
Worcester Co. militia, 1794. Covington. P. 162. MHS.
Sir George Yeardley. Upshur. P. 14. MHS.
See Bordley-Abbott-Laird-Winder.
See Gillis-Winder.
†**Winder, Gen.** Hist. of Md. Scharf. V. 3, pp. 65, 95. MHS.
Winder, Gov. Levin. Founders of Anne Arundel and Howard Cos. Warfield. P. 256. MHS; DAR.
†Governor of Md. Buchholz. P. 76. MHS.
†Hist. of Md. Scharf. V. 3, p. 36. MHS.
†**Winder, Wm.** Balto., hist. and biog. Richardson and Bennett. 1871, pp. 541–44. MHS; DAR.
Winder Family. Chart, photos. MHS.
*Some rec. Md. O. R. Soc. 1913, Bull., no. 3, pp. 5–19. MHS.
Written from Bible rec. Amer. Hist. Mag., Nashville, Tenn., v. 1, p. 257. MHS.
†**Windsor.** Med. Annals Md. Cordell. 1903, p. 627. MHS.
*Wicomico Co. families. Tilghman. Ms., p. 117. DAR.
†**Winebrenner.** Hist. of Frederick Co. Williams. V. 2, pp. 708, 1341. MHS; DAR.
Winecaff. Steiner geneal. Steiner. 1896. MHS.
Winegardner. Haugh's Lutheran Church, Carroll Co., tombstone rec. Md. Geneal. Rec. Com., 1939–40. Mss. DAR.
Wingart. *See* Wengert.
Wingate. Tombstone rec. of Dorchester Co. Jones. DAR.
Wingate, Md. and Ky. Mrs. E. W. Poe chart. MHS.
Winged. Somerset Co. Court Book. Tilghman. 1937. Ms. DAR.
Wingert. Zion Reformed Church, Hagerstown. Md. Geneal. Rec. Com., 1934–35. Mss. DAR.
Wingod. Somerset Co. Court Book. Tilghman. 1937. Ms. DAR.
†**Winn.** Bench and bar of Md. Sams and Riley. 1901, v. 1, p. 81. Lib. Cong.; MHS; Peabody Lib.
Bolton chart. MHS.
(40 rec.) St. Paul's Parish, Balto. V. 2, 3. Mss. MHS.
***Winn-Jarvis.** Ancestors and descendants of John Quarles Winn and his wife Mary Liscome Jarvis. Incl. also descendants of their parents. D. W. Winn and Elizabeth Jarvis Winn. Containing Va. families, Barclay, Bassett, Bedell, Burwell, Cary, Cole, Higginson, Lambert, Lear, Martiau, Martin, Roscow, Smith, Wills, Wilson, etc. Balto., Lord Baltimore Press, 1932. MHS.
*Geneal. Rev. David Watson Winn and Elizabeth Jarvis Winn. Balto., 1932. MHS.
***Winright.** Wicomico Co. families. Tilghman. Ms., p. 110. DAR.
Winsatt. *See* Abell-Smith-Winsatt.
Winsatt, St. Mary's Co. Marriages. Md. Geneal. Soc. Bull., v. 2, p. 5.
Winsett Family, St. Mary's Co. Marriages from Jan. 20, 1795, to May 16, 1846. Ms. MHS.
Winslow. Abr. Compend. Amer. Geneal. Virkus. V. 4, p. 691. MHS.
†Biog. sketches of Dr. Nathan Winslow and Dr. John Randolph. Pamph. MHS.
†Med. Annals Md. Cordell. 1903, pp. 627–28. MHS.
Tatum-Winslow families. Tatum. 1927.
†**Winslow, Randolph.** Men of mark in Md. Johnson. V. 2. DAR; Enoch Pratt Lib.
Winslow Line. See Williams. Balto., its hist., its people. Hall. V. 2, p. 240. MHS; DAR.
Winslow Line, Mass. (1629). N. W. Williams pedigree chart. Soc. Col. Wars, Md. Johnston. 1905, p. 127. MHS.
Winslow-Williams. Sanford chart. MHS.
Winsor. Rec. of Stepney Parish. MHS; DAR.
Winston. Burton ancestry. Ms. MHS.
*Winston of Va. Clayton Torrence. Incl. over thirty Va. families. Charts of the Bacon, Cary, Littlepage, Robinson and Todd families. In pocket in back of book: charts of Ann Lovelace, wife of John Gorsuch and Hon. John West. Richmond, Va., Whittet & Shepperson, 1927. MHS; DAR.
Wintabury. *See* Winterberry.
Winter. Balto., its hist., its people. Hall. V. 3. MHS; DAR.
Winterberry, Wintabury. St. Stephens Parish, Cecilton, Md. MHS; DAR.
***Winterbottom.** Hist. Dorchester Co. Jones. 1902. 1925, p. 495. MHS; DAR.
Winters, Frederick Co. Data. D. A. R. Mag., v. 67, no. 3, p. 145.
†**Winterson.** Med. Annals Md. Cordell. 1903, p. 628. MHS.
Winthrop. Christ P. E. Church cemetery, Cambridge. Steele. 1936. MHS; DAR.
Rev. Joseph Hull (1595) and some of his descendants. Hull. 1904. MHS.
***Winthrop Family.** Arch. of Georgetown Univ., Wash., D. C., v. 274, no. 3.
Wintkle. St. Paul's Parish, Balto. V. 2. Mss. MHS.
Wintour. Papers relating to early hist. of Md. Streeter. 1876. MHS.
Wirgman. St. Paul's Parish, Balto. V. 2. Mss. MHS.
Wirley, Worley, Pa. Bible rec. Md. Geneal. Rec. Com., 1932, p. 203. DAR.
†**Wirt.** Account of last illness and death of William Wirt. (Born in Bladensburg, Prince George Co., 1772; died in Wash., D. C., 1834.) By his daughter. Boston, 1834, pamphlet. Enoch Pratt Lib.
Ames Geneal. Coll. Ms. MHS.
†Bench and bar of Md. Sams and Riley. 1901, v. 1, p. 293. Lib. Cong.; MHS; Peabody Lib.
†Biog. cyc. of rep. men of Md. and D. C. P. 273. MHS; DAR.
†Memoirs of life of William Wirt, Atty. Gen. of U.S. John P. Kennedy. N. Y., Putman, 1849, 2 vols.; 2nd ed., 1872. MHS; Enoch Pratt Lib.
Monumental City. Howard. MHS; DAR.
†**Wirt, Wm.** (1772–1834). Balto., hist. and biog. Richardson and Bennett. 1871, p. 545. MHS; DAR.
†Eight great Amer. lawyers. Hagan. 1923. MHS.
***Wirtz.** Frederick Co. families. Markell. Ms. Personal list.

Wise. Abr. Compend. Amer. Geneal. Virkus. V. 6, p. 647. DAR.
Catonsville pioneers of Luth. faith. Natl. Geneal. Soc. Quart., v. 9, no. 2, p. 29.
*Frederick Co. families. Markell. Ms. Personal list.
†Hist. of Balto. City and Co. Scharf. P. 875. MHS.
*Wises of Va. D. A. R. Mag., April and Aug., 1927, v. 61.
*Col. John Wise of Eng. and Va., 1617–95; his ancestors and descendants. J. Cropper Wise. Richmond, Va., Bell Book and Stationery Co., 1918. MHS.
Zion Reformed Church, Hagerstown. Md. Geneal. Rec. Com., 1934–35. Mss. DAR.
See Weise.
Wise, Accomack Co., Va. D. A. R. Mag., April and Aug., 1927, v. 61.
Wise, Weise. Patriotic Md. Md. Soc. of S. A. R., 1930. MHS; DAR.
Wiseman. See Roach. Abr. Compend. Amer. Geneal. Virkus. V. 1, p. 800. DAR.
Wisenatt. Steiner geneal. Steiner. 1896. MHS.
Wisewell. Peale Geneal. Coll. Ms. MHS.
***Wisner.** Wisners in Amer., and their kindred. Charts. G. F. Wisner. (Over 5000 names in Amer. since 1714.) Balto., 1918. MHS.
With. St. Paul's Parish, Balto. V. 1. Mss. MHS.
†**Withers.** Hist. of Allegany Co. Thomas and Williams. V. 2. MHS; DAR.
Witherspoon. Mrs. J. Pleasants chart. MHS.
*Witherspoon family of Society Hill, S. C. J. W. Dubose. Bulletin of Dee Pee Hist. Assoc., pamph., 1910. MHS.
†**Witmer.** Hist. of West. Md. Scharf. V. 2, p. 1151. MHS; DAR.
Witten. Eiler-Anderson-Boon-Sothoron-Witten. Eiler. 1929, pamph. MHS.
***Witter.** Frederick Co. families. Markell. Ms. Personal list.
See Nicholson-Witter.
†**Witzenbacher.** Geneal. and mem. encyc. of Md. Spencer. V. 2, p. 431. MHS; DAR.
†Men of mark in Md. Johnson. V. 2. DAR; Enoch Pratt Lib.
Woelff. Diffenderfer family, arrived in Phila., 1727. Ms. File case, DAR.
Woelper. St. Paul's Parish, Balto. V. 2. Mss. MHS.
Wohringin. Hagerstown tombstone inscriptions. Gruder. Natl. Geneal. Soc. Quart., 1919, v. 8, nos. 1, 2.
Wolf. *See* Zug-Wolf.
Wolf, Carroll Co. Cemetery rec. Ms. MHS.
†**Wolf, Wolfe.** Hist. of Frederick Co. Williams. V. 2, pp. 1408, 1414. MHS; DAR.
Mountain Democrat, Garrett Co., Nov. 1, 1934. Newsp. clipp. MHS; DAR.
The Pilot, Union Bridge, Md., Nov. 1, 1935. Newsp. clipp. MHS.
***Wolfe.** Frederick Co. families. Markell. Ms. Personal list.
See Wolf.
Wolfe-Perrie-Wailes Line. Welsh-Hyatt and kindred. Supplement. Welsh. P. 17. MHS; DAR.
Wolfersberger. Zion Reformed Church, Hagerstown. Md. Geneal. Rec. Com., 1934–35. Mss. DAR.
Wolfersperger. Hagerstown tombstone inscriptions. Gruder. Natl. Geneal. Soc. Quart., 1919, v. 8, nos. 1, 2.
†**Wolford.** Hist. of Allegany Co. Thomas and Williams. V. 2. MHS; DAR.
†**Wolgamot.** Hist. of West. Md. Scharf. V. 2, p. 1036. MHS; DAR.
***Wollen, Woolen.** William Wesley Wollen, Thomas W. Wollen, Levin J. Wollen, all natives of Md. Cincinnato, Ohio, 1880. MHS.
Wolseley. Chart, photos., 2 sheets. Cary Geneal. Coll. Ms. MHS.
Woltz. Frederick Co. tombstone inscriptions. Gruder. Natl. Geneal. Soc. Quart., 1919, v. 8, nos. 1, 2.
†**Woltz, George.** Md. cabinet-maker. Mag. Antiques, Mar., 1939, v. 35, no. 3, p. 124.
***Woltz (Waltz) Family,** Hagerstown. (Complete.) Wilson Mss. Coll., no. 77. MHS.
Wood. Bible rec., 1818–99. Contributed by Mrs. H. B. Hudson, Chestertown. Md. Geneal. Rec. Com., 1937–38, pp. 78–79. Mss. DAR.
Col. families of U. S. A. Mackenzie. V. 7. MHS; DAR.
*Frederick Co. families. Markell. Ms. Personal list.
Griffith geneal. Griffith. MHS; DAR.
Mrs. C. C. Hall chart. MHS.
†Hist. of Frederick Co. Williams. V. 1, pp. 11, 326; v. 2, pp. 716, 1008. MHS; DAR.
Lloyd family hist. of Wales, Pa., and Md. DAR.
†Med. Annals Md. Cordell. 1903, p. 629. MHS.
M. E. Church South cemetery, near Poolesville, Montgomery Co. Md. Geneal. Rec. Com., 1926. Mss. DAR.
Monnet family geneal. Monette. MHS.
Pedigree of Garner Wood Denmead. Soc. Col. Wars Md. Culver. 1940. MHS; DAR.
St. Paul's Parish, Balto. V. 1, 2. Mss. MHS.
St. Stephens Parish, Cecilton, Md. MHS; DAR.
Somerset Parish. Abs. of rec. Turner Geneal. Coll. Ms. MHS.
Turner Geneal. Coll. Ms. MHS.
William and Mary Quart., 1st series, v. 6, p. 94.
Wood, Charles Co. Rev. Joseph Hull (1595) and some of his descendants. Hull. 1904, p. 20. MHS.
***Wood,** Va. The Sun, Balto., Feb. 17, 24 (Va.), 1907.
Wood, Aaron. Revolutionary pension abs. Natl. Geneal. Soc. Quart., v. 24, p. 28.
Wood, Frederick William. Pedigree. (New Eng. rec., mostly Mass.) Soc. Col. Wars Md. Culver. 1940. MHS; DAR.
Wood, Henry. Pedigree. Soc. Col. Wars Md. Culver. 1940. MHS; DAR.
Wood, Henry H. D. A. R. Mag., v. 70, no. 6, pp. 573–74.
Wood, Henry Hobbs. Bible rec. Md. Geneal. Bull., v. 11, no. 2, p. 23. MHS; DAR.
Wood, Peter Bryson. Md. Soc., War of 1812, v. 1, no. 105. Ms. MHS.
Woodall. Bible rec. Upper Penins. East. Shore, p. 230–35. MHS.
Crumpton graveyard. Md. Geneal. Rec. Com., 1933–34, pp. 193–203. Mss. DAR.
See Moody-Woodall.
Woodard. Keene family. Jones. MHS; DAR.
Wooden. Segrave chart. MHS.
St. Paul's Parish, Balto. V. 1. Mss. MHS.

Woodford. Md. families. Culver. Ms. Personal list.
Woodland. Bible rec. Md. Geneal. Rec. Com., 1939–40, pp. 112–13. Mss. DAR.
Woodley. Woodleys of Isle of Wight Co., Va. James F. Crocker. (Md. ref.) Portsmouth, Va., Fiske's Printery and Bindery, 1914, pamph. MHS.
***Woodruff.** Jemmes Geneal. Coll. Ms. MHS.
Woodruff, Caldwell, Balto. de Forest (Walloon) family in Amer. Forest. Md. ref., v. 2, p. 281. MHS.
Pedigree. (Mostly Conn. rec.) Soc. Col. Wars Md. Culver. 1940. MHS; DAR.
Woodruff (George Egleston) Family. Chart. MHS.
Woodruff Family. Ms. MHS.
†**Woods.** Hist. of West. Md. Scharf. V. 1, p. 616. MHS; DAR.
Machen chart. MHS.
†Med. Annals Md. Cordell. 1903, p. 630. MHS.
†Men of mark in Md. Johnson. V. 2; v. 4. DAR; Enoch Pratt Lib.
Woodson. Cary Geneal. Coll. Ms. MHS.
*The Sun, Balto., Feb. 2, 1908.
See Bassett-Du Puy-Woodson.
***Woodville.** Pennington Papers. Ms. MHS.
Woodward. Amer. Clan Gregor Year Book, 1909–10, p. 60; 1913, p. 62. MHS; DAR.
Ances. rec. and portraits. Col. Dames of Amer., 1910, v. 1, pp. 81, 85, 87, 384, 638. MHS; DAR.
Anne Arundel Co. tombstone inscriptions. Ms. DAR.
Autobiography of Summerfield Baldwin. Pp. 49–55. MHS; DAR.
Sara R. Baldwin chart. MHS.
†Balto. Richardson and Bennett. 1871, p. 551. MHS; DAR.
Cary Geneal. Coll. Ms. MHS.
Christ P. E. Church cemetery, Cambridge. Steele. 1936. MHS; DAR.
Col. families of U. S. A. Mackenzie. V. 3, p. 457; v. 7, p. 254. MHS; DAR.
Darby geneal. Darby. MHS.
Dorsey chart. MHS.
Dundas-Hesseluis. P. 119. MHS.
*Founders of Anne Arundel and Howard Cos. Warfield. Pp. 63, 123–27. MHS; DAR.
Hamill chart. MHS.
*Hist. of Dorchester Co. Jones. 1925, p. 295. MHS; DAR.
Hist. graves of Md. and D. C. Ridgely. MHS.
Howard-Govane-Woodward-Law Bible rec. Ms. MHS.
Jackson family gathering. 1878.
Lineage Bks., Natl. Soc. of Daughters of Amer. Col., v. 4, p. 38. MHS; DAR.
Md. families. Culver. Ms. Personal list.
Monumental City. Howard. MHS; DAR.
See Mullikin-Anderson-Woodward Hall. DAR.
*Mullikin family Bible rec. Mss., in Binder. DAR.
Pedigree of Charles Gambrill Baldwin. Soc. Col. Wars Md. Culver. 1940. MHS; DAR.
See Phelps. Abr. Compend. Amer. Geneal. Virkus. V. 1, p. 636. DAR.
Prentice chart. MHS.
St. Paul's Parish, Balto. V. 1, 2. Mss. MHS.
*The Sun, Balto., June 7, 1908.
†Tercentenary hist. of Md. Andrews. V. 3, p. 598; v. 4, p. 838. MHS; DAR.
See Woodward-Brown-Warfield. Abr. Compend. Amer. Geneal. Virkus. V. 4, pp. 343–44. MHS.
*Woodward family of Md., Va., and Tenn. Arkansas Geneal. Rec. Com., 1937, v. 15, pp. 355–56. Typed, bd. DAR.
See Baldwin-Woodward.
See Young-Woodward-Hesselius.
Woodward, Wm. Amer. Armory and Blue Bk. Matthews. 1908, p. 131. DAR.
†Balto., hist. and Biog. Richardson and Bennett. 1871, pp. 551–53. MHS; DAR.
Woodyear. St. Paul's Parish, Balto. V. 2. Mss. MHS.
***Wooford-Whiteley.** Hist. of Dorchester Co. Jones. 1925, pp. 486–95. MHS; DAR.
Woolcott, John. First will filed in Chestertown, Kent Co. Will Book, no. 1, p. 1. M. H. Mag., 1936, v. 31, no. 3, p. 264.
Woolen. *See* Wollen.
Woolen, Dorchester Co. Mrs. James McHenry chart. MHS.
Woolens. Andrew's Scrap Book. MHS.
Wooleyhan. Griffin family. Streets. P. 213. MHS.
Wooleyhand. Holdens Cemetery, Kent Co. Md. Geneal. Rec. Com., 1932, v. 5, p. 211. Mss. DAR.
Woolf. Naturalizations in Md., 1666–1765; Laws. Bacon. MHS.
Woolford. Ances. rec. and portraits. Col. Dames of Amer., 1910, p. 63. MHS; DAR.
Christ P. E. Church cemetery, Cambridge. Steele. 1936. MHS; DAR.
Dorsey and allied families. Ms. MHS.
*Lineage Bk., Daughters of Amer. Col., v. 4, p. 66. MHS; DAR.
Marriages. Dorchester Co. marriages, 1781–1807. Md. Geneal. Rec. Com., v. 4, p. 80. DAR.
†Med. Annals Md. Cordell. 1903, pp. 630–31. MHS.
Old Somerset. Torrence. MHS; DAR.
Patriotic Md. Md. Soc. of S. A. R., 1930. MHS; DAR.
Primitive or Old School Bapt. Church cemetery, Milton. Md. O. R. Soc. Bull., no. 3, p. 54.
St. Paul's Parish, Balto. V. 2. Mss. MHS.
Somerset Co. Court Book. Tilghman. 1937. Ms. DAR.
†Tercentenary hist. of Md. Andrews. V. 2, p. 835; v. 4, p. 302. MHS; DAR.
See Thompson, Dorchester Co. Abr. Compend. Amer. Geneal. Virkus. V. 1, p. 857. DAR.
Tombs by river, Church Creek, Dorchester Co. Md. O. R. Soc. Bull., no. 3, pp. 62–63. MHS.
Tombstone rec. of Dorchester Co. Jones. DAR.
Trinity Church cemetery, Dorchester Co. Md. O. R. Soc. Bull., no. 3, pp. 42–52.
Trinity Church burial ground, near Cambridge, Md. Md. Geneal. Rec. Com., 1937–38, pp. 93–104. Mss. DAR.
Young Bible rec. Ms. MHS.
Whiteley chart. MHS.
See Brooks-Woolford.
Woolford, Roger, Dorchester Co. Pedigree of Maurice Edward Skinner. Soc. Col. Wars Md. Culver. 1940. MHS; DAR.

†**Woolford-Whiteley.** Hist. of Dorchester Co. Jones. 1902, p. 398; revised, 1925, pp. 486–95. MHS; DAR.
***Woolford** or **Woolsford.** Hist. Dorchester Co. Jones. 1902. MHS; DAR.
†**Woolsey.** Portraits and biog. rec. of Harford and Cecil Cos. 1897. P. 198. MHS; DAR.
Woolsford. Portrait and biog. rec. of East. Shore of Md. 1898, pp. 542, 599, 882. MHS; DAR.
See Woolford.
***Wooten.** Ga. Geneal. Rec. Com. (in its family, church and court rec.), 1931, pp. 73–78. Typed, bd. DAR.
Somerset Co. Court Book. Tilghman. 1937. Ms. DAR.
†**Wooton.** Med. Annals Md. Cordell. 1903, p. 631. MHS.
Wootton. Col. families of U. S. A. Mackenzie. V. 2. MHS; DAR.
Work, Pa. Carey chart. MHS.
***Working.** Frederick Co. families. Markell. Ms. Personal list.
Worland. Centenary of Catholicity in Ky. Webb. 1884. MHS.
Worley. *See* Wirley.
Wormesley. Selden chart. MHS.
Worrel. St. Thomas' Parish, Balto. Co. Bd. ms. MHS. Also: Md. Geneal. Rec. Com., 1937, pp. 109–82. Mss. DAR.
†**Worrell.** Med. Annals Md. Cordell. 1903, pp. 631–32. MHS.
*Old Kent. Hanson. Pp. 164, 369. MHS; DAR.
Worthen, N. H. Bible rec. Md. Geneal. Rec. Com., 1930–31, v. 4, p. 8. DAR.
Worthington. Abr. Compend. Amer. Geneal. Virkus. V. 6, p. 36. DAR.
Amer. Armory and Blue Book. Matthews. 1911–12, p. 298.
Amer. of gentle birth, and their ancestors. Pittman. V. 1, pp. 392–93. MHS; DAR.
Ances. rec. and portraits. Col. Dames of Amer., 1910, v. 1, p. 252. MHS; DAR.
See Anderson. Abr. Compend. Amer. Geneal. Virkus. V. 1, p. 421. DAR.
Anne Arundel Co. tombstone inscriptions. Ms. DAR.
Balto. Herald, May 3, 1903. Newsp. clipp. MHS.
Barroll in Great Britain and Amer. Barroll. P. 102. MHS.
Bowies and their kindred. Bowie. MHS; DAR.
Britton Scrap Book. V. 1, 2. Ms. MHS.
*Burke's landed gentry. 1939. MHS.
See Carruth. Abr. Compend. Amer. Geneal. Virkus. V. 1, p. 540. DAR.
Chart, photos., 2 sheets. Cary Geneal. Coll. Ms. MHS.
Col. mansions of Md. and Del. Hammond. 1914. MHS.
Col. families of Amer. Lawrence. V. 2, p. 43; v. 3, p. 305; v. 5, pp. 287–301; v. 16, p.94. MHS.
Col. families of U. S. A. Mackenzie. V. 7, p. 60. MHS; DAR.
Descent of Lottie Repp Caldwell, from William the Conqueror. D. C. Geneal. Rec. Com., v. 34, pp. 30–33. Typed, bd. DAR.
Dorsey and allied families. Ms. MHS.
*Dorsey chart. Brown. MHS.
Dorsey chart. Lib. Cong.; MHS.
*Early comers to the Province. Georgians in Anne Arundel Co. Atlanta Jour., Sept. 22, 1906. Newsp. clipp. File case, MHS.
"Fairview," home of Gov. Oden Bowie, near Bowie, Prince George Co. Private burying ground, 1745–1904. Ms. MHS; DAR.
Ford and other lines. Md. Geneal. Rec. Com., 1932–33, pp. 7–20. Mss. DAR.
*Founders of Anne Arundel and Howard Cos. Warfield. Pp. 145–56, 319, 369, 525. MHS; DAR.
*Garrison Church. Allen. Pp. 147–50. MHS; DAR.
*Geneal. of family of Samuel Worthington, Balto. Co., 1734–1870. Md. Geneal. Rec. Com., 1934. DAR.
Griffith geneal. Griffith. MHS; DAR.
Harford Co. Hist. Soc. Mss. Coll. JHU.
†Hist. of Balto. City and Co. Scharf. Pp. 832, 862, 864. MHS.
†Hist. of Frederick Co. Williams. V. 1, pp. 166, 169, 596; v. 2, p. 728. MHS; DAR.
*Hoods-Worthington-Owings. Ms. MHS.
Hopkins chart. MHS.
Howard-Montague-Warfield geneal. chart. Culver and Marye. MHS.
Jenkins-Courtney chart. MHS.
Md. families. Culver. Ms. Personal list.
†Med. Annals Md. Cordell. 1903, pp. 632–33. MHS.
Merryman family. Culver. M. H. Mag., 1915, v. 10, pp. 176, 286.
Mt. Paran Pres. churchyard, Harrisonville, Balto. Co. Typed ms. MHS; DAR.
Patriotic Md. Md. Soc. of S. A. R., 1930. MHS; DAR.
Pedigree of Gustavus Warfield Evans. Soc. Col. Wars Md. Culver. 1940. MHS; DAR.
Pedigree of Edward Hambleton. Soc. Col. Wars Md. Culver. 1940. MHS; DAR.
Pedigree of Charles Worthington Hoff. Soc. Col. Wars Md. Culver. 1940. MHS; DAR.
Pedigree of Howard Hall Macy Lee. Soc. Col. Wars Md. Culver. 1940. MHS; DAR.
Pedigree of Tilghman Goldsborough Pitts. Soc. Col. Wars Md. Culver. 1940. MHS; DAR.
Pedigree of Townsend Scott, IV. Soc. Col. Wars Md. Culver. 1940. MHS; DAR.
Pedigree of Levin Gale Shreve. Soc. Col. Wars Md. Culver. 1940. MHS; DAR.
Pedigree of John Ogle Warfield, Jr. Soc. Col. Wars Md. Culver. 1940. MHS; DAR.
Pedigree of Andrew Jackson Young, Jr. Soc. Col. Wars Md. Culver. 1940. MHS; DAR.
Portrait and biog. rec. of East. Shore of Md. 1898, p. 912. MHS; DAR.
(30 rec.) St. Paul's Parish, Balto. V. 1, 2, 3. Mss. MHS.
St. Thomas' Parish, Balto. Co. Bd. ms. MHS. Also: Md. Geneal. Rec. Com., 1937, pp. 109–82. Mss. DAR.
Sarah Smith Hood Bible rec. Ms. MHS.
Sidelights on Md. hist. Richardson. V. 2, p. 255. MHS; DAR.
*The Day, Jan. 25, 1883. Scrap Book. MHS.
*The Sun, Balto., Dec. 20, 1903.
The Times, Balto., Jan. 3, 10, 24, 1886. Newsp. clipp. MHS.
Wallis chart. MHS.
Warfields of Md. Warfield. MHS.

Worthington. Worthington-Plaskitt families. J. Plaskitt Lamar. Pamph. with other Balto. families and additional ms. data. 1886. MHS.
See Andrews, Mo. Abr. Compend. Amer. Geneal. Virkus. V. 4, p. 543. MHS.
See Chew-Thomas-Worthington.
See Gosnell-O'Dell-Towson-Worthington.
See Hood-Worthington-Owings.
See Nelson-Worthington.
**See* John Calvin Wright.
Worthington, "Summer Hill," Crownsville, Anne Arundel Co. Graveyard, 1782-1853. Md. O. R. Soc. Bull., no. 1, p. 52.
Worthington, Edward. And his kin. MHS.
Worthington, Mrs. Ellicott (Katherine Graham Frick). Chart. Col. Dames, Chap. I. MHS.
Mrs. Henry Barton Jacobs chart. MHS.
Worthington, John. Bible rec. Ms. MHS.
Worthington, John, Balto. Co. The Day, Annapolis, Jan. 25, 1883.
Worthington, Capt. John. And his descendants. The Day, Annapolis, Jan. 29, 1883.
Worthington, R. Walker. Md. Soc., War of 1812, no. 289. Ms. MHS.
Worthington, Richard Walker. Pedigree. Soc. Col. Wars Md. Culver. 1904. MHS; DAR.
Worthington, Samuel, Balto. Co. Geneal., 1734-1815. Md. Geneal. Rec. Com., 1933-34, pp. 255-56. Mss. DAR.
Worthington, Thomas. Old N. W. Geneal. Soc. Quart., Columbus, Ohio, 1902, v. 5;1903, v. 6. MHS.
Worthington, Thomas Chew. Pedigree. Soc. Col. Wars Md. Culver. 1940. MHS; DAR.
Worthington, Thomas Chew, M.D. Md. Soc., War of 1812, v. 3, no. 288. Ms. MHS.
Worthington, Thomas Chew, III. Md. Soc., War of 1812, v. 4, no. 301. Ms. MHS.
***Worthington Family.** Anne Arundel Co. gentry. Newman. Pp. 309-46. MHS; DAR.
*Arch. of Georgetown Univ., Wash., D. C., v. 287.
Bible rec., 1811-49. D. C. Geneal. Rec. Com., v. 31, pp. 110-11. Typed, bd. DAR.
Md. Geneal. Rec. Com., 1933-34, pp. 27, 92-100. Mss. DAR.
*The Times, Jan. 3, 1886. MHS.
Worthington Line. Col. and Revolutionary lineages of Amer. 1939, v. 1, p. 287. MHS.
Worthington-Bowie. Bible rec. D. C. Geneal. Rec. Com., v. 31, pt. 1, pp. 82-87. Typed, bd. DAR.
Worthington-Wilson. Marriage certificate, 1769; and list of witnesses (33). Hist. of Harford Co. Preston. P. 273.
Wotton. Pedigree of Richard Walker Worthington. Soc. Col. Wars Md. Culver. 1940. MHS; DAR.
***Wotton,** Baltimore, Montgomery and Prince George Cos. The Sun, Balto., May 12, 19, 26, June 2, 1907.
***Wragg.** Pennington Papers. Ms. MHS.
Wrenn, Mrs. Harold Holmes (Elizabeth Cheney Jencks). Chart. Col. Dames, Chap. I. MHS.
Wright. Barroll chart. MHS.
†Bench and bar of Md. Sams and Riley. 1901, v. 1, p. 275. Lib. Cong; MHS; Peabody Lib.
Carbach-Wright. Ms. File case, DAR.
Cary Geneal. Coll. Ms. MHS.
†Chesapeake Bay Country. Earle. Pp. 338, 343. MHS.
Col. families of Amer. Lawrence. V. 3, p. 296. MHS.
Col. families of East. Shore and their descendants. Emory. 1900. MHS.
Col. mansions of Md. and Del. Hammond. 1914. MHS.
Dobbin chart. MHS.
Eldridge chart. MHS.
*Frederick Co. families. Markell. Ms. Personal list.
†Governors of Md. Buchholz. P. 64. MHS.
Griffith geneal. Griffith. MHS; DAR.
Hagerstown tombstone inscriptions. Gruder. Natl. Geneal. Soc. Quart., 1919, v. 8, nos. 1, 2.
Hist. Salisbury Wicomico Co. Truitt. P. 11. DAR.
Hopper family chart. Skirven. MHS.
Mrs. H. F. Johnston chart. MHS.
Md. families. Culver. Ms. Personal list.
†Med. Annals Md. Cordell. 1903, p. 633. MHS.
Patriotic Md. Md. Soc. of S. A. R., 1930. MHS; DAR.
Pattison wills. Md. Geneal. Rec. Com., 1929, pp. 7-42; 1930-31. Mss. DAR.
*Pennington Papers. Ms. MHS.
Pedigree of Nicholas Leeke Dashiell. Soc. Col. Wars Md. Culver. 1940. MHS; DAR.
Pedigree of Mark Alexander Herbert Smith. Soc. Col. Wars Md. Culver. 1940. MHS; DAR.
Rumsey-Smithson Bible rec. Md. Geneal. Rec. Com., 1932-33, v. 5, pp. 63-142. DAR.
Rumsey-Smithson family rec. bk. Md. Geneal. Rec. Com., 1932, pp. 63-158. DAR.
(46 rec.) St. Paul's Parish, Balto. V. 1, 4. Mss. MHS.
St. Stephens Parish, Cecilton, Md. MHS; DAR.
Smithsons of Harford Co. Md. Geneal. Rec. Com., 1932-33, pp. 152. Mss. DAR.
Somerset Co. Court Book. Tilghman. 1937. Ms. DAR.
Mrs. E. C. Venable chart. MHS.
*Wicomico Co. families. Tilghman. Ms., p. 124. DAR.
*Wright ancestry in Caroline, Dorchester, Somerset and Wicomico Cos. C. W. Wright. Balto. Baltimore City Printing and Bookbinding Co., 1907. MHS; DAR.
Peter Wright and Mary Anderson; family rec. Ernest Neall Wright. Ann Arbor, Mich., 1939, 135 pp. MHS.
Richard Wright, gentleman of London, Eng., and Northumberland Co., Va., 1655, and some descendants. Tyler's Quart. Mag., v. 1. (Md. connections, pp. 127-41, 177.)
See Addams-Robertson-Wright.
See Ball-Mahan-Pullen-Wright.
See Callahan-Lednum-Willis-Wright.
See Washington-Wright.
Wright, Anne Arundel Co. Mrs. C. L. Riggs chart. MHS.
Posey chart. MHS.
Wright, Queen Anne Co. Abr. Compend. Amer. Geneal. Virkus. V. 1, p. 623. DAR.
Wright, Somerset Co. Bible rec. of Dorchester and Somerset Cos. and Del. Pp. 92-93. DAR.
Wright, G. Mitchell. Md. Soc., War of 1812, v. 3, no. 231. Ms. MHS.

Wright, Miss Grace Eyre. Chart. Col. Dames, Chap. I. MHS.
***Wright, Henry De Courcy.** Burke's landed gentry. 1939. MHS.
Wright, J. R. Md. Soc., War of 1812, v. 1, no. 3. Ms. MHS.
***Wright, John Calvin.** Burke's landed gentry. 1939. MHS.
†**Wright, Riley E.** Men of mark in Md. Johnson. V. 3. DAR; Enoch Pratt Lib.
Wright, Gov. Robert. Founders of Anne Arundel and Howard Cos. Warfield. P. 253. MHS; DAR.
†Hist. of Md. Scharf. V. 2, p. 622. MHS.
Wright, Solomon, Queen Anne's Co. W. A. and S. W. Merritt pedigree charts. Soc. Col. Wars, Md. Johnston. 1905, pp. 68, 158. MHS.
***Wright Family.** Wilson Mss. Coll., no. 10; no. 36; no. 74; no. 81. MHS.
Wright Line. Col. and Revolutionary lineages of Amer., 1939, v. 3, pp. 232–35. MHS.
Geneal. and mem. encyc. of Md. Spencer. V. 2, p. 596. MHS; DAR.
Wright-Thom Line. Geneal. and memorial encyc. of Md. Spencer. V. 2, p. 596. MHS; DAR.
Wrights, N. J. Md. Geneal. Rec. Com., 1937. DAR.
Wrightson. Lambdin chart. MHS.
Wrightson, Talbot Co. H. Mullikin pedigree charts, plate 2. Soc. Col. Wars, Md. Johnston. 1905, p. 75. MHS.
Wroth. Md. Geneal. Rec. Com., 1934–35, p. 187. Mss. DAR.
†Med. Annals. Md. Cordell. 1903, pp. 510, 633–34. MHS.
St. Stephens Parish, Cecilton, Md. MHS; DAR.
Tombstone inscriptions, 1786–1836 (5 stones), near Chestertown. Md. Geneal. Rec. Com., 1938–39, p. 134. Mss. DAR.
See Baker-Reed-Young-Wroth.
See Page-Wickes-Wroth.
***Wroth Family.** Hist. of Cecil Co. Johnston. P. 243. MHS; DAR.
*Old Kent. Hanson. Pp. 199–202. MHS; DAR.
Wroton. Tombstone rec. of Dorchester Co. Jones. DAR.
Wuerschmidt. Southern Bapt. Church cemetery, Worcester Co. Md. Geneal. Rec. Com., 1937, Mrs. Lines. Mss. DAR.
Wyandt. Brief hist. of Andrew Putman, Christian Wyandt and Adam Snyder, Wash Co. E. C. Wyand. Hagerstown, Book-binding and Publishing Co., 1909.
*Putman family. MHS.
See Putman-Wyandt-Snyder.
Wyatt. Balto., its hist., its people. Hall. V. 3, p. 780. MHS; DAR.
Brooks chart. MHS.
Dorsey and allied families. Ms. MHS.
Hist. of Caroline Co., Va. Wingfield.
Lineage Bks., Natl. Soc. of Daughters of Amer. Col., v. 2, p. 298. MHS; DAR.
Md. families. Culver. Ms. Personal list.
†Memorial of Rev. William Edward Wyatt, D.D., rector of St. Paul's Church, Balto. (Born in Nova Scotia, 1789; died 1864.) Pub. by Vestry. Balto., John D. Toy, 1864, pamph. Enoch Pratt Lib.
†Men of mark in Md. Johnson. V. 1. DAR; Enoch Pratt Lib.
St. Paul's Parish, Balto. V. 2, 3, 4. Mss. MHS.
*The Sun, Balto., April 16, 1905.
Wyatt family of Balto. James Bosley Noel Wyatt. 1920, bklet. MHS.
See Dorsey-Wyatt.
†**Wyatt, Rev. Wm. E.** (born in Nova Scotia 1789; died 1864). Balto., hist. and biog. Richardson and Bennett. 1871, pp. 555–58. MHS; DAR.
***Wyatt Family.** Anne Arundel Co. gentry. Newman. P. 347. MHS; DAR.
Geneal.; Richard Wyatt Line, Md. to Tenn. Ms. MHS.
***Wyatt, Richard, Line.** Geneal. MHS.
***Wyatt, Nicholas-Dorsey, Edw.** Notes, from land rec. N. B. Nimmo. M. H. Mag., 1937, v. 32, pp. 47–51.
†**Wylie, D. M.** Geneal. and mem. encyc. of Md. Spencer. V. 2, p. 462. MHS; DAR.
Wyman Line. Balto., its hist., its people. Hall. V. 2, p. 295. MHS; DAR.
Clark chart. MHS.
Manly chart. MHS.
Mrs. H. De Courcy Wright Thom chart. MHS.
Wynants. *See* Winans.
†**Wynne.** Bench and bar of Md. Sams and Riley. 1901, v. 1, p. 80. Lib. Cong; MHS; Peabody Lib.
Pedigree of Coleman Randall Freeman. Soc. Col. Wars Md. Culver. 1940. MHS; DAR.
Wynnes. *See* Gwynn.
†**Wyse.** Med. Annals Md. Cordell. 1903, p. 634. MHS.
Wysham. St. Paul's Parish, Balto., V. 2, 3. Mss. MHS.
†**Wywill.** Med. Annals Md. Cordell. 1903, p. 635. MHS.

Y

Yager. Mt. Olivet Cemetery, Frederick. Md. Geneal. Rec. Com., 1934–35, p. 111. Mss. DAR.
Yalding. Somerset Co. Court Book. Tilghman. 1937. Ms. DAR.
Yardley. Cary Geneal. Coll. Ms. MHS.
See Yeardley.
Yardley Line. Turner family. Forman. Pp. 55, 68–70. MHS.
Yardley, Yeardley. Daughter of Md.; Mother of Texas. Bell. MHS; DAR.
Yarnall. White Geneal. Tree. MHS.
Yarnall, Pa. Dobbin chart. MHS.
***Yate Family.** Anne Arundel Co. gentry. Newman. Pp. 528–30. MHS; DAR.
Yates. Ances. rec. and portraits. Col. Dames of Amer., 1910, v. 2, p. 697. MHS; DAR.
Barber, "Luckland," St. Mary's Co. Bible rec. Natl. Geneal. Soc. Quart., v. 22, no. 4, pp. 89–92.
See Blue family. 24 mss. File case, DAR.
Mrs. D. G. Lovell chart. MHS.
Md. tombstone rec. Md. Geneal. Rec. Com., 1937, Parran, v. 9. Mss. DAR.
Ellen Emmerich Mears. Col. and Revolutionary families of Phila. Jordan. 1933, v. 1, pp. 412–15.
Patriotic Md. Md. Soc. of S. A. R., 1930. MHS; DAR.

Yates. Plummer family. A. P. H. Ms. MHS.
St. Paul's Parish, Balto. V. 1, 2. Mss. MHS.
Stirling chart. MHS.
Mrs. J. P. Thom chart. MHS.
Warfields of Md. Warfield. P. 65. MHS.

Yeakle, Yegley. Hagerstown tombstone inscriptions. Gruder. Natl. Geneal. Soc. Quart., 1919, v. 8, nos. 1, 2.

***Yeamans.** Pennington Papers. Ms. MHS.

***Yeardley.** Mrs. Charles Howard chart. Col. Dames Amer., Chap. I. MHS.
Mrs. Wm. L. Watson chart. MHS.
See Yardley.

Yeardley, Va. Pedigree of Gustav Wm. Lurman. Soc. Col. Wars Md. Culver. 1940. MHS; DAR.
Pedigree of James Donnell Tilghman. Soc. Col. Wars Md. Culver. 1940. MHS; DAR.
*The Sun, Balto., April 15, 22, 29, 1906.

***Yeardley-Scarborough-West.** The Sun, Balto., March 26, 1905.

Yeardley, Yardley. Sir George and temperance; Lady Yeardley; and some descendants, Bowdoin, Donnell, Gilmor, Handy, Hoffman, Lurman, Stewart, Teackle, Upshur, Winder and others. Thomas T. Uupshur. Amer. Hist. Mag., Nashville, Tenn., 1896, v. 1, pp. 339–74. MHS.

Yeates. Ames Geneal. Coll. Ms. MHS.
Descendants of Joran Kyn. Pa. Mag., v. 5, p. 334.
†Med. Annals. Md. Cordell. 1903, p. 635. MHS.
Shrewsbury churchyard, Kent Co. Md. O. R. Soc., v. 2, pp. 46–54. MHS.

Yeates, Col. Donaldson (Col. 27 Battalion, Md. Militia, 1778). Buried in Shrewsbury cemetery. Md. Geneal. Rec. Com., 1933–34, p. 232. Mss. DAR.

Yeatman. Marriages in Va. and Ky. D. A. R Mag., July, 1932, v. 66, no. 7, pp. 462–63.
Marriages in Va., Md. and D. C. Ms. MHS.
*Yeatmans in Amer. Pamph. DAR.

Yeatman-Peale. Amer. of gentle birth, and their ancestors. Pittman. V. 1, pp. 374–76. MHS; DAR.

Yegley. *See* Yeakle.

Yellott. Balto., its hist., its people. Hall. V. 3. MHS; DAR.
Col. families of U. S. A. Mackenzie. V. 1, p. 366; v. 2, p. 610. MHS; DAR.
Descendants of Valentine Hollingsworth, Sr. Stewart. MHS; DAR.
†Hist. of Balto. City and Co. Scharf. P. 906. MHS.
Maulsby family in Amer. Barnard. DAR; Peabody Lib.
Pedigree of Thomas Murray Maynadier. Soc. Col. Wars Md. Culver. 1940 MHS; DAR.
(19 stones, 1787–1937.) Trinity P. E. churchyard, Long Green. Typed ms. MHS; DAR.

†Yellott, Coleman. Men of mark in Md. Johnson. V. 4. DAR; Enoch Pratt Lib.

†Yellott, John I. Men of mark in Md. Johnson. V. 2. DAR; Enoch Pratt Lib.

†Yellott, Robt. E. Lee. Men of mark in Md. Johnson. V. 4. DAR; Enoch Pratt Lib.

Yeo. Selden chart. MHS.

Yerkes. Memorials of Reading, Howell, Yerkes, Watts, Latham and Elkins families. Leach.

Yieldhall. St. Paul's Parish, Balto. V. 2. Mss. MHS.

***Yingling.** Hornberger-Menges-Rahn-Yingling families. C. J. Rahn. 1930. MHS.
Rahn and allied families. Ms. MHS.
See Hornberger-Menges-Rahn-Yingling.

Yoe. See Henderson. Abr. Compend. Amer. Geneal. Virkus. V. 4, p. 575. MHS.

Yonson. Frederick Co. tombstone inscriptions. Gruder. Natl. Geneal. Soc. Quart., 1919, v. 8, nos. 1, 2.
Zion Reformed Church, Hagerstown. Md. Geneal. Rec. Com., 1934–35. Mss. DAR.

Yopp. Lambdin chart. MHS.

***Yost.** Frederick Co. families. Markell. Ms. Personal list.

Yost Family. Hist., 1712–1821; geneal. comp., 1924. Md. Geneal. Rec. Com., 1932–33, pp. 349–67. Mss. DAR.

Youle. St. Paul's Parish, Balto. V. 1. Mss. MHS.

Young. Ancestral beginnings in Amer. of McGregor, Magruder, Beall, Price, Phillips, Bland, McKisick, Young and related families. Caroline B. Price. 1928. DAR.
Balto., its hist., its people. Hall. V. 3. MHS; DAR.
Beall and Bell families. Beall. MHS; DAR.
*Bible rec., 1791–1900. Ms. MHS.
Bible rec. Ms. MHS.
Bible rec. Upper Penins. East. Shore, p. 115–20. MHS; DAR.
Children of Alex P. and M. C. Hill. Ms. MHS.
*Frederick Co. families. Markell. Ms. Personal list.
Geneal. and memorial encyc. of Md. Spencer. V. 2, p. 653. MHS; DAR.
Griffith geneal. Griffith. MHS; DAR.
Hist. graves of Md. and D. C. Ridgely. MHS.
†Hist. of Frederick Co. Williams. V. 2, pp. 707, 744, 931, 1120, 1331, 1590. MHS; DAR.
†Hist. of West. Md. Scharf. V. 2, p. 915. MHS; DAR.
Mansion and family of Notley Young. Rec. Columbia Hist. Soc., v. 16, pp. 1–24. (P. 23 contains Carroll and Notley chart.)
†Med. Annals Md. Cordell. 1903, pp. 635–36. MHS.
Mt. Carmel burial ground, Unity, Montgomery Co. Md. Geneal. Rec. Com., 1934–35, p. 85. Mss. DAR.
Mt. Olivet Cemetery, Frederick. Md. Geneal. Rec. Com., 1934–35, p. 111. Mss. DAR.
Naturalizations in Md., 1666–1765; Laws. Bacon. MHS.
Old cemetery, Denton, Caroline Co. Md. Geneal. Rec. Com., 1935–36, p. 168. Mss. DAR.
Patriotic Md. Md. Soc. of S. A. R., 1930. MHS; DAR.
Rec., Kent Co. Md. Geneal. Rec. Com., 1934–35, p. 178. Mss. DAR.
Rienhoff chart. MHS.
(96 rec.) St. Paul's Parish, Balto. V. 1, 3, 4. Mss. MHS.
St. Stephens Parish, Cecilton, Md. MHS; DAR.
Va. Mag. Hist. and Biog., v. 19, p. 95–100.
*Wicomico Co. families. Tilghman. Ms., p. 97. DAR.
Williamson Bible rec. Ms. MHS.
See Baker-Reed-Young-Wroth.

Young, Montgomery Co. Talbott of "Poplar Knowle." Shirk. MHS; DAR.

†**Young**, Pa. Hist. of Balto. City and Co. Scharf. P. 442. MHS.
Young, Andrew Jackson, Jr. Pedigree. Soc. Col. Wars Md. Culver. 1940. MHS; DAR.
Young, Arthur. Lukens chart. MHS.
Young, Charles Mervyn. Pedigree. (Mostly N. Y. and Conn. rec.). Soc. Col. Wars Md. Culver. 1940. MHS; DAR.
***Young, D. Eldred.** Geneal. and mem. encyc. of Md. Spencer. V. 2, pp. 653–58. MHS; DAR.
Young, Howard Edw. Md. Soc., War of 1812, v. 4, no. 346. Ms. MHS.
Young, Hugh. A Surgeon's Autobiography, with over 100 drawings by William P. Didusch and three color prints. Harcourt, Brace and Co. N. Y. 1940.
Young, James. Balto. actor. 14 personal scrap books. Enoch Pratt Lib.
†**Young, James P.** Men of mark in Md. Johnson. V. 3. DAR; Enoch Pratt Lib.
***Young, Notley.** Patriots of Revolutionary period interred in D. C. Balch. Rec. of Columbia Hist. Soc., v. 19, v. 20.
Young, Wm., Balto. D. A. R. Mag., v. 67, no. 2, p. 115.
Young-Woodward-Hesselius Family. Rec., 1737–1820. Photos. MHS.
Rec., 1737–1820. M. H. Mag., 1926, v. 21, no. 3, pp. 277–79.
Younker. Md. tombstone rec. Md. Geneal. Rec. Com., 1937, Parran, p. 24. Mss. DAR.
***Yountz.** Frederick Co. families. Markell. Ms. Personal list.
Yule. Bible rec. New Eng. Hist. and Geneal. Reg., v. 88, p. 92.

Z

Zacharias. Pa. geneal. Egle. P. 262. MHS.
Zackary. Trinity P. E. churchyard, St. Mary's City. Md. O. R. Soc. Bull., no. 3, p. 59.
Zealer. *See* Zieler.
Zehner. Catonsville pioneers of Luth. faith. Natl. Geneal. Soc. Quart., v. 9, no. 2, p. 29.
Zeigler. Tercentenary Hist. of Md. Andrews. V. 2, p. 129. MHS; DAR.
Zeigler, Washington Co. Md. Geneal. Bull., V. 3, p. 2. MHS; DAR.
Zell. Hist. of Washington Co. Williams. P. 589. MHS; DAR.
Tercentenary hist. of Md. Andrews. V. 3, p. 337. MHS; DAR.
Zeller. Hist. of Allegany Co. Thomas and Williams. V. 2, pp. 1201–02. MHS; DAR.
Hist. of West. Md. Scharf. V. 2, p. 1238. MHS; DAR.
†Med. Annals Md. Cordell. 1903, p. 636. MHS.
†Hist. of printing in Col. Md. Wroth. MHS.
Naturalizations in Md., 1666–1765; Laws. Bacon. MHS.
Zent Family. Carrollton Manor. Grove. 1921, p. 217. DAR.
Hist. of Frederick Co. Williams. V. 2, pp. 705–07, 918, 1457. MHS; DAR.
Md. Geneal. Rec. Com., 1930–31, v. 4, p. 11. DAR.
Zentz. Biggs family. Ms. DAR.
Zerbee Family. Tercentenary hist. of Md. Andrews. V. 2, p. 533. MHS; DAR.
Zermerman. *See* Zimmerman.
Ziegler. Md. Geneal. Bull., v. 3, p. 2. MHS; DAR.
See Zigler.
Zieler, Zealer. Frederick Co. tombstone inscriptions. Gruder. Natl. Geneal. Soc. Quart., 1919, v. 8, nos. 1, 2.
Zigler, Ziegler. St. Paul's Parish, Balto. V. 2, 4. Mss. MHS.
Zihlman Family. Hist. of Allegany Co. Thomas and Williams. V. 2, p. 738. MHS; DAR.
Zilch. Hist. of Allegany Co. Thomas and Williams. V. 2, pp. 1088–89. MHS; DAR.
Zillafrow, Zillefroe, Zillephro. St. Stephens Parish, Cecilton, Md. MHS; DAR.
Zillefroe. *See* Zillafrow.
Zillephro. *See* Zillafrow.
Zimmerly. Hist. of Allegany Co. Thomas and Williams. V. 2, p. 1203. MHS; DAR.
Zimmerman. Carrollton Manor. Grove. 1921, p. 94. DAR.
Clasping hands with generations past. Lloyd. MHS; DAR.
*Zimmerman-Edmonstone-Brooke. Lineage Bk., Daughters of Amer. Col., v. 5, p. 434. MHS; DAR.
Hist. of Carrollton Manor, Frederick Co. Grove. 1928, p. 124. DAR.
†Hist. of Frederick Co. Williams. V. 1, p. 596; v. 2, pp. 703, 724, 881, 934, 979, 997, 1002, 1042, 1089, 1163, 1167, 1190, 1198, 1294, 1401, 1406, 1409, 1411, 1496, 1567, 1586. MHS; DAR.
Hist. of Shriver family. Shriver. P. 66. MHS.
Hist. sketch of P. F. Eichelberger. Eichelberger.
Lineage Bks., Natl. Soc. of Daughters of Amer. Col., v. 4, p. 85. MHS; DAR.
*Pennington Papers. Ms. MHS.
Portrait and biog. rec., Sixth Cong. Dist. of Md., 1898, pp. 355, 451, 479, 787. MHS; DAR.
†Reminiscences after thirty years in ministry. L M. Zimmerman. (Born near Manchester, Carroll Co., 1860.) Balto., Myer & Thalheimer, 1917. Enoch Pratt Lib.
*Semmes Geneal. Coll. Ms. MHS.
Tercentenary hist. of Md. Andrews. V. 2, pp. 118, 832. MHS; DAR.
†**Zimmerman, Leander M.** Men of mark in Md. Johnson. V. 4. DAR; Enoch Pratt Lib.
†**Zimmerman, L. Seymour.** Men of mark in Md. Johnson. V. 3. DAR; Enoch Pratt Lib.
Zimmerman Family. Clasping hands with generations past. Emma Rouse Lloyd. Binder's title, Rouse family. Pp. 41–57. DAR.
*Wilson Mss. Coll., no. 21; no. 79; no. 126. MHS.
Zimmerman-Davis. Day Star. Newsp. clipp. MHS.
***Zimmerman-Waters.** Zimmerman-Waters and allied families. E. Zimmerman Allen. 1910. MHS; DAR.
Zimmerman, Zermerman. Frederick Co. tombstone inscriptions. Gruder. Natl. Geneal. Soc. Quart., 1919, v. 8, nos. 1, 2.
Zoller. Chart of Com. John Rodgers. DAR.
*Zoller-Anderson-Christie. Lineage Bk., Daughters of Amer. Col., v. 2, p. 187. MHS; DAR.

Zoller-Hall-Anderson-Christie. Lineage Bks., Natl. Soc. of Daughters of Amer. Col., v. 2, p. 187. MHS; DAR.

Zollickoffer. Graves, Uniontown Cemetery, Carroll Co. Hist. of West. Md. Scharf. V. 2, p. 859.

Griffith geneal. Griffith. MHS; DAR.

†Med. Annals Md. Cordell. 1903, p. 637. MHS.

Zollikofer. Chart. Cary Geneal. Coll. Ms. MHS.

Zollinger. Tercentenary hist. of Md. Andrews. V. 4, p. 415. MHS; DAR.

Zook. *See* Zug.

Zouch. Sir John Zouch and his descendants. Va. Mag. Hist. and Biog., v. 12, pp. 429–32.

***Zug.** Bible rec., Pa. and Md., 1760–1836. Natl. Geneal. Soc. Quart., Sept., 1937, v. 25, no. 3, p. 93.

Zug (Zook)-Wolf Family, Pa. and Md. Natl. Geneal. Soc. Quart., v. 25, no. 3, p. 93.

BIBLIOGRAPHY

* Genealogy. † Biography. ‡ History.

STATE RECORDS—GENERAL

Archives of Maryland. Published by authority of State, under direction of Maryland Historical Society; J. Hall Pleasants, editor; Louis Dow Scisco, assistant editor. Balto., 1883, v. 1.

Archives of Maryland, 1682–1785. Large portfolio, no. 87, copied by David Ridgely. Papers relative to Indian affairs, Pennsylvania boundary, government of Province, the currency, the Councils of Safety and Committees of Observation and various letters. 1 vol. Mss. Hall of Records.

Balance books, 1751–76. 7 vols.; index, 1 vol.; also 68 boxes of papers. Hall of Records.

Baltimore and Harford Tunrpike Company, 1816–1937. Various gaps; minutes; 1 ledger. MHS,

Baltimore and York Town Turnpike Road, 1807–13. 1861–1909. Minutes; Lists of 150 original subscribers to Company; 2 ledgers. MHS.

Board of Revenue, 1768–75. 1 vol. Hall of Records.

Calvert Papers, about 1000 documents, covering colonial period. (Original mss.) MHS.

Calender published in Proprietary Record Book, v. 1, p. 57. MHS.

Chapter 1. The Charter, 1632, and related papers.

Chapter 2. Colonization and plantation, 1633–1764.

Chapter 3. Government; proclamations, 1658–1729/30; orders, 1638–1756; commissions, 1753–61; Council records, 1638–1756; Assembly records, Upper House, 1717–62; Lower House, 1716–63; laws, 1638/9–1739.

Chapter 4. Land records, grants, etc., 1633–1754. (Original holders of land; dates of arrival and members of households.)

Chapter 5. Court records, wills, 1632–1770.

Chapter 6. Account books and related papers. Accounts of Lord Baltimore's revenues, 1731–61; papers (rent rolls, 1639–1725; debt books); letters (Land Office accounts, 1731, 1735–36, 1748, 1751–52, 1754–57, 1760–61; 11 vols.); Accounts of quit rents, 1753–61; earliest and latest dates of land grants (40 papers.); Eastern Shore quit rents, 1749–53, 1759.

Chapter 7. Indians.

Chapter 8. Virginia, 1623-86.

Chapter 9. Letters, 1621–1765.

Chapter 10. Boundary disputes, Delaware and Pennsylvania, 1629–1756.

Chapter 11. Extracts from records in England and America; Council records, 1659–85.

Chapter 12. Penn versus Lord Baltimore court proceedings, 1677–78; appointment commissioners, 1750–67; report of surveys, 1732–63; reports, 1751–69; maps, 1732; map of Taylors' and James Island, 1768, Dorchester County; letters, 1681–1763.

Chapter 13. Avalon.

Chapter 14. Calvert family grants, deeds, documents to land in England.

Chapter 15. Personal letters.

Chapter 16. Heraldic documents.

Calvert Papers, no. 1, with account of recovery and presentation to Society, Dec. 10, 1888. Together with calendar (by J. W. Lee, p. 57) of Papers recovered, and selections from Papers. M. H. S. Fund Pub., no. 28, Balto., 1889. MHS.

Calvert Papers, no. 2. Selections from correspondence. M. H. S. Fund Pub., no. 34, Balto., 1894. MHS.

Calvert Papers, no. 3. Brief relation of voyage into Maryland, and other papers. M. H. S. Fund Pub., no. 35, Balto., 1899. MHS.

Certificates and patents for land, 1634–date. Land Office.

Certificates and patents for land, of Eastern Shore of Maryland, 1796–1842. 8 vols. Land Office.

Chancery depositions, 1668–1789. Indexed. M. H. Mag., 1928, v. 23, pp. 101–54, 197–242, 293–343.

Chancery notes; index to depositions and testamentary proceedings (incomplete). W. F. Cregar. Bd. ms. MHS.

Chancery papers (original; 12,421 bundles) and plats. Card index, by case; all names. Land Office.

Chancery records and Chancery dockets, 1668–1852. 220 vols; index, name by name, name of tract. (Valuable genealogical matter, covering 31 vols., to 1791; 14 vols.) Land Office.

Charter of Maryland, granted by Charles the First, of England, to Cecil Calvert, Second Lord Baltimore (1606–75), June 20, 1632.

Calvert Papers, Chap. 1. Mss. MHS.

Hist. of Md. Scharf. V. 1, pp. 53–60.

Maryland, land of sanctuary. Russell.

Md. Manual. 1933.

Maryland charters. L. C. Wroth.

Md. colonization tracts, 1632–46. New Haven, 1929. Peabody Lib.

Colonial money, in denominations of one-half shilling to twenty shillings. Printed in Annapolis, 17—, but never used. 50 vols. Hall of Records.

Colonial records still retained in Court Houses of counties of Maryland. L. D. Scisco.

Anne Arundel County. M. H. Mag., Mar., 1927, v. 22, pp. 62–67.

Baltimore county. M. H. Mag., Sept., 1927, v. 22, no. 3, p. 245.

Calvert County. M. H. Mag., 1932, v. 27, pp. 36–41.

Caroline and Harford Counties. M. H. Mag., 1931, v. 26, pp. 135–38.
Cecil County. M. H. Mag., 1928, v. 23, pp. 20–26.
Charles County. M. H. Mag., 1926, v. 21, p. 261.
Dorchester County. M. H. Mag., 1928, v. 23, pp. 243–46.
Frederick County. M. H. Mag., 1930, v. 25, pp. 206–08.
Kent County. M. H. Mag., 1926, v. 21, pp. 356–61.
Prince George County. M. H. Mag., 1929, v. 24, pp. 17–23.
Queen Anne County. M. H. Mag., 1929, v. 24, pp. 224–28.
St. Mary's County. M. H. Mag., 1931, v. 26, pp. 58–59.
Somerset County. M. H. Mag., 1927, v. 22, pp. 349–56.
Talbot County. M. H. Mag., 1927, v. 22, pp. 186–89.
Worcester County. M. H. Mag., 1930, v. 25, pp. 28–29.

Convention journals, 1775–76. Hall of Records.
Counties of Maryland. Few scattered materials from counties, other than Anne Arundel and Baltimore Counties. Hall of Records.
Day Book, 1784–86. 1 vol. Hall of Records.
Debt books of colonial Maryland. Contain names of landholders, number of acres, and amount of quit rent due, some as early as 1733, some as late as 1775. 53 vols. Card index, by county and party names, 10 vols. Land Office.
Depositions in Land Office records, Annapolis, 1787–89. M. H. Mag., 1924, v. 19, no. 1, pp. 261–283; 1925, v. 20, no. 1, p. 42.
Ejectment plats. Index of lands recovered in ejectment. Hall of Records.
5 per cent stock, 1822; penitenary and university. 192 vols. Hall of Records.
General indexes to certificates and patents. 7 vols. Land Office.
Hagerstown balance book upon deceased persons' estates, 1775–1805. Natl. Geneal. Soc. Quart June, 1930, v. 18, no. 2, p. 31. MHS.
Hill Papers: V. 1, Calvert and Prince George Counties, surveys, 1670–1715. V. 2, Calvert County surveys, 1682–84. V. 3, Calvert and Prince George Counties, surveys, 1698–1715. (There are other mss. with this collection.) Mss. MHS.
House of Delegates, proceedings, 1804–50. 31 vols. Hall of Records.
Index to Libers 1, 2, 3. Patent records, 1633–58. Hall of Records.
Indexes to certificates of survey. 23 vols. Land Office.
Inventories, 1718–77. 126 vols.; indexes, 3 vols. Hall of Records.
Inventories and accounts, 1674–1718. 39 vols.; indexes, 2 vols. Hall of Records.
Inventories and accounts from Land Office (600 notes), dated 1674, 1682, 1696. (Remarriage of Maryland widows.) Mrs. J. B. Cotton. M. H. Mag., 1921, v. 16, pp. 279–98, 369–85; 1922, v. 17, pp. 60–74, 292–308.
Invoice books, 1771–76. 1 vol. Hall of Records.
Judgment records, W. T., 1699–1701. 31 vols. Hall of Records.
Ledger B., no. 2, 1780–82. 1 vol. Hall of Records.
Liber, 1700–01 (original). Hall of Records.
Liber B. L. C., 1731–52. Hall of Records.
Liber C. B., 1693–94. Hall of Records.
Liber C. and W. H., 1638–78; Liber W. H. L., 1640–92. 2 vols. Hall of Records.
Liber G. R., 1777–78. 1 vol. Hall of Records.
Liber H. D., 1694–97/8 (original). Hall of Records.
Liber H. S., no. 1, 1753–68. Hall of Records.
Liber L. L., no. 1, 1692. 1 vol. Hall of Records.
Liber L. L., no. 2, 1692–1704. 1 vol. Hall of Records.
Liber L. L., no. 3, 1704–10. 1 vol. Hall of Records.
Liber L. L., no. 4, 1711–23. 1 vol. Hall of Records.
Liber L. L., no. 5, 1724–31. 1 vol. Hall of Records.
Liber R. G., 1769–74. 1 vol. Hall of Records.
Liber X., 1697/8–1703. Hall of Records.
List of outlawries of Western Shore of Maryland. M. H. Mag., 1909, v. 4, pp. 287–80.
Lord Baltimore's bill book, 1766–69. Ms. MHS.
Lord Baltimore's receipt book, 1729–50. Calvert Papers. Mss. MHS.
Lower house journals, 1666–1776 (lapse 1702–1704). 14 vols. Hall of Records.
Lower House records, 1716–63. Calvert Papers. Mss. MHS.
Maryland notes. Henry H. Goldsborough. William and Mary Quart., 1897, v. 5. MHS.
Maryland State Department of Health, Bureau of Vital Statistics, 2411 N. Charles Street, Baltimore. Births, few births from 1878, official from 1898; death certificates, May, 1898–date. For marriages, refer to County Circuit Courts.
List of sextons of all graveyards in Maryland. Md. State Dept. of Health, Bureau of Vital Statistics.
Nearest of kin (two of whom were required to sign each inventory; records in Annapolis). Ancestral proofs and probabilities. Ljungstedt. No. 4, 24 pp. MHS.
Patent records and certificates, 1634–date (1679–81, originals; original certificates include plats). Cross index, giving name of tract and party names. Land Office.
Postage book, 1774–77. 1 vol. Hall of Records.
Proceedings of Assembly of Maryland, 1637–1774 (8 vols.), 1791–93 (1 vol.; original). Hall of Records.
Proceedings of Council of Maryland, 1636–1770, Archives of Md., vols. 3, 5, 8, 15, 17, 20, 25, 28, 31, 32.
Proceedings of Council of Maryland, 1636–1791 (original; 21 vols.). Council Book, Aug. 8, 1636–Dec., 1671 (imperfect), 1672–April, 1692 (no records). Hall of Records.
Proceedings of Council of Maryland, 1638–1756 (1659–85, England and America). Calvert Papers. Mss. MHS.
Proceedings of Executive, 1785–1825. 7 vols. Hall of Records.
Proprietary leases. 3 vols. Land Office.
Proprietary papers, 1701–76. 6. vols. Hall of Records.
Proprietary record books, 1637–58 (break in records, 1644–March 22, 1648). Two books of records of province of Maryland from Calvert Papers. V. 1, prepared by J. W. Lee. (Calendar on p. 57.) 2 vols. pub. 1889, 1904. MHS.
Proprietary record books, indexes to proper names taken from abstracts. Mss. MHS.

Record of duties on carriages, 1794-98. Mss. MHS.
Records of manors of Maryland. 186 cards. Mss. MHS.
Senate and House of Delegates journals, 1781-1851. 56 vols. Hall of Records.
Senate journals, 1773. 1 vol. Hall of Records.
Senate proceedings 1793-1837. 23 vols. Hall of Records.
Tax lists of Maryland, 1781-88. List of balances for taxes in several counties of Western Shore. Mss. MHS.
Tax list of Maryland, 1784. Arrears of tax due. Mss. MHS.
Tax lists (106) of Maryland, 1802-06, and sheriff's list of Chancery fees collected. Mss. Lib. Cong.
Tax lists of various counties of Maryland. Scharf Papers. Mss. MHS.
Tax Commissioners of Maryland, 1777. Natl. Geneal. Soc. Quart., v. 6, pp. 21-22. MHS.
Upper House journals, 1659-1777. (Original and contemporary copies.) 14 vols., mostly bd. Hall of Records.
Upper House records, 1717-62. Calvert Papers. Mss. MHS.
Upper and Lower House of Assembly and charter, 1722, 23, 24. Pub. by Lower House. Printed by Andrew Bradford, 1725.
Various English and American indentures, 1602-1770. Mss. MHS.
Warrants, 1634-date. Land Office.
General index to warrants. 5 vols. Land Office.
Warrants, assignments, etc., of Eastern Shore of Maryland, 1781-1842. 12 vols. Land Office.
Western Treasury. Mmo. of tobacco, July, 1782. Ms. MHS.

ACCOUNT BOOKS

Account books and related papers (accounts of Lord Baltimore's revenues, 1731-61). Calvert Papers. Mss. MHS.
Accounts. Old accounts of deceased persons, about 1635-1777. Hall of Records.
Accounts, 1674-1718. See Inventories and accounts. Hall of Records.
Accounts, 1718-77. 74 vols. Indexes, 2 vols. Also card index. Hall of Records.
Accounts of business concerns. 300 vols. Mss. Hall of Records.
Administration accounts of Maryland. A. W. Burns. Index to 1781-87, from records in Hall of Records. Annapolis, Md., 1936, 2 vols. typed, bd. DAR.
Ancestral proofs and probabilities. Occasional bulletin, 1935, 1936. Minor Ljungstedt, editor and publisher. MHS.
Annapolis records (early). M. L. Radoff. M. H. Mag., Mar., 1940, v. 35, no. 1, pp. 74-78.

BOUNDARIES

Boundary monuments of District of Columbia. Col. Hist. Soc. Rec., v. 1, pp. 215-24; v. 10, p. 63-87; v. 11. MHS.
Boundary of Maryland. William and Mary Quart., 1905, v. 13. MHS.
Concerning Delaware boundary disturbances, 1774. B. C. Steiner. M. H. Mag., 1915, v. 10, pp. 360-71.
Delaware and Pennsylvania disputes, 1629-1756. Calvert Papers. Mss. MHS.
Fight of century between Penns and Calverts, over three lower counties of Delaware, which resulted in making State of Delaware separate commonwealth, 1683-1767. W. A. Powell. M. H. Mag., 1934, v. 29, no. 2, pp. 83-101.
History of Mason and Dixon's line. John H. B. Latrobe. Hist. Soc. Pa., Phila., 1855, pamph.
Liber W. R. H. no. A. Maryland and Virginia boundary. Hall of Records.
Maryland boundaries. James Welch, 1808-79. Mason and Dixon's line; history. Peabody Lib.
Maryland and Pennsylvania boundaries. G. W. Archer. 1890. Peabody Lib.
Maryland and Pennsylvania boundaries. E. B. Mathews. Resurvey, 1909. Peabody Lib.
Maryland and Pennsylvania boundaries. Agreement between Lord Charles Baltimore and Penns, May 10, 1732. Hall of Records.
Maryland and Pennsylvania boundaries. Original astronomical observations and journal Mason and Dixon, Nov. 15, 1763-Oct. 4, 1767. Hall of Records.
Maryland, Pennsylvania and Delaware boundaries. Hall of Records.
Maryland and Virginia boundaries. J. H. Latané. Johns Hopkins Press, 1895. Peabody Lib.
Maryland and Virginia boundaries, 1718-90. (Fairfax Line, 1746.) J. Lewis. New Market, Va., 1925. Peabody Lib.
Maryland and Virginia boundary. T. S. Hodson. Resurvey, 1898. Peabody Lib.
Maryland and West Virginia boundary. L. Perry. Pamph. DAR.
Mason and Dixon line. M. H. Mag., 1907, v. 2, pp. 315-18.
Mason and Dixon line. Treatise of memoir on controversy between William Penn and Lord Baltimore, respecting boundaries of Pennsylvania and Maryland. Memoirs of Pa. Hist. Soc., Phila., 1864, v. 1, pp., 163-204.
Penn versus Baltimore. Journal of John Watson, 1750. Pa. Mag. Hist. and Biog., v. 38, p. 385.
Penn versus Lord Baltimore. Bounds, correspondence, disputes, expenses, surveys and commissioners, 1680-1768. Calvert Papers. Mss. MHS. Also: Pa. Hist. Soc. Mss. Coll.
Pennsylvania and Maryland boundaries. Pa. Mag. Hist. and Biog., v. 6, p. 412; v. 9, p. 241. Also: Hist. of Md. Scharf. V. 1, pp. 406-07. MHS.
Records in council chamber relative to dispute between government of New Netherlands and Lord Proprietary of Maryland, concerning title of Dutch to territories on Delaware, 1656-68. N. Y. Hist. Soc. Coll., v. 3.
Report of committee on west boundary of Maryland. M. H. S. Fund Pub., no. 29, Balto., 1890. MHS.
Virginia and Maryland boundaries, 1623-86. Calvert Papers. Mss. MHS.
Virginia commissioners of boundary lines. Report between States of Maryland, North Carolina, and Tennessee. Read in Senate, Jan. 17, 1872; with maps. MHS.

CALENDARS, REPORTS, ETC.

Annual report of Society for History of Germans in Maryland. Balto. MHS.
Calendar of Maryland papers in Public Record Office of London. Peabody index. Henry Stevens. Ms. MHS.

Calendar of State archives of Maryland. Archives of Md., v. 1, pp. 13-54; v. 2. Reference to Mss. V, Upper and Lower House and Council Proceedings in Hall of Records.

Calendar of State papers, 1574-1783. Preserved in State Paper Department of Her Majesty Public Record, London. America and West Indies, 1661-1712. 15 vols. V. 1, London, 1860. MHS.

Calendars of State papers. (England), colonial series. Preserved in Public Record Office. Edited by W. Noel Saintsbury. Pub. under direction of Master of Rolls, London, 1860, 1880. MHS.

Catalogue of Manuscripts in Maryland Historical Society. L. Mayer. 1854. MHS.

Index to calendar of Maryland state papers, in State Record Office, Annapolis. Compiled under direction of John H. Alexander. Balto., 1861. MHS.

Report of certain documents touching provincial history of Maryland. (Calendar.) John H. Alexander. Balto., 1860. Hall of Records; MHS.

Report on condition of public records (proprietary, Council and Assembly). Rev. Ethan Allen. Annapolis, 1860. Hall of Records; MHS.

Report of Maryland State Library, in relation to collection of documents and papers. D. Ridgely. Annapolis, 1836, pamph. MHS.

Report of Public Records Commission. Appendix; 1649-50; officers and dates; establishments of office, to 1776. F. C. Sparks. 1906. MHS.

Report of resources of Maryland. J. T. Scharf. MHS.

Report of Tercentennary Commission of Maryland, 1634-1934. 1935. DAR; Peabody Lib.

CANAL COMPANIES

Chesapeake and Delaware, 1799-1803. Hist. of Md. Scharf. V. 2, pp. 518-24.

Chesapeake and Ohio, 1762-1820, originally Potomac Company. Report, 1851. Hist. of Md. Scharf. V. 2, pp. 518-24.

Chesapeake and Ohio Canal Company. Executive communication, with report of Elwood Merris, chief engineer, Dec. 31, 1840. Annapolis, 1841, 63 pp.

Chesapeake and Ohio Canal conventions, 1823, 1826; proceedings. Wash., D. C., 1827, 112 pp.

Early development of Chesapeake and Ohio Canal project. G. W. Ward. J. H. Univ. Studies, Balto., 1899, series 17.

New chapter in early life of Washington in connection with narrative history of Potomac Company. John Pickell (member of board of Chesapeake and Ohio Canal Co.) N. Y., 1856.

Susquehannah, 1783, directors and proprietors. Hist. of Md. Scharf. V. 2, pp. 518-24.

CONSTITUTIONS OF MARYLAND

(First, November 10, 1776)

Constitution of Maryland, 1851 (second). J. W. Harry. J. H. Univ. Studies, 1902, series 20, nos. 7 and 8. MHS; Enoch Pratt Lib.

Constitution of State of Maryland, 1851. E. O. Hinkley. 1855. MHS; DAR.

Constitution of State of Maryland, 1864. E. O. Hinkley. Annapolis, 1864. MHS.

Constitution of Maryland, 1864 (third). W. S. Myers. J. H. Univ. Studies, 1901, series 19, nos. 8 and 9. MHS; Enoch Pratt Lib.

Constitution of State of Maryland, 1867. E. O. Hinkley. Balto. MHS.

Constitution of Maryland, 1867, with amendments to 1931. Md. Manual, 1933, pp. 417-93. (Full and complete index of Constitution of Md., pp. 407-16.) MHS.

Constitutional convention of Maryland, 1867 (fourth). J. H. Univ. Studies, 1909, series 27, p. 113. MHS.

COURTS

Catalogue mss. and printed matter in possession of the Court of Appeals of Maryland, Nov., 1926, Baltimore. Wm. Baxter. Daily Record Co. 1926. Lib. Cong.; Peabody Lib.

Court minutes and proceedings of March term, 1783-91. Mss. MHS.

Court of Appeals of Maryland. Records from 1695; consisting of dockets, judgments, of transcripts from below, opinions, briefs and miscellaneous matter, partly bound, but most unbound. In all, few million documents. Hall of Records.

Court of Oyer and Terminer, 1728-52. 1 vol. Hall Records.

General Court. Judgment records. 105 vols.; indexes, 3 vols. Hall of Records.

History of Court of Appeals of Maryland, 1695-1729. Chief Judge Carroll T. Bond. Pub. by Amer. Hist. Assoc., Wash., D. C., 1928.

Libers C, D, 1751-52. Original and perfect; 186 pp.; contains proceedings of Court of Delegates, begun Oct. 14, 1751, and ended Oct. 21, 1752. Hall of Records.

Maryland Court of Appeals. J. J. Harrod. Balto., 1831. Lib. Cong.; Peabody Lib.

Maryland Court of Appeals. Maryland reports containing cases adjudged during 1851-1938. Annapolis and Maryland, 1852-1939. Peabody Lib.

Maryland reports, 1700-99 (Provincial Court) Series of important law cases, argued and determined in Provincial Court, year 1700 [i.e., 1658] down to 1799. T. Harris, Jr., and J. M. Henry. Pub. by I. Riley, N. Y., 1809-18. Enoch Pratt Lib.

Maryland reports (Court of Appeals), 1800-26 1829, 1829-42, 1843-51. Enoch Pratt Lib.

Maryland's first courts. B. C. Steiner. Amer. Hist. Assoc., 1901, v. 1, pp. 211-29. Wash., D. C. Enoch Pratt Lib.

Proceedings of Court of Chancery of Maryland, 1669-79. Archives of Md., v. 51, Court series 5. High Court of Chancery established 1661, abolished 1851.

Proceedings of Provincial Court of Maryland, 1637-66. Archives of Md., vols. 4, 10, 41 and 49, Court series 1, 2, 3 and 4.

Provincial Court and General Court, series of judgments, 1679-1818. 110 libers. Index 3 vols. (New card index being made.) Hall of Records.

Provincial Court, "oldest appellate bench in United States." (Abolished, 1776.) Md. O. R. Soc. Bull., no. 3, p. 36.

Provincial Court proceedings. Item from Liber B and Liber B. 3. Items omitted from vol.

10, Archives of Md. M. H. Mag., 1913, v. 8 pp. 370–72.

Provincial Court, testamentary proceedings, 1657–1777, 47 vols. Testamentary indexes, 10 vols. Testamentary, 30 boxes of testamentary proceedings (over 70,000 names). Hall of Records.

Records of Court leet and court baron of St. Clement's Manor, 1659–72 (from mss. in MHS). Chronicles of col. Md. Thomas. P. 128. MHS.

Records of High Court of Chancery of Maryland, 1668–1851. Hall of Records.

Reports of Maryland courts prior to 1850, and as reported of Court of Appeals. Edited in 40 vols. W. T. Brantly.

Records of Vice-Admirality Court of Maryland, 1754–67. Contains two payrolls of portion of Invalid Regiment, Jan. and Feb., 1783. Mss. Lib. Cong.;

1754–72. Mss. MHS.

DEEDS

Deeds, 1634–date, or abstracts of same. Land Office.

Deeds, 1642–1786. "See list of counties that were formed previous to the extract system, and the number of books of deeds, that each of them contain."—Report of Commissioner of Land Office, 1917–19, p. 44. MHS.

Deeds. Portfolio of loose papers, 1632–1812; also contains Lord Baltimore deeds. Mss. Lib. Cong.

Early miscellaneous deeds. Provincial Court. Indexed. Hall of Records.

Index to deeds, 1658–1815. Hall of Records.

Miscellaneous deeds, mortgages and releases of mortgages. 1788–1823 and indexes (14 vols.); 1792–1812 and indexes (21 vols); 1815–49 and indexes (39 vols.) Land Office.

HISTORIC PAPERS, LETTERS, JOURNALS, DIARIES, ETC.

Correspondence of Gov. Sharpe, 1753–71. Archives of Md., vols. 6, 9, 14, 54.

Correspondence of Gov. Sharpe, 1763–68. Lib. Cong.

M. H. Mag., 1917, v. 12, pp. 370–83.

Correspondence of James McHenry, 1796–99. William and Mary Quart., 1905, v. 13. MHS.

Council correspondence, 1777–79, 1779–80, 1780–87, 1787–93. Hall of Records.

Dulany and Rousby papers. Letters, 1737. M. H. Mag., 1909, v. 4, pp. 388–90.

Dulany Mss Collection of Historical Papers. MHS.

Dulany papers, 1743–85. R. H. Spencer. M. H. Mag., 1919, v. 14, pp. 371–83; 1921, v. 16, pp. 43–50.

Eden, Gov. Robt. Correspondence. 1, 2, 3, 4. M. H. Mag., 1907, v. 2, pp. 1–13, 97–100, 227–44, 293–309.

Extracts from account and letter books of Dr. Charles Carroll of Annapolis. M. H. Mag., 1931, v. 26, pp. 230; 1932, v. 27, no. 3, pp. 215–30; no. 4, pp. 314–34.

Extracts from State papers, 1636–58. Mss. MHS.

Gilmor, Robert. Papers. Mss. collection, historical. MHS.

Gist, Gen. Mordeccai. Original papers. Correspondence, 8 orderly and account books. MHS.

Gist journal, 1703. Mss. DAR.

House of Delegates journal, 1777–80. 3 vols. Hall of Records.

Johnson, Gov. Thomas. State papers. M. H. Mag., 1910, v. 5, p. 180.

Journal of Charles Carroll of Carrollton, during visit to Canada in 1776, as commissioner from Congress; with memoir and notes. Brantz Mayer. Balto., John Murphy, 1846. MHS; DAR.

Journal of correspondence of Council of Safety, 1773–78. Archives of Md., vols. 11, 12, 16.

Journal of correspondence of State Council, 1773–84. Archives of Md., vols. 16, 21, 43, 45, 47, 48.

Journal of Latrobe. B. H. Latrobe. 1905. DAR.

Lafayette letters. M. H. Mag., 1906, v. 1, pp. 271–73.

Letter books. Calvert letters, 1753–58. Hall of Records.

Letter books, 1756–93. 8 vols. Hall of Records.

Letter books: Executive and Council, 1785–38 (91). Hall of Records.

Letter books: Lord Baltimore, Mr. Hamersley and Henry Harford, 1767–71. Hall of Records.

Letter books of Gov. Sharpe, 1761–71 (4 books; 1753–1761, 2 books missing). Hall of Records.

Letter from Charles Carroll of Carrollton to Gen. Washington. U. S. Catholic Hist. Mag., 1887, v. 1.

Letters of Charles Carroll, Barrister, 1755–69. M. H. Mag., 1936, v. 31, no. 4, pp. 293–32; 1937, v. 32, no. 1, pp. 35–46; no. 2, pp. 174–90; no. 4, pp. 348–68; 1938, v. 33, no. 2, pp. 187–202; no. 4, pp. 371–88; 1939, v. 34, no. 2, pp. 180–89; 1940, v. 35, no. 2, pp. 200–07; (to be continued).

*Letters between English and American branches of Tilghman family, 1697–1764. Harrison Tilghman. M. H. Mag., 1938, v. 33, no. 2, pp. 148–75.

Letters. Reverdy Johnson, Brantz Mayer, George Washington and others. M. H. Mag., 1921, v. 16, pp. 150–78.

Letters, 1621–1765. Calvert Papers. Mss. MHS.

Letters from two pioneers of Maryland and Kentucky, 1789–93. (John Wilmot to Benj. Wilmot of Talbot Co.) M. H. Mag., 1911, v. 6, pp. 352–57.

Letters (Land Office accounts, 1731, 1735–36, 1748, 1751–52, 1754–57, 1760–61. Calvert Papers. 11 vols. MHS.

Letters of County Committees of Safety. Mss. Lib. Cong.

Letters of Governor and Council, 1781. Archives of Md., v. 47.

Letters of Wm. Peaseley and wife on Maryland affairs. U. S. Catholic Hist. Mag., 1890, v. 3.

†Letters of James Rumsey, 1743–92. M. H. Mag., 1937, v. 32, pp. 10–28.

Letters of William Vans Murray to John Quincy Adams. Worthington C. Ford, ed. Wash., D. C., 1914.

Letters of Washington, Gist, Williams, and Smallwood. Brown Book, in Rainbow Series. Hall of Records.

Mayer, Col. Brantz. Miscellaneous correspondence and loose papers. Hall of Records.

McHenry, Dr. James. Letters and public papers. Mss. MHS.
McHenry letters, 1796–1817. South. Hist. Assoc. Pub., 1905, v. 9, pp. 99, 375; v. 10, p. 150.
McHenry papers. B. C. Steiner. South. Hist. Assoc. Pub., 1905, v. 9, p. 311.
Miscellaneous Papers, v. 11, p. 38. MHS.
Original letters of Gov. Horatio Sharpe. Lib. Cong.
Papers of Maryland State Colonization Society. (Md. in Liberia.) Wm. B. Hoyt, Jr. M. H. Mag., Sept., 1937, v. 32, no. 3, pp. 247–71.
Papers (portion) of Daniel Dulany, Judge Samuel Chase, Gov. Wm. Paca and Gov. Thomas Johnson. Mss. MHS.
Purviance Papers. Mss. MHS.
Reverdy Johnson papers. Lib. Cong.
Unpublished letters of Charles Carroll of Carrollton, and father, Charles Carroll of Doughoregan. Comp. and ed. with memoir by T. M. Field. U. S. Catholic Hist. Soc., N. Y., 1902.
Washington letter books. Lib. Cong.
Washington papers. Lib. Cong.
Washington's unpublished letters from Gist Papers, in Soc. Coll. M. H. Mag., 1906, v. 1, pp. 40–44.

LAND RECORDS

First land grants in Maryland. M. H. Mag., 1908, v. 3, pp. 158–69.
First land grants on Patapsco, 1652. M. H. Mag., 1908, v. 3, pp. 51–60.
Land grants, Eastern Shore of Maryland, 1682. Chesapeake Bay Country. Earle. P. 280.
Land notes of Maryland, 1634–55. from Land Office Records. Libers F. A. and B (described in Archives of Md., vol. 1.) M. H. Mag.; 1910, v. 5, pp. 166–74, 261–71, 365–74; Liber F, 1911, v. 6, pp. 60–70, 195–203, 262–70, 365–73; Liber A, 1912, v. 7, pp. 183–96, 307–15, 385–94; 1913, v. 8, pp. 51–65, 186–92, 257–70, 332–38. Liber B, 1914, v. 9, pp. 38–46, 170–82, 290–96.
Land policies and administrations in Colonial Maryland, 1753–69. P. H. Giddens. M. H. Mag., June, 1933, v. 28, no. 2, pp. 142–71.
Land records, 1634–date. Indexes. Land Office.
Land records, grants, etc., 1633–1754 (original holders of land, about date of arrival, and members of their household). Calvert Papers. Mss. MHS.
Land system in Maryland, 1720–65. C. P. Gould. J. H. Univ. Studies, series 33, no. 1, 1915. MHS; Enoch Pratt Lib.
Lord Baltimore's attempt at settlement on Delaware Bay, Durham County, Delaware, 1670–85. Lands, names of grantees, date of grants and location of properties in Cecil County. Debt Book, Land Office. P. G. Skirven. M. H. Mag., 1930, v. 25, pp. 157–67.
Original patentees of land, prior to 1700. Legal Archives of District of Columbia, Maryland, and Virginia. Bessie W. Gahn. Wash., D. C., Brentano's, 1936. MHS; DAR.

LAWS

Acts of Assembly of Maryland. Record. 1640–1927. (Original, engrossed, dating from 1732–1931.) Hall of Records.
Acts of Assembly of Maryland, 1698–1770. First parishes of Province of Maryland. Skirven. P. 171. MHS; DAR.
Acts of Assembly in reference to Montgomery County. Hist. of west. Md. Scharf. V. 1, p. 656. MHS; DAR.
Acts of Assembly of Province of Maryland. James Bisset. Phila., 1759.
Acts of General Assembly of Maryland on subject of attachment. Edward Hinkley. Balto., 1836.
Codified public general laws of Maryland. John P. Poe. 1905, 2 vols.
Compilation of Maryland laws of interest to women. E. Higgins. Balto., 1897.
Digest of decisions construing Statutes of Maryland. Lewis Mayer. Balto., 1866.
Digest of law and criminal procedure in Maryland. L. Hocheimer.
Digest of Maryland Chancery decisions. J. Raymond. N. Y., 1839.
English statutes in Maryland. St. G. L. Sioussat. J. H. Univ. Studies, Balto., series 21, 1903. MHS; Enoch Pratt Lib.
Handlist of Maryland laws, journals and documents, 1692–1800. J. W. M. Lee, at one time librarian of Maryland Historical Society. Priv. pr., Balto., 1878. MHS.
Labor Law of Maryland. M. H. Lauchmeimer. J. H. Univ. Studies, Balto., series 37, no. 2, 1919. MHS; Enoch Pratt Lib.
Law of wills of personal property in Maryland, prior to Aug. 1, 1884. A. J. Shriver.
Laws and resolutions of State of Maryland, 1800–13. John Kilty. Pub. by authority of State. Annapolis, T. Green, 1815. MHS.
Laws and resolutions of State of Maryland, 1818–25; 1826–31; 1832–37. John Kilty. Annapolis, Wm. McNeir, 1838. MHS.
Laws and resolutions of State of Maryland, 1838–45. John Kilty. Annapolis, Riley and Davis, 1846. MHS.
Laws and rules of the Land Office of Maryland. (List of officers and soldiers entitled to lots westward of Fort Cumberland, Allegany County, pp. 73–125; patented military lots, pp. 132–158.) J. M. Brewer and L. Mayer. Balto., Piet Co., 1871. MHS.
Laws of Maryland. Vol. 1: Original Charter, Bill of Rights, and Constitution. Vol. 2: Index to Private Acts, 1700-98, specifying persons and places named in them, and time of passing. John Kilty. Annapolis, Frederick Green, 1800. MHS.
Laws of Maryland. Laws prior to 1664 incomplete. Maryland Archives printed from manuscripts in Maryland and London much fuller, brought down to 1863. 1889.
Laws of Maryland. With index. Annapolis, William Parks, 1727.
Laws of Maryland, 1638–1739. (Copy of every law up to 1670, except those of 1634/5 and 1637/8, six acts 1647/8 and those of 1659/60, 1711–1718, Proprietary Record Book.) Clavert Papers. Mss. MHS.
Laws of Maryland, 1638–1927. Bound manuscripts; 1732–date; loose laws signed by Governor; 1836–1935; in folders and boxes. Hall of Records.
Laws of Maryland, 1700. M. H. Mag., 1910, v. 5, pp. 185–88.
Laws of Maryland, 1784. A. C. Hanson and S. Chase. Annapolis, Frederick Green. MHS.
Laws of Maryland, 1787. Maryland laws of Revolutionary period included in A. C. Han-

son's edition of Laws of Maryland, made since 1763. Annapolis, 1787. MHS.
Laws of Maryland. Index, 1800–10. Mss. MHS.
Laws of Maryland, December session, 1824. Rare item. MHS.
Laws of Maryland at large. Naturalizations in index, 1666–1765; prisioners 1724–56. Rev. Thomas Bacon, Annapolis, Jonas Green, 1765. MHS.
Maryland (Colony) laws, etc. Julia J. Alexander. Balto., 1870.
Maryland common law practice. H. Davy Evans. 1839.
Proceedings and Acts of Assembly, 1634–1758. Archives of Md., vols. 1, 2, 7, 13, 19, 22, 24, 26, 27, 29, 30, 33–40, 42, 44, 46, 50, 52, 55.
Proceedings and Acts of Assembly, 1694–1729. Archives of Md., v. 38. Hitherto unpub.
Proceedings and Acts of Assembly, 1714–26. Archives of Md., appendix, v. 36. Hitherto unpub.
Revised code of public laws of Maryland, with Constitution of State. Lewis Mayer. Balto., 1879.
Status of preferred stock of Baltimore and Ohio Rail Road Company. A. J. Shriver.
Statutory Testamentary Law of Maryland. Clement Dorsey. Balto., Fielding Lucas, Jr., 1838.
Treatise on Constitution and laws of United States. Wm. Vans Murray.

MARRIAGES

Delaware and Maryland marriages. In: Maryland marriages, 1777–1804. Ms. MHS.
Marriage notices for whole United States, 1785–94. Copies by C. K. Bolton. Salem, Mass., Putnam, 1900. MHS.
Marriage records, 1738–68. Loaned by Mrs. Beale Worthington. Ms. MHS.
Marriage references (10,000) prior to 1777. Collected by Mrs. George W. Hodges. Card form; cross index; 20,000 names. Hall of Records.
Marriages, 1756–1864. Md. records. Brumbaugh. V. 2, pp. 497–518. MHS; DAR.
Marriages, American records, before 1699. W. M. Clemens, editor of Genealogy. 12,000 names. N. J., 1926. MHS; DAR.
Marriages, mostly Delaware, Maryland and Virginia. Ancestral proofs and probabilities. Ljimgstedt. Bull. no. 2, 50 pp. MHS.
Marriages of Maryland and Maryland next of kin. (1000 items.) Ancestral proofs and probabilities. Ljimgstedt. No. 1. MHS.
Marriages of 1000 Maryland soldiers of Revolutionary War. Md. Revolutionary records. Newman. 1938.
Marriages performed by Phillip Courtney, minister of M. E. Church, Richmond, Va., 1816–65. Mss. DAR.
Marriages performed by Rev. George Moore (202 persons) 1789–1810, in Maryland (author states probably Kent and Cecil Co.) and Delaware. Md. records. Brumbaugh. V. 2, pp. 595–98. MHS; DAR.
Maryland and Delaware marriages, 1777–1804. Ms. MHS.
Md. records. Brumbaugh. V. 2, pp. 513–22. MHS; DAR.

MAPS

See Maryland card index file. Peabody Lib.
Army map of seat of War, showing battle fields, fortifications, etc., on and near Potomac River. I. G. Bruff. 1861. Peabody Lib.
Atlas of City of Baltimore. Made from surveys and official plans by Topographical Survey Commission. Joseph W. Shirley. Balto., 1914.
Atlas of City of Baltimore, from actual surveys and official plans. G. W. and W. S. Bromley. Phila., 1906.
Atlas of fifteen miles around Washington, including Montgomery County. G. M. Hopkins. 1879. DAR.
Baltimore County. Copy of atlas and census, 1870 (population and area, by districts). Md. Geneal. Rec. Com., 1937. Mss. DAR.
Baltimore public buildings, with map. Isaac Simmons. Balto., 1853. Colored.
Catalogue of old prints and maps of Baltimore. Property of late T. E. Hambleton. Typed. Peabody Lib.
Collection of maps of Cecil County. Photos. copies. MHS.
Dennis Griffith's map of Maryland, 1795.
Ground plot of City of Annapolis. 1718, blue print. DAR.
Jefferson's map of Virginia, Maryland, Pennsylvania and Delaware, 1787. MHS.
Map. Augustine Herman, Virginia and Maryland, 1670. London. (In book of old maps, by Emerson David Fite, Cambridge, 1926, 41½ x 30, p. 151.) Peabody Lib.
Map. Maryland Geological Survey, 1834. Peabody Lib.
Map of Calvert County, 1637–82, showing hundreds, manors and freeholders. H. J. Berkley. Ms. MHS; DAR.
Map of Delaware County with southern part of New Jersey, etc. T. Kitchin. 1757. Peabody Lib.
Map of manors of lower Patuxent River, 1640–63. H. J. Berkley. Mss. MHS; DAR.
Map of Maryland, 1801. M. Carey. Peabody Lib.
Map of Maryland (with inset plan of City of Baltimore). Fielding Lucas. 1819. Peabody Lib.
Map of Maryland. Fielding Lucas. 1822. Peabody Lib.
Map of Maryland. F. Lucas, Jr., engraver. By Cone & Freeman, Balto., 1824, colored, 15 x 21½.
Map of Maryland. Fielding Lucas. 1841. Peabody Lib.
Map of Maryland, showing ten counties and thirty parishes as laid out 1692–94, in accordance with law of 1692, establishing Church of England. Percy G. Skirven. Balto., Norman Remington Co., 1923. MHS.
Map of Maryland and Delaware, with canals, roads and distances (inset map of Baltimore). H. Schenck Tanner. 1833. Peabody Lib.
Map of Maryland, Delaware with parts of Philadelphia and Virginia, showing railroads. Fielding Lucas. Balto., 1852. Peabody Lib.
Map of Maryland and Virginia. H. Anderson. 1799. Peabody Lib.
Map of Newfoundland, Maryland and Virginia, 1715. Herman Moll. Peabody Lib.
Map of North America. Eman Bowen. 1763.

Map of Province of Maryland, 1780. Kuethe. M. H. Mag., 1937, v. 32, pp. 28–30.
Map of State of Maryland. L. Lewis. 1795. Peabody Lib.
Map of Virginia. Capt. John Smith. 1608.
Map of Virginia and Chesapeake Bay, 1608. Capt. John Smith. Hist. of Md. Scharf. V. 1, p. 6. MHS.
Map of Virginia and Maryland. J. Fry and P. Jefferson. 1775. Peabody Lib.
Map of Virginia and Maryland. (Rare.) Augustine Herman. Biographical account, with facsimile reproduction from copy in British Museum by P. Lee Phillips. Wash., D. C., Lowdermilk Co., 1911. Lib. Cong.; Peabody Lib.
Map of Virginia, Maryland, and improved parts of Pennsylvania and New Jersey. John Senex. 1719. Peabody Lib.
Map of Virginia, Maryland, North and South Carolina. J. B. Homams. 1759. Peabody Lib.
Map of Virginia, Maryland, Pennsylvania, East and West New Jersey. John Sellers. 1729. Peabody Lib.
Map, showing early Roman Catholic churches in Maryland. MHS.
Map showing part of Baltimore and Harford Cos. Mss. Peabody Lib.
Maps. 1732 (maps of Taylor's and James Island, 1768.) Calvert Papers. Mss. MHS.
Maps, 1861. Seat of War; birdseye view of Virginia, Maryland, Delaware and District of Columbia. J. Schedler. Peabody Lib.
Maps and map-makers of Maryland. Maryland Geological Survey. E. B. Mathews. (Herman's map, 1670, with family data, p. 368.) 1898, v. 2. Lib. Cong.; MHS; Enoch Pratt Lib.
Military map; Army of Potomac, on Virginia and parts of Maryland and Pennsylvania; 1864. G. R. Bechler. Peabody Lib.
Moale's map of Baltimore Town, 1752.
New and accurate map of Virginia and Maryland; showing Indian towns and lands, English plantations. Eman Bowen. London, 1747, Pictorial, 16 x 9¾.
New and enlarged map of Baltimore City. John F. Weishampel, Jr. 1872, 3¾ x 5½.
New series of Maryland maps, 1938. Lists every cemetery, church, fire house, hospital, hotel, school, town hall, every place of historical interest, every highway, amusement park or beach, all private dwellings, farms and factories. 5 maps of each county, 6 of State. To be kept up by periodical revision. Federal Bureau of Public Works, State Roads Commission, State Highway Planning Survey cooperating. Sale to general public.
Noua Terrae Mariae, tabula. Pictorial, 15 x 11½. John Ogilby. London, 1671. (Revision of first map of Maryland, 1635.)
Nova Virginae tabula (containing whole province of Maryland). Joan Blaen. In Grooten atlas, of wereltbeschryoing, 1648–50, v. 8. Redrawn from John Smith's map, 1606. Peabody Lib.
Panorama view of seat of War. Birdseye view of Virginia, Maryland, Delaware, and District of Columbia. J. Bachman. 1861. Peabody Lib.
Pitner's map of Baltimore. Wash., D. C., 1937, 36 x 50, on roller.
Plans of Fort Cumberland, 1755, from Kings' Mss. Library of British Museum. Hist. of Cumberland. Lowdermilk. P. 93.
Plat of Joppa, Baltimore County, 1725 (now Harford County). Hist. of Balto. City and Co. Scharf. P. 45.
Plat of St. Mary's City (original). Hall of Records. Copy. MHS.
Vaugondy's map, 1755.
War telegram, marking map of East Virginia, part of Maryland and Pennsylvania, 1862. Prang L. and Co. Peabody Lib.

RAINBOW SERIES

Manuscript Archives of Maryland. List of selected papers turned over to Maryland Historical Society in 1883, by Act of Assembly of Maryland, 1882. Papers cleaned, repaired, mounted and bound (all but 6 vols. in Red Book Series) by Maryland Historical Society and returned to Hall of Records, 1937. Black Book series, 11 vols.; Blue Book series, 6 vols.; Brown Book series, 10 vols.; Red Book series, 45 vols. (6 vols. to be bound) and 2 large portfolios of material too large to bind. (Letters in one Black Book portfolio.)
Black Book series, 1701–73 (few earlier dates; earliest 1636; few late as 1776). Proprietary papers, covering proprietary and royal period.
Blue Book series, 1775–1805. Printed broadsides of State of Maryland, and general government. Published papers relating to Maryland. Stock in Bank of England, 1783–1806; miscellaneous papers, 1778; papers concerning losses during Revolutionary War, 1781, and information about British property; oath of fidelity and support, 1778, of Charles, Somerset and Talbot Counties; militia of Maryland, 1813.
Brown Book series. Letters (62) and papers of George Washington, 1775-90; letters to Generals Gist and Williams, 1775–81; letters from Smallwood, 1777–82; military papers, 1777–83, 1790-97; executive papers (155), 1747–85; letters of foreign officers, 1778–82; letters of American officers and representatives of France, 1779–82.
Red Book series. Papers in case of Gov. Eden in 1776, his property and voyage to England, 1773–76; original minutes of Maryland Convention of July, 1775, and drafts of Revolution, etc.; minutes of Council of Safety and Legislative Council of 1776–77; Correspondence of Maryland delegates in Congress, 1776–78, 1778–81. William Goddard's case, 1779; Congress to Council and Governor of Maryland, 1775–89; Congress and War Office to Governor of Maryland, 1778–83, 1777–1803; miscellaneous and civil correspondence, 1775–90, 1780–1802; correspondence relating to War of 1812, 1800–30. Hall of Records.

RENT ROLLS

Accounts of quit rents, 1753–61. Earliest and latest dates of land grants, (40 papers). Calvert Papers. Mss. MHS.
Ground rents in Maryland. L. Mayer. Balto., 1883.
Lord Baltimore's quit rents, Eastern Shore of Maryland, 1749-53, 1759. Calvert Papers. Mss. MHS.

Quit rent system in Maryland. Beverly Bond. M. H. Mag., 1910, v. 5, pp. 350–56.
Rent rolls (additional) of Eastern Shore of Maryland, 1755–59, 1763, 1769–71 and 1774 (small). Mss. MHS.
Rent rolls (additional) of Western Shore of Maryland, 1752–70. Scharf Papers. Mss. MHS.
Rent rolls. Lords of Manor in colonial Maryland, and their original survey, taken from Lord Baltimore's rent rolls, 1639. Side lights on Md. Hist. Richardson. V. 1, pp. 263–66. MHS; DAR.
Rent rolls of Maryland, from earliest and latest dates of land grants in different counties, 1639–1725. Calvert Papers. 5 vols. Mss. MHS.
Rent rolls of Maryland, 1639–1725. Starting with St. Mary's County, 1639, card indexes complete by county and party names. 19 vols. Land Office.
Rent rolls of Maryland, 1658–1762. Description of rent rolls, with list covering different counties. M. H. Mag., 1924, v. 19, pp. 341–69; 1925, v. 20, pp. 23–33, 183–99, 273–96; 1926, v. 21, pp. 285–94, 336–56; 1928, v. 23, pp. 26–39, 182–93, 265–78, 373–78; 1929, v. 24, pp. 43–45, 132–45, 228–37; 1930, v. 25, pp. 209–18; 1931, v. 26, pp. 33–42, 171–82, 264–83.
Rent rolls of Maryland. List of lands returned by keeper of rent rolls, 1756 and 1757 (half year), 1758 (whole year). Mss. MHS.

WILLS

Abstracts of English wills. New Eng. Hist. and Geneal. Reg., v. 51, p. 297; v. 52, pp. 65–69. MHS.
Earliest wills. Index to certain Maryland, Virginia, South Carolina, and District of Columbia wills. Semmes Geneal. Coll. Mss. MHS.
Magruder's Maryland colonial abstracts, wills, accounts and inventories, 1772–77. James C. Magruder. 1934–39, vols. 1–5. Bd. Hall of Records; MHS; DAR.
Maryland calendar of wills, 1635–1743. Will Book, 1–23, 8 vols. Vols. 1–3 and 8, edited by Jane Baldwin Cotton; vols. 4–7, edited by Jane Baldwin Cotton and Roberta Henry. Balto., 1904–28. MHS; DAR.
Maryland gleanings in England. Wills. M. H. Mag., v. 2, pp. 179–85, 280–85, 375–78; v. 3, pp. 181–85; v. 4, pp. 193–97; v. 5, pp. 293–96.
Maryland Will Book, no 31, pts. 1 and 2. Abstracts, 1752–63. A. W. Burns. Typed, bd. Wash., D. C., 1937. Mss. DAR.
Maryland wills, court records, 1632–1770. Calvert Papers. Mss. MHS.
Index of Maryland colonial wills in Land Office, Annapolis, 1634–1777. James M. Magruder, Jr. 1933, 3 vols., mimeog. MHS; DAR.
Index to Maryland wills from cards, 1652–1705. 2 vols. W. F. Cregar. Bd. mss. MHS; DAR.
Maryland colonial statistics and indices. A. W. Burns. Will Book, no. 24, 1774. Indexed. Annapolis, 1938. MHS.
Probate of wills and administrating of estates, 1657–1777. Provincial Court indices. 47 vols. Hall of Records.
Some quaint wills of early Catholic settlers in Maryland, from Archives of Riggs Library in Georgetown. Amer. Catholic Hist. Soc. Phila. Rec., 1902, v. 2.
Will books, 1635–1777. 51 vols; indexes, 4 vols.; also new card index. 1777–1820. 6 vols.; indexes, 2 vols. Original; 1290 papers; 28 boxes; 2 vols.; index, 1 vol. Hall of Records

STATE RECORDS—COUNTY

ALLEGANY COUNTY

Erected 1789.

County seat: Cumberland.

Allegany County was formed from Washington County, and derives its name from Ollikhanna, meaning beautiful stream.

Court House: Cumberland.

Cumberland, the county seat developed from the settlement around Fort Cumberland, the old frontier Fort, laid out in 1749.

Allegany County (Cumberland) no. 1. Inventory of County and Town, Archives of Maryland. Prepared by Historical Records Survey, W.P.A. 86 mimeog. pp. Balto., 1937. Lib Cong.; Hall of Records; MHS; DAR; Enoch Pratt Lib.
Deeds, 1791–date. Court House.
Abstracts. Hall of Records.
Guardians accounts, 1791–date. Court House.
Indentures, 1796–1921. Court House.
Land records, 1791–date. Court House.
Marriages, 1791–date. (Marriage records in Court House destroyed by fire, 1893, but replaced from newspapers.) Court House.
Marriages, 1791–96. Natl. Geneal. Soc. Quart., v. 20, no. 2, p. 52. MHS.
Marriages, up to 1800. Hist. of Allegany Co. Thomas and Williams. V. 1, pp. 663–65. MHS; DAR.
Marriages, Aug., 1791–Nov., 1800. Hist. of west. Md. Scharf. V. 2, p. 1348. MHS; DAR.
Orphans' Court records, 1791–date. Court House.
Wills, 1790–date. Court House; 1790–1800. Hist. of west. Md. Scharf. V. 2, p. 1348.
Wills (decedents up to 1800). Hist. of Allegany Co. Thomas and Williams. P. 8. MHS; DAR.

ANNE ARUNDEL COUNTY

Erected 1650.

County seat: Annapolis.

Anne Arundel County was named for Lady Anne Arundel, wife of Cecilius Calvert, second Lord Baltimore, and daughter of Lord Arundel of Wardour Castle.

Annapolis, the capital of Maryland since 1694, is also the county seat.

Court House, built 1824, remodeled 1892.

Almshouse land records, Londontown, South River. (Land originally owned by Orrick family, later by Burgess family.) Wilson Mss. Coll., no. 109. MHS.
Certificates of surveys of lots in Annapolis, 1718–25. Liber T. H. no. 2. 2 vols., photos. MHS.

Debt books, 1753-74. Land Office.
Debt books, 1750. Calvert Papers, no. 903. Mss. MHS.
Deeds, few said to be copies from privately owned records lent by individuals after destruction of county records, lost in fire which destroyed State House in 1704. 1665-1787 (30 vols.); 1787-date. Court House.
Abstracts. Hall of Records.
Extracts from parish registers. Cary Geneal. Coll. Mss. MHS.
General index of wills, 1777-1917. M. R. Hodges. Compiled from original indices, multigraphed, bd. MHS; DAR.
Index of old Court House records. Mss. DAR.
Index of wills, 1777-1917. On sale through Carter Braxton Chapter, D. A. R. Balto., 1922, 149 pp. DAR.
Inquisitions taken before coroners, June 2, 1787-Sept., 1790. Hall of Records.
Judgments, 1702-1867. 96 vols. Hall of Records.
Land records, 1651-?. Land Office.
Land records, 1651-1774. Mss. MHS.
List of records transferred from Municipal Office, Annapolis, to Hall of Records: 1753-1806, mayor's office, 9 vols.; 1783-1877, journals, 6 vols.; 1789-96, by-laws; 1792-97, charter granted by Queen Anne to Annapolis (copy); 1814-1919, oaths of officers, etc.; 1819, list of real property in Annapolis, probably for tax assessment (paper bound); 1819-22, voters' names, election, etc. (paper bound); 1825-30, 1854, accounts, etc. (paper bound); 1826-28, 1838-1847, expense ledger; 1826-28, day book; 1826-48, by-laws; 1831-38, assessment book; 1846-51, cash book; 1848-89, ledger (record of accounts passed); 1852-58, ledger F; 1849-1861, ledger G, 2 vols.; 1850-53, resolutions and orders; 1851-56, corporation day book; 1852, names of voters of corporations; 1858-67, day book, etc.; 1899-1906, 1906-11, 1911-18, register of deaths, accounts, orders, etc.
Mss. and other records deposited by Rev. Charles W. Baldwin, D.D., in Hall of Records:
Tax lists 1827-31, 1841-49 (5 books).
Indexes received from register of wills. Court House.
Geneal. index of guardians' accounts, 1777 (6 vols.); inventories (6 vols.); inventories and sales, 1777 (1 vol.); wills, 1777-1820 (6 vols.); administration executors accounts, 1777-188-.
Index to record of receipts, 1896-1920. J. G. no. 2; Judgments, 1679-1791 (Provincial Court).
Marriages, 1777-1813, 1810-45, 1845-51 (3 books), 1851-date. Court House.
Marriages, 1767-70. (5800 licenses.) Md. records. Brumbaugh. V. 2, pp. 17-22. MHS; DAR.
Marriages, 1810-45. Photos. MHS.
Marriages, 1777-1850. D. A. R. Mag., Mar., 1913, v. 42, p. 132; Oct., 1913, v. 43, p. 612.
Marriages, 1796-98. Chronicles of col. Md. Thomas. Pp. 212-17. MHS; DAR.
Marriages: See also: Maryland marriages, 1799-1808. Mss. MHS.
Orphans Court records. Co. Court Note Book. Mrs. Milnor Ljungstedt. V. 3, pp. 38, 45. MHS; DAR.
Proceedings of Mayor's Court of Annapolis, 1720-22. Bd., photos. MHS.
Record of deeds and lots, Annapolis, 1722-41, Part 1; 1742-48, Part 2, Liber B. Photos., 2 vols. MHS.
Records. 94 vols. of bound documents and about 100 vols. of bound court dockets, etc. Hall of Records.
Records, 86 mss. volumes of miscellaneous documents from 1702-1840. Hall of Records.
Records of corporation of City of Annapolis, 1757-72. 2 vols., photos. MHS.
Rent roll, bearing Calvert and Harford book plates. Supplements rent rolls already owned by Maryland Historical Society. MHS.
Rent rolls, 1651-1718. Calvert Papers, no. 883. Mss. MHS.
Rent rolls, 1702-10. Land Office.
Rent rolls, 1707 (additional). Calvert Papers, no. 889. Mss. MHS.
Rent rolls, 1755 (additional). Calvert Papers, no. 899. Mss. MHS.
Rent rolls, 1707. M. H. Mag., 1927, v. 22, pp. 259-74; 380-90.
State of his Lordship's Manor, rent rolls and partial census, 1767-70. Md. rec. Brumbaugh. V. 2, pp. 17-22. MHS; DAR.
Tax lists, 1782: Annapolis, Broad Neck, Elkridge, Herring Creek, Huntington, Magothy, Patapsco, Patuxent, Road River, Severn, South River, Town Neck and West River. Mss. MHS.
Tax lists, 1783. Mss. MHS.
Wills, prior to Revolutionary War. Incorporated in Provincial Court records.
Wills, 1777-date. Court House, Annapolis.

BALTIMORE CITY

Laid out in 1730, incorporated in 1796.

Baltimore (Baltimore Town) was built on the Patapsco River, the fifth county seat of Baltimore County and retained the records until 1851, when a complete separation of county and city took place.

1801, account book of uncollected taxes. Mss. MHS.
1815, alphabetical list of assessed persons. Mss. MHS.
Baltimore City. Deptford Hundred or Patapsco, Gunpowder, Middle River, and that part of Bush Neck up to Susquehanna River, known as Baltimore Hundred. The migrations of Baltimore Town. Leakin. V. 1, p. 45.
Baltimore City and County marriage records, 1777-99. (6433 marriages, 12,866 names.) Copied by E. R. George. Md. Geneal. Rec. Com., 1937-38, pp. 39-41. Typed, bd. DAR.
Baltimore marriages and deaths, 1773-1840. F. Sidney Hayward, 508 Harwood Ave., Balto.
Charles Street Avenue Company, 1864—with breaks to 1936. Minutes; 1 ledger. MHS.
Court dockets from Court House, Baltimore, 1757-73. Mss. MHS.
Court proceedings, 1682-1799. Common pleas, 1761-62. Removed from Court House, Baltimore, to Hall of Records.
Court records, 1664-date (Colonial court books, 1664-1851, 54 vols.). Court House.
Debt books, 1764-71. Land Office.
Deeds (colonial), Baltimore City and County, 1659-1782 (57 vols.) removed to Hall of Records.

Deeds of Baltimore City and County, 1782–date. Court House, Baltimore.
Abstracts, 1782–date. Hall of Records.
1798, general assessments. Mss. MHS. Also: Md. Geneal. Bull., Oct., 1934, v. 5, no. 4. MHS; DAR.
Index of female names of Baltimore City and Count marriage records, 1777–99. Copied by E. R. George. Typed, bd., 1938. DAR.
Land records, depositions in Chancery records. Liber S. H. H. 1787–89. M. H. Mag., 1924, v. 19, pp. 261–63; 383–92; 1925, v. 20, pp. 42–57.
Marriage records of Baltimore, 1778. D. A. R. Mag., 1913, v. 43, no. 1, pp. 404–06.
Marriages, 1777–date. Court House, Room 310. (Marriage licenses not always recorded, hence lapses for one or several months at a time.)
100 marriages from Baltimore, 1777–1850. D. A. R. Mag., Sept., 1913, v. 43, pp. 402, 559–60.
Marriages, 1794–95 (list of 200). File case, DAR.
Marriages, 1837–38. Copied from The Sun, Balto. MHS.
Md. marriages, 1774-1804. Mss. list. MHS; City Hall Lib.
Marriages. Md. records. Brumbaugh. V. 2, pp. 513–22. MHS; DAR.
Tax lists, 1783. Back River Lower, East (likely Baltimore Town) and Mine Run Hundred. Mss. MHS.

BALTIMORE COUNTY

Erected 1659.
County seat: Towson.

Baltimore County was erected from Kent County, to the Chester River, part of Anne Arundel County and at that time included all of Harford and Cecil Counties, and was named for the Calverts' Irish estates.

August 24, 1861, an attempt was made to burn the Court House, Towson, and the civil dockets and papers in the Office of the Clerk of the Court were almost entirely destroyed. The late William Moore Isaac, while Clerk of the Court, was instrumental in erecting a fireproof building to prevent the loss of valuable records in the future.

Abstracts of old records, 1682–1768. M. H. Mag., 1923, v. 18, no. 1, pp. 1–22.
Debt book, 1750. Calvert Papers, no. 904. Ms. MHS.
Debt books, 1754–71. Mss. Land Office.
Depositions, 1785. M. H. Mag., 1924, v. 19, pp. 261, 383; v. 20, p. 42.
Founders of Baltimore County or Baltimore County's history in lands, 1699. 8 parts. Md. Geneal. Bull., vols. 5, 6, 7 and 11. MHS; DAR.
1798, general assessment of hundreds of Baltimore County. Mss. MHS.
Land records, 1661–1776–77. Hall of Records.
Land records, 1777–1851. Court House, Baltimore.
Land records, 1851–date. Court House, Towson.
Land records, 1682–1750. McHenry Howard. M. H. Mag., 1923, v. 18, pp. 1–22.
Land records (Colonial), Baltimore City and County, 1661–1776–77. 52 vols. Removed from Room 17, Court House, Baltimore, to Hall of Records. (Mss. index in Baltimore Court House.)
Land records, 1661–65 (with occasional entries of 1660–61). Louis Dow Scisco. M. H. Mag., 1929, v. 24, pp. 151–56.
Land records, 1665–67. Scisco. M. H. Mag., 1929, v. 24, pp. 342–48.
Land records 1668–69. Scisco. M. H. Mag., 1930, v. 25, pp. 255–62.
Land records, 1670. Scisco. M. H. Mag., 1931, v. 26, pp. 228–33.
Land records 1671. Scisco. M. H. Mag., 1932, v. 27, pp. 123–27.
Land records, 1672. Scisco. M. H. Mag., 1933, v. 28, pp. 44–48.
Land records, 1673. Scisco. M. H. Mag., 1933, v. 28, pp. 345–50.
Land records, 1674–75. Scisco. M. H. Mag., 1934, v. 29, pp. 116–20.
Land records, 1676–78. Scisco. M. H. Mag., 1934, v. 29, pp. 299–304.
Land records, 1679–80. Scisco. M. H. Mag., 1935, v. 30, pp. 271–77.
Land records, 1681. Scisco. M. H. Mag., 1936, v. 31, pp. 36–39.
Land records, 1682. Scisco. M. H. Mag., 1936, v. 31, pp. 242–47.
Land records, 1683. Scisco. M. H. Mag., 1937, v. 32, pp. 30–34.
Land records, 1684. Scisco. M. H. Mag., 1937, v. 32, p. 286.
Land records, 1685. Scisco. M. H., 1938, v. 33, p. 176.
Land records, 1686. Scisco. M. H. Mag., 1939, v. 34, p. 284.
1805, list of lands sold for taxes. Mss. MHS.
Marriages. For marriages in Baltimore County prior to 1851, see Baltimore City, 1851–date. Court House, Towson.
Marriages (300). Mss. DAR.
Notes on Baltimore County land records. M. L. Radoff. M. H. Mag., 1938, v. 33, no. 2, p. 183.
1798, particular assessment lists of North and Pipe Creek Hundreds, and tax list of Patapso. Mss. MHS.
Proceedings of Baltimore County Court, Liber D., 1682–86. 2 parts, photos. MHS.
Typed index to names in part, Liber D. Court records, Nov., 1682–Nov., 1684. Mss. MHS.
Rent rolls, 1658–1723. Calvert Papers, no. 883. Mss. MHS.
Rent rolls, 1700. Calvert Papers. Mss. MHS.
Rent rolls, 1700. M. H. Mag., v. 19, v. 20.
Rent rolls. M. H. Mag., 1925, v. 20, p. 273.
Taxables, 1699. (List from Soc. Coll.) M. H. Mag., 1917, v. 12, pp. 1–10.
May 6, 1818, tax assesments; list of sixth district of Baltimore County. Presented by Mordecai Gist Chapter, D. A. R. 1938–39. 402 names, 80 typed pp. DAR.
Tax lists, 1783, Back River Upper, Delaware Upper, Gunpowder, Middle River Lower and Upper, North Deptford and Pipe Creek Hundreds. Mss. MHS.
Wills, inventories and guardians' accounts, 1675–1780 (26 vols.), 1780–1851. Register of Wills Office, Balto. City Court House.
Wills, inventories and guardians' accounts, 1851–date. Court House, Towson.

CALVERT COUNTY

Erected 1654.
County seat: Prince Frederick.

Calvert County bears the family name of the Lords Baltimore.

Court House, Prince Frederick. Practically all records destroyed by fire, 1882.

Calvert County, surveys, 1682–84. Hill Papers, v. 2. Mss. MHS.
Calvert and Prince George Counties, surveys, 1670–1715. Hill Papers, v. 1. Mss. MHS.
Calvert and Prince George Counties, surveys, 1698–1715. Hill Papers, v. 3. Mss. MHS.
Colonial records of Calvert and Prince George Counties; duplication of more important deeds and wills, filed in Annapolis. Monette Book, pp. 300–409.
Debt books, 1753–74. Hall of Records.
Deeds, destroyed by fire, 1882. See Monette Book, pp. 300–409.
Abstracts. Hall of Records.
Land records. 1882–date. Court House.
See Land records of St. Mary, Charles and Calvert Counties, 1639–59. Calvert Papers, no. 880, p. 4. Mss. MHS.
Marriages, 1882–date. Court House.
See Md. marriages, 1777–1804. Mss. MHS.
See also: Marriages collected by Mrs. Hodges. Hall of Records.
Rent rolls 1651–1723. Calvert Papers, no. 882. Mss. MHS.
Rent rolls, 1707 (additional). Calvert Papers, no. 887. Mss. MHS.
Rent rolls, 1753. Calvert Papers, no. 895. Mss. MHS.
Rent rolls, 1759. Calvert Papers, no. 900. Mss. MHS.
Tax lists, 1733; list of taxables. Mss. MHS.
Tax lists, 1783, first district, Herring Creek and Lyons Creek Hundred. Ms. MHS.
Tax list, 1786. Ms. MHS.
Wills, Calvert County, prior to 1882, destroyed by fire. 1882–date. Court House.
See also: Monette Book, pp. 300–409. MHS.

CAROLINE COUNTY

Erected 1773.

County seat: Denton.

Caroline County was erected from portions of Dorchester, Queen Anne and Talbot Counties. It was named for Lady Caroline Calvert, sister of Frederick Calvert, the last Lord Baltimore, and wife of Sir Robert Eden, Governor of Maryland, 1769–1774.

Bridgetown was the county seat of Caroline County; then Edenton, built on the banks of the Choptank River. Edenton was named for the English Governor, but at the time of the Revolutionary War and on his return to England, the "E" was dropped and since has been known as Denton.

Deeds (colonial), 1773–86 (1 vol.); 1786–date. Court House.
Abstracts. Hall of Records.
Land records, March 15, 1774–date. Court House.
Marriages, April 6, 1774–date. Court House.
Marriages, 1774–1815 (367 marriages); 1776 missing. Pa. Mag. Hist. and Biog., Apr. 1904, v. 28, pp. 209–15, Oct., pp. 320–45, 428–55. Reprinted in pamph. by H. D. Cranor, 1904. MHS; DAR.
Marriages, 1774–81. Natl. Geneal. Soc. Quart., v. 23, no. 2, p. 33.
Marriages of Caroline, Charles and Worcester Counties. Mss. File case, DAR.
Tax lists, 1779, Choptank and Tuckahoo Hundreds. Ms. MHS.
Tax lists, 1783, Choptank District. Ms. MHS.
Tax lists, 1783, 1798, 1845. Mss. MHS.
Wills, 1774–date. Court House.
Wills, 1774–81. Natl. Geneal. Soc. Quart., v. 23, no. 2, p. 33. MHS.

CARROLL COUNTY

Erected January 19, 1837.

County seat: Westminster.

Carroll County was named for Charles Carroll of Carrollton and was formed from portions of Baltimore and Frederick counties. Westminster was incorporated in 1830 (originally called Winchester; laid out 1764).

Administrations on decedents, April, 1837–date. Court House.
Deeds, 1837–date. Court House.
Abstracts. Hall of Records.
Early settlers (as early as 1727) and land patents. Hist. of west. Md. Scharf. V. 2, pp. 789–90. MHS; DAR.
History of seventeen towns in northern part. Sketches of Englar, Garner, Plaine, Senseney and Shriner families. Taneytown Md., Carroll Record Print, 1894–96. Newsp. clipp., bd. MHS.
Land records, 1837–date. Court House.
Manchester District; earliest surveys. Hist. of west. Md. Scharf. V. 2, p. 883. MHS; DAR.
Marriages, 1837–date. Court House.
Marriages, April, 1837–May 4, 1839. Hist. of west. Md. Scharf. V. 2, pp. 798–800. MHS; DAR.
Orphan's Court records, 1837–date. Court House.
Wills, 1837–date. Court House.
Wills, 1837–39. Hist. of west. Md. Scharf. V. 2, p. 797. MHS; DAR.

CECIL COUNTY

Erected 1674.

County seat: Elkton.

Cecil County was erected from Baltimore County, and included all of Baltimore County on the Eastern Shore of Maryland, and was named for Cecil Calvert, Second Lord Baltimore.

Alphabetical alienation list; vendees and vendors, 1665–1755. Ms. MHS.
1781, assessors' returns of North Sassafras, North Susquehanna; report of James Fulton, commissioner. Ms. MHS.
1783, Back Creek, Bohemia Manor, Middle Neck, 2nd. district and South Milford Hundreds, 4th district. Mss. MHS.
Debt books, 1734–66. Mss. Land Office.
Deeds (colonial), 1674–1786 (15 vols.), 1786–date. Court House.
Abstracts. Hall of Records.
Draught of Township of Nottingham, according to survey made 1702, copied from original of page 55, Book no. 16, one of land record books of Cecil Co. Hist. of Cecil Co. Johnston. P. 149. MHS.

Marriages, 1777-date. Court House, Elkton.
Marriages, 1774-1816. File case; with Charles and Worcester Counties, mss.; DAR.
Marriages, 1777-1840. Pub. 1929. MHS; DAR.
Marriages, 1840-63. 1 vol., 85 pp., 733 items. Typed, bd. Md. Geneal. Rec. Com., 1935-36. Mss. DAR.
Marriages. See also: Md. marriages, 1777-1804. Ms. MHS.
Probate and land records, 1675-date. Court House.
Rent rolls, 1658-1724. Calvert Papers, no. 884. Mss. MHS.
Rent rolls, 1707. Calvert Papers, no. 890. Mss. MHS.
Rent rolls, 1737, abstracts. Index to early rent rolls. Ms. MHS.
1783, return of lands in Bohemia, Charlestown, North Susquehanna, South Susquehanna, West Nottingham and Octorara Hundreds. Mss. MHS.
1783, return of property in Bohemia, Elk, East Nottingham, North and South Milford, North and West Sassafras, North Susquehanna and Octarara Hundreds. Mss. MHS.
Tax lists, 1752; list of taxable persons. Ms. MHS.
Wills, 1675-date. Court House.

CHARLES COUNTY

Erected 1658.
County seat: La Plata.
Old Charles County, erected, 1650, abolished in 1654, is now in Calvert County; Charles County was named for Charles Calvert, Third Lord Baltimore.

Court House, La Plata, 1896. When the Court House at Port Tobacco burned in 1892, the land records had been removed to Annapolis; they were returned to the County in 1914.

Charles County is said to have very complete records. The records of births, marriages and deaths were often listed in the same book with the county's records.

Abstracts of wills, Charles and St. Mary Counties, 1444-72. A. W. Burns. Wash., D. C., 1937, 210 pp. DAR.
1793, assessment and general tax list. Mss. MHS.
1654-1726, births, marriages and deaths. Bd. mss. MHS.
Calverton Manor, Pangaiah Manor, Zachaiah Manor, state of his Lordship's Manor, rent rolls and partial census, 1767-68. Md. rec. Brumbaugh. V. 2, pp. 23-29. MHS; DAR.
Charles County. Story of first record book, 1649. B. C. Steiner. M. H. Mag., 1926, v. 21, pp. 270-73.
Charles County records, 1782-83. Ms. MHS.
Debt Book, 1750. Calvert Papers, no. 905. Mss. MHS.
Debt books, 1753-74. Hall of Records.
Deeds (colonial), 1658-1786 (71 vols.) 1786-date. Court House.
Abstracts. Hall of Records.
Depositions. Cary Geneal. Coll. Mss. MHS.
1782-83, folios of several hundreds, representing 7 districts, of real and personal property. Ms. MHS.
Land records, 1658-date. Court House.
Land records and depositions. Semmes Mss. Coll. MHS.
Marriages, 1777-date. Court House.
Marriages, 1789-1801. Md. records. Brumbaugh. V. 2, pp. 488-97. MHS; DAR.
Marriages, 1778-1801. D. A. R. Mag., 1927, v. 61, no. 3, pp. 233-36; no. 6, pp. 453-58.
Marriages, 1780-89. Md. O. R. Soc. Bull., no. 1. MHS.
Marriages. See also: Md. marriages, 1777-1804. Mss. MHS.
Proceedings of Court of Charles County, 1658-66, and Manor Court of St. Clements's Manor, 1659-72. Archives of Md., v. 53, Court series 6, 657 pp., complete index, 1936.
Rent rolls, 1642-1725. Calvert Papers, no. 885½. Mss. MHS.
Rent rolls, 1642-1725. Index. Calvert Papers, no. 897. Mss. MHS.
Rent rolls, (additional), 1753, 1762. Calvert Papers, no. 901, 902. Mss. MHS.
Rent rolls and partial census, 1767-68. State of his Lordship's Manor. Calverton, Pangaiah and Zachaiah. Md. records. Brumbaugh. V. 2. MHS; DAR.
Short history of beginning of Charles County, 1658, and detailed statement of old records. L. D. Scisco. M. H. Mag., 1926, v. 21, pp. 261-70.
Tax records, 1733; taxables. Ms. MHS.
Wills, 1665-date. Court House.

DORCHESTER COUNTY

Erected 1668.
County seat: Cambridge.
Dorchester County was named for the Earl of Dorset.
The Court House in Cambridge, third one erected there, was burned in 1851.

Abstracts of deeds, 1668-1719. Turner Geneal. Coll. Mss. MHS.
Alienations, 1798. Ms. MHS.
Bonds of trustees, 1815-date. Court House.
Corporation records, 1858-date. Court House.
Court of Chancery records 1820-51. Court House.
Debt books, 1734-70. Mss. Land Office.
Debt Book. Lands in debt book, 1798; more than in Muir's rent book, rendered in 1737. Ms. MHS.
Deeds (colonial), 1669-1786 (31 vols.), 1786-date. Court House.
Abstracts. Hall of Records.
Gunpowder Manor, Nanticoke Manor, state of his Lordship's Manor, rent rolls and partial census, 1767. Md. rec. Brumbaugh. V. 2, pp. 35-39. MHS; DAR.
Land and mortgage records, 1669-date; with index. (Records saved when Court House burned 1851.) Court House.
1798, list of all white taxables in Armitage Hundred. Mss. MHS.
Marriages, 1780-date. Court House.
Marriages, 1780-1865. 2 vols., photos. MHS.
Marriages, 1780-1886, inclusive. Dorset Chapter, D. A. R., 1935, typed, bd. DAR.
Marriages, 1780-89. Md. O. R. Soc. Bull., no. 1, pp. 56-64. MHS.
Marriages, 1790-1802 (800). Pub. Geneal. Soc. Pa., v. 8, no. 3, pp. 252-60; v. 9, no. 1, pp. 85-87, no. 2, pp. 130-40.

Marriages, 1734–1814, with St. Martin's parish register, Worcester County. Typed, bd. DAR.
1782, proceedings of commissioners of tax. Ms MHS.
Rent rolls, 1659–1723. Calvert Papers, no. 885. Mss. MHS.
Rent rolls, 1707 (additional). Calvert Papers, no. 891. Ms. MHS.
Rent rolls. List of lands held by papists, 1758. Unindexed. M. H. Mag., 1910, v. 5, p. 202.
Rent rolls and list of persons from Western Shore of Maryland, 1798, who owned land in Dorchester County. Ms. MHS.
Return of valuation of lands, 1783. Mss. MHS.
Tax lists, 1721–22, Fishing Creek and Little Choptank Hundreds. Mss. MHS.
Wills, prior to 1853. Md. Geneal. Rec. Com., 1929, v. 3, pp. 26–29; 32–38. DAR.
Wills, inventories of estates, administration accounts, disributions, receipts and releases, and guardian accounts, prior to 1852, destroyed by fire. 1852–date. Court House.

FREDERICK COUNTY

Erected 1748.
County seat: Frederick.
Frederick County was named for Frederick, Sixth and last Lord Baltimore. Frederick Town, as the county seat was originally called, was laid out in 1745.
The first Court House was erected in 1756, the second erected in 1785, burned in 1861.
Court House: Frederick.

Administration accounts, 1750–date. Court House.
Conocheague Manor, Monocacy Manor, state of his Lordships' Manor, rent rolls and partial census, 1767, 1768. Md. rec. Brumbaugh. V. 2, pp. 43–60. MHS; DAR.
Debt books (original) of 1753–73. Land Office.
Debt book of Prince George and Frederick Counties, 1750. Calvert Papers, no. 906. Mss. MHS.
Deeds (colonial), 1748–86 (27 vols.), 1786–date. Court House.
Abstracts. Hall of Records.
Frederick County representatives of hundreds, appointed to raise fund to purchase arms and ammunitions for army, Jan., 1775. Hist. of west. Md. Scharf. V. 2, pp. 175–76. MHS; DAR.
Marriage records of Frederick County. 3 vols. Collected by Mrs. Francis H. Markell. (Known as Dick Papers.) Md. Geneal. Rec. Com., v. 1, 503 records, 940 names, 34 pp., typed, bd., 1937–38; v. 2, 616 names 21 pp., typed, bd., 1938–39; v. 3, 1939–40. DAR.
Marriages, 1756–date. Court House, Frederick.
Marriages, 1756–1864 (52 persons). Md. records. Brumbaugh. v. 2., pp. 497–513. MHS; DAR.
Marriages, 1778. File case, DAR.
Marriages, March, 1778–March 1781 (fragmentary) Hist. of west. Md. Scharf. V. 1, pp. 425–30. MHS; DAR.
Marriages, 1866–69. G. W. Glassner. DAR.
Marriages. Geneal. Mag., v. 2, p. 111.
Monocacy Manor, belonging to Daniel Dulany, containing 8983 acres. Granted to soldiers of Maryland line, 1780, giving list of tenants and purchasers. Hist. of west Md. Scharf. V. 1, pp. 618–19. MHS; DAR.
Original patents on surveys, in Clerk's Office, and resurvey's since their issuance, 1749–1800. Hist. of west. Md. Scharf. V. 1, pp. 373–80. MHS; DAR.
Redemptioners, 1771–73. Pa. Germans in settlement of Md. Nead. P. 117. MHS; DAR.
Rent rolls and partial census of his Lordship's Manor, 1767–68. Conecocheaque and Monocacy of Frederick County. Md. Records. Brumbaugh. V. 2, pp. 43–48, 51–60. MHS; DAR.
Tax lists, 1778, Middle Monocacy. Mss. MHS.
Tax lists, 1781, Monocacy. Mss. MHS.
Tax lists, 1782, Frederick Town and Piney Creek. Mss. MHS.
Wills, 1744–date. Court House, Frederick.
Wills, 1745–77. Hist. of west. Md. Scharf. V. 1, p. 431. MHS; DAR.

GARRETT COUNTY

Erected April 1, 1872.
County seat: Oakland.
Garrett County was formed from Allegany County and was named in honor of John W. Garrett of Baltimore.

Court records, 1873–date. Court House.
Deeds, 1872–date. Court House.
Abstracts. Hall of Records.
First Orphan's Court, 1873.
Garrett County (Oakland). Inventory of County and Town Archives of Maryland, no. 11. Hist. Rec. Survey, W.P.A., 1938–39. Lib. Cong.; Hall of Records; MHS; DAR; Enoch Pratt Lib.
Land records, 1873–date. (First mortgage, Feb. 12, 1873.) Court House.
Marriages, April, 1872–date. Court House.
Marriages, April, 1872–August, 1873. Hist. of west. Md. Scharf. V. 2, p. 1522. MHS; DAR.
Wills, 1872–date. Court House.

HARFORD COUNTY

Erected 1773.
County seat: Belair, 1782.
Harford County was formed from a portion of Baltimore County and was named for Henry Harford, the last proprietary Governor of Maryland.
The Colonial county seat was Harford Town or Bush.

Deeds (colonial), 1774–86 (6 vols.), 1786–date. Court House.
Abstracts. Hall of Records.
Early settlers and their land patents, 1659–1808. Hist. of Harford Co. Preston. Pp. 29–38. MHS.
1798, general assessment book. Mss. MHS.
Land records, 1773–date. Court House.
Marriages, 1779–1865 (very irregular), 1867–date (complete). Court House.
Marriages, 1779–1838 (very irregular). Geneal. Soc. Pa. Pub., v. 8, no. 2, pp. 151–63.
Orphans Court, recording of wills and closing ot estates, 1774–date. Court House.
1783, return of property. Mss. MHS.

Tax lists, 1774–75, 1776; list of all free male taxables in several hundreds (Lower Bush River Hundred missing). Hist. Soc. of Harford Co. Mss. Coll. JHU.
Wills, 1774–date. Court House.

HOWARD COUNTY

Erected 1851.
County seat: Ellicott City.
Howard County was erected from a portion of Anne Arundel County and was named for one of Maryland's generals in the Revolutionary War, John Eager Howard.

Deeds, 1851–date. Court House.
Abstracts. Hall of Records.
Howard County (Ellicott City), no. 13. Inventory of the County and Town. Archives of Maryland, by the Historical Records Survey, W.P.A. Lib. Cong.; Hall of Records; MHS; DAR; Enoch Pratt Lib.
Land and mortgage records, 1851–date. Court House.
Marriages, 1851–date. Court House.
Wills, 1851–date. Court House.

KENT COUNTY

Erected 1642.
County seat: Chestertown.
Kent County was named for Kent County, England. Kent County, prior to 1706, was known as Isle of Kent County, and the first Court was held there, 1642.
First Court House, 1698; present Court House, 1860, Chestertown. Chestertown was laid out in 1706, on grant known as Stepney.

Administration accounts, 1709–date. Court House.
Court records. Libers A, B, C, 1655–56, 1656–62; 1668–71, 1675–76. 3 vols., photos. MHS.
Debt book, 1733–69. Land Office.
Debt book, alterations, 1752–53. Ms. MHS.
Deeds (colonial), Kent County, 1642–1786 (29 vols.), 1786–date. Court House.
Abstracts. Hall of Records.
First will filed in Chestertown, 1669. Book 1, p. 1. M. H. Mag., 1936, v. 31, pp. 264–65.
Inventories, 1709–date. Court House.
Isle of Kent County (now Queen Anne County), 1640–58. Calvert Papers, no. 880, pt. 2. Ms. MHS.
Kent County and Kent Island, 1656–62. Sketch of some old court cases. B. C. Steiner. M. H. Mag., 1913, v. 8, pp. 1–33.
Kent County and Kent Island land notes, 1656–62. M. H. Mag., v. 8, no. 1, p. 10.
Land records, 1636, continuous and complete to date. Court House.
Land records, 1783, Ms. MHS; Land Office.
List of taxables of Chester Hundred, March 23, 1721. Mss. MHS.
Marriages, 1796–1801, 1816–date. Court House.
Marriages, 1796–1866 (7000). Copied by Sarah Stuart. Bd. mss. MHS; DAR.
Marriages, 1796–1802. Md. Geneal. Rec. Com., 1934–35, pp. 203–40. Mss. DAR.
Marriages, 1796–1802. Md. O. R. Soc. Bull., no. 1, pp. 65–73. MHS.
Proceedings of Courts of Kent County, 1648–76, Talbot County, 1662–74, and Somerset County, 1665–68. Archives of Md., v. 54, Court series 7, 816 pp., complete index, 1937.
Rent rolls, 1658–1723. Calvert Papers, no. 884. Ms. MHS.
Rent rolls, 1707. Calvert Papers, no. 892. Ms. MHS.
Rent rolls, 1736, abstracts. Ms. MHS.
State of his Lordship's Manor, rent rolls and partial census, 1776. Md. rec. Brumbaugh. V. 2, pp. 4–14. MHS; DAR.
Tax lists, 1721–22. Mss. MHS.
Tax lists of East Neck, 1722. Mss. MHS.
Tax lists, 1783; return of property (including slaves). Mss. MHS.
Tombstone inscriptions and marriages, 1796–1802. Mss. MHS.
Wills, 1669–date. Originals and copies. Court House.

MONTGOMERY COUNTY

Erected September 6, 1776.
County seat: Rockville.
Montgomery County was formed from a portion of Frederick County and was named for Maj. Gen. Richard Montgomery, a hero of the Revolutionary War.
The Court House, first built in 1777, in Rockville, originally called Williamsburg.

Deeds (colonial), Montgomery County, 1776–86 (3 vols.), 1786–date. Court House.
Abstracts. Hall of Records.
Earliest land grants, in each neighborhood: Berry, 1688; Cracklin, 1688; Clarksburg, 1775; Medley, 1775, and Rockville, 1775. Centennial celebration of erection of Montgomery Co., pp. 15–19.
Inventories, 1779. Hist. of west. Md. Scharf. V. 1, p. 661. MHS; DAR.
Land patents, 1688–1766. Hist. of west. Md. Scharf. V. 1, pp. 647–52. MHS; DAR.
Land records, 1777–date. Court House.
Marriages, 1798–date. Court House, Rockville.
Marriages, 1777–1804. Md. records. Brumbaugh. V. 2, pp. 513–22.
Marriages, 1798–1800. (3 marriages in 1812, 1818 and 1844). Hist. of west. Md. Scharf. V. 1, pp. 662–64.
Marriages, 1797–1844. Photos., bd. DAR.
Marriages, 1796–98. Chronicles of col. Md. Thomas. Pp. 209–12. MHS.
Marriages. Wilson Mss. Coll., no. 31. MHS.
Montgomery County (Rockville), no. 15. Inventory of the County and Town. Archives of Maryland, by the Historical Records Survey, W.P.A. 1939, 319 pp. Lib. Cong.; Hall of Records; MHS; DAR; Enoch Pratt Lib.
Tax lists, 1780, Lower Land, Lower Potomac, Middle Potomac, North West, Upper Potomac and Rock Creek Hundreds. Mss. MHS.
Test book, 1790; several books to 1815. Typed, bd. MHS;
Test book, 1790. Md. Geneal. Rec. Com., 1932–33. Mss. DAR.
1783, Upper Potomac and Sugar Land Hundreds. Mss. MHS.
Wills, 1777–date. Court House.
Wills, May, 1777–May, 1780. Hist. of west. Md. Scharf. V. 1, p. 661. MHS; DAR.

PRINCE GEORGE COUNTY

Erected 1695.
County seat: Upper Marlboro.
Prince George County was erected from a portion of Charles County. It was named in honor of Prince George of Denmark.
Its Colonial county seat was Mt. Calvert.
Court House: Upper Marlboro (laid out anew, 1732). Bacon's Laws.

Assessments, Queen Anne District, 1813. Natl. Geneal. Soc. Quart., v. 22, no. 3, pp. 65-69. MHS.
Calvert and Prince George Counties, surveys, 1670-1715. Hill Papers, v. 1. Mss. MHS.
Calvert and Prince George Counties, surveys, 1698-1715. Hill Papers, v. 3. Mss. MHS.
Colonial records of Calvert and Prince George Counties; duplication of more important deeds and wills, filed in Annapolis. Monette Book, pp. 300-409.
Court records, 1746-47. 2 vols. Mss. MHS.
Debt Book, 1753-72. Land Office.
Debt book of Prince George and Frederick Counties, 1750. Calvert Papers, no. 906. Ms. MHS.
Deeds (colonial), 1695-1786 (22 vols.), 1786-date. Court House.
Abstracts. Hall of Records.
Index to wills, 1698-1832. W. C. Davis. DAR.
Land records, 1696-date. Court House.
Land records, 1696-1834. Mss. DAR.
1696-1808, list of early records in office of Register of Wills. Mss. MHS.
1783, Lower Potomac and Potomak Hundreds. Mss. MHS.
Marriages, 1777-date. Court House.
Marriages, 1777-1824. Bd. ms. MHS.
Marriages, 1777-1824. New Eng. Hist. Register, v. 73, pp. 134-54, 217-32, 261-79.
Marriages, 1777-1800. (Over 2800 names.) Md. records. Brumbaugh. V. 1, pp. 93-173. MHS; DAR.
Marriages, 1777-1850. D. A. R. Mag., June and July, 1913, v. 24, p. 332.
1798, particular assessments book and general tax list. Mss. MHS.
Rent rolls, Prince George and Calvert Counties, 1650-1723. Calvert Papers, no. 882. Mss. MHS.
Tax lists, 1722, Mattapony Hundred; list of taxables. Mss. MHS.
Wills, Prince George County, 1696-date. Court House.

QUEEN ANNE COUNTY

Erected April 6, 1706.
County seat: Centreville.
Queen Anne County was named for Queen Anne, consort of James I, of England, and was formed from Kent and Talbot Counties. Kent Island was given to Queen Anne County.
Queenstown was the Colonial county seat.

Debt book, 1734-75. Land Office.
Debt book, 1734-47, 1776 (abstracts). Ms. MHS.
Deeds (colonial), 1706-86 (16 vols.), 1786-date. Court House.
Abstracts. Hall of Records.
Isle of Kent County, land records, 1640-58. (Was Kent Co.) Bd. ms. MHS.
1783, Kent Island tax list. Ms. MHS.
Land records, 1706-date. Court House.
1756-58, land tax. Ms. MHS.
Marriages; certificates to marry, Jan. 1, 1817-1850; since 1850-date, regular marriage records. Court House.
Marriages, January 1, 1817, to January 11, 1838 (1151 marriages), from vol. 1, in Court House Records. Md. Geneal. Rec. Com., v. 3, pp. 91-103. Mss. DAR.
Marriages, 1829-38 (436 marriages). Md. Geneal. Rec. Com., v. 4, pp. 70-78. Mss. DAR.
1767, miscellaneous tax list. Ms. MHS.
1798, particular and general assessment lists. Ms. MHS.
Rent rolls, 1658-1722. Calvert Papers, no. 881. Mss. MHS.
Tax list, 1722, Upper Hundred. Ms. MHS.
Wills, 1706-date. Court House.

ST. MARY'S COUNTY

Erected 1637.
County seat: Leonardtown.
St. Mary's County was the birthplace of the Province of Maryland; named for the Blessed Virgin. St. Mary's City was the first capitol of the Province and Colonial county seat. First charter, 1668.
St. Mary's County record office destroyed by fire when Court House burned, 1831.

Abstracts of wills of Charles and St. Mary's Counties, 1744-72. A. W. Burns. Wash., D. C., 1937, 210 pp. DAR.
Debt books, 1753-74. Mss. Land Office.
Deeds, prior to 1830, destroyed by fire. 1830-date. Court House.
Abstracts. Hall of Records.
Index of wills. On sale through Carter Braxton Chapter, D. A. R. Balto., 1939. DAR.
Index of wills, 1633-1900, from original indices. Compiled by Margaret Hodges. Balto., 1922, multigraphed, bd. Hall of Records, MHS; DAR.
Land records, St. Mary's, Charles and Calvert Counties, 1639-59. Calvert Papers, no. 880, pt. 4. Mss. MHS.
Marriages, 1795-date. Court House.
Marriages, 1794-1864 (7532 persons). Md. records. Brumbaugh. V. 1, pp. 313-405. MHS; DAR.
Marriages, 1777-83. Md. records. Brumbaugh. V. 2, pp. 535-36. MHS; DAR.
Rent rolls, 1639-1725. Calvert Papers, no. 885½. Mss. MHS.
Rent rolls, 1707. Calvert Papers, no. 887. Mss. MHS.
Rent rolls and partial census, 1767-68. (Beaverdam, Chaptico, Mill, Snow Hill, West St. Mary's and Woolsey Manors.) Md. Records. Brumbaugh. V. 2, pp. 63-78. MHS; DAR.
Survey record book. Photos. from original, 1874-92. G. B. Dent. Bd. MHS.
Tax lists, 1783; 1798, particular and general assessments of Upper and Lower St. Clements Hundred; 1795. Photos. Ms. MHS.
Wills, 1658-1831. Court House.

SOMERSET COUNTY

Erected 1666.
County seat: Princess Ann.
Somerset County at the time of its erection, included all the territory that is now Wicomico and Worcester Counties. It was named for Lady Mary Somerset, sister of Lord Baltimore.

Accounts, 1714–17; bonds of counties, 1777; inventories, 1668–1732; wills, 1742. Md. Geneal. Rec. Com., 1911–15. Mss. DAR.
Administration accounts, 1663–date. Court House.
Alienations, 1748; vendees from vendors. Ms. MHS.
Court records, 1665–68. Photos. MHS.
Court records, 1665–date. Court House.
Court records on file at Princess Ann. Libers D. B. I. K. L. Natl. Geneal. Soc. Quart., Jan., 1918, v. 6, no. 4, pp. 74–76. MHS.
Debt books, 1733–74. Land Office.
Deeds (colonial), 1665–1786 (1665–68 irregular) (29 vols.), 1786–date. Court House.
Abstracts. Hall of Records.
1798, general tax book of general and particular assessment list. Ms. MHS.
Land and mortgage records, 1665–date. Court House.
Land Office accounts, 1744. Ms. MHS.
1672–1720. Libers D. B. I. K. L. Contain births, marriages and deaths. Mss. copy. MHS.
Marriages, 1668–date (incomplete). Court House.
Marriages, 1650–1720. See Old Court Book of Old Somerset, Liber I. K. C., in Court House. Also: Ms copies. MHS; DAR.
Marriages, 1796–1831; from original records at Princess Ann. Mimeog. MHS.
Marriages, 1797–1830 (5600 marriages). May, 1805–May, 1807, lost. Typed, bd. DAR.
1722, Nanticoke Hundred (now Wicomico County). Ms. MHS.
Old Court Book, 1650–1720. Libers I. K. L. Irma Bounds Tilghman. Abstracts of births, marriages and deaths. Md. Geneal. Rec. Com., 1937, typed, bd., 248 pp. DAR.
Orphan's Court records, 1800–date. Court House.
Patentees of land in Old Somerset area, 1662–66. Old Somerset. Torrence. Pp. 469–73. MHS; DAR.
Proceedings of Courts of Kent County, 1648–76, Talbot County, 1662–74, and Somerset County, 1665–68. Archives of Md., v. 54, Court series 7, 816 pp., complete index, 1937.
Rent rolls, 1663–1725. Calvert Papers, no. 885. Ms. MHS.
Rent rolls, 1707 (additional). Calvert Papers, no. 894. Ms. MHS.
Rent rolls, 1744, abstracts. Ms. MHS.
Rent rolls, 1749–53, 1756–58. Mss. MHS.
1783, return of Joseph Cottman, assessor of Nanticoke and Wicomico Hundreds. Ms. MHS.
1783, return of Thomas Handy, Jr., assessor of Great and Little Annemessex, Pocomok, and Dividing Creek Hundreds. Ms. MHS.
1783, return of Thomas Irving, assessor of Princess Ann and Manokin Hundreds. Ms. MHS.
1783, return of John Weatherby, assessor of Rewastica District. Ms. MHS.
Takers up of lands, in Somerset County, 1663–1723. Ms. MHS.
Tax lists, 1721–22, Pocomoke Hundred (now Worcester County). Ms. MHS.
Wills, 1667–date. Indexed. Court House.

TALBOT COUNTY

Erected 1661.
County seat: Easton.
Talbot County was named for Grace Talbot, wife of Sir Robert Talbot and daughter of George Calvert, first Lord Baltimore. Talbot County at one time embraced all of Caroline and Queen Anne, and a portion of Kent Counties.

Account of lands held by Papists, 1756. Ms. MHS.
Alphabetical list of names of persons, owning lands and names of lands of Bay, Bollingbrooke, Island, King Creek, Mill, Third Haven and Tuckahoe Hundreds, 1783. Ms. MHS.
Collectors' accounts, 1726–1811; registers, 1731–32, 1740–42. Port of Oxford. Mss. MHS.
Debt books, 1733–72. Land Office.
Deeds (colonial), 1662–1786 (22 vols.), 1786–date. Court House.
Abstracts. Hall of Records.
Land grants; earliest 1658–72. Hist. of Talbot Co. Tilghman. V. 2, pp. 11–13. MHS; DAR.
Land records, 1662–date. Court House.
Lands charged on Debt Book, 1757. Ms. MHS.
Marriages, 1794–date (complete). Court House.
Marriages, 1738–51. Leed's list. Mimeog. MHS.
Marriages, 1794–1810 (1000 marriages). Mimeog. MHS; DAR.
Marriages, 1796–1917. DAR.
1783, proceedings of commissioner of tax. Ms. MHS.
Proceedings of Courts of Kent County, 1648–76, Talbot County, 1662–74, and Somerset County, 1665–68. Archives of Md., v. 54, Court series 7, 816 pp. complete index, 1937.
Rent rolls, Talbot and Queen Anne Counties, 1658–1722. Calvert Papers, no. 881. Mss. MHS.
Rent rolls, 1707. Calvert Papers, no. 893. Mss. MHS.
Survey book, 1750. Ms. MHS.
Tax lists, 1721–22, Bollingbrooke, Mill and Third Haven (Tred Avon) Hundreds. Mss. MHS.
Tax lists, 1771. Third Haven Hundred. Ms. Lib. Cong.
Tax lists, 1779, unidentified. Ms. MHS.
Tax lists, 1782, balance due. Ms. MHS.
Wills, 1665–1716, 1722–date. Court House.
Wills, 1658–72. Hist. of Talbot Co. Tilghman. V. 2, p. 11. MHS; DAR.

WASHINGTON COUNTY

Erected September 6, 1776.
County seat: Hagerstown.
Washington County is said to have been the first county named for George Washington; was originally part of Frederick County and was erected at the same time as Montgomery County, and included at that time all that is now Allegany and Garrett Counties.
Hagerstown, the county seat, was originally called Elizabethtown; name was changed January 26, 1814.

Copy of earliest will book of Washington County, 1777–1850 (3000 names). Typed, bd., 120 pp. DAR.

Extracts of wills, 1778–91. Natl. Geneal. Soc. Quart., v. 23, no. 1, pp. 28–32; no. 2, p. 65. MHS.
Deeds (colonial), 1777–86 (3 vols.), 1786–date. Court House.
Abstracts. Hall of Records.
Land grants, surveys, etc., prior to 1800. Hist. of west. Md. Scharf. V. 2, pp. 982–86. MHS; DAR.
Land records, 1776–date. Court House.
Marriage bonds, 1792–1825. Mss. MHS.
Marriages, 1791–1860; index of names of two contracting parties, and date issued (some early records destroyed by fire). Court House, Hagerstown.
Marriages, 1791–1825 (fragmentary), Hagerstown District. Hist. of west. Md. Scharf. V. 2, pp. 1302–03. MHS; DAR.
Marriages, 1792–1825. Ms. MHS.
Marriages, 1777–1804. Md. records. Brumbaugh. V. 2, pp. 522–34. MHS; DAR.
Marriages, Jan., 1804–June, 1804. Natl. Geneal. Soc. Quart., June, 1935, v. 23, no. 2, pp. 65–67. MHS.
Washington County, Hagerstown, no. 21. Inventory of the County and Town. Archives of Maryland, by Historical Records Survey, W.P.A. 1937, 145 mimeog. pp. Lib. Cong.; Hall of Records; MHS; DAR; Enoch Pratt Lib.
Wills, 1777–date. Court House.

WICOMICO COUNTY

Erected 1867.
County seat: Salisbury.
Wicomico County was formed from Somerset and Worcester Counties and was named for the Wicomico River.
The old town of Salisbury, the county seat, 1732, was built on its banks.

Deeds, 1867–date. Court House, Salisbury.
Abstracts. Hall of Records.
Land records, 1867–date. Court House.
Marriages, 1867–date. Court House.
Wills, 1867–date. Court House.

WORCESTER COUNTY

Erected 1742.
County seat: Snow Hill.
Worcester County was formed from the eastern part of Somerset County, and was named in honor of the Earl of Worcester.
Snow Hill, the county seat, was founded 1642.

1799–1820, abstracts of marriages. C. H. B. Turner Geneal. Coll. Mss. MHS.
Alienations, 1748. Ms. MHS.
Assessments, 1776. Gilmor Papers. Mss. MHS.
Debt books, 1745–74. Land Office.
Debt books, 1771. Ms. MHS.
Debt books; list of alterations, 1748. Ms. MHS.
Deeds (colonial), 1742–86 (11 vols.), 1786–date. Court House.
Abstracts. Hall of Records.
Index of Orphans Court records of Worcester Co. Pub. Geneal. Soc., Pa., v. 7, p. 125.
Land records, 1742–date. Court House.
Marriage licenses (16,000) issued by Clerk of Circuit Court, Worcester County, April 14, 1795–July 1, 1865. (Law did not require ministers to make returns prior to July 1, 1865.) Copied by M. F. Hudson. 1927, mimeog. MHS; DAR.
Marriage records, 1795–97. D. A. R. Mag., Nov., 1914, v. 45, pp. 249–50.
Marriages, 1795–date. Typed copies, not indexed. Court House.
Marriages, 1795–99 (208 marriages). Md. records. Brumbaugh. V. 2, pp. 590–95. MHS; DAR.
Marriages (207), 1795–98; Charles County, 1788–99; Caroline County, 1774–1816. Ms. File case, DAR.
Marriages, 1797–1865. Md. Geneal. Bull., vols 1–8.
Marriages, 1823–33, from Snow Hill Messenger and Worcester County Advertiser. Lib. Cong.
Memorandum list of early records, in Court House, from Register of Wills of Somerset County; accounts, 1714–17; inventories, 1668–1732; wills, 1742. Mss. DAR.
Records of Orphan's Court, 1799–date. (Records prior to 1799, burned.) Court House.
Rent rolls, 1744, abstracts. Ms. MHS.
Tax lists, 1722, East Neck, Manny, Mattapanny, Pagatmorton (Pagatinocton) and Pocomoke Hundreds. Mss. MHS.
Tax lists, 1783, Acquango, Boquetemorton, Buckingham, Mattapany, Pitts Creek, Pocomoke, Queponeo, Snow Hill, Wicomico and Worcester Hundreds. Mss. MHS.

BIBLIOGRAPHY

*American genealogist. Bibliography of American genealogy, or list of title papers and pamphlets of family history, 1777–1900. Joel Munsell and Son. 1906.
American Historical Societies. Bibliography. (Listing contents.) Appleton P. Clark Griffin. Amer. Hist. Assoc., Wash., D. C., Annual Rept., 1905, v. 2. (M. H. S. Rept., p. 266.)
Baltimore in American literature. (Bio-bibliographical study made from M. H. S. Coll. of Md. authors.) David C. Holly. MHS.
Bibliographer's manual of American history. Thomas L. Bradford. 5 vols. Phila., Maurice H. Power, 1907–1910.
Bibliography. Hon. John W. Sabin. Catalogue of Americana. MHS.
Bibliography of American history. Amer. Hist. Assoc., Annual Repts., Wash., D. C., 1909, 1910, 1911. Indexed.
Bibliography of American Historical Societies. Annual Report of American Historical Association. First edition, 1895; second edition, 1895–1905, 2 vols.; revised and enlarged, March, 1907. Government Printing Office, Wash., D. C. MHS.
Bibliography of American newspapers. Clarence S. Brigham.
Bibliography of Baltimore and Ohio Railroad Company, 1827–79. J. W. M. Lee.
Bibliography on Confederate history. The South to posterity. D. S. Freeman. 1939.
Bibliography on German settlements in Colonial North America; especially on Pennsylvania Germans and their descendants, 1683–1933.

8000 titles. Edited by Emil Meynen. Leipzig, Otto Harrassowitz, 1937. MHS.

Bibliographia hopkinsiensis, 1876–91. J. H. Univ., pt. 1, Balto., 1892.

Bibliography of Maryland during time of Gov. Horatio Sharpe, 1753–69. P. H. Giddens. M. H. Mag., 1936, v. 31, no. 1, pp. 6–16.

*Bibliography of Maryland sources. Dr. Jean Stephenson. Pub. Natl. Geneal. Soc., pamph. MHS.

Bibliographies (7500) in American Historical Guide to Materials for Research. Covering guides to sources as well as to secondary material. (Contains 39 Md. bibliographies.) N. Y., H. W. Wilson Co., 1938, 339 pp. MHS.

Catalogue of historical and genealogical works in National Society of D. A. R. Library, Washington, D. C., 1920. (Catalogue is incomplete today; they have over 200,000 volumes, specializing in histories and genealogies. Card indexing system, by families and States. Certified copies of court, church and family records; remarkable collection of manuscripts, mainly genealogical.)

Guide to resources of American Antiquarian Society. 1937. DAR.

Handbook of manuscripts in Library of Congress, Washington. Govt. Print. Office, 1918.

Index to authors and titles of records of Columbia Historical Society. Vols. 1–33/34 inclusive. 1897–1932. E. J. Morrison. Mss. DAR.

Index to local history of Maryland. G. W. McCreary. Ms. DAR.

Index to titles and subjects and book reviews in Maryland Historical Magazine. Vols. 1–30. W. S. Meyer, director, WPA in Md. MHS.

Latrobe bibliography. M. H. Mag., 1936, v. 31, no. 2, p. 151.

List of publications of Charles Carroll of Carrollton, 1737–1832. Agnes C. Storer. U. S. Catholic Hist. Soc., Hist. Rec. and Studies, N. Y., Jan., 1903, v. 3, pt. 1.

Maryland bibliography. W. T. Coyle. (Balto. and Md. section.) City Lib. Balto.

Maryland imprints. Annotated bibliography of books, broadsides and newspapers printed in Maryland, 1689–1776. Hist. of printing in Col. Md. Wroth. Pp. 157–256. MHS.

Maryland press, 1777–90. (Continuation of Lawrence C. Wroth's Hist. of printing in Col. Md.) J. T. Wheeler. Pub. by M. H. S., 1938, indexed and detailed bibliography, 226 pp. MHS; DAR; Enoch Pratt Lib.

St. Mary's City press. (New chronology of American printing.) 1684. L. C. Wroth. M. H. Mag., 1936, v. 31, pp. 91–111.

Selected list of books dealing with American Colonial and Revolutionary period. Wm. Homer Ames. Sesquicentennial Exposition, Phila. DAR.

Seventeenth century books relating to Maryland. John W. Garrett. M. H. Mag., Mar., 1939, v. 34, no. 1, pp. 1–39.

BIOGRAPHY

†American biographical directories. H. B. F. Macfarland. Wash., D. C., 1908. DAR.

†American biographical and historical dictionary. Wm. Allen.

American Historical Magazine. Nashville, Tenn., quarterly, Jan., 1896–1904, 9 vols. MHS.

†America's old masters. J. T. Flexner. 1939.

†Appleton's cyclopaedia of American biography. Edited by James G. Wilson and John Fiske. N. Y., 1888, v. 1.

Authors today and yesterday. Companion volume to Living authors. N. Y., H. W. Wilson Co., 1933.

†Biographical directory of railway officials of America. T. Addison Busbey. Chicago, Railway Age Co. MHS.

†Biographical dictionary of United States. Edited by J. H. Brown. Boston, James H. Lamb Co., 1900, v. 1.

†Biography of signers of Declaration of Independence. John Sanderson. Phila., Pomeroy, 1820–27.

†Biographical dictionary of American Congress, 1774–1903. John Engart. Wash., D. C.

†Biographical sketches of eminent American statesmen. B. F. Perry. 1887.

†Century book of famous Americans. E. S. Brooks. 1896.

†Century dictionary of names. (Sketches under names of persons.) Century Encyclopedia, v. 7.

†Cyclopaedia of biography. Park Godwin. 1867.

†Cyclopedia of Virginia. Lyon G. Tyler, editor. N. Y., Lewis Hist. Pub. Co., 1915.

†Dictionary of American authors. 1905. Enoch Pratt Lib.

†Dictionary of American biography, including men of the time. F. S. Drake. Boston, 1872.

Dictionary of American biography. (Under auspecies of American Council of Learned Societies.) Allen Johnson. N. Y., Charles Scribner's Sons., 1928, v. 1, to 1936, v. 20. MHS.

†Dictionary of national biography. Twentieth Century Supplement, 1, 2, 3; 1901, 1912, 1921; with Index 1901–12. London, Smith, Elder Co.

†Dictionary of United States Congress. Charles Lanman. 1864.

†Eight great American lawyers. H. H. Hagan. Oklahoma City, 1923. MHS.

†Eminent Americans. Benson Lossing. 1886.

†Encyclopedia Americana. (Sketches found under names of persons.) Americana Co., 30 vols.

Encyclopedia Britannica.

Encyclopedia of American biography. Pub. Amer. Hist. Soc. MHS; DAR.

Encyclopedia of American biography. New series, 1934, v. 1. Under editorial direction of Winfield Scott Downes; address Amer. Hist. Soc., Inc., Eighth Avenue, New York City. MHS; DAR.

†Encyclopedia of Pennsylvania. J. W. Leonard, editor. New York, Lewis Hist. Pub. Co., 1914.

†Genesis of United States. Narrative of movement in England, 1605–16, which resulted in plantation of North America; contains biographies of Virginia Company. Boston and N. Y., Riverside Press, 1890, 2 vols.

†Harper's encyclopedia of United States history. 1902. (For local biography see name of person.)

†Historical register. E. C. Hill. N. Y., 1921, 1922, 2 vols. MHS.
†Historical register and biographical record of men and women of our time who have contributed to the making of America. Bella J. Porter.
†Index. Encyclopedia of American biography. V. 1, 1917, to v. 50. Amer. Hist. Soc., N. Y., 343 pp. DAR.
†Ladies of press. Ishbel Ross. Harper, 1936.
†Lamb's Biographical dictionary of United States. MHS.
†Lives of Catholic heroes. John O. Murray. N. Y., Sheehy, 1882. Enoch Pratt Lib.
Magazine of American History, 1877–93, vols. 1–29. N. Y. and Chicago, A. S. Barnes Co. MHS.
Memorials of Huguenots in America. A. Stapleton. 1901. DAR.
†Men of America. Biographical dictionary of contemparies. John W. Leonard, editor.
†National cyclopaedia of American biography. Compiled by George Berby. N. Y., James T. White & Co., 1906.
†National cyclopaedia of American biography. Containing complete indexes of National cyclopaedia of American biography, compiled by George Berby, 1906. N. Y., James T. White and Co., 1927.
†National cyclopedia of American biography. Enoch Pratt Lib. card, indexed vols. 1–24; all but vols. 1–12 checked.
†National portrait gallery of eminent Americans. 2 vols. DAR.
†New biographical Congressional directory.
†New biogographical Congressional directory. (List of names.) M. H. Mag., 1925, v. 20, pp. 388–89.
†New dictionary of American biography.
†Portraits of eminent Americans. J. Livingston. 1854. DAR.
†Portraits of persons born abroad who came to Colonies in North America before year 1701. (Biographical.) Chas. K. Bolton. 1919–26, 3 vols.
†Sketches of national portrait gallery of distinguished Americans. 1834–37, 4 vols. Longacre and Herring.
†United States Congress. Joint Committee on Printing Biographical Directory of American Congress. 1774–1927. Enoch Pratt Lib.
†Who's who among North American authors. A. Lawrence. (178 Md. biog.) Los Angeles, Golden Syndicate, 1936–39, 1220 pp.
Who's who in Maryland. Biographical dictionary of leading living men and women of Maryland, Pennsylvania, New Jersey, Delaware and West Virginia. Chicago, A. N. Marquis, 1939, v. 1, 1056 pp. (Brief sketches of over 2000 residents of Maryland are included.)
†Women of South distinguished in literature. Julia D. Freeman. (Contains sketches of many Balto. and Md. women.) 1861. Enoch Pratt Lib.

HISTORY, BIOGRAPHY, AND TRAVEL

Acadians (French neutrals) transported to Maryland. M. H. Mag., 1908, v. 3, pp. 1–21.
Acadians, transported into Maryland. Basil Sollers. M. H. Mag., 1908, v. 3, pp. 1–21.
Account of ceremony of laying corner stone of new building at St. John's College, Annapolis. Jeremiah Hughes. 1835.
†All Maryland eleven. Baltimore Evening Sun, Nov. 4, 1931.
American antique furniture. Book for amateurs. Edgar G. Miller, Jr. (Majority of illustrations are articles of furniture owned in Maryland.) Balto., Lord Baltimore Press, 1937, 2 vols. MHS.
American history of colonial period. (Two chapters deal with proprietary governments of Barbados and Maryland.) C. M. Andrews. 1935, 1936.
Ancient and Honorable Mechanical Company of Baltimore. H. W. McCreary. Balto., 1901.
Annacostin Indian Fort. Wm. B. Marye. M. H. Mag., June, 1938, v. 33, p. 134.
Annals of Annapolis, 1649 to War of 1812. David Ridgely. Balto., 1841. MHS.
Annals of Siler Spring. Gist Blair. Records Columbia Hist. Soc., v. 21, pp. 155–85.
Annapolis. Pamph. on Carvell Hall. DAR.
Annapolis, 1754–1840. (Descriptive.) M. H. Mag., 1919, v. 14, pp. 258–71.
Annapolis, ancient city, 1649–1887. E. S. Riley. Annapolis, 1887, 395 pp. MHS; DAR.
Annapolis and Elk Ridge Railroad Company. Annapolis, 1841.
Annapolis and its early American homes. E. R. Ramsburg. D. A. R. Mag., 1925, v. 61, pt. 1, no. 9, pp. 652–59; pt. 2, no. 10, pp. 735–42.
Annapolis and its early homes. See Brice and allied families. Mss. DAR.
Annapolis and Kent Island. Mrs. S. A. Shafer. In Powell's Historic towns. Peabody Lib.
Annapolis, Annals, 1649–1812. David Ridgley. Balto., 1841, 283 pp. DAR.
Annapolis. Anne Arundel's Town. W. O. Stevens. N. Y., 1937. DAR.
Annapolis, celebration of 200th anniversary of removal of Capitol of Maryland from St. Mary's to Annapolis. E. S. Riley. Annapolis, 1894. MHS.
Annapolis Convention of 1786. New Jersey Hist. Soc. Proceedings, first series, v. 10.
Annapolis. Guide book of United States Naval Acad.my. 1924. DAR.
Annapolis. Guide to Annapolis and United States Naval Academy. Ruby R. Duvall. Balto., 1926, Maps, illus.
Annapolis. Handbook of City of Annapolis and United States Naval Academy. Prepared and published by Anne Arundel Co. Hist. Soc., Annapolis, 1888.
Annapolis, historical sketch of United States Naval Academy. James R. Soley. 1876.
Annapolis. History of Annapolis. Oswald Tilghman. 1914. MHS.
Annapolis. History of Capital of Maryland, with full history and description of United States Naval Academy. O. M. Taylor. Balto., 1872.
Annapolis, its colonial and naval story. W. B. Norris. N. Y., 1925, 323 pp. MHS.
Annapolis. Outline history of Annapolis and Naval Academy. M. C. Dugan. Balto., 1902.

Annapolis. Pictorial Annapolis and United States Naval Academy. 1906. DAR.

Annapolis. Plan of City of Annapolis. 1718. Mss. DAR.

Annapolis. Records of Corporation of City of Annapolis, 1757–72. Photostats of original records. MHS.

Annapolis; three centuries of glamour. E. M. Jackson, Jr. Capital Gazette Press, 1937. DAR.

Annapolis today. (Chronological record of notable events in Annapolis and naval history.) Kendell Banning. Funk and Wagnalls, 1938, 376 pp.

Annapolis, ye ancient capital, Maryland, 1649–1901. E. S. Riley. Annapolis, 1901.

Annapolitan Library at St. John's College. Ford K. Brown. Annapolis, 17 pp.

Anne Arundel County. Londontown on South River, 240th anniversary of founding, 1638–1923. M. H. Mag., 1924, v. 19, pp. 134–43.

Antietam and its bridges. Helen A. Hays. N. Y., Putnam, 1910 (out of print). Western Maryland river, its bridges, and country through which it flows.

Appeal for establishment of free library in City of Baltimore. John D. Toy. Balto., 1856.

Archives of Maryland. Calendar and report. Pub. Committee of M. H. S., 1883, pamph. MHS; Hall of Records.

Ark and *Dove*, beginnings of civil and religious liberties in America. J. M. Ives. London, N. Y., etc., 1936. DAR.

†Art and artists in Baltimore. Latrobe Weston. M. H. Mag., Sept., 1938, v. 33, no. 3, pp. 213–27.

Article descriptive of Baltimore and trip through portion of State, 1791. F. M. Bayard. In Descriptions of Maryland. Steiner. Johns Hopkins University Studies, series 22. Peabody Lib.

Article descriptive of Deer Creek. Susanna Mason. Peabody Lib.

Authentic history of Cokesbury College, with sketches of its founders and teachers. G. W. Archer, M.D., Belair, Md., 1894. Harford Co. Hist. Soc. Coll. J. H. Univ. Lib.

Authors of Maryland. H. F. Shepherd. N. Y., 1911. MHS; Peabody Lib.

Babylon's fall in Maryland. Langford's refutation. M.H. Mag., 1909, v. 4, pp. 42–64.

Baltimore. St. G. L. Sioussat. In Powell's Historic towns. Peabody Lib.

Baltimore, 1846. H. Stockbridge, Jr. M. H. Mag., 1911, v. 6, pp. 20–34.

†Baltimore: Album of notable Baltimoreans. Balto., 1900–01.

Baltimore and Harford Counties. Place-names. Wm. B. Marye. M. H. Mag., 1930, v. 25, pp. 321–65.

Baltimore and Ohio in Civil War. I. P. Summers. N. Y., Putnam, 1939, 304 pp. MHS.

Baltimore and Ohio Rail Road, personal recollections. J. H. B. Latrobe.

Baltimore and Ohio Rail Road. Picturesque Baltimore and Ohio; historical and descriptive. J. G. Pangborne. Chicago, 1883.

Baltimore-Annapolis sketch book. F. P. Stieff.

†Baltimore Association of Commerce. Speaking of Baltimore (excellent sketches.) Issued monthly, 1910 to date. Enoch Pratt Lib.

Baltimore beauty. J. W. Palmer. Lippincott, v. 8, p. 11.

Baltimore book. W. H. Carpenter. 1838.

Baltimore centennial, 1829. M. H. Mag., 1929, v. 24, pp. 237–45.

Baltimore City government. T. P. Thomas. Johns Hopkins University Studies, 1896, series 14.

Baltimore Clearing House. Charles A. Hales. Johns Hopkins University Studies in Historical and Political Science. MHS; Enoch Pratt Lib.

Baltimore Clearing House, 1858 to present. C. Hales. Johns Hopkins University Press, 1939.

Baltimore Clipper and Old Baltimore shipbuilder. J. E. Hancock. M. H. Mag., v. 30, pp. 48, 62, 138–49.

Baltimore: complete view of Baltimore, with statistical sketch. Charles Varle. Balto., 1833.

Baltimore during time of Peale Museum. Raphael Semmes. M. H. Mag., 1932, v. 27, pp. 115–22.

†Baltimore Federation of Labor. (Includes photographs and biographies of citizens and officers.) Enoch Pratt Lib.

Baltimore: financial history. J. H. Hollander. Balto., Johns Hopkins University Press, 1899.

Baltimore: financial history, 1900–26. L. O. Rea. Johns Hopkins University Studies, series 47, p. 339. MHS.

Baltimore Fire Department. Official history, 1747–1898. C. H. Forrest. 1898. MHS; Enoch Pratt Lib.

Baltimore: guide. John Murphy Co., 1902, illus. MHS.

†Baltimore: history and biography. F. A. Richardson and W. A. Bennett. 1871. MHS; DAR.

Baltimore. History of city, its men and institutions. Balto., 1902, illus.

Baltimore. History of our police. From first watchman to latest appointee. de F. Folsom. Balto., 1888. MHS.

Baltimore homes. List of extant mansions. Mss., newspaper clipping and photographs collected by J. H. Maynard. Bd. MHS.

Baltimore in eighties and nineties. Meredith Janvier. 1933. MHS.

Baltimore memorial celebrations, 1730. Memorial volumes, 1880; account of municipal celebration of 150th anniversary of settlement of Baltimore. Edw. Spencer. Illus. by F. B. Mayer. Balto., 1881.

Baltimore: not too serious history. L. Stockett. Balto., 1928. MHS; DAR.

Baltimore: or a long time ago. W. B. Buchanan. Balto., Murphy and Co., 1853. MHS.

Baltimore: oriole and brief sketch of Audubon. R. S. Payne. Balto., Norman Remington Co., 1923.

†Baltimore: past and present. Brantz Mayer. Balto., 1871.

Baltimore (1824) reminiscences. J. H. B. Latrobe. M. H. Mag., 1906, v. 1, pp. 113–24.

Baltimore, the Monumental City—the Liverpool of America. Baltimore American, 1894.

Baltimore yesterdays. Meredith Janvier. Balto., 1937, illus.

Baltimore's yesterdays: exhibition at Municipal Museum. M. H. Mag., Sept., 1939, v. 34, p. 266.

†Baltimoreans in American literature. D. C. Holly. 1933. Enoch Pratt Lib., card index.

Battle of Severn, 1651–55. B. B. Browne. M. H. Mag., 1919, v. 14, pp. 154–57.

Beginnings of Maryland, 1631–39. B. C. Steiner. Johns Hopkins University Studies, series 21, nos. 8, 10, 1903; series 24, nos. 10, 12; series 25, nos. 4, 5. MHS; Enoch Pratt Lib.

Beginnings of Maryland in England and America. Ruthella M. Bibbins (Mrs. Arthur B.). 1934, pamph. MHS; DAR.

Belvedere of Baltimore. Maria Briscoe Crocker. D. A. R. Mag., 1939, v. 73, no. 10, pp. 48–51.

†Bench and bar of Maryland, 1634–1900. Conway W. Sams and Elihu S. Riley. Chicago, 1901, 2 vols., 678 pp. Lib. Cong.; MHS; Enoch Pratt Lib; Peabody Lib.

Bentztown Bard. Folger McKinsey (born at Elkton, 1866; poems appear daily in The Sun, Balto.) Balto. and London, Doxey Book Shop Co., 1907.

Bible in iron. C. H. Mercer. Contains list of early iron foundries in Maryland. MHS.

Bibliography of Maryland, Colonial and Revolutionary period. Waller Irene Bullock. Typed, bd. MHS.

Biennial report of commissioner of Land Office of Maryland. MHS; DAR.

†Biographical cyclopedia of representative men of Maryland and District of Columbia. Balto., 1879, portraits, 716 pp. MHS; DAR; Enoch Pratt Lib.

†Biographical file of Maryland. (Over 40,000 cards.) Md. Room, Enoch Pratt Lib.

†Biographical sketches of distinguished Marylanders. Esmeralda Boyle Kelly. Balto., Piet Co., 1877. MHS; DAR; Enoch Pratt Lib.

†Biographical sketches of eminent American patriots and early history of Maryland. J. Taggart. Kansas City, Mo., 1907. MHS.

†Biographical sketches of State officers of Maryland. Members of Senate; members of House of Delegates, January session, 1906. (From Md. Manual) Enoch Pratt Lib.

†Biographies and annals of Yale, 1804–15. V. 6. Prof. Franklin B. Dexter. MHS.

List of Marylanders. M. H. Mag., 1912, v. 7, p. 334.

†Biography—bibliography. Typed list (Md.). Enoch Pratt Lib.

Birds of Maryland farm. Sylvester D. Judd. Wash., D. C., 1902.

Blooded horses of colonial days. F. B. Culver. MHS.

Board of Trade and Plantations. Reports of British while Maryland was royal province. B. C. Steiner. M. H. Mag., 1907, v. 2, pp. 363–67.

Bohemia Manor. The Sun, Balto., Sept. 9, 1885.

Bohemia Manor, Cecil County. Historical collection of Rev. Charles Payson Mallery, containing memoranda and journal of Augustine Herman. Mss. MHS.

Book of Maryland men and institutions. Maryland Biographical Association, Balto., 1920. MHS.

Braddock memorial. D. A. R. Mag., Oct., 1913, pp. 573–76.

Braddock's Road. Story of Thomas Cresap. MHS.

Braddock's Road. Military map. J. K. Lacock. Pa. Mag. Hist. and Biog., v. 38, pp. 1–38.

Braddock trail. C. C. Magruder. D. A. R. Mag., Oct., 1913, pp. 578–83.

Brief account of settlement of Ellicott's Mills. Martha E. Tyson. M. H. S. Fund Pub., no. 4, Balto., 1871. MHS.

Brief history of bank (Western National Bank). Raymond Tompkins. Balto., 1938, 68 pp. MHS.

Brief history of establishment of Floating School of City of Baltimore. Rev. J. N. McJilton. Balto., 1860.

Brief relation of voyage into Maryland, 1634. From Father White's original narrative in Archives of Society of Jesus. 2 vols. Vol. 1, edited by Col. Brantz Mayer; republished in Shea's Early Southern Tracts, no. 1, 1865. Vol. 2, edited by Francis L. Hawks; republished with map, Joseph Sabin, N. Y., 1865. Narratives of early Maryland, Hall, 1910. History of Maryland, Scharf, v. 1, pp. 69–77. MHS.

Broadside relative to condition of sale of Right Hon. Lord Baltimore's manors and reserved lands. MHS.

Callister Papers, 1751. Mss. Md. Dioc. Lib.

Calvert County manors and hundreds. M. H, Mag., 1932, v. 27, pp. 237, 240; corrections, p. 335.

Captains and mariners of early Maryland. Raphael Semmes. Appendices contain list of officers who commanded rangers or troops, commanders of Kent Island, etc. Johns Hopkins University Press, 1937. MHS; DAR.

Carroll County. History of 10 towns. Newspaper clippings, 125 columns. MHS.

Carrollton Manor. Wm. Jarboe Grove. 1921. DAR.

Catalogue of coins, tokens, medals in Collection of United States Mint of Philadelphia. (Lord Baltimore's coins are listed and some from Annapolis, 1783.) M. H. Mag., 1912, v. 7, p. 334.

†Catonsville biographies. G. C. Keidel. M. H. Mag., 1921, v. 16, pp. 299–313; 1922, v. 17, pp. 74–89.

Causes of Maryland revolution in 1689. F. E. Sparks. Johns Hopkins University Studies, 1896, series 14, nos. 11, 12. MHS; Enoch Pratt Lib.

Cecil County and early settlement around head of Chesapeake Bay. G. Johnston. 1881. MHS; DAR.

Centennial celebration of foundation of University of Maryland, May 30, 31 and June 1, 2, 1907. Balto., 1908.

Character of Province of Maryland. George Alsop. 1666 (original). Balto., M. H. S. Fund Pub., no. 15, 1880.

Charles' Gift, or Preston-on-Patuxent. Salute to Maryland house of 1650. Hulbert Footner. Harper, 1939, 200 pp.

Check list of American newspapers in Library of Congress. A. B. Slauson. 1901.

Check list of biographical directories and general catalogues of American colleges, 1636–1910. Eva A. Cole, of Columbia Univ. Lib. N. Y. Geneal. and Biog. Records, 1915, v. 46, no. 1.

Chesapeake Bay. J. W. Palmer. Century, v. 25, pp. 251–70.

Chesapeake Bay and its tributaries. L. Webb-Peploe. 1923, pamph. DAR.

‡Chesapeake Bay country. Tales of old homes and their far-famed hospitality. Swepson Earle. Balto., 1934, 1938, 250 illus. MHS; DAR.
Chesapeake Bay region, extinct river towns of 1680. M. H. Mag., 1924, v. 19, pp. 125–34.
Chesapeake Bay section. Colonial ruins, colonial architecture and brickwork, 1650–1830. M. H. Mag., 1924, v. 19, pp. 1–10.
Chesapeake peninsula. G. A. Townsend. Scribner's Monthly, 1872, v. 3. Peabody Lib.
†Chronicles of Baltimore, 1659–1874. J. T. Scharf. Balto., Turnbull Bros., 1874. MHS; DAR.
Chronicles of colonial Maryland. J. W. Thomas. Cumberland, Eddy Press, 1913 (first edition 1900). MHS; DAR.
Citizenship and suffrage in Maryland. B. C. Steiner.
City government of Baltimore. T. P. Thomas. Johns Hopkins University Studies, 1896, series 14, no. 2. MHS.
City rambles or Baltimore as it is. J. C. Godright. Balto., 1857.
Claiborne and Kent Island in Maryland history. De Courcy W. Thom. Pamph. MHS.
Cole's Harbor. M. H. Mag., 1924, v. 19, pp. 261–83, 383–92; 1925, v. 20, pp. 42–57.
Collected poems of Virginia Woodward Cloud. Foreword by Ellen Duvall, editor. Henry Harrison, 1939, 93 pp.
Colonial and historic homes of Maryland. 100 etchings by Don Swann. Text by Don Swann, Jr. Etchcrafters Art Guild, 1938, 2 vols., 126 pp.
Colonial mansions of Maryland and Delaware; those who lived in them. J. M. Hammond. Phila., Lippincott, 1914, 65 illus. MHS.
Colonial men and times. Lillie Du P. Van C. Harpe. MHS.
Colonial recipes of Virginia and Maryland. M. A. Bomberger. Wash., D. C., 1907.
Colonial St. John's College, Annapolis, 1696–1928. Annapolis, 1928.
Colonial trade of Maryland, 1689–1715. M. S. Morriss. Johns Hopkins University Studies, 1914, series 32, no. 3, p. 443. MHS; Enoch Pratt Lib.
†Colonial women of Md. Mrs. A. M. L. Sioussat. Balto., 1891.
Commissary in colonial Maryland. (Sketch of different commissaries of Md., 1672–1764.) E. S. MacQueen. M. H. Mag., 1930, v. 25, pp. 190–206.
Complete view of Baltimore. C. Varle. Balto., 1833.
Cooperation in Maryland and South. Daniel R. Randall. Johns Hopkins University Studies, 1888, series 6, nos. 11–12. Balto. MHS; Enoch Pratt Lib.
Correspondence, with history of Gov. Eden's administration in Maryland. C. Carroll. 1902. Peabody Lib.
Counties of Maryland. Their origin, boundaries and election districts. Edward B. Mathews. Illustrated with maps of each county as it developed. Md. Geological Survey, Special Pub., v. 6, pt. 5. Johns Hopkins University Press. 1907. MHS; DAR; Enoch Pratt Lib.
County Court note book. Mrs. Milnor Ljungstedt. (Review.) M. H. Mag., 1922, v. 17, p. 230.
County seats of Baltimore County before removed to Baltimore, 1768, and to Towson, 1851. M. H. Mag., 1906, v. 1, nos. 1 and 2.
Creeks and manors of old Kent. R. H. Swain. Pamph. MHS.
Crime and punishment in early Maryland. Law and order in Lord Baltimore's colonial period. Raphael Semmes. Balto., 1938. MHS.
Cruises; mainly on Chesapeake. R. Barrie and G. Barrie, Jr. Phila., Franklin Press, 1909.
Cruising on Chesapeake Bay, 1781. M. H. Mag., 1910, v. 5, pp. 123–31.
Cumberland and vicinity. View album of photographs. Booklet pub. by Cresap Chapter, D. A. R. DAR.
Daniel Dulany's considerations. M. H. Mag., 1912, v. 7, p. 26.
Declaration of Lord Baltimore's plantation in Maryland; London, 1633. Reprinted in facsimile, 8 pp., limited edition, 125 copies, Baltimore, Lord Baltimore Press, 1929. Lib. Cong.; MHS; Peabody Lib.
M. H. Mag., 1930, v. 25, pp. 95–96.
Deer Park, 3000 feet above sea. J. G. Pangborn. Chicago, 1884.
Deer Park and Oakland, twins of Alleghanies. T. Scharf. Balto., 1887.
De La Brooke Manor. H. J. Berkley. 1935. DAR.
Delaware Finns, or first permanent settlements in Pennsylvania, Delaware, western New Jersey and eastern part of Maryland. E. A. Louhi. N. Y., 1925. MHS.
Deputy commissary's guide within Province of Maryland. Elie Valette. Annapolis, printed by Catharine Green and Son, 1774.
Descendants of signers of Declaration of Independence. Year Book, 1936–39. Pamph. DAR.
Descriptions of Maryland. Johns Hopkins University Studies, 1904, series 22, nos. 11–12. Bibliography, 1526–1905. MHS; Enoch Pratt Lib.; Peabody Lib.
Descriptive catalogue of minerals occurring in vicinity of Baltimore. Robt. Gilmor, Jr. 13 pp.
Descriptive sketch of Maryland (poem) from Newport Mercury, June 28, 1790. M. H. Mag., 1924, v. 19, pp. 196–97.
Diamond-back terrapin. Ferdinand C. Latrobe. Twentieth Century, 1940, bklet, 29 pp.
Diary of Thomas Parkin, Baltimore, eighteenth century, 1794–95. M. H. Mag., 1912, v. 7, pp. 356–74.
Diary of R. H. Townsend, 1804–79. Works Progress Administration, 3 vols. MHS; Enoch Pratt Lib.
Discovery of Maryland, or Verazzano's visit to Eastern Shore. Harry F. Covington. M. H Mag., 1915, v. 10, no. 3, p. 199.
Disfranchisement of Maryland 1861–67. Wm. A. Russ, Jr. M. H. Mag., 1928, v. 28, pp. 309–28.
Dismemberment of Maryland. Historical and critical essay. G. W. Archer. Also Maryland manor. Gen. James G. Wilson. M. H. S. Fund Pub., no. 30, Balto., 1890. MHS.
†Distinguished men of Baltimore and Maryland. Balto. American Pub., Balto., 1914. Enoch Pratt Lib.
Down Eastern Shore of Maryland. B. Taylor. Harper's Mag., 1871, v. 43, p. 702. Peabody Lib.
Down historic Susquehanna. C. W. Bump. 1899.
Early county seats of Baltimore County. Judge Albert Ritchie. M. H. Mag., 1906, v. 1, pp. 3, 99.

Early county seats of Baltimore County. History of Baltimore City and County. Scharf. P. 42. MHS.
Early German settlements in Maryland. A. B. Faust. N. Y., 1927, 2nd edition.
Early German settlements (1730) in Western Maryland. L. P. Henninghausen. Soc. for Hist. of Germans in Md., 6th Annual Rept., 1892. MHS.
Early history of Baltimore American. T. D. Penniman. M. H. Mag., Sept., 1933, v. 28, no. 3, pp. 272–78.
Early manor and plantation houses of Maryland. Architectural and historical compendium, 1634–1800. H. C. Forman. Easton, Md., 1934, illus., 500 homes. MHS; DAR.
Early Maryland poetry. (Works of Ebenezer Cook, laureate of Maryland.) M. H. S. Fund B. C. Steiner. M. H. S. Fund Pub., no. 36, 1901. MHS.
Early missions among Indians. M. H. Mag., 1906, v. 1, pp. 293–316.
Early relations between Maryland and Virginia. J. H. Latené. Johns Hopkins University Studies, series 13, nos. 3, 4, 1895. MHS; Enoch Pratt Lib.
Eat, drink and be merry in Maryland. Frederick P. Stieff. N. Y., 1932.
Economic history of Baltimore and Ohio Rail Road, 1827–53. Milton Reizenstein. Johns Hopkins University Studies, 1897, series 15.
Economic studies of Maryland. Issued by Planning Commission, 1939. Enoch Pratt Lib.
Economics and politics in Maryland, 1720–50, and public services of Daniel Dulany, the Elder. St. G. L. Sioussat. Johns Hopkins University Studies, 1903, series 21. MHS; Enoch Pratt Lib.
Eddis, Wm., late surveyor of customs, Annapolis. "Letters from America, 1769–77." Tell of administration of last provincial governor, Capt. Robert Eden, social life at Annapolis, etc. London, 1792. MHS; St. John's College Lib.
†Eight great American lawyers. (Biographical.) H. H. Hagan. Oklahoma City, 1923. MHS.
Electoral college for Senate of Maryland, and nineteen Van Buren electors. B. C. Steiner Amer. Hist. Assoc., Wash., D. C., Annual. Report, 1895.
Ellicott's Mills. Brief account of settlement, with fragments of history therewith connected. Martha E. Tyson. M. H. S. Fund Pub., no. 4, Balto., 1871. MHS.
Encyclopedia of American biography. 1915, v. 1, to 1932, v. 50. Amer. Hist. Soc., N. Y. MHS.
English ancestral homes of noted Americans. Anne H. Wharton. (Mostly relates to Maryland, Pennsylvania and Virginia.) First edition, 1915.
English in Maryland. W. T. Brantly. In: Winsor's Narrative and critical history of America. Boston, 1882.
English in Virginia, Maryland and Carolinas. J. A. Doyle. London, 1882.
Extinct river towns of Chesapeake Bay region. M. H. Mag., 1924, v. 19, pp. 125–41.
Financial history of Baltimore. Jacob H. Hollander. Johns Hopkins University Studies, Balto., 1899, extra v. 20.
Financial history of Maryland. H. S. Hanna. Johns Hopkins University Press, 1907.
First commander of Kent Island. S. F. Streeter. M. H. S. Fund Pub., no. 2. MHS.
First Lord Baltimore and his colonial projects. B. C. Steiner. Amer. Hist. Assoc., Wash., D. C., Annual Rept., 1905, v. 1.
†First settlement of Germans in Maryland. Biographical sketches. E. T. Schultz. Frederick Md., David H. Smith, 1896, 60 pp. MHS.
Fleets' journal of voyage in Virginia and Maryland.
Flowering of idea. Dr. Alan M. Chesney, Dean of Johns Hopkins Medical School. Play, presented at celebration of fiftieth anniversary of founding of Johns Hopkins Hospital. Johns Hopkins Press, 1939, 87 pp.
Formation of old counties of Maryland. In History of Maryland. Scharf. V. 1, pp. 271–72.
Fort Frederick. M. H. Mag., 1923, v. 18, pp. 101–08.
Fort Frederick, Washington County, 1756. L. H. Wilson. Pamph. DAR.
Fort Frederick: its ownership and how title was twice acquired by Maryland. W. McC. Brown. M. H. Mag., 1929, v. 24, pp. 176–81.
Founders of Maryland. Rev. Edward D. Neill. Albany, Joel Munsell, 1876.
Founding of Maryland, 1634–1934. From embarkation from Cowes, England, and first sixty years in Colony. Matthew Page Andrews. Balto., Williams & Wilkins Co., 1933, 367 pp. MHS; DAR.
Frederick County Agricultural Society. List of officers, 1821–1900. History of western Md. Scharf. V. 1, p. 446. MHS; DAR.
Frederick-Town, Maryland: the hive; or collection of thoughts on civil, moral, sentimental and religious subjects. Privately printed by John P. Thomson, 1804.
Garrison, Baltimore County, and old Garrison roads, 1675. Wm. B. Marye. M. H. Mag., 1921, v. 16, pp. 105–49, 207–59.
Gazette of State of Maryland. R. S. Fisher. N. Y. and Boston, 1852.
Gazetteer of Maryland. Henry Gannett. Government Printing Office, 1904 (U. S. Geologial Survey). Lib. Cong.; MHS; Peabody Lib.
Gazetteer of Maryland, 1673. J. C. Kuethe. (Compiled from Maryland's portion of Augustine Herman's map of Maryland and Virginia, published in London, 1673.) M. H. Mag., 1935, v. 30, pp. 310–25.
Geographical description of States of Maryland and Delaware. J. Scott. Phila., 1907.
German-American families in Maryland. C. F. Raddatz. Soc. for Hist. of Germans in Md., 6th Annual Rept., 1892, pp. 41–50. MHS.
German Society of Maryland. L. P. Hennighausen. Pub. by German Soc. of Md., 1909. MHS; DAR.
Germans in Baltimore. Rev. J. G. Morris. 1879; Soc. for Hist. of Germans in Md., 8thAnnual Rept., 1894. MHS.
Germans of Maryland, 1812–14. Pamph. DAR.
Glades of Alleghanies. J. G. Pangborn. Balto., 1882.
†Godefroy, Maximilian, Papers. Mss. MHS.
Governor of Maryland. Colonial executive; evolution of governor's position in Constitution, 1776, 1851, 1864. C. J. Rohr. Johns Hopkins University Studies, series 50, no. 3, 1932. MHS; Enoch Pratt Lib.
†Governors of Maryland. From Gov. Thomas Johnson (1777) to Gov. Austin Lane Crothers

(1908). H. E. Buchholz. Balto., Williams & Wilkins Co., 1908.

†Governors of Maryland (1777–1903). Founders of Howard and Anne Arundel Counties. Warfield. Pp. 224–301.

Great Seal of Maryland. C. C. Hall. M. H. S. Fund Pub., no. 23, Balto., 1886. MHS. Also: M. H. Mag., 1915, v. 10, pp. 109–14.

Guide to Baltimore and environs. A. K. Bond. Balto., 1926, map; illus. MHS.

Guide to Baltimore, with account of geology, environs and maps. G. H. Williams, editor.

Hagerstown, 1735–1935. L. H. Wilson. Pamph. DAR.

†Hagerstown Bank at Hagerstown. Annals of 100 years, 1807–1907. 1910. Enoch Pratt Lib.

Hall of Records from archivists' point of view. Dr. James A. Robertson. MHS.

Hammond versus Heamans. Heamans' narrative reprinted in M. H. Mag., 1909, v. 4, pp. 236–57. Originals in Bodleian Library and British Museum, London. Pamph. 1655.

*Handbook of heraldry. J. E. Cussaus. Enoch Pratt Lib.

Harrison Manuscript Collection. Largely relating to history of Talbot County. MHS.

Highway legislation in Maryland and its influence in economic development in State. St. G. L. Sioussat. Balto., 1899.

Hill Papers. Collection chiefly correspondence of Clement Hill, of Upper Marlborough, Prince George County, with London merchants receipts and accounts, etc. Mss. MHS.

Historic American building survey: Maryland. Works Progress Administration. (Over 100 photographs.) J. H. Scarff. Lib. Cong.; MHS; Hall of Records; Enoch Pratt Lib.

Historic Fort Washington. Amy C. Clinton. M. H. Mag., Sept., 1937, v. 32, no. 3, pp. 228–47.

†Historic Salisbury, Wicomico Co. C. J. Truitt. N. Y., 1932. DAR.

Historic sketch of Union Mills. J. Switzer. MHS.

Historical records survey of writers' project under Works Progress Administration in Maryland. Master inventory to be placed in Lib. Cong., DAR, Enoch Pratt Lib., and Hall of Records.

Historical sketch of Carroll County. Hon. J. K Longfellow. Book of photostats. MHS.

Historical sketch of University of Maryland, School of Medicine, 1807–90. E. F. Cordell. Balto., 1891.

Historical sketches of Harford County. Samuel Mason, Jr. Darlington, Md., privately printed, 119 pp.

Historical view of government of Maryland. John Van Lear McMahon. (J. V. L. McMahon born in Cumberland, Md., 1800; died 1871.) Balto., 1831. MHS.

Historical view of government of Maryland from its colonization to present day. John V. I. McMahon. Balto., Lucas and Deaver, 1837, 555 pp. MHS.

History and description of Baltimore and Ohio Rail Road; with an appendix. By citizen of Baltimore (Wm. Prescott Smith). Balto., 1853, illus., map, six original portraits.

†History of Allegany County. J. W. Thomas and T. J. C. Williams. L. R. Titsworth Co., 1923, 2 vols. MHS; DAR.

History of American city government. Colonial period. E. S. Griffith. (Ref. to Annapolis, Baltimore and St. Mary's City.). 1938. Enoch Pratt Lib.

History of Anne Arundel County. Mss. MHS.

History of Anne Arundel County. Ancient churches, homes, illustrious citizens, towns, State House and establishment of United States Naval Academy, 1845. E. S. Riley. Annapolis, Chas. F. Feldmeyer, 1905, 169 pp. MHS; DAR.

History of Baltimore. Lewis Hist. Pub. Co., 1912. DAR.

†History of Baltimore City and Baltimore County, from earliest period to present time. J. T. Scharf. Balto., 1874; Phila., 1881. MHS; Enoch Pratt Lib.

History of Baltimore County. Real stories. Data obtained by children of Baltimore County schools. Revised and adopted by Isobl Davidson. Balto., 1917, 282 pp. Enoch Pratt Lib.

History of Braddock's Road. (Expedition started from Maryland, 1755.) Mss. DAR.

History of Calvert County, 1634–1738. Dr. H. J. Berkley. (Contains rent rolls, surveys, tax returns, etc.) Typed, bd., 307 pp., map. MHS.

†History of Caroline County. From its beginning; material largely contributed by teachers and children of Caroline County Schools. (Contains militia lists, land holdings and church history.) E. M. Noble, editor. Federalsburg, Stowell Co., 1920. MHS.

History of Carrollton Manor, Frederick Co. Wm. Jarboe Grove. 1928. DAR; Enoch Pratt Lib.

†History of Cecil County. Early settlements around head of Chesapeake Bay and Delaware River. George Johnston. Pub. by author, Elkton, Md., 1881, map. MHS; DAR.

History of Confederate States Navy, from its organization to surrender of its last vessel. J. T. Scharf. N. Y., 1887.

History of coöperation in United States (Maryland and South). D. R. Randall. Balto., 1888, series 6, nos. 11–12.

†History of Cumberland. (Including Fort Cumberland, Battle of Fort Necessity, Braddocks, expedition, Civil War period, etc., 1728–1878.) W. H. Lowdermilk. Wash., D. C., 1878, 554 pp. MHS; DAR.

History of dentistry. Dr. A. W. Lufkin. Enoch Pratt Lib.

†History of Dorchester County. Elias Jones. Revised, Balto., 1925. MHS; DAR.

History of education in Maryland. B. C. Steiner. Wash., D. C., 1894.

History of Emmitsburg, Frederick County. J. A. Helman. 1906. MHS; DAR.

History of Frederick County. J. T. C. Williams and F. McKinsey. 1910. Mss. index of above. M. Holdcraft. Typed, bd., 135 pp. Balto., Jan. 1, 1936. MHS.

History of Frederick County. Pictorial Scrap Book. Frederick Chapter, D. A. R. DAR.

History of Frederick County. H. E. Gilbert. Frederick College Journal, Oct., Nov., Dec., 1889, Feb., 1890. Newspaper clipping. In envelope in History of Frederick County, Williams. MHS.

†History of Frederick County. From earliest time to War between States. J. T. C. Williams. Continued from beginning of year 1861 down to

present time by F. McKinsey. Hagerstown, L. R. Titsworth Co., 1910, 2 vols. MHS; DAR; Enoch Pratt Lib.
History of Free Masonry in Maryland. Edw. T. Schultz. 1884. Enoch Pratt Lib., card indexed.
History of General Assembly of Maryland, 1635–1904. Elihu S. Riley. Balto., 1905.
History of Goucher College, 1892–1934. Anna H. Knipp and T. P. Thomas. Balto., 1938, 659 pp. illus.
†History of Harford County. From Smith expedition, 1608, to close of War of 1812. W. W. Preston. (Includes enrollment of County militia in Revolution, etc.) Balto., Sun Book Office, 1901. MHS; DAR; Enoch Pratt Lib.
History of Howard County. Mss. MHS.
History of Kent County, 1630–1916. F. G. Usilton. Chestertown, Md., 1916. MHS; DAR.
History of Know Nothing party in Maryland. L. F. Schmeckebier. Johns Hopkins University Studies, 1899, series 17, nos. 4 and 5. MHS; Enoch Pratt Lib.
†History of Leitersburg District, Washington County. H. C. Bell. (Including its original land tenure, first settlements, etc.) Leitersburg, Md., 1898. DAR.
History of Maryland. E. H. Butler. 1886. DAR.
History of Maryland. (School text.) L. M. Passano. Balto., Dulany Co., 1901.
History of Maryland, 1634–1848. J. McSherry. Balto., 1849, 437 pp. Reprint 1904, edited and continued by Bartlett B. James.
History of Maryland. From founding through World War. M. P. Andrews. N. Y., Doubleday, 1929, 721 pp., map. MHS.
History of Maryland. Prepared for use of schools. Browne and Scharf. 1877–78. MHS.
History of Maryland, 1600–1880. J. T. Scharf. Balto., 1879, 3 vols., maps. MHS.
History of Maryland, 1632–1896. W. J. C. Dulany. 1896. DAR.
History of Maryland. Henry Onderdonk. Balto. 1868. MHS.
History of Maryland, its agricultural products, commerce, manufactors and statistics. A. Leo Knott.
History of Maryland bar. Charles Warren. MHS.
History of Maryland State. Society, D. A. R., 1892–1933. Mrs. Edward B. Passano. Typed, bd. DAR.
†History of Maryland to which are added brief biographies of distinguished statesmen, philanthropists, theologians, etc. Phila., 1866. DAR.
†History of Montgomery County, 1650–1879. T. H. S. Boyd. Clarksburg, Md., 1879. MHS.
History of Montgomery County, 1650–1879. Balto., W. K. Boyle and Son, 1880.
History of Montgomery County. Mss. MHS.
History of Newtown, Maryland. (Name changed by Legislature, to Pocomoke City, 1878–79.) Rev. James Murray. 1883. DAR.
History of Old Baltimore Conference from planting of Methodism in 1773 to division of Conference in 1857. J. E. Armstrong. 1907. DAR.
History of Palatinate. Maryland, 1634–1776. Wm. Hand Browne. Boston, 1912, copyright 1884. MHS; DAR.
History of Piscataway. Indians. Wm. B. Marye. M. H. Mag., 1935, v. 30, pp. 183–240.
History of Pocomoke City. Irving R. Spence.
History of printing in colonial Maryland, 1686–1776. Lawrence C. Worth. Typothetae of Balto., 1922. MHS.
History of Queen Anne County. Pub. in Centreville Observer, 1886. Typed copy, bd. MHS.
History of reincarnation of Easton, Talbot County. M. M. Higgins. Easton Star Democrat, 1926.
History of State banking in Maryland. A. C. Bryan. Johns Hopkins University Studies, v. 17, Balto., 1899.
†History of Talbot County, 1661–1861. Oswald Tilghman. Balto., 1915, 2 vols. MHS; Enoch Pratt Lib.
History of university education in Maryland. B. C. Steiner. Johns Hopkins University Studies, series 9, nos. 3 and 4, Balto., 1891. MHS.
†History of Washington County. From earliest settlement to present, containing history of Hagerstown; also biographical record of representative families. T. J. C. Williams. 1906, 2 vols. MHS; DAR.
History of Western Maryland. Frederick, Montgomery, Carroll, Washington, Allegany and Garrett Counties. J. T. Scharf. Phila., 1882, 2 vols. (Western Maryland, 1688–1700, was all Charles County; 1700–48, was all Prince George County; 1748–77, was all Frederick County; 1777, Montgomery and Washington Counties were taken from Frederick.) MHS; DAR.
†History of Western Maryland Railway Company, including biographies of presidents. E. M. Killough. Balto., the author, 1938, 90 pp., mimeog. MHS.
History of Worsell Manor, Cecilton, Cecil County. Pamph. DAR.
Hollingsworth Papers. Mss. MHS.
Homes of Cavaliers, 1648–1800. Katharine Scarborough. N. Y., 1930. DAR.
Hundred years of Carroll County. B. G. Lynch. 1939, pamph. DAR.
Hundreds of different counties of Maryland. (Hundred in Maryland constituted political unit and military district, abolished in 1824.) Md. Archives, v. 23, pp. 23–25.
Hungerford Tavern, prior to 1771, Rockville. Md. O. R. Soc., v. 2, p. 39.
Illustrated history and guide book to St. Anne's Parish, Annapolis. Pamph. DAR.
†Index to biographical sketches published in The Friend, vols. 26 and 27. Pub. Geneal. Soc. Pa., v. 3, no. 2, pp. 109–34.
Index to Encyclopedia of American biography. Vols. 1–50. Amer. Hist. Soc., N. Y., 1932. MHS.
Indians. Aboriginal Maryland, 1608–89. Part 1. Raphael Semmes. M. H. Mag., 1929, v. 24, no. 2, pp. 157–72, 195–209.
Indians. Calvert Papers. Mss. MHS.
Indians of Chesapeake Bay. J. E. Hancock. M. H. Mag., 1927, v. 22, pp. 23–40.
Institutions and civil government of Maryland. B. C. Steiner. 1899.
Intimate glimpses of Old St. Mary's. G. M. Knight, Jr. (Data on old manors in St. Mary Co., 44 illus.) 1938.
Jamestown and St. Mary's buried cities of romance. H. C. Forman. Balto., 1938. DAR; Enoch Pratt Lib.
Johns Hopkins in its relation to Baltimore. Severn Teackle Wallis. Balto., 1883.

Johns Hopkins quarter century. The Spectator, N. Y., 1902, pp. 79–97.
Johns Hopkins University, 1876–91. Daniel C. Gilman. Johns Hopkins University Studies, series 9, Balto., 1891.
Johns Hopkins University Studies in Historical and Political Science. Herbert B. Adams, editor. 1882, v. 1. Johns Hopkins Press, Balto.
Index to series 1–40. 1922, series 40. MHS; Enoch Pratt Lib.
Joppa. Agreement to build Baltimore County Court House, 1709. M. H. Mag., 1909, v. 4, pp. 384–86.
Journal of Dutch embassy to Maryland (1615). Augustine Herman. In: Descriptions of Maryland. Steiner. Johns Hopkins University Studies, series 22.
Journal of travels of Uria Brown, from City of Baltimore to States of Pennsylvania, Ohio, Virginia and through parts of Maryland, 1861. M. H. Mag., 1915, v. 10, p. 262; 1916, v. 11, pp. 24, 142, 218, 348.
Journal of visit to New York, and tour in several American Colonies, 1679–80. Contains account of Labadist's of Bohemia Manor, Cecil County, Maryland. Jasper Dankers and Peter Sluyter of Wiewerd, in Friesland. Translated from manuscript in Dutch. Edited by H. C. Murphy. Brooklyn, 1867. MHS.
Journal relatio itineris in Maryland, 1635–77. From Father White's original narrative in Archives of Society of Jesus. Rev. W. McSherry. M. H. S. Fund Pub., no. 7, 1874. MHS.
Journeys to western Maryland, 1818–44. J. H. W. Hawkins.
Judicial administration in State of Maryland. Study. G. K. Reiblich. Johns Hopkins University Studies, series 47, no. 2, 1929. MHS; Enoch Pratt Lib.
Kent County. Government of Kent County. W. R. Howell. Pub. through coöperation of Washington College, Chestertown, Md., 1931. DAR.
Kent County. Old Kent of Eastern Shore of Maryland. Notes illustrative of most ancient records of Kent County, and parishes of St. Paul's, Shrewsbury and I. U., and genealogical history of old and distinguished families. G. A. Hanson. Balto., 1876, 1936. MHS; DAR.
Kent Fort Manor. B. C. Steiner. M. H. Mag., 1911, v. 6, pp. 254–55.
Kent Island. First commander. S. F. Streeter. M. H. S. Fund Pub., Balto., no. 2, 1868. MHS.
King Williams School. T. Fell. Containing list of presidents and representative alumni, 1790–1894. Annapolis, 1894. MHS.
†Ladies of press. Ishbel Ross. Harper, 1936.
Land-holder's assistant and Land office guide. John Kilty. Balto., 1808.
Land of epicure (Eastern Shore of Maryland). L. D. Wilson.
Land of legendary lore. Sketches of romance and reality on Eastern Shore of the Chesapeake. P. Ingraham. Easton, Md., 1898. MHS; Enoch Pratt Lib.
Land Office, of Maryland. Biennial reports of Commissioner. MHS; DAR.
Land policies and administrations in colonial Maryland, 1753–69. P. H. Giddens. M. H. Mag., 1933, v. 28, pp. 142–71.
Laws and ordinances relating to Baltimore and Ohio Rail Road. Balto., 1850.
Leading events in Maryland history. J. M. Gambrill. 1917.
Leah and Rachel, or two fruitful sisters of Virginia and Maryland. John Hammond. 1656, pamph., reprinted in Force's Tracts, v. 3, Wash., D. C., 1844.
Narrative and critical history of Maryland. Hall. 1910. MHS.
Legislature of State of Maryland. Study. H. J. Green. Johns Hopkins University Studies, series 48, no. 3, 1930. MHS; Enoch Pratt Lib.
Letter to inhabitants of Baltimore. Dr. George Buchanan. (Suggests registrations of deaths, formation of public parks, and organization of humane society.) Balto., 1790.
Liberty and property or beauty of Maryland displayed. Being brief and candid search and inquiry, into character and fundamental laws, by lover of this country. Written in latter part of seventeenth century. U. S. Catholic Hist. Soc. Mag., 1890, v. 3. MHS.
Life of Whittier's heroine, Barbara Fritchie; including brief but comprehensive sketch of historic "Old Frederick." H. M. Nixdorff.
Life on ocean or twenty years at sea, 1807–27. Personal adventures of author, George Little (born in Mass., 1791; service out of Port of Balto.). Boston, Waite, Pierce & Co., 1846, 12th edition. Enoch Pratt Lib.
List of Maryland mills, taverns, forges and furnaces, 1795. M. H. Mag., 1936, v. 31, no. 2, pp. 155–69.
†Little journeys, Salisbury, Maryland. Biographical—business. 1934–35. Enoch Pratt Lib.
Little madam. Henrietta Maria, Queen of King Charles I (in whose honor Lord Baltimore's settlement was called Maryland). Jane Mackay.
†Living authors. Biographies. N. Y., W. Wilson Co., 1931.
Local institutions of Maryland. L. W. Wilhelm. Johns Hopkins University Studies, series 3, nos. 5, 6, 7, p. 129, Balto., 1885.
Londontown on South River, Anne Arundel County; 240th anniversary. M. H. Mag., 1924, v. 19, pp. 134–43.
Long Shore poems of (Chesapeake) Bay. Joel D. Barber. Derrydale Press, 1939, 124 pp.
Lord Baltimore's case. From Calvert Papers. Reprint of pamphlet. M. H. Mag., 1909, v. 4, pp. 171–82.
Lord Baltimore's Maryland. Manors, undisposed of, in 1776. History of Maryland. Scharf. V. 2, pp. 104–05. MHS.
Lords Baltimore. John G. Morris. M. H. S. Fund Pub., no. 8, Balto., 1874. MHS.
Lords Baltimore and Maryland Palatinate. C. C. Hall. Balto., 1904, 27 pp. MHS; DAR.
Lords Baltimore; exhibition of their portraits at War Memorial. Catalogue and history of paintings, owned by Dr. Hugh Young. Pamph. MHS; DAR.
Making of Maryland. Elmer and M. Green. Balto., 1934. DAR.
Manors and hundreds of Prince George County. M. H. Mag., 1934, v. 29, no. 3, p. 37; corrections, no. 4.
Marshall Hall and Potomac points. In: Story and picture. Minnie Kendall-Lowther. 1925, pamph. MHS; DAR.

Martin. Luther Martin. Speech to House of Delegates, 1788. B. C. Steiner. M. H. Mag., 1910, v. 5, pp. 139-50.
Martin. Luther Martin and Constitution. M. H. Mag., Dec., 1932, v. 27, no. 4, pp. 190, 280.
Maryland. American Guide Series (Works Progress Administration). Oxford Press, 1940, 561 pp., maps, illus.
Maryland and France, 1774-89. K. Sullivan. 1936. DAR.
Maryland and thoroughbred. D. Sterett Gittings. Balto., 1932.
Maryland and Virginia. Justin Winsor. (With critical essay on sources of information.) In his Narrative and critical history of America. (Maryland, 1887, v. 5, pp. 259-84.) Boston and N. Y., 1884-89, illus., maps. Peabody Lib.
Maryland as palatinate. Constance Lippincott. 1902.
Maryland as proprietary province. N. D. Mereness. N. Y., Macmillan Co., 1901. MHS; Peabody Lib.
†Maryland biography. R. H. Spencer. Amer. Hist. Soc., 1919. Peabody Lib.
Maryland business corporations, 1782-1852. J. G. Blandi. Johns Hopkins University Studies, 1934, series 52, no. 3. MHS; Enoch Pratt Lib.
Maryland composers. Compiled by Doris G. Wright, chairman of American Music, Elizabeth R. Davis, chairman State Composers' Research, and Virginia McNeill, editor of Maryland Bulletin. Pub. by Md. Federation of Music Clubs. Bklet., 1940.
Maryland during English Civil Wars. B. C. Steiner. Johns Hopkins University Studies, 1906, series 24, pt. 1, nos. 11, 12; 1907, series 25, pt. 2, nos. 4, 5. MHS; Enoch Pratt Lib.
Maryland General Assembly. H. Dawson. Peabody Lib.
Maryland gardens and houses. Elizabeth Clapp, Charlton Gillet, Romaine Randall. Federated Garden Clubs of Md., 1938, map.
Maryland in 1720. From Calendar of State Papers. M. H. Mag., 1934, v. 29, pp. 252-55.
Maryland in 1773. M. H. Mag., 1907, v. 2, pp. 354-62.
Maryland in 1798. M. H. Mag., 1936, v. 31, pp. 247-53.
Maryland in Liberia. J. H. B. Latrobe. M. H. S. Fund Pub., no. 21, Balto., 1885. MHS.
Maryland in Liberia. Brief statement of facts showing origin, progress and necessity of African colonization. J. D. Toy. Balto., 1836. Enoch Pratt Lib.
Maryland in Liberia. Colonization Society Committee of Board of Managers. John D. Toy. Balto., 1837. Enoch Pratt Lib.
Maryland in Liberia. Constitution and laws of Maryland in Liberia. John D. Toy. Balto., 1837, 215 pp. Enoch Pratt Lib.
Maryland in Liberia. History of Colony planted by Maryland State Colonization Society under auspices of State of Maryland, at Cape Palmas, south coast of Africa, 1833-53. J. H. B. Latrobe. Balto., 1885. Enoch Pratt Lib.
Maryland in Liberia. Laws, statutes, etc. John D. Toy. Balto., 1847, 2nd edition. Enoch Pratt Lib.
†Maryland in national politics. J. Fred Essary. 1915. DAR; Peabody Lib.
Maryland in poetry. Under this heading are entered poems about Maryland. Catalogue list, Md. Room, Enoch Pratt Lib.
Maryland in prose and poetry. E. M. Noble. E. T. Tubbs. Balto., 1909. Enoch Pratt Lib.
Maryland independence and Confederation. W. I. Hull. M. H. S. Fund Pub., no. 31, Balto., 1891. MHS.
Maryland's influence upon land cessions to United States. With minor papers on George Washington's interest in western lands, Potomac Company and national university. Herbert B. Adams. Johns Hopkins University Studies, series 3, no. 1, p. 102, Balto., 1885.
Maryland influence in founding national commonwealth or history of accession of public lands by old Confederation. H. B. Adams. M. H. S. Fund Pub., no. 11, Balto., 1877. MHS.
Maryland: its resources and industries and institution. W. H. Browne and others. Balto., 1893.
Maryland manor. F. Emory.
Maryland manor. J. G. Wilson. M. H. S. Fund Pub., no. 3, Balto., 1890. MHS.
Maryland manual. Compendium of legal, historical and statistical information relating to State of Maryland, 1631-date. Compiled by Secretary of State. Pub. annually, 1896-date. MHS; DAR; Enoch Pratt Lib.
Maryland memories. J. Edgeworth.
†Maryland men and institutions. Md. Biog. Assoc., 1920. Enoch Pratt Lib.
Maryland mutual savings bank. R. W. Thom, Jr. Johns Hopkins University Studies, series 53, no. 3, 1935. MHS; Enoch Pratt Lib.
Maryland, my Maryland, and other poems. James Ryder Randall. Balto., 1908.
Maryland or Rhode Island: which was first? Rev. Lucien Johnston. N. Y., 1904.
Maryland pilgrimage. G. H. Grosvenor. 1927.
Maryland poets. Foreword by Maria Briscoe Crocker. N. Y., 1932.
Maryland's primary bridge program. John E. G. Griener. 1938, 2 vols.
Maryland records. Colonial, Revolutionary, county and church. G. M. Brumbaugh. 1915, 1928, 2 vols. MHS; DAR; Enoch Pratt Lib.
Maryland silversmiths, 1715-1830. With illustrations of their silver and their marks, with facsimile of design book of William Faris. J. Hall Pleasant and Howard Sill. Balto., 1930. MHS.
Maryland State flag and colonial county colors. F. B. Culver. 1934. DAR.
Maryland State House. Memorial to John Appleton Wilson. (1674, capital was removed from St. Mary's City to Annapolis, under Gov. Francis Nicholson, also transfer of provincial records; 1696, foundation of first State House laid; 1704, destroyed by fire; 1706, second State House completed; 1772, torn down and foundation laid by Gov. Eden, for third State House; 1774, completed, dome added after Revolution; 1879, repaired; 1904, annex added.) Soc. Col. Wars of Md. 1931. MHS.
Maryland. Stories of her people and her history. L. M. Passano. Balto., 1905.
Maryland. Two hundred years ago. S. F. Streeter. Balto., 1852. MHS.

Maryland under Commonwealth, 1649–58. B. C. Steiner. Assembly, 1650; proprietor and colonists, 1650–51; proprietors struggle in England to retain this Province, Gov. Stone, 1652–53; Stone's breach with Commonwealth, Md. Civil War, 1654; conditions after War, Josias Fendall Governor, 1655; restoration of proprietary government, 1657; Appendix, p. 117, summary of proceedings of Provincial Courts, 1649–58. Johns Hopkins University Studies, series 29, no. 1, 1911. MHS; Enoch Pratt Lib.

†Maryland women. Biographical sketches. M. H. Luckett. Balto., 1931, 1937, 1939, 3 vols. MHS; DAR; Enoch Pratt Lib., card indexed.

†Marylanders I have known, some distinguished. H. P. Goddard. M. H. Mag., 1909, v. 4, pp. 24–41.

Maryland's adoption of Federal Constitution. B. C. Steiner. MHS.

Maryland's attitude in struggle for Canada. J. W. Black. Johns Hopkins University Studies, series 10, Balto., 1892.

Maryland's colonial charm portrayed in silver. Comdr. Harry W. Hill, U.S.N. (Account of sconses on famous service on U. S. S. Maryland. 300 pp., 40 illus. Newport, R. I., Naval War College, 1938.

Maryland's colonial Eastern Shore. Nine counties and their people. S. Earle and P. G. Skirven. Pub. under auspices of East. Shore Soc., Balto., 1916.

Maryland's first capital. Pamph. DAR.

Maryland's greatest politician, Cecilius Calvert's career as index to history of Palatinate. Edward Ingle. Southern Hist. Assoc. Pub., 1898, v. 2, p. 203.

Maryland's most historic spot, St. Mary's City. D. A. R. Mag., July, 1931, v. 65, no. 7, p. 415.

Maryland's part in founding Federal Government. Columbia Hist. Soc. Records, v. 19, p. 140.

†Mayors of Baltimore, 1797–1919. Biographical sketches. W. F. Coyle. Reprint from Balto. Municipal Journal, 1919. City Hall Lib.

†Medical annals of Baltimore, 1608–1880. J. F. Quinan. 1884. Enoch Pratt Lib.

†Medical annals of Maryland, 1799–1899. E. F. Cordell. Contains brief biographies of 2000 members of Medical and Chirurgical Faculty, giving place and date of birth and death. List of incorporators (pp. 22–25); list of members admitted since 1899–1902. Balto., Williams & Wilkins Co. 1903. MHS.

Memoranda in reference to German emigration (early) to Md. F. B. Mayer. Soc. for Hist. of Germans in Md., 5th Annual Rept., 1890–91. MHS.

†Memorials of several ministers and other deceased of Religious Society of Friends, within limits of Baltimore Meeting. 1875. DAR.

†Men of mark in Maryland. Biographical sketches of leading men. 4 vols., Johnson, Wynne Co., 1907; B. F. Johnson Co., 1912; Washington, D. C. DAR; Enoch Pratt Lib.; Peabody Lib.

†Men of Maryland. Collection of portraits of representative men in business and professional life in State of Md. Journalists Club, 1905. Enoch Pratt Lib.

†Men of Maryland specially honored by State and United States. Col. C. Chaille-Long. M. H. Mag., 1917, v. 12, pp. 201–53, 283–85; corrections and additions, 1918, v. 13, p. 76.

Men of Maryland since Civil War. V. 1, all published. Paul Winchester. Balto., 1923.

†Mercantile Trust Company of Baltimore. Early eighties. 1924. Enoch Pratt Lib.

Merion in Welsh Tract. Thomas Allen Glenn. Norristown, Pa., 1896. History of Cecil County. Johnston. "Most of original Welsh settlers on Welsh Tract, 1701, lived in Chester County, Pa.," p. 61. "Part of Welsh Tract is in Cecil County, Md.," p. 160.

Migrations of Baltimore Town. Rev. G. A. Leakin. M. H. Mag., 1906, v. 1, pp. 45–49.

Minerals of Maryland. C. W. Ostrander and W. E. Price, Jr. Natural History Society of Maryland, 1940.

†Modern encyclopedia. Complete in 1 vol. Edited by A. H. McDannald. N. Y., Wise & Co., 1933.

Money and transportation in Maryland, 1720–65. Economic history. C. P. Gould. Johns Hopkins University Studies, series 33, no. 1, 1915. MHS; Enoch Pratt Lib.

Montgomery County. Annals of Sandy Spring, or twelve years of rural community. Eliza N. Moore. 1884, 1902, 2 vols. MHS; DAR.

Montgomery County. Annals of Sandy Springs, or twelve years of rural community. Rebecca T. Miller. Balto., 1909.

Montgomery County. Annals of Sandy Spring. Two hundred and twenty years history of rural community in Maryland. Wm. Henry Farquhar. Balto., 1884.

†Montgomery County. Centennial celebration of erection of Montgomery County into separate municipality. Held at Rockville, Sept. 6, 1876. Contains earliest patents, 1688–1775; list of citizens and biographies. C. C. Saffel. Balto., 1887. MHS.

Montgomery County. Home community of nation's capitol. Wash., D. C., Greater Montgomery County, Inc., 1932.

Monumental City or Baltimore guide book. 1858.

†Monumental City. Its past history and present resources. Biographical. George W. Howard. Balto., J. D. Ehlers Co., 1873, maps, illus., 3 vols. MHS; DAR; Enoch Pratt Lib.

Mother St. Urban. Life of Mother St. Urban of Congregation of Sisters of Bon Secours of Paris. Rev. T. D. Williams. (Balto., p. 119.) Balto., John Murphy Co., 1936. Enoch Pratt Lib.

Mountain Lake Park, summit of Alleghanies. J. G. Pangborn. Chicago, 1884.

Mt. Royal and its owners, 1792. M. H. Mag., 1931, v. 26, pp. 311–15.

Moyaone and Piscataway Indians. A. L. L. Ferguson. Wash., D. C., pub. by author, 44 pp. MHS.

My Maryland. J. M. Gambrill. DAR.

My Maryland. Text book for intermediate grades. B. Kaessmann, H. R. Manakee and J. L. Wheeler. 1934. DAR.

Nanticoke. Dedicated to those born on its banks, birth place of author. Wm. M. Marine.

Nanticocke Manor. M. H. Mag., 1910, v. 5, pp. 252–54.

Narrative and critical history of America. (English in Maryland, Brantly, v. 3, p. 517.) Justin Winsor, editor. 8 v. Amer. Hist. Soc., N. Y., 1887.

Narrative of Col. Henry Darnall. From Public Record Office. America and West Indies, no.

556, London, Dec. 31, 1689. History of Maryland. Scharf. V. 1, p. 338. MHS.

Narratives of early Maryland, 1633–84. C. C. Hall. Contains account of Lord Baltimore's case, 1653; Baltimore case, uncased and answered, 1655 (Va., and Md.); Babylon's fall in Maryland, 1655, reprinted. M. H. Mag., v. 3, p. 228; refutation of Babylon's fall, p. 254, reprinted from pamphlet, by John Langford, 1655; Journal of George Fox, 1672–73, p. 391; Baltimore and Penn, 1682–84, p. 414; names of the gentlemen adventurers to Maryland, 1634, p. 101; etc. Scribner's Sons. N. Y., 1910. Lib. Cong.; MHS.

Natural and industrial resources and advantages of Maryland. J. T. Scharf. Annapolis, 1892.

Negro in Maryland. Johns Hopkins University Studies, series 23, 1889, extra v. 6. MHS; Enoch Pratt Lib.

New Hall of Records at Annapolis. Lawrence Fowler and Arthur Trader. M. H. Mag., 1935, v. 30, p. 62.

New light on Maryland history from British Archives. Bernard C. Steiner. M. H. Mag., 1909, v. 4, pp. 251–56.

New light on Maryland Loyalists. M. H. Mag., 1907, v. 2, pp. 133–37.

New Yarmouth. The ancient capital of Kent County. Md. O. R. Soc., v. 2, p. 100.

New Yarmouth, Kent County. Peregin Wroth. M. H. Mag., 1908, v. 3, pp. 273–76.

Notes on colonial free school (King William's) in Anne Arundel County, 1696. M. H. Mag., 1923, v. 18, pp. 248–56.

*Notes on history. Quarterly. Robt. Hayes, 3526 Roland Avenue, Balto. V. 1, 1940, multigraphed. MHS; DAR.

Notes on history, Hampden-Woodberry and other parts of Baltimore. V. 1. Pamph. DAR.

Notes on progress of colored people of Maryland, since War. J. R. Brackett. Balto., 1890, series 8, nos. 7, 8, 9, p. 96.

Old Baltimore, 1729–1829. A. L. Sioussat. Pub. under auspices of Md. Soc. of Colonial Dames of America. N. Y., Macmillan, 1931. MHS; DAR.

Old Bay Line, 1840–1940. (Story of steamboats that plied Chesapeake for last century.) Alexander Crosby Brown. 1940, illus. Enoch Pratt Lib.

Old Catholic Maryland. W. P. Treacy. DAR.

Old homes and ways in Maryland. J. W. Palmer. Century, v. 49, p. 244.

Old homes in and around St. Mary's City and County. J. Spence Howard. MHS.

Old houses of Harford County. J. Alexis Shriver. Ms. MHS.

Old Indian Road (18th century). Descriptive and map of some roads as early as 1661. Wm. B. Marye. 1920, v. 15, pp. 107–24, 208–29, 345–95.

Old manors in Colony of Maryland. 1st and 2nd series. A. L. Sioussat. Balto., Lord Balto. Press, 1911, pamph. MHS; DAR.

Old Maryland manors, with record of court leet and court baron. John Johnson. Johns Hopkins University Studies, series 1, no. 7, p. 38, Balto., 1882.

Old Senate Chamber. DeCourcy W. Thom. M. H. Mag., 1907, v. 2, pp. 326–35.

Old Senate Chamber, 1772. M. H. Mag., 1930, v. 25, pp. 365–84.

*Old Somerset on Eastern Shore of Maryland. Study in foundations and founders. Clayton Torrence. Richmond, 1935, 582 pp., with index. MHS; DAR.

Old South. W. E. Dodd. 1st vol. of forthcoming series of 4, Md., Va. and Carolinas. N. Y., Macmillan Co. DAR.

One hundred and fiftieth anniversary of founding of Baltimore, 1730–1880. "Oration" delivered Oct. 11, 1880, by J. T. Scharf. 1880, 20 pp. DAR.

Origin and growth of civil liberty in Maryland. J. D. Toy. M. H. S. Pub., Balto., 1850, v. 2, no. 10.

Origin and growth of civil liberty in Maryland. (Discourse before Maryland Historical Society.) G. W. Brown. Balto., 1850, 40 pp.

Original narratives of early American history. Reproduced under auspices of American Historical Society. J. Franklin Jameson, general editor.

Otho Holland Williams Papers. 7 vols. Mss., several hundred loose papers. MHS.

Otho Holland Williams Papers. Calendar. Historical Records Survey. MHS.

Paper money in Maryland, 1727–89. K. L. Behrens. Johns Hopkins University Studies, series 41, no. 1, 1923. MHS; Enoch Prabb Lib.

†Papers relating to early history of Maryland. S. F. Streeter. Contains First Assembly, journal of proceedings, and members. Fund Pub., no. 9, Balto., Jan., 1876. MHS.

Patapsco and other poems. C. Scran. Fielding Lucas, Jr., 1842.

Patowmeck above ye inhabitants. 2 pts. Wm. B. Marye. (With land notes, p. 135, and map by Lloyd; about 1721 mss. MHS.) M. H. Mag., 1935, v. 30, pp. 1–11, 114–37.

Patriotic Marylander. Published by Maryland State Society, Daughters of American Revolution. Issued quarterly, 3 vols., Sept., 1914, to June, 1917. MHS; DAR.

Patuxent and other poems. L. F. Matthews. Balto., 1907.

Pennsylvania Germans in settlement of Maryland. Daniel Wunderlich Nead. Lancaster, Pa., 1914. MHS; DAR.

Pennsylvania Rail Road. Summer excursion routes. Phila., 1879, 166 pp., illus.

Personal narrative of travels in Virginia and Maryland, 1817–18. E. P. Fordham. 1906. Peabody Lib.

Pictorial history of Frederick County. Frederick Chapter, D. A. R. Mss. DAR.

Pioneers of early days of Westminster, Carroll County, Maryland, 1721–1898. Mary B. Shellman. Contains inhabitants, 1822–32. 1924. MHS; DAR.

Piscataway. Wm. B. Marye. M. H. Mag., 1935, v. 30, no. 3, pp. 183–240; land notes, p. 233.

Plains of Parran, Baltimore County. Natl. Geneal. Soc. Quart., Dec., 1938, v. 26, no. 4, p. 27. MHS.

Plan of City of Baltimore. N. Y., J. H. Colton Co., 1855.

Plan of Fort McHenry, 1794. M. H. Mag., 1913, v. 8, pp. 286–90.

Poems of late Francis S. Key, Esq., author of Star Spangled Banner. With introduction by Chief Justice Taney. N. Y., 1857.

Poets and poetry of Cecil County. Collected and edited by George Johnston. Elkton, Md., the editor, 1887. DAR.

†Poets and prose writers of Maryland. George Perine. MHS.
Poets and verse writers of Maryland, 1754–1869. G. C. Perine. Cincinnati, Publishing Company, 1869. MHS.
Political. Book in opposition to "Knownothingism" as place of politics in State of Maryland. J. Raymond.
Politics in Maryland, 1720–50, and public service of Daniel Dulany, the Elder. St. G. L. Sioussat. 1903, Johns Hopkins Press, 84 pp. MHS.
†Portrait and biographical record of Eastern Shore of Maryland. N. Y. and Chicago, Chapman Publishing Company, 1898. MHS; DAR; Enoch Pratt Lib.
†Portrait and biographical record of Harford and Cecil Counties. N. Y. and Chicago, Chapman Publishing Company, 1898. MHS; Enoch Pratt Lib.
†Portrait and biographical record of Sixth Congressional District of Maryland. (Western Maryland, including Allegany, Frederick, Garrett, Montgomery and Washington Counties.) N. Y., Chapman Publishing Company. 1898, 873 pp. MHS; DAR; Enoch Pratt Lib.
Potomac landings. Author's travels and research in Maryland and Virginia. P. Wilstach. N. Y., Garden City, 1921. Reprint, N. Y., 1931. DAR.
Pratt, Enoch. Mss. MHS.
Principio company. Historical sketch of first iron work in Maryland. W. G. Whitely. Pa. Mag. Hist. and Biog., 1887, v. 11. MHS.
Proceedings of conventions of Province of Maryland, held at Annapolis 1774–76. Pub. at Annapolis, repub. in Balto., 1836. (Original mss. in MHS.) MHS.
Progress of colored people in Maryland. J. R. Brackett. Johns Hopkins University Studies, series 8, nos. 7 and 9, 1890. MHS; Enoch Pratt Lib.
Proprietary manors and hundreds of St. Mary's, Old Charles, Calvert, New Charles and Prince George Counties. H. J. Berkley. M. H. Mag., 1934, v. 29, no. 3, pp. 237–45; corrections, no. 4, p. 335.
Provincial flag of Maryland. R. H. Spencer. M. H. Mag., 1914, v. 9, pp. 218–25.
Provincial government of Maryland, 1774–77. J. A. Silver. Johns Hopkins University Studies, series 13, no. 10, 1895. MHS; Enoch Pratt Lib.
Public educational work in Maryland. Herbert B. Adams. Johns Hopkins University Studies, v. 17, Balto., 1899.
Public parks of Baltimore. Annual rept., no. 1, Sept. 1, 1927. MHS; DAR.
Puritan colony in Maryland. Daniel R. Randall. Johns Hopkins University Studies, 1886, series 4, no. 6. MHS; Enoch Pratt Lib.
†Quynn, Wm. Letters of Maryland medical student in Philadelphia and Edinburgh, 1782–84. M. H. Mag., 1936, v. 31, pp. 181–215.
Recollections. Wm. Cabell Bruce. 1931. DAR.
Recollections of Baltimore. Robt. Gilmore. M. H. Mag., 1912, v. 7, pp. 233–42.
Recollections of Baltimore. J. H. Neff. M. H. Mag., 1910, v. 5, pp. 104–23.
Records of City of Baltimore. Issued by W. F. Coyle, city Librarian. 1909, v. 1, supplement, 1729–1813. 1905, v. 2, first records of Baltimore Town and Jones Town, plat of lots and lot holders, 1729–97. 1909, v. 3, special commissioners, 1782–97. 1906, v. 4, city commissioners, 1797–1813. V. 5, commissioners, eastern precincts, 1812–17, and western precincts, 1810–17. Balto., 5 vols. MHS; DAR; City Hall Lib., Enoch Pratt Lib.
Records of Joppa Town, 1724. Accompanied by plat showing lot owners and more important buildings. Dr. Wm. Stull Holt. Mss. MHS.
Relation of Colony of Lord Baron of Baltimore in Maryland, near Virginia, 1558. Rev. Andrew White.
Relations of successful beginnings of Lord Baltimore plantation on Maryland. Brantz Mayer.
†Representative authors of Maryland, earliest time to present day. H. E. Sherpherd. 1911, Peabody Lib.
Restoration of Homewood and customs in colonial times in Maryland. Dr. R. T. H. Halsey. MHS.
Restoration of Proprietary of Maryland and legislation against Roman Catholics during governorship of Capt. John Hart, 1714–20. B. C. Steiner. MHS.
Restoration of Senate Chamber, 1876. M. H. Mag., 1927, v. 22, pp. 54–62.
Rich Neck Manor, 1684–1790. M. H. Mag., 1914, v. 9, pp. 226–32.
Rinehart letters. W. S. Rush. M. H. Mag., 1936, v. 31, pp. 225–42.
†Roads to success by Maryland's men and women of achievement. K. Z. Donellan. Calvert Text Book Co., 1927. Enoch Pratt Lib.
Rose Croft in Old St. Mary's. H. C. Forman. M. H. Mag., Mar., 1940, v. 15, no. 1, pp. 26–31.
Rose Hill Manor, Frederick Co. Rose Hill ballot box. Helen Urner Price. D. A. R. Mag., June, 1940, v. 74, p. 28.
Routes traveled by George Washington in Maryland. J. A. Shriver. Photos., maps. MHS; DAR.
Royall's (Mrs. Anne) articles about many people in Annapolis, Baltimore, Frederick, and Hagerstown, and on St. John's College and State House, Annapolis.
Sailor of fortune. Life and adventure of Commodore Barney. Herbert Footner. Harper, 305 pp.
Second general report of board of managers to proprietors and lot holders of Greenmount Cemetery, 1846. MHS; DAR.
Select bibliography of English genealogy, with brief list of Wales, Scotland and Ireland. Howard Guy Harrison. London, 1937. Peabody Lib.
Settlers in Havre de Grace, 1658. Sketch of them, with names and dates. Wm. B. Maryer. M. H. Mag., 1918, v. 13, pp. 197–214.
†Seven great Baltimore lawyers. Wm. Cabell Bruce. Pamph. MHS.
Siege of Baltimore and Battle of La Tranche; with other original poems. A. Umphraville. Balto., 1817.
Six historic homesteads. I. B. Oakley. (Mount Clare, Baltimore, owned by Charles Carroll, barrister, being one.) Phila., University of Pennsylvania Press. DAR.
Sizes of plantations in seventeenth century Maryland. V. J. Wyckoff. M. H. Mag., Dec., 1937, v. 32, no. 4, pp. 331–39.
Sketch of early currency in Maryland and Virginia. Banker's Mag., Aug., 1851, new series, v. 1, pp. 85–90. See also: Historical Mag., N. Y., 1858, v. 11, pp. 42–44.

Sketches of early history of Maryland with Annals of Baltimore, 1660–1821. T. W. Griffith. 1821, 1824. MHS; DAR; Enoch Pratt Lib.
Sketches of history of Maryland, 1633–60. John Leeds Bozman. 2 vols. First edition, 1811. Balto., 1837. MHS.
Snow Hill, Maryland. Charter, Acts of Assembly, and ordinances up to May, 1912. Contains plat, 1793, and maps, 1794–1894; some officials, 1894–1912. Published by authority of Mayor and Council of Snow Hill. Pamph. MHS.
Soil exhaustion as factor in agricultural history of Virginia and Maryland. A. O. Craven. University of Illinois. Studies in Social Sciences, Urbana, 1925, v. 13.
Soldiers Delight Hundred, Baltimore County. M. H. Mag., 1906, v. 1, pp. 141–54.
Some colonial mansions and those who lived in them. T. A. Glenn. 2 vols. 1st series, 1897; 2nd series, 1900. MHS.
†Some early colonial Marylanders. McHenry Howard. M. H. Mag., 1919, v. 14, pp. 384–99; 1920, v. 5, pp. 65–71, 168–80, 292–304, 312–24; 1921, v. 16, pp. 9–18, 179–89.
Some economic problems of seventeenth century Maryland. V. J. Wyckoff. MHS.
Some historic houses; their builders and their places in history. Dr. John C. Fitzpatrick, editor. Forword by Mrs. Charles E. Reiman, Baltimore, chairman. (Mount Clare, Balto., owned by Charles Carroll, barrister, being one.) Natl. Soc. of Colonial Dames of Amer. Enoch. Pratt Lib.
†Some Maryland statesmen in Continental Congress. F. Braxton. Enoch Pratt Lib., card indexed.
Some old historical landmarks of Virginia and Maryland. W. H. Snowden. Alexandria, Va., 1910.
Songs of Chesapeake. L. M. Thurston. With decorations by Margaret M. Piggott. Balto., no date.
Sot-weed factor or a voyage to Maryland. Ebeneezer Cook. Describing along Piscataway on Eastern Shore and to Annapolis. (Written in verse.) London, 1708, reprinted N. Y., 1865. MHS; Lib. Cong.
Sot-Weed Redivious. E. C. Gent. Annapolis, William Parks for author, 1730.
South American trade of Baltimore. F. R. Rutter. Johns Hopkins University Studies, series 15, no. 9. MHS; Enoch Pratt Lib.
Southern Spectator of Maryland, Virginia and District of Columbia. MHS; DAR.
Spirit of Maryland, as revealed in her twenty-three counties. From provincial days to 1929. E. E. Lantz. Balto., 1929. DAR.
Spring House, Goodloe-Harper estate, Roland Park. R. Buckler. MHS.
State administration in Maryland. Public education, public health, charities, finance, general economic welfare. J. E. Donaldson. Johns Hopkins University Studies, series 34, no. 1, p. 1916. MHS; Enoch Pratt Lib.
State banking in Maryland. A. C. Bryan. Johns Hopkins University Studies, series 17, nos. 1, 2, 3, 1899. MHS.
State government in Maryland, 1777–81. Beverly W. Bond, Jr. Johns Hopkins University Studies, series 23, nos. 3–4, Balto., 1905.
State House repairs, 1792. M. H. Mag., 1910, v. 5, pp. 188–91.
Story of Baltimore and Ohio Rail Road, 1827–1927. E. Hungerford. N. Y., 1928, 2 vols.
Story of Maryland politics. Political history of State, from Civil War to 1910. Frank R. Kent. 1911. MHS.
Story of thirteen colonies. H. A. Guerber. 1898.
Stricker letters. Alice H. Brent. M. H. Mag., Mar. 1, 1939, v. 34, no. 1, p. 67.
Supplementary report of taxation in Maryland. In: Report of Maryland tax commission to General Assembly. R. T. Ely. Balto., 1888.
Tah-Jah-Jute, or Logan the Mingo Chief. H. Jones. 1937. DAR.
Tah-Jah-Jute or Logan and Captain Michael Cresap. Historical essay. Brantz Mayer. (Considerably enlarged from address of same title before Maryland Historical Society in 1851.) Albany, 1867.
Talbot County. Recollections of a Long Life on the Eastern Shore. J. B. Seth and Mary W. Seth. Easton, Md. 1926.
Tales of Chesapeake. N. Y., 1880.
Tales of Old Maryland. History and romance of Eastern Shore of Maryland. J. H. K. Shannahan, Jr. Balto., 1907. MHS; Enoch Pratt Lib.
Taneytown. Founder. (Correction of Scharf's History of western Maryland.) M. H. Mag., 1916, v. 11, pp. 74–75.
Tangier Island; study of isolated group. S. Warren Hall, III. Phila., University of Pennsylvania Press, 1939. 122 pp.
Taxation in Maryland. T. Sewall Adams.
Tench Filghman's ride. (Poem.) Latrobe Weston. M. H. Mag., 1933, v. 28, pp. 139–41.
†Tercentenary history of Maryland. M. P. Andrews. 4 vols. Contain hundreds of biographical sketches of Maryland men. Balto., 1925. MHS; DAR; Enoch Pratt Lib., card indexed.
Terra mariae or threads of Maryland history. E. B. Neill. Phila., Lippincott & Co., 1867. MHS.
Thoroughbred horse and Maryland. W. Woodward. M. H. Mag., 1922, v. 17, pp. 139–62.
Three French visitors to Baltimore. Century ago. Gilbert Chinard. MHS.
†Three hundred years. Poets and poetry of Maryland. L. Raley. 1937. MHS; Enoch Pratt Lib., card indexed.
Tidewater Maryland. Jaunts through bay-front counties along tidal creeks and Coves; charm of old estates and legends of tidewater people. P. Wilstach. Indianapolis, 1931. DAR.
Tobbaco trade in Maryland, 1700–25. (History with poem, by Ebenezer Cooke.) Paul R. Kelbaugh. M. H. Mag., 1931, v. 26, pp. 1–33.
Towns erected in Maryland, prior to Revolution. History of Maryland. Scharf. 1683–1751, v. 1, p. 411; 1732–57, v. 2, p. 54. MHS.
Trade and industry in colonial Maryland. P. H. Giddens. MHS.
Traditions of St. Mary's. M. B. Crocker. Pamph. DAR.
Tragic scenes in history of Maryland and Old French War. Jos. Banvard. Boston, 1856. MHS.
Transportation of felons to Colonies, 1756–68. M. H. Mag., 1932, v. 27, pp. 263–74.
Transportation of prisoners to Maryland, 1719. M. H. Mag., 1926, v. 21, p. 394.

Transported convict laborers in Maryland during colonial period. M. H. Mag., 1907, v. 2, pp. 17–47.

True relation of Virginia and Maryland, 1667. N. Shrigley. Force's Tracts, 3. Wash., D. C., 1844.

Two hundredth anniversary of Baltimore, 1729–1929. Balto. Municipal Journal. Robt. Irwin, editor. Balto., 1929. DAR.

†Two Maryland heroines. M. H. Mag., 1908, v. 3, pp. 133–41.

Unpublished manuscript of Baltimore Town and Baltimore County. Bd. ms. DAR.

Virginians and Marylanders at Harvard College in seventeenth century. (Bennett, Brooke and Utie of Maryland.) In: William and Mary Quart., 2nd series, v. 13, no. 1, p. 1.

Visit to Bohemia Manor, Rev. Geo. A. Leakin. M. H. Mag., 1907, v. 2, pp. 143–46.

Voyage of the *Ark* and the *Dove*. From Public Record Office, London. M. H. Mag., 1906, v. 1, pp. 352–53.

Washington monument. Robert Mills and Washington monument. M. H. Mag., June, 1939, v. 34, no. 2, pp. 144–60; June, 1940, v. 35, no. 2, pp. 178–89; (to be continued).

Washington Monument and Square. M. H. Mag., 1918, v. 13, pp. 179–82.

Washington prints, list and description. M. H. Mag., 1919, v. 14, pp. 205–58.

Washington's relation to Eastern Shore of Maryland. M. H. Mag., 1926, v. 21, pp. 170–78.

When the Hopkins came to Baltimore. A. K. Bond. Brief mention of men connected with Johns Hopkins University. Pegasus Press, 1927. Enoch Pratt Lib.

White servitude in Maryland, 1634–1820. E. J. McCormac. Johns Hopkins University Studies, series 22, nos. 3–4, Balto., 1904. MHS; Enoch Pratt Lib.

Who were early settlers of Maryland. Ethan Allen. Paper read before Maryland Historical Society, Oct. 5, 1865. Amer. Quart. Church Review, 1866.

Who's who in America. Biographical dictionary of notable living men and women of United States. John W. Leonard. A. N. Marquis Co.

Winter journeys in South. J. M. Hammond. Phila., 1916.

†Women of Maryland (colonial). M. H. Mag., 1907, v. 2, pp. 214–26, notes, p. 379.

Work among working women in Baltimore. (Notes supplementary to Johns Hopkins University Studies, no. 6.) H. Baxter Adams.

Workmen's compensation in Maryland. E. E. Singleton. Johns Hopkins University Studies, series 53, no. 2, 1935. MHS; Enoch Pratt Lib.

Wye Island. Lippincott. V. 9, pp. 466–74. (Refers to Bordley, Floyd and Paca families.)

Wye House, Talbot County. (Descriptions with pictures.) M. H. Mag., 1923, v. 18, pp. 293–99.

GENEALOGY

MARYLAND

*Abstracts from Journal of Bishop Christian Newcomer, 1795–1830. N. H. Betts. 1935, pamph. MHS; DAR.

Allegany County. Births, 1865–1900. Court House, Cumberland.

Allegany County. Deaths, 1790. 8 vols. Court House, Cumberland.

Allegany County. Necrology, 1813–81. Hist. of west Md. Scharf. V. 2, pp. 1456–57. MHS; DAR.

Ancestral pilgrimage along life's pathway. Cartwright, Galloway, Gay, King, Mitchell, Stevenson and Waters families. (Very little Md.) 1940. MHS.

*Ancient families of Bohemia Manor, their homes and their graves. C. P. Mallery. Pub. Hist. Soc. Del., Wilmington, 1888. MHS.

*Andrews' Scrap Book. MHS.

Anne Arundel and Calvert Counties. Early Quaker records, 1665–1889. Pub. Geneal. Soc. Pa., v. 3, no. 3, pp. 197–200. MHS.

*Anne Arundel County gentry: Twenty-two pioneers and their descendants; historical and genealogical. H. W. Newman. Balto., 1933, Lord Baltimore Press, 668 pp. MHS; DAR.

Baltimore City and County. Necrology, 1781–1881. Hist. of Balto. City and Co. Scharf. Pp. 794–811. MHS.

*Baltimore: its history, its people. Clayton C. Hall. Vol. 1: History. Vols. 2 and 3: Genealogies and biographies. Index in vol. 3. N. Y., Lewis Publishing Co., 1912, illus., map. MHS; DAR.

*Baltimore. Marriages and deaths. (Over 10,000.) Baltimore American, 1771–1840. Federal Gazette, 1790–1820. Collected and owned by F. Sidney Hayward, 508 Harwood Avenue, Govans, Balto.

Baptismal and marriage records. Extracted from journal of Rev. John Sharpe, 1704–14. Start at Love Point, Maryland. Pa. Mag., v. 23, p. 104. MHS.

Carroll County. Births and deaths, 1837–98. Court House, Westminster.
1898–date. State Department of Health, Balto.

Carroll County. Names of persons, 1879, who were 70 years old. Hist. of west. Md. Scharf. V. 2. Freedom District, p. 875; Manchester District, p. 889; Myers District, p. 869; New Windsor District, p. 908; Westminster, p. 961; Woolery District, p. 869. MHS; DAR.

Charles County. Early people, 1658–62. Index of Liber A, court records. L. D. Scisco. M. H. Mag., 1928, v. 23, pp. 344–63. Also photos. MHS.

*Charles County. Vital records, 1654–1726. Bd. Mss. MHS.

Coats of arms. Wilson Mss. Coll., no. 91. MHS.

*Colonial families of Eastern Shore and their descendants. Dedicated to Wright family. Mrs. Mary Burke Emory. Balto., 1900. MHS; DAR.

Dorchester County families. Genealogical notes. C. H. B. Turner Geneal. Coll. Mss. MHS.

Dorchester and Somerset Counties, Md. and Del. Bible records. (Some families were pioneers to West.) Collected by Nanticoke Chapter, D. A. R. Md. Geneal. Rec. Com., 1938–39, 1 vol., 93 pp., 2582 names. Typed, bd. DAR.

*Eight family Bibles. Containing records of Buck, Simmonds, and Trew families. 8 vols. MHS.

*English letters and family notes. (Md. pedigrees.) McHenry Howard. M. H. Mag., 1914, v. 9, pp. 107–56.
*Extracts from diary of Wm. Faris, Annapolis, Jan. 4, 1792–Aug. 15, 1804. Births, marriages and deaths. M. H. Mag., 1933, v. 28, no. 3, p. 197–244.
Extracts from Maryland Gazette published at Annapolis. E. L. Henry. DAR.
*Family Bible records of Kent County. Md. Geneal. Rec. Com., Parran, 1937, pp. 182–202. Typed, bd. DAR.
*Family Bible records of Kent County. Francis and Sarah E. Stuart and others. Md. Geneal. Rec. Com., 1933–34, pp. 215–31. Mss. DAR.
Family histories and biographies in Maryland. Bibliography on German settlements in col. North Amer. Meynen. Pp. 431–38. MHS.
*Founders of Anne Arundel and Howard Counties, 1654–1905. J. D. Warfield. Genealogical and biographical review from wills, deeds and church records. Balto., Kohn & Pollock, 1905. MHS; DAR.
*Frederick County families. Genealogy (complete) of about three hundred families, containing all births, marriages, deaths, court, land, military records, wills and administrations, available in Frederick County. Mrs. Francis H. Markell, 116 W. Church Street, Frederick. Personal list.
Frederick County. Necrology, 1749–1881. Hist. of west. Md. Scharf. V. 1, pp. 470–76. MHS; DAR.
Frederick County. Vital records. Natl. Geneal. Soc. Quart., Mar., 1939, v. 27, pp. 12–16; June, pp. 53–56. MHS.
Frederick Town, Frederick County. Birth, marriages and deaths from newspaper clippings. N. Niecum. Natl. Geneal. Soc. Quart., 1937, v. 25, pp. 56–59, 79–84, 126–30; 1938, v. 26, pp. 11–12. MHS.
*Garrett County pioneer families. Asby, Bittinger, Custer, Drane, Frazee, Garlitz, Hoye, Savage and Stanton. Charles E. Hoye. Pub. in Mountain Democrat, Oakland, Md., 1935. Newsp. clipp., photos. MHS; DAR.
*Genealogical ancestral charts of each member of John Eager Howard Chapter. D. A. R. Balto. 55 records, 1088 items, 454 families represented. M. Knight. 1935–36, 1 vol., 58 pp. Typed in Binder. DAR.
*Genealogical and memorial encyclopedia of State of Maryland. R. H. Spencer. Amer. Hist. Soc., N. Y., 1919, 2 vols. MHS; DAR; Enoch Pratt Lib., card indexed.
Genealogical sources of Maryland. G. W. McCreary. Ms. MHS.
*German American records. Gathered from Niles Weekly. Dorethea Nuth. German Amer. Annals, Phila., new series, 1904, v. 2, pp. 83–105.
Harford County Historical Society. Incorporated 1886. Contents: Family genealogies (about 150); church histories of Harford County; John Archer's medical ledger, 1767–83; land papers, surveys, letters; list of non-associators; list of non-jurors; militia lists; oath of allegiance. Mss. Coll. JHU.
Index (card) of births, marriages, deaths (over 100,000) from newspapers, church registers, etc. Collected and compiled by Louis H. Dielman, Librarian of Peabody. In: Mr. Dielman's office, Peabody Institute.
*Index to Genealogies and sketches of some old families. B. T. Van Meter. 1901. Ms. DAR.
Index to Maryland and Virginia families as published in Baltimore Sun. Ms. list. MHS; DAR.
Index to Wilson Collection of Manuscript Records MHS. Arranged and indexed by Esther Ridgely George (Mrs. Thomas S.). Towson, Md., Feb. 1, 1940.
*Kent County. Bible and gravestone records. Md. Geneal. Rec. Com., 1934–35, pp. 176–202. Mss. DAR.
Kent County. Vital records, 1654–56. Old Kent. Hanson. P. 109. MHS; DAR.
1681–85. Natl. Geneal. Soc. Quart., v. 10, no. 2, p. 84. MHS.
Kith and kin. W. N. Dixon. 1922. DAR.
*Letters of Molly and Hetty Tilghman. (Genealogical data.) M. H. Mag., 1926, v. 21, pp. 12, 123, 219.
List of titles of genealogical articles in American periodicals and kindred works. Albany, N. Y., Joel Munsell's Sons, 1899. MHS.
Maryland and New Jersey. Unpublished family and court records. E. Henry. 1933. Mss. DAR.
*Maryland families (317) investigated. Francis B. Culver, genealogist. (Also miscellaneous data on 250 other Md. families.) Personal list.
*Maryland Gazette. Genealogical news, 1728–50. M. H. Mag., 1922, v. 17, pp. 364–78; 1923, v. 18, pp. 22–37, 150–83, 273–90.
*Maryland Genealogical Bulletin. R. F. Hayes, editor, 3526 Roland Avenue, Baltimore. 1930, v. 1, to 1937, v. 7. MHS; DAR.
Maryland Genealogical Bulletin and Revolutionary War Journal, 1934, v. 5, no. 1. DAR.
*Maryland Genealogical Records Committee. Annual Reports, 1925–date. Typed, bd. DAR.
*Maryland items in Sussex County, Delaware, records. Deeds, 1712–1804. C. H. B. Turner. M. H. Mag., 1923, v. 18, pp. 52–54, 184–86.
*Maryland journal extracts. Cary Geneal. Coll. Mss. MHS.
Maryland notes from Virginia records. L. A. Burgess. (Abstracts of wills and warrants.) M. H. Mag., 1936, v. 31, no. 3, pp. 254–59.
*Maryland Original Research Society of Baltimore. A. L. Richardson, editor. Baltimore, Bull. no. 1, 1906; no. 2, 1910; no. 3, 1913. MHS; DAR.
Maryland parish registers. Extracts. Cary Geneal. Coll. Mss. MHS.
*Maryland's next of kin. Mrs. Geo. W. Hodges. 1922. DAR.
Montgomery County. Births and deaths records. Natl. Geneal. Soc. Quart., 1919, v. 7, no. 4, p. 58. MHS.
Montgomery County. Necrology, 1799–1877. Hist. of west. Md. Scharf. V. 1, p. 685. MHS; DAR.
Montgomery County. Vital records. Hezekiah Wilson's diary, 1777–1803. Natl. Geneal. Soc. Quart., v. 6, no. 1, pp. 27–31. MHS.
*Obituaries and pedigrees from Baltimore Sun. Cary Geneal. Coll. Mss. MHS.
Old Kent, Eastern Shore of Maryland. Most ancient records of Kent County, and parishes of St. Paul's, Shrewsbury and I. U., with genealogical history of old and distinguished

families. George A. Hanson. Balto., J. P. Des Forges, 1876, 383 pp. MHS.
*Patriotic Marylander. MHS; DAR.
*Pedigrees published in The Sun, Baltimore. Cary Geneal. Coll. Mss. MHS.
Personal notes from Maryland Gazette, 1728–65. William and Mary Quart., 1895, v. 3. MHS.
Piscataway records. G. M. Brumbaugh. Natl. Geneal. Soc. Quart., Apr., 1914, v. 3, no. 1, p. 2.
Register of Maryland's heraldic families, 1634-1935. Alphabetical order preserved; no index. Alice Norris Parran. Balto., 1935, v. 1; 1938, v. 2. MHS; DAR.
*Series of historical, biographical, and genealogical studies in American history, 1760–89. Signers of Declaration of Independence, and their contemporaries in Continental Congress, 1774–83, from Pennsylvania, New Jersey, Maryland and Virginia; family history of each, both ancestors and descendants. Thomas F. Nelson. Wash, D. C.
*Seven pioneers of colonial Eastern Shore. Percy G. Skirven. M. H. Mag., v. 15, no. 3, p. 230; no. 4, p. 395.
*Side lights on Maryland history. Hester Dorsey Richardson. Coats of arms. V. 2: Genealogical sketches of more than one hundred Md. families. Balto., Williams & Wilkins Co., 1913, 2 vols. MHS; DAR; Enoch Pratt Lib.
Some old English letters. References to Calvert, Key, Lowe, Maynadier, Ross, Sewall, Taney, Wetenhall and other families. M. H. Mag., 1914, v. 9, no. 2, pp. 107–56.
Somerset County. Bible records of families of Somerset and Dorchester Counties. Md. Geneal. Rec. Com., 1938–39. Mss. DAR.
*Somerset County. Old Court Book, Liber I. K. L., 1650, 1719–20. Abstracts of births, burials, and marriages (259 families). Copied by Mrs. Wm. H. Tilghman. Md. Geneal. Rec. Com., 1937. Mss. DAR.
Somerset County and Hungers Parish, Northampton County (was Accomac County, Va.) Records, 1660–61. Jour. of Amer. Hist., New Haven, Conn., v. 24, p. 209. MHS. Also: Ms. records MHS.
Somerset and Worcester Counties, Md., and Kent and Sussex Counties, Del. Genealogical notes. In: Mss. Coll., Geneal. Soc. Pa.
Somerset Parish, Somerset County. Abstracts of records. Turner Geneal. Coll. Mss. MHS.
*Talbot County. Vital records, 1657. Liber no. 2 (written in back of book). Court House, Easton.
*The Sun, Baltimore. Complete photostat file of Maryland and Virginia families published in The Sun, May, 24, 1903–08. One set bound for readers; one set reserved for use of making reproductions of articles to fill orders. Periodical Division, Lib. of Cong.; Herbert Putman, librarian.
*The Sun, Baltimore. Genealogies and heraldry, published in The Sun, 1903–1908. Compiled by Hester Dorsey Richardson and Emily E. Lantz. Also some Virginia families compiled by E. C. Meade and Pecquet du Bellet. MHS.
*Upper Peninsula of Eastern Shore of Maryland. Bible (287) and tombstone records. Copied and indexed by Miss Sarah E. Stuart. Bd. mss. MHS; DAR.
Washington County. Births, 1900–date. Court House, Hagerstown.
Washington County. Necrology, 1791. Hist. of west. Md. Scharf. V. 2, pp. 1045–47. MHS; DAR.
Wicomico County family records. Mrs. W. H. (Irman Bounds) Tilghman. (Wicomico County, formed in 1867; therefore all old records go back to Somerset and Worcester Counties. Compiler has endeavored to copy only such records as are now found in Wicomico County.) Md. Geneal. Rec. Com., 1935, 129 pp. Typed, bd., indexed. DAR.
Wicomico County. List of births of Wicomico County; some as early as 1809; some as late as 1853; taken from Atlas by Lake, Griffing and Stevenson, Philadelphia, owned by Mrs. Wm. H. Tilghman, Salisbury. Md. Geneal. Rec. Com., 1939–40, pp. 151–60. Mss. DAR.
*Wilson Collection of Manuscript Records. 700 names, 146 envelopes. MHS.
Worcester County, Snow Hill. Parish records; marriages, 1828–34. From Snow Hill Messenger and Worcester County Advertiser in Library of Congress. Md. O. R. Soc. Bull., no. 3, pp. 22–26. MHS.
*Worcester County. Vital records. Girdletree diary. C. H. B. Turner. Geneal. Coll. Mss. MHS.
Wye Island. Bordley, Lloyd and Paca families. Lippincott Mag., v. 19.

AMERICAN

Abridged compendium of American genealogy. First families of America. F. A. Virkus, editor. 1925–1937, 6 vols., 45,000 lineages, 375,000 names. Chicago, Ill., A. N. Marquis and Co. Vol. 4, MHS; vols. 1, 2, 3, 5, 6, DAR.
America Heraldica. Compilation of coats of arms, crests and mottoes of prominent American families, settled in country before 1880. Edited by L. de V. Vermont. N. Y., Brentano Brothers, 1886.
*American ancestry, giving name and descent in male line of Americans whose ancestors settled in United States previous to Declaration of Independence. Albany, N. Y., Joel Munsell's Sons, 1877–99, 12 vols.
*American and English genealogies in Library of Congress. Gov. Print. Office, Wash., D. C., 1919. MHS; DAR.
*American armory and blue book. 4 parts, 1911, 1913, 1915, 1923. John Matthews, genealogist, 93/4 Chancery Lane, London, Eng.
*American Clan Gregor Year Book. Includes genealogies, biographical sketches, births, marriages, deaths, wills, etc., 1696–date. 1909–date. MHS; DAR.
*American family antiquity. Albert Wells. N. Y., 1880.
American Genealogist. Monthly magazine of genealogy and local history. T. A. Glenn, editor, 1897.
*Americans of gentle birth and their ancestors. Genealogical encyclopaedia. Mrs. H. D. Pittman, editor. St. Louis, Buxton and Skinner, 1903, v. 1; 1907, v. 2. MHS; DAR.
*Americans of royal descent. C. H. Browning. Phila., 1894, 3rd edition. Peabody Lib.
*[The] Ancestor. Quarterly review of county, family history, heraldry and antiquities. V. 1, p. 1902.

*Certain comeovers. H. H. Crapo. New Bedford, Mass., 1912, 2 vols. MHS.

Colonial and Revolutionary families of Pennsylvania. New series, 1932, v. 4. Wilfred Jordan, editor. N. Y., 1934. MHS.

Colonial and Revolutionary families of Philadelphia. Genealogy and personal memoirs. 1938, v. 1. Wilfred Jordan, editor. N. Y., Lewis Hist. Pub. Co., Inc., 1933. MHS; DAR.

Colonial and Revolutionary lineages of America. N. Y., Amer. Hist. Co., 1939, 3 vols. MHS.

*Colonial families of America. Ruth Lawrence, editor. Natl. Americana Soc., N. Y., 1928–1936, vols. 1–16. MHS.

*Colonial families of United States of America. In which is given history, genealogy and armorial bearings of colonial families who settled in America from settlement of Jamestown, 1607, to Battle of Lexington, 1775. 7 vols., representing an individual index of about 200,000 names. G. N. Mackenzie. 1907, v. 1. MHS; DAR.

Crozier's General armory. Register of American families entitled to coats of arms. Wm. A. Crozier. Geneal. Assoc., N. Y., Fox Duffield & Co., 1904. DAR.

*Encyclopedia of American Quaker genealogy. Wm. W. Hinshaw. 1936, v. 1: North Carolina Monthly Meeting. 1938, v. 2: Philadelphia Meeting; Monthly Meetings of Burlington (1678), Salem, New Jersey (1676), Fall (1683), Philadelphia (1682). Virginia and Maryland Meetings to be published. MHS; DAR.

English list of American families of note. Natl. Geneal. Soc. Quart., Apr., 1914, v. 3, no. 1, p. 8. MHS.

*Family records; being collection of family histories. W. M. Clemens, pub. 4 vols.

*Family references. Consult American Genealogical Foundation. Card index. MHS; most large libraries.

Genealogical Association Publication. W. M Crozier, editor. Hasbrouck Heights, N. J., 3 vols.

Virginia county record publications.

Southern pedigrees. Colonial ancestry of Ala., Ga., Ky., Md., N. C., S. C., Tenn., Va., v. 3.

Genealogical research among Pennsylvania German and Huguenot families. C. R. Robert. Geneal. Pub. Natl. Geneal. Soc. Quart.

*Genealogies. 3000 printed and 700 mss. D. A. R. Lib., Wash., D. C., 1940.

Genealogist's reference journal. 1935, pamph., v. 1, pt. 2. DAR.

*Genealogy. Magazine of American ancestry. N. Y., W. M. Clemens, pub., 1916.

*Genealogy of signers of Declaration of Independence. F. W. Leach. Mss. (copies), vols. 1–20. S. A. R. Lib., Wash., D. C.

*Genesis of U. S. Brown's and Browning's "Americans of royal descent, 1894.

*Grafton Magazine of History and Genealogy. Quarterly. Geneal. Pub., N. Y., Boston, Grafton Press, 1908–09, v. 1.

*Grafton index of titles of books, magazine articles, on history, genealogy and biography in United States. The Grafton Press, 1910.

*Handbook of American genealogy. T. A. Virkus, ex-Director. Guide to genealogical work known to kin progress, with names and addresses of professional genealogists. 1932, v. 1; 1934, v. 2. Institute of American Genealogy, 440–42 S. Dearborn Street, Chicago, Ill. MHS; DAR.

*Huguenot pedigrees. C. E. Lart. 1924, 2. vols. DAR.

*Index to American genealogies and genealogical material. Contains 50,000 references to local town and county history, biographies (alphabetical). Joel Munsell & Sons, 1908. MHS.

*Index to American genealogies and genealogical material contained in all works. Albany, N. Y., Joel Munsell's Sons, 1900, 5th edition. MHS.

*Supplement, 1900–08, to Index to genealogies (published, 1900). Albany, N. Y., Joel Munsell's Sons, 1908.

*Index to genealogical periodicals. D. L. Jacobus. 1932. MHS; DAR.

*International genealogical directory. Chas. A. Bernan, editor. 1910.

*Magazine of American genealogy. Lists of immigrants to all Colonies before 1750; soldiers and sailors of Revolution; index to Amer. lineages, and bibliography of Amer. genealogies. Institute of American Genealogy, 440–42 Dearborn Street, Chicago, Ill.

*Mayflower families. Histories carried down five and six generations. Wilson Mss. Coll., no 122. MHS.

*Moravian Church. Register of members of Moravian Church and of persons attached to this Church in this country and abroad, 1727–54. From manuscript of Araham Reincke. 1858, v. 1. Trans. of Moravian Hist. Soc., Nazareth, Pa., 2 vols. MHS.

*Savage's Genealogical dictionary.

Scoins of aristocracy of America. H. D. Richardson. North Amer. Review, 1906, v. 182, p. 761. Peabody Lib.

Searching for your ancestors. Why and how of genealogy. G. H. Doane. N. Y., McGraw-Hill Book Co., Inc., 1937. DAR.

*Some notable families of Southern States. 4 vols. Zella Armstrong. Chattanooga, Tenn., 1918, v. 1. DAR.

*Index to some notable families of Southern States. Zella Armstrong. 1926, v. 3. DAR.

GREAT BRITAIN

Alphabetical dictionary of coats of arms, belonging to families in Great Britain and Ireland; forming extensive ordinary of British armorials. John W. Papworth.

*Annals of Kingdom of Ireland. John D. O'Donovan, L.L.D. Births, marriages and deaths. Edited from manuscripts in Library of Royal Irish Academy and Trinity College, Dublin. 1851. Peabody Lib.

Armorial families. Directory of gentlemen of coats of armor, showing which arms now in use are born by legal authority. Arthur C. Fox-Davis. Grafton Press, pub., 5th edition.

Bristol and America. Record of first settlers in Colonies of North America, 1654–85. Names with places of origin of more than 10,000 servants to foreign plantations who sailed from Port of Bristol to Virginia, Maryland and other parts of Atlantic Coast, also West Indies. London, R. Hargreaves-Mawdsley. MHS.

British Public Record Office and material in it for early American history. W. Noel Sainsbury. Worcester, Amer. Antiquarian Soc., 1893.

Brydge's Biographical peerage.

Burke's Dormant peerages. 1883.
Burke's Encyclopedia of heraldry. General armory of England, Scotland, Ireland and Wales.
Burke's Family records. 1897.
*Burke's Landed gentry, including American families, with British ancestry. Illus. with heraldic color plates (290). Pub. by Burke's Peerage, Ltd., London, 1939. MHS.
Burke's Peerage and baronetage.
*Caribbeana. Quarterly. Vere Langford Oliver, M.R.C.S., editor. Record of British West Indies; land grants, parish register, marriages, wills, indentures, pedigrees, Bible records of Colonies. London, Mitchell, Hughes and Clarke. Complete file in Peabody Lib.
Dictionary of English and Welsh surnames. Charles W. Bardsley.
Encyclopedia heraldic. Wm. Berry.
England. Wills, Prerogative Court of Canterbury. Wills, sentences and probate acts 1661–70, arranged and numbered in alphabetical order of testators; with separate indexes of places, ships, trades and conditions. London, J. H. Morrison, 1935.
Fairbairn's Book of crests of families of Great Britain and Ireland. New edition, revised by Arthur Charles Fox-Davies. 2 vols. (Book of plates, v. 2.) T. C. and E. C. Jack. Edinburgh, Grange Pub. Works, 1892. MHS.
Falaise roll of companions of William the Conqueror. M. J. Crispin and L. Macary. London, Butler-Tanner, 1938. MHS.
Genealogical gleanings in England. H. F. Waters. New. Eng. Hist. Soc., Boston, 1901, 2 vols.
Genealogist. Quarterly, new series. Messers W. Pollard & Co., 39–40 North Street, Exeter, England.
*Genealogist's guide (for British records). George W. Marshall. Privately printed for author, Billings & Sons, Guilford, 1903.
German exodus to England, 1709. F. R. Diffenderfer. Lancaster, Pa., 1897.
Germans. List of Germans from Palatinate, who came to England, 1709. From original documents preserved in British Museum Library, London. N. Y., Geneal. and Biog. Record, Apr., July, Oct., 1909, v. 40, pp. 49, 93, 160, 241.
Homes of family names in Great Britain. H. B. Guppy. 1890. DAR.
Lodge's Peerage and baronetage of British Empire. London, 1879.
*Monumental histories of counties of England. Births, marriages and deaths. 100 vols. Peabody Lib.
*Parishes of England. Registers of christenings, weddings and burials of practically all parishes of England, 1538–1900. Parish Record Soc. of England. Peabody Lib.
Peerage of England. A. Collins. 1768, vols. 1–7. DAR.
References to English surnames, 1601. Index to 19,650 surnames in printed registers. F. K. and D. Hitching. England, Charles A. Bernan.
*St. Mary's, Whitechapel, London. Weddings, 1616–25. N. Y. Geneal. and Biog. Rec., v. 22, pp. 52, 75, 204; v. 23, pp. 42, 151.
*Scotish Record Society, Scotland, Great Britain. Christenings, weddings and burials. Peabody Lib.
Sulgrave Manor and Washingtons. H. C. Smith. 1933. DAR.

MAGAZINES, NEWSPAPERS

Baltimore American. First newspaper published in Baltimore; originally called Maryland Journal and Daily Advertiser. First issue Aug. 20, 1773. No files in office, Commerce and Pratt Streets, Balto. Complete files in Enoch Pratt Lib.
†Baltimore American. Early history (ref. to Bose, Dobbin and Murphy). M. H. Mag., 1933, v. 28, p. 272.
Bibliography of American newspapers, 1690–1820. Pt. 3, Maryland, Apr., 1915. Clarence Brigham. In: Proceedings of Amer. Antiquarian Soc.
Hagerstown Town and County Almanac. (J. Gruder's Almanac.) Established 1797; continued to date.
List of early newspapers (titles). Geo. C. Keidel. M. H. Mag., 1933, v. 28, pp. 119–37, 244–75, 328–44; continued in vols. 29 and 30.
Maryland Historical Magazine. James W. Foster, editor. 1906, v. 1, to date. Pub. by Maryland Historical Society. Complete card index of persons, places and subject matter. MHS.
Maryland magazines. Ante Bellum, 1793–1861. M. H. Mag., 1934, v. 29, no. 2, pp. 122–31.
†Newspapers and newspaper men of Maryland, Past and present. Paul Winchester and Frank D. Webb. Frank L. Silbey & Co., 1905. MHS.
†Niles Weekly Register, Baltimore. Historical and biographical material relating to Maryland. Editor, Hezekiah Niles (born Chester Co., Pa., 1777; died in Del., 1839; editor of 32 vols., 1811–36). Continued by son, W. O. Niles, 1837–49. Balto., 76 vols. MHS; DAR; City Hall Lib.
Patriotic Marylander. Pub. by Md. State Soc., D. A. R. MHS; DAR; Enoch Pratt Lib.
Sunpapers of Baltimore, 1837–1937. Centennial hist. of The Sun, The Evening Sun and the Sunday Sun. Written jointly by Gerald W. Johnson, Frank R. Kent, H. L. Mencken, and Hamilton Owens. Pub. by Alfred A. Knopf, 1937.
The Confederate Veteran. Monthly. File practically complete in MHS.
The Evening Sun, Balto. First issue, Apr., 18, 1910. Complete index of contents, 1910 to date, in Sun Office, Balto.
The Maryland Gazette. First newspaper printed in Province of Maryland. Annapolis, 1727. William Parks, public printer of Province, 1727–42. Jonas Green, 1745. Complete file in Md. State Lib., Annapolis.
The Maryland Gazette. M. C. Howard. M. H. Mag., 1934, v. 29, no. 4, p. 295.
The Sun, Baltimore. First issue, May 17, 1837. Complete index of contents, 1892 to date, in Sun Office, Balto. Complete file in Sun Office, Lib. Cong., MHS, Enoch Pratt Lib., and Peabody Lib.
Two hundred years with Maryland Gazette, 1727–1927. C. M. Christian. Annapolis, Capital Gazette Press. Supplement, 1927. DAR; Enoch Pratt Lib.

FICTION

Adventure in Maryland. Scare-Crow murders. F. A. Kummer.

Adventure in Maryland. Twisted face. F. A Kummer. Dodd-Mead, 1938, 223 pp.

Alice of Maryland. T. C. Harbaugh.

As I remember. Recollections of American society during 19th century. (Civil War and life in Md., etc.) Marian Gouverneur. N. Y., 1911.

Bones of Napoleon. Mystery story, scene laid on Eastern Shore of Maryland. James Warner Bellah. Appleton-Century Co., 266 pp.

Boston Public Library. Chronological index to historical quarto fiction, including prose fiction, plays and poems. Boston, 1892, 3rd enlarged edition. (Md. fiction, v. 1.) 2-page mss. inserted, p. 305. Enoch Pratt Lib.

Buried rose legends of old Baltimore. Five tales recreate Baltimore of 1800–1812. Sidney Nyburg. N. Y., 1932.

Chesapeake Bay log canoes. M. V. Brewington. Newport News, Mariners Museum, 113 pp. (Museum Pub., no. 3, pts. 1 and 2.) MHS.

Clairborne the rebel. Roman of Maryland, under proprietary. W. H. Carpenter. N. Y., 1845. Enoch Pratt Lib.

Clement Falconer or memoirs of young Whig. Wm. Price. Balto., N. Hickman, 1838. Enoch Pratt Lib.

Colonial Cavalier or southern life before Rebellion (Life in Maryland and Virginia.) Maud W. Goodwin. Boston, Little, Brown & Co.

Day before yesterday. Janet Laura Scott (Mrs. H. (Coale) Crew). 1925, illus. Enoch Pratt Lib.

Doings in Maryland or Matilda Douglas. Phila., 1871, J. B. Lippincott and Co. Enoch Pratt Lib.

Down in Maryland. G. W. Stowell. Federalsburg, Pub. Co., 1929. Enoch Pratt Lib.

Eat, drink and be merry in Maryland. F. P. Stieff. 1932.

Entailed hat or Patty Cannon's times. Romance. George Alfred Townsend. "Gath." Exclusive sales rights, C. H. Monsees, Salisbury, Md., 1912, 5th edition.

Flag is still there. Neil H. Swanson. 1933.

For Maryland's honor. Story of war for Southern independence. L. T. Everett. Boston, 1922.

Forty-four years of life of hunter. Pioneer life in western Maryland, over one hundred years ago. Meshach. Browning, reprint, 1928.

Fun and facts behind counter; with verses written at random. H. Donaldson. Hagerstown, 1897.

Glimpses of Baltimore. Latrobe Weston. Balto., H. G. Roebuck & Son, 1935. (Poetry.)

Grandma stories. Stories and anecdotes of ye olden times. Sister Mary Xavier Queen (S. M. X.). Balto., Visitation Academy; Boston, 1899. MHS.

Grandmother stories from land of used to be. Mrs. Howard Meriwether Lovett. A. B. Caldwell. MHS.

His Baltimore Madonna. (Volume of short stories.) C. W. Bump. 1906.

Horse-Shoe Robinson. Tale of Tory Ascendency. John P. Kennedy. N. Y., 1852.

House of de Mailly. Novel by Potter. Brings in life at Annapolis about 1744.

John Montcalm, heretic. Tale of Maryland hills. F. A. Rupp. Reading, Pa., 1908. Enoch Pratt Lib.

Katy of Catoctin or chain breakers. National romance. G. Townsend. "Gath." N. Y., Appleton, 1887. Enoch Pratt Lib.

Kennedy Square. Francis Hopkins Smith. 1911.

Land of legendary lore. (Chiefly Talbot Co.; with references to Earle family.) Prentiss Ingraham. Easton, Gazette Pub. House, 1898. MHS.

Maryland June jaunt, with some wanderings in footsteps of Washington, Braddock, and early pioneers. B. Mayer. Harper's Mag., 1857, v. 14, p. 592. Peabody Lib.

Maryland manor. Novel of plantation aristocracy and its fall. F. Emory. N. Y.. 1901. 3rd edition. Enoch Pratt Lib.

Mermaid of Druid Lake. (Short Stories.) C. W. Bump. 1906.

Miss Susie Slagle's. Story of medical boarding house opposite Johns Hopkins Hospital. Augusta Tucker. Harper's, 1939, 332 pp.

Mistress Brent. Story of Lord Baltimore's Colony in 1638. Lucy M. Thruston. Boston, Little, Brown & Co., 1901.

More than bread. Tale of southern Maryland. Hulberg Footner. Lippincott, 1938, 365 pp.

Murder on Ghost Tree Island. Katherine S. Daiger. (Scene laid near Balto. and Annapolis.) 1934.

Old Post Road. Margaret G. McClelland. N. Y., Merriam Co., 1894.

Past hours. Random collection of tales and addresses. W. C. Coleman. Balto., Lord Baltimore Press, 152 pp. MHS.

Pilate and Herod. Tale illustrative of early history of Church of England in province of Maryland. Rev. H. Stanely. Phila., H. Hooker, 1854. Enoch Pratt Lib.

Regeneration. Novel. H. B. Stimpson. Wash., D. C., W. Neale, 1869–1891.

Richard Carvel. Winston Churchill. (Scene laid at Carvel Hall, Annapolis.) 1899.

Rob of the Bowl. Legend of St. Inigoe's; story of early Maryland. J. P. Kennedy. 1838; reprint, 1856. N. Y., A. L. Burt Co. Enoch Pratt Lib.

Sally Cary. Long hidden romance of Washington's life. Wilson Miles Cary. N. Y., privately printed, 1916, 104 pp. MHS.

Sir Christopher. Romance of Maryland manor, 1644. Maud W. Goodwin. Boston, Little, Brown & Co.

Some of our people. L. R. Meekins. Balto., Williams & Wilkins Co.

South Mountain magic. Legendary lore of Md. mountaineers. Madeline V. Dahlgren. 1882.

Swallow Barn. John P. Kennedy. 2 vols.

Tackroom tattles. John McKenney. 1934.

Tales and traditions of Old St. Mary's. Maria Briscoe Crocker. 1934, pamph. DAR.

Tales of Chesapeake. Geo. Alfred Townsend. "Gath." N. Y., 1880.

Tales of old Maryland. Legends concerning Eastern Shore of Maryland. J. H. K. Shannahn, Jr. 1907.

Test tubes and dragon scales. (Marylanders in China.) George C. Basil in collaboration with Elizabeth Forman Lewis. Illus. by Raymond Creekmore. J. C. Winston Co., 1940, 316 pp.

Tory maid. Account of adventures of James Frisby of Fairlee, in County of Kent on Eastern

Shore of Md., and sometime officer in Md. line of Continental Army during Revolutionary War. H. B. Stimpson. N. Y., 1899.
Tower of Wye. Wm. H. Babcock. 1901.
Two Maryland girls. A. E. Blanchard. 1903.
Victorian village: Reminiscences of other days. Old Baltimore and village of Waverly. Lizette Woodworth Reese. 1929.
Wonders will never cease; and other stories. Sister Mary Xavier Queen (S. M. X.). Balto., Gallery and McCann, 1898.
York Road. Lizette Woodworth Reese.

CHURCH RECORDS

GENERAL CHURCH HISTORY OF MARYLAND

Act of Religion (Maryland Toleration Act). Signers, April 21, 1649. Side lights on Maryland history. Richardson. V. 1.
Allen Memorial Baptist Church, Salisbury, Wicomico County, 1859-1937. Pamph. DAR.
American Presbyterian beginnings. Francis Makemie, pioneer of 1683. W. I. Clarke. General Assembly Publicity Dept., Presbyterian Church, U.S.A., Witherspoon Bldg., Phila. Pamph., 1933. MHS.
American Presbyterianism. C. A. Brigg, D.D.
Annals of American pulpit. Wm. B. Sprague, D.D.
Answer of Joseph Wyeth to Dr. Bray, 1700. Edited by B. C. Steiner. Balto., 1901.
Archiepiscopal Archives, Baltimore. Mss.
Associators of Calvert County, Protestant rebellion, 1689. Hist. of Md. Scharf. V. 1, pp. 309, 319-20, 331, 334. MHS.
Baltimore Catholic Review. Tercentenary of Maryland, June 15, 1934. Pamph. DAR.
Baltimore Yearly Meeting. Old days and new. Bertha Janney. (Article in Friends Intelligence, Dec., 1936.) Newsp. clipp. MHS.
Baptist Church in Maryland. History from Sater's Church, in Baltimore County, first Baptist Church in Maryland, 1742-1885. J. F. Weishampel. Pub. by Md. Baptist Union Assoc., Balto., 1885. MHS; DAR; Peabody Lib.
Calvert and Penn, or growth of civil and religious liberty in America, as disclosed in planting of Maryland and Pennsylvania. Brantz Mayer. M. H. S. Pub., Balto., pamph., 1852. MHS.
Catalogue book of record. Baltimore Yearly Meeting and meetings thereunto belonging. Friends Meeting House, Park Ave., Balto.
Cathedral records from beginning of Catholicity in Baltimore to present time. Rev. M. J. Riordan. Balto., 1906.
Catholic and Puritan settlers of Maryland. A. P. Dennis.
Catholic clergy in Maryland, 1642. (Letter.) M. H. Mag., 1909, v. 4, pp. 262-65.
Catholic colonial Maryland. H. S. Spalding. Milwaukee, 1931. DAR.
Catholic Mission in Maryland. Amer. Hist. Review, Apr., 1907, p. 584.
Cecil County. Notes on parishes of Maryland, 1706-1857. Rev. Ethan Allen. M. H. Mag., 1914, v. 9, pp. 315-26.
Central Presbyterian Church, Baltimore. Embracing history of Presbyterianism in Baltimore. J. T. Smith. Includes much on dissensions within church during Civil War period. Phila., 1899. MHS; DAR.
Chronicles and sketch of St. Ignatius of Loyola, Baltimore, 1856-1906, within account of celebration of jubilee, April, 1907. Rev. J. J. Ryan. Balto., 1907.
Church and State in early Maryland. T. O'Gorman. Cath. Univ. Bull., 1896, v. 2, p. 461.
Church and State in early Maryland. George Petrie. Johns Hopkins University. Studies, 1892, series 10, no. 4. MHS; Enoch Pratt Lib.
Church life in colonial Maryland. T. C. Gambrall. 1885. MHS.
Church of England in Maryland, 1632-92. First sixty years. L. C. Wroth. M. H. Mag., 1916, v. 11, pp. 1-41.
Church vestry papers of various periods. 2 vols. Hall of Records.
Churches and religious institutions of Maryland, etc. C. W. Bump. In Maryland: its resources. W. Hand Browne and others. Balto., 1893. Peabody Lib.
Clergy in Maryland, of Protestant Episcopal Church, since independence, 1783-1860. Rev. Ethan Allen. MHS; DAR.
Clergy of Province of Maryland, summoned by Rev. Dr. Bray, May 23, 1700, to general visitation at Annapolis (First Ecclesiastical legislation in America). History of Maryland. Scharf. V. 1, p. 366. MHS.
Clergymen of Church of England in Maryland, prior to 1693. Also printed form and additional notes in Ethan Allen Papers. MHS.
Contributions to ecclestiastical history of United States. (Narrative of events connected with rise and progress of Protestant Episcopal Church in Md., 1632-1828. V. 2.) Francis L. Hawks. N. Y., 1839. MHS.
Dark chapter in Catholic history of Maryland. E. I. Devitt. U. S. Catholic Hist. Soc. Mag., 1887, v. 1. MHS.
†Day-Star of American Freedom or birth and early growth of tolerance in Province of Maryland. G. L. L. Davis. Balto., 1855. MHS; DAR.
Days of Makemie or vine planted, 1680-1708. Rev. L. P. Bowen. Phila., 1885. DAR.
Department of history of Presbyterian Church, organized 1852. Witherspoon Bldg., Phila. Extensive collection of biographies, church histories (nearly 200 Maryland churches) and miscellaneous collection.
Diary of Mary Spence, Snow Hill, 1779-82.
Early Christian missions in Maryland. M. H. Mag., Dec., 1906. V. 1, pp. 293-316.
Early churches of St. Mary's County. Chronicles of colonial Maryland. Thomas. Chap. 9. MHS.
Early Maryland clergy (17th century). M. H. Mag., 1910, v. 5, pp. 289-91.
Early movement for incorporation of Presbyterian Church in Baltimore; with petition of Protestant dissenters in Baltimore County, 1774. M. H. Mag., 1909, v. 4, pp. 228-35.
Early Presbyterianism in Maryland. J. W. McIlvain. Johns Hopkins University. Studies, 1890, series 8, no. 5. Notes, Supplementary no. 3.

Early records of church and parish of All Faith's, St. Mary's County, 1692–1835. H. F. Berkley. M. H. Mag., Dec., 1935, v. 30, pp. 326–63; 1936, v. 31, pp. 16–36.
Early religious history of Maryland, Rev. B. F. Brown. Balto., 1876. MHS.
Edithweston rectors of England (data from England). Reference to Peale. Ms. MHS.
Eighty years embracing history of Presbyterianism in Baltimore. Rev. J. Tate Smith. Phila., 1899. MHS.
Episcopal churches and parishes of Maryland, before Revolution of 1776. Map. Dr. H. J. Berkley. Typed, bd. MHS.
Evangelical Lutheran synod of Maryland. History of United Lutheran Church in America, 1820–1920. A. R. Wentz. Illus., port., biog., 641 pp. Harrisburg, Pa., 1920. MHS; DAR.
Every man's history of our church in Maryland. C. Torrence. Maryland Churchman, Jan., 1937, v. 51, no. 4; continued in nos. 5, 6, etc.
Faith of our fathers. Cardinal James Gibbons. Balto., 1895.
First parishes of Province of Maryland. Historical sketches of ten counties and thirty parishes in Maryland, 1692. Plates and folding map. Percy G. Skirven. Balto., 1923. MHS; DAR.
Foundation of Maryland, and origin of Act concerning Religion, April 2, 1649. Bradley T. Johnson. M. H. S. Fund Pub., Balto., 1883, no. 18. MHS.
Garrison Church. Sketches of history of St. Thomas' Parish, Garrison Forest, Baltimore County, 1742–1852. Rev. Ethan Allen. Edited by Rev. Hobart Smith. N. Y., James Pott Co., 1898. MHS; DAR.
Gladstone and Maryland toleration. R. H. Clarke. The Catholic Pub. Soc., N. Y., 1875. MHS.
Historical sketch of early Christian missions among Indians of Maryland. U. S. Catholic Mag., 1848, v. 7, pp. 529–35, 581–86.
History of Head of Christiana Church. H. C. Welbon. Pamph. DAR.
History of Maryland classics of Reformed Church in United States. Rev. Guy P. Bready. Taneytown, Md., 1938. MHS.
History of Md. Manuscripts of late Dr. Ethan Allen, historiographer of Diocese of Maryland. 4 vols. (1st v. photostated). In vault of Md. Diocesan Lib. in Peabody, Balto.
History of Old Baltimore Conference. Planting of Methodism, 1773. Division of Conference, 1857. J. E. Armstrong. Balto., 1907. MHS.
History of some churches in Baltimore City. History of Baltimore City and County. Scharf. Pp. 519–92. MHS.
History of Church of Brethren in Maryland. J. M. Henry. 1936. MHS; DAR; Enoch Pratt Lib.
History of establishment of Carmelites of Maryland. U. S. Catholic Mag., 1890, v. 3. MHS.
History of Old Catholic Chapel of Priest's Ford, in Harford County. G. W. Andrews. U. S. Catholic Hist. Mag., 1890, v. 3, pp. 41–46. MHS.
I. U., a historic shrine in Old Kent. Percy G. Skirven. Balto., 1931. 100 copies.
Illustrated history of Methodism. Methodist Mag. Pub. Co., 1900.
Jesuits in Maryland. In Jesuits of Middle United States. Garrahan. Enoch Pratt Lib.
Journal of annual convention of Protestant Episcopal Church of Maryland. Contains lists of parishes, congregations, clergy and lay delegates. 1784, v. 1, to date (corrected to Jan., 1936). Diocesan Church House, Monument Street, Balto.
Journal of Rev. Francis Asbury, Bishop of Methodist Episcopal Church, from August 7, 1771 to December 7, 1815. 1821, 3 vols. MHS; DAR.
Jubilee at Mt. St. Mary's. McSherry and others. 1856.
*Kaskaskia Parish register. In Archives of Georgetown University, Wash., D. C. V. 34. 1.
Kent County. Colonial St. Paul's Parish. Robt. L. Swain, Jr. Pamph. MHS.
Land of sanctuary. History of religious toleration in Maryland, 1634–1776. Rev. W. T. Russell. Balto., T. H. Furst Co. 1907. DAR; Enoch Pratt Lib.
Life story of Rev. Francis Makemie. Rev. I. Marshall Page, Berlin, Md. (Francis Makemie's grave located in Accomac County, Va., and monument erected May 14, 1908.) Enoch Pratt Lib.
Light thrown by Jesuits upon hitherto obscure points on early Maryland history. Edward Ingle. Pa. Mag. Hist. and Biog., 1881, v. 5, p. 51. MHS.
Light thrown by Jesuits upon hitherto obscure parts of early Maryland history. Rev. E. D. Neill. St. Paul., 1881.
Labadists of Bohemia Manor. G. A. Leakin. M. H. Mag., 1906, v. 1, pp. 337–45.
Labadists of Bohemia Manor, 1681–1720. M. H. Mag., v. 1, no. 4, p. 337.
History of Md. Scharf. V. 1, pp. 429–31. MHS.
History of Cecil County. Johnston. P. 84. MHS.
Ancient families of Bohemia Manor, their homes and their graves. Mallory. P. 31.
"First settlement of Germans in Maryland, 1681, were those among the Dutch and French Labadist, located at Bohemia Manor, Cecil County, scattered and mixed, 1720–1722." First settlement of Germans in Maryland. Schultz. 1896.
Labadist colony in Maryland. B. B. James. Johns Hopkins University. Studies, 1899, series 17, no. 6. MHS; Enoch Pratt Lib.
Labadist colony in Maryland. Bibliography on German settlements in colonial North America. Meynen. P. 65. MHS.
Labadist colony in Maryland. B. B. James. Amer. Soc. Church Hist. Papers. N. Y., 1897, v. 8.
Letters on early history of Presbyterian Church. Irving Spence.
Life and travels of Rev. Michael Schlatter, German Reformed Congregations in Maryland, 1753, first regularly organized. H. Harbaugh. Phila., 1857.
List of clergy ordained and licensed for American Colonies, 1699–1710. (Md. clergy: Adams, Bethum, Baron, Cordiner, Edwards, Glen, Gray, Hindman, Jennings, Jones (Hugh), Keith, Macqueen, Marsden, Owen, Ransford, Scot, Sharpe, Tibbs, White (Jonathan) Wagener and Wolton.) Va. Mag. Hist. and Biog., 1900, v. 7, no. 3, pp. 310–12.

List of clergymen of Church of England, 1632–92, in Maryland. Land of Sanctuary. Russell. 1907, p. 595.
List of emigrant ministers (Protestant Episcopal) to America, 1690–1811. (Mostly to Georgia, Maryland, North Carolina, South Carolina, and Virginia.) Gerald Fothergill. London, 1904, 65 pp.
List of parishes in Maryland and incumbents, 1738–78. Mss. Lib. Cong.
Living church annual. Year book of Protestant Episcopal Church in United States. Alphabetical index.
Lord Baltimore's struggle with Jesuits, 1634–49. Alfred P. Dennis. Amer. Hist. Assoc. Rept., 1900, v. 1.
Lord revive Thy Church. S. B. Russell. Restoration of Mt. Carmel Roman Catholic Church and St. George's and Trinity Protestant Episcopal churches of southern Maryland. D. A. R. Mag., v. 73, no. 4, pp. 2–8.
*Macknian baptismal records, 1747. In Archives of Georgetown University, Wash., D. C., v. 34. 1.
Makemieland memorials. Rev. L. P. Bowen. MHS.
Manor chapel of St. Augustine Church, St. Augustine parish, Cecil County. Historical sketch. E. DeC. Le Fevre. Easton, 1932. Peabody Lib.
Manuscripts from Fulham Palace relating to provincial Maryland (churches). B. C. Steiner. M. H. Mag., 1917, v. 12, pp. 115–41.
Maryland Baptist, Oct., 1935, v. 18, no. 10. DAR.
Maryland Catholics in penal days, 1759. U. S. Catholic Mag., 1890, v. 3. MHS.
Maryland. Early history studies, civil, social and ecclesiastical. Rev. T. C. Gambrall. N. Y., Whittaker Co., 1893. DAR.
Maryland in beginning. Rev. E. B. Neill. Balto., 1884.
Maryland. Not Roman Catholic colony. Rev. E. D. Neill. Minneapolis, 1875.
Maryland parish notes. M. H. Mag., 1914, v. 9, p. 315.
Maryland parishes, into which Maryland is divided, with names of rectors. In Robt. Gilmor Papers. MHS. (Maryland parish records contained births, marriages and deaths and were public records before the formation of counties.)
*Maryland parish registers. Extracts. Cary Geneal. Coll. Mss. MHS.
Maryland. Pioneer of religious liberty, only Catholic colony of Thirteenth and First, and first to establish civil and religious freedom. E. S. Riley. Annapolis, 1917. Hist. Series, no. 3. Peabody Lib.
Maryland toleration or sketches of early history of Maryland, to year 1650. Rev. Ethan Allen. Printed by Protestant Episcopal Church, James S. Waters, Balto., 1855, pamph. MHS.
Methodism in Old Waverly and its environment for last sixty years. Anna Cole. Balto., 1933. MHS.
Methodism of peninsula. Robert W. Todd. Phila., 1886.
Methodist sesqui-centennial, Oct. 10–14, 1934. 1934. DAR.
Methodists in United States of America, 1766–1809. Extracts from short hist., with brief account of their rise in England, 1729. Jesse Lee. Ms. MHS.
Moravians who moved to North Carolina from Maryland. See Pub. of North Carolina Hist. Com., v. 2. (from Carroll Manor, Frederick Co., p. 719), and v. 4. MHS.
Old brick churches of Maryland. Helen W. Ridgely. N. Y., 1894, 1906. MHS.
Old Buckingham by the Sea, on Eastern Shore of Maryland. One of seven churches established by Francis Mackemie, 1683. J. M. Page, pastor, Berlin, Md. Phila., Westminster Press, 1936. MHS.
Old Catholic Maryland and its early Jesuit missionaries. Rev. Wm. P. Treacy. N. J., 1889. Peabody Lib.
Old historic churches of America. Their romantic history and their traditions. E. F. Rines. (Illustration of Old Quaker Meeting House, Easton, oldest building for public worship now standing in Maryland.) Nat'l. Soc. C.D.A. N. Y., Macmillan Co., 1938.
Old silver service of America. E. Alfred Jones. M. H. Mag., 1914, v. 9, p. 89.
Old silver in American churches, prior to 1800. Mr. E. Alfred Jones, of England wrote preface, illustrated and containing genealogical account of each donor, record of silversmiths and reproductions of arms engraved on vessels, photographed and catalogued. Pub. by Nat'l. Soc. Colonial Dames of Amer., Letchworth. Arden Press, 1913. MHS.
Old Trinity Church, built prior to 1690, Dorchester Parish, Dorchester County. History. 1937, pamph. Md. Geneal. Rec. Com., 1937–38. DAR.
One hundred and seventy-fifth anniversary of Immanuel Luthern Church, Manchester, Md. MHS.
Our Baptist heritage. E. F. Ruark. (Wicomico County families.) 1934. DAR.
Our Christian heritage. James Cardinal Gibbons. Balto., 1889.
Our Quaker Friends of ye olden times. J. Bell.
Papers relating to history of church in Maryland, 1694–1775. W. S. Perry. 1878, privately printed. V. 4. DAR.
Parish institutions of Maryland. E. Ingle. Johns Hopkins University. Studies, 1882, series 1, no. 6. MHS; Enoch Pratt Lib. See also pamph. Balto., 1883. MHS; DAR.
Parish records of Maryland. H. T. Thompson. M. H. Mag., 1907, v. 2, pp. 126–33.
Parishes of Maryland, as of Act laid out. Md. Archives, v. 23, pp. 17–23. Diocese of Maryland, 1784, originally comprised whole of State and District of Columbia. Diocese of Easton, erected in 1868, took from it Caroline, Cecil, Dorchester, Kent, Queen Anne, Somerset, Talbot, Wicomico and Worcester Counties. Diocese of Washington, erected in 1895, included District of Columbia and Charles, Montgomery, Prince George and St. Mary's Counties.
Parochial clergy of Maryland. Proceedings, 1753. Calvert Papers. M. H. Mag., 1908, v. 3, pp. 257–73, 364–84.
Parsons of Islands Anecdotes of Rev. Joshua Thomas, and Methodism in early days on Tangier and Deal's Islands and Eastern Shore. Adam Wallace. Methodist Home Journal, Phila., 1870 (?). Enoch Pratt Lib.

Petition of Friends in Cecil County, from Land Records of Cecil County, 1696, Book 1, p. 153. M. H. Mag., 1912, v. 7, p. 328.
Pioneers of Ulster and America, Scotch-Irish. Mentions number of early Presbyterian ministers of Somerset County. M. H. Mag., 1913, v. 8, p. 304.
Port Tobbaco Parish, 1692–1869. M. H. Mag., 1927, v. 22, p. 303.
Presbyterian beginning in Baltimore. (North-Point), 1714. M. H. Mag., 1920, v. 15, pp. 305–11.
Protestant rebellion, 1689. Associators: Baltimore, Cecil, Charles, Kent, St. Mary's, Somerset, and Talbot Counties. History of Maryland. Scharf. V. 1, pp. 309–34. MHS.
Protestant revolution in Maryland. B. C. Steiner. Amer. Hist. Assoc., Wash., D. C., Annual Rept., 1897, v. 2, pp. 279–353.
Protestants in Lord Baltimore's Council, May 13, 1682. History of Maryland. Scharf. V. 1, p. 288. MHS.
*Pumfrey pew rent book. In Archives of Georgetown University, Wash., D. C., v. 118.
Puritan Colony in Maryland. D. R. Randall. Johns Hopkins University. Studies, 1886, series 4, no. 6. MHS; Enoch Pratt Lib.; Peabody Lib.
Quaker education in Baltimore and Virginia. Yearly meetings, with account of certain meetings of Delaware and Eastern Shore of Maryland. Affiliated with Philadelphia. W. C. Dunlop. Phila., 1935. MHS.
Quakers of American Colonies. Rufus M. Jones.
Reichel's early history of Church of United Brethren (Moravians) in America.
Religion under Barons of Baltimore. C. E. Smith. Balto., 1899.
Religious history of Maryland, 1639–1896. B. C. Steiner. M. H. Mag., 1926, v. 21, pp. 1–20.
Religious liberty in early Maryland. L. B. Bowen. Md. Churchman, 1906. MHS.
Religious organizations of Frederick County. History of Frederick County. Williams. Pp. 400–506. MHS; DAR.
Restoration of proprietary of Maryland, and legislation against Roman Catholics during governorship of Capt. John Hart, 1714–20. Bernard C. Steiner. Amer. Hist. Assoc., Wash., D. C., Annual Rept., 1899 (1900), v. 1.
Rise of Episcopal Church, in District of Columbia; dissensions in Maryland; charter to Lord Baltimore revoked and Church of England made official church. Piscataway Parish, St. John's Church on Broad Creek. Columbia Hist. Soc. Records, v. 9, p. 63.
Rule of proportion according to which God maketh increase of His church. Ethan Allen. Balto., 1855.
St. John's Church, Queen Caroline Parish, Howard County. History of mother church, Christ, 1832. M. H. Mag., 1926, v. 21, pp. 179–81.
St. Paul's Roman Catholic Church and parish, Ellicott City, Maryland. Brother Fabrician of Jesus. MHS.
Sermon preached in First Independent Church in Baltimore, after death of Rev. George W. Burnap. Balto., 1859.
Signers of Protestant Declaration, April 17, 1650. History of Maryland. Scharf. V. 1, p. 181. MHS.
Society of Friends in Maryland. D. L. Thornbury. M. H. Mag., 1934, v. 29, pp. 101–15.
Southern Quakers and slavery. S. B. Weeks. Johns Hopkins University. Studies, 1896, series 25. MHS; DAR.
Story of Baltimore's yearly meeting of Friends, 1672–1938. Anna B. Thomas. Weant Press, 1938, 152 pp. Enoch Pratt Lib.
Teachers' souvenir to members of Presbyterian Sabbath School of Lonaconing. 1889, pamph. DAR.
Thomas Bray and Maryland parochial libraries (established, 1699). J. T. Wheeler. M. H. Mag., 1939, v. 34, no. 3, p. 246.
Toleration Act, 1649. Gov. Stone and members of his council, who passed Act concerning Religion. History of Maryland. Scharf. V. 1, 1770.
  Side lights on Md. history. Richardson. V. 1, p. 104. MHS; DAR.
Toleration Act, 1649. Original from Calvert Papers. M. H. Mag., 1909, v. 14, pp. 377–79.
Trinity Parish, Charles County, 1744. M. H. Mag., 1906. V. 1, pp. 324–30.
*Trinity Roman Catholic Church baptismal records. In Archives of Georgetown University, Wash., D. C., v. 175.
Two hundred and fiftieth anniversary celebration of founding of Baltimore yearly meeting of Friends, 1672–1922. Pamph. DAR.
Two hundred and fiftieth anniversary of old Third Haven Meeting House, October 23, 1932. DAR.
United States Catholic Historical Magazine. U. S. Catholic Hist. Soc., quarterly, 1885, v. 1. N. Y., 1885.
United States Roman Catholic Church records. Cora C. Curry. 1935. (Genealogies publication of Nat'l. Geneal. Soc. Records of R. C. Church in U. S., as source of authentic genealogical and historical material.) Address Jean Stephenson, Apt. 1000, The Conrad, 13th and I. Streets, Washington, D. C.
Visit to Bohemia Manor. G. A. Leakin. M. H. Mag., 1907, v. 2, p. 143.
Westminster Presbyterian Church, Georgetown, Maryland. 50th anniversary, July 24, 1921. Ms. MHS.

BAPTIST CHURCHES

Baltimore City

First Baptist Church, established 1785, now 4200 Liberty Heights Avenue. Members manual, 1836, 1843. Historical sketch, 1785–1935. Leaflet. MHS.
Second Baptist Church, established 1798. Historical sketch. Phila., 1911. MHS.

Baltimore County

Black Rock Baptist Church, 1828, Butler. Records of baptisms and deaths, 1829– date, in custody of Rev. J. T. Rowe, 704 Deepdene Road, Roland Park, Balto.
Mettam Memorial Church, 1835, Pikesville. Unable to secure information of records; services held yearly; old cemetery in church yard.
Sater's Baptist Church, 1742, originally known as Chestnut Ridge, first Baptist church in Maryland and fifth in United States. No records located.
  Membership 1742, in Lane-Smith families. Photos. MHS.

Frederick County

Baptist Cemetery, 1802–74, on highway between Taneytown and Emmitsburg, (16 records). Md. Geneal. Rec. Com., 1932–33, p. 69. Mss. DAR.
Baptist Church, established July 10, 1790. Church still standing, on All Saints Street, Frederick. No records of births, marriages and deaths extant. List of members, 1790–1831, in Hist. of west. Md. Scharf, v. 1, p. 517. MHS; DAR.
Emmitsburg Baptist Church, tombstone records, 1755–1911. Md. Geneal. Rec. Com., 1932–33. Mss. DAR.
Pleasant Hill German Baptist Church Cemetery, Bush Creek near New Market. Tombstone inscriptions, 1845–1924, earliest birth 1801. Md. Geneal. Rec. Com., 1932–33, pp. 212–17. Mss. DAR.

Harford County

Old School Baptist Meeting House, 1754, near Jarrettsville. No records of baptisms and marriages, from 1754–1803 (records burned); records 1803 to date, in custody of Meeting House. List of members, 1803, in Hist. of Harford Co., Preston, pp. 190–93.

Montgomery County

Silver Spring Baptist Church. No records extant.
Rockeville Baptist Church. Tombstone inscriptions, 1845–78; earliest birth 1788 (fragmentary). Scharf. V. 1, p. 752.

Wicomico County

Allen Memorial Baptist Church, 1859–1937, Salisbury. Pamph. DAR.
Members of Old School Baptist, or Primitive Baptist Church, 1766–99, Salisbury. Wicomico Co. records. Mrs. Wm. Tilghman. Bd. mss. DAR.

CHRISTIAN CHURCH

First Christian Church, Baltimore. A. W. Gottschall. 1932, pamph. DAR.

CHURCH OF GOD

Churches of God in Carroll County: Barkhill Church, Union Bridge, Carrollton Church, Patapsco, Frizellburg Church, Uniontown, Mayberry Church, Union Bridge, Uniontown Church, Uniontown, Wakfield Church, Uniontown, Westminster Church, Westminster, Winfield Church, Patapsco. Churches under Maryland and Virginia eldership of Harrisburg, Pennsylvania; eldership does not require keeping of records. Tombstone inscriptions of Uniontown, 1814–81; earliest birth 1754. Hist. of west. Md. Scharf. V. 2, pp. 857–58. MHS; DAR.

CHURCHES OF THE BRETHREN

Carroll County

Churches of the Brethren: Beaver Dam, 1762, Taneytown; Meadow Branch, 1848, Westminster; New Windsor, 1891, New Windsor; Piney Creek, 1900, Taneytown; Pipe Creek, 1780, New Windsor; Sam's Creek, 1860, New Windsor; Westminster, 1878, Westminster; Linwood, Linwood.
Church of the Brethren, or German Baptists or Dunkards, established in Carroll County since 1762. Only records are secretary's book of each congregation; have no baptismal records (only adult baptism). Each church is under an elder, and is assisted by other elders in congregation; these elders can perform marriage ceremony in Maryland without license to preach and are not required to keep records; they may have kept personal records, but it would be impossible to tabulate them. Information given by Rev. Early of Westminster Church.

Frederick County

Agenda Church of the Brethren, Rock Ridge Records of births, marriages and deaths, 1882–date, in custody of Samuel R. Weybright, Detour, Md.
Beaver Dam Church of the Brethren, 1829, Beaver Dam 2½ miles north of Johnsville. No records extant; oldest tombstone in cemetery, 1829. Date of building, in Hist. of Frederick Co., Williams, p. 461.
Grossnickle Church of the Brethren, 1837, near Myersville. No early records; earliest tombstone, 1848.
Monrovia Church of the Brethren (originally part of Bush Creek Congregation), organized 1846. Records burned 1816; oldest tombstone in cemetery, 1818.
Thurmont Church of the Brethren (originally part of Union Chapel, 1831). No records prior to 1921.
Church of the United Brethren Theological Seminary. Dayton. Dr. A. W. Drury, historian, is unable to give any information regarding records.

DUNKARD, DUNKER OR TUNKER CHURCHES

Washington County

Dunker Burial Grounds records, 1813–63. Ms. MHS.
Dunker Church, Funkstown. Tombstone inscriptions, 1798–1862; earliest birth 1741 (7 stones). Hist. of west. Md. Scharf. V. 2, p. 1282. MHS; DAR.
Emmert's Dunker Church, near Tilghmanton. Tombstone inscriptions, 1839–79; earliest birth, 1770 (12 stones). Hist. of west. Md. Scharf. V. 2, p. 1287. MHS; DAR.
Tunker Church, Beaver Creek District, near Smoketown. Tombstone inscriptions 1794–1880; earliest birth 1775. Hist. of west. Md. Scharf. V. 2, pp. 1300–01. MHS; DAR.
Tunker Church, Conocheague District. Tombstone inscriptions, 1861–76; earliest birth, 1798. Hist. of west. Md. Scharf. V. 2, p. 1291. MHS; DAR.
Welty's Tunker Church, Ringgold District. Tombstone inscriptions, 1844–77, earliest birth 1780 (few stones). Hist. of west. Md. Scharf. V. 2, p. 1292. MHS; DAR.

LUTHERAN CHURCHES

Allegany County

St. Luke's Lutheran Church, Cumberland. Register of births, marriages and deaths, 1849–date, in custody of Church.

St. Paul's Lutheran Church, Cumberland. Records of births, marriages and deaths, 1794–date, in custody of Church.

Trinity Lutheran Church, Cumberland. Register of births, marriages and deaths, 1853–date, in custody of Church.

Baltimore City

First English Lutheran Church. Register of baptisms, marriages, deaths, confirmations and communicants, Feb., 1827–Mar., 1859. F. A. Hanzsche. Balto., 1859. MHS.

Records of proceedings of First English Evangelical Lutheran Church, 1823–26. MHS.

Grace English Evangelical Lutheran Church Golden anniversary, 1885–1935. MHS.

Baltimore County

Catonsville Lutheran Church, 1842. Records of births, marriages and deaths, 1842–date (complete) are in office of Argus, Catonsville.

Catonsville Lutheran Church. G. C. Keidel. 1919, priv. pr. MHS.

Catonsville pioneers of Lutheran Faith. Natl. Geneal. Soc. Quart., v. 9, p. 29. MHS.

St. Michael's Lutheran Church, Perry Hall. Records of births, marriages and deaths, 1861–date (practically complete), in custody of pastor.

St. Paul's Evangelical Lutheran Church, Upperco. History. Ms. MHS.

St. Paul's Lutheran Church, 1838 (first church called Algires, 1769), Arcadia. Records of baptisms, marriages and deaths from about 1902, in custody of pastor at Hampstead. (In 1926 number of records were destroyed by fire.) Names of members, Annual Report, 1939.

Salem Lutheran Church Yard, 1786–1880, near Catonsville. Natl. Geneal. Soc. Quart., v. 9, no. 2, p. 30. MHS.

Carroll County

Emmanuel Evangelical Lutheran Church, established Feb. 12, 1760, Manchester. Records of baptisms, marriages, and deaths, 1760–1839 (written in German script) in custody of Rev. John Hollenback, Manchester. No records extant, 1839–62; 1862–1908 in safe in church; 1908–date in custody of Rev. L. H. Rehmeyer. (Oldest Lutheran congregation in Carroll County; first church was built of logs, owned and used jointly by Lutherans and Reformed Churches, second church was also union church, known as Zion Church, 1798; parted 1863.

Zion Lutheran Church, 1798, Manchester. For original records, see Emmanuel Evangelical. Records of births, marriages and deaths, 1760–1850. Typed, bd., indexed. Ms. MHS.

Lutheran and Reformed Cemetery, 1760–1880, Manchester District. Hist. of west. Md. Scharf. V. 2, p. 886, MHS; DAR.

Grace Lutheran Church, organized 1846, Westminister. Record of births, marriages and deaths, 1884–date, in custody of church. Services held prior to 1846 at St. Benjamin's and at Union Meeting House.

History of Grace Lutheran Church, Westminster, 1868–94. Rev. P. H. Miller. Pub. by E. J. Lawyer, Westminster. MHS.

Hampstead charge. St. Mark's Lutheran Church, 1878, Hampstead. Records of baptisms and marriages, 1877–date, also partial list of church members 1879, in custody of Rev. F. H. Shraden, Westminster.

North Carroll charge. Jerusalem Evangelical Lutheran Church, 1797, Gemeinde, Bachman's Valley. Original records of births, marriages, deaths and communicants, 1793–1800, in custody of Mr. George Tracy, Westminster.

Records 1793–1880. Mss. Index. MHS.

Records 1881–date, in custody of Rev. J. B. Lau, Westminster, R.F.D.

North-Carroll charge. Lazarus Lutheran Church, 1853. Records of births, marriages and deaths 1853–date, in custody of Rev. J. B. Lau, Westminster, R.F.D.

Union Bridge charge. Keyesville Lutheran Church, 1872. Records of births, marriages and deaths, 1900–date, in custody of Rev. P. H. Williams, Union Bridge.

Union Bridge charge. St. James Lutheran Church, 1883, Union Bridge. Records of baptisms, marriages and deaths, 1885–date, in possession of church.

Uniontown charge. St. Luke's Lutheran Church, 1756, New Windsor. Baust or Emanuel Church, 1794, between Taneytown and Westminster; Mount Union Church, 1858, near Middleburg; St. Paul's Church, 1870, Uniontown.

Uniontown charge. Baust or Emanuel Lutheran Church, 1794. Records incomplete. Tombstone inscriptions (125) 1794–1907. Md. Geneal. Rec. Com., 1935–36, pp. 51–57. Mss. DAR;

Tombstone inscriptions, 1798–1800. Hist. of west. Md. Scharf. V. 2, pp. 862–68. MHS; DAR.

Uniontown charge. Mt. Union Lutheran Church, 1858. Records incomplete.

Uniontown charge. St. Luke's Lutheran Church, 1766. Original records of births, marriages and deaths, 1783–date, in vault at Seminary, Gettysburg, Pa.

Uniontown charge. St. Paul's Lutheran Church, 1870. Records of births, marriages and deaths, from 1876, in vault at Seminary, Gettysburg, Pa.

Salem charge. St. Benjamin's (Krider's), 1761; St. John's (Leister's), 1775, Westminster. Records of baptisms (including date of birth), Mar. 30, 1834–Nov. 10, 1859; lapse 1869–1887; marriages Apr. 7, 1842–Aug. 3, 1845; lapse 1845–1879. Records 1924–date (complete). In custody of Rev. J. E. MacDonald, Westminster.

Salem charge. St. Benjamin's (Kreider's) Union Church, 1761; Lutheran and Reformed Cemetery (oldest burying ground in county) near Westminster, 1753–1875. Earliest birth, 1742. Hist of west. Md. Scharf. V. 2, p. 923. MHS; DAR.

Silver Run charge. St. Matthew's Lutheran Church, 1879, Taneytown. St. Mary's Church, 1762. Records not located.

Trinity Lutheran Church, 1788, Deer Park Road, Taneytown. Records of births, marriages and deaths (with exception of one book, date not given), 1792–1934, in custody of Rev. A. T. Sutcliffe, Taneytown.

Tombstone inscriptions, 1792–1867. Hist. of west. Md. Scharf. V. 2, pp. 842–45. MHS; DAR.

Woodbine charge. Calvary Lutheran Church, 1889, Woodbine. Records of births, marriages and deaths, 1891–date (complete), in the custody of Church.

Woodbine charge. Messiah Lutheran Church, 1882, Berrett. Records of births, marriages and deaths, 1882–date, in custody of Rev. Carl Mumford, Ellicott City.

Frederick County

Bethel Evangelical Lutheran Church, 1838, Bethel. Records of births, marriages and deaths, 1838–date (complete), in the custody of Church.

Elias Evangelical Lutheran Church, 1757. (First log church at Tom's Creek, Emmitsburg.) Records of births, marriages and deaths, 1757–1850, are lost; 1850–date, in custody of Church.

Tombstone inscriptions, 1749–1929, in Md. Geneal. Rec. Com., 1932–33, pp. 104–21. Mss. DAR. (Tom's Creek M. E. Church bought old Lutheran Church, 1797; removed 1904, many graves as early as 1720 are unmarked.)

Evangelical Lutheran Church, 1743 (occasional service as early as 1734; usually accepted date 1737; church building begun 1742), Frederick. (Church is daughter of Monocacy congregation, Gemeinde Monakes, 1732.) Records of births, marriages, deaths and communicants (complete), also earliest record book of Gemeinde Monakes, 1734–date, in custody of Church; 1742–1885, translated from German. 5 vols. Mss. MHS.

Lutheran Cemetery, 1800–51, Frederick. Hist. of west. Md. Scharf. V. 1, pp. 524–25. MHS; DAR.

Lutheran Church of Frederick. Records Aug. 22, 1737. (First baptism, George Frederick Unsult, born Aug. 6, 1737, baptised Aug. 22, 1737.) Rev. Mr. Wolf. MHS.

Lutheran Church of Frederick, 1738–1938. A. Ross Wentz. Harrisburg, 1938, 375 pp. MHS.

Lutheran Church of Frederick. G. Diehl. 1856. Pamph., 23 pp. DAR.

Lutheran Church of Frederick. Hist. of Frederick Co. Williams. P. 420. MHS; DAR.

Lutheran Church of Frederick. Hist. of west. Md. Scharf. V. 1, p. 511. MHS; DAR.

Lutheran Church of Frederick: Early members. First settlement of Germans in Md. Schultz. Pp. 12–13. MHS; DAR.

Monocacy Congregation. Pa. Germans in settlement of Md. Nead. P. 93. MHS; DAR.

Evangelical Lutheran Church, Sept. 21, 1873, Petersville. Records of births, marriages and deaths, 1873–date, in custody of Church.

Jerusalem Lutheran Church, Jerusalem, Middletown Valley, few miles north of Myersville. Records are lost. Oldest tombstone, still legible is that of Rebecca, wife of Tobias Horine, died Dec. 6, 1790. Hist. of Frederick Co. Williams. P. 499. MHS; DAR. Following is inscription on stone shaft, which marks site of Old Jerusalem Church: "The first churches of western Maryland were built on or near this site. Dutch Congregation, 1711–1786; Lutheran and Reformed, 1786–1806; United Brethren, 1806–1852. Erected in memory of those who established Churches of Christ under great difficulties."

Lutheran cemeteries, Middletown Valley. Hist. west. Md. Scharf. Old graves, 1805–26, v. 1, p. 577; new graves, 1840–52, v. 1, p. 578.

Lutheran Church, 1768, near Sharpesburg, torn down after 1862. Records lost, list of families. Pa. Germans in settlement of Md. Nead. P. 102. MHS; DAR.

Mt. Moriah Lutheran Church, 1829, Foxville, P.O. Lantz. Records of births, marriages and deaths (complete) 1829–date, in custody of Church.

Mt. Tabor Reformed and Lutheran Church, Rocky Ridge. Lutheran congregation organized 1873. Only records date from 1900, in custody of Rev. P. H. Williams, Union Bridge.

Mt. Zion Church, 1819, about four miles southwest of Frederick. Oldest tombstone, 1822. Register of births, marriages and deaths, 1819–date, in custody of Church.

Mt. Zion (or Haugh's) Lutheran Church, 1799, near Ladiesburg. Records kept (incomplete).

Rocky Hill (or Grace) Lutheran Church, 1767, near Woodsboro. Register of births, marriages and deaths, 1767–1853, translated and transcribed from German by Mrs. Jacob Kintz, 1930, for Frederick Chapter D. A. R.; records in custody of Chapter historian.

St. John's Evangelical Church, 1760, Thurmont. Records of births, marriages and deaths, 1760–date, in custory of Church.

St. John's Evangelical Lutheran Church, 1770 (present Church, 1908–09), Creagerstown. Some records of births, marriages, 1789–date, in custody of Church.

Records, 1742–89. Ms. MHS.

List of members, 1790. Pa. Germans in settlement of Md. Nead. P. 105. MHS; DAR.

Souvenir history of St. John's Evangelical Lutheran Church, Creagerstown, 1732–1932. Rev. F. R. Seibel, Jr., pastor. Pamph., 40 pp. (List of pastors and pastorates, 1732–1932, pp. 35–36.) MHS.

St. John's Lutheran Church, 1830, near Myersville. Records of births, marriages and deaths in custody of M. L. Rice, Esq. (in case of Mrs. Edgar Warrenfeltz, Church Hill). Some of oldest records not in existence.

St. Mark's Lutheran Church, 1840, Wolfsville. Register of births, marriages and deaths, 1840–date, in custody of A. E. Sensenbaugh, Smithburg, R.F.D. 2.

St. Matthew's Lutheran Church (Church-on-the-Manor), 1768, Church Hill. Register of births, marriages and deaths, 1768–date, in custody of Church. Number of tombstones in churchyard date back to 1700's.

St. Paul and St. Matthias, Ladiesburg. Church book, Reformed and Lutheran. Births, baptisms (giving parents and witnesses), 1799–1834; communicants, 1806; children confirmed, 1806; adults confirmed, 1801–34. Mss. Dept. of Hist. of Presbyterian Church, Witherspoon Bldg., Phila.

St. Paul's Evangelical Lutheran Church, 1829 (rebuilt 1859), Burkittsville. Baptisms, 1846–date; deaths, 1846–date; marriages, 1866–date; in custody of Church; none destroyed by fire.

St. Paul's Evangelical Lutheran Church 1838, Utica. Register of births, marriages and deaths, 1838–date, in custody of Church.

St. Paul's Lutheran Church, 1825, Jefferson. Records of births, marriages and deaths, 1825–78 are lost; 1878-date in custody of Church. Tombstones in churchyard date back to 1810.

St. Paul's Lutheran Church, 1856, Myersville. Records of births, Marriages and deaths, 1856–date, in custody of Wm. S. Wachtel, Esq.

Solomon's Evangelical Lutheran Church, Feb. 10, 1805, Woodsboro. Records kept (incomplete).

Tom's Creek Lutheran Cemetery, Emmitsburg. Tombstone inscriptions, 1719-1929. Md. Geneal. Rec. Com., 1932–33, pp. 73–75. Mss. DAR.

Trinity Evangelical Lutheran Church, Knoxville (now closed); formerly Evangelical Church of Weaverton; originally known as Paines Hill Congregation; organized 1848. Records of baptisms and deaths, no marriages, in custody of St. Paul's Church, Burkittsville.

Union Chapel, Lutheran and Reformed, 1805, near Libertytown. Records kept (incomplete).

Zion Lutheran Church, 1772 (first log church, 1750), one mile southwest of Middletown. Lutheran and Reformed worshipped here. Records of births, marriages and deaths, 1819-?, transcribed from German, indexed, bd. MHS; DAR.

Record of Lutheran Congregation of Zion Church, Middletown, 1779–1853. C. T. Zahn. Westminster, Md., 1934, 107 pp., typed, bd. DAR.

Zion Lutheran Church, 1750. Hist. of Frederick Co. Williams. P. 500. MHS; DAR.

Washington County

Beard's Lutheran graveyard, Chewsville District' Washington County. Md. Geneal. Rec. Com.' 1935–36. Mss. DAR.

Lutheran Cemetery, near Mangansville. Tombstone inscriptions, 1846-81. Hist. of west. Md. Scharf. V. 2, p. 1290. MHS; DAR.

Lutheran Church, Beaver Creek. Tombstone inscriptions, 1851–81; earliest birth 1793. Hist. of west. Md. Scharf. V. 2, p. 1300. MHS; DAR.

Mt. Calvary Evangelical Lutheran Church, Sharpsburg. Tombstone inscriptions. Hist. of west. Md. Scharf. (Old cemetery 1812–66, earliest birth 1773, v. 2, p. 1207; new cemetery 1845–77, earliest birth 1785, v. 2, p. 1208.) MHS; DAR.

Mt. Tabor Lutheran Church, Conococheague. Tombstone inscriptions, 1859-73; earliest birth, 1786. Hist. of west. Md. Scharf. V. 2, p. 1291. MHS; DAR.

Mt. Zion Evangelical Cemetery, 1788–1865, near Cearfoss. Hist. of west. Md. Scharf. V. 2, p. 1290. MHS; DAR.

Salem Evangelical Lutheran Church, 1854. Tilghmanton District, Bakersville. Tombstone inscriptions, 1813–80; earliest birth, 1760. Hist. of west. Md. Scharf. V. 2; p. 1287. MHS; DAR.

St. John's Evangelical Lutheran Church. Hagerstown. 2 vols. V. 1: List of organizers; list of elders; church wardens, 1806. Tombstone records, Rose Hill Cemetery, Hagerstown, taken from St. John's Lutheran graveyard; burials and marriages. V. 2: Births and baptisms, 1767–1900. 598 pp., 11, 663 items or dates prior to 1850. 1935–1936, typed, bd. DAR.

Tombstone inscriptions, 1831–71; earliest birth, 1767. Hist. of west Md. Scharf. V. 2, p. 1091. MHS; DAR.

St. Paul's Lutheran Church, Clear Spring. Tombstone inscriptions, 1811–80; earliest birth, 1750. Hist. of west. Md. Scharf. V. 2, p. 1250. MHS; DAR.

St. Paul's Lutheran Church, 1826, Leitersburg. Tombstone inscriptions, 1832–80; earliest birth, 1780. Hist. of west Md. Scharf. V. 2, p. 1278. MHS; DAR.

St. Peter's or Beard Lutheran Church, 1787, Smithsburg. St. Peter's joined with Trinity Lutheran, 1817–80; united with St. Paul's, Leitersburg, 1800–date. Records in Church from 1791. Infant baptisms, 1789–1828 (complete) in Church.

Tombstone inscriptions, 1777–1874. Hist. of west Md. Scharf. V. 2, pp. 1272–73. MHS; DAR.

Md. Geneal. Rec. Com., 1935–36. Mss. DAR.

Trinity Lutheran Church, Hagerstown. Historical sketch and directory. J. S. Wenner. 1891, News print.

METHODIST CHURCHES

(Organized in Maryland, 1784)

Allegany County

Bedford Street Methodist Episcopal Church, 1838, Cumberland. Records of births, marriages and deaths, 1852–date, in custody of Church.

Center Street Methodist Episcopal Church, 1783, Cumberland. Records from 1783 (?) in custody of Church.

Frostburg Circuit Methodist Episcopal Church. List of pastors, 1839–81. Hist. of west. Md. Scharf. V. 2, p. 1479. MHS; DAR.

Anne Arundel County

Anne Arundel Methodist Protestant circuit. Register of baptisms, marriages and list of male members, 1830–94. Mss. MHS.

Md. Geneal. Bull., v. 4. MHS; DAR.

Holly Run Methodist Protestant Church, 1828, Fort Meade Boulevard and General's Highway. Oldest church building of denomination now standing in U. S. (therefore in world). Provisional organization effected under title of "The Associated Methodist Church," Nov. 12, 1828, Baltimore; general conference met in St. John's Church, Baltimore, Nov. 2, 1830, and title "Methodist Protestant Church" substituted—quoted from history of Holly Run Methodist Protestant Church, by Rev. T. H. Lewis, pamph.

Baltimore City

Eutaw Street Methodist Episcopal Church, 1808–1908. List of members, 1808–68. Plant never repotted. Pp. 59–61. MHS. (Bishop Asbury first buried under pulpit of Eutaw Street Methodist Episcopal Church; later removed to Preacher's Lot.)

First Methodist Episcopal Church (old Light Street Church); St. Paul and 22nd Streets. Baptisms, 1794–1835; marriages, 1799–1835. 2 vols. Mss. MHS.

Burial records, 1823–33. Md. Geneal. Bull., v. 4. MHS; DAR. Also: Mss. MHS.

List of local elders and preachers of Methodist Episcopal Church, in Baltimore Town, 1799. 2 vols. Mss. MHS.

Marriages solemnized by ministers of Methodist Episcopal churches, Baltimore City Station, 1807-66. Records of baptisms, 1821-56. Bd. mss. MHS.

Mt. Vernon Place Methodist Episcopal Church. Register in custody of Church.

Strawbridge Methodist Episcopal Church, 1836-1932. Contains complete list of preachers and others, 1836. Susanna A. Forsythe. Bd. mss. MHS.

Baltimore County

Dover Methodist Episcopal Church, 1845 (first services held in schoolhouse, 1823). Records of births, marriages and deaths (fragmentary) in parsonage, Monkton.

Epsom Chapel, 1839, Towson. No records extant (originally community church.)

Falls Road Methodist Episcopal Church (originally built by United Brethren Church, purchased by Methodist Episcopal Church, 1885). Records of births, marriages and deaths, 1885-date, in parsonage, Hereford.

Gatch Methodist Episcopal Church, 1772. Records not located.

Hereford Methodist Episcopal Church, 1871 (originally Foster's, 1824). Records of births, marriages and deaths, 1824-71, not located; 1871-date, in parsonage, Hereford.

Foster's Cemetery records, 1787-1876. Md. Geneal. Rec. Com., 1932-33, p. 370. Mss. DAR.

History of Methodist churches in Baltimore County, 1843-93. Anniversary, May 21, 22, 23, 1893, held at Bosley Church. Circuit of Bosley, 1808; Dover, Falls Road Chapel; Foster's, now Hereford, Jessop, 1808; Monkton, 1871; Mt. Nebo, Pearce's, 1846 (now Clynmalyra), near Hereford; Phoenix, 1889; Shaw's (now Wesley Chapel, 2nd) church, 1844; Warren, 1835. List of names of preachers and stewards during fifty years. Md. Geneal. Rec. Com., 1935-36, p. 247. Copy of pamph. DAR.

Hunt's Methodist Episcopal Meeting House, 1772, 1828, 1873, 1933. Records, ? to date, in parsonage, Riderwood.

Mt. Carmel Methodist Episcopal Church, 1851-52 (originally called Mt. Nebo, 1808). Records of births, marriages and deaths, ? to date, in parsonage, Monkton.

Mt. Olive Methodist Episcopal Church, 1858, Old Court Road. Records of births, marriages, deaths and membership, 1858-date, in custody of Church.

Tombstone inscriptions (22), 1798-1849. Md. Geneal. Rec. Com., 1932-33. Mss. DAR.

Old Fork Methodist Episcopal Meeting House (erected chiefly by Gorsuch family), Manor and Joppa Roads. Tombstone inscriptions, 1781-1871. Hist. of Balto. City and Co. Scharf. P. 922. MHS.

Stone Methodist Episcopal Chapel, 1786 (remodeled 1862), between Owings Mills and Reisterstown. Tombstone inscriptions. Focke Geneal. Coll. Mss. MHS.

Towson Methodist Episcopal Church, 1871 (first worshipped in Epsom Chapel, 1839). Records of baptisms and marriages, 1837-70, not located; 1870-date, in parsonage, Towson.

Towson Methodist Protestant Church, 1832. Records of births, marriages and deaths, destroyed prior to April, 1870, except membership 1832-date. In parsonage, Towson.

Caroline County

Methodist Episcopal Church, 1867, Denton (first church called Moore's Chapel, built in 1816). Tombstone inscriptions, 1828-1905. Md. O. R. Soc. Bull., no. 1, p. 50. MHS.

Methodist Episcopal Church, Hillsboro. Tombstone inscriptions; earliest birth 1795; first death, 1853 (few stones). Md. O. R. Soc. Bull., no. 1, p. 50. MHS.

Carroll County

Bethesda Methodist Episcopal Church, 1810, Pleasant Gap. Tombstone inscriptions, 1837-78; earliest birth, 1773. Hist. of west. Md. Scharf. V. 2, p. 875. MHS; DAR.

Bethany Methodist Episcopal Church, Franklinville. Tombstone inscriptions, 1854-78; earliest birth, 1799. Hist. of west. Md. Scharf. V. 2, p. 895. MHS; DAR.

Carrollton Methodist Episcopal circuit, Finksburg. Pleasant Grove Church, 1856; Patapsco, 1890. Records of births, marriages and deaths, 1856-90, not located; 1890-date, in custody of Rev. John Dawson.

Centenary Methodist Episcopal Church, 1868, Westminster. Records of baptisms and marriages, 1870-date, in custody of Church.

Deer Park Methodist Protestant Church, 1853. Records (original) lost; recent ones incomplete.

Grace Methodist Episcopal Church, 1856, Hamstead. Records of baptisms, marriages and deaths, 1858-date, in custody of Rev. W. I. Randle, Hampstead.

Grave Run Methodist Episcopal Church, 1856. Records of baptisms and marriages, 1858-date, in custody of Rev. W. I. Randle, Hampstead.

Hampstead Methodist Episcopal circuit, Hampstead. St. John's Church, 1800; Shiloh Church, 1883. Records of births marriages and deaths, 1800-53, not located; 1853-date, in custody of Rev. M. E. Lederer.

Tombstone inscriptions, 1848-1900; earliest birth, 1795. Hist. of west. Md. Scharf. V. 2, p. 892. MHS; DAR.

Methodist Episcopal Church cemetery, between Freedom and Eldersburg, 1825-80. Earliest birth, 1812. Hist. of west. Md. Scharf. V. 2, p. 878. MHS; DAR.

Methodist Episcopal Churches, South, circuit. Bethany, 1871; Freedom, 1866; Oakland, 1866; Salem, 1867; St. James, 1870.

Bethany: Records of baptisms, 1907-date, in custody of Rev. Conrad N. Jordan, Sykesville. Older records in custody of H. L. Coffman, Esq., Mt. Airy. Earliest tombstone inscriptions 1790.

Freedom: Records of baptisms and marriages, 1866-date; earliest tombstone inscriptions, 1824; in custody of Rev. Conrad N. Jordan, Sykesville.

Oakland: Records of baptisms and marriages, 1866-date; earliest tombstone inscription 1832; in custody of Rev. C. N. Jordan, Sykesville.

Salem: Records of baptisms and marriages, 1867–date, in custody of Rev. Conrad N. Jordan, Sykesville.

St. James: Records of births, marriages, 1907–date, in custody of Rev. Conrad N. Jordan, Sykesville. Records prior to 1907 in custody of Rev. H. L. Coffman, Mt. Airy. Earliest tombstone inscription 1790.

Methodist Episcopal Church, South. Tombstone inscriptions, 1804–71 (7 stones). Hist. of west. Md. Scharf. V. 2, p. 878. MHS; DAR.

New Windsor Methodist Episcopal circuit. Bethel Church, 1821, rebuilt 1860; Ebenezer Church, 1851; New Windsor Church, 1844; Stone Chapel, 1783; Salem Church, 1832. Records of births, marriages and deaths, 1866–date, in custody of Rev. Hoxter (book was printed in 1866, containing records from 1764 (?)).

Bethel Cemetery, Parrsville: Tombstone inscriptions, 1811–78; earliest birth, 1786. Hist. of west. Md. Scharf. V. 2, p. 895. MHS; DAR.

Cemetery (opposite Stone Chapel), 1793–1873. Hist. of west. Md. Scharf. V. 2, p. 904. MHS; DAR.

Ebenezer Cemetery, New Windsor: Tombstone inscriptions, 1857–78; earliest birth, 1818. Hist. of west. Md. Scharf. V. 2, p. 894. MHS; DAR.

Log Meeting House, 1764, Pipe's Creek, first Methodist church erected in America, was in New Windsor circuit; was known by following names: Strawbridge, Log Meeting House, Sam's Creek or Pipe's Creek; was built by Robert Strawbridge, who arrived in Frederick Co. about 1760 and who was first preacher of American Methodism. Log Meeting House gave place to Bethel Chapel, 1801. Another successor was Poulson's Chapel, torn down 1783, rebuilt 1800, and named Stone Chapel.

Stone Chapel, 1783, rebuilt 1800. Small graveyard, 1833–73; first birth, 1790. Hist. of West. Md. Scharf. V. 2, p. 904. MHS; DAR.

Old Union Methodist Episcopal Meeting House, 1760, located in center of Westminster Cemetery, used until 1839, abandoned in 1891. No information about records.

Pipe Creek Methodist Protestant Church, 1829, Uniontown. Records of births, marriages and deaths, 1829–82, not located; 1882–date, in custody of Church. Oldest tombstone in cemetery, 1827.

Providence Methodist Protestant Church, 1828, Westminister, Records not located.

Ridgeville Methodist Protestant Church, 1851. Records not located.

Sandy Mount Methodist Protestant Church, 1827, Finksburg. Cemetery attached to Church; records not located.

Union Bridge Methodist Episcopal circuit, Union Bridge. Middleburg Methodist Episcopal Church, 1889. Records of births, marriages and deaths, 1889–date, in custody of Rev. W. W. Culp.

Tombstone inscriptions, 1850–80; earliest birth, 1793. Hist. of west. Md. Scharf. V. 2, p. 899. MHS; DAR.

Uniontown Methodist Protestant Church, 1829, Uniontown. No information about records.

Wesley Methodist Episcopal Church, 1797 (present Church, 1922), near Houcksville. (Brown's Meeting House, 1800–78.) No information about records.

Westminster Methodist Protestant Church, 1837. Few records prior to 1857; 1857–83, incomplete; complete records of births, marriages and deaths, 1883–date, in custody of Church.

Historic sketch of Westminster Methodist Protestant Church. Joshua W. Herring. Pamph.

Cecil County

Asbury Methodist Episcopal Church, 1829, 1859, Aikim. No information about records.

Bethel Methodist Episcopal Church, prior to 1790. Records of births, marriages and deaths (incomplete) in custody of Church.

Harts Chapel, 1830, Elk River Neck. Records (?) prior to 1794 (incomplete) in custody of Church.

Methodist Episcopal Church, 1740, 1813, 1859, Elkton. History. Molly Ash. Md. Geneal. Rec. Com., 1937, pp. 87–89. Mss. DAR.

Northeast Methodist Episcopal Church. Records of births, marriages and deaths (incomplete; some records burned in 1875) in custody of Church. Northeast Methodist Episcopal cemetery, 1795.

Port Deposit Methodist Episcopal Church. Records (incomplete) in custody of Church.

Principio Methodist Episcopal Church, organized 1843 (church built 1845), Principio Furnace. Records of baptisms and marriages, 1875–date, in custody of Church. Records prior to 1875 were probably burned in fire at Northeast.

Rock Run Meeting House, 1782. No records of births, marriages or deaths extant.

St. John's Methodist Episcopal Church, 1822 (rebuilt 1856), Charlestown. Records of baptisms and marriages, 1875–date, in custody of Church. (Prior to this date, Church was on circuit of six or more charges; assumption is older records are in Wilmington, Del. Oldest stone in present churchyard, 1852.

Dorchester County

Bethlehem Methodist Episcopal Church, South, Taylor's Island. Register of births, marriages and deaths, 1863–date, official roll of trustees, 1787, and roll of members, 1795, in custody of Mr. Duncan L. Noble, Taylor's Island.

Zion Methodist Episcopal Church, 1806, Cambridge. Register of births, marriages and deaths, 1850–date, in custody of Church. Records of meetings of board of trustees since organization, in custody of Benj. S. Insley, Cambridge.

Frederick County

Bennett's Creek Methodist Episcopal Chapel (House's Chapel), 1853, Hyattstown. Records of births, marriages and deaths, 1853–date, in custody of pastor of Montgomery County circuit, Clarksburg.

Brook Hill Methodist Episcopal Church, 1851, Yellow Springs. No. records available.

Brunswick Methodist Episcopal Church, 1851, Brunswick. Records of births and marriages, 1851–date, in custody of Church. Earliest death record, 1863. No cemetery connected with Church.

Buckeystown Methodist Protestant Church, 1864, Buckeystown. Register of births, marriages and deaths, 1864–date, in custody of Church.

Calvary Methodist Episcopal Church, 1771, Frederick. No records of births, marriages and deaths prior to 1861; bodies from old cemetery transferred to Mt. Olivet cemetery; oldest stone 1814.

Central Methodist Protestant Church, 1844, New London. Records of births, marriages and deaths, 1844–date, in custody of Church.

Epworth Methodist Episcopal Church, 1867, Point of Rocks. Records of births, marriages and deaths; 1867–date, at parsonage, Doubs, Frederick Co.

Flint Hill Methodist Episcopal Church, South, 1865. Records of births, marriages and deaths, 1865–date, in Trinity methodist Episcopal parsonage, Frederick, and in Clarksburg.

Forest Grove Methodist Episcopal Church, South, 1874, Forest Grove. No records prior to 1883; 1883–date in custody of Church. No cemetery.

Ijamsville Methodist Episcopal Church, 1852. Records of births, marriages and deaths, 1852–date, in custody of Church.

Israel's Creek Methodist Episcopal Meeting House, 1817 (rebuilt, 1855; moved to Walkersville, 1885). No records extant. See Shiloh Methodist Protestant Church and Methodist Protestant Church cemetery, near Walkersville.

Johnsville Methodist Protestant Church, 1842, Johnsville. Records may be at parsonage, Libertytown. Oldest tombstone in cemetery, 1842.

Libertytown Methodist Episcopal Church, 1812, Libertytown. No records extant. No church cemetery; all burials in common cemetery, Libertytown.

Libertytown Methodist Protestant Church, 1827–28, Libertytown. Records of births, marriages and deaths, 1828–date, in custody of Church.

Linganore Methodist Episcopal Church, Unionville. No records extant. Rev. Henry J. Miller, pastor, states: "Church antedates Revolution as Episcopal church, bought by Methodists after Revolution." Headstones in graveyard date back to 1700's.

Methodist Episcopal Church cemetery, Middletown Valley. Tombstone inscriptions, 1773–1867. Hist. of west. Md. Scharf. V. 1, p. 587. MHS; DAR.

Methodist Protestant churches of Frederick County now closed: Agenda Mission, 1859–78, Frederick; Burkittsville, 1828, Burkittsville; Catoctin, near Lander; Harmony Grove, Harmony Grove; Jefferson, Jefferson; Knoxville, Knoxville; Lewiston, Lewiston; Woodvale, 1828 (location not given, not on any map). "Above eight churches were organized, 1828–59, and are now closed. Their records of births and marriages and partial list of deaths, 1850–90, are in custody of pastor of Methodist Protestant Church, Buckeystown, and are only data that exists"—Rev. C. E. Dryden, pastor.

Mt. Carmel Methodist Protestant Church, 1854, near Woodsboro. Records of births, marriages and deaths, 1854–date, in custody of pastor, Rev. G. E. Wunder, New Market.

Tombstone inscriptions, 1722–1929. Md. Geneal. Rec. Com., 1932–33, pp. 210–11. Mss. DAR.

New Market Methodist Episcopal Church, 1840, New Market. Records of births, marriages and deaths, 1840–date, in custody of Church.

Shiloh Methodist Protestant Church, 1856, Walkersville (now sewing factory). No records of births, marriages or deaths. Pastor says they may be found in Methodist Protestant parsonage at Libertytown. Dr. J. O. Nicodemus, who owns property, says, 1817 is oldest grave in cemetery, connected with Old Israel's Creek Methodist Episcopal Church.

Tombstone inscriptions of Methodist Protestant Church cemetery, near Walkersville, 1818–1924 (now abandoned). Md. Geneal. Rec. Com., 1932–33. Mss. DAR.

Thurmont Methodist Episcopal Church, 1851, Thurmont. Records of births, marriages and deaths, 1851–date, in custody of Church.

Tom's Creek Methodist Episcopal Church, 1797, near Emmitsburg. Records of births, marriages and deaths, 1797–date, in custody of Church.

Tombstone inscriptions, 1796–1921. Md. Geneal. Rec. Com., 1932–33, p. 70. Mss. DAR.

Trinity Methodist Episcopal Church, South, established Dec. 16, 1866, Frederick. Records of births, marriages and deaths, 1866–date (complete), in custody of Church.

Waesche Methodist Episcopal Chapel, 1835, Detour (Detour in Carroll Co. but Chapel in Frederick County). Records of births, marriages and deaths are lost. List of legible tombstone inscriptions, 1839–1934 (complete) in custody of Mrs. Wm. Slemmer, historian of Frederick Chapter, D. A. R.

Harford County

Calvary Methodist Episcopal Church, 1834. Old records burned; more recent ones in possession of Pastor.

Churchville Methodist Episcopal Church, 1859. Records of baptisms, marriages and deaths, 1862–date, in custody of Church.

Cokesbury Church, Abingdon. No records of births, marriages or deaths extant. (Cokesbury College, 1783, was first Methodist college in world.)

Dublin Methodist Church, 1790, Dublin. No records of births, marriages or deaths extant.

Methodist Episcopal Harford circuit: Records of births, marriages and deaths, 1809–76. Mss. MHS. Also: Md. Geneal. Bull., no. 4. MHS; DAR.

Hopewell Methodist Protestant Church, 1859. Records of baptisms, 1861–date, and marriages, 1862–date (incomplete), in custody of Church.

Smith's Methodist Episcopal Chapel. Records of baptisms, marriages and deaths, 1857–date, in custody of Rev. C. E. Subrack, Jr.

Thomas Run (Watters) Meeting House, 1782. No records of births, marriages or deaths extant. History of founding of Thomas Run Meeting House. Md. Geneal. Rec. Com., 1929, p. 62. Mss. DAR.

Wesleyan Methodist Protestant Chapel, 1826. Records of baptism, marriages and deaths, 1826–61, destroyed; 1861–date, in parsonage.

Howard County

Emory Methodist Episcopal Church, Ellicott City. Records in Church date back to Jan. 18, 1838.

Kent County

Bond Methodist Episcopal Chapel, near Pomona. Tombstone inscriptions, 1847–1907 (complete). Md. O. R. Soc. Bull., no. 2, p. 78. MHS.

Christ Methodist Protestant Church, Chestertown. No information about records.

Galena Methodist Episcopal Church. Tombstone inscriptions, 1812–87. Md. Geneal. Rec. Com., 1932–33, pp. 302–10. Mss. DAR.

•Methodist Protestant Church, Lynch. No information about records.

Old Dudley's Methodist Episcopal churchyard. Md. Geneal. Rec. Com., 1932–33, 267. Mss. DAR.

Old Kent circuit, Philadelphia Conference, Methodist Episcopal churches: Bond, Chestertown, Kennedyville, Locust Grove, Salem, Fairlee, Sudlersville and Union at Worton. Records of baptisms and marriages, 1853–69, copied by Sarah E. Stuart. Bd. ms. MHS. Also: Md. Geneal. Bull., v. 4. MHS; DAR.

St. James Methodist Protestant Church, Fairlee. No information about records.

Union Methodist Episcopal Church, Worton. Tombstone inscriptions, 1852–1929. Md. Geneal. Rec. Com., 1932–33, pp. 328–34. Mss. DAR.

Wesley Chapel Methodist Episcopal churchyard. Md. Geneal. Rec. Com., 1932–33, pp. 268–75. Mss. DAR.

Montgomery County

Methodist Episcopal Church, Barnesville. Tombstone inscriptions, 1848–74; earliest birth, 1777. Hist. of west. Md. Scharf. V. 1, p. 731. MHS; DAR.

Methodist Episcopal Church cemetery, Hyattstown. Tombstone inscriptions, 1824–79; earliest birth, 1761. Hist. of west. Md. Scharf. V. 1, p. 723. MHS; DAR.

Methodist Episcopal Church, Clarksburg. Tombstone inscriptions, 1794–1879. Hist. of west. Md. Scharf. V. 1, p. 720. MHS; DAR.

Methodist Episcopal Church, Laytonsville. Tombstone inscriptions, 1794–1932; earliest birth, 1720. Md. Geneal. Rec. Com., 1934–35, p. 69. Mss. DAR.

Tombstone inscriptions, 1812–79 (6 stones). Hist. of west. Md. Scharf. V. 1, p. 718. MHS; DAR.

Methodist Episcopal Church, Poolesville. Tombstone inscriptions, 1839–64; earliest birth, 1782. Hist. of west. Md. Scharf. V. 1, p. 734. MHS; DAR.

Methodist Episcopal Church, Silver Spring. Register of births, marriages and deaths, 1872–date, in custody of Church.

Methodist Episcopal Church, South, Poolesville. Cemetery, 1833–1916 (abandoned). Md. Geneal. Rec. Com., 1926–27, p. 74. Mss. DAR.

Record books of Churchville circuit (Rockingham), 1826–1901, and Huntersville circuit, 1846–52, in possession of Nolan B. Harmon, Jr.

Queen Anne County

Dudley Meeting House, 1783. Old Dudley churchyard records. Md. Geneal. Rec. Com., 1932–33. Mss. DAR.

Queen Anne circuit and Church Hill circuit. See Kent circuit (Methodist Episcopal Church), Kent Co.

Washington County

Boonsboro Methodist Episcopal Church. Tombstone inscriptions, 1832–62; earliest birth, 1769. Hist. of west. Md. Scharf. V. 2, p. 1265. MHS; DAR.

Sharpsburg Methodist Church. Tombstone inscriptions, 1828–79; earliest birth, 1793 (fragmentary). Hist. of west. Md. Scharf. V. 2, p. 1210. MHS; DAR.

Smithsburg Methodist Episcopal Church. Tombstone inscriptions, 1811–78; earliest birth, 1736 (fragmentary). Hist. of west. Md. Scharf. V. 2, p. 1275. MHS; DAR.

Wicomico County

Asbury Methodist Church, Wicomico County, 150 years old. Jay Williams. 1928. DAR.

History of Methodism. Jay Williams. (Mss. list of Methodists listed in booklet will be found in Wicomico Co. Records, Mrs. Wm. Tilghman, bd. mss., DAR.)

History of Methodist Protestant church. Edna A. Elderdice. (References to Wicomico Co. families.) DAR.

Quantico circuit. No records of births, marriages or deaths, but deeds and records of early Church from 1784, when Bishop Asbury and Freeborn Garrettson preached in Quantico, in custody of Ira Dishroon, Quantico; also book of minutes of Quarterly Meeting, 1851–76, of following churches: Jones, Masses, Mezicks, Moores, Mt. Pleasant, Quantico and Sharptown.

Salisbury circuit. Register of births, marriages and deaths, 1850–79, of several churches—Forktown, Melsons, Rockawalking, Salisbury, Shad Point, Union and Zion—in custody of Asbury Methodist Episcopal Church, Salisbury; are only vital records to be found of this circuit in Wicomico Co. covering these years.

Salisbury Methodist Protestant Church, 1842. No complete register of births, marriages and deaths in earliest records.

Trinity Southern Methodist Church, Salisbury, organized in 1866 when there was separation in Methodist Episcopal church. No information of records.

MORAVIAN CHURCH

Frederick County

Moravian Church, established Oct. 8, 1758, Graceham. Records of births, marriages and deaths, 1758–date, in custody of Church. Baptisms (few), 1759–67; tombstone records, oldest legible, 1749; Siess graves; list of ministers, 1745–1873. Hist. of west. Md. Scharf. V. 1, pp. 633–34; MHS; DAR.

Moravian Church records, Graceham, Frederick Co. Positive photos., bd., vols. 1 and 2. MHS.

Moravian Church cemetery. Tombstone inscriptions. 2 vols. MHS.

Moravians who moved to North Carolina from "Carroll's Manor," Frederick County. Pub. North Carolina Hist. Com., v. 2, p. 719; v. 4, p. 265. MHS.

PRESBYTERIAN CHURCHES

Allegany County

First Presbyterian Church, 1806, Cumberland. Register of baptisms, marriages and deaths, 1837-date, in custody of Church. Records of Southminster Church, 1906, Cumberland, and Ellerslie Church supplied in connection with Frostburg, dissolved and members added to Cumberland, Oct. 22, 1881.

Baltimore City

Faith Presbyterian Church, Broadway and Gay Streets. Register of births, marriages and deaths, 1768–1866. Ms., indexed. MHS.
  Tombstone inscriptions (Glendy graveyard), 1807–1902; first birth, 1768. Mss. MHS; DAR.
  Presbyterians of Baltimore. Bouldin. Pp. 71–84.
  Faith Presbyterian Church (Glendy graveyard), Broadway and Gay Streets. Balto., 1928, 25 pp., mss. MHS.
  Glendy churchyard. Commercial burial ground and tombstone inscriptions of soldiers of Revolution and War of 1812 buried there. Patriotic Marylander, v. 2, no. 4, pp. 54–60. MHS; DAR.
  Tombstone Records of Glendy Burying Ground, Broadway and Gay Streets. Md. Geneal. Rec. Com., 1933–34, pp. 171–78. Mss. DAR.

First Presbyterian Church, Park Avenue and Madison Street. Records of births, marriages and deaths, 1768-date (original), in custody of Church.
  Records, 1768–1866. Ms. copy. MHS.
  List of officers and members, 1764–1879. Dept. of Hist., Witherspoon Bldg., Phila.
  Directory, 1860; register and yearbooks, 1881–1924, 17 numbers (some missing). MHS.
  First Presbyterian Church. W. Reynolds. History and list of Church officers, 1763–1913. MHS; DAR.
  M. H. Mag., 1913, v. 8, p. 383.
  Manual; contains roll of communicants and directory of members, 1818–76. Baltimore, 1877. MHS.
  M. H. Mag., 1934, v. 29, pp. 50, 206.
  Membership, 1766–1783 (304 persons). M. H. Mag., Sept., 1940, v. 35, no. 3, pp. 257–61.

Franklin Square Presbyterian Church, 1836, Fayette and Cary Streets. Withdrew from Presbytery, 1866. Records of earlier Presbyteries stored in Library of Union Theological Seminary, in Richmond.

Franklin Street Presbyterian Church, 1847, Franklin and Cathedral Streets. Formed by colony from First Church, 1847; withdrew from Presbytery, 1866. See First Church for earlier records.

Historic notes of First Presbyterian Church, 1761–1936. Balto., pamph. MHS.

Manual of Presbytery of Baltimore. (History of formation of early Presbyterian churches of Md.) Rev. John P. Carter, stated clerk, 1870. Balto., 1907. Rare volume; kept with records in vault. Rev. A. Brown Caldwell, pastor of Walbrook Church, is custodian of records.

One hundred years of history, 1802–1902. Second Presbyterian Church of Baltimore. T. H. Walker. 1902. DAR.

Presbyterians of Baltimore: their churches and historic graveyards. J. E. Boulden. Incomplete list of graves in Westminster and Glendy. Balto., W. K. Boyle and Son, 1875. MHS.

Westminster Presbyterian Church, Fayette and Green Streets. Directory, 1859; tombstone inscriptions. Presbyterians of Balto. Bouldin. Pp. 59–69. MHS.
  Westminster churchyard. Plat of original owners of lots. Patriotic Marylander, v. 2, no. 4, pp. 54–60. MHS; DAR.

Baltimore County

Chestnut Grove Presbyterian Church, 1842, Sweet Air. No records of marriages and deaths, but complete records of baptisms and members, 1842-date, in custody of Church. (Franklinville Church, from 1874–91, was on same pastoral charge.)

Granite Presbyterian Church, Granite. Records of infant and adult baptisms, marriages and deaths, 1845-date (incomplete), in custody of Church. See Mt. Paran Church.

Mt. Paran Presbyterian Church, 1715 (first called Patapsco; second Soldier's Delight, Harrisonville). Early records not found. Infant and adult baptisms, marriages and deaths, 1841-date, includes also records of Granite (The Quarries) and Springfield churches, Carroll Co., 1845–61; in custody of Paul O'Dell, Hernwood.
  Cemetery records, 1705–1850. Typed. MHS; DAR.
  History of Mt. Paran Church, 1715–1915. Typed. DAR.
  Tombstone inscriptions. Natl. Geneal. Soc. Quart., June, 1937, pp. 59, 60. MHS.

Parkton Presbyterian Church, organized in 1850, dissolved in 1873, Parkton. Now Bethel. No information about records.

Carroll County

New Windsor Presbyterian Church, 1838, New Windsor. No information about records. Tombstone inscriptions, 1768–1876. Hist. of west. Md. Scharf. V. 2, pp. 911–12. MHS; DAR.

Piney Creek Presbyterian Church, 1771, north of Taneytown. No information about births and marriages. Tombstone inscriptions. Hist. of west. Md. Scharf. V. 2, pp. 835–36. MHS; DAR.
  1777–1925 (279 records). Md. Geneal. Rec. Com., 1932–33, pp. 87–95. Mss. DAR.;
  List of communicants, 1824, and subscribers to pastor's salary, 1817. Department of Hist. of Presbyterian Church, Witherspoon Bldg., Phila.

Springfield Presbyterian Church, 1842. For records of baptisms, marriages and deaths, 1842–67, see Mt. Paran Church, Balto. Co., 1867–1934 (records complete) and 1933-date, in custody of Howard Warfield, Sykesville.

Tombstone inscriptions, 1849–78 (fragmentary); earliest birth, 1791. Hist. of west. Md. Scharf. V. 2, pp. 879–80. MHS; DAR.

In graveyard are buried many prominent people of Freedom District, including Browns, Carrolls, Hewitts, Pattersons, Warfields and others. Hundred years of Carroll Co. Lynch. P. 66.

Taneytown Presbyterian Church, 1828, Taneytown. No information about records.

Cecil County

Rock Presbyterian Church, 1720. Records, 1720–date, in custody of Church.

West Nottingham Presbyterian Church, 1724, Colora. No records in Church prior to 1858.

West Nottingham Academy, opened in connection with Church, 1741; one of oldest educational institutions in Maryland; founded by Dr. Samuel Finley, who later (1761) became president of Princeton University.

Zion Presbyterian Church, 1850, Northeast. Records of births, marriages and deaths, 1850–date, in custody of Church.

Frederick County

Emmitsburg Presbyterian Church, 1867 (or Tom's Creek Church, 1761). Records of marriages, 1806–21; list of ministers, 1775–1837; list of communicants, 1824; (other records destroyed by fire). Mss. Dept. of Hist. of Presbyterian Church, Witherspoon Bldg., Phila.

Tombstone inscriptions, 1739–1931. Md. Geneal. Rec. Com., 1932–33, pp. 96–103. Mss. DAR.

Note: Emmitsburg Presbyterian Church (or Tom's Creek), Frederick County, and Piney Creek Church, Carroll County, were for 52 years, under united pastorage of Rev. Robert Gieer.

Frederick Presbyterian Church, 1780, Frederick. Records of births, marriages and deaths, 1780–1881, lost, destroyed or never kept; 1881–date, in custody of Church.

Tombstone inscriptions, 1804–50; earliest birth, 1775 (fragmentary). Hist. of west. Md. Scharf. V. 1, p. 527. MHS; DAR.

Garrett County

Garrett Memorial Presbyterian Church, 1868, Oakland. No information about records.

St. Matthew's Parish, 1874: St. Matthew's Church, 1872, Oakland; Anderson Chapel, Swanton. No information about records.

Harford County

Belair Presbyterian Church, 1852. No early records of baptisms or marriages extant.

Bethel Presbyterian Church, 1769, Upper Node Forest. No early records of baptisms or marriages. List of subscribers to minister's salary, 1796. Hist. of Harford Co. Preston. Pp. 171–75. (Several Revolutionary soldiers buried there. Rev. John Clark, first pastor.)

Bethel Presbyterian Church, Harford County. Sketch. J. Cairnes. Bklet. MHS.

History of Bethel Presbyterian Church. Rev. Andrew B. Cross. (In wilderness of Upper Node Forest, Balto. Co., before 1769, now Harford Co.) Balto., 1886. DAR.

List. of pastors and subscribers to pastor's salary, Dec. 27, 1769, with family data. Hist. of Bethel Presbyterian Church. Cross. Pp. 16–50. DAR.

Churchville Presbyterian Church, first called Whitefield's Meeting House, 1738. No early records of baptisms or marriages. Records from Jan. 20, 1876, in custody of W. W. Finney, Secretary, 3070 Overhill Road, Baltimore.

List of pastors, 1796–1870. Hist. of Harford Co. Preston. Pp. 180–82. MHS; DAR.

Bicentennial program, 1738–1938. Pamph. MHS.

Franklinville Presbyterian Church, 1839. Records, 1852–date, in possession of Alfred Schutz, Upper Falls. None destroyed by fire but earlier records lost; on same charge as Chestnut Grove Church, Baltimore Co., 1874–91.

Grove Presbyterian Church, 1862, Aberdeen. No early records of baptisms or marriages.

Harmony Presbyterian Church, Glenville, organized Jan. 18, 1837. No early records of baptisms or marriages.

Havre de Grace Presbyterian Church, 1841. No early records of baptisms or marriages.

Slate Ridge Presbyterian Church, 1750, Cardiff. No information of records. Sketch. A. Lawis Hyde. Harford Democrat, Aug. 27, 1909. MHS.

Slatville Presbyterian Church, 1750, Cardiff. No early records of baptisms or marriages.

Montgomery County

Bethesda Presbyterian Church (prior to Revolution called Captain John, later Cabin John), 1716. Records from Sept. 18, 1723, and list of charter members and organizers in custody of Church.

List of members past and present. Hist. of west. Md. Scharf. V. 1, pp. 767–68. MHS; DAR.

Outline history of Cabin John Presbyterian Church, from Sept. 18, 1723. G. S. Duncan, pastor, 1896–1926. Hermon and Cropley.

"Bethesda and Rockville originally had one bench of elders, one communion roll. Two distinct congregations with two churches." Hist. of west. Md. Scharf. MHS; DAR.

Darnestown Presbyterian Church. Tombstone inscriptions, 1847–80; earliest birth, 1809. Hist. of west. Md. Scharf. V. 1, p. 761. MHS; DAR.

Huntersville Presbyterian Church, 1787. Tombstone inscriptions, 1741–1890 (230 stones). Md. Geneal. Rec. Com., 1932–33. Mss. DAR.

Somerset County

Francis Makemie came to America and organized Presbyterian churches: Buckingham, Berlin; Makemie Memorial, Snow Hill; Manokin, Princess Ann; Pitts Creek (few miles from Pocomoke City); Rehobeth, Rehobeth; Wicomico (four miles west of Salisbury)—all in what was Somerset County. These churches are believed to date back to 1683, but there are no records in existence to verify exact dates of founding. It is generally thought earliest records were destroyed by fire in home of Rev. William Stewart at Princess Ann), pastor of Manokin, Rehobeth and Wicomico churches.

Manokin Presbyterian Church, 1683, Princess Ann. Records of baptisms and marriages (few regular baptisms, 1769–1843); 1840–date; three (original) sessional records, 1747–1934; committee book, 1825–74, in custody of Church and kept in Bank of Somerset.

Baptisms, 1843–69. Ms. MHS.

Sessional records, 1747–1856. (Earlier minutes lost.) Ms. copy. MHS.

Tombstone inscriptions, 1786–1900. Md. O. R. Soc. Bull., no. 1, pp. 32–35. MHS.

History of Manokin Presbyterian Church. H. P. Ford. Phila., 1910. DAR.

Rehobeth Presbyterian Church, 1683, rebuilt 1706. No records of baptisms, marriages or deaths prior to 1892. Sessional book, Lewes, Delaware, may contain some records.

Tablet in Rehobeth Church: "Francis Makemie, Father of the American Presbyterian Church, His first and favorite Child founded 1683, These sacred grounds given by him."

Rehoboth by the river. (Has been called "Mother of Ten Thousand Churches.") Hermann Bischof. Courtesy of Rev. John S. Howk. Contains list of Rehoboth ministers, 1683–1920. 1st ed., 1897; 2nd ed., 1933; bklet. DAR.

Washington County

Hagerstown Presbyterian Church, Potomac Street, Hagerstown. List of subscribers to building fund, 1816. Natl. Geneal. Soc. Quart., v. 20, p. 27. MHS.

Tombstone inscriptions, 1818–79; earliest birth, 1762. Hist. of west. Md. Scharf. V. 2, p. 1097. MHS; DAR.

Wicomico County

Wicomico Presbyterian Church. Records dating back to 1750. No early records of births, marriages and deaths. Baptismal records, 1825–date, and list of pew holders, 1759, in custody of Church.

Records of baptisms, 1825–51; members, 1827; pew holders, 1759; subscribers, 1759, 1770. Mss. DAR.

List of elders, 1750–1876. Dept. of Hist. of Presbyterian Church, Witherspoon Bldg., Phila.

Worcester County

Buckingham Presbyterian Church, 1683, Berlin. No early records of births, marriages and deaths extant.

Tombstone inscriptions. Worcester Co. tombstone inscriptions. Hudson. Bd. mss. MHS; DAR.

List of parishoners of Buckingham Presbyterian Church, prior to 1798, and communicants, 1823. Old Buckingham by the sea, East. Shore of Md. Page. Pp. 61, 74–75. DAR.

List of pew holders of Buckingham Presbyterian Church, Berlin. Calvin R. Taylor Bank, Berlin.

Ministers and elders of Buckingham Presbyterian Church, 1683–1936. Old Buckingham by the sea, East. Shore of Md. Page. DAR.

Old Buckingham by the sea, on East. Shore of Md. Rev. I. M. Page, pastor, Berlin. Phila., Westminster Press, 1936. DAR.

Makemie Memorial Presbyterian Church, 1683, Snow Hill. No early records of births, marriages and deaths. Tombstone inscriptions, 1754–1831. Old burial grounds of Worcester Co. Md. Geneal. Rec. Com., Lynes, 1937. Mss. DAR.

Worcester County tombstone inscriptions. Hudson. Bd. mss. MHS; DAR.

Presbyterian Dissenting Congregation, near Snow Hill. Original minutes (kept by Spence family) begin Jan. 11, 1745, and end Feb., 1752; meeting of session, 1764–99, and copy of meeting of session, 1801. Dept. of Hist. of Presbyterian Church, Witherspoon Bldg., Phila.

PROTESTANT EPISCOPAL CHURCHES

Allegany County

(Diocese of Maryland)

Emmanuel Parish, 1803. Emmanuel Church, 1817, 1853, built on site of Fort Cumberland. Register of births, marriages and deaths, 1830–date, in custody of Church.

St. George's Parish, 1875. St. George's Church, 1852, Mt. Savage. Tombstone inscriptions, 1850–80; earliest birth, 1781. Hist. of west. Md. Scharf. V. 2, p. 1408. MHS; DAR.

St. James' Church, 1875, 1894, Westernport. No information about records.

St. John's Parish, 1896. St. John's Church, 1841, Frostburg. No information about records.

St. Peter's Protestant Episcopal Church, 1839, Lonaconing. No information about records.

Anne Arundel County

(Diocese of Maryland)

All Hallows Parish (South River), 1692. All Hallows Church, 1690, 1727; All Hallows Chapel, 1869, Davidsonville. Chapel of St. Andrew the Fisherman. Register (original) of births, marriages and deaths, 1685–1858. 2 vols. Md. Dioc. Lib. Also: Mss. copy, in MHS.

Index to register of All Hallows Parish, 1685–1858. 1 vol. Ms. MHS. (No copies of early registers in Church.)

Vestry proceedings, 1761–1844. Md. Dioc. Lib. 1761–1844, 1846–99. 2 vols. MHS.

Inhabitants of All Hallows Parish, 1776. Md. rec. Brumbaugh. V. 1, p. 407–16.

Mss. Hall of Records.

All Hallows Church, All Hallows Parish and St. Margaret's Church, Westminister Parish, Anne Arundel County. Rev. Geo. A. Leakin.

Hist. of Amer. P. E. Church. Perry.

Queen Caroline Parish, 1728. Christ Church, 1809, Howard and Anne Arundel Counties. See Howard County.

Severn Parish, 1845. St. Stephen's Church, 1838. St. Paul's Chapel, Crownsville; St. John's Chapel, Gambrill. Registers and vestry proceedings destroyed by fire prior to 1865. Few deaths recorded in current index to graveyard lots copied from tombstones, as early as 1829, are in custody of Church.

Manuscript hist. of country parish, Severn, Anne Arundel County, 1838–90. MHS.

St. Ann's Parish (Middle Neck), 1692. St. Ann's Church, 1699, 1792, 1858, Annapolis; St. Luke's Chapel, 1899. Register of births, marriages and deaths, 1704–date (some pages lost about 1800), in custody of Church.

1687–1796. 2 vols. Mss. MHS.
Register and vestry proceedings, 1820–48. 1 vol., photos. Vestry index in same book. MHS.
Index to register of births, marriages and deaths, 1687–1848. Vols. 1, 2, 3. MHS.
Vestry proceedings, 1704–67, 1767–1818: 2 vols. Index in same book. MHS.
St. Ann's churchyard, 1699–1817, Annapolis. Md. O. R. Soc. Bull., no. 3, p. 55. MHS.
Endowment guild of St. Ann's Parish. John Wirt Randall. Annapolis, 1909.
Historical notes of St. Ann's Parish, 1649–1857, with biographical sketches. Rev. Ethan Allen. Contains list of rectors, 1696–1850, and vestrymen, 1704–1817. Balto., J. P. Des Forges, 1857, 131 pp. MHS; DAR.
St. Ann's Parish. Vestry proceedings, 1712–77. M. H. Mag., v. 6; contd. in vols. 7, 8, 9 and 10.

St. James Parish (Herring Creek), 1692. St. James Church, 1692, 1765; St. Mark's Chapel, 1876; Tracey's Landing; James the less, Owingsville. Register (original) of births, marriages and deaths, 1682–1869. Md. Dioc. Lib.
1682–1869. Ms. copy. MHS.
Index of register, 1682–1869. 1 vol. MHS. (Registers in Church, 1850–1900, destroyed by fire.)
Vestry proceedings, 1695–1740, 1740–60, 1761–70, 1770–92. Md. Dioc. Lib.
Vestry proceedings, 1695–1792, with index in same book. MHS.
List of families of St. James Parish, 1695–1855. Md. Dioc. Lib.
Census, 1776, of St. James Parish. Md. rec. Brumbaugh. V. 1, pp. 417–31.
List of inhabitants of St. James' Parish, 1776. Hall of Records.

St. Peter's Parish, 1869. St. Peter's Church, 1843; Epiphany Chapel, Odenton. Register of births, marriages, deaths, confirmations and communicants, 1848–1916. (St. Peter's taken over by government when Camp Meade was established; congregation since worshipped in Epiphany Chapel, 1869, Odenton.) Md. Dioc. Lib.

Trinity Parish, 1869. See Howard County.

Westminster Parish (Broad Neck), 1692. St. Margaret's Church, built prior to 1692, burned 1803, Severn Heights; Marley Chapel, 1727, Curtis Creek. Register (original) of births, marriages and deaths in Farmer's National Bank, Annapolis.
1673–1885. 1 vol. Ms. copy. MHS.
Index to register, 1673–1885. 1 vol. MHS.
"Part of St. Paul's Parish, Baltimore County, united to Westminster Parish, Anne Arundel County, 1722, remaining part in Anne Arundel County, to Queen Caroline Parish in 1728."—Bacon's laws, 1765.

Baltimore City

(Diocese of Maryland)

Bishop Kemp's record book, list of confirmations, 1817–27. Mss. Md. Dioc. Lib.

Bishop William Paret's private record book. Baptisms, 1876–81. Mss. Md. Dioc. Lib.

Christ Church, 1828, 1870, Chase and St. Paul Streets. Register of births, marriages and deaths, 1828–71. 1 vol.; index in same book. MHS. For earlier records, see Old St. Paul's registers.

Church of Ascension, 1839; Prince of Peace, 1899; Church of Ascension and Prince of Peace, 1931, Walbrook. Register of births, marriages and deaths, 1839–May 2, 1873, destroyed by fire; 1873–date in custody of Church.

Church of Holy Communion, 1854, Griffith's Mount. Ladies church associations, and list of active members and officers. Balto., Sherwood Co., 1869, pamph. MHS.

Church of Messiah, 1875, Harford Road and White Avenues. First Church (Old Christ, 1828), Gay and Fayette Streets. Register of births, marriages and deaths, 1873–date, in custody of Church. For earlier records, see Christ Church registers.

Church of Our Saviour (Cranmer Chapel), 1844, 1871. No information on records.

Church of Redeemer, 1855. Charles Street Avenue. No information on records.

The Church of St. Michael and All Angels, 1877.

Emanuel Protestant Episcopal Church, 1853, Cathedral and Read Streets. Register of births, marriages and deaths, 1853–date, in custody of Church. (Emanuel Church built by large portion of congregation of Christ Church, residing in northwestern section of city.) For earlier records, see Christ Church.

Grace and St. Peter's Church, 1912, Monument and Cathedral Streets. St. Peter's Church, 1802, 1870; first church, Sharpe and German Streets; second church, Druid Hill Avenue and Lanvale Street. Grace Church, cornerstone laid July 20, 1850, by rector of St. Peter's. Registers of births, marriages and deaths, 1803–date, in custody of Church.
1803–85. 1 vol. Ms. copy. MHS.
Index to register, 1803–85. 1 vol. Ms. MHS.
Statistics of St. Peters Church. Lists of ministers, wardens, vestrymen, confirmations, communicants, Sunday-School teachers, members of church societies. Balto., Innes & Macguire, 1865, pamph. MHS.
Grace and St. Peter's year books, 1919–20, 1925–26. MHS.

Holy Comforter Church. (Defunct.) Register of births, marriages and deaths, 1880–1922. 2 vols. Md. Dioc. Lib.

Holy Innocence. (Defunct.) Register of births, marriages and deaths, 1899–1925. Md. Dioc. Lib.

Memorial Protestant Episcopal Church, 1860, Lafayette Avenue and Bolton Street. Register of births, marriages and deaths, 1860–date, in custody of Church.

Mt. Calvary Church, 1843, Madison Avenue and Hamilton Terrace. No information on records.

Record Book, convocation of Balto., 1886–97. Md. Dioc. Lib.

Record book, election of ministers, 1841–95. Md. Dioc. Lib.

Record book, St. Andrews, Lauraville, and St. Clements, Rosedale, 1905–17. Md. Dioc. Lib.

St. Andrews Protestant Episcopal Church. Vestry records, 1860–80. Bd. ms. Md. Dioc. Lib.

St. Barnabas Church, Curtis Bay. (Defunct.) Register of births, marriages and deaths. Md. Dioc. Lib.

St. John's Church, 1845, Huntingdon. No information on records.

St. Luke Church, 1853. No information on records.

St. Mark's Church, 1848, Lombard and Parkin Streets. (Defunct.) Registers of births, marriages and deaths, 1865–1917. 5 vols. Md. Dioc. Lib.

Vestry proceedings, 1800–94. 2 vols. Md. Dioc. Lib.

Diary and register, St. Mark's Church, 1858–61. Md. Dioc. Lib.

St. Mary's Church, 1855, Hampden.

St. Matthew's Chapel and Memorial Church of Holy Comforter. (Defunct.) Register of births, marriages and deaths, 1875–81. Md. Dioc. Lib.

St. Paul's or Patapsco Parish, 1692, Baltimore City and County. St. Paul's Church, 1739, 1856, Charles and Saratoga Streets. Register of births, marriages and deaths, 1710–1808. 1 vol., 262 pp. Mss. MHS.

Index to register, 1710–1808. MHS.

Register, 1808–30; also 175 marriages of 1776. 1 vol., 445 pp. Mss. MHS.

Index to register, 1808–30. 1 vol. MHS.

Register, 1832–78; index in same book. 1 vol., 448 pp., photos. MHS.

Register of baptisms, 1878–1925. 1 vol., 152 double pp., photos. MHS.

Register of marriages and burials, 1878–1925. 1 vol., 155 double pp., photos. MHS.

List of original records of Old St. Paul's, deposited in vault in MHS, and much damaged by dampness.

Registers, 1723–1868, 1878; vestry proceedings, 1878–88, 1905–15. MHS.

List of communicants of St. Paul's Church, 1813. Md. Dioc. Lib.

List of vestrymen and parishioners, 1726–97. Hist. of Balto. City and Co. Scharf. Pp. 517–21. MHS.

Ancient Churchyards. (St. Paul's churchyard, Balto.) Mrs. Helen W. Ridgely. Grafton Mag., Mar., 1909, v. 1, no. 4, p. 8; v. 2, p. 105.

St. Paul's graveyard, Baltimore. Plat made April, 1911 from old book; original burned 1904. MHS.

St. Paul's Protestant Episcopal graveyard, Baltimore. Patriotic Marylander, v. 2, no. 4, pp. 54–60. MHS; DAR.

Sunday School records of St. Paul's Parish, 1817, 1827, 1876–81. Md. Dioc. Lib.

St. Paul's Parish, Baltimore. Brief hist. J. W. Poultney and J. E. Sinclair. Pamph. MHS.

St. Paul's Parish. See Westminster Parish, Anne Arundel Co.

History of St. Paul's Parish. Ethan Allen. Mss. MHS.

(Note: St. Paul's Church, 1702, first erected on Clopper's or Colgate Creek, 4 miles east of City; removed to Baltimore, 1739, and was first church built in Baltimore City.)

St. Stephens Church. (Defunct.) Register of births, marriages and deaths, 1857–92. Md. Dioc. Lib.

Vestry proceedings, 1857–92. Md. Dioc. Lib.

St. Thomas' Church, 1858. Homestead. No information on records.

Trinity Church, 1806, Trinity Street. (Defunct.) Register of births, marriages and deaths, 1805–1903. 3 vols. Md. Dioc. Lib.

Copy, 1805–18. Index in same book. MHS.

Vestry Proceedings 1879-1903. Md. Dioc. Lib. (Note: Vestry of First Trinity, 1806, built St. Andrews' P. E. Church, 1837.)

Baltimore County

(Diocese of Maryland)

Holy Apostles, 1866–1913, Halethorpe. Register of births, marriages and deaths, 1884–date (complete), in custody of Church.

Holy Comforter Church, Rossville, Baltimore Co. (?). (Defunct.) Register of births, marriages and deaths. Md. Dioc. Lib.

Holy Cross Church, Freeland, Baltimore Co. Register of births, marriages and deaths, 1910–23. Md. Dioc. Lib.

Parishes and Hundreds of Baltimore County, 1776. Hist. of Balto. City and Co. Scharf. P. 812. MHS.

Reisterstown Parish, 1871–86. All Saints' Church, 1894, Reisterstown. St. Michael's Chapel, 1853, Hannah More Academy, Reisterstown. Register of baptisms and confirmations (complete), 1854–date; burials, 1853–date; in custody of Church.

Sherwood Parish, 1859. Sherwood Church, 1836, Cockeysville. Register of births, marriages and deaths, 1836–date (with exception of one record that was lost), in custody of Church.

Tombstone inscriptions (incomplete), as early as 1790. Hist. of Balto. City and Co. Scharf. P. 879. MHS.

Sherwood Parish, Cockeysville, Baltimore Co., 1830–90. Rev. G. E. Kagey. 1930, pamph. MHS; DAR.

St. George's Parish, 1692. See Harford Co.

St. James Parish, 1777. St. James Church, 1752–55, My Lady's Manor. St. James Chapel, 1912, Parkton.

(Note: St. James Church was Chapel of Ease of St. John's Parish; became Parish Church of St. John's and St. James Parishes, 1752.)

Register of baptisms and marriages, 1812–date; deaths, 1792–date (there are lapses in records, 1821–1902), in custody of Church.

Register (original) of St. James Parish; births, marriages and deaths, 1819–60. Md. Dioc. Lib.

Register of St. James and St. John's Parishes; births, marriages and deaths, 1787–1815, 1809–1902. 2 vols. Mss. MHS.

Index to register, 1787–1815. 1 vol. Ms. MHS.

Index to register, 1809–1902, in same book.

Marriage licenses of St. James and St. John's Parishes, 1820–56, kept by John Reeder Keech, rector. Md. Dioc. Lib.

Vestry proceedings of St. James' Parish, 1778–1892. Index in same book. 1 vol. Ms. MHS.

List of subscribers (112) to rector's salary, 1790. Hist. of Balto. City and Co. Scharf. P. 911. MHS.

St. James Church shared its rector with St. John's, until 1777, when Rev. John Coleman became rector. Copies from diary of Rev. Coleman, 1792, in possession of Church.

St. John's Parish (Copley) 1692. St. John's Church, 1815, Kingsville. (First church was erected at Joppa, prior to 1691; few tombstones are near site of old church.)

St. John's Parish. Register of births, marriages and deaths only of recent date in custody of Church. (Some records lost prior to 1916).
1700–1760 (original). Md. Dioc. Lib. Ms. copy in MHS.
St. John's Parish and St. George's Parish (Harford Co.). Register (original) of births, marriages and deaths, 1696–1780. Md. Dioc. Lib.
1696–1851. 1 vol. Ms. copy. MHS.
Index to register of St. John's Parish and St. George's Parish (Harford Co.), 1696–1851. 1 vol. MHS.
See also Registers of St. James Parish.
Vestry proceedings of St. John's Parish, 1735–83. 1 vol. Md. Dioc. Lib.
1708–1777. 1 vol. Index in same book. MHS.
List of rectors of St. John's Parish, 1680–1881; list of vestryman and wardens, 1693–1799. Hist. of Balto. City and Co. Scharf. Pp. 920–21. MHS.

St. Paul's Parish or Patapsco, 1692, Baltimore City and Co. See Baltimore City.
St. Paul's Parish, Baltimore Co. Historical sketch. Rev. Ethan Allen. Contains list of pewholders, 1784. 2 vols. Balto., 1855. MHS.

St. Thomas' Parish, 1744. St. Thomas Church, 1743, Garrison Forest. (Note: St. Thomas' Church was built as Chapel of Ease of St. Paul's Parish, Baltimore City and Co.
Register of births, marriages and deaths, 1728–date, in custody of Church.
1712–1819. 1. vol. Ms. copy. MHS.
Index to register, 1712–1819. 1 vol. MHS.
1702–1824. Md. Geneal. Rec. Com., 1937, Parran, pp. 109–80. Mss. DAR.
Vestry proceedings, 1744–date, in custody of Church.
1744–89. Ms. copy. Index in same book. MHS.
Tombstone inscriptions, 1740–1868 (incomplete). Hist. of Balto. City and Co. Scharf. P. 864. Ms. in MHS. DAR.

Garrison Church. Sketches of history of St. Thomas' Parish, 1742–1852. Rev. Ethan Allen. Edited by Rev. Hobart. Smith. Contains list of contributors, 1743, toward building Church; list of rectors, 1745–1888; list of wardens and vestrymen, 1745–1898; list of taxable bachelors, 1745–63; biographical sketches of some of members. N. Y., James Pott Co., 1898.

St. Timothy's Church, 1844, Catonsville. Register of births, marriages and deaths, 1845–date (incomplete), in custody of Church.

Trinity Church, 1862, Long Green. Register of births, marriages and deaths, 1875–date, in custody of Church.
(Note: Only record prior to 1875 is one contained in minutes of vestry, giving account of building of Church and list of subscribers.)
Tombstone inscriptions, 1754–1936 (complete, with exception of few unmarked stones). Typed. MHS; DAR.

Trinity Church, 1859, Towson. Register of births, marriages and deaths, 1858–date; also register, 1887–date, Chapel of Holy Comforter, 1887, Lutherville, in custody of rector, Rev. Henry B. Lee, Jr., Towson.
Trinity Protestant Episcopal Church, Towson. History. Contains biographical sketches. Jackson Piper, M.D. Ms. MHS.

Western Run Parish, 1854. St. John's Church in the Valley, 1816, 1869, Worthington Valley, near Reisterstown. (Rev. Joseph Jackson was first rector.) Register (original) of births, marriages and deaths, 1816–69 (first baptism 1810) in custody of Church.
1820–99. 1 vol. Ms. copy in MHS.
Vestry proceedings, 1820–99. 1 vol. Md. Dioc. Lib. Ms. copy in MHS.
List of vestrymen (first) and subscribers of St. John's Church, 1804. Hist. of west. Md. Scharf. P. 865. Md. Dioc. Lib.
List of vestrymen, 1850–92. MHS.
Western Run Parish Book. Notes gathered from various sources, especially adjoining parishes; also some Methodist and German records, etc.; in handwriting of Rev. Ethan Allen. Contains register of births, marriages and deaths, 1823–92; births, 1689–1889; vestry proceedings, 1879–92; subscribers to building fund; list of rectors, 1816–23; family data. Bd. ms. MHS.

Calvert County

Diocese of Maryland

All Saints Parish, 1692. All Saints Church, 1815, Sunderland. Register of births, marriages and deaths lost in several fires. Vestry proceedings, 1702–20, 1720–1854. Md. Dioc. Lib.
1720–1853; containing typed list of pew holders, after fire of 1800. MHS.

Christ Church Parish, 1692. Christ Church, 1692 (Brick Church, 1732, 1772), Port Republic; Middleham Chapel, 1699, rebuilt 1748; St. Leonard's Chapel. Register in custody of Church.
First baptism, 1840; first marriage, 1759, and confirmations, 1794. Register of births, marriages and deaths, 1688–1819. Md. Dioc. Lib.
Register, 1688–1747. 1 vol. MHS.
Index to register, 1688–1747; also Queen Anne's Parish, Prince George Co. MHS.
Vestry proceedings, 1781–1813. Md. Dioc. Lib.; MHS.
Christ Church register, 1700–1811. Monette Book, p. 287. MHS.

St. Paul's Parish, 1842. St. Paul's Church, Prince Frederick. Register of marriages and burials, 1850–date, in custody of Church. Earlier registers burned.

Caroline County

(Diocese of Easton, 1885)

Holy Trinity Parish. Holy Trinity Church, Greensboro. No information on records.

St. John's Parish. St. Paul's Church, 1st church 1748; present church, 1858, Hillsboro. (Tuckahoe Chapel, prior to 1750, Tuckahoe Bridge.) Register (original) of births, marriages and deaths, 1752–date, in custody of Mrs. H. Lay Brown, Hillsboro.
1746–1858. 1 vol. Ms. copy. MHS.
Index to register, 1746–1858. 1 vol. Ms. MHS.
Vestry proceedings, 1752–82. Index in same book. MHS.
Tombstone records, 1833–1905 (complete). Md. O. R. Soc. Bull., no. 1, p. 48.

St. Mary's White Chapel Parish, 1725, divided from Great Choptank, takes in all of Caroline Co. east of Choptank River. St. John's Church, Denton. No information on records.

Carroll County

(Diocese of Maryland)

Ascension Parish, 1844. Ascension Church, 1846 (first a mission of Holy Trinity, Eldersburg), Westminster. Register of births, marriages and deaths, 1846-date, in custody of Church.
Cemetery records, 1847-74. Hist. of west. Md. Scharf. V. 2, p. 941. MHS.
Holy Trinity Parish, 1843, established from St. Thomas Parish, Baltimore Co. Holy Trinity Church, 1771, Eldersburg. St. Barnabas Chapel, 1851, Sykesville. Register of births, marriages and deaths, 1771-1843, 1852-65, burned.
Ware Register, 1871-1901, contains history of St. Barnabas, and complete records of baptisms, marriages and deaths, 1865-date, in custody of Rev. — Albaugh, Sykesville.
Register of Holy Trinity Parish, 1870-1901. Md. Dioc. Lib.
Register of St. Barnabas Chapel, 1902-30. Md. Dioc. Lib.
Vestry records, 1843-1920. Md. Dioc. Lib.
Tombstone inscriptions of Holy Trinity Cemetery, 1811-72 (fragmentary); earliest birth, 1769. Hist. of west. Md. Scharf. V. 2, p. 882.
St. Barnabas Chapel cemetery, 1788-1876. Hist. of west. Md. Scharf. V. 2, p. 889. MHS; DAR.
Financial report, Holy Trinity Parish, 1892-1900. Md. Dioc. Lib.

Cecil County

(Diocese of Easton, 1885)

North Elk Parish, 1706, or St. Mary Anne's Parish, 1742, North East. St. John's Chapel, Perryville. Register of birth, marriages and deaths, 1713-99. 1 vol. Mss. MHS.
Index to register, 1713-99. Ms. MHS.
Register of births, marriages and deaths, 1713-71. Typed, bd. DAR.
Marriages, 1840-63. Typed, bd. DAR.
Register of births, marriages and deaths. St. Mary Anne's Parish, Cecil Co. Mary E. Ford. DAR.
Vestry proceedings, 1713-99. 2 vols. Index in each book. Mss. MHS.
Notes on Maryland parishes, North Elk and St. Mary Anne Parishes, Cecil County. Ethan Allen. M. H. Mag., 1914, v. 9, pp. 315-26.
North Sassafras Parish, 1692. St. Stephen's Church, Earleville. (Chapel of Ease St. John's Manor, 1698.) St. Stephen's Chapel, Cecilton. Register of births, marriages and deaths, 1691-1837. 1 vol. Ms. MHS.
Index to register, 1691-1837. 1 vol. Ms. MHS.
Vestry proceedings, 1693-1804. Index in same book. Ms. MHS.
Tombstone inscriptions. Ms. MHS.
South Sassafras Parish, 1692 (Shrewsbury). See Kent Co.
St. Augustine Parish, 1744. Erected from North Sassafras Parish. St. Augustine Church (Good Shepherd), Chesapeake City. No early records; tradition says they were burned, but there is no proof of this. Miss Molly Ash, of Elkton, says they are probably incorporated with St. Stephen's Church or St. Mary Anne's.
Manor Chapel or St. Augustine Church. Pamph. DAR.
St. James Church, Port Deposit.
St. Mary Anne Parish.
St. Stephens Parish (Episcopal), Cecilton. Register of births, marriages and deaths, 1692-1837. Copied by D. C. Daughters of Amer. Colonists. Indexed, typed, bd. DAR.
(Note: St. Stephen's Parish or North Sassafras Parish, 1692, St. Stephen's Church.)
St. Stephen's Parish records, Cecil Co. Carbon copy, presented by Nanticoke Chapter to the D. A. R., 1939. DAR.
St. Stephen's graveyard, Cecil Co. Md. Geneal. Rec. Com., 1934-35, pp. 213-14. Mss. DAR.
Susquehanna Parish, 1913, formerly part of North Elk Parish, 1706. St. Mark's Church, 1844, Aikin. Register of births, marriages and deaths, 1844-1913, in North Elk Parish. 1913-date, in custody of Church.
Tombstone inscriptions from 1815.
Trinity Parish, 1832, erected from St. Mary Anne's Parish, 1742. Trinity Church, 1832, 1860, 1896, Elkton. St. Andrew's (Goldsborough Memorial Church), 1895. Registers (original) of births, marriages, deaths and vestry proceedings, 1832-date, in custody of Church.
Trinity Parish, Elkton. History. Miss Molly Ash. Md. Geneal. Rec. Com., 1937, pp. 78-86. Mss. DAR.

Charles County

(Diocese of Washington)

Durham Parish, 1692. Christ Church, 1692, 1734, 1791, Nanjemoy. St. James Chapel, Grayton. Register of births, marriages and deaths, 1842-43. 1 vol. Ms. MHS.
Journal of vestry (original), Easter Monday, 1774, to May, 28, 1824. Natl. Cathedral. Photostat copy in Lib. Cong.
Photostat copy (few baptisms included) with Ms. index. Ms. MHS.
History of Durham Parish, Charles Co. P. W. Pusey. 1894. DAR.
Port Tobacco Parish, 1692. Christ Church, La Plata; St. Paul's Chapel, Piney; St. James Church, St. Barnabas Mission, Waldorf. All parish registers prior to 1862 were destroyed by fire.
History, containing list of rectors, 1692-1928. Hist. sketches of Md. parishes, and missions in Diocese of Washington. P. 189.
List of rectors. M. H. Mag., 1927, v. 22, no. 3, p. 303.
Trinity Parish, 1744 (consisted of those portions of King and Queen and All Faiths' Parishes, which lay in Charles Co. Trinity Church, Newport; Trinity Chapel, 1769, Oldfields; rectory, Hughesville. Register of baptisms and vital statistics, Sept., 1792-Jan. 1, 1830, 1830-50; Treasurers account, 1794-1856; journal of vestry, May 6, 1729-April 17, 1797. Natl. Cathedral.
Register, 1729-1826; also vestry proceedings, in same book, 1749-97. 1 vol. Ms. MHS.

Register of Trinity Chapel (called Old Fields), 1799–1852. Index in same book. 1 vol. Ms. MHS.

Trinity Parish, Charles Co. J. N. Barry. M. H. Mag., 1906, v. 1, no. 4, pp. 324–30.

History, containing list of rectors, 1751–1927. Hist. sketches of parishes, and Missions in Diocese of Washington. P. 193.

Dorchester County

(Diocese of Easton)

Dorchester Parish, 1692. Trinity Church, Church Creek; Grace Church, Taylor's Island. Register (original) of births, marriages and deaths, 1743–1896, kept at County Trust Company Bank, Cambridge.

1738–1903. Ms. copy. MHS.

Index to register, 1738–1903. 1 vol. Ms. MHS.

Register of births, 1743; marriages, 1817–39; deaths, 1847–54. Md. Dioc. Lib.

Vestry proceedings, 1818–92. Index in same book. MHS.

Tombstone inscriptions, 1800–1909. (268 names). Md. O. R. Soc. Bull., no. 3. MHS.

Tombstone inscriptions. Md. Geneal. Rec. Com., 1937–38, pp. 93–104. Typed, bd. DAR.

Great Choptank Parish, 1692. Christ Church, Cambridge; St. John's Church, Cornersville. Register (original) of births, marriages and deaths, 1790–date, in custody of Church.

1734–1903. Bd. ms. MHS.

Index of register, 1734–1903. 1 vol. Ms. MHS.

1796–1812 (in handwriting of Bishop Kemp, and certified by him). Md. Dioc. Lib.

Register of Great Choptank Parish. Mss. Coll. Geneal. Soc.

Scattered items from Great Choptank Parish. Md. Geneal. Rec. Com., 1932–33. Mss. DAR.

Vestry proceedings, March 24, 1788–date, in custody of Church.

1788–1886. Mss. copy. Index in same book. MHS.

Christ Church, grave stone records, prior to 1850; oldest stone, 1793. Md. Geneal. Rec. Com., 1929, v. 3, pp. 39–42. DAR.

Historical records of Christ Protestant Episcopal Church cemetery, Cambridge. Dr. Guy Steele. Edited by Dorset Chapter, D. A. R. 1935–36, 438 items, pamph. MHS; DAR.

West Choptank Parish. List of births copied from register. Turner Geneal. Coll. 2 vols. Mss. MHS.

St. Stephen's Parish, 1836. St. Stephen's Church, East New Market; St. Andrew's, Hurlock; Epiphany Mission, Preston. Register of births, marriages and deaths, prior to 1914, destroyed by fire; 1914–date, in custody of Church.

Vienna Parish, 1836. St. Paul's Church, Vienna. Built as Chapel of Ease of Great Choptank Parish. Register of births, marriages and deaths, 1866–date, in custody of Mr. James A. Higgins, Vienna.

List of petitioners, 1728. Hist. of Dorchester Co. Jones. P. 83.

Frederick County

(Diocese of Maryland)

All Saints' Parish, 1742–92. Erected from Prince George Parish. All Saints Church, 1750, 1855, Frederick; St. Timothy's Chapel; St. Barnabas Chapel. Register of births, marriages, deaths, communicants and list of families, 1727–1801 (incomplete); 1801–date (complete), in custody of Church.

1727–1863. 1 vol. Ms. MHS.

Index to register, 1727–1863. 1 vol. Ms. MHS.

Births and marriages of All Saints' Parish, 1727–81. Md. rec. Brumbaugh. V. 1, pp. 258–62.

1727–1781. Mag. Amer. Ancestry. Clemens. V. 6, no. 7, p. 111.

1727–1781 (fragmentary). Pub. Geneal. Soc. Pa., v. 7, no. 3, pp. 245–50.

Tombstone inscriptions from original churchyard (later 324 bodies removed to Mt. Olivet, and only 70 stones identified), 1753–1850 (complete). Md. rec. Brumbaugh. V. 1, pp. 263–70.

Tombstone inscriptions, 1807–1880 (fragmentary). Hist. of west. Md. Scharf. V. 1, p. 525.

List of petitioners for establishment of All Saints Parish, 1742. Hist. of west. Md. Scharf. V. 1, pp. 501–02. MHS; DAR.

List of petitioners to divide All Saints Parish, 1760. Hist. of west Md. Scharf. V. 1, pp. 503–04. MHS; DAR.

List of rectors, assistant clergy and lay delegates to Diocesan Convention, for All Saints Parish, 1742–1873. Hist. of west. Md. Scharf. V. 1, p. 508. MHS; DAR.

Historical notes of All Saints Parish, 1742–1908. Ernest Helfenstein. 1908. MHS; DAR.

All Saints' Parish. Ethan Allen Papers. Mss. MHS.

All Saints Parish. Newspaper article. DAR.

Catoctin Parish, 1855. Harriott Chapel, 1833, Catoctin Furnace; St. Stephen's Chapel, 1894, Thurmont. Register of births, marriages and deaths, prior to 1896, destroyed by fire. No cemetery connected with chapel.

Linganore Parish, 1889, Frederick and Carroll Cos. Grace Protestant Episcopal Church, 1870, New Market. Register of births, marriages and deaths, 1870–date, in custody of Church.

St. Mark's Parish, 1800, Frederick and Washington Cos. St. Mark's Church (between 1800–06), Petersville; St. Luke's Chapel, 1856, Pleasant Valley; Grace Church, 1893, Brunswick; St. John's Chapel, 1896, Burkittsville.

St. Mark's Church register of births, marriages and deaths from about 1800–date, in custody of Church. (Many old tombstones in churchyard.)

St. Luke's Chapel register of births, marriages and deaths, 1837–date, in custody of Church.

St. Paul's Parish, 1841. St. Paul's Church, 1843 (now closed), Point of Rocks; Holy Trinity, 1886–1911; St. Luke's Church, 1882–1893, Adamstown. Register of births, marriages and deaths, 1843–75, in custody of St. Mark's Parish; later records in rectory in Adamstown.

Church grounds were incorporated in public cemetery in 1891. Mr. McGill Belt, Dickerson, Md., supt. of St. Paul's cemetery, has burial records from 1880–date.

Zion Parish, 1804. Zion Church, 1770, 1804, Urbana (recently added to defunct churches). Register of births, marriages and deaths, 1802–1912. 2 vols. Vestry proceedings 1802–90. Md. Dioc. Lib.

Tombstone inscriptions of Zion Church cemetery, 1772–1900. Md. Geneal. Rec. Com., 1932–33, pp. 201–05. Mss. DAR.

Harford County

(Diocese of Maryland)

Chapel of Prince of Peace, Fallston. No information about records.

Christ Church, 1805–1877, Rock Spring. Register of births and marriages, 1819–61; few entries as late as 1864. Md. Dioc. Lib.

Churchville Parish, 1869. Holy Trinity Protestant Episcopal Church, Churchville. Register of births, marriages and deaths, 1869–date, in custody of Rev. G. W. Thomas, Perryman. Oldest tombstone, 1868.

Deer Creek Parish, 1859. Grace Memorial Church, 1874, Darlington; Church of Ascension, 1876, Scarboro. Register of births, marriages and deaths, 1877–date, in custody of Church. Earliest tombstones date back to Revolution.

Emmanuel Protestant Episcopal Church, 1868, Belair. Register of births, marriages and deaths, 1868–date, in custody of Church.

Havre de Grace Parish, 1809. St. John's Protestant Episcopal Church, Havre de Grace. Register of births, marriages and deaths, burned in 1832.

1832–59. Md. Dioc. Lib.

1859–date, in custody of Church.

Holy Cross Chapel, 1888, The Rock. No information about records.

Rock Spring Parish. Grace Chapel, 1874, Hickory. Register of births, marriages and deaths, 1874–1920, in Emmanuel Church, Belair.

1920–date, in custody of Rev. J. E. Thompson, Forest Hill, Harford Co.

(Note: Few entries are in Christ Church register, Rock Spring.)

St. George's Parish, 1692. St. George's Church, 1851 (Spesutie, 1671), Perryman. Register (original) of births, marriages and deaths, 1696–1795, 1795–1850. Note: Register was kept by John Allen, rector, and contains records of following Parishes: Havre de Grace, 1811; St. James, 1807–09; St. John's, 1795–1814; St. Paul's, 1798–1806; St. Thomas', 1813–15. Md. Dioc. Lib.

Register, 1681–1799. MHS.

Register of St. John's (Joppa) and St. George's Parishes, 1696–1851. 1 vol. MHS.

Register and vestry proceedings, 1739–1850. 1 vol. MHS.

Index to register, 1739–1850. MHS.

Vestry proceedings, 1718–74. MHS.

List of pew holders. Ms. MHS.

List of rectors, 1680–1854. Hist. of Balto. City and Co. Scharf. P. 918. MHS.

List of rectors and vestrymen, 1718–1845. Hist. of Harford Co. Preston. P. 156. MHS; DAR.

List of taxable bachelors in St. George's Parish, 1760. Hist. of Harford Co. Preston. P. 151.

(Note: Rev. John Yeo was first rector and first Church of England clergyman in Baltimore County, 1676; he died in 1686.)

St. James Chapel, 1761–1874, Trappe. (Defunct.) No information about records.

Tombstone inscriptions. Md. Geneal. Rec. Com., 1934–35. Mss. DAR.

(Note: Capt. J. A. Greene, Frenchman, served on staff of Gen. Lafayette, in Revolutionary war, is buried in Trappe graveyard.)

St. Mary's Protestant Episcopal Church, 1848, Emmorton. Register of births, marriages and deaths, 1850–date, in custody of Church.

Howard County

(Diocese of Maryland)

Grace Protestant Episcopal Church, 1845, Elk Ridge Landing. No information about records.

Mt. Calvary Church, 1860, Glenwood. (Defunct.) Register of births, marriages and deaths, 1854–1936. Md. Dioc. Lib.

Mt. Calvary Church burial ground, on Cooksville Pike. Md. Geneal. Rec. Com., 1934–35. Mss. DAR.

St. John's Protestant Episcopal Church, 1830, near Ellicott's City. Register of births, marriages and deaths, 1830–date, in custody of Church.

Brief history of St. John's Church. M. H. Mag., 1926, v. 21, p. 179.

St. Mark's Protestant Episcopal Church, 1874, Clarksville. No information about records.

St. Paul's Church, 1885, under charge of Linganore Parish, Mount Airy. No information about records.

History of St. Paul's Church, 1838–1938. Bklet. MHS.

Queen Caroline Parish, erected, out of part of St. Paul's, Baltimore Co., and All Hallow's and St. Anne's Parishes, Anne Arundel Co., 1728. Christ Church, 1809; Trinity Church, Washington Road. Register of births, marriages, deaths and vestry proceedings, 1711–1857. Ms. MHS.

Index to register, 1711–1857. Ms. MHS.

List of vestrymen and church wardens, 1779–1870; list of parishioners, Oct. 5, 1771. Mss. Md. Dioc. Lib.

St. John's Church. Brief history of Queen Caroline Parish, and Mother Church, Christ. M. H. Mag., 1926, v. 21, pp. 179–81.

St. Peter's Protestant Episcopal Church, 1842, Ellicott's City. Register of births, marriages and deaths, 1842–date (?), in custody of Church. (Practically destroyed by fire, Oct. 14, 1939.)

Trinity Parish, 1869, Howard and Anne Arundel Cos. Trinity Church, 1857; Trinity Chapel, 1871, Dorsey; St. Mary's Chapel, 1873, Jessup. Register of births, marriages and deaths of St. Mary's Chapel, 1904–20. Md Dioc. Lib.

Kent County

(Diocese of Easton)

Chester Parish, 1765. Emmanuel Church, 1770, Chestertown (first built as Chapel of Ease of I. U. Church). Register of births, marriages and deaths, 1765–1862. Photos. Md. Dioc. Lib.

Register and vestry proceedings, 1765–1841. 1 vol., photos. Index in cover of book. MHS.
(Note: Registers contain few entries from Shrewsbury Parish.)
Chester Parish records, 1760-date are being copied at present time and will be placed in DAR.

I. U. or Christ Church Parish, 1862. I. U. or St. Peters Church, 1768 (first built as Chapel of Ease of St. Paul's Parish), near Worton Station; St. John's by the Bay, Betterton. Register of baptisms, 1812–44. Ms. MHS.
I. U. Churchyard records. Bible rec. Upper Penins. of East. Shore. P. 103. MHS; DAR.
I. U. Church, near Worton Station. Tombstone inscriptions, 1802–1907 (complete to Jan., 1907). Md. O. R. Soc. Bull., June, 1910, no. 2, pp. 76–78.
I. U. Parish. Vestrymen, 1766–1811, 1863. Old Kent. Hanson. Pp. 373–80.
I. U.: Historic shrine of Old Kent. History of Chester and I. U. Parishes of Kent Co., 1766–1931. Percy G. Skirven. Balto., 1931. MHS.

North Kent Parish. St. Clements Church, Massey. Holy Cross Church, Millington. No information about records.
Protestant Episcopal Church cemetery, Massey. Tombstone inscriptions, 1821–81, 1866–1926. (2 items). Md. Geneal. Rec. Com., 1932–33. Mss. DAR.

Shrewsbury Parish, 1692. Shrewsbury Church, 1729, Kennedyville; St. Andrews', Galena. Register of births, marriages and deaths, 1699–1860. 1 vol. Ms. MHS.
Vestry proceedings, 1702–30, 1745–99, 1799–1841. Mss. MHS.
Tombstone inscriptions, 1749–1907 (complete). Md. O. R. S. Bull., no. 2, p. 6.
Extracts from Shrewsbury Parish, 1701–79; contain list of clergymen and vestrymen. Old Kent. Hanson. Pp. 354–63. MHS; DAR.

St. Paul's Parish, 1692. St. Paul's Church, 1713, Fairlee, Chestertown, R.F.D. Register (original) of births, marriages, deaths and vestry proceedings, in custody of Church.
Register, 1690–1797. Ms. MHS.
Index to register, 1690–1797. Ms. MHS.
Vestry proceedings, 1693–1728. Ms. MHS.
Tombstone inscriptions, 1729–1907 (complete). Md. O. R. S. Bull., no. 2, pp. 54–65. MHS.
St. Paul's Parish, Kent Co., 1693–1893. Small book prepared for 200th anniversary of St. Paul's Parish; contains records from registers. (Note: copy in custody of rector.)
1893. Extracts from St. Paul's Parish, Jan. 30, 1693–April 11, 1726; contains list of vestrymen and list of pew holders, 1720. Old Kent. Hanson. P. 345.
St. Paul's and Shrewsbury Parishes. Act for better division, 1698. Bacon's Laws, 1765. MHS.
St. Paul's Parish. Church record, 1693–1726. Old Kent. Hanson. Pp. 344–56. MHS.
Souvenir history of Parish of St. Paul's, Kent Co. C. T. Denroche. 1893. Peabody Lib.

Montgomery County

(Diocese of Washington)

Prince George Parish, 1726, erected from Piscataway or St. John's Parish, 1692. Christ Church, Rockville; Ascension Chapel, 1887, Gaithersburg. Register (original) of marriages and deaths, Jan. 14, 1796–April 18, 1839. Natl. Cathedral.
Register, 1792–1845. Ms. MHS.
Index to register, 1792–1845. Ms. MHS.
Vestry proceedings, 1726–1829. Ms. MHS.
Ministerial records of Rev. Thomas Reed; baptisms, 1792–1845. Md. rec. Brumbaugh. V. 2, pp. 539–56.
Marriages and funerals, 1796–1808. Md. rec. Brumbaugh. V. 2, pp. 557–71.
Rockville Cemetery (formerly Protestant Episcopal Church cemetery). Tombstone inscriptions, 1752–1876. Hist. of west. Md. Scharf. V. 1, p. 749. MHS; DAR.
Tombstone inscriptions, 1761–1845 (few stones). Natl. Geneal. Soc. Quart., v. 6, no. 1, p. 32. MHS.
Prince George Parish. Register of earliest records of births, baptisms, marriages, deaths, funerals, vestrymen, wardens, communicants, clerks and items from Parish minutes. D. C. Geneal. Rec. Com. Typed, bd. DAR.
History of Prince George Parish. Edw. Waylen. 1845.

St. Bartholomew's Parish, 1812, erected from Prince George Parish, 1726. St. Bartholomew's Church, 1817 (first church known as Hawling's River Church, 1761), Laytonsville; St. John's Protestant Episcopal Church, Olney. Register of births, marriages and deaths destroyed by fire. For earlier records, see Christ Church, Rockville.
Petition to levy on taxables of Prince George Parish, for new chapel (Hawling's River). Hist. of west. Md. Scharf. V. 1, p. 445. MHS; DAR.

St. Peter's (or Eden) Parish, 1792, erected from All Saints Parish, 1747. St. Peter's Protestant Episcopal Church, 1847, Poolesville. Register of births and baptisms, 1798–1830; marriages, 1793–1830. Mss. copy. MHS.
Register. Md. Geneal. Rec. Com., 1932–33. Mss. DAR.
Register, 1799–1801. Md. Geneal. Bull., vols. 3, 4, and 5.
Earlier records. See All Saints Parish, Frederick.
History and list of rectors, 1799–1928. Hist. sketches of Md. parishes and missions in Diocese of Washington. P. 150.
St. Peter's Church. Marriages, 1822–54. Geneal. Rec. Com., 1934–35, pp. 203–45. File case, DAR.

Silver Spring Parish, erected 1864, from Prince George Parish, 1726. Grace Church, 1863, Woodside; St. Mary's Chapel, 1896, Aspen. Register of births, marriages and deaths, 1869–date, in custody of Church.
Tombstone inscriptions, 1791–1929. Md. Geneal. Rec. Com., 1932–33. Mss. DAR.
Tombstone inscriptions, 1793–1877. Hist. of west. Md. Scharf. V. 1, p. 760. MHS; DAR.
List of bachelors of Silver Spring Parish, 1756–26. Hist. of west. Md. Scharf. V. 1, p. 744. MHS; DAR.
St. Mark's Memorial Chapel (Paint Chapel, prior to 1748) was transferred to Zion Parish, in 1888.

Prince George County

Addison Parish, 1919. St. Matthew's Church, 1801 (?) (Addison Chapel, 1696), Seat Pleasant. For registers, see St. Matthew's Parish, 1811.
In cemetery next to Church are many grave stones, dating back to Revolution.

Holy Trinity Parish, 1844, erected from Queen Anne's Parish, 1704. Holy Trinity Church, 1836, Collington; St. George's Chapel, 1873, Glendale; St. James Chapel, Bowie. Register of births, marriages, deaths and vestry proceedings 1844–99. 1 vol. Ms. MHS.
Index to register, 1844–99. 1 vol. Ms. MHS.
Index to vestry proceedings, 1844–99. Photos. MHS.

List of communicants. (Protestant Episcopal Churches) of Prince George County, 1831–44. Md. Dioc. Lib.

Ministerial records of Prince George and Montgomery Cos. Md. rec. Brumbaugh. V. 2. MHS; DAR.

Piscataway or St. John's Parish, sometimes called King George's Parish, 1692 (included Washington, at that time). St. John's Church, Broad Creek (first church built in 1695; present and third church, 1723; is known as Mother Church of District); St. Barnabas' Chapel, 1830, Oxon Hill. Register of births, marriages and deaths, 1697–1786. Natl. Cathedral.
Register, 1701–1805. 1 vol. Mss. MHS.
Vestry proceedings, 1693–1789. Mss. MHS.
Vestry proceedings, 1784–1823. Natl. Cathedral.
(Note: All records of Piscataway Parish, 1823–90, destroyed in great Baltimore fire, 1904, where they had been forwarded for rebinding.)
Piscataway Parish records, 1702–12 (fragmentary). Natl. Geneal. Soc. Quart., v. 3, no. 1, p. 12. MHS.
Marriages, 1786–94. Geneal. Quart. Mag. (Putman), v. 1, pp. 39, 246.
St. John's or Piscataway Parish. Register of births, marriages and deaths, from oldest records; also list of clerks, vestrymen and wardens, and items from Parish minutes. D. C. Geneal. Rec. Com. Bd. mss. DAR.

Prince George Parish, 1726, Scotland Hundred. Ms. copy. From Ethan Allen's Papers. MHS. (Note: For records, see Montgomery Co.)

Queen Anne's Parish, 1704, erected from St. Paul's Parish, 1692. St. Barnabas' Church, 1772–76, Leeland. Register (original) of births, marriages, deaths and vestry proceedings, Jan. 15, 1705–July 17, 1770. Natl. Cathedral.
Register of births, marriages and deaths, 1689–1771. 1 vol. Ms. MHS.
Index to register, 1689–1771. 1 vol. Ms. MHS.
Vestry proceedings, 1705–70. Index on loose leaves in same book. 1 vol. Ms. MHS.
Records from 1770 until recent date (1894), destroyed by fire.
Tombstone inscriptions, 1787–1924 (incomplete). Typed. MHS; DAR.
History of St. Barnabas Church, 1704–74. C. C. Magruder. Contains list of subscribers, vestrymen and wardens. Clan Gregor Year Book, 1924–25, pp. 10–25.
Historic sermon in connection with St. Barnabas (Brick) Church, Queen Anne Parish, 1907. Peabody Lib.

St. John's Parish, 1823, erected from Piscataway Parish, 1692. Christ Church, 1745, 1857, Accokeek, Prince George Co. (Note: Christ Church built 1745; partially destroyed by fire, Dec. 28, 1855; rebuilt and consecrated June 18, 1857.) St. John's Chapel, 1834; rebuilt, 1902, Pomonkey, Charles Co. Register of births, marriages and deaths, 1691–1801. 1 vol. Ms. MHS.
Index to register, 1691–1801. 1 vol. Ms. MHS.
Vestry proceedings, 1693–1775. Index in same book. Ms. MHS.
Historical notes of St. John's Parish, 1823, from unpublished manuscripts. Ethan Allen. Ms. copy. MHS.

St. Matthew's Parish, 1811, erected from Piscataway or St. John's Parish, 1692. Pinkney Memorial, 1912, Hyattsville; St. Luke's Church, 1846, Bladensburg; St. John's Church, Mount Rainier. Register of births, marriages and deaths, 1831–1900. Md. Dioc. Lib.
History of St. Matthew's Parish; list of rectors 1815–1927. Hist. sketches of parishes and missions in Diocese of Washington. P. 126.

St. Paul's Parish, 1692. St. Paul's Church, prior to 1692, present Church 1732, Baden; St. Mary's Chapel, 1848, Aquasco (Woodville). Register of births, marriages, deaths and vestry proceeding, Oct. 10, 1733–June 22, 1819. 2 photos. copies. Washington Cathedral.
Registers, 1846–49, 1884–92, in custody of Church.
(Note: Records prior to 1832, in Church, destroyed by fire.)
Vestry proceedings, 1723-1823. 1 vol. Ms. MHS.;
Vestry proceedings, Oct. 1773-June 22, 1819. Natl. Cathedral.
Tombstone inscriptions, 1750–1929 (incomplete). Md. Geneal. Rec. Com., 1932–33, pp. 184–200. Mss. DAR.
History of St. Paul Parish, with list of rectors, 1727–1919. Hist. sketches of parishes and missions in Diocese of Washington. P. 174.
Brief history of St. Paul's Protestant Episcopal Church, Prince George Co. C. E. Crusoe. 1930, pamph. DAR.
Historical notes of St. Paul's Christ and St. Barnabas Protestant Episcopal Churches, 1692–1751. From unpublished manuscripts by Ethan Allen. Ms. copy. MHS; DAR.
St. Paul's Parish. Clan Gregor Year Book, 1929, p. 76.

St. Philip's Parish, 1848. St. Philip's Church, 1848, Laurel. Register of births, marriages and deaths, 1846–68. 1 vol. Ms. MHS.
List of rectors, 1847-1926. Hist. sketches of parishes and missions in Diocese of Washington. P. 159.

St. Thomas' Parish, 1851. St. Thomas' Protestant Episcopal Church, Croome (formerly called Page Chapel, erected 1732, as Chapel of Ease of St. Paul's Parish); Chapel of the Atonement, 1871 (services discontinued, 1925), Cheltenham; Chapel of Incarnation, 1917, Brandywine. For register of births, marriages and deaths, prior to 1850, see St. Paul's Parish.
History of St. Thomas' Parish; containing list of rectors, 1850–1926. Hist. sketches of parishes and missions. Diocese of Washington. MHS.

Trinity Church, 1810, present church 1847, Marlboro. Register of births, marriages and deaths mutilated by soldiers of British Army, in War of 1812; others burned;

Vestry proceeding, 1880–date, in possession of Church.

History of Trinity Church. Hist. sketches of parishes and missions in Diocese of Washington. P. 108. MHS.

(Note: in churchyard will be found graves of Belt family and others.)

Zion Parish, 1811. St. John's Church, 1857, 1868, 3rd and present church 1878, Beltsville. St. Mark's Memorial Chapel, 1875. (Paint Chapel, prior to 1748.) Columbia Pike, near Fairland. For register of births, marriages and deaths, 1811–30, see Queen Caroline Parish in Howard Co.

1830–36. See St. Matthew's Parish, Prince George Co.

From 1858 records are fairly complete (lapse 1860–64, 1866–68), in custody of Church.

Queen Anne County

(Diocese of Easton)

Kent Island or Christ Church Parish, 1692. Christ Church, 1885 (Broad Creek Church, 1652), Stevensville. Register of births, marriages and deaths lost or not kept. Those extant are no earlier than 1870, except in few instances. Mr. J. Fred Stevens, registrar, has older records.

(First church service held in Maryland was held on Kent Island, near Fort Point Manor, 1631, by Rev. Richard James, of Church of England. Little church was soon built, and later this was succeeded by another, located on Broad Creek. All that is left is crumbling foundation surrounded by old graveyard. Oldest tombstone inscription that can be read is that of Robert Young, who died in 1746. Church was torn down in 1885; old bricks and material removed to Stevensville where they were used in building of Christ Church.)

St. John's Parish, 1748, Queen Anne and Caroline Cos. St. Paul's Church (Tuckahoe Chapel, which has passed away), Hillsboro. See Caroline Co.

St. Luke's Parish, 1728. St. Luke's Church, (Up River Chapel, 1733), Church Hill; St. Andrew's Church, Sudlersville. Register of births, marriages and deaths, 1722–1850. 1 vol. Ms. MHS.

Vestry proceedings, 1727–1850. Ms. MHS.

Mr. Ernest Brown, Church Hill, has present records.

St. Andrew's Church, Sudlersville. Register of births, marriages and deaths, 1879–date, in custody of Mr. Ernest Brown, Church Hill.

List of petitioners for New Parish, division of St. Paul's and St. Luke's Parishes, in vestry proceedings of St. Luke's Church.

St. Paul's Parish, 1692. St. Paul's Church, 1835 ("Old Chester," 1698, rebuilt 1765, torn down 1835, old bricks used in building St. Paul's), Centreville. Register of births, marriages and deaths, 1835–date, in safe of St. Paul's Parish.

1754–94. Ms. copy. 1 vol. MHS.

Vestry proceedings, 1693–date, in safe of St. Paul's Parish.

1695–1762, 1762–1819. 2 vols. Indexed. Mss. MHS.

(St. Paul's Parish, 1692, embraced all of Queen Anne's Co. (except Kent Island), Caroline and part of Talbot. "Old Chester," 1698, near Hybernia, about 1 mile from Centreville, was Parish Church.)

History of St. Paul's Parish, 1650–1934. Rev. Alward Chamberlaine, rector. E. S. Churchman. V. 12, Jan. and Feb., 1934.

Wye Parish, 1860, erected from St. Paul's Parish, 1692. St. Luke's Protestant Episcopal Church, Queenstown; St. Luke's (Wye Chapel, 1722, restored 1854, Wye Mills, over line in Talbot Co.). Register of births, marriages, deaths and vestry proceedings, 1840-date, in custody of Parish, Queenstown.

Old Wye Church of Old Wye Parish. De Courcy W. Thom. Aug. 10, 1930. MHS.

St. Mary's County

(Diocese of Washington)

All Faith Parish, 1692. All Faith Church, 1692 1765, Mechanicsville; Dent Memorial Chapel, 1884, Charlotte Hall. Register of births, marriages and deaths not in existence prior to 1875.

Vestry proceedings 1692–1754 (lapse 1756–date), in custody of Church.

1692–1754, 1756–1817. 2 vols. Ms. copy. MHS.

List of first vestrymen. Chronicles of Col. Md. Thomas. P. 217. MHS.

Early records of Church and Parish of All Faiths, 1692–1835. H. J. Berkley. M. H. Mag., 1935, v. 30, no. 4, p. 326; 1936, v. 31, no. 1, p. 16.

List of clergymen of All Faiths, 1694–1776. Chronicles of Col. Md. Thomas. P. 204. MHS.

All Saints Parish, 1892, erected from King and Queen Parish, 1692. All Saints Chapel, 1844, Tomakokin. For register of births, marriages and deaths, 1844–92, see King and Queen Parish.

1892–date, in possession of Church.

Graveyard near site of first Episcopal Church, St. Mary's Co. Md. O. R. Soc. Bull., no. 3, p. 59. MHS.

King and Queen Parish, 1692. Christ Church, 1736, Chaptico; All Saints Chapel, 1844–1892, Tomakokin. No register of births, marriages and deaths prior to 1844; destroyed by fire. 1844–date, in custody of Church.

Vestry proceedings, May 17, 1799–Oct., 1838; Jan. 2, 1839–July 12, 1881. Natl. Cathedral, Washington.

List of rectors, 1692–1928. Hist. sketches of parishes and missions in Diocese of Washington. 1928, p. 199.

List of vestrymen, 1692. Chronicles of Col. Md. Thomas. P. 200. MHS.

St. Andrew's Parish, 1744. St. Andrew's Church, 1767, Leonardtown. Register of births, marriages and deaths, and list of parishoners. 1728–1886. Index in same book. 1 vol. Ms. MHS.

Vestry proceedings, 1754–99. Index in same book. 1 vol. Ms. MHS.

St. Mary's Parish, 1851, erected from William and Mary Parish. Trinity Church, 1829, St.

Mary's City; St. Mary's Chapel, The Ridge. Register of births, marriages and deaths, 1851–date, in custody of Church.

Tombstone inscriptions, 1791–1850. Md. rec. Brumbaugh. V. 2, pp. 572–79.

1803–1856. Md. O. R. Soc. Bull., no. 3, p. 59.

(After removal of Capital from St. Mary's City to Annapolis, Old State House was used as Church for over one hundred years. 1720: State House and grounds are vested in "the rector and vestry of William and Mary Parish, and their successors in fee simple, for use of Parish forever." 1829: Trinity Church erected from bricks of Old State House.)

William and Mary Parish, 1692. St. George's Protestant Episcopal Church, 1750 (or Poplar Hill Church, 1640), Valley Lee, near Leonardtown; St. Thomas's Chapel. Register (original) of births, marriages, deaths and vestry proceedings, 1798–1925, in custody of Church.

Photos. copies (429 pp.). Natl. Cathedral; Lib. Cong.; MHS. (Earlier records destroyed by fire.)

List of first vestrymen, 1692. Chronicles of Col. Md. Thomas. P. 215. MHS.

History of William and Mary Parish, containing list of rectors, 1650–1798. Hist. sketches of churches and missions of Diocese of Washington. 1928, pp. 202–04.

Somerset County

(Diocese of Easton)

*Coventry Parish, 1692, Upper Fairmount. St. Paul's Church, Annemessex; St. Stephen's Church, 1863, Dividing Creek, Worcester Co.; St. Mary's the Virgin, Newtown; St. Mark's Church, 1845, Kingston. Register (original and oldest extant) of births, marriages and deaths, 1742–date, with some references to earlier dates, in custody of Church.

1724–1821, 1837–86. Index in same book. 2 vols. Mss. MHS.

Coventry Parish records, 1736–1828, Somerset County. M. T. Layton and H. B. Clary. 1936, pamph. DAR.

1747–1800. Ms. Land Office.

Additional births, 1832–66. Coll. Geneal. Notes. Turner. 2 vols. Mss. MHS.

Parish abstracts. Turner Geneal. Coll. Mss. MHS.

Communicants in Coventry Parish. Revised list. P. 225. Ms. MHS.

Vestry proceedings, 1772–1830, index in same book. 1821–99; index in same book. 2 vols. Mss. MHS.

(Ruins of Old Rehobeth Church, near Pocomoke City, in Coventry Parish; service is held there once a year.)

Tombstone inscriptions of Rehobeth Churchyard. Old burial grounds of Worcester Co. Md. Geneal. Rec. Com., Lines, 1937. Mss. DAR.

Parishes in Somerset County. History of Coventry, Snow Hill and Stepney; with notes on Chapels of Ease. Old Somerset. Torrence. Pp. 131–208. MHS; DAR.

St. Bartholomew's Parish, Crisfield, erected from Coventry Parish. St. Paul's Church, 1848, Marion; St. John's Memorial, 1889, Crisfield. Register of births, marriages and deaths, 1889–date (lapse 1921–23); registers of Coventry, St. Bartholomews and Pocomoke Parishes, in custody of Rev. Hugh V. Clary, rector of three parishes.

Somerset Parish, 1692, Princess Anne. All Saints Church (Old Monie); St. Andrew's Church, 1771, Princess Anne (Kings Mill Chapel, rebuilt as St. Andrew's); 1st register, births, marriages and deaths, 1690–1760 (fragmentary); 2nd register, 1796–1850 (into this record have been copied some records of baptisms, etc., of earlier period, 1690–1700); 3rd register, 1838–95 (also confirmations); 4th register, 1895–1920; 5th register, 1920–date. Information given by Rev. Clayton Torrence. Registers in custody of Mr. C. M. Dashiell, registrar, Princess Anne.

Registers of Somerset Parish, births, marriages and deaths, 1717–1847. 2 vols. Mss. MHS.

Abstracts, 1697–1852. C. H. B. Turner Geneal. Coll. 2 vols. Mss. MHS.

Vestry proceedings of Somerset Parish, 1777–1886. 2 vols. Mss. MHS.

St. Andrew's Church cemetery, Princess Anne. Tombstone inscriptions, 1787–1905. Md. O. R. Soc. Bull., no. 1, pp. 29–32.

1816–1913. MHS.

Stepney Parish, 1692. See Wicomico Co.

Talbot County

(Diocese of Easton)

All Saints Parish, Longwoods. No information about records.

Church of Holy Trinity, 1852, near Oxford. No information about records.

Holy Innocents, Claiborne. No information about records.

Miles River Parish, Easton. All Faith Church, Tunis Mills.

St. Luke's Protestant Episcopal Church (Old Wye), Wye Mills. For register, see St. Paul's Parish, Centreville, Queen Anne Co.

St. Michael's Parish, 1692. Christ Church, 1690, 1736, 1812, St. Michael's; St. John's Church, Miles River Ferry; St. John's Church, Royal Oak. Register of births, marriages and deaths, 1672–1704 (lapse 1704–1823); 1829–date, in custody of Church.

1672–1704, 1829–59. Mss. MHS.

Index of register, 1672–1704, 1829–59. Mss. MHS.

1672–1704. Pa. Mag. Hist., 1905. V. 29, pp. 427–38.

Vestry proceedings, 1731–1836. Index in same book. Ms. MHS.

Tombstone inscriptions, 1805–1905 (incomplete); oldest stones under Church and not listed. Md. O. R. Soc. Bull., no. 1, pp. 54–55. MHS.

St. Peter's Parish, 1692. Christ Church, 1840, Easton. (White Marsh Ruins, Trappe, now in White Marsh Parish, 1857.) Register of births, marriages and deaths, 1681–date, in custody of Church.

1681–1855. 1 vol. Ms. MHS.

Index to register, 1681–1855. 1 vol. Ms. MHS.

Vestry proceedings, 1706–date, in custody of Church.

1706–1806. Ms. MHS.

List of pew holders, 1728. Hist. of Talbot Co. Tilghman. V. 2, pp. 287–88. MHS; DAR.

Washington County

(Diocese of Maryland)

Antietam Parish, 1899. St. Paul's Church, 1879, Sharpsburg. No information about records.
St. Andrew's Church, 1839, Clear Spring; St. Clement's Chapel, Indian Spring. No information about records.
St. Anne's Church, 1875, Smithsburg. No information about records.
St. John's Parish, 1806–29. St. John's Church, 1806, 1876, Hagerstown. Register of births, marriages, deaths and vestry proceedings, 1781–83. Photos. 1 vol. (Vestry proceedings not indexed.) MHS.
Register, 1816–93. Photos. 1 vol. MHS.
Register of births, baptisms, marriages, funerals, confirmations and communicants, 1816–1940. 69 pp., 1168 names, 1717 rec. Md. Geneal. Rec. Com., 1939–40. Mss. DAR.
Index to register, 1816–93. Type script. 1 vol. MHS.
List of rectors and vestrymen, 1787–1873. Hist. of west. Md. Scharf. V. 2, p. 1082. MHS; DAR.
Tombstone inscriptions, 1795–1867; earliest birth, 1737. Hist. of west. Md. Scharf. V. 2, p. 1087. MHS; DAR.
(Note: Original records of St. John's Parish supposed to have been burned about 1870.)
St. Mark's Church, 1849, Lappan's Cross Road; St. James' Chapel; St. James School. No information about records.
St. Mark's Parish, Frederick and Washington Cos. St. Mark's Church, Petersville; St. Luke's Chapel, 1856, Pleasant Valley; Grace Church, 1893, Brunswick; St. John's Chapel, 1896, Burkittsville. No information about records.
St. Thomas' Parish, 1891. St. Thomas' Church, 1835–1891, Hancock; Epiphany Chapel, Millstone. No information about records.
History of St. Thomas' Parish. Pamph. MHS.
Washington County parishes. Ethan Allen. Ms. copy. MHS.

Wicomico County

(Diocese of Easton)

Spring Hill Parish, 1827, from Stepney Parish, 1692. St. Paul's Protestant Church, 1765, Spring Hill; Spring Hill Chapel, 1761, or Goddard's Chapel, Quantico, rebuilt in Salisbury, as St. Peter's Church, Salisbury, now Salisbury Parish, 1848. Register (original) of births, marriages and deaths, 1829–1917, in custody of Church.
Copy, Md. Geneal. Rec. Com. Mss. DAR.
Stepney Parish, 1692. St. Bartholomes Church (Old Green Hill Church, 1733), Bivalve; St. Mary's Church, Tyaskin. Register (original) of births, marriages and deaths, July 4, 1738–date (some earlier copied from family and Bible records). In Vault of Bank in Princess Anne; in custody of Mr. C. M. Dashiell, registrar.
1703–1890. 1 vol. Ms. MHS.
Index to register, 1703–1890. 1 vol. Ms. MHS.
1700–1800 (2000 items, complete). Md. Geneal. Rec. Com., 1935–36. Mss. DAR.
Vestry proceedings, 1769–1889. Index in same book. 1 vol. Ms. MHS.
Old graveyard record. Mss. MHS.
St. Mary's churchyard records, Tyaskin, 1768–1937. Md. Geneal. Rec. Com., 1938–39, pp. 187–92. Mss. DAR.
History of Stepney Parish. C. M. Dashiell.
Wicomico Parish, 1845. Grace Church, Mt. Vernon. Register of births, marriages and deaths, 1845–date, in custody of Church.

Worcester County

(Diocese of Easton)

All Hallow's or Snow Hill Parish, 1692. All Hallows' Church, 1748, Snow Hill; Holy Cross, Stockton. No old registers; they were burned.
Abstracts from register, 1844–94. C. H. B. Turner. Geneal. Coll. Ms. MHS.
D. A. R. Mag., v. 60, no. 9.
William and Mary Quart., 1st series, v. 15, p. 211.
Tombstone inscriptions of All Hallows Protestant Episcopal churchyard. Tombstone inscriptions of Worcester Co. Hudson. Bd. MHS; DAR.
All Hallows' churchyard burial ground. Md. Geneal. Rec. Com., 1935–36, pp. 24–32. Mss. DAR.
All Hallows' Church, 1692–1892. Two hundredth anniversary. Bicentennial discourse. Address by Rev. Robert Scott. Pamph. MHS.
Early history of All Hallows Parish, Worcester Co. H. F. Covington. 1924, pamph. MHS.
Parish records of Worcester Co. From Snow Hill Messenger and Worcester Advertiser. Marriages and deaths, 1828–34. Lib. Cong.
Pocomoke Parish, 1855, Somerset and Worcester Cos., established from Coventry Parish, 1692. St. Mary's Church, 1845, Pocomoke City. For register of births, marriages and deaths, 1845–date, see Coventry and St. Bartholomew's Parishes, Somerset Co.
St. Mary's Protestant Episcopal churchyard records. Tombstone inscriptions of Worcester Co. Hudson. Bd. mss. MHS; DAR.
Worcester Parish, 1744. St. Paul's Church, Berlin; St. Martin's Church, 1756, Friendship, near Berlin; St. Paul's by the Sea, Ocean City.
St. Martin's register of births, marriages and deaths (original), in Exchange Bank, Berlin.
1722–1839. 1 vol. Mss. MHS.
1722–1816. Md. rec. Brumbaugh. V. 2, pp. 579–89.
1734–1814. Typed, bd. DAR. Also. M. O. R. Soc. Bull., no. 3, pp. 20–26. MHS.
Tombstone inscriptions of St. Martin's and St. Paul's churchyards. Old burial grounds of Worcester Co. Lynes. 1937. Mss. DAR.
Tombstone inscriptions of St. Paul's churchyard. Tombstone inscriptions of Worcester Co. Hudson. MHS; DAR.
Vestry proceedings of St. Martin's Church, 1722–1839. Index in same book. 1 vol. MHS.

QUAKER MEETINGS

Baltimore City—Homewood Friends Meeting House

Homewood Friends Meeting House, 3107 N. Charles Street. Separation of Friends in Baltimore, 1828. Index of records given through courtesy of Mrs. A. Viola Horisburg, custodian of records, Baltimore Yearly Meeting.
List of members of Baltimore Monthly Meeting, 1848–82; giving parents, dates of birth, mar-

riages and deaths; marriage certificates from Feb. 18, 1830–1932; minutes, 1828–1933 (several years' records destroyed by fire about 1840). This record contains also records of: Bush Creek, Frederick County (9 miles from Frederick), established, 1736, under Fairfax, Virginia; and Fawn Meeting, York County, Pa. (14 miles northwest of Broad Creek), established 1780, under Gunpowder.

Deer Creek Meeting, attached to Baltimore, Homewood Meeting House, 1855. Births, 1805; burials, 1822; marriage certificates, 1827; certificates of removal, 1805–1923; members, 1805–1923.

Gunpowder Meeting, Baltimore County. Deaths (10 or 12), Jan. 1, 1791; Preparative Meetings, 1829–52.

Indian Spring: Preparative Meeting, July, 1829–41, when Meeting closed and joined Baltimore Preparative.

Virginia Meetings under Homewood Friends:

Cedar Creek, Hanover County (originally Cambell County, 1755). Monthly Meeting minutes, 1781–1805.

Gravelly Run, Lower Virginia. Minute book. Births and deaths, 1760–1810; marriage certificates, 1760–1810; members, 1760–1810. Mss. copy.

Hopewell Monthly Meeting. Minutes and proceedings of elders, 1828–87; births and deaths, 1828–87; marriages, 1828–87; members, 1828–87.

Lower Virginia. Minute books. Register of births, marriages and deaths, 1673–1767, 1781–1805, 1856–86, 1879–1906. Photos.

Nansemond (Nanzemond?), Isle of Wight County, Va., and Henrico County, Va. Record books. Births, marriages and deaths, 1673–1767; 1781–1805. Photos.

Nansemond, Isle of Wight County, Va. Births and marriages, 1673–87; marriages, 1673–87. (Kept by order of George Fox.)

South River, Henrico County. Births and deaths, 1761–1838; marriage certificates, 1699–1757, 1761–1838.

Wainoke Meeting. Births and deaths, 1780–93; marriage certificates, 1780–93.

White Oak Swamp, Henrico County, Va. Monthly Meeting, 1781–1805; births and deaths, 1781–1805; marriage certificates, 1781–1805; members, 1781–1805. Photos.

Baltimore City—Park Avenue Friends Meeting House

Bibliography of records in fire proof vault of Baltimore. Yearly Meeting of Friends, Park Avenue, Baltimore. Bibliography is through courtesy of Committee on Records (Lombard Street), now Vault Committee, Park Avenue, Yearly Meeting of Friends. Dr. James Warner Harry, chairman. Compiled by Harriet P. Marine, custodian of records.

1658—Quakers first settled in Maryland.

1661—records of births and deaths begin.

1667—minutes begin.

1672—first Yearly Meeting in Maryland. Called by John Burnyeat. "To which came George Fox and many Friends." This was before the London Yearly Meeting, where Society of Friends first saw light through their founder George Fox.

Yearly Meetings, 1672–1790, in Maryland, held alternately at West River on Western Shore of Maryland, and Fred Haven on Eastern Shore of Maryland.

1790. Yearly Meeting removed to Baltimore, at which time Fairfax and Hopewell Monthly Meeting, Virginia and Warrington, Pennsylvania (which belonged to Concord Quarter, Philadelphia Yearly Meeting, were attached to Baltimore.

Meetings on Eastern Shore of Maryland were united to Philadelphia. Yearly Meeting, Susquehanna River and Chesapeake Bay being dividing line. (Did not include Meeting in Cecil County.)

General Yearly Meeting of Friends, held at West River, Third Haven and Baltimore Town.

Minutes, 1682–1758 (Third Haven only).

Minutes, 1754–89, West River, Third Haven and Baltimore.

1790. Yearly Meetings held in Baltimore.

1790–1921. Classified proceedings of minutes and book of general extracts from proceedings, 1677–1921.

1806–18. Extracts were published in the form of journal.

1819–87. Extracts published in pamphlet form.

1887–1931. Changed to "Minutes of proceedings of Baltimore Yearly Meeting of Friends," 1931–date.

The Annual Sessions has been included in title page. 2 perfect sets in Vault, Park Avenue, and 1 imperfect set in IIV. Baltimore Yearly Meeting of Friends.

Minutes and proceedings, 1790–1883, 1890–98 (Women's Branch). For other minutes see publications of Yearly Meetings beginning 1819–date.

Miscellaneous records of Cliffs, Herring Creek, Indian Spring, Patapsco, Sandy Spring and West River Meetings, so interwoven it would be difficult to separate them as older Meeting began to wane and Sandy Spring to grow stronger, they became Preparative Meetings under Sandy Springs, and eventually went out, leaving Sandy Springs to continue alone.

Yearly Meeting minutes:

Cliffs meeting, Calvert County, established prior to 1660, independent. Register of births, deaths and burials, 1662–1782; marriage certificates, 1682–1824; register of births and deaths in minutes of Sandy Spring, 1758–1895.

Deer Creek Meeting, Harford County, established 1736, under Nottingham. Register of births, deaths, and burials, 1662–1782. (See Homewood Meeting for records, 1805–1923.)

Gunpowder Meeting, Balto. County (two meetings). Perhaps oldest meeting in Maryland. Register of births, deaths, and burials, 1662–1782. (See Homewood Meeting for records, 1791.)

Herring Creek Meeting, Anne Arundel and Calvert County, established prior to 1660 from West River. Register of births, deaths and burials, 1662–1782; marriage certificates, 1682–1824.

Indian Spring Meeting, Prince George County, established prior to 1660, independent (for 22 years kept no minutes. Men's minutes, 1772–1867; births and deaths in minutes of Sandy Spring book, 1758–1895; marriage certificates, 1682–1824; Preparative Meeting, 1829–41. See Homewood Meeting House.

Joppa Meeting. Harford County. Register of births, deaths and burials, 1662–1782.

Patuxent Meeting, Calvert and Prince George Counties, established 1680, under Cliffs. Marriage certificates, 1682–1824.

Sandy Spring, Montgomery County (18 miles from Washington), established 1750, under West River. Minute book, with some earlier meetings, 1758–1895; births and deaths, 1758–1895.

West River, Anne Arundel County, established prior to 1659, independent. Register of births, deaths and burials, 1662–1782. Register of births and burials of Friends that belonged to men's and women's meetings at West River, 1674–1809 (reverse book for testimonials, 1675–79; marriage certificates, 1682–1824. Register of births and deaths, in minutes of Sandy Spring, 1758–1895.

Baltimore Yearly Meeting of Friends. Following Meetings are not mentioned in Miss Marine's bibliography, but names and location given and Meeting under which each was established.

Back Creek Meeting, Frederick County, Va. (9 miles northwest of Winchester), established 1777, under Hopewell, Va.

Fawn Meeting, York County, Pa. (14 miles northwest, of Broad Creek), established 1780, under Gunpowder, Baltimore County.

Little Elk Meeting, Chester County, Pa. (5 miles from East Nottingham), established 1825, under East Nottingham.

Ridge Meeting, Frederick County Va. (5 miles northwest of Winchester), established 1791, under Hopewell, Va.

Winchester (Center) Meeting, Winchester, Va., established 1777, under Hopewell, Va.

York Meeting, Borough of York, York County, Pa., established prior to 1786, under Warrington and Baltimore.

Quarterly Meetings, held in 1710–1822, at Baltimore, Cliffs, Gunpowder, Herring Creek, and West River (1790, West River only).

Monthly Meetings held in 1677–1771, at Cliffs, Herring Creek, Indian Spring and West River:

Cliffs Meeting, Calvert County, established prior to 1660, independent. Births and deaths, 1758–1895, in Sandy Spring book.

Indian Spring Meeting, Prince George County, established prior to 1660, independent. Men's minutes, 1772–1867; women's minutes, 1776–1845; register of births and deaths, 1758–1895, in Sandy Spring book.

Sandy Spring Meeting, Montgomery County, established, 1750, under West River. Men's minutes, 1817–1867; women's minutes, 1776–1880 (in book with Indian Spring); births and deaths, 1758–1895.

West River Meeting, Anne Arundel County, established prior to 1659, independent. Births and deaths, 1758–1895, in Sandy Spring book.

Baltimore Quarterly Meetings, (first held at home of Ann Chew). 1680–88, West River; 1682–1709, Herring Creek; 1710–1822, Baltimore, Gunpowder, Herring Creek, Indian Spring and West River. Men's minutes, 1822–1925; women's minutes, 1807–1849; minutes of Herring Creek, 1736–49; ministers and elders, 1759–1915.

Baltimore Monthly Meeting, established 1807. Records consist of books of minutes, births, deaths, marriages, and certificates of removal. Composed of: Eastern District, Aisquith Street; Western District, Lombard Street; Diamond Ridge, Baltimore County, established in 1851, under Baltimore; Mt. Washington, Baltimore, established 18—, under Baltimore; and York, Pa., established, 1786, under Warrington and Baltimore. (This was not first Monthly Meeting near Baltimore. In 1730, with consent of Gunpowder, Patapsco Meeting was established in 1780. Patapsco removed to their Meeting House in Baltimore Town (Aisquith Street) where Monthly Meeting was established in 1792, laid down in 1819). Minute books in Vault, 1792–1819. Certificates of removal, 1792–1807.

Eastern District, Aisquith Street (Old Town), Baltimore established 1792. Removal of Patapsco. Minute book, 1792–1819; births and deaths, 1793–1812 (63 pp. missing); certificates of removal, 1792–1819; marriages, 1793–1812; membership, 1793–1812.

Western District, Lombard Street, Baltimore, established under Baltimore Quarter, 1807. Minutes 1807–1930; Women's Branch, 1792–1930; births, marriages and deaths, 1807–1934; certificates of removal, 1807–1928, 1928–34 (embodied in minutes); membership, 1807–1934.

Deer Creek Monthly Meeting, Harford County (4 miles southwest of Conowingo Bridge), established 1736, under Nottingham. Men's minutes, 1760–1881 (1771–86 missing); covered by women's minutes, 1760–1895; births and deaths 1761–1823; marriage certificates, 1761–1822.

Broad Creek, Harford County, established, 1828, under Deer Creek. Preparative Meeting minutes 1871–76. (Bush Creek and Deer Creek proposed holding meetings together, 1754. In 1760 Deer Creek became Monthly Meeting. For records prior to 1760, see Nottingham.)

Elk Ridge Monthly Meeting, Howard County, established 1680, under West River. 1739, under West River Monthly Meeting, built new house at Ellicott's Mills. 1756, made Preparative Meeting. 1780, joined Indian Spring Meeting. 1807, Baltimore Monthly Meeting. Minutes, 1795–1801, in Vault, Park Avenue.

Gunpowder Monthly Meeting, established 1739, branch of West River Quarterly Meeting. (This meeting is perhaps oldest meeting belonging to Yearly Meeting, precise time of establishment has not been ascertained.)

Men's minutes, 1739–1920; women's minutes, 1742–1819; register of births and deaths, 1716–1855; marriage certificates, 1757–79, 1794–1855; certificates of removal, 1757–1855.

Gunpowder Monthly Meeting, composed of Preparative Meetings of Elkridge, Howard County, established 1680, under West River. Forest Hill, Harford County, established 1814, under West River. Little Falls, Harford County, established 1738, under Gunpowder. Patapsco, Baltimore County, established 1729, under West River.

Elk Ridge, joined Gunpowder 1747, made Preparative Meeting 1756, joined Indian Spring 1780, and Baltimore. Monthly Meeting, Western Division 1807. Minutes, 1795–1801, in Vault, Park Avenue.

Little Britain Monthly Meeting, Fulton Township (formerly Little Britain), Lancaster County), Pa., established 1745, under West Nottingham. Men's minutes, 1804–1923; women's minutes, 1804–74; Preparative Meeting, ministers and elders, 1853–87; births, deaths and burials, 1775–1881. (For records prior to 1804, see Nottingham books.

Little Falls Monthly Meeting, 1815, Harford County, established 1738, under Gunpowder. Men's minutes, 1815–1924; women's minutes, 1815–89; certificates of removal, 1815–70; marriage certificates, 1818–73; membership, 1738–1881. (This Monthly Meeting composed of Little Falls and Forest Hill Preparative Meetings.)

Little Falls Preparative Meeting. Ministers and elders, 1815–1911; women's minutes, 1839–72.

Forest Hill Meeting, Harford County, established 1814, under West River Preparative Meeting. Men's minutes, 1851–192-, women's minutes, 1865–89.

Nottingham Monthly Meeting, established 1730, under Chester, Pa. Composed of: East Nottingham (brick meeting house), Cecil County, established 1700, under Concord, Pa.; West Nottingham, established 1710. Other meetings in this section under Nottingham (from time to time) were Bush, Frederick County, established 1736, under Fairfax Meeting, Va.; Deer Creek, Harford Co., established 1736, under Nottingham Meeting; Octoraro, near Conowingo Bridge, Cecil County, established 1823, under West Nottingham; Drumore, Lancaster County, Pa., established 1818, under Little Britain; Eastland, Pa.; Little Britain, Fulton Township (formerly Little Britain), Lancaster County, Pa., established 1745, under West Nottingham and Oxford, Pa. (Records from 1700–30, in Concord and Chester Monthly Meetings minutes.)

Chester Meeting, Pa. Preparative Meeting minutes, 1801–11, in Vault, Park Avenue.

Nottingham Monthly minutes. Men's minutes, 1730–1904; women's minutes, 1730–1892; births, 1713–1888; marriage certificates, 1730–1889; certificates of removal, 1764–1855.

Nottingham Quarterly. Ministers', and elders' minutes, 1819-30; women's minutes, 1819-77; Preparative Meeting minutes, 1795–1801, 1819-1918.

*Nottingham. Notes and reminiscences of Nottingham. By James Trimble. Book in script. Consists of classified subjects, based on minutes of Meeting. In back of book is genealogy of each family as far as minutes and his knowledge allowed. In front is map of survey of Nottingham lots, with name of each owner thereon. Oxford, Pa. History of Oxford Meeting of Religious Society of Friends. Vault, Park Avenue.

Pipe Creek Monthly Meeting, Frederick County (1 mile from Union Bridge), established 1735, under Fairfax, Va. Minutes, 1772–1889; women's minutes, 1832-85; rough minutes, 1810–17; births and deaths, 1773–1880; marriage certificates, 1773–1895. (Prior to 1772, records of Pipe Creek, Bush Creek and Monococy, Frederick county, 1746–72, in Fairfax Meeting, Va.)

Iowa Meetings of Baltimore Yearly Meeting:

Highland, Johnson County (32 miles north of Prarie Grove), established 1856, under Fairfax, Va.

Honey Grove, established after 1856, under Fairfax, Va.

Marietta Meeting, Marshall County, established 1869, under Fairfax, Va.

Prarie Grove, Henry County (first branch of Baltimore Yearly Meeting in Iowa), established 1856, by Friends from Fairfax, Va.

Tama City, Tama City, Marshall County, established 1874, under Marietta Meeting, Iowa, of Baltimore Yearly Meeting.

Wapsinonoc, near West Liberty, Iowa, established 1856, under Fairfax Quarter, Va., Baltimore Yearly Meetings of Friends.

For minutes, see report in extracts of Baltimore Yearly Meeting of Friends, 1865.

Ohio Yearly Meeting formed from Baltimore Yearly Meeting, 1812. Ceasar's Creek Monthly Meeting, Ohio. Births and deaths, 1810-95; marriage certificates, 1810-95.

Pennsylvania Meeting of Baltimore Yearly Meeting of Friends, 1803. Prior to this date Centre Monthly Meeting was part of Menallen Monthly Meeting, Centre Quarter and Warrington Quarter.

Centre Quarterly Meeting was composed of: Centre Monthly Meeting (Centre Meeting, Half Moon Valley, Centre County, Pa., established 1800, under Warrington); Dunning Creek, Bedford County, established 1795, under Menallen, West Branch, Clearfield County, Pa., established 1833, under Centre Monthly Meeting; Bald Eagle, Unionville, Centre County, Pa., established 1800, under Centre. In Vault, Park Avenue are following Quarterly Meetings (not all sent in); Men's minutes, 1835-72; women's minutes, 1835–1916; men's monthly minutes, 1803–42; women's monthly minutes, 1803–85; women's monthly minutes, 1803–87 (Dunning Creek); men's minutes 1896–1910 (West Branch); women Friends, 1833–82.

Menallen Monthly Meeting, in 1875, was composed of Menallen Preparative Meeting (Menallen Meeting, Adams County, Pa. 9 miles from Gettysburg), established 1748, under Warrington; Huntingdon Preparative Adams County, Pa. (10 miles from Oxford), established ——, under Menallen; Newberry Meeting, York County, Pa., established 18—, under Warrington. Men's minutes, 1780–1890; women's minutes, 1780–1835; births and deaths, 1733–1884; marriage certificates, 1781–1931; certificates of removal, 1786–1854.

Redstone Monthly Meeting, Pa. Minutes, 1793–1843; births and deaths, 1793–1843; marriage certificates, 1793–1843; certificates of removal, 1793-1843.

Warrington Quarter, York Co., Pa., established 1730, individual large meeting (once combined with Fairfax, Va., separated 1787).

Warrington Quarterly minutes. Joint session, men and women, 1776-1813; men's minutes, 1803–88; women's minutes, 1776–1873; ministers' and elders' minutes, 1806–1924.

Warrington Monthly Meeting. Men's minutes, 1747–1856; women's minutes, 1753–1857; births and deaths, 1739–1810; marriage certificates, 1745–1851, 1788–1857; certificates of removal, 1788–1859.

Virginia Meeting of Baltimore Yearly Meeting of Friends:

Cane Creek, South Carolina, Monthly Meeting. Births and deaths, 1789–1806; marriage certificates, 1789–1806.

Alexandria Meeting, City of Alexandria, Va., established 1802, under Fairfax Monthly Meeting. In 1875, composed of Preparative Meeting of Alexandria, Woodlawn (settled by Friends from Pennsylvania and New Jersey, on Mt. Vernon estate, Alexandria, 1847); and Washington, now (1939) 2 Meetings, established 1750, under Indian Spring. Men's minutes, 1802–1916; ministers and elders' minutes, 1829–82; births and deaths, 1823–81; marriage certificates, 1803–19; certificates of removal, 1803–19; membership, 1823–81.

Crooked Run, Va., Monthly Meeting (attached from time to time to Hopewell Monthly Meeting). Men's minutes, 1782–84; women's minutes, 1782–89; births, deaths, marriages, 1783-1803; certificates of removal, 1783–1807.

Fairfax Meeting (Waterford), Loudon County, Va., at Fairfax, established 1745, under Concord Quarterly Meeting in Pennsylvania, with approbation of Hopewell. Held alternately at Fairfax, Va., and Monocacy, Frederick County, until 1776, when Monocacy was attached to Pipe Creek. Men's minutes, 1746–1929 (imperfect); women's minutes, 1745–1889.

Fairfax Quarterly Meeting. Men's minutes, 1787–1850; women's minutes, 1787–1889; ministers' and elders' minutes 1820–27, 1845–56, 1861–82. Fairfax and Warrington men's minutes, 1776–87 (separated in 1787); women's minutes, 1776–87; women's minutes, 1787–1813 (Warrington only); ministers' and elders' minutes, 1806–18.

Fairfax Monthly Meeting. Births and deaths (reverse book), 1740–1880; marriage certificates, 1760–1893, 1898–1924; certificates of removal, 1783–1909.

Goose Creek, Loudon County, Va. (9 miles West from Leesburg), established 1785, under Fairfax Monthly Meeting. Men's minutes, 1785–1920; womens minutes, 1785–1885; births, burials, 1785–1880; marriage certificates, 1785–1880; certificate of removal, 1785–1875.

Hopewell Meeting, Frederick County, Va. (5 miles north of Winchester), established, 1735, under Concord, Pa.

Hopewell Monthly Meeting. Minute books, 1735–58, lost by fire; men's minutes, 1759–1913; women's minutes, 1829–35, 1847–66.

Hopewell Preparative Meeting, 1832–49. Books of births, deaths and marriages, in safe of Daniel Lupton, Esq., Winchester, Va. Marriages, in brief form, copies in Park Avenue. Certificates of Removal, 1778–1805.

Baltimore County

Gunpowder Quaker Meeting House. Second meeting house erected 1772; present one 1821; Beaver Dam Road, near Oregon. First marriage recorded, 1740. Balto. Meeting House, Park Avenue, and Homewood Meeting House, Baltimore.

See also Jeffersonian, June 22, 1934.

161st anniversary of Gunpowder Meeting House; dedication. Md. Geneal. Rec. Com., 1935–36, p. 276. Mss. DAR.

Anne Arundel and Calvert Counties

West River Quaker Meeting. Records of Anne Arundel and Calvert Counties. Births, marriages and deaths, 1655–1882. Pub. Geneal. Soc. Pa., v. 3, no. 3, pp. 197–200.

Abstracts of records. Mss. MHS.

Thomas-Chew-Lawrence families. Thomas. 1883. Park Avenue Meeting House.

Calvert County

West River Quaker Meeting. Records of Anne Arundel and Calvert Counties. Births, marriages and deaths, 1655–1882. Pub. Geneal. Soc. Pa., v. 3, no. 3, pp. 197–200.

Caroline County

List of family names of Nicolite Quakers of Caroline County, 1752–1800, supplied by Miss Julia M. Kelly, Route 1, Preston, Md., custodian of Nicolite Friend records and of the North West Fork Quaker Meeting, 1799.

Records of marriages and deaths of Caroline and Dorchester Counties. Md. Geneal. Rec. Com., 1931–32, p. 87. Mss. DAR.

List of members (Nicolite Quakers) still in Caroline County. Hist. of Caroline Co. P. 110.

Nicolite Friends (141) who received membership, 1798, in Third Haven Meeting, Talbot County. Pa. Mag. Hist. and Biog., v. 27, p. 76.

Carroll County

Pipe Creek Quaker Meeting House, 1772, Union Bridge. Record of marriages and deaths, 1772–date, in custody of Mr. W. Morris Haines, Linwood.

Mss. copy. DAR.

Tombstone records, 1833–79. Hist. of West. Md. Scharf. V. 2, p. 971. MHS; DAR.

Early families of Pipe Creek Quaker Meeting were Benedums, Cooksons, Haines, Hibbards, Hurseys, Rineharts, Shepherds, Thomas, Wolfes and Wrights. Hundred years of Carroll Co. Lynch. P. 62.

Cecil County

Bicentennial of Brick Meeting House, Calvert, Cecil County, 1701–1901. 1902. DAR.

Brick Meeting House, 1701, Calvert, Cecil County. For records, see Park Avenue Friends Meeting House.

East and West Nottingham and Octoraro Quaker records from, 1700. See Park Avenue Friends Meeting House.

Harford County

Broad Creek, 1828, near Dublin. Bush Creek, Deer Creek, Forest, and Little Falls, Fallston Friend's Meeting records. Baltimore Yearly Meeting, Park Avenue.

Deer Creek Friends' Meeting House, founded 1737, rebuilt 1784, restored 1888, Darlington. For records prior to 1823 see Park Avenue Meeting, and after 1823, see Homewood Meeting House, Baltimore.

Howard County

Elkridge Meeting, established, 1739, and Meeting House, 1798, Ellicott's City (now laid down). For records see Park Avenue Friends Meeting House.

Kent County

Cecil Monthly Meeting of Friends, originally in Cecil County, resurvey took in Kent County. Records of births, marriages and deaths (original), 1682–1820; minutes, 1698–1840, in Friends Yearly Meeting House, 15th and Race Streets, Philadelphia. Photos. copy, 1672–1848, 7 vols., indexed. MHS.

Cecil Monthly Meeting, Kent County. 700 family names, from 7 books of records. Md. Geneal. Bull., v. 2, no. 3, pp. 19–21. MHS; DAR.

Montgomery County

Sandy Springs Quaker Meeting House, 1750. Records of births, marriages and deaths, 1758–1895. For records see Park Avenue Friends Meeting House; also Bank at Sandy Springs (no burial records there prior to 1870).

Burial records, 1789–1867. Hist. of west. Md. Scharf. V. 1, p. 776. MHS; DAR;

Centennial of Sandy Springs, 1817–1917. MHS; DAR.

Quaker Records, Montgomery County. Births and deaths. Natl. Geneal. Soc. Quart., v. 7, no. 4, p. 58. MHS; DAR.

Prince George County

Indian Spring Quaker Meeting, established, prior to 1660, laid down May 6, 1846. Records in Park Avenue Friends Meeting House.

Talbot County

Third Haven or Tred Avon Friends Meeting House, 1684. Minutes of Monthly Meetings contain records of births, marriages and deaths, 1676–date, in custody of Mr. James Dixon, Easton.

1676–1764, 6 vols. of photos., with mss. index. MHS.

1668–1755. Mss. Collection of Geneal. Soc. Pa.

Extracts from records, 1680. Pa. Mag. Hist. and Biog., 1893, v. 17, p. 88.

Extracts from records. Natl. Geneal. Soc. Quart., v. 11, no. 1, pp. 9–14. MHS; DAR.

List of surnames. Md. Geneal. Bull., no. 2, p. 30, no. 3, pp. 7, 12. MHS; DAR.

Nicholite Friends of Caroline County. List (141) of those who received membership, 1798, in Third Haven Meeting, Talbot County. Pa. Mag. Hist. and Biog., v. 27, pp. 76–79.

250th anniversary of Old Third Haven Meeting House, Oct. 23, 1932. DAR.

Third Haven Friends Meeting House, 1684, is still standing and is said to be oldest frame house on Eastern Shore. Second Meeting House is built on grounds near old building, and is used today.

Miscellaneous Quaker Records

Baltimore Yearly Meeting (1883). Extracts of minutes of proceedings. Mss. MHS.

Books of burials, 1792–1934, Baltimore Yearly Meeting of Friends. Mss. Park Avenue Friends Meeting House.

Earliest London epistles, 1675–1759. Park Avenue Friends Meeting House.

Early Friends (Quakers) in Maryland. Balto., J. D. Toy, 1862. MHS.

First discipline of Friends, of Baltimore Yearly Meeting, 1759. (Script.) Park Avenue Friends Meeting House.

Friends (or Quakers) settled in Maryland, about 1658, and it was at West River, Anne Arundel County, the second Yearly Meeting of Friends in United States was held, 1672, at which time George Fox preached. Mrs. Ridgely in her "Old brick churches of Maryland," says: "First house built for the yearly meeting of Friends was at West River, Anne Arundel County" (p. 70); Mr. Jufus M. Jones states in his book, "Quakers of American Colonies": "First meeting house built in Colony was at Bettie's Cove, on the Eastern Shore of Maryland, from minutes of a Men's Meeting held at Wenlock Christison in 1678."

Journals of members (gift of two original volumes of Journal of George Fox) by J. W. Harry. Park Avenue Friends Meeting House.

List of records of meeting constituting the Yearly Meeting of Society of Friends at 15th and Race Streets, Philadelphia. Minutes and records of births, marriages and deaths. 7 vols., photos. MHS.

Lodging lists (registers) of all persons attending Yearly Meetings, 1888–date. Park Avenue Friends Meeting House.

Memorials of deceased Friends, 1786–1889. (Script.) Park Avenue Friends Meeting House.

Miscellaneous records (over 1000 books, 600 pamphlets and manuscripts) presented to Park Avenue Vault Committee, from estate of late Kirk Brown, by his son Clemson Brown. This is only small portion of bequest, as late Mr. Brown, genealogist, Quaker historian, and long custodian of records of Baltimore Yearly Meeting, indexed about all Monthly Meetings of Maryland and Virginia.

Treasurer's accounts. Pasture lot, 1792–94, Yearly Meeting of Stock, 1788–90, 1794–1818. Park Avenue Friends Meeting House.

Westland Monthly Meeting. Minutes, 1786–1836. Mss. Park Avenue Friends Meeting House.

REFORMED CHURCHES

(All Reformed Churches early established in America called German Reformed; in 1863, Officially changed to Reformed Church of United States)

Baltimore City

Associate Reformed Congregation. Register of births, marriages, deaths and members, 1812–65. 4 vols. Mss. MHS.

Evangelical Alliance for Baltimore. Church directory, prepared 1888. Pamph. MHS.

First German Reformed Church, 1897, Calvert Street, South of Read Street. Register of births, marriages and deaths, 1768–1856. Ms. MHS.

Lutherans and German Reformed worshipped together and built second church in Baltimore, 1758, opposite St. Paul's Protestant Episcopal Church.

Otterbein (German Evangelical Reformed Church), 1785, Conway and Sharp Streets. (Oldest church standing in Baltimore.) Register of baptisms, marriages and deaths (partly in German script), 1798–date, kept in safe in parsonage. (Death records incomplete.)

Register of baptisms, 1798–1850; marriages, 1801–50; deaths, 1798–1826; names of members. Ms. MHS.

Records, 1798–1850. Md. Geneal. Bull.

History of Otterbein Church. Md. O. R. Soc. Bull., no. 2, pp. 27–29. MHS.

Zion German Lutheran Church, Gay Street and Court House Plaza. Register of births, marriages and deaths, 1786–1849. 2 vols. Mss. MHS.

Zion Church of Baltimore. Soc. for Germans in Md., 2nd annual report. MHS.

History of Zion Church, 1755–1897. Julius Hofman, pastor. Balto., 1905. MHS.

Carroll County

Baust Reformed Church, 1868 (Emmanuel, 1794; Reformed, 1815; Lutheran, 1907), near Westminster. No records of births, baptisms or deaths prior to 1850; 1895–1913, incomplete; 1913–date, complete; list of communicants, in custody of Rev. Miles Reifsnider.

Tombstone records, 1794–1907. Md. Geneal. Rec. Com., 1935–36, pp. 51–57. Mss. DAR.

Cemetery records of Lutheran and Reformed, 1798–1880. Hist. of west. Md. Scharf. V. 2, p. 862. MHS; DAR.

Grace Reformed Church, 1770, 1821, Taneytown. Register of births, marriages and deaths, 1770–1893, not located; 1894–date, in custody of Rev. Guy Brady.

Cemetery (Taneytown) tombstone inscriptions, 1777–1879; earliest birth, 1722. Hist. of west. Md. Scharf. V. 2, pp. 840–42. MHS; DAR.

Jerusalem Reformed Church (first known as Bowers Church), 1797, Bachman's Valley. For history, see Hist. manual of Reformed Church in U. S. J. H. Dubbs, D.D.

Keyesville Reformed Church, 1820, Taneytown. Records of baptisms, marriages and deaths not kept prior to 1904; 1904–date, in custody of Rev. Guy Brady.

Manchester charge. Lazarus Reformed Church, 1853, Lineboro. Records of baptisms, Marriages and deaths (complete), 1856–date, in custody of Rev. John Hollenbach, Manchester.

Manchester charge. Trinity Reformed Church, 1760, Manchester. Worshipped jointly with Lutherans until 1862, when each congregation built own church (Lutherans built on old site). Records (both congregations) of baptisms, marriages and deaths, 1760–1839, written in German script, and complete records of Trinity Church, 1839–date, in English, in custody of Rev. John Hollenbach.

Lutheran and Reformed Church cemetery, Manchester District. Tombstone inscriptions, 1760–1863; earliest birth, 1730. Hist. of west. Md. Scharf. V. 2, p. 886. MHS; DAR.

Old Union Meeting House cemetery, 1790; oldest burying ground in county; now Westminster Cemetery, organized 1864; 1788–1878. Earliest birth, 1710. Hist. of west. Md. Scharf. V. 2, p. 935. MHS; DAR.

*St. Benjamin's (Old Carroll; Krieder's) Union Church, 1763; present Church, 1807; Lutheran and Reformed, located on Gettysburg Turnpike, 1½ miles from Westminster. Records of births, baptisms, marriages and deaths, 1763–date (fragmentary), in custody of Rev. C. E. Robert, Westminster.

Records, 1763–1836. Ms. MHS.

Records of business meetings of classes, in custody of Rev. Guy Brady, Taneytown.

First record book, Reformed Congregation of St. Banjamin's or Kreider's Church, Pipe Creek. C. T. Zahn. 1934. Typed in binder, 26 pp. DAR.

St. Mary's Reformed Church, 1762, 1821, 1893, Silver Run. Records of baptisms, marriages and deaths, 1762–1848, lost; 1848–date (complete), in custody of Rev. F. B. Peck. Earliest tombstone, 1789.

Review of history of St. Mary's Reformed Church, Silver Run, 1762–1912, and St. Mary's Lutheran and Reformed Church, Westminster. Congregations organized May 31, 1762, under same constitution. Union church constitution in full. Original records and documents, written in German. Owned by Leland Johnson.

St. Mary's Reformed Church. S. C. Hooker.

St. Matthew's Reformed Church, 1879, Pleasant Valley. Records of baptisms, marriages and deaths, 1882–date, in custody of Rev. C. E. Robert, Westminster.

St. Paul's Reformed Church, 1868, Westminster. Records of baptisms, births, confirmations, 1868–date, in custody of Rev. H. N. Bassler

Frederick County

Apple Reformed Church, established April 15, 1770, Thurmont. Records of births, marriages and deaths, 1770–1933, in custody of Miss Sarah Dotterer, Graceham.

Tombstone inscriptions, 1719–1919 (322 graves). Md. General. Rec, Com., 1932–33. Pp. 76–86. Mss. DAR.

Christ Reformed Church, about 1756, Middletown. Records of births, marriages and deaths, 1756–1830; incorporated in Evangelical Reformed Church Frederick; 1830–76 (incomplete) and 1876–date, in custody of Church.

Church of Incarnation (Reformed), erected 1868, organized 1782, Emmitsburg records of baptisms, births, marriages and deaths, 1782–1851, lost; 1851–date, in custody of Church. Early interments made in cemetery, now Lutheran property.

Church of Resurrection, 1829, Burkittsville. Records of births, marriages and deaths, 1829–date (complete), in custody of Church.

Prior to building of Resurrection Church, 1829, Elias Willard, an old resident and early settler, kept in family Bible record of marriages and deaths of community. German script, translated; manuscript now in possession of descendant, Mrs. Ida Markey (103 E. Second Street, Frederick), who is making copy to present to Church. (Records begin in 1763; while not voluminous probably cover whole of community.)

Trinity Chapel, 1868, Adamstown. Erratum. Register of births, marriages and deaths, 1868-80, lost; 1880-date, in custody of B. Clark Gibson, Adamstown. Burials in Mt. Olivet.

Evangelical Reformed Church, 1740, Frederick. Records of baptisms, 1746-date, marriages, 1756-date, deaths, 1788-date, and confirmations, 1753-date, in custody of Church.

Register, 1753-1875. 3 vols. Mss. MHS.

Marriages (700), copied from register. Md. Geneal. Rec. Com., 1932-33. Mss. DAR.

Marriages, 1756-1894 (52 persons). Md. records. Brumbaugh. V. 2, pp. 498-513.

Glade Reformed Church, 1750, Walkersville. Early records of births, marriages and deaths apparently incorporated with those of Evangelical Reformed Church, Frederick, on same circuit, 1833; congregation united with St. John's (Creagerston), St. John's (Woodsboro) and Rocky Hill. 1874-date, in custody of Church. Oldest legible stone in cemetery, 1805.

Jefferson Reformed Church, 1825, Jefferson. Register of births, marriages and deaths, 1825-40, lost; 1840-date (complete), in possession of Church.

Mt. Pleasant Reformed Church, 1870, Mt. Pleasant. Register of births, marriages and deaths 1870-date, in custody of Church.

Mt. Tabor Reformed and Lutheran Church, 1873, Rocky Ridge. Records of births, marriages and deaths, 1873-1900, lost; 1900-date, in custody of Rev. P. H. Williams, Union Bridge.

St. John's German Reformed Church, 1843, disbanded 1912, Frederick. Records borrowed by officers (now deceased) from vault of Evangelical Reformed Church, Frederick; never returned; not located.

German Reformed cemeteries, 1748-1867, Frederick. (Oldest tombstone that of Jacob Steiner, born 1713, died 1748. First one on record that of Magdalind Schmidt, born 1713, died 1748.) Hist. of west. Md. Scharf. V. 1, pp. 525-26. MHS; DAR.

German Reformed graveyard, Frederick. (On site now stands Memorial Park to World War Heroes. Bodies removed to Mt. Olivet Cemetery. Barbara Fritchie buried here. Oldest stone, that of Casper Mantz, born April 8, 1718, died Feb. 28, 1791.) Hist. of west. Md. Scharf. V. 1, p. 526. MHS; DAR.

St. John's Reformed Church, May 8, 1747, Creagerstown. Records of births, marriages and deaths, 1747-date, in custody of Russell Seiss, Creagerstown.

St. John's Reformed Church (formerly St. John's German Reformed), 1855, remodeled 1893, Sabillasville (originally built by Harbaugh families). Records of baptisms, marriages and deaths, 1855-date, in custody of Church.

Ms. copy. MHS.

St. John's (Solomon's) Reformed Church, 1802, organized prior to 1760, Woodsboro. Records of births, marriages and deaths apparently incorporated with those of Evangelical Reformed Church, Frederick. Oldest legible tombstone, 1803.

St. Matthews Church (on-the-Manor), organized April, 1831, Church Hill (now closed). Records of births, marriages and deaths, in custody of G. F. Thomas, Adamstown. Burials in Mt. Olivet Cemetery, Frederick.

Trinity Chapel. Names and dates on monument in Trinity Chapel yard, Frederick. (Erected by Evangelical Reformed Church.) Md. Geneal. Rec. Com., 1934-35. Mss. DAR.

Washington County

Associate Reformed Church, Hagerstown. List of contributors to building fund, 1817. Natl. Geneal. Soc. Quart., v. 20, no. 1, pp. 28-31. MHS.

German Reformed Church, Cavetown. Tombstone inscriptions, 1828-79; earliest birth, 1780. Hist. of west. Md. Scharf. V. 2, p. 1270. MHS; DAR.

Reformed Church, Hagerstown. Records of births and list of heads of families, 1766-1809. Mss. MHS.

Reformed Church, Sharpsburg. Records of Church lost. Tombstone inscriptions, 1811-78; earliest birth, 1734. Hist. of west. Md. Scharf. V. 2, p. 1209. MHS; DAR.

Salem German Reformed Church, Conococheague District. Records of births, marriages, deaths and parents' names, 1744-83 (fragmentary; some destroyed by fire). Mss. MHS.

Tombstone inscriptions, 1796-1875; earliest birth, 1763. Hist. of west. Md. Scharf. V. 2, pp. 1289-90. MHS; DAR.

St. Paul's Reformed Church, 1748, Clear Spring, Conococheague District. Records of baptisms and marriages, 1807-41. Mss. MHS.

Tombstone inscriptions, 1813-80. Hist. of west. Md. Scharf. V. 2, p. 1250. MHS; DAR.

Trinity Reformed Church, 1750, Boonsboro. Tombstone inscriptions, 1806-78; earliest birth, 1753. Hist. of west. Md. Scharf. V. 2, p. 1264. MHS; DAR.

Zion Reformed Church, prior to 1770, Hagerstown. Tombstone inscriptions, 1713-1920 (complete). Md. Geneal. Rec. Com., 1934-35, p. 31. Mss. DAR.

Tombstone inscriptions, 1800-72. Hist. of west. Md. Scharf. V. 2, p. 1094. MHS; DAR.

Cemetery inscriptions of Westmoreland County, Pennsylvania, and Zion Reformed Church cemetery, Hagerstown. Mrs. R. N. Bergen. Pamph. DAR.

ROMAN CATHOLIC CHURCHES

Allegany County

St. Patrick's Roman Catholic Church, Cumberland. Register of births, marriages and deaths, 1792-date, in custody of Church.

St. Peter's and St. Paul's Roman Catholic German Church, Cumberland. Register of births, marriages and deaths, 1841-date, in custody of Church.

Tombstone inscriptions, 1839-1900; earliest birth, 1781. Hist. of west. Md. Scharf. V. 2, pp. 1418-20. MHS; DAR.

Baltimore City

Cathedral burial records, 1793-1874. Typed, bd., 3 vols. MHS.

St. Patrick's Roman Catholic Church, Broadway and Bank Streets. Cemetery, Philadelphia Road, tombstone inscriptions, 1746-1896. Md. Geneal. Rec. Com., 1932-33, pp. 124-33. Mss. DAR.

St. Patrick's Roman Catholic Church. Register. Amer. Catholic Hist. Soc. of Phila. Rec., 1887, v. 1, p. 387.

St. Peter's Roman Catholic Church. Register. Amer. Catholic Hist. Soc. of Phila. Rec., 1887, v. 1.

Tombstone inscriptions, 1737–1917 (practically complete). Md. Geneal. Rec. Com., 1934–35. Mss. DAR.

Carroll County

Catholic Cemetery, Westminster. Tombstone inscriptions, 1802–81; earliest birth, 1742. Hist. of west. Md. Scharf. V. 2, pp. 938–39. MHS; DAR.

St. John's Roman Catholic Church, 1789, 1804, 1866 (formerly Christ Church), Westminster, mission of Taneytown Church. Records of baptisms, marriages and deaths, 1853–date, in custody of priest in charge.

St. Joseph's Roman Catholic Church, first church 1796, 1804, Taneytown. No records prior to 1904. Cemetery records, 1792–1867; earliest birth, 1758. Hist. of west. Md. Scharf. V. 2, pp. 845–47. MHS; DAR.

St. Joseph's Roman Catholic Church, established prior to Civil War, completed 1867, Sykesville. Records of baptisms, marriages and deaths, 1892–date, in custody of Rev. Father Martin, Harrisonville, Balto. Co.

For records prior to 1892, see Woodstock College, Balto. Co.

Cecil County

Bohemia pew rent book. Archives of Georgetown Univ., Wash., D. C., v. 7. 6; v. 53. 9.

Charles County

Records of Roman Catholic Congregation of Upper and Lower Zachiah, Mattawoman and St. Mary's Bryantown. Records of baptisms, marriages and deaths, 1793–1861 (4000 entries). 1 vol., 276 pp. Ms. (Pp. 178–204, colored people, not indexed.) MHS; DAR.

*St. Mary's Roman Catholic Church records, Bryantown. Archives of Georgetown Univ., Wash., D. C., v. 242. 3.

*Roman Catholic Church records, Mattawoman. Archives of Georgetown Univ., Wash., D. C., v. 242. 3.

Roman Catholic Church records, Waldorf. Archives of Georgetown Univ., Wash., D. C., v. 242. 3.

Dorchester County

Roman Catholic records in Dorchester County, prior to 1892. Will be found in Easton, at Church of St. Peter and St. Paul, under jurisdiction of priest in charge.

Frederick County

Roman Catholic Chapel of Immaculate Conception, 1808, Mt. St. Mary's College, Emmitsburg. Records of baptisms, marriages and burials, 1808–date, in custody of priest in charge.

Roman Catholic Church of Our Lady of Mt. Carmel, established May 8, 1857, Thurmont. Records of baptisms, marriages and burials, 1857–date, now at Shrine of St. Anthony, Emmitsburg. Oldest tombstone, 1859.

St. John's Roman Catholic Church, first built in 1763, Frederick. Records of baptisms, marriages and burials, 1811–date, at St. John's rectory, 116 E. Second Street, Frederick. Oldest tombstone, 1794.

Catholic Cemetery, Frederick. Tombstone inscriptions, 1831–75 (incomplete); earliest birth, 1776. Hist. of west. Md. Scharf. V. 1, p. 52. MHS; DAR.

St. Joseph's Roman Catholic Church, about 1764, Carrollton Manor, Buckeystown. Register of baptisms, marriages and burials, prior to 1902, are in St. John's rectory, 116 E. Second Street, Frederick; 1902–date, at St. Joseph Church.

St. Joseph's Roman Catholic Church, 1793, Emmitsburg. Records of baptisms, marriages and burials, 1793–date, in custody of priest in charge.

Tombstone inscriptions, 1795–1887. Md. O. R. Soc. Bull., no. 3, pp. 64–66. MHS.

St. Mary's Roman Catholic Church, 1826, Petersville. Register of baptisms, marriages and burials, 1826–date, at St. John's rectory, 116 E. Second Street, Frederick.

St. Peter's Roman Catholic Church, 1821, Libertytown (mission of St. John's until 1881 or 1882). Records of baptisms, marriages and burials, 1821–date, at St. John's rectory, Frederick.

Harford County

Priest's Ford Chapel, 1747 (mission of St. Joseph's, sold in 1814). G. W. Archer. Pamph. Harford Co. Hist. Soc. Coll. JHU.

St. Ignatius Roman Catholic Church, 1779. Early records of baptisms, marriages and burials lost. List of few Catholics to take up lands and settle at Deer Creek. Hist. of Harford Co. Preston. P. 160. (Col. Ignatius Wheeler, prominent in Revolution, buried there in 1793.) MHS; DAR.

Howard County

Roman Catholic Chapel, Doughorean Manor. No records in Chapel. (Charles Carroll of Carrollton buried in Chapel in 1832.)

St. Paul's Roman Catholic Church, 1838, Ellicott City. Register of births, marriages and deaths, 1838–date, in custody of priest in charge.

History of St. Paul's Roman Catholic Church, 1838–1938, Ellicott City. MHS.

Montgomery County

St. John's Roman Catholic Church (Carroll Chapel), 1770, Forest Glen, Montgomery Co. (Parish includes Barnstown, Rockville and Seneca, also some Prince George Co. families.) Register of births marriages, and deaths, 1813–date, in custody of priest in charge.

Register of births and marriages, 1813–50. Ms. DAR.

Tombstone records. Ms. MHS.

Tombstone records, 1804–1924. Md. Geneal. Rec. Com., 1926–27. Mss. DAR.

Tombstone records, 1796–1876; earliest birth, 1750. Hist. of west. Md. Scharf. V. 1, p. 759.

(John Carroll (1735–1815), first Roman Catholic bishop in United States, 1789, archbishop of Baltimore, 1808, was at one time stationed at Forest Glen.)

St. Mary's Roman Catholic Church, 1808, Barnesville. Tombstone inscriptions, 1820–78; earliest birth, 1789. Hist. of west. Md. Scharf. V. 1, p. 731. MHS; DAR.

St. Mary's Roman Catholic Church, Rockville. Tombstone inscriptions, 1842–80; earliest birth, 1798. Hist. of west. Md. Scharf. V. 1, p. 750. MHS; DAR.

St. Mary's County

Sacred Heart Roman Catholic churchyard, Bushwood. Tombstone inscriptions, St. Mary's County. 1828–93. Md. Geneal. Rec. Com. 1929. Bd. mss. DAR.

St. Francis Roman Catholic Chapel, 1767, near Leonardtown. No information about records.

St. Inigoes Roman Catholic Church. No information about records. Tombstone inscriptions, 1787–1854. Md. O. R. Soc. Bull., no. 3, p. 58. MHS.

St. Inigoes churchyard, 1787–1854. Tombstone inscriptions St. Mary's County. Md. O. R. Soc. Bull., no. 3, p. 58. MHS.

Priest's House, 1661 (ruins), Priest Point, St. Inigoes Creek. Old cemetery; no information about inscriptions.

Plundering of St. Inigoes, St. Mary's County. U. S. Catholic Hist. Soc. Mag., 1890, v. 3. MHS.

Talbot County

Roman Catholic Church. Records of baptisms and funerals, 1818–33, White Marsh. Archives of Georgetown Univ., Wash., D. C., v. 215. 2.

Records of baptisms, 1818–22, White Marsh. (Partial copy of Georgetown Univ. Archives, v. 215. 2, pp. 1–54.) D. C. Geneal. Rec. Com., 1937–38. Bd. mss. DAR.

St. Joseph's Roman Catholic Church, 1762, second Catholic church built on Eastern Shore of Maryland, still in use. No information about records; very old tombstones.

St. Peter's and St. Paul's Roman Catholic Church, Easton, 1868, Chapel on Miles River, about 1803. Records of births, marriages and deaths, in possession of priest in charge.

SWEDENBORGEN CHURCH

New Jerusalem (Swedenborgen) Church, Baltimore. Register of births, marriages and deaths, 1793–1862. Ms. MHS.

UNITARIAN CHURCH

First Unitarian Church, Franklin and Charles Streets, Baltimore. Register of births, marriages and deaths, 1818–1925. Photos. MHS.

UNITED BRETHREN IN CHRIST CHURCHES

Carroll County

Greenmount United Brethren Church, 1851, Greenmount. Records of baptisms, marriages and deaths, 1863-date, in custody of Rev. D. K Reisinger.

Manchester charge. Bethel United Brethren Church, 1845, Manchester. No information on records. Tombstone inscriptions, 1830–69; earliest birth 1752 (9 stones). Hist. of west. Md. Scharf. V. 2, p. 886. MHS; DAR.

Note: Pastor, Rev. Ivan S. Nagle says there are many old stones moved from private burying ground, to Manchester.

Manchester charge. Bixler's United Brethren Church, 1877. No information on records.

Manchester charge. Miller's United Brethren Church, 1877. No information on records.

Meadow Branch Dunkard Church, 1847, near Westminster. No information about records. "Here spring and autumn, semi-annual feasts of Brethren are held, and people assemble from distances to witness unique service." Spirit of Md. Lantz. P. 64.

Pleasant Valley United Brethren Church, 1872, Route 7, Westminster. No records available.

Taneytown United Brethren Church, 1850. No information about records.

Frederick County

Deerfield United Brethren Church, 1871, Deerfield. Records of births and marriages, 1871–date, in custody of United Brethren Church, Thurmont.

Eyler's Valley United Brethren Church, 1857, Eyler's Valley. Records lost, not destroyed by fire.

Mt. Olivet United Brethren Church, 1867, Pleasant Walk, near Myersville. No records extant. Oldest tombstone inscription that of Daniel Burns, 1867.

Mt. Vernon United Brethren Church, 1874, Daysville. Records of births, marriages and deaths 1874-date, in custody of Church.

Mt. Zion United Brethren Church, 1852, Myersville. (Congregation organized, 1827; worshipped first in Old Jerusalem Church; records lost; early burials must have been made at cemetery at Jerusalem; oldest tombstone inscriptions that of Abraham Doub, Mar., 1853.)

Oterbein United Brethren Cemetery records, Harbaugh Valley. Ms. MHS.

Otterbein Chapel (originally Baulus Chapel), 1801, Middletown. Erected by United Brethren and Methodist Episcopal churches. No records found, none destroyed by fire.

Rocky Ridge United Brethren Church, 1853 (Monocaly Congregation), Rocky Ridge, Detour. No marriages recorded in the Church book; each minister kept his own. Tombstone inscriptions, 1853-1934, in custody of Mrs. Wm. Slemmer, Historian of Frederick Chapter, D. A. R.

United Brethren Cemetery, Sabillasville. Natl. Geneal. Soc. Quart., v. 61. MHS.

Walkersville United Brethren Church, 1875 (originally known as Georgetown Chapel) Walkersville. Records of births, marriages and deaths, 1857-date (complete), in custody of Church (Congregation over 100 years old; worshipped in old Retreat School House, destroyed several years ago; no records of that organization located.)

Weller United Brethren Church, 1831, Thurmont. Records of births, marriages and deaths, 1831–date, in custody of Church.

Washington County

United Brethren Church, Chewsville. Tombstone inscriptions, 1819–78; earliest birth, 1750. Hist. of west. Md. Scharf. V. 2, p. 1305. MHS; DAR.

United Brethren Church, Keedysville. Mt. Hebron Cemetery, 1798–1872. Earliest birth, 1761. Hist. of west. Md. Scharf. V. 2, p. 1307. MHS; DAR.

United Brethren Church. Mt. Tabor Cemetery. Tombstone inscriptions, 1855–79 (fragmentary). Hist. of west. Md. Scharf. V. 2, p. 1290. MHS; DAR.

United Brethren Church, Rohresville. Tombstone inscriptions, 1842–77; earliest birth, 1769. Hist. of west. Md. Scharf. V. 2, p. 1277. MHS; DAR.

TOMBSTONE INSCRIPTIONS

GENERAL TOMBSTONE RECORDS

Tombstone records of Anne Arundel, Prince George and Queen Anne Counties. Md. O. R. Soc. Bull., no. 1, p. 52. MHS.

Beaver Creek epitaphs. Hist. of west. Md. Scharf. V. 2, pp. 1300–01. MHS; DAR.

Tombstone inscriptions of Caroline, Dorchester, Frederick, Talbot and Queen Anne Counties. Mss. MHS.

Tombstone inscriptions of Cemetery Creek, 1790–1890, Annapolis. Founders of Anne Arundel and Howard Counties. Warfield. Pp. 333–35. MHS; DAR.

Collection of American epitaphs and inscriptions. Rev. Timothy Alden. New York, 1814, 5 vols. MHS.

Tombstone inscriptions. From Pennington Papers. Mss. MHS.

Historic graves of Maryland and District of Columbia, with inscriptions appearing on tombstones in most of counties in State, in Washington and Georgetown. Helen W. Ridgely. Grafton Press, 1908. MHS.

*Maryland tombstone records, 1699. (Only 67 family names.) Md. Geneal. Rec. Com., Parran, 1937, pp. 1–34. Mss. DAR.

Memoirs of dead and tomb's remembrances. Compiled by Wm. C. Cochran. Printed by editors. Balto., 1806, 300 pp. (very rare item). MHS; DAR; City Hall Lib.

Records of gravestones of Delaware, Maryland, Pennsylvania and West Virginia, with complete index. Md. Geneal. Rec. Com., Parran, 1937. Typed, bd. DAR.

St. Paul's Church notes. Churchyards of Baltimore. Ancient. Helen W. Ridgely. Grafton Mag., Nov., 1909. Also: M. H. Mag., 1910, v. 5, p. 201.

Tombstone and Bible records of lower Delaware-Maryland-Virginia peninsula. 514 names, 37 pp., indexed. Md. Geneal. Rec. Com., 1938–39, p. 218. Mss. DAR.

Tombstone inscriptions of southern Maryland. Md. O. R. Soc. Bull., no. 3, pp. 56–67. MHS.

*Trinity Roman Catholic Church graveyard records, 1817–33. Archives of Georgetown Univ., Wash., D. C., v. 175, pp. 1–66.

West Virginia, tombstone records at Hancock, Maryland. Md. Geneal. Rec. Com., Parran, 1937, pp. 36–42. Typed, bd. DAR.

ALLEGANY COUNTY

Allegany Cemetery, 1842–78, Frostburg. First birth, 1790. Hist. of west. Md. Scharf. V. 2, p. 1486. MHS; DAR.

Percy Cemetery, 1848–77, Frostburg. Earliest birth, 1772. Hist. of west. Md. Scharf. V. 2, p. 1485. MHS; DAR.

Catholic Cemetery, 1808–80; Frostburg District. Earliest birth, 1808. Hist. of west. Md. Scharf. V. 2, p. 1486. MHS; DAR.

Methodist Episcopal Cemetery, 1844–75, Mount Savage District (few stones). Earliest birth, 1779. Hist. of west. Md. Scharf. V. 2, p. 1497. MHS; DAR.

Mount Savage Cemetery. Hist. of west. Md. Scharf. V. 2, p. 1498. MHS; DAR.

Philos Cemetery, 1859–78, Western Port District. Earliest birth, 1792. Hist. of west. Md. Scharf. V. 2, p. 1464. MHS; DAR.

Rose Hill Cemetery, 1777–1880, Cumberland. Hist. of west. Md. Scharf. V. 2, pp. 1422–24. MHS; DAR.

Shaw's Cemetery, 1818–76, Moscow (16 stones). Earliest birth, 1716. Hist. of west. Md. Scharf. V. 2, p. 1511. MHS; DAR.

St. Gabriel's Roman Catholic Cemetery, 1800–74. Hist. of west. Md. Scharf. V. 2, p. 1472. MHS; DAR.

ANNE ARUNDEL COUNTY

All Hallows churchyard. Bd. mss. DAR.

Baldwin Memorial churchyard. Bd. mss. DAR.

Bascom Chapel. Bd. mss. DAR.

Burials. Founders of Anne Arundel and Howard Counties. Warfield. Pp. 333–35. MHS; DAR.

St. Ann's churchyard, Annapolis, 1699–1817. Md. O. R. Soc. Bull., no. 3, pp. 55–56. MHS.

St. Anne's churchyard, Annapolis. Bd. mss. DAR.

St. Stephens Church, Millersville. Bd. mss. DAR.

Tombstone inscriptions (mostly prior to 1830). 1913, typed, bd. DAR.

BALTIMORE CITY

Tombstone inscriptions around Baltimore. Notes on History, v. 1, pp. 44–46. MHS; DAR.

Greenmount Cemetery, charter, dedication and lot holders, 1839. Balto., 1885, pamph. MHS.

One hundredth anniversary, 1838–1938. Baltimore, Proprietors of Greenmount Cemetery, 1938, 96 pp. 39 illus. of hist. graves and monuments. MHS.

Second general report of board of managers to proprietors and lot holders. 1848, pamph. MHS; DAR.

Some graves and monuments, from 1839. J. T. King. Balto., 1876, pamph. MHS.

Loudon Park Cemetery Company. By-laws, regulations, map-fold, list of lot holders, 1872. (Several thousand Union and Confederate soldiers buried here.) Pamph. Balto., Sherwood. 1872, pamph. MHS.

Methodist Episcopal Church burial grounds, lot holders, records of interments in southern precincts of Baltimore City. Mss. MHS.
Mt. Olivet Methodist Episcopal Cemetery, 1761–1849. Md. Geneal. Rec. Com., 1932–33. Mss. DAR.
Notes on burial grounds of Baltimore. W. L. Holmas. Ms. MHS.
Presbyterians of Baltimore, their churches and historic graveyards. J. E. P. Boulden. Balto., 1875. MHS.

BALTIMORE COUNTY

Drumquhasle (now Anneslie). MHS.
Foster's cemetery, seventh district, Baltimore County. Markings of gravestones, 1780–1869. Md. Geneal. Rec. Com., 1932–33, p. 370. Mss. DAR.
Gray Rock, Reisterstown Road. Focke Geneal. Coll. Mss. MHS.
Mt. Paran Presbyterian churchyard, 1707–1850, Harrissonville. Mss. MHS. Also: Md. Geneal. Rec. Com., 1937–38, pp. 215–19. Bd. mss. DAR.
Pierpont burying ground, Catonsville. Lib. Cong. Also: Reprint in Natl. Geneal. Soc. Quart., July, 1918, v. 7, p. 25. MHS.
Salem churchyard, Catonsville, 1796–1880. Catonsville pioneers of Lutheran faith. Natl. Geneal. Soc. Quart., v. 9, no. 2, p. 29. MHS.
Trinity Protestant Episcopal churchyard, Long Green, 1754–1850. Mss. MHS. Also: Md. Geneal. Rec. Com., 1937–38, pp. 207–14. Mss. DAR.

CAROLINE COUNTY

Caroline County tombstone inscriptions. Mss. DAR.
Catholic Cemetery, 1828–1905, Denton. Md. O. R. Soc. Bull., no. 1, p. 51. MHS.
Denton Cemetery. Md. O. R. Soc. Bull., no. 1, p. 50. MHS.
Old churchyard, 1773–1849, Greensboro. (5 stones). Md. Geneal. Rec. Com., 1935–36, p. 168. Bd. mss. DAR.

CARROLL COUNTY

Baust or Emanuel Reformed churchyard records, 1798–1850, Westminster. Earliest birth, 1737. Md. Geneal. Rec. Com., 1935–36. Bd. mss. DAR.
Brucevill Cemetery, 1806–1829 (5 stones, over grown). Earliest birth, 1732. Hist. of west. Md. Scharf. V. 2, p. 901. MHS; DAR.
Cassell Cemetery rec., near Westminster. L. H. Dielman. Ms. MHS.
Eldersberg epitaphs. Hist. of west. Md. Scharf. V. 2, pp. 878–79. MHS; DAR.
German Baptist Cemetery, 1825–77, Pipe Creek. Earliest birth, 1753. Hist. of west. Md. Scharf. V. 2, pp. 824–26. MHS; DAR.
German Baptist Cemetery, between Westminster and Friggellbery. Hist. of west. Md. Scharf. V. 2, p. 824. MHS; DAR.
Haugh's Lutheran Church, tombstone records, 1751–1841. Md. Geneal. Rec. Com., 1939–40, pp. 173–74. Mss. DAR.
Lutheran and Reformed Cemetery, 1760–1868, Manchester District. Hist. of west. Md. Scharf. V. 2, pp. 886–87. MHS; DAR.
Nusbaum Cemetery, 1785–1853, Tyrone. Earliest birth, 1732. Hist. of west. Md. Scharf. V. 2, p. 863. MHS; DAR.
Pipe Creek epitaphs. Hist. of west. Md. Scharf. V. 2, p. 824. MHS; DAR.
Union Bridge Cemetery, 1790–1880 (8 stones). Hist. of west. Md. Scharf. V. 2, p. 972. MHS; DAR.
Uniontown Cemetery, 1827–80. Earliest birth, 1762. Hist. of west. Md. Scharf. V. 2, p. 859. MHS; DAR.
Westminster Cemetery. Interments to 1880. Ms. MHS.
Winter's Cemetery, New Windsor. Lutheran and Reformed, 1731–1880. Earliest birth, 1723. Hist. of west. Md. Scharf. V. 2, pp. 906–07. MHS; DAR.
Wolfe Cemetery. Ms. MHS.

CECIL COUNTY

Bible and gravestone records. Collected by head of Elk Chapter, D. A. R., Elkton. 847 names, indexed. Md. Geneal. Rec. Com., 1938–39, pp. 90–140. Mss. DAR.
St. Francis Xavier's Church, founded 1704. Old Bohemia. Md. Geneal. Rec. Com., 1934–35, pp. 188–94. Mss. DAR.
West Nothingham Cemetery, 1758–1851, Rising Sun. M. H. Mag., 1923, v. 18, p. 55.
Old West Nothingham Cemetery, 1739–1851, Rising Sun. St. Mary's Ann Parish. Bd. mss., p. 337. MHS.

CHARLES COUNTY

Marshall Hall private burying ground, Marshall Hall (land grant 1651). Natl. Geneal. Soc. Quart., v. 15, no. 1, p. 11; corrections and additions, no. 3, pp. 40–41; Bible records, no. 3, pp. 36–40. MHS.
Burial register of Roman Catholic Church, Newport. Archives of Georgetown Univ., Wash., D. C., v. 118.
St. Charles Roman Catholic churchyard, Indianhead. Md. Geneal. Rec. Com., 1933–34, p. 137. Bd. mss. DAR.
Stonestreet Place, 1782–1879. Md. Geneal. Rec. Com., 1932–33. Bd. mss. DAR.

DORCHESTER COUNTY

Christ Protestant Episcopal Church cemetery, Cambridge. Historical records. Dr. Guy Steele. List of rectors, 1697–1935; index of graves. Edited by Dorset Chapter, D. A. R. 1936, pamph. MHS; DAR.
Tombstone inscriptions of Dorchester County. Mss. MHS.
Primitive Baptist or Old School Baptist Church cemetery, 1862–1910 Milton (complete). Md. O. R. Soc. Bull., no. 3, p. 54. MHS.
Tombstone records of Dorchester County. Collected by Elias Jones. (Inscriptions in private burying grounds and farms; 350 names.) 1938–39, 48 pp., indexed, typed, bd., DAR.
Trinity Church cemetery, 1800–1909 (268 graves). Md. O. R. Soc. Bull., no. 3, pp. 42–52. MHS.
Trinity Protestant Episcopal Church, prior to 1690, Dorchester Parish, near Cambridge. Records from old burial ground. Md. Geneal. Rec. Com., 1937–38, pp. 93–104. Bd. mss. DAR.

FREDERICK COUNTY

Bliss Churchyard, 1747–1929. Md. Geneal. Rec. Com., 1932–33. Mss. DAR.
Cemetery records. Md. Geneal. Rec. Com., 1932–33, pp. 69–121; 194; 210–11. Mss. DAR.
Cemetery records. Pa. Geneal. Rec. Com., 1932–34, v. 1, pp. 213–24. Typed, bd. DAR.
Creagerstown old graveyard, 1731–1854 (5 stones). Hist. of west. Md. Scharf. V. 1, p. 580. MHS; DAR.
Epitaphs of Frederick. Hist. of west. Md. Scharf. V. 1, pp. 524–27. MHS; DAR.
Frederick County tombstone inscriptions. M. A. Gruder. German and Reformed cemeteries; also appendix A from official poll of presidential electors of Frederick County; 207 persons born prior to 1800. Natl. Geneal. Soc. Quart., April and July, 1919, v. 8. MHS.
German Reformed Cemetery, 1794–1862, Middletown Valley (few stones). Earliest birth, 1732. Hist. of west. Md. Scharf. V. 1, p. 578. MHS; DAR.
Jacob Harbaugh cemetery. Mss. MHS.
Moravian Cemetery, Graceham. Murial records. 2 vols. Mss. MHS.
Methodist Protestant Cemetery, 1755–1924, Walkersville. Md. Geneal. Rec. Com., 1932–33. Mss. DAR.
Mt. Olivet Cemetery, Frederick, incorporated 1852. (Partial list.) Md. Geneal. Rec. Com., 1933–34, pp. 179–82; 1934–35, pp. 111–22. Mss. DAR. Many reinterments from other grounds, All Saints Protestant Episcopal; Mt. Calvary Methodist Episcopal; St. John's German Reformed, and others (very early dates). Robt. A. Kemp is Secretary-Treasurer of Mt. Olivet and has records of all transfers.
Mt. Olivet Cemetery. Some graves. Hist. of Frederick County. Williams. V. 1, p. 227. MHS; DAR.
Names on monument in yard of Trinity Church, Frederick (persons buried). Md. Geneal. Rec. Com., 1934–35, p. 110. Mss. DAR.
Old Fundenburg Farm burial ground, 1759–1836, Lewiston. Md. Geneal. Rec. Com., 1932–33. Bd. mss. DAR.
Otterbein United Brethren at Harbaugh Valley. Burial records. Mss. MHS.
St. John's Reformed Church, Sabillasville. Burial records. Mss. MHS.
St. Joseph's Roman Catholic Church cemetery. Mss. MHS.
St. Joseph's Roman Catholic churchyard records, Emmitsburg. Md. O. R. Soc. Bull., May, 1913, no. 3, pp. 64–66. MHS.
United Brethren Cemetery, Sabillasville. H. J. Young. Natl. Geneal. Soc. Quart., Sept., 1938, v. 26, no. 3, p. 61. MHS.

GARRETT COUNTY

Grantsville (old) Cemetery, 1831–80. Hist. of west. Md. Scharf. V. 2, p. 1532. MHS; DAR.
Methodist Episcopal Cemetery, 1847–79, Grantsville District. Hist. of west. Md. Scharf. V. 2, p. 1532. MHS; DAR.

HARFORD COUNTY

Edgewood Arsenal, 1810–63. Mss. MHS.
Tombstone inscriptions. Ms. MHS.
Trap Church burial records. Md. Geneal. Rec. Com., 1934–35, p. 108. Mss. DAR.

HOWARD COUNTY

Ellicott City records, 1820–80. M. H. Mag., 1924, v. 19, p. 200.
Tombstone records, Howard and Montgomery Counties. Ms. MHS.
Mt. Calvary Church burial ground. Md. Geneal. Rec. Com., 1934–35, pp. 95–99. Mss. DAR.

KENT COUNTY

Airy Hill Farm burial ground. Bible rec. of Upper Penins. East. Shore. P. 97. Bd. mss. MHS.
Andover Farm burial ground, Millington. Mss. DAR.
Blackiston churchyard, near Millington. Mss. DAR.
Catholic Cemetery, 1860–1929. Lambson's Station. Md. Geneal. Rec. Com., 1932–33, pp. 262–64. Mss. DAR.
Chestertown Cemetery, 1700–1905 (complete). Md. O. R. Soc. Bull., no. 1, pp. 18–29.
Chesterville Cemetery, 1843–1916. Md. Geneal. Rec. Com., 1932–33, pp. 265–66. Mss. DAR.
Dulaney churchyard, 4 miles east of Massey. Md. Geneal. Rec. Com., 1933–34, pp. 210–12. Mss. DAR.
Holdens Cemetery, 1828–1920, near Millington. Md. Geneal. Rec. Com., 1932, v. 5, p. 211–13. Mss. DAR.
Tombstone inscriptions and marriages, 1796–1802. Mss. MHS.
Millington Cemetery, 1817–1924. Md. Geneal. Rec. Com., 1932–33, pp. 283–301. Mss. DAR.
Old Grove Cemetery, 1806–81. Massey. Md. Geneal. Rec. Com., 1932, v. 5, p. 215. Mss. DAR.
Quaker Cemetery, Millington. Md. Geneal. Rec. Com., 1932–33, p. 209. Mss. DAR.
Shrewsbury churchyard, 1749–1907. Md. O. R. Soc. Bull., no. 2, pp. 46–54. MHS.
Still Pond churchyard and cemetery, 1776–1907 (complete). Md. O. R. Soc. Bull., no. 2, pp. 65–75. MHS.
St. Paul's Protestant Episcopal churchyard, 1735–1905 (complete). Md. O. R. Soc. Bull., no. 2, pp. 54–65. MHS.
Trumpington of Chesapeake, 1729–1853. Md. Geneal. Rec. Com., 1937, p. 203. Mss. DAR.
Wesley Methodist Episcopal Chapel cemetery, Rock Hall, 1816–1924. Md. Geneal. Rec. Com., 1932–33. Mss. DAR.
"Worton Manor" graveyard. Md. O. R. Soc. Bull., no. 2, p. 80. MHS.

MONTGOMERY COUNTY

Baptist Church cemetery, Rockville. Ms. DAR.
Beallsvill epitaphs. Hist. of west. Md. Scharf. V. 1, p. 736. MHS; DAR.
Cemetery near Carroll Chapel, Forest Glen. Md. Geneal. Rec. Com., v. 2, pp. 27–38. Mss. DAR.
Christian Church cemetery, 1813–74, Hyattstown, on Frederick Road. Earliest birth, 1763. Hist. of west. Md. Scharf. V. 1, p. 722. MHS; DAR.

Darnestown Baptist Church, 1846–73. Earliest birth, 1786. Hist. of west. Md. Scharf. V. 1, p. 762. MHS; DAR.

Family burial plots in Momtgomery County. Ms. DAR.

Lay Hill burial ground, between Glenmount and Norwood, on Sandy Spring Road. Md. Geneal. Rec. Com., 1934–35, pp. 66–67. Mss. DAR.

Laytonsville Methodist Episcopal churchyard, 1794–1932. Earliest birth, 1720. Md. Geneal. Rec. Com., 1934–35, pp. 69–82. Mss. DAR.

Methodist Episcopal Cemetery, Boyd Station. Hist. of west. Md. Scharf. V. 1, p. 725. MHS; DAR.

Methodist Episcopal Church, South Cemetery near Poolesville (now adandoned). Md. Geneal. Rec. Com., 1926, v. 2. Mss. DAR.

Monocacy Cemetery, on site of Old St. Peter's Church, 1814–77, Beallsville. Earliest birth, 1762. Hist. of west. Md. Scharf. V. 1, pp. 736–38. MHS; DAR.

1754–1914. Md. Geneal. Rec. Com., 1926–27, v. 2, pp. 70–73. Mss. DAR.

1806–1914. Md. Geneal. Rec. Com., 1925. Mss. DAR.

Cemetery records, Montgomery and Howard Counties. Also: Md. Geneal. Rec. Com., 1934–35, p. 63. Mss. DAR.

Tombstone inscriptions (few). Natl. Geneal. Soc. Quart., April, 1917, no. 6, p. 32. MHS.

Mt. Calvary Church burial ground, Cooksville Pike, near Roxbury Mills, five miles north of Brookeville. Md. Geneal. Rec. Com., 1934. Mss. DAR.

Mt. Carmel burial ground, one mile from Old Triadelphia. Md. Geneal. Rec. Com., 1934–35, p. 85. Mss. DAR.

Old German Baptist church, near Germantown. Md. Geneal. Rec. Com., 1934–35, p. 83. Mss. DAR.

Old Baptist church lot, Rockville (now abandoned). Ms. MHS. Also: M. H. Mag., v. 29, p. 54.

Private cemetery on Humphrey Cissel's farm near Poolesville. Md. Geneal. Rec. Com., v. 2, p. 75. Mss. DAR.

Salem Methodist Protestant Church, 1769–1872. Brookville. Hist. of west. Md. Scharf. V. 1, p. 781. MHS; DAR.

Union Cemetery, 1779–1860, Spencerville (17 stones). Hist. of west. Md. Scharf. V. 1, p. 757. MHS; DAR.

St. John's Roman Catholic Church, 1804–1924 (Carroll Chapel, 1790), Forest Glen. Md. Geneal. Rec. Com., 1927, p. 27. Mss. DAR. Also (incomplete): Hist. of west. Md. Scharf. V. 1, p. 759. MHS; DAR.

Stones on hilltop, near Laytonsville on Hawlings Creek. Md. Geneal. Rec. Com., 1932–33, p. 206. Bd. mss. DAR.

Worthington Place, one mile west of Unity, private burial ground. Md. Geneal. Rec. Com., 1934–35, p. 90. Bd. mss. DAR.

PRINCE GEORGE COUNTY

Marlboro; gravestone inscriptions, near school. Mss. DAR.

Private burying ground, near Berwin, 1806–54 (few stones). Md. O. R. Soc. Bull., no. 1, p. 52. MHS.

St. Barnabas Protestant Episcopal churchyard, Leeland. Typed mss. MHS. Also: Md. Geneal. Rec. Com., 1937–38. Mss. DAR.

QUEEN ANNE COUNTY

Centreville Cemetery, 1815–1905 (incomplete). Md. O. R. Soc. Bull., no. 1, pp. 41–47. MHS.

Crumpton graveyard records. Md. Geneal. Rec. Com., 1933–34, pp. 193–200. Bd. mss. DAR.

Newman's Wharf graveyard. Upper Penins. East. Shore. Pp. 95–96. Bd. ms. MHS.

Queen Anne County records. Mss. MHS.

Queenstown Cemetery, 1760–1835, Queenstown (few stones). Md. O. R. Soc. Bull., no. 1, p. 53. MHS.

Ring's End private burying ground, near Millington. Md. Geneal. Rec. Com., 1933–34, p. 203. Mss. DAR.

ST. MARY'S COUNTY

Corn Field Harbor. Md. O. R. Soc. Bull., no. 3, p. 57. MHS.

Ellenborough burial ground, near Leonardtown, 1771–1867 (few stones). Md. O. R. Soc. Bull., no. 2, pp. 80–81. MHS.

*St. Mary's County, list of dead, 1806–43. Archives of Georgetown Univ., Wash., D. C., v. 138. 1.

"The Plains," St. Mary's County, tombstone records. Chronicles of colonial Md. Thomas. MHS; DAR.

SOMERSET COUNTY

Tombstone inscriptions, Somerset County. Mss. MHS.

St. Andrews Protestant Episcopal churchyard, Princess Anne, 1788–1905. Md. O. R. Soc. Bull., no. 1, pp. 29–32. MHS.

Princes Anne and Snow Hill records (miscellaneous), 1816–1913. Turner Geneal. Coll. Mss. MHS.

Rehobeth Protestant Episcopal churchyard, oldest stone, 1748. Md. Geneal. Rec. Com., Lines, 1937. Md. mss. DAR.

TALBOT COUNTY

Talbot County tombstone inscriptions. Ms. MHS.

Spring Hill Cemetery, 1800–91, Easton (incomplete). Md. O. R. Soc. Bull., no. 1, pp. 35–41. MHS.

WASHINGTON COUNTY

Antietam National Cemetery, East Sharpsburg (4667 graves). List of Maryland soldiers, 1862–64. Hist. of west. Md. Scharf. V. 2, p. 1213. MHS; DAR.

Beard's Lutheran graveyard, 1810–1900, Chewsville District. First birth, 1758. Md. Geneal. Rec. Com., 1935–36. Bd. mss. DAR.

Boonsboro public cemetery, 1818–81. Earliest birth, 1763. Hist. of west. Md. Scharf. V. 2, p. 1265. MHS; DAR.

Brethren in Christ or River Brethren Church (only one in Md.), 1821–77, Village of Ringgold. Earliest birth, 1775; few stones. Hist. of west. Md. Scharf. V. 2, p. 1292. MHS; DAR.

Catholic Cemetery, 1822–79, W. Bethel Street, Hagerstown. Earliest birth, 1768. Hist. of west. Md. Scharf. V. 2, p. 1098. MHS; DAR.

Church of Disciples, 1817–72, Hagerstown. Earliest birth, 1777. Hist. of west. Md. Scharf. V. 2, p. 1099. MHS; DAR.

Disciples of Christ Church, 1846–79, Beaver Creek. Earliest birth, 1781 (fragmentary). Hist. of west. Md. Scharf. V. 2, p. 1300. MHS; DAR.

Fahrney's Cemetery, 1815–69, Smoketown, Beaver Creek District. Earliest birth, 1763. Hist. of west. Md. Scharf. V. 2, pp. 1301–02. MHS; DAR.

Fairview Cemetery, 1814–80, Keedysville. Earliest birth, 1771. Hist. of west. Md. Scharf. V. 2, pp. 1306–07. MHS; DAR.

Funkstown public cemetery, 1782–1881. Earliest birth, 1741. Hist. of west. Md. Scharf. V. 2, pp. 1282–84. MHS; DAR.

Hagerstown tombstone inscriptions, 1754–?. M. A. Gruder (Washington, D. C.: copyrighted). Hagerstown Cemetery (118); Lutheran Cemetery (302); Reformed Cemetery (59). Natl. Geneal. Soc. Quart., 1919, v. 8, nos. 1 and 2. MHS.

Hancock cemeteries, 1822–80. Earliest birth, 1786. Hist. of west. Md. Scharf. V. 2, p. 1253. MHS; DAR.

Mennonite Cemetery, 1798–1877, Mangansville. Hist. of west. Md. Scharf. V. 2, p. 1290. MHS; DAR.

Mt. Hebron United Brethren Cemetery, Keedysville District. Hist. of west. Md. Scharf. V. 2, p. 1307. MHS; DAR.

Mt. Tabor United Brethren Cemetery, 1855–79 (fragmentary). Hist. of west. Md. Scharf. V. 2, pp. 1290–91. MHS; DAR.

Mt. Vernon Reformed Cemetery, in Fairview Cemetery, Keedysville District. Hist. of west. Md. Scharf. V. 2, p. 1306. MHS; DAR.

New Mennonite or Franzite Church (only one in Md.), 1824–80, Ringgold District, near Pennsylvania state line. Earliest birth, 1764. Hist. of west. Md. Scharf. V. 2, p. 1292. MHS; DAR.

Rose Hill Cemetery, 1800–76, Clear Spring (5 stones). Hist. of west. Md. Scharf. V. 2, p. 1250. MHS; DAR.

Rose Hill Cemetery, 1806–79, Hagerstown. Earliest birth, 1759. Hist. of west. Md. Scharf. V. 2, pp. 1100–02. MHS; DAR.

Trinity Church Cemetery, 1824–78, Smithsburg. Hist. of west. Md. Scharf. V. 2, p. 1274. MHS; DAR.

United Brethren Cemetery, 1789–1876, Chewsville. Hist. of west. Md. Scharf. V. 2, p. 1305. MHS; DAR.

Williamsport Cemetery, 1764–75. Hist. of west. Md. Scharf. V. 2, pp. 1221–22. MHS; DAR.

Winebrennerian Church cemetery, 1844–75, Cearfoss (few stones). Hist. of west. Md. Scharf. V. 2, p. 1291. MHS; DAR. (John Winebrenner, born in Frederick, 1797; died in Harrisburg Pa., 1860; established new denomination, which he called "Church of God", 1830; members known as Winebrennerians; he became its first Bishop.)

Zion Reformed Church, 1770, Hagerstown. Burial ground records (complete copy), 1713–1920. One record, 15 pp. 581 items. Md. Geneal. Rec. Com., 1934–35, p. 31. Mss. DAR.

WORCESTER COUNTY

All Hallows Protestant Episcopal churchyard, 1786–1928, Snow Hill. First birth, 1717. Tombstone inscriptions of Worcester County. Hudson. Bd. mss. MHS; DAR. Also: Md. Geneal. Rec. Com., 1935–36, p. 24. Md. mss. DAR.

Baptist Cemetery, Pocomoke City. Tombstone inscriptions of Worcester County. Hudson. Bd. mss. MHS; DAR.

Bates Memorial Methodist. Old burial grounds of Worcester County. Md. Geneal. Rec. Com., Lines, 1937. Bd. mss. DAR.

Berlin churchyard. C. H. B. Turner Geneal. Coll. 2 vols. Mss. MHS.

Buckingham Presbyterian churchyard, Berlin. Tombstone inscriptions of Worcester County. Hudson. Bd. mss. MHS; DAR.

Evergreen Cemetery, undenominational, about one mile southeast of Berlin. Tombstone inscriptions of Worcester County. Hudson. Bd. mss. MHS; DAR.

Graveyard, Bishopville. Tombstone inscriptions of Worcester County. Hudson. Bd. mss. MHS; DAR.

Makemie Memorial churchyard, 1754–1831, Snow Hill. Tombstone inscriptions of Worcester County. Hudson. Bd. mss. MHS; DAR.
Old burial grounds of Worcester County. Md. Geneal. Rec. Com., Lines, 1937. Bd. mss. DAR.

Methodist Episcopal Cemetery, Pocomoke. Tombstone inscriptions of Worcester County. Hudson. Bd. mss. MHS; DAR.

Methodist Episcopal churchyard, Snow Hill. Tombstone inscriptions of Worcester County. Hudson. Bd. mss. MHS; DAR.
Old burial grounds of Worcester County. Md. Geneal. Rec. Com., Lines, 1937. Bd. mss. DAR.

Methodist Protestant Cemetery, Pocomoke City. Tombstone inscriptions of Worcester County. Hudson. Bd. mss. MHS; DAR.

Methodist Protestant Cemetery, Snow Hill. Tombstone inscriptions of Worcester County. Hudson. Mss. MHS; DAR.

Mt. Olive Methodist Protestant. Old burial grounds of Worcester County. Md. Geneal. Rec. Com., Lines, 1937. Bd. mss. DAR.

Mt. Zion, Protestant. Old burial grounds of Worcester County. Md. Geneal. Rec. Com., Lines, 1937. Bd. mss. DAR.

New cemetery, Bishopville. Tombstone inscriptions of Worcester County. Hudson. Bd. mss. MHS; DAR.

Newark (Queponco) Cemetery. Tombstone inscriptions of Worcester County. Hudson. Mss. MHS; DAR.

Old burial grounds of Worcester County. Mrs. Edna P. Lines. Md. Geneal. Rec. Com., 1937. Bd. mss. DAR.

Old cemetery (known as Levin D. Collins). Tombstone inscriptions of Worcester County. Hudson. Bd. mss. MHS; DAR.

Pocomoke Presbyterian churchyard, Pocomoke. Tombstone inscriptions of Worcester County. Hudson. Bd. mss. MHS; DAR.

Rehobeth Protestant Episcopal churchyard. Old burial grounds of Worcester County. Md. Geneal. Rec. Com., Lines, 1937. Bd. mss. DAR.

Rehobeth Presbyterian churchyard. Old burial grounds of Worcester County. Md. Geneal. Rec. Com., Lines, 1937. Bd. mss. DAR.
Riverside Cemetery, Libertytown. Tombstone inscriptions of Worcester County. Hudson. Bd. mss. MHS; DAR.
Sinepuxent Presbyterian Cemetery, near Berlin. Tombstone inscriptions of Worcester County. Hudson. Bd. mss. MHS; DAR.
Snow Hill and Princess Anne miscellaneous tombstone records, 1816–1913. C. H. B. Turner Geneal. Coll. Mss. MHS.
Southern Baptist Cemetery records, between Snow Hill and Pocomoke. Old burial grounds of Worcester County. Md. Geneal. Rec. Com., Lines, 1937. Bd. mss. DAR.
St. Martin's Protestant Episcopal (from old book). Burials and marriages. Old burial grounds of Worcester County. Md. Geneal. Rec. Com., Lines, 1937. Bd. mss. DAR.
St. Mary's Protestant Episcopal churchyard, Pocomoke City. Tombstone inscriptions of Worcester County. Hudson. Bd. mss. MHS; DAR.
St. Paul's Protestant Episcopal churchyard, Berlin. Tombstone inscriptions of Worcester County. Hudson. Bd. mss. MHS; DAR.
Old burial grounds of Worcester County. Md. Geneal. Rec. Com., Lines, 1937. Bd. mss. DAR.
Tombstone inscriptions of Worcester County. M. F. Hudson. Bd. mss. MHS; DAR.
Whaley Cemetery, Whaleyvill. Tombstone inscriptions of Worcester County. Hudson. Bd. mss. MHS; DAR.
Zion Methodist Episcopal or St. Martin's Church cemetery, East Bishopville. Tombstone inscriptions of Worcester County. Hudson. Bd. mss. MHS; DAR.

CENSUS, LISTS, COMMISSIONS, ETC.

GENERAL

Census of 1790: 12 original states available. DAR.
Kentucky. Census (19) of various counties, 1810. Mrs. A. K. Burns. Mss. DAR.
Maine census, 1790. DAR.
Massachusetts census, 1790. DAR.
North Carolina census, 1790. DAR.
Ohio, Green County, census of 1820. Natl. Geneal. Soc. Quart., v. 5; Dec., 1936, v. 26, p. 126.
Ohio, Homes County, census, 1830. D. A. R. Mag., April, 1934, v. 68, no. 4, pp. 250–51; no. 8, p. 504.
Pennsylvania census, 1790. MHS.
Rhode Island census, 1790. MHS.
Tennessee census, 1820 (8 counties). DAR.
Virginia census, 1624–25. Va. Mag. Hist. and Biog., 1900, v. 7. MHS.
Virginia census, 1790. DAR.

CENSUS OF MARYLAND

Census, Allegany County, 1800. 1936, typed, bd. DAR.
Census, City of Annapolis and Anne Arundel County, April 25, 1801. Mimeog. copy. MHS.
Census (Provincial), Anne Arundel County, 1776, including All Hallows' and St. James Parishes. Mss. Hall of Records.
Md. records. Brumbaugh. V. 1, pp. 407–31. MHS; DAR.
Census, Anne Arundel County, 1800. 1936, typed, bd. DAR.
Census, Baltimore City, 1800. R. E. L. Hall. 1937, typed, bd. DAR.
Census, Baltimore County, 1800, burned.
Census, Calvert County, 1800. 1936, typed, bd. DAR.
Census, Caroline County, 1776 (700 men), 18 or more years old. 1939, typed, bd. DAR.
Census, Caroline County, 1776. Bridge Town Hundred. Md. records. Brumbaugh. V. 2, pp. 79–85.
Census, Caroline County, 1776. Bridgetown Hundred. Ms. Hall of Records.
Census, Caroline County, 1800. 1936, typed, bd. DAR.
Census, Cecil County, 1800. 1937, typed, bd. DAR.
Census (constable's), Charles County, 1775–78. (1800 persons.) Md. records. Brumbaugh. V. 1, pp. 297–312.
Census, Charles County, 1800. 1937, typed, bd. DAR.
Census, Dorchester County, 1776. Nantacoake, Straight's and Transquakin Hundreds. Md. records. Brumbaugh. V. 2, pp. 87–110.
Census, Dorchester County, 1800. 1936, typed, bd. DAR.
Census, Fells' Point or Deptford Hundred, Baltimore City, 1776. (130 names.) M. H. Mag., Mar., 1930, v. 25, pp. 271–74.
Census (Provincial), Frederick County, 1776. Md. records. Brumbaugh. V. 1, pp. 177–257.
Census, Frederick County, 1790. Hist. of Frederick Co. Williams. V. 1, pp. 623–47. MHS; DAR.
Census, Frederick County, 1800. 1936, typed, 226 pp. DAR.
Census, Harford County, 1776. Broad Creek, Bush River Lower, Deer Creek, Harford Lower, Spesutia Lower and Susquehanna Hundreds. Md. records. Brumbaugh. V. 2, pp. 113–94. Mss. Hall of Records.
Census, Harford County, 1800. 1937, typed, bd. DAR.
Census, Kent County, 1800. 1936, typed, bd. DAR.
Census (first), Maryland, 1790. Heads of families. Baltimore City and County, alphabetical. Wash., D. C., Government Printing Office, 1907. Lib. Cong.; MHS; DAR.
Census, Maryland, North Carolina, South Carolina and Virginia, 1790. DAR.
Census, Maryland, 1790. (Allegheny County missing.)
Census, Maryland, 1790. (Calvert County missing.)
Census, Maryland, 1790. (Somerset County missing.)
Census (Provincial), Prince George County, August 31, 1776. (St. John's and Prince George's Parishes.) Mss. Hall of Records.
Md. records. Brumbaugh. V. 1, pp. 1–89.

Census, Prince George County, 1800. 1936, typed, bd. DAR.
Census, Montgomery County, 1800. 1936, typed, bd. DAR.
Census, Queen Anne County, 1776. Kent Island, Town, Upper and Wye Hundreds. Mss. lists. Hall of Records.
Md. records. Brumbaugh. V. 2, pp. 197-214.
Census, Queen Anne County, 1800. 1936, typed, bd. DAR.
Census, St. Mary County, 1800. R. E. L. Hall. 1937, typed, bd. DAR.
Census, Somerset County, 1800. 1937, typed, bd. DAR.
Census, Talbot County, 1776. Bay, Mill, and Tuckahoe Hundreds. Mss lists. Hall of Records.
Md. records. Brumbaugh. V. 2, pp. 217-30.
Census, Talbot County, 1800. 1937, typed, bd. DAR.
Census, Washington County, 1776. Elizabeth Hundred (formerly Frederick County). Md. records. Brumbaugh. V. 1, p. 235.
Census, Washington County, 1800. 1937, typed, bd. DAR.
Census, Worcester County, 1800. 1937, typed, bd. DAR.
Population, Maryland, 1775. Mss. Lib. Cong.

COMMISSIONS, LISTS, DIRECTORIES, ETC., IN MARYLAND

Adjutants general, 1794-1920. Md. manual. 1933, p. 376. MHS.
American medical directory. 1925, 9th edition.
Assembly men of Maryland, 1649. Day-Star of Amer. Freedom. Davis. 1855.
Attorneys general of Maryland, 1778-1931. Md. manual. 1933, p. 376.
Authors who have lived and worked in Maryland. Bernard C. Steiner. Typed list in Md. Room, Enoch Pratt Lib.; pub. in Sun, Sunday, Oct. 27, 1908.
Baltimore City business directory, 1889-90. Issued by R. L. Polk and Co., Balto., 1889.
Baltimore City directories, 1796-date. MHS; Enoch Pratt Lib.; Peabody Lib.
Baltimore City directory, 1807. James McHenry. 1807. MHS.
Baltimore commanders of privateers engaged in South American enterprises, 1794. Hist. of Md. Scharf. V. 2, p. 582.
Baltimore directory. Cary Geneal. Coll. Mss. MHS.
Baltimore society directory, 1878. Names of 5000 women. Balto., H. Durfee Co., 1878. MHS.
Baltimore Town, 1797. Incorporated to divide city into eight wards. List of councilmen. Chronicles of Balto. Scharf. P. 280.
Baltimore tradesmen and merchants, April 11, 1789. Photos. MHS.
Barons of Baltimore and lords proprietary of Maryland, 1632-1776. Mss. list, prepared by Bernard Steiner. Enoch Pratt Lib.
Md. Manual. 1933, pp. 360-65.
Hist. of Md. Scharf. V. 3, p. 776.
Hist. of Balto. City and Co. Scharf. P. 195.
Blue book. Society visiting list. Pub. annually, Balto., 1888-date.
Business directory and Baltimore almanac. D. H. Craig. 1842. Enoch Pratt Lib.
Cabinet appointments from Maryland. (From James McHenry, Jan., 1796, to Chas. J. Bonaparte, Dec., 1906.) Md. manual, 1933, p. 380.
Cabinet appointments, 1796-1869. Hist. of Md. Scharf. V. 3, p. 775.
Caroline County. Poll list, 2nd district, 1800. Ms. MHS.
Chancellors of Maryland, 1777-1854. Hist. of Md. Scharf. V. 3, p. 760.
Civil list, 1641. Henry Hollyday Goldsborough. Md. Geneal. Bull., v. 11, no. 2, p. 18. MHS; DAR.
Civil Officers of Maryland, 1637-1888. Hon. Henry Holliday Goldsborough. Mss, 4 vols. MHS. Also ms. notes, in back of book of Hanson's Laws of Md., in MHS.
1638-1759. Md. Geneal. Rec. Com., 1932-33. Mss. DAR.
William and Mary Quart., first series, v. 5, pp. 47-50, 131-34.
Civil officers of State, 1777-98 (original), from Governor's (Thomas Johnson) and Council Proceedings. Hall of Records.
Commission book, 82, 1733-73. Record book of Council of Maryland. M. H. Mag., 1931, v. 26, pp. 138-58, 244-63, 342-61; 1932, v. 27, pp. 29-36.
Commission book (original), 1743-45. Ms. MHS.
Commission books, 1812-38. 6 vols. Hall of Records.
Commissioners of Anne Arundel County, 1650. Hist. of Md. Scharf. V. 1, p. 206.
Commissioners of Land Office, from John Lewger, 1637, to G. G. Brewer, 1827. Md. manual. 1933, p. 379. (Land Office created 1680, with register in Eastern and in Western Shore. Eastern Shore office abolished 1841, and transfered to Western Shore. Office of Commissioner of Land Office created 1851.)
Commissions, 1753-61. Calvert Papers. Mss. MHS.
Commissions, civil appointments, 1825-39. Hall of Records.
Commissions issued by Lord Proprietary and Governor, 1733-50, 1761-73. Hall of Records.
Commissions issued by Provincial Court, 1726-86. Hall of Records.
Mss. copy, indexed, typed, bd. MHS.
Congressmen from Maryland, 1789-1933. Md. manual. 1933, p. 385.
Coroners of Maryland. Hist. of Md. Scharf. V. 3, p. 760. MHS.
Delegates to Colonial Congress. Hist. of Md. Scharf. V. 1, pp. 537-38.
Delegates, 1765. Hist. of Md. Scharf. V. 3, p. 752. MHS.
Md. manual. 1933, p. 381. MHS; DAR.
Deputies elected to Provincial Conventions Meeting, Annapolis, 1774-76, of Baltimore Town, and various counties of Md. Hist. of Md. Scharf. Pp. 150-86.
Md. manual. 1933, pp. 365-66.
Chesapeake Bay country. Earle. P. 284.
Directory of Frederick City and County, 1886 (business directory). C. W. Miller. DAR.
Directory of Mongomery County, 1650-1879. T. H. S. Boyd. 1879. DAR.
Duellists of Maryland, 1781-1852. Hist. of Md. Scharf. V. 3, p. 85. MHS.

Early Maryland apothecary, 1638–85. R. H. Swain, Jr. Pamph. MHS.
Early medicine in Maryland. T. S. Cullen. Brief mention of names connected with its history. 1927. Enoch Pratt Lib.
Electors of Presidents and Vice-Presidents from Baltimore City, 1789–1881. Hist. of Balto. City and Co. Scharf. P. 195.
Executive officers (chief) of Maryland, during Provincial period; with commissions and dates of commissions. M. H. Mag., 1912, v. 7, pp. 321–28.
Governor's council, 1776–1837. Md. manual. 1933, pp. 372–74.
Governors of Maryland, 1633–1875. Hist. of Md. Scharf. V. 3, p. 776. MHS.
  Governors, 1777–1933. Md. manual. 1933. MHS; DAR.
Judges of Court of Appeals of Maryland, 1778–1926. Md. manual. 1933, pp. 377–79.
  Judges, 1778–1924. M. H. Mag., 1925, v. 20, pp. 375–78.
  Judges, 1778–1806. Hist. of Md. Scharf. V. 3, p. 773. MHS.
Judges of General Court, 1777–1808. Hist. of Md. Scharf. V. 3, p. 756. MHS.
Justices of county courts, 1790. Hist. of Md. Scharf. V. 2, pp. 573–75.
  Justices, 1777. Hist. of Md. Scharf. V. 3, pp. 757–58.
Justices of Orphans Courts, 1777. Hist. of Md. Scharf. V. 3, p. 759.
Justices of Supreme Court, 1836–61. Hist. of Md. Scharf. V. 3, p. 775.
Justices of United States District Court, 1789–1880. Hist. of Md. Scharf. V. 3, p. 775.
Justices of United States Supreme Court from Maryland, 1789–1864. Md. manual. 1933, p. 381.
Librarians of Maryland, 1827–1931. Md. manual. 1933, p. 380.
List of board of trustees, 1696, of King William School, Annapolis, established 1694. (Progenitor of St. John's College, 1784; consolidated, 1786.) Ancient City. Riley. P. 40.
  Founders of Anne Arundel and Howard Co. Warfield. P. 219.
  King William's School. Fell. 1894, p. 40.
List of civil officers of Maryland, 1749–1891. Ms.
List of distinguished Marylanders who claim St. John's College as their alma mater, 1789–95. (First name on register is Right Rev. Thomas J. Claggett, D.D., First Bishop of Protestant Episcopal Church, consecrated on American soil.) M. H. Mag., v. 29, no. 4, p. 305.
List of executive officers of Maryland, during Provisional period. M. H. Mag., Sept., 1912, v. 7, no. 3, p. 321.
List of Huguenot refugees in America. Monette Book. P. 35. MHS.
List of members of Legislature of Maryland, whose names or families have been mentioned, 1674–1768, from Annapolis and Charles, Cecil, Dorchester, Kent, Queen Anne, Somerset, Talbot and Worcester Counties. Old Kent. Hanson. Pp. 380–83.
List of those who governed Maryland before it was made royal province. B. C. Steiner. Pa. Mag. Hist. and Biog., 1898, v. 22. MHS.

EARLY SETTLERS OF AMERICA; PASSENGERS; SHIPS

American colonists in English records, 1597–1773. Guide to direct references in authentic passenger lists, not in Hottens, etc. George Sherwood, 210 Strand W.C., London. First series, 1932; second series, 1933. MHS; DAR.
Clipper ships of America and Great Britain, 1833–69. Thirty-seven wood engravings by Jacques La Grange. Text by Helen La Grange. N. Y., G. P. Putnam and Sons, 1936.
Colonial ships and their masters. Md. O. R. Soc. Bull., 1913, no. 3, pp. 27–33. MHS.
Early eighteenth century palatine emigration. W. A. Knittle. 1937. DAR.
Emigrants from England, 1773–76. Repr. from New Eng. Hist. and Geneal. Reg., 1913.
Emigrants from England to America, 1774–75. Gerald Fothergill, London, Eng. New Eng. Hist. Reg., v. 62, pp. 320–32; v. 63, pp. 16–31 134–46, 234–44, 342–55; v. 64, pp. 18–25, 106–15, 214–27; 314–26; v. 65, pp. 20–35, 116–32, 232–51. To Md.: v. 62, pp. 321–32; v. 63, pp. 18–19, 22–26, 134, 144, 234–40; 342–48, 354; v. 64, pp. 19–23, 25, 106–09, 112–15, 214, 220–21, 321–26; v. 65, pp. 21–31, 33–35, 117–22, 125–32; 232–43. MHS.
Emigrants from Liverpool, 1697–1707. Repr. from New Eng. Hist. and Geneal. Reg., 1913.
Emigrants from Scotland to America, 1774–75. Viola R. Cameron. N. Y., 1930.
Emigrants' guide to western and southwestern States and territories. W. Darby. 1818. DAR.
Emigrant ministers to America, of Church of England, from December, 1690 to 1811. Alphabetical list of 1200 names. (Many born in Colonies and returned to England for Holy Orders.) Gerald Fothergill. London, 1904. MHS.
German element in United States. Albert B. Faust. N. Y., Houghton Mifflin Co., 1909, 2 vols.
German emigration to American Colonies, its cause and distributing of emigrants. Pa. Mag. Hist. and Biog., 1886, v. 10, pts. 1, 2, pp. 241, 375.
German immigration into Pennsylvania, through Port of Philadelphia, 1700–75. German Soc. Proceedings, 1896, v. 7.
Grandchildren of Mayflower passengers. Complete list. Natl. Geneal. Soc. Quart., Oct., 1915, v. 4, pp. 37–41, 54–57; v. 5, pp. 6–10, 20–23; corrections and additions, v. 5, p. 23; v. 10, pp. 125–27; v. 11, pp. 1–2.
History of Mennonites emigration to Pennsylvania. Pa. Mag. Hist. and Biog., v. 2, p. 117.
History of Huguenot emigration in America. C. W. Baird. N. Y., Dodd, Mead and Co., 1885, 2 vols. DAR.
*Huguenot emigration to Virginia, and settlements at Manakin, with appendix of genealogies, Chastian, Cocke, Dupuy, Fontaine, Marye, Maury, Traub and other families. R. A. Brock. Pub. Va. Hist. Soc., Richmond, 1886, new series, v. 5, no. 1.
Huguenots in America, with special reference in their emigration to Pennsylvania. A. Stapleton. 1901. MHS.
Immigrants to Pennsylvania, 1727–76. Collection of 30,000 names of German, Swiss, Dutch, French and others, with names of ships, date of

sailing, date of arrival in Philadelphia. Chronologically arranged. I. D. Rupp. 1927, 2nd edition. MHS; DAR.

Immigrants to Pennsylvania, 1726–76. Rupp. Index to same, Ernest Wecken. 1931. DAR.

Immigrants to Pennsylvania (30,000 names). Natl. Geneal. Soc. Quart., 1929, v. 17, p. 8.

Immigration of Irish Quakers into Pennsylvania, 1682–1750. A. C. Myers. Swarthmore College, Swarthmore, 1902.

Koger index of 3000 immigrants, 1727–76, German, Dutch and French into Pennsylvania. DAR.

List of emigrants from Liverpool, 1697–1707, copied by Miss Elizabeth French. New Eng. Hist. Reg., v. 64, pp. 158–66, 252–63 (some to Md.). MHS.

Lists of emigrants to all Colonies, before 1750. Mag. Amer. Geneal., Institute of Amer. Geneal., Chicago.

List of foreigners who arrived in Philadelphia, 1791–92. Pa. Archives, second series, v. 17.

List of foreigners who arrived in Philadelphia, 1791–92 (additional to those printed in Pa. Archives, second series, v. 17). Pa. Mag. Hist. and Biog., v. 24, pp. 187–94, 334–42.

List of Swiss emigrants. Pa. Mag. Hist. and Biog., 1926, v. 5, pp. 191–92.

List of Swiss emigrants. N. Y. Geneal. and Biog. Rec., Apr., 1926, v. 57, no. 2, p. 198.

List of Swiss emigrants in eighteenth century, to American Colonies, Zurich, 1734–44. From Archives of Switzerland. Albert B. Faust. Geneal. Pub. Natl. Geneal. Soc. Quart., Wash., D. C., 1920, v. 1.

List of Swiss emigrants (over 2310) in eighteenth century, to American Colonies. From State Archives of Bern and Basel, Switzerland, 1734–44. A. B. Faust and G. M. Brumbaugh. Geneal. Pub. Natl. Geneal. Soc. Quart., Wash., D. C., 1925, v. 2. MHS; DAR.

Mayflower passengers. Colonial families of United States of Amer. Mackenzie. V. 5, pp. 607–14. MHS; DAR.

Natl. Cyc. Amer. Biog. Berby. 1906, p. 144. Peabody Lib.

(104 passengers.) Natl. Geneal. Soc. Quart., Oct., 1917, v. 6, no. 3, p. 56.

Memoranda in regard to several hundred emigrants to Virginia during Colonial period. W. G. Stanard. Richmond, 1915, 2nd edition, enlarged.

Moravian immigration, 1734–65. Pa. Mag. Hist. and Biog., v. 33, pp. 228–48.

Moravian immigration, 1742–63. English and German settlers (500) who came through Port of New York. 1899.

Original list of persons of quality, 1600–1700. Emigrants, religious exiles, political rebels, serving men sold for term of years, etc., from Great Britain to America, giving ages, location in Mother Country, name of ships they embarked on, etc. J. C. Hotten. N. Y., 1874, 580 pp. Repr. from mss. in State Paper Dept., of Her Majesty Public Record Office, London, 1874, 1931. MHS; DAR; Enoch Pratt Lib.

Partial list of families who arrived in Philadelphia, 1682–1787. From mss. in Pa. Hist. Soc. Pa. Mag. Hist. and Biog., v. 8, pp. 328–40.

Passenger lists, bibliography, passenger ships coming to North America, 1607–1825. A. H. Lancour. N. Y., N. Y. Pub. Lib., 1937, 24 pp. DAR.

Passenger lists, 1620–1836; passengers bound for what is now the United States. Filing case, drawer A, DAR.

Passenger ships to America, 1803–06. Gerald Fothergill. New Eng. Hist. Reg., v. 60, pp. 23–28, 160–64, 240–43, 346–49; v. 61, pp. 133–39, 265–70, 347–53; v. 62, pp. 78–81, 168–71; v. 66, pp. 30, 306. To Md., v. 60, pp. 163, 240–41; v. 62, p. 168. MHS.

Protestant exiles from France. D. C. Agnew. London, 1871.

Record of names of passengers on Good Ship *Mayflower*, Dec., 1620. H. Folger. Pamph. DAR.

Register of officers and agents, civil, military and naval in service of United States, Sept. 30, 1825. Together with names, force and condition of all vessels, belonging to United States, when and where built. Wash., D. C., 1825. MHS.

Register of persons who journeyed, 1709, from Germany to America. U. Simmendinger. 1934. DAR.

Scotch Irish. Scot in northern Britain, northern Ireland and North America. New York and London, The Knickerbocker Press, G. P. Putman's Sons, 1900, vols. 1 and 2.

Scotch Irish in Amerca. H. J. Ford.

Scotch Irish in America. S. W. Green. Worcester, Mass., 1895.

Scotch-Irish pioneers in Ulster and America. Chas. K. Bolton. 1910.

Ships and their masters of Colonial period, 1751–56. Md. O. R. Soc., v. 3, pp. 27–33. MHS.

Virginia immigrants, 1623–66. G. C. Greer. DAR.

Washington, D. C., Bureau of Immigration. See for information on vessels, crew, owners and passenger lists.

Welcome passengers, 1682 (William Penn). Natl. Cyc. Amer. Biog. Berby. 1906, p. 145. Peabody Lib.

Welsh emigration to Pennsylvania. Pa. Mag. Hist. and Biog., 1877, v. 1. MHS.

EARLY SETTLERS OF MARYLAND; PASSENGERS; SHIPS

Alphabetical record of arrival of ships in Province of Maryland, 1634–79. Original mss. Hall of Records.

M. H. Mag., 1910, v. 5, pp. 339–41.

Baltimore customs, 1780–1933. Entrances and clearances. Port of Chester, Harve de Grace and others.

Baltimore immigration, Baltimore City register. Proceeding list entered by authority of Charter and public local laws of Baltimore City, 1927. Page 327, section 519. Filed in Bureau of Archives, fourth floor, City Hall. Number of foreign passengers arriving in port of Baltimore, 1833–74. Ledger record giving name of vessel, country of origin, port of sailing, total number of passengers on vessel and number under five years. List filed by ships' masters containing name of ship, number of passengers, occupation, origin, destination, sex, from 1833–66. Bureau of Archives, City Hall, Baltimore.

Baltimore. Privateers (248), name, captain, owner, date of commission, 1777–83. Hist. of Balto. City and Co. Scharf. Pp. 100–03.

Log of *Chasseur*. Town journal of Com. Thomas Bogle. M. H. Mag., 1906, v. 1, pp. 168–80, 218–40.

Early comers to Province. Georgians in Anne Arundel County. Atlanta Journal, Sept. 22, 1906. Newsp. clipp. File case, MHS.

Early settlers of Allegany County, 1788, located on lands lying west of Fort Cumberland. Hist. of west. Md. Scharf. V. 2, p. 1343.
Hist. of Cumberland. Lowdermilk. P. 264. MHS; DAR.

Early settlers of Anne Arundel County, with land grants, 1651–63. Hist. of Anne Arundel Co. Riley. 1905. MHS; DAR.

Early settlers of Baltimore. Chronicles of Balto. Scharf. Settlers, 1659, pp. 9–11; settlers, 1756–59, pp. 49–54; settlers, 1771, p. 71; settlers, 1778, p. 170; settlers, 1783, p. 209; settlers, 1793, p. 267. MHS.

Early settlers of Calvert Co., 1700. Monette Book. Pp. 240–51. MHS.

Early settlers of Cecil County. Brief notes on Augustine Herman, Col. Nathaniel Utie, Col. Thomas Cresap, and the Hollingsworth, Key, Lee, Mauldin, Ramsay, Rudulph and Talbot Families. Patriotic Marylander, v. 1, no. 4. MHS; DAR.

Early settlers of Creagerstown, Graceham and Monocacy, Frederick County. First settlement of Germans in Md. Schultz. Pp. 16, 23, 24. MHS.

List of early settlers (Moravians) in village of Graceham, Frederick Co. Pa. Germans in settlement of Md. Nead. MHS; DAR.

Early settlers (English speaking) in Frederick County. Hist. of Frederick Co. Williams. V. 1, pp. 10–11. MHS; DAR.

Early settlers (pioneer German families) in Frederick County. Hist. of Frederick Co. Williams. V. 1, p. 8. MHS; DAR.

Early settlers of Maryland 1633–80. (20,000 names.) Indexed. Ms. Land Office.

Early settlers list. Mss. MHS; DAR.
Md. Geneal. Bull., vols. 1–8. MHS; DAR.

Early settlers of Maryland 1639–1707 (1000 names), with their earliest land surveys, from Lord Baltimore's rent, in various counties of Maryland. Sidelights on Md. hist. Richardson. V. 1, pp. 287–355. MHS; DAR.

Early settlers of Maryland. Culver. M. H. Mag., 1917, v. 12, p. 198.

Early settlers, Maryland. (Land records, etc.) Liber A. B. H. A. W. Burns. 1936, pamph. DAR.

Early settlers of Maryland. (Land records, etc.) Liber W. C. 2. A. W. Burns. 1937. Mss. DAR.

Early settlers and surveys of Allegany County, 1774. Hist. of Allegany Co. Thomas and Williams. V. 1, pp. 3–9. MHS; DAR.

Early settlers of site of Havre de Grace, 1658. Wm. Marye. M. H. Mag., 1918, v. 13, no. 3, p. 197.

Early settlers of Williamsburg District, 1746–1900. Hist. of Dorchester Co. Jones. P. 97. MHS; DAR.

Emigrants to America, 1699. Gerald H. Fothergill. New Eng. Hist. and Geneal. Register, v. 64, pp. 260, 262. (To Md.) MHS.

Emigrants to America, 1774–75. Gerald H. Fothergill. New Eng. Hist. and Geneal. Register, v. 63, pp. 18, 22–26, 130–32, 134, 144, 234–35, 237–41, 337–43, 346–48; v. 64, pp. 19–20, 22, 25, 106, 108–09, 112, 114–15, 214, 220–23, 235, 321–23, 324–26; v. 65, pp. 21, 22–26, 29, 30, 31, 33, 117, 119–21, 125, 128–32, 144, 232–33, 235–38, 243. Over 50 vessels. (To Md.) MHS.

Emigrants to America, 1803. Gerald H. Fothergill. New Eng. Hist. and Geneal. Register, v. 60, pp. 163–240, 247. (To Md.) MHS.

Emigrants to America, 1804. Gerald H. Fothergill. New Eng. Hist. and Geneal. Register, v. 61, p. 347; v. 62, p. 168. (To Md.) MHS.

Entry book, 1771. 1 vol. Hall of Records.

Families living in Cambridge, 1715. Hist. of Dorchester Co. Jones. P. 62.

First permanent settlement in Frederick County, of Germans from Pennsylvania. Hist. of west. Md. Scharf. List of families, 1732–34, v. 1, p. 58; earliest emigrants, 1745–1881, pp. 485–86. MHS.

First settlers of Anne Arundel County. Founders of Anne Arundel and Howard Cos. Warfield. P. 5.

Heads of families in Worcester County, 1790. M. F. Hudson. Pamph. DAR.

List of Huguenot refugees in Calvert County. Monette Book. Pp. 35–43, 134–57.

List of inhabitants of Allegany County, 1802–06 Ms. Lib. Cong.

List of inhabitants of Anne Arundel County, 1802–06. Ms. Lib. Cong.

List of inhabitants of Baltimore County, 1802–06. Ms. Lib. Cong.

List of inhabitants of Baltimore Town, 1752. Hist. of Balto. City and Co. Scharf. P. 58.

List of inhabitants of Calvert County, 1802–06. Ms. Lib. Cong.

List of inhabitants of Caroline County, 1802–06. Ms. Lib. Cong.

List of inhabitants of Cecil County, 1802–06. Ms. Lib. Cong.

List of inhabitants of Dorchester County, 1776. (Broad Creek, Nanticoke, Straight's and Transquakin.) Mss. Hall of Records.

List of inhabitants of Dorchester County, 1802–06. Ms. Lib. Cong.

List of inhabitants of Frederick County, 1776. (Elizabeth, Lower District, Lower Potowmack, North West and Sugar Land Hundreds.) Mss. Hall of Records.

List of inhabitants of Georgetown, Md., 1808. Geneal. Mag. of Amer. Ancestry, N. Y., 1916.

List of inhabitants of Harford County, 1802–06. Ms. Lib. Cong.

List of inhabitants of Isle of Kent County (now Queen Anne Co.) 1647. Hist. of Md. Scharf. V. 1, p. 194.

List of inhabitants of Kent County, 1802–06. Ms. Lib. Cong.

List of inhabitants of Kent Island, who took oath of fealty to Lord Baltimore, April 16, 1647. Hist. of Md. Scharf. V. 1, p. 194.

List of inhabitants of Montgomery County, 1802–06. Ms. Lib. Cong.

List of inhabitants of Prince George County, 1802–06. Ms. Lib. Cong.

List of inhabitants of Queen Anne County, 1802–06. Ms. Lib. Cong.

List of inhabitants of St. Mary's County, 1802–06. Ms. Lib. Cong.

List of inhabitants of Somerset County, 1802–06. Ms. Lib. Cong.

List of inhabitants of Talbot County, 1802–06. Ms. Lib. Cong.
List of inhabitants of Washington County, 1802–06. Ms. Lib. Cong.
List of inhabitants of Westminster, 1815–98. Pioneers of early days of Westminster. Shellman. 1934, pp. 24–31.
List of inhabitants of Worcester County, 1802–06. Ms. Lib. Cong.
List of lot holders of Baltimore Town, 1730. Hist. of Balto. City and Co. Scharf. P. 53.
List of lot holders of Jones' Town, 1732. Hist. of Balto. City and Co. Scharf. Pp. 55–56.
List of lot holders of Joppa, Baltimore County, now Harford County. Hist. of Md. Scharf. V. 1, p. 414.
List of lot owners in Rockville, Montgomery County, 1793. Hist. of west. Md. Scharf. V. 1, p. 740. MHS.
List of lot holders of Joppa. Hist. of Harford Co. Preston. P. 45.
List of names of persons in Montgomery County, 1692–1790. Ms. MHS.
List of prominent citizens of Queen Anne County, 1775, 1776. Patriotic Marylander, v. 3, no. 3, pp. 159–66. MHS; DAR.
List of residents of Calvert County, 1689. Monette Book. Pp. 240–51. MHS.
List of residents of Monocacy, Frederick County, 1767. Photos. In Binder's title Monocacy. DAR.
List of ships at Annapolis, 1748. Hall of Records.
List of those who governed Maryland before 1776. B. C. Steiner. Md. manual. 1933, pp. 360–65.
List of vessels arriving in Province of Maryland, 1637–71. (Supplementing list, pp. 339–41.) M. H. Mag., 1910, v. 5, p. 392.
Log of ship *Submission*, 1682, arrived in Choptank River, Eastern Shore of Maryland. Pub. Geneal. Soc. Pa., v. 1, p. 1.
Lord Baltimore's Maryland. Manors, undisposed of 1776. Hist. of Md. Scharf. V. 2, pp. 104–05. MHS.
Lords proprietary of Maryland, 1632–1776. Md. manual. 1933, p. 360.
Managers of Washington monument, 1815. Chronicles of Balto. Scharf. P. 377.
Maryland collectors of money, etc., for Continental treasury, 1780. Nat'l. Geneal. Soc. Quart., v. 23, no. 1, p. 22.
Maryland manors and early settlers. Hester Dorsey Richardson. Pub. Natl. Geneal. Soc., Wash., D. C., pamph.
Maryland oaths of office, 1757, 1769 and 1773. Mss. MHS.
Maryland register, 1856–76. Legal, political and business manual; lists of attorneys, civil officers, executives, physicians and members of Congress and Legislature. James Wingate. Balto. MHS; DAR; Enoch Pratt Lib.
Maryland state gazetteers and business directory, 1867–68. G. W. Hawes. Balto. Peabody Lib.
Masons in Maryland. Member Book, 1773–80 MHS.
Matchett's Baltimore directory corrected up to June, 1829. R. J. Matchett. 1829.
Matchett's Baltimore directory or register of householders corrected up to June, 1842. Balto. 1842.
Mayors of Baltimore, 1797–1878. Hist. of Md. Scharf. V. 3, p. 779. MHS.
†Mayors of Baltimore, from Calhoun, 1797, to Broening 1919. Illus. with portraits from City Hall. Enoch Pratt Lib.
†Medical profession in Maryland. Lists and biographical sketches. Hist. of Balto. City and Co. Scharf. Pp. 729–57. MHS.
†Members of bar in Maryland, with biographical sketches. Hist. of Balto. City and Co. Scharf. Pp. 698–728. MHS.
Members of Constitutional Conventions of Maryland, 1776, 1778, 1851, 1864, 1867. Hist. of Md. Scharf. V. 3, p. 750. MHS.
Hist. of Balto. City and Co. Scharf. P. 194.
Members of Assembly of Maryland. Hist. of Md. Scharf. V. 1, p. 130 (Feb. 25, 1639), p. 203 (Apr., 1650), p. 342 (1692). MHS.
Members (27) of first Anti-Slavery Society in Maryland, 1798. Chronicles of Balto. Scharf. P. 255. MHS.
Members of Honor Roll of American Clan Gregor Society in World War. Amer. Clan Gregor Year Book, 1919, pp. 23–34. MHS; DAR.
Members of House of Delegates from Baltimore City, 1776–1880. Hist. of Balto. City and Co. Scharf. P. 194.
Members of House of Delegates from Baltimore County, 1659–1880. Hist. of Balto. City and Co. Scharf. P. 818.
Members of House of Delegates from Harford County, 1786–1900. Hist. of Harford Co. Preston. Pp. 352–57.
Members of House of Representatives from Maryland, 1789–1935. Md. manual. 1933, pp. 385–89.
Membership (750) of American Clan Gregor Society (221 different families). Amer. Clan Gregor Year Book, 1937, pp. 91–105. MHS; DAR.
Members (over 100) of Maryland. Society for Promoting Abolition of Slavery, 1789. Hist. of Md. Scharf. V. 3, pp. 306–07. MHS.
Members of Provincial Conventions of Baltimore Town, 1774 and 1775. Chronicles of Balto. Scharf. P. 130 (1774), p. 136 (1775).
Members of United States Congress Meeting at Annapolis, Dec. 13, 1873, and Jan. 1789. Hist. of Md. Scharf. V. 2, pp. 495–96 (1873), p. 500 (1789). MHS.
Men of Maryland since Civil War. Winchester. Enoch Pratt Lib.
Ms. civil list, 1749–1891. Hon. Henry Goldsborough. MHS.
Ms. list of Baltimoreans listed in Who's Who. Clipp. Enoch Pratt Lib.
Ms. list of names of outstanding men in Maryland history. Enoch Pratt Lib.
Names of early settlers in Somerset County, 1666–1700. Old Somerset. Torrence. Pp. 464–60; founders, pp. 545–53; Church of England families, p. 468; from Virginia, 1661–62, pp. 279–80; Presbyterian families, p. 468; Quaker families, p. 467.
Naturalized citizens of Maryland (176), 1666–1750. Hist. of Md. Scharf. V. 2, p. 11.
Naturalizations. County Court Note Book. Ljungstedt. MHS.
Naturalizations during Court Session, Jan. 1, 1798, Washington County. Natl. Geneal. Soc. Quart., Dec., 1935, v. 23, no. 4, pp. 111–13.
Naturalizations (early) in Maryland. Kilty's Laws. V. 2. (Naturalizations in Dist. U. S.

Courts, all Balto. City Courts of Civil Jurisdiction and Circuit Courts in counties of Md.)
Naturalizations (early). Md. records. Brumbaugh. V. 2, pp. 311-13.
Naturalizations in Maryland, 1666-1765. Laws of Md. Rev. Thomas Bacon. (In Index.) Annapolis, 1765. (Augustine Herman and family naturalized 1666, first foreigners naturalized in Md.)
Naturalizations of Maryland settlers (23) in Pennsylvania (mostly York), 1767-72. M. H. Mag., 1910, v. 5, p. 72.
Origin of surnames of Baltimore. S. G. Oliphant. Newsp. clipp. from The Sun, Balto., 1906-08. Indexed, bd. MHS.
Passenger lists of *Ark* and *Dove*, 1633. Col. families of U. S. of Amer. V. 5, pp. 593-606.
Passenger list of *Ark* and *Dove*, 1633. Hist. of Md. Scharf. V. 1, p. 66. MHS.
Passenger list of *Ark* and *Dove*, 1633. Md. Geneal. Rec. Com., 1932-33, p. 335. Mss. DAR.
Passenger list of *Ark* and *Dove*, 1633. Md. Unpub. Rev. Rec. Hodges. V. 2. Mss. DAR.
Passenger list of *Ark* and *Dove*. Sidelights on Md. hist. Richardson. V. 1, pp. 7-10.
Payne's ledger, 1758-61. List of names (some from Maryland) found in ledger of Daniel Payne, merchant of Dumfries, Prince William County, Virginia. William and Mary Quart. Mag., v. 4 (series 2), p. 117.
Petition of inhabitants of Calvert County. Photos. MHS. (Original in Public Record Office, London.)
Port of entry books, Annapolis, 1754-74. Mss. MHS.
Port of Oxford records. Chamberlain. Mss. MHS.
Portraits of Maryland Historical Society. F. B. Mayer. M. H. Mag., 1906, v. 1, pp. 330-36.
Presidential electors of Maryland, 1789-1877, 1805. Hist. of Md. Scharf. V. 3, p. 753 (1789-1877); v. 2, pp. 549, 613 (1805). MHS.
Presidents of Senate of Maryland, 1777-1933. Md. manual. 1933, p. 390.
Proprietaries of Maryland and their representatives, 1634-1776. Sidelights on Md. hist. Richardson. Pp. 260-62. MHS; DAR.
Proprietary Council of Maryland, 1773-74. Hist. of Md. Scharf. V. 2, p. 430. MHS.
References to English surnames, 1601. Index, 19,650 surnames, in printed register of 778 English parishes, during first year of seventeenth century. Charles A. Berman. 1910. MHS.
Register of civil appointments, 1777-1825, 1825-35. 2 vols. Hall of Records.
Register of cabinet makers and allied trades of Maryland, 1746-1820 (about 500 persons). M. H. Mag., Mar., 1930, v. 25, pp. 1-27.
Register of vessels, 1774-97. Manifest of departures, 1745-1849; vessels entering, 1801-12. Bureau of Customs, Treasury Dept., Annapolis.
Register of vessels, Port of Nottingham, beginning 1789. Hall of Records.
Registers of wills in Maryland. Hist. of Md. Scharf. V. 3, p. 760. MHS.
Representatives to Congress of United States from Maryland. 1789-1935. Md. manual. 1933, pp. 385-89.
Scotch exiles, who settled in Prince George County. Sidelights on Md. hist. Richardson. V. 1, p. 214.
Scottish prisoners on ship *Johnson* of Liverpool, arrived at Oxford Eastern Shore of Maryland, July 20, 1747. Hist. of Md. Scharf. V. 1, p. 435. MHS.
Secretaries of State of Maryland, 1838-1931. Md. manual. 1933, p. 371.
Ship entry book, 1773-76. Mss. Hall of Records.
Ship *Friendship* of Belfast. Rebels transported into Province of Maryland, Aug. 20, 1716. Hist. of Md. Scharf. V. 1, pp. 386-87. MHS.
Ship *Good Speed*. Rebels transported into Province of Maryland, Oct. 18, 1716. Hist. of Md. Scharf. V. 1, pp. 388-89. MHS.
Ships and other vessels. List of entries inward for Patuxent District, Maryland, June 25, 1745-June 2, 1757. Ships and other vessels. Ms. book. Hall of Records.
Ships and their masters of Colonial period. Md. O. R. Soc. Bull., v. 3, p. 27. MHS.
Ship's logs. Naval Academy, Annapolis.
Signers of Articles of Confederation, 1781. (For Maryland, Daniel Carroll and John Hanson.) Hist. of Md. Scharf. V. 3, p. 752.
Md. Manual. 1933, p. 381.
Signers of Declaration of Independence from Maryland, 1776. (Carroll, Chase, Paca and Stone.) Hist. of Md. Scharf. V. 3, p. 752.
Md. manual. 1933, p. 381.
Signers of Federal Constitution from Maryland, 1787. (Daniel Carroll, Daniel of St. Thomas Jenifer, and James McHenry.) Md. manual. 1933, p. 381.
Hist. of Md. Scharf. V. 2, p. 546.
Social register, Baltimore, vols. 1-54, no. 10 (1940). N. Y., Social Register Assoc.
Speakers of House of Delegates of Maryland, 1777-1933. Md. manual. 1933, pp. 392-94.
Suburban directory of Maryland and Virginia, of towns adjacent to District of Columbia. Justus C. Nelso. Wash., D. C., 1913. DAR.
Subscribers, 1805, Frederick and Baltimore Turnpike. Ms. MHS.
Surveyors of Maryland. Hist. of Md. Scharf. V. 3, p. 759. MHS.
Tax commissioners of Maryland, 1777. Natl. Geneal. Soc. Quart., v. 6, no. 1, pp. 21-22.
Hist. of Md. Scharf. V. 2, p. 508.
Maryland medical recorder, 1829-33. H. G. Jameson. Balto.
Tobacco growers of Maryland, 1784. Pa. Mag. Hist. and Biog., v. 18, pp. 261-62.
Treasurers of Eastern and Western Shores of Md., 1775-1852. (Two offices consolidated, 1851.) 1852-1931. Md. manual. 1933, p. 375.
1775-1878. Hist. of Md. Scharf. V. 3, pp. 777-78. MHS.
United States Senators from Maryland, 1780-1931. Md. manual. 1933, p. 383.
United States senators from Maryland, 1789-1878. Hist. of Md. Scharf. V. 3, p. 755.
Works Progress Administration, Customs Service in Baltimore. Index of records to be placed in National Records. Records date 1790 to World War. Name of ship, date of arrival, and passenger lists.

MARYLAND LISTS

Allegany County:
List of attorneys, 1791-1893. Hist. of Allegany Co. Thomas and Williams. Pp. 669-73. MHS; DAR.

List of civil officers, 1791–1881. Hist. of west. Md. Scharf. V. 2, p. 1349. MHS; DAR.
List of civil officers and local incidents, 1822–62. Hist. of Cumberland. Lowdermilk. Pp. 307–87.
List of judges, 1791–1915. Hist. of Allegany Co. Thomas and Williams. P. 673.
List of postmasters of Cumberland, 1795–1878. Hist. of Cumberland. Lowdermilk. P. 435.
List of property holders of Cumberland, 1813. Hist. of west. Md. Scharf. V. 2, p. 1374. MHS; DAR.
Hist. of Cumberland. Lowdermilk. Pp. 293–95, 299.
List of residents of Cumberland, 1787, 1790–1800. Hist. of Cumberland. Pp. 262, 278.

Anne Arundel County:
List of civil officers, 1650–92, 1847–95. Founders of Anne Arundel and Howard Cos. Warfield. Pp. 37–40, 537–40.
List of distinguished men, 1793–1846. Founders of Anne Arundel and Howard Cos. Warfield. P. 318. MHS; DAR.

Baltimore City:
List of civil officers, 1659–1881. Hist. of Balto. City and Co. Scharf. Pp. 812–15. MHS.
List of collectors, naval officers and surveyors of customs, of Baltimore District, 1794–1877. Hist. of Balto. City and Co. Scharf. P. 498. MHS.
List of mayors, city councilmen and registers, 1797–1881. Hist. of Balto. City and Co. Scharf. Pp. 187–93. MHS.
List of officers of fire companies, 1831–64. Hist. of Balto. City and Co. Scharf. Pp. 240–56.
List of State Senators, 1776–1881. Hist. of Balto. City and Co. Scharf. P. 193. MHS.
List of subscribers for building Town Hall, Market Place, 1751. Ms. MHS.
List of subscribers for keeping up and repairing fence (stockade) around Baltimore Town, prior to 1749. (Original.) Ms. MHS. Also: Hist. of Balto. City and Co. Scharf. P. 37.
List of subscribers for opening Calvert Street, 1784. Ms. MHS.

Baltimore County. Members of House of Delegates, 1659–1800. Hist. of Balto. City and Co. Scharf. P. 818.

Calvert County. List of some early land holders. Md. Geneal. Bull., vols. 1, 2, 3 and 4. MHS; DAR.

Caroline County:
List of commissioners, 1774–98. Hist. of Caroline Co. Pp. 11–12.
List of commissioners appointed to survey Denton. Hist. of Caroline Co. P. 224.

Carroll County:
List of attorneys, 1837–81. Hist. of west. Md. Scharf. V. 2, pp. 815–20. MHS; DAR.
List of judges, county clerks, State's attorneys and officers, 1837–80. Hist. of west. Md. Scharf. V. 2, pp. 806–15. MHS; DAR.
List of mayors and officers of Westminster, 1839–81. Hist. of west. Md. Scharf. V. 2, p. 931. MHS; DAR.

Cecil County:
List of commissioners of Charleston, 1750. Hist. of Md. Scharf. V. 2, p. 64.
List of petition of inhabitants of Octorara Hundred, June 1, 1795. Mss. MHS.
List of petitioners of inhabitants of Elk Neck Hundred, signed May 30, 1796, requesting road from Turkey Point to head of Elk River. Md. Geneal. Rec. Com., 1932, v. 5, p. 192. Mss. DAR.
Lists. 16 mss. petitions of inhabitants (in different hundreds) of Cecil County for repair or new roads from 1794–1833. MHS.
List of petitioners of tenants of Susquehanna Manor for titles in fee of their respective holdings, December, 1779. (108 names.) M. H. Mag., 1910, v. 5, pp. 58–60.

Dorchester County.
List of Assembly delegates and burgesses, 1669–1773, and delegates, 1774–1924. Hist. of Dorchester Co. Jones. Pp. 501–06. MHS; DAR.
List of collectors of Port of Vienna, 1791–1866. Hist. of Dorchester Co. Jones. P. 88. MHS; DAR.
List of Maryland deputies and delegates, 1774–1924. Hist. of Dorchester Co. Jones. Pp. 501–06. MHS; DAR.
List of members of bar; Cambridge, 1692–1924. Hist. of Dorchester Co. Jones. P. 176. MHS; DAR.
List of county officers, 1669–1924. Hist. of Dorchester Co. Jones. Pp. 506–35. MHS; DAR.
List of office holders and United States Senators, 1789–1901. Hist. of Dorchester Co. Jones. P. 535. MHS; DAR.
List of residents of Vienna, 1840. Hist. of Dorchester Co. Jones. P. 86. MHS; DAR.

Frederick County:
Civil lists. Hist. of Frederick Co. Williams. V. 1, pp. 599–607. MHS; DAR.
List of commissioners, mayors, immigrants, physicians and innkeepers, 1745–1881. Hist. of west. Md. Scharf. V. 1, pp. 485–89. MHS; DAR.
List of commissioners of Middletown, 1834–81. Hist. of west. Md. Scharf. V. 1, p. 575. MHS; DAR.
Constable's list and names of hundreds, 1750–51. Hist. of west. Md. Scharf. V. 1, pp. 419–21. MHS; DAR.
List of civil officers, 1777–1880. Hist. of west. Md. Scharf. V. 1, pp. 478–83. MHS; DAR.
List of Orphans. County Court Note Book. Mrs. Milnor Ljungstedt. V. 2, pp. 94, 102; v. 3, pp. 7, 11, 22, 30. MHS; DAR.
List of publishers, editors and printers connected with press, 1785–1875. Hist. of west. Md. Scharf. V. 1, pp. 537–38. MHS; DAR.
List of subscribers to Frederick and Baltimore Turnpike Company. Ms. MHS.
List of those admitted to bar at Frederick, 1749–1881. Hist. of west. Md. Scharf. V. 1, p. 416. MHS; DAR.
Medical society lists. Hist. of Frederick Co. Williams. V. 1, pp. 580–97. MHS; DAR.
Meetings of inhabitants, November 18, 1774. Hist. of Frederick Co. Williams. V. 1, pp. 84–86. MHS; DAR.
Members of bar, 1749–1907. Hist. of Frederick Co. Williams. V. 1, pp. 597–99. MHS; DAR.
Names from ancient letter book of John Hoffman. Md. Geneal. Rec. Com., 1934–35. Mss. DAR.

Poll list of presidential election, November 9–12, 1796 (1917 voters). Md. records. Brumbaugh. V. 1, pp. 271-95. MHS; DAR.

Garrett County. List of civil officers, 1873–81. Hist. of west. Md. Scharf. V. 2, p. 1523. MHS; DAR.

Harford County:

List of civil officers, 1774-1889. Hist. of Harford Co. Preston. Pp. 357–69. MHS; DAR.

List of jurors (943 names). Harford Co., 1774-91. 1798-1806, Hist. Soc. Coll. J.H.U.

List of jurors. Hist. of Harford Co. Preston. Chaps. 4, 5 and 10. MHS; DAR.

List of commissioners of Harve de Grace, 1800-50. Hist. of Harford Co. Preston. P. 251. MHS; DAR.

Kent County. List of judges, 1777, 1788. Md. Geneal. Bull., v. 2, no. 1. MHS; DAR.

Montgomery County:

List of civil officers, 1777-1881. Hist. of west. Md. Scharf. V. 1, pp. 664-68. MHS; DAR.

Civil officers, 1780-82. Natl. Geneal. Soc. Quart., 1917, v. 6, p. 11. MHS; DAR.

Commissioners (first) of Montgomery and Washington Counties. Hist. of west. Md. Scharf. V. 2, p. 270. MHS; DAR.

List of members of bar, 1777-1881. Hist. of west. Md. Scharf. V. 1, p. 667. MHS; DAR.

List of overseers of roads, 1771. Hist. of west. Md. Scharf. V. 1, p. 696. MHS; DAR.

Queen Anne County. List of signers (66) pledging allegiance to Commonwealth of England, Isle of Kent, April 5, 1652. Old Kent. Hanson. Pp. 59-60. MHS; DAR.

St. Mary's County. List of alderman, councilmen and freemen of City of St. Mary's and signers of petition to Governor (1694) to reconsider action of removing capitol from St. Mary's to Annapolis. Hist. of Md. Scharf. V. 1, p. 347. MHS; DAR.

Chronicles of Col. Md. Thomas. Pp. 61-62. MHS; DAR.

Somerset County. Officials, member of Lower House of Assembly, justices of peace, and militia commissions, before 1700. Old Somerset. Torrance. Pp. 393-96. MHS; DAR.

Talbot County:

List of civil officers, 1692-1915. Hist. of Talbot Co. Tilghman. V. 2, p. 21. MHS; DAR.

List of members of House of Burgesses, 1661-1776. Hist. of Talbot Co. Tilghman. V. 2, p. 6. MHS; DAR.

List of slave holders, 1790. Hist. of Talbot Co. Tilghman. V. 2, p. 138. MHS; DAR.

Washington County:

List of attorneys, 1805-80. Hist. of west. Md. Scharf. V. 2, p. 1131. MHS; DAR.

List of business men in Williamsport (originally called Conecocheague), 1801-12. Hist. of west. Md. Scharf. V. 2, pp. 1224-25. MHS; DAR.

Commissioners (first) of Montgomery and Washington Counties. Hist. of west. Md. Scharf. V. 2, p. 270. MHS; DAR.

List of commissioners, mayors and members of Common Council of Hagerstown, 1814-81. Hist. of west. Md. Scharf. V. 2, p. 1065. MHS; DAR.

List of civil officers, 1778. Natl. Geneal. Soc. Quart., 1917, v. 6, pp. 12-21. MHS; DAR.

List of public officials, 1777-1880. Hist. of west. Md. Scharf. V. 2, pp. 987-94. MHS; DAR.

List of residents, Boonsboro and Mt. Pleasant District, 1800-18. Hist. of west. Md. Scharf. V. 2, p. 1260. MHS; DAR.

List of residents, Funkstown, 1804. Hist. of west. Md. Scharf. V. 2, p. 1280. MHS; DAR.

List of residents, Hagerstown and immediate vicinity, 1800-05. Hist. of west. Md. Scharf. V. 2, pp. 1061-65. MHS; DAR.

List of residents, Sharpsburg, 1812. Hist. of west. Md. Scharf. V. 2, p. 1206. MHS; DAR.

Wicomico County. List of commissioners and property owners of Salisbury, 1817. Historic Salisbury. Truitt. Pp. 43-50. DAR.

Worcester County:

List of decedents in unindexed bond book, in office of Registrar of Wills, Snow Hill, Worcester Co. (Old Somerset), 1667-1742. Contributed by Mrs. O. A. Ljunstedt. Geneal. Soc. Pa. Pub., v. 7, pp. 192-94. Mss. MHS.

List of men under 25 years, 1756 and 1762. Md. Geneal. Rec. Com., 1911-15. Mss. DAR.

NATIONAL LISTS

Cabinet officers, 1789-1905. Natl. Cyc. of Amer. Biog. Berby. 1906, pp. 4-6. Peabody Lib.

Committee that prepared Articles of Confederation. Natl. Cyc. of Amer. Biog. Berby. 1906, p. 1. Peabody Lib.

Delegates to first Colonial Congress, New York, May 6, 1690. Natl. Cyc. of Amer. Biog. Berby. 1906. P. 1. Peabody Lib.

Delegates to first Continental Congress, Philadelphia, 1774. Natl. Cyc. of Amer. Biog. Berby. 1906, p. 1. Peabody Lib.

Delegates to Federal Convention that prepared Natl. Constitution, Philadelphia, May 2, 1787. Natl. Cyc. of Amer. Biog. Berby. 1906, p. 2. Peabody Lib.

Delegates to second Colonial Congress, New York, 1754. Natl. Cyc. of Amer. Biog. Berby. 1906, p. 1. Peabody Lib.

Delegates to Stamp Act, 1765. Natl. Cyc. of Amer. Biog. Berby. 1906, p. 1. Peabody Lib.

Directors of astronomical observatories in United States, 1840-1905. Natl. Cyc. of Amer. Biog. Berby. 1906, p. 43. Peabody Lib.

Governors, chief justices, 1776-1905. Natl. Cyc. of Amer. Biog. Berby. 1906, pp. 75-115. Peabody Lib.

Heads of departments in Washington, 1775-1903. Natl. Cyc. of Amer. Biog. Berby. 1906, p. 71. Peabody Lib.

Judiciary of United States, 1696-1900. Natl. Cyc. of Amer. Biog. Berby. 1906, p. 73. Peabody Lib.

Presidents of American universities, 1640-1904. Natl. Cyc. of Amer. Biog. Berby. 1906, pp. 117-23. Peabody Lib.

Presidents of Continental Congress of United States, 1774-78. Natl. Cyc. of Amer. Biog. Berby. 1906, p. 2. Peabody Lib.

Presidents of national scientific and learned societies, 1780-1905. Natl. Cyc. of Amer. Biog. Berby. 1906, pp. 133-38. Peabody Lib.

Presidents of religious organizations in United States, 1814–1905. Natl. Cyc. of Amer. Biog. Berby. 1906, p. 74. Peabody Lib.

Presidents of United States 1789–1901. Natl. Cyc. of Amer. Biog. Berby. 1906, p. 3. Peabody Lib.

Roll of honor in American biographies, Hall of Fame, Congressional medals, society and university medals, 1776–1905. Natl. Cyc. of Amer. Biog. Berby. 1906, pp. 139–42. Peabody Lib.

Roman Catholic hierarchy in United States, 1810–1904. Natl. Cyc. of Amer. Biog. Berby. 1906, pp. 129–32. Peabody Lib.

Signers of Articles of Confederation, adopted by Congress November 15, 1777. Natl. Cyc. of Amer. Biog. Berby. 1906, p. 2. Peabody Lib.

Speakers of House of Representatives of United States. Natl. Cyc. of Amer. Biog. Berby. 1906, p. 2. Peabody Lib.

Succession of American bishops of Protestant Episcopal church, 1784–1904. Natl. Cyc. of Amer. Biog. Berby. 1906, pp. 129–32. Peabody Lib.

Vice-Presidents of United States, 1789–1904. Natl. Cyc. of Amer. Biog. Berby. 1906, p. 3. Peabody Lib.

United States ambassadors, envoys extraordinary and ministers plenipotentiary, 1703–1901. Natl. Cyc. of Amer. Biog. Berby. 1906, pp. 67–70. Peabody Lib.

United States Congressmen, 1789–1907. Natl. Cyc. of Amer. Biog. Berby. 1906, pp. 27–65. Peabody Lib.

United States Senators, 1789–1905. Natl. Cyc. of Amer. Biog. Berby. 1906, pp. 11–25. Peabody Lib.

POPULATION CENSUS

Population census records, 1790–date. Commerce Building, Room 6016, Wash., D. C.

1790. First census, only name on schedule was that of head of family.

1850. Seventh census (known as first modern census), carried for first time name of every person enumerated; also foreign-born persons first enumerated separately.

1880. Ninth census, first census to give country or state of birth of parents.

1790–1870. Census schedules open to public. Later records not accessible to public, and information given out only upon request or with approval of person to whom it relates. Entries cannot be found unless exact place of abode at time of census is known. Records now used for retirement, old age pensions, war pensions, working papers, citizenship, passports, settling of estates, insurance, annuities, genealogy, etc.—excerpts from article by C. E. Batschelet, geographer, Bureau of Census. Pub. in D. A. R. Mag., Aug., 1933, v. 67, no. 8, pp. 482–85. Permission given by editor.

WAR RECORDS

GENERAL AND MISCELLANEOUS WAR RECORDS

†Adjutants General of Maryland, 1794–1904. Biographical sketches. With particular references to military service. F. B. Culver. Rept. of Adjutant General of Md., 1906–07, p. 285. MHS.

Army register of United States (complete), 1776–1887. Alphabetical list of all officers of army and navy. T. H. S. Hamersly. N. Y., 1888. MHS.

Baltimore County militia, 1779. M. H. Mag., 1912, v. 7, p. 90.

Battle flags of Maryland, 1777–1917, in Flag Room, State House, Annapolis. Rept. of Adjutant General of Md., 1906–07, p. 304.
  Md. manual. 1933, p. 353–56. MHS.

Commanders of armies and navies of United States in time of war (Revolutionary and Civil, etc.) Natl. cyc. of Amer. biog. Berby. 1906, p. 145. Peabody Lib.

Decorations. United States Army, 1862–1926. War Dept., Office of Adjutant General. Govt. Print. Office, Wash., D. C., 1927. MHS.

Dictionary of all officers who have been commissioned or have been appointed and served in Army of United States, 1789–Jan. 1, 1853, and distinguished officers, volunteers and militia of States, Navy and Marine Corps. C. K. Gardener. N. Y., Putnam, 1853. MHS.

Frederick County. Two companies of rifleman, 1764. Pa. Germans in settlement in Md. Nead. P. 161. MHS; DAR.

Historical register and dictionary of United States Army, from organization, Sept. 29, 1789, to Mar. 2, 1903. F. B. Heitman. 2 vols. Govt. Print. Office, Wash., D. C., 1903. MHS.

†Historical sketch of militia of Maryland. F. B. Culver. Rept. of Adjutant General of Md., 1906–07, p. 265. MHS.

Historical sketch of militia of Maryland. F. B. Culver. 1908.

History of Fifth Regiment, from organization to present time, 1889–99. G. A. Meekins. Balto.

History of navy. James Fenimore Cooper. 1847. MHS.

Independent Greys, 3rd Regiment, 1841–48. Ms. MHS.

List of Flying Corps of Maryland. Hist. of Md. McSherry. 1849; appendix. MHS.

Lives of distinguished American naval officers. Jas. Fenimore Cooper. 1846.

Maryland militia lists, 1794–1808, 1814, 1821–45. Mss. MHS.

Maryland officers during Whiskey Insurrection, 1794. Hist. of Md. Scharf. V. 2, p. 583. MHS.

Memoirs of Maryland volunteer in War with Mexico, 1846–48. Maj.-Gen. J. R. Kenly. (Old Balto. Battalion, pp. 22–23.) Lippincott 1873. MHS.

Military records in custody of Bureau of Pensions, Interior Department, Washington, D. C. (Write to U. S. Commissioner of Pensions.)

Navy register of United States, general and complete, 1776–1887. Record of each officer as on file at Navy Department, date of entry, progress and rank, and in what manner they left service. T. H. S. Hamersly. N. Y., 1888. MHS.

Officers of Baltimore City Home Guard, 1835–42. Ms. MHS.

Officers of provisional army of United States in war with France, 1798–1800. Pa. Mag. Hist. and Biog., v. 38, pp. 129–82. (Md., pp. 151–52.) MHS.

Organization of provisional army of United States in anticipated war with France, 1798–1800. (Roster of officers.) Dr. Carlos E. Godfrey. Bklet. MHS.

Pension Papers. Vols. 1–133, 1937–38. DAR.

Pension Papers. Office of Adjutant General, War Department, Wash., D. C.

Pension Papers. Navy Department, Wash., D. C.

Pension rolls of United States, 1818. DAR.

Prince George County. Militia, 1799, two muster rolls, French War, giving date of birth of soldiers. Md. rec. Brumbaugh. V. 1, pp. 173–75. MHS; DAR.

Records from office of Adjutant General; containing some material relating to War of 1812, draft records of Civil War, and some Spanish American War records. Also much miscellaneous material. Hall of Records.

Register of commissioned and warrant officers of Navy of United States and Marine Corps, 1827. Govt. Print. Office, Wash., D. C., 1896. S. A. R. Lib.

Report of Secretary of War; containing list of pensioners, under various Acts of Congress. 1835, 3 vols. DAR.

War with Mexico. List. of distinguished Marylanders. Hist. of Balto. City and Co. Scharf. P. 114. MHS.

War records of Maryland sailors and soldiers. Service records of men who served in Civil, Mexican, Revolutionary and Spanish American Wars, War of 1812 and World War. Records pertaining to Mexican, Revolutionary Wars and War of 1812 (due to methods used in those days), incomplete. Address: Commanding General, Md. Natl. Guard, Annapolis.

Washington County. List of those draughted at Elizabethtown (now Hagerstown), Aug., 27, 1794 (Whisky Insurrection). Hist. west. Md. Scharf. V. 1, p. 165. MHS; DAR.

Worcester County militia, 1794. H. F. Covington. Reprinted from M. H. Mag., June, 1926, v. 21, p. 149, pamph. MHS.

COLONIAL AND FRENCH AND INDIAN WARS

Calvert County. Muster rolls of companies of militia, 1749. (Officers Grant, Isaacks, Sappington and Sollers.) Hall of Records.

Capt. Dagworth's list of Maryland troops in French and Indian War, 1757, 1758–59. Mss. MHS.

Capt. Elias Delashmut's muster roll, August, 1757–58. M. H. Mag., 1914, v. 9, pp. 260–80.

Col. John D. Dagworth's ledger, 1762–63, French and Indian War. Calvert Papers. Mss. MHS.

Colonial Militia of Anne Arundel County. Mss. MHS.

Colonial Militia of Maryland, 1732, 1740, 1748–49. Lists (original). Mss. Hall of Records.

Colonial Militia of Maryland, 1740, 1748. Sidelights on Md. hist. Richardson. V. 1, pp. 265–68. MHS; DAR.

Colonial Militia of Maryland, 1740, 1748. M. H. Mag., 1911, v. 6, pp. 44–59, 180–95. (Calvert Co., 1740, pp. 51–53; Cecil Co., 1740, p. 45; Charles Co., 1748, pp. 54–55; Dorchester Co., 1748, p. 54; Prince George Co., 1748, pp. 55–59; Queen Anne Co., 1748, p. 180; Somerset Co., 1747, 1748, pp. 183–89, 193–95; St. Mary's Co., 1748, pp. 181–83; Talbot Co., 1748, pp. 189–93.)

Earl Loudon of Maryland. (Story of defense of Maryland's frontier, 1755–58.) P. H. Giddens. M. H. Mag., 1934, v. 29, pp. 268–94.

French and Indian War. M. H. Mag., Dec. 1909, v. 4, pp. 344–53.

French and Indian War. Roster of Maryland troops, 1757–59. M. H. Mag., Sept., 1910, v. 5, pp. 271–89; Sept., 1914, v. 9, pp. 260–80; Dec., pp. 348–70.

French and Indian War in Maryland, 1753–56. P. H. Giddens. M. H. Mag., 1935, v. 30, pp. 281–310.

Lafayette in Harford County, 1781. J. Alexis Shriver. M. H. Mag., 1931, v. 26, p. 203.

List of bachelors taxed by Assembly, for Defense of Maryland, 1756–63. Hist. of Balto. City and Co. Scharf. P. 38. MHS.

List of officers killed and wounded in Braddock's Retreat. (From Gentleman's Mag., Aug., 1755.) Hist. of west. Md. Scharf. V. 1, p. 89.

Hist. of Cumberland. Lowdermilk. Pp. 164–66. MHS.

List of persons from Dorchester County, who received pay, who had served or had aided troops, in Campaign, 1678, against Nanticoke Indians. Hist. of Dorchester Co. Jones. P. 40. MHS; DAR.

List of Maryland soldiers in War with France, 1690. Hist. of Md. Scharf. V. 1, p. 355. MHS.

Maryland troops killed at Fort Duquesne, 1758. Ms. Lib. Cong.

Muster rolls, companies of militia, of Maryland, 1732, 1740, 1748. Mss. Hall of Records.

Muster rolls of Maryland, 1757–59. Calvert Papers. Mss. MHS.

Naval officers accounts, 1753–61. Calvert Papers (16 papers). Mss. MHS.

Pioneers of Maryland and Old French War. Joseph Banvard. Boston, 1875. MHS.

Roster of Maryland troops, 1757–59. Hist. of Frederick Co. Williams. V. 1, pp. 660–70; appendix no. 3. MHS; DAR.

Washington County (was Frederick County). Sharpsburg muster rolls, 1755, 1757. Hist. of west. Md. Scharf. V. 1, p. 100; v. 2, p. 1211. MHS; DAR.

REVOLUTIONARY WAR—MARYLAND

Anne Arundel County. Commissions issued by Council of Safety, 1776. Founders of Anne Arundel and Howard Cos. Warfield. Pp. 222–24. MHS; DAR.

Ante Revolutionary and Revolutionary Papers of Maryland (2000). Partly bound and partly unbound. Hall of Records.

Association of Freeman of Maryland (facsimilie of signatures), July 26, 1775. Hist. of Md. Scharf. V. 2, p. 184. MHS.

Associations and associators of Maryland in Revolution. M. H. Mag., 1911, v. 6, pp. 241–45.

Associators of Frederick County, 1775. M. H. Mag., 1916, v. 11, pp. 163–75.

Associators of Harford County, 1775-76. Harford Co. Hist. Soc. Coll. J. H. Univ. Lib.
Hist. of Harford Co. Preston. P. 263. MHS; DAR.
Associators, Patuxent. Minutes. M. H. Mag., 1911, v. 6, pp. 305-17.
Background of Revolutionary movement in Maryland. C. A. Barker. Mss. Yale Univ. Lib.
Baltimore independent cadets, 1774. M. H. Mag., 1909, v. 4, pp. 372-74.
Baltimore subscribers, 1781, to fund raised by Gen. La Fayette for clothing suffering Army. Chronicles of Balto. Scharf. P. 414. MHS.
Barges in Chesapeake; action between American and British, 1782. M. H. Mag., 1909, v. 4, pp. 115-33.
Battle of Long Island. Thomas W. Field. (Marylanders, p. 199.)
Battle of Long Island. List, (incomplete) of wounded officers, Maryland battalion. Hist. of Md. Scharf. V. 2, p. 247. MHS;
Chronicles of Balto. Scharf. P. 148. MHS.
Battle of Long Island. "Maryland's Four Hundred." (Aug. 2, 1776, First Company, Maj. Mordecai Gist, commanding.) List of soldiers. M. H. Mag., 1919, v. 14, pp. 110-120.
British and American prisoners of war, 1778. Pa. Mag. Hist. and Biog., v. 17, pp. 159-74. MHS.
British Campaign of 1777 in Maryland, prior to Battle of Brandywine. Dr. G. H. Wells. MHS.
British confiscations. (Several volumes only, and no general index.) Hall of Records.
British property, 1792, confiscated. (Property of Anthony Stewart.) M. H. Mag., 1913, v. 8, pp. 369-70.
Calendar of Otho Holland Williams Papers in Maryland Historical Society. Historical Records Survey. MHS.
Capt. John Kershner's Company, Fort Frederick, July 27, 1778. Pa. Germans in settlement of Md. Nead. MHS; DAR.
Caroline County troopers, 1780. Md. O. R. Soc. Bull., no. 3, p. 41. MHS.
Chronology of American Revolution; with special reference to Maryland's participation. Patriotic Md., S. A. R., Balto., 1930, pp. 53-64. MHS; DAR.
Colonial and Revolutionary soldiers (500). Ancestral proofs and probabilities. Ljungstedt. Bull. no. 3. MHS.
Committee of Correspondence. Hist. of Md. Scharf. Annapolis, v. 2, p. 144; Anne Arundel County, v. 2, pp. 150, 163; Baltimore County and Town, 1774, v. 2, pp. 144, 147; Calvert County, v. 2, p. 164; Caroline County, v. 2, pp. 153-54; Charles County, v. 2, pp. 152, 153, 165; Frederick County, 1775, v. 1, pp. 128-29; v. 2, pp. 151, 154, 167, 175; Harford County, 1774, v. 2, pp. 151-52; Kent County, v. 2, pp. 149-50; Prince George County, v. 2, pp. 166, 172; Queen Anne County, 1774, v. 2, pp. 148-49. MHS.
Committee of Observation, Anne Arundel County, 1775. Founders of Anne Arundel and Howard Cos. Warfield. P. 222. MHS; DAR.
Hist. of Md. Scharf. V. 2, pp. 170-86. MHS.
Committee of Observation, Baltimore County. Hist. of Md. Scharf. V. 2, pp. 173, 185. MHS.
Committee of Observation, Baltimore County, 1774-76. Record book. Ms. Lib. of Cong.
Committee of Observation, Baltimore Town and County, 1774-76. Roster. Md. Geneal. Rec. Com., 1932-33. Photos. DAR.
Committee of Observation, Charles County. Hist. of Md. Scharf. V. 2, pp. 170-86. MHS.
Committee of Observation, Frederick County, 1775-76. Hist. of west. Md. Scharf. V. 1, p. 132.
Pa. Germans in settlement of Md. Nead. Pp. 190, 257. MHS; DAR.
Hist. of Md. Scharf. V. 2, pp. 174, 185. MHS.
Frederick County and Elizabeth Town (now Washington County). M. H. Mag., 1916, v. 11, pp. 50-66; 157-75; 237-60, 304-21; 1917, v. 12, pp. 12-21, 142-63, 261-75; 324-47; 1918, v. 13, pp. 28-53, 227-48.
Middle District of Frederick County. M. H. Mag., 1915, v. 10, pp. 320-21.
Middle and Upper District of Frederick County. Hist. of west. Md. Scharf. V. 1, p. 185. MHS; DAR.
Committee of Observation, Harford County. Hist. of Harford Co. Preston. P. 336. MHS; DAR.
Committee of Observation, Harford County, Mar. 22, 1775. Mss. MHS.
Committee of Observation of Maryland, 1775. Side lights on Md. hist. Richardson. V. 1, pp. 373-74. MHS; DAR.
Committee of Observation, Prince George County. Hist. of Md. Scharf. V. 2, p. 172. MHS.
Committee of Safety of Baltimore Town and County, 1774. Chronicles of Balto. Scharf. P. 129. MHS.
Committee of Safety of Baltimore Town and County, 1775-76. Gilmor Papers. Mss. MHS.
Commutation warrants issued to 2201 Revolutionary War officers. Including rank, regiment and State. G. M. Brumbaugh. (Md. names in list.) Natl. Geneal. Soc. Quart., April and July, 1920, v. 9, nos. 1 and 2. MHS.
Company lieutenants or Continental agents appointed in Maryland, 1777, 1779, to purchase supplies for Army. Hist. of Md. Scharf. V. 2, pp. 379-80. MHS.
Confiscation of British property in Baltimore City, and purchasers. Chronicles of Balto. Scharf. P. 188. MHS.
Contributions to annals of medical progress, and medical education in United States, before and during War of Independence. (Early physicians and surgeons of Md., pp. 86-90.) Gov. Printing Office, Wash., D. C., 1874, pamph.
Council of Safety, of Eastern Shore of Maryland. Chesapeake Bay Country. Earle. P. 285;
M. H. Mag., 1910, v. 5, pp. 153-60.
Cresap's muster roll, 1775. (No muster roll ever found; names of officers in Scharf's Hist. of west. Md.) M. H. Mag., 1927, v. 22, p. 399.
*Declaration of Independence. (Maryland signers, Carroll, Chase, Paca and Stone, with genealogical notes.) Historical Register. Hill. P. 13.
Deputies elected by freemen of Maryland to Provincial Conventions Meeting at Annapolis, 1774 and 1775. Hist. of Md. Scharf. Anne

Arundel Co., v. 2, pp. 163, 170–71; Baltimore Town and Co., v. 2, pp. 166–67, 173; Calvert Co., v. 2, p. 164; Charles Co., v. 2, pp. 165, 169–70; Frederick Co., v. 2, pp. 164, 174–75; Prince George Co., v. 2, pp. 165–66, 171–72. MHS.

Diary of Tench Francis Tilghman. A. J. Hanna. Pamph. DAR.

Eastern Shore of Maryland field officers, 1775. Chesapeake Bay Country. Earle. P. 285.

Enlistment papers (original), Revolutionary War. Black cloth binding, 163 pp. Index to names in front of book. (Collection of individual enlistments mounted in Scrap Book.) Hall of Records.

Frederick County. List of lots sold and purchasers (sale, Oct. 10, 1781). Monocacy Manor belonged to Daniel Dulany, granted to soldiers of Maryland line. Hist. of Frederick Co. Williams. V. 1, pp. 327–28. MHS; DAR.

Frederick County. List of substitutes, 1778. M. H. Mag., 1911, v. 6, pp. 256–61.

Frederick County. Maryland line. Petition of officers (grievances), 1779. Pa. Germans in settlement of Md. Nead. P. 257. MHS; DAR.

Frederick County militia, 1775. Pa. Germans in settlement of Md. P. 203. Lower District (now Montgomery Co.), pp. 208–12; Middle District, pp. 213–18; Upper District (now Washington Co.), pp. 218–23. MHS; DAR.

Frederick County militia, 1779. Revolutionary War pay roll of Capt. Christ. Myer's company. Md. Geneal. Bull., v. 5, pp. 37–38. MHS; DAR.

Frederick County. Muster roll. Capt. Thomas Price's company of riflemen, in service of United States. (The Lost Legion.) One of two companies from Frederick to join Army at Boston (Cresap's, other). From Soc. Coll. M. H. Mag., 1927, v. 22, pp. 275–83.

Frederick County. Revolutionary records. County Court note book. Ljungstedt. V. 2, p. 94; v. 3, p. 37. MHS; DAR.

French troops in Maryland, 1782. From Rochambeau Papers. M. H. Mag., 1910, v. 5, p. 229.

Fort Frederick Guard, 1778. Pa. Germans in of Md. Nead. P. 174. MHS; DAR.

German regiments in Frederick County, June 27, 1776. Pa. Germans in settlement of Md. Nead. Pp. 224–40. MHS; DAR.

Harford County. List of non associators and non enrollers of 1775–76. Harford Co. Hist. Soc. Coll. J. H. Univ. Lib.

Hist. of Harford Co. Preston. Pp. 344–51. MHS; DAR.

Harford County. List of solicitors of subscribers of Association of Freeman, 1776. Hist. of Harford Co. Preston. P. 262. MHS; DAR.

Harford County. Revolutionary Committee. Original minutes of proceedings, Dec. 8, 1774–Sept. 11, 1776. (Contain many names.) Harford Co. Hist. Soc. Coll. J. H. Univ. Lib.

Hist. of Harford Co. Preston. Pp. 278–344. MHS; DAR.

Harford County. Revolutionary soldiers (10) drawing pensions in census, 1840. Harford Co. Hist. Soc. Coll. J. H. Univ. Lib.

Hist. of Harford Co. Preston. P. 262. MHS; DAR.

Harford County. Signers of Bush Declaration of Independence, Mar. 22, 1775. Harford Town or Bush. Harford Co. Hist. Soc. Coll. J.H. Univ. Lib.

Hist. of Harford Co. Preston. P. 34.

Md. Geneal. Rec. Com., 1932–33, p. 156. Mss. DAR.

Patriotic Md. S. A. R., Balto., 1930, p. 34. MHS.

Independent companies of Maryland. Officers, 1776. Hist. of Md. Scharf. V. 2, p. 192. MHS.

Index of House and Senate Journals, 1777–1837. Used for private bills of Revolutionary soldiers. 3 vols. Published by State of Md., 1866–67.

Index to Revolutionary War militia lists of Maryland. 1926. Bd. mss. MHS; DAR.

Journal of Capt. Wm. Beatty, 1776–81. From Soc. Coll. M. H. Mag., 1908, v. 3, pp. 104–19.

Journal of correspondence of Council of Safety, Aug. 26, 1775–Mar. 20, 1777. Original mss. Hall of Records.

Archives of Md. Vols. 11, 12, 16.

Journal of Council of Safety. Journal of draughts on treasury Jan. 18–May 7, 1776. Account of money drawn out of treasury by governor and council (200,000 pounds), 1781. Ms. Hall of Records.

Lafayette in Harford County. Memorial Monograph, 1781–1931. J. Alexis Shriver. Belair, Md., 1931. DAR.

Last blood shed in Revolution. F. B. Culver. M. H. Mag., 1910, v. 5, p. 329.

List of men blown up in barges, 1781. Md. O. R. Soc. Bull., no. 3, p. 40. MHS.

List of officers before Maryland Assembly, Mar., 1779, asking for relief and just provision for support of Army. Hist. of Md. Scharf. V. 2, p. 352. MHS.

List of physicians of Revolutionary period in Maryland, 1775–83. M. H. Mag.; 1929, v.24, no. 1, pp. 1–17.

List of principal officers (87) of Maryland regiments, 1779. Hist. of Md. Scharf. V. 2, pp. 352–53. MHS.

Maryland and France, 1774–89. Kathryn Sullivan. Phila., Univ. of Pa. Press, 1936. DAR.

Maryland and North Carolina in Campaign, 1780–1781. With preliminary notice of earlier battles in Revolutionary War, in which two States won distinction. E. G. Davis. M. H. S. Fund Pub., no. 33, Balto., 1893. MHS.

Maryland and Stamp Act controversy. P. H. Giddens. MHS.

*Maryland during Revolution. M. H. Mag., 1929, v. 24, pp. 325–42.

Maryland line at Eutaw Springs, South Carolina, Sept. 8, 1781. Wm. Wilmott, captain. List of officers killed and wounded. (Lieut. Zedekiah Moore, said to have been last soldier wounded in Revolutionary War.) Patriotic Marylander. MHS; DAR.

Maryland line during Revolution. Seventy-Six Soc. Pub., T. Balch, Phila., vols. 1–4, 1855–57.

Maryland line. Grievances from Gist Papers. M. H. Mag., 1909, v. 4, pp. 262–68.

Maryland line. Pay lists and officers, 1783. Mss. MHS.

Maryland line. Record of pay, after Revolutionary War. (Original.) Md. Room, Enoch Pratt Lib.

Maryland Loyalists. Orderly book of Maryland Loyalist's regiment, June 18-Oct. 12, 1778. Kept by Capt. Caleb Jones. P. L. Ford. Brookline, N. Y., 1891.
Maryland officers appointed to command Flying Camp, 1776-77. Ms. MHS.
Maryland Revolutionary records. Data obtained from 3050 pension claims and bounty land applications, including 1000 marriages of Maryland soldiers and list of 1200 proved services of soldiers and patriots of other States. H. W. Newman, 1701 H Street, Wash., D. C., 1938, 155 pp. MHS; DAR; Enoch Pratt Lib.
Maryland's Declaration of Independence, July 3, 1776. Ms. (original). Hall of Records.
Hist. of Md. Scharf. V. 2, p. 232. MHS.
Maryland's distressed soldiers' families and half-pay officers. Earliest date, 1782. Mss. MHS.
Maryland's Navy, 1775-79. Privateers and their commanders. Hist. of Md. Scharf. V. 2, pp. 201-07.
Hist. of Balto. City and Co. Scharf. P. 99. MHS.
Maryland soldiers on half pay and soldiers receiving bounty land. Md. unpublished Revolutionary War records. Hodges. V. 4. Mss. DAR.
Maryland troops. Payrolls of independent companies, 1788. Mss. Lib. Cong.
Maryland troops, 1st Regiment (Gen. Mordecai Gist). Return of six independent companies, 1776. Mss. Lib. Cong.
Maryland troops, 6th Regiment, 1780. Ms. Lib., Cong.
Maryland troops (Gen. Smallwood), 1776. Ms. Lib. Cong.
Maryland troops in War of Revolution. From Public Record Office, London. M. H. Mag., 1909, v. 4, p. 288.
Medical men of Revolution; with history of Medical Department of Continental Army. J. M. Toner. Phila., 1876, 140 pp. DAR.
Meeting of Freemen of Frederick County, Nov. 18, 1774, and Jun. 24, 1775. Hist. of west. Md. Scharf. V. 1, pp.127-29. MHS; DAR.
Members of Assembly of Maryland, June, 1780, who subscribed to support of Army. Hist. of Md. Scharf. V. 2, p. 352. MHS.
Members of Senate and House of Delegates, who were subscribers to fund to supply soldiers with necessaries for campaign, 1780 ($25,000 and 120 hhds. tobacco). Chronicles of Balto. Scharf. Pp. 187-89. MHS.
Memoirs of my times. James Wilkinson, soldier of Revolutionary War and War of 1812.
Merchants of Baltimore, 1781, who subscribed to support of Army. Hist. of Md. Scharf. V. 2, p. 445. MHS.
Military papers, 1777-83, 1790-97. Rainbow Series, Brown Book. Mss. Hall of Records.
Militia list of Maryland, Revolutionary War. 1926. Bd., indexed, mss. MHS; DAR.
Patriotic Marylander, v. 3, pp. 57, 122, 231. MHS; DAR.
Militia officers and commissions of Maryland, 1778-79. Bd. ms. MHS.
Militia officers of Maryland. Names and other data of Maryland militia officers which do not appear in America Revolution, 1776-83, recently published by State. Pa. Mag. Hist. and Biog., 1901, v. 25, p. 583. MHS.
Militia of Anne Arundel County. Md. unpublished Revolutionary War records. Hodges. V. 2. Mss. DAR.
Md. Geneal. Records, v. 4, p. 9. MHS; DAR.
Patriotic Marylander, v. 3, pp. 57, 122. MHS; DAR.
Militia of Baltimore in defense of Baltimore, with list of company lieutenants, June, 1777. Hist. of Md. Scharf. V. 2, p. 453.
Battalion, 1779. Patriotic Marylander, v. 3, no. 2, p. 111. MHS; DAR.
Militia of Baltimore County. Md. unpublished Revolutionary records. Hodges. V. 2. Mss. DAR.
1779. From original roll presented by F. B. Culver. M. H. Mag., 1912, v. 7, p. 90.
Militia of Calvert County. Md. unpublished Revolutionary War records. Hodges. V. 2. Mss. DAR.
Militia of Caroline County. Hist. of Caroline Co. List of officers, p. 62; 1777, pp. 67-68; list of officers and privates (incomplete), pp. 74-75. MHS.
Militia of Charles County. Md. unpublished Revolutionary War records. Hodges. V. 2. Mss. DAR.
Militia of Dorchester County, Dec. 1, 1776-1781. Hist. of Dorchester Co. Jones. Pp. 215-46. MHS; DAR.
Militia of Eastern Shore of Maryland; with officers stationed on Chesapeake and its tributaries, July, 1776. Hist. of Md. Scharf. V. 2, p. 268. MHS.
Militia of Frederick County, 1779. Md. Geneal. Bull., v. 6, p. 15. MHS; DAR.
Militia of Harford County, 1775-83. Hist. of Harford Co. Preston. Pp. 105-37, 265-68. MHS; DAR.
Militia of Kent County, Revolutionary War, 1778. P. G. Skirven. Patriotic Marylander, 1917, v. 3, no. 4, pp. 57-62, 230-35. MHS; DAR.
1776. Mss. MHS.
Md. unpublished Revolutionary War records. Hodges. V. 2. Mss. DAR.
Militia of Maryland. Return of 33rd Battalion, 1777. From Soc. Coll. M. H. Mag., 1909, v. 4, pp. 379-81.
Militia of Montgomery County. Md. unpublished Revolutionary War records. Hodges. Mss. DAR.
Md. Geneal. Bull., v. 7, p. 52. MHS; DAR.
Militia of Somerset County, 1780. Md. Geneal. Bull., v. 2, p. 25. MHS; DAR.
Militia of St. Mary's County. Md. unpublished Revolutionary War records. Hodges. V. 2. Mss. DAR.
1794. Mss. MHS.
Militia of Talbot County. Mss. MHS.
Some names of officers and privates, 1778-81. Md. O. R. Soc., v. 3, pp. 86-105. MHS.
Minutes of Council of Safety. Instructions and correspondence to Maryland delegates in Congress, etc., 1776-90. 32 vols. Hall of Records.
Montgomery County. List of Revolutionary graves (50). Md. Geneal. Rec. Com., 1932-33. Bd. mss. DAR.
Montgomery County. Revolutionary pensioners. Hist. of west. Md. Scharf. V. 1, p. 683. MHS.

Muster roll, Capt. James Hindman's company of Maryland independent regular troops, Sept. 1776. Pa. Mag. Hist. and Biog., 1897, v. 21, pp. 503–04. MHS; DAR.

Muster roll, Capt. Thomas Prices's company of riflemen, in service of United States, 1775. M. H. Mag., 1927, v. 22, p. 275.

Muster roll, Capt. Sterett's independent company of Baltimore merchants, 1777. Hist. of Balto. City and Co. Scharf. P. 77. MHS.

Muster roll of Kent County, 1778. P. G. Skirven. Patriotic Marylander, v. 2, no. 1, pp. 57–62. MHS; DAR.

Muster rolls and other records of service of Maryland troops in Revolution, 1775–83. Archives of Md. V. 18. Also civil and military lists, vols. 11, 12, 16, 22, 43 and 45. MHS.

Muster rolls of year 1782, of six companies of Loyalists recruited in Maryland. Coll. of historic papers. Soc. Col. Wars, State of Md. MHS.

Names of those who served on Washington's staff. (From Md., Hanson, McHenry and Tilghman.) Notes and queries. Egle. 1898.

Narrative of events which occurred in Baltimore Town during Revolutionary War. Robert Purviance. Balto., 1849. MHS; DAR.

Narrative of Campaign of 1780. Otho Holland Williams, Adjutant General. In appendix to William Johnson's Sketches of life and correspondence of Nathaniel Green. William's original correspondence. MHS.

National Genealogical Society. Quarterly, v. 6, no. 1. Revolutionary number issued April, 1917; devoted to Maryland items. M. H. Mag., 1917, v. 12, p. 196.

Oath of Allegiance of Anne Arundel County, Mar., 1778. Merriweather Book (Test Book). Ms. Hall of Records.
- D. A. R. Mag., July, 1917, v. 51, pp. 49–55; Aug., 1917, pp. 84–87.
- Md. unpublished Revolutionary War records. Hodges. V. 3. Mss. DAR.
- Scharf Papers. Mss. MHS.

Oath of allegiance of Baltimore County. (Original.) Hall of Records.
- Photos. copy. MHS.
- 23 returns. From Scharf Papers. Mss. MHS.
- Md. unpublished Revolutionary War records. Hodges. V. 3, v. 6. Mss. DAR.
- M. H. Mag., 1916, v. 11, p. 163.

Oath of Allegiance of Baltimore Town. Original. Hall of Records.
- Liber, 1772–1780, of Court Sessions. Court House, Balto.
- Photos. MHS.
- Md. unpublished Revolutionary War records. Hodges. V. 6. Mss. DAR.

Oath of Allegiance of Calvert County. Original. Hall of Records.
- Photos. copy. MHS.
- 9 returns. Mss. MHS.
- Revolutionary record of Md. Brumbaugh and Hodges. P. 37, pt. 1. MHS; DAR.
- Md. unpublished Revolutionary War records. Hodges. V. 6. Mss. DAR.
- 1778. Monette Book. P. 422. MHS.

Oath of Allegiance of Caroline County. Wilson Mss. Coll., no. 30. MHS.
- 9 returns. Mss. MHS.
- Revolutionary records of Md. Brumbaugh and Hodges. P. 7. MHS; DAR.

Oath of Allegiance of Cecil County. Crude little booklets (original), yellowed by age, irregular size. Court House, Elkton.
- Signers of Oath of Allegiance sworn by County Justices, March 2, 1778. Miss Molly Ash. Elkton, Author, 1940, 41 pp. MHS; DAR.
- Signers (330 names), with genealogical notes. Miss Molly Ash. D. A. R. Mag., Sept., 1928, v. 62, no. 9, p. 561. See also D. A. R. Mag., Aug. and July, 1917, v. 51, pp. 49, 84.

Oath of Allegiance of Charles County. Blue Book, Rainbow Series. Bd. mss. Hall of Records.
- Photos. copy. MHS.
- Md. unpublished Revolutionary War records. Hodges. V. 5. Mss. DAR.
- List of Signers. C. R. Morehead. Pamph. DAR.

Oath of Allegiance of Dorchester County. Original. Hall of Records.
- Photos. copy. MHS.
- 8 returns. Mss. MHS.
- 8 returns. Mss. MHS.
- Md. unpublished Revolutionary War records Hodges. V. 6. Mss. DAR.
- Md. O. R. Soc., v. 3, pp. 115–190. MHS; DAR.
- List of persons taking Oath of Fidelity of Dorchester County, 1778. Baltimore Imprint. MHS.

Oath of Allegiance of Frederick County, 1788. Revolutionary records of Maryland. Brumbaugh and Hodges. Pp. 22–24.
- Md. unpublished Revolutionary War records. Hodges. V. 3. Mss. DAR.
- M. H. Mag., 1916, v. 11, p. 163.
- 1 return. Ms. MHS.
- Natl. Geneal. Soc. Quart., July, 1917, v. 6, no. 2, pp. 33–35. (337 men.)

Oath of Allegiance of Harford County. Original. Hall of Records.
- Photos. copy. MHS.
- 10 returns. Mss. MHS.
- Md. records. Brumbaugh. V. 2, pp. 233–48.
- Md. unpublished Revolutionary War records. Hodges. V. 3. Mss. DAR.
- Harford Co. Hist. Soc. Coll. (1500 names.) J. H. Univ. Lib.

Oath of Allegiance of Montgomery County. Original. Hall of Records.
- Photos. copy. MHS.
- 9 returns. Mss. MHS.
- Revolutionary records of Md. Brumbaugh and Hodges. Pp. 1–11. MHS; DAR.
- Natl. Geneal. Soc. Quart., Apr., 1917, v. 6, no. 1, pp. 1–11. (1598 men.)
- Mar., 1780–Mar., 1782. Typed, bd., 4 pp. DAR.

Oath of Allegiance of Prince George County. Original. Hall of Records.
- Photos. copy. MHS.
- 20 returns. Mss. MHS.
- Md. records. Brumbaugh. V. 2, pp. 251–308.
- Md. unpublished Revolutionary War records, Hodges. V. 3. Mss. DAR.

Oath of Allegiance of Queen Anne County. 9 returns. Mss. MHS.

Oath of Allegiance of St. Mary's County. 1 return. Ms. MHS.
- Md. unpublished Revolutionary War records. Hodges. V. 6. Mss. DAR.

Oath of Allegiance of Somerset County. Blue Book, Rainbow Series. Bd. mss. Hall of Records.

Md. unpublished Revolutionary War records. Hodges. Mss. DAR.
Oath of Allegiance of Talbot County. Blue Book, Rainbow Series. Bd. mss. Hall of Records.
Photos. copy. MHS.
1 return. Mss. MHS.
Md. unpublished Revolutionary War records. Hodges. V. 6. Mss. DAR.
Md. O. R. Soc., v. 3, pp. 106–14.
Oath of Allegiance of Washington County. 12 returns. Scharf Papers. Mss. MHS.
Md. unpublished Revolutionary War records. Hodges. V. 3. Mss. DAR.
Revolutionary records of Md. Brumbaugh and Hodges. Pp. 12–21.
Natl. Geneal. Soc. Quart., 1917, v. 6, no. 1, pp. 12–21. (1485 men.)
Oath of Allegiance of Worcester Co. 8 returns. Mss. MHS.
Oaths of Allegiance of Maryland. Wilson Mss. Coll., no. 131. MHS.
Officers and organizations of military forces of Maryland, Jan., 1776. Hist. of Md. Scharf. V. 2, pp. 191–95. MHS.
Officers and privates. Hist. of Md. Scharf. V. 3, pp. 760–63. MHS.
Olive Branch Petition. Maryland Signers: Matthew Tilghman, 1718–90; Samuel Chase, 1741–1811; Thomas Johnson, 1732–1819; William Paca, 1740–99. D. A. R. Mag., v. 66, no. 5, p. 293; no. 6, p. 346.
Facsimile "Olive Branch Petition, 8 July, 1775," in Collotype, from original in Museum of Public Record Office, London. MHS.
Original commissions, 1775–82. Officers of Maryland State militia. Md. unpublished Revolutionary War records. Hodges. Typed, bd. DAR. (V. 1: Anne Arundel, Baltimore, Calvert, Caroline, Cecil, Dorchester, Frederick, Harford, Kent, Montgomery, Prince George, Queen Anne, Somerset, St. Mary's, Talbot, Washington and Worcester Counties.)
Original enlistment papers (Revolutionary War). Scrap Book, Black Cloth binding, 163 pp. Index to names in front of book. (Collection of individual enlistments mounted in Scrap Book.) Hall of Records.
Orphans Court lists, Western Maryland, 1788; half-pay for maimed officers, soldiers, seamen and children of deceased. Hist. of west. Md. Scharf. V. 1, pp. 475–76. MHS.
Papers concerning losses during Revolutionary War, 1781, and information about British property. Rainbow Series, Blue Book. Mss. Hall of Records.
Papers relating to Maryland line during Revolution. Seventy-Six Soc., Thomas Balch, Phila., 1857, v. 4, pp. 218.
Pay roll of Capt. John Jones' Company, 1778 (Md.) Mss. MHS.
Payrolls (2) of portion of Invalid Regiment, Jan. and Feb., 1783. Records of Vice-Admiralty Court of Maryland, 1754–67. Ms. Lib. Cong.
1754–72. Mss. MHS.
Pensions:
List of 153 soldiers from Maryland. Pensioners who served in War of Revolution, residing in Kentucky, 1818–40. Mss. MHS.
Maryland pensioners on Mississippi pension rolls of United States, under Act of Congress, approved 1818, 1828, 1832. D. A. R. Mag., v. 69, no. 11, p. 685.
Pensioners of State of Maryland, 1800–12. Mss. MHS.
Pension records of Revolutionary War. National Archives Building, Washington.
Pensions of Revolutionary War. Abstracts of original on file in Pension Office, 1910–29. Washington, 142 vols. Typed, bd. DAR.
Pensions, Revolutionary War, Oct., 1778. Hall of Records.
Revolutionary War pension abstracts. (Containing numerous Bible records and other family data, some of Md.) Natl. Geneal. Soc. Quart., vols. 17, 18, 19, 20 and 23. MHS.
Revolutionary War pensioners in Baltimore City. Census, 1840. Md. Geneal. Bull., v. 2, no. 2, p. 25. MHS; DAR.
Revolutionary War pensions. From Kilty's Laws, some original commissions. Md. rec. Brumbaugh. V. 2, pp. 314–411. MHS; DAR.
United States census of pensioners, 1840, for Revolutionary or military services, with names, ages and place of residence. (Md. census, pp. 127–28.) Wash., D. C., Blair & Rivers, 1841. MHS.
Prince George County. Loyal civil service, Apr. 19, 1775–Sept. 8, 1793. Md. unpublished Revolutionary records. Brumbaugh and Hodges. Pp. 25–36. MHS.
Privateers in American Revolution of Maryland. B. C. Steiner. M. H. Mag., 1908, v. 3, pp. 99–103.
Prominent citizens of Queen Anne County, at dawn of Revolution. Patriotic Marylander, v. 3, no. 3, pp. 159–66. MHS; DAR.
Propaganda of Maryland's entrance into American Revolution. E. Meredith. 1936. Typed, bd., 149 pp. MHS.
†Pulaski's legion roll, 1778–79. (Biog. of Count Casimir Pulaski.) R. H. Spencer. M. H. Mag., 1918, v. 13, pp. 214–26.
Records of Revolutionary War. Wm. T. R. Saffell, counsellor and agent for Revolutionary claims. Contains names of officers and privates in Maryland; list of distinguished prisoners of war; officers entitled to half-pay; commutation and lands; officers and privates with dates of their commissions and enlistments. 1858. MHS; DAR.
Register (partial) of officers under Washington, July, 1778. (Md., pp. 68–69.) Pa. Mag. Hist. and Biog., v. 18, pp. 64–72. MHS.
Resistance of Stamp Act. From Public Record Office, London. M. H. Mag., 1909, v. 4, pp. 134–39.
Revolutionary committee of Bladensburg, Prince George County. (Copied from Md. Gazette, Jan. 5, 1775.) Md. O. R. Soc. Bull., no. 3. MHS.
Revolutionary letters, Charles Carroll to Gist, 1781. M. H. Mag., 1907, v. 2, pp. 344–45. Gist to Charles Carroll. Pp. 345–46.
Revolutionary letters, Patrick Henry to Thomas Johnson, 1777. M. H. Mag., 1910, v. 5, p. 255.
Revolutionary letters, Thomas Jefferson to Thomas Sim Lee, 1779. M. H. Mag., 1910, v. 5, pp. 182, 256–57.
Revolutionary officers and soldiers, entitled to lots westward of Fort Cumberland, Allegany

County, 1788. Hist. of west. Md. Scharf. V. 1, pp. 145-46. MHS.
Laws and rules of Land Office, Maryland. Brewer. Pp. 73-125; patented military lots, pp. 132-58.
Revolutionary officers' and soldiers' lots of Maryland. Liber A. Indexed. (Original.) Ms. Hall of records.
Ms. copy. MHS.
Revolutionary officers of Maryland. Hist. of Md. McSherry. Appendix. 1849. MHS.
Revolutionary records in reference to bounty lands. (Original.) 150 plats of military lots and others, with indexes. 8 vols. Land Office.
Revolutionary records of Maryland. G. M. Brumbaugh and Mrs. M. R. Hodges. Wash., D. C., 1924. Lib. Cong.; MHS; DAR.
Revolutionary soldiers' graves. Friends, Glendy, Greenmount, Louden Park, St. Paul's and Westminster churchyards, Balto. Patriotic Marylander, v. 2, no. 4. Pp. 54-60. MHS; DAR.
Revolutionary War commissions, militia officers. Photos. and mss. 142 pp., 30 pp. index. Bd. MHS.
Revolutionary War heroes. A. Cole. Pub. by Westminster Presbyterian Church, Balto., bklet. DAR; Enoch Pratt Lib.
Revolutionary War militia lists. 256 pp. Bd. mss. MHS.
St. Mary's County. List of delegates, to several Provincial Conventions of Maryland, 1774-76. Chronicles of Md. Thomas. Pp. 278-81. MHS.
St. Mary's County. Revolutionary committees of importance. Copied from Md. Gazette, Jan. 5, 1775. Md. O. R. Soc., v. 3, pp. 126-27. MHS.
Sixth Regiment, Maryland line, in command of Otho H. Williams; and list of officers, Sept. 8, 1779. Hist. of Md. Scharf. V. 2, p. 332. MHS.
Some Revolutionary correspondence of Dr. James McHenry. B. C. Steiner. Pa. Mag. Hist. and Biog., 1905, v. 29. MHS.
Somerset and Worcester Counties. Signers of Declaration of Association of Freemen. Side lights of Md. hist. Richardson. V. 1, p. 377. MHS; DAR.
Historic Salisbury. Truitt. Pp. 38-39.
Stamp Act Papers. From Coll. of Soc. M. H. Mag., 1911, v. 6, pp. 282-305.
Tories and non-jurors of Revolution in Talbot County. Harrison Mss. Coll. MHS.
Tories of Maryland (100). Hist. of Md. Scharf. V. 2, pp. 387-88. MHS.
Tories of Somerset and Worcester Counties. Hist. of Md. Scharf. V. 2, pp. 300, 302. MHS.
Twelth Battalion of Charles County; 1777. Md. Geneal. Bull., v. 4, p. 25. MHS; DAR.
Unpublished Revolutionary records of Maryland. Natl. Geneal. Soc. Quart., Apr., 1917, v. 6, no. 1; Jan., 1918, no. 1, pp. 1-22. MHS.
Unpublished Revolutionary records of Maryland. V. 1: contains original commissions, 1775-82; officers of State militia. V. 2: passengers of *The Ark* and *The Dove*; Maryland militia. V. 3: Oath of Allegiance, 1778, of Frederick, Harford, Montgomery and Washington Counties. 247 pp. V. 4: soldiers of half-pay and families of distressed soldiers. 215 pp. V. 5: Montgomery County militia; Charles County Oath of Allegiance. 170 pp. V. 6: Oath of Allegiance, 1778, of Calvert, Baltimore, Talbot, Dorchester and St. Mary's Counties, 174 pp. Copied by Margaret R. Hodges. Original in DAR. Copies have been made under auspices of Maryland State Society, D. A. R., and presented by Mrs. Arthur W. Lambert, State Librarian, to Hall of Records and MHS. Typed, Bd. 1939, 1940.
Washington County. List of members of military companies, organized 1776. Hist. of west. Md. Scharf. V. 2, pp. 1189-90. MHS.
Washington County. List of surviving veterans of Revolutionary War granted pension certificates, Aug., 1820. Hist. of west. Md. Scharf. V. 2, p. 1190. MHS.
Western Maryland soldiers in Revolutionary War. B. C. Steiner. Johns Hopkins University Studies, series 20, no. 1, 1902. MHS; Enoch Pratt Lib.

REVOLUTIONARY WAR—GENERAL

Aides to Washington. Notes and queries. Egle. 1898, p. 86. MHS; DAR.
Alabama. Revolutionary soldiers. T. W. Owen. 1911. DAR.
†American Loyalists. Lorenzo Sabine. Biographical sketches to adherents to British Crown, in War of Revolution. Alphabetically arranged. Boston, 1847, 1864. MHS.
American prisoners of Revolution. Danske Dandridge. 1911. DAR.
American Revolution. W. E. H. Lecky. 1922. DAR.
American Revolution. J. Thacher. 1859. DAR.
American Revolutionary patriots, who are interred in District of Columbia. Col. Hist. Soc., 1918, v. 21.
Chaplains and clergy of Revolution. J. I. Headley. DAR.
Colonial merchants of American Revolution, 1776-93. A. M. Schlesinger. 1918. DAR.
†Commander-in-Chief's Guard. Revolutionary War. C. E. Godgrey. Biog. (Biographical records of officers and men, pp. 113-274.) Wash., D. C., Stevenson and Smith, pub., 1904.
Commutation warrants issued to 2201 Revolutionary War officers, including rank, regiment and State. Natl. Geneal. Soc. Quart., v. 8, no. 4, pp. 49-55; v. 9, no. 1, p. 1; no. 2, p. 1. MHS.
Complete Navy register of United States, 1778-81. T. S. Hammersly. MHS.
Connecticut men in War of Revolution, War of 1812 and Mexican War. 1889. DAR.
Connecticut men in Revolution. Pub. by State of Connecticut. See also: Coll. Conn. Hist. Soc., v. 8, v. 12. DAR.
Delaware. Colonial and Revolutionary records. 5 vols. DAR.
Delaware. Oaths of fidelity, 1771, 1778, 1784, 1785. 10 photos. DAR.
Delaware. Papers of Historical Society of Delaware. Brief account of Delaware regiments in War of Revolution. Also personal memoirs of officers, rolls of same. Oration before Delaware, Cincinnati on death of Washington. Henry H. Bellas. Paper no. 13. Wilmington, 1895.
Delaware. Revolutionary soldiers. Hist. Soc. of Delaware Papers, no. 14. Wilmington, 1896.

Delaware. Revolutionary soldiers. (Taken from Milford, Delaware, Herald, May 30, 1895.) G. W. Marshall. 1895. DAR.

*District of Columbia in American Revolution and patriots of Revolutionary period, who are interred in District or Arlington. Dr. Stephen Balch. Rec. Columbia Hist. Soc., v. 19, v. 20. MHS.

District of Columbia in American Revolution, and patriots of Revolutionary period who are interred therein. S. M. Ely. 1918.

District of Columbia. Revolutionary dead, place of burial, lot number, date of birth and death. Consult Daughters of American Revolution, Annual Rept. to Smithsonian Institution, Wash., D. C. (Especially long list in 3rd, 5th, 17th, and 21st repts.) These reports are in many large libraries.

District of Columbia, Revolutionary graves. Natl. Geneal. Soc. Quart., July, 1918, v. 2, p. 27. MHS.

First issue of Declaration of Independence, printed with names of Signers. Mary Goddard, printer, Balto., 1777. Lib. Cong.

Generals of Continental line in Revolutionary War, 1775–83. Pa. Mag. Hist. and Biog., v. 27, no. 4, pp. 385–403. MHS.

Georgia. Obituary notices of Revolutionary soldiers buried in Georgia. From Milledgeville, Ga., Journal, 1819. Mss. DAR.

Georgia. Revolutionary graves. Consult Daughters of American Revolution, annual Repts. to Smithsonian Institution, nos. 3 and 5, Wash., D. C.

Georgia. Revolutionary records of State. L. L. Knight. 1918. DAR.

Georgia. Revolutionary records. A. D. Chandler. 3 vols. DAR.

Georgia. Revolutionary soldiers (600) living in Georgia, 1827–28. M. L. Houston. 1932. DAR.

Georgia. Revolutionary soldiers: receipts from Georgia county grants. 1928. DAR.

Georgia. Roster of Revolution. L. L. Knight. 1920. DAR.

Heroes of American Revolution and their descendants; Battle of Long Island. Henry Whittemore. 1897. Supplement, 1899. DAR.

Historical register of officers of Continental Army, April, 1775–Dec., 1783. F. B. Heitman. Alphabetical lists of officers, military secretaries, aides-de-camp to Washington, French officers, troops at Valley Forge, 1777–78 as given to Congress by War Department. 1827. Rare Book Shop, Wash., D. C., 1914. MHS; DAR.

History of American Revolution. P. Allen. 1819, 2 vols. DAR.

Illinois. Revolutionary soldiers buried in Illinois. H. H. Walker. 1917. DAR.

Index to medical men in Revolution, 1775–83. From War Department Medical Field Service School. Wash., D. C., Pamph. DAR; SAR Lib.

Indiana. Soldiers and patriots of American Revolution buried in Indiana. Mrs. Roscoe C. O'Bryne. Indiana Geneal. Rec. Com., 1938. Typed, bd. DAR.

Kentucky, Collins' History of Kentucky, has list of Revolutionary soldiers who settled in Kentucky. DAR.

Kentucky, Fayette County. Index to abstracts of Pension Papers of soldiers, who resided in Fayette County in Revolutionary War, War of 1812 and Indian Wars. A. W. B. Burns. Pamph. DAR.

Kentucky Society of Sons of American Revolution Year Book, and Catalogue. Contains list of Revolutionary soldiers of Virginia to whom State gave military warrants (land bounty warrants for services, pp. 190–272). 1913. DAR.

Les combattant's francais de la guerre americaine, 1778–83. Imprimerie Nationale, Wash., D. C., 1905. MHS.

List (complete) of generals of Revolutionary War, according to rank and seniority, with respective terms of service in each rank. Pa. Mag. Hist. and Biog., v. 27, pp. 397–403. MHS.

List of names of Washington's staff. Notes and queries. Egle.

Lives of Signers. Rev. G. A. Goodrich. Hartford. 1841.

Lives of Signers. N. Dwight. N. Y., 1895. DAR.

Maine. Revolutionary soldiers of Maine. Pub. by Sons of American Revolution of Maine. DAR.

Marine officers in American Revolution, 1776. Maj. E. N. McClellan, U. S. Marine Corps. D. A. R. Mag., June, 1921, v. 55, no. 6, pp. 303–12; Jan., 1922, v. 56, no. 1, pp. 23–33; July, 1923, v. 57, no. 7, pp. 409–17; Sept., 1932, v. 66, no. 9, pp. 560–68.

Massachusetts soldiers and sailors of Revolution, from Blandford. S. G. Ward. 1933. DAR.

Mecklenburg militia, 1775–78. D. A. R. Mag., July, 1927, v. 61, no. 7, pp. 547–51.

Medal list of Sons of American Revolution who served in War with Spain. 1900. DAR.

Medical men in American Revolution, 1775–83. L. C. Duncan. From Office of Surgeon General, U.S.A. 1931, pamph. DAR.

Medical men of Revolution. Contains names of nearly twelve thousand physicians. J. M. Toner, M.D. Phila., Collins, printer, 1876.

Missouri soldiers of Revolution. Mrs. J. Short. 1938. DAR.

Names of about eight thousand persons; small portion of number confined on board British prision ships during War of Revolution. 1888. DAR.

Naval records of American Revolution, 1775–88. C. H. Lincoln. Pub. Lib. Cong., 1906. Lib. Cong.; DAR.

New Hampshire Revolutionary War pension records. Natl. Geneal. Soc. Quart., Sept., 1938, v. 26, pp. 33–35; Mar., 1939, v. 27, p. 22. MHS.

New Hampshire Revolutionary War rolls. J. W. Hammond. DAR.

New Hampshire soldiers of American Revolution. L. M. Cate. 1932. DAR.

New Hampshire State Papers. Revolutionary records. V. 30. DAR.

New Jersey in Revolutionary War. Official register of officers and men. W. S. Stryker. 1872. DAR.

New Jersey. Records of 331 soldiers who fought in New Jersey, during Revolutionary War. M. E. Doolittle. New Jersey Geneal. Rec. Com., 1939, v. 5. Typed, bd. DAR.

New Jersey. Revolutionary soldiers. New Jersey Geneal. Rec. Com., vols. 1, 2, 3 and 6, 1935–36–37–40. Typed 1, bd. DAR.

New Jersey. Revolutionary history. V. 1: Extracts from newspapers, 1776–77. Edited by W. M. Stryker, Trenton, N. J., 1901. V. 2: 1778. Edited by F. B. Lee, Trenton. Under direction of New Jersey Hist. Soc., 1903. DAR.

New Jersey. Revolutionary soldiers. F. E. Young. 1936, pamph. DAR.

New Jersey, Warren County. Soldiers of American Revolution; their wives and daughters. 2 vols. DAR.

New York. Copies from London, of American Loyalists; history of each; testimony; confiscation of property, etc. New York Public Lib., New York City, kept in metal cases.

New York. Grave records of Revolutionary soldiers buried in New York. New York State Committee of Hist. Research and Preservation of Records. 1938, 11 vols. DAR.

New York in Revolution. New York State Archives, v. 1. Includes roster of State troops. Berthold Fernow. 1887. DAR.

New York. Mather's "Refugees of 1776," from Long Island to Connecticut. DAR.

New York Muster and pay rolls of War of Revolution, 1775–83. New York Hist. Soc. Coll., 1916, v. 47, v. 48. Includes troops of Maryland, North Carolina, NewYork, Pennsylvania, Virginia, etc. DAR.

New York Public Papers of George Clinton, first governor of New York, 1777–95, 1801–04. Military. V. 1–8, 1899–1904. V. 9–10, index, 1911, 1914. DAR.

North Carolina. Roster of soldiers in American Revolution. (With appendix containing collection of miscellaneous records.) North Carolina Soc. D. A. R., publisher, 1932. DAR.

North and South Carolina. Officers killed in Revolutionary War. Mss. MHS.

Ohio. Early settlers and Revolutionary soldiers of Preble County, Ohio. From Maryland: Allabaugh, Barton, Eby, Etzler, Gift, Locke, Loy, Norris, Parker, Prugh, Ridenour, Ruple, Saylor, Teal and Wimmer. D. A. R. Mag., Sept., 1935, v. 69, no. 9, pp. 568–71.

Ohio. Names and location of burial of 800 Revolutionary soldiers in Ohio. W. L. Curry. 1913. DAR.

Ohio. Official roster of soldiers of American Revolution buried in State of Ohio. 1929. DAR.

Ohio. Official roster of soldiers of American Revolution who lived in Ohio. Mrs. O. D. Dailey. 1938, 2 vols. DAR.

Ohio. Revolutionary soldiers buried near Portsmouth, Ohio. Ohio Geneal. Rec. Com., 1903, p. 251. Bd. mss. DAR.

Ohio. Revolutionary soldiers records of Richland County. H. A. Frank. Pamph. DAR.

Ohio. Roster of Revolutionary soldiers residing in Ohio, 1840. W. L. Curry. 1913. DAR.

Ohio, Washington County. Revolutionary soldiers buried there. 1923. DAR.

Old time list of soldiers of Revolutionary War. E. D. Hunter. Pamph. DAR.

Pension records of Revolutionary War. National Archives Building, Washington.

Pennsylvania Allegany County. Soldiers of Revolutionary buried there. D. A. R. Mag., Dec., 1914, v. 45, p. 343.

Pennsylvania Archives, v. 10–11, 2nd series; also vols. 2, 3, 5, 6 and 7. Series contain names and services of thousands of Revolutionary soldiers. DAR.

Pennsylvania, Berks County. Soldiers who fought in American Revolution, 1775–84. Jean G. Maurer. DAR.

Pennsylvania, Butler County. Revolutionary soldiers buried there. Hist. of Butler County, 1895, pp. 217–20. (Soldiers of War of 1812, p. 221.)

Pennsylvania, Erie County. Soldiers of American Revolution. 1929. DAR.

Pennsylvania in War of Revolution; battalions and line; 1775–83. 1886, 2 vols. DAR.

Pennsylvania. Names of persons who took oath of allegiance, 1777–89, to State of Pennsylvania. Thompson Westcott. 1865. DAR.

Pennsylvania pensioners of Revolutionary War. Pa. Mag. Hist. and Biog., v. 41, v. 42. MHS.

Pennsylvania Revolutionary War pensioners. Giving name, rank and other details, under Act of Congress, Mar. 18, 1818. Geneal. Mag. Amer. Ancestry. Clemens. N. Y., 1912, v. 1; 1916, v. 2. MHS.

Pennsylvania. Soldiers of Revolution; obituary notices. Collected by W. Summers. Pa. Mag. Hist. and Biog., v. 38, p. 443. MHS.

Pennsylvania, Warren County. List of Revolutionary soldiers. Wilson Mss. Coll., no. 141. MHS.

Pictorial Field Book of American Revolution. B. J. Lossing. 2 vols.

Records of Revolutionary War. C. C. Saffell. MHS; DAR.

Revolutionary records from Congressional Reports. Collection of number of reports of committees on pensions and Revolutionary claims. 4 vols. DAR.

Revolutionary War. Hist. of Md. Scharf. V. 1, chap. 7, p. 121. MHS; DAR.

Revolutionary War pensions. Abstracts of original pension applications. 137 vols. Typed, bd. DAR. (Note: Abstracts are being compiled by member of staff of D. A. R. Lib.) Card Index. DAR.

†Sages and heroes of American Revolution. L. C. Judson. Enoch Pratt Lib., card indexed.

Signers of Declaration of Independence. B. J. Lossing. 1860.

Signers of Declaration of Independence. C. W. Heathcote. 1932. DAR.

*Signers of Declaration of Independence. Complete geneal. Homer P. Rogers. Pendleton; Oregon.

*Signers of Declaration of Independence. Register, with brief family data. D. A. R. Mag., v. 60, July, Aug., Oct.

Signers of Declaration of Independence, July 4, 1776. Natl. Cyc. Amer. Biog. Berby. 1906, p. 1. Peabody Lib.

South Carolina. History of South Carolina's records of Revolution. A. S. Salley. D. A. R. Mag., v. 71, no. 4, p. 283.

South Carolina in Revolution. See Ramsay's History of South Carolina.

South Carolina. List of officers of South Carolina's Continental establishment. Charleston, Year Book, 1893, Pp. 208–37. DAR.

South Carolina. Revolutionary necrology. South Carolina Hist. Geneal. Mag., 1904, v. 4. MHS.

South Carolina. Revolutionary soldiers. D. A. R. Mag., Sept., Oct., Nov., 1913, v. 43, pp. 550–55, 605–06, 657–62.

South Carolina. Revolutionary soldiers. South Carolina Hist. and Geneal. Mag., 1904, v. 4. MHS.

South Carolina. Roster of Geneal Sumter's Brigade. Daughters of American Revolution. Rept. to Smithsonian Institution, Wash., D. C.

Story of Revolution. H. Cabot Lodge. 1919. DAR.

Tennessee. Pensioners (2400) of Revolutionary and War of 1812. Z. Armstrong. 1937. DAR.

Tennessee. Revolutionary soldiers who were granted land in Tennessee for services in that War. E. Whitley. 1939. DAR.

Tennessee, Roane County. Revolutionary soldiers buried there. (Acree, Brakshears and Chapman of Md.) D. A. R. Mag., v. 68, no. 11, p. 688.

Tennessee. Some Tennessee heroes of Revolution. Compiled from pension statements. Pamph. DAR.

Vermont. Goodrich's Revolutionary rolls of Vermont. DAR.

Vermont. Revolutionary soldiers buried in Vermont. Pamph. DAR.

Vermont. Revolutionary War records. DAR.

Virginia, Accomack County. Revolutionary soldiers and sailors. S. Nottingham. Onancock, 1927, 101 pp. DAR.

Virginia, Albemarle County. Dissenters' petition. Amherst and Buckingham Counties, 1776. v. 18, pp. 255–58, 263. MHS; DAR.

Virginia, Albemarle County. Mss., Public Claim Paper, May, 1782. DAR.

Virginia, Albemarle County. Oath of allegiance, 1779. Hist. of Albemarle Co. 1901, pp. 365–76. DAR.

Virginia, Albemarle County. Papers military and political, 1775–78. Va. Hist. Soc. Coll., v. 6, pp. 71–140. DAR.

Virginia, Albemarle County. Pay roll of Capt. B. Harris's company militia, 1781. Va. soldiers of 1776. Burgess. DAR.

Virginia, Augusta County. Partial list of early settlers, Revolutionary soldiers and graves, located to date. Mrs. W. W. King. 1935, pamph. DAR.

Virginia, Augusta County. Revolutionary soldiers. J. A. Waddell. 1886; 2nd edition, 1902. DAR.

Virginia, Augusta County. Revolutionary soldiers who died between 1835 and 1848. DAR.

Virginia, Botetourt County. Revolutionary claims (returned, 1782). D. A. R. Mag., 1935, v. 69, no. 8, p. 471.

Virginia, Brunswick County. Revolutionary patriots (600 soldiers, 46 officers). D. A. R. Mag., Apr., 1934, v. 68, no. 4, pp. 244–47.

Virginia, Chesterfield County. Revolutionary War public service. Ethel C. Clarke. 1937, v. 1. DAR.

Virginia. Colonial militia, 1651–1776. W. A. Crozier. N. Y., 1905, 144 pp. DAR.

Virginia, Culpeper County. List of classes, Jan., 1781, for recruiting State's quota of troops in Continental Army. DAR.

Virginia, Franklin County. Pensioners, 1832–33. Complete from Order Book, 1831–34. A. L. Worrell. Mss. DAR.

Virginia, Henry County. Revolutionary muster roll: Col. Abram Penn's. D. A. R. Mag., Oct., 1914, v. 45, p. 206.

Virginia, Henry County. Revolutionary patriots. A. L. Worrell. Mss. DAR.

Virginia. Historical register of Virginia, in Revolution. Soldiers, sailors and marines, 1775–83. J. H. Gwathmey. Richmond, Va., 1938. DAR.

Virginia. Index to Saffell's list of Virginia soldiers in Revolutionary War. J. T. McAllister. Hot Springs, Va., McAllister Pub. Co., 1913. MHS; DAR.

Virginia. Index to Virginia land warrants for service in Continental and State lines and State Navy during Revolution. Pub. by Natl. Geneal. Soc., Wash., D. C. MHS.

Virginia. Journals of Virginia House of Delegates, 1833–35, inclusive; contain many important lists of Revolutionary officers and soldiers. DAR.

Virginia, Lancaster County. Revolutionary soldiers and sailors. S. Nottingham. 1930. DAR.

Virginia. List of claims for bounty land for Revolutionary services, acted upon by governor since April 1, 1834. 20 pp. (House of Delegates Journal, Dec. session, Dec. 25, 1834.) DAR.

Virginia. List of officers, sailors and marines of Virginia Navy, in American Revolution. Va. Mag. Hist. and Biog., v. 1, pp. 64–75. MHS; DAR.

Virginia. Militia in Revolutionary War; includes militia of West Virginia. J. T. McAllister. Hot Springs, Va., J. T. McAllister Pub. Co., 1913. MHS; DAR.

Virginia. Militia in Revolutionary War. Va. Mag. Hist. and Biog., 1899, v. 6; 1901, v. 8; 1902, v. 9; 1903, v. 10; 1904, v. 11; 1905, v. 12; 1905, v. 13, nos. 1 and 2. MHS.

Virginia. Navy of Revolution. R. A. Stewart. 1933. DAR.

Virginia. Revolutionary records gathered from court records in South West Virginia. A. L. Worrell. 1936. Mss. DAR.

Virginia. Revolutionary service data of Virginia, not found in Adjt. Gen.'s Office, War Department, Navy Department, Washington, D. C., in addition to those found in Pension Bureau. D. A. R. Mag., May, 1928, v. 62, no. 10, pp. 625–29.

Virginia. Revolutionary soldiers and sailors to whom land bounty warrants were granted by Virginia for military service. S. A. R. of Ky. Soc., Year Book, 1913, p. 191.

Virginia. Revolutionary War records. Army and Navy forces, with bounty land warrants for Virginia military district of Ohio and Virginia. Military scrip from Federal and State archives. (Original census and muster rolls of 1775, recently discovered.) G. M. Brumbaugh. Vol. 1. Pub. by author, 905 Massachusetts Ave., N.W., Wash., D. C., 1936, 707 pp. (88 pp. index). DAR.

Virginia soldiers of 1776. Louis A. Burgess. Complete index. V. 1, v. 2, 1927; v. 3, 1929. Richmond, Va., Richmond Press. DAR.

Virginia soldiers in Revolutionary War (over 40,000). Va. State Lib., 8th and 9th Annual Repts., 1912, 1913. MHS; DAR.

Virginia. Valuable Revolutionary service data. List of pension papers and Virginia half pay claims in office of Adjutant General in Navy Department, Wash., D. C., additional to those found in Pension Bureau. D. A. R. Mag., v. 62, no. 10, pp. 625–29.

Washington and his aides-de-camp. Emily S. Whitely. N. Y., Macmillan Co. DAR.

West Virginia, Monongalia County (was Virginia). List of public Revolutionary claims. D. A. R. Mag., 1934, v. 68, no. 9, p. 559.

West Virginia, Monongalia County. Revolutionary soldiers buried there. Geneal. Rec. Com., v. 1, Col. John Evans Chap. Typed, bd. 1940. DAR.

West Virginia. Monongalia County. Revolutionary soldiers' graves (75) with family data. D. A. R. Mag., June, 1940, v. 74, pp. 36–37.

West Virginia. Pension declarations made in counties of West Virginia, that were Virginia. DAR.

WAR OF 1812

Address delivered at celebration of Battle of North Point, by Association of Defenders of Baltimore. E. Higgins. Balto., 1879.

Allegany County. Militia, officers and men, two companies of infantry, 1814. Hist. of Cumberland. Lowdermilk. Pp. 292–99. MHS; DAR.

Baltimore. Citizen soldiers of Baltimore at North Point and Fort McHenry, Sept. 12 and 13, 1814. Chares C. Saffell. Contains muster roll. Reprint, Balto., 1889. MHS; DAR.

Baltimore, 1814. Defense of Capt. James Piper. M. H. Mag., 1912, v. 7, pp. 375–84.

Baltimore. Delegates to Democratic Convention, May, 1812, protesting conduct of Great Britain. Hist. of Md. Scharf. V. 2, p. 634. MHS.

Baltimore. Germans in defense of Baltimore, War of 1812–14. Soc. for Hist. of Germans in Md., 16th Annual Rept., 1907, pp. 57–60. MHS.

Baltimore City. Roll of artillery, Company of Fencibles, immediately after bombardment of Fort McHenry, on Sept. 13, 1814. Capt. Joseph H. Nicholson, commanding. Composed of gentlemen of Baltimore City. Md. O. R. Soc., v. 2, pp. 20–21. MHS.

Baltimore City. Committee of Vigilance and Safety, War of 1812. Hist. of Balto. City and Co. Scharf. P. 89. MHS.

Baltimore City. Committee of Vigilance and Safety, Aug. 24, 1814. Invasion of Md. Marine. Pp. 133-34. MHS.

Battle of Bladensburg, Aug. 24, 1814. M. H. Mag., 1906, v. 1, pp. 155–67, 197–210; 1910, v. 5, pp. 341–49.

Battle of Caulk's Field, Aug. 13, 1814. P. G. Skirvin. List of officers and men, from list published in Easton, Talblt Co., Aug. 31, 1814. Patriotic Marylander, v. 2, no. 3, pp. 20–38. See also V. 1, no. 1. MHS; DAR.

Battle of North Point. W. M. Marine. 1901. MHS.

Battle of North Point. M. H. Mag. 1907, v. 2, pp. 111–25; 1929, v. 24, pp. 356–64.

†British attack on Baltimore. Biographical memoir of late Sir Peter Parker, Capt. of Menelaw, killed in action while storming American Camp at Belair, Md., Aug. 31, 1814. London. 1815.

British invasion of Maryland, 1812–15. Wm. M. Marine. Edited with appendix by Louis H. Dielman, containing 11000 soldiers. (Md. roster, pp. 195–495.) Pub. by Soc. of War of 1812 in Md. Balto., 1913, 507 pp. MHS.

Caroline County. Militia officers. Hist. of Caroline Co. P. 130. MHS.

Col. Veazey and defense of Fredericktown; names of militia who remained within Fort, 1814. Hist. of Cecil Co. Johnston. P. 421–22. MHS; DAR.

Defenders list of 1814. Ms. MHS.

Dorchester County. List of those receiving money from Congress, 1817, for gallant service. Hist. of Dorchester Co. Jones. P. 256. MHS; DAR.

Dorchester County. Partial list of officers. Hist. of Dorchester Co. Jones. P. 259. MHS; DAR.

First Baltimore Horse Artillery, 1814. Ms. MHS.

Index to certified copy of list of American prisoners of war, who died at Princeton, Dartmoor, England, 1812–15 (187 Marylanders). Comp. by Mrs. Henry J. Carr. Pub. by Natl. Soc. Daughters of 1812. Pamph. MHS.

Journal kept on board U. S. Frigate *Constitution*, 1812. A. A. Evans, Surgeon U.S.N. Elkton, Md., 1895, 43 pp. Reprint from Pa. Mag. Hist. and Biog., 1895, v. 19, pp. 152–69. MHS. DAR.

List of non-commissioned officers and privates killed in bombardment of Fort McHenry. Hist. of Balto. City and Co. Scharf. P. 95. MHS.

List of officers of Forty-second Regiment, War of 1812. Hist. of Harford Co. Preston. P. 246. MHS; DAR.

List of officers under Major Armistead, War of 1812. Hist. of Balto. City and Co. Scharf. P. 91. MHS.

List of those killed and wounded at Fort McHenry, Sept. 13, 1814. Patriotic Marylander, v. 1, no. 1, pp. 41–42. MHS; DAR.

Maryland roster, War of 1812. L. H. Dielman. In British invasion of Maryland, 1812–13. W. M. Marine. Pp. 195–502. MHS; DAR.

Men of marque. (Account of Baltimore Privateers in War of 1812.) John Philips Cranwell and William Bowers Crane. Remington, Putnam, Balto., 1940.

Militia of Maryland, 1813. Rainbow Series, Blue Book. Mss. Hall of Records.

Muster roll of "A" Company, Maryland militia, under command of Capt. John Owings, 1812–14. M. H. Mag., 1936, v. 31, pp. 260–64.

Muster roll of Company "A", Maryland militia, stationed at Fort Armisted, Sept., 1813. 103 officers and privates (many names unknown in former lists.) Photos. copy. MHS.

Muster roll of Capt. John Brengle's Company, War of 1812. Hist. of Frederick Co. Williams. V. 1, p. 167. MHS; DAR.

Muster roll of Capt. Nicholas Turnbull's Company. Volunteer infantry, from Frederick County to Baltimore, 1814. Hist. of Frederick Co. Williams. V. 1, pp. 169–70. MHS; DAR.

Muster rolls of western Maryland in War of 1812. Hist. of west. Md. Scharf. V. 1, pp. 192–94. MHS; DAR.

Names of Maryland privateers, War of 1812. Ms. MHS.
Naval history of Baltimore in War of 1812. Chronicles of Balto. Scharf. Pp. 354–76. MHS.
Officers and citizens killed and wounded in defense of Baltimore at Fort McHenry, Sept. 13, 1814. Patriotic Marylander, v. 1, no. 1, p. 41.
Hist. of Md. Scharf. V. 3, pp. 103–05 113. MHS.
Pay roll, 12th Regiment, April, 1814. Ms. MHS.
Pay roll detachment of 23rd Regiment, 1814. Ms. MHS.
Pension records of War of 1812. National Archives Building, Washington.
Pictorial Field Book of War of 1812. (See p 158.) B. J. Lossing. 1868. DAR.
Return of effective men composing rifle battalion, Aug., 20, 1814. Ms. MHS.
Returns of officers and privates attending at Fort Defiance, Cecil County, from 29th unto 24th May, 1813. Hist. of Cecil Co. Johnston. P. 411. MHS; DAR.
Riot of 1812, Baltimore. M. H. Mag., 1910, v. 5, pp. 191–94.
Soldiers and widows of soldiers of War of 1812, who were on U. S. pension list, Jan. 1, 1883. Copied by Elizabeth F. Fischer and Martha L. Houston. Pub. by Natl. Geneal. Soc., Wash., D. C. Pamph.
War of 1812. Speech in Hagerstown, Md., 1843. Autobiographical and historical. Jesse D. Elliott, Com. U.S.N. Phila., 1844. MHS.
Washington County. Muster roll of officers and men, 1813. Hist. of West. Md. Scharf. V. 2, p. 1213. MHS; DAR.

CIVIL WAR

Allegany County. List of young men, who joined Confederate Army. Hist. of Cumberland. Lowdermilk. P. 406. MHS; DAR.
Allegany County. Military organizations, 1861–64. Hist. of west. Md. Scharf. V. 2, p. 1386. MHS; DAR.
Allegany County. Muster rolls of officers in United. States service, 1861. Hist. of Cumberland. Lowdermilk. P. 405. MHS; DAR.
Baltimore and nineteenth of April, 1861. G. W. Brown. J. H. Univ. Studies, series, extra, v. 3, N. Murray, pub. agent, Balto., 1887.
Baltimore City and County. Commissioned officers in Volunteer Force of United States, 1861–65. Hist. of Balto. City and Co. Scharf. Pp. 151–56. MHS.
Baltimore County. Gov. Bradford's private list of Union men in Baltimore, 1861. W. S. Meyers. M. H. Mag., 1912, v. 7, no. 1, pp. 83–90.
Baltimore and Ohio in Civil War. F. Summers. Putnam, 1939.
Baltimore. List of those killed in riot in Baltimore, April 19, 1861. Hist. of Md. Scharf. V. 3, p. 409. MHS.
Baltimore. Memoirs and History of Capt. F. W. Alexander's Baltimore Battery of Light Artillery, U.S.V., 1862–65. F. W. Wild. Balto., 1912.
Baltimore. Muster roll of Purnell's Legion and Baltimore home guards, 1863. Ms. MHS.
Brengle Home Guard, 1861. M. H. Mag., 1912, v. 7, pp. 196–200.
Caroline County, Greensboro District. Roster of soldiers, Company D, 1861. Hist. of Caroline Co. Pp. 171–74. MHS.
Civil War bibliography of State participation, 1861–65. U. S. War Dept. Lib.
M. H. Mag., 1913, v. 8, p. 382.
Civil War maps (145). Robert E. Lee Russell. Placed on exhibition in M. H. S. gallery, Apr. 1–13, 1940.
Photos. Lib. Cong.
Civil War records. Wilson Mss. Coll., no. 101. MHS.
Commissioned officers of Baltimore City and County in Volunteer Force of United States Army, 1861–65. Hist. of Balto. City and Co. Scharf. Pp. 156–61. MHS.
†Confederate military history. Evans. Enoch Pratt Lib., card indexed.
Correspondence between S. T. Wallis, of Baltimore and John Sherman, Senator, concerning arrest of members of Maryland Legislature, and Mayor and police commissioners of Baltimore in 1861. Wrappers, 1863, 31 pp.
Dorchester County. Roster of Confederate soldiers. Hist. of Dorchester Co. Jones. P. 265.
Roster of volunteers, with casualty list. Hist. of Dorchester Co. Jones. Pp. 537–67. MHS; DAR.
Four years in saddle. C. H. Gilmor. 1866. MHS; DAR.
Frederick County. Commissioned officers of Union Army. Hist. of west. Md. Scharf. V. 1. p. 326. MHS; DAR.
Frederick and Carroll Counties. List of commissioned officers, War of Rebellion. Hist. of west. Md. Scharf. V. 1, pp. 326–29. MHS; DAR.
Gov. Thomas Hicks of Maryland and Civil War. G. L. P. Radcliffe. J. H. Univ. Studies, series 19, nos. 11, 12, Balto., 1901. MHS; Enoch Pratt Lib.
Historical record, First Regiment, Maryland Infantry, 1861–65. C. Camper and J. W. Kirkley. 1871. DAR.
History and roster, Maryland volunteers, War of 1861–65. Pub. under authority of General Assembly of Md., Balto., 1898, 2 vols. MHS.
Immediate emancipation in Maryland; proceedings of Union State Central Committee at meeting held in Temperance Temple. Balto., 1863, 20 pp.
Man power of Civil War in Maryland. 400 vols. Mss. Hall of Records.
Maryland Guard, battalion, 1860–61. Isaac Nicholson. M. H. Mag., 1911, v. 6, pp. 117–31.
Maryland line in Confederate States Army, 1861–65. W. W. Goldsborough. Balto., 1869, 1900. MHS.
Memoirs of service afloat during War between States. Admiral Raphael Semmes. Balto., 1869.
Personal reminiscences of Maryland soldier, in War between States, 1861–65. G. W. Booth.
Recollections of Maryland Confederate soldier. McHenry Howard. Campaigns and personalities, during Civil War. Out of print; see Remington, Putnam Co., Balto.
Reminiscence of troublous times, April, 1861, based on interviews at Washington, touching movement of troops through Baltimore. Hon. J.

Morrison Harris. M. H. S. Fund Pub., no. 31, Balto., 1891. MHS.

Reminiscences and documents relating to Civil War, during 1865. J. A. Campbell. Balto., 1887.

Riot. Passage of Sixth Massachusetts Regiment through Baltimore, April 19, 1861. M. P. Andrews. M. H. Mag., 1919, v. 14, pp. 60–76, 1932, v. 27, pp. 274–79.

Second Maryland Regiment, 1861. Hist. of Cumberland. Lowdermilk. Pp. 403–05.

Second Regiment, Maryland Volunteers, Infantry. M. H. Mag., Mar., 1917, Infantry. v. 12, no. 1, p. 41–45.

Secret correspondence illustrating conditions of affairs in Maryland. Balto., 1863, 42 pp.

Self-reconstruction of Maryland, 1864–67. W. S. Myers. J. H. Univ. Studies, series 27, no. 9, 1909. MHS; Enoch Pratt Lib.

Service afloat or remarkable career of Confederate cruisers *Sumter* and *Alabama*. Admiral Raphael Semmes. Balto., 1887.

Southern side, or Andersonville Prison. R. R. Stevenson. List of Federal soldiers who died and were buried at Andersonville, Ga. (Md. soldiers, p. 318.) Balto., 1876. MHS.

†Trimble, Gen. Isaac Ridgeway. Civil War diary of 1862–63. M. H. Mag., 1922, v. 17, pp. 1–20.

True history of War between States. G. Carleton Lee. 1903.

Union in Maryland, 1859–61. (Narrative of part Gov. Hicks played in keeping Maryland in Union.) M. H. Mag., 1920, v. 24, pp. 210–24.

Volunteers of western Maryland, in War of 1812. Hist. of west. Md. Scharf. V. 1, p. 192. MHS; DAR.

War of Rebellion. Official records of Union and Confederate Armies. Prepared under direction of Secretary of War. Series 1, 2, 3. Govt. Print. Office., Wash., D. C.

Washington County. List of commissioned officers, Union Army. Hist. of west Md. Scharf. V. 1, p. 327. MHS; DAR.

WORLD WAR

Allegany County. Mortality list of Allegany County in World War. Hist. of Allegany Co. Thomas and Williams. V. 1, pp. 676–79. MHS; DAR.

Caroline County. List of inducted men furnished, by local board of Caroline County, in Great War, to Adjutant General of Maryland. Hist. of Caroline Co. Pp. 338–42. Honor roll, p. 346. Roster of enlisted men, p. 343. MHS.

Wicomico's honor roll in World War. Historic Salisbury. Truitt. Pp. 173–89.

World War history of State of Maryland, 1917–19. Contains special chapters of dead and wounded; those receiving decorations and citations; muster rolls of American Army, Navy, Marine Corps, National Guard, officers, enlisted men, drafted men and nurses; Twenty-ninth and Seventy-ninth Sectors, in different phases of Meuse-Argonne struggle. Prepared by American Battle Monument Commission. Here given by special permission; first publication. K. Singerwald and others. War Record Commission, 1933, 2 vols. MHS.

†World War. In memoriam. M. H. Mag., 1919, v. 14, pp. 101–10, 293–303, 322–29; 1920, v. 15, pp. 20–27.

World War: Roster of soldiers and casualty lists from Dorchester County. Hist. of Dorchester County. Jones. Pp. 549–67. MHS; DAR.

STAR SPANGLED BANNER

Incidents of War of 1812. (Night Star Spangled Banner was composed.) M. H. Mag., Dec., 1937, v. 32, no. 4, pp. 340–47.

National Anthem, the Star-Spangled Banner, and Patriotic lines. E. Higgins. Balto., 1898.

National Star-Spangled Banner centennial, Baltimore, Sept. 6–13, 1914. W. F. Coyle. DAR.

Spangled Banner. Story of Francis Scott Key. V. Weybright. 1935. DAR.

Star Spangled Banner. Words and music. Issued between 1814–64. J. Muller. 1936. DAR.

Star Spangled Banner. O. H. T. Sonneck. Wash., D. C., 1914, portraits, facsimiles.

PATRIOTIC CLUBS AND SOCIETIES

American historical register and monthly gazette of patrotic hereditary societies in America. From Sept., 1894, to Feb., 1896. C. H. Browning, editor. Phila., 2 vols. MHS.

Ancestry. Giving objects and requirements relating to membership in various hereditary societies. Eugene Zieber. Bailey-Banks-Biddle Co.

Ark and Dove ceremonies. Pamph. DAR.

*Ark and Dove Society records. Leaflets. MHS.

Colonial Dames of America.

- *Ancestral records and portraits. Compilation from Archives of Colonial Dames of America, Chapter I. Roster and family data. N. Y., Grafton Press, 2 vols. MHS; DAR; Enoch Pratt Lib.
- *Colonial Dames of America, Chapter I. Pedigree books. 2 vols. V. 1, A–M; v. 2, N–Z. 250 mss. charts. Wm. B. Marye, genealogist. MHS.
- Eligibility list of Colonial Dames of America. (Md., p. 6.) Privately printed, Oct., 1911. MHS.
- History and register of ancestors and members of Society of Colonial Dames in State of Virginia, 1892–1930. 1930. DAR.
- Maryland Society of Colonial Dames of America. Register, 1891–1915. 1915. MHS; Peabody Lib.
- Maryland Society of Colonial Dames of America. Register, 1915–38. 1940. MHS.

Delphian Club, Baltimore, 1861. History and list of members. M. H. Mag., 1925, v. 20, pp. 305–46.

Maryland Society of Sons of American Revolution. "Patriotic Maryland." Roster of members, pp. 90–153; roster of ancestors, pp. 154–258. Pub. by Md. Soc., S. A. R., Waverly Press, Balto., 1930. MHS; DAR.

Members of Continental Congress, 1774–89. List prepared for Society of Descendants. Pamph. MHS.

*National Society of Daughters of American Colonists. Lineage book. 1929, v. 1–1936, v. 5. (V. 5, Missouri.) MHS; DAR.

*National Society of Daughters of American Revolution. Lineage book. 1908, v. 1–1938, v. 166 (1000 records in each vol.). MHS; DAR.

Index of Rolls of Honor (index of ancestors). Vols. 1–40. Press of Pierpont Switer Co., Pittsburg, Pa., 1916. MHS; DAR.

Index of Rolls of Honor. Vols. 41–80. Press of Judd and Detweiler, Inc., Wash., D. C., 1926. MHS; DAR.

Index of Rolls of Honor. Vols. 81–166, being printed at this time. (Over 300,000 women's ancestral records permanently filed with Natl. Soc., D. A. R., Wash., D. C.)

*National Society of Daughters of Barons of Runmeade. Year Book, 1935–36.

*National Society of Daughters of Founders and Patriots of America. Lineage book. MHS; DAR.

National Society of Magna Charta Barons. Magna Charta Barons and their American descendants. C. H. Browning. Phila., 1898. DAR.

*National Society of Magna Charta Dames. Year Book.

National Society of War of 1812:

Constitution and register of membership of General Society of War of 1812, June 1, 1908. 1908. DAR.

*Maryland Society of War of 1812. Association of descendants of defenders of Baltimore. Including supplements. Compiled by Ira H. Haughton, secretary. 1929. Members' application papers (nos. 1–350) in State of Md. 4 vols. Mss. MHS.

Members of National Society of Daughters of War of 1812. British invasion of Md. Marine. Pp. 502–07. MHS.

Members of Society of War of 1812, in Maryland. British invasion of Md. Marine. Pp. 496–501. MHS.

National Society of United States Daughters of 1812. Records of National members.

Society of Army and Navy of Confederate States in Maryland. Roster of officers and members. Balto., 1883. MHS.

Society of Cincinnati:

Autograph list of Society of Cincinnati. D. A. R. Mag., v. 60, no. 9, p. 550.

History of Delaware State Society of Cincinnati, from its organization to present time; to which is appended brief account of Delaware register of War of Revolution. H. T. Bellas. Hist. Soc. Delaware Papers, no. 13. Wilmington, 1895.

Members of Society of Cincinnati (original). Kentucky Society of Sons of Revolution, Year Book. 1913. (Md., p. 297.)

Papers of Society of Cincinnati in State of Virginia, 1783–1824. Lieut. Col. Edgar E. Hume. Richmond, Va., 1939, 495 pp. (Reproduction of original roll of membership.)

Roster of Delaware State Society of Cincinnati. Amer. Hist. Register, 1894, v. 1, pp. 203–12. MHS.

Roster of Maryland State Society of Cincinnati. Hist. of Md. McSherry. 1849. Appendix.

Roster of original members of Maryland State Society of Cincinnati. Side lights on Md. hist. Richardson. V. 1, pp. 390–91.

Roster of Pennsylvania State Society of Cincinnati. 1937. DAR.

Roster of Virginia State Society of Cincinnati. 1937. MHS.

Society of Cincinnati. Marcus Benjamin. Leaflet. MHS.

Society of Cincinnati of Maryland. Founded Nov. 21, 1783; organized May 13, 1783. Maj.-Gen. Smallwood, first president; list of hereditary members brought down to Feb. 22, 1935. Pub. by Society. MHS.

Society of Daughters of Cincinnati, 1894. N. Y. Geneal. and Biog. Soc. Lib., pamph.

*Society of Colonial Daughters of Seventeenth Century. Membership, pp. 51–169; index of ancestors and descendants, pp. 170–341. Brooklyn, 1923. MHS.

*Society of Colonial Wars of State of Maryland. Pedigree charts of members and records of ancestors. Christopher Johnston, editor. Balto., 1905, v. 1. MHS; DAR.

*Pedigrees of members (277) and records of ancestors. Francis B. Culver, editor. Balto., 1940, v. 2. MHS; DAR.

Index of ancestors and honor roll. Pub. by authority of General Assembly, N. Y., 1922. MHS.

*Society of Descendants of Colonial Clergy. First Record Book, 1934.

*Society of Descendants of Continental Congress. Founded 1930. Descendants of Continental Congress. Frank Clay Cross, general secretary 1537 Lafayette Street, Denver, Colorado.

*Society of Descendants of Signers of Declaration of Independence. Organized, July 4, 1907. Year Book.

*Order of Washington. Lineage book. J. G. B. Bulloch. MHS; DAR.

South River Club. Membership, 1742–1872. Founders of Anne Arundel and Howard Cos. Warfield. Pp. 201–02. MHS; DAR.

Membership, 1742–1903 (complete). Side lights on Md. hist. Richardson. V. 1, pp. 202–04. MHS; DAR.

Tuesday Club. Organized by Alexander Hamilton, M.D., and Jonas Green, editor, Maryland Gazette, 1745–55. Proceedings. MHS.

Tuesday Club, Annapolis. M. H. Mag., 1906, v. 1, pp. 59–65. (From original manuscript in MHS.)

Virginia Daughters of American Revolution. Roster, 1892–1936 (giving Revolutionary Ancestor, date and place of birth). Ida J. Lee, 2701 North Avenue, Richmond, Va. DAR.

EARLY EASTERN COLLEGES

(Few in England)

†Amherst College, Mass., 1821–1896. Obituary, 1864–1913.

†Andover Theological Seminary, Mass., 1808–1908.

Baltimore City College. One hundred years of Baltimore City College. J. C. Leonhart. 307 pp.

†Brown University, Providence, R. I. Historical catalogue, 1764–1914. Pub. by University, Providence, R. I., 1914.

Charlotte Hall Academy, Charlotte Hall, St. Mary's County, Md. Established, 1793. List of first board of trustees, 1794; list of principals, 1796. Chronicles of col. Md. Thomas. Pp. 275–76.

List of trustees. Hist. of Md. Scharf. V. 2, p. 514. MHS.

Cokesbury College, Abingdon, Harford County, Md. Established by Methodist Episcopal Church, 1784 (first Methodist institution for higher education in world). Authentic history. Harford Co. Hist. Soc. Mss. Coll. 1894, pamph. J. H. Univ. Lib.

List of trustees. Hist. of Md. Scharf. V. 2, p. 515.

Columbia University, New York City. Alumni register, 1754–1931. Compiled by Committee on General Catalogue. (100,000 names.) N. Y., Columbia Univ. Press, 1932.

Officers and alumni, 1754–1857. M. H. Thomas. N. Y., Columbia Univ. Press, 1936. DAR.

Cornell University, Ithaca, N. Y. Ten Year Book, 1864–1908.

†Dartmouth College, Hanover, N. H., 1769–1911.

Davidson College, Davidson, N. C. Semi-Centennial Catalogue, 1837–87.

Dickinson College, Carlyle, Pa. Catalogue of faculty and students, Dec., 1811. Broadside. MHS.

Eden School, Somerset County, Md. Established, 1770. List of trustees. Hist. of Md. Scharf. V. 2, p. 512.

Fair School, Baltimore, Md. Its origin and use. Subscription book, 1815–1927. Park Avenue, Friend's Meeting House, Balto.

First Free School in Queen Anne County, Md., 1724. E. H. Brown, Jr. M. H. Mag., 1911, v. 6, pp. 1–15.

First uniform school system of Maryland, 1865–68. History. M. H. Mag., 1931, v. 26, pp. 205–27.

Georgetown University, Washington, D. C. List of graduates, 1909. Historical catalogue, 1821–91.

Harvard University, Cambridge, Mass. Quinquennial catalogue, 1636–1910.

Catalogue, 1830. Signature and notes by J. Bozman Kerr. Pamph. MHS.

Quinquennial catalogue of Law School of Harvard University, 1817–1914. Pub. by Law School, Cambridge, 1915. MHS.

Virginians and Marylanders at Harvard College in seventeenth century. Samuel Eliot Morison. Reprint from William and Mary Quart. Mag., Jan., 1933. Pamph., 11 pp. MHS.

†Haverford College, Haverford, Conn. Catalogue, 1833–1900.

Hillsboro Academy, Caroline County, Md. Established, 1797. First board of trustees. Hist. of Caroline Co. P. 291.

Irish school masters in American Colonies, 1640–1775. John C. Lineham and T. H. Murray. American-Irish Hist. Soc., Wash., 1898.

Johns Hopkins University, Baltimore, Md. Established, 1867. List of graduates and fellows, 1876–1913. 1914. Enoch Pratt Lib.

Half-century directory. Compiled by W. Norman Brown. Balto., 1926.

Register, 1878–1934. MHS.

When the Hopkins came to Baltimore. Allen Kerr Bond.

King William's School, Annapolis, Md., 1696. First public free school in North America, progenitor of St. John's College, Annapolis. Thomas Fell. 1894. MHS.

List of board of trustees, 1696. Ancient city. Riley. Pp. 40–41.

List of visitors and trustees. Hist. of Md. Scharf. V. 1, pp. 350, 352.

†Lafayette College, Easton, Pa. Catalogue, 1832–1912.

List of seven visitors in each of twelve counties in Maryland, 1723. Hist. of Md. Scharf. V. 1, p. 353.

Massachusetts Institute of Technology, Boston, Mass. Register of former students, 1864–1911. 1912.

McDonogh Educational Fund and Institute. Annual Reports, 1859–74. Bd. in Balto.

McKim Free School, 1820, Baltimore, Md. One of two first free schools in Baltimore. Record, 1821–58; with complete list of pupils. Park Avenue Friends Meeting House, Balto. 1889.

†New Brunswick Theological Seminary, New Brunswick, N. J. Catalogue, 1784–1911.

†New York University, New York City. Catalogue, 1833–1907.

†Pennsylvania University, Philadelphia, Pa. Catalogue, 1749–1893.

Presbyterian School, Somerset County, Md. Established, 1779. List of trustees. Hist. of Md. Scharf. V. 2, p. 514.

†Princeton University, Princeton, N. J. General catalogue, 1746–1906. 1908.

Biographical catalogue, 1815–1932.

Public education in Maryland. Abraham Flexner. N. Y., F. P. Bachman, 1916.

Public educational work in Maryland. Johns Hopkins University Studies, series 17, no. 2, 1899. MHS; Enoch Pratt Lib.

Rutgers College, New Brunswick, N. J. General catalogue, 1766–1909. 1909.

St. Charles College, Catonsville, Md. Land given by Charles Carroll of Carrollton; cornerstone laid 1831; first scholastic year, Oct. 31, 1848. Catalogue.

St. John's College, Annapolis, Md. Incorporated, 1784. List of professors, teachers, and students 1790–95; survivors of classes, 1789, in Jan. 1, 1849. M. H. Mag., 1934, v. 29, pp. 305–09.

Commemoration of 100th anniversary, 1789–1889. Balto., 1890.

Letter on St. John's College. Rev. E. J. Stearns, professor at St. John's College. Also articles for reviews. 3 vols.

List of distinguished Marylanders, who claim St. John's College as their alma mater. Founders of Anne Arundel and Howard Cos. Warfield. Pp. 316–18.

St. John's College upholds American tradition. D. A. R. Mag., v. 62, no. 10, pp. 609–12.

Society of Alumni. John C. Herbert. Register of visitors and governors, 1784–1873 (first name on list is Right Rev. Thomas J. Claggett, DD.); list of faculty and instructors; graduates and alumni, 1793–1853. Annapolis, Jeremiah Hughes, printer, 1828. Lib. of St. Johns College.

Schools and some of schoolteachers of Maryland, 1696–1803. Hist. of Md. Scharf. V. 2, pp. 508–17.

†Smith College, Northampton, Mass. Catalogue, 1875–1910.

†Swarthmore, Swarthmore, Pa. Catalogue, 1873–92.

†Union Theological Seminary, New York City. Catalogue, 1836–1908.

†United States Military Academy, West Point, N. Y., 1802. Register of officers and graduates, 1802–1920. Brevet Maj.-Gen. George Whillum, U. S. A. 6 vols.

1910–20. Supplement. Col. Wirt Robinson, U.S.A. Vols. 6A and 6B.

Rolls of cadets from establishment to present time. 1810, pamph. DAR.

†Alumin Association report. Biographical sketches for 200 years.

United States Naval Academy, Annapolis, Md. Established, 1845. Registers.

Annual Alumni Association registers. 1845–date.

*United States Navy and Naval Academy registers. Source of bibliographical and genealogical information. G. H. Preble. New England Geneal. Soc. Reg., v. 27, p. 147.

†United States Navy Year Book, 1883–1912. Woodbury Pulsifer. 1912.

†University of Cambridge, Cambridge, England. Alumni Cantabrigienses. Biographical list of all known students, graduates, and holders of office at University of Cambridge, 1751–1896. John Venn. 1922, 3 pts. MHS.

University of Maryland, Baltimore Md. (Maryland Agricultural College, 1856, College Park, Prince George County, and University of Maryland College, of Medicine, Baltimore, (Merged in 1920).

Alumni record. 1907.

†University of Maryland, and others, 1807–1907. E. F. Cordell. N. Y. and Chicago, 2 vols. DAR; Enoch Pratt Lib; card indexed.

University of Maryland Law School, Baltimore. Annual catalogue of students at close of session.

University of Maryland School of Medicine, Baltimore. Historical sketch, 1807–90; with catalogue of alumni. E. F. Cordell. Balto., 1891.

University of Maryland School of Medicine Library, Baltimore. Skilling-Doyle memorial volume. Ruth Lee Briscoe, librarian.

†University of Maryland School of Medicine Library. Collection of portraits of gold star men and women, their biographies, and mortality roll of alumni.

University of North Carolina, Chapel Hill, N. C. Catalogue of officers and students, 1789–1889. 1889.

University of Oxford, Oxford, England. Alumni Oxonienses. Members of University of Oxford, giving parentage, birthplace, year of birth, with record of degree, 1500–1714. First series, 1887–88, 4 vols.

1714–1886. Second series, 1891–92, 4 vols. MHS.

University of Virginia, Charlottesville, Va. Historical catalogue. 2 vols, 1904 pp.

†Vassar College, Poughkeepsie, N. Y. Catalogue, 1861–1910.

Washington College, Chestertown, Md. Incorporated, 1782. Account of Washington College in State of Maryland; list of board of visitors, governors and donors. Judge Crukshank. Pub. in Phila., 1784, pamph. Lib. of Washington College.

Catalogue, 1903–04. List of distinguished alumni. Ms. copy in Lib. of Washington College.

Catalogue, 1910–11. Minutes of board of visitors and governors, 1783, 1816–49. Lib. of Washington College.

Catalogue, 1913–14. List of graduates, 1783–1913. Not biographical. Lib. of Washington College.

List of visitors. Hist. of Md. Scharf. V. 2, p. 515.

List of subscribers and visitors. M. H. Mag., v. 2, pp. 164–79.

Washington College, 1783. L. W. Barroll. M. H. Mag., 1911, v. 6, pp. 164–69.

†Washington and Jefferson College, Washington, Pa. Catalogue, 1802–1902.

Wellesley College, Wellesley, Mass. Catalogue, 1875–1912.

Wesleyan University, Middleton, Conn. Catalogue, 1831–1911.

West Nottingham Academy, Cecil County, Md. Oldest school in State. Newspaper sketch. DAR.

Williams College, Williamstown, Mass. General catalogue of alumni and officers, 1795–1910.

†Yale University, New Haven Conn. Biographical sketches of graduates, Oct., 1701–1745. (438 biographies.) N. Y., 1885. Peabody Lib.

Biographies and annals, 1701–1815; obituary records, 1860–1914; catalogue of officers, 1701–1910. Franklin B. Dexter. 6 vols. MHS.

Biographical notices of graduates later than 1815, who are not in annual obituary records. Supplement of record. Franklin B. Dexter. New Haven, Conn., 1913.

BIBLIOGRAPHY OF OTHER STATES, CONTAINING REFERENCES TO MARYLAND FAMILIES

CALIFORNIA

Records of families of California pioneers. Pub. by California Geneal. Rec. Com., D. A. R. MHS; DAR.

CONNECTICUT

*Connecticut families. Records collected in commemoration of three hundredth anniversary of settlement of Connecticut. Gift of Md. Daughters of Founders and Patriots of America MHS.

DELAWARE

*Allied families of Delaware. E. J. Sellers. Phila., 1901. MHS.
Biographical and genealogical history of Delaware. 1899, 2 vols. DAR.
Crane Hook Church, predecessor of old Swedes Church, Wilmington. Pennock Pusey. Hist. Soc. of Delaware Papers, no. 11, 1895.
Delaware County marriage bonds, 1832–65. Del. Geneal. Rec. Com., 1940, 2 vols. Typed, bd. DAR.
Delaware Finns or first permanent settlement in Pennsylvania, Delaware, West New Jersey and eastern part of Maryland. E. A. Louli. 1925.
Dulany churchyard, Kent County, Delaware. Md. Geneal. Rec. Com., 1934, pp. 210–12. Typed, bd. DAR.
Dutch and Swedes on Delaware, 1609–64. C. Ward. 1930. DAR.
History of Delaware. T. J. Scharf. DAR.
Holy Trinity (Old Swedes) Church, Wilmington, 1698; Lutheran, 1698–1791; Episcopalian, 1791–date. Register compiled from Dr. Barr's Works, 10,500 names. Geneal. Soc. Pa. Mss. Coll.
Kent County. Early marriages, births and deaths from deed book. Pub. Geneal. Soc. Pa., v. 7, p. 107.
*Kent County. Genealogical material relating to Lord Collection. Geneal. Soc. Pa. Mss. Coll.
Kent County. Marriages and births from deeds. M. S. Hart. 1939, pamph. DAR.
*Kent County. Some allied families. T. H. Streets, U.S.N. Phila., 1904, pamph. MHS.
Marriages, 1789–1810. Md. Rec. Brumbaugh. V. 2.
New Sweden on Delaware. C. Ward. Univ. of Pa. Press, 1938, 160 pp.
Records of Holy Trinity (Old Swedes) Church, Wilmington, Del., 1697–1773, from original by Horace Barr; with abstract of English records, 1773–1810. Hist. Soc. of Delaware Papers, no. 9. Wilmington, 1890.
Roster and ancestral roll. Delaware D. A. R. Pamph. DAR.
*Some records of Sussex County, Delaware. C. H. B. Turner. Contains Bible, court, marriage, tombstone records, and wills; some as early as 1681 (many Md. refs.). Phila., Allen-Lane-Scott, 1909. MHS.
St. Ann's Church (dated 1705) cemetery, near Middletown, Del. Md. Geneal. Rec. Com., 1934–35, p. 213. Typed, bd. DAR.
Sussex County. Abstracts of will book "B". M. S. Hart. 1935, typed, bd. DAR.
Sussex County. Index to wills. M. S. Hart. 1934. Ms. DAR.
Sussex County (at one time Maryland). Cemetery records, Millard F. Hudson, specialist in Eastern Shore records (Del., Md., and Va.) 2 vols., 718 pp. Typed, bd. MHS.
Sussex County. Will book "A." 1935. Mss. DAR.
Sussex County. Wills 1694–1799. M. S. Hart. Typed, bd. 1934. DAR.
Swedish settlements on Delaware, 1638–64. A. Johnson. 2 vols. 1911. DAR.
Tombstone inscriptions. Blakiston churchyard, Kent County, Del., near Millington. Md. Geneal. Rec. Com., 1933–34,. pp. 204–07. Typed, bd. DAR.

DISTRICT OF COLUMBIA

American biographical directories of District of Columbia. H. B. F. Macfarland. DAR.
Assessments and tax lists, 1798. Mss. MHS.
Bible records from all portions of United States. Photostatic copies from original Bible records (even entire Bibles) filed. See Bureau of Pensions, Interior Department, Wash., D. C.
Catholic churches in District. (Md. in 1634–1791.) Records of Columbia Hist. Soc., v. 15, pp. 1–58.
Cemeteries of Washington and contiguous territory. M. P. Wright. 1938–39, pamph. DAR.
Congressional Cemetery, 1812. Copies of first four books of records of interments and removals, April 25, 1820–Feb. 5, 1865. D. C. Geneal. Rec. Com., 1937. Indexed, typed, bd. DAR. See also: V. 23, 26, 1934–35. Bd. mss. DAR.
Congressional Cemetery interments. Natl. Geneal. Soc. Quart., July, 1918, v. 7, pp. 27–28; Oct., pp. 40–41. MHS.
Commissioners appointed to lay off District, Jan., 1791, and main owners of site. Hist. of west. Md. Scharf. V. 2, p. 568. MHS; DAR.
County Court note book. Little bulletin of history and genealogy, 1921–31. Mrs. Milnor Ljungstedt. (Last issue 1931.) Columbia Printing Co. MHS; DAR.
Court House records. Wills and Bible records. N. G. Ross. D. C. Geneal. Rec. Com., 1938–39, v. 49. Typed, bd. DAR.
Dumbarton Avenue Methodist Episcopal Church, 1772. (First church of this denomination in District.) Records copied from original 9 vols. date back from 1772. Marriages, 1823–66; deaths, some few since 1870; list of members, some from 1823; list of preachers, members, prominent women and brief history of Church. Copied by D. C. Geneal. Rec. Com., 1934–35, v. 14, pp. 1–75. Typed, bd. DAR.
Earliest proprietors of Capitol Hill. Margaret Brent Downing. Col. Hist. Soc. Rec., 1918, v. 21, pp. 1–23.
Earliest Wills. Scrap Book. MHS.
†Early days of Washington. S. S. Mackall. 1899. DAR.
Episcopal Church in District. Records of Columbia Hist. Soc., v. 9, p. 631.

Family bible and cemetery records of District of Columbia, northern Virginia and Jefferson County, West Virginia. D. C. Geneal. Rec. Com., 1938–39, v. 51. Indexed, typed, bd. DAR.

Foundry Methodist Episcopal Church. Records of baptisms, 1818–37; marriages, 1818–62; list of members and brief history of Church. Copied by D. C. Geneal. Rec. Com., v. 15, part 1, 76 pp. Typed, bd. DAR.

Georgetown. Christ Church Parish, 1818. Christ Church, 31st. and O Streets. (Church organized Nov. 10, 1817, by group of former members of St. John's Church, Georgetown.) Baptisms, 1820–60; burials and funerals, 1820–60; list of communicants, 1844–56; confirmations, 1840–64. D. C. Geneal. Rec. Com., 1937. Index, typed, bd. DAR.

Georgetown. List of principal municipal authorities, 1751–1871. Records of Columbia Hist. Soc., v. 24, pp. 89–117.

Georgetown. Mayor and aldermen, 1789. Hist. of Md. Scharf. V. 2, p. 572. MHS; DAR.

Georgetown. Oak Hill Cemetery records. Register of interments from Aug. 13, 1849–June 29 1869, with additional records of notable and distinguished persons who have been buried there; also some removals. Brief history. D. C. Geneal. Rec. Com., 1936, v. 17. Indexed, typed, bd. DAR.

Georgetown Parish, 1809. St. John's Church, 1794, abandoned 1831, reopened in 1838, Potomac and O Streets; St. Johns Chapel, 33 Street, near P Street. Baptisms, 1821–31, 1841–69; burials and funerals, 1821–69; marriages, 1821–28, 1841–67; list of communicants (394 names), Sept. 16, 1841; list of rectors, 1804–67; earliest pew holders, 1804, also 1821; subscribers to building fund, 1796, 1843; vestrymen, 1806–38. Contains brief history. Copied from original registers. D. C. Geneal. Rec. Com., 1937, v. 27, 103 pp. Typed, bd. DAR.

List of rectors, 1794–1925; with sketch of Parish. Historical sketches of parishes and missions of Diocese of Washington. P. 67.

Georgetown University Archives. List of genealogical records to be found at Georgetown University. D. C. Geneal. Rec. Com., Mrs. Harry M. Howard, State Chairman, 1937–38, v. 47. Typed, bd. DAR.

Glenwood Cemetery records. D. C. Geneal. Rec. Com., 1938–39, v. 48, p. 1. DAR.

Historical sketches of parishes and missions in Diocese of Washington. Compiled by Committee of Hist. of Diocese, Mrs. Marcus Benjamin, chairman. Wash., D. C., 1928.

†History of national capital. W. B. Bryan. 1914. DAR.

Holy Cross Protestant Episcopal Church. Register, 1875–94. Natl. Cathedral.

List of Maryland Parish records in National Cathedral, Washington. MHS; DAR.

List of principal municipal authorities, 1791–1920; executives and voters. Records of Columbia Hist. Soc., v. 23, pp. 180–87.

Marriage index of Supreme Court. Copy nos., 1 and 2, letters A–L, vols. 19 and 20; letters L–Z, Dec. 23, 1811–Sept. 1, 1858, vols. 21, and 22. D. C. Geneal. Rec. Com., 1936–37, 4 vols. Typed, bd. DAR.

Marriage licenses of Supreme Court. Mss. MHS.

Marriages of District of Columbia, 1801–20. Natl. Geneal. Soc. Quart., Oct., 1918, v. 7, no. 3, pp. 33–39; Jan., 1919, v. 7, no. 4, pp. 49–53; v. 8, no. 1, pp. 27–31; Jan., 1920, v. 8, no. 4, pp. 55–57. MHS.

Maryland patriots interred in District of Columbia, 1793. Natl. Geneal. Soc. Quart., v. 7, no. 2, p. 27. MHS.

Mayors of Corporation of Washington. Allen C. Clark. Reprint from Columbia Hist. Soc., 1916, v. 19, pamph. File Case, DAR.

National Genealogical Society Quarterly, v. 1, no. 1, 1912. Pub. Natl. Geneal. Soc., Dr. G. M. Brumbaugh, editor, Wash., D. C. MHS; DAR.

Office of Comptroller General. General Accounting Office, Records Division. Among other information, records of all pensions paid, records of pensioners' deaths, wills, and places of residence, etc.

Old Georgetown on Potomac. H. R. Evans. DAR.

Portrait of Old Georgetown, 1933. Ecker. Grace Dunlop. DAR.

Records of Columbia Historical Society, Washington. Compiled by Committee of Publications and Recording Secretary. Aug., 1895–97, v. 1. MHS; DAR.

Records of Columbia Historical Society. Index to authors and titles of records. Ella J. Morrison. 1897–1932, vols. 1–33–34 incl. MHS; DAR.

Register of Georgetown, District of Columbia, 1830. People and places of Old Georgetown. Columbia Hist. Soc. Rec., vols. 33, 34, pp. 133–162. See also v. 18, pp. 70–91.

Reminiscences of Georgetown. Rev. S. B. Balch. 1859.

Rock Creek Parish, 1811, erected from Prince George Parish. St. Paul's Church; Rock Creek Cemetery; Holy Comforter Chapel, Georgia Avenue. Register (original) of births, marriages and deaths, 1726–98. Natl. Cathedral.

1711–1829. 1 vol. MHS.

Index to register, 1711–1829. 1 vol. Mss. MHS.

Vestry proceedings, 1719–1829. Natl. Cathedral.

1719–1829. Index in same vol. MHS.

Rock Creek Church Parish register. Births, baptisms, communicants, confirmations, deaths, funerals, marriages, from earliest dates; rectors, 1712–1937. Extracts from minutes of vestry (some date back to 1693), containing history of Parish. D. C. Geneal. Rec. Com., 1934–36, v. 16. Indexed, typed, bd. DAR.

Marriages of Rock Creek Parish, 1778–1800. Hist. of west. Md. Scharf. V. 1, pp. 662–64. MHS; DAR.

1796–1807 (fragmentary). Chronicles of col. Md. Thomas. 1st edition, pp. 225–32; 2nd edition, pp. 209–12. MHS; DAR.

Marriage and funeral, 1796–1808 (ministerial records of Rev. Thomas Reed). Md. records. Brumbaugh. V. 2, pp. 556–72.

Tombstone inscriptions in Rock Creek Cemetery; Section A–I, inclusive. D. C. Daughters of Amer. Colonists, 1935, 289 pp. DAR.

Rock Creek Cemetery interments. Natl. Geneal. Soc. Quart., Oct., 1918, v. 7, p. 41.

List of rectors of Rock Creek Parish, 1709–1926, and history. Hist. sketches of parishes and missions in diocese of Washington. P. 109.

List of taxable bachelors of Rock Creek, 1756–62. Hist. of Md. Scharf. V. 1, p. 744. MHS; DAR.

St. John's Parish, 1816. St. John's Church, 16th and H. Streets. Register of marriages from May 20, 1817–Sept., 1870; names of brides and grooms, dates of marriages, names of witnesses, and places of marriage. D. C. Geneal. Rec. Com., pencil copy, 62 pp.; to be indexed, typed, bd. 1937. DAR. (It is hoped by this Committee to include baptisms and funerals.)

List of rectors of St. John's Church, 1816–1922. Hist. sketches of parishes and missions of Diocese of Washington. P. 81.

History and Reminiscenses of St. John's Protestant Episcopal Church. Hon. A. B. Hagner. Records of Columbia Hist. Soc., v. 12, p. 89.

Trinity Church, Georgetown. Records of marriages and baptisms, 1795–1807. Archives of Georgetown Univ., v. 175, pp. 1–50. DAR.

Vital records extracted from National Intelligencer, Wash., D. C., 1805, 1806, 1807 and 1808. Natl. Geneal. Soc. Quart., June, Sept., Dec., 1938, v. 26; March., 1939. (Many Md. ref.) MHS.

Washington, D. C. Library of Surgeon General, established 1836. Contains over million medical books. Abstracts and catalogues of every medical book and every Medical journal printed.

Washington Parish. St. James Protestant Episcopal Church, organized June 26, 1873, 8th Street North West, between Massachusetts Avenue and C Street. Register of births, marriages and deaths, 1873–1901; list of rectors, communicants and members with brief history of Parish. D. C. Geneal. Rec. Com., 1934–35, v. 15, pt. 2. Indexed, typed, bd. DAR.

Washington Parish, 1794. Christ Church, Navy Yard. Early register of old Christ Church copied, typed, with index partly made, and vestry proceedings, 1800–36. D. C. Geneal. Rec. Com., 1937. Will be bd. DAR.

Washington Parish, 1794. Christ Church marriages, 1795–1812. Scrap Book. MHS.

History of Washington Parish. Contains list of rectors. Hist. sketches of parishes and missions of Diocese of Washington. P. 106.

Washington past and present. J. C. Proctor. 1930, 2 vols. DAR.

KENTUCKY

Adair County. Wills, 1801–51. A. W. Burns. 1936. DAR.

Anderson County. Marriages, 1827–51. A. W. Burns. DAR.

Bath County. Marriages, 1811–50. A. W. Burns. 1937. DAR.

Bath County. Wills. A. W. Burns. 1936. Mss. DAR.

Barron County. Marriages, 1852–62. Mss. DAR.

Bracken County. Abstracts of wills, 1796–1851. A. W. Burns. Mss. DAR.

Breckenridge County. Marriages. A. W. Burns. DAR.

Calvary baptismal records, Holy Mary Church, 1807–35; marriages, 1828–29. Mss. MHS.

Carter County. Marriages, 1852–62. A. W. Burns. Mss. DAR.

Centenary of Catholicity in Kentucky. Hon. B. J. Webb. Contains account of sixty catholic families from Md., mostly residents of St. Mary's Co., pledged to emigrate to Ky., and list of twenty-five families who did leave Md., 1785, p. 57. Louisville. Charles A. Rogers, 1884. MHS.

Christian County. Wills, 1797–1812. A. W. B. Bell. 1935. DAR.

Clark County. Marriages, 1792–1851. A. W. B. Bell. Mss. DAR.

Clay County. Marriages, 1807–51. A. W. Burns. DAR.

Early wills and inventories. J. E. King. 1936. DAR.

Fayette County. Birth, marriages and deaths, 1852–62. A. W. Burns. DAR.

Fayette County. Historical Records Survey. Inventory of County Archives. Works Progress Administration, 1937. DAR.

Fayette County. Marriages, 1801–53. A. W. Burns. DAR.

Franklin County. Marriage bonds, 1852–54. E. Crager. Mss. 1940. DAR.

Franklin County. Marriages, 1794–1851. A. W. Burns. 1931. DAR.

Gerrard County. Marriages, 1796–1851. A. W. Burns. 1932. Mss. DAR.

Gerrard County. Wills, 1796–1851. A. W. Burns. 1931. DAR.

Hardin County. Marriages, 1815–40. A. W. Burns. DAR.

Hardin County. Marriages, 1792–1815. A. W. Burns. 1932. DAR.

Harlan County. Marriages, 1818–51, 1870–73. DAR.

Henderson County. Wills, 1819–50. A. W. Burns. 1935, pamph. DAR.

Henry County. Marriages. A. W. Burns. 1936. DAR.

Hopkins County. Marriages, 1807–68. A. W. B. Burns. 1935. DAR.

Hopkins County. Wills. 1801–51. Mss. DAR.

Hopkins County. Wills, 1806–40. A. W. Burns. 1935, pamph. DAR.

Jefferson County (formerly Virginia). Marriages (2336), 1800–26. Natl. Geneal. Soc. Quart., v. 4, no. 1, p. 15.

1783–1813. Natl. Geneal. Soc. Quart., v. 6, no. 3, p. 47. MHS.

Johnson County. Marriages, 1818–51, 1870–73. DAR.

Kentucky pioneer and court records. Mrs. H. K. McAdams. Lexington.

Knox County. Early marriages, 1800–19. D. A. R. Mag., 1935, v. 69, no. 2, p. 122; no. 4, p. 248.

Knox County. Inventory of County Archives. Historical Records Survey. Works Progress Administration, 1937, no. 61. DAR.

Knox County. Marriages, 1799–1819. A. W. B. Bell. Mss. DAR.

Laurel County. Marriages, 1825–51. A. W. Burns. DAR.

Laurel County. Wills, 1824–51. A. W. B. Bell. Mss. DAR.

Lawrence County. Marriages and wills, 1821–51. A. W. Burns. DAR.

Letcher County. Marriages, 1842–51. A. W. Burns. DAR.
Lewis County. Marriages, 1806–77. A. W. Burns. Mss. DAR.
Lincoln County. Abstracts of wills, 1780–1823. A. W. Burns. DAR.
Lincoln County. Marriages, 1780–1823. A. W. Burns. Pamph. DAR.
Livingston County. Wills, 1799–1815. A. W. Bursn. DAR.
Logan County. Abstracts of wills, 1792–1851. A. W. Burns. 1932. DAR.
Madison County. Marriages, 1785–1851. A. W. Burns. 1932, pamph. DAR.
Mason County. Marriages, 1788–1851. A. W. Burns. 1932, pamph. DAR.
Mason County. Supplemental list of marriage bonds. Limestone Chap., D. A. R. Mss. DAR.
Mason County. Wills, 1813–23. A. W. Burns. Pamph. DAR.
Mercer County. Will book, no. 7. M. Menaugh. 1940. Mss. DAR.
Morgan County. Marriages, 1818–51, 1870–73. Mss. DAR.
Nelson County. Abstracts of wills, 1792–1851. A. W. Burns. DAR.
Nelson County. Bardstown. 1851–1932. A. W. Burns. 1932. Mss. DAR.
Nicholas County. Record of marriages and settlement of estates. A. W. Burns. 1936, pamph. DAR.
Ohio County. Marriages, 1799–1851. A. W. Burns. DAR.
Old Kentucky entries and deeds. W. R. Jillson. DAR.
Owen County. Marriages, 1819–51. A. W. Burns. DAR.
Pike County. Marriages and wills, 1821–51. A. W. Burns. DAR.
Powell County. V. 1: marriages, 1818–51, 1870–73. V. 2: marriages and abstracts of wills. A. W. Burns. DAR.
Pulaski County. Marriage records. A. W. Burns. DAR.
Records of deaths, 1852–62. A. W. B. Bell. 3 vols. Mss. DAR.
Scott County. Marriages. A. W. Bell. DAR.
Spencer County. 1824–51. A. W. Burns. DAR.
Systematic index of all land grants, recorded in State Land Office, Frankfort, 1782–1924. W. R. Jillson. 1925. DAR.
Warren County. Marriages, 1796–1871. V. 1: mss. and wills. V. 2: Pamph. A. W. B. Bell. DAR.
Warren County. Wills. B. and D. Kentucky Geneal. Rec. Com. Typed, bd. DAR.
Washington County. Marriages, 1783–1813. Natl. Geneal. Soc. Quart., v. 6, no. 3, p. 47; v. 19, no. 4, p. 101. MHS.
Washington County. Marriages, 1792–1825. Mss. MHS.
Washington County. Wills, 1792–1858. A. W. Burns. DAR.
Woodford County. Wills, 1788–1851. A. W. Burns. 1934. DAR.

NEW ENGLAND

New England Historical and Genealogical Register. New Eng. Hist. and Geneal. Soc., Boston. Index of persons, vols. 1–50. 1906. MHS; DAR.
Index to places, vols. 1–50. 1911. MHS; DAR.
Index to subjects, vols. 1–50. 1908. MHS; DAR.
New England Historical and Genealogical Register and Antiquarian Journal, Quarterly, 1847–date. New Eng. Hist. and Geneal. Soc., Boston. MHS; DAR.

NEW JERSEY

Calendar of New Jersey wills, 1670–1750. 1901, 1918, 2 vols.
First settlers of ye plantation of Piscataway and Woolbridge, Olde East New Jersey, 1664–1714. O. E. Monette. 5 pts. MHS.
Index to wills, inventories etc., in office of Secretary of State, prior to 1901. 1912–1913, 3 vols. DAR.
Marriages, 1665–1800. N. J. Hist. Soc. Proceedings, 1904, v. 22. DAR.
New Jersey Historical Society Proceedings. W. A. Whitehead, editor (and others). DAR.
Wills of New Jersey, 1670–1730. N. J. Hist. Soc. Proceedings, v. 23. DAR.

NEW YORK

Calendar of wills in file, Albany, 1626–1836. B. Fernow. 1896. DAR.
Cemetery, church and town records. 1939, 119 vols. DAR.
Collection of Huguenot Society of America. Pub. by Huguenot Soc., N. Y., 1886. (Contains births, marriages and deaths of New York, French Church.) N. Y., Douglas Taylor, printer.
Early settlers of New York State. Their ancestors and descendants; from original manuscripts, tombstones, newspapers and Bibles. Monthly Mag., 1934–37. Indexed. DAR.
Marriage licenses. R. H. Kelly. 1916. DAR.
Marriage licenses, prior to 1784. Printed by order of G. J. Tucker, Secretary of State. Albany, 1860, 480 pp. DAR.
Marriages. N. Y. Geneal. and Biog. Rec., 1639–75, 1875, v. 6; 1686–88, 1874, v. 5; 1691–93, 1873, v. 4; 1692–1701, 1871, v. 2; 1693–1702, 1872, v. 3; 1702–03, 1870, v. 1; 1703–06, 1871, v. 2; 1756–58, supplemental list, 1871, v. 2. MHS.
Marriages. Supplemental list of marriage licenses. 1898. N. Y. State Lib. Bull., no. 1. DAR.
Marriages from Friends records in Philadelphia, 1686–1763. W. J. Potts. N. Y. Geneal. and Biog. Rec., 1872, v. 3. MHS.
New York Bible records (unpublished) and genealogical notes. 1922–1929, 44 vols. DAR.
New York genealogical and biographical record. Pub. N. Y. Geneal. Soc. Quart., N. Y., 1870, v. 1. MHS; DAR.
New York genealogical and biographical record. Subject index, vols. 1–38. F. E. Young. 1907.

NORTH CAROLINA

Bible records of North Carolina. 1937, pamph. DAR.
Brunswick County. Marriages. A. W. B. Bell. 1935, pamph. DAR.
Carteret County. Marriages. A. W. B. Bell. 1935, pamph. DAR.
Cravin County. Marriages. A. W. B. Bell. 1935, pamph. DAR.

Cumberland County. Marriage bonds. E. T. Howard. North Carolina Geneal. Rec. Com. 1937–38, v. 43, v. 44. Typed, bd. DAR.
Cumberland County. Marriages. A. W. Burns. 1935, pamph. DAR.
Duplin County. Cemetery records. 1938, pamph. DAR.
Duplin County. Marriages, 1780–1865. Letters A–O, pamph. DAR.
Edgecombe County. Marriage bonds. Geneal. Soc. of Utah. 1938. DAR.
Gates County. Marriages, prior to 1825. A. W. Burns. 1935, pamph. DAR.
Green County. Tombstone records. Pamph. DAR.
Guilford County. Tombstone records. Pamph. DAR.
Hoke County. Marriages, 1906–37. Pamph. DAR.
Index to marriages and wills in vol. 1 of North Carolina Historical and Genealogical Register. Catherine B. Brumbaugh. 1919. Typed, bd. DAR.
Johnson County. Marriage bonds. E. T. Howard. North Carolina Geneal. Rec. Com., 1937–38, v. 4. Typed, bd. DAR.
Lincoln County. See Tryon County.
Marriage bonds. D. A. R. Mag., 1935, v. 69.
New Hanover County. Marriages, 1779–1825. A. W. B. Bell. 1935. DAR.
North and South Carolina Marriage records from earliest colonization days, to Civil War. (About 15,000 names.) Wm. M. Clemens. E. P. Dutton Co., 1927, 295 pp. DAR.
North Carolina and Texas Marriages. Rev. Watson M. Fairley. 1937, pamph. DAR.
North Carolina Historical and Genealogical Register, 1900–03, 3 vols., all published.
Onslow County. Marriage records, prior to 1825. MHS.
Onslow County. Marriages, prior to 1825. A. W. Burns. 1935, pamph. DAR.
Orange County. Marriages. E. T. Howard. North Carolina Geneal. Rec. Com., 1938, v. 46, pt. 2. Typed, bd. DAR.
Person County. Tombstone records. 1937, pamph. DAR.
Richmond County. Tombstone records. 1937, pamph. DAR.
Rowan County. Marriage bonds, 1762–99. D. A. R. Mag., Sept., Nov., 1913.
Rowan County. Marriage bonds. E. T. Howard. North Carolina Geneal. Rec. Com., 1937–38, v. 41, v. 42. Typed, bd. DAR.
Rutherford County. Public officials, 1779–1934. C. Griffin. 1934, pamph. DAR.
Sampson County. Tombstone records. 1937, pamph. DAR.
Some North Carolina vital records, from Raleigh Star, 1810. D. A. R. Mag., 1933, pt. 1, v. 67, no. 2, p. 119–22; pt. 2, no. 3, pp. 149–53.
State records. Vols. 9, 10, 11, 12, 13, 16, 17 and 22. Contain civil and military service. Index to same has been published. DAR.
Tombstone records. North Carolina Geneal. Rec. Com., 46 vols. Typed. DAR.
Tryon and Lincoln Counties. Marriage bonds. C. Bynum. 1929. DAR.
Wills. 1938, pamph. DAR.
Wills and inventories. Compiled from original and recorded wills in office of Secretary of State. J. B. Grimes. 1912. DAR.

OHIO

Allen County. Marriages, 1831–45. A. W. B. Bell. 1934. DAR.
Allen County. Shawnee Township. St. Matthews Lutheran Church records. Photos. DAR.
Athens County. Marriages, 1805–65. Ohio Geneal. Rec. Com. Typed, bd. DAR.
Brown County. Marriage records. Ohio Geneal. Rec. Com., v. 1. Typed, bd. DAR.
Butler County. Marriages, 1803–17. Ohio Geneal. Rec. Com., 1938. Typed, bd. DAR.
Champaign County. Marriage bonds, 1849–65. Ohio Geneal. Rec. Com., 1936. Typed, bd. DAR.
Clark County. Marriage bonds, 1818–65. Ohio Geneal. Rec. Com., 4 vols. Typed. DAR.
Columbiana County. Marriages 1804–35. Ohio Geneal. Rec. Com. Typed, bd. DAR.
Cuyahoga County. Early marriages, 1838–49, 1850–57. Ohio Geneal. Rec. Com., 3 vols. Typed. DAR.
Cuyahoga County. Historical Records Survey. Works Progress Administration, 1937, no. 18. DAR.
Cuyahoga, Fulton, Medina, Lorain and Wayne Counties. Cemetery records. Ohio Geneal. Rec. Com. Typed, bd. DAR.
Delaware County. Marriage bonds, 1832–65. Ohio Geneal. Rec. Com. (Delaware City Chap.), 1940, 2 vols. Typed, bd. DAR.
Defiance County. Index to marriages. Ohio Geneal. Rec. Com., 1940. Typed, bd. DAR.
Defiance county. Wills. Ohio Geneal. Rec. Com. Typed, bd. DAR.
Early marriage bonds. 1936, 39 vols. DAR.
Erie County. Cemetery records. Ohio Geneal. Rec. Com. Typed, bd. DAR.
Erie County. Marriage records, 1838–64. Ohio Geneal. Rec. Com., 3 vols. Typed. DAR.
Fairfield County. Marriage records, 1803–65. Ohio Geneal. Rec. Com. (Elizabeth Sherman Reese Chap). 1940, 2 vols. Typed, bd. DAR.
Family register, West Branch Monthly Meeting, Niami County, Ohio. D. A. R. Mag., Sept., 1934, v. 68, no. 9, pp. 560–61; Oct., 1934, v. 68, no. 10, pp. 628–34; Dec., 1938, v. 68, no. 11, pp. 691–21.
Fayette County. Bloomingburg Church and 29 cemetery records, wills and guardianships. Ohio Geneal. Rec. Com. Typed, bd. DAR.
Fayette County. Marriage records, Ohio Geneal. Rec. Com. Typed, bd. DAR.
Franklin County. Early Bible and family records. Ohio Geneal. Rec. Com. Typed, bd. 1940. DAR.
Franklin County. Marriages, 1803–40. Old Northwest Geneal. Soc., 1898, v. 1; 1899, v. 2; 1901, v. 4. MHS.
Franklin County. Marriage bonds, 1803–65. Ohio Geneal. Rec. Com., 6 vols. Typed, bd. DAR.
Franklin County. Wills, 1803–65. Ohio Geneal. Rec. Com., 1939. Typed, bd. DAR.
Fulton County. Cemetery records. Ohio Geneal. Rec. Com. Typed, bd. DAR.
Gallia County. Early marriages. V. 1, A–L; v. 2, L–Z. French Colony Chap., D. A. R. Typed. DAR.
Geauga County. Cemetery records. DAR.

Geauga County. Marriage records, 1805–24, 1852–65. Ohio Geneal. Rec. Com. Typed, bd. DAR.
Geaugo County. See Lake County. DAR.
Greene County. Census, 1820. Natl. Geneal. Soc. Quart., Oct., 1916, v. 5, p. 47; Dec. 1938, v. 26, p. 126. MHS.
Greene county. Index to marriage bonds. Mss. DAR.
Greene County. Marriage bonds. Ohio Geneal. Rec. Com., 2 vols. Typed. DAR.
Hamilton County. Marriage records. Mss. DAR.
Hardin County. Marriage records, 1833–65. Ohio Geneal. Rec. Com., 1 vol. Typed, bd. DAR.
Historical Collection of Harrison County. C. A. Hanna. Contains first land owners, 1841; marriages and wills to 1861; burial records and numerous genealogies. Privately printed, 1900.
Huron County. Marriage bonds. Old series, 1846–55. Copy of vol. 3. Ohio Geneal. Rec. Com., 1936. Typed, bd. DAR.
Jackson County. Marriages, 1816–26. Old Northwest Geneal. Soc., 1904, v. 7. MHS.
Jackson County. Marriage records, 1818–65. Ohio Geneal. Rec. Com. Typed, bd. DAR.
Jefferson County. Marriage bonds, 1789–1839. Ohio Geneal. Rec. Coms., M. D. Sinclair, 1940, 2 vols. DAR.
Lake and Geaugo Counties. Marriages, 1817–27. Pamph. DAR.
Lake, Licking and Logan Counties. Marriage bonds, 1840–65. Ohio Geneal. Rec. Com. Typed, bd. DAR.
Lorain County. Cemetery records. Ohio Geneal. Rec. Com. Typed, bd. DAR.
Lorain County. Marriage records, 1825–65. Ohio Geneal. Rec. Com. Typed, bd. DAR.
Lucas County. Marriage bonds, 1835–66. Ohio Geneal. Rec. Com., 1936. Typed, bd. DAR.
Lucas County. Toledo. Inventory of County. Archives of Ohio. 1937, no. 48. DAR.
Mahonning County. Early marriages. Ohio Geneal. Rec. Com. Typed, bd. DAR.
Mayhonning County. Wills. Ohio Geneal. Rec. Com. Typed, bd. DAR.
Marion County. Early marriages, 1824–65. Ohio Geneal. Rec. Com., 2 vols. Typed. DAR.
Marion County. Marriages, 1824–26. Old Northwest Geneal. Soc., 1904, v. 7. MHS.
Medina County. Cemetery records. Ohio Geneal. Rec. Com. Typed, bd. DAR.
Medina County. Marriages, prior to 1850. Mss. DAR.
Medina County. Marriages, 1818–65. Ohio Geneal. Rec. Com., 2 vols. Typed. DAR.
Montgomery County. German inhabitants, 1806. Natl. Geneal. Soc. Quart., v. 25, pp. 64–65. MHS.
Montgomery County. Index to county marriages, 1803–27. Mss. DAR.
Montgomery County. Marriage records, 1803–27. Ohio Geneal. Rec. Com. Typed, bd. DAR.
Niami County. Family register, West Branch Monthly Meeting. 1805 records. (Contains Hoover family records, Md. ref.) D. A. R Mag., Sept., 1934, v. 68, no. 9, p. 560; no. 10, p. 628; no. 11, p. 691.
Noble County. Marriages, 1852–65. Ohio Geneal. Rec. Com., 1939. Typed, bd. DAR.
Ohio Valley genealogies. C. E. Hanna. 1900. DAR.
Old Northwest Genealogical Society Quarterly, Columbus, Ohio. MHS.
Pickaway County. Index to inscriptions from grave stones. Pickaway Chap., D. A. R. Geneal. Rec. Com., 1936. Typed, bd. DAR.
Pickaway County. Marriages, 1813. Old Northwest Geneal. Soc., July, 1905, v. 8, no. 3. MHS.
Pickaway County. Marriage records. Book 5. Ohio Geneal. Rec. Com. Typed, bd. DAR.
Pioneer settlers of Ohio. S. P. Hildreth. Cincinnati, 1852.
Portage County. Marriage bonds. A–K, v. 2. Ohio Geneal. Rec. Com., 1936. Typed, bd. DAR.
Preble County. Early settlers. D. A. R. Mag., Sept., 1935, v. 69, p. 568.
Preble County. Marriage bonds, 1808–60. Ohio Geneal. Rec. Com., 3 vols. Typed. DAR.
Richald County. Birth certificates. DAR.
Richland County. Data on cemeteries, with records of first burials and location of cemeteries. Pamph. DAR.
Richland County. Death certificates, 1856–70. Pamph. DAR.
Richland County. Wills. Ohio Geneal. Rec. Com. Typed, bd. DAR.
Ross County. Index to marriage records, 1840–90. 2 vols. Typed, bd. DAR.
Ross County. Marriage records, 1840–90. Ohio Geneal. Rec. Com., 2 vols. Typed. DAR.
Ross County. Marriages, 1804–06. Old Northwest Geneal. Soc., 1905, v. 8, no. 2. MHS.
Sandusky County. Marriage records. Ohio Geneal. Rec. Com., 2 vols. Typed. DAR.
Scioto County. Marriage records, 1804–65. Ohio Geneal. Rec. Com., 3 vols. Typed. DAR.
Seneca County. Marriage records, 1841–65. Ohio Geneal. Rec. Com., 2 vols. Typed, bd. DAR.
Shelby County. Early marriage records. Ohio Geneal. Rec. Com., 2 vols. Typed. DAR.
Stark County. Marriage records, 1808–85. Ohio Geneal. Rec. Com., 5 vols. Typed. DAR.
Trumbull County. Marriage records, 1803–65. Ohio Geneal. Rec. Com., 2 vols. Typed. DAR.
Trumbull County. Warren. Inventory of County Archives of Ohio, no. 78. DAR.
Vinton County. Marriages. Ohio Geneal. Rec. Com. Typed, bd. DAR.
Washington County. Death records, 1811–65. Ohio Geneal. Rec. Com. Typed, bd. DAR.
Washington County. Early Bible and family records. Ohio Geneal. Rec. Com., 1940. Typed, bd. DAR.
Washington County. Marriages, 1780–1825. Mss. DAR.
Washington County. Marriages, 1789–1822. Old Northwest Geneal. Soc., 1900, v. 3; 1901, v. 4; 1902, v. 5. MHS.
Wayne County. Cemetery records. Ohio Geneal. Rec. Com. Typed, bd. DAR.
Wilderness trail or ventures and adventures of Pennsylvania traders ofAllegheney path. C. A. Hanna. N. Y., G. P. Putnam's Sons, 1911, 2 vols. Peabody Lib.

Wood County. Marriages, 1820–65. Ohio Geneal. Rec. Com., 1936–37. Typed, bd. DAR.
Wyandot County. Marriages, 1845–65. Ohio Geneal. Rec. Com. Typed, bd. DAR.

PENNSYLVANIA

Adams County. Mummerts Dunkard Meeting House cemetery; 1743–1898. Md. Geneal. Rec. Com., 1932–33, pp. 122–25. Mss. DAR.
Allegheney County. Abstracts of wills. Geneal. Soc. Pa. Pub., Mar., 1920, v. 7, no. 3, p. 226.
Beaver County. Cemetery records. Pa. Geneal. Rec. Com., 1938, v. 2, pp. 56–61, 66–72. Typed, bd. DAR.
Beaver County. Cemeteries; grave records. Pa. Geneal. Rec. Com., 1939. Typed, bd. DAR.
Beaver County. Mortuary list of aged persons, 1817–86. Hist. of Beaver Co., Pa. 1888, p. 108. DAR.
Berks County. Mennonite cemetery records. Hereford Congregation in Borough of Bally. Mss. DAR.
Burials and tombstone inscriptions collected in Pennsylvania. DAR.
†Byberry in County of Philadelphia. Sketches of history of Byberry. I. Comly. Memoirs. Hist. Soc. Pa., v. 2. MHS.
Cemetery records of western Pennsylvania. Pa. Geneal. Rec. Com., 1939. Typed, bd. DAR.
Center County. Center Quaker records. Wilson Mss. Coll., no. 81. MHS.
Center County. Marriage records, 1804–72, Society of Friends Center Meeting Halfmoon, Township. Md. Geneal. Rec. Com., 1939–40. Typed, bd. DAR.
Center County. Marriages of Center Friends Meeting. Wilson Mss. Coll., no. 146. MHS.
Chester County. Collections. Anderson and Darlington. Bureau of Historical Research, nos. 1–8. DAR.
Chester Co. Collections. Bureau of Historical Research, nos. 9–16. DAR.
Chester County. Quaker records. Gilbert Cope. DAR.
Erie County. Abstracts of first book of wills. D. A. R. Mag., Nov. 1928, v. 62, no. 11, pp. 706–09.
Exquisite siren, romance of Peggy Shippen and Major John André. E. Irvine Haines. Phila., N. Y., London, J. B. Lippincott Co., 1938. MHS.
Fayette County. Wills. Pa. Geneal. Rec. Com., 1 vol. Typed. DAR.
Franklin County. Records of Salem Reformed Church, 1787–1807. D. A. R. Mag., 1935, v. 69, no. 8, pp. 502–06.
Genealogical map of counties of Pennsylvania. J. H. Campbell. 1911, blue print. MHS.
Genealogical register. W. M. Mervine. Lancaster, Pa., Wickersham Printing Co., 1913, v. 1. MHS.
Genealogical research among Pennsylvania German and Huguenot families. C. R. Roberts. Pub. Natl. Geneal. Soc., Wash., D. C.
Genealogical Society of Pennsylvania. Mss. Coll.
Genealogical Society of Pennsylvania Publications. V. 1, nos. 1–4, Jan., 1895–date. Phila., Pa.
Harrisburg. Marriage bonds, 1784–86 (1 in 1791). Pa. Mag. Hist. and Biog., v. 55, pp. 259–76.
History of Townships of Byberry and Moreland in Philadelphia, from earliest settlement to present time. (Mostly Quaker records.) J. C. Martindale. Phila., 1867. MHS.
Immigration of Irish Quakers into Pennsylvania, 1682–1750. A. C. Myers. Swathmore, Pa., 1902. MHS.
Lancaster. First Reformed Church. Births and baptismal records, 1736–69. Pa. German Soc. Pub., 1894, v. 4.
1769–1800. Pa. German Soc. Pub., 1895, v. 5.
Lancaster. Trinity Lutheran Church. Birth and baptismal records, 1747–74. Pa. German Soc. Pub., 1893, v. 3.
1774–86. Pa. German Soc. Pub., 1894, v. 4.
1786–92. Pa. German Soc. Pub., 1895, v. 5.
1793–99. Pa. German Soc. Pub., 1896, v. 6.
Lancaster County. Copy of intestate records, 1730–1850. Pa. Geneal. Rec. Com., 1936. Typed, bd. DAR.
Lancaster County. Copy of will book, 1720–1850. Pa. Geneal. Rec. Com., 1936. Typed, bd. DAR.
Lancaster County Court House. Abstracts of wills. D. A. R. Mag., Oct., 1939, v. 73, pp. 72–74; Nov., pp. 61–62; Jan., 1940, p. 47; Feb., pp. 36–39; Mar., pp. 39–43.
Lancaster County. Index to intestate records and will books, 1729–1850. E. J. Fulton and B. K. Mylin. 1936. MHS; DAR.
Lancaster County tax lists, 1751, 1756, 1757, 1758. A. H. Gerberich, Dr. G. M. Brumbaugh. Geneal. Pub. Natl. Geneal. Soc. Quart. Pamph. DAR.
*List of records of meeting constituting Yearly Meeting of Society of Friends, held at 15th and Race Streets, Philadelphia. Morgan Bunting. Darby, Pa., 1904. MHS.
Marriage licenses, 1742–48. Pa. Mag. Hist. and Biog., v. 39, pp. 176, 364, 434. MHS; DAR.
1748–52. Pa. Mag. Hist. and Biog., v. 32, pp. 71, 233, 345, 471. MHS; DAR.
1762–68. Pa. Mag. Hist. and Biog., v. 40, pp. 104, 208, 319, 436. MHS; DAR.
1769–76. Pa. Mag. Hist. and Biog., v. 41, pp. 224, 334, 489. MHS; DAR.
Marriages. Lynn. Lib. Cong.
Marriages, prior to 1810. 2 vols. 1880.
Menallen Quaker records. Wilson Mss. Coll., no. 81. MHS.
Merion in Welsh tract, in Province of Pennsylvania. T. A. Glenn. 1896.
Montgomery County. Augustus Lutheran and St. Luke's Reformed Churches, Abington Presbyterian, and Lehman Memorial Methodist Episcopal Churches. Tombstone inscriptions. Pa. Geneal. Rec. Com., 1938. Typed, bd. DAR.
Montgomery County. Mennonite Churches (Wentz's Reformed and Yellow). Tombstone inscriptions. Pa. Geneal. Rec. Com., 1938. Typed, bd. DAR.
Montgomery County. New Goshenhopper Congregation, 1731–61. D. A. R. Mag., 1913, v. 43, Mar., Apr., May, June and July.
Moravian Church of York. Register of 1780. Pub. Geneal. Soc. Pa., v. 4, pp. 324–69.
Moravian Historical Society, Nazareth, Pa. Transactions. 1858–1891, v. 1–3; v. 4, pt. 1.
Notes and queries. Annual. W. H. Egle, editor. (History, biography and genealogy, relating mostly to Pa.) 1894–1900. Harrisburg, Pa., 1898, 1932. MHS; DAR.
Index to contents. Pa. State Lib., 1932.

Of narrative and critical history. Prepared at request of Pa.-German Soc. Lancaster, Pa., 1894, 13 pts.
Pennsylvania, distributing center. Pa. Mag. Hist. and Biog., v. 45, pp. 143–69. MHS.
*Pennsylvania genealogies. Scotch, Irish and German. Wm. H. Egle. Harrisburg, Pa., Lane S. Hart, 1886, 720 pp. MHS.
Pennsylvania German pioneers. R. B. Strassburger and W. J. Hinke. 1934, 3 vols. DAR.
Pennsylvania-German Society, Lancaster. 1891, v. 1. (Proceedings and addresses.)
Pennsylvania Magazine of History and Biography. Pub. Fund of Hist. Soc. of Pa., Phila., 1887, v. 1, no. 1. MHS; DAR.
Pennsylvania Society of Colonial Governors. V. 1. MHS.
Pennsylvania Yearly Meeting (Friends), Philadelphia. Marriages and deaths. See Quaker records, Baltimore.
Perry County. Abstracts from will book. A, 1820–35. Pa. Geneal. Rec. Com., v. 1, Typed, bd. DAR.
Philadelphia folks. C. Waygandt. Appleton, 1938.
Provincial Councillors of Pennsylvania, 1883. C. P. Keith. 1883. DAR.
Quarterly Review of Evangelical Lutheran Church. Gettysburg.
Rouzerville. Harbaugh Reformed Church. Burial records. Mss. MHS.
Snyder County. Marriages, 1835–99. G. W. Wagenseller. (7000 marriages, 1800 different surnames.) Middleburg, Pa., 1899. DAR.
Some Pennsylvania cemetery records. 1938. DAR.
*Tombstone records at Hancock, Maryland. Md. Geneal. Rec. Com., Parran, 1937, pp. 44–50. Mss. DAR.
Washington County. Marriages, 1811–45. DAR.
Welsh settlements in Pennsylvania. C. H. Browning. 1912. DAR.
Western Pennsylvania genealogies, with affiliated branches. Pa. Geneal. Rec. Com., 1939. Typed, bd. DAR.
York. Marriages of Christ Lutheran Church. Wilson Mss. Coll., no. 78. MHS.

RHODE ISLAND

Civil and military lists, 1647–1850. J. J. Smith. 1900–07, 3 vols. DAR.
Genealogical dictionary of Rhode Island. J. O. Auston. 1887.
Index to vital records of Rhode Island, 1636–1850. 3 vols. MHS; DAR.
Vital records of Rhode Island, 1836–50. 21 vols. First series complete; v. 1, 1891. Providence R. I. MHS; DAR.

SOUTH CAROLINA

Abstracts of wills. S. R. Reese. 1940, pamph. DAR.
Church records. 1938, pamph. DAR.
Death notices, 1732–1801. A. S. Salley, Jr. 1902. DAR.
Death notices from South Carolina Gazette, 1732–75. A. S. Salley, Jr. Printed for Hist. Commission, Columbia, South Carolina, 1917, State Co. MHS.
Huguenot Society of South Carolina, Charleston, S. C. Transactions, no. 1, 1889–date.
Inscriptions from South Carolina cemeteries. S. C. Geneal. Rec. Com., 1939, 3 vols. Typed, bd. DAR.
Marriage licenses. M. H. Mag., Oct., 1914.
Marriage licenses. D. A. R. Mag., v. 45, pp. 208–09.
Marriage notices in Royal Gazette, 1781–82. A. S. Salley, Jr. Printed for Hist. Commission, Columbia, South Carolina, 1919, State Co. MHS.
Marriage records. W. M. Clemens.
St. Phillips Parish Register, Charles Town, 1720–58. A. S. Salley, Jr. Charleston, South Carolina, 1904. MHS.
South Carolina Historical and Genealogical Magazine. Pub. S. C. Hist. Soc. Quart., Charleston, v. 1, no. 1, Jan., 1900. MHS; DAR.

VIRGINIA

Abstracts of Virginia land patents. Va. Mag. Hist. and Biog., 1901, v. 8. MHS; DAR.
Accomac County. Certificates and rights, 1663–1709. S. Nottingham. Onancock, 1929, 91 pp. DAR.
Accomac County. County Court Note Book, v. 2, pp. 25–33. DAR.
Accomac County. County notes. G. E. Callahan. William and Mary Quart., Coll. A, v. 18, p. 108. DAR.
Accomac County. Land causes, 1727–1826. S. Nottingham. Onancock, 1930. DAR.
Accomac County. Land grants (Va. Co. rec.). V. 6, pp., 95, 129; v. 7, p. 1; v. 10, p. 4. DAR.
Accomac County (was Northampton County). Marriages, 1774–1806. S. Nottingham. Onancock, 1927, pamph., 40 pp. DAR.
Accomac County. Marriages. Genealogy Mag., v. 7, p. 10. MHS; DAR.
Accomac County. Records. In: Virginia County records. Crozier. V. 7, p. 152.
Accomac County. Wills and administrations, 1663–1800. S. Nottingham. Onancock, 1931, 2 vols. DAR.
Accomac County. Ye Kingdom of Accawmacke, or Eastern Shore of Virginia, in seventeenth century. J. C. Wise, 1911, 406 pp. MHS; DAR.
Albemarle County. Christ Church, Charlottesville, Parish register. Typed. In Binder. DAR.
Albemarle County. Records. In: Virginia County records. Crozier. V. 7, p. 111. DAR.
Albemarle County. Marriage records. Gleanings of Va. hist. Boogher. 1903, p. 384. DAR. Also: Mss. in DAR.
Albemarle County. Marriages. Va. Mag. Hist. and Biog., v. 31, p. 333; v. 32, p. 365. MHS; DAR.
Albemarle County. Tombstone records. 10 pp. Mss. DAR.
Alexandria. List of vestry books and registers at library, Alexandria.
Alexandria. Records from Alexandria Herald. (Md. refs.) Natl. Geneal. Soc. Quart., v. 5, no. 2, p. 1. MHS.
Amelia County. Marriage bonds, 1739–1849. Copied by J. D. Eggleston. D. A. R. Mag., 1932, v. 66, nos. 8, 9, 10; 1933, v. 67, nos. 1, 2, 3, 4, 6, 9.

Amelia County. Marriage performed by Rev. Timothy Howe, 1833–90. Va. Geneal. Rec. Com. Typed, bd. DAR.
Amherst County. Bonds and other marriage records, 1763–1800. W. M. Sweeny. Astoria, L. I., N. Y., 1937, 102 pp. DAR.
Amherst County. Marriage bonds, 1768–1800, 1800–25. Va. Geneal. Rec. Com., 1931, pp. 17–30. Typed, bd. DAR.
Annals of South West Virginia, 1769–1800. L. P. Summers. Abingdon, 1929, 757 pp.
Annual report of Virginia State Library.
Antiquary. Lower Norfolk County Va. Edited by E. W. James. Richmond, Va., 1895–1906, vols. 1–5. MHS.
Augusta County. Extracts from records of 1754–1800. L. Chalkley. 1912, 3 vols. DAR.
Augusta County. First marriages, 1785–1813. Pub. by Col. Thomas Hughart Chap., D. A. R. DAR.
Augusta County. Gleanings of Virginia history. W. F. Boogher. 1903, 289 pp. DAR.
Augusta County. Marriages, 1749–1843. Va. Mag. Hist. Biog., 1900, v. 7; 1901, v. 8. MHS.
Augusta County. Marriages, 1785–1812. A. W. B. Bell. 1935, pamph., vols. 1–4. DAR.
Barbour County. Marriage bonds, 1843. H. B. Grant. Mss. DAR.
Bedford County. Marriage bonds, 1755–1800. E. S. Dennis and J. E. Smith. 1932. DAR.
Botetourt County. Marriage bonds, 1769–1800. Pamph. DAR.
Brief history of Tangier Island. C. P. Swain. Pamph. MHS.
Brunswick County. Abstracts of wills, 1732–97. D. A. R. Mag., July, 1935, v. 69, no. 7, pp. 438–43.
Bruton Parish Church. Brief history with map and key list of tombstones in churchyard. DAR.
Buckingham County. Marriage bonds, 1785–94. Wilson Mss. Coll., no. 124. MHS.
Calendar of Virginia State Papers.
Campbell County. Bible records, chiefly Campbell County. J. Fauntleroy. 1938, pamph. DAR.
Campbell County. Marriages. D. A. R. Mag., v. 64.
Campbell County and other counties of Virginia. Tombstone inscriptions. J. Fauntleroy. 1938, pamph. DAR.
*Caroline County. History. Marshall Wingfield.
Caroline County. Marriage bonds. Tyler's Quart. Mag., v. 14, p. 164. MHS.
Caroline County. Marriage bonds, 1787–52. Mss. DAR.
Catalogue of Books, no. 56. (Va., W. Va. genealogy; South; Civil War; with other Americana.) Dayton, Va., Joseph K. Ruebush Co.
Cavaliers and pioneers. Abstracts of Virginia land patents and grants, 1623–1800. N. M. Nugent. 1934, 5 vols. (V. 1, Richmond.) MHS; DAR.
Charles County. Marriages. William and Mary Quart., 1890, v. 8. MHS.
Charlotte County. Marriage bonds, 1767–80. Tyler's Quart. Mag., v. 5, pp. 67–71. MHS.
Chesterfield County. Court records. S. A. Thompson. 1934, pamph. DAR.
Chesterfield County. Marriages, 1771–99. W. W. Barnes, Jr. Mss. DAR.
Chesterfield County. V. 1: Revolutionary War, public service claims. V. 2: index to marriage bonds. V. 3: index to wills. Ethel C. Clarke. Richmond, 1937. DAR.
Clark County. Tombstone records from Old Chapel Cemetery, Berryville. Pamph. DAR.
Counties of Virginia. Natl. Geneal. Soc. Quart., July, 1917, v. 6, no. 2, p. 46. MHS.
Culpeper County. Property tax lists and names of slaves, 1783. DAR.
Cumberland County. Marriage bonds. J. D. Eggleston. (Mr. Eggleston says probably 60 per cent are lost.) D. A. R. Mag., v. 65, nos. 2, 5, 7, 10 and 12.
Cumberland County. Records. Natl. Geneal. Soc. Quart., Jan. and Apr., 1915, v. 3, v. 4. MHS.
Douglas register. Detailed account of births, marriages, deaths, and other interesting notes kept by Rev. Wm. Douglas, 1750–97. Contains besides parish register of Goochland, index of Goochland wills, notes on French Huguenot refugees who lived in Manakin Town. Compiled by W. M. Jones. Richmond. MHS; DAR.
Early marriages. Virginia County records. N. Y., 1907, v. 4.
Early Quaker records. Pub. Southern Hist. Assoc., v. 1, p. 17; continued through v. 2, v. 3; concluded in v. 7.
Elizabeth City. Marriages, 1689–99. William and Mary Quart., 1894, v. 2. MHS.
Essex County. Marriage bonds, 1783–89. Tyler's Quart. Mag., v. 13, pp. 99–100. MHS.
Executive journals of colonial Virginia. From Va. State Library. DAR.
Fairfax County. Abstracts of wills and inventories, 1742–1810. J. E. S. King. Calif., 1936. DAR.
Fairfax County. Marriages, 1759–90. William and Mary Quart., 1904, v. 12. MHS.
Families of Virginia. G. W. Chappelean. 2 vols. DAR.
Fauquier County. Marriage returns. Cary Geneal. Coll. Mss. MHS.
Fauquier County. Marshall. Tombstone inscriptions. Natl. Geneal. Soc. Quart., Mar., 1939, v. 27, p. 21. MHS.
Fauquier County. Wills administration and marriages, 1759–1800. J. H. S. King. 1939. DAR.
Fluvanna County. Marriages, 1783–1809. Mss. DAR.
Fluvanna County. Marriage bonds. Kate S. Curry. Wash., D. C.
Franklin County. Marriage bonds, 1786–1858. M. Wingfield. 1939. DAR.
Frederick County. Marriage records. Natl. Geneal. Soc. Quart., 1931, v. 19, no. 3, p. 68. MHS.
Frederick County. History. Shenandoah Valley pioneers and their descendants, 1738–1908. T. K. Cartmell. Winchester, 1909.
Fredericksburg. Marriage bonds, 1782–1824. G. H. S. King. 1939. Mss. DAR.
Genealogy. Bibliographies relating to Virginia. C. Shepard. Pub. Natl. Geneal. Soc. Quart., June, 1931. MHS.

German element in Shenandoah Valley, Virginia. J. W. Wayland. Pub. by author, 1907. DAR.
German New River settlement, Virginia. U.S.A. Heavener. Md. Geneal. Rec. Com. (Janet Montgomery Chap.) Typed, bd. DAR.
Gloucester County. Marriage bonds, 1777–78. Tyler's Quart. Mag., v. 5, pp. 57–58. MHS.
Gloucester County. Old tombstones. William and Mary Quart., 1894, v. 2. MHS.
Goochland County. Marriages, 1739–84. William and Mary Quart., 1899, v. 7; 1900, v. 8. MHS.
Goochland County. See Douglas register.
Greensville County. Marriages, 1781–1801. D. A. R. Mag., May, 1933, v. 67, no. 5, pp. 294–96.
Greensville County. Marriage bonds, 1781–1808. Tyler's Quart. Mag., v. 2, pp. 248–56; v. 3, pp. 58–66, 194–210; v. 6, pp. 177–87, 285–90.
1809–1827. Tyler's Quart. Mag., v. 7, pp. 57–59.
Guide to genealogical research in Virginia. K. C. Gottoschalk, genealogist. 1931. DAR.
Halifax County. Marriage bonds. Tyler's Quart. Mag., v. 4, pp. 58–64.
Hennings' statutes.
Henrico Parish and Old St. John's Church, Richmond, 1611–1904. J. S. Moore. 1904. DAR.
Henrico County. Marriage bonds, 1780–1861. Mss. DAR.
Historic Virginia homes and churches. Robert A. Lancaster, Jr. Phila., Lippincott, 1915, 36 illus.
Historic Lower Shenandoah, Virginia. J. E. Norris. 1890. DAR.
Historical Collection, Virginia Company, 1619–24. Richmond, 1889.
History of Old Virginia, and her neighbors. J. Fiske. (Much of Md. and N. C.) Boston 1897, 2 vols., maps.
Huguenot Church, Manakintown, on James River. Register, 1707–50. Va. Mag. Hist. and Biog., 1904, v. 11.
Huguenot exile in Virginia. Durand, 1685–87. N. Y. Press of Pioneers, Inc., 1934. (3 Md.) Peabody Lib.
Huguenot founders of Manakin in Colony of Virginia. (Pedigrees of Cabaniss, Marye, Maupin, Michaux, Pasteur, Reamy, Witt and others.) Pub. by Huguenot Soc. MHS.
Index to Bishop Meade's old churches, ministers and families of Virginia. J. C. Wise. 1910. DAR.
Index to Bishop Meade's old churches, ministers and families of Virginia. J. M. Toner. 1898. DAR.
Index to Virginia notes. T. Nimmo. Vols. 1–5. DAR.
Index to Virginia printed genealogies, including key and bibliography. R. A. Stewart. Richmond, Va., 1930. MHS.
Isle of Wight County. Abstracts of more important deeds, wills, lists of justices, vestrymen, militia officers, land grants, officers of the counties, etc. William and Mary Quart., Apr., 1899, v. 7. MHS.
Isle of Wight County. Births. Tyler's Quart. Mag., v. 9, pp. 118–22.
Isle of Wight County. Early deeds and wills, 1733–1898. Va. Mag. Hist. and Biog., 1898, v. 5. MHS.
Isle of Wight County. Marriages, 1628–1800. Mrs. B. A. Chapman, genealogist. Smithfield, Isle of Wight Co., 1933. DAR.
Isle of Wight County. Marriage bonds. Tyler's Quart. Mag., v. 8, pp. 266–269.
Isle of Wight County. Wills and administrations, 1647–1800. Mrs. B. A. Chapman, genealogist. 1938, v. 1, bk. 3, 152 mimeog. pp. DAR.
Journal of House of Burgesses. MHS.
Journals of Council of State of Virginia, Oct. 6, 1777–Nov. 30, 1781. V. 2. DAR.
*King and Queen County. History and genealogy. A. A. Bagby. N. Y., 1908.
King and Queen County. Virginia colonial abstracts, eighteenth century records. B. Fleet. DAR.
Kith and kin. Written for children of Mr. and Mrs. John Russell Sampson at their urgent request, by their mother. 25 pedigree charts. Richmond, 1922, 247 pp. MHS.
Lancaster County. Land causes, 1759–1848. See Northampton County, Nottingham, 1931.
Lancaster County. Marriages, 1701–1848. S. Nottingham. 1927. DAR.
Lancaster County. Marriages, 1717–47. William and Mary Quart., 1898, v. 6. MHS.
1721–79. William and Mary Quart., 1904, v. 12. MHS.
Lancaster County. Tithables, 1654, with notes. Va. Mag. Hist. and Biog., 1898, v. 5. MHS.
Lancaster County. Virginia colonial abstracts, 1654–66. B. Fleet. V. 1, Rec. Bk., no. 2. DAR.
Land records. Lib. Cong.
List of early land patents and grants in Virginia. Va. Mag. Hist. and Biog., v. 5, pp. 173–80, 241–44.
List of House of Burgesses, 1683–48. Va. Mag. Hist. and Biog., 1903, v. 10. MHS.
1688. Va. Mag. Hist. and Biog., 1902, v. 9. MHS.
1766–75. Va. Mag. Hist. and Biog., 1897, v. 4. MHS.
List of members of Virginia Assembly, 1641. Va. Mag. Hist. and Biog., 1902, v. 9. MHS.
Loudoun County. Marriages, 1793–96. D. A. R. Mag., Sept., 1914, v. 45, pp. 152–53.
Loudoun Co. Marriages, 1793–95. Natl. Geneal. Soc. Quart., v. 9, no. 3, pp. 47–48. MHS.
Lower Norfolk County. Virginia Antiquary. 5 vols. MHS.
Lunenburg County. Marriage bonds. Tyler's Quart. Mag., v. 8, pp. 37–39.
Lynchburg will book, A. 1809, pamph. DAR.
Mecklenburg County. Marriage bonds, 1765–1810. S. Nottingham. 1928, pamph. DAR.
Middlesex County. Marriages. William and Mary Quart., 1896, v. 4. MHS.
1759–1803. William and Mary Quart., 1899, v. 7. MHS.
Middlesex County. Parish register of Christ Church, 1663–1812. Pub. Grafton Press.
Minutes of Council and General Court of colonial Virginia. MHS.
Monongalia County (formerly Virginia). Marriage bonds. See West. Virginia.
Nansemond County. Records have been lost.
New Kent County. Records. Martha Washington Chap., D. A. R. 1938, v. 1. DAR.
New Kent County. Register of St. Peter's Parish, 1680–1787. Pub. by Soc. C. D. A. of State of Va. Grafton Press. DAR.

Norfolk City. Marriage bonds, 1797–1850, and other genealogical data. G. H. Tucker. 1934. DAR.
Norfolk County. Marriage bonds, Oct. 5, 1706–Dec. 31, 1850. DAR.
Norfolk County. Abstracts of marriages. Lower Norfolk Co. Antiquary. V. 2, pp. 39, 46, 94, 116; v. 3, pp. 8, 57, 74, 95, 107, 124, 133; v. 4, pp. 54, 100, 170; v. 5, pp. 18, 47, 114. (Some as early as 1706; some as late as 1802.) MHS.
Norfolk County. Abstracts of wills. See Westmoreland County.
Norfolk County. Births and baptisms. William and Mary Quart., 1893, v. 1. MHS.
Norfolk County. Brief abstract of wills, 1710–53. C. F. McIntosh. Pub. by Soc. C. D. A. of State of Va., 1922. DAR.
Norfolk County. Marriage bonds from Oct. 5, 1706–Dec. 31, 1850. 1933. Mss. DAR.
Norfolk and Lower Norfolk County. Wills, 1637–1710. C. F. McIntosh. Pub. by Soc. C. D. A. of State of Va., 1914. DAR.
Northampton County. Abstracts of records. Va. Mag. Hist. and Biog., 1897, v. 4; 1898, v. 5. MHS.
Northampton County. Land causes, 1731–1868. (Lancaster County, 1759–1848.) S. Nottingham. 1931. DAR.
Northampton County (now accomac County). Marriage bonds, 1706–1800. Tyler's Quart. Mag., v. 1, pp. 129–211; v. 2, pp. 338–356.
Northumberland County. Marriages, 1783–1850. S. Nottingham. 1929. DAR.
Northumberland County. Records, 1652–55. Virginia colonial abstracts. B. Fleet. V. 2. DAR.
Northumberland County. Records of births, 1661–1810. Virginia colonial abstracts. B. Fleet. V. 3. DAR.
*Old churches, ministers and families of Virginia. Bishop Meade. Including Wise's index. Phila., 1931, 2 vols., 490 and 610 pp., illus. MHS; DAR.
Old King William homes and families. P. N. Clarke. 1897. DAR.
Old plantation and what I gathered there in an autumn month. J. Hungerford. 1859. Lib. Cong.; Enoch Pratt Lib.
Orange Co., Virginia. Marriage bonds, 1757–1803, 1810–65. Mss. DAR.
Payne's ledger, 1758–61. List of names (some of Md.) found in ledger of Daniel Payne, merchant of Dumfries, Prince William Co., Va. William and Mary Quart., v. 4, pp. 117–19 (2 series).
Pittsylvania County. Marriage bonds, 1767–87. D. A. R. Mag., July, 1936, v. 70, no. 7, pp. 722–29.
Pittsylvania County. Marriage bonds (few). Tyler's Quart., 1936–37, v. 17, p. 88. MHS.
Prince George County. Marriages and wills, 1801–50. A. W. B. Bell. 1935, pamph. DAR.
Prince George County. Records, with information on families. Va. Mag. Hist. and Biog., 1897, v. 4. MHS.
Princess Ann County. Abstracts of marriages. Lower Norfolk County Antiquary. V. 3, pp. 19, 117; v. 4, pp. 40, 147; v. 5, pp. 1, 139. (Some as early as 1798, some as late as 1856.) MHS.
Princess Ann County. Marriage bonds. William and Mary Quart., 1893, v. 1. MHS.
1756–66. William and Mary Quart., 1894, v. 2. MHS.
Restoration of Virginia county records, giving list of counties, number of volumes with dates of records. D. A. R. Mag., Aug., 1937, v. 71, no. 8, pp. 725–26.
Richmond County. Marriage bonds. A. W. Reddy and A. L. Riffe. 1929, v. 1. DAR.
Richmond County. Marriage records, 1709–15. From Parish registers. Cary Geneal. Coll. Mss. MHS.
Roanoke County. Salem. Marriage bonds, 1838–40. Natl. Geneal. Soc. Quart., June, 1939, v. 27, pp. 34–37. MHS.
Rockbridge County. Marriage bonds, 1783–89. Tyler's Quart. Mag., v. 13, pp. 261–263. MHS.
Rockingham County. Marriages, 1778–1816. (10,000 names.) H. M. Stricker. 1928. DAR.
Shenandoah County. Marriage bonds, 1772–1850. 1939. Mss. DAR.
Some prominent Virginia families. L. P. Du Bellet. 1907. DAR.
*Some Virginia families. Genealogies of Kinney, McCormick, McIlhany, Milton, Rogers, Snickers, Stribling, Tate, Taylor, and other families. H. Milton McIlhany, Jr. Staunton, Va., 1903.
Spotsylvania County. Marriage licenses. Va. Mag. Hist. and Biog., 1897, v. 4. MHS.
Spotsylvania County. Marriages, 1726–44. William and Mary Quart., 1893, v. 1. MHS.
Spotsylvania County. Virginia county records, 1727–1800. W. A. Crozier. 1905. DAR.
Stafford County. Abstracts of wills. From book M, 1729–48. A. W. B. Bell. 1935. Typed, bd. DAR.
State historical markers of Virginia. Colonial, Revolutionary and nineteenth century. 1937, 4th edition. DAR.
Story of Virginia's first century. Mary N. Stanard. Phila. and London, 1928. DAR.
Sussex County. Marriage bonds, 1739–75. Tyler's Quart. Mag., v. 7, pp. 111–18, 178–79.
Sussex County. Parish register. William and Mary Quart., v. 14, p. 1.
*Times Dispatch, Richmond. Genealogies by E. C. Meade, Mrs. Sally Robins and others.
Two hundred and seventy years of Virginia history. C. M. Long. Neale Pub. Co., 1908.
*Valentine Papers. Edited by Clayton Torrence. Indexed by Miss Mary Garland. Virginia history of counties, cities and families. Ballard, Brassieur (Brashear), Cary, Crenshaw, Dabney, Fontaine, Hardy, Pleasants, Randolph, Valentine and many others. Pub. by Valentine Museum, Richmond, 1929, 4 vols. MHS.
Virginia. American Guide Series. Works Progress Administration Writers' Project. 728 pp., maps, Oxford.
Virginia Almanac, 1774. "List of parishes and ministers in them." Counties of Virginia in which parishes are located. D. A. R. Mag., June, 1938, v. 72, no. 5, pp. 75–76. Reprint from William and Mary Quart., 1897, v. 5, p. 200. MHS.
Virginia colonial register. W. G. and M. N. Stanard. 1902. MHS.

Virginia County. Tombstone records. William and Mary Quart., 1901, v. 9. MHS.
Virginia county records. Virginia Heraldica. Wills, deeds, administrations, guardians, accounts, marriages, licenses and Revolutionary pensions. W. A. Crozier. Pub. by Geneal. Assoc. Quarterly, N. Y., 1912, 10 vols. MHS; DAR.
*Virginia families; some prominent. L. P. Du Bellet. Lynchburg. 1904, 4 vols.
Virginia frontier, 1740–83. F. B. Kegley. 1938, 2 vols. DAR.
Virginia genealogies. 4th annual report of Library Board, 1906–07. Richmond, Va., 1907, Appendix D, pp. 102–33. DAR.
Virginia genealogies. Contains history of Glassell family of Scotland and Ball, Brown, Bryan, Conway, Daniels, Ewell, Holladay, Lewis, Littlepage, Moncure, Peyton, Robinson, Scott, Taylor and Wallace families of Virginia and Maryland. Horace E. Hayden. Wash., D. C., 1931, 759 pp. Facsimilie of 1891 edition. Indexed. MHS; DAR.
Virginia Historical Index. Analysis of information that relates to Virginia and Virginians, in following books:
E. G. Swem, librarian of College of William and Mary. V. 1, A–K, 1934; v. 2, L–Z, 1936. Roanoke, Va. MHS; DAR.
Va. Mag. Hist. and Biog., 1893–1930, vols. 1–38.
William and Mary College Quarterly, 1892–1919, vols. 1–27; second series, 1921–1930, vols. 1–10.
Va. Hist. Reg. and Literary Advertiser, 1848–1853, vols. 1–6.
Lower Norfolk Co. Antiquary, 1895–1906, vols. 1–5.
Henning Statutes at Large of Va. Collection of all laws of Va., 1619–1792, vols. 1–13.
Virginia Historical Index. Calendar of Virginia State Papers and other manuscripts preserved in capitol of Richmond, 1652–1869, vols. 1–2. Specific index, arranged alphabetically.
Virginia Magazine of History and Biography, June, 1894, v. 1, to 1938, v. 46.
Virginia notes. T. Nimmo. 1938, 10 vols. DAR.
Virginia Valley records. J. W. Wayland. 1930, Shenandoah Pub. House. DAR.
*Virginia and Virginians. Dr. R. A. Brock.
Virginians at St. John's College, Annapolis, 1793–94. William and Mary Quart., 1897, v. 5. MHS.
Westmoreland County and Norfolk County. Abstracts of wills, 1654–1800. Md. Geneal. Rec. Com., 1933–34. Mss. DAR.
Westmoreland County. Marriages, 1786–1850. S. Nottingham. 1928. DAR.
Westmoreland County. Wills, 1654–1800. A. B. Fothergill. 1925. DAR.
Wills. N. C. Geneal. Rec. Com. Typed, bd. DAR.
Wills, before 1790. (Complete abstract of names mentioned in over 600 wills in various counties.) Wm. M. Clemens. Pompton Lakes, N. J., Biblio Co., Inc., 1924.
Wills and administrations, 1632–1800, recorded in local courts of Virginia. (11,000 surnames, 5000 entries.) Clayton Torrence. Pub. by Natl. Soc. C. D. A., 1931, paper bd. DAR.
York County. Charles Parish. History; register of births, 1648–1789; deaths, 1665–1787. DAR.
York County. Marriage licenses. William and Mary Quart., 1893, v. 1. MHS.

WEST VIRGINIA

Cabell County. Marriages, 1809–60. 1934. DAR.
Hardy County. Marriages. Natl. Geneal. Soc. Quart., Dec., 1930, v. 18. MHS.
Hardy County, Virginia (now West Virginia). Wills, 1786–1807. D. A. R. Mag., June, 1940, v. 74, pp. 32–34.
Jefferson County, West Virginia, Northern Virginia and District of Columbia Bible and family records. N. G. Ross. D. C. Geneal. Rec. Com., 1938–39, v. 51. Typed, bd. DAR.
Monongalia County (was Virginia). Marriage bonds, 1798–1800, 1802, 1823. D. A. R. Mag., Jan., 1933, v. 67, no. 1, pp. 49–52; Aug., 1933, v. 67, no. 8, pp. 518–22.
Pendleton County. Marriage bonds. Natl. Geneal. Soc. Quart., Apr., 1920, v. 9, no. 1, p. 14. MHS.
Tombstone inscriptions. Natl. Geneal. Soc. Quart., June, 1931, v. 19, p. 37. MHS.
Vital records of West Virginia. From birth and death reports, marriages, cemetery records, wills, inventories. Historical Records Survey. Inventory of County Archives. Works Progress Administration. DAR.
West Virginia Historical Magazine. West Virginia Historical and Antiquarian Soc. Quart., Charleston, W. Va., 1901, v. 1.